# 解读 世界经济发展

林毅夫　付才辉　著

# DEMYSTIFYING
## THE WORLD ECONOMIC DEVELOPMENT

高等教育出版社·北京

内容简介

本书集林毅夫出任世界银行首席经济学家十年来与其同仁关于世界经济发展研究之大成！如果说林毅夫所著的经典教材《解读中国经济》是新结构经济学在分析中国由盛而衰再由衰而盛的一个初步运用，那么本书则是新结构经济学在分析世界各国贫富分流以及如何走向共同繁荣的一个初步应用和检验。本书的基本目标是用最简洁的新结构经济学理论工具获取对世界经济结构变迁的历史、轨迹、现状、趋势与中国在其中的角色及其背后规律和政策方案最多的理解。本书配有大量史料、数据、案例与政策实践，可作为世界经济、全球经济治理与新结构经济学等专业教材，也可作为一般读物供读者了解世界经济发展的来龙去脉与“一带一路”等中国新时代的全球化形势。

**图书在版编目（CIP）数据**

解读世界经济发展 / 林毅夫，付才辉著 . -- 北京：高等教育出版社，2020.6

ISBN 978-7-04-053602-7

Ⅰ. ①解… Ⅱ. ①林… ②付… Ⅲ. ①世界经济 - 经济发展 - 研究 Ⅳ. ① F112

中国版本图书馆 CIP 数据核字 (2020) 第 023741 号

**解读世界经济发展**

JIEDU SHIJIE JINGJI FAZHAN

策划编辑 于 明 刘清田　责任编辑 赵 鹏 王 琼　书籍设计 赵 阳
插图绘制 于 博　责任校对 吕红颖　责任印制 赵义民

出版发行 高等教育出版社
社 址 北京市西城区德外大街4号
邮政编码 100120
印 刷 北京盛通印刷股份有限公司
开 本 787mm × 1092mm 1/16
印 张 48
字 数 970 千字
购书热线 010-58581118
咨询电话 400-810-0598
网 址 http://www.hep.edu.cn
http://www.hep.com.cn
网上订购 http://www.hepmall.com.cn
http://www.hepmall.com
http://www.hepmall.cn
版 次 2020 年 6 月第1版
印 次 2020 年 6 月第1次印刷
定 价 148.00元


物 料 号 53602-00

# 作者简介

## 林毅夫

北京大学新结构经济学研究院教授、院长，南南合作与发展学院院长，国家发展研究院名誉院长。发展中国家科学院（原第三世界科学院）外籍院士、英国科学院外籍院士。1994年创立北京大学中国经济研究中心（现北京大学国家发展研究院），并担任主任一职。2008年被任命为世界银行首席经济学家兼负责发展经济学的高级副行长，成为担此要职的发展中国家第一人，2012年任满返回北大，继续教学研究工作。现任全国政协常委、经济委员会副主任，国务院参事，国家"十三五""十四五"规划专家委员会副主席，"一带一路"国际合作高峰论坛咨询委员会主席。2018年荣获党中央、国务院授予的改革先锋称号，并被誉为经济体制改革理论的探索者。

## 付才辉

北京大学新结构经济学研究院研究员，教材课程与报告案例研发中心主任。2014年起协助林毅夫教授创办北京大学新结构经济学研究中心（现新结构经济学研究院），开展新结构经济学的学科建设与智库建设工作。除了本书之外，还与林毅夫教授合著或主编了多部新结构经济学学术著作以及一些影响广泛的智库报告。每年春季学期在北京大学开设"新结构经济学导论"公共课程、秋季学期在清华大学开设"新结构经济学分析"通识课程。

# 序言

2018年11月，美国前国务卿基辛格博士造访中国，这是他过去半个世纪里近百次访问中国的最近一次。他在与我们所在的北京大学的师生座谈交流时表示，亲眼目睹中国发生了翻天覆地的变化。基辛格在他的名著《大外交》一书中开宗明义地指出，世界每隔百年会出现一个新的全球大国。[①]2018年11月10日与基辛格会谈的中国国务院副总理刘鹤，在其所著的《两次全球大危机的比较研究》一书中，认为基辛格的这个判断可能被两次危机所证实。大萧条后世界经济重心由欧洲转向美洲，美国在世界经济中发挥主导作用，美元占据支配地位，联合国、国际货币基金组织和世界银行诞生，世界经济政治格局发生重大变化。2008年危机发生后，全球发展的重心向亚太地区转移，二十国集团（G20）平台产生，世界实力对比正在急剧变动，国际经济秩序正在发生变化。[②]

从2008年的全球经济金融危机至今，中国经济是世界经济的压舱石，每年对世界经济增长的贡献超过30%。中国经济之所以在世界经济中有如此举足轻重的地位，得益于新中国70年尤其是改革开放40年所取得的发展成就。差不多与基辛格出版《大外交》同时，

---

① Henry Kissinger, *Diplomacy*. Simon & Schuster, 1995.

② 刘鹤，《两次全球大危机的比较研究》，中国经济出版社，2013年版。

林毅夫和其合作者蔡昉、李周在1994年出版了《中国的奇迹：发展战略与经济改革》(简称《中国的奇迹》)，成功预测了到2015年按购买力平价计算，中国的经济规模将超过美国。[①]林毅夫赴任世界银行首席经济学家前夕，根据《中国的奇迹》后续十余年的研究成果在剑桥大学出版社出版了两部著作：一部是《解读中国经济》，是他在北京大学从1996年开设至今的"中国经济专题"课程的讲义；[②]另一部是《经济发展与转型：思潮、战略与自生能力》(简称《经济发展与转型》)，是他2007年在剑桥大学马歇尔年度讲座上的讲稿，总结了他对经济发展与转型的理论和经验研究。[③]这两部著作奠定了新结构经济学的基础。

2009年，林毅夫在世界银行首席经济学家任期一周年时，根据他多年深入研究东亚和中国发展经验的心得，提出"新结构经济学"的理论体系框架，[④]倡导在市场经济中，政府发挥因势利导的作用，克服软硬基础设施的瓶颈，助力企业按照一个经济体在每个时点的要素禀赋结构所决定的比较优势，充分利用后来者优势来发展经济；在经济危机时则采用实施积极财政政策投资于基础设施建设，创造就业，消除增长的瓶颈，平稳经济并为未来发展创造条件的超越凯恩斯

---

① 林毅夫、蔡昉、李周，《中国的奇迹：发展战略与经济改革》，上海三联书店，1994年版。Lin Justin Yifu, Cai Fang, Li Zhou, *China Miracle: Development Strategy and Economic Reform*. revised ed. Hong Kong: The Chinese University of Hong Kong Press, 2003. [First Chinese edition, Shanghai: Shanghai Sanlian Press, 1994; First English edition, Hong Kong: The Chinese University of Hong Kong Press, 1996; Japanese edition, Tokyo: Nihon Hyo Ron Sha, 1996; Korean edition, Seoul: Baeksan Press, 1996; Vietnamese edition, Ho Chi Minh City: Saigon Times, 1999; French edition, Paris: Economica, 2000; revised Chinese edition: Chinese version, Shanghai: Shanghai Sanlian Press,1999; revised Korean edition, Seoul: Baeksan Press, 2000; Traditional Chinese edition, Taipei: Lian Jing Press, 2000 (with the title *China's Economic Reform and Development*); Russian Version, Moscow: Far Eastern Institute Press, Russian Academy of Sciences, 2001.]

② Lin Justin Yifu, *Demystifying the Chinese Economy*. Cambridge University Press, 2012.

③ Lin Justin Yifu, *Economic Development and Transition: Thought, Strategy and Viability*. Cambridge University Press, 2009.

④ Lin Justin Yifu, *New Structural Economics: A Framework for Rethinking Development Policy*. World Bank, 2012.

主义的政策主张，以应对世界发展与经济危机的挑战。[①]2011年，林毅夫首次提出，中国的经济转型升级和比较优势的转移，会给低收入的发展中国家创造巨大的工业化、现代化的发展机会；中国会从一只跟随的雁成为引领之龙（from a following goose to a leading dragon）。[②]八年之后的今天，由于中国的改革开放和时势的变化，中非合作、“一带一路”迅猛发展，成千上万的企业走出去，在成百个经济特区和产业园内外，为东道国创造了上百万工作岗位，许多当时的预测正在变为现实。[③]

2017年5月14日至15日，万物并秀的北京迎来一场历史性盛会——首届“一带一路”国际合作高峰论坛，140多个国家、80多个国际组织与会。[④]林毅夫被授任“一带一路”国际咨询委员会主席。我们在首届“一带一路”高峰论坛前夕发布了首部应用新结构经济学的思想、理论、思路、视角以及实践来观察世界经济结构变迁以及中国在其中的方位、力量、方案与机遇的智库旗舰报告——《世界经济结构转型升级报告——新结构经济学之路》。[⑤]让我们高兴的是，不少师生也将该智库报告作为了解世界经济以及学习新结构经济学相关学科的教辅资料，并建议我们将其修改成解读世界经济发展的教材。我们欣然接受了来自师生们的好建议，以新结构经济学为理论框架，集结林毅夫出任世界银行首席经济学家以来十年间关于世界经济的相关研究精华和智库实践，同时综合国内外沿用新结构经济学所做的最新相关研究，在2019年4月第二届“一带一路”国际合作高峰论坛前夕形成了这部《解读世界经济发展》的初稿。本书共10章，主要内容依次在世界经济结构变迁的历史、现状、趋势与方案层面上

---

① Lin Justin Yifu, “Beyond Keynesianism: The Necessity of a Globally Coordinated Solution”, *Harvard International Review,* 2009, Vol.31, No.2, pp. 14–17. Lin Justin Yifu, *Against the Consensus: Reflections on the Great Recession*. Cambridge University Press, 2013.

② Vandana Chandra, Lin Justin Yifu and Wang Yan, “Leading Dragons Phenomenon: New Opportunities for Catch-Up in Low-Income Countries”, *World Bank Policy Research Working Paper 6000*, 2012.

③ 林毅夫、王燕，“以比较优势作为南南合作互利共赢的指南”，《区域与全球发展》，2018年第5期，第5–23页。

④ “首届‘一带一路’国际合作高峰论坛——让各国人民更好共享发展成果”，http://www.gov.cn/xinwen/2018–12/18/content_5349820.htm，2018年12月18日。

⑤ 林毅夫、付才辉，《世界经济结构转型升级报告——新结构经济学之路》，北京大学出版社，2018年版。

延续了《新结构经济学》《繁荣的求索》《从西潮到东风》《超越发展援助》《战胜命运》等新结构经济学系列著作的核心内容。

第1章概述了世界经济秩序、格局、理论与思路的变迁，作为全书的绪论。中国人常讲，“三十年河东、三十年河西”，用来感叹世事兴衰更替。马克思主义讲经济基础决定上层建筑，世界经济变迁莫不验证了这一原理。第二次世界大战以后，美国的国内生产总值占据了世界的约一半，诞生了唯美国马首是瞻的“布雷顿森林体系”。20世纪70年代的石油危机让七国集团（G7）取而代之，更新了世界经济秩序，但G7依然只是一个封闭的富国俱乐部，当时七国的国内生产总值超过了世界的3/5。改革开放40年让中国经济腾飞，带动新兴经济体一起撼动了由发达国家主导的世界经济格局，2008年全球金融危机之后，G20逐步取代G7。中国的经济奇迹，不但会改变世界经济的秩序与机遇，而且也会改变世界经济发展的理论和思路。在这样的背景下，本章介绍了新结构经济学作为取代第二次世界大战后旧结构主义与新自由主义的第三代发展经济学的理论与思路，概括性介绍了经济结构变迁的新结构经济学理论框架。归结起来，发展经济学的前两代都是以发达国家为参照系，来看发展中国家缺什么（如第一代结构主义所强调的现代资本、技术密集产业），或发展中国家做得不好的地方（如第二代新自由主义所强调的市场制度和治理，即“华盛顿共识”所推动的私有化、市场化、自由化），并以此作为改造发展中国家的依据。与前两代发展思潮相反，新结构经济学主张应该从发展中国家现在有什么（其要素禀赋）出发，规划在此基础上能做好什么（其比较优势），把现在能做好的在政府的因势利导和企业家的共同努力下把它做大做强，以此加速资本积累，改变禀赋结构，为产业、技术、软硬基础设施的改善创造物质条件，实现逐步赶上甚至超越发达国家的目标。

第2章在更广阔的世界历史视野下，论述了经济结构变迁是发展的关键，既是对第1章所介绍的新结构经济学框架的理论深化，也是历史检验。经济结构变迁重要到可以按照其根本特征给世界历史进行断代。尽管经济结构变迁是连续不断的，但工业革命是世界经济变迁最关键的分水岭。在工业革命之前，人类社会处于“马尔萨斯陷阱”之中，存在上限的自然资源禀赋支配着其结构变迁特征。让人类跳出“马尔萨斯陷阱”的是工业革命，但其本质是技术持续创新带来的经济结构的不断转型升级而非几项耀眼的科技成就。工业革命造就了当今的发达国家，但也造成了世界经济的大分流。未能实现持续的经济结构转型是发展中经济体的顽疾。亚当·斯密的经济学是总结于地理大发现之后工业革命全面爆发之前经验的理论，其后的经济学大师虽不断总结发达国家的经验提出新的理论，这些理论不可避免地内嵌于产生这些理论的发达国家的技术、产业、社会、政治、文化结构之中，并以此发达国家的各种结构为理论的暗含前提，如此的主流理论难以指导具有结构本质差异的发展中国家的经济结构转型升级。第二次世界大战后第一代发展经济学（结构主义）虽然强调了经济结构转型的重要性，但是忽视了结构的内生性，主张违背比较优势去发展和发达国家相同的、先进的资本密集型大产业，拔苗助长的结果却适得其反。在这样的背景下，本章深化了第1章介绍的新结构经济学理论框架，认为古典经济学通过边际革命形成了新古典经济学，对新古典经济学进行结构革命便形成了新结构经济学。新古典经济学是给定经济结构求解最优的资源配置。新结构经济学恰恰相反，是给定要素禀赋求解最优经济结构。按此理论框架，本章量化核算了第二次世界大战后至今世界各个经济体的经济结构变迁对经济增长的影响，确认了经济结构转型升级是发展的关键。更进一步，本章简要梳理了作为上层建筑的各种制度结构如金融、法律等如何随作为经济基础的技术、产业的变迁而变迁，再一次在世界经济层面验证了马克思历史唯物主义所揭示的作为经济基础的生产力和生产关系，决定作为上层建筑的各种制度安排，同时也驳斥了流行的新制度经济学派所主张的制度决定论的观点。

第3章应用新结构经济学的基本原理追踪了世界经济结构变迁的历史轨迹。造就当今发达国家的工业革命并不是一夜之间爆发的，英美工业革命其实是非常漫长的循序渐进的结构变迁过程。不论在三次产业层面，还是在细分制造业层面，甚至在产品与技术层面，生产结构的变迁都是一个随发展阶段（禀赋结构）拾级而上的过程。在世界经济发展的历史上，那些遵循产业发展次序的经济体取得了成功经验，而那些颠倒产业发展次序的经济体却遭受了惨痛教训，全球各个经济体的经验实证支持了结构扭曲导致经济停滞的这个宝贵经验教训。据此，本章追踪测算了近半个世纪以来近两百个经济体的经济结构变迁轨迹，并归纳了前沿发达经济体、发展中经济体以及陷入低收入陷阱和中等收入陷阱的经济体的结构变迁轨迹特征。

第4章探寻了第二次世界大战后发展典范的经济结构变迁规律。第二次世界大战以后，有13个经济体实现了连续25年超过7%的经济增长，堪称发展典范。它们分别是中国内地、中国香港、中国台湾、韩国、新加坡、日本、印度尼西亚、马来西亚、泰国、阿曼、马耳他、博茨瓦纳、巴西。它们有5个典型特征：对外开放、宏观稳定、禀赋积累、有效市场、有为政府。[①]本章通过一一复原其经济结构转型升级的历程，以案例形式展现了新结构经济学所揭示的按照比较优势进行结构变迁的规律，统一解释了它们的典型特征事实。有效市场和有为政府是按照比较优势发展的制度前提，对外开放、宏观稳定和高储蓄高投资是按照比较优势发展的必然结果，按照比较优势不断转型、加速禀赋结构升级是快速发展的关键之道。新结构经济学也揭开了成功经济体的高储蓄率之谜。然而，这些发展典范的高储蓄率却为流行思潮所诟病，甚至被无端指责为美国经济失衡的原因——其实美国在高速结构转型的19世纪也曾出现过高储蓄现象。[②]

第5章以第二次世界大战后这13个发展典范的经济结构转型升级轨迹而非发达国家作为标杆，测评了世界各个经济体结构转型升级的达标程度及其效果。遵循比较优势的发展方法对于发展中国家的经济发展而言看起来或许是缓慢而令人沮丧的，但事实上，这种办法却是积累资本、提升要素禀赋结构和产业结构，以小步快跑的方式推动经济包容性可持续发展的最好方法；并且，按此办法还能积极参与全球化，发挥后来者优势，从更为发达的国家引进技术和产业，利用外资和外贸，而取得比发达国家更为快速的产业结构升级和经济发展。与之相反，违背比较优势的发展方式则将错失全球化发展机遇，跌入包括低收入陷阱和中等收入陷阱在内的发展陷阱。本章再一次以详细的世界经济结构变迁历程论述了新结构经济学的基本原理和发展思路。

第6章以制造业及其就业结构变迁为焦点分析了世界经济结构变迁中的发展机遇。中国有句俗话说，“无农不稳，无工不富，无商不活”。制造业是世界财富的发动机和就业的水池。就业是发展的基石，中国伟大的脱贫成就源于发挥比较优势由制造业带动创造了大量的就业，而人类艰难的反贫困斗争则根源于制造业就业的缺失。本章继续运用新结构经济学的基本原理探索了全球制造业就业结构随禀赋结构变化而变化的一般规律与特征，并估算了其缺口。就全球各地区制造业就业结构变迁的基本趋势而言，持续不断的亚洲雁行模式是东亚奇迹的秘密，南亚与撒哈拉以南非洲地区亟须发展劳动力密集型制造业来脱贫，中东与北非以及拉美需要转型升级制造业以摆脱中等收入陷阱，欧洲和中亚地区需要调整违背

---

① Commission on Growth and Development, *The Growth Report: Strategies for Sustained Growth and Inclusive Development.* World Bank, 2008.

② Lin Justin Yifu, *Against the Consensus: Reflections on the Great Recession.* Cambridge University Press, 2013.

比较优势的制造业重获竞争优势，美国这样的高收入经济体则需要持续创新拓展世界产业前沿。与此同时，世界经济结构变迁过程中的工作性质也发生了变迁，就业结构也可能出现极化，需要加以应对才能创造更包容平等的社会。全球制造业的差序格局是南北合作与南南合作的产业基础，与过去的雁阵模式不同，中国在南南合作中的地位则是“领头龙模式”。本章最后以日本和中国重庆如何把握全球电子信息产业转移的机遇为例，说明世界任何经济体只要找准自身的比较优势均可以在政府的因势利导下，助力企业家在市场中创造竞争优势，利用全球化的机遇加速发展。

第7章以制约经济结构转型升级的瓶颈为焦点分析了世界基础设施建设。软硬基础设施“瓶颈”是经济结构转型升级的障碍，也是随手可牵的“替罪羊”。基础设施落后的确是经济表现的主要约束因素，但并不是经济转型不可逾越的障碍。经济发展和基础设施建设可以并行发展、相助互济。流行思潮认为在经济增长动态过程启动之前，所有的软硬基础设施障碍都需要排除，这既不现实也不必要。在过去的20年里增长最快的30个经济体的证据表明，那些用流行指标衡量的营商环境质量似乎都不重要，因为除了新加坡和马来西亚，其余经济体的营商指标评分居然都相当差！一个更务实的做法是政府将有限的资源和执行能力用于打造工业园、加工出口区、经济特区，在园区里实行一站式服务，即在整体的基础设施和商业环境不善的国家创造局部有利条件，充分挖掘和利用经济体的潜在比较优势，为企业家创造条件，促进有竞争力产业的兴起，然后积累物质条件，提升执行能力，逐步改善全国的软硬基础设施和营商环境。基于此，本章介绍了从局部到整体渐进式改善软硬基础设施的中国经验，概括了世界各地区的水、电、交通、电信、互联网、能源等基础设施随发展阶段而变化的建设状况，介绍了已经认识到基础设施重要性的二十国集团的全球基础设施倡议，归纳了发达国家与发展中国家的基础设施建设差异。

第8章梳理了中国与世界经济结构转型升级的关系。与流行的偏见相反，中国经济的崛起不但不会给世界产生两难困境，[1]反而既会给发达国家带来继续的繁荣，也会给发展中国家创造机遇。中国在世界经济结构转型升级中有着独特的方位：按购买力平价计算，中国的经济体量已经重回世界第一，但中国的整

---

① Dani Rodrik, “Making Room for China in the World Economy”, *American Economic Review*, 2010, Vol.100, No.2, pp. 89–93.

体经济发展水平却处于世界居中的位置，并且中国从低到高的地区发展差异巨大。这造就了中国与世界经济结构的深度耦合，以及中国的差异化全球化，与发达国家和发展中国家的不同耦合方向，中国与世界经济联系的多样性。中国在世界经济结构转型升级中有着巨大的力量：中国依然是世界经济增长的引擎，中国的工业化依然保持强劲的态势，中国拥有全球最具活力的庞大消费市场，中国依然是全球最大的贸易国，中国依然是全球最具投资吸引力的国家，中国拥有全球最庞大的产能，中国拥有全球最具实力的基础设施建设能力，中国已经成为净资本输出国并位居对外投资流量大国。中国在世界经济结构转型升级中独特的方位与力量是中国与世界大同的根源。基于此，本章梳理了中国与发达国家和发展中国家经济结构转型升级的匹配状况。发达国家依然是中国通过学习利用后来者优势的对象，需要充分利用中国与其他不同收入经济体互补的比较优势深化合作，中国去发达国家投资能够促进中国与发达经济体的经济结构转型升级，从发达国家"引进来"也能够促进中国与发达经济体的经济结构转型升级，同时中国有带给发展中经济体产业转移的机会与基础设施建设的能力。新时代，中国能够建设融入世界的开放型经济新体制。

第9章专门讨论了"一带一路"倡议如何助推世界经济发展。从世界经济结构变迁以及中国在其中的方位可以看到，"一带一路"倡议可以互利双赢的方式助推中国和沿线各国经济结构转型升级。基于此，本章梳理了过去五年来"一带一路"倡议的主要进展，包括对外投资、经贸合作区、经贸投资成效、企业转型升级、人民币国际化等重要方面。为降低金融风险，需要提高"一带一路"沿线基础设施投资回报率与"耐心资本"。最后，本章梳理了"一带一路"沿线各国与中国各地区如何发挥比较优势参与"一带一路"。"一带一路"倡议不同于给世界人民带来痛苦的殖民主义全球化，也不同于未能给世界人民带来福音的新自由主义全球化，是包容性的新型全球化，[①]有助于实现"百花齐放春满园"的人类命运共同体。

第10章总结了新结构经济学的世界经济繁荣稳定之路，提供了一套推动世界各国经济结构快速、包容、可持续转型升级的新结构经济学措施，并附上了一份联合国工业发展组织开发的新结构经济学"增长甄别与因势利导"（GIFF）技

① 刘卫东、Michael Dunford、高菠阳，"'一带一路'倡议的理论建构——从新自由主义全球化到包容性全球化"，《地理科学进展》，2017年第11期。

术手册，以及一套覆盖近200个经济体的新结构经济学全球包容性可持续转型指数。我们相信，一个国家即便深陷贫困陷阱的泥沼长达数个世纪，沿着新结构经济学的道路，改变发展思路，在市场经济中政府发挥因势利导的作用，助力企业家将潜在比较优势转化为竞争优势，就能够骤然改变命运，踏上快速发展转型的繁荣之路，在一两代之间摆脱贫困，实现工业化、现代化。本书的第一作者于第二次世界大战结束不久后的20世纪50年代初期生于中国台湾，当时的台湾与多数非洲国家一样贫穷落后。本书的第二作者于20世纪80年代中期生于中国四川，当时的中国大陆与本书第一作者出生时的中国台湾一样贫穷落后，甚至人均收入水平大约为撒哈拉以南非洲地区平均水平的一半，而那时的中国台湾已经成长为一个新兴工业化经济体。当我们今天阅读本书时，中国已经是一个人均GDP超过一万美元的中等偏上收入经济体了。世界经济格局在短短四十年间发生剧变。如此梦幻般的亲身经历让我们确信贫困并非宿命。虽然任何理论都有前提条件，但是，一个国家只要发展思路正确，在任何起始条件下实现包容可持续发展都是可能的。正如中国国家主席习近平在联合国成立70周年发展峰会上所阐述的世界发展的中国方案："发展归根结底要靠本国自身努力。中国人讲：'量腹而受，量身而衣。'各国要根据自身禀赋特点，制定适合本国国情的发展战略。"

如果说《解读中国经济》是新结构经济学理论在分析中国由盛而衰再由衰而盛的一个初步运用，那么《解读世界经济发展》则是新结构经济学理论在分析全球各国贫富分流以及如何走向共同繁荣的一个初步应用和检验。我们的基本目标是，用最少的新结构经济学理论工具获取对世界经济结构变迁现象和政策方案最多的理解。因此，作为本书的配套读物，林毅夫和付才辉所著的《新结构经济学导论》教材有助于读者更全面了解新结构经济学的学科体系，[①]其他专著则有助于读者更深入了解本书的相关议题，比如对中国经济的深入介绍可参考林毅夫、蔡昉、李周所著《中国的奇迹》以及文一所著的《伟大的中国工业革命》，对发展中国家发展与转型的深入介绍可参考林毅夫所著《经济发展与转型》，对发展思潮的深入反思可参考林毅夫所著《新结构经济学：反思经济发展与政策的理论框架》，对南南合作的深入探讨可参考林毅夫、王燕所著《超越

① 林毅夫、付才辉，《新结构经济学导论》（上、下册），高等教育出版社，2019年版。

发展援助》[①]，对在充满制度扭曲的经济体中推动结构转型与发展的深入探讨可参考林毅夫和孟加所著的《战胜命运》[②]，对新结构经济学政策举措的深入浅出介绍可参考林毅夫所著《繁荣的求索》[③]，对非洲发展中经济体的详细探讨可参考林毅夫和Célestin Monga主编的工具手册*The Oxford Handbook of Africa and Economics(Ⅰ/Ⅱ)*[④]，对波兰等已经达到高收入水平的转型经济体发展政策的详细探讨可参考林毅夫和Alojzy Z. Nowak等著的*New Structural Economics for Less Advanced Countries*[⑤]以及*New Structural Policy in an Open Market Economy*[⑥]，对产业政策更详细的探讨可参考林毅夫和Joseph E. Stiglitz主编的*Industrial Policy Revolution(Ⅰ/Ⅱ)*[⑦]，对经济结构转型更详细的探讨可参考林毅夫和孟加主编的*The Oxford Handbook of Structural Transformation*[⑧]。此外，尽管本书已经颇为冗长地整理了非常多的最新相关数据和案例资料，但是当今中国与世界经济结构变迁的速度之快令人目不暇接，读者有必要紧跟时事去了解最新的相关数据和案例。

除了上述著作以及我们过去研究的合作者与支持者的研究成果外，本书也吸纳了诸多沿用新结构经济学开展的相关研究的成果和资料，感谢这些志同道合的朋友，贡献是他们的，不足是我们的。例如，本书第3章中关于英美工业革命历程的梳理与第4章中对我们开发的一个追踪结构变迁轨迹工具（付－林图）的进一步案例应用就来自文一教授的工作，第9章中关于“一带一路”倡议对企业转

---

① Lin Justin Yifu, Wang Yan, *Going Beyond Aid: Development Cooperation for Structural Transformation*. Cambridge University Press, 2016.

② Lin Justin Yifu, Célestin Monga, *Beating the Odds: Jump-Starting Developing Countries*. Princeton University Press, 2017.

③ Lin Justin Yifu, *The Quest for Prosperity: How Developing Economies Can Take Off*. Princeton University Press, 2012.

④ Lin Justin Yifu, Célestin Monga, *The Oxford Handbook of Africa and Economics (I/II)*. Oxford University Press, 2015.

⑤ Lin Justin Yifu, Alojzy Z. Nowak, *New Structural Economics for Less Advanced Countries*. University of Warsaw Faculty of Management Press, 2017.

⑥ Lin Justin Yifu, Alojzy Z. Nowak, *New Structural Policy in an Open Market Economy*. University of Warsaw Faculty of Management Press, 2019.

⑦ Joseph E. Stiglitz, Justin Yifu Lin, *Industrial Policy Revolution (I/II)*. Palgrave Macmillan, 2013.

⑧ Lin Justin Yifu, Célestin Monga, *The Oxford Handbook of Structural Transformation*. Oxford University Press, 2019.

型升级影响的实证研究就来自王桂军博士的工作，第9章和第10章中一些关于新结构经济学增长甄别与因势利导工具（GIFF）的应用案例来自刘文革教授、孙瑾博士和赵秋运博士等同仁的工作，等等，不一而足。2017年5月，本书的雏形《世界经济结构转型升级报告——新结构经济学之路》作为智库旗舰报告发布时，有来自海内外各界数百名与会者交流讨论，大家的热情给予了我们在此基础上推进进一步研究工作的动力。也特别感谢师生朋友，本书作为专著性质的教材的进一步修改完善则源于他们的建议。2019年4月，在本书初稿的研讨会上，来自国内外数十所兄弟院校师生的意见建议尤为宝贵，特别是中国科学院刘卫东研究员、中国人民大学范志勇教授、辽宁大学刘文革教授、广东外语外贸大学韩永辉教授、北京大学王勇教授等同仁提出了具体的修改建议。北京师范大学的郑飞虎教授在教学应用上也提出了有益建议。高等教育出版社的诸多同仁，尤其是赵鹏编辑为本书付出了很多心血。一并表示感谢！也欢迎大家继续将任何意见建议反馈给我们（fucaihui@nsd.pku.edu.cn），以便下一版进一步改进。

最后，我们也非常期待着以《解读世界经济发展》为讲义开设相关课程（北京大学新结构经济学本科实验班将以此为教材开设同名课程），和广大师生以及各界朋友一起探讨基于中国经济和发展中经济体实践经验的新结构经济学理论视角下的世界经济发展与新时代中国的全球化。就在本书即将定稿付梓之际，爆发了肆虐全球的新冠疫情（COVID-19），世界已然一家，我们任何人都没有理由不去认识她，让她变得更美好！

林毅夫　付才辉

于北京大学

2020年春

# Preface

In November 2018, former US Secretary of State, Henry Alfred Kissinger visited China, the latest of nearly 100 visits he has made in the past half century. 'We've seen the earth-shaking changes in China, 'he said during a panel discussion with students and faculty at Peking University, where we are. In his famous book, *Diplomacy*, Kissinger begins by pointing out that every hundred years a new global power emerges.[①] Liu He, Vice Premier of the State Council of China, who met with Kissinger on November 10, 2018, pointed out in a comparative study on the two global crises that "Henry Kissinger stated clearly in his book *Diplomacy* that a new global power emerges for every century in the world. The judgment could be confirmed by the two crises." After the "Great Depression", the center of world economy moved from Europe to America. The US played the leading role in the world economy and the US dollar secured the dominant position. The United Nations, the International Monetary Fund, and the World Bank were founded. The world economic and political pattern changed significantly.

① Henry Kissinger. *Diplomacy*. Simon & Schuster, 1995.

After the crisis in 2008, the focus of global development shifted to the Asia-Pacific region and the G20 platform emerged. With such drastic changes to the strength of world powers, the international economic order has been undergoing great change.①

Contributing to over 30% of global economic growth annually, the Chinese economy has been a cornerstone of the world economy since the global financial crisis in 2008. Attaining such a pivotal position for the Chinese economy in the world is based on the achievements, developments, and reform that have taken place over the last 70 years since the founding of the People's Republic of China, in particular, the past 40 years since the reform and opening up. In *China Miracle: Development Strategy and Economic Reform* published in 1994, Justin Lin Yifu, Cai Fang, and Li Zhou successfully predicted that China's economy would surpass the US economy in 2015 based on the purchasing power parity (PPP). ②Before his appointment as the chief economist to the World Bank, Justin Lin Yifu published two works to show the achievements of his research in a decade after the book *China Miracle*. One is *Demystifying the Chinese Economy*, which contains the lecture notes from 1996 until the present, on "Chinese economics" from Peking University. ③ The other is *Economic Development and Transition: Thought,*

---

① Liu He. *A Comparative Study of the Two Great Global Crises*. China Economic Press, 2013 (In Chinese).

② Lin Justin Yifu, Cai Fang, Li Zhou, *China Miracle: Development Strategy and Economic Reform*. revised ed. Hong Kong: The Chinese University of Hong Kong Press, 2003. (First Chinese edition, Shanghai: Shanghai Sanlian Press, 1994; First English edition Hong Kong: The Chinese University of Hong Kong Press, 1996; Japanese edition, Tokyo: Nihon Hyo Ron Sha, 1996; Korean edition, Seoul: Baeksan Press, 1996; Vietnamese edition, Ho Chi Minh City: Saigon Times, 1999; French edition, Paris: Economica, 2000; revised Chinese edition: Chinese version, Shanghai. Shanghai Sanlian Press,1999; revised Korean edition, Seoul: Baeksan Press, 2000; Traditional Chinese edition, Taipei: Lian Jing Press, 2000 (with the title *China's Economic Reform and Development*); Russian Version, Moscow: Far Eastern Institute Press, Russian Academy of Sciences, 2001. )

③ Lin Justin Yifu, *Demystifying the Chinese Economy*. Cambridge University Press, 2012.

*Strategy, and Viability,* which covers lecture notes from Marshall Lectures at Cambridge University delivered by him in 2007, in which he summarized his research on theories and experience in economic development and transformation.[①] These two books laid the foundation of New Structural Economics.

One year after Justin Lin Yifu served as the chief economist to the World Bank, he put forward the theoretical framework of "new structural economics" according to his in-depth several year-long study of development experience in China and other countries in East Asia.[②] He advocated that governments should effectively play their facilitating role to overcome bottlenecks in hard and soft infrastructure in the market economy and help entrepreneurs take advantage of the latecomer advantage to promote economic development on the basis of comparative advantage determined by the factor endowment structure of each economy at different times. Facing economic crisis, the adoption of positive fiscal policy beyond Keynesianism is needed in order to invest in the construction of infrastructure so as to eliminate "bottleneck" economic growth and job creation to stabilize the economy and create conditions for future development. Such policies could be adopted to cope with the challenges of global development and economic crisis.[③] In 2011, Justin Lin Yifu proposed, for the first time, that economic transformation, upgrading, and change of comparative advantages in China would create great development opportunities for low-income or developing countries who are undergoing industrialization and modernization, and China would change its role from "being a following goose to a leading dragon".[④] Eight years have passed. The China-Africa Cooperation and the Belt and Road Initiative (BRI) have been promoted vigorously during this time of reform and opening-up in China. Tens of thousands of enterprises

---

① Lin Justin Yifu, *Economic Development and Transition: Thought, Strategy and Viability*. Cambridge University Press, 2009.

② Lin Justin Yifu, *New Structural Economics:* A *Framework for Rethinking Development Policy*. World Bank, 2012.

③ Lin Justin Yifu, "Beyond Keynesianism: The Necessity of a Globally Coordinated Solution", *Harvard International Review,* 2009, Vol.31, No.2, pp.14–17. Lin Justin Yifu, *Against the Consensus: Reflections on the Great Recession*. Cambridge University Press, 2013.

④ Vandana Chandra, Lin Justin Yifu and Wang Yan, "Leading Dragons Phenomenon: New Opportunities for Catch-Up in Low-Income Countries", *World Bank Policy Research Working Paper 6000,* 2012.

have gone abroad and created millions of job vacancies for hosting countries in and around hundreds of special economic zones and industrial parks. Many of his predictions are coming true.[①]

From May 14 to 15, 2017, the first Belt and Road Forum for International Cooperation of great historical significance was held in Beijing when every living thing was full of energy. Over 140 countries and 80 international organizations attended the event.[②] Justin Lin Yifu was appointed chairman of the International Advisory Board of the Belt and Road Forum for International Cooperation. Right before the first Belt and Road Forum for International Cooperation was held, the *Report on the Structural Transformation and Upgrading of the World Economy—The Path of New Structural Economics*, as the flagship think tank report using the ideas, theories, thoughts, perspectives, and practices of the newly structured economics to observe changes in the world economic structure, as well as the position, strength, plan, and opportunities of China, was published for the first time.[③] It is pleasant that many teachers and students use the report as supplementary teaching material for such subjects as world economy and new structural economics and have suggested to revise it into a textbook for demystifying the world economic development. This excellent suggestion from teachers and students is accepted. Taking the new structural economics as the theoretical framework, the essence of research of Justin Lin Yifu on world economy and his practice in think tanks in the past decade since he served as the chief economist of the World Bank have been collected and the latest research

---

① Lin Justin Yifu, Wang Yan, "Comparative Advantage to Guide South-South Cooperation and Development", *Area Studies and Global Development*, 2018, No.5, pp. 5–23.

② *The first Belt and Road Forum for International Cooperation--Sharing the Achievements of Development with People from all around the Globe,* www.gov.cn/xinwen/2018–12/18/content_5349820.htm, December 18, 2018.

③ Lin Justin Yifu, Fu Caihui, *Report on the Structural Transformation and Upgrading of the World Economy—The Path of New Structural Economics*, Peking University Press, 2018.

relevant to new structural economics at home and abroad have been included to form the first draft *Demystifying the World Economic Development* in April 2019 before the Second Belt and Road Forum for International Cooperation.

The book consists of 10 chapters. The major content continues with the theme of the core concepts in the series of works about new structural economics, including *New Structural Economics*, *The Quest for Prosperity*, *Against the Consensus*, *Going Beyond Aid*, and *Beating the Odds*, in terms of the history, status quo, trend, and program for change to global economic structure.

As the introduction to the book, Chapter I introduces the change of the order, pattern, theory, and concepts of world economy. The Chinese often say that "the pendulum has swung back to express their reflection on the fluctation of history". According to Marxism, the economic basis determines the superstructure, which has been verified by the changes in the world economy. After World War II, the US GDP accounted for about half of the world's total and the "Bretton Woods System" leading by the US was established. In the 1970s the oil crisis forced the US to update its economic standing and create the G7, yet the G7 was merely an exclusive club of seven rich countries with a total GDP surpassing 3/5 of the world's total. The Chinese economy has taken off in the forty years of reform and opening-up, thus driving emerging economies to challenge the global economic environment dominated by developed countries. After the global financial crisis in 2008, the G7 was gradually replaced by the G20. China's economic miracle changes not only the order and opportunities of the world economy but also the theories and concepts of the world's economic development. Within this context, this chapter introduces the theories and concepts of new structural economics as being the third generation of economics, thus replacing the structuralism and neo-liberalism of Post-World War II and summarizes the theoretical framework of new structural economics showing the change of economic structure. In short, the first two generations of development economics take developed countries as the frame of reference. The deficiencies (like modern capital and technology-intensive industries emphasized by the first generation of structuralism), or shortcomings (like market system and governance emphasized by the second generation of neoliberalism, namely the privatization, marketization, and liberalization promoted by "Washington Consensus") of developing countries are highlighted and used as the basis for transforming developing countries. Contrary to the first two waves of development trends, the new structural economics advocates a start from the local condition of developing countries (namely the factor endowment) and search for what can be achieved on this basis (namely comparative advantage). In this way, the economy of developing countries should make what they can do well bigger and stronger, so that they can make it bigger and stronger with the joint efforts of the government and the entrepreneurs, so as to speed up the capital accumulation and change the endowment structure. Therefore, they will create material conditions for the improvement of Industries, technologies, soft and hard infrastructure, and then gradually catch up and even surpass that of developed countries.

Chapter II elaborates on the change of economic structure as the key to development with a broader view as to world history. It expands on the theory of new structural economic frameworks as introduced in Chapter I and provides historical proof for it. The change of economic structure is so important that world history could be divided into different periods with fundamental characteristics. Although the change of economic structure is a continuous process, industrial revolution is the most critical watershed for world economic development. Before the industrial revolution, human society was in the "Malthusian trap". The limited natural resources endowment dominated the characteristics of its structural change. It is the industrial revolution that lifted mankind out of the "Malthusian trap", yet its essence lies in continuous transformation and upgrading of economic structure rather than several shining technological achievements. The industrial revolution has raised up the currently developed countries, yet it has also caused a great diversion of the world economy. Developing economies face long-lasting economic transformation structural failure. Adam. Smith's economics was also little more than a theory based on experience before the industrial revolution, after the discovery of geography. While the economic masters who followed continued to sum up the experience of the developed countries and put forward new theories, these theories were inevitably embedded in the technological, industrial, social, political and cultural structures of the developed countries that produced them, and take the various structures of the developed countries as the implicit premise of the theory, such a mainstream theory is difficult to guide economic restructuring and upgrading of the developing countries with the structural differences. Although the first generation of economic development (structuralism) after World War II highlights the significance of the transformation of economic structure, it neglects the structural endogeneity and the development path against comparative advantage goes opposite to what it wished. In this context, the theoretical framework of new structural economics as introduced in Chapter I is deepened, proposing that neoclassical economics comes from a marginal revolution of classical economics while new structural economics results from a structural revolution to neoclassical economics. Neoclassical economics aims to provide optimal resource allocation for the given economic structure. On the contrary, new structural economics searches for the best economic structure for the given resource endowment. Under this theoretical framework, the influence of economic structural changes of various economies in the world on their economic growth since the end of World War II is quantified in this chapter and it is confirmed by the transformation and upgrading of economic structure which is key to development. Moreover, the change of various institutional structures like finance, law, and so on, which are the superstructure and development of technology and industry as the economic basis is briefly sorted out, proving what Marxism historical materialism revealed productivity and relations of production economic base determined superstructure's various institutional arrangements from the perspective of world economy again, and refuting the popular institutional determinism as advocated by the neo-institutionalism school of thought.

Chapter III tracks the historical trajectory of changes to a global economy with the basic principles of new structural economics. The industrial revolution that created the currently developed countries didn't break out overnight. In fact, the industrial revolution in the US and the UK is a long and gradual process of structural change. For no matter the thrice industrial structure, the segmented manufacturing, or even products and technology, the production structure is a process of step-by-step development following a development stage (endowment structure). In the history of world economy, all those economies that follow the order of industrial development have succeeded while those reversing that order have learned painful lessons. The empirical experience of various economies around the globe supports the valuable theory that structural distortions would result in economic stagnation. Based on this, the chapter tracks the trajectories and economic structural changes of nearly 200 economies in the past half-century and summarizes corresponding characteristics in leading developed economies, developing economies, and economies that are trapped in low and middle incomes.

Chapter IV explores the laws of economic structural change by typical examples of development after World War II. After World War II, 13 economies had realized an economic growth of over 7% for 25 consecutive years and became typical examples of development. They are mainland China, Hong Kong SAR of China, Taiwan of China, South Korea, Singapore, Japan, Indonesia, Malaysia, Thailand, Oman, Malta, Botswana, and Brazil. They share five typical characteristics, including opening-up to the outside world, stable macroeconomy, endowment accumulation, effective markets, and promising government. [①]Through economic restoration, transformation, and one by one structural upgrading, this chapter reveals the law of structural change according to the comparative advantage in new structural economics and explains their typical characteristics in a unified way. Effective market and promising government are institutional prerequisites for development

① Commission on Growth and Development, *The Growth Report: Strategies for Sustained Growth and Inclusive Development*. World Bank, 2008.

based on comparative advantage. Opening-up to the outside world, stable macroeconomy, high investments, and savings are the inevitable outcomes. The key to rapid development lies in the continuous transformation and acceleration of endowment structure upgrading according to the comparative advantages. New structural economics also unveils the mystery of high savings rates and of successful economies. However, the high savings rate of these typical examples of economic development in East Asia is criticized by popular thoughts and even falsely blamed as the cause of economic imbalance in the US. In fact, the US also experienced a period of high savings during its fast structural transformation in the 19th century.[①]

Chapter V evaluates structural transformation by degree and effect, and the upgrading of different economies worldwide based on the trajectory of economic transformation and upgrading as set by the 13 typical examples of development post World War II. It seems that the development based on comparative advantage is slow and frustrating for developing countries. Nevertheless, it is, in fact, the best way to capital accumulation as well as factor endowment structure and industrial structure improvement to promote inclusive and sustainable development to an economy by fast iteration. Moreover, it could promote globalization, give latecomers an advantage, introduce technology and industry from more developed countries, and use foreign capital and foreign trade to achieve faster upgrading of industrial structure and economic development than developed countries. In contrast, development against the comparative advantage would miss the development opportunity in globalization and fall into these development traps including, low and middle-income trap. This chapter elaborates on the basic principles and development concepts of new structural economics with a detailed process of the change in world economic structure once again.

Focusing on manufacturing and the change in its employment structure,

---

① Lin Justin Yifu, *Against the Consensus: Reflections on the Great Recession*. Cambridge University Press, 2013.

Chapter VI analyzes the development opportunities based on global economic structural change. As an old Chinese saying goes, “agriculture is for stability, industry is for prosperity, and commerce is for flexibility.” Manufacturing is the engine of global wealth and the pool of employment. Employment is a cornerstone for development and success. Chinese achievements to alleviate poverty comes from the creation numerous job vacancies driven by manufacturing with its comparative advantage, while the arduous struggle of mankind against poverty is rooted in a lack of manufacturing employment. This chapter continues to explore the general laws and characteristics of the change in employment structure for the manufacturing industry with the change of endowment structure worldwide under the guidance of the basic principles of new structural economics and estimates the employment gap. In terms of the basic trend of structural change needed for employment in the manufacturing industry worldwide, the continuous flying geese paradigm is the secret of the East Asian miracle. South Asia and sub-Saharan Africa urgently need to develop labor-intensive manufacturing to alleviate poverty. Middle East, North Africa, and Latin America should transform and upgrade its manufacturing industry to get out of the middle-income trap. Europe and Central Asia should adjust the manufacturing industry against comparative advantage to regain competitive advantage, and high-income economies, like the US, need to continuously innovate and expand into global industry frontiers. Meanwhile, the nature of work would change and the employment structures may also be polarized during the change of world economic structure, which should be addressed to create a more inclusive and egalitarian society. The pattern of difference sequence for global manufacturing is the industrial basis for both North-South cooperation and South-South cooperation. Different from the flying geese paradigm in the past, China becomes the “leading dragon” as with South-South cooperation. The chapter concludes with the example of Japan and Chongqing in China for grasping the opportunity in the transfer of global electronic information industry to prove that all economies in the world could accelerate globalization development with their competitive advantages and the facilitation of government to helping entrepreneurs in a market economy after finding their own comparative advantages.

Chapter VII discusses global infrastructure construction with emphasis laid on the "bottleneck" of transformation and upgrading of economic structures. The "bottleneck" of "hard" and "soft" infrastructure is an obstacle to the transformation and upgrading of economic structure and a "scapegoat" that could be easily taken. Backward infrastructure is indeed the major constraint to economic performance, yet it is by no means an insurmountable obstacle to economic transformation. Economic development and infrastructure construction can be promoted simultaneously with mutual support. According to popular trend of thought, all infrastructure barriers should be removed before launching the dynamic process of economic growth, which is neither realistic nor necessary. The situation of 30 economies with the fastest growth in the past 20 years shows that the quality of a business environment being evaluated by popular indicators seems not so important since the ratings for business environments of most of them are very poor except for Singapore and Malaysia. A more pragmatic approach is to concentrate the limited resources and governance capacity of government on the building of industrial parks, export processing zones, and special economic zones,and implemente one-stop service in the park. Although the overall infrastructure and business environment are not satisfactory, favorable conditions could be created regionally to fully exploit and utilize the potential comparative advantages of the economy, created the conditions for entrepreneurs to promote the rise of competitive industries, and then gradually improve the "hard" and "soft" infrastructure and business environments nationwide. Based on this, this chapter introduces the Chinese experience to gradually improve the infrastructure from parts to a whole. It summarizes the changes made in the construction of such infrastructure as water, power supply, transportation, telecommunications, the Internet, and energy in different regions of the world at different development stages, the G20's global infrastructure initiative, which recognizes the importance of infrastructure, and concludes the differences of developed countries and developing countries in infrastructure construction.

Chapter VIII analyzes the relationship between China and the transformation of the world's economic structure. Contrary to popular prejudices, China's economic rise will not create a dilemma for the world,[①] but will bring continued prosperity to the developed countries as well as development opportunities to the developing countries. China has a unique position in the transformation and upgrading of the global economic structure. The size of China's economy will raise it to be a global leader, yet the overall level of global economic development has great room for improvement and there is still great disparity in the development of different regions within China. As a result of the in-depth coupling of China and the world's economic structure, as well as China's differentiation and globalization go in different directions from those of developed countries and other developing countries. There are the diversity of China's economic links with the world. China shows great strength via its transformation and upgrading of the world economic structure. China is still a global engine of world economic growth. China's industrialization continues to maintain strong momentum. Boasting a tremendously healthy consumption market, China is still the biggest trader and the most attractive region for investment worldwide. China has the largest production capacity and the most powerful infrastructure construction capability. China has become an exporter of net-capital and a major overseas investor. China's unique position and strength in the transformation and upgrading of the world economic structure is the root of the great harmony between China and the world. Based on this, this chapter looks into and compares the economic structure and transformation of China with that seen by developed and other developing countries. Developed countries are still the object for China to use as a model to study. In order to deepen cooperation between China and other different income level economies, it is necessary

① Dani Rodrik, "Making Room for China in the World Economy" , *American Economic Review*, 2010, Vol. 100, No. 2, pp. 89–93.

to take full advantage of China's comparable advantages. Investment in developed countries can promote the transformation and upgrading of economic structure for both China and developed economies, so can "bringing in" investment from developed countries. Meanwhile, China is capable of providing opportunities for developing economies in terms of industrial transfer and infrastructure construction. In this new era, China can build an open economic system facing the world.

Chapter IX expounds on the promotion of the development of the world's economy through the Belt and Road Initiative. It can be seen from the change of world economic structure, and China's position in it, that the Belt and Road Initiative can mutually promote the transformation and upgrading of economic structure in China and other Belt and Road countries. Based on this, this chapter reviews the major progress of the Belt and Road Initiative in the past five years, discussing outbound investment, economic cooperation zones, the effects of trade and investment, transformation and upgrading of enterprises, the internationalization of the Chinese yuan (RMB), and other important aspects. In order to lower the financial risks, it is necessary to improve the rates of returns on investment into infrastructure along the Belt and Road and the patient capital. Finally, this chapter discusses how can the Belt and Road countries and different regions in China become fully engaged and make full use of their comparative advantages from the Belt and Road Initiative. The Belt and Road Initiative is different from the globalization of colonialism which had brought such suffering to the people in the world, and from the globalization of neoliberalism which also failed to bring happiness to the people in the world. It is a new type of inclusive globalization that is conducive to the realization of a community who share the same hope for the future of mankind, [①]characterized by the old Chinese saying "all flowers in full blossom make a beautiful spring."

---

① Liu Weidong, Michael Dunford, Gao Boyang, "Discursive Construction of the Belt and Road Initiative: From Neoliberal to Inclusive Globalization", *Progress in Geography*, 2017, No. 11.

Chapter X summarizes how the "road" of new structural economy will lead to prosperity and stability for the global economy. This chapter provides a series of measures for the new structural economy for promoting the fast, inclusive, and sustainable transformation and upgrading of the economic structure of countries worldwide. While is also including the Growth Identification and Facilitation (GIFF) technical manual of the new structural economy as developed by the United Nations Industrial Development Organization, as well as a set of global inclusive and sustainable transformation indexes for the new structural economics covering nearly 200 economies. We believe that even a country stuck in the trap of poverty for centuries could change its destiny and step on the road to prosperity with fast development and transformation under the guidance of the new structural economy to change development thinking, the government in the market economy to helping entrepreneurs to transform potential comparative advantage into competitive advantage. And so, it is easy to get rid of poverty and realize industrialization and modernization within one or two generations. The first author of the book was born in Taiwan, China in the early 1950s, shortly after the end of World War II when Taiwan was as poor and backward as most regions in Africa. The second author of the book was born in Sichuan, China in the mid-1980s. At that time, the Chinese mainland was as poor and backward as Taiwan, China when the first author was born. The per capita income of mainland China was merely half of the average for sub-Saharan Africa, while Taiwan, China had already developed into an emerging industrialized economy. When we read this book today, China is already an upper middle income economy with a per capita GDP of more than $10,000. The world economic pattern has changed dramatically in just four decades. Such fantastic personal experience assures us that poverty is not a fate. Although there are preconditions for any theory, it is possible for any country, regardless of their starting conditions, to realize inclusive and sustainable development. During the summits marking the 70th anniversary of the United Nations, Chinese President Xi Jinping elaborated on the Chinese solution for world development. "Development, in the final analysis, is the job of individual countries. We Chinese say, 'Eat according to the size your own stomach and dress according to your own figure.' It is, therefore necessary for each country to formulate its own development strategies that fit its strengths and national conditions."

*Demystifying the Chinese Economy* is about the application of the new structural economics theory for analysis of the decline and rising of China. *Demystifying the World Economic Development* is about the application and testing of the new structural economics theory for analysis of the polarization between the rich and poor for countries worldwide, and provides a way for them to achieve common prosperity. Our fundamental goal is to use the least theoretical tools of new structural economics to obtain the most understanding of the change of world economic structure and policy. Therefore, as the supporting reading material, the textbook *Introduction to New Structural Economics* by Justin Lin Yifu and Fu Caihui can help readers gain a more comprehensive understanding of the system of new structural economics.[①] Other monographs can also help readers better understand relevant topics in the book. For example, *China Miracle: Development Strategy and Economic Reform* by Justin Lin Yifu, Cai Fang, and Li Zhou, as well as *Great Industrial Revolution of China* by Wen Yi, provide an in-depth introduction to the economy in China. *Economic Development and Transition: Thought, Strategy, and Viability* by Justin Lin Yifu contains an in-depth introduction to the development and transformation of developing countries. *Going Beyond Aid:Development Cooperation for Structural Transformation* by Justin Lin Yifu and Wang Yan provides an in-depth exploration into the South-South cooperation[②]. *Beating the Odds: Jump-Starting Developing Countries* by Justin Lin Yifu and Célestin Monga provides an in-depth analysis of the promotion of structural transformation and development in economies

---

① Lin Justin Yifu, Fu Caihui, *Introduction to New Structural Economics* (1st half and 2nd half). Higher Education Press, 2019.

② Lin Justin Yifu, Wang Yan, *Going Beyond Aid: Development Cooperation for Structural Transformation*. Cambridge University Press, 2016.

full of institutional distortions[1]. *The Quest for Prosperity: How Developing Economies Can Take Off* by Justin Lin Yifu provides an introduction to the policies of the new structural economics in simple language[2]. *The Oxford Handbook of Africa and Economics* by Justin Lin Yifu contains a detailed discussion on developing economies in Africa[3]. *New Structural Economics for Less Advanced Countries*[4] and *New Structural Policy in An Open Market Economy*[5] by Justin Lin Yifu and Alojzy Z. Nowak discusses the development policies of transition economies reaching high-income levels like Poland. *Industrial Policy Revolution* by Justin Lin Yifu and Joseph E. Stiglitz provides detailed discussion on industrial policies.[6] *The Oxford Handbook of Structural Transformation* by Justin Lin Yifu and Célestin Monga provides detailed material on the transformation of economic structure.[7] Although this book contains the most recent data sets and cases, the speed of economic structural change in China and worldwide is so dazzling that readers should keep up with the current events to learn current information.

Apart from the previously mentioned works, our collaborators, and supporters of past research, the book also absorbs the achievements and materials of researches relevant to the new structural economics. I'd like to express my gratitude to all like-minded friends. Their contribution is theirs, but our deficiency is ours. For example, further case studies in Chapter 3 on

---

① Lin Justin Yifu, Célestin Monga, *Beating the Odds*: *Jump-Starting Developing Countries*. Princeton University Press, 2017.

② Lin Justin Yifu, *The Quest for Prosperity: How Developing Economies Can Take Off*. Princeton University Press, 2012.

③ Lin Justin Yifu, Célestin Monga, *The Oxford Handbook of Africa and Economics (I/II)*. Oxford University Press, 2015.

④ Lin Justin Yifu, Alojzy Z. Nowak, *New Structural Economics for Less Advanced Countries*. University of Warsaw Faculty of Management Press, 2017.

⑤ Lin Justin Yifu, Alojzy Z. Nowak, *New Structural Policy in An Open Market Economy*. University of Warsaw Faculty of Management Press, 2019.

⑥ Joseph E. Stiglitz, Justin Yifu Lin, *Industrial Policy Revolution (I/II)*. Palgrave Macmillan, 2013.

⑦ Lin Justin Yifu, Célestin Monga, *The Oxford Handbook of Structural Transformation*. Oxford University Press, 2019.

the history of the Anglo-American Industrial Revolution and in Chapter 4 on a tool we developed to track the trajectory of structural change (Fu-Lin Map) come from the work of Professor Wen Yi, and the empirical research on the impact of the "Belt and Road" initiative on enterprise transformation and upgrading in Chapter 9 comes from the work of Dr. Wang Guijun, and some examples in Chapters 9 and 10 of the application of the Growth Identification and Facilitation Framework (GIFF) in new structural economics come from the work of colleagues such as Professor Liu Wenge, Dr. Sun Jin and Dr. Zhao Qiu yun, and so on. In May 2017, the prototype of the book—*The Road to Structural Transformation and Upgrading of the World Economy*—was released as the flagship report of the think tank, with hundreds of participants from all walks of life at home and abroad, their enthusiasm gave us the impetus to build on this foundation for further research. Special thanks also to the teachers and students, the book as a monograph of the nature of the further improvement of the textbook is derived from their suggestions. In April 2019, at a workshop on the first draft of this book, the comments and suggestions from the teachers and students from dozens of sister colleges and universities at home and abroad were particularly valuable, in particular, Professor Liu Weidong of Chinese Academy of Sciences, Professor Fan Zhiyong of Renmin University of China, Professor Liu Wenge of Liaoning University, Professor Han Yonghui of Guangdong University of Foreign Studies, Professor Wang Yong of Peking University and other colleagues have put forward specific proposals for revision. Professor Zheng Feihu of the Beijing Normal University also offers helpful advice on teaching applications. Many of his colleagues at the Higher Education Press, especially editor Zhao Peng, have put a lot of work into the book. And thank you! You are also welcome to continue to send any comments and suggestions to fucaihui@nsd.pku.edu.cn for further improvement in the next edition.

Finally, we are also very much looking forward to the introduction of the course "Demystifying the World Economic Development" , which will be used as the textbook for an undergraduate program of new structural economics at Peking University (Justin Lin Yifu Program), to discuss with teachers, students and friends from all walks of life the development of the world economy and the globalization of China in the new era from the perspective of new structural economics. Just as the book was about to be finalized, a new global epidemic broke out (COVID-19). The world is one, and there is no reason for any of us not to get to know her and make her better!

Lin Yifu, Fu Caihui
At Peking University
Beijing, China
Spring, 2020

# 目录
# Contents

## 第1章 剧变的年代
## Chapter I The Age of Drastic Changes

# 第2章 经济结构转型升级是发展的关键

# Chapter II Transformation and Upgrading of Economic Structure is the Key to Development

# 第3章 追踪世界经济结构转型升级的轨迹

# Chapter III Tracing the Trajectory of the Transformation and Upgrading of the World Economic Structure

## 第4章 寻找经济结构转型升级路径的典范

## Chapter IV Searching for Typical Examples of Economic Structural Transformation and Upgrading

# 第5章 监测世界经济结构变迁的轨迹

# Chapter V Monitoring the Trajectory of Global Economic Structural Transformation

## 第 6 章 世界经济结构转型升级中的机遇

## Chapter VI Opportunities in Global Economic Structural Transformation and Upgrading

## 第7章 克服世界经济结构转型升级的瓶颈

## Chapter VII Breaking the “Bottleneck” to Global Economic Structural Transformation and Upgrading

# 第8章 世界经济结构转型升级中的中国

# Chapter VIII China in the Global Economic Structural Transformation and Upgrading

# 第9章 "一带一路"助推世界经济发展
# Chapter IX Promotion of Global Economic Development through the Belt and Road Initiative

# 第10章 世界经济的繁荣稳定包容之路

# Chapter X The Road to Prosperity, Stability, and Inclusiveness in the World Economy

第 1 章

# 剧变的年代

清代吴敬梓的《儒林外史》是中国古代讽刺小说的高峰，该书第四十六回有这么一句话："大先生，'三十年河东，三十年河西'！就像三十年前，你二位府上何等优势，我是亲眼看见的。"后来"三十年河东，三十年河西"成为形容世事盛衰兴替、感叹世事变化无常的俗语。

《儒林外史》成书于1750年前后，恰逢中西方大分流之际："康乾盛世"只不过是深陷马尔萨斯陷阱的回光返照（参见第2章第2小节），而英国因为爆发了工业革命而成为统治世界的"日不落帝国"（参见第3章第2小节）。第二次世界大战不但使得很多殖民地摆脱了英国的统治，而且也击垮了这个不可一世的"日不落帝国"。1944年7月，盟国代表在美国新罕布什尔州布雷顿森林会晤，确立了第二次世界大战后（简称战后）西方国家唯美国马首是瞻的国际经济秩序——"布雷顿森林体系"。这反映了战后美国的超级经济实力。按1990年国际元的购买力平价计算，1950年，美国的国内生产总值（GDP）占全球的比重约为1/4。战后欧洲和日本的复兴，虽然冲击了美国的霸主地位，但也加速了西方国家集团在冷战中的胜利，在苏联解体后将美国送上了并不稳固的世界秩序的顶点。即便如此，到20世纪70年代就连一场石油危机也无法让任何一个发达国家独善其身。1975年11月，为共同研究世界经济形势、协调各国政策及重振西方经济，法、美、德、日、英、意六国领导人在法国巴黎郊外的朗布依埃举行了首次最高级经济会议。1976年6月，六国领导人在波多黎各首府圣胡安举行第二次会议，加拿大应邀与会，形成七国集团（G7）。会议每年一次轮流在各成员国召开，G7峰会宣告诞生。G7集团给人的第一印象是"富人"俱乐部。当年七国集团的GDP占全球的比重高达63.49%。以G7为首的西方发达国家主宰了全球的经济版图和治理规则以及发展思想。

在G7峰会诞生的40年后，2016年9月在中国杭州召开了二十国集团（G20）峰会。中国国家主席习近平在G20峰会上就全球的发展思想、发展动力以及治理规则发出了新的倡议：第一，创新发展方式。各国要创新发展理念、政策、方式，重视基础设施建设对经济的拉动效应，将互联互通作为核心议题，中国支持二十国集团成立全球基础设施中心，支持世界银行成立全球基础设施基金，并将通过建设丝绸之路经济带、21世纪海上丝绸之路、亚洲基础设施投资银行、丝路基金等途径，为全球基础设施投资做出贡献。第二，建设开放型世界经济。各国要维护多边贸易体制，构建互利共赢的全球价值链，培育全球大市场，反对贸易和投资保护主义，推动多哈回合谈判。第三，完善全球经济治理。各国要致力于建设公平公正、包容有序的国际金融体系，提高新兴市场国家和发展中国家的代表性及发言权，确保各国在国际经济合作中权利平等、机会平等、规则平等。

2015年3月28日，中国发布了《推动共建丝绸之路经济带和21世纪海上丝绸之路的愿景与行动》（以下简称《愿景与行动》），正式启动了具有划时代意义的"一带一路"倡议。

《愿景与行动》指出，共建“一带一路”致力于亚欧非大陆及附近海洋的互联互通，建立和加强沿线各国互联互通伙伴关系，构建全方位、多层次、复合型的互联互通网络，实现沿线各国多元、自主、平衡、可持续的发展。“一带一路”的互联互通项目将推动沿线各国发展战略的对接与耦合，发掘区域内市场的潜力，促进投资和消费，创造需求和就业，增进沿线各国人民的人文交流与文明互鉴，让各国人民相逢相知、互信互敬，共享和谐、安宁、富裕的生活。当前，中国经济和世界经济高度关联。中国将一以贯之地坚持对外开放的基本国策，构建全方位开放新格局，深度融入世界经济体系。推进“一带一路”建设既是中国扩大和深化对外开放的需要，也是加强和亚欧非及世界各国互利合作的需要，中国愿意在力所能及的范围内承担更多的责任义务，为人类的和平发展做出更大的贡献。2017年5月在北京举办的“一带一路”国际合作高峰论坛标志着这一影响全球的合作倡议向纵深方向推进。2019年4月又在北京举办了第二届高峰论坛。我们将在第9章讨论“一带一路”如何促进世界经济发展。

2016年年底，中国外交部部长王毅在接受《人民日报》记者专访时指出：“当今世界正面临开放与保守、合作与封闭、变革与守旧的重要抉择。在此形势下，我们在以习近平同志为核心的党中央坚强领导下，攻坚克难、开拓进取，在全球治理变局中引领方向，在国际形势乱象中把握大局，在激烈复杂博弈中维护利益，在世界经济转型中助力发展，开创了中国特色大国外交全面推进的新局面。中国正在以更为成熟、稳健的步伐，走近世界舞台中央，成为乱局中的稳定器、变局中的正能量。”历史就这样在逐步改写，世界经济格局将会出现千年未有之大变局。

# 1.1

# 规则在更换

## 1.1.1 从G1到G7

第二次世界大战让美国取代曾经的“日不落大英帝国”成为世界的头号强国（第3章将介绍让英美成为世界强国的工业化历程）。为避免诱导两次世界大战的经济纷争再次发生，1944年7月，盟国代表在美国新罕布什尔州布雷顿森林会晤，确立了以美元为中心、美元和黄金挂钩、各国货币和美元挂钩的国际货币体系，即布雷顿森林货币体系（Bretton Woods system）。①“布雷顿森林体系”建立了国际货币基金组织（IMF）和世界银行（WB）两大国际金融机构。前者负责向成员国提供短期资金借贷，目的是保障国际货币体系的稳定；后者提供中长期信贷来促进成员国经济复苏。关税总协定（WTO的前身）作为1944年布雷顿森林会议的补充，连同布雷顿森林会议通过的各项协定，统称为“布雷顿森林体系”，构成以美国为首的西方发达经济体在战后世界经济秩序的核心内容，我们不妨称之为“G1”。②

美国的好景不长。1973年，在由欧佩克引发的石油危机的冲击下，美元和黄金脱钩，布雷顿森林体系土崩瓦解，美国和依赖石油的主要工业国家出现了宏观经济学中称为“滞胀”的高通货膨胀和高失业率的现象，描述通货膨胀与失业之间存在权衡取舍的菲利普斯曲线因此折断。凯恩斯宏观经济学也因此被20世纪70年代由芝加哥大学经济学家提出的理性预期学派取而代之。石油危机对美国造成了严重影响，如表1.1所示。欧洲也不例外，这一时期标志

① 布雷顿森林会晤其实审视了两个国际货币体系计划，即美元和黄金挂钩、各国货币和美元挂钩的“怀特计划”（美国版）和以与一篮子商品价值挂钩的“班柯”为国际货币的“凯恩斯计划”（英国版）。“怀特计划”和“凯恩斯计划”的目标基本相同，即以设立国际金融机构、稳定汇率、扩大国际贸易、规避诱导两次世界大战的经济金融冲突，但运营方式有所不同。毫不奇怪，当然是美国版胜出。由于美国在两次世界大战后登上了资本主义世界盟主地位，美元的国际地位因其国际黄金储备的实力得到稳固，双方于1944年4月达成了反映“怀特计划”的“关于设立国际货币基金的专家共同声明”。建立布雷顿森林体系的关键人物是美国财政部前助理部长哈里·怀特，凭借战后美国拥有全球3/4黄金储备和强大军事实力的大国地位，他力主强化美元地位的提议力挫英国代表团团长、宏观经济学之父凯恩斯，“怀特计划”成为布雷顿森林会议最后通过决议的蓝本。这鲜活地说明了经济实力是塑造规则的根本性力量，而不见得是当时的理论权威。

② 可参考：本·斯泰尔，《布雷顿森林货币战：美元如何统治世界》，机械工业出版社，2014年版。

着欧洲高失业的开始。[①]为了避免重蹈20世纪30年代经济大萧条的覆辙，西方发达国家的领导人都急于寻找平息危机的出路，于是产生了本章开篇提到的G7集团。其实，G7取代以美国为中心的国际治理也反映了美国在发达国家中霸主地位的衰落，这源于欧洲和日本战后的迅速复兴。例如，1972年日本超过德国成为全球第二大经济体，人均GDP已达美国的67.3%。1979年，哈佛大学教授傅高义出版《日本第一：对美国的启示》[②]，加剧了日本与美国的竞争，于是1985年就出现了广场协议（Plaza Accord）。[③]1991年欧盟的成立又进一步加剧了欧洲国家与美国的竞争。

表1.1 石油危机与美国的滞胀

| 年份 | 石油价格变动（%） | 通货膨胀率（CPI）（%） | 失业率（%） |
|---|---|---|---|
| 1973 | 11.0 | 6.2 | 4.9 |
| 1974 | 68.0 | 11 | 5.6 |
| 1975 | 16.0 | 9.1 | 8.5 |
| 1976 | 3.3 | 5.8 | 7.7 |
| 1977 | 8.1 | 6.5 | 7.1 |
| 1978 | 9.4 | 7.7 | 6.1 |
| 1979 | 25.4 | 11.3 | 5.8 |
| 1980 | 47.8 | 13.5 | 7.0 |
| 1981 | 44.4 | 10.3 | 7.5 |
| 1982 | −8.7 | 6.1 | 9.5 |
| 1983 | −7.1 | 3.2 | 9.5 |
| 1984 | −1.7 | 4.3 | 7.4 |
| 1985 | −7.5 | 3.6 | 7.1 |
| 1986 | −44.5 | 1.9 | 6.9 |
| 1987 | 18.3 | 3.6 | 6.1 |

资料来源：N.格里高利·曼昆，《宏观经济学》，中国人民大学出版社，2018年版，第235页。

① 当今，石油价格的波动对发达国家宏观经济波动的影响已经没有20世纪70年代那么严重了，从新结构经济学的角度来讲，其主要原因是欧美发达国家发生了进一步的产业转型升级，从依赖石油的工业转型到了服务业，与此同时节能技术的进步也使得GDP的单位能耗大幅度下降。这也意味着，其实在石油危机的20世纪70年代之前，石油价格的波动也在发达国家的经济波动中起到了主要作用（James D. Hamilton, “Oil and the Macroeconomy since World War II”, *Journal of Political Economy,* 1983, Vol. 91, pp.228−248.）。按此道理，石油危机也对当时采取重工业赶超战略，原来就外汇储备不足的发展中经济体产生了严重影响，为后来的债务危机埋下隐患。

② Ezra F. Vogel, *Japan As Number One: Lessons for America.* Harper Colophon, 1979（中文版可参考：傅高义，《日本第一：对美国的启示》，谷英、张柯、丹柳译，上海译文出版社，2016年版。）

③ 广场协议签订后，日元大幅升值，泡沫急剧扩大，最终由于房地产泡沫的破灭造成了经济长期停滞。对广场协议的一项回顾性研究可参考：Frankel, Jeffrey A., “The Plaza Accord, 30 Years Later (December 2015)”, *NBER Working Paper NO. w21813*。

20世纪70年代美国霸主地位逐渐衰落之后，发达国家用一种相互协调形式的“软体制”替代“布雷顿森林体系”时代的“硬体制”来为国际经济金融提供秩序。然而，G7不但治理能力不足，而且是一个封闭的富国俱乐部，不但无法为全球经济金融起到“稳定器”的作用，而且还与发展中经济体的利益存在冲突，引发了如表1.2所示的诸多区域性金融危机。①即便如此，G7至今依然是发达经济体内部“争吵的房间”，不时也会“以邻为壑”。

表1.2 G7治理下全球主要的区域性金融危机

| 金融危机 | 时间 | 受影响的主要国家和地区 |
|---|---|---|
| 拉美债务危机 | 1982—1983年 | 集中在拉美地区 |
| 英镑危机 | 1992年9月 | 英国、德国、意大利、芬兰、法国 |
| 墨西哥金融危机 | 1994年12月—1995年3月 | 墨西哥 |
| 东亚金融危机 | 1997年7月—1998年2月 | 泰国、菲律宾、印度尼西亚、马来西亚、新加坡、日本、韩国、中国香港、中国台湾 |
| 俄罗斯金融危机 | 1997年10月—1998年8月 | 俄罗斯，波及欧美、拉美等地区 |
| 阿根廷金融危机 | 2001年年底 | 阿根廷、乌拉圭、巴西 |

资料来源：崔志楠和邢悦（2011）。

## 1.1.2 从G7到G20

1997年东亚金融危机爆发，它是20世纪末最严峻的一场金融危机，充分暴露了G7治理下的全球经济金融治理体系的弊端，再也无法将新兴经济体排除在外了，因此出现了“G7时代”全球经济金融治理体系改革的第一波浪潮。②首先，1991年开始就应邀参加G7首脑峰会的部分会议的俄罗斯，在1997年被接纳为成员国，正式成立了八国集团。同时，1999年6月，为防止类似亚洲金融风暴的重演，让有关国家就国际经济、货币政策举行非正式对话，以利于国际金融和货币体系的稳定，G20财长会议在德国柏林成立。后于2008年国际金融危机爆发后在华盛顿举办了第一届G20峰会，属于非正式对话的一种机制，由原8国集团以及其余12个重要经济体组成（中国、阿根廷、澳大利亚、巴西、加拿大、法国、德国、印度、印度尼西亚、意大利、日本、韩国、墨西哥、沙特阿拉伯、南非、土耳其、英国、美国、俄罗斯以及欧盟）。其宗旨是

① 崔志楠、邢悦，“从‘G7时代’到‘G20时代’——国际金融治理机制的变迁”，《世界经济与政治》，2011年第1期，第134–154页。

② Safeguarding Prosperity in a Global Financial System: The Future International Financial Architecture, Council on Foreign Relations Task Force. Carla Hills, Peter Peterson. 1999.

为推动已工业化的发达国家和新兴市场国家之间就实质性问题进行开放及富有建设性的讨论和研究，以寻求合作并促进国际金融稳定和经济的持续增长。按照以往惯例，国际货币基金组织与世界银行等国际发展机构列席该组织的会议。G20成员涵盖面广，代表性强，人口占全球人口的67%，国土面积占全球的60%，国内生产总值占全球的90%，贸易额占全球的80%，构成兼顾了发达国家和发展中国家以及不同地域利益平衡。

2008年由美国引爆的金融危机是“大萧条”以来最严峻的全球金融危机，G20部长会议全面升级为首脑会议以加速各国协调来应对危机。甚至在2009—2010年每年举行两次G20峰会，这足以说明此次全球金融危机对全球治理体系变革的紧迫性。此后，G20全面取代G8，全球治理开始从“西方治理”向“西方和非西方共同治理”转变。[①]不过，这种全球性制度变迁并非一帆风顺。在G20创建前后，G7仍显示出抵制变革的巨大“惰性”。非G7国家目前正通过议题置换、集团化等方式谋求在G20内部发展中国家的更大影响力，以平衡G7。然而，G7向G20转变的根本原因在于“新兴经济体”的崛起及由此引发的世界经济结构变迁（见1.2小节）。[②]因此，全球治理规则更换势不可当。

---

① G20目前依然属于非正式论坛，旨在促进工业化国家和新兴市场国家就国际经济、货币政策和金融体系的重要问题开展富有建设性和开放性的对话，并通过对话，为有关实质问题的讨论和协商奠定广泛基础，以寻求合作并推动国际金融体制的改革，加强国际金融体系架构，促进经济的稳定和持续增长。此外，G20还为处于不同发展阶段的主要国家提供了一个共商当前国际经济问题的平台。同时，G20还致力于建立全球公认的标准，如在透明的财政政策、反洗钱和反恐怖融资等领域率先建立统一标准。

② 李因才，“结构变迁与治理制度的演化:从G7到G20”，《当代世界社会主义问题》，2011年第4期；Dale W. Jorgenson; Khuong Minh Vu, “The emergence of the new economic order: Growth in the G7 and the G20” , *Journal of Policy Modeling*, 2013, Vol.35, pp. 389–399。

# 1.2

# 版图在更替

## 1.2.1 多元世界经济格局的形成："1+100"的历史意义

据世界银行发布的统计报告，2015年全球GDP总量达74万亿美元。虽然美国依然雄踞世界第一的经济霸主地位，以官方汇率计算，经济总量占世界的比重高达24.32%，但是整个世界经济结构的格局在不断更替。[①]1972年，日本超过德国成为世界第二大经济体，并一直延续至2009年。从2010年开始，中国取代日本成为全球第二大经济体。2015年，中国GDP总量占全球的比重为14.84%；排名第三、第四的国家是日本、德国，占比分别为5.91%、4.54%。如图1.1所示，从各大洲的排名看，当前亚洲正开始处于领先地位，占全球GDP的33.84%。亚洲的重心又在东亚，中国、日本和韩国的GDP之和几乎与美国一样多，"东亚奇迹"当之无愧，绝非"纸老虎"。[②]排名第二、第三的区域是北美和欧洲，GDP分别占比27.95%、21.37%。前三大洲的GDP占据全球约83%的份额。受困于中等收入陷阱和贫困陷阱之中，南美洲和非洲当前依然未能在全球经济中占据更大比重。南美洲四大经济体中，巴西、阿根廷、委内瑞拉和哥伦比亚的GDP之和只占全球GDP的4%，而非洲三大国家南非、埃及和尼日利亚的GDP之和只占1.5%。超过100个太小而无法单独显示的经济体被集中在一起，成为"世界其他地区"，其GDP正好是美中之间的差距，我们不妨称之为"1+100"。在中国强劲的带领下，新兴经济体、欠发达的发展中经济体以及亚非拉经济体的经济体量日益在加速，正在改写过去一直由欧美发达经济体主导的世界经济版图。

① 如果按购买力平价（PPP）衡量的GDP（2011年不变价国际元），根据世界银行的数据，中国占全球的比重在2013年就已经超过美国，2017年中国的比重为18.21%，美国为15.16%。

② 诺贝尔经济学奖得主保罗·克鲁格曼（Paul Krugman）于1994年在国际上甚有影响的《外交》杂志上的文章指出，东亚的经济增长完全可以用要素投入的增加来解释，全要素生产率没有贡献，因此只是不堪一击的"纸老虎"。

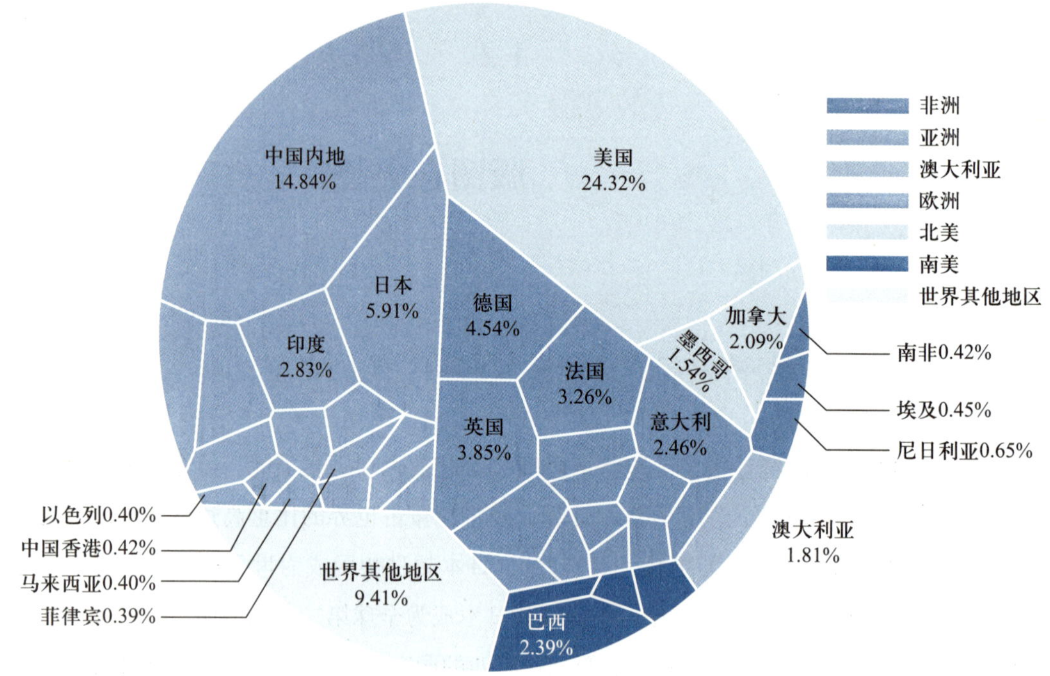


**图1.1 2015年世界各国、各地区GDP占比**

资料来源：世界银行报告。

### 1.2.2 新兴经济体的崛起：新兴经济体对老牌工业强国经济总量的超越

世界经济格局的第一个重大变化是新兴经济体的崛起。如图1.2所示，2012年，按照2011年不变价的购买力平价计算的经济总量（GDP），中国、俄罗斯、印度、巴西四个金砖国家加上墨西哥、印度尼西亚和土耳其七个新兴经济体（N7），已经超过G7集团的七个老牌工业强国。在21世纪尤其是2008年全球金融危机之后，N7以超过G7的增长势头在增长，这意味着已经更变的全球经济版图不会再逆转。如图1.3所示，2013—2017年这五年间N7比G7的人均GDP增长率平均高出1.86个百分点。与此同时，新兴经济体依然处于中等偏上的收入阶段，具备充足的后来者优势，增长空间巨大。如图1.4所示，2017年N7的平均人均GDP为7 805美元，只有G7的18.36%。

正如G7不能代表所有的发达经济体一样（目前一般以OECD国家概括），N7也不能完全概括新兴经济体。一些学者提出了E30的概念扩大了新兴经济体的数量，包括亚洲的中国、印度、印度尼西亚、伊朗、哈萨克斯坦、马来西亚、巴基斯坦、菲律宾、沙特阿拉伯、泰国、土耳其、乌兹别克斯坦、越南，非洲的埃及、加纳、摩洛哥、南非、突尼斯，拉丁美洲

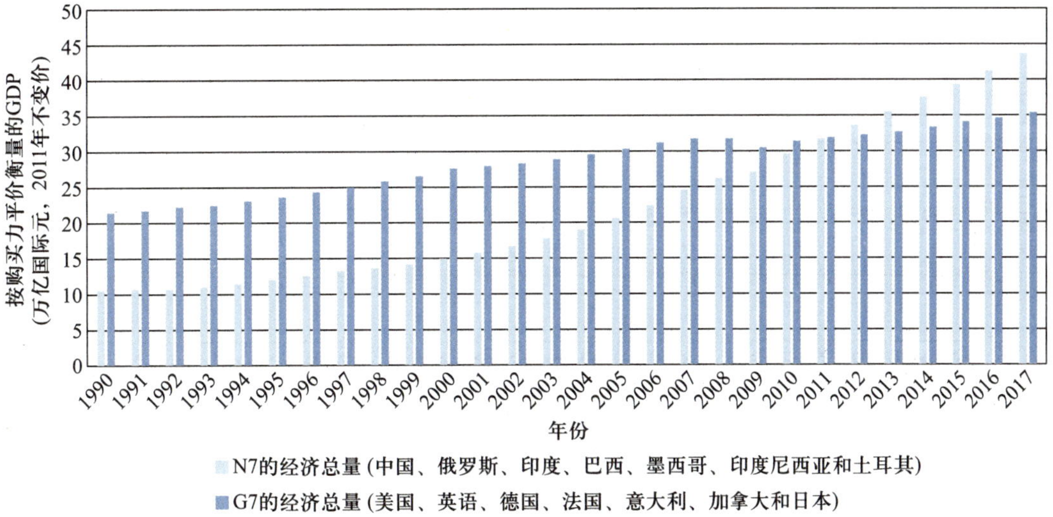


**图1.2 新兴经济体的崛起：新兴经济体与老牌工业强国的经济总量比较**

注：图中数据是按购买力平价衡量的GDP（2011年不变价国际元）。

资料来源：世界银行。

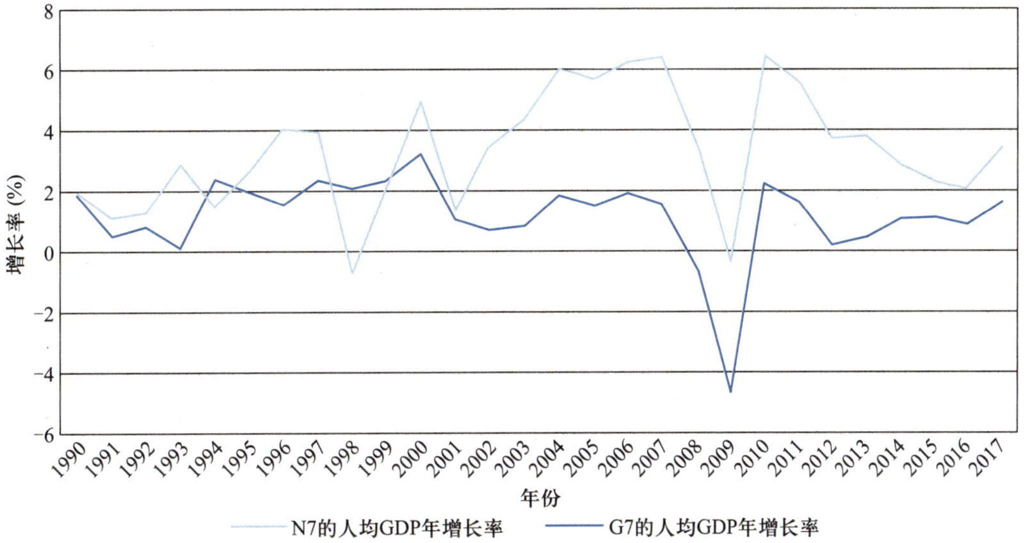


**图1.3 新兴经济体的崛起：新兴经济体与老牌工业强国的经济增长率比较**

注：图中数据是基于不变价本币的人均GDP年增长率，七个经济体的算术平均。

资料来源：世界银行。

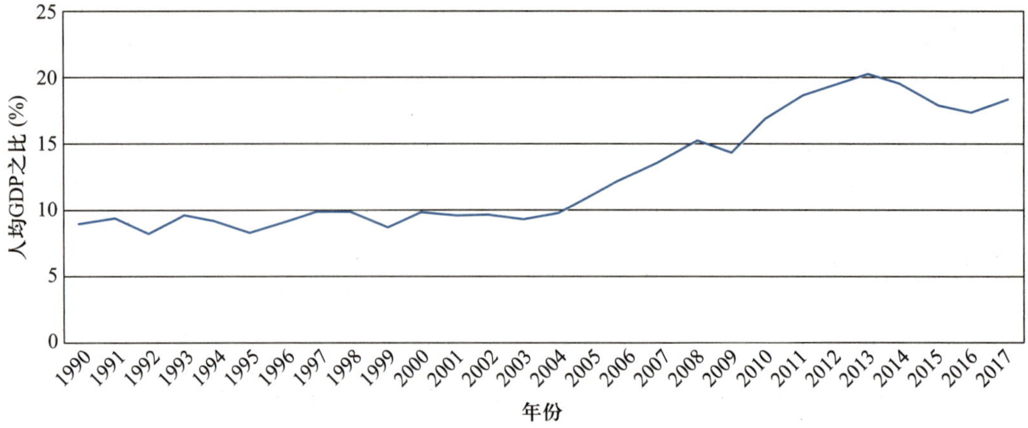


**图1.4 新兴经济体的后来者优势：新兴经济体与老牌工业强国的人均GDP比较**

注：图中数据是基于现价美元的人均GDP，7个经济体的算术平均。

资料来源：世界银行。

的阿根廷、巴西、智利、哥伦比亚、多米尼加、厄瓜多尔、危地马拉、墨西哥、秘鲁，欧洲的波兰、罗马尼亚、俄罗斯。①如表1.3所示，这30个新兴经济体与34个发达经济体的经济体量约占全球的九成；在2008年全球金融危机之后，这30个新兴经济体的体量超过了34个发达经济体的体量，2015年前者全球占比超过了后者约6个百分点。2008年全球金融危机之后，发达经济体增长疲软，新兴经济体成为全球经济增长的引擎。如表1.4所示，2015年34个发达经济体对全球经济增长的贡献率约31%，而30个新兴经济体的贡献率将近60%。这里可以鲜明地看到，始于2008年的全球金融危机是上述全球经济格局历史性变动的标志性事件。

表1.3 近20年来不同类型国家（地区）按购买力平价计算的GDP全球占比变迁（%）

| 不同类型国家（地区） | 1998—2002年 | 2003—2007年 | 2008—2012年 | 2013年 | 2011年 | 2015年 |
|---|---|---|---|---|---|---|
| 发达国家(34) | 55.37 | 51.23 | 45.02 | 42.10 | 41.48 | 41.06 |
| 新兴市场国家（E30) | 35.34 | 38.96 | 44.60 | 47.39 | 48.03 | 47.31 |
| 亚洲(13) | 20.96 | 24.53 | 30.02 | 33.02 | 33.95 | 33.69 |
| 非洲(5) | 1.91 | 1.92 | 2.00 | 1.98 | 1.95 | 1.95 |
| 拉丁美洲(9) | 7.96 | 7.55 | 7.58 | 7.57 | 7.40 | 7.17 |
| 欧洲（3） | 4.51 | 4.96 | 5.00 | 4.82 | 4.73 | 4.50 |
| 其他发展中国家(119) | 7.60 | 8.11 | 8.58 | 8.60 | 8.44 | 7.86 |

资料来源：胡必亮等（2018）。

① 胡必亮、唐幸、殷琳、刘倩，"新兴市场国家的综合测度与发展前景"，《中国社会科学》，2018年第10期，第59-85页。

表1.4 近20年来不同类型国家（地区）按购买力平价计算的GDP增量对全球GDP增量的贡献率（%）

| 不同类型国家（地区） | 1998—2002年 | 2003—2007年 | 2008—2012年 | 2013年 | 2014年 | 2015年 |
|---|---|---|---|---|---|---|
| 发达国家(34) | 51.72 | 35.92 | 0.78 | 32.78 | 27.29 | 31.33 |
| 新兴市场国家（E30） | 38.14 | 52.16 | 87.52 | 55.60 | 62.67 | 58.93 |
| 亚洲(13) | 27.42 | 36.76 | 74.05 | 49.29 | 51.79 | 57.14 |
| 非洲(5) | 2.10 | 1.96 | 2.73 | 1.70 | 1.53 | 1.93 |
| 拉丁美洲(9) | 5.16 | 7.36 | 6.14 | 6.69 | 4.74 | 0.28 |
| 欧洲（3） | 3.46 | 6.08 | 4.60 | −2.08 | 4.61 | −0.42 |
| 其他发展中国家(119) | 7.95 | 9.79 | 9.59 | 9.65 | 7.70 | 6.74 |

资料来源：胡必亮等（2018）。

### 1.2.3 第三世界[①]的崛起：中低收入经济体对高收入经济体经济总量的追赶

世界经济格局的第二个重大变化是第三世界的崛起。尽管在工业革命之后，发达经济体与低收入经济体之间出现了长期的大分化[②]，但是在新千年之后，中低收入经济体整体上开启了如图1.5所示的快速增长之路。如图1.6所示，2013年按照2011年不变价的购买力平价计算的经济总量（GDP），中等收入国家已经超过了高收入国家。战后，广大发展中国家受到不当的以追赶发达国家产业结构为主要目标的结构主义发展思潮的引导，采取了错误的赶超战略，发展违反比较优势的资本密集型现代化大产业，在开放竞争的市场中企业没有自生能力，为了把这样的产业建立起来，导致系统性的经济体制扭曲，经济效率低下，增长停滞，危机不断。如图1.7所示，在20世纪60—80年代发展中经济体的人均收入水平与高收入国家的差距并没有缩小。80年代以后发展中国家纷纷放弃了结构主义的政策框架，以克服政府失灵、建立完善的市场经济体系为主要内容的“新自由主义”为指导，进行了结构性改革，但是，大多数发展中经济体遭遇了“迷失的二十年”，经济增长率比在结构主义时低，危机

① 第三世界（the third world）泛指全世界的欠发达经济体。1973年9月，不结盟国家在阿尔及尔通过的《政治宣言》中正式使用了“第三世界”这个概念。毛泽东在1974年2月22日同赞比亚共和国总统卡翁达的谈话中曾提出：“我看美国、苏联是第一世界。中间派，日本、欧洲、澳大利亚、加拿大，是第二世界。……亚洲除了日本，都是第三世界。整个非洲都是第三世界，拉丁美洲也是第三世界。”

② Lant Pritchett, “Divergence, Big Time”, *Journal of Economic Perspectives*, 1997, Vol.11, No.3, pp.3–17.

发生的频率比在结构主义时高。如图1.7所示，在20世纪80年代到20世纪末，发展中经济体的人均收入水平与高收入国家的差距不但没有缩小反而在扩大。战后，韩国以及中国台湾等极少数未按照主流发展经济学理论来制定发展政策的经济体却大获成功，从低收入经济体进入高收入经济体行列。中国大陆、越南等极少数未按照“新自由主义”进行改革的经济体也大获成功，通过快速的经济增长走出了贫困陷阱。得益于新千年对第一波结构主义发展思潮和第二波新自由主义发展思潮的反思，广大发展中经济体逐步调整发展战略，渐进开启了动态经济增长之路。①相信未来广大低收入经济体在吸取了经验教训之后，在正确的发展和转型战略指引下，充分发挥各自的比较优势利用后来者优势（如图1.7所示，2017年即便是中高等收入经济体的人均GDP也只有高收入经济体的20.89%），积极把握世界经济结构变迁中的机遇（第6章将以制造业及其就业结构变迁为例阐述这一机遇），积极有为地消除各自面临的经济结构转型升级瓶颈（第7章将以软硬基础设施瓶颈为例阐述这一瓶颈），就会逐步实现对高收入经济体的追赶。

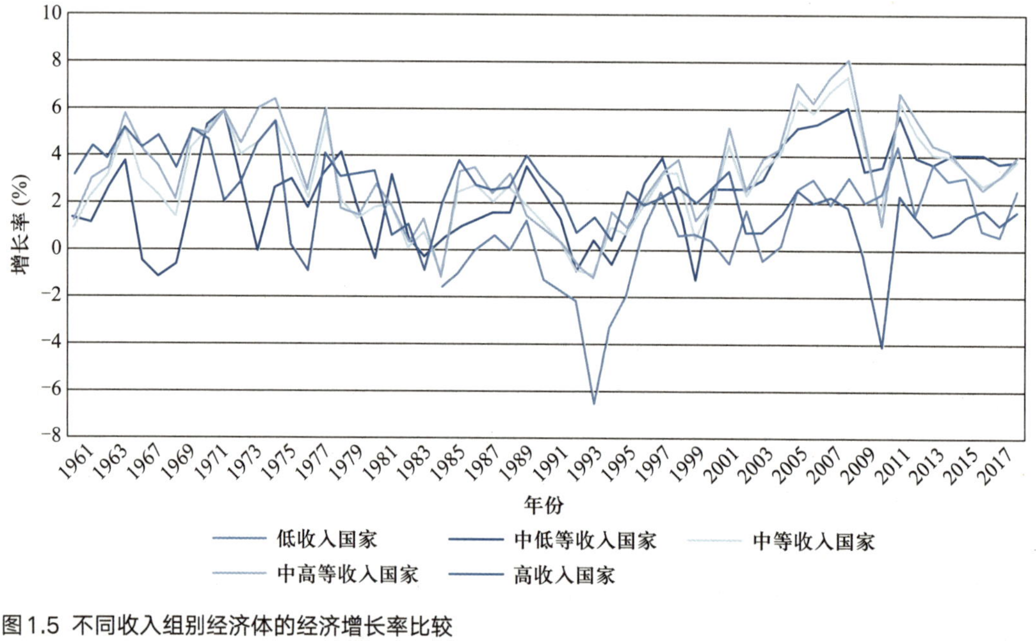


图1.5 不同收入组别经济体的经济增长率比较

注：图中数据是基于不变价本币的人均GDP年增长率。

资料来源：世界银行。

① 关于战后发展中经济体的经济发展与转型的新结构经济学理论研究可参考：林毅夫，《经济发展与转型：思潮、战略与自生能力》，北京大学出版社，2008年版（英文版Lin Justin Yifu, *Economic Development and Transition: Thought, Strategy and Viability*. Cambridge University Press, 2009）。

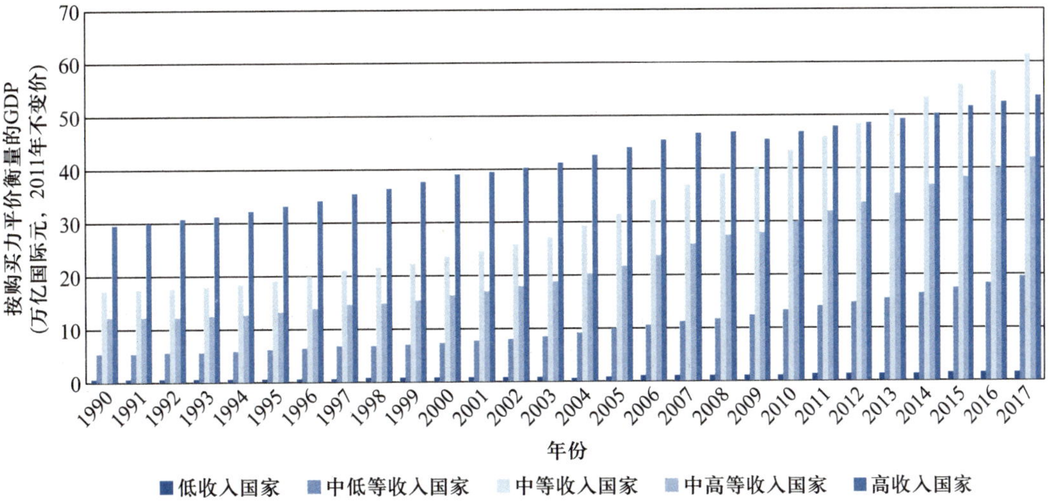


**图1.6 第三世界的崛起：高收入国家、中等收入国家与低收入国家的经济总量比较**

注：图中数据是按购买力平价（PPP）衡量的GDP（2011年不变价国际元）。

资料来源：世界银行。

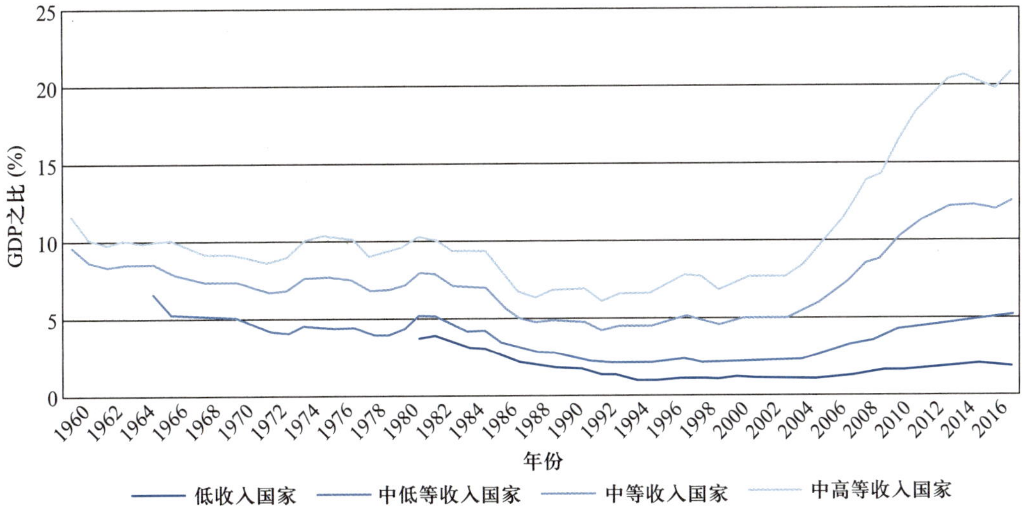


**图1.7 发展中经济体的后来者优势：发展中国家与高收入国家的人均GDP之比**

注：图中数据是基于现价美元的人均GDP。

资料来源：世界银行。

### 1.2.4 亚非拉的崛起：亚非拉对欧美经济总量的超越

世界经济格局的第三个重大变化是亚非拉的崛起。在前述几个格局的变迁之下，世界经济的地区板块也悄然变动。在东亚奇迹的带动下，东亚和太平洋地区的经济总量急速飙升。南亚、中东和北非、撒哈拉以南的非洲地区以及拉美也得益于新世纪之后的快速增长。①欧洲和北美在新世纪之后由于增长疲软，经济总量相对下滑（见图1.8、图1.9）。尽管亚非拉的经济体量占全球的比重在不断上升，但是相对于北美这样富足的地区而言，依然具有巨大的后来者优势（如图1.10所示）。例如，2017年撒哈拉以南非洲地区的人均GDP只有北美的2.71%，拉丁美洲与加勒比海地区的人均GDP只有北美的15.97%，东亚与太平洋地区的人均GDP只有北美的17.86%。世界经济的地域板块变动对于中国推行诸如"一带一路"之类带有明显地缘色彩的全球化倡议有着重要的影响。"一带一路"倡议覆盖了东亚、南亚、北非和中东等非欧美发达地区，对推动这些地区的迅速发展作用巨大，也将进一步改变全球地缘经济板块。

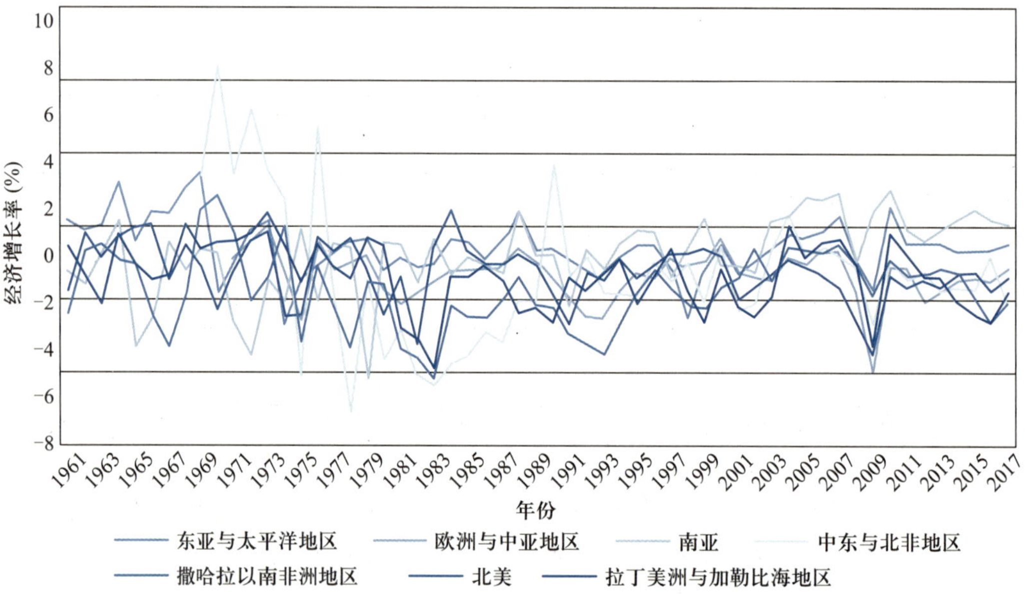


**图1.8 世界各个区域的经济增长率比较**

注：图中数据是基于不变价本币的人均GDP年增长率。

资料来源：世界银行。

① 如果从消费角度看，亚非拉的发展成绩可嘉。例如，基于耐用品所有权的实际消费、住房的质量、儿童的健康和死亡率、青年的教育和女性在家庭的时间配置，均表明撒哈拉以南非洲地区的生活水平，在过去的20年里，每年增长3.4%到3.7%。这成绩被一些经济学家称为过去20年"非洲的增长奇迹"（Alwyn Young, "The African Growth Miracle", *Journal of Political Economy,* 2012, Vol. 120, No. 4, pp. 696–739.）。

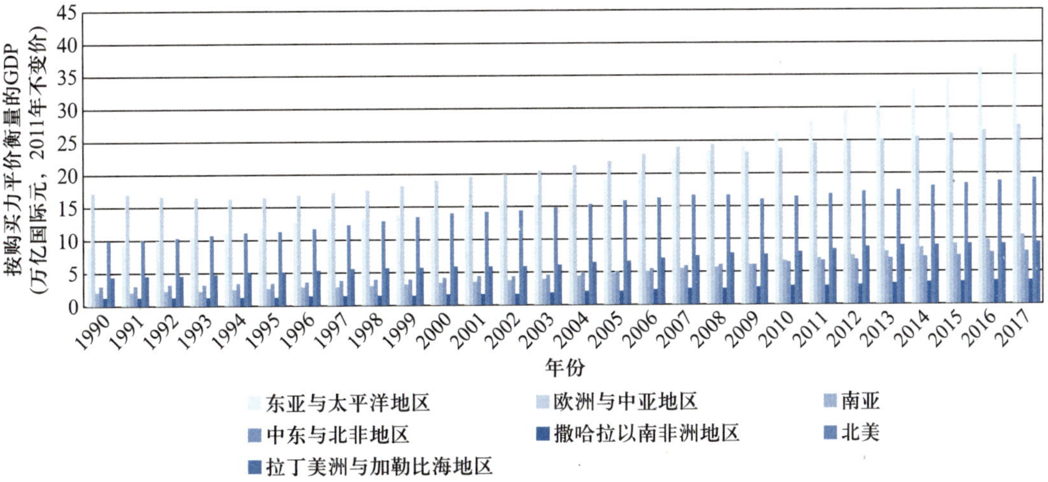


**图1.9 亚非拉的崛起：全球主要经济板块的经济总量比较**

注：图中数据是按购买力平价（PPP）衡量的GDP（2011年不变价国际元）。

资料来源：世界银行。

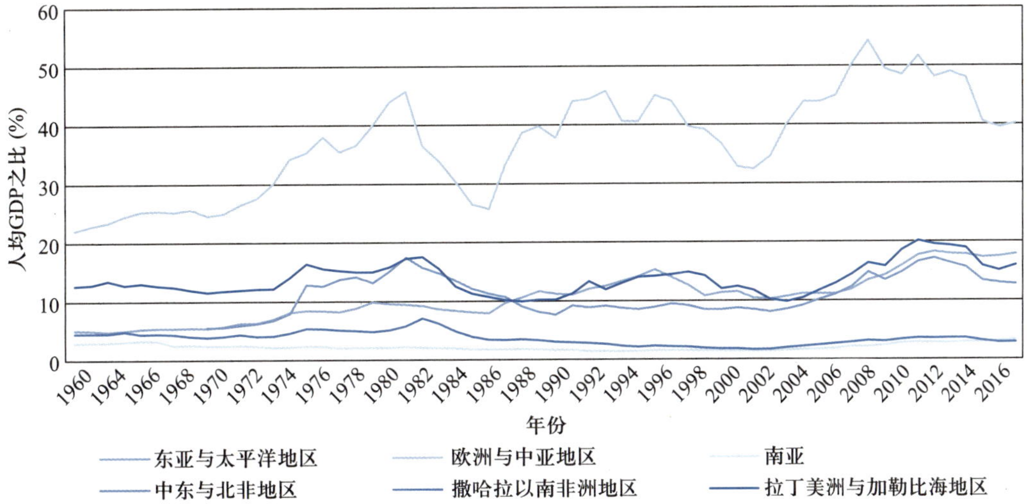


**图1.10 亚非拉的后来者优势：各地区与北美的人均GDP之比**

注：图中数据是基于现价美元的人均GDP。

资料来源：世界银行。

### 1.2.5 中国的崛起：中国对老牌工业强国经济总量的超越

世界经济格局的第四个重大变化便是中国的经济总量按照购买力平价计算已经逐步赶超G7成员国，如图1.11所示。而且，中国经济依然保持着强劲的增长，势头远超过G7，如图1.12所示。并且，中国经济增长的空间远未耗尽，后来者优势依然巨大，如图1.13所示。2018年中国的人均GDP虽然达到9 608美元，但是依然只有美国的15.3%、英国的22.6%、德国的19.9%、法国的22.4%、意大利的28.0%、加拿大的20.8%、日本的22.4%。① 虽然按照汇率计算，中国是仅次于美国的全球第二大经济体，但是按照国际货币基金组织（IMF）最新的数据，中国按照购买力平价计算的经济总量在2013年已经超过美国。即便是按照汇率计算，中国在2030年前后超过美国成为全球最大经济体也已经是没有争议的趋势。中国在改革开放之后的超高速发展是前面三个全球重大经济格局变化的基本动力。如图1.14所示，中国30多个省份过去30多年的经济增长速度远远超过全球其他180多个经济体，各个省份的经济体量已经与世界上一些较大经济体的体量不相上下（见图1.15）。

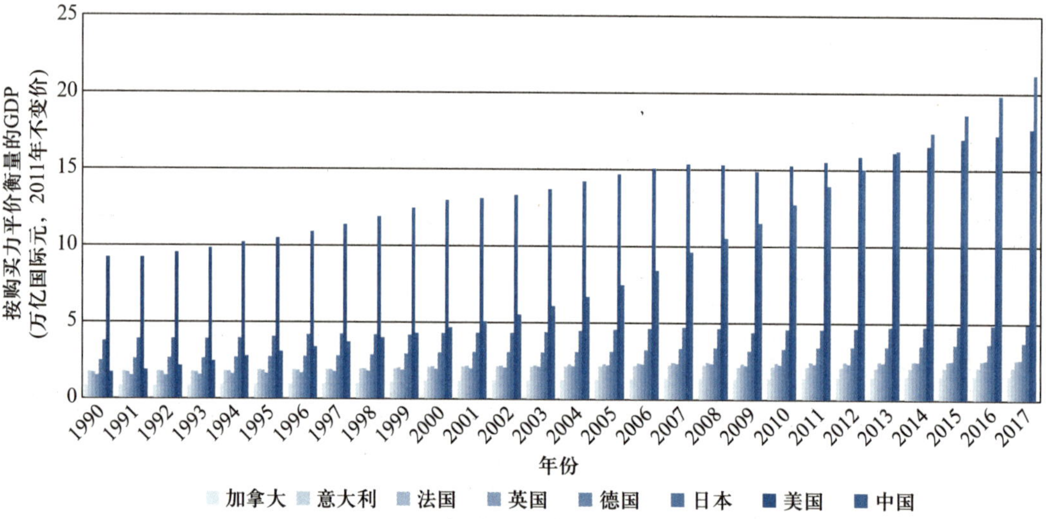


**图1.11 中国的崛起：中国与G7经济总量比较**

注：图中数据是按购买力平价（PPP）衡量的GDP（2011年不变价国际元）。

资料来源：世界银行。

---

① 林毅夫早在2012年就预测，从2008年起中国还有20年8%的增长潜力，其估算方法是：根据安格斯麦迪森研究院的研究，按照购买力平价计算，2008年中国人均GDP是美国的21%，这是1951年日本、1967年新加坡、1977年韩国的水平。这些东亚经济体恰恰是利用后来者居上的优势，实现了连续20年的8%~9%的年均GDP增长率（Lin Justin Yifu, Wan Guanghua and Peter J. Morgan, “Prospects for a Re-acceleration of Economic Growth in the PRC”, *Journal of Comparative Economics*, 2016, Vol.44, No.4, pp.842–853）。根据世界银行的数据，2008—2017年中国的实际GDP（基于不变价本币计算）的增长率是8.26%，过去10年中国实现的经济增长已经超过了林毅夫预测的潜在增长，尽管近期受外部经济周期的影响有所下滑。（第8章将讨论）

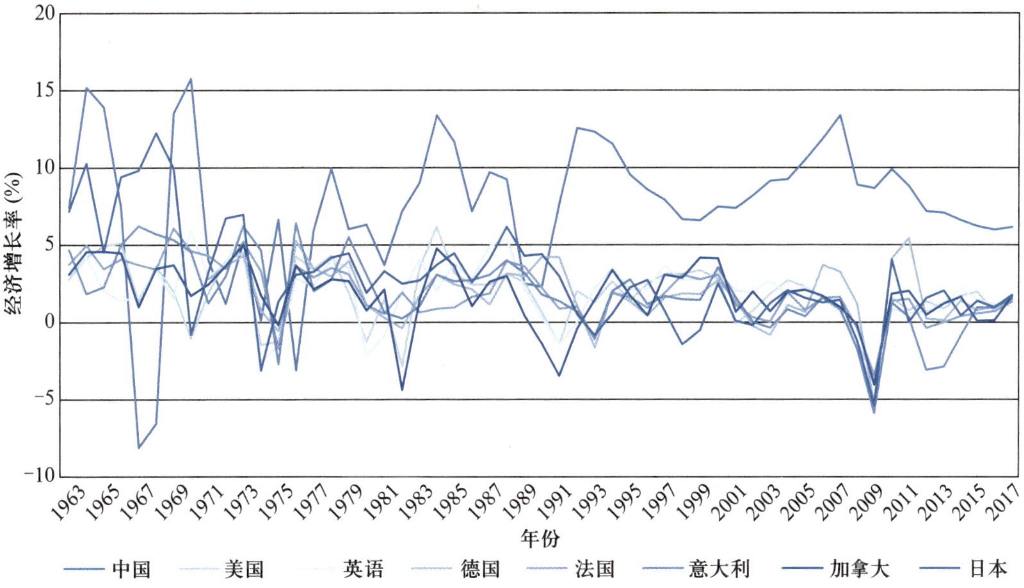


**图 1.12 中国与 G7 的经济增长率比较**

注：图中数据是基于不变价本币的人均 GDP 年增长率。

资料来源：世界银行。

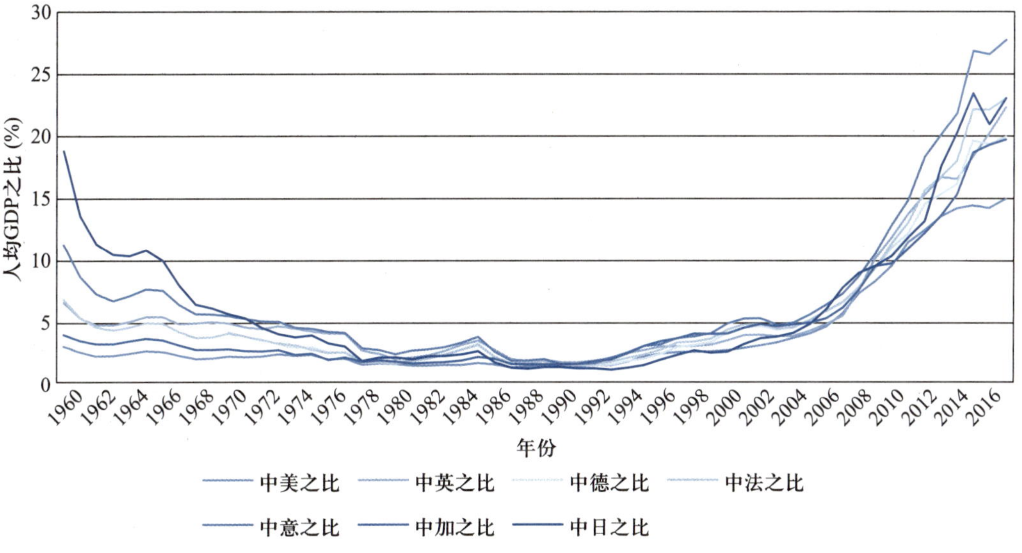


**图 1.13 中国的后来者优势：中国与 G7 的人均 GDP 之比**

注：图中数据是基于现价美元的人均 GDP。

资料来源：世界银行。

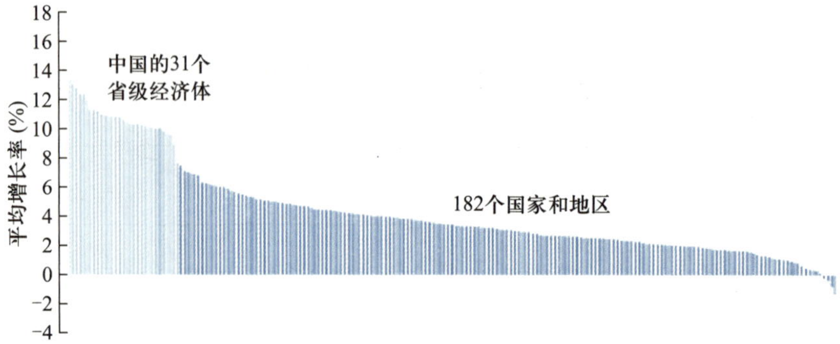


**图1.14 1980—2010年中国各个省份与一些经济体经济平均增长率比较**

资料来源：世界银行和历年《中国统计年鉴》。

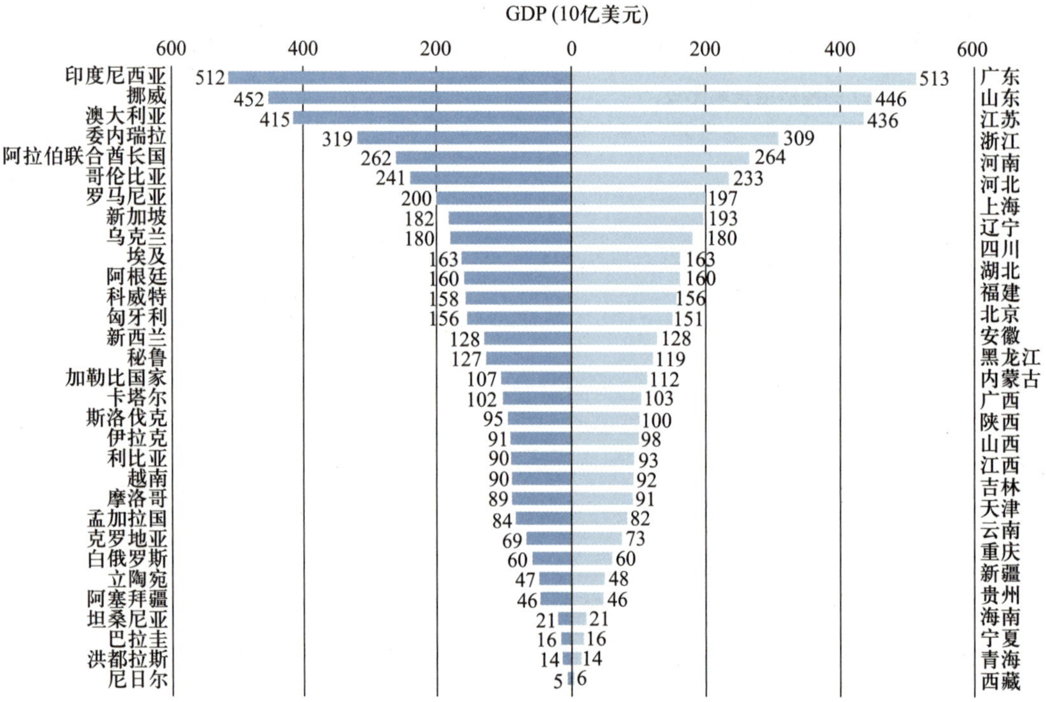


**图1.15 中国的崛起：2008年中国部分省份与一些经济体的经济体量比较**

资料来源：世界银行和中国国家统计局。

## 1.2.6 中国带给世界经济结构转型升级的机遇与方法

### 1.2.6.1 中国是世界经济发展与稳定的中流砥柱

与中国在经济体量上挑战美国经济霸主地位的趋势很不相同（图1.11），中国的经济发展水平还难以望其项背。2015年中国的人均GDP在统计的232个国家中居于第81位，低于欧美发达经济体（图1.13），但又高于印度和非洲等诸多发展中经济体（图1.16）。正是中国这种发展阶段位居中等、经济体量庞大、快速发展的大国特征，让中国成为推动世界经济结构转型升级的中流砥柱。自2008年国际金融危机以来中国每年贡献了世界1/3的经济增长，几乎达到所有发达国家所贡献的增长总和。对于老牌的发达国家来讲，中国将成为其高质量产品与服务的全球最大市场，以及高端产业投资与技术转移的最为重要的目标国和廉价优质商品的来源地，如图1.17所示；对于发展中经济体来讲，中国将成为其初级产品以及劳动力密集型产业最为重要的市场，以及符合当地比较优势的劳动力密集型产业转移和投资的来源地。因此，这种形势对世界经济形势甚至政治形势而言都是令人欣喜的，不论是对于发达国家还是发展中国家，中国经济由于处于中高等收入水平阶段（即便迈入高收入国家行列甚至达到日韩的收入水平），整体上的经济结构与二者形成的都是互补性的比较优势，合作共赢的机会大于竞争。在全球经济息息相关的今天，中国经济的发展态势将直接影响全球经济发展的走势。这种极强的经济互补的世界经济结构是世界和平的根基，①这与引爆两次世界大战的背后实际上是列强之间相互争夺有限的原材料和市场极为不同。综上，中国是世界经济发展与稳定的中流砥柱，通过贸易和投资给各个不同发展程度的国家带来双赢的机会（第8章将讨论）。

### 1.2.6.2 中国工业革命的方法值得全世界发展中国家借鉴

让中国拥有改变世界经济格局的高速经济增长动力的正是其成功的工业化。然而，1979年改革开放之初，中国的人均GDP按当时的市场汇率计算仅为182美元，低于撒哈拉以南非洲地区平均数的1/3。事实上，如图1.16所示，中国在改革开放前后与世界各个收入水平国家的发展差距都是巨大的。但是，中国在改革开放之后一代人的时间内几乎取得了西方国家几百年的工业成就，探索出了发展中国家成功工业化的“秘密”。在短短一代人的时间里，

---

① Feldman, Noah, *Cool War: The Future of Global Competition*. Random House, 2013.

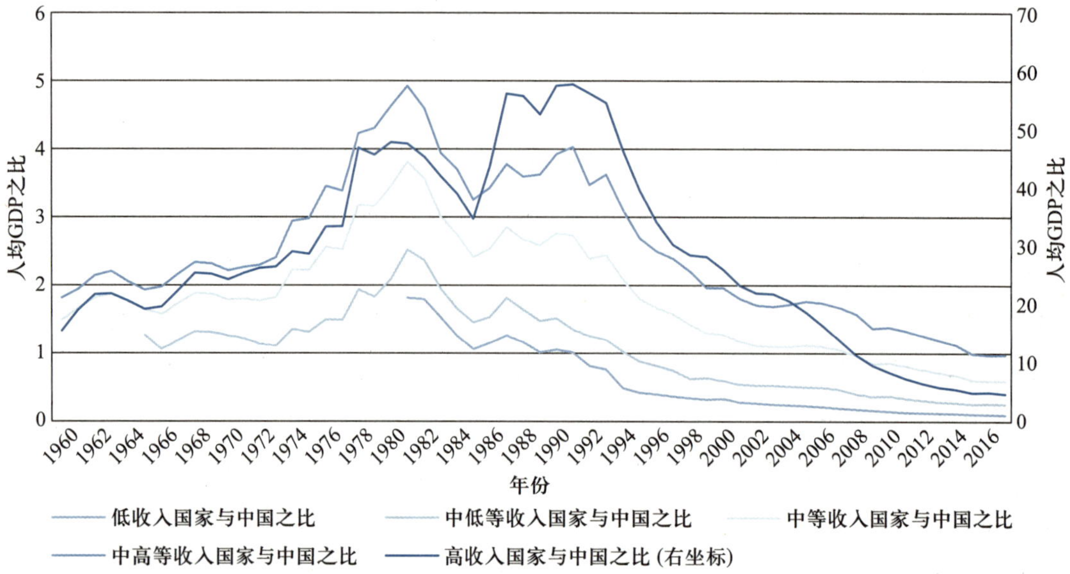


图1.16 中国在世界中的南北方位：右边是高收入国家与中国的人均GDP之比，左边是其他国家与中国的人均GDP之比

注：图中数据是基于现价美元的人均GDP。

资料来源：世界银行。

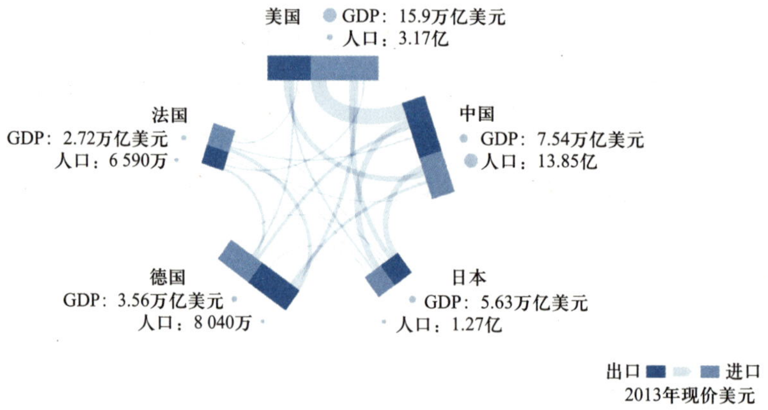


图1.17 2013年中国与主要发达国家（美国、日本、德国、法国）间的经济体量和贸易流量

资料来源：UN Comtrade.

中国创造的社会生产力比它过去五千年所创造的总和还要多，从一个贫穷落后的农业国一举变成了全球最大和最具活力的制造业中心。中国目前的工业产能①，一年里可以生产500亿件T恤衫（世界人口的7倍）、100亿双鞋、8亿吨粗钢（美国的8倍）、24亿吨水泥以及4万亿吨煤炭（占全球的一半）。中国还是全球最大的汽车、高速列车、轮船、机床、手机、计算机、机器人、空调、冰箱、洗衣机、家具、化肥、粮食、鱼、肉、蛋、棉花、铜、铝和电视节目的制造商，建设了全球最多的桥梁、隧道和高速公路，出版了全球最多的书籍、杂志，同时还不断培养着全球规模最大的大学生群体。中国在2011—2013年三年内消费的作为最基础的工业和建筑材料的水泥达65亿吨，超过美国整个20世纪使用量的50%。另外，中国还是世界上首屈一指的工业专利申请国。2014年，仅中国一国的工业专利申请数量就超过了美国和日本两国之和。②与改革开放之前计划经济时期的重工业赶超战略不同，改革开放之后遵循比较优势循序渐进的工业化看似缓慢而实际速度却惊人，这种经验值得许多尚未成功开启工业化的发展中经济体借鉴。除此之外，中国经济发展阶段与诸多发展中经济体类似，中国的发展经验以及基于中国发展经验总结的理论较之发达国家的经验与基于发达国家经验总结的理论更适合于广大发展中经济体。总之，中国不但能够为世界经济结构变迁提供经济机遇，还能够提供新的经验和理论。③

---

① 我们这里再详细看看中国近20年来日常所用的家用电器产量及其变化，这标志着中国已经完成了轻工业革命并处于世界领先的地位：家用电冰箱产量2016年是8 481.57万台，是2008年4 799.95万台的1.77倍，是1998年1 060万台的8倍；房间空气调节器产量2016年是14 342.37万台，是2008年8 147.37万台的1.76倍，是1998年1 156.87万台的12.4倍；家用电风扇产量2016年是17 631.87万台，是2008年13 890.74万台的1.27倍，是1998年6 724.49万台的2.62倍；家用吸排油烟机产量是3 180.31万台，是2008年1 633.15万台的1.95倍，是1998年258.15万台的12.32倍；家用洗衣机产量2016年是7 620.85万台，是2008年4 447万台的1.71倍，是1998年1 207.31万台的6.3倍；家用吸尘器产量2016年是8 765.79万台，是2008年6 367.53万台的1.37倍，是1998年519.18万台的16.88倍；彩色电视机产量2016年是15 769.64万台，是2008年9 187.14万台的1.72倍，是1998年3 497万台的4.51倍。我们也不妨看看表1.6中日常所用的产品例子的出口量：皮鞋出口数量2016年是69 039万双，2008年是112 586万双，1998年是64 894万双；橡胶或塑料底布鞋出口数量2016年是266 940万双，2008年是138 050万双，1998年是59 016万双；电视机出口数量2016年是8 029万台，2008年是5 138万台，1998年是1 021万台；电话机出口数量2016年是136 405万台，2008年是70 023万台，1998年是10 686万台。

② 文一，《伟大的中国工业革命："发展政治经济学"一般原理批判纲要》，清华大学出版社，2016年。

③ 可进一步参考国际知名学术出版商Taylor & Francis于2017年3月在其官方网站报道的林毅夫发表在*Area Developmentand Policy*上的文章"The Rise of China and Its Implications for Economics and Other Developing Countries"。

# 1.3

# 理论的演进

## 1.3.1 西潮并没有改变中国和广大发展中国家的命运

中国的成功不容易：它不仅没有可遵循的经济学理论做指导（因为这样的理论并不存在），而且还有很多错误的经济学理论来误导[①]，只能以“解放思想、实事求是、与时俱进、求真务实、实干兴邦”的务实精神，摸索着前进。与战后发展中经济体一样，中国在改革开放之前不但与发达经济体的发展水平差距越来越大，而且与发展中经济体的发展水平差距也越来越大。例如，1960年，中等收入国家的人均GDP与中国之比是148.63%，高收入国家这一比例是1 550.94%；1978年，中等收入国家的人均GDP与中国之比上升到319.03%，高收入国家这一比例也上升到惊人的4 706.33%。然而，改革开放近40年后的2017年，中等收入国家的人均GDP只有中国的58.61%，高收入国家这一比例也缩小到466.91%。中国的成败经验给当今的发展中经济体提供了巨大的启示与信心，只要思路正确，在一代人之内就可以彻底改变国家命运。[②]

中国从1978年开始的经济改革并不是中国近代史上第一次雄心勃勃地尝试启动工业化。在这之前，中国进行了多次工业化尝试，包括第二次鸦片战争后在大城市办工业的洋务运动，辛亥革命后新共和政府通过全面模仿美国的政治制度推动的工业化进程，以及中华人民共和国成立后模仿苏联的计划经济建设。所有这些工业化尝试的一个共同特点就是政府花大力气去发展先进产业，创造的就业少，未能将广大的农村人口纳入工业化进程。[③]

作为一个农村人口占总人口90%以上的农业大国，成功的经济发展需要自下而上地培育市场需求和企业组织，逐渐把农村剩余劳动力引入劳动密集型制造业，按次序进行产业升级。中华人民共和国成立后，中国选择了与苏联类似的工业化道路，利用农村浅薄的积累来优先

---

① 文一，《伟大的中国工业革命：“发展政治经济学”一般原理批判纲要》，清华大学出版社，2016年版。

② 关于中国的故事请参阅另一部教材：林毅夫，《解读中国经济》，北京大学出版社，2018年增订版（英文版Lin Justin Yifu, *Demystifying the Chinese Economy*. Cambridge University Press, 2011）。

③ 近现代知识分子对国家命运的探索可参见：梁漱溟，《乡村建设理论》（原版1934年），上海人民出版社，2011年版。

发展重工业。自“一五”计划起，中国在苏联的帮助下，建立起了许多的城市型工业中心，生产资本密集型产品和重工业产品，如汽车、钢铁、机床和大型精密仪器等。为了提高钢铁产量，“大跃进”时期，在“以钢为纲，全面跃进”的口号下，全国人民开展了空前规模的大众炼钢运动，以支援重工业建设。这种优先发展重工业的政策一直持续到“文化大革命”结束，导致了轻工业与重工业的比率不断下降。1952—1978年，无论是中国轻工业与重工业的增加值之比，还是这两个产业之间的劳动力比率与资本比率都呈现了明显的下降趋势，尤其在第一个五年计划期间下降最快。虽然工业增加值在“大跃进”失败以后经过1962—1964年的短暂调整有所恢复，但是从劳动力和资本构成来看这种重工业化的趋势一直在继续。其中，轻工业与重工业增加值之比由最初的1.4降到了1978年的0.6，劳动力比率从接近2.5降到了0.5，固定资产比由0.5降到了0.18。中国这种重工业优先的大推进发展战略是低效率的和难以为继的（见表1.5）。

表1.5 欲速不达：新中国采取的赶超战略（“赶英超美”）并未改变自身的禀赋结构

| 年份 | 中国的人均资本（美元） | 中国的人均资本占其他国家的人均资本的比重（%） | | | |
|---|---|---|---|---|---|
| | | 美国 | 英国 | 法国 | 日本 |
| 1952 | 1 537.59 | 1.77 | 3.07 | 4.18 | 16.72 |
| 1953 | 1 573.59 | 1.77 | 3.09 | 4.12 | 16.49 |
| 1954 | 1 611.14 | 1.73 | 3.13 | 4.10 | 16.29 |
| 1955 | 1 659.93 | 1.77 | 3.15 | 4.07 | 15.98 |
| 1956 | 1 749.84 | 1.79 | 3.18 | 4.05 | 15.51 |
| 1957 | 1 798.37 | 1.79 | 3.20 | 3.98 | 14.85 |
| 1958 | 1 806.76 | 1.75 | 3.22 | 3.85 | 14.18 |
| 1959 | 1 965.46 | 1.89 | 3.43 | 3.98 | 14.33 |
| 1960 | 2 255.86 | 2.15 | 3.92 | 4.31 | 15.06 |
| 1961 | 2 310.35 | 2.16 | 3.99 | 4.23 | 13.95 |
| 1962 | 2 301.17 | 2.14 | 3.93 | 4.00 | 12.73 |
| 1963 | 2 289.60 | 2.09 | 3.83 | 3.82 | 11.61 |
| 1964 | 2 291.62 | 2.06 | 3.72 | 3.63 | 10.62 |
| 1965 | 2 344.39 | 2.05 | 3.68 | 3.48 | 10.02 |
| 1966 | 2 426.63 | 2.07 | 3.68 | 3.39 | 9.67 |
| 1967 | 2 439.68 | 2.05 | 3.50 | 3.21 | 8.87 |
| 1968 | 2 462.78 | 2.01 | 3.36 | 3.01 | 7.95 |
| 1969 | 2 503.65 | 1.99 | 3.26 | 2.88 | 7.10 |
| 1970 | 2 699.71 | 2.09 | 3.30 | 2.89 | 6.59 |
| 1971 | 2 830.26 | 2.09 | 3.46 | 2.87 | 6.14 |
| 1972 | 2 978.16 | 2.14 | 3.68 | 2.85 | 5.75 |
| 1973 | 3 150.47 | 2.20 | 3.94 | 2.87 | 5.52 |
| 1974 | 3 354.76 | 2.26 | 4.20 | 2.89 | 5.23 |

续表

| 年份 | 中国的人均资本（美元） | 中国的人均资本占其他国家的人均资本的比重（%） | | | |
|---|---|---|---|---|---|
| | | 美国 | 英国 | 法国 | 日本 |
| 1975 | 3 586.65 | 2.28 | 4.47 | 2.91 | 5.01 |
| 1976 | 3 737.98 | 2.39 | 4.57 | 2.87 | 4.91 |
| 1977 | 3 982.82 | 2.49 | 4.73 | 2.85 | 4.81 |
| 1978 | 4 266.83 | 2.60 | 4.88 | 2.83 | 4.67 |

数据来源：根据PWT8.0计算。

首先，计划经济时期中国资本积累有限，大力发展钢铁、汽车、机械制造等资本密集型行业，不符合中国的要素禀赋结构所决定的比较优势，重工业企业在竞争的市场中缺乏自生能力。政府为支持重工业建设，把没有自生能力的企业建立起来并维持其生存，采取了价格扭曲体制，造成资源严重错配，极大地降低了经济效率。一方面，政府对农产品课以重税，并压低农产品与原材料的价格，间接补贴重工业企业。另一方面，政府给予重工业企业垄断地位，甚至使用行政手段直接向大型重工业企业配给资源。这导致农业、轻工业部门投入严重不足，发展滞后，国民经济比例严重失衡。[①]其次，重工业属于资金技术密集型，初始投资巨大，只有依靠规模化大生产才能够自负盈亏，而重工业规模化大生产需要规模化大市场和零部件规模化生产以及相应的交通运输网络，并保障原材料源源不断地供应，才能积累和增长。在20世纪50年代，中国工业刚刚起步，国民经济各行业对钢铁、机床、汽车等重工业品的需求十分有限。不仅这些重工业的中间产品和零件无法在国内得到大规模的生产，而且原材料无法保障，最终产品的产出水平也往往低于其潜在产能的30% ~ 50%。这种企业若要盈利或者哪怕仅仅覆盖投资和固定运营成本，市场规模要相当大才行，至少要达到潜在产能的70% ~ 80%，而且上下游产业链需要相对完善并能够推向国际市场。中国当时占全国人口90%的“一无所有”的农民和广袤的“一穷二白”的黄土地不可能提供这种大市场和购买力以及相应的产业链。由于不符合比较优势，生产成本高，除了政治和当时面临的国际环境的原因外，也不可能在国际市场与具有比较优势的发达国家同类产品竞争。中国计划经济遇到的发展障碍表明，战后第一波旧结构主义提出的在落后国家由政府主导发展资本密集型生产方式的大推进发展模式，无法在落后农业国家推动可持续的工业化、现代化。采取类似发展方式的一些市场经济国家同样陷入困境。例如，在进口替代政策下过早进入重工业化阶段的拉美国家长期陷入了中等收入陷阱。相反，自1978年起，中国以双轨渐进的方式开启了改

① 王丽莉、文一，“中国能跨越中等收入陷阱吗？——基于工业化路径的跨国比较”，《经济评论》，2017年第3期。更详细论述参见：林毅夫、蔡昉、李周，《中国的奇迹：发展战略与经济改革》，上海三联书店，1994年版。

革开放，在继续给予不具比较优势的重工业必要的转型期保护补贴以维持稳定的前提下，放开市场准入，以工业园、经济特区、招商引资的方式因势利导具有比较优势的劳动密集型产业的发展，使其变成竞争优势，资本开始积累后，充分利用后来者优势，从轻工业到重工业的循序渐进，从而成功实现了工业化，变成制造业大国，迅速缩小了和发达国家的差距。因此，在具备一定市场竞争要素的前提下，按照要素禀赋结构的比较优势展开工业化的进程，实施以充分利用国内国际两种市场和两种资源为目的的发展战略，开展由产业链低端向高端逐步拓展的产业升级步骤，是工业化成功的关键，也是一条中国自身和其他成功实现工业化、现代化国家的结构变迁道路（第4章将更详细地介绍中国的结构变迁案例）。①

由此可见，中国不仅在近代就开始向西方学习（洋务运动、辛亥革命、社会主义革命）而且在战后推行的发展思路也与深受当时流行的发展思潮（旧结构主义）的影响的广大发展中国家一样而遭遇挫折。改革开放之后中国没有盲目全盘接受当时流行的新自由主义改革思潮，不是试图以休克疗法一次性地消除各种扭曲，而是采取符合中国实际的渐进式改革，在维持稳定的前提下，将违背比较优势的赶超战略调整为符合比较优势的发展战略，而大获成功（表1.6）。总之，来自西方的思潮并没有改变中国的命运，也没有改变广大发展中国家的命运（专栏1.1）。②

表1.6 中国与东欧的巨大转型反差：人均收入水平及其增长率比较

| 国家 | 1990年排名 | 2017年排名 | 排名变化 | 1990年比中国 | 2017年比中国 | 增长倍数 | 1990—2017年年均增长率 |
|---|---|---|---|---|---|---|---|
| 中国 | 159 | 73 | 86 | 1.0 | 1.0 | 27.8 | 12.6 |
| 斯洛伐克 | 72 | 43 | 29 | 7.6 | 2.0 | 7.4 | 7.4 |
| 波兰 | 86 | 57 | 29 | 5.5 | 1.6 | 8.0 | 7.7 |
| 罗马尼亚 | 87 | 61 | 26 | 5.3 | 1.2 | 6.4 | 6.9 |
| 捷克 | 57 | 40 | 17 | 12.4 | 2.3 | 5.2 | 6.1 |
| 斯洛文尼亚 | 45 | 37 | 8 | 33.7 | 2.7 | 2.2 | 2.9 |
| 匈牙利 | 61 | 56 | 5 | 10.6 | 1.6 | 4.2 | 5.3 |
| 塞尔维亚 | 94 | 91 | 3 | 6.9 | 0.7 | 2.7 | 3.6 |
| 克罗地亚 | 61 | 59 | 2 | 15.1 | 1.5 | 2.8 | 3.7 |
| 保加利亚 | 76 | 76 | 0 | 7.5 | 0.9 | 3.4 | 4.5 |
| 俄罗斯 | 59 | 62 | −3 | 11.0 | 1.2 | 3.1 | 4.1 |
| 白俄罗斯 | 82 | 92 | −10 | 6.7 | 0.6 | 2.7 | 3.6 |
| 乌克兰 | 91 | 130 | −39 | 4.9 | 0.3 | 1.7 | 1.9 |

注：斯洛文尼亚、克罗地亚、塞尔维亚的数据自1995年开始，匈牙利的数据自1991年开始。
数据来源：根据世界银行数据测算。

① 林毅夫，《新结构经济学：反思经济发展与政策的理论框架》，北京大学出版社，2012年版；文一，《伟大的中国工业革命："发展政治经济学"一般原理批判纲要》，清华大学出版社，2016年版。

② 林毅夫，"对新文化运动的反思：经济学的视角"，《北京大学学报（哲学社会科学版）》，2015年第52卷第6期。

### 1.3.2 从西潮到东风

#### 1.3.2.1 第一代发展经济学：结构主义

Rosenstein-Rodan和Prebisch的开创性研究激发了第一波被称为结构主义的发展经济学思潮[①]。他们强调由于结构刚性的存在，市场有着难以克服的缺陷而无法自发实现产业结构的现代化变迁，在加速经济发展方面，政府是一个强有力的手段；由于贸易条件的恶化以及无力竞争的幼稚产业，避免被发达国家剥削的唯一途径就是采取进口替代战略和保护主义手段发展与发达国家相抗衡的制造业。伴随着强烈的国家主义情绪，第二次世界大战后的许多亚非拉国家采纳了结构主义的发展思潮：以进口替代优先发展违反比较优势的资本、技术密集型重工业；企业缺乏自生能力，依靠政府的动员来投资，依靠保护、补贴来生存，这样导致了资源错配、寻租和腐败等一系列问题。这种结构主义模式以斯大林计划经济模式为样板，拉丁美洲国家、南亚国家都受到了影响。结构主义建议发展中国家优先发展资本密集、技术先进的大型重工业，而这些国家当时的条件是资本相当短缺，以农业经济为主。因此，在资本短缺的农业经济的基础之上建立现代化的产业违背当时的要素禀赋结构所决定的比较优势。在这种状况下，优先发展产业中的企业在开放竞争的市场中没有自生能力，投资靠政府动员，继续生产经营靠政府的保护补贴。这些保护补贴来自于政府的各种干预扭曲，产生了很多租金，导致了资源错配、寻租和腐败等一系列的问题。计划经济时代的中国和其他发展中国家的失败就是这一发展思路所导致的结果。

#### 1.3.2.2 第二代发展经济学：新自由主义

随着结构主义发展思潮与政府主导的经济发展战略在许多国家的惨败，以及20世纪70年代开始的“理性预期”宏观经济理论对凯恩斯主义的革命，结构主义发展观主张的政府干预市场的理论基础遭到了摒弃，第二波被称为新自由主义发展观的发展经济学思潮在许多多边机构的推动下盛行，并推行于许多面临债务危机的发展中国家（史称“华盛顿共识”）。新自由主义强调了系统性的政府干预产生的扭曲是制约发展的顽疾，需要进行私有化、市场化以及去管制化的激进改革，一步到位地消除政府对市场的干预，以建立和发达国家相同的完

---

① P. N. Rosenstein-Rodan, “Problems of Industrialisation of Eastern and South Eastern Europe”, *Economic Journal*, 1943, 53; R. Prebisch, *The Economic Development of Latin America and Its Principal Problems*. United Nations, 1950.

善市场制度。但“华盛顿共识”很快就被认为是“位于华盛顿的一些国际金融机构施加于那些不幸国家，并使这些国家走向危机和痛苦的一套新自由主义政策”。20世纪80年代以后，绝大多数发展中国家按照新自由主义的“华盛顿共识”进行改革和转型。这些转型中国家一般都有许多在结构主义政策时期建立起来的缺乏自生能力的企业，“华盛顿共识”忽视了这种原来存在的扭曲的内生性，按照“休克疗法”把这些保护补贴一下子都取消掉，导致大量破产、失业和社会政治不稳定。同时，“华盛顿共识”强调政府失灵，主张由市场来解决一切问题，反对政府发挥因势利导的作用去帮助企业克服产业升级、技术创新伴随的外部性和协调相应软硬基础设施完善必然存在的市场失灵问题。因此，“华盛顿共识”推行的结果，使发展中国家经济的绩效比20世纪六七十年代按照结构主义发展时的绩效还要差，经济增长率低于转型前，危机发生的频率则高于转型前。绝大多数转型国家因为遵循了这一转型思潮而失败。经济学家Easterly因此将推行“华盛顿共识”改革的20世纪八九十年代称为发展中国家“失去的20年”。①诺贝尔经济学奖得主斯蒂格利茨在“后华盛顿共识”中就指出，“华盛顿共识”错把工具当目标，低估了政府在发展中的作用。苏联、东欧“休克疗法”的失败就是因为遵循了这一改革思路。②

### 专栏1.1
### 为什么要反思来自发达国家的主流的发展理论

在全球长期经济发展中，跨国收入差距的历史呈现出“大分流”模式。据Pritchett估计，从1870年至1990年，最富裕的国家和最贫穷的国家之间生活标准的差距比例增长了5倍以上。③根据Maddison的估计，从1950年至1998年，最富裕的群体和最贫穷的群体之间的人均收入差距比例增长了1.75倍④，而按照Mayer-Foulkes的估计，这个比例增长了2.6倍⑤。从第二次世界大战以后到2008

---

① William Easterly, “The Lost Decades: Developing Countries Stagnation in Spite of Policy Reform 1980—1998”, *Journal of Economic Growth*, 2001, Vol.6, No.2, pp.135-157.

② Lin Justin Yifu, “The Washington Consensus Revisited: a New Structural Economics Perspective”, *Journal of Economic Policy Reform,* 2015, Vol.18, No.2, 96-113.

③ L. Pritchett, “Divergence, Big Time”, *Journal of Economics Perspectives*, 1997, Vol.11, No.3, pp.3-17.

④ A. Maddison, *The World Economy: A Millennial Perspective*, Paris. OECD, 2001.

⑤ D. Mayer-Foulkes, “Global Divergence”, Documento de Trabajo del CIDE, SDTE, 2002.

年，全世界有两百多个发展中经济体，只有中国台湾地区和韩国两个经济体从低收入进入到中等收入再进一步发展成为高收入经济体；在1960年的101个中等收入经济体中到2008年只有13个经济体从中等收入经济体发展成为高收入经济体，其中只有日本和亚洲“四小龙”不是原本和发达经济体差距就不大的西欧周边经济体或石油产国；28个经济体人均收入和美国的差距缩小了10个百分点或更多，其中，不少是石油等资源输出国家；另外，有18个经济体人均收入和美国的差距不仅没有缩小，反而扩大了10个以上百分点。上述数据说明第二次世界大战以来，绝大多数发展中经济体仍深陷低收入或中等收入陷阱。① 如图1.18所示，整体上看，战后结构主义发展思潮引导下的30年（1950—1980年）与新自由主义引导下的30年（1980—2010年），世界上大多数经济体的发展水平并没有多么显著的改善。

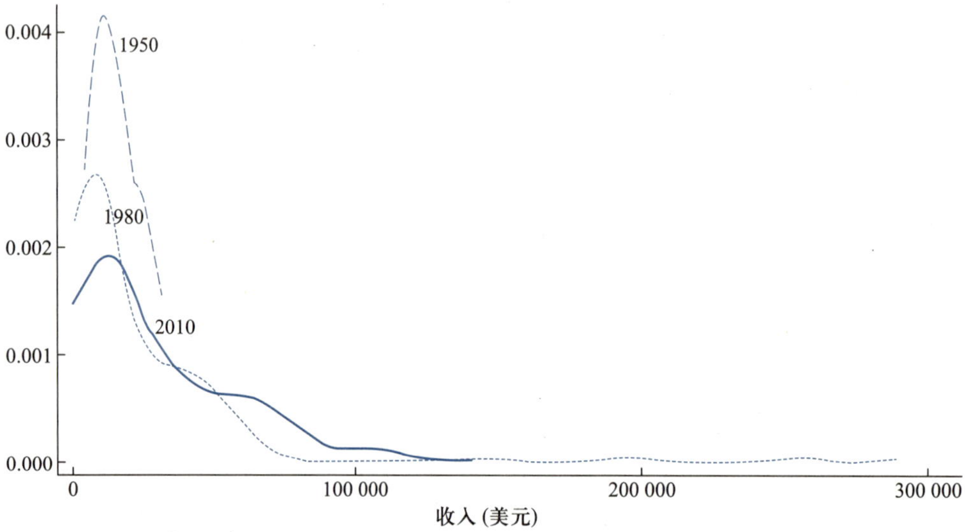


**图1.18 1950年、1980年、2010年世界各个经济体人均收入分布**

资料来源：PWT8.0.

面对如此糟糕的发展绩效，经济学家Easterly以散文家的口吻写道：“50年前，第二次世界大战刚刚结束，经济学家们就开始了热切的寻宝之旅，我们希望可以找到灵丹妙药，让热带雨林国家也能像欧洲和北美的富国一样富有。穷国人

① Pierre-Richard Agenor, Otaviano Canuto, and Michael Jelenic, “Avoiding Middle-income Growth Traps”, *Economic Premise*, 2012, No.98.

民的苦难和富国人民的享乐形成鲜明的反差，这激励我们一定要完成任务。如果能够成功，这将是人类思想史上的一大辉煌。同过去的寻宝者一样，经济学家试图找到一个法宝能让穷国变富。许多次，我们都认为已经找到了灵丹妙药，从外国援助到直接投资，从扶持教育到控制人口，从根据改革状况提供贷款到根据改革状况减免贷款，遗憾的是，一切都没有收到预期效果。那些接受我们药方的穷国没有取得意料中的进步。在我们最花力气的地区——非洲撒哈拉，经济根本没有增长；拉丁美洲和中东一度有增长，但20世纪80年代和90年代重新陷入贫困的陷阱；南亚是另一个备受经济学家们关注的地区，无规律的经济增长使那里集聚了大量的贫困人口；最近，东亚，我们曾为之欢欣鼓舞的经济新星，也陷入了增长泥潭（一些国家但并非全部国家正在复苏）。除了热带雨林贫困国家，我们还试图将一些做法应用于前社会主义国家，但结果也非常令人沮丧。就像很多宣称找到仙丹的无稽之谈一样。”①

理论是用来帮助人们认识世界、改造世界的，当根据理论的认识去改造世界无法成功时，需要改变的是理论。如林毅夫所回忆的：“发展中国家的发展实践让我感觉到迫切需要对现有的主流经济学理论进行反思。第一次世界大战后民族主义风起云涌，第二次世界大战以后发展中国家纷纷摆脱了西方列强的殖民地半殖民地枷锁，取得了政治独立，在第一代革命家的领导下开始进行工业化和现代化的建设。在20世纪五六十年代，主流理论思潮建议发展中国家迎头赶上，建立起当时发达国家所拥有的那种资本密集型的先进现代化大产业。这种思潮的逻辑似乎令人信服：除非劳动生产率达到发达国家的水平，否则没有哪个国家能够达到和发达国家同样的收入水平，发展现代化的资本密集型大产业被认为是任何发展中国家要达到和发达国家同一劳动生产率水平所必需的前提条件。在当时，市场失灵被认为是发展中国家未能建立起这些先进的大产业的原因。因此，主流的经济学理论，也就是后来被称为结构主义的第一版发展经济学理论，建议政府克服市场失灵，以进口替代战略的方式，通过直接动员和配置资源来发展这些资本密集型的大产业。推行该战略的国家通常会出现一个短时期的投资拉动的快速增长，但之后，经济便会出现停滞并危机不断。少数几个实现奇迹式发展的东亚经济体则是采取出口导向战略，从发展传统小规模的劳动力密集型产业起步，根据当时的主流理论，这种战略是错误的。构建或学习理论是为了认识世界、改造

---

① 威廉·伊斯特利，《在增长的迷雾中求索——经济学家在欠发达国家的探险与失败》，中信出版社，2005年版，第1–2页。

世界。不容讳言的事实是，现代的主流理论基本上都是由生活在发达国家的学者根据他们所观察到的发达国家的现象和经验构建的。但是，从1987年回国后的切身体验以及对西方主流理论演进史的学习，让我认识到发达国家其实并不存在一本‘放诸四海而皆准，百世以俟圣人而不惑’的真经。为什么呢？一个显而易见的理由是，理论的适用性取决于前提条件的相似性，发展中国家由于条件和发达国家有差异，即使在发达国家适用的理论在发展中国家也不见得适用。更何况发达国家盛行的理论就像时尚一样，不断被新的理论所扬弃，也就是说，发达国家的理论即使在发达国家也不见得总是适用。倘若发展中国家的政府、企业或个人根据发达国家盛行的理论来做决策，经常会有‘淮南为橘，淮北为枳’的遗憾。这个认识让我幡然醒悟，为何第二次世界大战以后的两百多个发展中国家为了追赶发达国家，也和我国一样都做了许许多多艰苦卓绝的努力，但是尚未有根据发达国家的主流理论制定政策而取得经济发展成功的例子，少数几个成功的发展中经济体的政策在推行时从当时的主流理论来看则是错误的。”①

除了对这样的发展实践的反思，新结构经济学的萌芽也基于对转型实践的反思。据林毅夫回忆：“回国后我发现，我国政府从计划经济向市场经济转型过程中推行的各项政策，基本上都违背了我在芝加哥大学博士课程中学到的一个运行良好的市场经济应该有的基本原则。20世纪八九十年代西方经济学界的主流是新自由主义，认为有效的经济体系必须建立在私有产权的基础上，由市场决定价格，配置资源，政府的作用则仅限于保护产权、推行法治、维护社会秩序。当时经济学界的共识是，计划经济不如市场经济，计划经济向市场经济的转型应该执行根据新自由主义所形成的‘华盛顿共识’，以‘休克疗法’的方式一步到位地推行私有化、市场化、自由化，消除经济中政府各种不当干预所形成的扭曲。当时还有一个共识，渐进的、双轨制的转型不仅会导致资源错误配置，而且还会滋生腐败、恶化收入分配，是比计划经济还要糟糕的制度。我国推行的却是这种被学界认为最糟糕的转型方式。我是应该像众多国内外经济学家那样，以现有的主流理论为依据，把转型中出现的诸多问题都归咎于中国政府过度干预，未能彻底地推行私有化、市场化、自由化，一次性地消除所有的扭曲，还是应该放弃现有的主流理论，以开放的心态把中国政府当作一个以实现稳定和发展为目标而面临

① 林毅夫，《新结构经济学：反思经济发展与政策的理论框架》（增订版），北京大学出版社，2014年版。该书第二章“增长报告与新结构经济学”解释了战后13个发展典范的特征事实。

各种现实约束条件的理性决策者，构建新的理论体系来分析中国在转型过程中取得的成绩和出现的问题？我选择了后者。1994年，我和蔡昉、李周合作出版了《中国的奇迹》一书，通过该书的分析，我理解到，中国转型前政府对市场的各种干预、扭曲旨在保护那些违背比较优势的重工业优先发展部门中缺乏自生能力的企业。渐进、双轨的改革一方面为先前优先发展部门中的国有企业提供了转型期的保护和补贴；另一方面放开准入并因势利导民营和外资企业进入符合比较优势的劳动力密集型部门。这种方式使得中国经济在转型期同时实现了稳定和快速增长，但是因为扭曲的继续存在从而会伴随着收入分配恶化和腐败，所以，这本书的分析建议中国应该放弃赶超战略，改为实行比较优势战略，并在转型过程中创造条件解决传统部门中企业自生能力的问题，消除双轨制遗留下来的扭曲，以建立完善的市场经济体系。”①

《中国的奇迹》一书也预测到，如果像“华盛顿共识”主张的那样试图通过私有化、市场化和自由化一次性地消除所有的扭曲，势必导致先前优先发展的部门中缺乏自生能力的企业的破产，引起大规模失业和社会、政治不稳定。出于对这种严重后果的担忧或是对那些仍然被认为是因国防安全与民族自豪感需要而必须存在的“先进产业”的考虑，政府可能不得不在推行了“休克疗法”、取消了先前“明”的扭曲所给予的保护补贴后，再度引入各种“暗”的扭曲和干预以保护已经私有化了的企业。私有企业对这种隐性保护补贴寻租的积极性会比国有时更高，代价会更为高昂，腐败和收入分配恶化的程度也会较之双轨、渐进的改革更为严重。20世纪八九十年代发生在社会主义和非社会主义国家的转型结果与《中国的奇迹：发展战略与经济改革》一书的预言一致。不管采取何种转型方式，收入分配恶化和腐败的情形都将存在。总的来讲，在推行“休克疗法”的国家会更加严重。少数几个在转型期实现了稳定和快速发展的经济体，在20世纪70年代末80年代初开始转型的中国、越南和老挝，以及70年代初就开始转型的印度洋中的非洲小岛国毛里求斯，都采取从主流经济学理论来看最糟糕的渐进双轨式转型（图1.19）。那些遵循主流经济学理论主张的“休克疗法”的国家却经历了“失去的二十年”，它们在20世纪八九十年代的年均增长率还不如六七十年

① 林毅夫，《新结构经济学：反思经济发展与政策的理论框架》（增订版），北京大学出版社，2014年版。

代，且危机频仍。①图1.20反映了一些不同转型方式的代表性经济体鲜明的绩效反差，也反映了中国与东欧的巨大转型反差。②

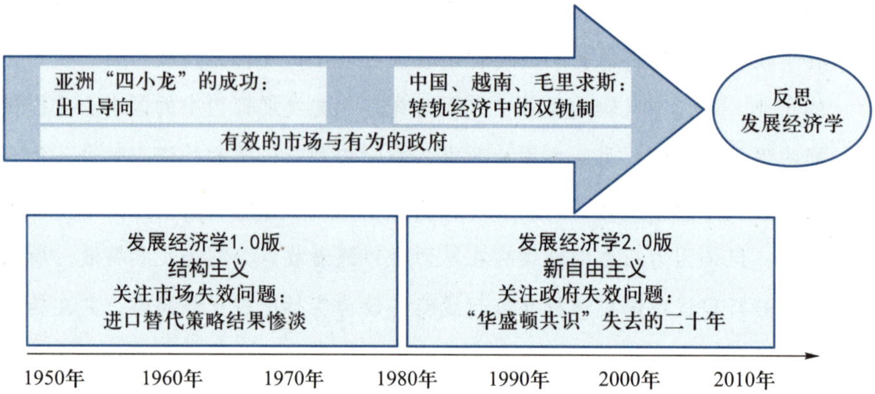


图1.19 发展理论急需反思

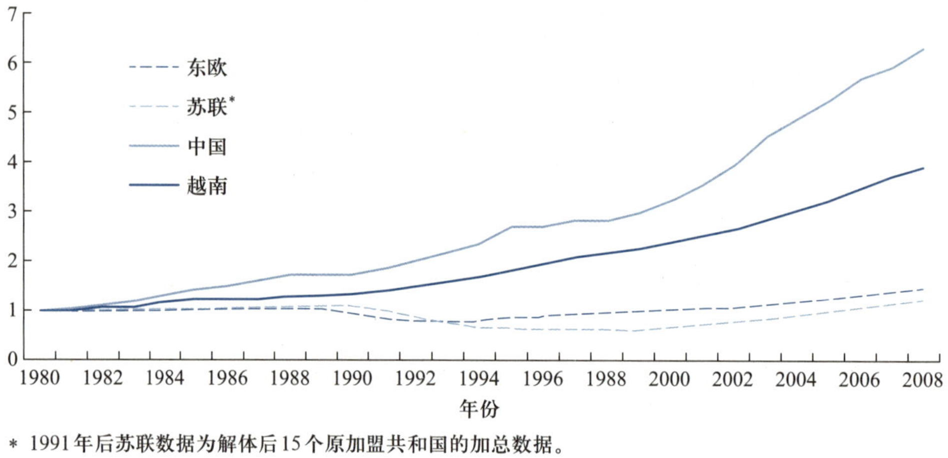


图1.20 渐进式转型与“休克疗法”转型绩效比较（1980年人均GDP为1，以1990年国际元计价）
资料来源：根据Maddison所著的*Historical Statisticsof the World Economy*：*1-2008AD*计算。

---

① 20世纪90年代初期苏联和东欧国家的转型却出现了经济急速下滑以及社会发展的普遍恶化。欧洲开发银行和世界银行2006年在对包括东欧、东南欧、波罗的海国家及独联体国家和蒙古在内的29个国家29 000人进行的调查中发现，只有30%的人认为自己的生活水平好于1989年。（European Bank for Reconstruction and Development, EBRD, 2007; *Life in Transition: A Survey of People's Attitude and Experiences*. European Bank for Reconstruction and Development）

② 渐进式转型优于休克疗法的根本原因是，社会主义国家和转型经济中的大部分现存企业都没有自生能力（除了少数当时扭曲并不太深的经济体，如斯洛伐克、波兰、罗马尼亚、捷克，其没有自生能力的企业所占比重不大）。如果自生能力问题不解决，如果政府不愿意或不能够让没有自生能力的企业破产，那么根据现有新古典经济学理论消除扭曲和改革制度安排可能将这些安排从次优降为第三优。因此，最优的改革可能达不到预期效果，但却可能恶化最糟的处境。所以，毫不奇怪以企业具有自生能力为暗含前提的现有新古典经济学理论难以处理社会主义经济和转型经济中的问题。关于新结构转型经济学的更深入讨论可参考：林毅夫、付才辉，《新结构经济学导论》（上、下册），高等教育出版社，2019年版。

中国走的是渐进双轨制道路，事实证明取得了成功。如前所述，成功的原因是：一方面继续给予原来优先发展部门中缺乏自生能力的企业暂时性的保护补贴，以维持稳定；另一方面放开原来受抑制部门的准入，并发挥因势利导的作用以取得经济的快速增长。对原来抑制的符合比较优势的劳动力密集型的产业部门开放，允许三资企业、民营经济进入。但是，这也付出了一定的代价，即双轨制保留了不少扭曲，保护原来没有自生能力的企业。这些扭曲主要体现在：金融结构的扭曲（金融行业的大银行，只能给大企业和富人提供服务）、资源税费的扭曲（主要体现为资源价格非常低）和服务业（如电信、交通部门）的垄断导致分配不均，收入向富人和大企业倾斜；富人和大企业消费倾向低，导致消费和储蓄不均衡；和为了获得更多那些扭曲所带来的租金的寻租行为和腐败现象等问题。不过，快速的发展，带来了资本的迅速积累和比较优势的变化，使得原来违反比较优势的产业逐渐变成符合比较优势，企业由没有自生能力变为有自生能力，保护补贴从“雪中送炭”变为“锦上添花”，渐进双轨的转型所遗留下来的各种扭曲和干预也就可以取消，完成从计划和市场并存的双轨经济向完善的市场经济转型。

总之，正是由于西方主流的发展与转型理论同战后发展与转型经验形成的强烈反差，尤其是中华人民共和国成立之后赶超战略同改革开放之后渐进式转轨为比较优势战略形成的强烈反差，构成了新结构经济学的萌芽和发展与转型经验背景。

### 专栏1.2
### “华盛顿共识”的最新反思：斯德哥尔摩陈述[①]

2016年9月16—17日，包括4位前世界银行首席经济学家在内的13名经济学家，于瑞典斯德哥尔摩举行了为期两天的会议，讨论当今经济政策制定者面临的挑战。本次会议由瑞典国际发展署和世界银行主办，会议参加者包括Sabina Alkire（牛津），Pranab Bardhan（伯克利），Kaushik Basu（纽约），Haroon Bhorat（开普敦），Francois Bourguignon（巴黎），Ashwini Deshpande（德里），Ravi Kanbur（伊萨卡），林毅夫（北京），Kalle Moene（奥斯陆），Jean-Philippe Platteau（纳摩尔），

① “斯德哥尔摩陈述：关于当代世界政策制定原则的共识”，SIDA官方网站。

Jaime Saavedra（利马），Joseph Stiglitz（纽约）和Finn Tarp（赫尔辛基和哥本哈根）。会议结束时，与会者决定发布他们达成的共识，即下述的“斯德哥尔摩陈述”。“斯德哥尔摩陈述”被视为“华盛顿共识”关于政策制定原则的替代版。[①]

**发展的挑战**

当今世界正处于动荡的时代，在全球化的浪潮下，希望与危机并存。前所未有的技术进步促进了生活质量的提高，但也带来了劳动力被替代和青年失业的危险。贸易与跨国投资的扩张推动了经济增长，使得一些低收入国家迈入中等收入国家行列，而这些国家中的许多群体并未从中获益。即使在发达经济体中也是如此，全球化对不少群体产生了不利影响。此外，那些陷于冲突和战争困境的国家，生活质量在降低。国内不断加剧的不平等威胁着整个社会的凝聚力和经济进步，环境恶化和气候变化威胁着我们的地球，并亟待全球性的一致举措来应对迫在眉睫的危机。至于快速的城市化进程，它通过集聚效应使生产力得到提高，但也可能加剧城市贫民窟、贫困和冲突的问题。

当然，上述一切问题都不能抹杀世界在收入增长、改善卫生和加强教育方面取得的巨大进步。我们庆贺这些成就，并且展望政策制定者面临的无可置疑的挑战。成功应对这些挑战在于利用好全球化的发展力量，以导向一条充满希望而非危机四伏的道路。这也就需要在政策设计中对发展目标有一个清晰的认识，并以史为鉴，从过去的成功及错误中吸取经验，从过去相当长一段时间积累下来的经济理论、统计分析中学习。现在一些较为传统的经济学建议显然已经无效。政策制定者不能依照简单的政策指南，如维持财政收支平衡、用货币政策来控制通货膨胀、保持宏观经济的稳定，依赖市场来解决其他一切挑战。以为这样就能促进经济增长并惠及穷人的看法实际上是不成立的。当前世界的一些困扰恰恰是过去太过于坚持上述建议的结果。

---

① 林毅夫作为“斯德哥尔摩陈述”的起草人之一，在2016年第二届新结构经济学冬令营上介绍了“斯德哥尔摩陈述”为何被视为“华盛顿共识”关于政策制定原则的替代版的背景：这次会议的主要目的是对现代国际上盛行的“华盛顿共识”进行反思。“华盛顿共识”认为一个国家只要财政取得平衡，通货膨胀得到控制，政府维持社会稳定，市场就能够解决包括收入分配、环境以及产业升级等一切问题。但是，事实并非如此。例如，“华盛顿共识”中的一条原则强调政府的财政预算必须平衡，政府财政预算的平衡从长期来看是应该的，因为政府的赤字最后总是要有人买单。但是“华盛顿共识”主张每一期的预算都必须平衡则不适合，因为经济的发展有周期波动，如果在经济下滑时政府财政也需要平衡，可能会造成这个国家的经济难以复苏。所以，这个政策主张从长期来看是对的，但是短期来看就不完全恰当。另外，“华盛顿共识”所关注的范围也太局限，比如忽视了环境、收入分配等问题。但是现在发现这些问题对一个国家、一个社会的发展都至关重要。因此，需要对“华盛顿共识”不太正确之处进行修正，对其不完全的地方给予补充，以此来形成一个新的、可供每个国家在政策制定时参考的原则，这也正是这次会议的目的。

这份陈述并不是一张政策制定的蓝图，而是一系列的原则，我们希望这些原则有助于制定国家政策、促进全球对话以及设计多边政策。在当下这个日新月异的全球化世界，这些原则将愈发重要。

1. GDP增长本身并不是目的

我们认为，固然需要有促进GDP增长的政策，但GDP本身不该作为目的，而应作为一种手段，以创造资源来实现一系列社会目标，包括改善卫生、教育、就业、安全以及消费。个人福利是多维的，这也就意味着政策应旨在改善社会所珍视的方方面面，而不仅仅是提高收入。例如，应当向所有学龄前儿童提供更好的营养，确保每个人都有基本的医疗保障，并认识到这些其实都在可企及的范畴之内。如果正确的政策无法到位，GDP增长可能以福利损失为代价，包括当地环境以及全球气候恶化。同样值得注意的是，GDP增长本身并不能消除对弱势群体的不公正行为及歧视性做法，这通常需要采取有意的干预措施。

我们认识到，应当承认并不存在一个普遍适用于所有经济体的“药方”。文化、社会以及历史背景千差万别，这也就带来了不同社会的不同追求，并决定了何种政策有效、何种政策无效。过去，存在一种一些高收入国家试图为所有国家制定统一的政策规范的倾向。固然有些政策原则我们都应该遵守，但同时我们必须为多样性和因时因地的决策留出一定的空间。

2. 发展必须具有包容性

我们认为，政策应确保发展在社会及经济层面上具有包容性，任何人群都不会因为性别、种族或其他社会标识而被忽视。我们应当关注福利遭受严重损害的许多维度，尤其是那些福利正遭受多方面伤害的个人。然而，我们对最受剥夺者的关注仍然不够。并且，贫富之间以及主要社会群体间的差距同样值得关注。近几十年来，收入和财富的不平等程度加剧，包括卫生、教育在内的基本服务的获取机会都存在可见的、在道德上不可辩护的严重不平等。这不仅破坏了社会凝聚力，更让精英团体有机会通过政策制定来进一步加剧这种不平等。高度不平等反过来又会剥夺穷人的发言权，进而弱化民主。为女性及历史上受歧视的群体赋权的重要性不言而喻，而且这也同时为经济效率提供了坚实的基础。当出现政治动荡和社会冲突时，发展不再可能。发展政策若无法做到包容，则可能滋生社会冲突。总之，发展只有具有包容性才是在社会及经济层面上可持续的发展。

3. 环境可持续性是必需，而非一道选项

尽管在目标和执行上每个国家及区域因条件不同而不尽相同，但我们认为，发展政策制定必须将环境可持续性作为一个核心目标。在环境质量退化的地方，收入增长将会是福利及进步的虚假指标。此外，对资源的争夺以及因环境而引起的人口迁移将危及安全并引发冲突，进而抑制发展。从全球层面来看，气候变化对地球的生存构成长期的威胁，在短期至中期则会危及许多国家的生计、农业及生态环境。首先需要采取缓解措施，并且应当在全球层面上实施；适应性政策则需要在国家及地方层面上采取积极的干预与支持。显然，自由市场是解决不了这些问题的，国家的监管干预乃至多国的政策协调不可或缺。

4. 应当平衡市场、政府与社会团体的作用

对于我们所要达到的目标及世界各地所面临的全球性挑战，一项发展政策需要建立在市场、政府及社会团体作用的明智平衡之上。要认识到，市场本身是一种社会制度，需要存在有效的监管体系，市场才能实现有效配置资源的功能。此外，即便在一些领域市场能带来效率，但正如我们所知道的，饥荒可以存在于一个有效的自由市场，市场本身不会有实现包容和公平的自发倾向。在过去的四分之一世纪里，向着不受约束的自由市场发展的趋势，导致了当前世界面临的金融危机，使得不平等达到了难以维持以及发展到了不可持续的程度。

然而，认识到了市场作用的局限性，我们同样要求政府的运行本身必须有效。一个国家在许多方面可以超越市场：不同层面的政府可以发挥许多重要的作用，公民社会的许多组织形式包括合作社、协会、非政府组织等也可以发挥重要作用。如果一项事务由市场或社会团体来运作更好，那么政府就不应该掺和进去。通常，各个制度发挥的作用具有互补性。在某些情况下，最贫困者的福利能通过社区团体获得极大的提升。尽管我们知道有些地方社会机构被一些不良势力控制，但各级公民社会组织对促进和维持社会凝聚力起到了重要作用。

在此我们重申，在制定规则并建立监管体系方面政府是不可或缺的，也只有基于此，市场和社会组织才能蓬勃发展。一套好的规则体系能带来更强的社会凝聚力和信任度，从而减轻不平等程度、促进增长并在各个方面提升福利水平。此外，在那些市场无法有效发挥作用的领域，尤其是金融、卫生和环境方面，以及基于包容性要求而需要干预的问题，如女性赋权、保护弱势群体及解决过度的收入不平等，政府需要发挥责无旁贷的作用。在制定产业政策及有效的农业、服务业政策上，政府同样需要发挥作用。最后，政府必须防止因为不平等的加重导致自身被挟持，从而进一步加剧社会、政治及经济层面不平等程度的恶性循环。

5. 提供宏观经济的稳定

许多传统政策建议集中于维持宏观经济稳定的必要性。一个更稳定的经济体能实现更高速的增长，并进一步提升福利。达到宏观经济稳定需要政策管理，使

整个经济保持在平稳发展的根基上，并关注当前政策的长期影响，尤其是保证财政与外部金融的可持续性。各国应当在高增长时期储备财政资源，以便应对不时之需。尽管就长期而言财政纪律是重要的，这一点传统经济学强调的并没有错，然而结果是政策制定者往往对预算平衡有着拜物教式的崇拜。

我们必须认识到，在债务受到审慎管理且货币化带来的通货膨胀结果得到控制的情况下，财政刺激和公共投资通常对摆脱经济停滞的陷阱至关重要。公共投资对基础设施建设以及绿色技术非常重要，这些项目通常只有在长期施行时才能获得收益，因而很难吸引私人投资。此外，宏观审慎措施可以作为货币政策的补充，以遏制泡沫的发展、缓解可能带来不稳定的资本流动并防止过度的对外负债。

6. 关注全球技术和不平等带来的影响

随着近年来的技术进步，政策制定领域出现了一项特殊的挑战。技术进步连接了全球劳动市场，使得发展中国家的劳动者无须流动就得以在当地为全球市场和消费者工作。这固然为劳动者提供了新的机遇，但同时也加剧了国内的不平等程度。高收入国家倾向于将此看作一个劳动力竞争的问题，即发达国家与发展中国家的劳动者存在利益冲突。然而，遗憾的是这忽视了一个更现实的问题，即劳动与资本的竞争问题。在自动化、机器人技术的兴起以及劳动力市场的全球化进程中，替代劳动者收入的是公司和机器所有者的更高额利润。这些后果是我们必须解决的问题，而非将此转化为全球劳动力间的角力问题。

由此，我们提出三项必要的应对政策。首先，在技术进步的同时，必须加大提升技能和技术互补的人力资本投资，从而使劳动收入得以随着技术进步而提高。其次，必须创造新的政策工具来进行国内的收入转移。工资占GDP比重的下降，不应当被看作技术进步不可避免的结果，政府必须建立税收及利益分配制度来打破这种趋势，并制定一系列的法规，如强制执行的竞争法则以及提升工人在社会和公司中话语权的劳动法。最后，这种趋势使得多国间的政策制定尤为必要。多边机构有责任鼓励各国政策的协调，并且倡导不仅考虑高收入工业化国家的利益而且保障新兴经济体利益的政策，后者在国际决策中经常被剥夺话语权。

7. 社会规范与思维模式至关重要

在传统经济学看来，社会规范和思维模式对于我们的经济生活无关紧要。然而越来越多的研究表明，事实并非如此。我们的价值观和文化不仅本身具有意义，还影响着经济的运行。一个人与人之间相互信任的社会，它的经济表现会比一个人与人之间缺乏信任的社会要好。例如，对同一组选项，当它们以不同次序或不同的默认选项呈现给人们时，人们最终选择的结果会有所差异。各国政府需要开始利用这些新的知识和措施以更有效地推行政策。事实上，私营公司长久以来经常利用对人类心理学和社会偏好的了解，来提升它们自身的利益和利润。在致力于提升公共利益时，如果政府希望有效地提供教育和卫生服务，那么公平征税和加深对社会规范的理解也应当纳入政策制定中。社会规范和思维模式在遏制腐败方面也能发挥重要作用。腐败问题在各国存在重要的特定情境差异，因为社会规范和思维模式正是一个社会历史和经验的产物。

8. 全球政策和国际社会的责任

全球化的力量越来越制约着各国政府的发展政策选择，这些力量给各国带来限制和机会，并且，它们本身取决于其他国家的行动。

高收入国家的货币政策会影响流向发展中国家的资本。正如2008年金融危机所充分表明的，富国的金融管制政策虽然首先影响富国自身，但最终还会对新兴经济体及发展中国家产生深远影响。对避税天堂采取的政策与管制，会影响所有国家尤其是低收入国家的政府为包容和可持续发展政策筹集资金的能力。一国的贸易政策会影响其他国家的出口预期。高收入国家的移民政策则会影响低收入国家公民改善其自身生活，并通过汇款和知识转移来帮助其祖国发展的可能性。如上种种，在当下这个全球化的世界，任何一个国家的行为都会对其他国家产生连带影响。也正因如此，所有国家都有责任把这个世界上最困苦的人们考虑在内，提升他们的发展机遇。

跨国协议与制度对解决我们当下迫在眉睫的问题至关重要。然而，这些协议与制度却也是最难以建立和维持的。尽管巴黎气候变化协定有了一个好的开头，全世界都在等着所有国家对排放问题采取措施所做的承诺的落实，以及高收入国家给低收入国家采取适应气候变暖和减排措施提供帮助的承诺的落实。近年来，我们见证了来自传统渠道的发展援助的下降以及许多新建的双边和多边发展机构的出现，然而几十年前向国际社会承诺的达到国内生产总值0.7%的官方发展援助的目标越来越难以实现。国际社会有责任确保这些援助用于发展中国家及发展中国家内部受到边缘化的群体，确保发展中国家在国际机构的治理结构中得到更好的代表，而这也会反过来保证国际协定及公约能充分考虑发展中国家的诉求。

**展望**

在应对发展带来的挑战中，如果各国采取平衡市场、政府和社会的务实政策，并且国际社会共同努力减轻全球化带来的约束并抓住新的机遇，那么当下的技术进步，将切实转化为包括最底层在内的所有人的福利提升。我们可以实现一个繁荣共享的世界，过去的错误和成功给我们提供了一套各国乃至全球层面的政策制定应当遵循的原则。现在是系统性地应用这些原则以制定经济发展政策的时候了！

#### 1.3.2.3 第三代发展经济学：新结构经济学[①]

由“斯德哥尔摩陈述”的起草人之一林毅夫倡导的新结构经济学是在反思战后结构主义和1980年代的新自由主义的基础上提出的第三代发展经济学的代表。“新结构经济学”的雏形是林毅夫、蔡昉和李周于1994年出版的《中国的奇迹》一书。对于该书的写作背景，林毅夫回忆道：“在二次世界大战后，东亚是世界上最为贫穷的地区，人多、自然资源少，曾被认为是世界上最不具发展希望的地区。然而日本在战后迅速恢复，到了20世纪60年代成为第一个非白种人的高收入经济体。接着亚洲‘四小龙’——中国台湾、中国香港、韩国、新加坡——到了70年代也成为充满活力的新兴工业化经济体。在这些事实面前，世界银行作为世界上最为重要的多边发展机构，自20世纪90年代初起每隔4年对东亚经济进行一次主题研究，概括其独特的发展经验与教训，揭示既定时期的问题与挑战。这个系列研究中的第一个报告发表于1993年，题为《东亚奇迹：经济增长与公共政策》，首次系统研究了东亚8个经济发展表现卓尔不群经济体的成功原因。这8个经济体除日本和亚洲‘四小龙’外还包括印度尼西亚、马来西亚和泰国。虽然从1978年年底开始改革开放到1993年，中国已经取得了15年年均9.7%的高速增长，在一个底子薄、人口超10亿又处于转型期的国家取得这样的成绩在人类经济史上前所未有，但是《东亚奇迹》有意无意地忽略了中国经济增长的故事，作为中国的经济学者，我们义不容辞地以‘中国的奇迹’为题，分析了中国转型期经济增长奇迹背后的道理，预测了这个奇迹是否有可能持续，探讨了如何深化改革才可以将之继续保持下去。”[②]

《中国的奇迹》一书系统阐述了中华人民共和国成立以后我国重工业赶超战略与当时中国人多资本少的禀赋特征之间的政府干预矛盾，揭示了扭曲价格的宏观经济政策、资源计划配置与剥夺微观主体自主权“三位一体”的计划经济体制的内生形成机制，用比较优势战略对东亚奇迹进行了重新解释，分析了改革开放之后发展战略转轨为比较优势战略与当时劳动力相对资本富裕的禀赋特征之间的相容，总结了发展战略渐进式转型的经验。可以说，《中国的奇迹》这本书基本上构建了以要素禀赋结构为分析的切入点，关于发展与转型以及政府

① 对于前两波发展思潮存在的问题的评论可参见：杰拉尔德·迈耶：“老一代发展经济学家和新一代发展经济学家”，载于杰拉尔德·迈耶、约瑟夫·斯蒂格利茨，《发展经济学前沿：未来展望》，中国财政经济出版社，2004年版。

② 林毅夫，《中国的奇迹：发展战略与经济改革》（增订版），格致出版社，2014年版。

作用的新结构经济学的基本理论框架。《经济发展与转型》一书是以林毅夫2007年在英国剑桥大学的马歇尔讲座的内容为基础出版的，该书以《中国的奇迹》的理论框架为基础，将基于中国经验提炼的理论推广到全球历史背景下，以发展战略遵循还是违背比较优势为出发点提出了发展与转型一系列可验证的假说，如发展战略对经济增长、经济波动、收入分配、制度扭曲等的影响，并用战后发展中国家的经验数据对各个假说做了经验检验，绝大部分实证结果符合理论预期。新结构经济学的一般理论成型之作产生于2009年6月林毅夫教授于其出任世界银行高级副行长兼首席经济学家一周年的一个内部研讨会上，以他1994年出版的《中国的奇迹》和2007年出版的《经济发展与转型》两本书的理论框架为基础，反思了自第二次世界大战以后发展经济学成为一门学科以来的理论进展和发展中国家发展与转型的成败经验，指出第一代的"结构主义"发展经济学忽视了产业结构的内在性，重视政府的作用而忽视市场的作用，第二代的"新自由主义"发展经济学重视市场而忽视政府作用的偏颇，提出以"新结构经济学"作为第三代发展经济学，强调经济发展是一个产业、技术、基础设施、制度结构不断内生变迁的过程，在这个过程中既要有"有效的市场"根据市场竞争和价格决定具有比较优势的产业，给企业家的作用提供空间，也要有"有为的政府"来克服经济发展转型中必然存在的外部性和软硬基础设施完善的协调等市场失灵问题。2011年3月，林毅夫应邀到耶鲁大学做著名的库茨涅茨年度讲座，以"新结构经济学：反思发展问题的一个理论框架"为题阐述了新结构经济学理论的基本框架和主要观点，演讲全文发表于2011年出版的《世界银行研究观察》第26卷第2期，向经济学界正式宣告了新结构经济学的诞生。2012年林毅夫在世界银行的工作结束前将新结构经济学的有关论文结集为《新结构经济学：反思经济发展与政策的理论框架》一书，系统论述了新结构经济学的基本理论分析框架、所依赖的经验特征事实、政府在结构变迁动态机制中的因势利导作用及其应用案例等新结构经济学的核心内容。基于在世界银行的工作经验以及对广大发展中国家的观察，林毅夫又出版了《繁荣的求索：发展中经济如何崛起》《超越发展援助：在一个多极世界中重构发展合作新理念》《战胜命运：跨越贫困陷阱，创造经济奇迹》等书，对新结构经济学的理论和应用进行了深入浅出的阐述。林毅夫等著述的《新结构经济学文集》《新结构经济学新在何处》等则系统探讨了新结构经济学各个子领域的相关研究。

正如新制度经济学的命名者威廉姆森所言，契约多样性可谓"资本主义经济制度研究无数谜团的起源"。并且，相对于新古典经济学的"选择的科学"（the science of choice），威廉姆森也将新制度经济学称为"缔约的科学"（the science of contract）。同样，在新结构经济学看来，结构多样性可谓发展中经济体经济发展与转型以及政府作用研究无数谜团的起源。顺理成章，在我们看来，新结构经济学可以被称为"结构的科学"（the science of structure），而不仅局限于发展经济学一隅，更不限于关于发展战略的比较优势学说，有着极其重要的理论范式突破。

新结构经济学的理论出发点遵循了经济学之父亚当·斯密在《国民财富的性质和原因的研究》(简称《国富论》) 一书中所倡导的研究方法，也就是从现代经济增长的本质及其决定因素入手，即人均收入水平提高的不断加速，而这主要取决于技术不断创新和产业不断升级所推动的劳动生产率的不断提高。[①]随着生产结构（产业结构与技术结构）的升级，对应的金融结构、人力资本结构、区域结构（包括城市化）、开放结构（国际金融与国际贸易）、周期结构、制度结构、人口资源环境结构以及相应地降低交易费用的软硬基础设施结构等结构安排也需要随之升级。任何经济体的经济结构变迁都是一个连续的动态过程，每一发展阶段都是这条连续谱上的一点。尽管人类社会经济发展的本质相同，但是处于不同发展阶段的国家，由于禀赋结构不同，相应也会有不同的生产结构及其对应的其他经济结构安排。例如，处于初级发展阶段的国家，其要素禀赋结构一般会呈现出劳动力或自然资源相对丰裕，同时资本相对稀缺的特点，因而生产也多集中于劳动力或资源密集型产业（主要有维持生存的农业、畜牧业、渔业和采矿业），采用传统的、成熟的技术，生产"成熟的"和"绿色的"产品。除了矿业和棉花等少数农产品的庄园种植，这些生产活动很少有规模经济。这些国家的企业规模一般而言相对较小，市场交换往往也不正规，通常仅限于在当地市场上跟熟人进行交易。这种生产和交易对硬件和软件基础设施的要求不高，只需要相对简单、初级的基础设施就可以了。与之相反，位于发展阶段谱系另一端的高收入国家，则呈现出一幅完全不同的禀赋结构图景。这些国家相对丰裕的要素不是劳动力，也不是自然资源，而是资本，因而在资本密集型产业中具有比较优势，这些产业具有规模经济的特征。各种硬件（电力、通信、道路、港口等）和软件（法律法规体系、文化价值系统等）基础设施也必须与全国性乃至全球性的市场活动相适应，这种情形下的市场交易是远距离、大容量、高价值的。人类社会的经济发展就是这些经济结构不断变迁的过程。因此，处于全球结构变迁前沿的发达经济体的结构安排实际上只是全球整个连续谱的一个经验特例。

现有的主流理论大都来自发达国家的经验总结，而从工业革命以后发达国家的技术和产业都处于世界的最前沿，对于它们来说，技术创新和产业升级都只能自己发明，而发展中国家的产业和技术大多处于世界的前沿之内，它们的技术创新和产业升级可以有后来者优势。并且，发达国家和发展中国家可以动员的资源，面对的各种要素价格、风险因素和软硬件基

---

① 经济快速增长的现象是在18世纪以后才出现的。根据经济史学家麦迪森的研究，18世纪以前西欧国家人均收入的年平均增长率只有0.05%，人均收入需要1 400年的时间才能翻一番。18世纪以后到19世纪中叶，其人均收入年平均增长率提高到1%，人均收入翻一番所需要的时间缩短到70年。从19世纪中叶到现在，人均收入年平均增长率为2%，人均收入翻一番的时间降至35年。上述增长加速的现象是18世纪中叶开始的工业革命的结果。

础设施的瓶颈限制也不一样，适用的产业结构和技术结构以及基础设施结构也不一样，不同的产业结构和技术结构由于其特性不同，适宜的金融结构、人力资本结构、区域结构（包括城市化）、开放结构（包括国际金融与国际贸易）、周期结构、制度结构、人口资源环境结构等各种结构安排也不相同。所以，适宜于前沿发达经济体的经济结构安排不见得适用于发展中国家。忽视了这些环环相扣的结构性差异，因而，从第二次世界大战以后按西方主流理论来制定发展政策的国家没有一个成功，而极少数成功国家的发展政策从西方主流理论来看却是错误的。如结构主义与“新自由主义”都因忽视了经济体的禀赋结构、生产结构以及对应的其他结构安排环环相扣的内生差异性而失败。所以说，单单基于处于人类社会整个连续谱结构变迁前沿的发达经济体的结构安排这一经验特例的西方主流理论，对于处在整个连续谱结构变迁不同阶段的广大发展中经济体而言却是理论陷阱。一个国家陷入低收入陷阱或中等收入陷阱是由于其结构未能有动态的变迁。按照新结构经济学的基本主张，遵循一国每一时点的要素禀赋结构所决定的比较优势来选择技术、发展产业，这样的经济会有最大的竞争力，可以创造最多的剩余，进行最快的资本积累以提升要素禀赋结构，进而升级产业结构、促进收入增长、消除贫困的最好办法。发展中国家的适宜性目标不一定非得是最前沿发达经济体的经济结构，以后者为标杆甚至会适得其反。既然结构变迁是一个连续的动态过程，每一阶段都是这条连续谱上的一点，基于整个连续谱结构变迁前沿的发达经济体这一特例的西方主流理论不具有普遍性，那么新结构经济学就试图构建一门具有普遍意义的结构科学，来理解人们在结构变迁过程中观察到的、关于持续增长的各种特征事实背后的因果关系。因此，可以说基于经济结构前沿的发达经济体经验（如卡尔多特征事实）的主流理论其实只是基于整个世界经济结构变迁谱系经验特征的新结构经济学的理论退化特例。换言之，新结构经济学在理论上更为高阶。[①]

### 1.3.3 新结构经济学学科理论体系概要[②]

新结构经济学理论与西方主流经济学理论的本质差别在于，后者以发达国家的结构为其暗含的唯一结构，并且为了数学建模的方便，经常用一个生产函数来描述发达国家和发展中

① 可进一步参考：林毅夫、付才辉、王勇，《新结构经济学新在何处》，北京大学出版社，2016 年版。

② 想了解新结构经济学的学科全貌可参见教科书：林毅夫、付才辉，《新结构经济学导论》（上、下册），高等教育出版社，2019 年版。

国家，在这样的模型设定下就没有结构的概念，发达国家和发展中国家也就只有量的差异而没有质的区别，前者则倡导以新古典的现代经济学方法来研究经济发展过程中经济结构（包括技术、产业、硬的基础设施、软的制度环境等）及其变迁的决定因素和影响，主张在每一时点的经济结构内生决定于该时点给定的、决定该经济体总预算和相对价格的要素禀赋和其结构①。因此，新结构经济学实际上是使忽视了发达国家和发展中国家结构差异的现代主流经济学理论成为其理论体系的一个退化特例。用现代经济学的术语和模型来表述这种差别就是：西方主流经济学理论（新古典经济学）是以给定不变的代表特定技术集的生产函数求解最优资源配置，在这种模型中发展中国家和发达国家只有量的差异而没有质的区别；新结构经济学则全部颠覆过来——以给定的禀赋结构求解最优的代表特定产业和其相应技术集的生产函数及其动态变化，在这种模型中发达国家和发展中国家既有量的差异也有质的区别。②这种范式的转变实际上是参照系的转变：西方主流理论是以最发达国家或地区作为参照，看发展中国家或地区和发达国家相比缺什么（产业技术）或有什么做得不好（市场制度），以此来改造发展中国家；而新结构经济学则完全颠覆过来了，从发展中国家或地区自身有什么（禀赋条件）出发，在此基础上把现在能够做好的（比较优势）产业，发挥政府因势利导的作用帮助产业中的企业在市场中做大做强，逐步实现发展。③

---

① 按经济学的命名规则，以新古典经济学的方法来研究一个经济体的结构和结构变迁的决定因素及其影响，应该取名为结构经济学，为了和结构主义区分，故取名为新结构经济学。

② 付才辉，“最优生产函数理论——从新古典经济学向新结构经济学的范式转换”，《经济评论》，2018年第1期，第3-44页。

③ 与新结构经济学的结构范式不同，发展经济学乃至一般性的经济学领域目前主要的范式还是非结构性的，即可以称之为“X理论范式”。在刚刚步入21世纪的时候，世界银行组织了几代发展经济学先驱们对发展的思想进行了回顾与反思，其中阿德尔曼在“发展理论中的误区及其对政策的含义”一文中深刻地指出：“没有哪个经济学领域像经济发展那样在其主要范式上经历了那么多意外的变化。发展经济学的曲折经历对发展政策产生了深刻的影响。特别是，主要的发展范式决定了与政府在经济中的理想作用、政府干预的程度、干预的形式和方向以及政府—市场互动的实质等问题有关的政策处方”（杰拉尔德·迈耶、约瑟夫·斯蒂格利茨，《发展经济学前沿：未来展望》，中国财政经济出版社，2004年版，第73页）。“发展经济学的主要范式之所以存在很多突然的变化，其根本原因一直就在于人们总是想为不发达找出一个单一的原因（从根本上说，这是错误的），并由此找到一种单一的解决办法，即发展理论。根据‘简单，否则就是愚蠢’的原则，一种特殊的论证方式被创造出来了，而且这种方式基本上不曾变化，即不发达是由于要素X的制约，解决了X，发展就是必然的结果。但是随着时间的推移，由于从过去的失败和成功中吸取的历史经验和教训不同，以及对上面所列的范式变化的其他根源所做出的反应也不同，因此对什么是要素X，答案是大不同的……人们关于最佳形式的政府—市场互动关系和一些主要的政策杠杆建议也是如此。寻找发展的唯一法宝从根本上说是错误的，因为它的基础是一种简单的机械主义发展观和体制观。但是在过去半个世纪中，人们像炼金术士寻找点金石一样寻找着要素X，这种现象一直左右着经济发展中的理论和实证研究……X等于有形资本（1940—1970年）、X等于企业家精神（1958—1965年）、X等于不正确的相对价格（1970—1980年）、X等于国际贸易（1980— ）、X等于强有力的政府（1980—1996年）、X等于人力资本（1988— ）、X等于无效政府（1997— ）”（杰拉尔德·迈耶、约瑟夫·斯蒂格利茨，《发展经济学前沿：未来展望》，中国财政经济出版社，2004年版，第74—

新结构经济学这种思想与理论范式的革新反映了马克思历史唯物主义所揭示的经济基础决定上层建筑，上层建筑反作用于经济基础的道理。新结构经济学从一个经济体每一时点的要素禀赋这一物质存在为出发点，来探讨决定其生产力水平和生产方式的技术和产业的内生选择，并进而探讨适应于产业和技术的软硬基础设施，这一分析方式源于马克思主义经济基础决定上层建筑的历史唯物主义。[①]不过，新结构经济学应用国际通用的现代科学研究方法继承和发展了马克思历史唯物主义。实际上，新结构经济学为新古典经济学和马克思主义经济学的分析范式找到了一条融合的道路。

经过近30年来林毅夫教授及其弟子以及学界追随者的不断开拓，新结构经济学理论体系日趋完善。由于将结构及其变迁引入现代经济学并用现代经济学的科学方法体现马克思主义政治经济学的“经济基础决定上层建筑，上层建筑反作用于经济基础”的理论内核，新结构经济学的理论体系非常庞大，涵盖了经济发展过程中经济结构及其变迁现象的方方面面，新结构经济学的中心思想可以概括为围绕发展、转型以及市场和政府在经济运行中发挥作用的基本原理。

在发展问题上，新结构经济学的切入点是现代经济发展、收入不断提升的本质，即决定劳动生产率水平的技术不断创新、产业不断升级，以及决定交易费用的硬的基础设施和软的制度环境不断完善的结构变迁的过程。由于不同发展程度的国家经济结构内生决定于该国家的要素禀赋结构，一个国家实现快速包容可持续发展的最优方式是按照该国每一时点给定的要素禀赋结构所决定的比较优势来选择所要发展的产业和所要采用的技术。由此，在具有合适的软硬基础设施的条件下，该国将会以最低的要素生产成本和交易成本、最大的竞争力，创造出最大的经济剩余，投资会有最大的回报，积累的积极性会最高，资本禀赋增加和要素禀赋结构提升，产业结构和技术升级的速度也会最快。一个发展中国家按此路径来发展，在技术变迁、产业升级和软硬基础设施的完善上也可以享有后来者优势，取得比发达国家更快的经济增长，实现向发达国家收入水平的收敛。企业家在经济发展过程中会自发按照要素禀赋结构所决定的比较优势来选择产业和技术的前提是要素相对价格必须反映要素的相对稀缺

---

82页）。实际上，这种X理论如今依然主导着关于发展的前沿学术文献和主流教材。例如，对于如何解释为什么有的国家富裕有的国家贫穷这一基本的问题，一些标准化的X要素就至少包括物质资本、人力资本、技术与效率等直接要素，政策、法律规则、腐败、制度、文化、地理、气候、运气乃至一些最新前沿文献强调的种族和遗传基因等间接要素甚至具有贫困本身等宿命性的因素。例如，关于基因与发展的所谓的最新前沿研究（Oded Galor and Omer Moav, “Natural Selection and the Origin of Economic Growth”, *The Quarterly Journal of Economics*, 2002 Vol. 117, No. 4, pp. 1133–1191; Q. Ashraf, and O. Galor, “The ‘Out of Africa’ Hypothesis, Human Genetic Diversity, and Comparative Economic Development”, *American Economic Review*, 2013, Vol.103, No.1, pp.1–46.）。这与林毅夫和孟加所著的《战胜命运：跨越贫困陷阱，创造经济奇迹》（北京大学出版社，2017年版）一书的思想迥然不同。

① 林毅夫，“我在经济学研究道路上的上下求索”，北京大学新结构经济学研究中心网站，2016年版。

性，这样的相对价格只能存在于充分竞争的市场，因此，按照比较优势发展经济是以存在充分竞争的市场为制度前提的。由于经济发展不是静态的资源最优配置，而是一个技术不断创新、产业不断升级以及硬的基础设施和软的制度环境不断完善的结构变迁过程，在这个过程中必须对技术创新和产业升级的先行者给予外部性的补偿，协调相应的软硬基础设施的完善，这些工作仅能由政府来做，因此，也必须有一个“有为的政府”，经济结构才能顺利按照要素禀赋结构和比较优势的变化变动。所以，“有效的市场”和“有为的政府”是经济快速可持续发展的两个最重要的制度前提。

在转型或改革问题上，新结构经济学的切入点是企业自生能力，即企业所在行业是否符合要素禀赋结构所决定的比较优势。由于对一个国家在某一时点上的产业和技术结构内生决定于该时点的要素禀赋结构缺乏认识，在第二次世界大战以后，许多发展中国家摆脱了殖民地、半殖民地身份，出于快速追赶发达国家的主观良好愿望，试图在资本短缺的要素禀赋结构条件下去发展和发达国家相同的资本密集型现代化大产业。第二次世界大战后发展经济学的第一代——结构主义，为这种发展战略提供了理论支撑。但是政府想优先发展的这种产业违反要素禀赋结构所决定的比较优势，企业在开放竞争的市场中要素生产成本会比在该产业上具有比较优势的企业高，没有竞争力，因而缺乏自生能力，政府必须靠对各种要素价格的扭曲和对市场的干预，给予这些企业保护补贴才能把这种“先进”的产业建立起来，结果导致资源错误配置和寻租。虽然先进的产业建立起来了，但是经济发展的绩效低下，发展中国家和发达国家的差距继续扩大。

由于对政府的各种扭曲和干预是内生决定于保护补贴赶超产业中不具备自生能力的企业的需要缺乏认识，发展经济学的第二代——新自由主义，倡导以华盛顿共识的“私有化、市场化、稳定化”，用“休克疗法”的方式一次性地把各种保护补贴取消掉，来进行从政府主导的经济向市场经济转型。在20世纪八九十年代，绝大多数社会主义国家和非社会主义发展中国家，遵循华盛顿共识的建议，用“休克疗法”来进行转型，结果不是新自由主义所预期的经济稍微下滑后快速的“J”形复苏，而是“L”形的经济崩溃、停滞、危机不断，出现了所谓的“失去的20年”。然而，中国和少数几个国家采用的被主流理论认为是最糟的渐进的双轨制改革，其实是一个务实的、比较好的转型策略。这种转型方式一方面给予旧的违反比较优势产业中缺乏自生能力的企业必要的转型期保护补贴；另一方面放开对原来受到抑制的产业的准入，并在软硬基础设施普遍不好、政府可用资源有限的条件下，以工业园、加工出口区等方式局部改善基础设施和营商环境以因势利导符合比较优势产业的发展，这种方式在转型过程中能够同时取得稳定和快速发展的绩效。快速的发展则能够不断积累资本，使许多原来违反比较优势的产业逐渐变得符合比较优势，企业由不具有自生能力变得具有自生能力，旧体制下遗留下来的保护补贴也就从“雪中送炭”变为“锦上添花”，能够取消掉也应取消掉以完成从计划经济向市场经济的过渡。

上述旨在揭示发展与转型以及市场和政府在其中作用的新结构经济学基本原理，事实上已经重构了发展经济学与转型经济学，并以此为突破口更一般地、系统地运用现代经济学的方法将结构全面引入了有关经济运行但忽视发展中国家和发达国家结构内生差异性的主流理论体系中，使其成为新结构经济学的退化特例。因此，新结构经济学理论方法和视角的创新可以自成体系地将结构差异的内生性及其分析逻辑引入各个传统的经济学子领域，构建起诸如新结构增长经济学、新结构产业经济学、新结构创新理论、新结构金融学、新结构劳动经济学、新结构区域经济学、新结构国际经济学、新结构货币和财政理论（宏观经济学）、新结构制度经济学、新结构人口资源环境经济学等子学科领域，这些领域便构成了整个新结构经济学完整的学科体系。①

图1.21直观地描述了新结构经济学整个学科架构的内在逻辑体系。整个新结构经济学理论体系的“牛鼻子”便是每一个时点给定、随时间可变的要素禀赋结构，由其内生决定每个时点的产业结构，并据此派生出对基础设施以及其他上层建筑结构安排的需求，比如产业结构的金融特性、教育特性、空间特性、开放特性、波动特性、环境特性与制度特性等。②因此，按照新结构经济学的理论，处于不同发展阶段的国家或地区由于要素禀赋结构不同，最优产业结构也不同，对应的最优金融结构、教育结构、空间结构、开放结构、环境结构、制度结构以及财政货币等宏观经济政策结构也必然不同。那么，我们就不能以处于世界经济发展前沿的发达国家作为参照系，认为发展中国家的这些经济结构安排及其运行特征不同于发达国家就是扭曲的结果，更不能据此要求发展中国家向发达国家整齐划一地看齐。这种做法如战后世界经济的实践所表明的那样，其效果往往南辕北辙。例如，金融系统的发展对于经济持续增长至关重要，但对其在这一过程中起到了怎样的具体作用却众说纷纭。人们观察到，发展中国家经济发展的主要约束之一是缺乏资本积累。从这一点出发，第一波旧结构主义发展思潮认为欠发达国家金融体系无法为资本密集型产业动员足够的资本源自人民缺乏储蓄习惯的文化倾向所造成的市场失灵，这些市场失灵无法单靠市场自身的力量来克服。他们建议政府插手干预这一资本积累过程，动员储蓄，压低利率，配置信贷，以支持先进的资本密集型产业的发展。然而，这种以压低利率的金融抑制来发展违背比较优势的产业的发展战略往往导致发展中国家绩效差，发展不可持续，出现债务危机。吸取这些教训后，第二波新自由主义发展思潮提倡自由化，主张取消政府的各种干预、扭曲和补贴，认为官僚们通常既无激

---

① 相关内容可以参考：付才辉，“构建我国自主创新的新结构经济学学科：综述、架构与展望”，《制度经济学研究》，2015年第4期，第1–80页。

② 详细的教材可参考：林毅夫、付才辉，《新结构经济学导论》（下册），高等教育出版社，2019年版。

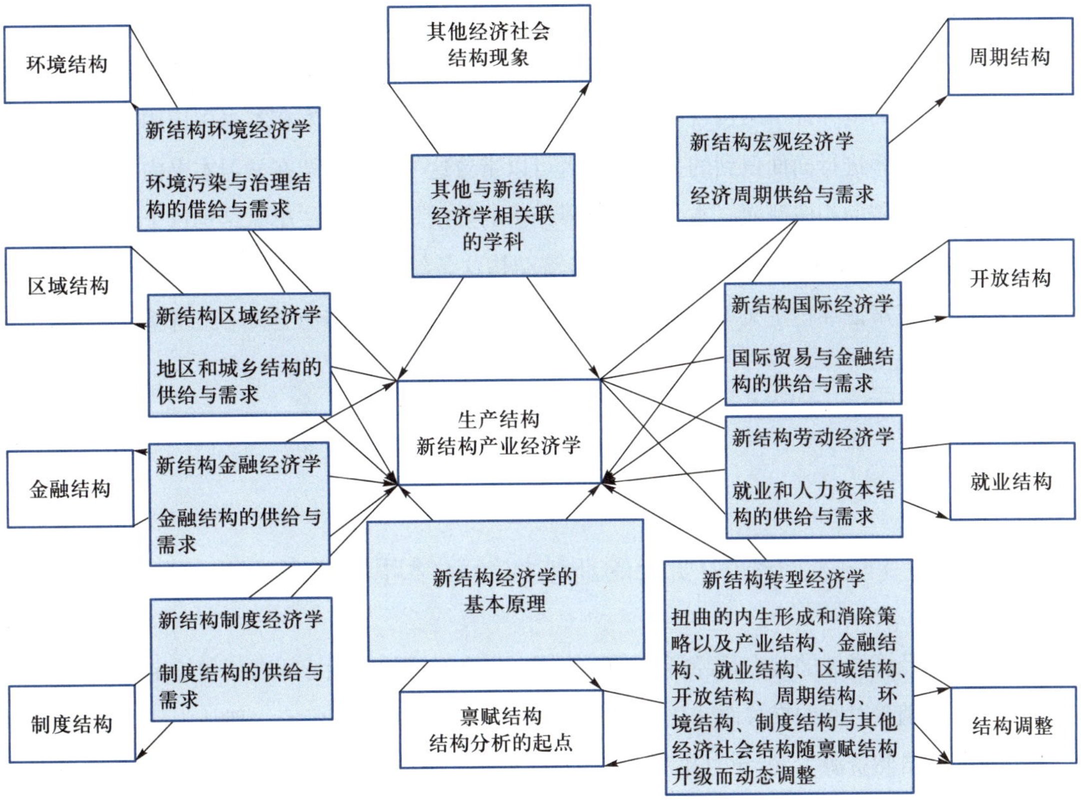


图1.21 新结构经济学学科架构的内在逻辑体系：结构的科学

励也无能力有效地干预信贷和各种资源的配置及定价，而界定清晰的产权体系、运作良好的合约制度安排以及竞争会为一个健全的市场系统的出现创造条件。他们建议政府放弃对银行和各种国有企业的所有权，去除对信贷和各种物资的政府定价和计划配置，并放开资本账户让资本在国际上自由流动。新结构经济学尽管也同意金融抑制、价格扭曲和政府干预的负面效果，却强调如下事实：那些扭曲和干预是人为设计出来的，目的是保护发展中国家优先部门中缺乏自生能力的企业，那些企业有的和国防安全有关，有的和国计民生有关，并且提供了大量的就业，即使私有化以后，为了国家的安全和社会的稳定也不能让其破产倒闭，私有的、不能让其倒闭的、需要政府补贴的企业所有者反而有更强的寻租动机。新结构经济学强调，要在转轨过程中同时实现经济稳定和快速增长，进行自由化改革时的政策顺序就很重要。新自由主义指导下的改革不但未能结束发展中国家的债务危机，反而加剧了发展中经济体的金融危机。不仅发展中国家如此，这种自由化的思潮也为发达国家的金融危机、收入分配差距扩大、社会矛盾恶化埋下隐患。总之，新结构经济学将不同发展程度的国家结构差异的内生性引入现代经济学的各个领域而产生了不同于旧结构经济学和新古典经济学在发展、转型和经济运行上的各种新的见解。

这个分析体系为我们解读世界经济的发展、转型与运行提供了一个全新的分析框架。然而，现实中的世界经济结构现象丰富多彩，我们不可能也没必要在本书中应用新结构经济学这个理论体系进行面面俱到的分析，读者可以带着这一分析框架在学习本书内容的基础上去理解世界经济的相应侧面。本书解读世界经济的红线是牢牢抓住禀赋结构这个新结构经济学的“牛鼻子”，来分析其所内生决定的经济结构这条新结构经济学的基本原理。这种分析范式也反映了辩证唯物主义（要素禀赋这一物质存在）和历史唯物主义（经济基础决定上层建筑）的精髓。

### 1.3.4 理解经济结构变迁的新结构经济学理论要点①

分析经济发展的起点是经济的禀赋特征。一个经济的禀赋特征在任何给定的时间是给定的，但会随着时间的推移而变化。遵循古典经济学的传统经济学家一般认为一国的禀赋仅由土地（或自然资源）、劳动力和资本（包括物质和人力资本）构成。这些实际上是要素禀赋，是企业在生产中使用的。应该指出的是，新结构经济学强调资本劳动比的动态变化。这是因为，在实事求是地讨论一国的经济发展时，土地都是外生给定的，而自然资源的存量是固定的。理论上说，也应将基础设施作为一个经济体的禀赋的一部分。基础设施包括硬件（有形的）基础设施和软件（无形的）基础设施。硬件基础设施的例子包括高速公路、港口、机场、电信系统、电网和其他公共设施等。软件基础设施包括制度、条例、社会、资本价值体系以及其他社会和经济安排等。基础设施影响每个企业的交易成本和投资的边际收益。

经济发展要求在现有产业中不断引入新的、更好的技术。低收入国家的绝大多数人都以农业为生。农业技术的改进对于增加农民收入和减贫是必不可少的。然而，经济发展也要求经济不断地从现有附加值低的产业向新的、附加值高、资本密集度更高的产业扩展，从而实现产业多样化和产业升级。如果没有这样的结构变迁，人均收入持续增加的余地就很小。

发展中国家的产业位于国际产业前沿的内部，在产业升级过程中，具有后来者优势，资本密集度从小到大的所有产业都可供选择。然而，要实现向具有比较优势的资本更密集产业

① 这一部分的内容主要引自Lin Justin Yifu, “New Structural Economics: A Framework for Rethinking Development”, *World Bank Research Observer*, 2011, Vol.26, No.3, pp.193–221；更详细的内容可参见：林毅夫，《新结构经济学：反思经济发展与政策的理论框架》，北京大学出版社，2012年版，第1、2、3章。

升级，发展中国家首先需要升级其要素禀赋结构，而这就要求资本积累速度高于劳动力增长速度。当一个国家在经济发展过程中顺着产业阶梯拾级而上时，由于资本设备的不可分性，该国生产的规模效应也在扩大。该国企业的规模越大，需要越大的市场，这些都反过来要求基础设施（比如电力、交通、金融以及其他软件基础设施）的相应变化。产业升级和产业多样化的过程也增加了企业所面临的风险。企业离世界科技前沿越近，就越难从发达国家引进成熟技术，也就越需要自主研发新技术和新产品，从而面对的风险就越大。根据风险的来源，一个企业独有的风险可以分为三类：技术创新风险、产品创新风险和管理才能风险。在发展的初级阶段，企业倾向于使用成熟的技术为成熟的市场生产成熟的产品。此时企业面临的主要风险来自企业所有者和管理者的管理才能。当发展到了更高水平，企业往往需要发明新技术以向新市场生产新产品。此时，除管理才能风险以外，企业还会面临技术创新是否成功和市场是否接受其生产的新产品的风险。因此，虽然技术创新、产品创新和管理才能都影响企业的总体风险，但三者之间的相对重要性却因产业和发展阶段的不同而大不相同。随着企业规模、市场范围和风险性质的变化，以及产业结构的升级，经济对基础设施（包括硬件和软件）的要求也在发生变化。倘若软硬基础设施无法同时改善，各个产业的升级过程都将面临莱本斯坦讨论过的X无效率问题①。在任何给定时点，一个经济体的产业结构内生决定于该时点上劳动力、资本和自然资源的相对丰裕程度。因此，随着资本的积累或人口的增长，经济的要素禀赋结构也会发生变化，使其产业结构偏离原来发展阶段下的最优产业结构。

当企业所选择的产业和技术都与经济体要素禀赋所决定的比较优势相符时，其要素生产成本会在国际比较中处于最低水平，如果同时也有和产业相适应的软硬基础设施，交易成本也会处于低的水平，这个经济体在国内国际市场将会有竞争优势。随着这些充满竞争力的企业和产业不断成长，它们将占有更大的国内、国际市场份额，同时也将最大限度地创造经济剩余（表现为各个企业的利润和超过工人生存所需的工资水平）。而且，产业结构在那个要素禀赋结构下是最优的，因此如果把这些经济剩余重新投资的话，其回报也将最大。随着时间的推移，经济体将不断积累实物和人力资本，不断提升自身的要素禀赋结构、具有比较优势的产业和技术的资本相对密集度。

企业家关注的是利润。要想使企业自发进入和选择符合要素禀赋结构的产业和技术，该经济的价格体系就必须反映要素的相对稀缺性，而只有竞争性的市场才能做到这一点。因此，无论在哪一个发展水平上，市场都应被作为基础性的资源配置机制。这种遵循比较优势的发展方法对于贫穷国家的经济发展而言看起来或许是缓慢而令人沮丧的。但事实上，这种办法

---

① H. Leibenstein, “Allocative efficiency vs. ‘X-efficiency’”, *American Economic Review*, 1966, Vol.56, No.3, pp.392-415.

却是积累资本、提升要素禀赋结构、改变比较优势的最快方法。并且，只要能得到更为发达的国家已经开发出来且依然存在于这些国家的技术，并进入这类产业，发展中国家的产业结构升级速度还可加快。在每一个发展水平上，发展中国家的产业和技术由于和世界前沿存在差距，其企业在技术创新和产业升级上都可以选择已经存在的、适合该阶段要素禀赋结构的技术（并进入相关产业），而不用自己重新研发。

随着发展中国家沿产业和技术阶梯拾级而上，其他许多变化都随之而至。企业所采用的技术越来越复杂，资本需求增加，生产和市场规模也有了变化。远距离市场交易越来越多。因而，为了给新升级的产业中的企业降低交易成本，使其达到生产可能性边界，一个灵活、平稳的产业和技术升级过程就需要教育、金融、法律和硬件基础设施方面同时做出相应的改进。显而易见，单个企业无法有效地内部化所有这些变革成本，而多个企业之间为了应对这种挑战进行的自发协调往往也不可能实现。基础设施的改善需要集体行动，至少需要基础设施服务的提供者与工业企业二者之间协调行动。这样，就把政府拉了进来，政府要么自己进行这些基础设施的改善，要么就需要积极协调各方的行动。当一个经济体的禀赋结构发生变化之后，其潜在比较优势也会发生变化，那么哪些新产业符合这一新的比较优势呢？这就出现了信息不足的问题。要想进行产业升级，就要求有一些先驱企业去尝试解决这一问题。这些先驱成功企业不管成功还是失败，它们的经验教训都会带来有价值的信息外部性。因此，除了在改善硬件和软件基础设施中发挥积极作用，发展中国家的政府，跟发达国家的政府一样，还需要对先驱企业产生的信息外部性进行补偿。

### 专栏 1.3
### 新结构经济学的运用：在最不发达非洲的案例[①]

从第二次世界大战后开始，在第一代发展经济学（结构主义）和第二代发展

① 本专栏根据相关资料整理而成。关于新结构经济学视角下非洲经济发展的详细论述可参考如下的两卷工具书：Lin Justin Yifu, Célestin Monga, *The Oxford Handbook of Africa and Economics (I/II).* Oxford University Press, 2015。新结构经济学关于波兰的研究和应用可参考如下两部著作：Lin Justin Yifu and Alojzy Z. Nowak, *New Structural Economics for Less Advanced Countries.* University of Warsaw Faculty of Management Press, 2017; Lin Justin Yifu and Alojzy Z. Nowak, *New Structural Policy in An Open Market Economy*. University of Warsaw Faculty of Management Press, 2018。

经济学（新自由主义）的理论指导下制定政策，广大发展中经济体未能摆脱贫困，缩小和发达国家的差距。出于黔驴技穷的无奈与人道主义的考虑，西方发达国家与世界各发展机构越来越多地把发展议题转向以教育和健康为重点项目的援助。国际援助的有效性也越来越令人失望[①]，使得人们开始对发展项目和方案的效果进行更严格地评价。这就产生了发展研究的一条新思路，由麻省理工学院贫困研究室的2019年诺贝尔经济学奖获得者巴纳吉（Banerjee）和迪弗洛（Duflo）领衔推动，其目的是通过随机化控制试验来检验这些人道主义项目，以基于科学证据的政策来减贫。该趋势可以被称为是在现有的发展思路下，提高援助效率的“发展经济学2.5”版本。然而，作为第三代发展经济学的新结构经济学，与简单的国际援助不同，主张通过研究“授之以渔”而非“授之以鱼”的造血方法帮助发展中经济体脱贫致富。

在全球产业周期变化背景下，每个不同发展水平的经济体都可以识别其面临的全球产业窗口机遇期，通过工业园区的局部渐进式改革消除瓶颈，承接符合禀赋结构决定的潜在比较优势的产业转移，充分利用后来者优势迅速登上持续的经济发展之路。以中国为例，在1979年向市场经济转型时，营商环境差，基础设施落后，投资环境糟糕。按照“华盛顿共识”的建议，应该没有地区或产业偏好，一步到位地改善全国的基础设施、市场环境等，而不能优先支持特定部门和地区。相反，中国政府动员其有限的资源和实施能力建立了经济特区、加工出口区和工业园等。在特区和园区内部，基础设施瓶颈得以缓解，实施一站式服务，营商环境也变得富有竞争力。虽然在转型初期有低成本的劳动力，但是中国缺乏利用这个优势生产具有合格质量的劳动力密集型出口产品的知识。为了克服这些困难，中国各个地区的各级政府四处寻求外国投资者，鼓励他们在经济特区和工业园区内投资。采取这种办法，中国迅速建立起了劳动力密集型的轻工业，成为“世界工厂”。在局部地区取得的成功，增加了税收，为政府改善其他地方的基础设施和消除扭曲提供了资源和条件。这不仅是中国，而且也是东亚其他经济体发展成功的奥秘。

华坚鞋厂在埃塞俄比亚的快速成功生动地表明前述奥秘在其他发展中国家照样管用。根据林毅夫在世界银行领导开展的《非洲的轻工业》研究，埃塞俄比亚制鞋业的工资率只有中国同行业的1/10到1/8，将近越南同行业的一半；埃塞

① 林毅夫、王燕，《超越发展援助：在一个多极世界中重构发展合作新理念》，北京大学出版社，2016年版。

俄比亚的劳动生产率则大约为中国的70%，与越南大体相当。由于劳动成本大约只有中国总成本的1/4，埃塞俄比亚在制鞋业上应该很有竞争力。但是，2010年，中国的制鞋行业工人有1 900万，越南有120万，而埃塞俄比亚只有区区8 000人。2011年3月，埃塞俄比亚总理梅莱斯·泽纳维在林毅夫的建议下，于同年8月来到深圳招商引资，邀请中国的制鞋厂商去埃塞俄比亚投资。华坚公司的管理层应邀于2011年10月访问了埃塞俄比亚的首都亚的斯亚贝巴后，决定投资，2012年1月便在亚的斯亚贝巴附近的东方工业园开设了鞋厂。最初只有两条生产线，雇佣550个埃塞俄比亚工人，2012年12月迅速扩充到1 800人，使埃塞俄比亚的鞋业出口翻番，2013年12月达到3 500人，2016年达到6 500人，2018年达到8 000人。2012年之前，埃塞俄比亚和绝大多数非洲国家都很难在轻工业中吸引到出口导向型的外国直接投资。华坚鞋厂立竿见影的成功使外国投资者看到了埃塞俄比亚成为一个面向全球市场出口的轻工业基地的潜力。在世界银行的资金支持下，埃塞俄比亚政府在亚的斯亚贝巴新建了一个名叫博莱拉明（Bole Lamin）的工业园区。2013年仅仅用了3个月便有8栋建筑拔地而起、14栋在建。这些建筑租赁给出口导向型厂商，目前已有22家工厂入驻。按照世界银行的营商指数排名，埃塞俄比亚从2012年的125位跌到了2013年的127位，尽管如此，上述非凡的成功故事还是发生了。2017年埃塞俄比亚政府以10个月的时间在亚的斯亚贝巴以南275千米的哈瓦萨镇（Hawassa）建立一个新的工业园，迅速成为一个纺织和成衣加工出口的产业集群，到2018年8月时已经雇用了1万多名工人，预计到2022年时可达5万名工人。2018年按世界银行的营商指数排名，埃塞俄比亚排名进一步下滑至161位，但它却成为非洲国家中吸引外资在制造业直接投资最多的国家。在2012—2017年，埃塞俄比亚的年均增长速度高达9.8%，为非洲乃至全世界增长最快的国家。第10章我们将简要介绍埃塞俄比亚如何使用新结构经济学的“GIFF”进行转型的案例。

如表1.7所示，近十年来，尽管全球经济金融危机的阴霾并未完全散去，但是埃塞俄比亚取得了非凡的结构转型和经济增长。相对于全球金融危机爆发后的2009年，2017年埃塞俄比亚的制造业增加值占GDP的百分比提高了1.7个百分点，2016年制造业出口占商品出口的百分比提高了3.88个百分点，2017年农业就业人员占就业总数的百分比下降10.5个百分点。2009—2017年制造业增加值年增长率平均高达13.57%，人均GDP年增长率平均高达7.28%。这个案例告诉我们，包括撒哈拉以南非洲在内的发展中国家无须坐等所有的发展条件都具备了才行动。如果政府能够采取前述务实的发展方法，那么，随着中国的发展，工资增长，比较优势变化，来自中国潜在的8 500万的劳动力密集加工出口制造业工作机会将使几乎所有低收入国家实现如中国和其他东亚国家在过去数十年那样的动态增长。中国也正在和埃及、埃塞俄比亚、毛里求斯、尼日利亚与赞比亚建立经贸合作区。中国逐渐失去比较优势的巨大的劳动力密集型产业是广大低收入经济体新一轮国际发展的窗口机遇期，中国发展经验就是它们把握住发展机遇的方法。

表1.7 埃塞俄比亚与撒哈拉以南非洲地区近十年来的经济结构转型与经济增长：希望与挑战

| 指标 | 年份 | | | | | | | | | |
|---|---|---|---|---|---|---|---|---|---|---|
| | 2008 | 2009 | 2010 | 2011 | 2012 | 2013 | 2014 | 2015 | 2016 | 2017 |
| 埃塞俄比亚 | | | | | | | | | | |
| 制造业增加值占GDP的百分比 | 4.11 | 3.88 | 3.97 | 3.68 | 3.42 | 3.70 | 3.99 | 4.40 | 5.58 | 5.59 |
| 制造业进口占商品进口的百分比 | 60.18 | 71.53 | 68.69 | 65.27 | 67.13 | 73.22 | 71.02 | 75.97 | 78.79 | — |
| 制造业出口占商品出口的百分比 | 9.01 | 8.65 | 8.91 | 10.37 | 8.77 | 8.61 | 6.77 | 7.33 | 12.53 | — |
| 农业就业人员占就业总数的百分比 | 79.21 | 78.71 | 77.15 | 75.51 | 74.95 | 72.68 | 71.38 | 69.89 | 68.99 | 68.22 |
| 制造业增加值年增长率（%） | 9.26 | 8.62 | 9.21 | 9.24 | 11.80 | 16.93 | 16.64 | 18.22 | 18.39 | 17.41 |
| 人均GDP增长年增长率（%） | 7.88 | 5.96 | 9.62 | 8.28 | 5.83 | 7.73 | 7.45 | 7.62 | 4.90 | 7.56 |
| 撒哈拉以南非洲地区 | | | | | | | | | | |
| 制造业增加值占GDP的百分比 | 10.23 | 10.11 | 9.45 | 9.38 | 9.51 | 9.95 | 10.19 | 10.19 | 10.09 | 10.10 |
| 制造业进口占商品进口的百分比 | 65.41 | 68.37 | 67.82 | 61.81 | 64.07 | 62.42 | 61.80 | — | 64.41 | 62.52 |
| 制造业出口占商品出口的百分比 | 26.36 | 21.43 | 22.59 | 20.33 | 21.31 | 21.84 | 23.91 | — | — | — |
| 农业就业人员占就业总数的百分比 | 61.09 | 60.33 | 58.44 | 58.29 | 58.38 | 58.51 | 57.92 | 57.50 | 57.40 | 57.36 |
| 制造业增加值年增长率（%） | 3.55 | −2.89 | 4.71 | 7.08 | 5.40 | 7.71 | 5.05 | 1.42 | 1.19 | 1.55 |
| 人均GDP增长年增长率（%） | 2.52 | 0.24 | 2.73 | 1.73 | 1.72 | 2.16 | 1.87 | 0.19 | −1.46 | −0.17 |

数据来源：世界银行。

# 1.4

## 思路的转变

### 1.4.1 主流发展思潮视角下的发展指南

#### 1.4.1.1 主流发展思潮的陈规：以发达国家作为标杆

归结起来，前两代的发展经济学都是以发达国家为参照系，来看发展中国家缺什么（如第一代结构主义所强调的现代资本、技术密集产业），或发展中国家做得不好的地方（如第二代新自由主义所强调的完善的市场制度，即华盛顿共识所推动的私有化、市场化、稳定化，以及营商环境、透明度等），并以此作为改造发展中国家的依据。结构主义忽视发展中国家禀赋结构特征所决定的比较优势的重要影响，低估了市场在结构变迁中的力量，高估了政府在结构变迁中的作用；新自由主义没有意识到，发展中国家的系统性扭曲，内生于违背比较优势的发展战略，为缺乏自生能力的资本密集大企业生存的前提，低估了政府因势利导在结构变迁中的必要性，高估了市场在结构变迁中的作用。这两波发展思潮均未能有效地指导绝大多数发展中国家成功地实现转型升级；少数成功地实现追赶发达国家和转型升级的经济体，也都未遵循这两波主流发展思潮。

#### 1.4.1.2 主流发展指南的代表：瑞士达沃斯论坛的《全球竞争力报告》

当今风靡全球的瑞士达沃斯世界经济论坛[①]的《全球竞争力报告》(*The Global Competitiveness Report*）便是“发展因素/结果导向”思想的经典之作，其以最发达的经济体作为参照，通过12个标杆从各个方面来评价各个经济体（见图1.22），来看发展中国家

① 世界经济论坛（World Economic Forum）是以研究和探讨世界经济领域存在的问题、促进国际经济合作与交流为宗旨的非官方国际性机构，总部设在瑞士日内瓦。其前身是1971年由现任论坛主席、日内瓦大学教授克劳斯·施瓦布创建的“欧洲管理论坛”。1987年，“欧洲管理论坛”更名为“世界经济论坛”。论坛会员是遵守论坛“致力于改善全球状况”宗旨，并影响全球未来经济发展的1 000多家顶级公司。由于在瑞士小镇达沃斯首次举办，所以日后也称其为“达沃斯论坛”。

缺什么，或发展中国家做得不好的地方，其评价结果便是将发展阶段分为三个阶段两次转型。[①]新版本的《全球竞争力报告》由经典经济学教科书《经济增长》[②]的作者之一萨拉伊马丁（Sala-i-Martin）作为世界经济论坛前首席经济学家领衔按X理论范式下跨国回归的思路设计。[③]

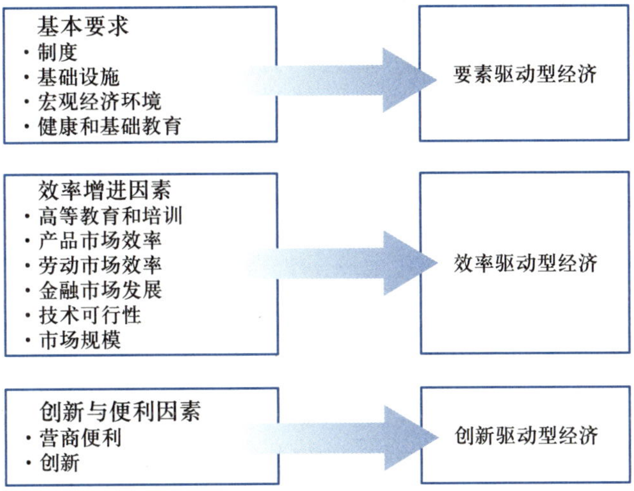


**图1.22 以发达国家作为参照系：发展因素/结果导向**

资料来源：《全球竞争力报告2011—2012》，第9页。

---

① 经济增长论文通常都是先提出一个理论，紧接着是实证部分。实证部分将证明，当其他变量不变时，刻画该理论强调的现象的变量与增长相关。论文一般还会接着证明，即便当解释变量出现变动时，理论强调的变量也具有显著性，即理论的稳健性。那么，究竟哪些变量应被纳入回归分析中呢？可惜现有的经济增长理论还没有精确到足以指出增长确切决定因素，几乎没有什么变量是特别稳健的，甚至时常出现“王婆卖瓜”乃至相互矛盾的估值。

② 另一作者是新古典宏观经济学大家罗伯特·巴罗（Robert J. Barro, Xavier Sala-i-Martin, *Economic Growth* (2nd Edition). MIT Press, 2003）。

③ 萨拉伊马丁等利用古典经济学估计的贝叶斯平均（BACE）方法对含有67个变量集合的跨国横截面回归基准估值（可参见巴罗和萨拉伊马丁的教科书《经济增长》）。这恰恰是前述阿德尔曼讽刺的发展经济学X理论范式在理论与实证研究中的体现（参见第1.3.3节的脚注对X理论的描述）。

### 1.4.2 新结构经济学视角下的发展指南

#### 1.4.2.1 新结构经济学的发展思想：从每个国家自身出发

与前两波发展思潮不同，新结构经济学主张应该从发展中国家现在有什么（即其要素禀赋）出发，规划在此基础上能做好什么（即其比较优势），把现在能做好的产业在市场经济中由政府的因势利导协助企业家将其做大做强，以此实现逐步赶上甚至超越发达国家的目标。与以发达国家作为标杆分析发展与转型的因素及结果的研究范式不同，突出发展与转型方法和过程的新结构经济学的研究范式更加实事求是地分析发展中国家经济现象的成因，提出求真务实的对策，而非“一刀切”。

#### 1.4.2.2 新结构经济学的发展指南：新结构经济学之路

与主流发展思潮指南下的《全球竞争力报告》不同，新结构经济学视角下的研究报告则以“发展方法/过程导向”追踪各个经济体结构转型升级的路径。从每个经济体在每个时点的自身禀赋特征出发，从事符合此时由禀赋结构决定的比较优势的生产活动，生产活动产生的剩余便最多，最有利于禀赋结构的提升；当禀赋结构升级之后，比较优势发生变化，再从事更高级的符合变化了的比较优势的活动；如此循序渐进、小步快跑地顺利实现经济结构转型升级。这种遵循比较优势的发展方法对于贫穷国家的经济发展而言看起来或许是缓慢而令人沮丧的，但事实上，这种办法却是积累资本、提升要素禀赋结构和产业结构，推动经济包容性可持续发展的最快方法；并且，按此办法还能发挥后发优势，从更为发达的国家引进技术和产业，而取得比发达国家更为快速的产业结构升级和经济发展。图1.23概括了新结构经济学的核心思路：任意阶段的最优生产结构内生于其禀赋结构，在转型升级的过程中都需要“有效市场”和“有为政府”，后面的诸多章节都是在此图的框架中展开。我们将在第10章结合世界经济结构变迁形势和案例来详细介绍新结构经济学发展思路下的可操作性方法。

对比可以发现，发展因素只是发展方法选择的对象，发展结果只是发展过程的结局。如图1.24所示，韩国之所以取得了如此成功的发展，孟加拉国却数十年都未走出低收入陷阱，原因在于前者在经济结构转型升级过程中吻合了新结构经济学的发展方法，而后者却远离了新结构经济学之路。中国的发展轨迹介于二者之间，改革开放之前远离了新结构经济学之路，而之后大致遵循了新结构经济学的方法。

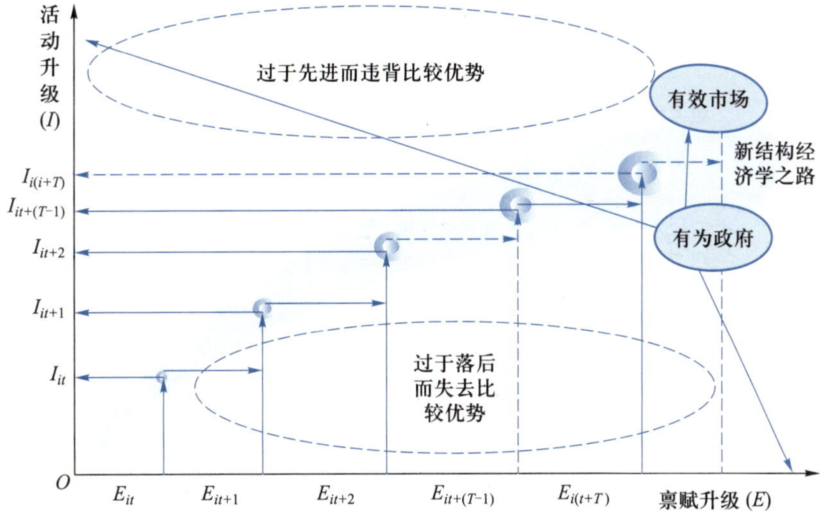


图1.23 从发展中国家自身出发：发展方法/过程导向

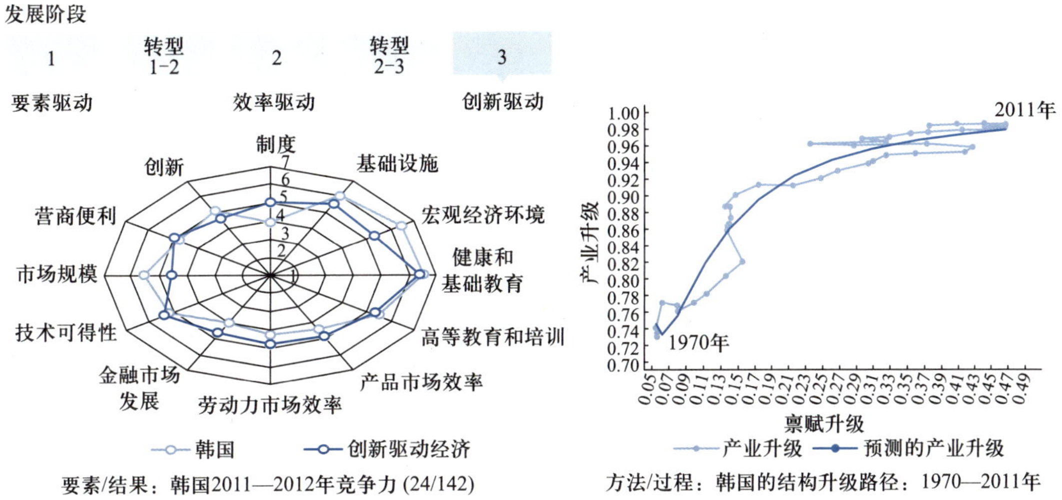

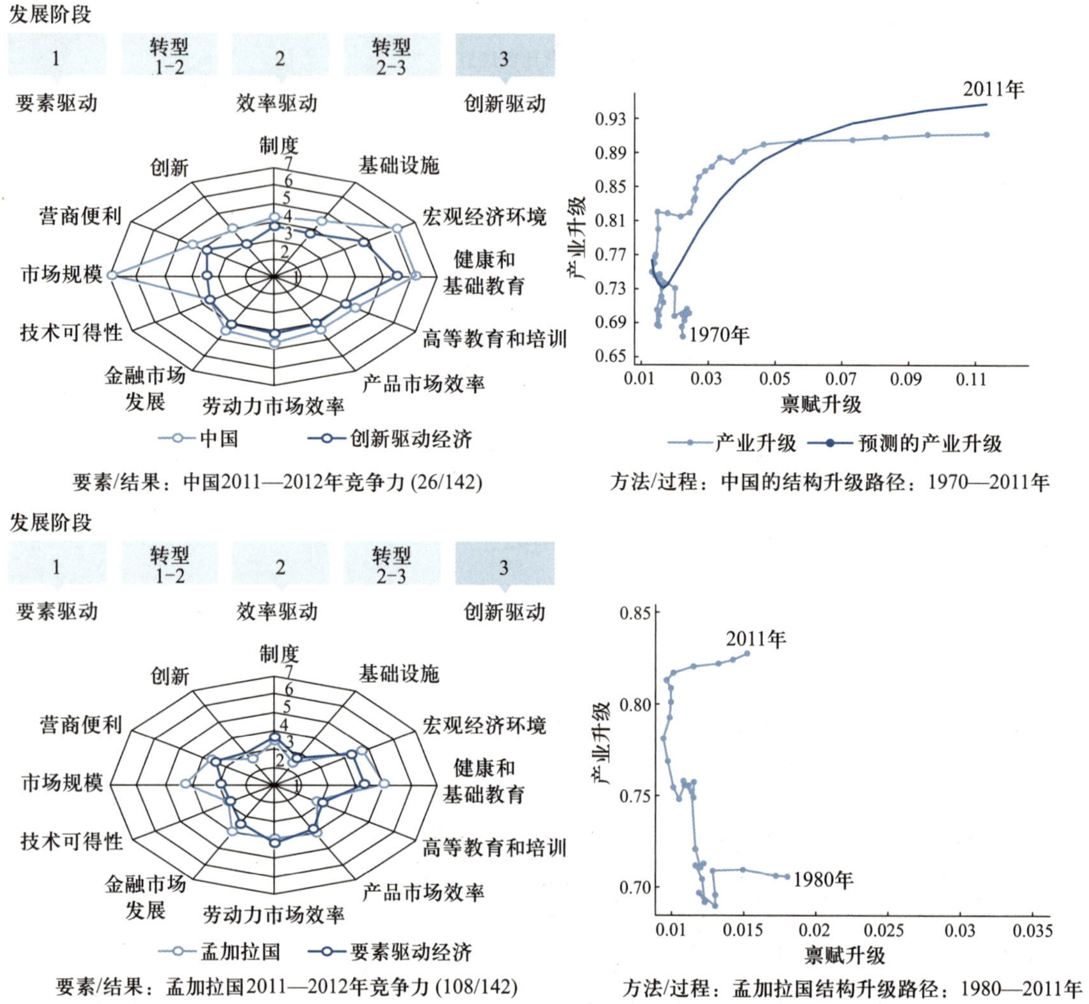


**图1.24 发展要素/结果与发展方法/过程之间的比较：以韩国、中国、孟加拉国为例**

注：右边结构升级路径的横轴是以实际人均GDP度量的禀赋结构，纵轴是以非农产值占GDP的比重度量的生产结构。见第3章的详细说明。

资料来源：左边的竞争力排名资料来自瑞士达沃斯世界经济论坛的《全球竞争力报告2011—2012》，右边的升级路径来自林毅夫和付才辉所著的《世界经济结构转型升级报告》[1]。

① 林毅夫、付才辉，《世界经济结构转型升级报告——新结构经济学之路》，北京大学出版社，2018年版。

### 1.4.3 人类发展思想的最大挑战：布隆迪如何转型升级为瑞士[①]

每年的达沃斯论坛，来自世界各地的数千名各界领袖云集于欧洲内陆的瑞士小镇，见证其繁华。论坛期间，这些意见领袖就世界经济的各项议题发表各种有影响力的看法。然而，正当这些全球的意见领袖们谈笑风生之时，同样身处内陆的非洲国家布隆迪的人民却在为摆脱贫困和短命而苦苦挣扎。[②]为何两个人口量级相当的内陆国家发展水平差距如此大？布隆迪能否实现瑞士那样的发展水平？

我们既可以按照前述达沃斯论坛发布的《全球竞争力报告》的发展思路，以当今最发达的经济体瑞士作为参照系，以成百上千条标准（X理论范式）来批评当今最不发达经济体布隆迪的普遍“落后性”。[③]例如，布隆迪之所以落后，是因为没有瑞士那样“先进”的资本积累、产业结构、教育结构、金融结构、城市化与全球化等，如表1.8所示。按此思路，布隆迪基本上“无可救药”，因为这些思路从战后至今都付诸了实践，收效寥寥。我们也可以按照前述新结构经济学的发展思路，从布隆迪和瑞士自身的禀赋结构出发，来理解二者之间在产业结构、教育结构、金融结构、城市化与全球化等经济结构方面的巨大差异的根源以及实现经济结构转型的路径，求索出一条让布隆迪达到瑞士那样繁荣的发展之路。

表1.8 布隆迪与瑞士的收入、人口、资本、产业结构、城镇化、就业、教育、金融与贸易等方面的简要比较（人均GDP和资本形成总额以2010年不变价美元计价）

| 指标 | 国家 | 1960年 | 1980年 | 1990年 | 2016年 |
|---|---|---|---|---|---|
| 人口总数 | 布隆迪 | 2 786 106 | 4 116 817 | 5 415 415 | 10 524 117 |
| | 瑞士 | 5 327 827 | 6 319 408 | 6 715 519 | 8 373 338 |
| 人均GDP | 布隆迪 | 214.14 | 279.96 | 329.16 | 218.28 |
| | 瑞士 | — | 54 891 | 64 344 | 76 683 |
| 布隆迪资本形成总额与瑞士之比（%） | | — | — | — | 0.27 |
| 农业占GDP比例（%） | 布隆迪 | — | 57.57 | 51.06 | 36.36 |
| | 瑞士 | — | — | 2.24 | 0.65 |
| 工业占GDP比例（%） | 布隆迪 | — | 11.67 | 17.33 | 15.15 |
| | 瑞士 | — | — | 31.07 | 25.01 |
| 城镇人口占总人口比例（%） | 布隆迪 | 2.08 | 4.34 | 6.27 | 12.39 |
| | 瑞士 | 70.92 | 74.48 | 73.93 | 73.74 |

① 应用新结构经济学对布隆迪和瑞士的比较案例分析可进一步参考：林毅夫，《繁荣的求索》，北京大学出版社，2012年。（英文版Lin Justin Yifu, *The Quest for Prosperity: How Developing Economies Can Take Off*. Princeton University Press, 2012.）

② 布隆迪与瑞士在预期寿命上的差距令人咋舌：2016年布隆迪只有57岁，而这一年瑞士高达83岁。

③ 世界银行WDI数据库是目前最为翔实跨国可比数据库，从中可以下载瑞士和布隆迪的所有数据集。瑞士和布隆迪都有1 600个指标变量，时间跨度为1960—2017年。尽管部分数据有缺失，但足够我们从上千个维度对比瑞士和布隆迪的差别。

续表

| 指标 | 国家 | 1960年 | 1980年 | 1990年 | 2016年 |
|---|---|---|---|---|---|
| 农业就业比重（%） | 布隆迪 | — | — | — | 91.37 |
| | 瑞士 | — | — | — | 3.36 |
| 工业就业比重（%） | 布隆迪 | — | — | — | 2.41 |
| | 瑞士 | — | — | — | 20.59 |
| 高等院校入学率（%） | 布隆迪 | — | 0.46 | 0.72 | — |
| | 瑞士 | — | 17.82 | 25.51 | 57.87 |
| 国内信贷与GDP之比（%） | 布隆迪 | — | 6.89 | 8.61 | 16.74 |
| | 瑞士 | 95.99 | 98.17 | 148.61 | 175.26 |
| 瑞士股票交易总额与GDP之比（%） | | — | 66.52 | 155.20 | 125.20 |
| 贸易额与GDP之比（%） | 布隆迪 | 25.89 | 32.10 | 35.65 | 38.16 |
| | 瑞士 | 54.52 | 96.49 | 83.70 | 120.40 |

数据来源：世界银行。

在新结构经济学看来，布隆迪和瑞士之间经济结构的巨大差异很容易理解。虽然目前布隆迪和瑞士的人口量级相当，2017年布隆迪人口1 086万，瑞士846万，但两个国家过去半个多世纪的人口增长轨迹却十分迥异：布隆迪遵循典型的欠发达经济体快速的人口增长轨迹，从1960年的279万人增长整整4倍；瑞士遵循发达经济体的缓慢的人口增长轨迹，从1960年的533万人只增加了6%。欠发达经济体的总收入的增长都被快速增长的人口所吸收了，导致人均收入水平停滞不前，1960年布隆迪的人均GDP只有214.14美元（2010年不变价美元），到2017年依然只有212.55美元，这足以说明布隆迪深陷马尔萨斯陷阱。与布隆迪极端贫困又停滞不前的境地截然相反，1980年瑞士的人均GDP就达到54 891美元，到2017年又上升到76 667美元，是当今世界上最富裕的经济体之一。人口数量和人均收入水平的这种差异也直接折射出布隆迪和瑞士禀赋结构的差异：布隆迪相对而言人多资本少，瑞士相对而言人少资本多。例如，近二十年来，布隆迪的资本形成总额不足瑞士的0.5%，这两个经济体的资本丰腴程度简直不可同日而语。禀赋结构的不同又导致产业结构的不同。布隆迪在1970年农业占GDP的比重高达65.33%，过去近半个世纪虽然农业比重逐步下降，但到2016年依然高达36.36%，依然是一个传统的农业经济体。与此相反，瑞士在1990年农业占GDP的比重只有2.24%，到2017年只有微不足道的0.65%。这折射出布隆迪艰难的工业化进程。1970年布隆迪工业占GDP的比重只有9.40%，其中制造业占GDP比重只有更低的6.73%，到2016年缓慢地上升到15.15%，但制造业占GDP比重依然只有9.21%，近半个世纪制造业比重仅提升了2个多百分点。而瑞士在1990年的工业占GDP比重为31.07%，服务业占比为67%，早已步入后工业社会，尽管如此，瑞士依然有着强大的制造业能力，2017年其制造业占GDP的比重为18.15%。与产业结构相呼应，布隆迪和瑞士在城市化、就业结构、教育结构、金融结构、开放结构等方面也呈现出完全不同的风景。1960年的布隆迪大地一片乡野，城镇只是零星的点缀，城镇人口占总人口的比例只有2.08%，也就说100个人只有2个人是城里人。到2017年，布隆迪依然是乡村社会，农村人口占比依然高达87.29%。在瑞士的大地上则是另外一幅风景，1960年瑞士的城镇人口占总人口的比例就超过70%。即便是当下的2017年，布隆迪的农业就业比重依然高达91.44%，换言之，10个人有9个人靠传统农业维持生计。与此相反，二十年多前的1997年瑞士的农业就业比重只有区区4.60%，这一极低的比重也超过了布隆迪2017年工业就业比重的2.46%，今天瑞士超过75%的人从事服务业。这种就业结构也必然意味着瑞士的国民教育程度非常高，2016年高等院校入学率达到近58%，而布隆迪在2014年只有5.3%，二者在比例上相差十倍之剧。除了教育差距惊人之外，金融也如出一辙。例如私营部门的国内信贷占GDP的百分比，2016年瑞士高达175.26%，而布隆迪不足16.74%，二者在比例上也相差十多倍。瑞士2017年股票交易总额占国民生产总值（GDP）的比例高达140%，而布隆迪连股市都没有。在参与全球化方面二者差距也惊人，以贸易为例，2016年瑞士贸易额占国民生产总值（GDP）的比例为120.40%，而这一年布隆迪只有38.16%。很显然，对应于布隆迪农业经济的出口大多是原材料和资源型产品，而瑞士高度发达的工业化和服务经济出口的是高技术商品和知识密集型技术，例如2016年瑞士高科技出口占制成品出口的比重就高达27%，而布隆迪2017年食品出口占商品出口的比重将近80%、矿石和金属出口占商品出口的比重将近8%。

在新结构经济学看来，布隆迪也能够战胜命运。[①]事实上，瑞士人民在历史上也曾贫困到以当雇佣军为生（著名的垂死狮子像诉说着这段苦难的历史），历经19世纪和20世纪的漫长奋斗而实现了今天的繁荣，20世纪一些起飞前与布隆迪处于相同发展水平的发展典范也战胜了命运，如图1.25所示（中国、韩国与爱尔兰这些发展典范的故事将陆续在后面的章节予以介绍）。对于像布隆迪这样的发展中国家而言，它的禀赋结构可以从劳动力相对充裕变为像瑞士那样资本相对充裕，但只有通过每一个生产周期中产生的经济剩余所形成的资本积累才能实现。因此，一个国家要想保持经济持续增长，必须循序渐进地提升自身的产业基础，逐步达到像瑞士这样的高收入国家的水平。如何才能以一种连贯一致、可靠和可持续的方式做到这一点呢？这也许是人类发展思想面临的最大挑战。一个有用的发展理论必须能够解释产业、技术筛选和战略选择的模式，还能够诠释瑞士企业从曾经像布隆迪现有企业一样的规模变为全球领导者，并且国家成为人类历史上最成功的经济体之一的这种禀赋升级的动态过

① 林毅夫、塞勒斯汀·孟加，《战胜命运》，北京大学出版社，2017年版。（英文版Lin Justin Yifu, Célestin Monga, *Beating the Odds: Jump-Starting Developing Countries*. Princeton University Press, 2017.）

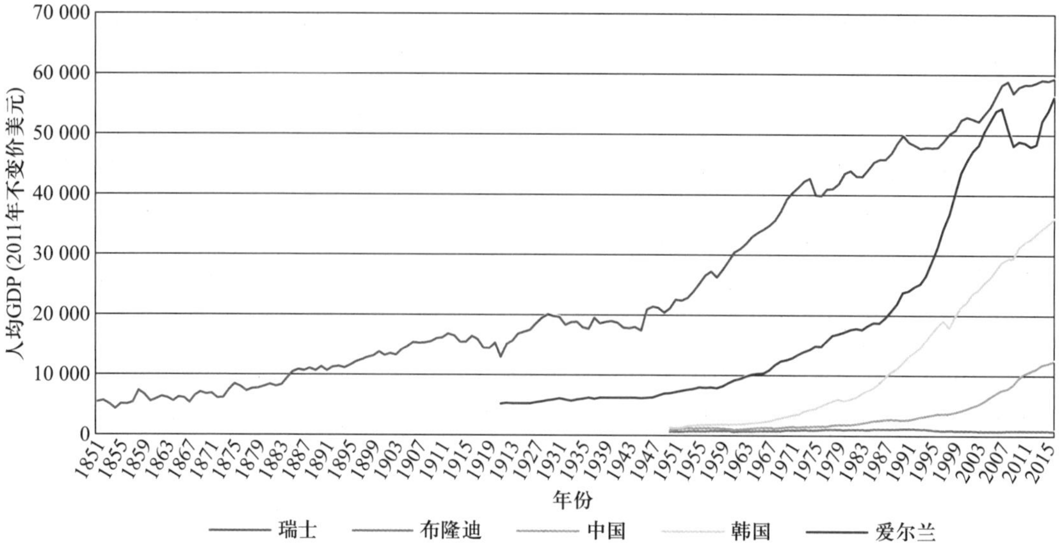


**图1.25 20世纪一些起飞前与布隆迪处于相同发展水平的发展典范**

资料来源：Maddison Project Database (MPD) 2018。

**垂死狮子像是位于瑞士城市卢塞恩的一座负伤狮子的雕像。这座雕像由丹麦雕塑家巴特尔·托瓦尔森设计，用以纪念在1792年保卫巴黎杜伊勒里宫的战斗中的约1 100名瑞士雇佣兵，大约760名战死，350名生还。在石像的上方刻有拉丁文"HELVETIORUM FIDEI AC VIRTUTI"，意为"献给忠诚和勇敢的瑞士"。美国著名作家马克·吐温一生游历了无数的地方，唯独对这座纪念碑雕塑赞赏有加，称其为："世界上最令人难过、最让人动情的石头。"**

程。[①]在本书接下来的章节里，我们便开始运用这样的发展理论（新结构经济学）来认识世界经济结构的变迁，并为身处其中的国家寻求繁荣之道。

---

① 林毅夫，《繁荣的求索》第5章，北京大学出版社，2012年版。（英文版Justin Yifu Lin, *The Quest for Prosperity: How Developing Economies Can Take Off*. Princeton University Press, 2012.）

# 第2章

# 经济结构转型升级是发展的关键

- 2.1 按经济结构特征断代的世界历史
- 2.2 前现代社会的经济结构变迁
- 2.3 工业革命造就了当今的发达经济体
- 2.4 未能实现持续的经济结构转型是发展中经济体的顽疾
- 2.5 如何实现持续的经济结构转型升级以获得经济增长
- 2.6 结构转型升级的方向与道路：新结构经济学
- 2.7 “上层建筑”如何随经济基础变迁而变迁
- 2.8 制度前提决定论的谬误

## 2.1

## 按经济结构特征断代的世界历史①

人类作为一个物种起源于旧石器时代中期，即大约25万年前到5万年前之间的某个时间。在旧石器时代，人类的生产生活方式主要是为了生存从环境中收集食物和其他生活必需品，即采集活动。这个时期的产业活动的生产率水平很难量化，但也不是不可能。例如，在全新世界早期的欧洲，采集生活方式供养一个人需要大约10平方千米土地，在早期农业社会，同样大小的土地可以养活50到100人。旧石器时代的采集生产生活极具流动性，使得人类遍布除了南极之外的世界。②由于各个大陆自然环境的不同，对动植物的驯化难易程度不同，就导致了世界各地定居的农业产业结构变迁不同。③表2.1是按照人类社会主要依赖的生产活动方式（分别以采集、农业和工业为标志）断代的世界历史的三大主要时代。前现代世界各地的产业结构及其生产力水平差别不大。工业化是现代化的标志，也是全球大分化的标

① 对于产业结构的重要性，17世纪古典政治经济学家配第（1672年《政治算术》）就察觉到工业比农业收入（附加值）多，商业有比工业收入（附加值）多，蕴含三次产业分类雏形；马克思（1867年《资本论》）在魁奈（1766年《经济表》）的基础上进一步提出社会资本再生产Ⅰ、Ⅱ部门，即明确提出生产资料部门（重工业）和消费资料部门（轻工业）；霍夫曼1931年《工业化的阶段和类型》在此基础上提出了二者比例关系的霍夫曼定理。费希尔1935年《安全与进步的冲突》首次明确提出三次产业分类，其将人类经济活动分为三个阶段分别对应不同的产业：第一阶段是以农业和畜牧业为主的初级生产阶段，对应的第一产业便是农业和畜牧业，同时也包括了劳动对象为自然界天然物品的采掘业；第二阶段是以工业生产活动大规模发展为标志，对应的第二产业主要以制造业为核心，是对原材料进行加工，并提供物质资料的生产部门；第三阶段是以资本和劳动力大量流向服务领域为特征，对应的第三产业向社会提供物质产品以外的服务需求。克拉克1940年《经济进步的条件》应用三次产业分类方法对经济发展与产业结构变化之间的关系进行了研究，提出三次产业变化的一般化规律被称之为"配第－克拉克定理"，三次产业分类有时也被称之为"克拉克大分类法"。

② 大卫·克里斯蒂安，《极简人类史：从宇宙大爆炸到21世纪》，王睿译，中信出版社，2016年版。

③ 贾雷德·戴蒙德，《枪炮、病菌和钢铁：人类社会的命运》，谢延光译，上海译文出版社，2006年版。

志，如图2.1所示。[①]工业革命以后近两百年来，当今一些发达经济体随着工业化的不断深入，服务业不断上升，逐步步入后工业化社会。首先提出“后工业社会”概念的社会学家丹尼尔·贝尔就是根据上述经济结构特征把人类社会发展的历史简单地分为三个阶段：第一个阶段为前工业社会（或称农业社会），人们依赖于自然界提供的原料和人的体力，经济主要由农业、矿业、渔业和林业部门构成；第二阶段为工业社会，人们对自然界的依赖减少，用能源代替体力，依靠技术和机器从事大规模的商品生产；经济主要由制造业、交通运输业和

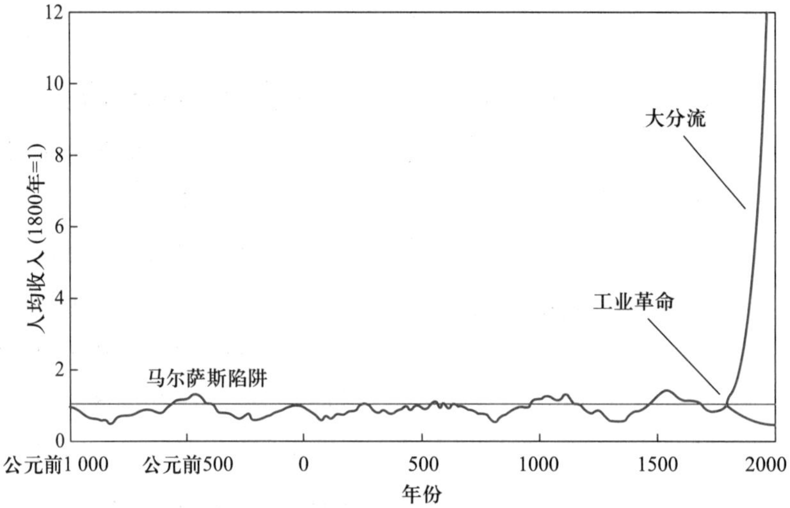


图2.1 人类极简经济史

资料来源：乔治·克拉克，《应该读点经济史：一部世界经济简史》，李淑萍译，中信出版社，2009年版。

---

① 将工业化作为现代化的标志尽管内容显得单一，但却是最根本的。如北京大学已故的罗荣渠先生在《现代化新论》一书中所认为的：“从历史的角度来透视，广义而言，现代化作为一个世界性的历史过程，是指人类社会从工业革命以来所经历的一场急剧变革，这一变革以工业化为推动力，导致传统的农业社会向现代工业社会的全球性的大转变过程，她使工业主义渗透到经济、政治、文化、思想各个领域，引起深刻的相应变化；……作为人类近期历史发展的特定过程，把高度发达的工业社会的实现作为现代化完成的一个主要标志也许是合适的”（罗荣渠，《现代化新论——中国的现代化之路（增订本）》，华东师范大学出版社，2018年版）。除了工业化之外，著名的政治学家亨廷顿归纳了现代化的九个特征：现代化是革命的过程。从传统社会向现代社会的转变，只能与人类起源的变化和从原始社会向文明社会的变化相比拟。现代化是复杂的过程。它实际上包含着人类思想和行为一切领域的变化。现代化是系统的过程。一个因素的变化将联系并影响到其他各种因素的变化。现代化是全球的过程。现代化起源于15世纪和16世纪的欧洲，但现在已经成为全世界的现象。现代化是长期的过程。现代化所涉及的整个变化，需要时间才能解决。现代化是有阶段的过程。一切社会进行现代化的过程，有可能区别出不同的水平或阶段。现代化是趋同的过程。传统社会以很多不同的类型而存在，现代社会却基本是相似的。现代化是不可逆的过程。虽然在现代化过程中某些方面可能出现暂时的挫折和偶然的倒退，但在整体上现代化是一个长期的趋向。现代化是进步的过程。在转变时期，现代化的代价和痛苦是巨大的；从长远看，现代化增加了人类在文化和物质方面的幸福。（塞缪尔·P.亨廷顿，《现代化：理论与历史经验的再探讨》，张景明译，上海译文出版社，1993年版。）

商业等部门构成。第三阶段为后工业社会，人们依赖于信息，将致力于发展服务业。[①]很显然，后工业社会对于当今的广大发展中经济体而言还是非常遥远的社会，如何实现工业化是首要的任务，如图2.2所示。

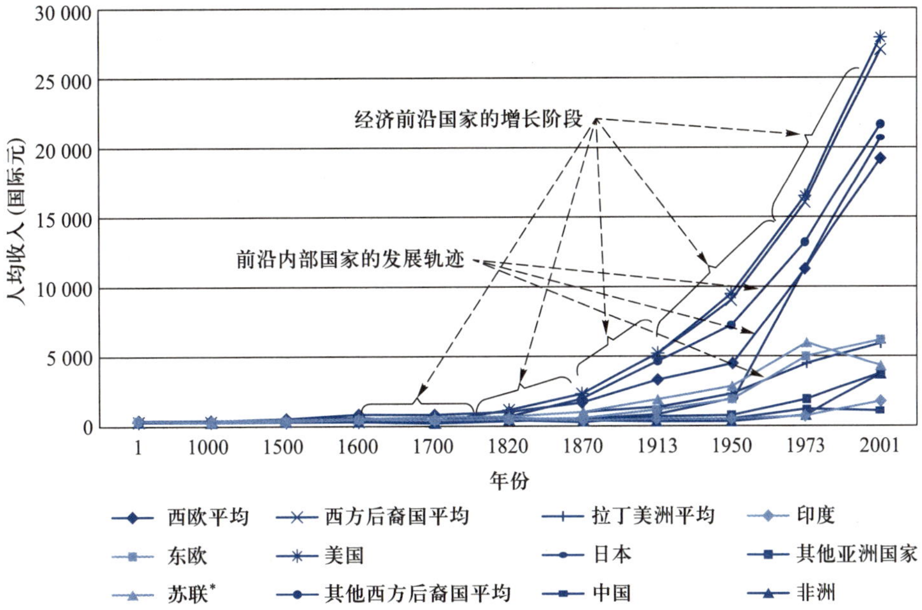


* 1991年后苏联数据为解体后15个原加盟共和国的加总数据。

**图2.2 世界经济发展历史概况（图中人均收入水平，单位是国际元）**

数据来源：安格斯·麦迪逊，《世界经济千年统计》，伍晓鹰、施发启译，北京大学出版社，2008年版。

表2.1 按照人类社会主要依赖的生产活动方式断代的世界历史的三大主要时代

| 主要时代 | 从属时期 |
| --- | --- |
| 采集狩猎时代<br>距今250 000至100 000年<br>人类社会主要依赖于采集狩猎 | 距今250 000至100 000年<br>起源于非洲 |
| | 距今100 000年至10 000年<br>全球迁徙 |
| 农耕时代<br>公元前8000年至公元1750年<br>（距今10 000年至250年）<br>人类社会主要依赖于农业生产 | 公元前8000年至前3000年<br>（距今10 000年至5 000年）<br>城市出现之前的农业社会 |
| | 公元前3000年至前500年<br>农业社会、最早的城市和国家 |
| | 公元前500年至公元1000年<br>农业、城市与帝国 |
| | 公元1000年至1750年<br>现代革命前夕的农业社会 |

① 丹尼尔·贝尔，《后工业社会的来临》，江西人民出版社，高铦等译，2018年版。除了贝尔之外，还有一些所谓的“未来学家”也热衷于研究人类社会未来的结构变迁方向，比较著名的代表有托夫勒（《第三次浪潮》作者）和奈斯比特（《大趋势》作者）。

续表

| 主要时代 | 从属时期 |
| --- | --- |
| 近现代<br>1750年至今<br>人类社会主要依赖于现代工业 | 1750年至1914年<br>工业革命 |
| | 1914年至1945年<br>20世纪危机 |
| | 1945年<br>当代社会 |

资料来源：大卫·克里斯蒂安，《极简人类史：从宇宙大爆炸到21世纪》，王睿译，中信出版社，2016年版。

## 2.2 前现代社会的经济结构变迁

### 2.2.1 马尔萨斯陷阱

如表2.1所概括的那样，1750年至今也不过两百多年而已，相对于人类前现代社会而言只不过是短暂的一瞬。从图2.2中我们也可以一目了然地看到，世界各地在工业革命之前的发展水平其实大同小异，都处于马尔萨斯陷阱的漫漫黑夜之中，尽管有许多璀璨的古代文明。[①] 除了世界横向比较之外，历史纵向比较也一目了然，如图2.3和图2.4所示。在图2.3中，我们会惊讶地看到，其实20世纪70年代末期中国改革开放时的人均生活水平不见得比秦汉时期高多少。很多人可能无法理解，中国那时已经成功试爆了原子弹，卫星也已升空，怎么可能人均生活水平还不如古代。事实上，决定人均生活水平的不是几项耀眼的科技成就，而是收入水平的持续提高。图2.4也直观地反映了工业革命前英国的马尔萨斯陷阱。

① 著名历史学家汤恩比（Arnold Joseph Toynbee）的《历史研究》可供参考。

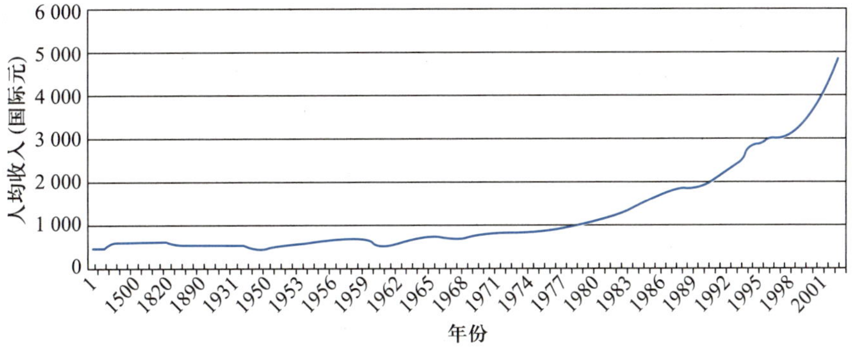


**图2.3 中国经济千年史**

数据来源：安格斯·麦迪逊，《世界经济千年统计》，伍晓鹰、施发启译，北京大学出版社，2009年版。

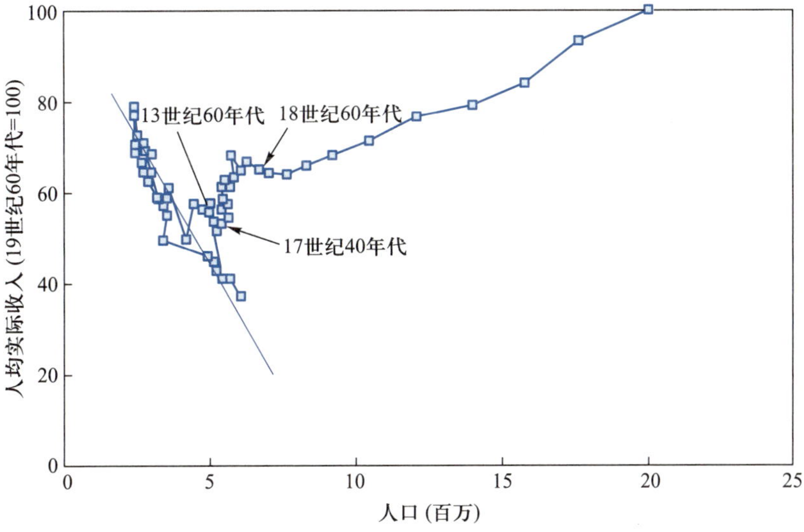


**图2.4 英国经济千年史**

资料来源：乔治·克拉克，《应该读点经济史：一部世界经济简史》，李淑萍译，中信出版社，2009年版。

人口学家马尔萨斯于1798年发表的《人口学原理》中，他做出了一个著名的悲观预言：人口增长超越食物供应，会导致人均占有食物的减少。马尔萨斯的这一原理非常简单，但却是支配前工业社会整个人类社会最强大的结构变迁机制——马尔萨斯陷阱。① 如图2.4所示，工业革命前英国社会的结构变迁的基本特征是，人口增长与人均收入水平增长负相关。换言

① 马尔萨斯陷阱也是自然界的法则，这意味着前现代社会其实人类并未从根本上摆脱自然的控制。马尔萨斯理论对现代进化论创始人达尔文和阿尔弗雷德·华莱士产生关键影响。达尔文在他的《物种起源》一书中说，他的理论是马尔萨斯理论在没有人类智力干预的一个领域里的应用。达尔文终生都是马尔萨斯的崇拜者，称他为“伟大的哲学家”。华莱士称马尔萨斯的著作是“我所阅读过的最重要的书”，并把他和达尔文通过学习马尔萨斯理论，各自独立地发展出进化论，称作“最有趣的巧合”。

之，所有提高收入的努力都被人口吸收了，而无法提高人均收入。前现代社会人们所有的努力，努力寻找新的土地资源、努力开发新的农耕技术、努力掌握自然世界的新规律等，虽然能够养活更多的人口，但是却无法同时改善每个人的生活水平。这一机制已经得到一些实证研究的有力支持，如图2.5和图2.6所示。[①]1800年的世界人均福利并不比公元前10万年前高，甚至世界大部分人口都要比他们的原始祖先更为贫困。例如，1800年世界人口的预期寿命为30岁，比狩猎－采集社会时的35岁还要短。[②]

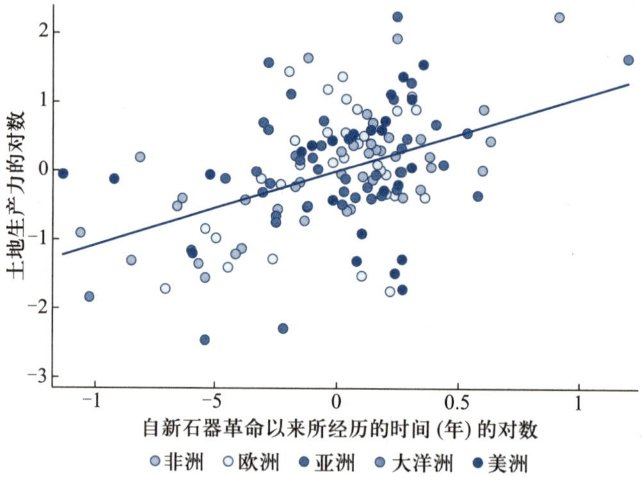


(a) 自新石器革命以来所经历的时间对1500年人口密度的边际影响

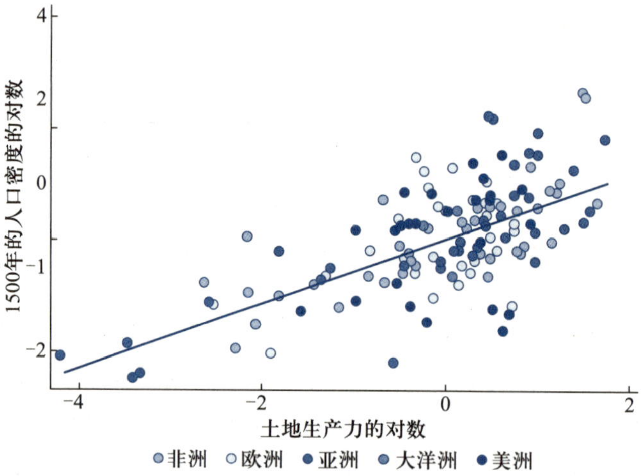


(b) 土地生产力对1500年人口密度的边际影响

**图2.5 自新石器革命以来所经历的时间和土地生产力对人口密度的影响**

资料来源：Ashraf和Galor（2011）。

① Quamrul Ashraf, Oded Galor, "Dynamics and Stagnation in the Malthusian Epoch", *American Economic Review*, 2011, Vol.101, No.5, pp.2003–2041.

② 大卫·克里斯蒂安，《极简人类史：从宇宙大爆炸到21世纪》，中信出版社，2016年版。

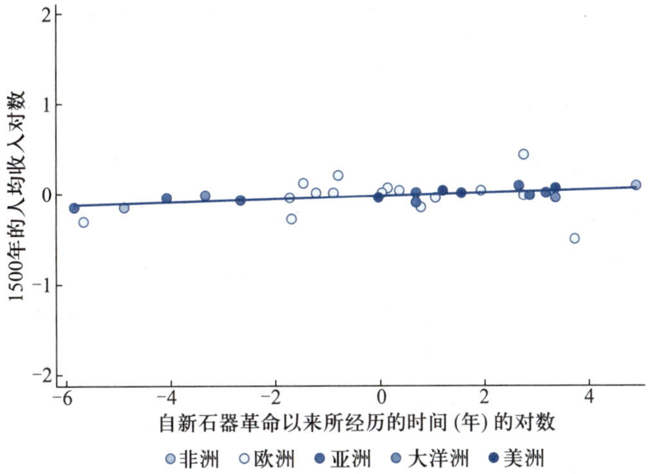


(a) 自新石器革命以来的经历的时间对1500年人均收入的边际影响

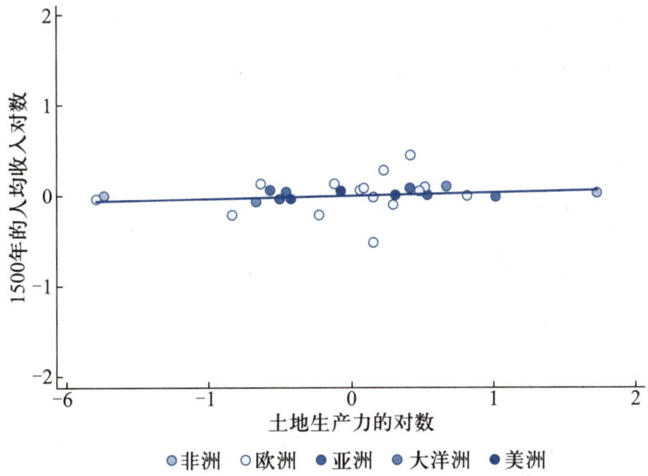


(b) 土地生产力对1500年人均收入的边际影响

**图2.6 自新石器革命以来所经历的时间和土地生产力对人均收入的影响**

资料来源：Ashraf和Galor（2011）。

## 2.2.2 马尔萨斯陷阱的新结构经济学

马尔萨斯不但解释了前现代社会的结构变迁机制，而且他提出的“边际递减律”对经济学也产生了难以估量的（正反面）影响。边际报酬递减律后经过大卫·李嘉图发扬并经过边际学派被阿尔弗雷德·马歇尔引进新古典经济学。正是因为边际报酬递减律，新古典增长理论无法获得长期的内生增长。因此，经济学被称为“忧郁的科学”（The Dismal Science）。

后来一些社会学家和经济学家认为马尔萨斯陷阱的机制源于土地的边际报酬递减律，用所谓的“内卷化”重新概括马尔萨斯陷阱的社会经济变迁机制。内卷化一词源于美国人类学家吉尔茨（Chifford Geertz）《农业内卷化》（*Agricultural Involution*）。根据吉尔茨的定义，“内卷化”是指一种社会或文化模式在某一发展阶段达到一种确定的形式后，便停滞不前或无法转化为另一种高级模式的现象。经济史的加州学派代表人物黄宗智在《长江三角洲小农家庭与乡村发展》中，把内卷化这一概念用于中国经济发展与社会变迁的研究，他把通过在有限的土地上投入大量的劳动力来获得总产量增长的方式，即边际效益递减的方式，称为没有发展的增长即“内卷化”。因此，中国灿烂的古典文明也被称为“高水平均衡陷阱”。①

然而，正如我们在第1章第3节所介绍的，新结构经济学不同于新古典经济学。②源于马尔萨斯边际报酬递减的新古典经济学其实是没有结构变迁的，只不过是给定的农业生产结构（即给定生产函数）下的资源配置，没有效率更高的产业出现推动结构变迁就会出现资源配置的边际报酬递减。在新结构经济学中，如果结构持续变迁，资源配置的边际报酬递减效应会被结构升级效应抵消，就不会出现边际报酬递减。在新结构经济学看来③，前工业社会的结构变迁之所以会由马尔萨斯陷阱所支配的根本原因在于没有技术不断创新，生产活动局限在土地密集的产业，其主导的禀赋结构是人均自然资源（$n=N/L$），自然资源（土地$N$）禀赋的根本特征是上限原则，不能像在工业社会，新的产业不断涌现，资本的边际报酬不降，剩余多，储蓄的积极性高，物质资本（$K$）可以无限积累——这一点被马克思在《资本论》中视为资本主义工业社会的根本法则。前工业社会占主导的生产方式是依赖于土地的农业生产方式，如柯布-道格拉斯生产函数 $f(n)=n^{\beta}=n^{1-\frac{1}{\ln n}}$，最优生产函数的结构变迁方程是 $\beta=1-\frac{1}{\ln n}$。④然而，由于适合农业生产的土地是有限的，不可像物质资本一样积累，随着人口$L$的增加，前工业社会的禀赋结构$n=N/L$是不断萎缩的，因此生产方式的土地密集度（$\beta$）越来越小，也即在有限的土地上耕作方式越来越劳动密集（$1-\beta$越来越大）（也即所谓的“内卷化”），从而导致人均产出水平 $y=f(n)=n^{\beta}=n^{1-\frac{1}{\ln n}}$ 越来越低；当人均产出水

① Mark Elvin, *The Pattern of the Chinese Past*. Stanford University Press, 1973.也可以参见林毅夫对该假说的不同意见：林毅夫，《解读中国经济》，北京大学出版社，2018年版，第2讲。

② 更详细的内容请参考：林毅夫、付才辉，《新结构经济学导论》（上、下册），高等教育出版社，2019年版。

③ 付才辉，“前工业社会的结构变迁——马尔萨斯陷阱的新结构经济学”，北京大学新结构经济学研究院工作论文，2018年。

④ 关于结构变迁方程的详细推导可参见：付才辉，“最优生产函数理论”，《经济评论》，2018年第1期。

平越低就越难以养活现有人口，人口就会越来越少，人口越少，前工业社会的禀赋结构水平 $n = N/L$ 就变高，从而又通过结构变迁方程 $\beta = 1 - \frac{1}{\ln n}$ 使得最优的生产方式的土地密集度（$\beta$）变大，从而又使得人均产出水平 $y = f(n) = n^{\beta} = n^{1-\frac{1}{\ln n}}$ 得以恢复提高；人均产出水平提高到一定程度又使得人口不断增长……。①前工业社会的结构变迁就这样停留在“马尔萨斯陷阱”均衡中，人均收入和人口长期处于较低的不变水平，土地资源的扩大只会导致人口规模的变大而不会提高人均收入水平，恰如图2.5和图2.6的实证结果所示。因此，可以看到我们的解释与加州学派的解释有所不同，农业社会内生的生产函数 $y = f(\beta) = n^{\beta} = n^{1-\frac{1}{\ln n}}$ 即便不出现边际收益递减，也会导致内卷化而无法走出马尔萨斯陷阱，如图2.7所示的历史情况。

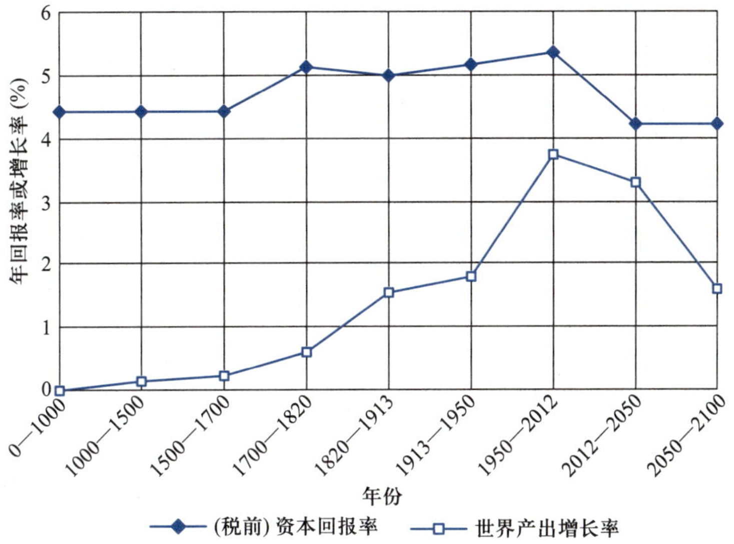


**图2.7 人类社会的经济增长率与资本回报率**

资料来源：Thomas Piketty. *Capital in the Twenty First Century*. Harvard University Press，2014.

---

① 如果由于外生的禀赋结构的变化而存在其他有利于人口结构转型的生产方式选择，那么就有利于内生地为跳出马尔萨斯陷阱创造条件。例如，Voigtländer和Hans-Joachim研究了中世纪晚期的黑死病（the Black Death in 1348—1350）对英国的深远影响：黑死病导致人口外生地锐减，人口锐减改变人、地禀赋结构（从土地稀缺变成劳动稀缺），人、地禀赋结构改变导致农业结构变迁（土地密集的畜牧业相对劳动密集的种植业占比变大）；种植业相对畜牧业而言是体力活，女性在畜牧业上相对更有比较优势；农业结构变迁导致女性就业结构变迁，进而导致其婚姻结构变迁（女性开始变得晚婚晚育），婚姻结构变迁又导致人口结构变迁（女性晚婚晚育导致人口出生率下降）；人口结构变迁又反过来导致禀赋结构变迁，工资水平变得越来越高。更详细的实证研究可参考：Nico Voigtländer and Hans-Joachim Voth, “How the West ‘Invented’ Fertility Restriction”, *American Economic Review*, 2013, Vol.103, No.6, pp.2227–2264。高工资，加上后来英国意外发生煤炭引发的能源结构变化，加速催化了英国原始工业革命，随着资本的原始积累和殖民掠夺，英国社会支配性的禀赋结构由土地转变为资本，为后来的英国工业革命埋下伏笔（第3章将进一步讨论）。

### 2.2.3 大航海与康乾“番薯盛世”的人口大爆炸

当英国通过工业革命跳出马尔萨斯陷阱之时，中国正处于所谓的“康乾盛世”。[①]之所以有“康乾盛世”之说，主要源于当时的领土和人口达到了空前的水平。康乾盛世时期，清朝的领土几经扩张。到乾隆年间平定新疆，整个清帝国版图空前，仅次于元。北起自外兴安岭以南，东北至北海，东含库页岛，西至巴尔喀什湖以东，继承了1758年准噶尔汗国的边界，形成了空前“大一统”的多民族国家，史称“汉、唐以来未之有也”。不过，康乾盛世最主要的表现却在人口的增长上，在康熙六十一年（1722年），全国人口突破1.5亿，乾隆五十五年（1790年）突破3亿大关，约占当时世界人口的1/3。如图2.8所示，康乾盛世确实是中国千年来人口规模的转折期。

徐扬所作《盛世滋生图》，又名《姑苏繁华图》，全长1 225厘米，宽35.8厘米，以苏州当时繁华景象为背景。该图从苏州城西灵岩山起，由山下的木渎镇东行，过横山，渡石湖等，再入姑苏城；再自葑盘、胥门、出阊门外，转入山塘街，至虎丘而止。整个画面包括太湖至虎丘近百里的风光山色、地理民俗、政治经济、文化艺术、建筑园林等极为丰富的内容，重点描绘了一村、一镇、一城、一街的景况。妙笔丹青，画出了江南的湖光山色、水上人家、水运漕行、田园村舍、商贾云集等繁盛图景。全图构思巧妙，疏密有致，重点突出，笔墨精道，气势宏大。虽不免有粉饰之处，但与历史文献相印，不失其实，故不愧为一件写实的杰作，是研究“乾隆盛世”的形象资料。

① 中国近代的很多日常用品的名称都要加个洋字，如“火柴”叫“洋火”，深刻地反映了工业化的落后性。孙玉璋所撰写《异闻琐录》（同治九年四月刻本），有这样一段文字：“道光间，英夷所贡杂物，多谣巧好玩。中有自来火者，长仅盈寸，一端五色洋药，擦之而火爆发。士大夫见之莫不惊奇，以为鬼物。今各大商埠均有市者，唯索值斤昂，非豪商显宦无力求之耳。”

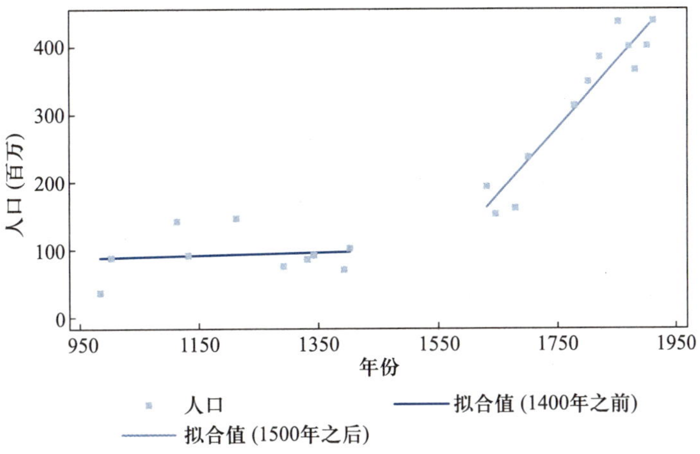


**图2.8 中国人口的千年变迁：980—1910**

数据来源：Kang Chao, *Man and Land in Chinese History: An Economic Analysis*, Stanford University Press, 1986.

然而，“康乾盛世”根本无法与同一时期的英国工业革命相比，只不过是中国古代封建王朝的最后一个盛世的回光返照而已。如图2.3所示，“康乾盛世”虽然人口剧增，但是人均收入水平却并没有任何改善，依然深处马尔萨斯陷阱。为什么这一时期人口会出现千年来的剧增呢？这其实源于大航海之后美洲新大陆的马铃薯、番薯（地瓜）、玉米等易种的高产物种的传入，大大提高了食物产量，尤其帮助人们度过饥荒年月。因此，清代的“康乾盛世”也被称之为“番薯盛世”。①陈硕等通过对18世纪中叶前后中国玉米种植的双重差分分析（DID），发现玉米能够解释在1776—1910年间中国人口增长的18%。同时，他们的实证结果也支持前述马尔萨斯陷阱假说：一项新的农业技术（如新物种）只能带来人口，而不能带来经济增长。②其实，这一结论对于大航海之后的全球人口大爆炸和快速的城市化都成立。Nunn和Qian利用马铃薯适宜种植的区域差异，以及马铃薯从美洲传入东半球的时间差异，来估计马铃薯对东半球人口和城市化的影响。他们的研究结果表明，在18世纪和19世纪的人口增长和城市化进程中，土豆的引进是一个显著的原因。根据最保守的估计，1700年至1900年间，旧大陆人口和城市化的增长中，土豆的引进能够解释约占1/4。③

---

①《农政全书》详细记述了番薯的种植、贮藏、加工法。讲到番薯育苗越冬、剪茎分种、扦插、窖藏干藏等技术，是最早系统介绍番薯种植法的著作。此后清人陈世元撰《金薯传习录》记述了冷床育苗，包世臣《齐民四术》中记述了翻蔓技术，番薯种植技术逐渐完善。

② Shuo Chen and James Kai-Sing Kung, “Of Maize and Men: The Effect of a New World Crop on Population and Economic Growth in China”, *Journal of Economic Growth*, 2016, Vol.21, No.1, pp.71–99.

③ Nathan Nunn, Nancy Qian, “The Potato’s Contribution to Population and Urbanization”, *The Quarterly Journal of Economics*, 2011, Vol. 126. No.2, pp.593–650.

### 2.2.4 全球化与当今穷国的“超前城市化”

从经济结构上讲，当今的很多欠发达国家其实还处于前现代社会。然而，在当今的全球化时代，还是有一些不一样的特征。例如与前述研究中所发现的马铃薯的全球传播有助于城市化一样，当今很多欠发达国家也可以依靠食物国际贸易养活更多的城市人口。如果按照英美城市化历史的标准，那么其实当今很多贫穷经济体在类似发展阶段的城市化水平都超过了英美当年的城市化水平。二战后全球的城市化率对收入水平的时间序列回归系数为0.25左右，而欠发达经济体的这种关系系数大得多。Glaeser对人均收入水平低于5 000美元的经济体做了估算，发现城市化率关于人均GDP对数的回归系数，在1960年的横截面数据中是3.6（标准差为0.24），2010年的横截面数据中是5.3（标准差为0.35）。尤其是相对于1960年，2010年这种关系系数变得更大而且标准差更大，反映了欠发达经济体更加超前的城市化以及收入水平更低但城市化水平更高的经济体更多。[①]表2.2是当今一些欠发达经济体的超前城市化的例子。从中可以看到，2017年，相对于世界人均GDP平均16 940国际元所对应的54.83%的城市化率，这些经济体的人均GDP远低于世界平均水平，但是其城市化水平却并不逊色。这些超前的城市化人口大都涌入了少数城市，使得其人口规模剧增。例如，巴基斯坦的卡拉奇人口远超千万。对于农业经济而言，出现如此大规模巨型城市只能是一个庞大帝国的首都才有能力征集维持城市需要的资源。例如，中国古代的长安、开封与杭州，以及罗马帝国时期的罗马，阿巴斯王朝时期的巴格达。在封闭经济中，只要靠农业生产力达到一定水平才能养活巨大的城市人口，然而在全球化时代这些中下收入型经济体靠进口食物才能够养活城市人口。

表2.2 全球化与贫穷经济体的超前城市化（2017年数据）

| 经济体 | 总人口（万人） | 最大城市人口（万人） | 城市化率（%） | 百万人以上大城市人口比例（%） | 人均GDP（国际元） | 进口占GDP比重（%） |
|---|---|---|---|---|---|---|
| 刚果民主共和国 | 8 134 | 金沙萨 840 | 43.88 | 23.87 | 887 | 39.44 |
| 津巴布韦 | 1 653 | 哈拉雷 150 | 32.24 | 9.13 | 2 086 | 37.40 |
| 马里 | 1 854 | 巴马科 190 | 41.57 | 12.77 | 2 211 | 41.05 |
| 海地 | 1 098 | 太子港 210 | 54.35 | 23.39 | 1 815 | 56.49 |
| 巴基斯坦 | 19 702 | 卡拉奇 1 350 | 36.44 | 20.97 | 5 527 | 17.55 |

① Edward L. Glaeser, “A World of Cities: the Causes and Consequences of Urbanization in Poorer Countries”, *Journal of the European Economic Association*, 2014, Vol.12, No.5, pp. 1154–1199.

续表

| 经济体 | 总人口（万人） | 最大城市人口（万人） | 城市化率（%） | 百万人以上大城市人口比例（%） | 人均GDP（国际元） | 进口占GDP比重（%） |
|---|---|---|---|---|---|---|
| 塞内加尔 | 1 585 | 达喀尔 290 | 46.74 | 18.32 | 2 712 | 42.75 |
| 科特迪瓦 | 2 429 | 阿比让 415 | 50.33 | 19.71 | 3 953 | 19.40 |

资料来源：根据世界银行数据库整理。

# 2.3

# 工业革命造就了当今的发达经济体

## 2.3.1 工业革命与西方发达国家的崛起[①]

图2.4也非常直白地告诉我们，英国之所以能够跳出马尔萨斯陷阱得益于工业革命；图2.3也非常直白地告诉我们，中国之所以能够在改革开放之后跳出马尔萨斯陷阱也得益于我们在第1章第2节已经提到并且后面章节还会继续讨论的工业革命。不仅如此，工业革命的威力巨大，造就了当今的发达经济体。我们在第1章第1小节介绍了曾经支配世界经济秩序

① 新制度经济学家诺思认为，工业革命可以追溯到1688年的光荣革命，其原因是此后确定了议会之上的基本原则，对皇室特权加以约束，承诺保障私有产权，产权保护有助于激励投资和发明创造，于是工业革命应运而生。一些历史学家发现真实的历史并没有产生其声称的功能。例如通过对银行业发展史和利率波动史的研究并不能核实在1688年后出现过任何结构性的剧变，产权的激励功能并没有被证实。恰恰相反，法国的工业化进程却受制于良好的对地主的产权保护。本章第7和第8小节将进一步讨论。

的G7老牌工业强国，图2.9到图2.15展示了这个7个国家的经济简史，可以一目了然地发现工业革命不但让他们跳出了马尔萨斯陷阱（人均收入与人口同时持续提高），而且奠定了支配世界经济结构的力量。第3章我们将归纳回顾英美等发达国家的工业革命的结构变迁历程，以验证第1章第3小节提出的新结构经济学关于结构转型升级分析理论框架。

如图2.16所示，1750年，世界上的大多数产品由中国（占全世界总量的33%）和印度次大陆（25%）生产。亚洲的人均产量低于更为富裕的西欧国家的人均产量，但差距很小。到1913年时，世界格局发生了翻天覆地的变化。中国和印度次大陆占世界总产量的比重分别下降到4%和1%。英国、美国和欧洲占到世界总产量的3/4。英国的人均产量是中国的38倍，是印度的58倍。这不仅是因为英国的产量迅猛增长，中国和印度次大陆制造业的大幅衰落也是原因之一，因为西方各国的机械化生产将这两个国家的纺织业和冶金业驱逐出了市场。在19世纪，亚洲各国从世界制造业中心变成了只会生产并出口农产品的典型的不发达国家。图2.16展示了世界历史进程中的若干重大转折点。从1750年至1880年，英国工业革命是主要事件。在这一阶段，英国占世界制造业的份额从2%上升到23%，正是来自英国的竞争摧毁了亚洲的传统制造业。从1880年至第二次世界大战这一阶段，标志性事件是美国和欧洲大陆（尤其是德国）的工业化。到1938年，它们占世界总产值的份额分别提高到33%和24%。英国被这些竞争者抢占了部分市场，它所占的份额下降到13%。从二战结束后到20世纪80年代，苏联占世界总产值的份额迅速上升，但随着苏联解体后各成员国陷入经济衰退，这一地区所占的比重又大幅下降。东亚奇迹见证了日本、中国台湾地区和韩国的崛起，它们占世界总产值的份额提高到17%。从20世纪80年代起，中国大陆地区也一直在进行工业化。2006年，中国大陆地区生产的产品占世界总量的9%。中国大陆地区正在追上西方国家的前进步伐，世界格局将重新回到原点（艾伦，2015）。①

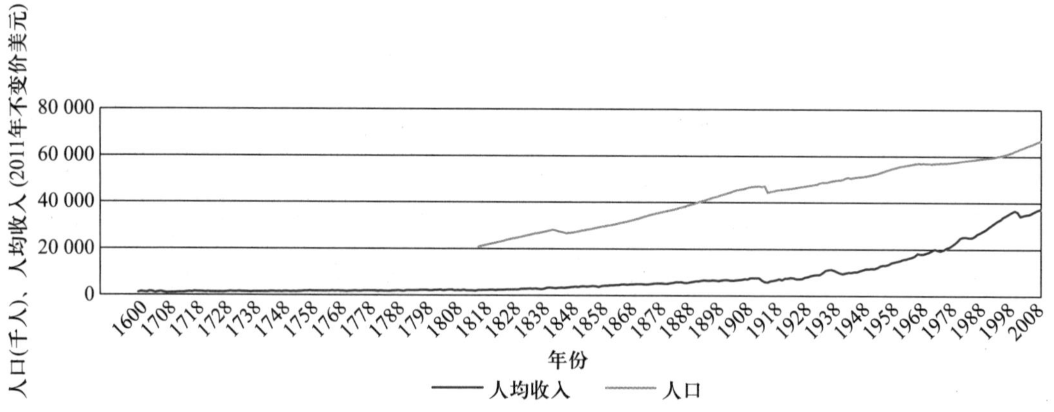


**图2.9 英国人均收入（2011年不变价美元）与人口（千人）的历史变迁轨迹**

资料来源：Maddison Project Database (MPD) 2018.

① 罗伯特·艾伦，《全球经济史》，陆赟译，译林出版社，2015年版，第8页。

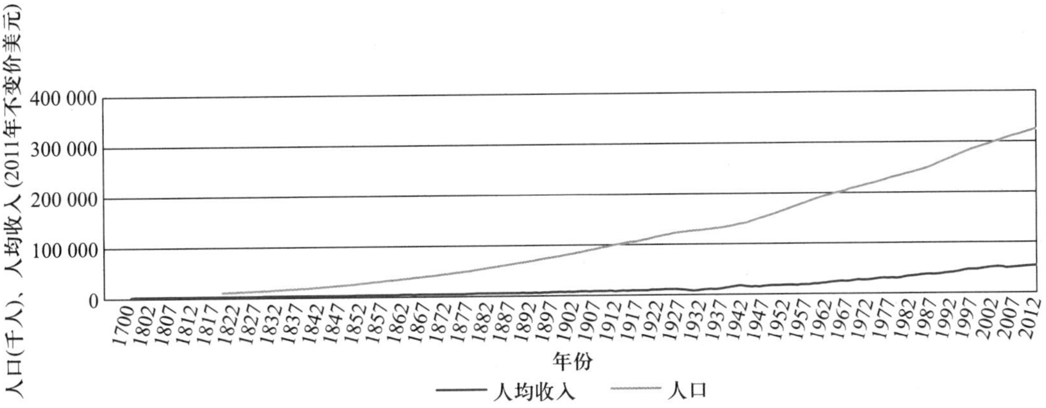


图2.10 美国人均收入（2011年不变价美元）与人口（千人）的历史变迁轨迹

资料来源：Maddison Project Database（MPD）2018.

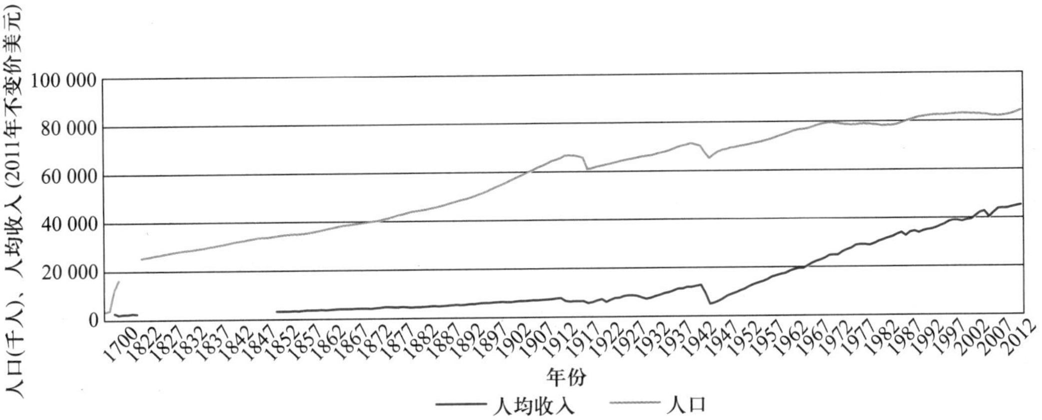


图2.11 德国人均收入（2011年不变价美元）与人口（千人）的历史变迁轨迹

资料来源：Maddison Project Database（MPD）2018.

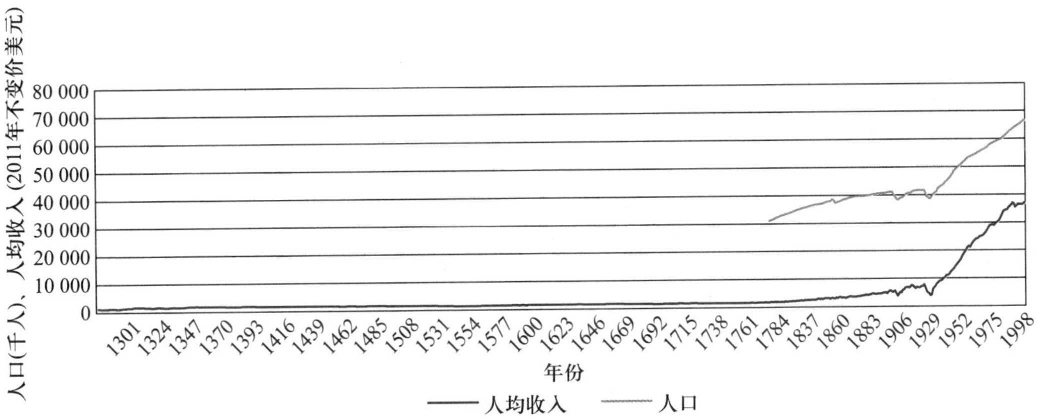


图2.12 法国人均收入（2011年不变价美元）与人口（千人）的历史变迁轨迹

资料来源：Maddison Project Database（MPD）2018.

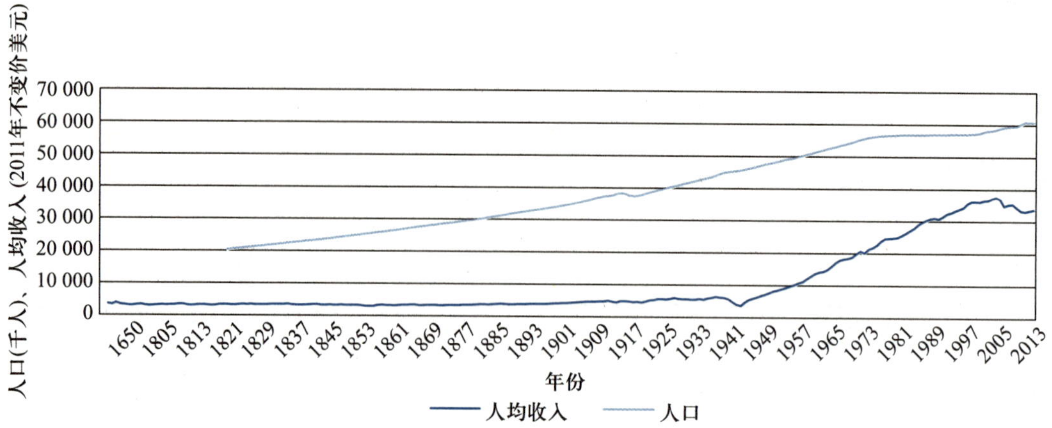


**图2.13 意大利人均收入（2011年不变价美元）与人口（千人）的历史变迁轨迹**

资料来源：Maddison Project Database (MPD) 2018.

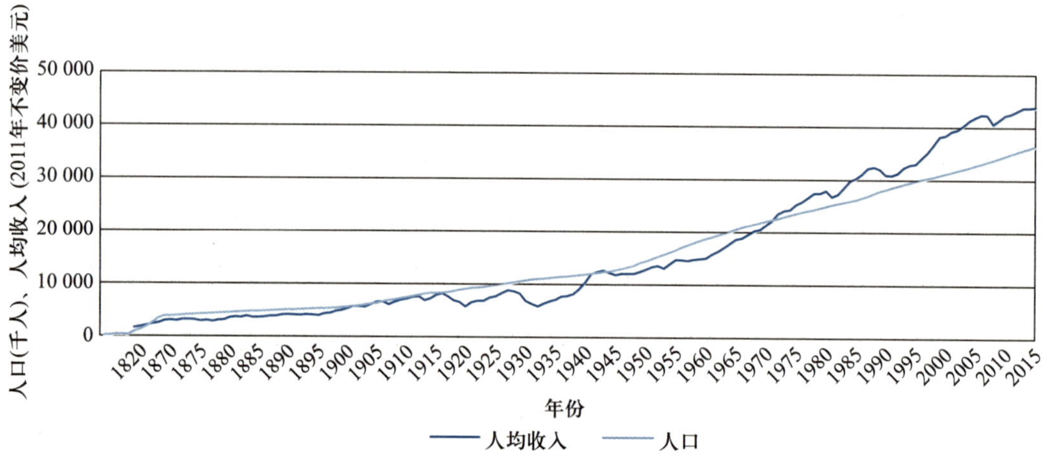


**图2.14 加拿大人均收入（2011年不变价美元）与人口（千人）的历史变迁轨迹**

资料来源：Maddison Project Database (MPD) 2018.

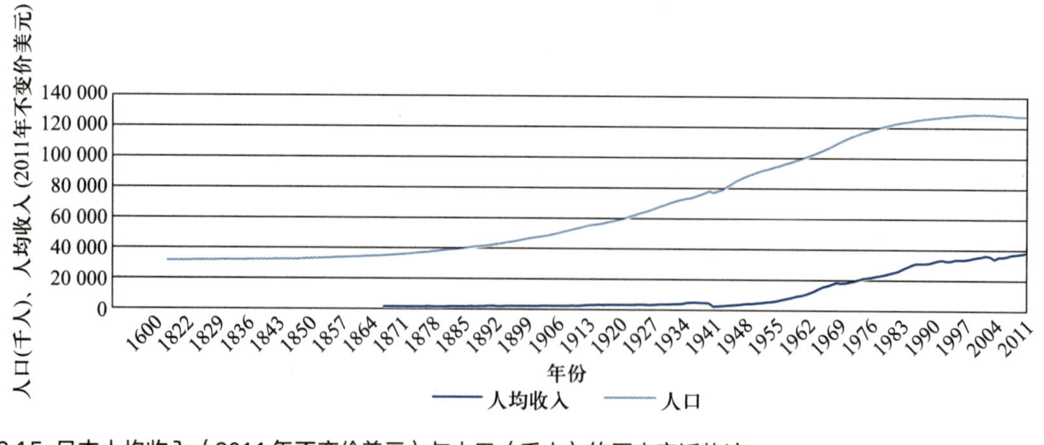


**图2.15 日本人均收入（2011年不变价美元）与人口（千人）的历史变迁轨迹**

资料来源：Maddison Project Database (MPD) 2018.

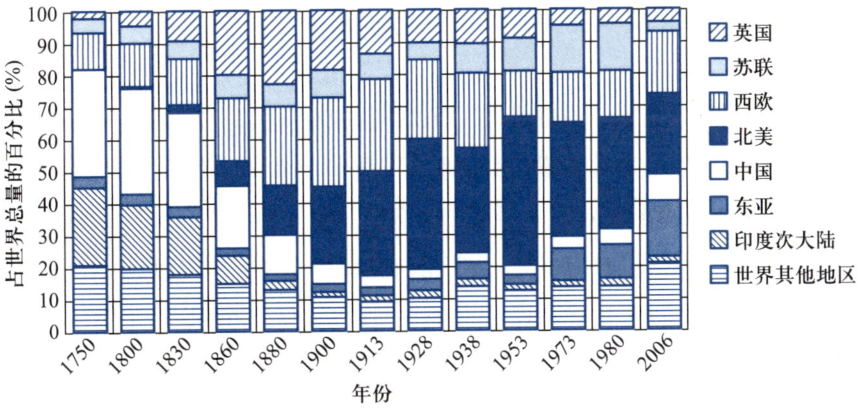


**图2.16 世界产量分布的变迁**

资料来源：罗伯特·艾伦，《全球经济史》，陆赟译，译林出版社，2015年版，第7页。

## 2.3.2 持续的结构转型升级是工业革命的本质

既然工业革命如此重要，我们得先了解一下“工业革命”是什么含义。对很多人来说，工业革命意味着蒸汽机的应用、纺织工业的机械化与钢铁使用的普遍化。但这不是一个好的定义。因为如果一个经济体只有这三样创新，他们只会经历一次大幅度的生产率提高，却不会有持续的经济发展。在18世纪之前，西方国家平均每年国民年收入的增长率仅为0.05%。这意味着要用1 400年，才使得人均收入翻倍。18世纪之后，增长率提高了近20倍。国民平均收入增长率从0.05%提高到1%，人均国民收入增长一倍所花费的时间也从1 400年减少到70年。在西方，从19世纪中叶至今，国民平均收入增长率再度翻倍至2%。收入翻倍的时间也从70年减少至35年。这种加速的经济增长并不是因为那三样新技术的运用，而是因为科学技术日新月异，带来的经济增长一日千里。技术创新的速度和产业升级速度的提高才是工业革命的本质和更重要的内涵。[①]下一章我们将介绍英美工业革命的详细历程，以及发达经济体的产业结构变迁特征。

① Lin Justin Yifu, “The Needham Puzzle: Why the Industrial Revolution Did Not Originate in China?” , *Economic Development and Cultural Change*, 1995, Vol.43, No.2, pp.269–292.

### 2.3.3 亚当·斯密及其继承者的学说远离了工业革命

从上述历史我们可以看到，虽然亚当·斯密因为探寻国民财富的性质与原因而被称为经济学之父，但是国民财富的爆炸性增长实则来自工业革命而非工业革命之前的劳动分工。现代新古典经济学的DNA脱胎于亚当·斯密《国富论》中“看不见的手”所描述的自由市场图景，然而《国富论》出版于1776年，是斯密研究西方地理大发现以后、工业革命尚未全面发生前，国际贸易盛行时期的经济现象的著作，所以他强调市场、分工等。而现代的快速经济增长则是工业革命以后才出现的现象，斯密不可能超乎时代，对现代经济增长的本质和原因有先见之明。

一些学者曾非常仔细地考证了《国富论》中最著名的关于劳动分工的例子，18世纪最为驰名的一项手工业“别针制造业”的素材其实来源于落后的法国传统手工业而不是英国现代工业。斯密很可能是通过法国狄德罗等主编的《百科全书》获得了该行业的相关生产知识，因为两者在各自的叙述中都将生产过程划分为18个阶段，这当然不可能是一种巧合。这可能与斯密在撰写《国富论》之前游历法国结识了狄德罗等人有关。这使得经济史学家艾伦感慨道：“可惜亚当·斯密却置技术水平明显领先的英国企业于不顾，反而从技术水平相对落后的法国人撰写的《百科全书》当中寻找所谓的‘领先’技术，实在令人遗憾；假若他能够跟着亚瑟·杨周游欧洲，实地观摩考察一番，想必会大有收获。”艾伦还以此为例，用禀赋结构的差异解释了为何英法两个制针行业所采取的技术差异：“《百科全书》对相关生产技术的描述取材于位于法国诺曼底地区雷格镇的工厂，而这里采用的生产技术相对落后，根本无法和英国通行的那一套先进的生产技术同日而语。1692年，多克拉铜业公司牵头组建了英国首家采用先进技术手段制造别针类产品的工厂，到了18世纪50年代，在布里斯托尔附近又出现了一家新型制针厂——沃姆利公司。布里斯托尔此前是闻名遐迩的旅游胜地，亚瑟·杨就曾造访过此地。这两家生产针类产品的工厂皆以机械化水平高而著称于世，不过这两家工厂获取生产所需动力的方式与位于诺曼底的那家法国工厂大为不同。在雷格镇，由工人们一起手工推动飞轮旋转来带动生产机器运转，这里的飞轮在外观上同纺织机械上的齿轮相似。相比之下，沃姆利公司则采用水力驱动机器运转。不过由于天然状态下的水流不是一种在任何季节都很可靠的动力源，于是该工厂特意装备了一台纽卡门式蒸汽机，用于将顺着水轮机叶片流下的水抽回至位于其上方的水池当中再次使用，这样就可以使有限的水流实现循环利用，不断为水轮机提供动力。据亚瑟·杨的考察，全部机器和轮轴都是依靠水力驱动保持连续运转的；为了将下泄的水流抽回至上方水池反复利用，该厂还配有一台大型燃煤抽水机。如果位于雷格镇的那家法国工厂也采用这种方式来驱动机器运转，那么那批负责推动飞轮旋转的工人将立刻失业（这里不要忘了支付给这批推轮工的工资会占将铜条加工成别针这一整套生产流程总支出的1/6），其他工种的工人也可能面临无事可做乃至终遭裁撤的命运。例如法国那家工厂里，有很多工人专职负责将别针打磨擦洗干净。而在同期英国的很多制针厂里，此类工序已采用由水力驱动的大型机械设备自动完成。亚瑟·杨曾仔细考察过沃姆利公司采用的那套生产设备，并称赞这套设备‘令人大开眼界，值得认真观摩’。通过上述比较我们发现英国工厂同法国工厂的经营模式差别很大，那么英国人为什么更倾向于采用一种资本密集型且高能耗的技术来进行生产呢？法国雷格镇坐落在一条河流边上，当地有一家锻造厂就利用了该河流提供的水力作为工厂所需的动力源，可见就雷格镇所处的地理区位而言，使用水力驱动机器运转不存在太大障碍（况且从沃姆利公司采用蒸汽机抽水实现水利资源的循环利用这一成功实例来看，只要工厂能够负担起运转一台蒸汽机的费用，那么几乎在任何地方都可以利用水力作为驱动机器运转的动力源）。18世纪50年代，有一位来自瑞典的工程师安格斯坦亲自造访了沃姆利公司，并留下了对该公司经营状况的记录，‘这个工厂每周要耗费5 000蒲式耳煤炭，不过由于该工厂拥有自己的专属煤矿，因此1蒲式耳煤炭的成本仅值3瑞典斯蒂弗’，可见该工厂用于燃料的开支很低，燃料的单位成本仅为纽卡斯尔市场上通行的煤炭价格水平的一半。此外，这一时期英法两国的劳动力成本也极为悬殊，英国人的工资水平比法国人高得多。综上所述，尽量减少价格昂贵的生产要素的消耗量这一机制指引着技术进步的方向，英国制针行业之所以会涌现出一系列新技术、新工艺，就是此机制发挥作用的结果。”[①]（罗伯特·艾伦，2012，第220—223页）。艾伦的分析事实上与第1章第3小节所介绍的新结构经济学的逻辑是一致的：英国煤炭资源丰富且工资水平高，法国恰好相反，这决定前述英法两个不同的生产方式，前者的生产方式是资本密集型而后者是劳动密集型的。

其实，斯密也并非没有强调资本对分工的作用。一般人，包括杨小凯、Alleyn Young等在读《国富论》时，只注意斯密强调了市场规模对分工程度的限制。[②]但是，在《国富论》中，斯密首先论述了资本积累是分工的前提，因为分工需要有更多的资本投入才可进行。斯密认为，对于国民财富的来源，与重商主义视之为金银不同，也与重农主义视之为土地不同，斯密强调劳动。他认为一个国家的财富即我们今天所称的国民收入取决于：劳动力生产力以及生产性劳动所占比例，劳动生产力取决于劳动分工，劳动分工取决于市场范围和资本积累，生产性劳动所占比例也取决于资本积累，图4.1概括了这个完整的思想逻辑框架。斯密建议，国家的财富应当按照人均指标来衡量，也即人均收入，而非国家的总财富或总收入——这个

---

① 罗伯特·艾伦，《近代英国工业革命揭秘》，毛立坤译，浙江大学出版社，2012年版，第220—223页。

② 虽然这些经济学家也零星提到资本与分工的关系，但是并未将其置于分析的中心位置（杨小凯，《经济学原理》，中国社会科学出版社，1998年版，第20章）。

建议此后一直被采纳至今。人均收入的提高取决于劳动生产力，《国富论》开篇就论述了劳动分工提高劳动生产力的三条基本途径：第一，劳动者的熟练程度因分工而提高；第二，工作之间因连接交换而损失的时间减少；第三，机械的发明为劳动提供了便利，简化了工作，劳动者的工作量随之得到极大提升。劳动分工又依次取决于市场范围和资本积累。市场范围越大，可销售的产品数量越多，劳动分工的机会就越多。反之，有限的市场则仅允许有限的劳动分工。劳动分工受到资本积累限制的原因在于生产过程是耗时的，即生产开始与产品最终销售之间有一个时间间隔。在自然经济中，一个家庭生产其消费所需的全部产品，劳动分工程度非常低，在此过程中只需要很少的资本来维持劳动力的衣食住行。随着劳动分工的深化，劳动者不再为其自身的消费生产产品，在耗时的生产过程期间需要保持一定的消费品储备——即斯密所说的资本来维持劳动者。资本家的作用便是为缩短生产过程的时间间隔提供手段。斯密断定，积累先于分工，所以劳动分工只能随此前积累的越来越多的储蓄而越来越细分。斯密甚至还论述了基础设施对于扩大市场范围的作用。斯密也按照他自己的价值判断标准区分了生产性劳动（资产阶级的生产活动）和非生产性劳动（比如地主阶级的家庭服务）。他认为经济作为一个整体来说，用于生产有形实际产品的劳动力份额越多，国家的财富就越多。资本被要求用来支持生产性劳动力，因此资本积累越多，卷入生产性劳动的总劳动力的比例越大。总之，斯密其实是非常强调资本积累在通过促进劳动分工提高国民财富的根本性作用的。[①]正如斯密在《国富论》导论中概括的：任何条件下，从事有用的生产性劳动人数都与推动劳动生产力发展的资本量大小及资本用途成一定比例。

然而，尽管斯密分析了资本积累与分工深化的关系，但遗憾的是，历史并没有按照斯密的预言前行。英国别针行业结构变迁的历史清楚地反映了分工只是传统劳动密集型生产方式下提高生产率的手段，资本密集型生产方式下机器的普及而非分工才是提高劳动生产力的关键，而且随着英国资本的积累，禀赋结构的变迁，别针行业也发生了剧烈变迁。斯密时代每个工人生产4 800根别针，但是今天的劳动生产率是80万根，这超乎了斯密的想象[②]，无法用分工解释，但却是新结构经济学的典型案例。

---

① 哈里·兰德雷斯、大卫·C.柯南德尔，《经济思想史》，人民邮电出版社，2014年版，第96页。从新结构经济学的视角来看，斯密对资本的重要性的论述还是有局限性的，因为在现代经济增长中，除了需要有资本来维持生产过程中劳动力的衣食住行之外，机器设备的投资、基础设施的完善、人力资本的提高和新技术的研发都需要投入资本。

② Clifford F. Pratten, “The Manufacture of Pins” , *Journal of Economic Literature*, 1980, Vol. 18, No.1, pp. 93–96.

# 2.4

# 未能实现持续的经济结构转型是发展中经济体的顽疾

## 2.4.1 发展中经济体艰难的结构转型

尽管没有历史学家和社会学家那样广阔的视野，早期的发展经济学家们，如库茨涅茨、钱纳里、罗斯托、格申克龙、赤松要等都非常关注不同经济结构的特征及其变迁，并记录了丰富的经济结构变迁内容。[①]尤其是诺贝尔经济学奖得主西蒙·库兹涅茨（Simon Kuznets），他试图通过一系列标准化事实来理解和描述长期的转型过程（但他并不关注从中总结出一套发展理论）。库兹涅茨的实证研究概括了现代经济增长的四个主要特征：经济体的部门构成的变化，非农产业比重提高，农业比重下降；部门构成的变化体现在就业构成的变化上；人口从乡村向城市迁移；非农产业的资本—劳动比提高。根据这些观察，库兹涅茨得出结论：不但在经济领域，还涉及社会制度和观念，都需要某些结构变迁，离开它们的话，现代经济增长不可能实现。后世将经济发展过程中的经济结构转型升级现象称为库茨涅茨特征事实。

图2.17至图2.19记录了近半个多世纪以来全球所处不同发展阶段的国家所经历的三次产业结构变迁情况，图2.20和图2.21则记录了对应的收入水平。基本的库兹涅茨特征事实也一样：低收入国家在很多基本方面是非常相似的，都有大量的人口住在乡村，从事农业生产，很多农业活动都是自给自足式生产；发展的起点就是资源从乡村地区的农业活动中转移出来。收入较高的国家，居住在乡村地区的人口比例更低，农业产值所占的比重更低，从事农业生产的人口比例也更低。领先国家和已经赶上它们的国家都经历了就业结构以及三次产业附加值结构的巨大变化。相反，低收入国家未能发生类似的结构变迁。因此，以工业化为核心的经济结构转型升级被视为经济增长最主要的推动力之一，尤其是在早期发展阶段。工业化的本质特征包括，制造业和全部第二产业在国民收入中所占的份额提高（商业周期中或许会出

① 代表性的著作可参考：西蒙·库兹涅茨，《各国的经济增长》，常勋等译，石景云校，商务印书馆，2018年版；罗斯托，《经济增长的阶段》，郭熙保、王松茂译，中国社会科学出版社，2001年版。

现例外）；从事制造业工作的人口比重提高；与此有关的人均收入的增加。很少有国家能在没有工业化的情况下取得经济发展的成功，仅有少数自然资源或土地极其丰富的国家例外。如图2.22所示，1993—2007年的制造业附加值增长率与人均GDP变化存在很强的正相关关系，在撒哈拉以南的非洲国家这一相关关系表现得比世界其他国家更为显著。我们将在第6章专门讨论制造业及其就业结构变迁。

然而，尽管经济发展的实质是一个经济结构转型升级的过程，在许多发展中国家，尤其是拉丁美洲和非洲国家，发展的努力没能带来持续的经济结构转型升级并带来经济增长。非洲国家今天面临的主要发展挑战显示出许多结构变迁受到局限的迹象，这可以解释为什么它

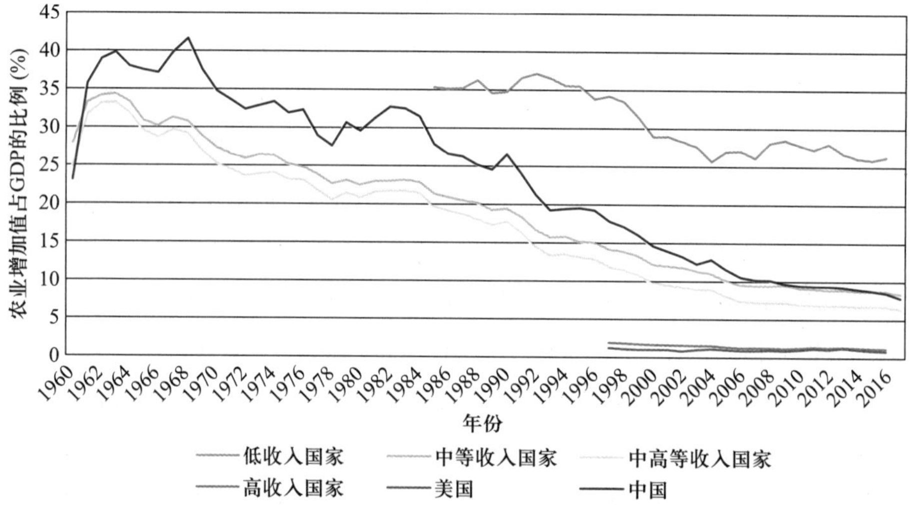


图2.17 不同发展阶段国家的农业增加值占GDP比重的趋势（1960—2017年）
资料来源：世界银行。

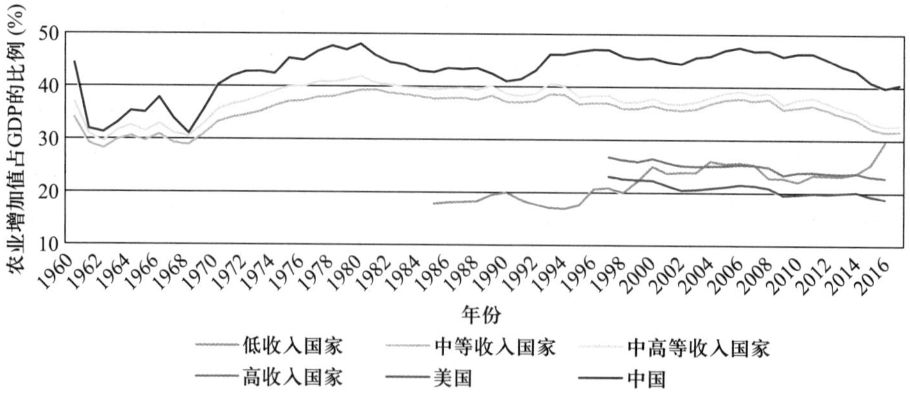


图2.18 不同发展阶段国家的工业增加值占GDP比重的趋势（1961—2017年）
资料来源：世界银行。

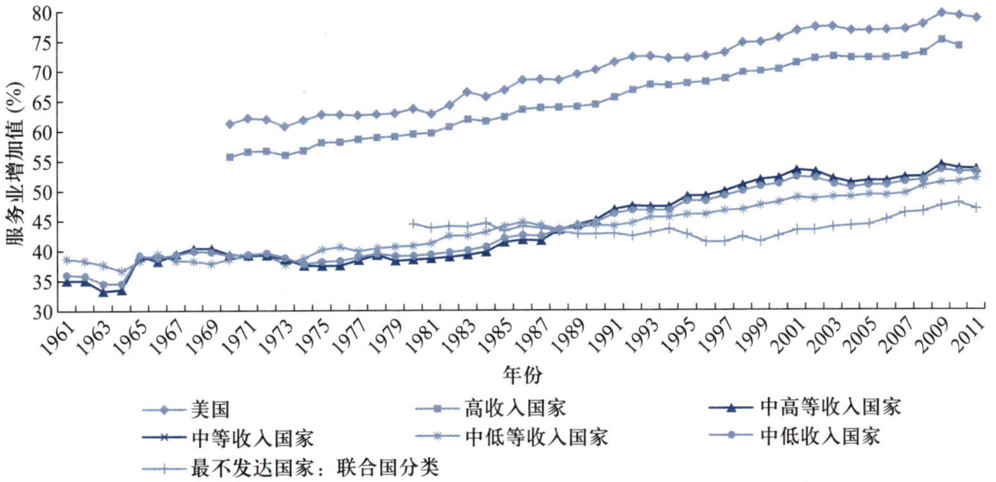


图2.19 不同发展阶段国家的服务业增加值占GDP比重的趋势（1961—2011年）

资料来源：世界银行。

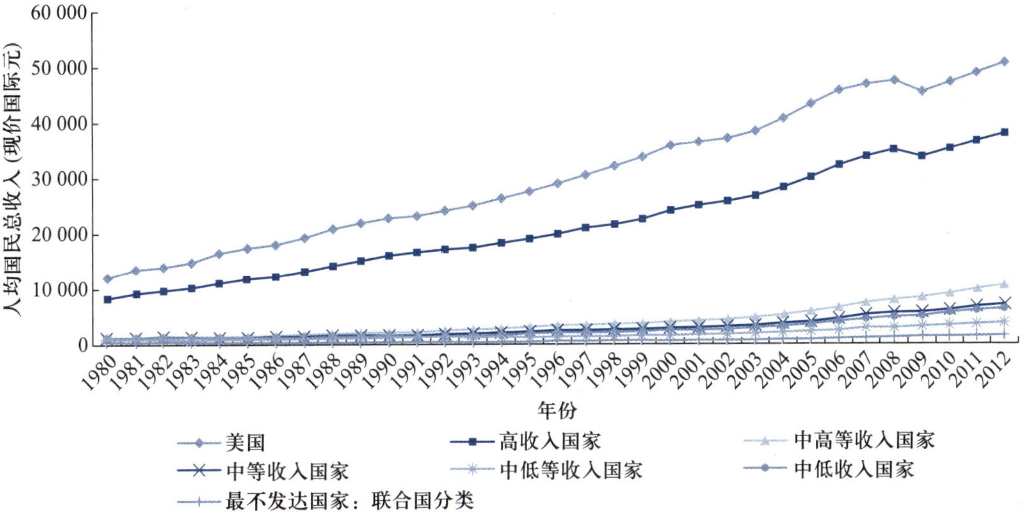


图2.20 不同发展阶段国家的人均国民总收入（GNI，PPP）（1980—2012年）

资料来源：世界银行。

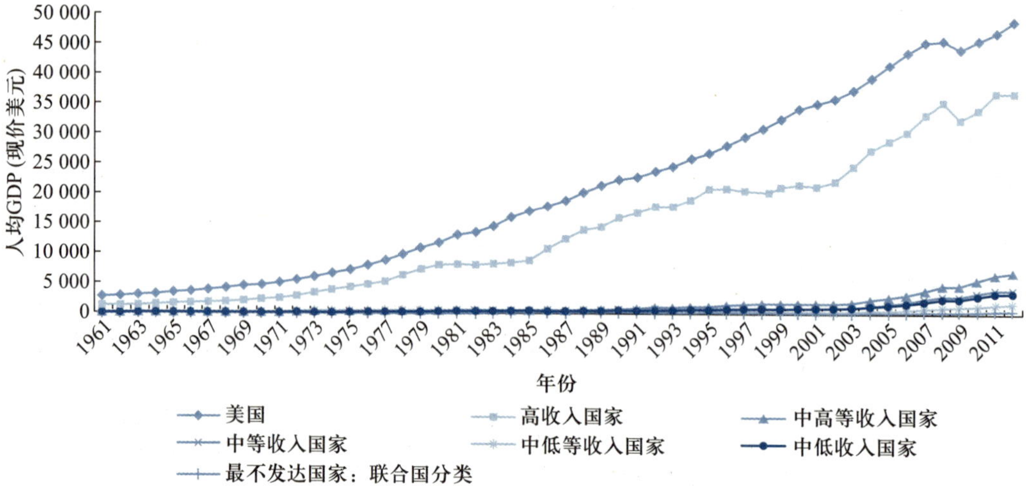


图2.21 不同发展阶段国家的人均GDP（1961—2012年）
资料来源：世界银行。

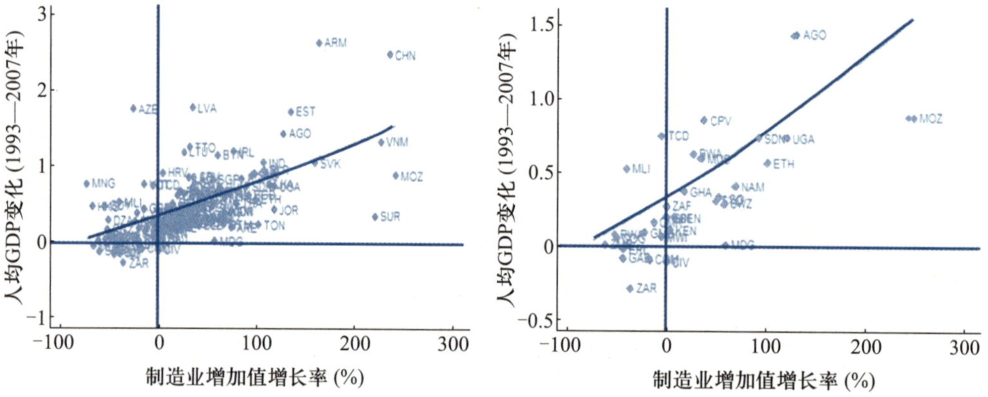


(a) GDP和制造业增加值增长率
(世界，1993—2007年)

(b) GDP和制造业增加值增长率
(非洲，1993—2007年)

图2.22 工业化成为增长的动力——制造业与收入增长的关系（1993—2007年）
资料来源：世界银行。

们自独立以来发展持续低迷。1965年，农业在撒哈拉以南非洲国家的GDP中占22%的份额，服务业为47%，工业为31%（其中制造业为17.5%）。到2005年，农业在这些国家GDP中的份额降至15%，服务业为52%，工业仅为33%（其中制造业不足15%）。在撒哈拉以南的非洲国家，通常伴随着经济发展出现的农业劳动力比例下降并未发生。该地区的经济在1960年以农业为主，农业劳动力占全部劳动力的85%。这个比例虽然在过去40年持续下降，但目前仍然很高，2009年为63%，比其他经济体在1960年的平均水平还略高一点。由于人口增长率很高，这样小的比例下降意味着农村的人口密度反而有大幅增加，人均的耕地面积非常吃紧。在一个封闭经济中，从事农业的劳动力比重下降时，只有农业的劳动生产率提高速度足够快，才能支撑不断增多的城市人口。在一个开放经济中，食品可以进口，但农业生产率依然是农业人口家庭收入和总体生活质量的决定性因素，而且是资本品进口所需要的外汇的重要来源。然而没有什么证据显示，非洲国家农业劳动力的少量转移主要是农业劳动生产率提高的结果。1960—2000年，撒哈拉以南非洲国家的单位员工农业附加值仅实现了0.5%的年均增长，不足其他发展中国家一般水平的三分之一。很自然，许多非洲国家的制造业发展非常落后，1993—2007年，在31个国家中有21个的工业化水平出现下降。撒哈拉以南非洲国家的经济多元化也受到限制，这反映在它们受到危机影响的脆弱性和年均增长率的波动性上面，其指标均大大高于其他发展中国家。许多非洲小国的经济主要依靠出口，但集中在价格波动剧烈的少数初级大宗商品上面，很多时候，随着矿产资源的开发扩大，出口的集中度进一步加强。因此，在亚洲各国已成功向高技术、高附加值产品转型的时候，非洲国家依然是大宗商品和低技术产品的出口国。非洲国家在产业结构升级和多元化方面的失败，尤其堪忧。与其他发展中地区不同，撒哈拉以南非洲国家在高收入国家的去工业化进程中获益很少。在创新和技术变革的推动下，日本、欧盟和美国的经济结构转向服务业占据主导地位，它们在这个过程中逐步退出了劳动密集型的工业领域。全球化进程，加上对竞争力和利润的追求，导致许多企业把劳动力密集型制造业搬迁到中低收入国家，这反映在近年来外国直接投资的流向变化中。但是除南非以外的撒哈拉以南非洲国家仅获得了其中很少一部分投资。McMillan和Rodrik的测算结果显示亚洲与拉丁美洲和非洲的发展中国家增长的差异的大部分可以归因于结构变迁对总体劳动生产率的贡献。[①]

总之，处于不同发展阶段的国家，禀赋结构存在巨大差异，高收入经济体的禀赋结构表现出资本相对劳动更加丰裕的特征，而低收入经济体的禀赋结构表现出劳动相对资本更加丰裕的特征，并且禀赋结构的分布不是只有这两个状态而是处于一个连续谱系。对应地，产业结构在不同的发展阶段也呈现出不同的特征，高收入经济体的产业结构表现出更加技术和资本密集，而低收入经济体的产业结构表现出更加劳动力密集。然而，并不是每个经济体都已经成功实现了这样的经济结构转型升级。

---

① Margaret S. Mc Millan, Dani Rodrik, “Globalization, Structural Change and Productivity Growth”, *NBER Working Paper*, 2011, No.17143.

## 2.4.2 结构转型与经济收敛[①]

西方经济学教科书中标准的新古典增长理论预言的经济体总量层面的收敛，在全球各个经济体之间的经验数据上是缺乏的，如图2.23所示。这也是建立在标准新古典总量生产函数基础上的新古典增长理论遭受质疑的原因。绝对收敛的缺失便出现了条件收敛的概念，指的是诸如OECD国家以及一个经济体内部的相对同质的地区之间出现的收敛。[②]在现有的增长理论文献中，条件收敛的“条件”相当含糊，泛指经济体之间存在异质性而不具有相同稳态位置。在新结构经济学中，明确指的是经济结构问题。OECD成员国是前沿的发达国家，其生产结构分布大同小异，所以退化后的总量生产函数接近于新古典总量生产函数，会出现收敛。同样，如果一个经济体内部各个地区之间的生产结构分布也大同小异，同样也会出现收敛。然而，真正的重要的是，按照生产单元（企业或行业）的标准，新古典生产函数是会出现绝对收敛的；但是加总之后由于包含了结构，因此总量生产函数并不意味着一定会出现绝对收敛。这与Rodrick整理的跨国经验证据惊人地一致，见图2.24到图2.25。在经济体的整体层面不存在绝对收敛，但在制造业行业层面存在非常稳健的绝对收敛，行业细分程度越细，收敛性越强。这种产业层面的绝对收敛在一个相对同质的经济体内部也是成立的。[③]

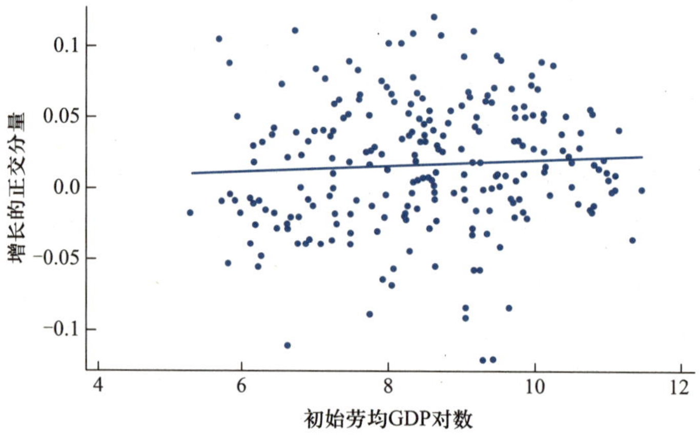


**图2.23 全球经济体总量层面缺乏收敛**

资料来源：Dani Rodrik, "Unconditional convergence in Manufacturing", *Quarterly Journal of Economics*, 2013, Vol.128, No.1, pp.165-204.

---

① Dani Rodrik, "Unconditional convergence in Manufacturing", *Quarterly Journal of Economics,* 2013, Vol.128, No.1, pp.165–204.

② R. J. Barro, X. Sala-i-Martin, Convergence Across States and Regions, *Brookings Papers on Economic Activity*, 1992, No.1, pp.107–182.

③ 戴觅、茅锐，“产业异质性、产业结构与中国省际经济收敛”，《管理世界》，2015年第6期。

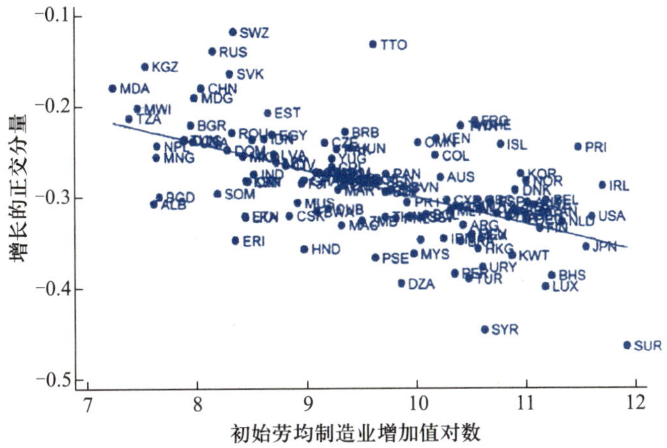


**图2.24 全球制造业层面存在绝对收敛**

资料来源：Dani Rodrik，“Unconditional convergence in Manufacturing”，*Quarterly Journal of Economics*，2013，Vol.128，No.1，pp.165-204.

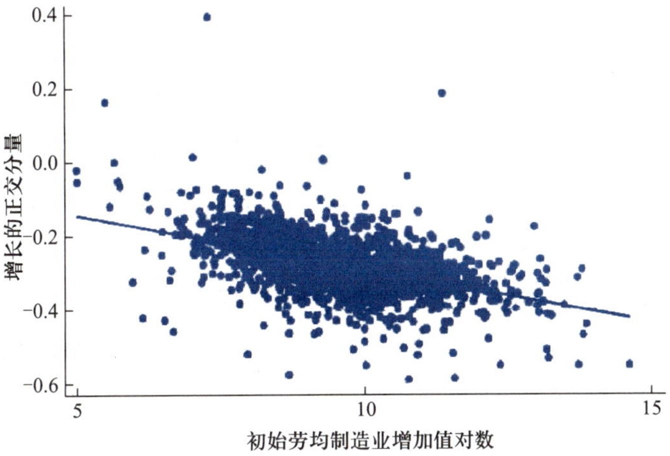


**图2.25 全球制造业2位数层面存在更加显著的绝对收敛**

资料来源：Dani Rodrik，“Unconditional convergence in Manufacturing”，*Quarterly Journal of Economics*，2013，Vol.128，No.1，pp.165-204.

## 2.5

## 如何实现持续的经济结构转型升级以获得经济增长[①]

### 2.5.1 没有结构差异的主流理论：方向错了道路对不了[②]

正如我们在第1章第3节介绍新结构经济学时所指出的，目前主流理论普遍缺乏不同发展程度国家结构的差异及其变迁，因此反映在经济增长核算框架上也如此。传统标准基本增长核算框架始于一个标准生产函数，其表达式为：

$$Y = F(A, K, L) \tag{2.1}$$

其中，$A$是技术水平，$K$是资本总量，$L$是劳动数量。尽管诸如Jorgenson和Griliches[③]这些增长核算的先驱们早就强调不同种类、不同质量的资本与劳动是不能直接简单加总的——这深刻地反映了结构的思想，但是处于简化的考虑，研究者们假定这些变量都是可以测量和加总的。然而这不是严重的问题，传统做法的麻烦在于用一个外生给定不变的生产函数$Y = F(\cdot)$来描述各种不同发展程度的国家。因此，按照目前经济学的传统思维，该生产函数明确表明，只有生产性投入增长，包括技术水平增长，GDP才能增长[④]。按照这种做法，产出的增长率可以被分解为与要素积累和技术进步相关的不同部分，对式（2.1）取对数并对时间求导，可得：

$$\frac{\dot{Y}(t)}{Y(t)} = x + \left(\frac{F_K K}{Y}\right) \times \frac{\dot{K}(t)}{K(t)} + \left(\frac{F_L L}{Y}\right) \times \frac{\dot{L}(t)}{L(t)} \tag{2.2}$$

---

① 关于这一小节更详细的内容可参考：付才辉，“新结构经济学：一场经济学的结构革命”，《经济评论》，2017年第3期。也可以参考：林毅夫、付才辉，《新结构经济学导论》（上、下册），高等教育出版社，2019年版。

② 对传统的基本经济增长核算框架的介绍可参考任意一本宏观经济学教科书，例如：巴罗与萨拉·伊·马丁所著的《经济增长》第10章第1节（R. J. Barro, X. Sala-i-Martin，*Economic Growth* (2nd Edition). MIT Press, 2004, pp.342.）。对于没有结构的增长模型基本框架的评论可参考：Justin Yifu Lin and Yong Wang, “Remodeling Structural Change”, *Oxford Handbook of Structural Transformation*, 2019。

③ D. W. Jorgenson, Z. Griliches, “The Explanation of Productivity Change”, *Review of Economic Studies*, 1967, Vol.34, No.3, pp.249–283.

④ R. J. Barro, X. Sala-i-Martin, *Economic Growth* (2nd Edition). MIT Press, 2004, pp.342.

其中，$F_K$、$F_L$分别表示投入要素资本和劳动的边际产出，由于一般在增长核算中采取的是总量生产函数，因此边际产出也是社会边际产出，$x=\left(\frac{F_A A}{Y}\right)\times\frac{\dot{A}(t)}{A(t)}$ 表示技术进步推动的经济增长——这种表达式将希克斯中性和劳动增强型技术进步作为特殊情况纳进来了，例如，如果是希克斯中性技术进步，那么 $x=\frac{\dot{A}(t)}{A(t)}$。

因此，式（2.2）将经济增长率分解为三种投入的增长率：资本、劳动与技术。从经验上讲，除了技术，其他几项都是可以直接观测的，因此技术进步对经济增长的贡献一般是通过将其视为“剩余”的方法倒推出来的，即 $x=\frac{\dot{Y}(t)}{Y(t)}-\left(\frac{F_K K}{Y}\right)\times\frac{\dot{K}(t)}{K(t)}-\left(\frac{F_L L}{Y}\right)\times\frac{\dot{L}(t)}{L(t)}$，这个被称为索洛剩余的变量便是著名的“全要素生产率”（TFP）增长率。可以看到，这种没有结构及其变迁的传统理论思维下，经济增长只不过是资本、劳动与技术等投入的增长而已，所以研究结构及其变迁在其中并不重要。

前面是一般性的目前经济增长核算框架的介绍。众所周知，现代西方标准化的经典增长模型源自Solow①，成于Cass②和Koopmans③，史称拉姆齐－卡斯－库普曼斯模型（或新古典增长模型）。为检验新古典模型分解的增长源泉，Solow利用如下不变的新古典总量生产函数开启了增长核算的先河：

$$y(t)=\frac{Y(t)}{L(t)}=\frac{F\left(A(t),K(t),L(t)\right)}{L(t)}=A(t)f\left(k(t)\right) \tag{2.3}$$

$F(\cdot)$满足新古典生产函数的全部性质。$A(t)$是技术水平或者全要素生产率。为了表述的直观和简单，我们不妨以整个经济学中最为著名的科布－道格拉斯生产函数为例，即 $F(A,K,L)=AK^{\alpha}L^{1-\alpha}$，那么式（2.3）可以改写为

$$y(t)=A(t)k(t)^{\alpha} \tag{2.4}$$

其中$\alpha$为外生的常数，$k=\frac{K}{L}$ 为人均资本。对式（2.4）两边取对数然后关于时间求导便可得到标准的增长核算公式：

---

① R. M. Solow, “A Contribution to the Theory of Economic Growth”, *Quarterly Journal of Economics*, 1956, Vol.70, No.1, pp.65–94.

② D. Cass, “Optimum Growth in an Aggregative Model of Capital Accumulation”, *Review of Economic Studies*, 1965, Vol.32, No.32, pp.233–240.

③ T. C. Koopmans, “On the Concept of Optimal Economic Growth”, *Cowles Foundation Discussion Papers*, 1965.

$$\gamma_y(t) = x + \alpha\gamma_k(t) \tag{2.5}$$

上式将人均收入增长率 $\left[\gamma_y = \frac{\dot{y}(t)}{y(t)}\right]$ 分解为来自（外生的）技术进步 $\left[x = \frac{\dot{A}(t)}{A(t)}\right]$ 和资本积累 $\left[\gamma_k = \frac{\dot{k}(t)}{k(t)}\right]$ 两个部分的贡献，资本积累的贡献大小由资本份额加权。

根据外生储蓄的新古典索罗增长模型中如下基本的资本运动或资本积累方程，即资本积累来源于投资减去折旧：

$$\dot{K}(t) = sY - \delta K \tag{2.6}$$

因此，根据式（2.6）进一步可以得到如下的人均资本增长率：

$$\gamma_k = \frac{\dot{k}(t)}{k(t)} = sA(t)k^{\alpha-1} - \delta - n \tag{2.7}$$

其中 $n$ 为（外生的）劳动力增长率。

按照新古典生产函数的性质，其要素边际产出是递减的，即 $0 < \alpha < 1$，因此如果没有技术进步，新古典模型中的人均资本增长率终将变为零。所以，长期经济增长就只能够依赖于技术进步 $x$，即TFP的增长。也因此，后续拓展新古典增长模型的各种版本的主流内生增长模型大都致力于研究全要素生产率。①更进一步地，新制度经济学则认为资本深化与技术进步只不过是增长本身而非原因（或可称为近因），制度才是潜在的根本原因。②因此，上述各种观点可以概括到下面这个公式中：

$$\underbrace{\frac{\dot{y}(t)}{y(t)}}_{\text{总经济增长率}} = \underbrace{\underbrace{\frac{\dot{A}(t)}{A(t)}}_{\text{技术的进步率}} + \alpha \underbrace{\frac{\dot{k}(t)}{k(t)}}_{\text{物质资本的增长率}} + (1-\alpha)\left[\underbrace{\frac{\dot{L}(t)}{L(t)}}_{\text{初级劳动力增长率}} + \underbrace{\frac{\dot{H}(t)}{H(t)}}_{\text{人力资本的增长率}}\right]}_{\text{保障技术、投资和劳动(知识)的产权等制度安排}} \tag{2.8}$$

前面是单个国家的增长核算，发展核算则在此基础上直接比较了不同国家的人均收入差距——“为什么有的国家富裕而有的国家贫穷”，这个问题被视为经济学家们的一生追求。考虑如下i、j两个国家不变的总量生产函数，即同样生产函数式（2.4）中的 $\alpha$ 为外生的（相同的）常数：

$$Y_{\mathrm{i}}(t) = A_{\mathrm{i}}(t)K_{\mathrm{i}}(t)^{\alpha} L_{\mathrm{i}}(t)^{1-\alpha} \tag{2.9}$$

$$Y_{\mathrm{j}}(t) = A_{\mathrm{j}}(t)K_{\mathrm{j}}(t)^{\alpha} L_{\mathrm{j}}(t)^{1-\alpha} \tag{2.10}$$

---

① D. Acemoglu, *Introduction to Modern Economic Growth*. Princeton University Press, 2009.

② D. Acemoglu, *Introduction to Modern Economic Growth*. Princeton University Press, 2009.

由式（2.9）和式（2.10）可知，这两个经济体的相对人均收入差距为：

$$\frac{y_{\mathrm{i}}(t)}{y_{\mathrm{j}}(t)}=\frac{Y_{\mathrm{i}}(t)/L_{\mathrm{i}}(t)}{Y_{\mathrm{j}}(t)/L_{\mathrm{j}}(t)}=\frac{A_{\mathrm{i}}(t)K_{\mathrm{i}}(t)^{\alpha}L_{\mathrm{i}}(t)^{-\alpha}}{A_{\mathrm{j}}(t)K_{\mathrm{j}}(t)^{\alpha}L_{\mathrm{j}}(t)^{-\alpha}}=\frac{A_{\mathrm{i}}(t)}{A_{\mathrm{j}}(t)}\left[\frac{k_{\mathrm{i}}(t)}{k_{\mathrm{j}}(t)}\right]^{\alpha} \tag{2.11}$$

对式（2.11）两边取对数得到：

$$\ln y_{\mathrm{ij}}(t)=\ln A_{\mathrm{ij}}(t)+\alpha\ln k_{\mathrm{ij}}(t) \tag{2.12}$$

其中，$y_{\mathrm{ij}}(t)=\frac{y_{\mathrm{i}}(t)}{y_{\mathrm{j}}(t)}$、$k_{\mathrm{ij}}(t)=\frac{k_{\mathrm{i}}(t)}{k_{\mathrm{j}}(t)}$、$A_{\mathrm{ij}}(t)=\frac{A_{\mathrm{i}}(t)}{A_{\mathrm{j}}(t)}$。

然后，对式（2.12）关于时间求导可得到流行的发展核算公式：

$$\gamma_{y_{\mathrm{ij}}}(t)=x_{\mathrm{ij}}+\alpha\gamma_{k_{\mathrm{ij}}}(t) \tag{2.13}$$

其中，$\gamma_{\mathrm{ij}}(t)=\frac{\dot{y}_{\mathrm{ij}}(t)}{y_{\mathrm{ij}}(t)}$、$\gamma_{\mathrm{ij}}(t)=\frac{\dot{k}_{\mathrm{ij}}(t)}{k_{\mathrm{ij}}(t)}$、$A_{\mathrm{ij}}(t)=\frac{\dot{A}_{\mathrm{ij}}(t)}{A_{\mathrm{ij}}(t)}$。

式（2.13）在思想上类似于式（2.5）。同样，按照新古典生产函数边际报酬递减的法则，人均资本积累速度长期终会降为零，因此长期跨国收入差距的动态主要依赖于跨国技术进步的差距。也因此，近二十多以来，旨在解释跨国收入差距的发展核算（及其对应的发展经济学）无一例外地崇拜TFP以及聚焦于影响TFP的因素。[①]通过上述增长核算与发展核算所展现的主流发展思潮在逻辑上似乎无懈可击，但为什么说其对于发展中国家来讲是找错了方向呢？事实很简单，主流发展思潮及其背后的理论的“阿喀琉斯之踵”在于：基于发达国家的TFP崇拜，忽视发展中国家的结构变迁——即在上述模型中总量生产函数自始至终保持不变。换言之，不论在理论模型，还是在增长核算与发展核算以及一些经验校准中，主流做法视$C$–$D$总量生产函数中的$\alpha$相对保持不变，大约为1/3。这个做法基本上吻合发达国家的情况——即著名的卡尔多特征事实，如图2.26所示的OECD国家的例子。但是，发展中国家总量生产函数中的资本相对劳动密度（$\alpha/1-\alpha$）变化非常大。总之，从全球的历史变迁角度来看，这种做法存在巨大问题。

---

① F. Caselli, “Accounting for Cross-country Income Differences”, in P. Aghion and S. Durlauf (eds), *Handbook of Economic Growth*, 2005; R. E. Hall and C. Jones, “Why Do Some Countries Produce so Much More Output Per worker than Others?”, *Quarterly Journal of Economics*, 1999, Vol.114, No.1, pp. 83–116; C-T Hsieh, P. J. Klenow, “Development Accounting”, *American Economic Journal: Macroeconomics*, 2010, Vol.2, No.1, pp.207–223.

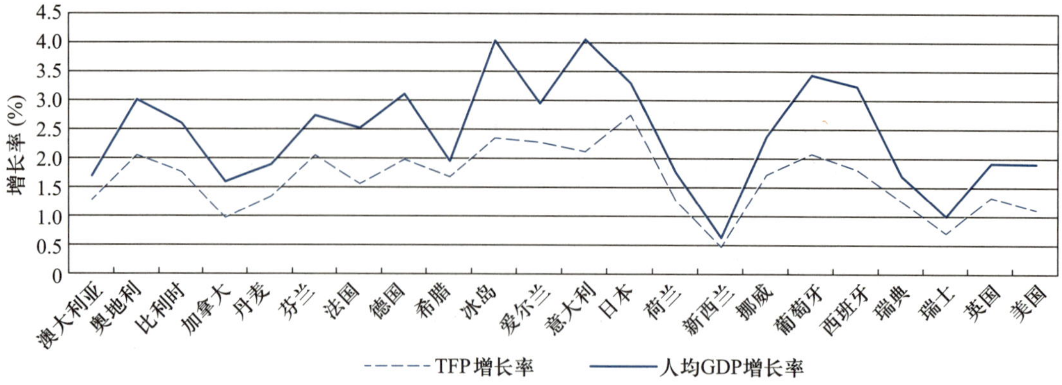


**图2.26 OECD国家的TFP增长率与人均GDP增长率：1960—2000年平均值**

资料来源：P. Aghion & P. Howitt, *The Economics of Growth*. MIT Press, 2009.

## 2.5.2 二战后的发展思想先驱：方向正确但道路错误

其实，早期拉美等国家的发展经济学家们就基于自身的体验意识到了落后经济体与发达经济体之间生产结构的根本性差异，战后衍生出的众多发展思潮被贴上了“结构主义”标签。结构主义发展思潮认为国家间巨大的收入差距根源于落后国家缺乏发达国家那样先进的（资本密集型）生产结构。

与经典的外生不变的新古典生产函数式不同，我们考虑一个可变的总量生产函数，其同样满足新古典生产函数的所有性质，如同样还是简便的科布－道格拉斯生产函数：

$$y(t)=A(t)k(t)^{\alpha(t)} \tag{2.14}$$

这与新古典生产函数不同之处在于，刻画生产函数的$\alpha(t)$是可变的（且内生于禀赋结构的）而非外生给定的常数。我们就用$\alpha(t)\in(0,1)$表征生产函数谱系。同样，对其取对数后关于时间求导可得到可变总量生产函数的增长核算公式：

$$\gamma_y(t)=x+\alpha(t)\gamma_k(t)+\big(\alpha(t)\ln k(t)\big)\gamma_\alpha(t) \tag{2.15}$$

其中，$\gamma_\alpha(t)=\dfrac{\dot{\alpha}(t)}{\alpha(t)}$便是生产函数的动态或者表示生产结构变迁。

通过对比标准的增长核算式（2.5），我们容易发现式（2.15）在形式上多了一项$\big(\alpha(t)\ln k(t)\big)\gamma_\alpha(t)$，这便是生产结构升级驱动的经济增长——这是发展中国家独特而关键的增长动力，然而遗憾的是，根据发达国家的卡尔多特征事实以及基于该事实的新古典模型（包括拓展的新增长理论）设定$\gamma_\alpha(t)=0$，这就把这股力量给假设没了。此外，由于$\alpha(t)$是可变的，式（2.15）的增长核算包含了新结构经济学的基本循环累积因果原理：禀赋结构驱动生产结构升级、生产结构升级反过来又驱动禀赋结构升级，经济发展就是如此往复。

同样，我们也可以在前述可变总量生产函数的基础上比较不同国家的人均收入差距进行发展核算。与式（2.9）、式（2.10）类似，考虑如下i、j两个国家可变的总量生产函数。

$$Y_{\mathrm{i}}(t)=A_{\mathrm{i}}(t)K_{\mathrm{i}}(t)^{\alpha_{\mathrm{i}}(t)}L_{\mathrm{i}}(t)^{1-\alpha_{\mathrm{i}}(t)} \tag{2.16}$$

$$Y_{\mathrm{j}}(t)=A_{\mathrm{j}}(t)K_{\mathrm{j}}(t)^{\alpha_{\mathrm{j}}(t)}L_{\mathrm{j}}(t)^{1-\alpha_{\mathrm{j}}(t)} \tag{2.17}$$

由式（2.16）和式（2.17）可知，这两个经济体的相对人均收入差距为：

$$\frac{y_{\mathrm{i}}(t)}{y_{\mathrm{j}}(t)}=\frac{Y_{\mathrm{i}}(t)\big/L_{\mathrm{i}}(t)}{Y_{\mathrm{j}}(t)\big/L_{\mathrm{j}}(t)}=\frac{A_{\mathrm{i}}(t)K_{\mathrm{i}}(t)^{\alpha_{\mathrm{i}}(t)}L_{\mathrm{i}}(t)^{-\alpha_{\mathrm{i}}(t)}}{A_{\mathrm{j}}(t)K_{\mathrm{j}}(t)^{\alpha_{\mathrm{j}}(t)}L_{\mathrm{j}}(t)^{-\alpha_{\mathrm{j}}(t)}}=\frac{A_{\mathrm{i}}(t)}{A_{\mathrm{j}}(t)}\frac{k_{\mathrm{i}}(t)^{\alpha_{\mathrm{i}}(t)}}{k_{\mathrm{j}}(t)^{\alpha_{\mathrm{j}}(t)}} \tag{2.18}$$

对式（2.18）两边取对数得到：

$$\ln y_{\mathrm{ij}}(t)=\ln A_{\mathrm{ij}}(t)+\alpha_{\mathrm{i}}\ln k_{\mathrm{i}}(t)-\alpha_{\mathrm{j}}\ln k_{\mathrm{j}}(t) \tag{2.19}$$

然后，再对式（2.19）关于时间求导稍做整理可得可变总量生产函数的发展核算公式：

$$\gamma_{y_{\mathrm{ij}}}(t)=x_{\mathrm{ij}}+\left[\alpha_{\mathrm{i}}(t)\gamma_{k_{\mathrm{i}}}(t)-\alpha_{\mathrm{j}}\gamma_{k_{\mathrm{j}}}(t)\right]+\left[\left(\alpha_{\mathrm{i}}(t)\ln k_{\mathrm{i}}(t)\right)\gamma_{\alpha_{\mathrm{i}}}(t)-\left(\alpha_{\mathrm{j}}(t)\ln k_{\mathrm{j}}(t)\right)\gamma_{\alpha_{\mathrm{j}}}(t)\right] \tag{2.20}$$

通过对比发展核算式（2.13），可看到式（2.20）也多了一项 $\left[\left(\alpha_{\mathrm{i}}(t)\ln k_{\mathrm{i}}(t)\right)\gamma_{\alpha_{\mathrm{i}}}(t)-\left(\alpha_{\mathrm{j}}(t)\ln k_{\mathrm{j}}(t)\right)\gamma_{\alpha_{\mathrm{j}}}(t)\right]$，这便是生产结构升级差异驱动的收入差距——这是发展中国家独特而关键的发展动力，然而遗憾的是根据发达国家的卡尔多特征事实以及基于该事实的新古典主流模型（包括拓展的新增长理论）设定 $\gamma_{\alpha_{\mathrm{i}}}(t)=\gamma_{\alpha_{\mathrm{j}}}(t)=0$，这就也把这股力量给假设没了。此外，由于 $\alpha_{\mathrm{i}}(t)\neq\alpha_{\mathrm{j}}(t)$，即生产结构在国家之间存在差异，式（2.20）的发展核算同样包含了新结构经济学的基本循环累积因果原理在跨国层面的差异。

总之，不变总量生产函数和可变总量生产函数假定下增长核算和发展核算之间的差异，表明结构变迁而非TFP可能才是发展中国家的关键问题所在。这也是早期发展经济学先驱们的真知灼见！① 然而遗憾的是类似于TFP崇拜一样，他们也免不了崇拜发达国家先进的资本密集型生产结构。为什么说结构主义作为发展经济学的先驱找对了方向但是道路错了呢？答案藏于式（2.15）和式（2.20）中结构变迁速度 $\gamma_{\alpha}(t)$、$\gamma_{\alpha_{\mathrm{i}}}(t)$、$\gamma_{\alpha_{\mathrm{j}}}(t)$ 的系数 $(\alpha(t)\ln k(t))$、$(\alpha_{\mathrm{i}}(t)\ln k_{\mathrm{i}}(t))$、$(\alpha_{\mathrm{j}}(t)\ln k_{\mathrm{j}}(t))$ 之中。这便是新结构经济学的灵魂所在——“比较优势”！在新结构经济学中比

① 可参见发展经济学先驱们的自述性评论：杰拉尔德·迈耶：“老一代发展经济学家和新一代发展经济学家”，载于杰拉尔德·迈耶、约瑟夫·斯蒂格利茨主编,《发展经济学前沿：未来展望》,本书翻译组译，中国财政经济出版社，2004年版。

较优势的实质是由禀赋结构决定的相对价格机制，或者说是不同生产结构选择的机会成本。在新结构经济学的最优生产函数模型中（参见本章2.6节），我们由利率的结构变迁弹性 $\eta_{r\alpha}=\frac{\partial r(t)}{\partial \alpha(t)}\frac{\alpha(t)}{r(t)}$ 可知 $\alpha(t)\ln k(t)=\eta_{r\alpha}-1$、$\alpha_{\mathrm{i}}(t)\ln k_{\mathrm{i}}(t)=\eta_{r_{\mathrm{i}}\alpha_{\mathrm{i}}}-1$、$\alpha_{\mathrm{j}}(t)\ln k_{\mathrm{j}}(t)=\eta_{r_{\mathrm{j}}\alpha_{\mathrm{j}}}-1$，可以将式（2.15）的可变总量生产函数的增长核算公式和式（2.20）的可变总量生产函数的发展核算公式改写为：

$$\gamma_y(t)=x+\alpha(t)\gamma_k(t)+(\eta_{r\alpha}-1)\gamma_\alpha(t) \tag{2.21}$$

$$\gamma_{y_{\mathrm{ij}}}(t)=x_{\mathrm{ij}}+\left[\alpha_{\mathrm{i}}(t)\gamma_{k_{\mathrm{i}}}(t)-\alpha_{\mathrm{j}}\gamma_{k_{\mathrm{j}}}(t)\right]+\left[(\eta_{r_{\mathrm{i}}\alpha_{\mathrm{i}}}-1)\gamma_{\alpha_{\mathrm{i}}}(t)-(\eta_{r_{\mathrm{j}}\alpha_{\mathrm{j}}}-1)\gamma_{\alpha_{\mathrm{j}}}(t)\right] \tag{2.22}$$

如第1章所述的新结构经济学关于发展与转型问题的基本论述，如果生产结构的选择违背禀赋结构决定的比较优势，那么就会扭曲禀赋结构的相对价格，即式（2.21）和式（2.22）中的利率的结构变迁弹性就会被扭曲，进而扭曲禀赋结构和生产结构，从而扭曲经济增长和经济发展。因此，可以说结构主义作为发展经济学的先驱，认为结构变迁是发展中国家的核心问题——找对了方向，但是幻想一步到位地建立起发达国家那样的先进生产结构——道路错了。这是因为不考虑禀赋条件的结构变迁必然破坏禀赋要素的相对价格，不利于经济结构升级，其后果适得其反，欲速则不达。①

① 在20世纪80年代中期，人们发现作为探索长期增长决定因素的理论工具，新古典增长模型还存在理论缺陷，因为其得出经济体最终将收敛到人均增长率为零的稳态而不符合卡尔多特征事实——人均产出持续增长。为克服新古典增长范式中递减的资本收益，外部性增长范式（AK模型）延伸了资本的概念，典型的做法是加入人力资本元素，然后假定收益递减不适用于这一更宽泛的资本范畴。然而，仅依靠额外的人力资本外溢作用支撑起长期增长并不令人信服。AK模型注定只是向内生增长的过渡。以罗默模型和熊彼特模型为代表的内生增长理论认为，长期来看以产生新思想的形式表现出来的技术进步是经济体得以摆脱收益递减的唯一方式，但是作为技术基石的思想是非竞争性的——这就彻底突破了新古典模型的范式。与前述20世纪80年代以后主流理论进阶方向完全不同，新结构经济学并不崇拜内生增长理论的瑰宝——表征技术进步的全要素生产率，而是牢牢抓住了结构变迁。最早是诺贝尔经济学奖获得者詹姆斯·赫克曼意识到了该理论进阶方向的不同。2001年，芝加哥大学设立了以D.盖尔·约翰逊教授命名的年度讲座，林毅夫做了题为“发展战略、自生能力和经济收敛”的首讲，该讲座是对林毅夫自1994年之后近十年来新结构经济学研究的总结（Lin Justin Yifu, “Development Strategy, Viability and Economic Convergence”, *Economic Development and Cultural Change*, 2003, Vol.53, pp.277–308）。会后詹姆斯·赫克曼在接受芝加哥大学的校报《芝加哥褐红色报》（*Chicago Maroon*，2001年5月15日）采访时称：“根据林毅夫的研究，过去15年出现的新发展理论是无用的……包括许多芝加哥大学的教授所做的研究是无用的。”他所说的新发展理论是20世纪八九十年代盛行的“内生增长理论”。

## 2.5.3 经济结构转型升级对经济增长贡献的核算结果

### 2.5.3.1 全球概况

我们利用PWT8.0的167个经济体1950—2011年收入、资本存量、就业与劳动份额数据对前述可变与不变总量生产函数设定下的新古典索洛模型（式2.5）与新结构经济学（式2.15）进行了核算比较。对比可以发现：新古典索洛标准核算严重高估了技术进步而低估了结构变迁的贡献；相对于可变总量生产函数核算，不变总量生产函数核算的禀赋驱动增长率平均被低估了125.53%，去掉大于0.5或小于−0.5的异常值之后仍被低估了65.99%，如表2.3和图2.27所示；技术进步率（TFP）平均被高估了113.14%，去掉大于0.5或小于−0.5的异常值之后仍被高估了74.57%，如表2.4和图2.28所示。图2.29和图2.30分别展示了新古典经济学和新结构经济学两种视角下经济结构核算结果以及经济增长贡献分解的比较。

表2.3 可变总量生产函数设定与不变生产函数设定下禀赋驱动增长率核算比较

| 禀赋驱动增长率比较 | 观测值 | 平均值 | 标准差 | 最小值 | 最大值 |
|---|---|---|---|---|---|
| 可变总量生产函数核算的禀赋驱动增长率 | 5 607 | 0.027 | 0.228 | −2.187 | 7.584 |
| 不变总量生产函数核算的禀赋驱动增长率 | 5 614 | 0.012 | 0.121 | −0.592 | 7.909 |
| 去掉大于1或小于−1的异常值 | | | | | |
| 可变总量生产函数核算的禀赋驱动增长率 | 5 565 | 0.020 | 0.150 | −0.984 | 0.995 |
| 不变总量生产函数核算的禀赋驱动增长率 | 5 565 | 0.010 | 0.023 | −0.592 | 0.327 |
| 去掉大于0.5或小于−0.5的异常值 | | | | | |
| 可变总量生产函数核算的禀赋驱动增长率 | 5 436 | 0.017 | 0.110 | −0.499 | 0.499 |
| 不变总量生产函数核算的禀赋驱动增长率 | 5 436 | 0.010 | 0.020 | −0.272 | 0.327 |

表2.4 可变总量生产函数设定与不变生产函数设定下技术进步率（TFP）核算比较

| 技术进步率比较 | 观测值 | 平均值 | 标准差 | 最小值 | 最大值 |
|---|---|---|---|---|---|
| 可变总量生产函数核算的技术进步率 | 5 607 | −0.002 | 0.360 | −4.511 | 20.070 |
| 不变总量生产函数核算的技术进步率 | 5 614 | 0.015 | 0.283 | −0.599 | 17.936 |
| 去掉大于1或小于−1的异常值 | | | | | |
| 可变总量生产函数核算的技术进步率 | 5 570 | −0.001 | 0.155 | −0.945 | 0.942 |

续表

| 技术进步率比较 | 观测值 | 平均值 | 标准差 | 最小值 | 最大值 |
|---|---|---|---|---|---|
| 不变总量生产函数核算的技术进步率 | 5 570 | 0.009 | 0.059 | −0.599 | 0.795 |
| 去掉大于0.5或小于−0.5的异常值 | | | | | |
| 可变总量生产函数核算的技术进步率 | 5 437 | 0.002 | 0.117 | −0.493 | 0.499 |
| 不变总量生产函数核算的技术进步率 | 5 437 | 0.009 | 0.055 | −0.500 | 0.495 |

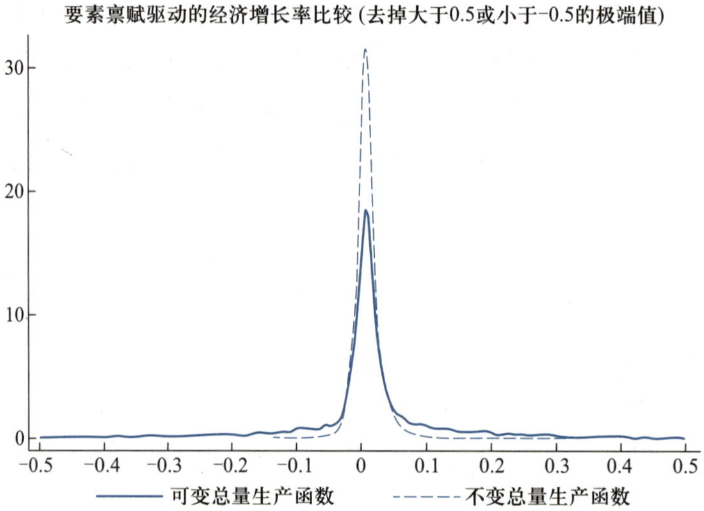


图2.27 可变总量生产函数设定与不变生产函数设定下禀赋驱动的增长率核密度分布

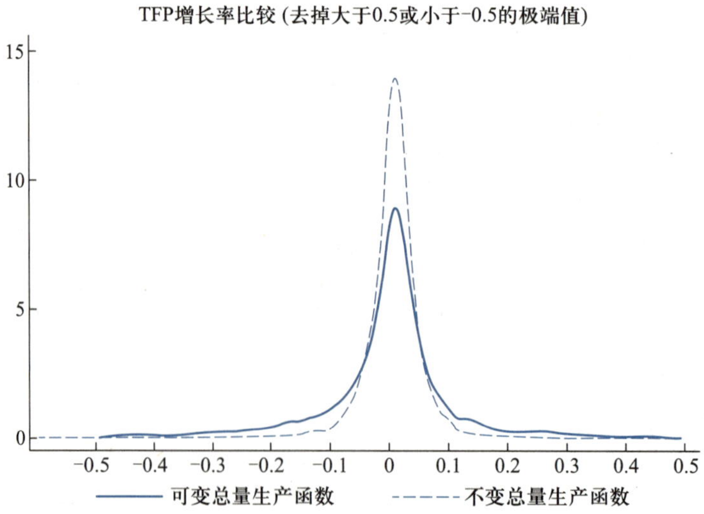


图2.28 可变总量生产函数设定与不变生产函数设定下技术进步率核密度分布

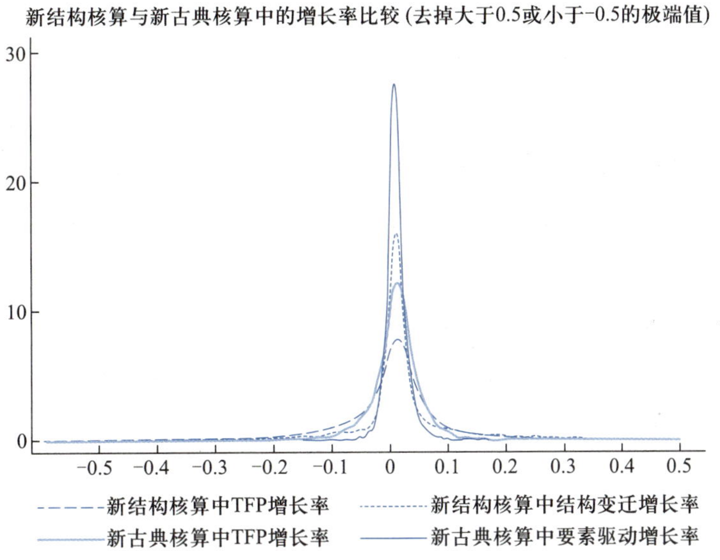


图2.29 经济增长率核算比较：新结构VS新古典

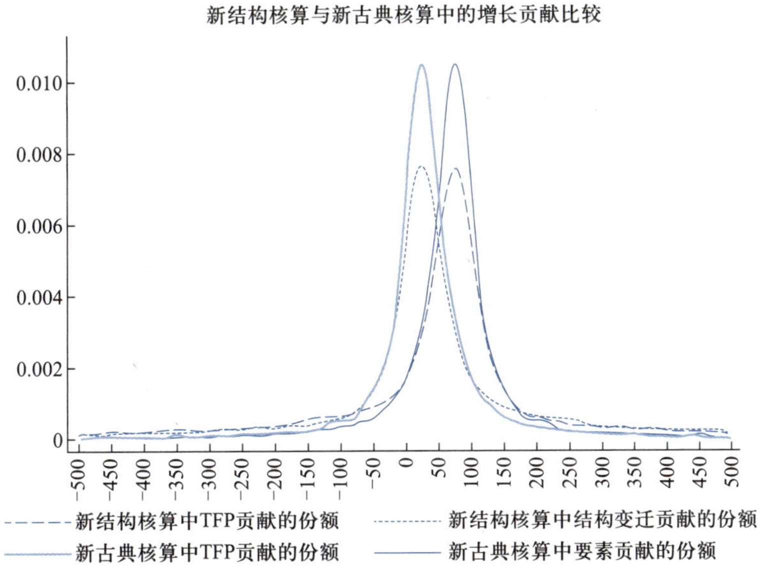


图2.30 经济增长贡献分解比较：新结构VS新古典

#### 2.5.3.2 前沿发达经济体的经济增长核算结果

前面的全样本核算比较彰显了经济结构转型升级对经济增长的重要性。新结构经济学也指出了前沿发达经济体和前沿内部发展中经济体在结构变迁特征上的差异，后面的章节在追踪各个经济体的经济结构变迁轨迹的特征时可以再次看到这一点。按照经济史统计学家麦迪森的分类，以澳大利亚、奥地利、比利时、加拿大、丹麦、芬兰、法国、德国、希腊、冰岛、爱尔兰、意大利、日本、荷兰、新西兰、挪威、葡萄牙、西班牙、瑞典、英国和美国这21个西欧及其后裔老牌工业化强国作为经济前沿发达经济体，样本中的其他经济体作为前沿内部经济体。如表2.5和图2.31所示，按照新古典传统的不变总量生产函数设定，前沿经济体平均技术进步率均大于平均要素驱动增长率，而按照新结构经济学的可变总量生产函数设定，前沿经济体平均技术进步率远低于平均禀赋驱动增长率。因此，即便是在经济前沿经济体中，结构转型升级对经济增长的贡献也大于技术进步或全要素生产率。与均值相对应，可变总量生产函数设定下的技术进步率与禀赋驱动增长率的标准差均大于不变总量生产函数设定，这从另一个方面也说明了结构变迁是经济波动的主要来源。

表2.5  21个西欧及其后裔老牌工业化强国（主要是OECD国家）人均收入水平增长率核算

| 指标 | 观测值 | 平均值 | 标准差 | 最小值 | 最大值 |
|---|---|---|---|---|---|
| 不变总量生产函数核算的禀赋驱动增长率 | 1 254 | 0.011 224 | 0.009 279 | −0.027 441 | 0.057 024 |
| 不变总量生产函数核算的技术进步率 | 1 254 | 0.013 254 | 0.025 692 | −0.088 193 | 0.296 411 |
| 可变总量生产函数核算的禀赋驱动增长率 | 1 254 | 0.024 688 | 0.134 970 | −0.743 866 | 2.268 931 |
| 可变总量生产函数核算的技术进步率 | 1 254 | −0.000 210 | 0.136 290 | −2.276 828 | 0.784 296 |

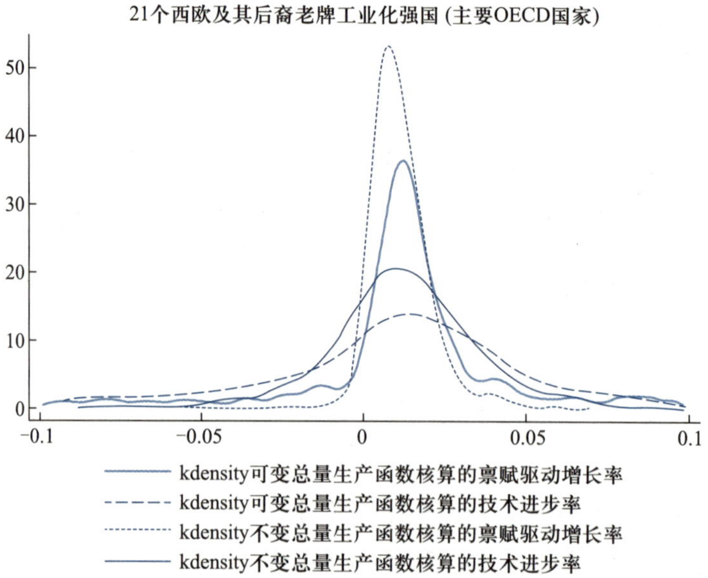


图2.31  前沿国家增长率核算：可变总量生产函数与不变总量生产函数比较

### 2.5.3.3 前沿内部的发展中经济体的经济增长核算结果

如表2.6和图2.32所示，不论是按照新古典传统的不变总量生产函数设定还是按照新结构经济学可变总量生产函数设定，前沿内部的发展中经济体平均技术进步率均小于平均要素驱动增长率。而且，在新结构经济学的可变生产函数设定中，技术进步率平均为负数，经济增长主要由结构变迁驱动。因此，在经济前沿内部经济体中，结构变迁对经济增长的贡献也远远大于技术进步率或全要素生产率。相对而言，前沿内部的发展中经济体的经济结构变迁对经济增长的贡献远大于前沿发达经济体。同样，与均值相对应，可变总量生产函数设定下的技术进步率与禀赋驱动增长率的标准差均大于不变总量生产函数设定，这也说明了结构变迁是发展中经济体经济波动的主要来源。

表2.6 前沿内部国家的人均收入水平增长率核算

| 指标 | 观测值 | 平均值 | 标准差 | 最小值 | 最大值 |
|---|---|---|---|---|---|
| 不变总量生产函数核算的禀赋驱动增长率 | 4 333 | 0.009 699 | 0.022 199 | −0.132 761 | 0.326 572 |
| 不变总量生产函数核算的技术进步率 | 4 333 | 0.008 428 | 0.061 391 | −0.598 792 | 0.519 716 |
| 可变总量生产函数核算的禀赋驱动增长率 | 4 333 | 0.029 217 | 0.206 052 | −1.011 791 | 4.521 481 |
| 可变总量生产函数核算的技术进步率 | 4 333 | −0.011 091 | 0.212 288 | −4.511 064 | 1.147 941 |

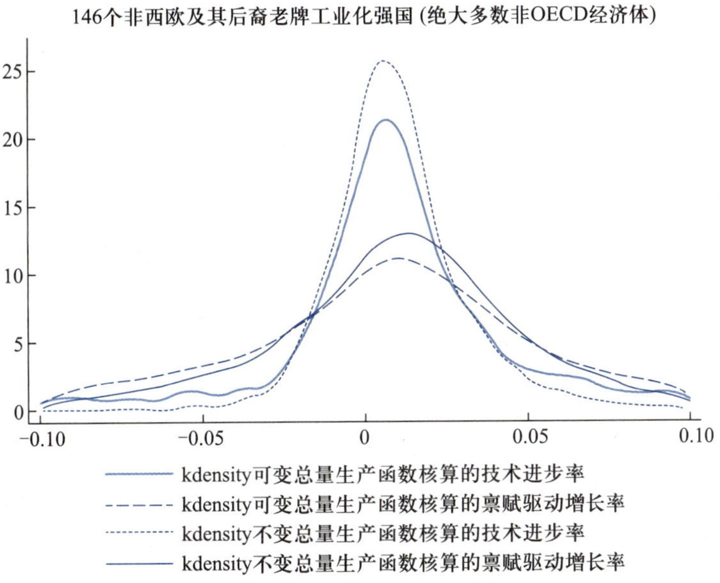


图2.32 前沿内部国家增长率核算：可变总量生产函数与不变总量生产函数比较

注：该核密度图去掉了小于−0.1与大于0.1的异常值。

# 2.6

# 结构转型升级的方向与道路：新结构经济学

## 2.6.1 由禀赋结构所支配的结构变迁方程

### 2.6.1.1 新古典经济学：古典经济学的边际革命

前面我们已经指出亚当·斯密及其继承者其实远离了工业革命这个人类历史上最重要的结构变迁。在亚当·斯密之后的古典经济学和新古典经济学家们抛开了斯密对国民财富性质和来源这类宏观增长问题的关注，转而探求价格的决定和资源配置以及收入分配等微观问题。让经济学发生这种转折的是大卫·李嘉图，而其理论体系的基础却是收益递减原理，这其实与斯密主张的分工提升劳动生产率的观点背道而驰。边际收益递减原理最早由法国经济学家杜尔哥于1765年提出，后被马尔萨斯用在其人口原理中。马尔萨斯认为，人口增长速度超过食物增长速度将导致我们在前面所讨论的马尔萨斯陷阱。李嘉图深受其影响，认为土地的边际产出递减更加理所当然。马尔萨斯所笼罩的悲观和李嘉图对斯密思潮的取代，使得整个19世纪主流经济学思潮对经济增长也充满悲观主义——更准确地讲是忽视，因为增长不再是其主要焦点。边际革命不但提出了边际效用论，还继续延续了边际产出递减原理。马歇尔将二者融合到新古典经济学中完成了资源配置的均衡分析。因此，新古典经济学其实可以被称为“马尔萨斯经济学”，是古典经济学经过边际革命之后形成的经济学。

### 2.6.1.2 新结构经济学：新古典经济学的结构革命

正如我们在第1章第3小节所概括的新古典经济学（NCE）与新结构经济学（NSE）的根本区别为：新古典经济学的基本公理是理性选择资源配置使得其价值（实现的效用或利润）最优；新结构经济学的基本公理是在最优资源配置的同时理性选择经济结构以使得其价值

（实现的要素禀赋价值/边际生产力）最优。[①]我们可以用如下的数学规划问题来刻画这种差异：

NCE：给定生产函数（技术状态），求解最优资源配置。

$$\max_{z} \pi(z) = y - wz \qquad (2.23)$$
$$\text{s.t.} f(z) = y$$

NSE：给定要素禀赋，求解最优生产函数（最优产业与技术）。

$$\max_{f} v(f) \qquad (2.24)$$
$$\text{s.t.} z = \bar{z}$$

注意，二者的分析空间是不同的：新古典经济学的资源配置空间 $(z, w) \in \mathrm{R}$ 是欧几里得空间，新结构经济学的结构变迁空间 $f \in \mathrm{C}$ 是函数空间。

以我们前面使用过的柯布–道格拉斯生产函数 $Y = F(K, L) = K^{\alpha} L^{1-\alpha}$ 为例，新古典经济学的资源配置公理，也即式（2.23）的求解结果就是所谓的边际革命的边际生产力理论[②]，即 $\frac{\partial f(z)}{\partial z} = w$。边际生产力理论说的是，其他要素数量不变，而增加或减少单位某种生产要素在生产过程中所引起的商品产值的减少（或增加）量，就等于该种生产要素一个单位的服务报酬或其他报酬。这些是经济学入门课程所学习的知识。新结构经济学的结构变迁公理，则是选择最优的生产函数使得给定禀赋结构的边际生产力最大化，即选择生产函数（$\alpha$）使得劳动生产力 $\frac{\partial F}{\partial L} = (1-\alpha) K^{\alpha} L^{-\alpha}$ 最大化，很容易求解得到结构变迁方程（参见图2.33）。

$$\alpha = 1 - \frac{1}{\ln\left(\frac{K}{L}\right)} \quad 当 \frac{K}{L} \geqslant e，否则 \alpha = 0 \qquad (2.25)$$

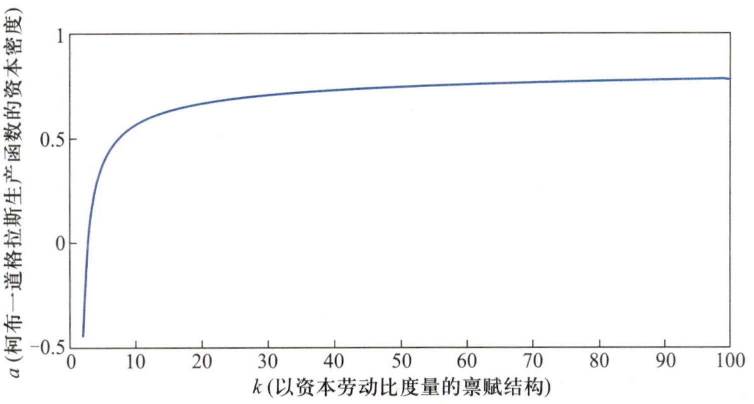


图2.33 结构变迁方程的图示

① 新制度经济学的基本公理是理性选择制度安排使得其价值（节约的交易费用）最优。

② 边际生产力理论由美国经济学家克拉克提出，对应于消费的边际效用理论。

## 2.6.2 用结构变迁方程来预测世界经济结构变迁

### 2.6.2.1 全球预测的情况

结构变迁方程 $\alpha=1-\frac{1}{\ln k}$ 刻画了新结构经济学的基本原理（比较优势原理）：任意时点上给定的要素禀赋结构（资本劳动比 $k$）便决定了最优的生产方式（生产结构）。这个结构变迁方程中没有任何其他外生的需要估算的校准参数，非常简单，预测的产出也没有需要估算的校准参数，这彰显了新结构经济学单单以禀赋结构作为理论分析和预测的能力。我们利用常用的跨国数据库PWT8.0中167个经济体从1950—2011年的长期数据来拟合，涉及的变量数据只有劳动、资本和产出三个，劳均变量也就只有人均资本（度量禀赋结构$k$）、人均GDP（度量产出$y$）。因此，利用人均资本数据通过结构变迁方程 $\alpha=1-\frac{1}{\ln k}$ 可以得到产出 $y=k^{1-\frac{1}{\ln k}}$ 的预测数据$\tilde{y}$。图2.34是人均产出的预测数据［的对数 $\ln(\tilde{y})$］与实际的人均GDP数据（对数）的拟合，相关系数高达0.913 9。

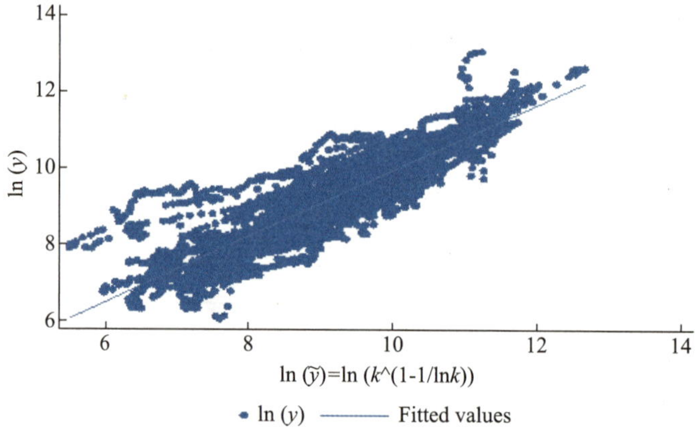


图2.34 产出拟合：全球167个经济体1950—2011年的数据

### 2.6.2.2 第二次世界大战后13个发展典范的预测情况

由两位诺贝尔经济学奖得主领衔的增长与发展委员会于2008年发布了对“最佳实践”的研究成果——《增长报告：持续增长和包容性发展战略》（简称《增长报告》），找到了战后能够以超过7%的增长率持续增长25年以上的13个高增长经济体，堪称战后的发展典范。[①]图2.35是战后13个发展典范的拟合，相关系数比全球的样本大幅提高，诸如中国台湾和韩国这样的发展典范中的典范的相关系数分别高达0.997 7和0.996 3，日本的相关系数高达0.992 5，新加坡的相关系数高达0.992 6，中国大陆也高达0.991 3。用上述结构变迁方程预测这些结构变迁符合其潜在比较优势而经济发展迅速的经济体当然更准，因为它们符合新结构经济学的发展主张，而那些违背比较优势的结构变迁自然发展不好。[②]

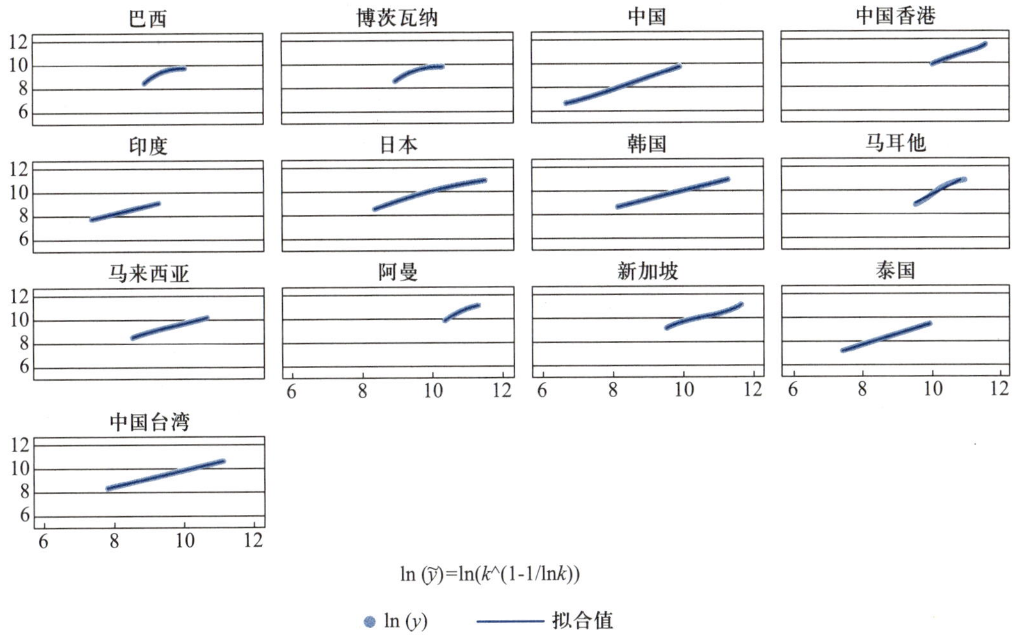


图2.35 最优产出拟合：战后13个发展典范1950—2011年的数据

我们不妨将战后发展典范中的中国的结构变迁轨迹放大，来仔细观察中国的结构变迁试验。一目了然，其结构变迁轨迹与我们所熟知的一些影响结构变迁轨迹的重大历史事件丝丝入扣。经过三年经济恢复工作，1952年年底，中共中央提出了党在过渡时期的总路线，明确规定："党在这个过渡时期的总路线和总任务，是要在一个相当长的时期内，逐步实现国家对农业、对手工业和对资本主义工商业的社会主义改造。"1953年之后，中国进入了重工业优先发展的计划经济时代。此后，中国的结构变迁轨迹严重违背比较优势，出现了严重的结构扭曲，进而使得实际的人均GDP低于结构变迁方程预测的人均产出水平，出现了较大的生产率缺口。1978年年底中国开始了改革开放，放开符合当时中国潜在比较优势的劳动力密集

① Growth Commission, *The Growth Report: Strategies for Sustained Growth and Inclusive Development,* Washington, D. C., 2008.

② 林毅夫，《新结构经济学》，北京大学出版社，2012年版。

型产业发展，使得结构变迁轨迹转轨到结构变迁方程所预测的轨迹上来。尽管改革开放至今中国也受到了一些内外部重要事件的影响，比如分税制改革、亚洲金融危机和世界金融危机，但结构变迁大体上是符合比较优势，使得其实际产出水平与结构变迁方程预测的潜在产出水平非常贴近。因此，改革开放之后，中国保持了近四十年年均近两位数的高速增长，也就不足为奇了。因此，在我们看来，战后中国至今最大的社会试验不是计划经济向市场经济的转轨，而是其背后从违背比较优势的赶超战略结构变迁向符合比较优势的结构变迁路径转轨。基于中国经验的新结构经济学雏形是林毅夫、蔡昉和李周于1994年出版的《中国的奇迹：发展战略与经济改革》一书，该书系统阐述了中华人民共和国成立以后我国重工业赶超战略与当时中国人多资本少的禀赋特征之间的政府干预矛盾，揭示了扭曲价格的宏观经济政策、资源计划配置与剥夺微观主体自主权三位一体的计划经济体制的内生形成机制，用比较优势战略对东亚奇迹（大多位列《增长报告》所列的战后发展典范之中）进行了重新解释，分析了改革开放之后发展战略转轨为比较优势战略与当时劳动力相对资本富裕的禀赋特征之间的相容，总结了在赶超战略下没有自生能力的企业在约束下的渐进式转型的经验。《经济发展与转型：思潮、战略和自生能力》一书则将基于中国经验提炼的逻辑推广到全球历史背景下。

### 专栏2.1
### 罗思义：新结构经济学应作为经济分析的重要基石[①]

新结构经济学的一个重要特征，是对“比较优势”理念进行了独创性和全面性的分析。大多数教材对比较优势理论的分析，往往把焦点集中在纯物质生产优势——拥有丰富石油供应的国家在能源生产上具有比较优势，气候炎热的国家在生产热带作物上具有比较优势，等等，来阐释大卫·李嘉图（David Ricardo）提出的理念。新结构经济学则重点对资本和劳动力等不同的生产要素的比较优势进行更全面的分析。比如，新结构经济学认为，随着经济的发展，经济结构会从劳动力密集型过渡到资本密集型：“一国的要素禀赋在任意特定的时刻是给定的，但随着时间推移是可变的。它决定了一国的比较优势，并从而决定了该国的最优

① 作者罗思义（John Ross）系英国伦敦经济与商业政策署前署长、中国人民大学重阳金融研究院高级研究员。本专栏的资料来源于罗思义刊于2017年10月9日新浪网的文章《新结构经济学应作为经济分析的重要基石》。

产业结构。一个特定国家产业结构的升级要求要素禀赋结构的升级（即由劳动力和自然资源相对丰裕的结构升级到资本相对丰裕的结构）。”新结构经济学的这一分析显然得出一个明确且经得起事实检验的结论：发达经济体资本密集型发展高于欠发达经济体。正如世界银行发布的涵盖占世界GDP比重99%的168个国家的资本密集型生产数据的《2017年世界发展指标》显示，此分析完全经得起实证检验。

资本密集型生产增加意味着，促进同样数量的经济增长所需的资本投入数量需要有所提高。这可通过增量资本产出率（ICOR）来衡量。ICOR是GDP增长1%所需投资总值占GDP总值的比重。增加产出所需的投资越低越好，即增量资本产出率越小，投资效率则越高。这用公式来表达就是：ICOR = GDP增长率/投资占GDP的比重。图2.36呈现的是以世界银行提供的最新国际可比数据为依据的2015年ICOR比较：世界ICOR平均水平为8.6，即世界GDP每增加一个百分点需要投资GDP的8.6%；发展中经济体ICOR为7.7，即发展中经济体资本密度低于世界平均水平；发达经济体ICOR为9.7，即高收入经济体资本密集型生产不仅高于世界平均水平，而且远高于发展中经济体水平；中国ICOR为6.3，不仅低于世界平均水平，而且也低于发达和发展中经济体水平。可以看出，世界银行提供的最新国际可比数据充分印证了新结构经济学的分析——发达/高收入经济体资本密集型生产多于发展中经济体。

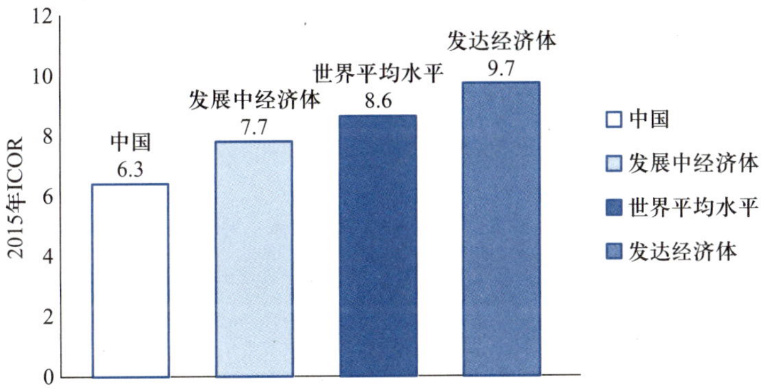


**图2.36 2015年ICOR比较**

资料来源：根据世界银行发布的《世界发展指标》数据计算。

应指出的是，单年的ICOR可能会受到经济周期波动，以及随之而来的GDP增速或减速所带来的影响。因此，为避免最新数据仅反映单年的非典型趋势之嫌，有必要进行交叉验证。图2.37呈现的是按照5年移动平均线计算的2010—2015

年ICOR比较。按照5年移动平均线计算：世界ICOR平均水平为8.5；发展中经济体ICOR为6.1，低于世界平均水平；高收入经济体ICOR为12.1，高于世界平均水平；中国ICOR为5.7，不仅低于世界平均水平，而且也低于发展中经济体。新结构经济学的分析——发达经济体资本密集型生产多于发展中经济体，再次得到充分印证。

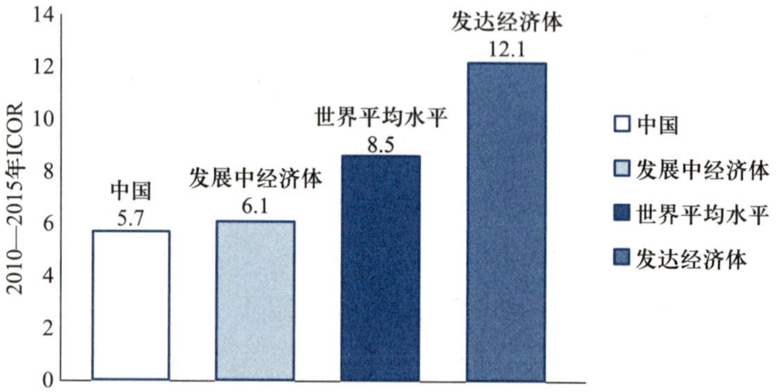


图2.37 2010—2015年ICOR比较（参照5年移动平均线计算）

资料来源：根据世界银行发布的《世界发展指标》数据计算。

最后，为体现长期框架以及结构特征，图2.38为大家呈现按照能消除经济周期波动影响的10年移动平均线计算的ICOR比较。可以看出，在整个比较期间，高收入经济体ICOR高于发展中经济体，正好吻合新结构经济学的分析。显然，从全球数据可以看出，无论按照什么样的时间框架计算，新结构经济学的基本前提——随着经济的发展，经济结构会从低资本密集型的增长过渡到高资本密集型的增长，均得到印证。

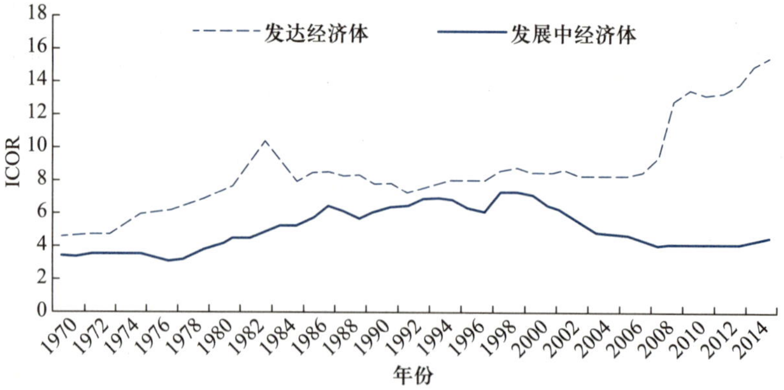


图2.38 长期ICOR比较（参照10年移动平均线计算）

资料来源：根据世界银行发布的《世界发展指标》数据计算。

# 2.7

# “上层建筑”如何随经济基础变迁而变迁

## 2.7.1 马克思历史唯物主义方法论

马克思在《〈政治经济学批判〉序言》中说：“人们在自己生活的社会生产中发生一定的、必然的、不以他们的意志为转移的关系，即同他们的物质生产力的一定发展阶段相适合的生产关系。这些生产关系的总和构成社会的经济结构，即有法律的和政治的上层建筑竖立其上并有一定的社会意识形式与之相适应的现实基础。”①恩格斯也说：“一切社会变迁和政治变革的终极原因，不应当到人们的头脑中，到人们对永恒真理和正义的日益增进的认识中去寻找，而应当到生产方式和交换方式的变更中去寻找；不应当到有关时代的哲学中去寻找，而应当到有关时代的经济中去寻找。”②

历史唯物主义方法论把唯物主义和辩证法的结合贯彻到了包括社会历史在内的一切领域中，揭示社会生活的本质、阐明社会发展的一般规律。这些基本原理包括：生产是历史一切社会进步的尺度，社会生产力的发展水平，决定人类社会的进程；与生产力一定发展相适应的生产关系，构成一定的社会形态和经济结构的现实基础，规定着社会形态的主要特征；一定的社会形态是一定的经济基础和一定的上层建筑的统一，经济基础的性质决定上层建筑的变更，上层建筑又服务和反作用于经济基础；一切社会制度、社会形态都是人类社会从低级到高级的无穷的发展过程中的一些暂时阶段，没有永恒的社会制度和形态，社会制度的发迹是社会基本矛盾发展的结果。社会关系要在一定的物质条件下从旧社会的基础中成熟，在它们的所容纳的全部生产力发挥出来之前，社会形态是不会灭亡的；现实存在的具体社会形态都是复杂的，人类社会发展的每一个阶段都既有占支配地位的社会形态，又存在其他社会形态的残余和萌芽；人类社会的一般总规律是从原始社会到奴隶社会、封建社会、资本主义社

---

①《马克思恩格斯选集》第2卷，人民出版社，2012年版，第2页。

②《马克思恩格斯选集》第2卷，人民出版社，2012年版，第797–798页。

会再到社会主义和共产主义社会。这是一个自然的历史发展过程，社会生产力是推动社会历史前进的根本动力。

可以从历史唯物主义关于社会发展一般规律中看到社会其实是一个复杂的有机体。[①]当然，历史唯物主义对社会有机结构的理解，与斯宾塞等人的社会有机论有所不同。后者抹杀社会同自然界的本质区别，把社会有机体同生物有机体做简单的机械类比，把社会矛盾归结于生物体的矛盾。马克思主义关于社会有机结构或社会有机体的理论则完全不同，它既看到社会与自然界的联系，又注意到社会与自然界的质的区别，指出社会是以生产方式为物质基础的有机体，有着自身所固有的生产力和生产关系、上层建筑和经济基础等特殊的矛盾。当然，历史唯物主义并不研究社会有机结构的各个细节，而只从整体上研究和把握社会系统，从理论上再现社会有机结构的普遍本质，主要是社会有机结构的物质性、整体性和变动性。社会有机体是有形的、现实的存在，并非什么虚无缥缈、不可捉摸的东西，就是说，它本质上是物质的。社会的物质性不能和实物意义上的物质性相等同。后者是指某种能被感觉器官感知的实体，而社会的物质性主要是指那种不以人的意志为转移的客观物质关系，或者叫作物质的社会关系，如生产力、生产关系、交换关系以及各阶级的经济关系等。同时，那些有形的、现实存在的诸社会要素，又是彼此联系、相互作用、有机统一的。它们始终在活动和发展着，而不是处于孤立、静止的状态。观察和研究社会必须从实际出发，着眼于各种社会要素的联系和发展。为此，必须首先对生产方式的内在矛盾运动，即生产力与生产关系的矛盾及其展开过程进行具体的分析。广义地讲，经济基础包括生产力和生产关系，生产力和生产关系也是统一的。经济基础决定上层建筑，是二者相互作用中最基本的方面。在此前提下，又必须承认上层建筑对于经济基础的反作用。上层建筑从经济基础中产生，其内容、性质均由经济基础所决定，这就注定了上层建筑的“天职”即根本职能是反映并服务于经济基础。上层建筑对经济基础的作用，就在于它一定要以各种方式为自己的经济基础服务，这种服务主要表现在以下几个方面：首先是服务的方向，其次是服务的方式，最后是服务的效果。从效果上看，上层建筑对经济基础的发展既可以起促进作用，也可以起阻碍作用。当上层建筑同自己的经济基础相适应，能够满足经济基础的要求时，就起促进作用；反之，如果上层建筑已不能满足经济基础的要求，它的活动就会同经济基础发生尖锐矛盾，就会对经济基础起某种破坏作用。上层建筑的反作用是巨大的，但并不是无限的，不是决定一切的。上层建筑的反作用是在经济基础起决定作用的前提下的反作用，因而是第二位的；它不能与经济基础

---

① 关于经济基础与上层建筑的辩证原理，有很多相关著作可资参考，这里主要参考：萧前、李秀林、汪永祥主编，《历史唯物主义原理》（第三版），北京师范大学出版社，2012年版。

的决定作用等同，更不能超过经济基础的决定作用。从发源或根源上看，上层建筑反作用于经济基础的可能性，得之于经济基础及其发展的力量，就是说，上层建筑的反作用归根到底是由经济基础赋予的；从结果即发展的最终结局上看，上层建筑的反作用只有同经济基础发展的趋势相适应而不是相违背时，才能持久地得到发挥。如果相反，这种反作用虽能延续或暂时阻碍经济发展的进程，却不能决定经济发展的总趋势。经济基础的决定性和上层建筑的能动性的统一，体现了历史观中唯物主义和辩证法的统一。总之，正如王沪宁等所言，历史唯物主义方法论应用到具体学科上并不排斥具体的分析方法，关键问题是所有具体方法的应用都应当在一个科学的总的方法论的指导下进行，没有一个科学的总的方法论的指导，具体方法的应用往往难以导致一个科学的结论。历史唯物主义方法的运用，为人类更好、更深刻、更科学地认识自身的社会现象的发展规律提供了科学的方法论。①

### 2.7.2 以历史唯物主义辩证法为指导避免“盲人摸象”与“本末倒置”

新结构经济学强调不同发展阶段由于禀赋结构的不同，因而对应的构成经济基础、决定生产力水平和生产关系的产业结构以及作为上层建筑的各种制度安排也不同，与马克思主义政治经济学如出一辙。恩格斯有一段精彩的论述，与新结构经济学丝丝入扣：“人们在生产和交换时所处的条件，各个国家各不相同，而在每一个国家里，各个世代又各不相同。因此，政治经济学不可能对一切国家和一切历史时代都是一样的。从弓和箭，从石刀和仅仅是例外地出现的野蛮人的交换往来，到上千马力的蒸汽机，到机械织机、铁路和英格兰银行，有一段很大的距离。火地岛的居民没有达到进行大规模生产和世界贸易的程度，也没有达到出现票据投机或交易所破产的程度。谁要想把火地岛的政治经济学和现代英国的政治经济学置于同一规律之下，那么，除了最陈腐的老生常谈以外，他显然不能揭示出任何东西。因此，政治经济学本质上是一门历史的科学。它所涉及的是历史性的即经常变化的材料；它首先研究生产和交换的每个个别发展阶段的特殊规律，而且只有在完成这种研究以后，它才能确立为数不多的、适用于生产一般和交换一般的、完全普遍的规律。同时，不言而喻，适用于一定的生产方式和交换形式的规律，对于具有这种生产方式和交换形式

① 王沪宁等主编，《政治的逻辑——马克思主义政治学原理》，上海人民出版社，2004年版，第27页。

的一切历史时期也是适用的”。①

一个经济体的经济系统不但是一个有机体，而且还是极其复杂变化的，越是发达的经济体其复杂性越高，如第1章第4小节所对比的布隆迪和瑞士的经济系统差异。不论是社会科学还是自然科学，都会对复杂的现实世界进行理论抽象，不论在物理学、生物学还是经济学中，科学思考的艺术就是做出使解释世界变得容易的假设。我们在第1章第3小节介绍新结构经济学的研究体系时，就将作为新结构经济学研究对象的经济结构系统划分为不同的结构安排类型，如禀赋结构、生产结构（产业结构与创新结构）、金融结构、劳动结构、空间结构、开放结构、波动结构、环境结构、制度结构等，并在图1.23中将这些不同的结构安排合作为一个统一的经济结构系统。然而，这个经济结构系统依然是一个理论系统，是对现实世界的理论抽象。任何理论，包括新结构经济学在内，都可能“盲人摸象”。对于复杂的现实世界，新古典经济学摸到了资源配置的部位，新制度经济学摸到了制度的部位，行为经济学摸到了行为的部位，而新结构经济学试图在更广阔的结构视角下将这些不同的部位统一起来。尽管如此，在学习或研究新结构经济学时，依然还会容易出现“盲人摸象”的问题，比如只顾及其中一种类型的结构安排而不考虑与其他类型的结构安排的前因后果。聚焦于金融结构的人可能只强调金融结构的重要性，聚焦于劳动结构的人可能只强调劳动结构的重要性，聚焦于空间结构的人可能只强调空间结构的重要性，聚焦于开放结构的人可能只强调开放结构的重要性，聚焦于波动结构的人可能只强调波动结构的重要性，聚焦于环境结构的人可能只强调环境结构的重要性，聚焦于制度结构的人可能只强调制度结构的重要性。尽管引入了结构的视角，但诸如此类的“盲人摸象”还是极有可能“本末倒置”。因为在新结构经济学中，这些结构安排都是第二位的，都是由禀赋结构所内生的生产结构所决定的，不能错把这些上层结构安排对作为经济基础的禀赋结构所决定的生产结构的反作用当成决定性作用。因此，单单引入结构视角还不是新结构范式，新结构范式需要从在每一个时点给定、随着时间可变、决定一个经济体总预算和要素相对价格的禀赋结构这一物质存在作为切入点，并且采取历史唯物主义辩证法的方法来分析作为经济基础的禀赋结构所内生决定的生产结构和生产关系，及与生产结构相适应的、内生的金融结构、教育结构、空间结构、开放结构、周期结构、环境结构、制度结构等上层结构安排之间的辩证关系，以及历史动态地看问题。只有采取了这样的新结构范式才可能避免“一叶障目不见泰山”。②

---

① “反杜林论”，《马克思恩格斯选集》第3卷，人民出版社，2012年版，第525–526页。

② 阿德尔曼，“发展理论中的误区及其对政策的含义”，《发展经济学前沿：未来展望》，杰拉尔德·迈耶和约瑟夫·斯蒂格利茨主编，中国财政经济出版社，2004年版。

# 2.8

# 制度前提决定论的谬误[①]

## 2.8.1 制度是重要的但更是内生的

本来20世纪60年代道格拉斯·诺斯刚提出新制度经济学时，还吸收了马克思主义的思想认识，认为制度是重要的，同时是内生的，也就是经济基础决定上层建筑，同时认为制度对经济绩效是有影响的，也就是上层建筑会反作用于经济基础。但是，到了20世纪80年代以后，诺斯本人及其后来的新制度经济学家则只强调制度对经济运行的影响，制度是内生的这一重要理论视角则被忽略了，并且把西方现行的制度作为各国都应该采用的制度。后来的新制度经济学的继承者们，如阿西莫格鲁在《为什么国家会失败》一书中，甚至唯发达经济体的制度安排是从，认为其他发展中国家经济不能发展好就是因为没有西方发达国家的制度安排。[②]事实上，不仅仅是新制度经济学如此，现代经济学中的宏观、金融、教育、财政、环境等领域的理论也直接把发达国家的相关经济制度作为暗含的前提，在运用于发展中国家时，通常认为发达国家与发展中国家只有量的差异没有质的不同。但是，实际上，并非如此。认为任何单一的制度安排都是在一个复杂的制度结构中发挥作用。所以，很难拿出一个单一的制度安排来谈这个制度结构的重要性。[③]单单强调某种制度安排的重要性的做法其实是我们在前面所讨论的“X理论”范式的加强版。“X理论”貌似得到了实证检验的支持，但实际上是同义重复。例如，在以收入水平为左手边变量（被解释变量），以各种“X要素”为右手边变

---

① 更深入的理论问题可参考：林毅夫和付才辉，《新结构经济学导论》（下册），高等教育出版社，2019年版。也可以进一步参考新结构学派对制度学派深入浅出的批判：文一，《伟大的中国工业革命》，清华大学出版社，2016年版；林毅夫、塞勒斯汀·孟加，《战胜命运》，北京大学出版社，2017年版。

② 该书的中译本可参考：德隆·阿西莫格鲁、詹姆斯·A. 罗宾逊，《国家为什么会失败》，湖南科学技术出版社，2018年版。

③ Lin Justin Yifu, “An Economic Theory of Institutional Change: Induced and Imposed Change”, *Cato Journal*, 1989, No.9, pp.1–33. 事实上，对于制度内生性，Acemoglu自己也强调，在下一阶段，更具挑战性的研究方向是，为什么各国的制度有那么大的差别，它们为什么会发生变化，以及为什么总是无法进行改革：Daron. Acemoglu. “Challenges for Social Sciences: Institutions and Economic Development” . American Economic Association, Ten Years and Beyond: Economists Answer NSF’s Call for Long-Term Research Agendas，2010.

量（解释变量）的回归模型中，以发达经济体为参照系，欠发达经济体不但收入水平较差而且各种“X要素”也较差。也恰如林毅夫和孟加在《战胜命运》一书中所指出的，[①]在经济学研究领域，由理论霸权造成的问题已被广泛认识到[②]。而当人们意识到“理论和假设是同义词”，而且“假设另外的同义词是假说、前提和推测”时，这些问题会变得更加尖锐。[③]经验实证主义的兴起（通常认为是源于约翰·洛克的思想，洛克认为，一个人获得任何真正的知识，主要是通过实践经验，而现在则反映在对随机对照试验的广泛依赖上，并已成为发展研究的主要工具）也导致了对数字游戏内在价值的宗教式信仰。然而，这些所谓的以证据为基础的方法，往往是“马后炮”。

### 2.8.2 当今发达经济体“先进制度”的演进史[④]

韩国经济学家张夏准在《富国陷阱》一书中非常精彩地梳理了当今人们认为的“先进制度”在发达经济体的演进历史，鞭辟入里地揭露了西方发达国家宣扬的制度谎言。他考察了被当今流行思潮视为“善政”必不可少的六大领域的“先进制度”——民主制度、官僚和司法制度、知识产权制度、公司治理制度、公私金融制度、福利和劳工制度——在发达国家的历史演进，发现无一例外都是工业化的产物而非原因。[⑤]这背后的原因就是前面所论述的制度变迁的基本原理：只有当这些先进的制度安排的收益超过其成本时才会出现，工业化的推进使得这些制度安排的收益大幅提升而成本相对下降，从而为这些先进的制度安排提供了巨大的激励，不论其变迁方式是诱致性变迁还是强制性变迁。当然，与经济社会政治福利相关的制度安排，也仅是工业化的福利结果，或者由其所推动的社会进步而已。

---

① 林毅夫、塞勒斯汀·孟加，《战胜命运》，北京大学出版社，2017年版（英文版Lin Justin Yifu, Célestin Monga, *Beating the Odds: Jump-Starting Developing Countries*. Princeton University Press, 2017）。

② Amartya K. Sen, “Rational Fools: A Critique of the Behavioral Foundations of Economic Theory”, *Philosophy and Public Affairs,* 1977, Vol.6, No.4 (Summer): 317–344.

③ Charles F. Manski, *Public Policy in an Uncertain World: Analysis and Decisions*. Harvard University Press, 2013: 11.

④ 本小节的主要史料内容主要参考：Ha-Joon Chang, *Kicking Away the Ladder: Development Strategy in Historical Perspective*. Anthem Press, 2002.

⑤ 下面的小节我们只转引了张夏准对这些制度梳理的部分内容。

#### 2.8.2.1 民主制度变迁简史

“一人一票”的普选制是最简单的也最流行的民主制。成人男子普选权首次出现在法国大革命爆发半个世纪后的1848年[①]，历经一个世纪之久才在发达国家普及，如表2.7所示。发达国家最初出现选举权的时候，仅限于极小的一部分有产的30岁以上的男性，而且通常会按照财产、教育状况和年龄来分配，每个人拥有的选举权各不相同。法国在1815—1830年期间，只有30岁以上、交纳直接税至少300法郎的男性才有选举权。而当时法国总人口近3 200万，只有0.25% ~ 0.3%的人，即8万到10万人才有选举权，到1848年之前这一比例也只有0.6%。1832年英国《改革法案》颁布之后，也只有18%的男性公民拥有选举权，没有财产或财产极少的工匠与劳工的选举权被剥夺。1882年的意大利虽然放宽了选民年龄下限和纳税额要求，但也只有占总人口7%的男性公民拥有投票权。直到1946年，表2.8所列的19个当今发达国家的大多数才实现了全民普选。澳大利亚于1903年、新西兰于1907年最早赋予妇女选举权，但1962年澳大利亚的非白种人才获得选举权。挪威1907年开始允许纳税妇女和纳税男子的夫人参加选举，1913年才实现全民普选。1920年的美国、1928年的英国才允许妇女投票。其他许多发达国家，如德国、意大利、芬兰、法国、比利时等，妇女在第二次世界大战后才被允许投票。在瑞士，男性于1879年就获得了普选权，而一个世纪后妇女才有此权利。如我们在第3章对美国结构变迁案例中也将提到的，直到1965年的民权运动才推动美国通过了《选举权法案》，这才保证了黑人的选举权。即使民主在当今发达国家得到了正式实施，但其质量也很差。例如，秘密投票直到20世纪才普及。挪威在1884年才开始实行秘密投票；德国在1919年选举改革之前投票不保密，雇主可以控制工人的投票。法国在1913年才出现选票封和写票间。拉选票和舞弊也司空见惯。英国在1853—1854年制定的《腐败行为法案》首次定义了贿选并规定了选举程序，但直到1883年通过的《腐败与非法行为法案》才大大减少了选举腐败，然而20世纪英国地方选举中依然如此。在美国，州议员公开卖选票的现象在19世纪六七十年代泛滥成灾。这些被称为“黑马骑士”的腐败的两党州议员对铁路议案的要价是1 000美元一票，但竞争使得每一票的价格涨到5 000美元。后来美国总统罗斯福感慨，纽约州那些把表决票公开出卖给游说团队的议员们“对待公职生涯和文官服务的态度就如同秃鹫对待死羊一般”。[②]

---

① 法国大革命始于1789年7月14日，这一天后来成为法国国庆日。

② G. Benson, *Political Corruption in America*. Lexington Books, 1978.

表2.7 当今发达国家的普选起始年份

| 国家 | 成年男子普选 | 全民普选 | 国家 | 成年男子普选 | 全民普选 |
|---|---|---|---|---|---|
| 澳大利亚 | 1903 | 1962 | 荷兰 | 1917 | 1919 |
| 奥地利 | 1907 | 1918 | 新西兰 | 1889 | 1907 |
| 比利时 | 1919 | 1948 | 挪威 | 1898 | 1913 |
| 加拿大 | 1920 | 1970 | 葡萄牙 | 不详 | 1970 |
| 丹麦 | 1849 | 1915 | 西班牙 | 不详 | 1977（1931） |
| 芬兰 | 1919 | 1944 | 瑞典 | 1918 | 1918 |
| 法国 | 1848 | 1946 | 瑞士 | 1879 | 1971 |
| 德国 | 1849 | 1946 | 英国 | 1918 | 1928 |
| 意大利 | 1919 | 1946 | 美国 | 1965（1870） | 1965 |
| 日本 | 1925 | 1952 | | | |

资料来源：张夏准（2003）。

表2.8 当今发达国家制度演化小结

| | 首次实行 | 多数实行 | 最后实行 | 英国 | 美国 |
|---|---|---|---|---|---|
| 民主成年男子普选 | 1848（法国） | 1907 | 1925（日本） | 1918 | 1870 |
| 全民普选 | 1907（新西兰） | 1946 | 1971（瑞士） | 1928 | 1965 |
| 现代官僚制度 | 约19世纪早期（普鲁士） | | | 19世纪中期 | 20世纪早期 |
| 现代司法知识产权 | | | | 20世纪30年代 | |
| 专利法 | 1471（威尼斯） | 19世纪40年代 | 1912（荷兰） | 1623 | 1793 |
| “现代”专利法 | 1836（美国） | 20世纪60年代 | 20世纪90年代（西班牙、加拿大） | 1852 | 1836 |
| “现代”版权法 | | | | | 1891（1988） |
| 商标法 | 1862（英国） | | | 1862 | |
| 公司治理制度 | | | | | |
| 定型的有限责任制 | 1844（瑞典） | | | 1856（1862） | |
| 破产法 | | | | 1542 | 1800 |
| “现代”破产法 | | | | 1849 | 1898 |
| “现代”审计和信息披露制度 | | | | 1948 | 1933 |
| 竞争法 | 1890（美国） | | | 1919 | 1890 |
| 有效的竞争法 | 1914（美国） | | | 1956 | 1914 |
| 金融制度 | | | | | |
| “现代”银行制 | 20世纪20年代中期（英国） | | | 20世纪20年代中期 | |
| 中央银行 | 1688（瑞典） | 1847 | 1913（美国） | 1694 | 1913 |

续表

| | 首次实行 | 多数实行 | 最后实行 | 英国 | 美国 |
|---|---|---|---|---|---|
| “现代”中央银行 | 1844（英国） | 1891 | 1929（美国） | 1844 | 1929 |
| 证券法规 | 1679（英国） | | | 1679 | 19世纪中叶 |
| “现代”证券法规 | | | | 1939 | 1933 |
| 所得税 | 1842（英国） | | | 1842 | 1913 |
| 工伤保险 | 1871（德国） | 1898 | 1930（美国、加拿大） | 1897 | 1930 |
| 医疗保险 | 1883（德国） | 1911 | 美国至今尚无 | 1911 | 尚无 |
| 国家养老金 | 1889（德国） | 1909 | 1946（瑞士） | 1908 | 1946 |
| 失业保险 | 1905（法国） | 1920 | 1945（澳大利亚） | 1911 | 1935 |
| 童工法规 | 1787（奥地利） | 1873 | 1913（葡萄牙） | 1802 | 1904 |
| “现代”童工法规 | 1878（英国、葡萄牙） | | | 1878 | 1938 |

资料来源：张夏准（2003）。

### 2.8.2.2 官僚和司法制度变迁简史

当今发达国家现代化的官僚制度同样是经过漫长而艰难的改革才得以实现的。普鲁士是现代官僚制度的先驱。德皇威廉一世于1713年发起了官僚制度改革，将分散于二十多个领地的权力和职责重叠的各部门的权力集中到中央，将官员的地位由过去的皇室仆役转变为国家公务员，按期领取薪水，同时建立起监督体系。到19世纪初，普鲁士甚至整个德意志各邦已经具备了现代官僚制度的各种特征——入职考试、等级组织、养老金体系、纪律规范和固定任期。这被马克斯·韦伯①加以研究总结，后世称之为“韦伯式官僚体系”。即便如此，裙带关系依然十分盛行，在19世纪早期大约31%的高级文官之父曾为精英行政人员，而到19世纪中期该比例依然高达26%。法国类似，在19世纪工业化崛起阶段，该比例也高达21%。英国在1780—1834年间推出的一系列改革消除了挂名职位，在19世纪上半叶薪金制取代基于服务费的官僚薪酬制度，政府各部门由私人机构转变为现代意义上的政府部门。在此之前，政府各部门都是不对议会负责的私人机构，只给雇员开服务费而不支付薪水。②直到1860年

① 马克斯·韦伯（Max Weber，1864—1920），德国社会学家、政治学家、经济学家、哲学家。他对于当时德国的政界影响极大，参与了《魏玛共和国宪法》的起草设计，对西方古典管理理论的确立做出杰出贡献，是公认的古典社会学理论和公共行政学重要的创始人之一，被后世称为“组织理论之父”。

② S. Finer, “Patronage and Public Service in Britain and America” , in Heidenheimer et al., *Political Corruption: A Handbook*. Transaction Publishers, 1989.

以后，英国才彻底实现现代文官制度。比利时是19世纪仅次于英国的第二大工业国，但其文官专业化直到1933年才完全实现。美国则在19世纪最后20年间初步实现官僚制度专业化，联邦政府中实行竞争选拔的职位比例由1883年《彭德尔顿法》刚颁布时的10%上升到1897年的将近50%。而在此之前，美国则是将公职委派给执政党支持者的“政党分赃制”，并未建立起无党派倾向的文官队伍。当今发达国家的法治在历史上也是“神话而已”。到19世纪末甚至更晚，发达国家的司法制度深受政治影响和任命或选举中腐败之苦，司法机构常常充斥着几乎未受任何法律培训却具有特权社会背景的人员，导致司法不公和缺乏专业精神。例如，英国在19世纪末的反腐败法案都没能纠正验尸官选举中的大量腐败和党派操纵，直到1926年此类职业才要求必须具备专业资格。在意大利，至少在19世纪后期之前，法官一般没有法律背景。德国在19世纪末才基本实现司法独立，但是对军人和中产阶级犯罪也马虎处理。英美等国普遍存在司法不平等。

#### 2.8.2.3 知识产权制度变迁简史[①]

知识产权制度最早可追溯到15世纪的欧洲，源于被授予的专营特权。1474年威尼斯授予新工艺和新机器发明者为期10年的专营权。到16世纪，以萨克森为代表的德意志邦国使用了专利。英国在1624年出台了《垄断法案》和1710年出台了《安妮法案》，建立了持续时间最长的现在依然生效的知识产权制度。法国于1791年、美国于1793年、奥地利于1794年分别通过了专利法。其他一些当今的发达经济体在19世纪上半叶制定了专利法，如俄国在1812年、普鲁士在1815年、比利时与荷兰在1817年、西班牙在1820年、瑞典在1834年、葡萄牙在1837年分别制定了专利法。日本的第一部专利法于1885年出台。除了技术发明的知识产权制度，英国在1709年也最早制定了版权法，在1862年制定了商标法。即便如此，这些知识产权制度也都极不完善，例如，信息披露缺失，申请专利成本过高，对专利保护者力度不够，多数专利疏于发明原创性的审查，各种虚假专利以及据此进行的专利勒索层出不穷。瑞士在1888年颁布了一个仅保护机械发明的专利法，一直不承认任何发明的知识产权。直到后来使用了德国化工和医药业的发明，在德国的威胁制裁下才于1907年制定了一部名副其实的专利法。19世纪后期国际知识产权公约陆续出台。1883年11个国家签署了《保护工业产权国际联盟巴黎公约》(以下简称《巴黎公约》)。1886年又签署了关于版权的《伯尔尼

---

① 关于英美知识产权制度历史更详细的史料可参考：B. Zorina Khan, The Democratization of Invention: Patents and Copyrights in American Economic Development, 1790—1920, *NBER Series on Long-Term Factors in Economic Development*. Cambridge University Press, 2009.

公约》。后来《巴黎公约》相继于1911年、1925年、1934年、1958年、1967年、1979年多次修订。[①]

#### 2.8.2.4 公司治理制度变迁简史

有限责任制是"风险社会化"最强有力的机制之一，因此成为现代公司治理的基石。然而，由于其可能造成"道德风险"，有限责任制从16世纪东印度公司开始采取到19世纪中叶都不受待见。亚当·斯密就指责过有限责任会导致管理者逃避责任。英国在1720年出台的《泡沫法案》就禁止成立新的有限责任公司。定型的有限责任制于1844年由瑞典首先推出。英国随后在1856年通过了《合股公司法案》。比利时第一家有限责任公司成立于1822年。德意志在19世纪60年代才打破传统的行会法，从而为有限责任制的完全制度化打开了大门。法国的有限责任制于1867年才定型。西班牙虽然在1848年出现了合股公司，但直到1951年才完全确立。美国第一部定型的有限责任制法规于1811年在纽约州制定，不过并没有引起人们的兴趣，被置之不用。其他各州直到1837年才开始允许成立有限责任公司，但是迟至19世纪60年代，从事制造业的公司大多还是采取非有限责任制，仍没有任何联邦法律对定型的有限责任制做出规定。与有限责任制一道发展起来的是破产法。虽然英国第一部破产法于1542年颁布，但只适用于负债达到一定额度的商人，1571年的立法使其进一步强化，但责任免除非常有限。直到1705—1706年，英国允许合伙破产者保留5%的资产，若债权人许可，甚至可以免除某些破产者日后的全部债务。不过，其后到19世纪中叶，英国破产法依然很不完善，全国也不统一，控告权依然掌握在债权人手中，破产委托人缺乏专业精神，腐败横行。1831年破产法院建立，1842年修正案规定法院而非债权人有权决定是否免除债务，1849年破产保护得以普及。美国早期的破产法模仿了英国早期的破产法，偏向债权人，但只在州一级执行。到19世纪，美国出台了几部联邦破产法，但于1878年均废止。直到1898年国会才得以通过一部持久的联邦破产法来保护破产者。然而，破产保护一直也有滥用的可能。直到2005年美国开始实行防止滥用破产及消费者权益保护法。与有限责任制和破产保

①《保护工业产权巴黎公约》（*Paris Convention on the Protection of Industrial Property*）简称《巴黎公约》，于1883年3月20日在巴黎签订，1884年7月7日生效。《巴黎公约》的调整对象即保护范围是工业产权，包括发明专利权、实用新型、工业品外观设计、商标权、服务标记、厂商名称、产地标记或原产地名称以及制止不正当竞争等。《巴黎公约》的基本目的是保证一成员国的工业产权在所有其他成员国都得到保护，该公约与《保护文学与艺术作品伯尔尼公约》一起构成了全世界范围内保护经济"硬实力"和文化"软实力"的两个"基本法"。1985年3月19日中国成为该公约成员国，我国政府在加入书中声明：中华人民共和国不受公约第28条第1款的约束。该公约最初的成员为11个，在该公约签署后130年，截至2014年12月2日，随着科威特的正式加入，使该公约缔约方总数达到176家。

护相对应的是审计、财务报告和信息披露，这种制度安排有助于缓解道德风险。英国1844年的《合股公司法案》要求公司必须实行外部审计，但1856年的《合股公司法案》不顾经济学家穆勒等批评者的建议又取消了这一强制条件。直到1900年颁布的《公司法案》才把外部审计定为强制要求，但其后到1928年的修正案才完善要求在年度股东大会前发布最新的资产负债表等详细信息。德国在1884年通过了公司法规范了公司上市。挪威直到1910年才立法规定公司向股东公开信息。美国在1933年颁布的《联邦证券法案》才强制要求向投资者完全公开与上市相关的公司信息。西班牙在1988年才把独立审计人审查公司账务列为强制要求。

#### 2.8.2.5 社会福利与劳工制度变迁简史

我们在第3章介绍英国和美国结构变迁史时将指出，英国在进入20世纪之后、美国在第二次世界大战之后才开始全面进入福利社会。实际上，德国才是社会福利领域的先驱，是第一个引入工伤保险（1871年）、医疗保险（1883年）和国家养老金（1889年）的国家。法国是第一个引入失业保险（1905年）的国家。在19世纪最后25年到20世纪最初25年这50年间，当今发达国家的社会福利制度取得了令人瞩目的成就。如表2.9所示的19个国家中，在1875年，除了德国于1871年引入了工伤保险外，其余国家都不具备表中所列的其他任何一项福利制度，但到了1925年，16个国家有了工伤保险，13个国家有了医疗保险，12个国家有了养老金体系，12个国家有了失业保险。与这些社会福利制度形成强烈反差的是童工制度。在工业化早期，童工现象在当今发达国家非常普遍。在19世纪20年代，英国童工每天工作12.5 ~ 16个小时。1840—1846年，14岁以下的儿童在德国工厂劳动力中的比例高达1/5。直到1837年在瑞典仍然可以雇佣6岁以下的儿童。美国在19世纪早期童工现象也非常普遍。19世纪20年代，棉纺业约有一半工人在16岁以下。到1900年，全职工作在16岁以下的美国童工有170万人。英国在1819年颁布的《棉布厂管理法案》禁止雇佣9岁以下的儿童，并限制童工的劳动时间。但是此法形同虚设，截至1825年只有两个案件适用了此法。英国管理童工第一次有实质性效果的尝试是1833年颁布的《工厂法案》，但只覆盖了棉织、毛纺、麻纤维和丝织业，严禁雇佣9岁以下的儿童，将9 ~ 13岁童工的工作日限制在8小时，将13 ~ 18岁的童工的工作日限制在12小时，也不准童工在夜间（晚上八点半到凌晨五点半）劳动。1853年起，其他一系列行业也被纳入该法案，不过煤矿雇佣童工的劳动时间直到1872年才纳入。直到1878年颁布的《工厂和工场法案》仍允许10岁以上的童工一周劳动长达30个小时以上。普鲁士在1839年颁布了童工法。法国于1841年颁布了童工管理规定。瑞典在1846年通过法律严禁雇佣12岁以下的儿童。丹麦在1873年颁布首部童工管理规定，禁止工业领域雇佣10岁以下的儿童。西班牙在1873年通过法律禁止雇佣10岁以下的儿童。在美国虽然在19世纪40年代一些州就颁布了童工管理规定，但直到第一次世界大战时各州才都颁布法律，禁止雇佣低龄童工，限制稍大一些的童工劳动的时间。1916年美国众议院通过了一部联邦童工法，但两年后最高法院宣布此法违宪。直到1938年严禁童工的联邦法律《公平劳动标准法案》才得以出台。如表2.10所示，在19世纪70年代之前，表中所列的15个国家中基本上没有童工法规，直到20世纪早期才执行了比较严格的童工法规。

表2.9 当今发达国家社会福利制度的起始年份

| 国家 | 工伤 | 医疗 | 养老金 | 失业 |
| --- | --- | --- | --- | --- |
| 德国 | 1871 | 1883 | 1889 | 1927 |
| 瑞士 | 1881 | 1911 | 1946 | 1924 |
| 奥地利 | 1887 | 1888 | 1927 | 1920 |
| 挪威 | 1894 | 1909 | 1936 | 1906 |
| 芬兰 | 1895 | 1963 | 1937 | 1917 |
| 英国 | 1897 | 1911 | 1908 | 1911 |
| 爱尔兰 | 1897 | 1911 | 1908 | 1911 |
| 意大利 | 1898 | 1886 | 1898 | 1919 |
| 丹麦 | 1898 | 1892 | 1891 | 1907 |
| 法国 | 1898 | 1898 | 1895 | 1905 |
| 新西兰 | 1900 | 1938 | 1898 | 1938 |
| 西班牙 | 1900 | 1942 | 1919 | 不详 |
| 瑞典 | 1901 | 1891 | 1913 | 1934 |
| 荷兰 | 1901 | 1929 | 1913 | 1916 |
| 澳大利亚 | 1902 | 1945 | 1909 | 1945 |
| 比利时 | 1903 | 1894 | 1900 | 1920 |
| 加拿大 | 1930 | 1971 | 1927 | 1940 |
| 美国 | 1930 | — | 1935 | 1935 |
| 葡萄牙 | 1962 | 1984 | 1984 | 1984 |

资料来源：张夏准（2003）。

表2.10 当今发达国家童工法规的颁布年份

| 国家 | 最初尝试管理童工的法规（大多无效） | 第一部“严肃的”法规 | 相对全面并得到有效执行的法规 |
| --- | --- | --- | --- |
| 奥地利 | 1787 | 1842 | — |
| 英国 | 1802 | 1833 | 1878 |
| 普鲁士 | 1839 | 1853—1854 | 1878 |
| 法国 | 1841 | — | — |
| 美国 | 1842 | 1904—1914 | 1938 |

续表

| 国家 | 最初尝试管理童工的法规（大多无效） | 第一部“严肃的”法规 | 相对全面并得到有效执行的法规 |
|---|---|---|---|
| 瑞典 | 1846 | 1881 | 1900 |
| 萨克森 | 1861 | — | — |
| 丹麦 | 1873 | 1925 | — |
| 西班牙 | 1873 | 1900 | — |
| 荷兰 | 1874 | — | — |
| 瑞士 | 1877 | — | — |
| 比利时 | 1878 | 1909 | 1914 |
| 挪威 | 1892 | — | — |
| 意大利 | 1902 | — | — |
| 葡萄牙 | 1913 | — | — |

资料来源：张夏准（2003）。

### 2.8.2.6 教育制度变迁简史[①]

同样，当今西方发达国家的教育体系并非一开始就有，而是缓慢形成的，而且主要是内生于工业化进程中教育的产业需求。[②]在工业革命第一阶段，人力资本在生产过程中的作用是有限的，只有在工业革命第二阶段，人力资本的作用才在工业革命的刺激下变得重要。在工业革命之前，教育往往是由非经济因素所推崇，尤其是文化传统和国家维持统一与稳定的需要。一些经济史学家考证，在工业革命之前和早期，虽然某些特定的工人，尤其是从事管理的文职人员必须识字以及掌握一些基本的算术操作，但是大部分工作都是由不识字的工人完成的。[③]例如，在英国工业革命的第一阶段（1760—1830年），投资产出比从1760年的6%上升至1831年的12%，而识字率在很大程度上保持不变，如1841年只有5%的男性工人和2%的女性工人受雇于那些对识字率有严格要求的职业。可以看到，在工业革命第一阶段，物质资本相对人力资本更加重要。在英国工业革命的第二阶段（1830—1900年），初级学校就读的5 ~ 14岁儿童所占的比例从1955年的11%上升到1870年的25%。10周岁儿童入学率从1870年的40%提高到1900年的100%。初等学校中年龄在5 ~ 14岁儿童的比例从1855

① 更详细的历史比较分析可参考：安迪·格林，《教育与国家的形成：英、法、美教育体系起源之比较》，教育科学出版社，2004年版。

② 关于工业化进程中教育的产业需求的概述性介绍可参考：O.盖勒，《统一增长理论》，中国人民大学出版社，2017年版。

③ David S. Landes, *The Unbound Prometheus: Technological Change and Industrial Development in Western Europe from 1750 to the Present*. Cambridge University Press, 1969.

年的11%上升到1900年的74%。1868年英国议会设立了议会科学教育特别委员会；1870年出台了《教育法案》；1880年实现义务教育（1884年之后才扩大普选权）；1890年的《地方税收法案》为可能的技术教育支出提供公共资金；1902年《Balfour教育法案》标志着免费义务教育的国民教育体系的形成。到1971年英国的中学入学率①达76.5%，20世纪90年代初已经达到100%左右。到1971年英国高等院校入学率②达14.56%，到21世纪初已经达到60%左右。欧洲大陆国家，比如德国、法国、瑞典和荷兰，早在工业革命之前公共教育就已经得到发展。然而，与英国的情况一样，欧洲大陆的教育的改革发展都是在19世纪下半叶由工业化进程导致对技能的需求增加而引发的。法国的工业化进程中，伴随对技能型劳动需求的上升以及传统学徒体系的衰落，显著地影响了政府对于教育的态度。在19世纪30年代，政府给予初等学校的拨款逐渐增加，一些相关的法律法规业已出现，涉及在所有地区提供初等教育、扩大高等教育以及开展教师培训和进行学校监管等。从1837年到1850年，没有学校的社区的数量减少了一半。随着实业界对教育结构的影响变强，教育越来越依据等级化的职业模式。资本家在进行教育改革方面的热情反映在产业社会的组织上，即其投资兴办学校专门培养化工、设计、机械纺织以及商业等领域的劳动力。20岁年龄组的应征测试者的文盲率逐渐从1851—1855年的38%下降到1876—1880年的17%，儿童去初等学校接受教育的比重从1820年的52%上升到1901的86%。③到1971年法国的中学入学率达74.31%，20世纪90年代初已经达到100%左右。到1971年，法国的高等院校入学率达到18.54%，到21世纪初达到60%左右。与法国类似，普鲁士在18世纪初期开始尝试义务教育，从1870年到1911年，中等学校总入学率提高了6倍。工业化也显著影响了德国的大学教育。工业家们认为高级技术是一种比较优势，开始为大学的运转改革游说，并提供资金将大学的职能重塑为技术培训以及基础研究的工业应用。④到20世纪90年代初，德国的高等院校入学率达到33.64%，到21世纪初也达到60%左右。尽管与欧洲教育融资结构方面存在一定差异，但是美国的教育体系一样随着工业化而演进。在19世纪末和20世纪初，工业、商业和贸易的发展增加了对经理人、文职员工以及受过教育的销售代表的需求，这些劳动力在会计、打字、速记、代数和商业方面都受过培训。到20世纪的头十年，技术上领先的产业进一步要求工人提高技能和知识水平，需要在

---

① 该指标指的是中学所有课程总入学率，是指不论年龄大小，中学在校生总数占符合中学官方入学年龄人口的百分比。总入学率可能超过100%，因为包含了较早或较晚入学及复读的超龄和小龄学生。

② 该指标指的是总入学率，大学（ISCED 5和6）入学百分比，是指不论年龄大小，大学（ISCED 5和6）在校生总数占中学之后5年学龄人口总数的百分比。

③ R. D. Anderson, *Education in France 1848–1870*. Clarendon Press, 1975.

④ C. MeClelland, *State, Society, and University in Germany, 1700–1914*. Cambridge Uniersity Press, 1984.

几何、代数、化学、机械制图以及工程技术方面接受系统培训。产业的发展改变了教育的结构。20世纪早期就连美国的高中也做出了改变以适应现代工厂的要求。高中毕业的年轻人比例从1915年到1940年从13%提升到50%。大学毕业的年轻男性的比例从1920年占不到同龄人的15%，增加到1950年的30%。[①]美国的教育革命其实也只是在第二次世界大战后才开始。在1910年，美国制造业中有27%的男性工人认为他们自己从事的是“体力劳动”，交通运输部门的比例也有30%。到1971年美国的中学入学率达84%，20世纪90年代初已经达到100%左右。到1971年，美国的高等院校入学率达到47.3%，到20世纪90年代达70%左右。可以看到美国的教育水平超过了欧洲。为了弥补与美国的教育差距，加大教育投资成为欧盟里斯本计划的一部分。欧盟2014年教育公共开支总额占GDP的比例达5.28%，而同年美国的比重不足5%。图2.39是全球金融危机前夕世界上主要发达经济体的教育投入结构，总的教育投入比重超过世界水平尤其是发展中经济体，然而中国此时的教育投入虽然较低但是也远超发达经济体历史上处于相同发展阶段的水平。另外值得强调的是，韩国此时由于发展水平赶上发达经济体所以其教育支出及其结构已经超过了OECD国家的平均水准。

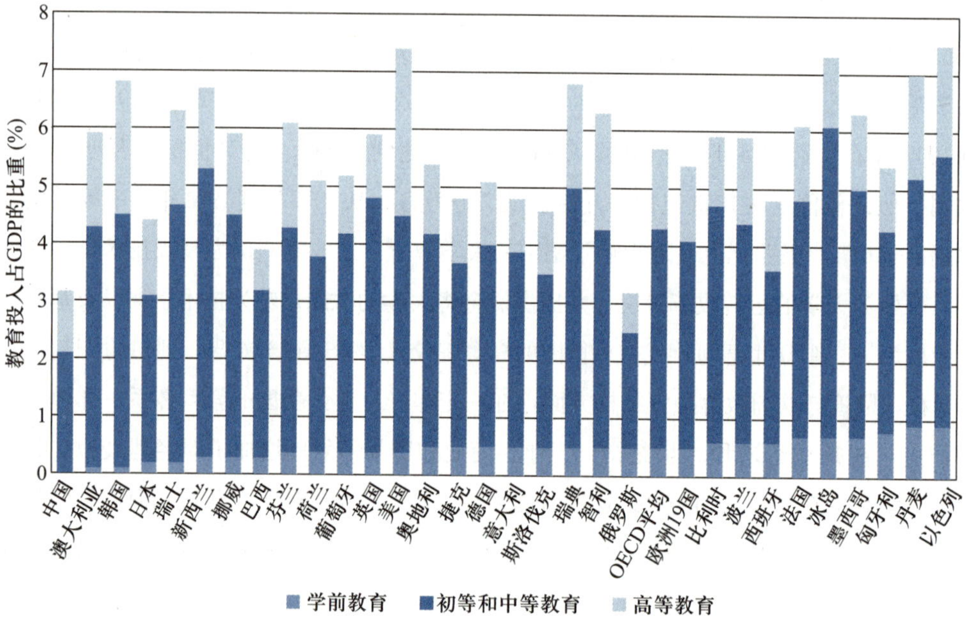


**图2.39 2008年中国与世界主要发达经济体的教育投入结构（占GDP的比重%）比较**

资料来源：世界银行。

---

① Claudia Goldin, “America’s Graduation from High School: The Evolution and Spread of Secondary Schooling in the Twentieth Century”, *The Journal of Economic History*, 1998, Vol. 58, No. 2, pp. 345–374. 也可以参考Goldin对美国20世纪劳动力市场的概括：斯坦利·L. 恩格尔曼、罗伯特·E. 高尔曼主编,《剑桥美国经济史：漫长的19世纪》(第三卷)，高德步等译，中国人民大学出版社，2018年版。

### 2.8.3 并未给发展中经济体带来繁荣的制度赶超：被高估的制度神话[①]

在考察完所谓“先进制度”在发达国家的演进历程之后，张夏准也对比了当今发展中经济体与处于类似发展阶段的发达国家制度发展水平。我们可以按照工业化的历程观察三个片段：1820年的时候当今最先进的发达国家都处于工业化的早期，或者用前面章节更详细地划分的话处于第一次工业革命的上半场。在此阶段，所有当今发达经济体的制度安排以今天的眼光来看不用说完善与否，甚至只初具雏形。到了1875年，当今比较先进的发达国家已经完成了第一次工业革命开启了第二次工业革命，工业化进程比较缓慢的发达国家的第一次工业革命也步入下半场。在此阶段，发达国家的各种制度安排应运而生或者进一步完善抑或执行效率大幅提升。到了1913年，基本上当今主要欧美发达国家已经完成了第二次工业革命，已经形成了成熟的工业化体系，形成了完整的现代化的制度体系，但是制度化并不如工业化那样成熟，依然存在很多不完善之处，而一个耀眼的制度成就是形成了福利社会制度。总之，从上一小节可以看到各种现代制度安排在发达国家的曲折而漫长的演进历史，许多“先进制度”并非我们想象的那样早已存在或一蹴而就。例如，法国和瑞士从成人男子普选跃升为全面普选几乎走过了一个世纪。从表2.10可以一目了然地看到，一种制度安排从出现到被大多数当今发达国家采用所需的时间在20年到150年之久。

表2.11对比了在要求发展中经济体广泛采取当今发达国家“先进制度”的“华盛顿共识”和新制度经济学盛行的20世纪90年代初，发展中经济体所处的发展水平与发达经济体历史上所处类似发展阶段的比较。20世纪90年代初的埃塞俄比亚、孟加拉国、缅甸的人均收入水平分别为300美元、720美元、748美元，其发展水平相当于19世纪20年代初的日本、芬兰、加拿大和爱尔兰，其人均收入水平分别为704美元、759美元、893美元、954美元。20世纪90年代初的加纳、肯尼亚、科特迪瓦、尼日利亚、印度发展中经济体的人均收入水平在1 000 ~ 1 500美元，大致相当于19世纪20年代初的挪威、西班牙、意大利、德国、瑞典、法国、丹麦、美国、比利时、奥地利，以及19世纪70年代中期的芬兰、挪威，与20世纪初的日本和葡萄牙。20世纪90年代初的巴基斯坦、埃及的人均收入水平在1 500 ~ 2 000美元，大致相当于19世纪20年代的澳大利亚、荷兰、英国，19世纪70年代的意大利、加拿大、瑞典、奥地利，与20世纪初的希腊。20世纪90年代初的菲律宾、摩洛哥、印尼的人均收入水平在2 000 ~ 3 000美元，大致相当于19世纪中期的丹麦、法国、德国、美国、比利

① 本小节的史料内容主要参考：Ha-Joon Chang, *Kicking Away the Ladder: Development Strategy in Historical Perspective*. Anthem Press, 2002。

时、荷兰，20世纪初的芬兰、西班牙、挪威、意大利、爱尔兰。20世纪90年代初期的秘鲁和中国的人均收入水平介于3 000 ～ 4 000美元，大致相当于19世纪70年代中期的新西兰和英国，以及20世纪初的瑞典、法国、奥地利、丹麦、德国、荷兰。20世纪90年代初期的土耳其、泰国、巴西的人均收入水平介于4 000 ～ 5 000美元，大致相当于19世纪70年代中期的澳大利亚，20世纪初的比利时、瑞士、加拿大。20世纪90年代的墨西哥和哥伦比亚在发展中经济体中收入水平较高，人均收入介于5 000 ～ 6 000美元，不过也大致相当于20世纪初的英国、新西兰、美国、澳大利亚。然后，我们将处于类似发展阶段的发展中经济体和当今发达国家的制度发展水平进行粗略比较，可以令人吃惊地发现：当今发达国家过去的制度总的来讲要比与之处于类似发展阶段的发展中国家的制度水平逊色得多，如表2.12所示。令人印象深刻的例子莫过于印度。1820年的英国相当于20世纪90年代的印度，但是相比之下印度在20世纪90年代的制度远比19世纪20年代英国的制度要完善得多。例如，20世纪90年代印度实现了普选民主制，建立了中央银行以及金融体系、财税制度、专业化的官僚制度以及公司法和破产法等法律制度，而这些现代意义上的制度不存在于19世纪20年代的英国。又如，第3章我们将提到的产品空间理论的创始人Hausmann在2016年第三届新结构经济学国际研讨会上也特别展示了人力资本投资未创造出所期望的效果，并向人力资本理论提出了质疑。Hausmann展示的几张PPT令人印象深刻，如图2.40所示：过去四十年间全球各个地区尤其是低收入的撒哈拉以南的非洲的人力资本都显著提高了，但其收入水平并未得到对应的显著提升。例如，1998年的加纳、2005年的泰国、1993年的墨西哥、1985年的法国，其教育年限均为7年，但是其人均GDP却有天壤之别，加纳只有1 015美元、泰国为6 751美元、墨西哥为10 544美元、法国为21 315美元；更甚的例子是加纳和泰国这两个非洲和亚洲的发展中国家，在20世纪70年代二者的收入水平相差无几，而从60年代开始加纳就迅速提升其教育年限，70年代其教育年限一直超过了泰国，但是其收入水平却一直远低于泰国而且二者的收入差距越来越大。这些例子看起来就像Pritchett质疑的，教育投资都打水漂吗？[①]

① Lant Pritchett, "Where Has All the Education Gone?" , *The World Bank Economic Review*, 2001, 15(3), pp.367–391.

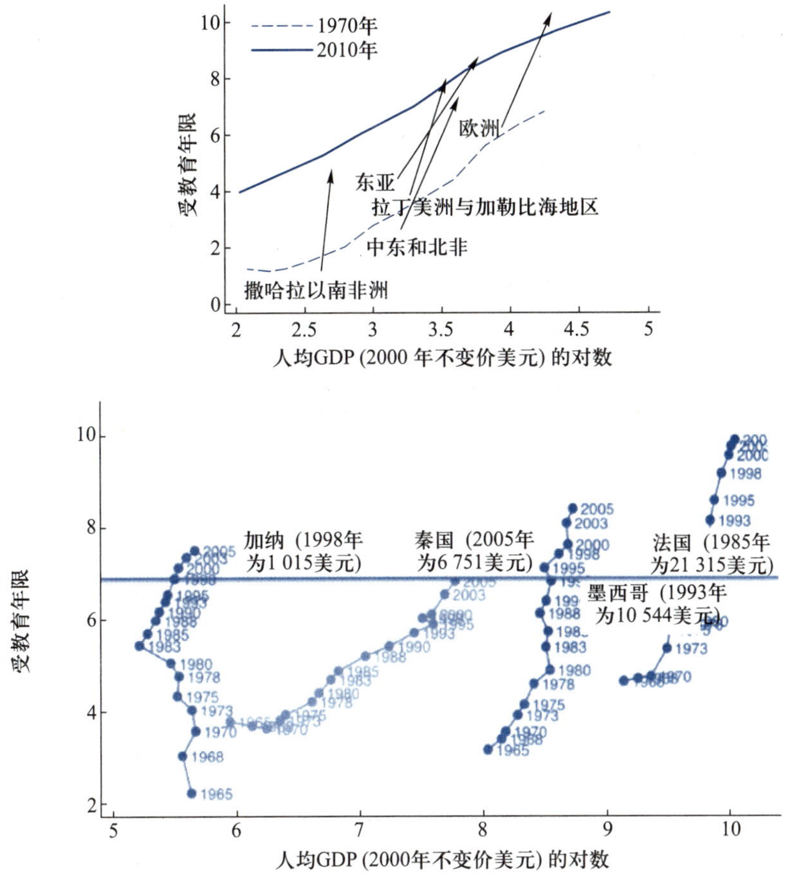


**图2.40 教育年限为何没带来经济发展？**

资料来源：Ricardo Hausmann, "How does diverification happen？", *The Third International Conference on New Structural Economics*, December 15–16, 2016, Beijing, P.R. China.

表2.11 当今发达国家在发展过程中的相对位置（收入数按1990年国际美元计算）

| 人均收入范围 | 当今发达国家 | | | | 发展中国家（1992年） |
|---|---|---|---|---|---|
| | 1750年 | 1820年 | 1875年 | 1913年 | |
| 1 000以下 | 法国（921） | 日本（704） | | | 埃塞俄比亚（300） |
| | | 芬兰（759） | | | 孟加拉国（720） |
| | | 加拿大（893） | | | 缅甸（748） |
| | | 爱尔兰（954） | | | |
| 1 000（含）~1 500 | 英国（1328） | 挪威（1002） | 芬兰（1176） | 日本（1334） | 加纳（1007） |
| | | 西班牙（1063） | 挪威（1469） | 葡萄牙（1354） | 肯尼亚（1055） |
| | | 意大利（1092） | | | 科特迪瓦（1134） |
| | | 德国（1112） | | | 尼日利亚（1152） |
| | | 瑞典（1198） | | | 印度（1348） |
| | | 法国（1218） | | | |

续表

| 人均收入范围 | 当今发达国家 | | | | 发展中国家（1992年） |
|---|---|---|---|---|---|
| | 1750年 | 1820年 | 1875年 | 1913年 | |
| 1 000（含）~1 500 | | 丹麦（1225） | | | |
| | | 美国（1287） | | | |
| | | 比利时（1291） | | | |
| | | 奥地利（1295） | | | |
| 1 500（含）~2 000 | | 澳大利亚（1528） | 意大利（1516） | 希腊（1621） | 巴基斯坦（1642） |
| | | 荷兰（1561） | 加拿大（1690） | | 埃及（1927） |
| | | 英国（1756） | 瑞典（1835） | | |
| | | | 奥地利（1986） | | |
| 2 000（含）~3 000 | | | 丹麦（2031） | 芬兰（2050） | 菲律宾（2213） |
| | | | 法国（2198） | 西班牙（2255） | 摩洛哥（2327） |
| | | | 德国（2198） | 挪威（2275） | 印尼（2749） |
| | | | 美国（2599） | 意大利（2507） | |
| | | | 比利时（2800） | 爱尔兰（2733） | |
| | | | 荷兰（2829） | | |
| 3 000（含）~4 000 | | | 新西兰（3707） | 瑞典（3096） | 秘鲁（3232） |
| | | | 英国（3511） | 法国（3452） | 中国（3098） |
| | | | | 奥地利（3488） | |
| | | | | 丹麦（3764） | |
| | | | | 德国（3833） | |
| | | | | 荷兰（3950） | |
| 4 000（含）~5 000 | | | 澳大利亚（4433） | 比利时（4130） | 土耳其（4422） |
| | | | | 瑞士（4027） | 泰国（4422） |
| | | | | 加拿大（4231） | 巴西（4862） |
| 5 000（含）~6 000 | | | | 英国（5032） | 墨西哥（5098） |
| | | | | 新西兰（5178） | 哥伦比亚（5359） |
| | | | | 美国（5307） | |
| | | | | 澳大利亚（5505） | |

资料来源：张夏准（2003）。

表2.12 实现全民普选时的人均收入

| 人均GDP（按1990年国际美元计） | 当今发达国家（实现全民普选的年份；人均GDP） | 发展中国家和地区（实现全民普选的年份；人均GDP） |
|---|---|---|
| <1 000 | | 孟加拉国（1947；585美元） |
| | | 缅甸（1948；393美元） |

续表

| 人均GDP（按1990年国际美元计） | 当今发达国家（实现全民普选的年份；人均GDP） | 发展中国家和地区（实现全民普选的年份；人均GDP） |
|---|---|---|
| <1 000 | | 埃及（1952；542美元） |
| | | 埃塞俄比亚（1955；295美元） |
| | | 印度（1947；641美元） |
| | | 印尼（1945；514美元） |
| | | 肯尼亚（1963；713美元） |
| | | 巴基斯坦（1947；631美元） |
| | | 韩国（1948；777美元） |
| | | 坦桑尼亚（1962；506美元） |
| | | 扎伊尔（1967；707美元） |
| 1 000（含）~ 1 999 | | 保加利亚（1945；1073美元） |
| | | 加纳（1957；1159美元） |
| | | 匈牙利（1945；1721美元） |
| | | 墨西哥（1947；1882美元） |
| | | 尼日利亚（1979；1189美元） |
| | | 土耳其（1946；1129美元） |
| 2 000 ~ 2 999 | 奥地利（1918；2572美元） | 哥伦比亚（1957；2382美元） |
| | 德国（1946；2503美元） | 秘鲁（1956；2732美元） |
| | 意大利（1946；2448美元） | 菲律宾（1981；2526美元） |
| | 日本（1952；2277美元） | |
| | 挪威（1913；2275美元） | |
| | 瑞典（1918；2533美元） | |
| 3 000 ~ 3 999 | 丹麦（1915；3635美元） | 中国台湾（1972；3313美元） |
| | 芬兰（1944；3578美元） | 智利（1949；3715美元） |
| | 法国（1946；3819美元） | |
| 4 000 ~ 4 999 | 比利时（1948；4917美元） | 巴西（1977；4613美元） |
| | 荷兰（1919；4022美元） | |
| 5 000 ~ 9 999 | 澳大利亚（1962；8691美元） | 阿根廷（1947；5089美元） |
| | 新西兰（1907；5367美元） | 委内瑞拉（1947；6894美元） |
| | 葡萄牙（1970；5885美元） | |
| | 英国（1928；5115美元） | |
| | 加拿大（1970：11758美元） | |
| >10 000（含） | 瑞士（1971；17142美元） | |
| | 美国（1965；13316美元） | |

资料来源：张夏准（2009）。

总之，新结构经济学对传统的发展思想和虚设的前提条件提出挑战，认为解决发展问题的传统方法——专注于诊断诸多影响发展的障碍和限制，如“治理不善”“人力资本不足”“金融落后”“基础设施匮乏”——纯属误导。当前经济发展的主流观点所倡导的方法，即对于发展中国家仍然推行线性的、目的论的路径，会使政策制定——即使可能——也很困难，最后是将结果交于随机性和偶然性。认为旨在改善贫穷国家“治理”和商业环境的结构改革可以带来持续的经济增长，从历史和概念的角度来看都是不现实的。缘于何故？这种方法是以高收入国家现在拥有的或高收入国家现在做得相对较好的地方作为参考，用以确定一个发展中国家所缺乏的或做得不好的方面。然后，他们建议发展中国家争取得到高收入国家所拥有的东西，或者做高收入国家所做的事情。这种方法往往没能完全考虑发展中国家和高收入国家在发展先决条件上的差异，从而出现“本末倒置”。例如，金融结构内生于由禀赋结构所决定产业结构，如果脱离产业结构的需求，过于“先进”的金融结构会造成诸多负面影响，甚至金融危机；培育人力资本的教育结构内生于由禀赋结构所决定的产业结构，如果脱离产业结构的需求，过于“先进”的教育结构会造成人才流失而为发达经济体做嫁衣，甚至因为众多拥有高教育水平的人才在国内找不到合适的工作而影响社会的稳定。因此，从一般原理层面需要破除以发达经济体为参照系的制度神话，强调即使是在制度和商业环境不利的贫穷国家，只要着眼于已有的基础，着手于自身擅长的方面，同样可以做得很好，并且也能够在发展过程中逐渐建立起适宜的制度体系和实现良好的国家治理。图 2.41 验证并说明了简单的历史真相，它清楚地显示了良好的政治治理认知和收入增长之间的相关关系。如果真是这样的话，那么在低收入国家打击腐败、改善治理的关键就是有一个能够减少政治俘获和

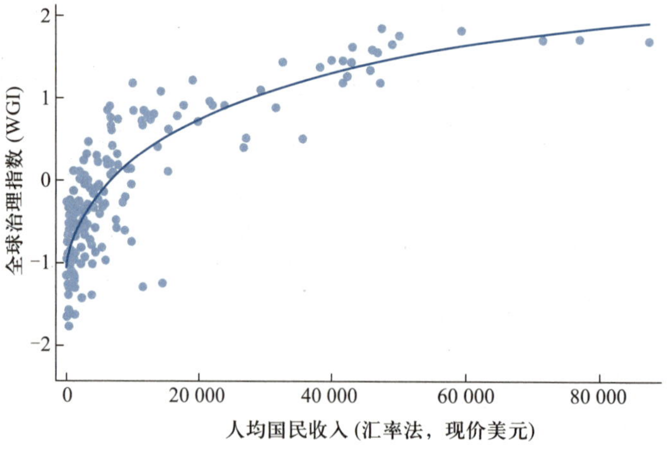


**图 2.41 治理表现和人均国民收入：代数解谜**

资料来源：Lin Justin Yifu and Célestin Monga, “Solving the Mystery of African Governance”, *New Political Economy*, 2012, Vol.17, No.5, pp. 659-666.

权力寻租活动机会的发展战略。换言之，解决腐败的主要方法是创造一个减少此类产生外部性活动的机会和相应收益的政策环境。如果政府采取遵循比较优势的战略，处在优先领域的企业将在一个开放、竞争的市场中有自生能力，因此政府就不需要通过各种形式的扭曲来保护或补贴它们，从而带来有力的增长以及寻租机会和租金的降低；相反，如果政府采取违背比较优势的战略，结果也只会相反。总之，“良好的政治治理”是一个难以操作化的概念，并没有一般的或普遍的处方可用。尽管有联合国言辞凿凿的条约以及来自世界各国政府对良好政治治理议程的承诺，却没有国际单位和研究机构有资格对他人的治理质量给出具有合法性的衡量。良好的政治治理应该是一个重要的公共政策目标，由各国人民和领导人自由设定。它不应该是好的经济表现的先决条件。持续的经济增长、就业的创造和贫困的减少，甚至可以在极为不良的治理环境下实现。此外，良好的政治治理总是一个无可穷尽的过程。

第3章

# 追踪世界经济结构转型升级的轨迹

# 3.1

# 工业革命不是一夜爆发的

## 3.1.1 1500—1750年西欧的经济结构变迁[①]

从第2章中我们知道了经济结构转型升级对世界发展的根本重要性，尤其是工业革命造就了当今的发达经济体。然而，回顾历史，造就“日不落帝国”的英国工业革命也并非一夜之间爆发的，而是自16世纪初大航海为全球贸易创造必要条件之后近300年漫长的原始工业化积累所带来的从量变到质变的结果。如表3.1所示，在1500—1750年西欧诸国的经济结构变迁中只有英国成功地实现了经济转型，农业人口比重下降到45%。在整个欧洲，英格兰是城市化速度最快的地区。1500年伦敦人口为5万人，1600年增加到20万人，1700年增加到50万人，最终在1800年超过100万人。1750年，英格兰人口中32%的人属于农村地区的非农业人口。这些人绝大多数从事制造业，他们所生产的商品被运往欧洲各地，有时甚至被运往世界各个角落。比如，牛津郡威特尼地区的工匠将毛毯出售给哈得逊湾公司，后者用这些毯子去和加拿大的土著人交易毛皮。低地国家有着类似的经济发展轨迹。荷兰的城市化程度甚至超过了英格兰，并且同样拥有大规模的、以出口为导向的乡村工业。

表3.1 1500—1750年西欧诸国的经济结构变迁

| 国家 | 1500年 | | | 1750年 | | |
|---|---|---|---|---|---|---|
| | 城市人口比重（%） | 农村非农业人口比重（%） | 农业人口比重（%） | 城市人口比重（%） | 农村非农业人口比重（%） | 农业人口比重（%） |
| 变化最大 | | | | | | |
| 英格兰 | 7 | 18 | 74 | 23 | 32 | 45 |
| 显著变化 | | | | | | |
| 荷兰 | 30 | 14 | 56 | 36 | 22 | 42 |
| 比利时 | 28 | 14 | 58 | 22 | 27 | 51 |

① 本小节的资料和内容主要来源于：罗伯特·艾伦，《全球经济简史》，译林出版社，2014年版；罗伯特·艾伦，《近代英国工业革命揭秘》，浙江大学出版社，2012年版。

续表

| 国家 | 1500年 | | | 1750年 | | |
|---|---|---|---|---|---|---|
| | 城市人口比重（%） | 农村非农业人口比重（%） | 农业人口比重（%） | 城市人口比重（%） | 农村非农业人口比重（%） | 农业人口比重（%） |
| 小幅变化 | | | | | | |
| 德国 | 8 | 18 | 73 | 9 | 27 | 64 |
| 法国 | 9 | 18 | 73 | 13 | 26 | 61 |
| 奥地利/匈牙利 | 5 | 19 | 76 | 78 | 32 | 61 |
| 波兰 | 6 | 19 | 75 | 4 | 36 | 60 |
| 几乎没变 | | | | | | |
| 意大利 | 22 | 16 | 62 | 22 | 19 | 59 |
| 西班牙 | 19 | 16 | 65 | 21 | 17 | 62 |

资料来源：罗伯特·艾伦，《全球经济史》，译林出版社，2015年版，第22–23页。

这种缓慢的经济结构转型产生了重大的影响，主要包括几个方面：第一，城市化和乡村制造业的发展增加了对于劳动力的需求，从而导致劳动力市场供不应求，工资水平居高不下。伦敦和阿姆斯特丹的生活水平较高（参见图3.1）。第二，发展中的城市和工资水平较高的经济体对于农业有着巨大需求，既需要大量食物，同时也需要大量劳动力。结果就是，在英格兰和荷兰两地都出现了农业革命。在这两个国家，农业劳动者的人均产量都增加了约50%，达到欧洲地区的最高水平。第三，不断增加的城市需求还使英格兰和荷兰两地出现了能源革命。在中世纪，城市中使用的主要燃料是木炭和木材。随着城市的发展，木材价格急速上涨，人们开发出替代能源。在荷兰，替代木材的是泥煤；在英格兰，则是煤炭。达勒姆和诺森伯兰地区的煤炭被开采出来，沿着海岸线运往伦敦。18世纪，英格兰是世界上唯一拥有大规模煤炭产业的国家，它因此得以享用世界上最便宜的能源。第四，工资水平较高的经济体通常能培养出具有良好读写能力、计算能力和技术水平的工人。欧洲各地民众的读写能力都在提高，但西北部地区的进步幅度最大。宗教改革常被当作读写能力提高的主要原因，但其实改革并不足以解释这一现象，因为在西欧东北部地区，比如法国、比利时和莱茵河流域（都奉行天主教），当地人的读写能力并不亚于荷兰人和英格兰人。读写能力提高的真正原因在于商业化经济体制之下的高工资。商业和制造业的扩展对教育提出了更高要求，因为当时教育在商业上具有重要价值。与此同时，工资水平较高的经济体为家长提供了足够的资金，用于支付子女的教育费用。

上述缓慢的结构转型带来了工业革命前夕的禀赋结构从量变到质变的飞跃。如图3.2所示，16世纪晚期，在英格兰南部、法国和奥地利（这些是欧洲大陆具有代表性的地区），工资与资本服务价格的比率大致相当。然而，到了18世纪中叶，英格兰的资本/劳动力比率比

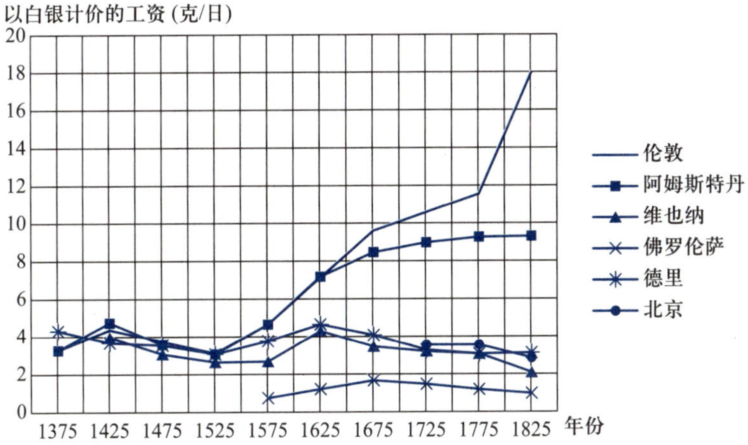


**图3.1 世界各地工人工资水平比较：1375—1825**

资料来源：罗伯特·艾伦，《全球经济史》，译林出版社，2015年版，第51页。

欧洲大陆要高出60%。到19世纪初，首次有了亚洲的数据。比较的结果是，印度的资本/劳动力比率比法国的或奥地利的更低。因此，印度更加缺乏经济激励，不愿意采取机械化方式进行生产。这一现象与能源的状况类似，如图3.3所示。英国（尤其是北部和中部的煤矿区）拥有世界上最廉价的能源。因此，相比世界上其他地区，在英国能源相对于劳动力要便宜许多。正是由于工资和价格的这些差异，英国企业发现采用新技术有利可图，通过增加相对廉价的能源和资本，可以节约昂贵的人力成本。有了更多资本和能源，英国工人就能生产出更多产品——这就是经济增长的秘诀。在亚洲和非洲，廉价劳动力造成了相反的结果。

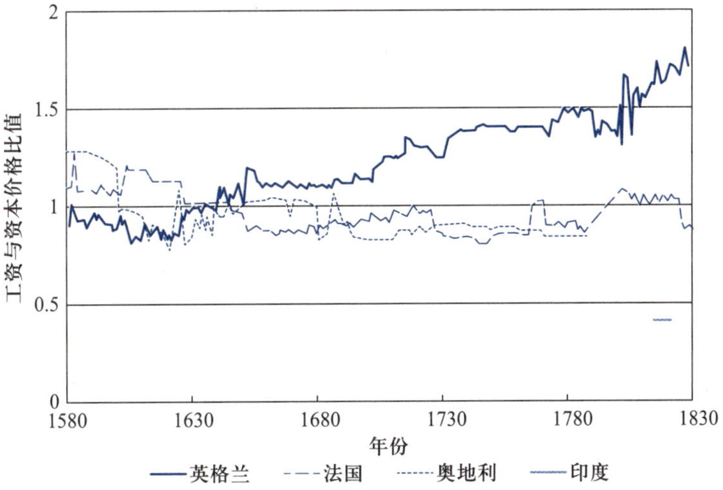


**图3.2 工资（劳动力价格）与资本价格比值示意图**

资料来源：罗伯特·艾伦，《全球经济史》，译林出版社，2015年版，第22–23页。

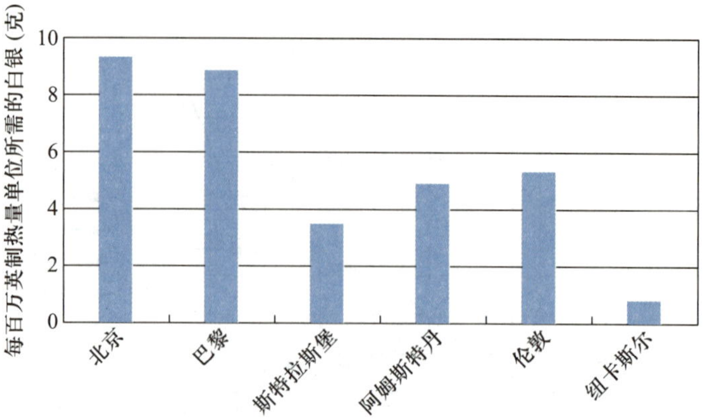


**图3.3 18世纪世界的能源价格比较**

资料来源：罗伯特·艾伦，《全球经济史》，译林出版社，2015年版，第22–23页。

### 3.1.2 资本的原始积累：圈地运动与奴隶贸易

改变其禀赋结构的资本主义的原始积累远非上面描述的那样春风化雨，水到渠成，而是充满血雨腥风。马克思就非常精彩地论述过，通过暴力血腥手段，对内对外的资本原始积累事实上成为资本主义生产方式的起点。资本主义生产方式的确立必须具备两个基本条件：一是出现了大批有人身自由但没有生产资料的劳动者，他们必须依靠出卖劳动力为生；二是积累起大量货币财富。在封建社会内部，通过自然经济的瓦解和小商品生产者的分化，已经逐渐形成了这两个条件，产生了资本主义生产关系的萌芽。然而，如果单靠这样来发展资本主义，那将是一个十分缓慢的过程，不能适应15世纪以来地理大发现所造成的市场需求。新兴资产阶级和新的土地所有者便使用掠夺的手段，加速了这两个条件的形成。如马克思所揭示的谎言：资产阶级编造出种种神话来解释资本原始积累，说什么人类天生就分为勤劳聪明和懒惰愚蠢两种人，前一种人克勤克俭，积累起大量的货币财富，后一种人懒惰贫穷，因而除了本人的劳动力外没有可以出卖的东西。历史表明，勤俭并不能积累一大笔开创资本主义企业所必需的财富，用懒惰更无法说明在人类历史上存在了几千年的小生产者何以突然沦为雇佣工人。实际上，资本原始积累是一个使用暴力剥夺劳动者、消灭以个人劳动为基础的私有制的过程，它不是田园诗式的过程，而“是用血和火的文字载入人类编年史的”[①]。

①《马克思恩格斯选集》第2卷，人民出版社，2012年版，第291页。

对农民土地的剥夺形成整个原始积累的基础。这个过程，在不同的国家具有不同的特点，但最典型的形式是英国的"圈地运动"。在15世纪以前，英国的生产主要还是以农业为主，纺织业在人们的生活中还是个附带的手工业。随着新航路的发现和海外贸易的扩大，在欧洲大陆的佛兰德斯地区，毛纺织业随之繁盛起来，尔后英国也被带动起来。毛纺织业的迅猛发展，使得羊毛的需求量逐渐增大，市场上的羊毛价格开始猛涨。英国本来是一个传统的养羊大国，这时除了满足国内的需要外，还要满足国外的羊毛需要。因此，养羊业与农业相比，就变得越来越有利可图，有钱的贵族开始投资养羊业。土地主便开始强行用篱笆、壕沟圈占农民的公有地。英国资产阶级革命胜利后，政府颁布了一系列圈地法令，使这一暴行合法化，圈地运动以空前的规模加速进行。资产阶级残暴地毁灭村庄，把农民赶走，变耕地为牧场，制造了历史上有名的"羊吃人"的凄惨景象。这个用暴力掠夺土地的运动长达300年之久，到18世纪末，农民公有地的最后痕迹也消灭了。也如表3.1所示，到1750年，农业人口占比降至45%。被掠夺了土地的广大农民，不可能马上适应新生产关系的秩序，忍受长达15~16小时的劳动，他们大批沦为乞丐或盗贼，到处流浪。同时，新的生产方式还不能单纯靠经济的方法把这些劳动者纳入自己的轨道。资产阶级用国家权力曾颁布了一系列惩治流浪者的"血腥法令"，强迫破产的农民忍受资本的残酷剥削。例如，16世纪英国的法律规定，身强力壮的流浪者要绑在马车后被鞭打到遍体流血为止，然后要发誓回原籍劳动。流浪者第二次被捕，不仅要受鞭打，还要被割去半只耳朵，第三次被捕就将被处死。

最初作为资本的货币财富也是通过劫掠取得的。新兴的资产阶级远渡重洋，进行血腥的殖民掠夺。美洲金银产地的发现，土著民族被剿灭、被奴役和被埋葬于矿井中，印第安人的累累白骨，变成了殖民主义者的满船金银。英国东印度公司对茶叶、盐、鸦片、槟榔和其他商品的贸易的垄断权，成为它取之不尽的财富源泉。海盗劫掠活动以及奴隶贸易也是进行原始积累的方法。①公债也是原始积累的有力手段之一，它使货币转化为资本，又用不着承担风险。国家发行公债券，使充当政府和人民之间中介人的金融家大发横财，公债

---

① Nunn和Wantchekon的量化历史实证研究发现，奴隶贸易导致了非洲内部的不信任文化，并持续到了现在。奴隶贸易的早期，几乎所有的奴隶都是通过大规模战争或袭击的手段从非洲掳来的。这导致了地方社区外部环境的极度不安定。这种不安定的外部环境反过来引发了社区内部的不安，因为这迫使非洲人通过欺骗、绑架甚至暴力将邻居、朋友甚至亲人贩卖给欧洲人或奴隶贩子，以换取枪支等武器保护自己。据统计，40%的奴隶是绑架得来的，20%是被亲友卖掉的。司法系统也是奴隶的来源之一，16%的奴隶来自于此。而通过指控他人有罪后将其判作奴隶，也成为社区领袖获得奴隶的一种主要方式。奴隶贸易导致的这种亲人和朋友之间的坑蒙拐骗，以及地方领袖的腐败，损害了他们对亲人的信任，并导致了对政治人物尤其是地方领导人的不信任。近500年的奴隶贸易滋生的不信任环境，塑造了一种文化规范并延续到了今天。见N. Nunn & L. Wantchekon, "The slave trade and the origins of mistrust in Africa", *American Economic Review*, 2011, Vol.101, No.7, pp.3221–3252。

的大部分落入包税者、商人和工厂主手中。现代税收制度成为国债制度的补充，国债是依靠国家收入来支付利息等开支，而国家收入则来自对居民的课税。这种课税实际上是对雇佣工人、农民、手工业者以及社会中下层居民的暴力掠夺。此外，国际信用制度也往往成为这个或那个国家原始积累的源泉之一。所有这一切都使资本以及与之相适应的生产方式形成所需要的货币财富迅速增长，而这些原始积累的因素没有不是通过暴力来实现的。正如马克思所指出的："资本来到世间，从头到脚，每个毛孔都滴着血和肮脏的东西"①。

## 3.2

## 英美工业革命的历程②

### 3.2.1 工业革命的"胚胎发育模式"③

文一将工业革命的历史过程概括为"胚胎发育模式"④，包括了前面英美工业革命所经历的几个阶段，这些阶段是结构变迁不可或缺以及颠倒的循序渐进的过程：

①《马克思恩格斯选集》第二卷，人民出版社2012年版，第297页。

② 这一小节关于英美国家的工业化历史概括主要转引自：文一、乔治·佛梯尔，"看得见的手:政府在命运多舛的中国工业革命中所扮演的角色"，《经济资料译丛》，2017年第2期，第1–42页（英文版：Yi Wen and George E. Fortier, "The Visible Hand: The Role of Government in China's Long-Awaited Industrial Revolution", *Federal Reserve Bank of St. Louis Review*, 2016, Vol. 98, No. 3, pp.189–226）。

③ 文一，《伟大的中国工业革命》，清华大学出版社，2016年版。

④ 文一教授在《伟大的中国工业革命》一书中将生物学的胚胎发育模式隐喻到经济社会发展，马歇尔当年在其《经济学原理》中也采取了这种做法。胚胎生物学发现，高等动物和人类个体的胚胎发育过程快速重复了整个生物进化过程的关键阶段，比如从单细胞到多细胞，从无脊椎到有脊椎，从低等脊椎动物再到高等脊椎动物。又如人类胚胎的早期阶段与低等脊椎动物（比如鱼类和鸟类）的晚期胚胎发育阶段也十分相似。人类的文化知识的获取与传播也服从这样一个胚胎发育原理。比如，人类通过几千年的研究积累起来的数学知识，是从数的概念开始的。原始人首先学会用手指数数，然后

第一个阶段，是工业革命之前的原始工业化阶段，这个阶段在欧洲经历了几百年的时间，也就是我们国家的乡镇企业高速发展阶段。与中国的乡镇企业繁荣类似的乡村企业，在16—18世纪的英国、荷兰、比利时、法国和其他西欧国家繁荣了几百年。这些欧洲乡镇企业也是在当时欧洲各国的重商主义政府的支持下繁荣的，不是自然爆发产生的。它们的特点是都以远距离贸易为其生产的目的，而不是以自给自足或满足当地需求为目的。换句话说，它们都以农村剩余劳动力为主力，以远距离的全球贸易为目标。这个乡镇企业繁荣阶段以各国政府修建人工运河和原始公路网络为契机，为引爆工业革命所需要的统一国内外市场和营销网络奠定了基础，为训练一支产业大军做好了准备。正是这个原始工业化阶段最终在政府正确的产业政策（尤其是全面扶持纺织业的产业政策）支持下启动了第一次工业革命。

第一次工业革命的特点就是用劳动密集型的规模化大生产方式（工厂体制），来生产终端的轻工消费品或小商品，主要是纺织品，把它们倾销到全球，但是机器和生产工具可能是手工造的，而不是量化（规模化）生产的。这个产业革命首先在英国发生，是因为英国历代王室和政府自16世纪起就开始以举国之力为本国乡镇企业提供和创造了全球最大的纺织品市场和棉花原材料供应基地（比如殖民印度、美洲、非洲的棉花产地），而不是因为英国的光荣革命和君主立宪。

随着第一次工业革命的不断推进，就产生了对新的能源、新的动力、新的交通运输方式的巨大市场需求，以加速商品的生产和运输，提高流通速度和单位总重量，因而使得老式的能源－动力－运输体系成为经济继续发展的瓶颈。这刺激了新型能源－动力－运输新技术的发明和工业应用，产生了一个工业“三位一体”的大繁荣，如像煤炭开采、蒸汽机的发明和改进、铁路和公路基础设施的繁荣。

这个能源－动力－运输“三位一体”繁荣是由市场需求驱动的，也是由强政府供给推动的。因为“三位一体”环节很大成分是公共产品，必须靠国家力量和有为政府来提供和提携。这个三位一体繁荣就自然会导致生产力水平的提高，市场的扩张和资本的快速积累，为重工业繁荣并诱发第二次工业革命提供了必要条件。大量采煤需要大量挖掘工具，大量制造蒸汽机需要规模化生产零部件和大量车床，大量铺设铁路轨道需要规模化炼铁、炼钢。而第二次工业革命的特征就是对所有生产资料、中间产品和生产工具的规模化大生产，包括钢铁、

---

发展到会用加减法、代数、微积分，用了几千年。今天作为人类个体的任何一个小孩想要学习数学，也必须重复整个人类当年走过的道路，即从扳指头学习数数开始，然后进入加减法，再到乘除法和代数，最后到微积分。无论多聪明的小孩也必须遵循这些阶段，不能跳跃，否则学不好数学。关键是他们还必须在父母、老师指导下或接受学校里的强化训练才能完成这个过程，他们不可能在原始森林里自己完成从数到微积分的发展。而这个学校教育过程就正好对应于工业化的产业政策和政府的作用，它起到胚胎发育过程里面的“酶”和“催化剂”的作用。

煤炭、铁路、机器、通信设施、轮船，与汽车等运输工具，这些都需要有大量的资本的投入。对这些新的生产方式所需设备的需求，也使得采用新技术和量化生产方式来生产这些重工业产品有利可图。所以第二次工业革命的特征就是在资本积累下一系列工业新技术的大爆发。每一个国家一旦引爆第二次工业革命，都立刻进入一个新技术大爆发时代，不管他们以前是如何模仿和引进英国先进纺织和铁路技术的，因为重工业的产业链特别漫长，零部件和生产环节非常多且复杂，产品多样化特别高，并且，产业和技术已经在世界的前沿，难于依赖于外国技术的引进，进一步的发展有赖于本国的自主创新。这就是为什么法国、德国、美国、日本，还有目前的中国都是到了第二次工业革命阶段才开始逐步摆脱对外国技术的依赖并大量涌现出自己的创新发明的。

第二次工业革命完成以后，一个经济体就完成了一个回路，不仅是终端产品能量化生产，连中间产品和生产工具都能量化生产。在这样的基础之上，生产力大大跃进，人类社会就有条件进入第五个阶段，即福利社会阶段。而这个阶段也是农业现代化的阶段，因为农业不可能是一开始就现代化（机械化）的，而是要等到一个国家能够规模化生产机器和生产工具的时代。比如农业技术在美国长期落后，直到美国快完成第二次工业革命的时候，即1920年，农业人口仍然占总人口的50%。只有等到资本变得廉价（也就是能够规模化生产所有农业机械和其他生产工具），人力变得昂贵，一个国家才能够全面开启实现农业现代化的进程，因为农业现代化需要大量资本，现代农业是资本密集型的。福利社会阶段有两个特点，一个是经济福利，比如免费教育、免费医疗、社会安全网、退休和失业保险，等等。还有政治福利，比如各种各样的天赋人权。人权这个东西在完成第二次工业革命之前都只是喊口号，从来没有真正实现过。比如美国是在完成第二次工业革命以后才开始由社会力量来推动各种政治福利的，包括妇女、儿童和黑人的各种基本人权，同性恋、残疾人甚至犯人的人权也得到保护，一人一票的民主选举才获得真正实施。这些都需要经济基础。

### 3.2.2 英国工业革命的历程[①]

作为第一个走上这条产业升级（“五阶段”）之路的国家，英国在所有欧洲老牌殖民主义者中是第一个成为现代意义上的民族国家的。无论是在工业革命前期和初期的“重商主义”

① 更详细的内容可参考：罗伯特·艾伦，《近代英国工业革命揭秘》，浙江大学出版社，2012年版。

时期，还是在开启工业革命后由于巨大产能过剩向全球推销“自由贸易主义”的时期，都是一个统一的、“全民皆商”的、向外扩张性的强权国家。

英国王室与其它欧洲王室（还有大清王朝）最大的不同之处，在于它从16世纪开始就长期坚持“重商主义”立国的国家发展战略。英国重商主义代表人物托马斯·孟（Thomas Mun）于1615年担任东印度公司董事时极力主张为实现国家贸易出超，国家必须要干预经济活动，其中主要是采取出口退税和进口纳税的国际贸易政策，以支持和保护本国原始制造业的发展。从15世纪开始直到20世纪上半叶的500多年间，从英国王室到所有立法机构都一直把国家当成是同世界其他地方做生意和竞争的一个统一行动者。国家的商业利益与每个国民在海外的商业利益是一致的。①

19世纪中叶美国政治经济学家皮塞·史密斯在研究英国崛起强大的秘密时就指出，英国整个国家就是一个（单一）商人。这种由国家主导的、建立在重商主义意识形态上的统一集体力量，使得英国在全球贸易和政治事务中所向披靡。约翰·威勒（John Wheeler）1601年（即英国第一次工业革命爆发一个半世纪前）发表的《商业论》（*A Treatise of Commerce*）可以认为是英国原始工业化——第一次工业革命助跑阶段——进入高潮的标志。在这本书中威勒系统地提出了大英帝国作为民族国家的振兴战略是靠商业和世界贸易立国，为此除需要鼓励私人和民间贸易以外，还需要建立政府直接干预、控制、保护和指导的大型商业公司（比如英国东印度公司）。威勒在书中为那些以盈利为目的的全民性商业活动进行了道德和伦理上的有力辩护。他把人类历史上被人看不起的商业逐利活动提到了高尚的、为国家谋利的道德高度，指出商人在外面代表的是国家和王室的利益，而不仅仅是私人利益。因此毫不奇怪，威勒的见解得到了伊丽莎白女王的无限欣赏和大力认同。这本书虽然学术性不强，但它的出版标志了近代政治经济学的诞生，比亚当·斯密的《国富论》早了160多年。但是英国成功的秘密还体现在其无意中“发现”和遵循的“制造业”市场培育和“制造业”产业升级的顺序上。与英国同时代竞争的其他欧洲列强（包括西班牙和荷兰），因为没有发

① 这种保护制造业的重商主义的产业政策和传统在英国历史上几乎无间断地延续了至少四五百年，最终成就了大英帝国的辉煌，而且直接促使了18世纪中叶的第一次工业革命的爆发。例如，都铎王朝的君主，尤其是亨利七世（1485—1509）和伊丽莎白一世（1558—1603），将英国从一个严重依赖向低地国家出口羊毛的国家转变成为当时世界上最强大的羊毛加工国家。为了保护英国的纺织工业免受低地国家的竞争，都铎王朝的君主在1489年、1512年、1513年和1536年通过了一系列法律，禁止出口未完成的衣服。到伊丽莎白一世（1587年）的时候，英国开始对其生羊毛制造业的国际竞争力有足够的信心，并完全禁止生羊毛出口。这最终把低地国家的制造业推向毁灭。为了开辟新的世界市场，伊丽莎白一世还派出贸易特使去见俄罗斯、莫卧儿和波斯的教皇和皇帝。这一长期坚持下来的产业政策和重商主义传统丝毫没有因为1688年的光荣革命而受影响。比如1699年的羊毛法令直到1867年才取消，那时英国早就完成了它的第一次工业革命，并处于第二次工业革命的高潮中。

现这条市场培育与产业升级道路而落伍甚至衰败了。而后来所有成功“复制”英国工业革命的国家都“无意中”遵从了这个工业化顺序，而亚洲、非洲、拉美其他企图采取“跨越式”发展方式的国家均遭到工业化失利。

原始工业化阶段：1550—1750年。这一阶段的特点是以远距离贸易为目的的乡村作坊工业的全国性繁荣。这些遍布农村的家庭小企业由一大批从事国内和全球贸易（比如大西洋三角奴隶贸易）的富裕商人来帮助融资和组织生产并负责销售（比如通过外包工制，putting-out system）。比如他们把英国农村作坊生产的纺织品集中起来卖到非洲换取奴隶，再把奴隶卖到美洲换取香料、蔗糖、咖啡，再把这些农副产品运回欧洲大赚一笔。为了在全球垄断这些贸易通道和市场，英国皇室颁布一系列航海法令严格禁止其他欧洲国家和英国殖民地的商船从事同样的贸易活动或在英国本土和领地靠岸。英国政府还设立一系列贸易保护主义关税政策来保护和扶持国内纺织业，并采用一切手段排挤、打击欧洲其他国家尤其是当时发达的低地国家的纺织业。这个漫长的原始工业化阶段最终帮助英国创造了全球最大的纺织品市场和销售网络。

开启第一次工业革命阶段：1750—1830年。英国第一次工业革命主要发生在棉纺织业，其技术代表是木制的珍妮纺纱机和后来对它的各种改进装置，开始主要由人力和水力推动，属于劳动密集型。这场技术革命是在原始工业化阶段所创造的全球性纺织品市场的基础上和政府产业政策的鼓励和保护下所催生的。由政府帮助建立的全球性纺织品大市场和原材料（棉花）供应链使得英国企业采用规模化生产方式更加有利可图，更能够击败国内外竞争对手。而由规模化生产方式催生的工厂体制开始把农村剩余劳动力从农村集中到靠近河流的工厂，形成人类历史上最早的“工业园区”和以此为基础的中小城市，因此实现了人类历史上第一次以远距离贸易和全球市场为目的的规模化大生产，也即第一次工业革命。这个规模化大生产方式不仅依靠规模庞大的全球市场和交通枢纽，而且还依靠那些能够保障源源不断的原材料（棉花）供给的殖民地（比如印度、非洲和美洲大陆，因为英国和其他欧洲国家都不盛产棉花）。值得一提的是，英国并非欧洲第一个开启原始工业化过程的国家。15—18世纪的意大利、西班牙、比利时、爱尔兰等国，尤其是荷兰，其乡村纺织业也十分发达。但是这些国家的乡村制造业由于缺乏政府持之以恒的大力支持和正确的产业政策引导（比如重点培育产业链漫长、劳动力需求多、全球市场巨大的纺织业，而不是香料产业），而最终没落、消亡了。英国开启第一次工业革命后首先摧毁的就是这些国家的手工纺织业。

开启克服能源-动力-运输（工业“三位一体”）的瓶颈结构的“煤-铁路-蒸汽机”时代：1830—1850年。由第一次工业革命产生的巨大物流需求，使传统的运输方式和能源形式严重短缺和落伍，从而促使新的能源（煤炭）、交通（铁路）、动力（蒸汽机）的采用和发明。其实关于这些新技术的知识和机械雏形早就存在，但是以前由于没有巨大的市场需求而没有被采纳和改进，因为实际利用这些技术来赚钱需要进一步付出巨大的投资和研发成本，只有大规模工业用途才能够刺激其需求。比如英国著名生产商博尔顿（Matthew Boulton）就曾经在给他的商业伙伴、蒸汽机发明和改良者瓦特（James Watt）的信中写道："如果仅为3个区县生产你的引擎，太不值得；但如果是为全世界生产你的引擎，那才叫值得！"而这巨大的蒸汽机市场只能通过第一次工业革命来培育，并依靠在世界其他国家开启铁路时代（资本输出）来巩固和维持。

进入以规模化方式生产所有生产工具、机械装备和中间品为特征的第二次工业革命阶段：1850—1900年。如果说第一次工业革命的特征是靠发明机器来规模化生产终极商品，那么第二次工业革命的特征就是以机器来生产机器，或以规模化生产方式来生产所有从事规模化生产的生产工具和生产资料。具体说来，对工业"三位一体"的需求进一步刺激了对资源开采、炼铁、铸造、机器零部件等一系列生产工具和中间产品的标准化、规模化生产的需求，从而引爆了第二次工业革命，而这些需求则建立在资本大量积累的前提条件之下才能实现。这个阶段是马克思和恩格斯生活和思考的年代。这个阶段的第一个主要特征是规模经济引发的大量产能过剩和由此产生的严重经济危机。为了缓解危机，英国政府在这一阶段积极向全世界推销亚当·斯密《国富论》里提出的所谓"看不见的手"，大力提倡自由贸易，以此来输出过剩产能，并由此形成全球产业链分工和对制造业的垄断。英国当时出口的很多产品充满假冒伪劣产品，甚至用木屑充当棉花，普遍采用降低质量的做法，以至于在国际市场上遭到强力抵制，迫使英国政府后来亲自出面采取措施对出口产品实行严格检查和监管。曾经帮助亚伯拉罕·林肯总统制定经济战略的美国经济学家亨利·凯里就说过，"很长时间以来，机械行业一直被英格兰垄断……她的企业都是大公司，随时准备挫败企图与其竞争的对手……让其他国家花几倍的价钱去购买英国生产的服装和钢铁。在英国，为了赢得国际竞争，妇女已经替代了男工，甚至大多数未成年的孩子替代了妇女，劳动时间也尽可能延长……。"英国在印度投资建设的亚洲最大铁路网也是在这一时期完成的。这一铁路系统的目的，第一是通过输出过剩产能为英国在亚洲从事殖民战争投送军事力量和后勤服务，第二是进一步保障英国庞大纺织业所需的大量棉花供应与按时运输。英国对中国的鸦片出口贸易和鸦片战争也是部分依靠这个铁路运输系统来实现。这个阶段的第二个特征是国内社会矛盾日益尖锐突出，广大知识分子同情工人阶级的痛苦，因此开始倒逼政府进行社会制度改良和福利社会建设。值得指出的是，还在1882年，时任英国海军上校的菲舍尔爵士，就提出研究如何让英国皇家海军舰队放弃使用煤炭作为动力燃料的现状，而代之以当时仍未普及的石油作为燃料。但是由于技术和成本限制，这个富有远见的计划直到1909年才开始实施，并于1911年由接替菲舍尔担任第一海军大臣的温斯顿·丘吉尔落实。这一军事领域的技术升级对英国控制全球石油产地、维护英国的世界霸权和赢得第一次世界大战功不可没。

全面进入福利社会阶段：1900年以后。第二次工业革命的完成意味着英国社会的各阶层形成了一个利益攸关的统一体，由于对资本设备实现了规模化生产，不仅工人依赖资本设备，而且资本设备更加依赖本国熟练工人，缺了谁都不行。由于产业升级和社会化大生产带来的劳动力的日益匮乏和资本的日益廉价，尤其是在马克思主义造成的工人罢工和社会主义运动潮流冲击下，为了维护社会稳定，保障和维护英国的全球地位、利益和形象，英国政府开始采取一系列措施来改进劳动生产安全条件和国内工人的福利待遇，比如提供失业保险、社会公共安全网覆盖、低收入家庭补贴、贫民窟改造等，并逐渐扩大广大人民对政治的参与程度。一人一票的全民选举制在1928年（即开启第一次工业革命170年后、完成以规模化方式生产重工业品为标志的第二次工业革命30年后）才顺利实现。顺便提醒一下，几乎所有老牌资本主义国家都是在完成第二次工业革命和进入福利社会后实现全民普选的。比如目前发达国家实现普选的时间分别为：澳大利亚1962年，比利时1948年，加拿大1970年，法国1946年，德国1946年，意大利1946年，日本1952年，葡萄牙1970年，瑞士1971年，英国1928年，美国1965年。即使在这些国家实现正式的全民普选制度之后相当一段时间，贿选和其他选举丑闻也一直屡见不鲜。

### 3.2.3 美国工业革命的历程①

原始工业化阶段：1600—1820年。美国原本是印第安人的地盘和家园。但是自从1492年哥伦布航海大发现以后，陆续来到现在的美国的英国和欧洲移民对本土印第安原住民实施有组织的驱赶、迁移和大规模屠杀。印第安原始部落组织的一次又一次自卫反抗都被残酷镇压和剿灭。因为这片土地极其辽阔，这个驱逐和歼灭印第安人的过程一直持续了300多年。在美国1776年靠“人权宣言”建国后的100年中更是达到高潮，原住民不仅仅是因为被传染上白种人携带的天花病毒而整村整村地集体死亡，而且常常是被集体性强迫搬迁、驱逐或斩尽杀绝。哥伦布来到这片大陆之前，印第安原住民估计有5 000万左右（也有史学家估计在1亿人左右）。1900年美国崛起成为全球制造业头号大国时，美国印第安人已经不足25万人。

为发财和新机遇移居现在的美国的英国和欧洲移民们，继承了他们祖国的殖民主义野蛮扩张“基因”和帝国主义文化。他们在白人至上主义信念的支配下，倚仗更加先进的武

① 关于美国经济史的详实研究可参考：斯坦利 · L. 恩格尔曼、罗伯特 · E. 高尔曼主编，《剑桥美国经济史》（全三卷），高德步等译，中国人民大学出版社，2019年版。

器、组织能力和生产方式，把一片比欧洲大陆还要广袤的肥沃土地变成了一个只属于白种人的新帝国。政府长期不断把抢占到的新土地用拍卖方式卖给新来移民，仅1815年就拍卖出超过100万英亩的黑土地，在随后的1818年这个数字达到250万英亩。与之伴随的是移民人口的急剧增长。比如密西西比州的白人移民人口在1810—1820的十年间翻了一番，路易斯安那州也是如此，而亚拉巴马州的移民人口在这期间增长了12倍。这些移民人口的增长全是以印第安原住民人口的急剧减少为代价的。英国和其他欧洲移民为美国带来了他们出生地的“重商主义”意识形态和农村原始工业化生产方式，使得美国人从一开始就主要是以商业交换为目的来从事农业生产的。也就是说，拥有土地（农业生产）的目的主要是商业交换和远距离贸易，而不是自给自足，这恰好反映了英国的“圈地运动”精神。唯一不同的是，东部和北部农业是依靠白人家庭为核心的小土地制度，而南方是农场主和黑奴种植为特征的大土地制度（以生产和向英国等欧洲国家出口棉花为主）。当时的黑奴等都是用铁链串起来从遥远的黑奴市场长途跋涉驱赶到目的地的。因为路途遥远，农场主更喜欢买进十几岁至二十几岁的年轻黑奴，无论男女都每天行军几十千米，饿了用干粮充饥，晚上就让他们直接睡在光秃的泥巴地上，睡觉时也拴着铁链。美国南方当时遍地是森林和沼泽地带，因此白人移民也靠黑人的双手把大面积森林和沼泽洼地改造成为良田。

美国的建国之父们都是商人，他们对欧洲国家间的战争计谋和祖先们的殖民主义扩张手段了然于胸，且对英国在亚洲和全球主导的贸易秩序心怀不满。美国国父之一亚历山大·汉密尔顿是美国第一任财政部长，他在建国之初就在《美国工业发展计划》里提出以制造业为基础的美国强国计划，告诫美国精英集团千万不要中了英国政府关于亚当·斯密自由贸易理论的“诡计”，这个自由贸易理论让美国只是永远出口农产品，进口英国制造的工业品。汉密尔顿主张依靠提高欧洲对美国的进口关税来保护美国本土制造业，并通过制造业崛起与英国在全球争雄，而不是依靠农业出口和制造品进口来受制于英国。汉密尔顿的制造业计划并没有立即被政府完全采纳，而是等到美国的乡村原始工业化接近完成的19世纪初叶才开始被全面认真采纳和执行。从这以后开始实行的长达一百多年的一系列工业品高关税政策不仅支撑了美国的一系列产业升级，也为19世纪中叶稍后的南北分裂埋下了种子，因为南方严重依赖同欧洲的自由贸易来支撑它巨大的棉花种植和出口。这也成为美国北方与南方后来的4年血腥内战的直接导火索。南方认为只有通过独立才能摆脱北方政府长期不顾南方反对而坚持采纳的高关税政策，这个政策使依赖自由贸易下的棉花出口的南方经济受到重创。而通过赢得南北战争，已经在轻纺工业完成第一次工业革命的北方，不仅可以继续维持对欧洲制造品的高额进口关税，直到美国开启第二次工业革命并出现大量产能过剩为止，而且可以把南方这个昔日全球最大的棉花出口基地，变成维系北方工业化所需要的内部供应基地和制造业产品倾销地，形成巨大国内统一市场和产业链，并因此而牢牢控制英国和欧洲的棉花需求，为今后争夺世界霸权奠定雄厚基础。棉花作为19世纪上半叶英国和欧洲各国工业化最重要的原材料（当时叫做“白金”或材料之“王”），先前主要靠亚洲（尤其是印度）进口，进入19世纪以后，全球棉花生产的霸主地位逐渐被美国取代。棉花在第一次工业革命中的作用一点也不亚于石油在第二次工业革命中的作用。当时谁垄断了棉花，谁就垄断了世界。这一论断在美国南北战争期间再一次应验，那期间英国的纺织工业和整个国民经济由于美国南部的棉花出口中断而坍塌，大批企业倒闭，工人失业，社会陷入前所未有的混乱。作为产棉超级大国，1801年美国出口的棉花占全球市场份额的9%，半个世纪后这个数字变为68%。仅1800—1820年的二十年期间，美国棉花产量就疯狂增长了十倍。1820年，美国出口总值的40%靠棉花，1840年这个份额变为60%。[①]

北美大陆与南美洲的不同之处在于，不断涌入北美的白人移民继承了英国的重商主义价值观和农村原始工业化生产方式，而霸占南美的西班牙移民继承的是西班牙的老式拜金主义，把南美洲仅仅当成像美国南方一样的自然资源出产（掠夺）基地，而没有去扶持制造业。依靠制造业立国的发展战略需要等到南美国家获得独立以后才有可能被采纳和实施。事实上，早在18世纪，美国的农民就已逐渐变得像企业家，从事着广泛的家庭消费品的生产和远距离商业交换。比如还在建国初期，美国就已经在重商主义政府主导下把全球贸易的触角伸向了中国，开始与英国竞争中国和亚洲的市场。在1812年，美国北部各州的乡村地区已经完全商业化了（与中国在20世纪80年代乡镇企业发展阶段类似）。依靠着瀑布为水车提供动力，周遭的小村落普遍从事着制造业活动。这是一个由农业商业化的兴盛而逐渐在自然的市场发酵过程中兴起的、自下而上的原始工业化过程。到了19世纪20年代，这种市场性的交易活动几乎全部被政府支持的由富裕商人阶层建立的有组织的商业活动所取代。领薪工人成为一种流行的农业就业形式，同时农业剩余也往往被用来投资于商业和工业事业而不是土地。本地商人就这样为新型乡村企业的形成提供了推动力。也就是说，美国在1820年左右就已经在它广袤的乡村轰轰烈烈完成了原始工业化进程。但是，这种即将在美国引起第一次工业革命和经济起飞的原始工业化过程完全没有被英国（甚至后来的马克思）注意到。原始工业化期间刺激的商品交换对物流运输网络不断提出进一步需求。于是联邦和地方政府也不断通过兴修运河与公路网络来满足和进一步刺激市场需求。美国最著名的运河是1817年开始修建的长达582千米的伊利运河。美国在1830年代以前建起的运河网络，超过70%的费用是由中央和地方政府支付的。

---

① 关于棉花塑造美国的历史及其全球化历史可参考：Sven Beckert, *Empire of Cotton: A Global History.* Alfred A. Knopf, 2015.

美国的第一次工业革命：1820—1865年。由原始工业化时期培育的统一市场和销售网络以及购买力，为美国此后进入劳动密集型大工厂生产方式创造了市场条件。进入19世纪20年代后，美国北方政府大力鼓励对英国机器的引进和美国产业升级，通过关税保护等一系列产业政策限制欧洲制造品进口，最终在美国引爆（复制）了英国的以工厂体系（劳动密集型生产方式）为特征的第一次工业革命。

像英国一样，美国的这次产业升级也肇始于纺织业。这一产业升级没有发生在当时已经较为发达的商业口岸和金融中心城市（比如波士顿、纽约、费城等），而且也不是靠首先引进当时先进的英国蒸汽机和铁路来开启的。然而对于欧洲而言，1820年代的美国仍然显得非常落后。那时美国90%的人口还居住在农村，这一点直到19世纪中叶也没有多大改变。当时的英国著名作家Sidney Smith在1820年嘲讽美国时写到，美国人虽然勇敢、勤劳，但他们连喝水的杯子和吃饭用的盘子也要靠从英国进口，他们根本不可能培育出像阿克莱特（Arkwright）和瓦特（Watt）这样的发明家。事实上，美国在整个第一次工业革命期间就一直是靠模仿、山寨、剽窃英国技术来推动工业化的，而不是靠自主研发和发明创新。甚至美国在19世纪80年代取代英国成为世界工厂之时也是如此。整个19世纪美国在炼钢和几乎任何其他以科学为基础的工业领域都是英国的学生。比如美国人崇拜的19世纪初期的英雄人物里面，就包括沙缪·斯拉特（Samuel Slate）和佛朗西斯·洛维尔（Francis Lowell）。由于英国第一次工业革命期间的关键技术是纺织技术，它们作为国家级机密受政府严格保护，泄密和盗密者甚至被处以死刑。早在1789年建国伊始，斯拉特就成功从英国把阿克莱特发明的纺织机技术偷偷带到美国发财赚钱。他于1793年在美国东部罗德岛建立了美国第一家纺线工厂，而且从此以后又开了多家工厂并帮助美国培育了一批技术人员，因而被尊称为“美国工业革命之父”（但他在英国却被称为“叛徒和卖国贼”）。不过他的纺线厂一开始十分原始，只雇用十几个童工用脚踏人力方式驱动纺车，以后才改为水力驱动。1813年，美国人洛维尔与其他人合伙成立了一个纺织公司，成为美国第一次工业革命史上的又一个里程碑。洛维尔在这之前花了整整两年时间潜伏在英国曼彻斯特的先进纺织工厂里偷学技术，把当时最先进的水力推动的织布机技术和组装原理弄得清清楚楚后偷渡回国。1814年，洛维尔就自豪地向公司公布了他组装的全世界最新式的联动纺纱织布机，它把美国纺织技术提高到了一个崭新阶段。不过，要到很多年以后这些先进纺织技术才在美国获得广泛工业应用和普及。1832年，美国第一次工业革命开始进入高潮，当时106家最大的企业里面纺织企业占了88家。1831年，美国共有120万台纺锤和33 500台织机，差不多每10个人就拥有一个纺锤（当时美国总人口约为1 300万）。到1860年，纺织业继续是美国工业的主要产业。当时美国拥有200万纺锤和3 700家纺织厂，其中1 200家棉纺织厂和1 500家羊毛纺织厂。不过这些机械设备仍然主要靠自然力量（水力）驱动。为了控制生产成本，妇女和儿童是这个产业就业人员的主要构成成分。由于对就连英国也不是直接通过蒸汽机、煤炭、钢铁和铁路从城市开启工业革命这个基本事实无知，美国作家Anthony F. C. Wallace在描写他的老家Rockdale这个美国小镇在19世纪中叶由美国第一次工业革命带来的经济繁荣时曾这样写道："和英国广泛采用蒸汽机作为动力并把制造业中心放在像曼彻斯特这样的大城市来开启工业化不同，美国当年开启工业化的制造业体系是遍布在乡村而且依赖于这个新兴国家的河流所产生的动力。Rockdale作为一个当年的制造业基地完全是位于自给自足的乡村，只不过却在经济上，通过不断买进棉花和卖出纱线和布匹，与遥远的世界市场和金融中心紧密相连。"这个发展阶段，美国还在爱国主义和扩张主义精神驱使下，通过战争从墨西哥手里夺走了德克萨斯和加利福尼亚两个全美最大的州，还把夏威夷收入囊中，并在与西班牙交战后接手了西班牙在亚洲和南美的很多殖民地。事实上，美国国父之一，托马斯·杰弗逊总统当年的美利坚帝国的梦想里面还包括吞并加拿大和古巴。后来美国政府通过主导跨洋铁路建设连接了西海岸和东海岸，帮助美国形成了全球最大、最具规模的统一国内市场。这个市场进一步刺激了规模化大生产和托拉斯企业的出现，为美国引爆第二次工业革命打下了基础。而在同一时期，美国最大最繁华的商业和金融中心纽约市，却并非治理良好的大都市，丝毫体现不出美国自吹的"人权和法治"精神。那里犯罪率极高，工厂女工和良家妇女经常遭到骚扰、合伙强奸和打劫。街头群殴现象比比皆是。由民怨和不公造成的地方暴动，还有暗杀、偷盗、抢劫。穷人和工人聚集区更是如此。形形色色的黑社会组织盛行，相互冲突。在稍微富裕的新兴市区，有组织的商业犯罪猖獗。比如1844年（马克思写作《1844年经济学哲学手稿》的年份）人们可以看到上万妓女合股成立的大妓院股份公司，实行规模化卖淫。由于工业污染使得空气极其污浊，家庭用煤、抽烟、供暖、油灯照明加上蒸汽机驱动的大小工厂使得市区住房伸手不见五指。火灾频频发生，居住条件和卫生环境极其恶劣，城市稀缺的饮水源也长期被垃圾、人类和宠物的排泄物污染得不像样。城区政府根本不关心居民的供水问题，人们被迫在自己居住的后院打井取水，尽管这些水资源已经被严重污染。每每遇到下雨，地下粪池到处溢出，垃圾粪便满街流淌，臭味熏天。即便在旱季，沿路到处都是马粪，让人无法抬头行走。从1830年代开始，由马匹牵引的运货车、载客车和旅行车增加了城市繁荣，但也更进一步增加了纽约满街的粪便和臭气。为了解决满城垃圾问题，城市官员把居民圈养的猪和鹅驱赶到小巷里面与那里的流浪狗、老鼠、秃鹫、蟑螂汇合，然后统一歼灭清除。街道上还能看到提醒父母的警示牌，警告他们无人照看的小孩随时可能被上面提到的生物围攻和吃掉。这个城市的死亡率不仅远远超过美国农村地区，甚至高于纽约市的出生率，以至于人均预期寿命才区区24岁！而美国黑奴在当时的预期寿命也不过30岁而已。

工业"三位一体"爆法式繁荣阶段：1865—1880年。由第一次工业革命开创的巨大市场和物流运输需求，使得已有能源驱动方式（主要是风力和水力）和基础设施（主要是运河与初级公路）严重不足，成为经济发展的瓶颈。这直接促使联邦政府对能源、运输、动力工业三位一体的重视和战略规划，鼓励了一系列产业政策以实现工业三位一体的现代化。其中最典型的就是铁路泡沫。为了刺激私有资本进入铁路建设，联邦政府用特许批准方式出售廉价土地给铁路公司并让铁路公司拥有沿线的垄断价格制定权。在巨大天然垄断利润前景的驱动下，美国各个铁路公司为了在交通行业获得足够市场份额，以非常激烈的速度竞争修建铁路。结果，“其中最大的十三条铁路线的里程在1865年到1880年期间增长了6倍，仅在1870年和1876年的6年间就增长了两倍……大干线是竞争最激烈的地方：这些公司经常过度铺设铁路线路并从事毁灭性的价格战争。例如，在1880年代，仅在圣路易斯和亚特兰大之间就有20条铁路线相互竞争”。1840—1900年美国GNP的部门分布如表3.2所示。

表3.2 1840—1900年美国GNP的部门分布（%）

| 部门 | 1840年 | 1850年 | 1860年 | 1870年 | 1880年 | 1890年 | 1900年 |
|---|---|---|---|---|---|---|---|
| 农业 | 41 | 35 | 35 | 33 | 28 | 19 | 18 |
| 制造业、采矿业和手工业 | 17 | 22 | 22 | 24 | 25 | 30 | 31 |
| 运输业和公共基础设施 | 7 | 4 | 6 | 6 | 8 | 9 | 9 |
| 商业和其他全部私有产业 | 23 | 26 | 26 | 26 | 29 | 32 | 32 |
| 政府和教育 | 2 | 2 | 2 | 2 | 2 | 3 | 3 |
| 救济 | 10 | 11 | 9 | 9 | 8 | 7 | 7 |

资料来源：斯坦利·L. 恩格尔曼、罗伯特·E. 高尔曼主编，《剑桥美国经济史：漫长的19世纪》（第二卷），高德步等译，中国人民大学出版社，2018年版，第47–48页。

第二次工业革命阶段：1880—1950年。铁路繁荣，尤其是跨洋铁路的建设，把整个美国连接成了一个统一而巨大的市场，这个市场催生了美国新一轮制造业大繁荣。遍及全国的基础设施建设和房地产繁荣催生了对所有生产资料（包括生铁、水泥、矿产、金属以及各种化工产品）和生产工具（包括铁路、蒸汽机、引擎、机器、机械零部件、轮船和其他运输和通信工具等）实现规模化生产的市场需求。这直接引爆了美国的第二次工业革命。在这场革命中，市场越大，其涌现出来的创新能力就越强。也正是在这个巨大市场条件下形成的规模化大生产时代，美国超越英国成为世界第一大制造业中心，开始逐渐在各个工程技术方面领先英国和欧洲，并产生了像爱迪生这样的发明家和卡内基（Andrew Carnegie）、福特（Henry Ford）、摩根（J. P. Morgan）、洛克菲勒（John D. Rockefeller）和范德比尔特（Cornelius Vanderbilt）这样的工业巨头。对美国而言，19世纪下半叶开启第二次工业革命以后是一个“需要巨人并能够产生巨人的时代”。得益于巨大的国内市场，美国在进入第二次工业革命以后成功超越了英国，成为第二次工业革命的领跑者。这个巨大的国内市场使得美国有能力不需要通过国际贸易就能够在自负盈亏的情况下，对所有英国能够规模化生产的产品和很多英国无法规模化生产的产品实现规模化生产并使得价格更低、更富有竞争力，比如除了纺织品、铁路、蒸汽机、轮船、坦克、大炮等以外还有包装食品、快餐、饮料、药品、医疗器件、住房、厨房用具、购物中心、好莱坞电影、汽车、高速公路、民用飞机等。但是有两个历史现象值得注意，因为它们都反映了经济发展的规律。

第一，美国即使在超越英国成为全球制造业大国以后，由于政府监管不到位，不仅法律沦为一纸空文，而且监管部门成为腐败的温床。各种假冒伪劣产品更是蒸蒸日上，比美国第一次工业革命时期更加泛滥。欧洲和其他国家都成了美国假冒伪劣产品的倾销市场，违反欧洲知识产权的事情在美国层出不穷，“美国制造”简直成了美国崛起期间劣质产品的代名词。比如，美国毫不尊重欧洲出版的书籍的版权，简直就是19世纪全球剽窃和盗版的温床，以至于英国著名作家狄更斯在美国各色书店都发现了他和同时代英国畅销作家的各种盗版作品，让他十分吃惊和恼火。又比如，美国当时的市场上和出口欧洲的食品中充满了掺假食品和有意误导消费者的标签、内容介绍和广告。从制造商到分销商再到零售商，无不层层在包装食品制作过程和包装销售过程中造假，以更低的成本获取更大的利润，包括对食品添加廉价填料，对过期、腐败食品注入对人体有毒的添加剂以掩盖异味和真相，或对食品涂上人工做的颜色和调味料。比如小孩吃的糖果被发现含有剧毒砷，并涂上氯化铜以让色彩更鲜艳；啤酒制造商在水里添加一种叫做“nux vomica”的树叶提取物，模拟啤酒花的苦味；供应商在腌制黄瓜的液体里面加入硫酸铜以让色彩逼真鲜艳；乳蛋白粉里面总能够找到铅的痕迹；白糖和面粉都混有大量石膏；牛奶里面总是大量掺水以后再添加上石灰粉和羊脑浆；靠对奶牛强制喂养由酒厂排出的有毒废物做成的饮食来增加牛奶的产量；号称原产地进口的一百磅一袋的咖啡，其实里面有五分之三是豌豆粉，五分之一是有咖啡气味的菊苣；“火腿”由牛肉脂肪、牛肚和小牛残余物混合制成；香肠由患结核病的猪的肉做成；猪肉产品含有屠宰场因事故死去的工人的尸体成分。这样的案例举不胜举。食品行业只是美国假冒伪劣产品泛滥的冰山一角，在一个又一个的行业中，19世纪的美国生产商不断把巨量的假冒伪劣产品投放到市场上，而且标榜他们能够在当地生产原装进口的几乎一切欧洲产品。专利药品的造假者特别臭名昭著。这有点讽刺，因为这些方法特别虚假，但这并没有阻止这种做法。最精明的计划涉及进口空瓶，用伪造的混合物填充它们，然后粘贴来自知名的欧洲公司的假标签。美国人还展示了伪造货币的特殊天赋。私有银行，而不是联邦政府，提供了这个国家的令人咋舌的各种各样假冒的所谓银行“票据”。仿造假币者的数量蓬勃发展到了一个如此惊人的数目，以至于1862年一位英国作家在考察了美国市面上流通的接近6 000种不同种类的假冒纸币和银行票据后，自信地向他的读者写道：“在美国，假币泛滥所达到的程度和规模简直令人觉得不可思议。”这一系列造假经济活动在19世纪上半叶美国的第一次工业革命期间就开始泛滥成灾，南北战争以后更是愈演愈烈。由于成为出口大国，这些假冒伪劣产品大量出口到了英国和欧洲，其结果是遭到这些国家的抵制和追究，开始危害美国出口。比如在1879年，德国指责美国出口受猪瘟病毒和霍乱感染的猪肉，这导致几个国家抵制美国猪肉。类似的对肺部感染的美国牛肉的恐慌加剧了这些贸易战。这最终促成已经成为全球制造业大国的美国联邦政府在19世纪末下决心出台一系列监管措施和惩罚制度，严厉打击假冒伪劣产品，整顿市场秩序，保障美国商品的世界市场份额和声誉。比如从1880年代开始，欧洲国家对美国肉类的抵制运动促使美国国会通过一系列联邦立法，旨在对肉类出口实施一些专门检查和质量控制。作为回应，欧洲国家再次向美国肉类敞开大门。在1891年，美国国会终于屈服于几十年的愤怒游说，通过了一个国际版权法来保护外国作家的著作版权。1905年美国联邦食品与药品法获得通过。不过要知道，这些违法造假现象在更早期的英国和欧洲都繁荣过，而且在19世纪末和20世纪初的日本也被大肆重复过。因此，所谓美国和西方国家都是依靠法制和民主才开启了工业革命的说法，简直就是对历史的无知。那些认为只有在不发达国家实行民主选举才能够遏制腐败、造假、环境污染的说法也不过是知识分子的天真幻想。那些鼓吹“企业家精神”只有在政府退出市场干预的情况下才能展现出来的人士，不过是现代西方“黑板经济学”训练出来的会学舌的鹦鹉而已。

第二，即使到了19世纪80年代，当美国已经完成第一次工业革命，开启了第二次工业革命，建成了世界上最大的铁路网络，并超越英国成为“世界工厂”的时候，它的高等教育和纯科学研究与当时的欧洲，尤其是英国、法国和德国相比仍然相当落后和原始。美国物理学会第一任会长和同时代最出色（但是在欧洲和全球科技历史上很不出名）的美国科学家之一，罗兰德（Henry Augustus Rowland，1848—1901），在1883年的学会年会上公开抱怨美国的极其落后的高等教育和大学的科学研究水平：“我面前放着一份教育局专员1880年的报告。按照这个报告，美国一共只有389或大约400所自称为学院和大学的高等研究机构！……其中三分之一称自己为大学，而在这些所谓的大学中，有一所只有2个教授和18个学生，还有一所有3个老师和12个学生！……然而这些并非只是个别情况，因为有太多小小的学校称呼自己为大学……但是谁能怀疑一个比如有800个学生和70个教授的大学不会比只有一二十个学生和两三个老师的大学更好、质量更高呢？”“然而这也不尽然，因为我还熟悉一个有500名学生的大学实际上只有高中水平。每个这样的大学都有所谓的教授，但是他们实际上只有中学老师水平……在这个国家，并非是那些工资最高、在最贵的学校教书的人最有能力从事科研：那些拿最高工资并霸占讲席教授位置的人却并不从事任何纯科学研究，只不过在为各种商业利益集团服务并用他们的知识为自己已经很高的收入争取更大的商业回报……”“但是危险正在逼近我们，即便在我们这样的科学协会中……当社会对科研的平均要求很低，当最高的学术荣誉被那些不学无术或平庸的人占据，当三流的学者被推为学术楷模，当微不足道的发现被吹捧为了不起的科学发明时，学术机构对社会的影响就得大打折扣……我们的国家科学院由来至全国的杰出科学家组成，但是它却没有办公楼和图书馆，而且除了发表一些对政府免费开放的信息以外不发表任何东西……它根本无法与英国皇家学会，或在巴黎、柏林、维也纳、圣彼得堡、慕尼黑，以及任何欧洲首都和大城市的科学院相比。”“一个自诩为大学但却在办公桌和图书馆书架上没有一本科学期刊的高等学府和研究机构，确实不是在为社会尽到它应尽的责任。……在美国的物理学领域，目前还没有发表或出版过或可能出版任何一本高于基础读物水平的书。”事实上，尽管罗兰德在19世纪80年代初对美国科学界发出的富有激情的恳求，美国要等到第二次世界大战后才在纯科学研究上开始引领世界，那时离美国成为世界工业霸主已经过了半个多世纪。比如从1851年到1900年，GDP比整个欧洲还大的美国所取得的重大科技成果远远不如欧洲的一个国家，比如法、英、德的重大科技成果分别为美国数量的227%、321%和612%。在1901年到1920年间，美国已经处于完成第二次工业革命的下半期并在工业技术上领跑第二次工业革命，其获得诺贝尔自然科学奖的人数远远逊于欧洲，获奖人数分别为2人（美）、8人（英）、11人（法）和20人（德）。事实上，美国哪怕在完成第二次工业革命后在科学方面的突飞猛进也十分得益于它的特殊移民政策。这说明科学理论与工业技术之间有很大的鸿沟和距离。难怪工业革命历史上很多伟大的发明家都没有受过正规教育，比如阿克赖特、瓦特、爱迪生等。又比如，虽然没有古希腊的形式逻辑和数学体系，中国古代在应用技术方面一直遥遥领先欧洲。再比如，美国在火箭技术方面的突破在很大程度要归功于二战后从德国引进的大批科学家。

全面进入福利社会阶段：1950年至今。第二次工业革命的完成为美国进入福利国家创造了经济基础。蛋糕做大了毕竟要分的，不是政府主动分就是被革命运动强迫分。福利社会包括政治福利和大众经济福利。随着第二次工业革命的逐步完成，美国逐步获得了规模化生产所需的几乎一切生产工具和生产资料的能力（当然也包括军事武器和动员全面战争的能力）。这个高度发达的生产力同时也意味着它具备了为社会所有公民成员全面地、廉价地提供基本政治和经济福利的能力，以及国家和政府职能的转换（从强势介入型变为服务型）。但是福利和政府职能转换不会自然、顺利到来，而需要靠工人阶级和底层人们去争取，有时甚至是流血牺牲才能换来。

首先，在政治福利方面，美国历史上通过的一系列对妇女、黑人、印第安人和其他外来移民（比如华人）的种族歧视性法案随着第二次工业革命的深入和完成逐渐得到废除。比如1920年通过了妇女选举权法案，在“人人生而平等”的建国宣言发布145年之后承认了妇女的选举权。1924年，在一万名印第安人为保卫美国参加了第一次世界大战之后，被剥夺土地几百年之后的美国印第安人终于被宣布可以合法获得美国公民身份。但是长期被剥削、压迫、奴役的印第安人昂首拒绝了这个具有侮辱性的“礼物”，因为他们从来就是这片土地的主人，但却已经被赶尽杀绝。1943年，美国国会为了表彰中国成为美国在第二次世界大战中的盟国，废除了历史上一系列歧视华人劳工和移民的法案，允许每年给予中国105个移民配额。1952年，美国历史上第一次没有发现黑人被白人处以私刑。1954年，美国最高法院宣布全国所有学校实行的种族隔离政策为非法。这个决定被认为是美国进入后工业化时代真正的人权运动开始的标志。但是这些立法并不意味着问题的真正结束。比如1955年8月28日，一个14岁黑人小孩仅仅因为在密西西比一个商店对一个白人女孩说了声“宝贝，再见！”就被殴打、枪击并处以死刑。同年12月1日，一个黑人妇女因为在公交车上拒绝为一个白人男人让座被逮捕并罚款。1957年，阿肯色州一所中学因为放弃种族隔离政策而发生骚乱，当时的州长甚至扬言如果黑人推动进行种族融合，那将会造成“血流成河”。1963年8月28日，25万人在首都华盛顿举行集会，聆听马丁·路德·金“我有一个梦想”的著名讲演。1965年，美国实现全民选举（但不包括原住民）。印第安人的基本人权要到1968年才获得美国政府承认，这些是印第安人长期在自己领土上为之浴血奋战的权利，它们包括：（1）言论、集会、新闻自由；（2）对被强加的不合理搜身和财产剥夺获得的应有保护；（3）在刑事被告时迅速进行审判的权利，和被告知有关指控以及面对任何不利的证人的权利；（4）在刑事案件中雇用律师的权利；（5）保护免受自我归罪的权利；（6）保护免受残酷和不寻常的惩罚、超额保释金、无指控情况下监禁一年以上和/或任何一项罪行的罚款超过5 000美元的权利；（7）保护免受双重犯罪惩罚或事后新建法律追究的权利；（8）可判处监禁的罪行获得陪审团审判的权利；（9）法律和程序面前人人平等的权利。但是即便如此，部落所在区的领土主权，狩猎和捕鱼以及投票等其他公民权利仍然是当今印第安原住民面临的问题，因为美国政府不希望原住民有任何争取独立自治的念头，如果敢于独立自治，一定是武力伺候。1966年，全国妇女协会正式成立，开始为妇女的平等权利而公开抗争。1967年在底特律发生一起由警察袭击演变而来的严重种族冲突，冲突中33名黑人和10名白人丧生。同一年的其他时期，美国还发生了另外164起种族冲突事件，包括好几个州的暴动，那些暴动导致83人被枪杀。1968年4月4日，人权领袖马丁·路德·金被暗杀，造成全美很多地方大规模骚乱。1969年6月27日的一次警察对同性恋酒吧的袭击导致了连续两天的骚乱，成为美国同性恋民权运动的发端。1973年，通过了残废工人休假权法案。1979年10月，发生有10万人参加的声势浩大的争取同性恋合法权利的游行。1982年，计划写进宪法的工作岗位反性别歧视法案没有获得通过。1990年，国会通过法案严禁对于残疾人的歧视并要求所有大楼和公共场所修建残疾人特殊通道。但是由于人口太少的原因导致的抗争乏力，美国印第安人获得的政治补偿却一直远远少于美国黑人。比如直到21世纪的2000年9月8日，美国印第安事务局才对美国政府在过去几百年中对印第安部落实施的种族清洗和屠杀正式道歉。

其次，一系列的经济福利计划逐步开始实施。比如，1935年1月17日，包括子女养育和失业救济在内的社会保障法案获得通过。1940年12月，美国36万个低收入家庭获得子女负担方面的补贴。获得这个补贴的家庭数在1950年代增加了11万，1960年代增加了80万。1962年，肯尼迪总统签署一项公共福利法案，鼓励州政府为促进自我就业提供更多社会服务。1964年，国会通过一项由约翰逊总统推动的“向贫困宣战”法案。这一法案成为美国二战后为建设“伟大社会”而颁布的一系列社会福利计划之一。截至1997年10月8日，大约1亿美国人享受社会经济福利。到1999年，大约还有670万个家庭生活在人均年收入低于4 000美元的贫困线以下。比如在缅因州，对三口之家的贫困家庭实施的最高福利补贴为每月461美元。

# 3.3

# –

# 生产结构随禀赋结构拾级而上的次序特征

## 3.3.1 当今一些发达经济体三次产业的历史变迁特征

按照第1章所介绍的经济结构转型升级的新结构经济学分析框架，处于不同发展阶段的国家，由于作为物质基础的禀赋结构不同，相应地也会有不同的经济结构。处于不同发展阶段的国家，禀赋结构存在巨大差异，西欧和北美的高收入经济体在工业革命以后，经济发展和资本积累加速，禀赋结构表现出资本相对劳动更加丰裕的特征，而低收入经济体的经济发展慢，剩余少，资本积累有限禀赋结构表现出劳动相对资本更加丰裕的特征，并且禀赋结构的分布不是只有这两个状态而是处于一个连续谱系。同样，对应的产业结构在不同的发展阶段也呈现出不同的特征，高收入经济体的产业结构表现出更加技术和资本密集，而低收入经济体的产业结构表现出更加劳动力密集。这是一个无法跳跃的连续谱系，经济发展就是这样的持续不断的经济结构转型升级的过程。经济发展要求在现有产业中不断引入新的、更好的

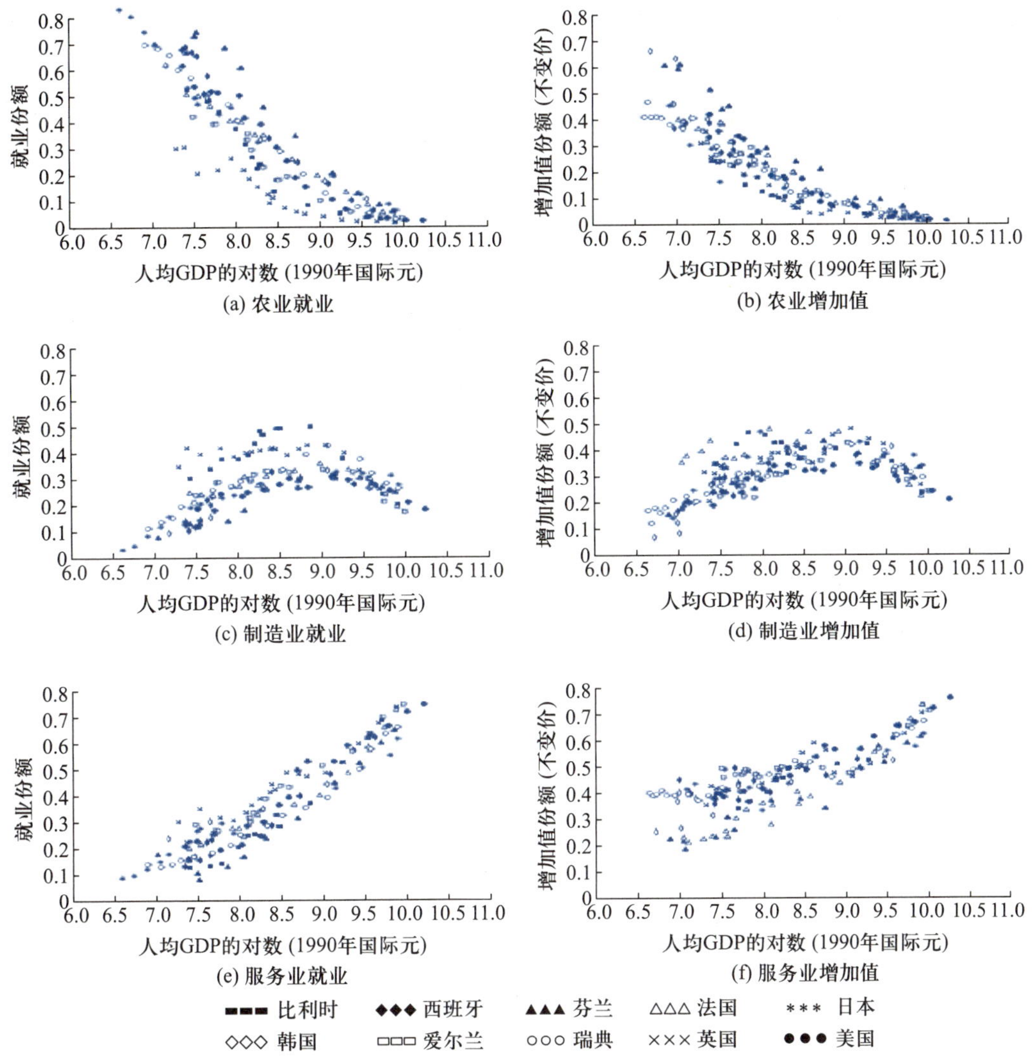


图3.4 当今一些发达经济体两百年间的三次产业结构变迁（1800—2000）

资料来源：Berthold Herrendorf，Richard Rogerson，Akos Valentinyi，“Growth and Structural Transformation”，*NBER Working Paper 18996*，2013.

技术，以及不断引进附加值更高、资本更密集、技术更先进的新产业。低收入国家的绝大多数人都以农业为生。农业技术的改进对于增加农民收入和减贫是必不可少的。然而，经济发展也要求经济不断地从现有产业向新的、资本密集度更高的产业扩展，从而实现产业多样化和产业升级。如果没有这样的结构变迁，人均收入持续增加的余地就很小。对应于这个基本的禀赋结构和产业结构的经济结构转型升级框架，第2章也介绍了全球三次产业结构随发展阶段而依次变化的特征。图3.4则记录了当今一些发达经济体过去两百年来的三次产业结构持续的转型升级。例如，在三次产业层面上经济结构转型升级的基本特征事实可以概括为：随着收入水平的提高，农业占比不断下降、工业占比不断提高然后逐步下降、服务业占比不断提高。[①]二战后，英美等发达经济体已经完成了工业化，农业在经济中的比重已经微不足道。以英国为例，在1851年农业就业人口已经下降到21%，到1911年进一步下降到7%，而到1995年只有微不足道的2%了。欧洲大陆的法国是个例外，1960年的农业占GDP比重依然还有10.52%，不过到2017年其比重只有微不足道的1.51%。正如第1章最后小节所对比的布隆迪和瑞士的经济结构系统差异，瑞士这样的发达经济体由于禀赋结构水平高，产业结构呈现出资本密集型制造业和人力资本密集型服务业的特征，与之相对应的其他经济结构安排，如金融结构、城市化、教育结构、开放结构等都完全不同于布隆迪这样的欠发达经济体。

### 3.3.2 制造业及其细分行业与细分产品的结构变迁特征

不同的发展阶段制造业的结构也是显著不同的。正如后面将对战后发展中经济体激进的工业化适得其反的数据所揭示的，如果制造业结构变迁过于激进也会适得其反，这正是我们在下一小节将使用的发展战略的代理变量TCI指数的构建依据。图3.5、图3.6以及图3.7展示了不同细分部门的制造业在不同发展阶段的变迁轨迹。服装、纺织、食品等劳动力密集型的轻工业往往是发展早期阶段的主导产业，而其他资本密集型的重工业和高技术产业往往是发展中后期阶段的主导产业。林毅夫等（2015）在实证上展示了美国制造业细分行业随禀赋结构变迁而变迁的规律。一般而言，制造业部门较高细分程度上的产业结构演化存在四大特征事实：第一，行业异质性，即不同行业之间存在要素禀赋差异（资本－劳动比衡量）；第二，行业生命周期呈现“驼峰状”（hump-shaped），即每一行业（增加值）经历增长—顶峰—下降的过程；第三，越是资本密集型产业，到达产业峰值的时间越迟；第四，资本要素密集度越是偏离经济体要素禀赋结构的产业，其规模越小。这些特征事实也可以概括为著名的“雁行模式”，我们在第6章将进一步讨论。如果我们进一步将产业细分到产品层面，依

---

① 如何解释产业结构变迁的这一经验事实，目前的研究从其出发点来看大致可以归纳为三类，基于恩格尔法则的结构变迁理论、基于鲍莫尔法则的结构变迁理论、基于林毅夫法则的结构变迁理论。由于恩格尔法则所依赖的收入弹性以及鲍莫尔法则所强调的技术创新偏向都无法解释收入水平为何会不断变动，从新结构经济学所主张的禀赋结构出发透过产业和技术选择，决定了生产率、收入和积累水平更具根本性。因此，可以将产业结构变迁的恩格尔法则和鲍莫尔法则视为新结构经济学对产业结构变迁分析的进一步延展。例如，随着由禀赋结构所驱动的产业结构不断升级，收入水平的不断提高通过偏好的非对称性就会反过来对产业结构产生影响，这是新纳入偏好结构对产业结构影响的一种重要方式（Piyabha Kongsamut, Sergio Rebelo, Danyang Xie, “Beyond Balanced Growth”. *The Review of Economic Studies 2001,* Vol.68, No.4, pp.869–882.）。

然可以观察到这一产品结构变迁的典型特征事实。图3.8和图3.9是豪斯曼提出的产品空间模型及其对全球各地区产品空间的测度。

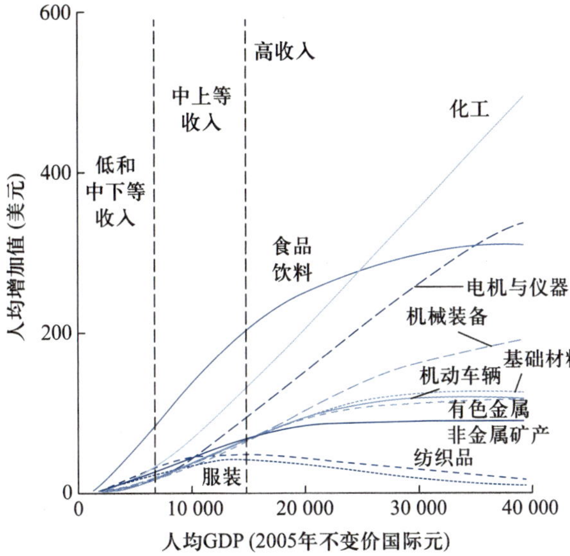


**图3.5 全球制造业细分行业结构变迁的特征事实**

注：图3.5为74个经济体的混合数据；图3.6为95个经济体的混合数据。

资料来源：UNIDO, Industrial Development Report 2013, *Sustaining Employment Growth*: *The Role of Manufacturing and Structural Change*.

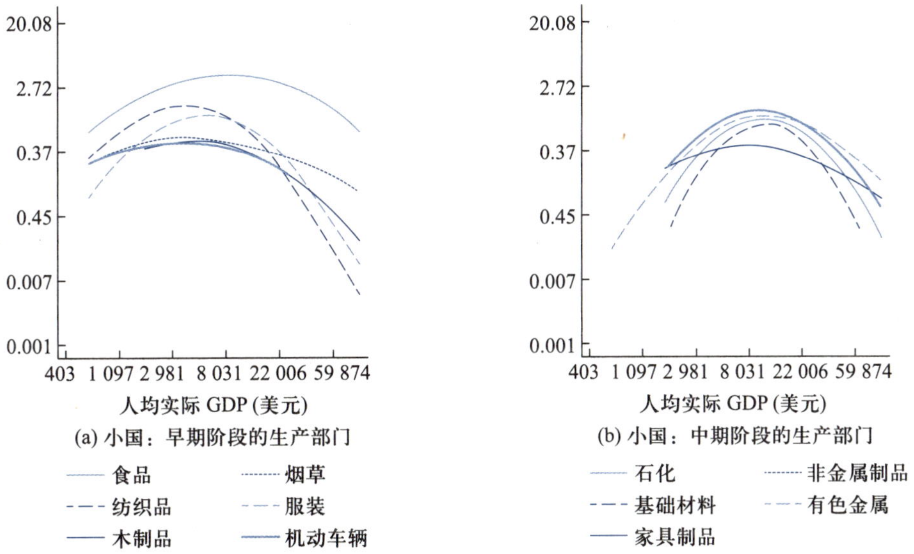

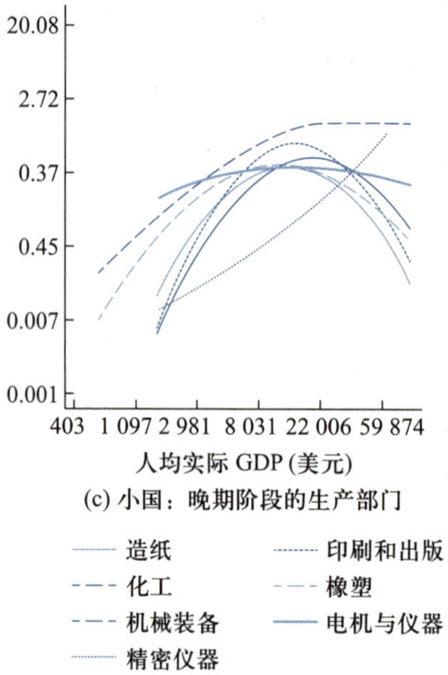


**图 3.6 全球 95 个经济体制造业细分行业结构变迁的特征事实**

资料来源：根据 N. Haraguchi，G. Rezonja，"Patterns of Manufacturing Development Revisited"，UNIDO Working Paper，2009 测算。

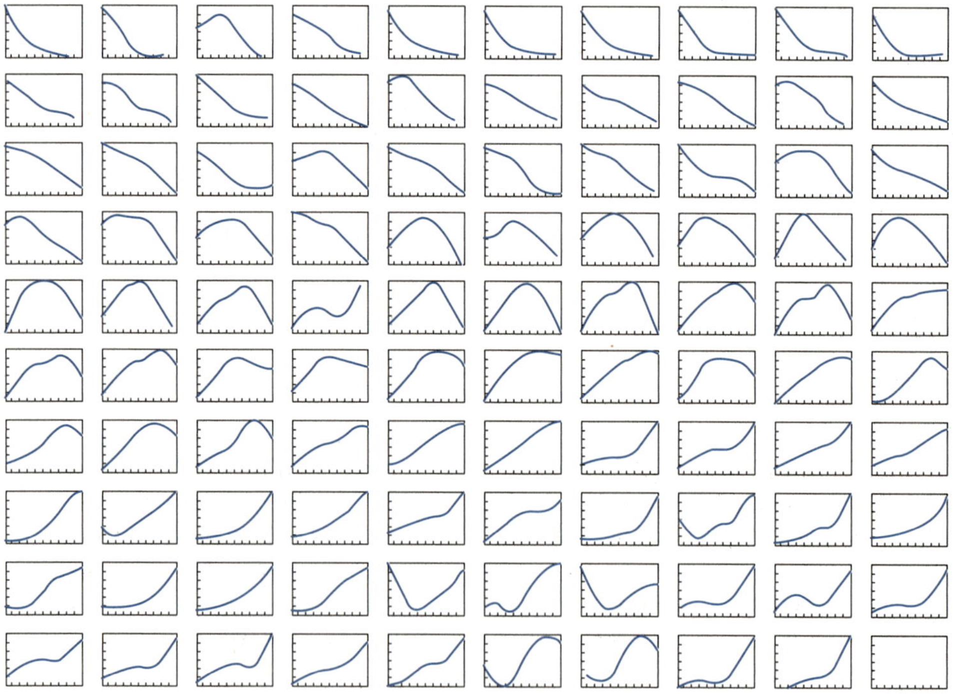

**图 3.7 美国细分制造业结构的转型升级特征：按照资本密集度划分的一百个行业从低到高的变迁情况**

资料来源：根据 Jiandong Ju，Justin Yifu Lin，Yong Wang，"Endowment Structure，Industrial Dynamics，and Economic Growth"，*Journal of Monetary Economics*，2015，Vol.76，pp.244–263 测算。

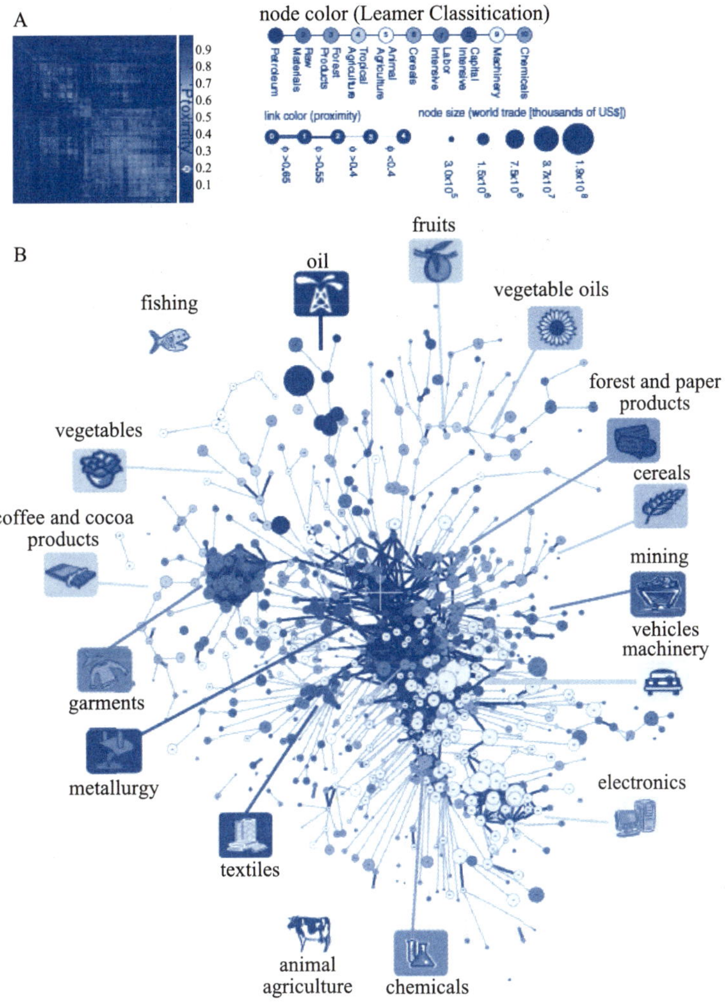


图A是反映1998—2000年间出口的775个SIIC4位数产品类别的分层集群近似矩阵。图B是产品空间的网络表示；连接线颜色按照其相近性值编码，圆点大小按照其占世界贸易中的份额大小编码。

图3.8 产品空间的图示

资料来源：C. A. Hidalgo, B. Klinger, A.-L. Barabasi, R. Hausmann, "The Product Space Conditions the Development of Nations", *Science*, 2007, Vol.317, No.5837, pp.482-487。

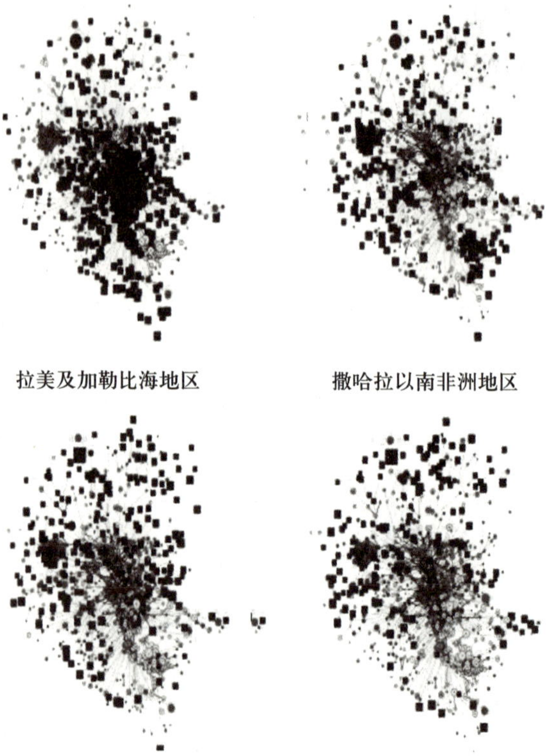


**图3.9 全球各地区的产品空间分布**[①]

资料来源：C. A. Hidalgo, B. Klinger, A.–L. Barabasi, R. Hausmann, "The Product Space Conditions the Development of Nations", *Science*, 2007, Vol.317, No.5837, pp.482–487。

### 3.3.3 全球技术创新结构随禀赋结构升级的特征[②]

与主流内生增长理论所强调的技术进步或技术创新不同，在本书中我们主要探讨产业结构随禀赋结构的转型升级，其实，技术进步或技术创新也有结构，而且也是内生于要素禀赋结构的。创新包含了发明创新和模仿创新，发明创新直接越过创新之前的最先进技术水平值，

---

① 关于更多的全球各个经济体产品空间变迁的内容可参考豪斯曼等编制的工具书：*The Atlas of Economic Complexity—Mapping Paths to Prosperity*。

② 更详细的内容可参考：林毅夫、付才辉，《新结构经济学导论》（上册）第6章"新结构创新理论"，高等教育出版社，2019年版。

而模仿创新始终处于全球技术前沿内部。发明创新所要求的投入大、不确定性高，而且在不同的禀赋结构与生产结构阶段其回报也是不同的。一个处在禀赋结构和产业结构水平较低阶段的经济体，其产业和技术处于世界产业和技术前沿之内，新产业和新技术可以靠引进现有的成熟产业和技术取得，对拓展世界技术前沿的发明创新的需求并不高，导致回报也就较低，同时发明创新对投入大，风险高，对资本的需求大，只有在禀赋结构较高时才能满足，而此时禀赋结构供给较低会导致较高的禀赋结构的相对价格，因此此时发明创新的利润并不高，甚至还会亏本。与此相反，在禀赋结构和生产结构较低阶段，对模仿创新的需求比较高导致回报比较高，同时模仿创新对投入的禀赋结构需求较低，在禀赋结构供给较低时禀赋结构的相对价格也就较低，因此此时模仿创新的利润较高而富有吸引力。所以，在禀赋结构与生产结构比较低的阶段，创新应该更多地偏向模仿创新。同理，在禀赋结构和生产结构比较高的阶段，创新应该更多地偏向发明创新。因此，在每一个发展阶段都有一个最优的技术进步或技术创新结构与之相对应，最优的创新结构随发展阶段的提高而不断升级。

付才辉、林炜和林毅夫的一项跨国实证研究支持上述最优创新结构（以专利结构即发明专利与其他类型专利数量之比度量创新结构）的理论，如图3.10所示。[①]以中美为例，这种创新结构的差异一目了然，如表3.3和表3.4所示：2011—2016年中美两国的专利结构差异巨大，中国发明专利比重只有1/3左右，而美国超过90%。与研发产出相对应，研发支出比重也展现类似的结论，发展水平越高研发支出比重也就越大。图3.12展现了近20多年来全球一些经济体的研发支出占GDP的比重的变化趋势比较。我们可以看到：欧美发达经济体的

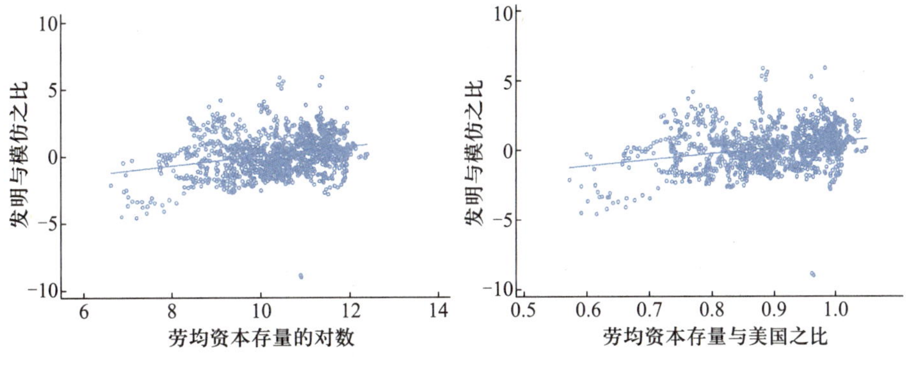


**图3.10 禀赋结构及其前沿距离与创新结构：1980—2011年全球所有样本观测值散点图**

资料来源：付才辉等（2015）。

① 付才辉、林炜、林毅夫，“The Optimal Innovation Structure: Theory and Evidence from World and China”，北京大学新结构经济学研究中心工作论文，2015年。

研发支出比重远超新兴发展中经济体；韩国这个我们反复举例的成功转型的经济体的研发支出比重在20世纪90年代初期远低于美国和日本，但是现阶段其比重已经超过后者；中国同样如此，在20世纪90年代初期远低于OCED经济体的平均水平，但时下已经超过后者。在付才辉、林炜和林毅夫的实证研究中，如果以OECD样本作为最优创新结构变迁轨迹的近似，那么对最优创新结构的偏离就不利于经济增长，如表3.5所示。按此回归，如中国在2005年之前存在创新赶超而此后存在创新不足。因此，在新的发展阶段，由于禀赋结构的改变，中国加大创新力度，尤其是增强发明专利比重的创新结构转型升级势在必行。如图3.11所示，与中国相反，俄罗斯存在严重的技术赶超。苏联的科技水平是众所周知的。在20世纪80年代末，苏联的科技人员有150万人，相当于世界总数的1/4，每年的新技术发明约占世界总数的1/3。然而，这些技术创新违背了当时苏联的要素禀赋结构所决定的比较优势，难以产生实际的经济效益，苏联的科技成果中只有1/4在经济中得以应用。①

表3.3 中国的专利结构

| 年份 | 专利申请 | | | | | |
|---|---|---|---|---|---|---|
| | 发明专利 | 所占比重（%） | 外观设计专利 | 实用新型专利 | 植物专利 | 总计 |
| 2016 | 133.850 3 | 38.6 | 65.034 4 | 147.597 7 | | 346.482 4 |
| 2015 | 110.186 4 | 39.4 | 56.905 9 | 112.757 7 | | 279.850 0 |
| 2014 | 92.817 7 | 39.3 | 56.155 5 | 86.851 1 | | 235.824 3 |
| 2013 | 82.513 6 | 34.7 | 65.956 3 | 89.236 2 | | 237.706 1 |
| 2012 | 65.277 7 | 31.8 | 65.758 2 | 74.029 0 | | 205.064 9 |
| 2011 | 52.641 2 | 32.2 | 52.146 8 | 58.546 7 | | 163.334 7 |

数据来源：国家知识产权局。

表3.4 美国的专利结构

| 年份 | 专利申请 | | | | | |
|---|---|---|---|---|---|---|
| | 发明专利 | 所占比重（%） | 外观设计专利 | 实用新型专利 | 植物专利 | 总计 |
| 2016 | 60.775 3 | 93.4 | 4.040 6 | | 0.118 0 | 64.933 9 |
| 2015 | 58.941 0 | 93.6 | 3.909 7 | | 0.114 0 | 62.964 7 |
| 2014 | 57.880 2 | 94.1 | 3.537 8 | | 0.106 3 | 61.524 3 |
| 2013 | 57.161 2 | 93.9 | 3.603 4 | | 0.140 6 | 60.905 2 |

① 萧国亮、隋福民，《世界经济史》，第400页，北京大学出版社，2007年版。

续表

| 年份 | 专利申请 | | | | | |
|---|---|---|---|---|---|---|
| | 发明专利 | 所占比重（%） | 外观设计专利 | 实用新型专利 | 植物专利 | 总计 |
| 2012 | 54.281 5 | 94.1 | 3.279 9 | | 0.114 9 | 57.676 3 |
| 2011 | 50.358 2 | 94.1 | 3.046 7 | | 0.113 9 | 53.518 8 |

数据来源：美国专利商标局（USPTO）。

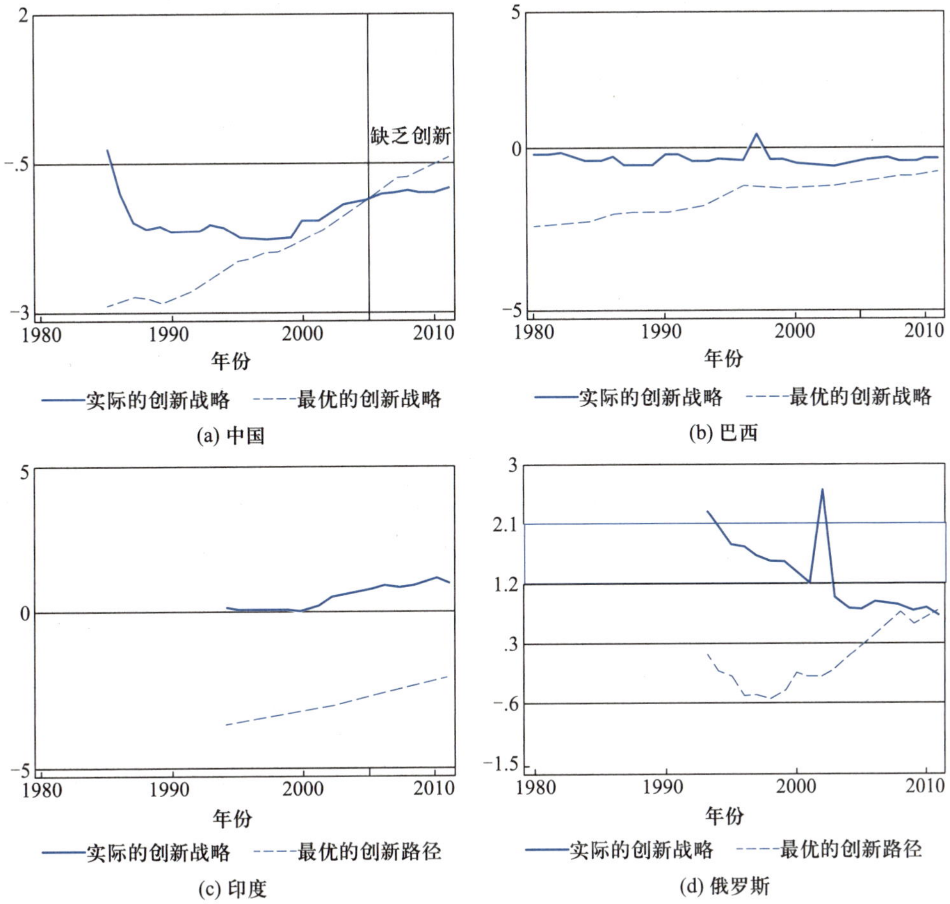


图 3.11 实际的创新结构与拟合的最优创新结构变迁轨迹比较

资料来源：付才辉等（2015）。

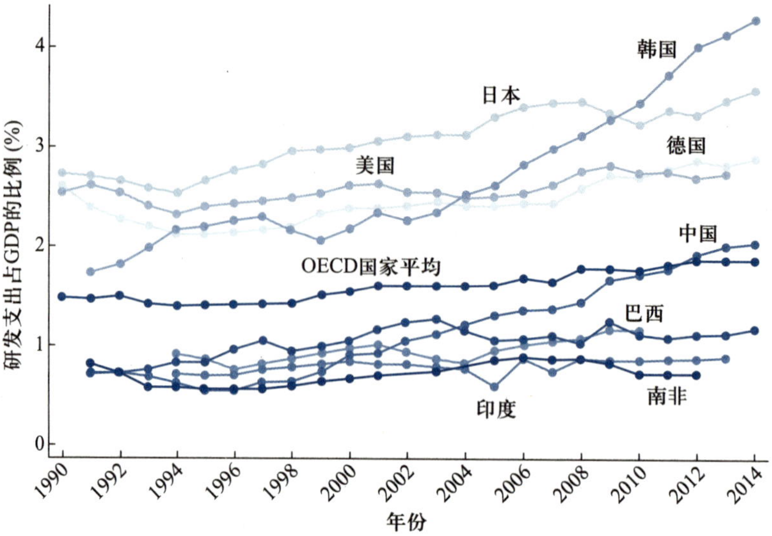


**图3.12 世界一些经济体的研发支出占GDP比重比较**

资料来源：Shangjin Wei, Zhuan Xie, Xiaobo Zhang, "From 'Made in China' to 'Innovated in China': Necessity, Prospect, and Challenges", *Journal of Economic Perspectives*, 2017, Vol.31, No.1, pp.49–70.

表3.5 对最优创新结构的偏离（*Gap*）与经济增长的回归结果

| 项目 | （1） | （2） | （3） | （4） |
|---|---|---|---|---|
| 被解释变量：经济增长率 | OLS（最小二乘回归） | QR_25（分位数回归） | QR_50（分位数回归） | QR_75（分位数回归） |
| 对最优创新结构的偏离程度的对数 | −0.004** | −0.003*** | −0.003*** | −0.002*** |
| | （0.002） | （0.000） | （0.000） | （0.000） |
| 前沿距离 | −0.348** | −0.169*** | −0.390*** | −0.213*** |
| | （0.160） | （0.000） | （0.000） | （0.000） |
| 人力资本 | 0.037 | 0.028*** | 0.031*** | 0.022*** |
| | （0.025） | （0.000） | （0.000） | （0.000） |
| 人口的对数 | −0.070** | 0.031*** | −0.013*** | −0.030*** |
| | （0.032） | （0.000） | （0.000） | （0.000） |
| 全要素生产率 | 0.104*** | 0.118*** | 0.022*** | 0.073*** |
| | （0.038） | （0.000） | （0.000） | （0.000） |
| 人均GDP的对数 | −0.004 | 0.005*** | 0.051*** | −0.001*** |
| | （0.024） | （0.000） | （0.000） | （0.000） |
| 国家效应 | Y | Y | Y | Y |
| 年份效应 | Y | Y | Y | Y |
| 常数项 | 0.361** | −0.164*** | −0.300*** | −0.025*** |
| | （0.170） | （0.000） | （0.000） | （0.000） |
| 样本量 | 1 228 | 1 228 | 1 228 | 1 228 |
| R-squared | 0.177 | | | |
| 国家数目 | 87 | | | |

注：Standard errors in parentheses*** $p < 0.01$，** $p < 0.05$，* $p < 0.1$.

### 3.3.4 经济结构变迁是一个连续的循序渐进过程

因此，将经济发展视为一个连续统一的过程，新结构经济学包含了对一国比较优势的理解，这种比较优势受制于要素禀赋结构的不断演化。[①]这意味着，与结构主义不同的是，新结构经济学强调，某时某地某个具体的发展中国家可供选择的产业结构不一定非得是经济前沿国家最先进、最发达的产业——后果可能适得其反。一个国家的资源要素禀赋结构决定了其比较优势，因此该国的最优产业结构也会因为发展水平的不同而存在差异。不同的产业结构意味着各个产业的资本密度、最优企业规模、产量规模、市场范围、交易复杂程度以及风险性质都存在差异。所以，对于发展中国家而言，要持续快速地资本积累，提升要素禀赋结构，改变比较优势，支持产业升级和经济增长、在国内外市场上形成竞争力，其最佳途径就是发展适应自身当前要素禀赋结构所决定的具有比较优势的产业。一个国家如果能够按照比较优势发展，就能够在自己的发展阶段创造最大的收入，使投资能获得最高可能的回报，产生最大的储蓄动力，则其资本也就能以最快的速度积累。这样，该国的要素禀赋结构就能从劳动力或资源富余向资本富余过渡，其比较优势也会变得相应更趋向于资本密集型，劳动生产率和收入水平也会相应不断提高。后进国家的产业升级可以发挥后来者优势，在技术创新、产业升级和经济发展方面比领先者拥有更大的潜力。然而，要使得企业家为了自身的利益自发在每一阶段按照禀赋结构决定的比较优势选择最优产业结构，禀赋结构的相对稀缺程度就必须被反映在各种要素相对价格的高低之上。而只有市场价格机制才能够产生这样的相对价格信息。与此同时，任何一种产业结构都要求相应的软硬件基础设施来使得其生产潜力得以发挥。硬件基础设施包括电力、交通和电信系统等，软件基础设施则包括金融体系及其监管、教育体系、法律体系、社会网络、价值观以及经济中的其他无形构造等。最优产业结构决定着一个国家的生产边界，实际产量能否达到这个边界，则取决于软硬基础设施是否完备。由于软硬基础设施具有公共品的特性，以及产业升级中的协调困难、信息外部性、风险等市场失灵的原因，因此就要求政府在完善软硬基础设施和产业升级中起到因势利导、克服

---

① 这是新结构经济学与早期结构变迁文献和旧结构主义重要的区别之处。罗斯托著名的增长阶段理论将所有国家都纳入五个增长阶段：传统社会、为发动创造前提条件阶段、发动阶段、向成熟推进阶段、大众消费时代。所有的发展中国家都要经历一个类似的发展水平序列和发展路径。与之不同，新结构经济学认为，从低水平到高水平的经济发展是一个连续过程，并非五个不同水平的机械序列。尽管一国产业结构的变迁反映了该国禀赋结构的变化，但是在禀赋结构类似的国家，产业发展的方式可以是不同的和非线性的。结构主义也将世界划分为“低收入的外围国家”和“高收入的中心国家”两类，也相应地用两分法来描述发展中国家和发达国家之间产业结构的差异。与之相反，新结构经济学则认为发展中国家和发达国家之间产业结构的这种差异反映了处于一整个谱线上的不同发展水平（W. W. 罗斯托，《经济增长的阶段：非共产党宣言》，中国社会科学出版社，2001年版）。

市场失灵的作用。总之，就像我们接下来将要揭示的全球近两百个经济体经济结构转型升级轨迹的情况那样，但凡产业发展次序颠倒紊乱者，无一例外惨遭失败。如果在经济结构转型升级过程中缺乏“有效市场”和“有为政府”，转型升级也无一成功。这就是我们在第1章的图1.21所示的经济结构转型升级的新结构经济学之路中，要标示“有效市场”和“有为政府”，也就是经济结构变迁的发展战略动态路径的两个方向盘的原因。

正如中国地方经济发展能手重庆市前市长黄奇帆在2017年的全国政协会议上所言：“产业升级没有捷径可走，现代服务业尤其是生产性服务业，必须依托工业特别是制造业的需求衍生开来，脱离制造业的服务业，永远只能囿于传统服务业的范畴，不可能成为真正的现代服务业。……服务业与制造业是相辅相成的，任何脱离实体经济‘卡拉OK’、自弹自唱的行为都不可持续，还会带来巨大伤害。”纵观整个工业革命以来的历史，除了几个矿产资源生产大国，任何成功国家经济结构的转型次序都需要遵从劳动力密集型产业到资本密集型产业、从轻工业到重工业、从低端制造业到高端制造业再到金融服务业，都需要从农村市场到城市市场、从消费品市场到生产资料市场，从高储蓄到高福利的这样一个循序渐进的经济结构转型升级次序。各个经济发展阶段都是从低收入农业国向高收入工业国连续演进过程的一个点，而不能把两个阶段——贫穷阶段和富裕阶段，发展中阶段和发达阶段，完全割裂开来。由于各个发展阶段的产业结构的内生性，发展中国家的产业和基础设施升级的目标与高收入国家未必相同。

# 3.4

## 历史上不同经济结构变迁方式的经验教训

### 3.4.1 历史上那些颠倒产业发展次序的惨痛教训①

在20世纪五六十年代，不少发展中国家的领导人制定了雄心勃勃的政策目标，为什么却导致了失败的发展战略设计？要回答这个问题，我们需要回到长期宏观经济分析的起点——对要素禀赋结构的主要特征进行回顾。通常来说，发展中国家拥有相对丰富的自然资源和非熟练劳动力，但人力资本和物质资本匮乏。在开放的竞争市场中，只有劳动力密集型或资源密集型产业才拥有比较优势。相反，对于资本丰富但劳动力相对稀缺的发达国家，资本密集型产业最有竞争力。只有承认这条基本事实，才能给制定有效的发展战略奠定坚实的基础。可是，第二次世界大战后大多数发展中国家领导人采用的发展模式却借鉴了20世纪五六十年代发展经济学的主流思想——结构主义，鼓励发展中国家兴办与高收入工业化国家一样的先进产业。这一思路通常显得非常冠冕堂皇，领导人拥有促进国家发展的远大理想，希望本国尽快加入国际技术前沿的竞争。但这是一个致命的错误。结构主义模式就是我们所说的违背比较优势的发展战略，因为它是在资本非常稀缺的时候，仍建议各国发展资本密集型的重工业。该战略意味着，与其他顺应比较优势而发展类似产业的国家相比，发展中国家的生产成本过高。这些生产成本过高的企业在开放的竞争市场中缺乏自生能力，因此，需要政府通过补贴和税收激励等措施提供大量保护。此类战略的例子包括：印度尼西亚在60年代兴办造船业，当时的人均GDP水平仅为主要竞争国的10%；刚果民主共和国（当时称扎伊尔）在70年代试图发展汽车产业，该国的人均GDP仅为产业领先国家的5%（见表3.6）。这些国家的战略的共同之处在于，它们希望发展的产业，是人均收入远高于自己的国家擅长的产业。由于生产这些产品不具备成本优势，它们难以在市场上有竞争力。为推行此类不符合比较优势的发展战略，这些国家的政府给大量亏损企业提供保护，减少其投资和运营成本，

① 可进一步参考林毅夫所著的《中国的奇迹：发展战略与经济改革》与《发展与转型：思潮、战略与自生能力》对中国和世界各个经济体赶超战略的详细论述。

包括授予市场垄断权、压低利率水平、高估本国货币价值，以及控制原材料价格等。干预导致资金、外汇和原材料的普遍短缺。结果，政府还不得不通过行政渠道给这些企业直接提供资源，包括社会主义国家实行的全国计划，以及其他发展中国家实行的信贷配额和投资、产业准入许可等。为便于实施，许多国家还依赖国有企业来发展目标产业。

表3.6 历史上那些不切实际的赶超战略

| 计划发展的产业 | 时间 | 后进国家 | 当时的主要生产国 | 后进国家的实际人均GDP | 领先国家的实际人均GDP | 后进国家人均GDP占领先国家的百分比（%） |
|---|---|---|---|---|---|---|
| 汽车 | 20世纪50年代 | 中国 | 美国 | 577 | 10 897 | 5 |
| 汽车 | 20世纪70年代 | 刚果民主共和国 | 美国 | 761 | 16 284 | 5 |
| 汽车 | 20世纪50年代 | 印度 | 美国 | 676 | 10 897 | 6 |
| 汽车 | 20世纪50年代 | 土耳其 | 美国 | 2 093 | 10 897 | 19 |
| 汽车 | 20世纪70年代 | 赞比亚 | 美国 | 1 041 | 16 284 | 6 |
| 钢铁、化工 | 20世纪50年代 | 埃及 | 美国 | 885 | 10 897 | 8 |
| 造船 | 20世纪60年代 | 印度尼西亚 | 荷兰 | 983 | 9 798 | 10 |
| 卡车 | 20世纪60年代 | 塞内加尔 | 美国 | 1 511 | 13 419 | 11 |

资料来源：根据Maddison的数据测算。

上述论断在战后的发展中经济体是非常普遍的，我们不妨再回到第2章的图2.17和图2.18中，可以一目了然。在世界银行有数据记录的战后15年的1960年，平均而言，即便是发展中经济体，农业占GDP的比重也下降到较低的水平，中低收入国家为28.04%，中等收入国家为27.95%，中高等收入国家为24.95%。在前现代社会农业文明巅峰的亚洲大陆也出现了类似情况，东亚与太平洋地区（不包括高收入）的农业比重下降到24.68%，南亚下降到42.70%。在世界银行有数据记录的经济体中，只有极少数农业比重依然超过50%的经济体，包括莱索托（88.18%）、尼日尔（75.32%）、索马里（64.45%）、孟加拉国（57.47%）、土耳其（54.92%）、多哥（54.88%）、苏丹（51.43%）；农业比重接近50%的经济体还有乌干达（49.87%）、马拉维（48.37%）、科特迪瓦（47.91%）、贝宁（46.16%）、毛里塔尼亚（46.00%）、马来西亚（43.72%）、巴基斯坦（43.68%）、博茨瓦纳（43.22%）、印度（41.79%）、加纳（40.85%）、乍得（39.72 %）、布基纳法索（38.48%）、泰国（36.44%）、韩国（36.23%）、肯尼亚（35.35%）、洪都拉斯（33.81%）、加蓬（32.19%）、斯里兰卡（32.10%）、斯威士兰（31.53%）。还有一些发展中经济体在1960年的农业比重下降得令人印象深刻：厄瓜多尔只有29.15%、菲律宾只有26.94%、哥斯达黎加只有26.03%、伊朗只有25.90%、刚果（布）只有23.60%、圭亚那只有23.58%、中国只有23.18%、塞内加尔只有22.11%、秘鲁只有19.05%、阿尔及利亚只有18.58%、巴西只有17.67%、赞比亚只有11.46%、南非只有10.66%、苏里南只有10.12%、智利只有9.91%，作为岛国的新加坡则只有微不足道的3.71%。这些发展中经济体在战后头15年的农业占比下降的快速的重要原因是“结构主义”发展思潮，其强调工业化赶超。然而，这种结构变迁方式是违背比较优势的，难以持续，因此我们在图2.15中可以明显看到整个20世纪60年代这些经济体的农业占比甚至又出现倒退。中国便是典型例子，1960年的农业占比虽然下降到23.18%，但是到1968年又回到41.64%。这种曲折的结构变迁便是激进的工业化的结果。1960年中国的工业比重高达44.39%，超过中等收入国家近10个百分点，超过中高等收入国家近7个百分点。显然，这样的工业化是不可持续的，因此到了1968年工业比重又退回到了31.11%。图2.16显示了发展中经济体出现的类似情况。图2.16还显示出了20世纪80年代以后的几个工业化结构变迁的典型特征事实：第一个严峻的特征事实是，低收入经济体依然尚未启动持续的工业化，到20世纪80年代中后期，低收入经济体工业比重依然不足20%。撒哈拉以南非洲地区甚至从20世纪80年代出现了不可思议的去工业化，1981—1989年其平均工业比重为41.84%，到20世纪90年代其平均工业比重下降到了33.06%、下降了约8个百分点。21世纪以后，撒哈拉以南非洲地区的工业化依然面临严峻的挑战，其比重从2000年的33.06%持续下降到2017年的23.29%。第二显著的特征事实是，一些低收入和中等收入经济体“过早去工业化”。[①]这实际上是在“华盛顿共识”思潮下发展中经济体在进口替代战略下建立起来的违反比较优势的制造业在取消补贴以后无法生存而退出生产，符合比较优势的制造业则缺乏政府积极有为的因势利导去克服软硬基础设施的瓶颈限制而无法涌现的结果。第三个显著特征是，高收入经济体出现了温和的后工业化，普遍开启了服务业占主导的经济结构，如图2.17所示，但是其依然具备坚实的工业化基础。例如，2017年高收入国家的工业比重依然高达22.9%，美国的工业比重也高达18.88%。

### 3.4.2 历史上那些遵循产业发展次序的成功经验[②]

与前述的颠倒产业发展次序而追赶失败的历史例子截然相反，19世纪西欧工业化的传播、第二次世界大战后经济的快速追赶以及20世纪80年代至90年代的东亚经济奇迹表明，凭借

---

① Dani Rodrik, “Premature Deindustrialization”, *Journal of Economic Growth*, 2016 Vol.21, No.1, pp. 1–33.

② 本小节的主要内容转引自：Vandana Chandra、林毅夫、王燕，“领头龙现象：低收入国家赶超式发展的新机遇”，《劳动经济研究》，2013年第1期；林毅夫，《从西潮到东风》，中信出版社，2012年版，第9章。

自身的比较优势去更好地利用后来者优势是发展中国家开启和维持动态增长路径并最终实现多样化和工业化的最佳途径。工业革命始于18世纪的英国，但是之后的约50年内，工业革命并没有传播到其他的国家。其原因主要是英国政府禁止输出机械、制造技术和熟练工人。最终，工业革命在19世纪才逐渐传播到西欧的其他国家。欧洲大陆最早的工业生产中心是煤、铁、纺织品、玻璃和其他装备的生产均很繁荣的比利时。到1830年，法国公司雇用了许多熟练的英国工人帮助建立纺织业，铁路也开始在西欧地区出现。而德国当时由于缺乏集权的中央政府，是工业发展的后来者。虽然英国人1804年就发明了第一台蒸汽机车，但是直到19世纪30年代，其他欧洲国家才开始修建铁路。比如，德国于1835年制成第一台机车，但其铁路建设由于缺乏中央集权政府而被一再拖延。1840年后德国的煤炭和钢铁产量大幅上升，到了19世纪50年代，德国开始修建铁路网。在1871年德国实现政治统一后，其新修建的铁路里程超过了英国，同时在生铁和其他行业也进入了一个快速的追赶通道。相对于英国，美国的工业化由于当时缺乏商业投资所需的基本要素禀赋——劳动力和资本，而被推迟了。但当其在19世纪20年代终于开始进行工业化时，其增长速度是爆炸性的。欧洲的政治革命使大量移民将劳动力和资本带入美国。1826年，美国开始出现机车；1837年，美国第一条铁路建成；1850年，美国的铁路总里程超过了英国，达到9 021英里；到1890年，铁路在美国西部地区的迅速扩张使其总里程达到129 774英里，这一距离比整个欧洲大陆的铁路总和还要长。随后，美国迅速进行了工业化和结构转型，农业人口的比重从1800年的85%下降到1860年的50%。著名经济史学家Gerschenkron观察到，快速工业化可以从不同层次的“经济落后”开始。事实上，越是经济落后的国家，那些特殊的制度性因素（如政府和银行）在向新兴产业增加资本时起到的作用越大。然而，以Gerschenkron为代表的结构主义发展思想存在不足，即没有强调一个后进经济体如果想拥有竞争力，必须发掘与它的比较优势相吻合的产业，或者说必须符合比较优势战略。工业化的确可以从低水平的经济发展期起步，但是如果发展水平太低，那些过于先进的产业不符合该经济体的比较优势，或者说这些产业是违背比较优势战略的，那么发展这些产业则需要大量的国家保护和政府补贴。通过政府的支持，先进产业的确有可能建立起来，但如果该产业是违背比较优势的，它将既没有自生能力也没有比较优势，只能靠政府以干预扭曲为代价的保护补贴才能生存，结果是资源配置低效和寻租腐败，即使把这样的产业建立起来也不可持续，最终导致经济停滞和各种危机。①

工业革命的历史经验提供了如下几点启示：第一，像英国这样处于技术前沿的国家可以

---

① Lin Justin Yifu, “The Latecomer Advantages and Disadvantages: A New Structural Economics Perspective”, in Martin Andersson and Tobias Axelsson eds. *Diverse Development Paths and Structural Transformation in Escape from Poverty*. Cambridge University Press, 2016, pp. 43–67.

发挥“领头雁”的作用，而后来者具有后来者优势，并在某些条件下能够赶超甚至取代“领头雁”的位置。第二，资本积累是经济发展取得成功的必要条件但不是充分条件，政治稳定、贸易开放和劳动力流动也是一个国家获取新技术和发展新产业的重要因素。第三，政府在发展的过程中必须起到促进作用，德国、日本和美国的发展就是很好的例证。如果德国1871年没有实现中央集权，贯穿全国的铁路或者工业革命就无从谈起。更为重要的是，要选择正确的目标国家进行追赶。一些欧洲国家之所以能够比较快地赶上英国，是因为它们的发展阶段离“领头雁”差得并不太远。根据Maddison的估计，法国、德国和美国在1870年的人均GDP是英国的60%至75%。在明治维新时期，日本的人均收入约是其目标国普鲁士（即后来的德国）的40%，这个目标是切合实际的。而在当时无论是英国还是美国，其发展阶段都大大超前于日本，选择那些国家作为追赶对象明显不切实际。尽管当时很多国家试图进行赶超，但日本最终成为亚洲第一个工业化国家，其成功的原因就在于选择了正确的赶超目标。

历史经验告诉我们，追赶型产业政策失败，通常是因为该国试图以人均收入5倍于本国或更高的国家的产业为学习样本。而成功的追赶国家的产业政策，基本都以其他要素禀赋结构类似、人均收入稍高国家的产业为学习样本（参考表3.7）：

- 16和17世纪，英国以荷兰的产业为样本，当时英国的人均GDP是荷兰的70%。
- 19世纪末，德国、法国、美国以英国的产业为样本；当时这些国家的人均收入是英国的60%~75%。
- 明治维新时期，日本以普鲁士的产业为样本，当时日本的人均GDP是普鲁士的40%左右；20世纪60年代，日本以美国的产业为样本，当时日本的人均GDP是美国的40%左右。
- 20世纪60—80年代，亚洲“四小龙”以日本的产业为样本，它们的人均收入是日本的30%左右。
- 20世纪70年代，毛里求斯以中国香港的纺织和服装业为样本，其人均收入大概是中国香港的50%左右。
- 20世纪80年代，爱尔兰以美国的信息、电子、化工、医药产业为样本，其人均收入大约是美国的45%。
- 20世纪90年代，哥斯达黎加以中国台湾的存储器封装和测试产业为样本，其人均GDP是中国台湾的40%，而中国台湾是该行业的主要生产地区。

表3.7 战前和战后时代的赶超（人均GDP以1900年国际元计价）

| | 欧陆国家以英国为目标 | | 明治维新时日本以普鲁士（后来的德国）为目标 | | | 第二次世界大战后日本以美国为目标 | | |
|---|---|---|---|---|---|---|---|---|
| | 1870年 | 相当于英国的比例（%） | 1890年 | 1900年 | 相当于普鲁士（后来的德国）的比例（%） | 1950年 | 1960年 | 相当于美国的比例（%） |
| 法国 | 1 876 | 59 | 2 376 | 2 876 | | 5 186 | 7 398 | |
| 德国 | 1 839 | 58 | 2 428 | 2 985 | 100 | 3 881 | 7 705 | |
| 英国 | 3 190 | 100 | 4 009 | 4 492 | | 6 939 | 8 645 | |
| 美国 | 2 445 | 77 | 3 392 | 4 091 | | 9 561 | 11 328 | 100 |
| 日本 | 737 | | 1 012 | 1 180 | 40 | 1 921 | 3 986 | 35 |

| | 20世纪60年代到80年代亚洲“四小龙”以日本为目标 | | | 中国内地以亚洲“四小龙”为目标 | | | 2000年后后来者以中国内地为目标 | | |
|---|---|---|---|---|---|---|---|---|---|
| | 1960年 | 1970年 | 相当于日本的比例（%） | 1980年 | 1990年 | 相当于韩国的比例（%） | 2000年 | 2008年 | 相当于中国内地的比例（%） |
| 英国 | 8 645 | 10 767 | | 12 931 | 16 430 | | 20 353 | 23 742 | |
| 美国 | 11 328 | 15 030 | | 18 577 | 23 201 | | 28 467 | 31 178 | |
| 日本 | 3 986 | 9 714 | 100 | 13 428 | 18 789 | | 20 738 | 22 816 | |
| 韩国 | 1 226 | 2 167 | 25 | 4 114 | 8 704 | 100 | 14 375 | 19 614 | |
| 中国内地 | 662 | 778 | | 1 061 | 1 871 | 23 | 3 421 | 6 725 | 100 |
| 印度 | 753 | 868 | | 938 | 1 309 | | 1 892 | 2 975 | 44 |
| 越南 | 799 | 735 | | 757 | 1 025 | | 1 809 | 2 970 | 44 |

资料来源：Vandana Chandra、林毅夫、王燕，“领头龙现象：低收入国家赶超式发展的新机遇”，《劳动经济研究》，2013年第1期。

### 3.4.3 结构扭曲与经济停滞：全球的经验实证①

战后至今绝大多数发展中经济体由于深受战后第一波结构主义发展思潮和第二波新自由主义发展思潮的影响而深陷发展陷阱中，只有少数不按当时主流思潮发展的经济体取得了成功。其原因是我们反复强调的，第一代结构主义主张的发展战略违背比较优势而扭曲经济结构，第二代新自由主义主张的改革忽视了扭曲的内生性并自废武功地消除了政府的因势利导

① 陈斌开、伏霖，“发展战略与经济停滞”，《世界经济》，2018年第1期，第52–77页。

作用。陈斌开和伏霖从结构变迁违背比较优势的角度对全球经济增长停滞进行了测算和实证检验（见表3.8）。结构变迁违背比较优势程度的常用测度指标是TCI指数。① 如图3.13和表3.9所示，经济结构变迁越是违背比较优势，后续的经济增长越乏力，尤其是对于发展中经济体而言。如果经济增长长期乏力，就会出现经济增长停滞（例如定义7年内人均GDP增长率低于1%则可视为增长停滞）。

表3.8 人均GDP达到美国1/4之后的经济体的增长情况

| 经济停滞经济体 | | | 经济持续增长经济体 | | |
|---|---|---|---|---|---|
| 经济体 | 25%年份 | 之后20年人均GDP增长率（%） | 经济体 | 25%年份 | 之后20年人均GDP增长率（%） |
| 阿根廷 | 1993 | 4.2 | 中国香港 | 1963 | 6.3 |
| 保加利亚 | 1975 | 2.3 | 日本 | 1957 | 7.5 |
| 巴西 | 1996 | 2.34 | 韩国 | 1986 | 6.77 |
| 阿尔及利亚 | 1987 | 1.9 | 中国台湾 | 1975 | 7.3 |
| 智利 | 1961 | 2.4 | 新加坡 | 1970 | 6.6 |
| 加蓬 | 1973 | 2.06 | 塞浦路斯 | 1975 | 7.26 |
| 格鲁吉亚 | 1991 | 1.45 | 西班牙 | 1950 | 5.9 |
| 牙买加 | 1970 | −1.06 | 葡萄牙 | 1960 | 4.7 |
| 墨西哥 | 1953 | 3.46 | 希腊 | 1956 | 5.96 |
| 墨西哥 | 1997 | 2.4 | 马耳他 | 1975 | 5.05 |
| 毛里求斯 | 1989 | 2.9 | 波兰 | 1989 | 4 |
| 马来西亚 | 1984 | 3.4 | 波兰 | 1994 | 4.87 |
| 匈牙利 | 1975 | 3.9 | 爱沙尼亚 | 1992 | 5.51 |
| 纳米比亚 | 1964 | −0.2 | 爱沙尼亚 | 1999 | 6.4 |
| 尼日利亚 | 1974 | −10.3 | 罗马尼亚 | 2007 | 6.4 |
| 泰国 | 2009 | 3.53 | 俄罗斯 | 2007 | 5.6 |
| 土耳其 | 1952 | 3.15 | 土库曼斯坦 | 2008 | 11.14 |
| 土耳其 | 1964 | 2.56 | 立陶宛 | 2000 | 6.64 |
| 土耳其 | 1998 | 3.47 | 拉脱维亚 | 2001 | 6.04 |
| 乌克兰 | 1992 | 1.13 | 哈萨克斯坦 | 2006 | 8.6 |
| 乌拉圭 | 1986 | 1.44 | 阿根廷 | 2002 | 4.53 |
| 委内瑞拉 | 1985 | 1.15 | 巴西 | 2009 | 4.96 |
| 委内瑞拉 | 2007 | 3.04 | 智利 | 1994 | 4.1 |
| 南非 | 1986 | 1.38 | 马来西亚 | 1992 | 4.46 |

数据来源：陈斌开和伏霖根据PWT9.0测算。

① TCI指数以工业的劳均GDP比上整个经济的劳均GDP，指数越大说明工业赶超程度越大。

表3.9 初始发展战略（TCI）对长期经济增长和经济停滞的影响

| 解释变量 | （1）<br>经济增长<br>全部 | （2）<br>经济增长<br>发展中 | （3）<br>经济停滞<br>全部 | （4）<br>经济停滞<br>发展中 | （5）<br>经济增长<br>全部 | （6）<br>经济增长<br>发展中 | （7）<br>经济停滞<br>全部 | （8）<br>经济停滞<br>发展中 |
|---|---|---|---|---|---|---|---|---|
| TCI_1965 | −0.632*** | −0.663*** | 0.159 | 0.085 4 | | | | |
| | （0.195） | （0.209） | （0.143） | （0.113） | | | | |
| 1965年人均GDP的对数 | −3.695*** | −3.484** | 0.974 | 0.57 | | | | |
| | （1.213） | （1.568） | （0.661） | （0.487） | | | | |
| TCI_1970 | | | | | −0.418*** | −0.426*** | 0.426*** | 0.407*** |
| | | | | | （0.084 4） | （0.085 6） | （0.154） | （0.131） |
| 1970人均GDP对数 | | | | | −2.306*** | −2.068*** | 1.941*** | 1.492** |
| | | | | | （0.504） | （0.571） | （0.642） | （0.650） |
| 地区变量 | 是 | 是 | 是 | 是 | 是 | 是 | 是 | 是 |
| 常数项 | 34.72*** | 37.77** | −10.23 | −6.282 | 23.87*** | 23.44*** | −18.82*** | −15.15*** |
| | （11.45） | （14.47） | （6.595） | （4.614） | （4.846） | （5.455） | （6.369） | （6.124） |
| 样本量 | 42 | 28 | 39 | 25 | 55 | 41 | 55 | 41 |
| $R^2$ | 0.318 | 0.28 | — | — | 0.406 | 0.391 | — | — |

注：本表第（3）和第（4）系数不显著的主要原因可能是样本量太少。
资料来源：陈斌开和伏霖（2018）。

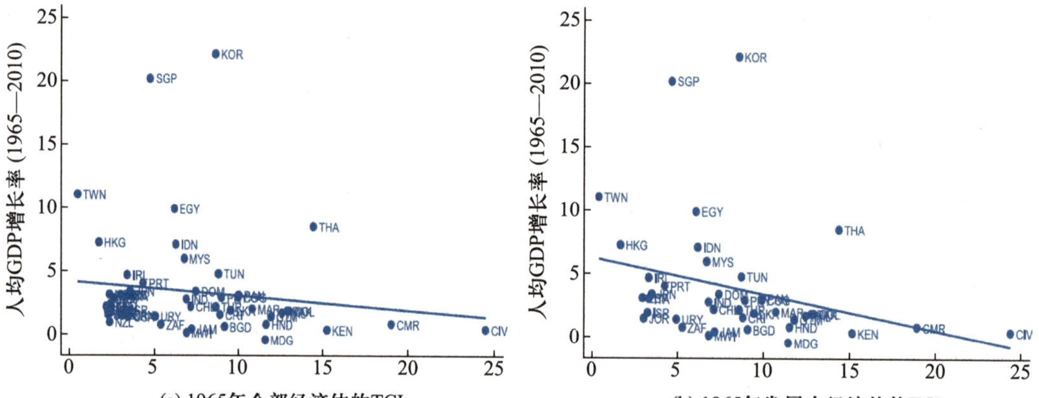


(a) 1965年全部经济体的TCI　　(b) 1965年发展中经济体的TCI

**图3.13 1965年的发展战略指数（TCI）与1965—2010年的经济增长率**

资料来源：陈斌开和伏霖（2018）。

## 3.5

## “付 – 林图”：测算经济结构变迁轨迹

按照前述产业发展的次序特征以及新结构经济学的基本原理，禀赋结构升级和产业结构升级是结构变迁的两条核心维度。并且，经济结构变迁是一个连续的动态过程，每一阶段都是这条连续谱上的一点。因此，在经济结构变迁连续空间中，一个经济体的经济结构转型升级轨迹或者发展战略路径可概括为：首先，在任意时点，给定的要素禀赋结构决定了其比较优势，进而决定了最优的产业结构；其次，按照比较优势进行的产业升级将使经济具有最强的竞争力，产生的剩余最大，进而禀赋结构升级最快；最后，禀赋结构升级之后，最优的产业结构也须升级。经济的发展就是如此往复的循序渐进过程。当然，在此过程中，其他软硬基础设施也需要随之升级，不然就会成为产业升级的瓶颈制约，影响现有产业在全球市场上的竞争力，难以将符合要素禀赋结构的潜在比较优势变成现实的比较优势①。这一新结构经济学的重要论断我们将在第7章讨论。因此，我们想重申的是“比较优势遵循型方法在本质上是动态的……这意味着一个国家的经济发展也该务实地利用现有的、嵌入在一国的比较优势领域中的机会，当那些领域的比较优势被充分利用后，同时也要认识到产业升级的潜力”②。这就是经济结构变迁的新结构经济学最核心的部分：包含了对一国比较优势的理解，这种比较优势受制于要素禀赋结构的不断演化。因此，图1.26中的经济结构变迁的轨迹或路径 $I_{it}=f(E_{it})$ 可描述如下：

$$\cdots\rightarrow \underbrace{E_{it}\rightarrow I_{it}}_{t\text{期的结构变迁轨迹}} \rightarrow \underbrace{E_{it+1}\rightarrow I_{it+1}}_{t+1\text{期的结构变迁轨迹}} \rightarrow\cdots\rightarrow \underbrace{E_{it+T}\rightarrow I_{it+T}}_{t+T\text{期的结构变迁轨迹}} \rightarrow\cdots \tag{3.1}$$

在式（3.1）刻画的经济结构转型升级路径中，如果每一阶段都采取遵循比较优势的发展战略 $I_{it}^{CAC}=f^{CAC}(E_{it})$，则其经济结构转型升级路径为

① 国际贸易理论中的比较优势一般只讨论生产成本，但是，在现实的经济中，市场的竞争还决定于软硬基础设施所决定的交易成本，若交易成本太高，在市场没有竞争力，这样的产业即使符合比较优势也不会存在。所以，要素禀赋结构所决定的比较优势只是潜在比较优势。

② 林毅夫，《新结构经济学：反思经济发展与政策的理论框架》，北京大学出版社，2012年版，第129页。

$$\cdots \to \underbrace{E_{it}^{\mathrm{CAC}} \to I_{it}^{\mathrm{CAC}}}_{t\text{期的结构变迁轨迹}} \to \underbrace{E_{it+1}^{\mathrm{CAC}} \to I_{it+1}^{\mathrm{CAC}}}_{t+1\text{期的结构变迁轨迹}} \to \cdots \to \underbrace{E_{it+T}^{\mathrm{CAC}} \to I_{it+T}^{\mathrm{CAC}}}_{t+T\text{期的结构变迁轨迹}} \to \cdots \tag{3.2}$$

反之，如果每一阶段都采取违背比较优势的发展战略$I_{it}^{\mathrm{CAD}} = f^{\mathrm{CAD}}(E_{it})$，则其经济结构转型升级路径为

$$\cdots \to \underbrace{E_{it}^{\mathrm{CAD}} \to I_{it}^{\mathrm{CAD}}}_{t\text{期的结构变迁轨迹}} \to \underbrace{E_{it+1}^{\mathrm{CAD}} \to I_{it+1}^{\mathrm{CAD}}}_{t+1\text{期的结构变迁轨迹}} \to \cdots \to \underbrace{E_{it+T}^{\mathrm{CAD}} \to I_{it+T}^{\mathrm{CAD}}}_{t+T\text{期的结构变迁轨迹}} \to \cdots \tag{3.3}$$

当然，实际的结构变迁轨迹或路径一般介于二者之间。因此，我们可以以遵循比较优势的结构变迁轨迹或路径（新结构经济学之路，即$I_{it}^{\mathrm{CAC}} = f^{\mathrm{CAC}}(E_{it})$）作为标杆来判断其偏离程度

$$\mathrm{Deviation}_{it} = I_{it} - I_{it}^{\mathrm{NSE}} = f(E_{it}) - f^{\mathrm{NSE}}(E_{it}) \tag{3.4}$$

如果$\mathrm{Deviation}_{it} > 0$，则说明在禀赋条件$E_{it}$下选择的产业结构$I_{it}$过于先进而违背了比较优势；如果$\mathrm{Deviation}_{it} < 0$，则说明在禀赋条件$E_{it}$下选择的产业结构$I_{it}$过于落后而失去了比较优势。如图1.26轨迹上下的区域所示。

为了定量刻画经济结构变迁轨迹或路径的特性，我们需要继续定义几个相关的概念。首先，我们定义结构变迁路径的斜率

$$\beta_{I_{it}E_{it}} = \frac{\partial I_{it}}{\partial E_{it}} = \frac{\partial f(E_{it})}{\partial E_{it}} = f'(E_{it}) \tag{3.5}$$

式（3.5）的含义是，在某一个时刻给定的禀赋条件$E_{it}$下，如果禀赋结构升级一单位，那么结构变迁路径斜率指的就是产业结构升级的程度。

其次，我们定义结构变迁路径的弹性

$$\eta_{I_{it}E_{it}} = \frac{\partial I_{it}}{\partial E_{it}}\frac{E_{it}}{I_{it}} = \frac{E_{it} \times f'(E_{it})}{I_{it}} = \frac{E_{it} \times f'(E_{it})}{f(E_{it})} \tag{3.6}$$

式（3.6）的含义是，在某一个时刻给定的禀赋条件$E_{it}$下，如果禀赋结构升级1%，那么结构变迁路径弹性指的就是产业结构升级的百分比。

结构变迁路径的斜率定量刻画了经济结构变迁步伐的大小，弹性定量刻画了经济结构变迁的敏感性。我们可以用这两个定量工具来测度新结构经济学主张的结构变迁的两个核心概念："比较优势"和"后来者优势"。

新结构经济学最重要也最饱受争议的是发展战略的比较优势分析方法。对于这一点，剑桥大学的张夏准评论道："实际上，我与毅夫的分歧主要在于，对比较优势何种程度的偏离在我们看来才是明智的。毅夫认为，攀登阶梯时对梯级的跳跃应非常小（以他的话来说，是'比较优势遵循型'的），但我相信跳跃可以而且有时不得不大一些（以他的话说，是'比较

优势违背型’的)。”[①]要争论和检验对比较优势是否应该偏离，我们首先得测度经济结构变迁轨迹偏离比较优势的程度。经济结构变迁路径斜率就是测度“攀登阶梯时对梯级的跳跃级数”，经济结构变迁路径弹性就是测度“攀登阶梯时跳跃的灵敏性”。如果结构变迁路径的斜率过大，则说明在攀登产业阶梯时跳跃的级数过多；如果结构变迁路径的弹性过大，则说明在攀登产业阶梯时跳跃的频度过大。此时二者均反映出可能违背了比较优势。

后来者优势可以用$\frac{\partial \beta_{I_{it}E_{it}}}{\partial E_{it}}<0$与$\frac{\partial \eta_{I_{it}E_{it}}}{\partial I_{it}}<0$两个性质来刻画：结构变迁路径的斜率和弹性会随着禀赋升级和产业升级而降低。如果处于经济结构变迁的前沿，斜率和弹性可能接近于零，表现出结构变迁路径随机游走的性质，说明经济发展的后来者优势逐渐消失。如果离经济结构变迁前沿越远，斜率和弹性越大，那就意味着经济发展的后来者优势越大。

在新结构经济学中，禀赋结构除了土地（或自然资源）、劳动力和资本（包括物质和人力资本），还包括（软硬件）基础设施。作为一个概括性的单一指标，我们记$y_{it}$为经济体（$i$）在某时刻（$t$）的禀赋水平（一般而言，可用人均国民收入或人均国内生产总值来综合性地概括）。我们以禀赋水平向世界前沿水平接近的程度来刻画禀赋结构升级程度，即

$$E_{it}=1-\mathrm{DE}_{it}=1-\left(1-\frac{y_{it}}{y_{\mathrm{USA},t}}\right)=\frac{y_{it}}{y_{\mathrm{USA},t}} \tag{3.7}$$

其中，$\mathrm{DE}_{it}=\left(1-\frac{y_{it}}{y_{\mathrm{USA},t}}\right)$为经济体$i$在时刻$t$与世界前沿的禀赋距离，$y_{\mathrm{USA},t}$为时刻$t$的世界前沿禀赋水平（一般而言，在第二次世界大战后可以美国作为世界前沿标杆）。

需要注意的是，如第1章第3小节和第4小节所介绍的，新结构经济学强调了禀赋结构升级（即发展阶段）是一个连续谱，即$E_{it}\in[0,1]\cup[1,\infty)$。如前一部分所言，处于初级发展阶段的国家（$E_{it}^{\mathrm{LDC}}\in[0,E_L]$），其要素禀赋结构一般会呈现出劳动力或自然资源相对丰富，同时资本相对稀缺的特点，也只有简单、初级的基础设施。位于发展阶段谱线另一端的高收入国家（$E_{it}^{\mathrm{DC}}\in[E_H,1]\cup[1,\infty)$），则呈现出一幅完全不同的禀赋结构图景。这些国家相对丰裕的要素不是劳动力，也不是自然资源，而是资本；各种硬件（电力、通信、道路、港口等）和软件（法律法规体系、文化价值系统等），基础设施也与全国性乃至全球性的市场活动相适应。当然，许多经济体大部分时候处于两端之间，即$E_{it}^{\mathrm{MDC}}\in[E_L,E_H]$。

在新结构经济学中，产业结构升级的核心内容是产业升级和产业多样性以及新技术的引入。作为一个概括性的单一指标，我们记$I_{it}$为经济体$i$在时刻$t$的产业结构水平。同样，我们

① 林毅夫,《新结构经济学：反思经济发展与政策的理论框架》，北京大学出版社，2012年版，第131页。

以产业结构水平向世界前沿水平接近的程度来刻画产业结构升级程度，即

$$I_{it}=1-\mathrm{DI}_{it}=1-\left(1-\frac{s_{it}}{s_{\mathrm{USA},t}}\right)=\frac{s_{it}}{s_{\mathrm{USA},t}} \tag{3.8}$$

其中，$\mathrm{DI}_{it}=\left(1-\frac{s_{it}}{s_{\mathrm{USA},t}}\right)$为经济体$i$在时刻$t$与世界前沿的产业距离，$s_{\mathrm{USA},\ t}$为时刻$t$的世界前沿产业结构水平（一般而言，在第二次世界大战后可以美国作为世界前沿标杆）。

同样，需要注意的是，新结构经济学强调了产业结构升级也是一个连续谱，即$I_{it}\in[0,\ 1]\cup[1,\ \infty)$。如前面的内容所讨论的，处于初级发展阶段的国家（$I_{it}^{\mathrm{LDC}}\in[0,\ I_L]$），生产也多集中于劳动力或资源密集型产业（如农业、畜牧业、渔业和采矿业），采用传统的、成熟的技术，生产"成熟的"产品。除了矿业和种植业，这些生产活动很少有规模经济。这些国家的企业规模一般而言相对较小，市场交换往往也不正规，通常仅限于在当地市场上跟熟人进行交易。位于发展阶段谱线另一端的高收入国家（$I_{it}^{\mathrm{DC}}\in[I_H,\ 1]\cup[1,\ \infty)$），则呈现出一幅完全不同的产业结构图景，具有资本密集与规模经济的特征，市场交易是远距离、大容量、高价值的。当然，许多经济体大部分时候处于两端之间，即$I_{it}^{\mathrm{MDC}}\in[I_L,\ I_H]$。

联立式（3.7）与式（3.8），我们可构建一个由禀赋升级和产业升级构成的二维连续空间

$$D_{it}=\left(E_{it},I_{it}\right)=\left(\frac{y_{it}}{y_{\mathrm{USA},t}},\frac{s_{it}}{s_{\mathrm{USA},t}}\right) \tag{3.9}$$

同样，需要注意的是，经济结构转型升级空间$D_{it}=$（$E_{it}$，$I_{it}$）的连续性反映了新结构经济学的要点之一："禀赋结构会随着发展阶段的不同而不同，产业结构也会随着发展阶段的不同而不同；经济发展阶段并非仅有'穷'与'富'（或'发展中'与'工业化'）这种两分的情况，而是从一条低收入水平的农业经济一直到高收入的后工业化经济的连续谱，经济发展的每一个水平都是这条连续谱上的一个点。"①

因此，尽管式（3.9）中的具体指标选择可以根据研究需要有一定的灵活性，但我们可以很方便地用其来追踪一个经济体在一定时期内的结构变迁轨迹，一目了然地观察其变迁路径的特征。文一教授将这个追踪结构变迁轨迹的工具称为"付-林图"。②

---

① 林毅夫，《新结构经济学：反思经济发展与政策的理论框架》，北京大学出版社，2012年版，第12页。

② 文一，"中国崛起的秘诀与挑战——'新制度经济学'批判"，《政治经济学报》第13卷，上海人民出版社，2018年12月；王丽莉、文一，"中国能跨越中等收入陷阱吗？——基于工业化路径的跨国比较"，《经济评论》，2017年第3期；Lili Wang & Yi Wen, "Escaping the Middle-Income Trap: A Cross-Country Analysis on the Patterns of Industrial Upgrading", Working Papers 2018-1, Federal Reserve Bank of St. Louis, revised 2018-01-01。

## 3.6

# 世界经济结构的变迁轨迹

### 3.6.1 禀赋结构升级与产业结构升级的指标

为了追踪结构变迁路径$D_{it}=(E_{it}, I_{it})$，我们必须测度禀赋结构升级和产业结构升级。如前所述，在新结构经济学中，禀赋结构除了土地（或自然资源）、劳动力和资本（包括物质和人力资本），还包括（软硬件）基础设施。作为一个概括性指标，可用人均国民收入或人均国内生产总值概括其发展水平或禀赋水平。[①]如图3.14所示，不同发展阶段的禀赋条件差距巨大。以购买力平价计算，美国2012年的人均国民总收入已超过50 000国际元，而最不发达国家的人均国民总收入却只有大约1 500国际元，二者相差30余倍。如果以现价美元计算，二者的差距会更大。根据式（3.8），我们用一个经济体$i$在时刻$t$的人均国内生产总值$y_{it}$与美国（USA）在时刻$t$的人均国内生产总值$y_{USA,t}$之比测度其禀赋升级程度：[②]

$$E_{it}=1-\mathrm{DE}_{it}=1-\left(1-\frac{y_{it}}{y_{\mathrm{USA},t}}\right)=\frac{y_{it}}{y_{\mathrm{USA},t}} \quad (3.10)$$

在新结构经济学中，产业结构升级的核心内容是产业升级与产业多样性，以及新技术的引入。秉承传统发展经济学的库兹涅茨事实，产业结构变迁具体可指经济体$i$在时刻$t$的非农业化（非农产业占比，即克拉克定律）、工业化（制造业占比）以及服务化（后工业化，即第三产业占比）。如图3.4以及上一章所刻画的产业结构变迁。鉴于大多数发展中国家的大多数人依然靠传统农业维持生计，以传统农业为主的农村部门和以非农产业为主的城市部门并存的城乡二元经济依然是发展中国家的基本特征，非农化首先需要成为产业结构升级的测度指标。根据式（3.9），我们用一个经济体$i$在时刻$t$的非农产业产值占比与美国（USA）在时刻$t$的非农产业产值占比$s_{USA,t}$之比测度其产业升级程度：

---

① 林毅夫，《新结构经济学：反思经济发展与政策的理论框架》，北京大学出版社，2012年版，第275页。

② 除了这个概括性的指标，在后续的研究可以分别将从自然资源、物质资本、人力资本与基础设施等分项指标测度禀赋结构升级。

$$I_{it}=1-\mathrm{DI}_{it}=1-\left(1-\frac{s_{it}}{s_{\mathrm{USA},t}}\right)=\frac{s_{it}}{s_{\mathrm{USA},t}} \tag{3.11}$$

除了非农化这个最重要的产业结构升级指标，我们也同时测度工业（包含制造业）、服务业的结构转型升级路径。同时，我们专门在第6章测算制造业结构变迁带来的就业机会，算是单独强调制造业结构变迁的重要性。

### 3.6.2 全球的经济结构分布概况①

诚如剑桥大学的张夏准所言："以购买力平价（PPP）计算的数据往往会夸大一个较贫穷国家的收入，购买力平价（PPP）数据在我们对衡量生活水平感兴趣时是可取的，但如果我们对国际贸易中的比较优势感兴趣，当前的美元数据，而不是购买力平价数据，将是更加适合使用的数据。"②因此，在测算禀赋升级时我们先用了各个经济体现价美元的人均国内生产总值，由于我们以美国作为世界前沿的标杆，其产业结构数据分布是1970—2011年，加之存在数据缺失情况，这个版本中的最终样本也就为世界180个经济体1970—2011年的非平衡面板数据。

表3.10是非农产业结构变迁的描述性统计，从中可以看到时间序列数据的缺失情况。禀赋升级数据在42年中平均缺失了约6年，产业升级数据平均缺失了约10年，因此样本使用5 786对观测值追踪到的结构变迁的发展战略路径轨迹平均大约是32年。在该样本中禀赋结构升级程度最大的观测值是2.395 8（卢森堡2008年的观测值），最小的观测值是0.002 4（利比里亚1995年的观测值），均值为0.221 1，标准差为0.320 9。标准差超过了均值，确实表明世界各个经济体禀赋条件差异巨大。任何不考虑现实禀赋差异的"一刀切"（one-size-fits-all）做法都很突兀。由图3.14禀赋结构升级的核密度分布可以看到，世界大部分经济体在1970—2011年内的大部分时期的禀赋水平都分布在0.2以内，换言之，不到美国禀赋水平的五分之一。因此，大部分经济体在大部分时期内依然是发展中国家，处于前沿的发达经济体的时期毕竟是少数。有意思的是，该密度图是右侧长尾分布，这意味着在禀赋结构上向上赶超的经济体也不在少数。在该样本中产业结构升级程度最大的观测值是1.047 8（科威特

① 除了特别说明，本书中测算世界各个经济体结构变迁路径的主要数据均来自世界银行"世界发展指标"数据库，第6章的制造业数据来自联合国工业发展组织。

② 林毅夫，《新结构经济学：反思经济发展与政策的理论框架》，北京大学出版社，2012年版，第125页。

1973年的观测值），最小的观测值是0.061 3（喀麦隆1981年的观测值），均值是0.837 5，标准差是0.155 4。相对而言，非农化刻画的产业结构分布差异没有禀赋结构分布差异那么大，但也相互迥异。由图3.15非农产业结构升级的核密度分布可以看到，世界大部分经济体在1970—2011年内的大部分时期的非农产业结构水平都分布在1之内，换言之都低于美国的产业结构水平，处于前沿内部。有意思的是，该密度图是左侧长尾分布，这意味着在前沿内部的产业结构上向上赶超是可能的，但在前沿外部赶超却很难。

表3.10 非农产业结构变迁样本的描述性统计

| 变量 | | 均值 | 标准差 | 最小值 | 最大值 | 观测值 |
|---|---|---|---|---|---|---|
| 禀赋升级（Endowment Upgrading） | 总体 | 0.221 149 8 | 0.320 921 6 | 0.002 400 | 2.395 800 | $N$ = 6 454 |
| | 组间 | | 0.288 264 0 | 0.006 025 | 1.421 917 | $n$ = 180 |
| | 组内 | | 0.106 636 2 | −0.497 266 | 1.573 690 | $T$-bar = 35.855 6 |
| 产业升级（Industry Upgrading） | 总体 | 0.837 488 6 | 0.155 384 6 | 0.061 300 | 1.047 800 | $N$ = 5 786 |
| | 组间 | | 0.142 002 7 | 0.389 042 | 1.021 624 | $n$ = 180 |
| | 组内 | | 0.059 458 0 | 0.391 733 | 1.295 620 | $T$-bar = 32.144 4 |

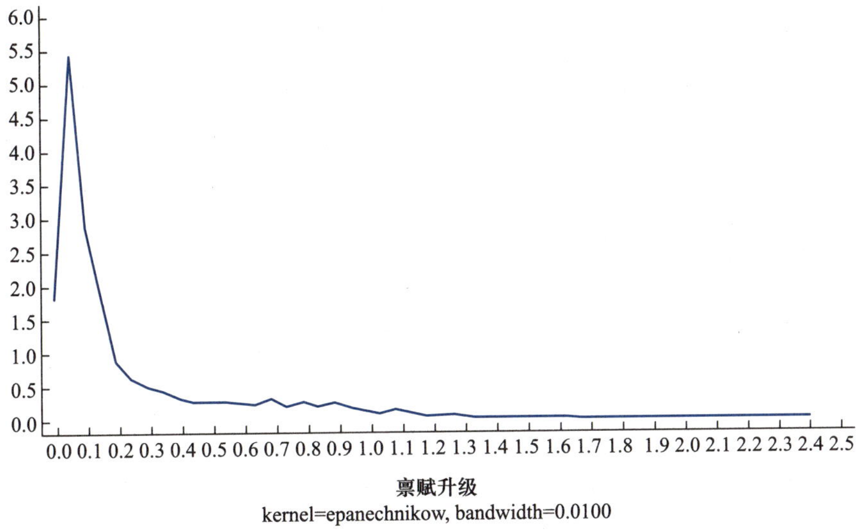


图3.14 世界180个经济体1970—2011年禀赋结构升级的核密度图

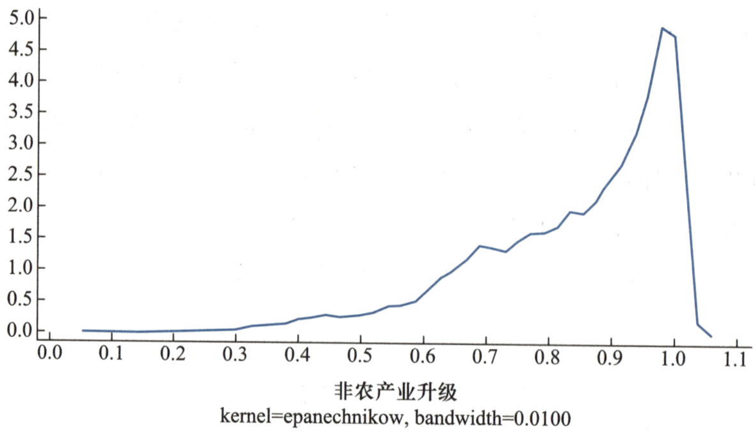


图3.15 非农产业结构升级的核密度图

表3.11是工业结构变迁的描述性统计。从时间序列数据缺失的情况来看，工业升级数据平均大约缺失了10年，因此样本使用5 795对观测值追踪到的结构变迁的发展战略路径轨迹平均也是32年。在该样本中工业结构升级程度最大的观测值是4.449 4（赤道几内亚2005年的观测值），最小的观测值是0.076 4（利比里亚1996年的观测值），均值为1.196 2，标准差为0.544 5。相对非农化刻画的产业结构分布差异而言，工业化描述的产业结构分布差异要更大一些。由图3.16可以看到，世界大部分经济体在1970—2011年间的多数时期内，其工业结构水平都分布在1以外，也就是说，都高于美国的工业结构水平，表明存在比较普遍的工业赶超现象。同时，该密度图是右侧长尾分布的，说明少数国家出现了较为严重的工业赶超现象。当然，这也反映了美国的后工业化升级，导致不少经济体相对美国的工业化过高。

表3.11 工业结构变迁样本的描述性统计

| 变量 | 观测值 | 均值 | 标准差 | 最小值 | 最大值 |
|---|---|---|---|---|---|
| 工业升级 | 5 795 | 1.196 195 0 | 0.544 471 6 | 0.076 407 | 4.449 423 |

表3.12是服务业结构变迁的描述性统计。服务业结构升级数据平均大约缺失了11.5年，因此样本使用5 486对观测值追踪到的服务业结构变迁发展战略路径轨迹平均是30.5年。在该样本中，服务业结构升级程度最大的观测值是1.279 7（巴哈马1984年的观测值），最小的观测值是0.012 3（乌兹别克斯坦1985年的观测值），均值为0.723 1，标准差为0.199 9。就其刻画的服务业结构分布差异而言，与非农化差异接近而比工业化差异小得多。由图3.17可以看到，大部分经济体在1970—2011年间的多数时期内，其服务业结构水平都分布在1以内，也就是说，都低于美国的服务业结构水平，处于前沿内部。总体而言，服务业结构的赶超程度不如工业结构。

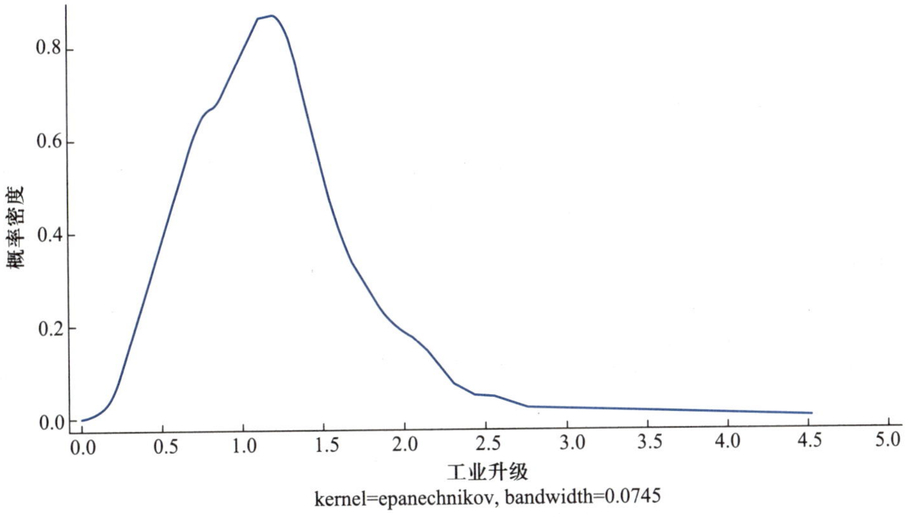


图3.16 工业结构变迁的核密度图

表3.12 服务业结构变迁样本的描述性统计

| 变量 | 观测值 | 均值 | 标准差 | 最小值 | 最大值 |
|---|---|---|---|---|---|
| 服务业升级 | 5 486 | 0.723 129 4 | 0.199 898 4 | 0.012 300 | 1.279 702 |

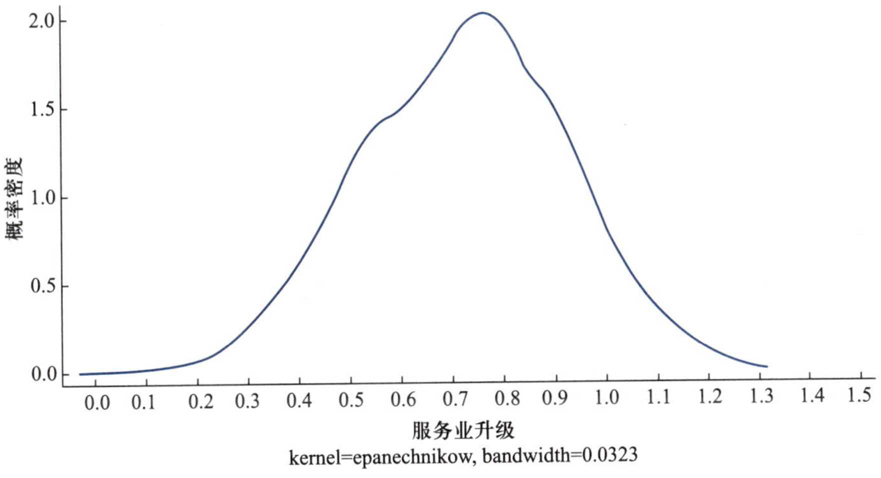


图3.17 服务业结构变迁的核密度图

### 3.6.3 经济结构变迁轨迹的全球概貌

根据对世界180个经济体1970—2011年的经济结构变迁轨迹或路径的测算结果，我们可以追踪出每一个经济体的经济结构变迁的轨迹。如后文图3.21所示的一些经济体的非农产业结构变迁轨迹的示例，犹如天上的星座一样，这180个经济体的经济结构变迁路径没有两个是完全相同的。经济结构变迁路径的多样性正是新结构经济学所要解释的核心问题。

图3.18是所有非农产业结构变迁样本观测值的混合散点图，用以反映全球整体的经济结构变迁的发展战略路径分布概貌。我们不妨由全球样本对经济结构变迁的路径做对数拟合（$R^2=0.64$）

$$I_{it}=f^{W}\left(E_{it}\right)=1.0483+0.0832\times\ln\left(E_{it}\right) \tag{3.12}$$

其斜率和弹性分别为 $\dfrac{\partial I_{it}}{\partial E_{it}}=\dfrac{0.0832}{E_{it}}$，$\dfrac{\partial I_{it}}{\partial E_{it}}\dfrac{E_{it}}{I_{it}}=\dfrac{0.0832}{I_{it}}$。可以看到，世界样本拟合的非农产业经济结构变迁路径的斜率和弹性均为正而且随禀赋升级和产业升级而递减。尽管我们不能判断这两个具体的数值是否最优地遵循了比较优势，但是我们可以看到斜率和弹性随着结构升级而递减的趋势蕴含了后来者优势和结构的动态调整。

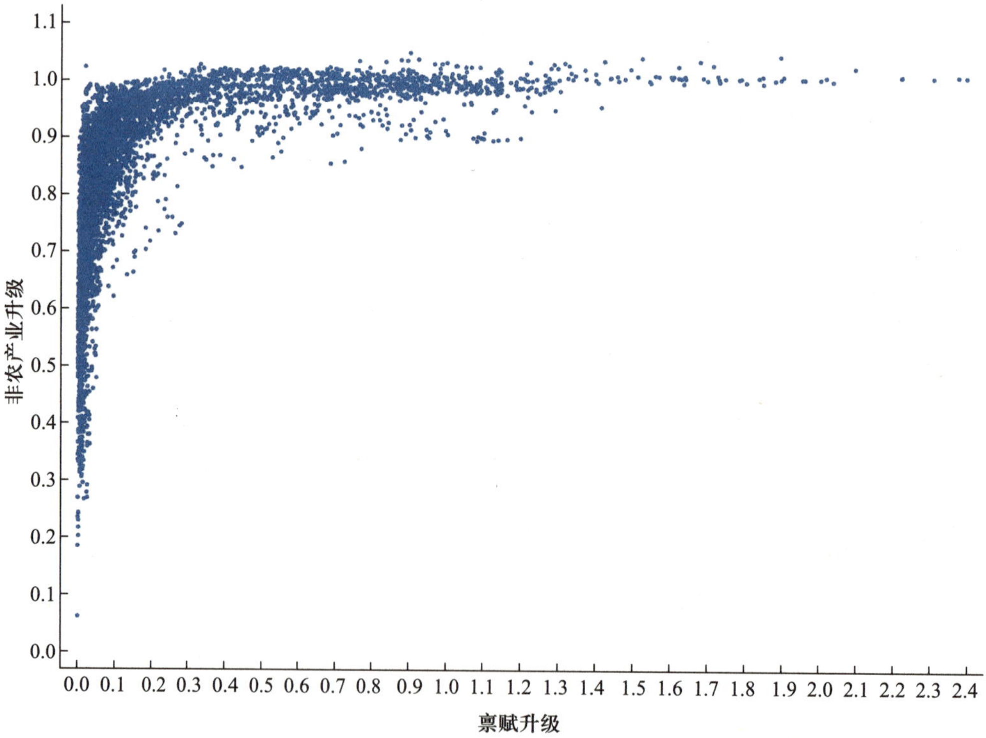


图3.18 全球所有非农产业结构变迁样本的散点图

图3.19是所有工业结构变迁样本观测值的混合散点图，反映了全球整体工业结构变迁径分布。考虑到在工业化进程持续一段时间后会逐渐出现去工业化的情况，不妨由全球样本对工业结构变迁路径做二次函数拟合（$R^2 = 0.037$）①：

$$I_{it} = f^{W}\left(E_{it}\right) = 1.101\,7 + 0.785\,6E_{it} - 0.512\,2E_{it}^{2} \tag{3.13}$$

拐点为$E = 0.766\,9$，顶点为$I = 2.006\,1$，其斜率为$\frac{\partial I_{it}}{\partial E_{it}} = 0.785\,6 - 1.024\,4E_{it}$（弹性表达式过于复杂因而不在此列出）。在工业化阶段（$E < 0.766\,9$），世界样本拟合的工业结构变迁路径的斜率为正，且随禀赋升级而递减。工业化也显示出后来者优势和结构的动态调整。

图3.20是所有服务业结构变迁样本观测值的混合散点图。同非农产业结构变迁路径拟合一样，我们采用对数拟合（$R^2 = 0.274$）：

$$I_{it} = f^{W}\left(E_{it}\right) = 0.915\,9 + 0.072\,5 \times \ln\left(E_{it}\right) \tag{3.14}$$

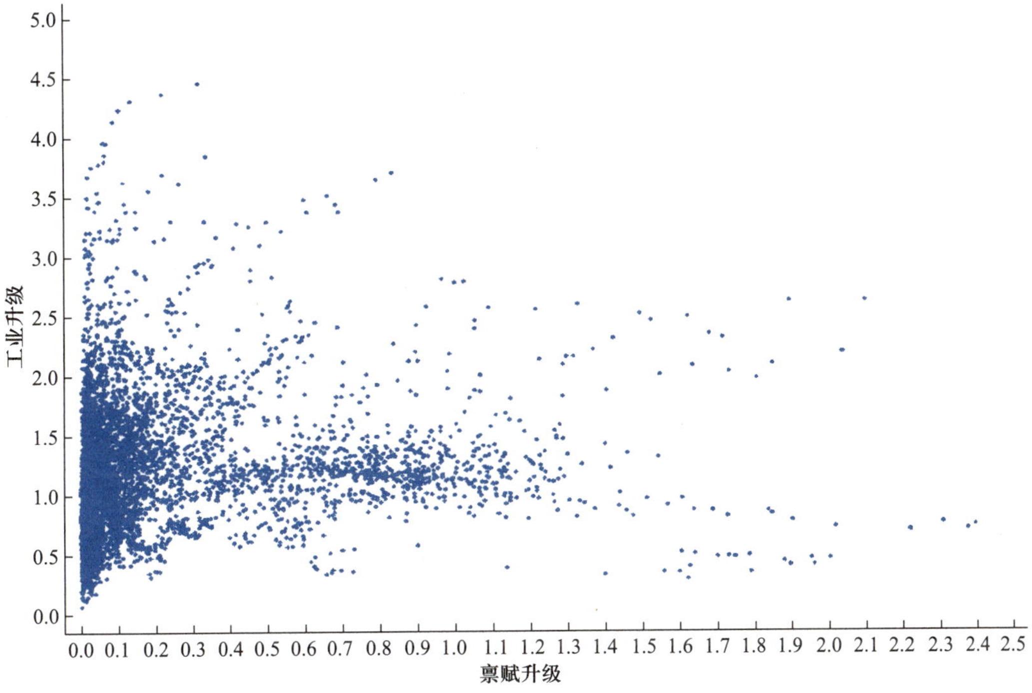


图3.19 全球所有工业结构变迁样本的散点图

① 需要说明的是，由于许多低收入国家工业发展存在严重的赶超现象，以及步入禀赋结构和工业结构前沿的国家其工业结构变迁发展战略路径显示出不确定性，因而模型的拟合优度不高。

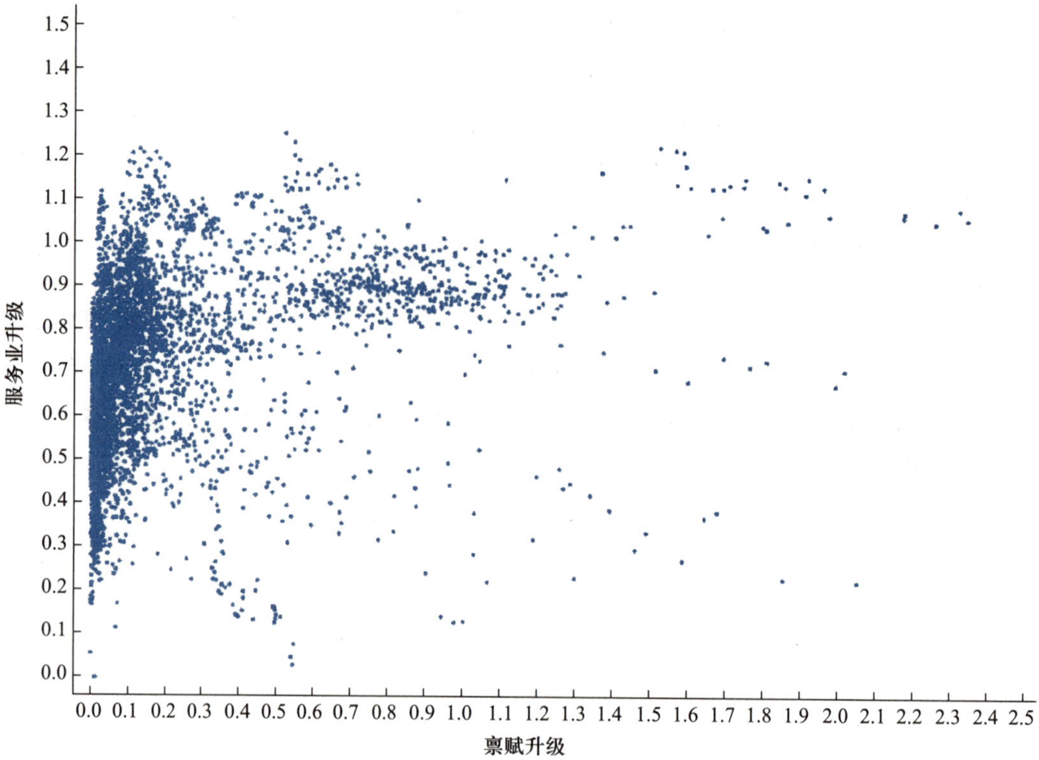


图3.20 全球所有服务业结构变迁样本的散点图

其斜率和弹性分别为 $\frac{\partial I_{it}}{\partial E_{it}}=\frac{0.0725}{E_{it}}$，$\frac{\partial I_{it}}{\partial E_{it}}\frac{E_{it}}{I_{it}}=\frac{0.0725}{I_{it}}$。可以看到，世界样本拟合的服务业结构变迁路径的斜率和弹性均为正，且随着禀赋升级和服务业升级而递减。这一结果再次表现出后来者优势和结构动态调整的特征。

图3.21向我们展示了一些经济体的非农产业结构变迁轨迹示例。

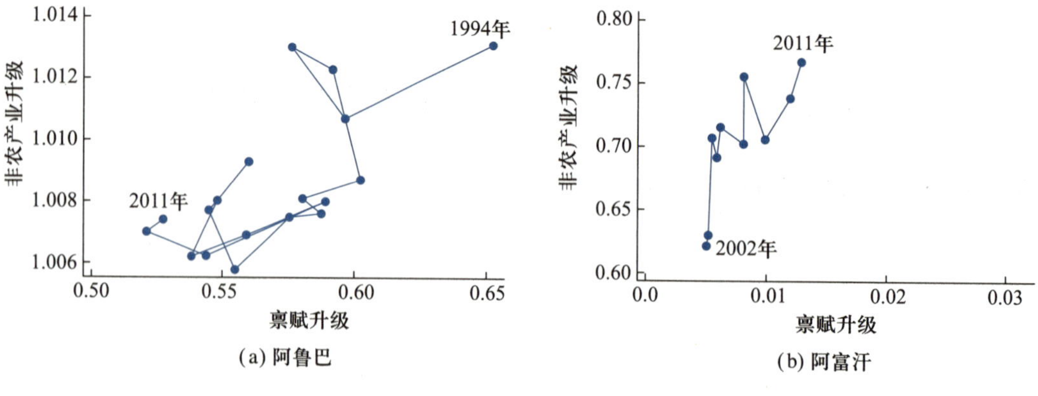

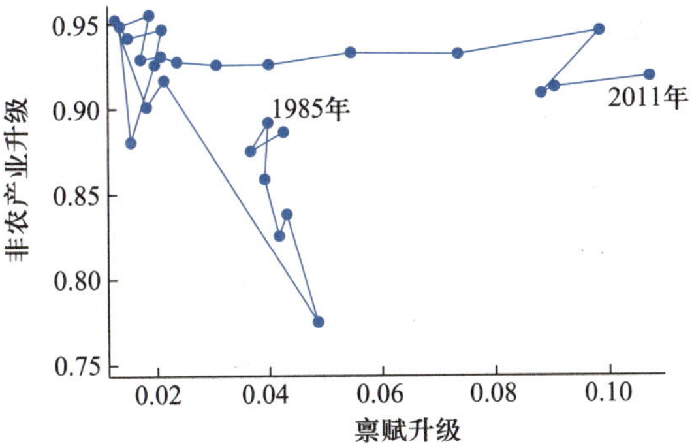

(c) 安哥拉

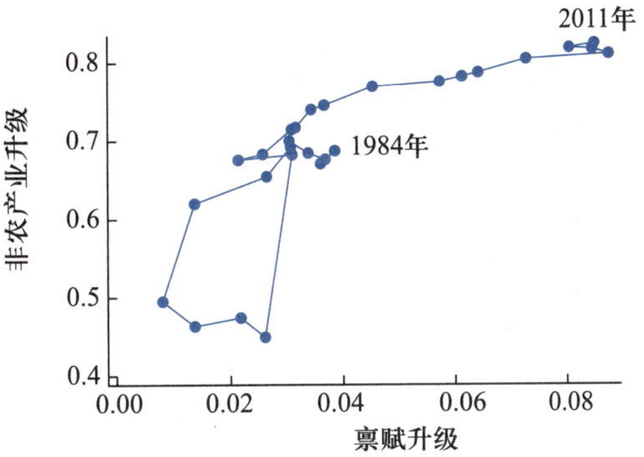

(d) 阿尔巴尼亚

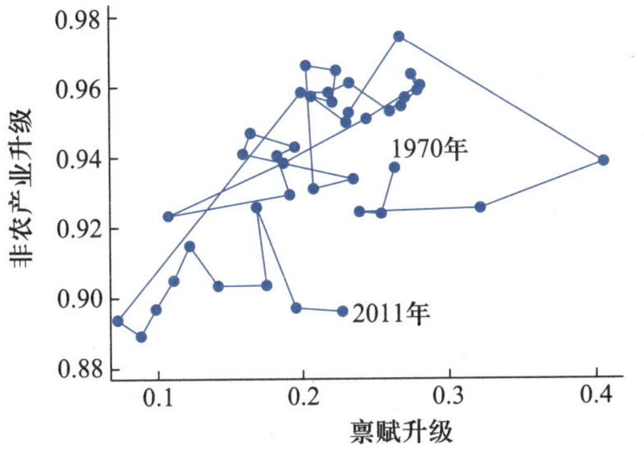

(e) 阿根廷

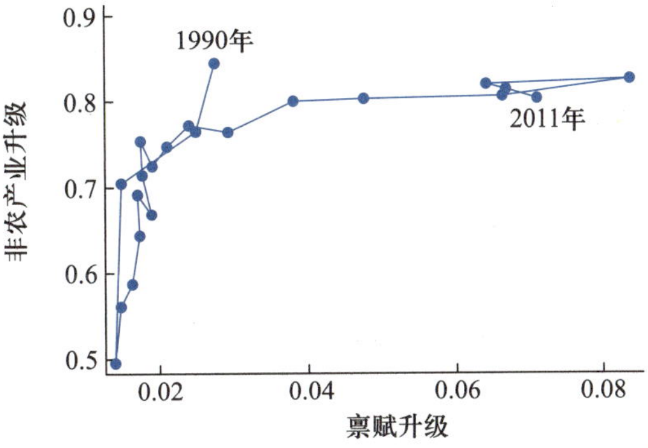

(f) 亚美尼亚

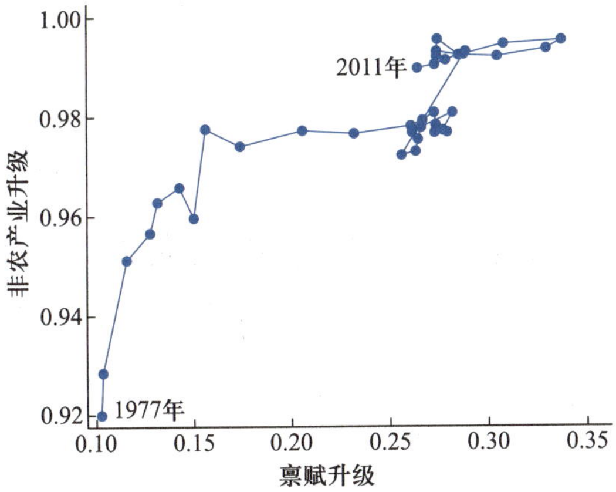

(g) 安提瓜和巴布达

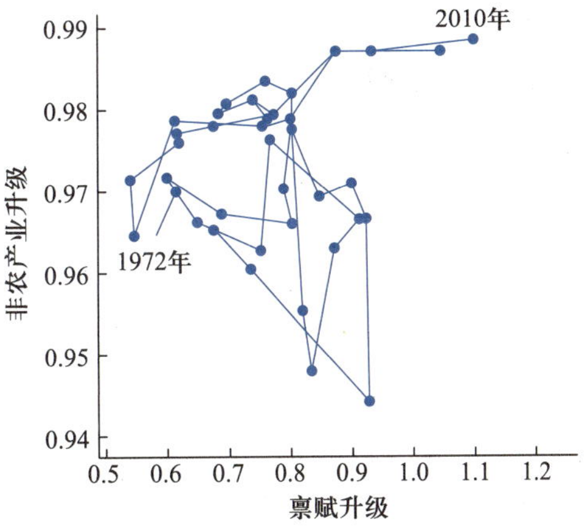

(h) 澳大利亚

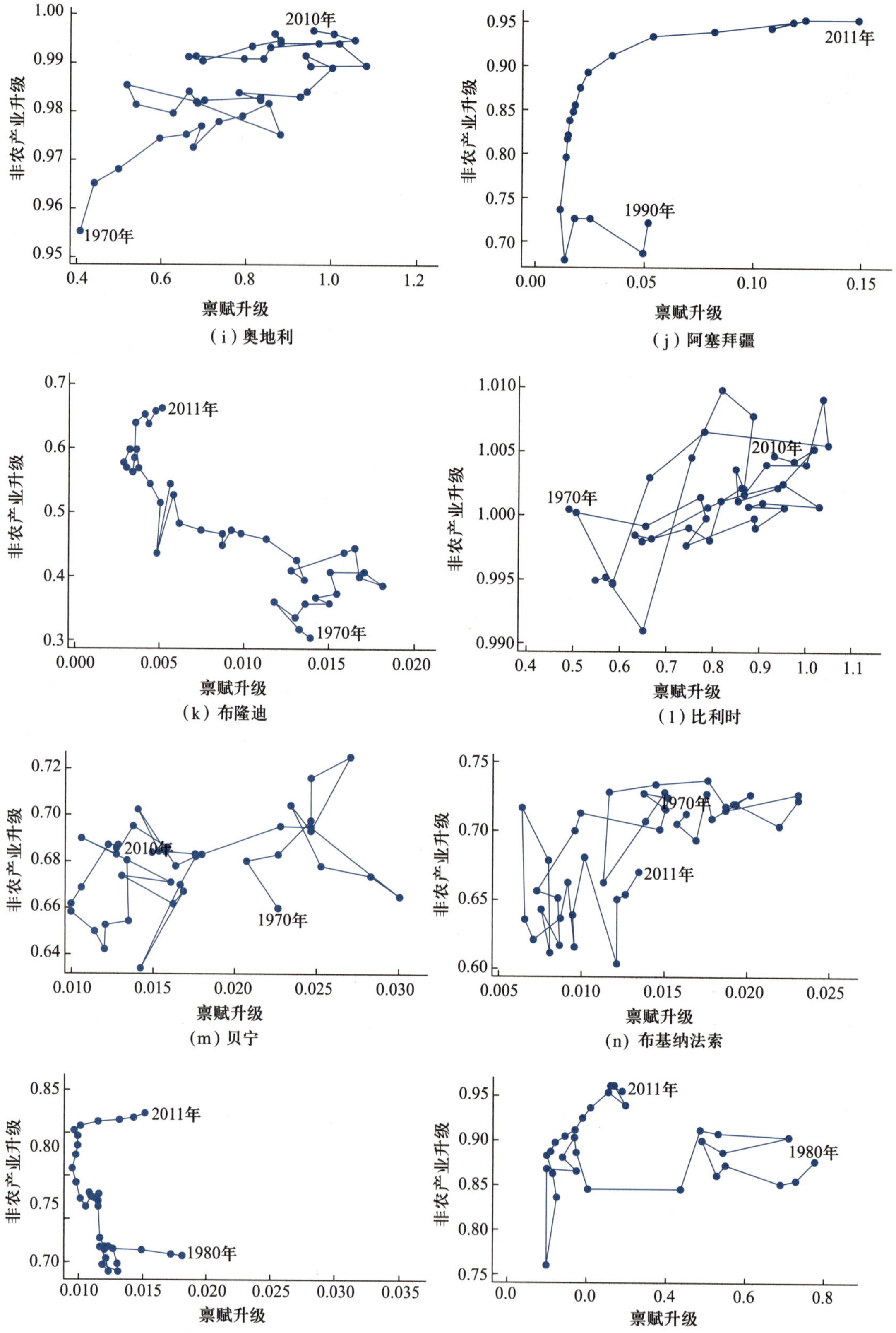


(i) 奥地利
(j) 阿塞拜疆
(k) 布隆迪
(l) 比利时
(m) 贝宁
(n) 布基纳法索
(o) 孟加拉国 (BGD)
(p) 保加利亚

图3.21 一些经济体的非农产业结构变迁轨迹示例

### 3.6.4 世界经济结构变迁前沿的特征：不确定性

进一步，我们来看看经济结构变迁前沿的经济结构变迁路径特征。根据全球样本的经济结构变迁路径的对数拟合式（3.10），当经济结构处于前沿时，$D_{it}=\{(E_{it}, I_{it})|E_{it}\geqslant 1, I_{it}\geqslant 1\}$，经济结构变迁路径的斜率 $\frac{\partial I_{it}}{\partial E_{it}}=\frac{0.083\,2}{E_{it}}\leqslant 0.083\,2$，结构变迁路径的弹性 $\frac{\partial I_{it}}{\partial E_{it}}\frac{E_{it}}{I_{it}}=\frac{0.083\,2}{I_{it}}\leqslant 0.083\,2$。二者均非常低，接近于0，这就反映出了经济结构前沿的结构变迁路径的随机特征，如图3.22和图3.23所示。这就是新结构经济学判断的，处于经济前沿国家的产业升级的机会是不可预期的，产业下一步的发展方向一般具有不确定性，除了需要政府进行基础研究领域的支持，还需要依赖于企业家的自我探索。

图3.24和图3.25分别是处于工业结构前沿和禀赋结构前沿的工业结构变迁路径。需要说明的是，由于许多低收入国家的工业结构发展存在较为严重的赶超现象，因而图3.25更能反映处于经济结构前沿的经济体工业结构变迁的路径。可以看到，当经济结构处于前沿时，工业结构变迁路径显示出强烈的随机游走特征。

类似于非农产业结构变迁，我们根据全球样本的服务业结构变迁路径的对数拟合式（3.12）可以发现，当服务业结构处于前沿外部时，$D_{it}=\{(E_{it}, I_{it})|E_{it}\geqslant 1, I_{it}\geqslant 1\}$，服务业结构变迁路径的斜率 $\frac{\partial I_{it}}{\partial E_{it}}=\frac{0.072\,5}{E_{it}}\leqslant 0.072\,5$，结构变迁路径的弹性 $\frac{\partial I_{it}}{\partial E_{it}}\frac{E_{it}}{I_{it}}=\frac{0.072\,5}{I_{it}}\leqslant 0.072\,5$，二者均接近于0，反映出服务业结构前沿变迁路径同样具备随机特征，如图3.26和图3.27所示。

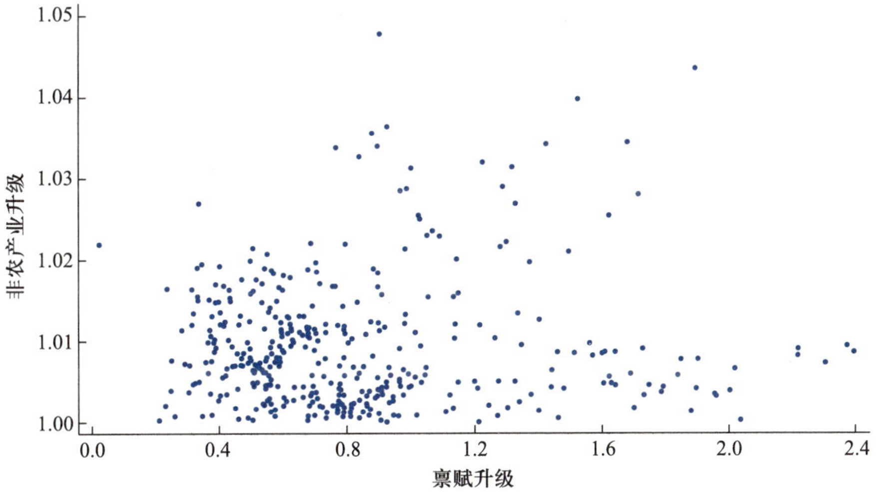


图3.22 非农产业结构前沿（Industry Upgrading > 1）的非农产业结构变迁路径散点图

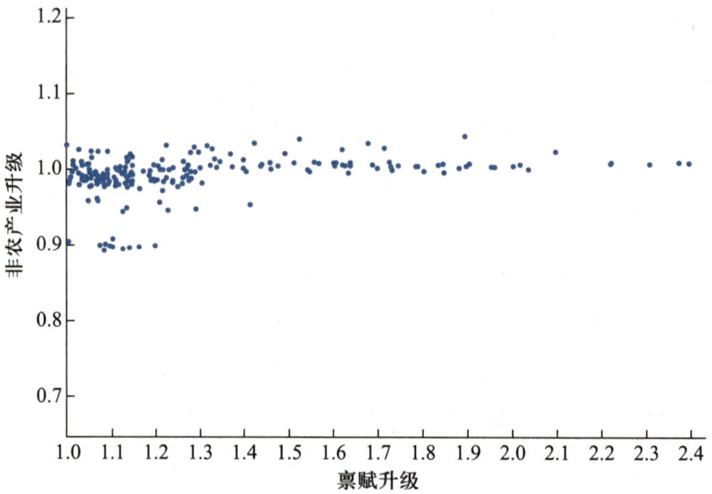


图 3.23 禀赋结构前沿（Endowment Upgrading > 1）的非农产业结构变迁路径散点图

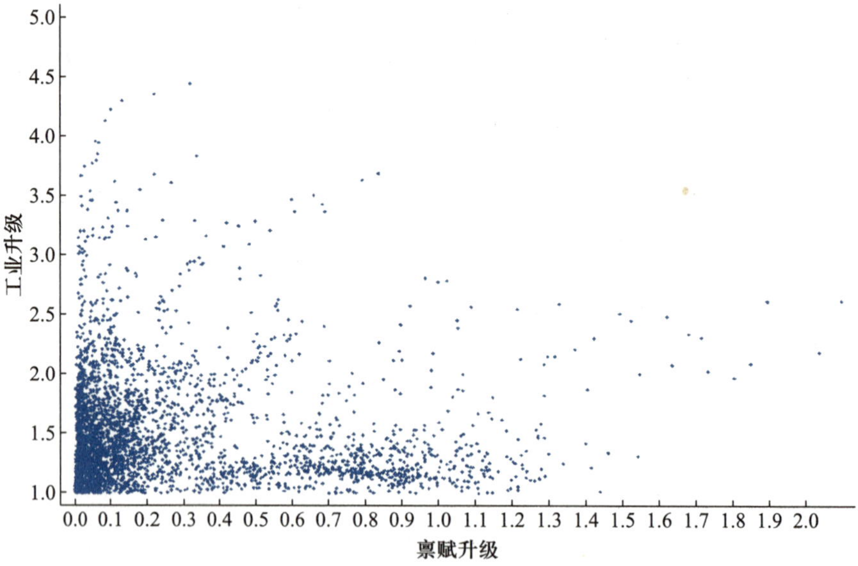


图 3.24 工业结构前沿（Industry Upgrading > 1）的工业结构变迁发展战略路径散点图

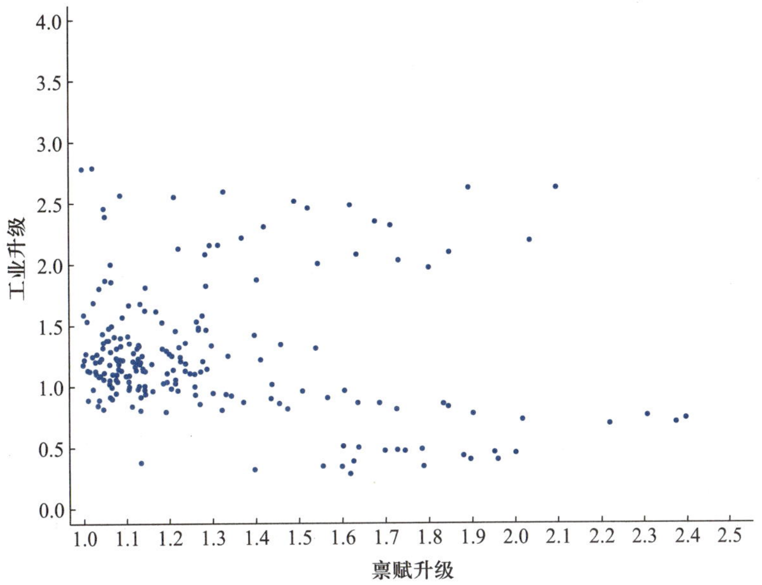


图3.25 禀赋结构前沿（Endowment Upgrading > 1）的工业结构变迁发展战略路径散点图

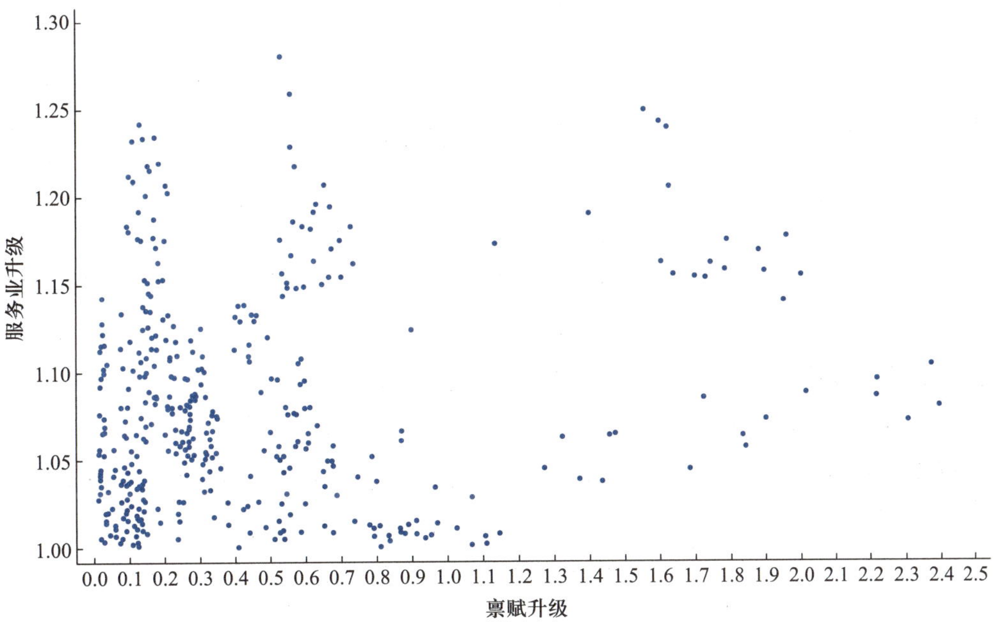


图3.26 服务业结构前沿（Service Upgrading > 1）的服务业结构变迁路径散点图

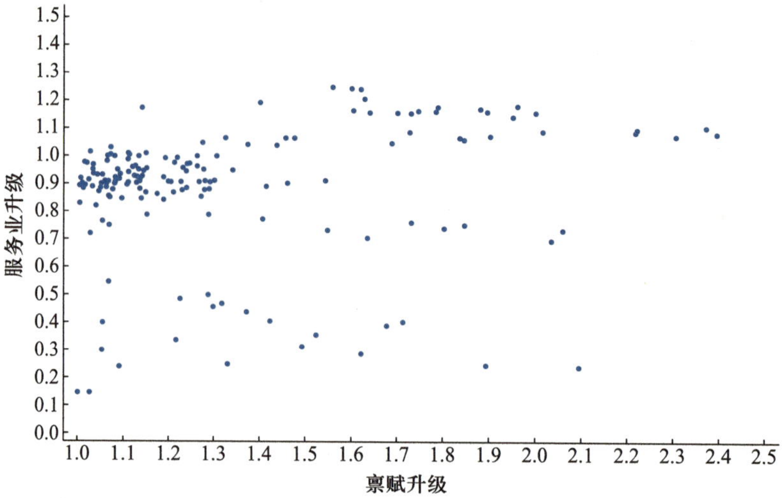


图3.27 禀赋结构前沿（Endowment Upgrading > 1）的服务业结构变迁路径散点图

## 3.6.5 世界经济结构变迁内部的特征：后来者优势

进一步，我们来看看经济结构前沿内部的发展战略路径特征。根据全球样本的发展战略路径的对数拟合式（3.11），当经济结构处于前沿内部时，$D_{it}=\{(E_{it},\ I_{it})\,|E_{it}<1,\ I_{it}<1\}$，结构变迁路径的斜率 $\frac{\partial I_{it}}{\partial E_{it}}=\frac{0.0832}{E_{it}}>0.0832$，结构变迁路径的弹性 $\frac{\partial I_{it}}{\partial E_{it}}\frac{E_{it}}{I_{it}}=\frac{0.0832}{I_{it}}>0.0832$。可见越远离经济结构前沿，结构变迁路径的斜率和弹性就越大，这就反映出了经济结构内部的后来者优势特征，如图3.28和图3.29所示。这就是新结构经济学判断的，处于经济前沿内部国家的产业升级的机会是可预期的，产业下一步的发展方向往往是明确的。

从工业结构前沿内部来看，在工业化阶段（$E<0.7669$），结构变迁路径的斜率 $\frac{\partial I_{it}}{\partial E_{it}}=0.7856-1.0244E_{it}>0$。可见越远离工业结构前沿，结构变迁路径的斜率就越大，如图3.30和图3.31所示。这同样反映出了工业结构前沿内部的后来者优势特征。

从服务业结构变迁来看，当服务业结构处于前沿内部时，$D_{it}=\{(E_{it},\ I_{it})\,|E_{it}<1,\ I_{it}<1\}$，结构变迁路径的斜率$\frac{\partial I_{it}}{\partial E_{it}}=\frac{0.0725}{E_{it}}>0.0725$，结构变迁路径的弹性$\frac{\partial I_{it}}{\partial E_{it}}\frac{E_{it}}{I_{it}}=\frac{0.0725}{I_{it}}>0.0725$。可见越远离服务业结构前沿，结构变迁路径的斜率和弹性就越大，如图3.32和图3.33所示。这表明服务业结构内部同样存在后来者优势特征。

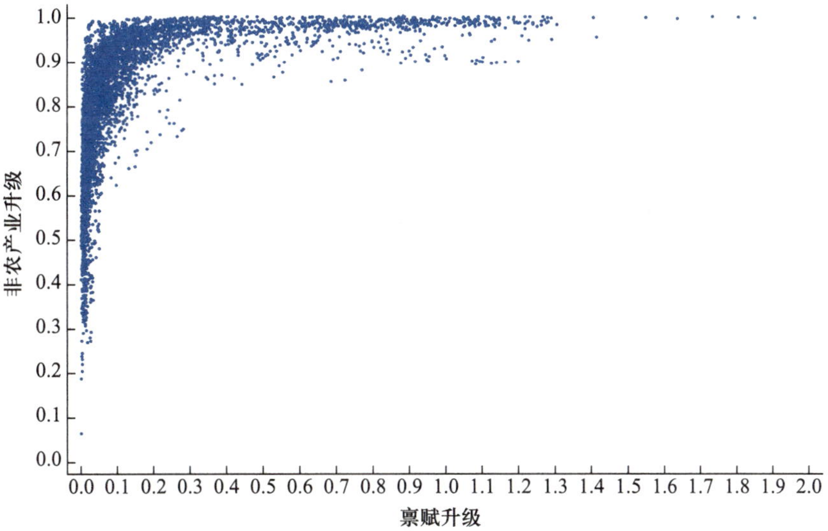


图3.28 产业结构前沿内部（Industry Upgrading < 1）的结构变迁路径散点图

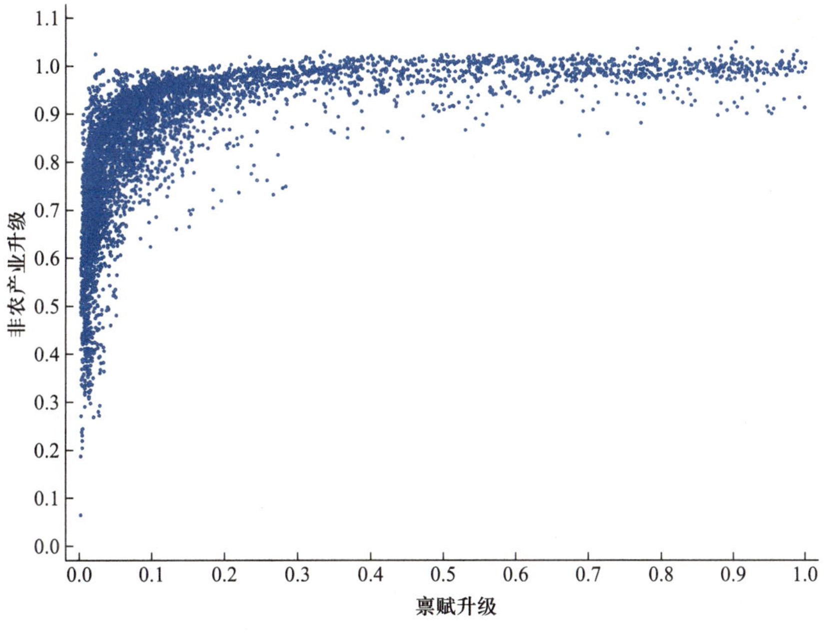


图3.29 禀赋结构前沿内部（Endowment Upgrading < 1）的结构变迁路径散点图

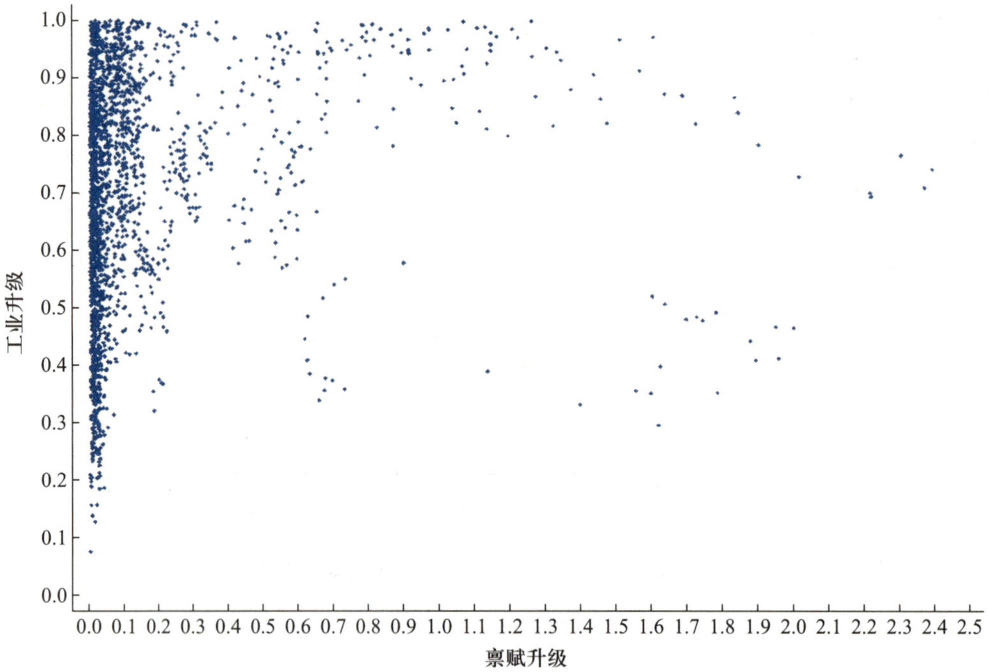


图 3.30 工业产业结构前沿内部（Industry Upgrading < 1）的工业结构变迁路径散点图

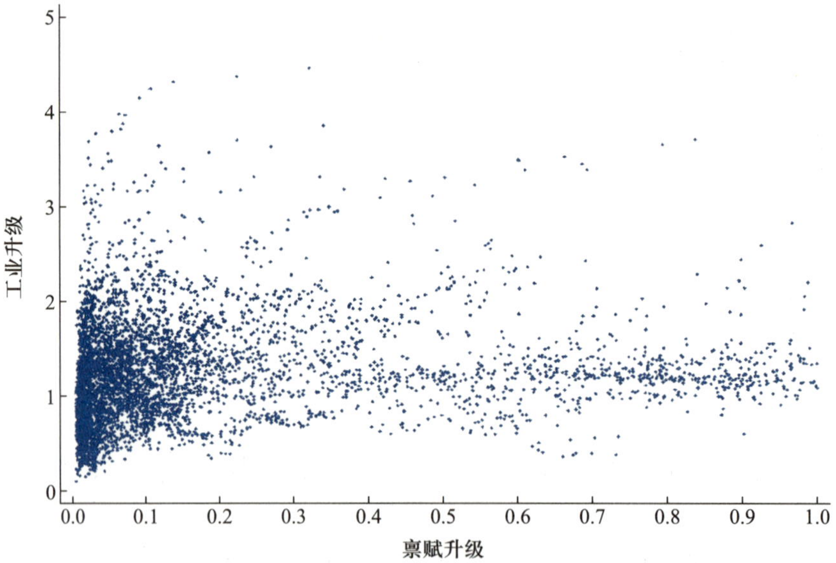


图 3.31 禀赋结构前沿内部（Endowment Upgrading < 1）的工业结构变迁路径散点图

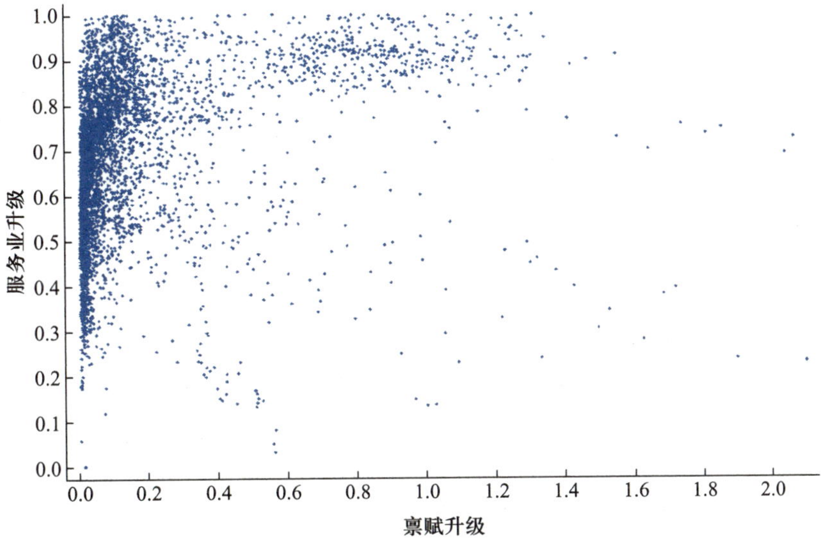


图3.32 服务业结构前沿内部（Service Upgrading < 1）的服务业结构变迁路径散点图

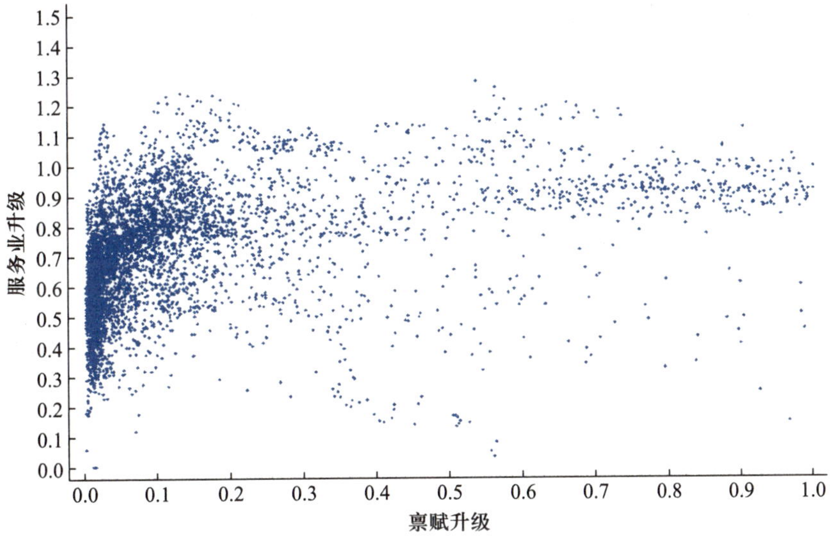


图3.33 禀赋结构前沿内部（Endowment Upgrading < 1）的服务业结构变迁路径散点图

### 3.6.6 落后经济体的特征：机会与障碍

落后经济体虽然均远离经济结构的前沿，但是其依然充满了发展机会和巨大的潜力。如果我们以$D_{it}=\{(E_{it},\ I_{it})|E_{it}<0.2,\ I_{it}<0.7\}$为落后经济体的结构变迁区域，那么根据全球样本的结构变迁路径的对数拟合式（3.11），落后经济体的结构变迁路径的斜率$\frac{\partial I_{it}}{\partial E_{it}}=\frac{0.0832}{E_{it}}>0.416$，结构变迁路径的弹性$\frac{\partial I_{it}}{\partial E_{it}}\frac{E_{it}}{I_{it}}=\frac{0.0832}{I_{it}}>0.119$。可以看到，其结构变迁路径的斜率和弹性均远大于经济前沿国家，如图3.34和图3.35所示。只要采取合理的结构变迁，落后国家便可以充分利用其面临的发展机会和拥有的巨大潜力。这也是新结构经济学以乐观积极的态度看待落后经济体发展的依据所在。

同对非农产业结构变迁的分析保持一致，我们以$D_{it}=\{(E_{it},\ I_{it})|E_{it}<0.2,\ I_{it}<0.7\}$为落后经济体的工业结构变迁区域。根据全球样本的工业结构变迁路径二次函数拟合式（3.13），落后经济体工业结构变迁路径的斜率为$\frac{\partial I_{it}}{\partial E_{it}}=0.7856-1.0244E_{it}>0.5807$。可以看到，其结构变迁路径的斜率同样远大于工业发展前沿国家，如图3.36和图3.37所示。

仍以$D_{it}=\{(E_{it},\ I_{it})|E_{it}<0.2,\ I_{it}<0.7\}$为落后经济体的结构变迁区域，那么根据全球样本的服务业结构变迁路径的对数拟合式（3.14），落后经济体的服务业结构变迁路径的斜

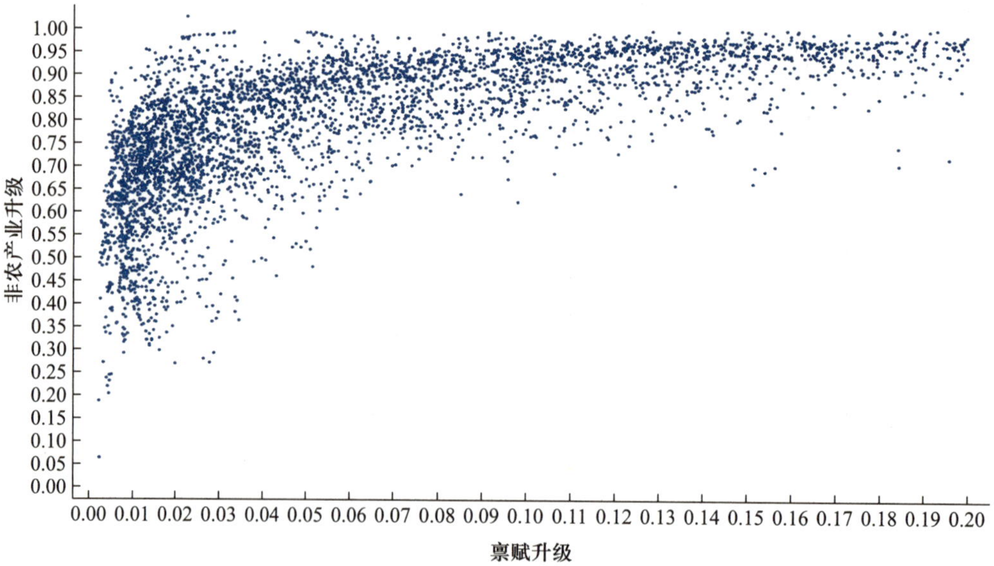


图3.34 低收入国家产业结构升级的后来者优势（Endowment Upgrading < 0.2）

率 $\frac{\partial I_{it}}{\partial E_{it}}=\frac{0.072\ 5}{E_{it}}>0.362\ 5$，结构变迁路径的弹性 $\frac{\partial I_{it}}{\partial E_{it}}\frac{E_{it}}{I_{it}}=\frac{0.072\ 5}{I_{it}}>0.103\ 6$。可以看到，其结构变迁径的斜率和弹性同样远大于经济前沿国家，如图3.38和图3.39所示。

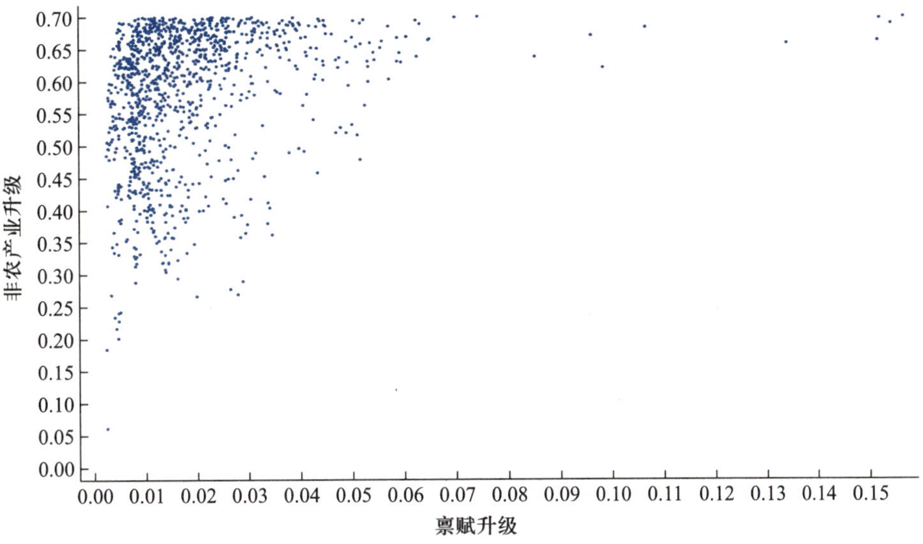

图3.35 低收入国家产业结构升级的后来者优势（Industry Upgrading < 0.7）

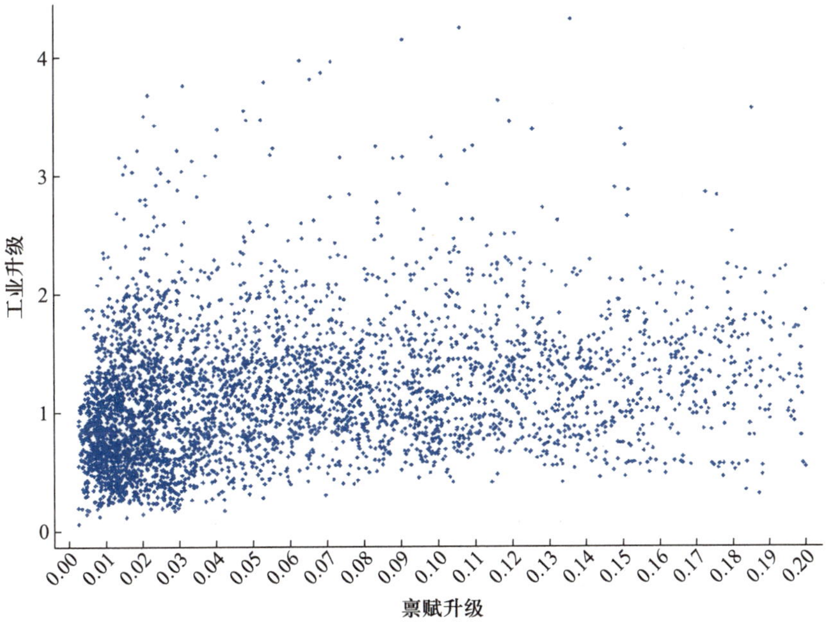

图3.36 低收入国家工业结构升级的后发优势（Endowment Upgrading < 0.2）

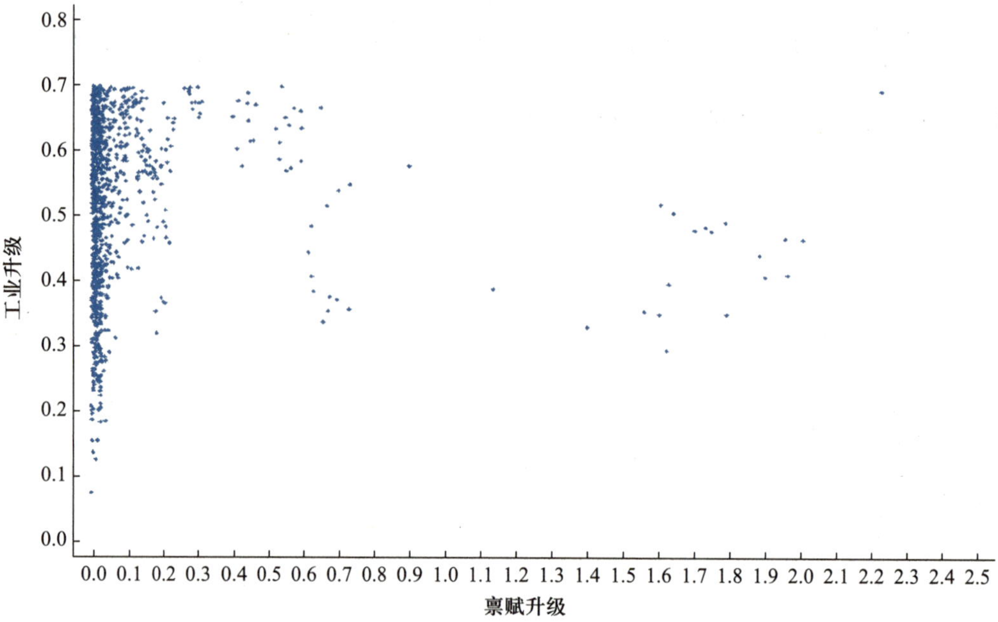


图3.37 低收入国家工业结构升级的后发优势（Industry Upgrading < 0.7）

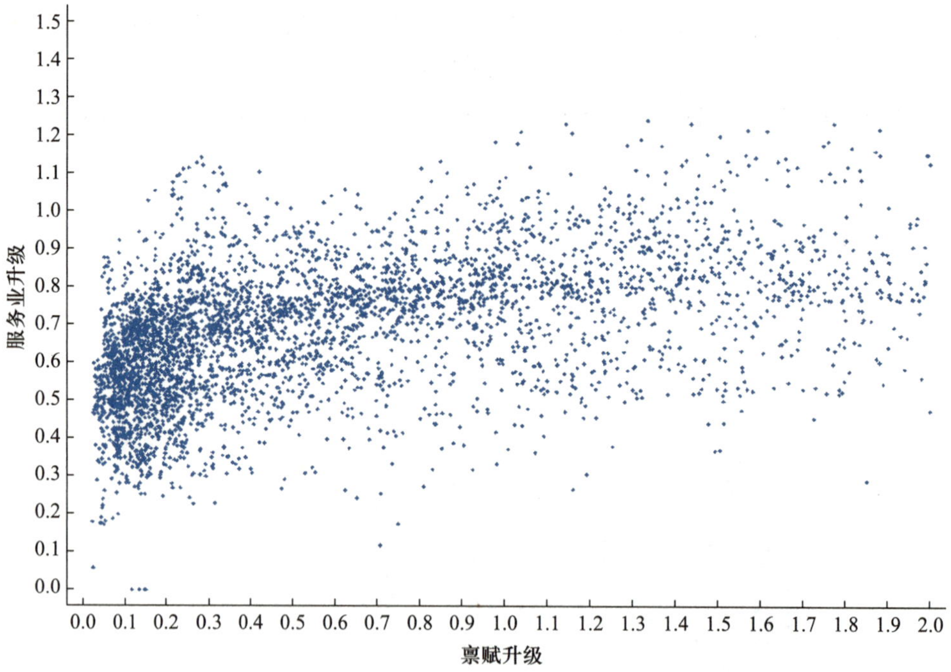


图3.38 低收入国家服务业结构升级的后来者优势（Endowment Upgrading < 0.2）

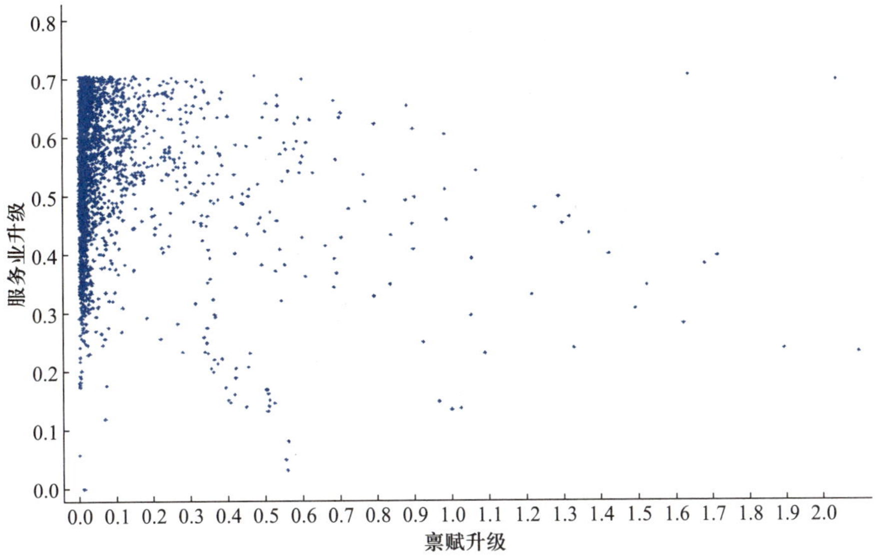


图3.39 低收入国家服务业结构升级的后来者优势（Service Upgrading < 0.7）

### 3.6.7 中等收入陷阱的特征：一团糨糊

按照世界银行的标准，如果人均收入在1 006到3 975美元之间，则是中等偏下收入国家；如果人均收入在3 976到12 275美元之间，则是中等偏上收入国家。令人惊奇的是，许多经济体长期处于中等偏上收入国家这一阶段，无法迈入高收入经济体的行列。例如阿根廷在1900年曾经是世界第六大经济体以及收入最高的国家之一。1950年的委内瑞拉也曾经是拉丁美洲人均收入排名最高的国家。然而，如今阿根廷和委内瑞拉的人均收入一直徘徊在中等收入国家行列，如图3.40所示。鉴于此，2006年，世界银行《东亚经济发展报告》首先提出“中等收入陷阱”（Middle Income Trap）的概念。这些陷入中等收入陷阱的经济体尽管已经脱贫，在社会发展方面也有不错的表现，例如成人识字率、婴儿死亡率、平均寿命相对于低收入国家都有大幅提升，但是相对于富裕国家而言，其人力和物质资本、技术水平和制度复杂性依然较低。除了少数行业，这些国家多数并没有为促进其产业升级以达到国际技术前沿，并与发达国家进行正面竞争而进行结构改革。与此同时，快速发展中积聚的问题集中爆发，造成贫富分化加剧、产业升级艰难、社会矛盾凸显等。

相对于成功跨越中等收入陷阱的经济体，如韩国、新加坡、中国香港等而言，这些典型

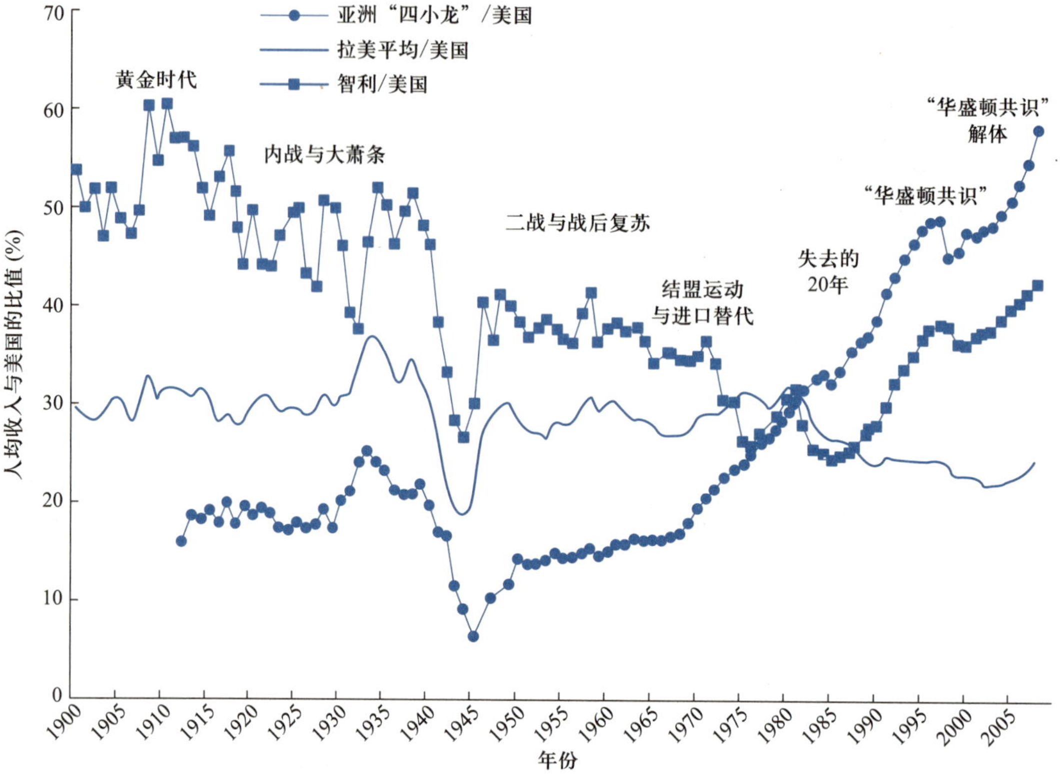


**图3.40 拉美陷阱与东亚奇迹的比较**

注：拉美是阿根廷、巴西、智利、哥伦比亚、墨西哥、秘鲁、乌拉圭和委内瑞拉的加权平均值。

资料来源：根据Maddison所著的*Historical Statistics of the World Economy*：*1-2008AD*和世界银行的数据计算。

的陷入中等收入陷阱的经济体的发展路径紊乱，并未成功实现持续的结构变迁。[①]其中最为直接的表现是未能成功应对低成本国家和高收入创新国家的夹击。背后的原因则是未能持续地向资本和技术密集更高的产业进行转型升级，而使其生产力和收入水平进入到高收入国家的行列。我们将在第5章评估经济结构转型升级的绩效时进一步分析陷入中等收入陷阱经济体的经济结构转型升级路径存在的问题。

图3.41至图3.43展示了陷入中等收入陷阱的一些国家的产业结构变迁轨迹。

① 请参阅第4章第4节对日本、韩国、新加坡、中国香港等13个成功典范发展路径的讨论。

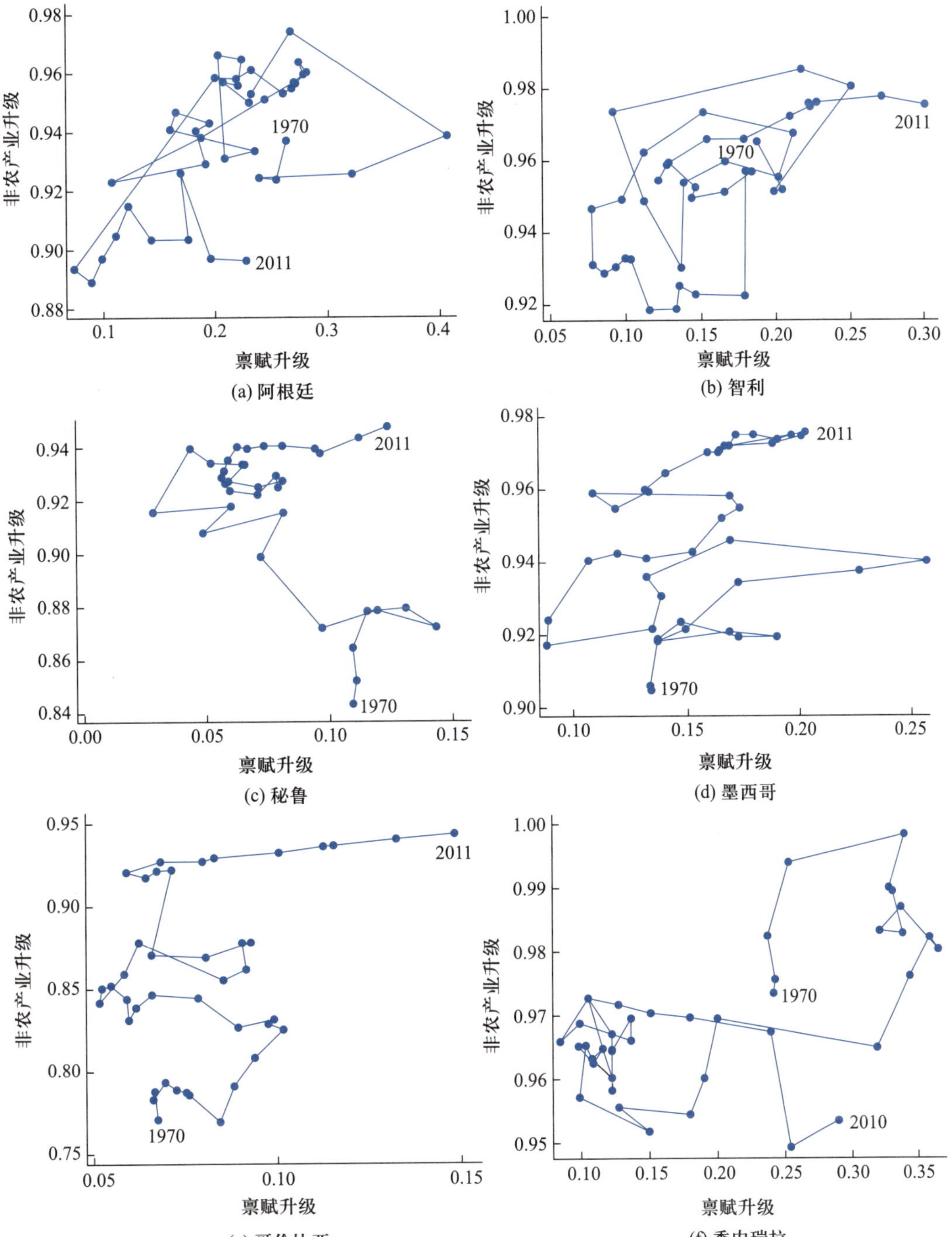


图3.41 陷入中等收入陷阱的一些国家的非农产业结构变迁轨迹

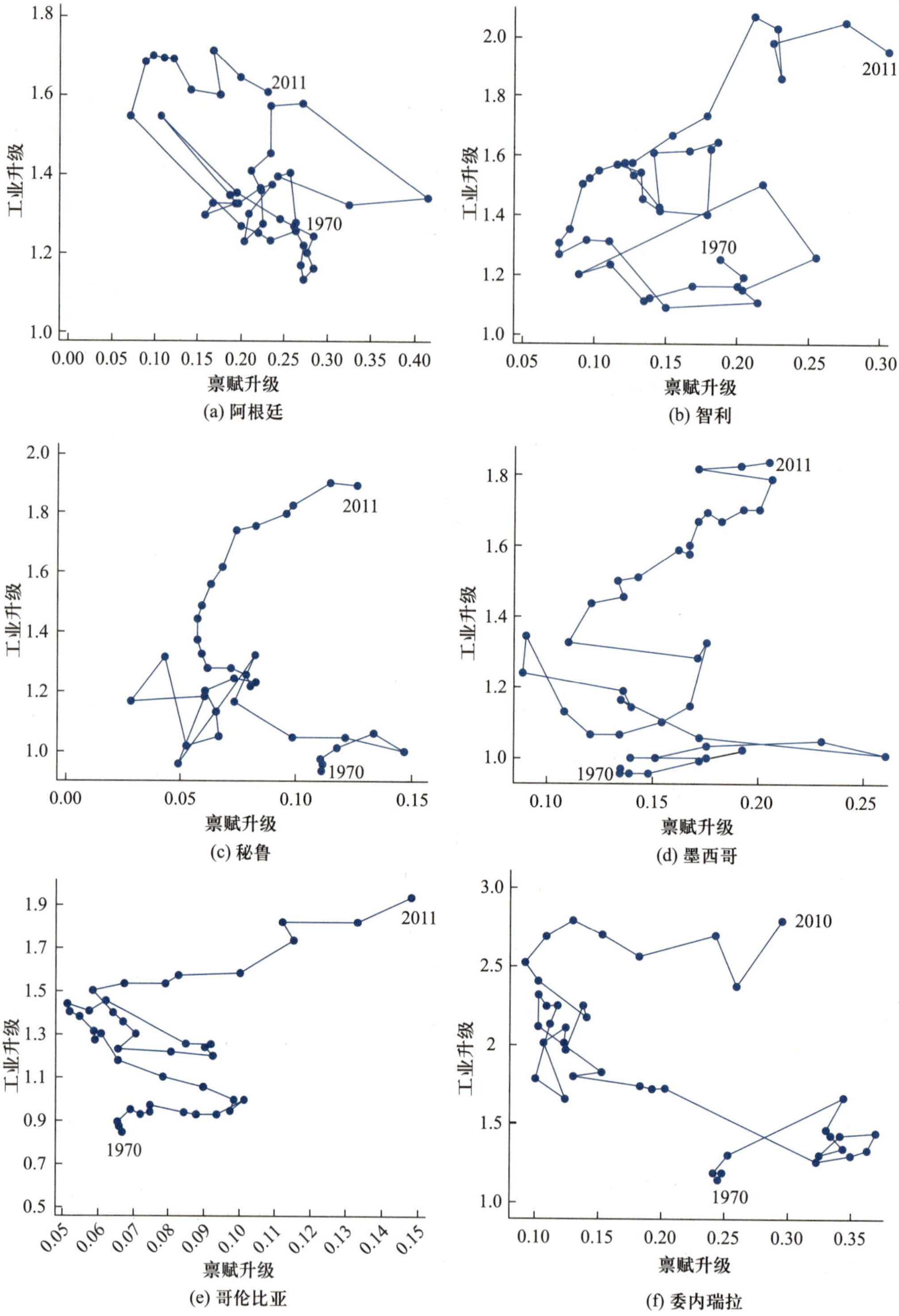


图 3.42 陷入中等收入陷阱的一些国家的工业结构变迁轨迹

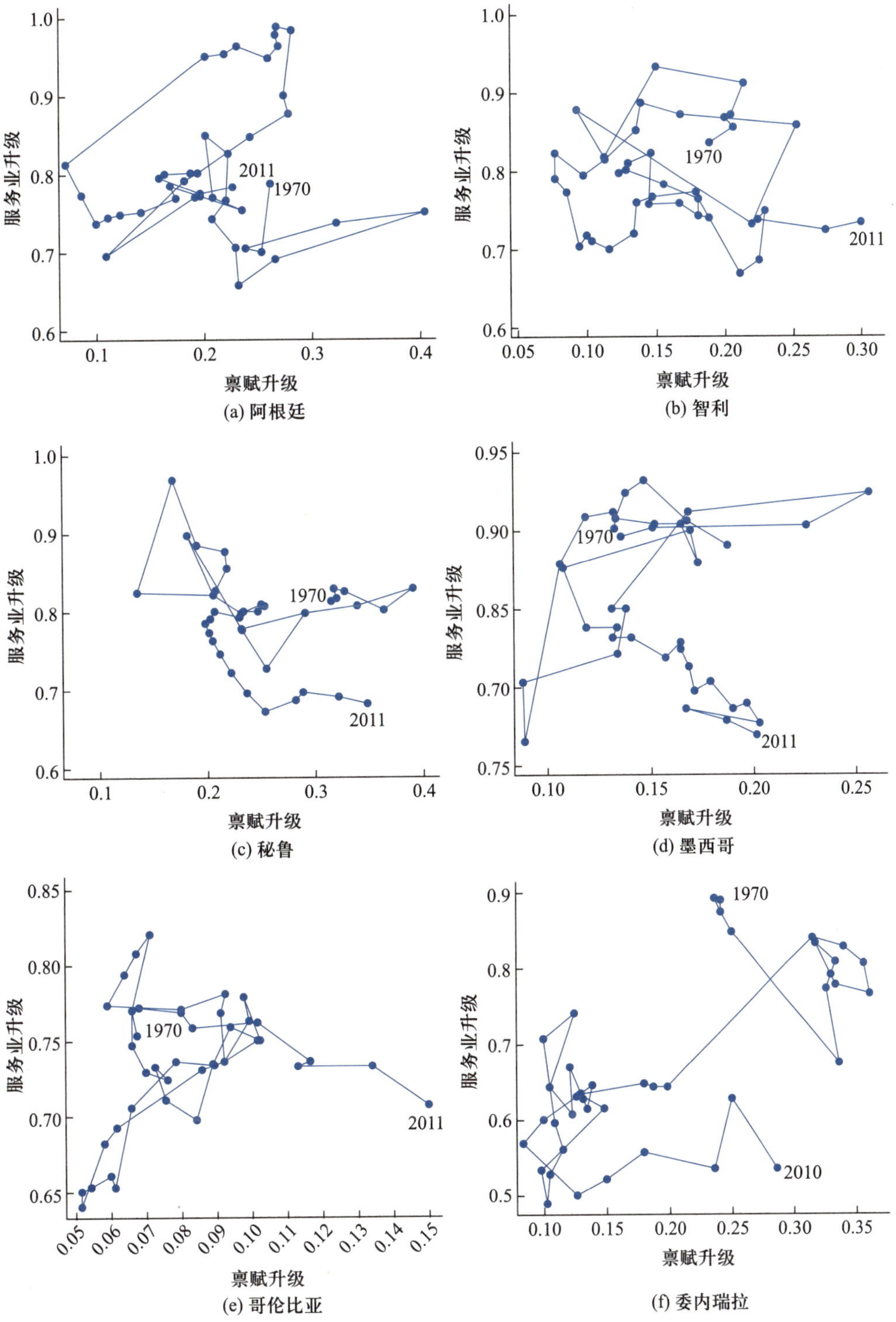


图3.43 陷入中等收入陷阱的一些国家的服务业结构变迁轨迹

第4章

# 寻找经济结构转型升级路径的典范①

① 关于本章的理论背景可以参阅：林毅夫，《新结构经济学：反思经济发展与政策的理论框架》，北京大学出版社，2012年版。

在一份关于20世纪90年代教训的具有里程碑意义的报告中，世界银行强调了经济增长的复杂性，并认识到它不是用简单的公式就能解决的。其中指出：许多发展中国家在20世纪90年代进行的改革重点过于局限在对资源的有效利用，而不是能力扩张和增长上。虽然它们致力于更好地利用现有能力，以建立长期持续增长的基础，但它们没有提供足够的激励来扩张这种能力。由此我们可以得到的结论是“不存在唯一的通用法则。……（我们）需要从公式中摆脱出来，寻求难以捉摸的‘最佳实践’”①。

在此背景下，增长与发展委员会于2006年4月召集了22位来自商界和政策制定领域的领导者，他们大多来自发展中国家，由诺贝尔经济学奖获得者迈克尔·斯宾塞（Michael Spence）和世界银行副行长丹尼·利浦泽格（Danny Leipziger）担任主席。在两年多的时间里，该委员会试图“汇集支持经济持续快速增长和减少贫困的政策和战略的最佳理解”。成立该委员会的目的是：对关于经济增长的现有理论和实证知识进行总结、评估和反思，希望得到一些政策建议，并避免陷入纯粹的理论探讨之中。该委员会认为具体原因如下：（1）他们感觉到减少贫困不能与经济增长相分离，而这一纽带在许多发展战略当中是缺失的；（2）越来越多的证据表明，人们对于快速持续的经济增长背后的经济和社会力量的理解远不如人们一般认为的那么多——对于给予发展中国家的经济建议来说，现有的知识不足以支持人们对它们的信心；（3）他们认识到过去20年高度相关的增长经验——包括成功和不成功的积累为人们提供了独特的学习源泉；（4）越来越多的人意识到，除了中国和印度以及其他快速增长的东亚经济体，发展中国家需要显著提高经济增长速度，以使其收入水平赶上工业化国家，并使得全世界的财富和机会分布更加平衡。增长与发展委员会于2008年发布了对“最佳实践”的研究成果《增长报告：持续增长和包容性发展战略》②（简称《增长报告》），归纳了第二次世界大战后能够以超过7%的增长率持续增长25年以上的13个高增长经济体的特征，试图为政策制定者提供一个设计发展战略的框架。

追随增长与发展委员会的步伐，我们将其选定的发展典范作为样本，用新结构经济学的基本原理分析其典型特征事实背后的逻辑，并拟合其经济结构变迁的路径，提炼一条最佳实践经济结构变迁轨迹或发展战略路径的标杆。

① World Bank, *Economic Growth in the 1990s: Learning from a Decade of Reform*, Washington, D.C., 2005.

② Growth Commission, *The Growth Report: Strategies for Sustained Growth and Inclusive Development*, Washington, D.C., 2008.

## 4.1

## 第二次世界大战后经济发展的典范

被增长与发展委员会视为发展典范的13个经济体是：博茨瓦纳、巴西、中国内地、中国香港、印度尼西亚、日本、韩国、马来西亚、马耳他、阿曼、新加坡、中国台湾和泰国。如表4.1和图4.1到图4.3所示。[①]以如此高的增长率，一个经济体差不多每十年甚至更短的时间GDP就可以翻一番。中国香港、日本、韩国、马耳他、新加坡和中国台湾这六个经济体就持续增长并进入到高收入行列。日本和新加坡成功实现了对世界前沿（美国）的赶超。其中如中国内地、印度尼西亚等人均收入水平最低的经济体也都进入中等收入行列。相对于低收入经济体的平均情况而言，这些发展典范在反贫困表现上也极为成功。中国这个世界上人口最多的国家在20世纪80年代之前几乎所有的人（1981年贫困人口为97%）都处于贫困境地，但今天2/3的人都已经脱贫（2009年贫困人口为27%）。尽管1979年爆发的第二次石油危机使巴西的高速经济增长戛然而止，时至今日仍未恢复元气，掉入了“中等收入陷阱”，但依然不失为一个曾经有过靓丽的快速持续发展的国家典范。

这13个发展典范之间差异显著。其中亚洲经济体占据了名单的大部分，但其他发展中地区（非洲、拉丁美洲、中东）也都有各自的代表。有的经济体（如博茨瓦纳、巴西、印度尼西亚、马来西亚、阿曼和泰国）自然资源丰富，而有的经济体则资源匮乏。其中既包括人口在10亿以上的国家（中国），也包括人口不足50万的国家（马耳他）。这13个发展典范样本的差异性很好地蕴含了发展规律的一般性。这些发展典范的成功经验告诉人们，快速的可持续经济增长是有可能的——毕竟已经有13个经济体成功地实现了这一目标。但它们同时也表明，经济快速持续增长并非唾手可得——毕竟还只有13个经济体做到了这一点。的确，有人将这些案例视为“经济奇迹”，因而无法解释也不能复制。增长与发展委员会认为并非如此：“我们不妨看看一些局外人是如何看待这个问题的。增长理论的代表人物、增长与发展委员会工作小组成员Paul Romer提醒我们：当年日本经济以这种速度增长时，评论家们也曾认为

① 由于世界银行发展指标中数据缺失的原因，本报告指数编制中没有中国台湾，只纳入了其他12个发展典范样本。

表4.1 13个持续高增长的经济体

| 经济体 | 高增长年份** | 高增长起始年份人均GDP*** | 2005年人均GDP*** |
|---|---|---|---|
| 博茨瓦纳 | 1960—2005 | 210 | 3 800 |
| 巴西 | 1950—1980 | 960 | 4 000 |
| 中国内地 | 1961—2005 | 105 | 1 400 |
| 中国香港* | 1960—1997 | 3 100 | 29 900 |
| 印度尼西亚 | 1966—1997 | 200 | 900 |
| 日本* | 1950—1983 | 3 500 | 39 600 |
| 韩国* | 1960—2001 | 1 100 | 13 200 |
| 马来西亚 | 1967—1997 | 790 | 4 400 |
| 马耳他 | 1963—1994 | 1 100 | 9 600 |
| 阿曼 | 1960—1999 | 950 | 9 000 |
| 新加坡* | 1967—2002 | 2 200 | 25 400 |
| 中国台湾* | 1965—2002 | 1 500 | 16 400 |
| 泰国 | 1960—1997 | 330 | 2 400 |

注：*已经达到工业化国家水平的经济体；**GDP每年增长率达到或超过7%的时期；***以2 000年美元不变价格计算。
资料来源：世界银行。

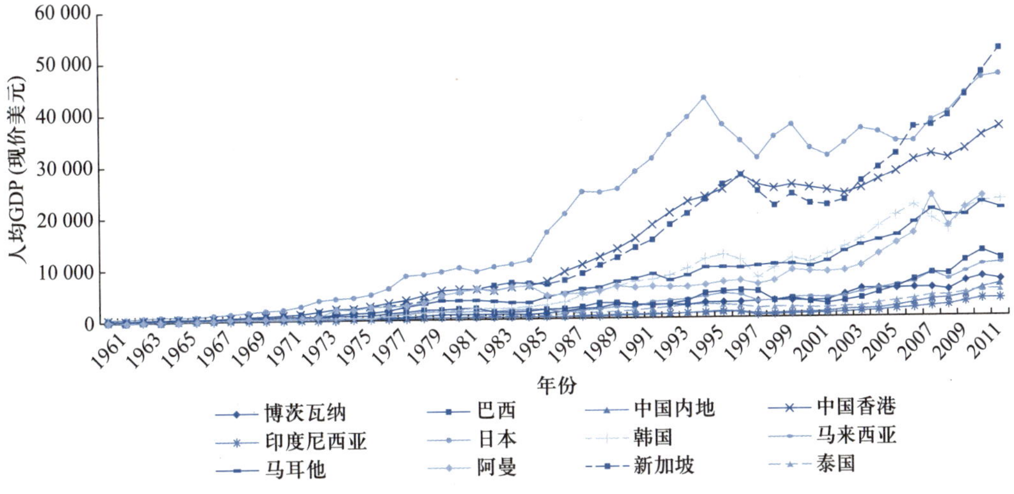


图4.1 发展典范的人均GDP（现价美元）变迁（1961—2012年）
资料来源：世界银行。

那只不过是战后复苏所催生的一个特殊案例；当亚洲‘四小龙’（中国香港、中国台湾、新加坡和韩国）追赶上来的时候，怀疑者们将其成功的原因归结为‘船小好掉头’；而当中国超越它们的时候，人们又把这解释为‘船大好扬帆’。”因此，我们也追随增长与发展委员会的步伐，通过对这些发展典范的特征归纳，寻找发展中经济体经济发展的“最佳实践”。

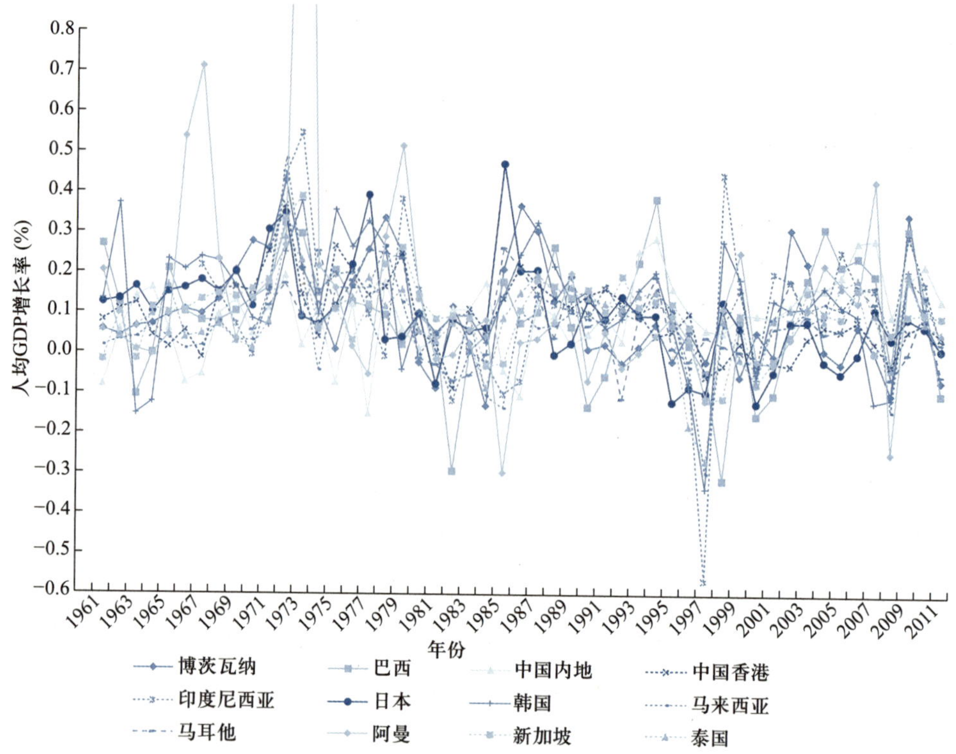


**图4.2 发展典范的人均GDP（现价美元）增长率（1961—2012年）**

注：图形未显示阿曼1974年的意外增长率（2.265 755）。

资料来源：世界银行。

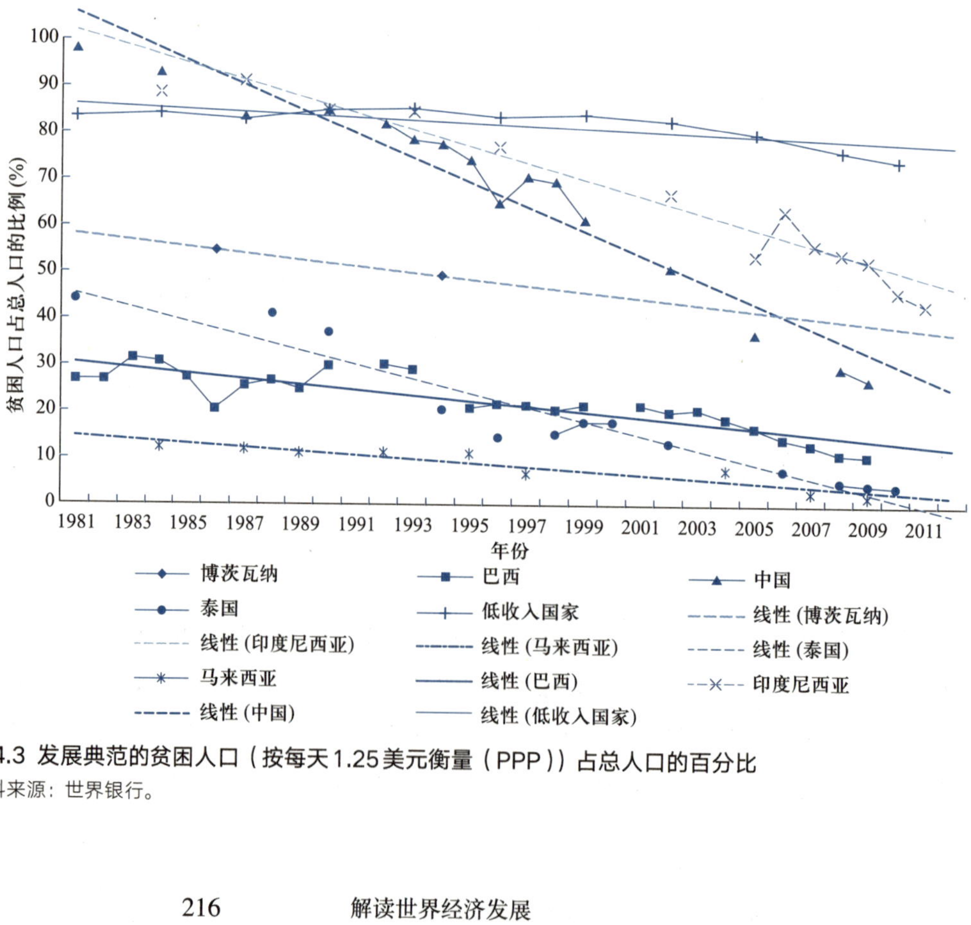


**图4.3 发展典范的贫困人口（按每天1.25美元衡量（PPP））占总人口的百分比**

资料来源：世界银行。

## 4.2

## 发展典范的特征事实①

这13个经济体虽然各有其特点，但我们不能就此断定其中没有一些共性的东西，更不能认为它们的增长之路不适用于其他经济体因而毫无可取之处。上述经济体自身就摒弃了这种态度。决策者们认真学习其他榜样，范例研究产生了深刻的影响，示范效应发挥了极其重要的作用。仔细观察这13个案例，《增长报告》归纳出了五个明显的共同之处或特征事实（见图4.4）：① 对外开放，充分利用了国际经济；② 保持了宏观经济的稳定；③ 维持了很高的储蓄率和投资率；④ 由市场来配置资源；⑤ 拥有敢作敢为、值得信赖和精明强干的政府。

### 4.2.1 对外开放

关于第一个特征事实，发展典范中的这些经济体在快速增长时期都对外开放，充分利用了世界经济，如图4.5、图4.6和图4.7所示。不论是货物与服务的进口还是出口，占GDP的比重都比较大，尤其是新加坡、中国香港，而且贸易开放度都在不断扩大。除了贸易，在大多数年份，发展典范的外国直接投资都是净流入，而且占GDP的比重也不小。对外开放的好处至少

① 通过归纳特征事实提取规律是从经验到理论的必经之路。例如，基于英美20世纪的情况，卡尔多归纳了（平衡）增长理论赖以生存的著名的卡尔多特征事实：劳动生产率的持续提高；人均资本的持续提高；资本回报率几乎恒定；劳动和资本报酬份额几乎恒定；人均产出增长率在各国差异较大。在新的时代背景下，Jones和Romer重新归纳了新卡尔多特征事实：通过全球化和城市化，市场化的程度提高；增长速度加快，从接近于零增长到相对较快的增长率；人均GDP增速随着与技术前沿的接近而降低；收入和全要素生产率的差距较大；工人人均人力资本的增加；相对工资的长期稳定。（Charles L. Jones, Paul M. Romer, "The New Kaldor Facts: Ideas, Institutions, Population, and Human Capital", *American Economic Journal: Macroeconomics*, 2010, Vol.2, No.1, pp.224–245）库兹涅茨也归纳了著名的库兹涅茨特征事实：现代经济增长的特征是，产业结构的快速转型，包括从农业到工业，再到服务业的转型，这一过程涉及城市化、从家庭作坊向雇佣关系的转变，以及正规教育日益增加的作用。库兹涅茨特征事实所强调的结构变迁一直都是传统发展经济学的主题，也是新近非平衡增长理论的分析对象。这里增长与发展委员会对战后发展典范特征事实的归纳也就成为第三波发展思潮的事实基础。

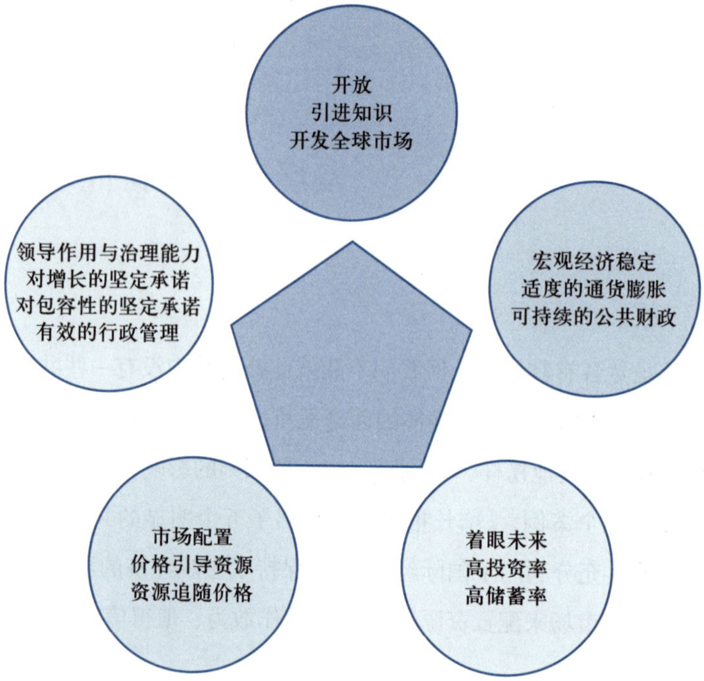


图4.4 发展典范的基本特征事实

资料来源：Growth Commission, *The Growth Report: Strategies for Sustained Growth and Inclusive Development*, Washington, D.C., 2008.

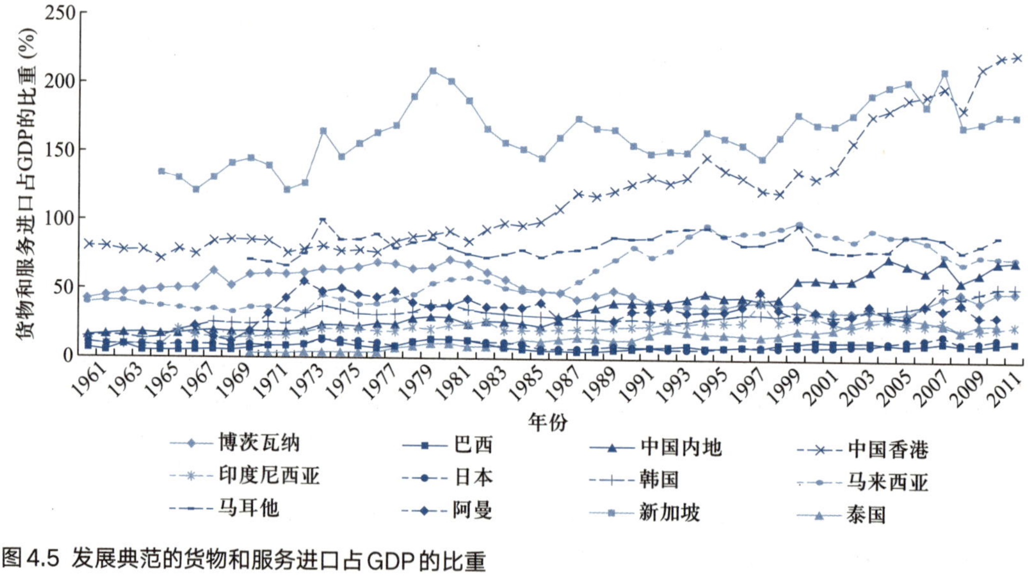


图4.5 发展典范的货物和服务进口占GDP的比重

资料来源：世界银行。

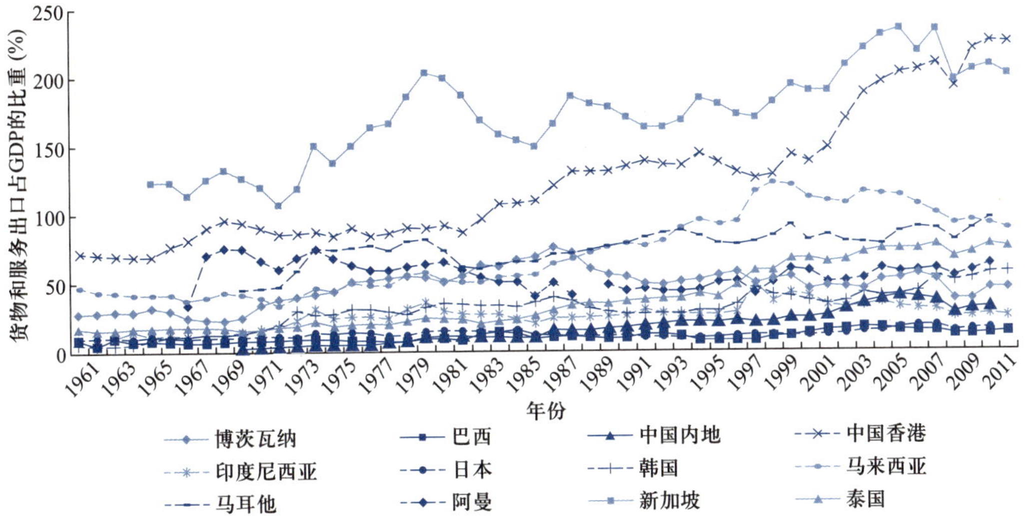


图 4.6 发展典范的货物和服务出口占 GDP 的比重

资料来源：世界银行。

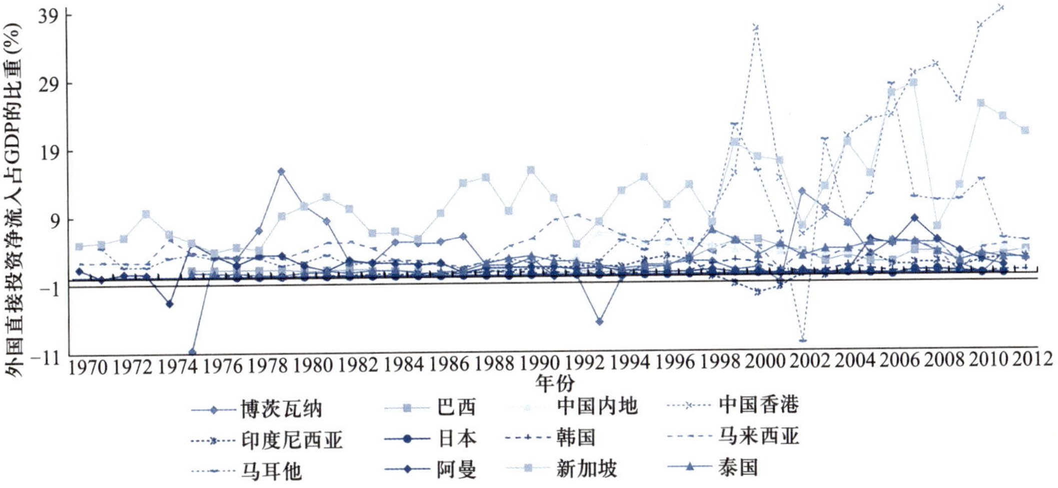


图 4.7 发展典范的外国直接投资净流入占 GDP 的比重（BoP/GDP，现价美元）

资料来源：世界银行。

可以体现在两个方面：首先，它们从世界其他地方引进创意、技术和专业技能。其次，它们开拓了全球的需求，为其产品提供了几乎无穷大的市场。总之，所有成功的经济体“都进口世界其他地方之所知，出口世界其他地方之所需”。而不成功的国家则与之背道而驰。这一点给我们的启发是清楚的：为了实现持续的动态高速增长，发展中国家必须依靠其比较优势（也就是说，出口世界其他地方之所需，并为保持经济竞争力，按照禀赋结构的改变一步步升级其产业结构），利用后来者优势的潜力（在产业升级过程中从世界其他地区引进创意、技术和专业技能）。

### 4.2.2 宏观稳定

发展典范经济体的第二个特征事实是它们维持了稳定的宏观经济环境。在它们最成功的时期，所有13个经济体都避免了可能损害私人部门投资的财政政策和货币政策的不可预知性。宏观经济动荡和变幻莫测会损害私人部门投资，从而殃及经济增长。在13个高速增长经济体最成功的时期，它们都在动荡面前化险为夷。尽管经济增长在一些地方有时伴随着温和的通货膨胀，例如20世纪70年代的韩国，90年代中期的中国内地，也有一些经济体有预算赤字或是较高的债务占GDP的比例，但这些公共债务仍在政府的掌握之中，因为它们经济增长的速度至少超过公共债务增长的速度。它们的通货膨胀率如图4.8、图4.9和图4.10所示。

### 4.2.3 禀赋积累

发展典范经济体的第三个特征事实是它们愿意放弃当期消费而追求未来更高水平的收入。高储蓄率和高投资率相匹配，如图4.11和图4.12所示。一些国家，例如新加坡和马来西亚，采取了强制储蓄计划，使得一些研究者强调政府有意的储蓄政策是这些国家高储蓄和投

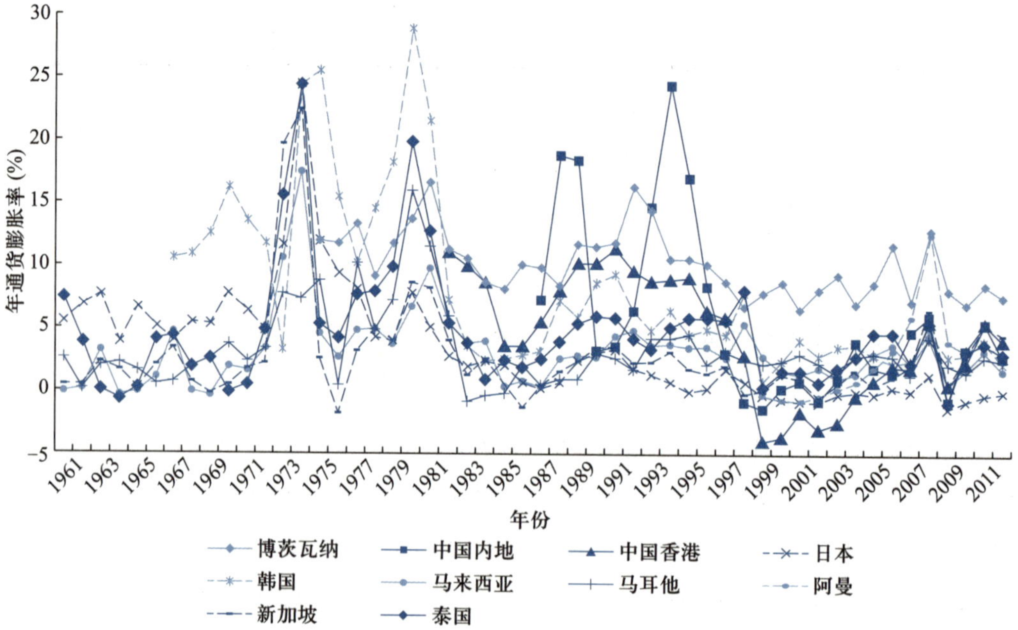


图4.8 发展典范按消费者价格指数衡量的通货膨胀（年通胀率）

资料来源：世界银行。

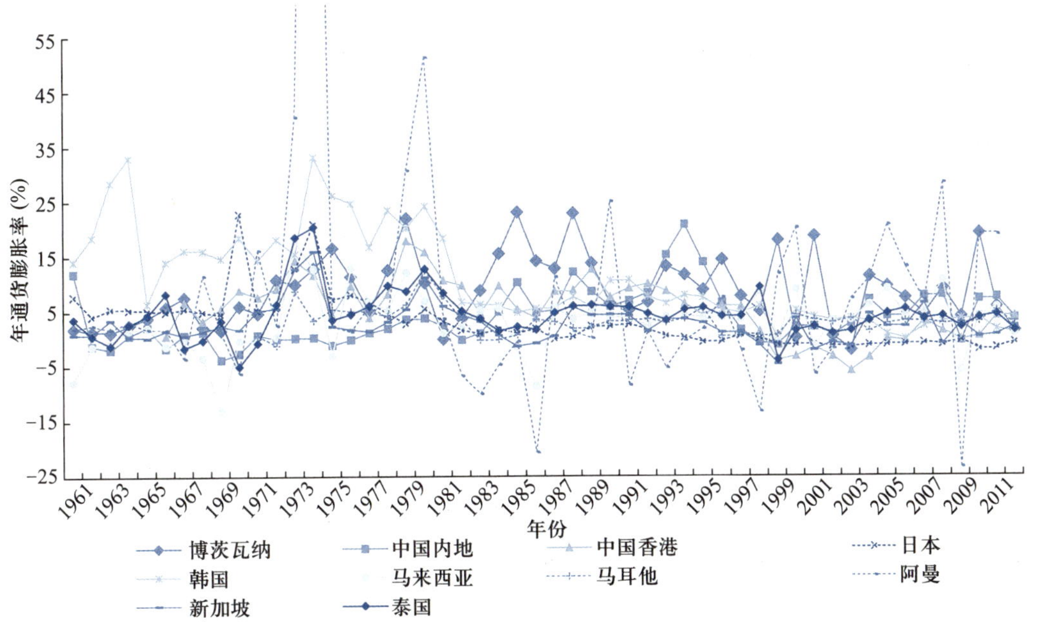


图4.9 发展典范按GDP平减指数衡量的通货膨胀（年通胀率）

注：图形未显示阿曼1974年的值（200.99）。

资料来源：世界银行。

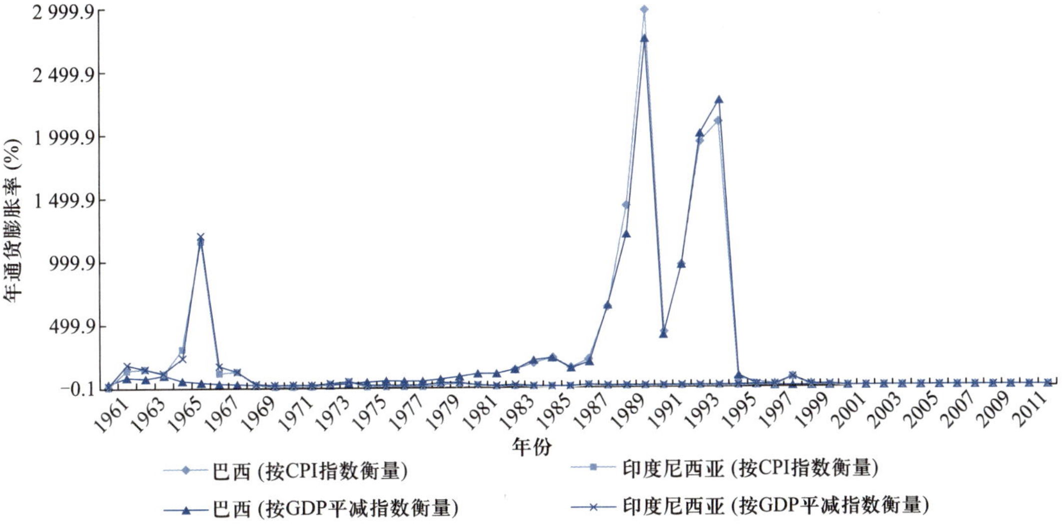


图4.10 两个经济体的几个意外时期：巴西和印度尼西亚

资料来源：世界银行。

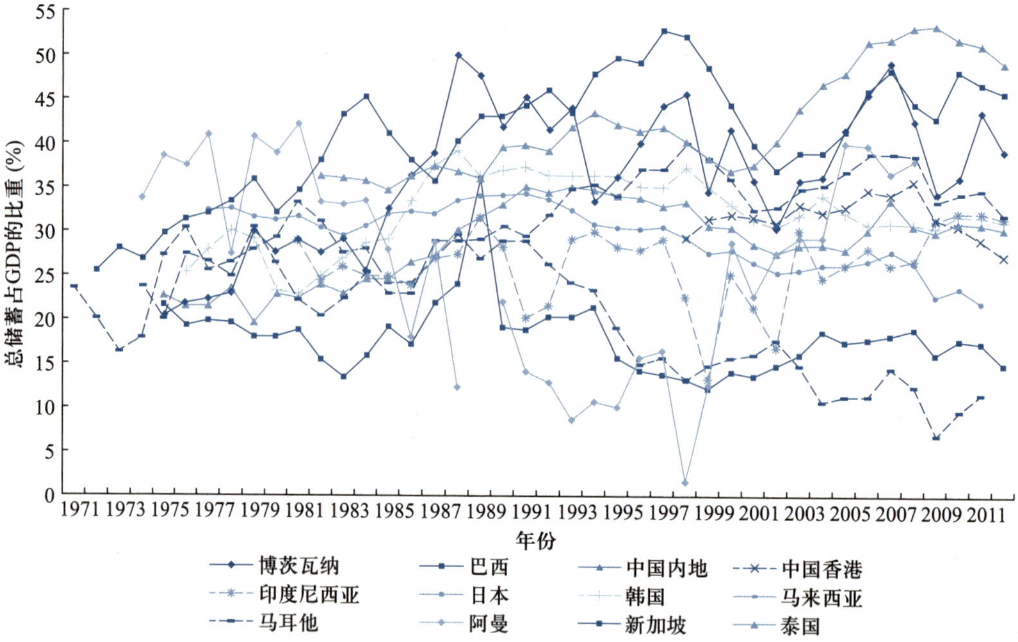


图 4.11 发展典范的总储蓄占GDP的比重

资料来源：世界银行。

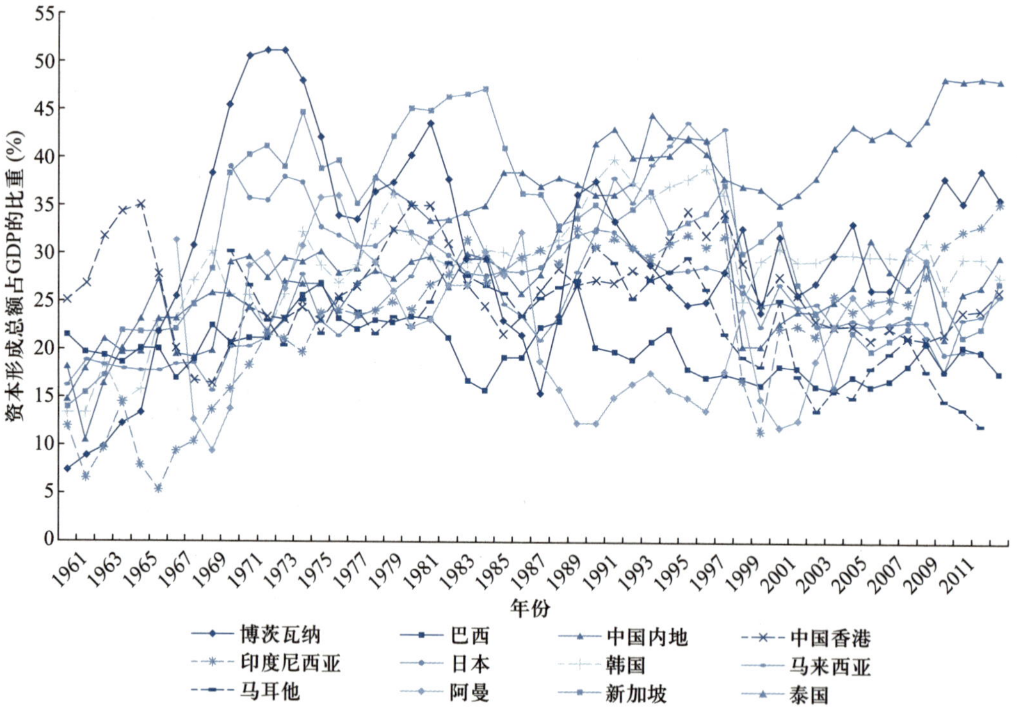


图 4.12 发展典范的资本形成总额占GDP的比重

资料来源：世界银行。

资率的主要原因。①事实上，主要的原因或许是这些国家能够生产大量的经济剩余，并产生足够高的投资回报率，从而为储蓄提供了强有力的激励。②在20世纪70年代，东南亚和拉丁美洲的储蓄率很接近，但20年之后东南亚的储蓄率比拉丁美洲高20个百分点。

### 4.2.4 有效市场

《增长报告》提到，20世纪曾经有很多企图替代市场体系的实验。最终，这些实验都失败了，都未能帮助发展中国家实现持续增长。尽管成功的国家在产权体系的强度和保护力度方面可能存在差异，但它们无一例外地都采纳了运转良好的市场机制。市场机制提供了适当的价格信号、透明的决策制定过程和良好的激励。在资本和劳动于不同部门、不同产业之间重新配置的过程中，这些国家的政府也没有妨碍市场机制的运转。以图4.13为例，在发展典范的经济体中，在经济增长的快速时期私人部门的国内信贷占GDP的比重较高而且不断攀升。因此，可以看出其要素市场化程度是在不断提高的。

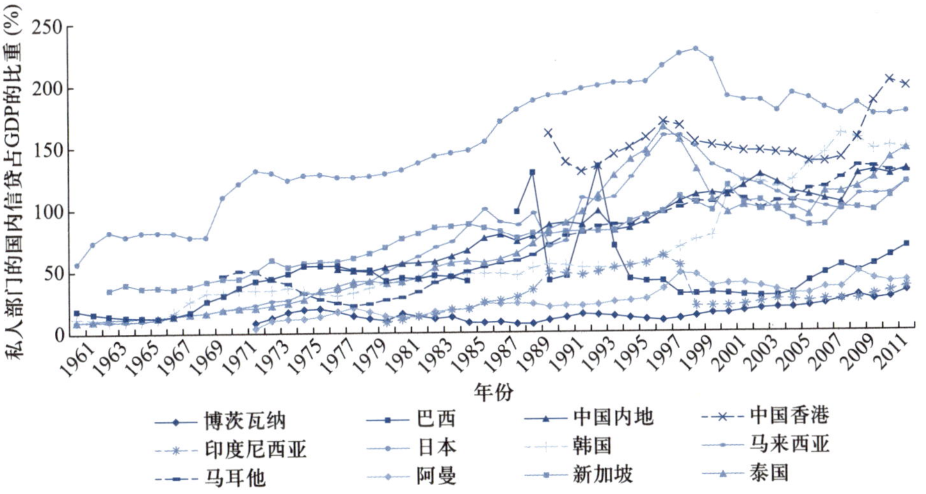


**图4.13 私人部门的国内信贷占GDP的比重**

资料来源：世界银行。

① P. Montiel and L. Serven, "Real Exchange Rates,Saving, and Growth: Is There a Link?" Background Paper, Commission on Growth and Development, Washington D.C., 2008.

② 付才辉，"最优生产函数理论：从新古典经济学向新结构社会学的范式转换"，《经济评论》，2018年第1期。

### 4.2.5 有为政府

《增长报告》指出的第五个特征事实是，成功需要有一个敢作敢为、值得信赖、精明强干的政府。高增长经济体的繁荣无一不是立足于坚实的政治基础之上的。它们的决策者深知经济增长不能靠侥幸，而是必须通过政府的领导力量有意识地制定一个宏伟的目标。增长与发展委员会委员、新加坡前国务资政吴作栋曾在一次演讲中介绍说，在过去40年里，该国始终把促进经济增长作为国家政治的一项组织原则。为保持经济增长的动力，政府和其他机构一直在进行着各种探索。新加坡的做法是否与众不同？实际上，大多数政治领导人都标榜自己对经济发展负有义不容辞的责任。然而一旦落实到行动上，许多政府往往都会为了维护政治上的太平而不愿看到经济发生裂变——这种裂变正是经济增长所必需的。有的政府为了它们自身的利益推行一些哗众取宠的改革，而一旦经济增长不能如期而至，它们绝不会另辟蹊径重新探索，而是干脆宣称大功告成，鸣金收兵。与之相反，快速增长经济体的决策者们深知，成功的发展需要数十年的不懈努力，需要在当前与未来之间做出正确取舍。一个低收入经济体即使以7% ~ 10%这样的高速度增长，要跃居较高收入经济体行列也必须花上数十年的功夫。而这种跨越几十年的过程，仅能发生于稳定和运转良好的投资环境当中。它需要适当的政治领导体制和有效的、奉行实用主义甚至有时奉行激进主义的政府。图4.14至图4.16罗列了一些反映政府行为的基础设施建设情况与政府财政支出占GDP的比重。《增长报告》同时列出了政策制定者在制定发展战略时应该避免的一系列“坏主意”。这些“坏主意”至少包括：对能源的补贴；依靠行政部门解决失业问题；通过减少基础设施投资支出降低财

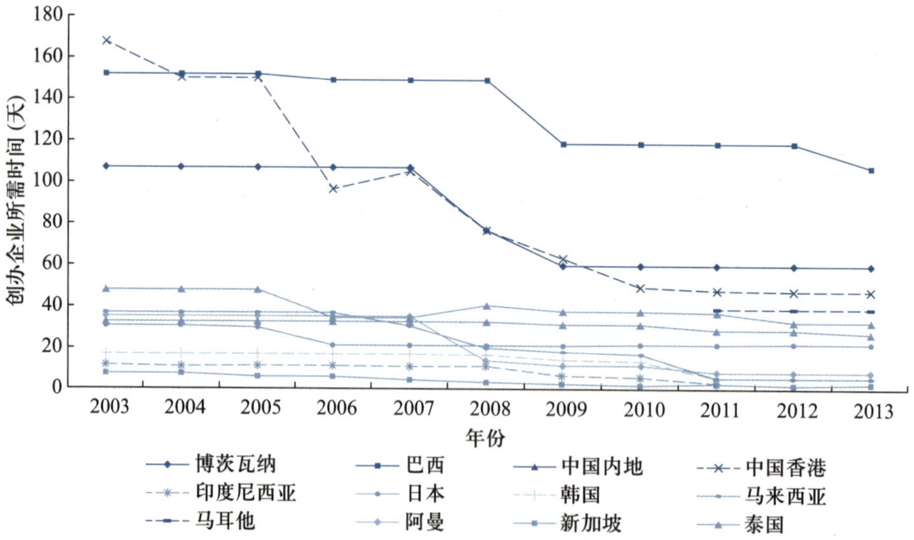


**图4.14 发展典范创办企业所需时间（天）的改进（软件基础设施）**

资料来源：世界银行。

政赤字；对国内企业提供无限制保护；利用价格管制来治理通货膨胀；长期禁止出口；抵制城市化，通过基础设施的变化衡量教育的发展；忽视环境问题，将其视为“付不起的奢侈品”；对银行系统采取管制；允许本币过度升值。

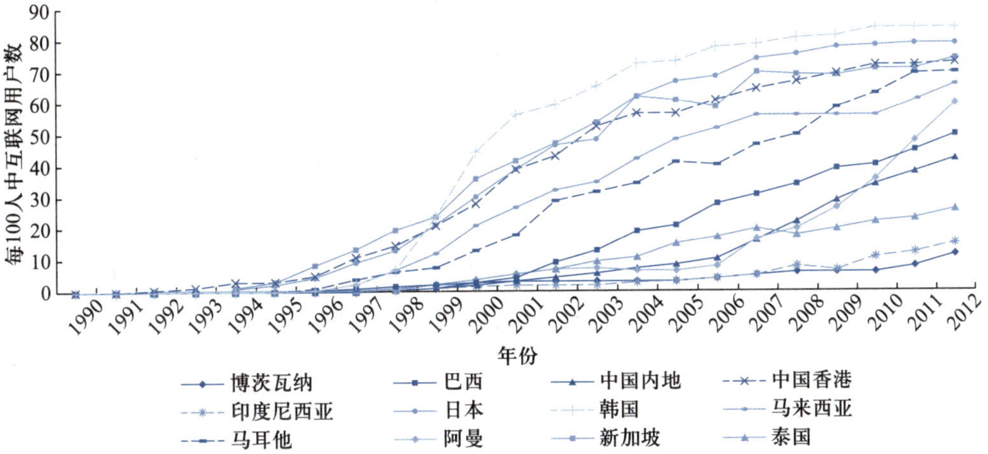


图4.15 发展典范的互联网用户（每100人）（硬件基础设施）

资料来源：世界银行。

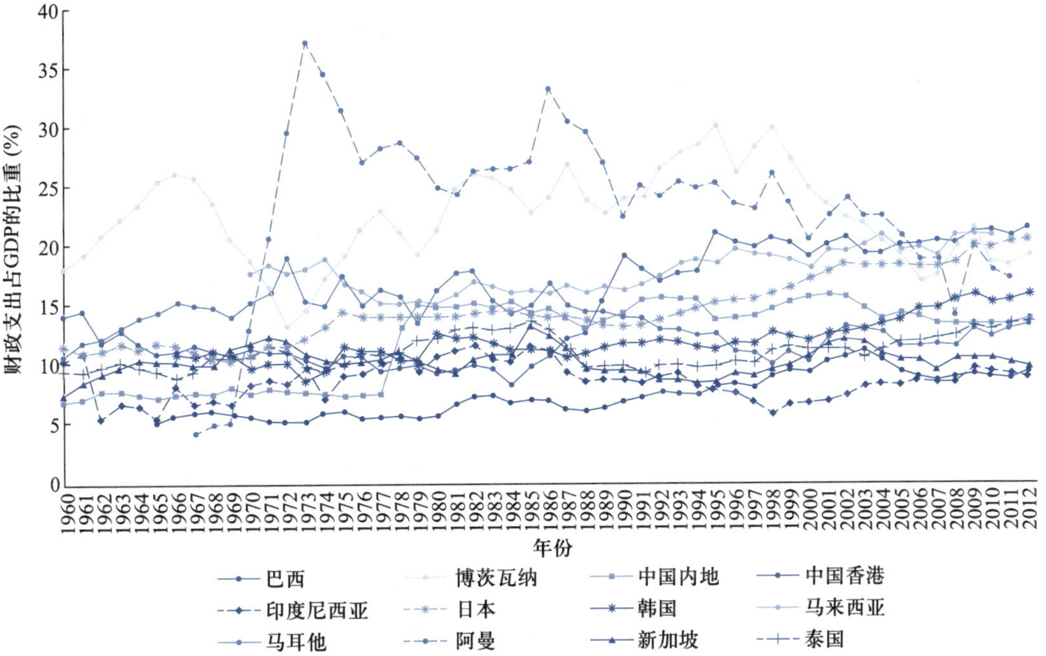


图4.16 发展典范财政支出占GDP的比重

资料来源：世界银行。

# 4.3

# 发展典范特征事实的新结构经济学诠释

以上五个方面便是增长与发展委员会报告给出的五个特征事实：（1）通过对外开放利用世界经济；（2）维持宏观经济稳定；（3）保持高储蓄率和投资率；（4）运用市场机制配置资源；（5）拥有坚定的、可信赖的和有能力的政府。围绕这五个特征事实，出现了一些外生性和内生性问题。新结构经济学为理解这些问题提供了一个分析框架。前三个特征事实是一个国家在发展的每个阶段按照由要素禀赋结构决定的比较优势发展经济时的合理结果。第四个特征事实，即市场机制，是资源有效配置，也是一个国家按照比较优势发展经济的必要的制度前提。最后一个特征事实，即一个坚定的、可信赖的和有能力的政府也是遵循比较优势发展的必要制度前提，因为经济在快速发展和结构转型中必然会出现各种市场失灵，需要一个有为的政府来克服才能顺利进行。在发展委员会的报告出版后，委员会主席迈克尔·斯宾塞常说，上述五个特征事实是成功的药材，但是，没有成功的药方。其实，药方就是新结构经济学所主张的要按照比较优势发展经济。

如果一个国家在发展战略中遵循自身的比较优势，那么它的经济就会是对外开放的，生产那些与现有禀赋结构相一致的产品和服务并出口至国际市场，进口那些不符合自身比较优势的产品和服务。这个经济体的贸易依存度内生于自身的比较优势，并将会大于其他任何情况下的贸易依存度。这个经济体将达到最有竞争力的状态，它的禀赋结构和产业结构将以可能的最快速度升级。在产业升级过程中，这个国家能够通过向发达国家借鉴技术和产业，充分挖掘自身的后来者优势，并实现比发达国家更高的经济增长率，因为它的创新成本和风险将小于那些已经处于全球技术前沿的国家。因而，这个经济体将能实现与高收入国家的收敛。从这个角度而言，通过对外开放利用世界市场（特征事实1）是按照由一个国家的禀赋结构决定的比较优势来推动产业升级的增长战略的结果。对外开放这一特征事实给我们的启示是清楚的：（1）依靠比较优势（即出口世界其他地方之所需，并为保持经济竞争力，按照禀赋结构的改变一步步升级其产业结构）；（2）利用后来者优势的潜力（在产业升级过程中从世界其他地区引进创意、技术和专业技能）。

宏观经济稳定（特征事实2）也是一个国家在发展战略中遵循比较优势的结果。如果一个国家能做到这一点，它的经济将会有竞争力，它的产业也能够在开放和竞争的市场中存活下来。它的产业升级将主要依赖于自身的资本积累过程。政府将会有健康的财政状况，原因如下：第一，它将从有力的经济增长中增加财政收入；第二，政府将没有必要补贴那些没有自生能力的企业；第三，经济增长将会创造更多的就业机会，失业较少，政府失业经济的财政开支较少。同时，这个国家将较少出现由于产业缺乏竞争力、货币错配或者财政危机而导致的内源性危机。由于该经济体的对外竞争力较强，经济增长对资本流入的依赖度不高，该国的对外收支状况也可能更好。因此，在全球性危机对该国经济产生外来冲击时，政府在采取反周期政策方面也将处于一个有利的地位。

发展与比较优势一致的产业的另外一个逻辑结果是高储蓄率和高投资率（特征事实3）。这样的一种发展战略使得发展中经济体达到最强的竞争力并生产出可能的最大经济剩余（利润），可以用来储蓄。有竞争力的产业同时也意味着高投资回报，这反过来又为储蓄和投资提供了额外的激励。此外，成功的公共投资能够提高经济的增长潜力，减少私人部门的交易成本，提高私人投资的回报率，并在未来产生足够的税收收入以清偿初始的投资成本。

采取市场机制来配置资源（特征事实4）是经济在发展当中遵循比较优势的必要条件。大多数企业是为追求利润而生的。如果相对价格能够反映禀赋结构中各种要素的相对稀缺性，企业在技术和产业选择上就会遵循经济的比较优势。而这个相对价格条件仅能在竞争性市场经济中成立。所以，在发展的每一个阶段，竞争性市场是按照比较优势发展的必要制度前提。

建立一个坚定的、可信赖的和有能力的政府（特征事实5），即创造一个具有因势利导作用的政府，也是经济发展过程中采取遵循比较优势战略的一个条件。在经济发展、产业升级过程中，要有先行者，先行者的成败都给后来者提供有用的信息，因此，必须对其外部性提供补偿，先行者的成功与否决定于是否有和新的产业相适应的软硬基础设施，需要政府来协调不同企业对软硬基础设施进行投资或由政府本身来提供，产业结构的升级才能顺利进行。因此，一个坚定的、可信赖的和有能力的政府是可持续增长的制度前提条件。然而，有能力的政府也可以看成是按照比较优势发展的一个结果：如果政府的目标是促进与国家比较优势一致的发展过程，那么，它对于经济的干预将更容易实施且更加成功，而这将增强政府的公信力。因此，一个坚定的、可信赖的和有能力的政府也被看作一个国家遵循其比较优势发展经济的结果。

总之，发展典范的这五个特征事实蕴含了新结构经济学的基本逻辑：发展中国家要根据自身的禀赋结构所决定的比较优势来选择最优的产业结构——这样其禀赋结构升级和产业结构升级才可能最快；然而，要使得发展战略在每一阶段按照禀赋结构决定的比较优势选择最优产业结构，有效市场产生的相对价格信息和激励约束机制是战略路径不发生严重偏离的保证；由于软硬基础设施这样的公共品的提供，以及产业升级中的协调、信息、外部性、风险等的补偿，就要求政府在产业升级中起到因势利导的作用。概言之，在禀赋结构升级和产业结构升级的二维结构变迁空间中，比较优势是发展战略路径的基准航道，有效市场和有为政府是发展战略路径的方向盘。如图4.17和图4.18所示，发展典范的产业结构和禀赋结构均实现了持续的转型升级。

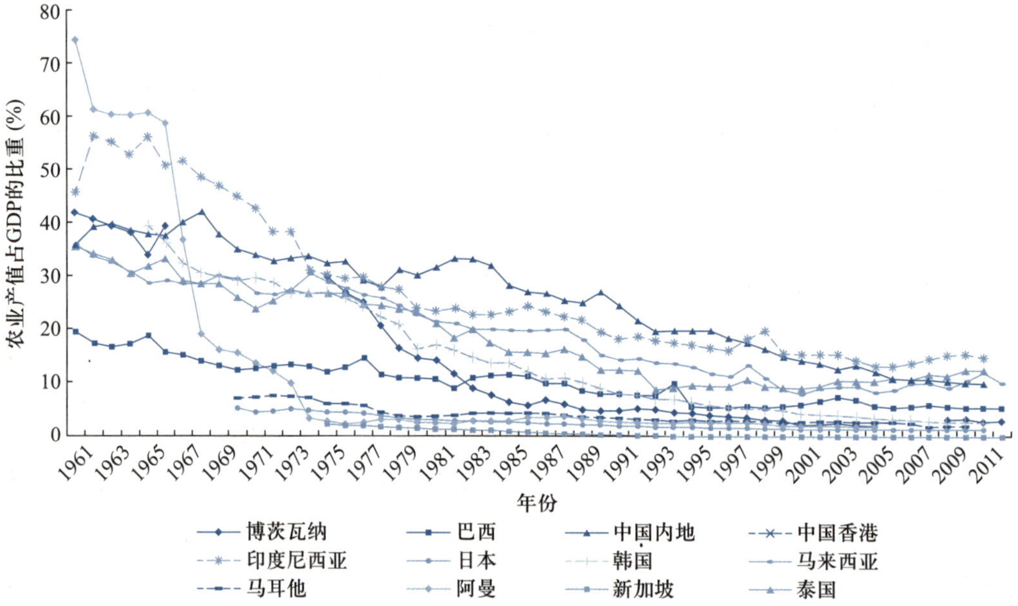


图4.17 发展典范的产业结构升级（1961—2012年）

资料来源：世界银行。

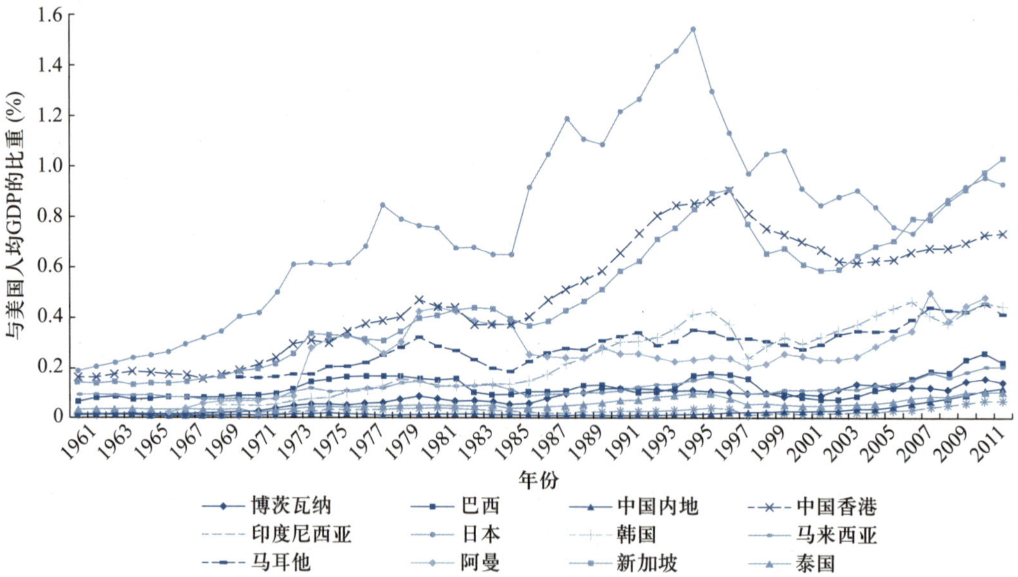


图4.18 发展典范的禀赋结构升级（1961—2012年）

资料来源：世界银行。

## 专栏4.1
## 世界银行不断对发展经济学进行反思的标志性研究报告[①]

世界银行（图4.19）是为发展中国家发展项目提供援助和贷款的国际金融机构。1945年12月27日，世界银行在布雷顿森林会议后正式宣告成立；1946年6月25日，世界银行开始运行，1947年5月9日，它批准了第一笔贷款，向法国贷款2.5亿美元。1947年11月，它成为联合国的专门机构，负责长期贷款。世界银行的最初目标是帮助欧洲国家和日本在第二次世界大战后的重建，此外辅助非洲、亚洲和拉丁美洲国家的经济发展。一开始，世界银行的贷款主要集中于大规模的基础建设，如高速公路、飞机场和发电厂等。日本和西欧国家“毕业”（达到一定的人均收入水平）后，世界银行的贷款便完全聚焦于发展中国家。从20世纪90年代初开始，世界银行也开始向东欧国家和原苏联国家贷款。1980年，中国恢复世界银行的成员国地位，次年接受了其第一笔贷款。

图4.19 世界银行徽标

世界银行的官方目标为消除贫困，根据其有关协定规定（修订并于1989年2月16日生效），其所有决定都必须旨在推动外商直接投资和国际贸易，以及为资本投资提供便利。世界银行由两个机构组成：国际复兴开发银行（IBRD）与国际开发协会（IDA）。世界银行与世界银行集团并不一样，后者包括世界银行、国际金融公司（IFC）、多边投资担保机构（MIGA）以及国际投资争端解决中心（ICSID）。按照《国际复兴开发银行协定》的规定，世界银行的主要工作任务包

① 世界银行既是发展思潮的引领者又是反思者，可参见杰拉尔德·迈耶和约瑟夫·斯蒂格利茨主编的《发展经济学前沿：未来展望》所记录的第一、第二代发展经济学先驱们的反思，以及尤素夫（Yusuf）主编的*Development Economics Through the Decades: A Critical Look at 30 Years of the World Development Report*。新结构经济学视角下对“华盛顿共识”的反思可进一步参考：Lin Justin Yifu, “The Washington Consensus Revisited: A New Structural Economics Perspective”, *Journal of Economic Policy Reform*, 2015, Vol.18, No.2, pp.96–113。

括：（1）通过对生产事业的投资，协助成员国经济的复兴与建设，鼓励不发达国家对资源的开发。（2）通过担保或参加私人贷款及其他私人投资的方式，促进私人对外投资。当成员国不能在合理条件下获得私人资本时，可运用该行自有资本或筹集的资金来补充私人投资的不足。（3）鼓励国际投资，协助成员国提高生产能力，促进成员国国际贸易的平衡发展和国际收支状况的改善。（4）在提供贷款保证时，应与其他方面的国际贷款配合。世界银行为全世界设定了到2030年要实现的两大目标：（1）终结极度贫困，将日均生活费低于1.25美元的人口比例降低到3%以下；（2）促进共享繁荣，促进每个国家底层40%人口的收入增长。然而，新千年开始之时，如果将中国排除在外，全球贫困人口不但没有减少反而增加的残酷现实与世界银行的宗旨背道而驰。其根源在于世界银行从成立之初就奉行从结构主义到“华盛顿共识”等当时主流学界的理论。面对不佳的现实，世界银行既是前两版发展经济学的主要倡导者，也在实践过程中不断对发展经济学进行反思（参见专栏1.1和专栏1.2）。世界银行根据发展中经济体的成败教训反思发展经济学的标志性研究报告主要有三部：《东亚奇迹》《第一个十年的经济增长》《增长报告》（见图4.20）。

第二次世界大战以后，许多发展中国家纷纷摆脱了殖民地半殖民地的束缚，走向政治独立，寻求自己的经济发展。由于人口数量多，耕地和自然资源的数量相对贫乏，东亚地区的发展前景并没有被普遍看好。当时，一些人预言资源丰富的非洲会有良好的发展前景。然而，40年之后，以亚洲“四小龙”为代表的东亚地区不仅克服了资源贫乏对经济增长的制约，而且通过经济起飞改善了人民生活，实现了社会进步。东亚经济发展所取得的骄人成就被誉为“东亚奇迹”，吸

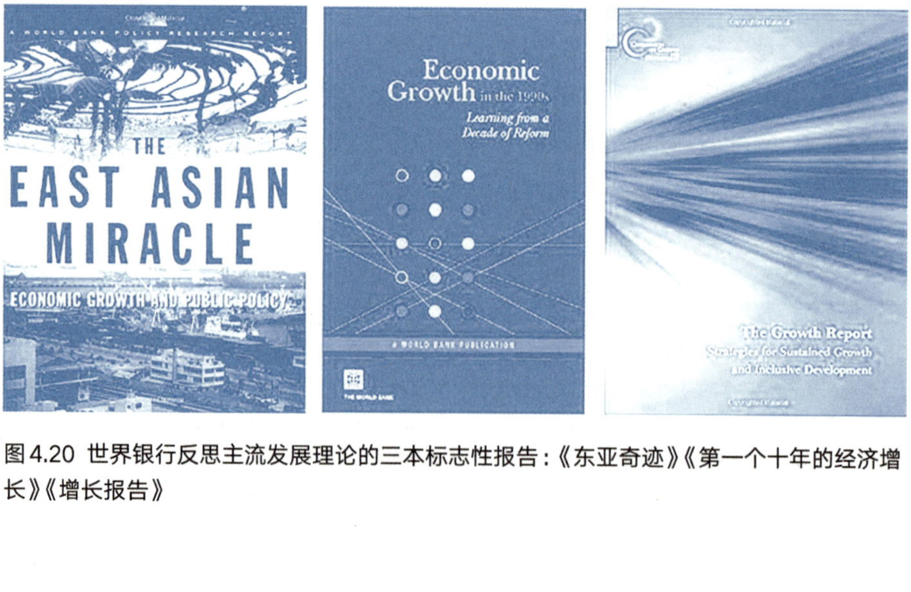


图4.20 世界银行反思主流发展理论的三本标志性报告：《东亚奇迹》《第一个十年的经济增长》《增长报告》

引着人们去探询它背后的故事。1991—1993年，世界银行组织有关专家对日本、韩国、新加坡、中国香港、中国台湾、印度尼西亚、马来西亚、泰国八个东亚国家和地区的经济发展进行了全面总结，在此基础上出版了题为“东亚奇迹”的报告。在这份报告中，世界银行认为，东亚经济异乎寻常的高速增长，不仅来自资金和人力资源的高速积累，而且还得益于市场化改革和有效的政策干预。“东亚奇迹”中三分之二归功于投资水平提高和人力资本积累等要素投入，三分之一归功于劳动生产率的改善。与其他发展中国家相比，东亚经济能够更好地配置物质和人力资源，并把它们用于高产出的投资领域和掌握先进技术。从这个意义上讲，东亚经济获得成功没有任何“奇迹”可言。但是，东亚经济之所以能够更好地配置物质和人力资源，在于它们实施了一系列共同的有利于市场经济发展的政策，并在保证宏观经济稳定的前提下，充分开发其丰富的人力资源。“东亚奇迹”的实质是不仅有经济的高速增长，而且实现了收入分配的均等化。总之，这份研究报告破除了结构主义对市场作用的漠视以及“华盛顿共识”对政府作用的漠视，归纳出“东亚奇迹”受益于出口导向且支持市场经济的政府。2003年世界银行发布的研究报告《第一个十年的经济增长》则声称世上没有万能药。2006年，世界银行又别开生面地邀请了19位实践经验丰富的国家前政要、时任或前任政府经济金融部门的主要负责人和2位诺贝尔经济学奖得主组成增长与发展委员会，集思广益，最终得到了《增长报告》这本里程碑式的研究报告。①这些领导人主要来自发展中国家，总结了二战后发展典范的实践经验，总结出发展典范的五个特征事实：开放；宏观经济稳定；高储蓄率、高投资率和有效市场；运用

① 增长与发展委员会成员包括：Montek Singh Ahluwalia，印度计划委员会副主席；Edmar Bacha，Casa Das Garças，巴西银行经济政策研究所所长、高级顾问，巴西财政部实施“黑奥计划”的前任高级顾问，巴西国家经济社会发展银行（BNDES）前任行长；Boediono，印度尼西亚银行行长，前经济统筹部部长，Gajah Mada大学经济学教授；John Browne勋爵，瑞通公司总裁，英国石油公司前任首席执行官；Kemal Derviş，联合国开发计划署署长，前土耳其经济部部长；Alejandro Foxley，智利外交部部长，前财政部部长；Goh Chok Tong，新加坡国务资政兼金融管理局主席、前总理；Han Duck-soo，韩国前国务总理、前副总理、前财政部部长；Danuta Hübner，欧洲委员会地区政策专员，前联合国欧洲经济委员会副秘书长和执行秘书，曾任欧洲事务委员会主席，欧洲统一部部长和外国事务部副部长，波兰共和国总统办公厅主任、贸易与产业部副部长；Carin Jämtin，瑞典前外援大臣；Pedro-Pablo Kuczynski，秘鲁前总理和前经济财政部部长；Danny Leipziger，世界银行经济管理与扶贫部副主任，委员会副主席；Trevor Manuel，南非财政部部长；Mahmoud Mohieldin，埃及投资部部长；Ngozi N. Okonjo-Iweala，世界银行常务副行长，尼日利亚前财政与外国事务部部长；Robert Rubin，花旗集团执行委员会董事长，美国前财政部部长；Robert Solow，诺贝尔经济学奖得主，麻省理工学院荣誉教授；Michael Spence，诺贝尔经济学奖得主，斯坦福大学荣誉教授，委员会主席；K. Dwight Venner爵士，圣基茨和尼维斯东加勒比中央银行行长；Ernesto Zedillo，墨西哥前总统，耶鲁大学全球化研究中心主任；周小川，中国人民银行行长。

市场机制配置资源；政府有决心，有信用，有能力。这本报告只归纳总结了特征事实，即药材，并没有给出如何使用药材的药方。而新结构经济学则对发展典范的特征事实做了理论升华。

## 4.4 发展典范的经济结构转型升级路径拟合及其特征

### 4.4.1 中国的经济结构转型升级路径拟合及其特征①

中国位于亚洲东部、太平洋西岸。陆地同14国接壤，与6国隔海相望。陆地面积约960万平方千米，大陆海岸线1.8万多千米。地势西高东低，地貌复杂多样，山地、高原和丘陵约占陆地面积的67%，盆地和平原约占陆地面积的33%。气候差异明显，从南到北跨越热带、亚热带、暖温带、中温带、寒温带气候带。人口主体为汉族，占全国总人口的91.51%，其余8.49%为55个少数民族。2014年全国人口总数为13.68亿。官方语言为汉语。在55个少数民族中，除回、满两个民族通用汉语外，其他53个少数民族都使用本民族的语言；有文字的民族有21个，共使用27种文字。1949年中华人民共和国成立，经过3年的恢复期后，从1953年开始实行计划经济，到1978年年底开始改革开放，并于2001年加入世界贸易组织。1978—2019年间年均增长率高达9.3%，是世界上经济增长最快的国家之一。2019年，中国人均GDP超过1万美元，很可能在2025年左右超过12 700美元，步入中等收入国家的行列。

① 这里对中国工业化路径阶段的归纳转引自：王丽莉、文一，“中国能跨越中等收入陷阱吗？——基于工业化路径的跨国比较”，《经济评论》，2017年第3期。更详细的论述参见：林毅夫、蔡昉、李周，《中国的奇迹：发展战略与经济改革》，上海三联书店，1994年；林毅夫，《解读中国经济》，北京大学出版社，2012年。

目前，中国是世界第二大经济体（仅次于美国）、第一大工业国和第一大贸易国。

中国在取得今天的成绩之前经历了曲折坎坷的探索。中国改革开放之前的工业化路径严重违背比较优势。中国1978年开始的经济改革并不是中国近代史上第一次雄心勃勃地尝试启动工业化。在这之前，中国进行了多次工业化尝试，包括第二次鸦片战争后在大城市兴办工业的洋务运动，辛亥革命后新共和政府通过全面模仿美国的政治制度推动工业化进程，以及中华人民共和国成立后模仿苏联的计划经济建设。这些自上而下的工业化尝试纷纷遇到困境，原因在于违背了按照要素禀赋条件所决定的比较优势发展，试图跳过劳动密集型的轻工业阶段直接发展资本密集型的重工业。作为一个农村人口占总人口90%以上的农业大国，成功的经济发展需要自下而上地培育市场需求和企业组织，逐渐把农村剩余劳动力引入劳动密集制造业，按次序进行产业升级。中华人民共和国成立后，中国选择了与苏联类似的工业化道路，利用农村浅薄的积累来优先发展违反比较优势的重工业。自“一五”计划起，中国在苏联的帮助下，建立起了许多的城市型工业中心，生产资本密集型产品和重工业产品，例如，汽车、钢铁、机床和大型精密仪器等。为了提高钢铁产量，“大跃进”时期，在“以钢为纲，全面跃进”的口号下，全国人民开展空前规模的大众炼钢运动，以支援重工业建设。这种优先发展重工业的政策一直持续到“文化大革命”结束，导致了轻工业与重工业的比率不断下降。1952—1978年，无论是中国轻工业与重工业的增加值之比，还是这两个产业之间的劳动力比率与资本比率都呈现明显的下降趋势，尤其在第一个五年计划期间下降最快。虽然工业增加值在“大跃进”失败以后经过1961—1964年的短暂调整有所恢复，但是从劳动力和资本构成来看，这种重工业化的趋势一直在继续。其中，轻、重工业增加值之比由最初的1.4降到了1978年的0.6，劳动力比率从接近2.5降到了0.5，固定资产比由0.5降到了0.18。

中国采取这种重工业优先的大推进发展战略，由于资金短缺，资金的价格太高，违反比较优势，生产成本必然高于符合比较优势的发达国家的同类产品，因此，在国内和国际市场缺乏竞争力，企业没有自生能力，只能靠政府的保护补贴才能存在，而且，在政府的保护补贴下，即使把这样的产业建立起来，由于国内的购买力低，最终产品的产出水平也往往低于其潜在产能的30% ~ 50%。其次，政府为支持重工业建设采取的价格扭曲体制，造成资源严重错配，大大降低了经济效率。一方面，政府对农产品课以重税，并压低农产品与原材料的价格，间接补贴重工业企业。另一方面，有限的资本由政府使用行政手段直接向大型重工业企业配给资源，这导致农业、轻工业部门投入严重不足，发展滞后，国民经济比例严重失衡。中国计划经济后来遇到的发展障碍和二战后第一波结构主义提出的在落后国家采用政府主导大推进模式发展资本密集型的大产业失败同出一辙，说明在落后农业国家无法成功实现工业化，其关键不在于计划经济，而在于违反比较优势，因为，采取类似发展方式的一些市场经济国家同样陷入困境。例如，在进口替代政策下过早进入重工业化阶段的拉美国家长期陷入了中等收入陷阱。相反，自1978年起，中国不仅吸收了市场经济元素，鼓励竞争和优胜劣汰，关键是采取了从轻工业到重工业的循序渐进的产业升级顺序，符合中国自身禀赋比较优势的结构变迁道路。

中国改革开放之后的工业化路径逐步转变到比较优势的轨道上来，大致经历了如下几个阶段：

乡村原始工业爆发阶段（1978—1988年）。1978年改革开放后，乡镇企业在中国异军突起。一方面，国内市场受到高关税保护，轻工业产品极端短缺，需求大，皇帝的女儿不愁嫁，只要生产得出来就能卖得掉，给农民致富提供了一条新的道路。另一方面，在中央政府的要求下，地方政府希望找到方法快速发展地方经济。以农村集体土地所有制为基础，村镇政府能够将土地、资金与农村剩余劳动力汇集起来，组建乡镇企业，进行小规模的小商品生产，但是以远距离贸易（而不是自给自足）为目的。改革开放前建立的农村合作社经验、社队企业模式、土地集体所有制、供销合作社、扫盲运动、地方社会治安和农村基础设施（原始公路、运河、机耕道、灌溉系统）也大大降低了乡村原始工业化的制度成本，乡镇企业如雨后春笋般在广大农村出现，并快速增长。在1978—1988年的十年间，农村工业总产值从515亿元增加到7 020亿元，增长超过12.5倍；农村工业的就业从2 800万人发展到9 500万人，增长超过2倍；农民总收入从87亿元提高到963亿元，增长10倍；乡镇企业总资本存量从230亿元增加到2 100亿元，增长超过8倍。1992年，乡镇企业部门已经吸收了从农业部门转移出来的约1.03亿劳动力，占乡村劳动力总数的24.2%。其中，农村工业吸收的劳动力占整个农村非农产业吸收劳动力总数的61.4%。从全国情况来看，在农村剩余劳动力的转移总量中，大约只有12%的劳动力转移到各类城镇部门，而约88%的劳动力在农村工业、商业和服务部门实现就业转移。[①]到了2000年，乡镇企业职工超过1.28亿人（不包括进城务工的农民工），占中国农村总劳动力的30%。农村工业总产值达到11.6万亿，是1988年的16.5倍，1978年的225倍。从1978年到2000年，扣除通胀因素后的乡村工业实际总产值年均增速为21%，至少增长了66倍，乡镇工业产值占全国工业总产值的比重呈直线上升。从1978年到1997年，乡镇工业总产值占全国工业总产值的比重由10%增长到接近60%。这一上升趋势直到90年代末才开始在现代轻工业和重工业的崛起中停止，让位于现代轻工业和重工业。乡村工业以食品、纺织、制鞋等劳动力密集型的小型企业为主。以乡村纺织业的增长为例，1985—1989年乡村纺织企业平均每年增加1 741个，职工人数平均每年增加33.06万人，按1980年不变价格计算的工业总产值年均递增31.98%，固定资产原值年均递增40%，产品销售收入年均递增32.36%。其中，整个20世纪80年代江苏乡村两级的纺织工业产值年均增长29.25%，其主

① 陈吉元、胡必亮，“中国的三元经济结构与农业剩余劳动力转移”，《经济研究》，1994年第4期。

要产品产量，棉纱提高了7.84倍，棉布提高了3.22倍，针棉织品提高了5.23倍，丝织品提高了10.35倍。

**劳动力密集型规模化轻工业繁荣阶段**（1989—1998年）。经过乡村原始工业化头十年的爆发式增长，国内外市场迅速扩大，供应与分销网络逐步建立起来，市场竞争也日趋激烈。因此，依赖流动农业人口的规模化大企业变得有利可图。在20世纪80年代末，中国开启了以规模化方式生产轻工业产品为特征的第一次工业革命，基于劳动分工原理的劳动力密集型大企业在沿海中小城市快速兴起。由于轻工业资本密集度较低，乡村原始工业化时期积累的资本能够满足轻工业规模化生产的需求。从1988年到1998年，纺织、服装、食品和家具等规模化轻工业部门高速增长，轻工业增加值由2 413亿元增长到11 753亿元，增长接近4倍；轻工业资本存量由3 661亿元增长到12 898亿元，增长超过2.5倍。改革开放后的前20年成为中国轻工业发展的黄金时期。据《中国工业经济年鉴》，这一时期轻工业与重工业的工业增加值、固定资产原值、资本与劳动投入的比值均呈现急速上升的趋势，彻底扭转了改革开放前30年的下降趋势。这个趋势直到完成以劳动力密集型轻工业为主导的第一次工业革命时期（即20世纪90年代中后期）才结束，中国才又重新进入重工业起飞阶段。从1978年到1998年，中国轻工业增加值增长了14倍，年均增长率约为14%。经过价格调整后，年均增长率约为11%。1978年轻工业劳动力人数为1 828万人，1998年增长到4 017万人，增长约1.2倍。与80年代相比，90年代轻工业行业的工业增加值比重大多上升，其中食品制造、服装业、电子工业等增长明显。而除交通设备制造业外，重工业行业的工业增加值比重大多下降，其中化学工业、石油加工业与黑色金属加工业的下降最为明显。在这一时期，作为第一次工业革命旗舰产业的纺织工业的增长最为突出。1978—1988年纺织工业（乡及以上）企业单位数由1.21万个增长到2.73万个，工业净产值由148亿元增长到407亿元。从乡镇小规模纺织企业，到大规模纺织工厂，纺织工业的生产能力迅速扩张。到1997年纺织业的工业增加值达到1 117亿元，与1978年相比，增长超过6.5倍。从1978年到1998年，纱的产量由232万吨增长到542万吨，布的产量由110亿米增长到241亿米。化学纤维产量在1988年后增速大大提高。1988年，化学纤维年产量是130万吨，1998年增长到510万吨。此外，作为我国重要出口品，纺织纱线、布及其制品在1984年的出口额为35亿美元，1998年增长到128亿美元。这些巨大变化都为中国加入WTO做好了充分准备。1995年，即中国加入WTO的约6年前，就已经超过美国成为世界最大的纺织服装品生产国和出口国，并且从此一直占据这个主导地位。

**重型基础设施建设和重化工业起飞阶段**（1999年—　）。轻工业部门的急剧膨胀终于为重工业的发展提供了条件和机会，因为它真正创造了重化工业产品所需要的资金积累和市场。随着经济的快速发展，资本迅速积累，要素禀赋结构发生变化，重工业逐渐从违反比较优势变成符合比较优势，企业逐渐变成拥有自成能力。同时，轻工业生产规模的扩大，工业企业对原材料、中间产品、机器以及分销网络的需求日益膨胀，能源、动力、交通运输在1990年中期成为巨大的发展瓶颈。有了在前一阶段积累的巨大资金和市场，对能源、动力与交通运输（工业“三位一体”）的产业升级便变得有利可图，从而在政府基础设施发展战略主导下开启了中国的第二次工业革命，开始进入重工业化阶段。根据《中国工业经济年鉴》数据，自20世纪90年代中期开始，轻工业发展相对于重工业达到顶峰。在1999—2011年间，中国轻工业与重工业的工业总产值、工业增加值、固定资产原值、资本与劳动投入的比值开始呈下降趋势，说明重工业开始起飞。而这次起飞与50—70年代计划经济时期的起飞有本质的不同：第一次起飞因为违反比较优势，企业缺乏自生能力，缺乏市场基础，一直处于亏本经营。而第二次起飞则靠国内的资本积累，比较优势变化储蓄托起，因而是盈利和可持续的。经过第一次（轻）工业革命，日益扩大的轻工业品贸易，对更大规模、更高效的交通运输方式产生了巨大的需求，快速的发展也为这些基础设施的建设积累了足够的资本。自20世纪90年代起，中国通过高速公路建设、铁路提速与高铁建设，日益完善了全国交通网络。中国航班里程、公路里程、铁路里程等在90年代末增速大大提高。“八五”期间中国建成通车的高速公路年平均为324千米，“九五”前三年达到年均1 372千米。到1998年年底，中国高速公路通车里程跃居世界第八位，在建高速公路项目总里程12 600千米。1996年年底，中国铁路运营里程达到了6.49万千米，中国横贯东西、沟通南北、干支结合的具有相当规模的铁路运输网络已经形成并逐步趋于完善。1997年到2007年，中国共进行了六次铁路大提速，一批时速超过200千米的旅客列车投入运营。而且货运列车时速也超过了120千米，时速比90年代初提高了3倍。2008年8月，中国开通运营第一条时速超过300千米的高速铁路——京津城际铁路，到2015年年底，中国高速铁路营业里程达1.9万千米。中国已经拥有全世界最大规模以及最高运营速度的高速铁路网。工业生产与远距离运输离不开能源的支持。家庭收入提高以后城市发展对能源的需求也急剧上升。1978年，中国能源生产总量为6.3亿吨标准煤，1998年能源生产总量大约翻一番，达到13亿吨标准煤。但自90年代末起，中国能源生产开始加速增长，达到一个新的拐点，标志着重化工业的崛起。到2015年，中国能源生产总量达到36.2亿吨标准煤，是1998年能源产量的2.8倍，1978年的5.8倍。煤炭是中国的主要能源。进入21世纪后，电力、冶金、化学和建材等主要耗煤行业均保持较快的发展速度，拉动煤炭需求强劲增长，煤炭价格持续攀升。从2002年开始，中国煤炭行业进入了一个史无前例的繁荣阶段，经历了“黄金十年”。中国原煤产量由2002年的11.4亿吨增长到2012年的26.7亿吨，年均增长8.9%。此外，自21世纪起，水电、核电、风电等清洁能源加速增长，在中国能源生产中的比重越来越大。2004年，中国水电装机容量突破1亿千瓦，超过美国成为世界水电第一大国。2010年，中国水电装机容量超过2亿千瓦。

自20世纪90年代末起，在能源、动力与运输的工业“三位一体”建设高潮的支持下，中国规模化重工业生产开始迅猛发展，资本进一步积累，比较优势进一步提高，引爆了以规模化方式生产基本生产工具和原材料（包括中间品和耐用消费品）为特征的第二次工业革命。1998—2011年，重工业增加值由11 943亿元增长到173 686亿元，增长了13.5倍，年均增长率为22.8%；重工业资本存量由31 099亿元增长到106 883亿元，增长了2.4倍；重工业劳动力人数由5 639万人增长到7 406万人。与1997年的工业结构相比，2007年重工业行业的工业增加值比重大多上升，钢铁行业和交通、电气、电子与通信设备制造业的增长尤其显著。而多数轻工业行业的增加值与总产值比重下降，特别是食品工业与纺织业。1995年中国汽车年产量约为145万辆，2012年汽车年产量增长到1 927万辆，平均每年增长16.4%。汽车行业的快速增长来自资本积累、比较优势变化和市场规模的扩大及重工业基础的增强。数据显示，中国民用汽车拥有量在20世纪90年代末开始加速上升。1995年中国民用汽车拥有量约为1 000万辆，到2012年，民用汽车拥有量超过1亿辆。同时，中国汽车出口量不断扩大。1995年，中国汽车出口仅有1.7万辆，2012年汽车出口增长到101.5万辆。从1978年至今，中国轻工业与重工业重要经济指标的比值呈现出重新工业化的特点，即对1978年以前的工业化道路纠偏，首先发展轻工业，然后再用轻工业积累的市场、技术和资金条件发展重工业。这种建立在以资本积累、比较优势变化基础上的，从轻工业到重工业、从生活消费品到生产资料、从劳动力密集型产品到资本密集型产品的升级过程符合新结构经济学所揭示的工业化的内在逻辑。在发展的初始阶段，资本积累不充足，无法支持资本密集型产品的大规模生产。相反，劳动力密集的轻工业产品则与本国的要素禀赋与比较优势相符。①

尽管存在各种不足，但中国这个世界上最大的发展中国家数十年的高速增长和脱贫成就堪称发展典范中的典范。尽管中国在1978年的改革开放之前也曾步履蹒跚，但其后的发展路径稳步推进。图4.21是1970—2011年中国内地的非农业结构转型升级的路径。对数拟合（$R^2 = 0.57$）的发展战略路径曲线为$I_{\mathrm{CHN},\,t} = 1.189+0.107\,8\times\ln(E_{\mathrm{CHN},\,t})$，斜率和弹性分别为$\dfrac{\partial I_{\mathrm{CHN},t}}{\partial E_{\mathrm{CHN},t}}=\dfrac{0.107\,8}{E_{\mathrm{CHN},t}}$，$\dfrac{\partial I_{\mathrm{CHN},t}}{\partial E_{\mathrm{CHN},t}}\dfrac{E_{\mathrm{CHN},t}}{I_{\mathrm{CHN},t}}=\dfrac{0.107\,8}{I_{\mathrm{CHN},t}}$。相对于世界整体而言，中国产业升级的步伐和弹性要大。因此，温和的渐进式升级似乎是中国式风格。

图4.22是1970—2011年中国内地的工业发展战略路径，二次函数拟合（$R^2 = 0.66$）的发展战略路径曲线为$I_{\mathrm{CHN},\,t} = 1.033\,09+34.584\,07\times E_{\mathrm{CHN},\,t}-203.846\,3\times E^2_{\mathrm{CHN},\,t}$，顶点和拐点分别为$I = 2.499\,95$和$E = 0.084\,83$。即便是相较于非洲的博茨瓦纳而言，中国内地工业升级的拐

① 林毅夫、蔡昉、李周，《中国的奇迹：发展战略与经济改革》，上海三联书店，1994年版。

点也出现得较早，而工业占比的顶点也偏高，说明中国内地的工业发展似乎比较迅猛。

图4.23是中国内地1970—2011年的服务业发展战略路径。对数拟合（$R^2=0.48$）的发展战略路径为$I_{CHN,t}=0.77782+0.08837\times\ln(E_{CHN,t})$，斜率和弹性分别为$\frac{\partial I_{CHN,t}}{\partial E_{CHN,t}}=\frac{0.8837}{E_{CHN,t}}$，

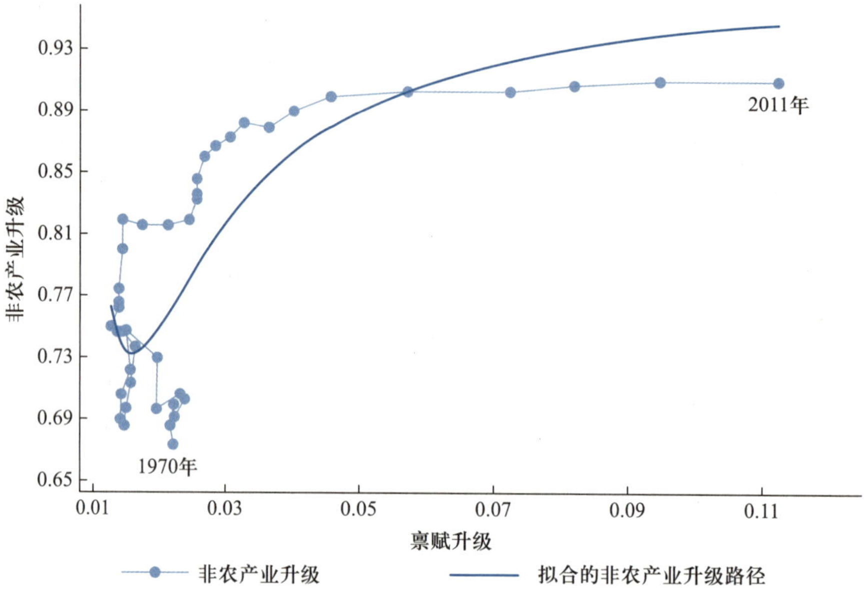


图4.21 中国内地的非农产业发展战略路径（1970—2011年）及其拟合

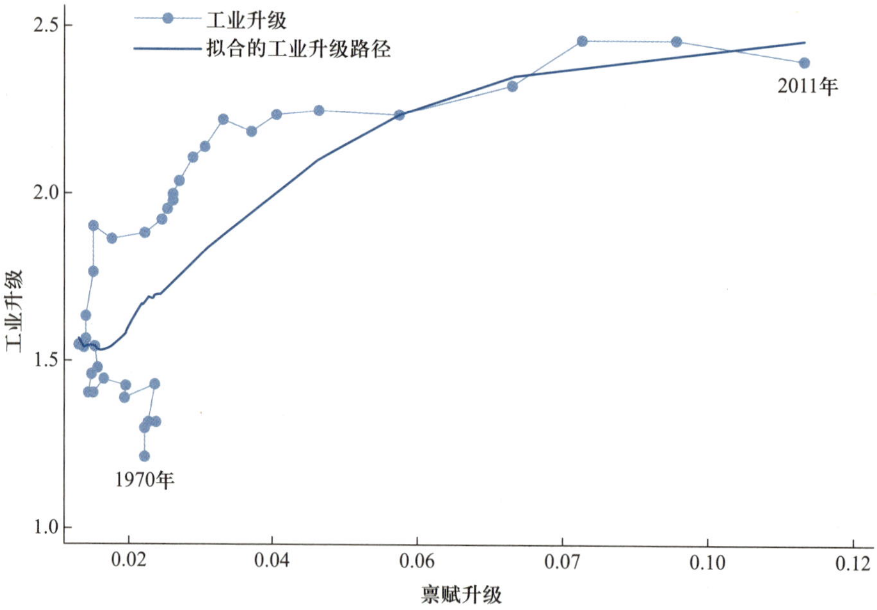


图4.22 中国内地的工业发展战略路径（1970—2011年）及其拟合

$\frac{\partial I_{CHN,t}}{\partial E_{CHN,t}}\frac{E_{CHN,t}}{I_{CHN,t}}=\frac{0.088\,37}{I_{CHN,t}}$。相对于世界样本而言，中国内地服务业升级路径的斜率和弹性要略大一点。

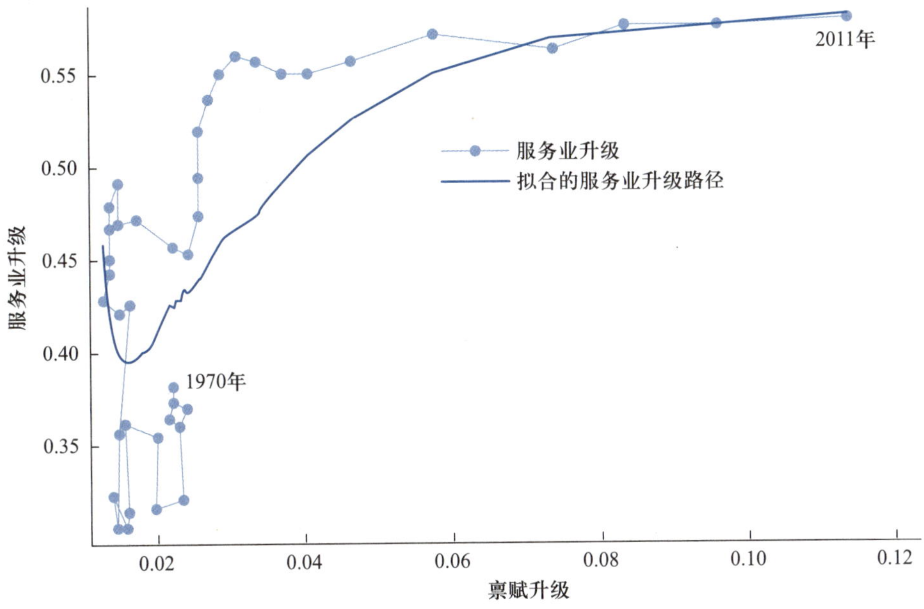


图4.23 中国内地的服务业发展战略路径（1970—2011年）及其拟合

### 4.4.2 中国香港的经济结构转型升级路径拟合及其特征

香港地处中国华南地区，北接广东省深圳市，西接珠江，与澳门和内地隔珠江口相望，其余两面与南海邻接。全境由香港岛、九龙半岛、新界三大区域组成，管辖陆地总面积1 104.32平方千米。属亚热带气候，全年气温较高，年平均温度为22.8℃。截至2014年年末，香港总人口约726.4万，人口密度居世界第三。1842年至1997年6月，香港为英国殖民地；第二次世界大战后的香港经济和社会迅速发展，东西方文化在此交汇，成为亚洲“四小龙”之一。1997年7月1日，中国正式恢复对香港行使主权，香港成为中国的特别行政区之一。香港素以治安优良、经济自由和法律制度健全等闻名于世，有“东方之珠”“美食天堂”和“购物天堂”等美誉，也是全球最富裕、经济最发达和生活水准最高的地区之一。香港是继纽约、伦敦后的世界第三大金融中心（三者合称为“纽伦港”），在世界享有极高的声誉，也是亚太地区乃至全球重要的航运枢纽和最具竞争力的城市之一。

如西谚所云，“罗马不是一天建成的”，香港也是近百年来不断通过经济结构转型升级才取得今天的成就。香港由于地理原因没有农业基础，最初主要依赖于转口贸易作为原始工业化阶段。如表4.2所示，从20世纪50年代开始到21世纪初，香港的对外贸易依存度一直在124%到252%之间，但是其贸易结构却历经了重要的转型变化。香港的经济结构转型升级依次经历了从“转口型”经济转向以轻纺工业为主的加工出口型经济，再由出口加工型劳动力密集型产业转型升级到技术和资金密集型制造业，最后才过渡到现代金融业，成为全球金融中心。香港在20世纪五六十年代完成了从转口贸易向出口加工型贸易的转型升级。1950年，香港对外贸易依存度为238.2%，但本港商品出口比重只有11%。到了本阶段末的1966年，对外贸易依存度略有下降，为124.1%，但本港产品出口比重上升到75.8%，绝对额为57.3亿港元，是1950年的14倍。这一时期的主要产业包括成衣和制鞋业，办公室、会计及计算器材制造业、收音机、电视机及通信设备与器材制造业、家庭电器用具及电子玩具制造业等劳动力密集型制造业。1952—1966年，制造业就业人数年均增长速度高达10.5%，该时期末的1966年就业人数达到346 990人。1952—1960年年均名义经济增长速度为8.9%，1961—1966年年均增长速度为10.9%。该时期是增长最快的时期之一，1966年人均GDP达到中上等国家（地区）低位收入水平，在亚洲紧随日本之后，位于第二位。香港在20世纪七八十年代完成了从出口加工劳动力密集型产业向技术和资金密集型制造业的转型升级。这一时期的主要产业包括计算机存储系统、电子计算器、集成电路、半导体元件等电子产品。如表4.3所示，香港的制造业发展到1971年时增加值达到59亿港元，然后一路高歌猛进，在1993年时达到934亿港元的峰值。香港在20世纪90年代开始逐步从制造业向现代金融服务业转型升级。这一过程中，先是从制造业向物流和酒店餐饮业等服务业转型，然后才向现代金融服务业转型升级。1988年，香港的批发零售和酒店餐饮业的增加值首次超过制造业，达到1 101亿港元，到1993年现代金融业达到2 200亿港元，是制造业的2倍多。至此，香港完成了现代经济转型。

表4.2 中国香港转口贸易占总出口额比例　　单位：亿港元

| | 1950年 | 1955年 | 1960年 | 1966年 | 1970年 | 1975年 | 1980年 | 1985年 |
|---|---|---|---|---|---|---|---|---|
| 进出口总额 | 75.03 | 62.53 | 98.01 | 176.60 | 328.45 | 633.04 | 2 098.93 | 4 665.272 |
| 对外贸易依存度（%） | 238.2 | 169.7 | 166.3 | 124.1 | 142.7 | 128.5 | 148.0 | 171.8 |
| 出口总额 | 37.16 | 25.34 | 39.38 | 75.63 | 152.38 | 298.33 | 982.42 | 2 351.52 |
| 本港出口额 | 4.09 | 7.30 | 28.67 | 57.30 | 123.43 | 228.52 | 681.70 | 1 298.00 |
| 本港出口比重（%） | 11.0 | 28.8 | 72.8 | 75.8 | 81.0 | 76.6 | 69.4 | 55.2 |

| | 1988年 | 1990年 | 1993年 | 1995年 | 1998年 | 2000年 | 2002年 |
|---|---|---|---|---|---|---|---|
| 进出口总额 | 9 918.70 | 12 824.10 | 21 188.50 | 26 854.10 | 27 767.41 | 32 306.51 | 31 799.36 |
| 对外贸易依存度（%） | 218.0 | 220.1 | 236.1 | 249.3 | 219.2 | 250.80 | 252.4 |

续表

| | 1988年 | 1990年 | 1993年 | 1995年 | 1998年 | 2000年 | 2002年 |
|---|---|---|---|---|---|---|---|
| 出口总额 | 4 930.69 | 6 398.74 | 10 462.5 | 13 441.3 | 13 476.59 | 15 726.89 | 15 605.17 |
| 本港出口额 | 2 174.43 | 2 258.76 | 2 228.51 | 2 311.90 | 1 884.54 | 1 808.59 | 14 295.90 |
| 本港出口比重（%） | 44.1 | 35.3 | 21.3 | 17.2 | 14.0 | 11.5 | 9.4 |

资料来源：滕光进等，“香港产业结构演变与城市竞争力发展研究”，《中国软科学》，2003年第12期。

表4.3 1961—2000年中国香港选定行业增加值结构变化情况　　单位：亿港元

| 行业 | 1961年 | 1971年 | 1975年 | 1985年 | 1988年 | 1993年 | 1998年 | 2000年 |
|---|---|---|---|---|---|---|---|---|
| 制造业 | | 59.13 | 99.54 | 562.29 | 900.95 | 933.62 | 726.01 | 716.55 |
| 所占比例（%） | 23.6 | 28.1 | 26.9 | 22.0 | 20.4 | 11.1 | 6.0 | 5.8 |
| 批发零售进出口酒店餐饮业 | | 37.55 | 76.63 | 581.07 | 1 100.62 | 2 288.03 | 3 016.93 | 3 246.22 |
| 所占比例（%） | 21.9 | 19.5 | 20.7 | 22.8 | 25.0 | 27.1 | 25.0 | 26.4 |
| 运输业、仓储及通信业 | | 14.58 | 26.57 | 207.49 | 401.97 | 800.45 | 1 114.09 | 1 257.24 |
| 所占比例（%） | 9.6 | 6.8 | 7.2 | 8.1 | 9.1 | 9.5 | 9.2 | 10.2 |
| 金融保险地产及商业服务 | | 28.55 | 62.83 | 412.00 | 837.73 | 2 199.76 | 2 963.52 | 2 910.62 |
| 所占比例（%） | 17.4 | 17.5 | 17.0 | 16.1 | 19.0 | 26.1 | 24.6 | 23.7 |
| 社区及个人服务业 | | 34.40 | 69.18 | 425.22 | 610.19 | 1 304.82 | 2 331.69 | 2 524.35 |
| 所占比例（%） | 15.3 | 18.9 | 18.7 | 16.6 | 13.8 | 15.5 | 19.3 | 20.5 |
| 本地生产总值 | | | 369.74 | 2 554.12 | 4 408.50 | 8 443.22 | 12 053.49 | 12 288.97 |

资料来源：滕光进等，“香港产业结构演变与城市竞争力发展研究”，《中国软科学》，2003年第12期。

图4.24是发展典范中的中国香港2000—2011年间的非农产业转型升级的发展战略路径。① 由于在此期间香港的禀赋结构水平接近世界前沿而产业结构水平已超过世界前沿，如前所述已经完成了现代经济结构的转型升级，因此其发展路径有非常强烈的随机游走特征。例如，对数拟合的曲线为$I_{HKG,t} = 1.011\ 1+0.000\ 3\times\ln(E_{HKG,t})$，斜率和弹性都近乎为0，而且拟合优度$R^2 = 0.000\ 3$也近乎为0。图4.25和图4.26分别是中国香港2000—2011年间工业和服务业的发展战略路径。前者的对数拟合（$R^2 = 0.12$）和后者的二次函数拟合（$R^2 = 0.09$）曲线分别为$I_{HKG,t} = 7.065-20.005\times E_{HKG,t}+15.024\times E^2_{HKG,t}$和$I_{HKG,t} = 1.14-0.102\times\ln(E_{HKG,t})$。二者的拟合优度均很低，具有非常强烈的随机游走特征。

① 世界银行WDI数据库中没有中国香港更长历史时期的数据，故不能追踪历史上其转型升级的轨迹。

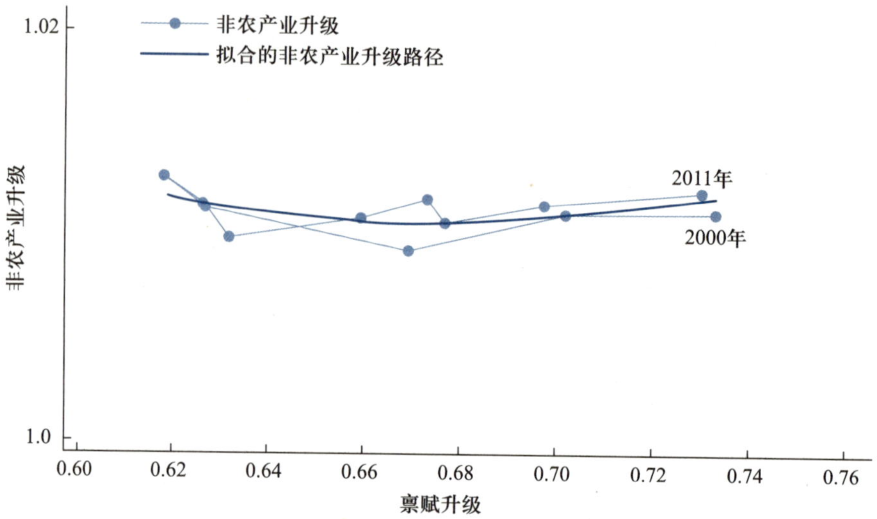


图4.24 中国香港的非农产业转型升级发展战略路径（2000—2011年）及其拟合

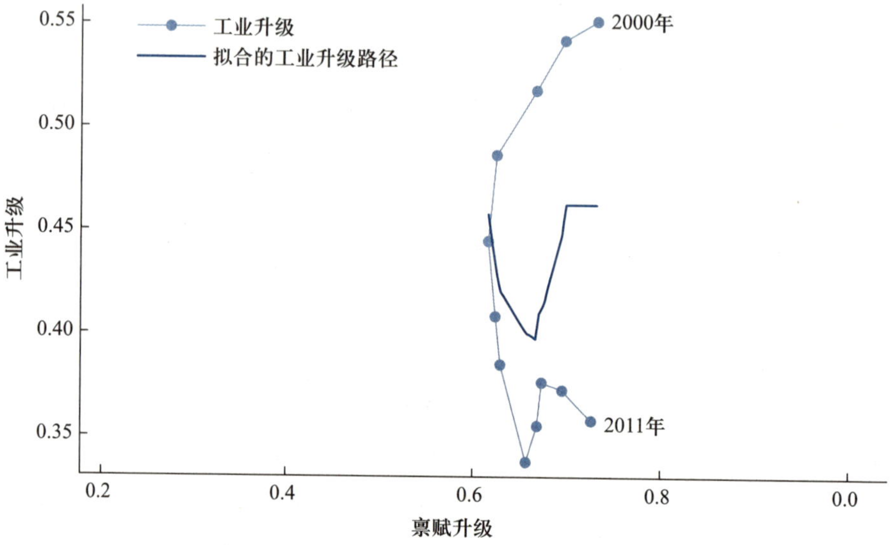


图4.25 中国香港的工业发展战略路径（2000—2011年）及其拟合

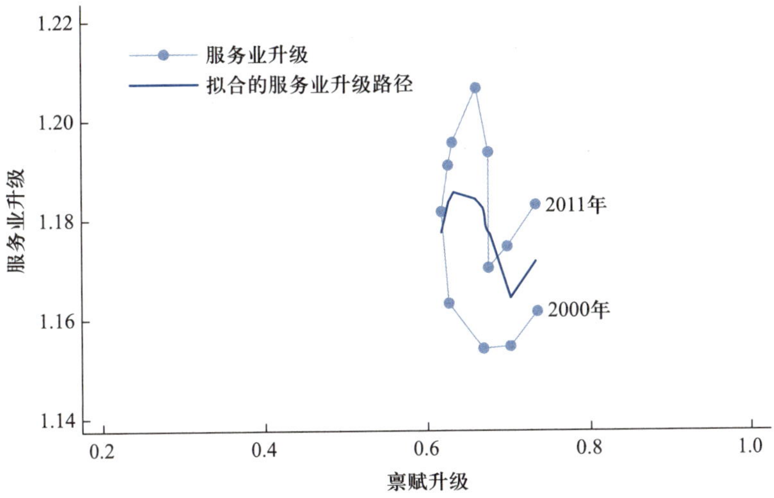


图4.26 中国香港的服务业发展战略路径（2000—2011年）及其拟合

### 4.4.3 中国台湾的经济结构转型升级路径特征[①]

中国台湾是目前仅有的两个从低收入农业经济持续转型升级到工业化高收入经济体的发展典范。按照Maddison的估计，中国台湾在1950年的实际人均所得为916美元，只有世界平均值的43%，不到当时美国水平的一成，仍是相对贫穷落后的经济体。而在半个多世纪之后的2008年，台湾人均所得增长了22.8倍，达到20 926美元，为世界平均值的2.75倍。依据Maddison的估计来计算全球所有经济体在1950—2008年间人均所得的成长倍数，并依此来排序（排除人口不及百万的小国和地区），韩国的23倍与中国台湾的22.8倍几乎不相上下，并列榜首（而排第三的中国大陆则是15倍），可称是第二次世界大战后后进经济体中成绩最优异的两个经济体。

中国台湾较早地启动了工业化阶段。在日据时期，特别是第一次世界大战之后，为满足日本市场的需求，台湾的制糖业、樟脑业等农副产品加工业得到发展。从1920年到1937年，台湾食品加工厂数由1 462家增长到5 386家，其职工人数由2.8万人增长到4.9万人。制糖业是食品加工业的主干，1914年砂糖产值占食品加工业产值的79%，1929年为83%。这一时期

① 鉴于世界银行WDI数据库中没有中国台湾的数据，因此我们在本书后面的指数编制中没有纳入中国台湾，这里对中国台湾经济结构转型升级特征的梳理资料转引自：王丽莉、文一，“中国能跨越中等收入陷阱吗？——基于工业化路径的跨国比较”，《经济评论》，2017年第3期。

的加工厂一般为雇用人数在30人以下的小型手工工场。因为农村地区靠近原材料与廉价劳动力，工厂大多分布在农村地区。1930年，台湾制造业就业在农村地区的比重为62.6%，采矿业就业在农村地区的比重达到84.8%。然而，根据台湾学者瞿宛文的研究，第二次世界大战结束时台湾经济仍是一个以出口米、糖为主的典型殖民经济，现代工业是由日本人主导的工业飞地。而米、糖所高度依赖的日本市场在战后消失，战后四年间虽有大陆市场为之替代，但又因国民党当局退居台湾后两岸隔绝而再度失去市场。1945—1949年间，战争的破坏、国民党当局接收上的缺失与解放战争的影响，造成台湾经济的动荡与混乱。在国民党当局于1949年迁台前后，台湾经济更为困难，百万人口的流入带来物资供给的压力，外汇与物资极度缺乏，财政赤字庞大而物价上涨压力犹存，稳定经济成为严肃的挑战。从1949年起，台湾当局施行多项重要政策，包括农村土地改革及设立经建机构总管物资及经济事务等，并以刚从大陆运台的黄金储备作为后盾发行了新台币，降低通胀压力。随后配合美国因朝鲜战争重启的援助计划，台湾当局戒慎恐惧地实行了较合宜的经济与产业政策，数年内稳定了经济，恢复了生产，并开启了战后快速的工业化。而正是工业化使得台湾很快脱离了对米、糖的依赖，其在台湾出口所占比例由1952年的74%降至1970年的3.2%。①

从20世纪50年代起，台湾工业开始起飞。1962年，台湾农村家庭的非农收入份额为25%。到1975年，非农收入份额增长到43%。1956—1966年，台湾农村劳动力从事农业生产的份额由73%下降到54%，农村劳动力制造业就业的份额由略低于7%增长到10%。1970年，至少从事30天非农劳动的台湾农村劳动力超过120万人，其中的26.5%从事工业和矿业，11.7%从事商业，5.8%从事家庭手工业。不在农场工作的台湾农村劳动力达到53.4万人，其中超过40%从事工业和矿业。在1956—1966年的十年间，台湾制造业职工人数总共增长了27.5万人，其中的46%被农村制造业吸收，农村制造业就业的年均增长率为7.2%，远远高于城市地区。1956—1966年，采矿业、制造业、建筑业、商业与交通通信业，都呈现出从城市向农村转移的趋势。其中，农村制造业就业占全部制造业就业的比重由37.2%增长到41.3%。到1971年，台湾农村制造业职工人数占全部制造业职工人数的比重达到50%，农村制造业增加值占全部制造业增加值的比重达到48%。与城镇工业企业相比，农村工业企业规模更小。例如，1971年，台湾农村制造业企业平均雇用15个工人，而城市企业平均雇用50个工人。此外，农村工业企业大多生产食品、纺织、家具等劳动力密集型产品，资本需求少，可以充分利用农村剩余劳动力，其增长速度快于城市地区。例如，1956—1966年，台湾农村纺织服装业就业的年均增长率为8.6%，而城市纺织服装业就业的年均增长率约为5%。台

① 瞿宛文，《台湾战后经济发展的源起：后进发展的为何与如何》，联经出版社，2016年版。

湾的乡村原始工业化，以进入国际市场的远距离贸易为目的，利用农村剩余劳动力“就地”生产。这有利于提高农民收入，发酵市场，培育企业家精神，以及发展供应链和商业分销网络，是台湾成功开启工业化必不可少的阶段。

台湾的产业升级遵循了从轻工业到重工业，从劳动力密集型工业到资本密集型工业的循序渐进的路径。与韩国的工业化类似，20世纪50年代初到70年代中期，台湾轻工业蓬勃发展。自20世纪70年代末起，台湾进入重化工业化阶段。1953—1960年，台湾的农副产品加工业、纺织、玻璃、造纸、皮革等消费品工业得到迅速发展。在此期间，台湾工业生产年均增长11.7%，工业生产比例由19.7%上升到26.9%，而轻工业增加值占全部工业增加值的比重在70%以上（见表4.4）。在20世纪50年代末期，内需趋于饱和，台湾当局利用工资低廉的比较优势，借助国际市场对轻工业品需求旺盛的有利时机，积极推行出口导向的经济战略，继续发展劳动力密集型消费品出口。除传统轻工业品外，电子工业也开始发展。1961—1973年，台湾工业生产年均增长率为16.4%，出口贸易由1.64亿美元增长到44.83亿美元，工业制品在出口贸易额中的比重由32.3%增长到84.6%。在台湾工业化初期，与农业关系密切的制糖、菠萝罐头等食品加工业增长最快。1952—1959年，食品工业就业占全部工业就业的比重保持在20%以上，是这一时期最大的工业部门。1952—1969年，食品工业增加值在全部工业中的比重最大。纺织服装业因其充分利用劳动分工与剩余劳动力的特性，在工业化过程中发挥着重要作用。1947年，台湾纺织服装业就业占全部制造业就业的比重仅为5.46%。到1952年，纺织服装业的就业比重增长到20.73%。1960年，纺织服装业的就业比重达到25.02%，超过食品工业，成为最大的工业部门。1970—1984年，纺织服装业增加值占全部制造业增加值的比重最大，平均在15%以上。1952年，台湾纺织服装业的出口额占全部出口额的比重仅为0.71%。到1970年，纺织服装业的出口比重增长到31.71%。1960—1970年的十年间，纺织服装业的平均出口比重为20.29%。由于消费品工业生产规模扩大，对原材料、零部件、能源与机器设备的需求急剧增长。到20世纪70年代中期，台湾积累了资金和技术实力，居民储蓄与外汇收入都有了较大增长，已具备了发展资本密集型工业的条件。台湾当局适时推动中上游工业发展，逐步建立和发展了钢铁、机器制造、交通设备制造、石油化工等重化工业。1974—1981年，台湾工业生产年均增长14.1%，重工业的增长速度大大超过轻工业。如表4.4所示，1960年，台湾重工业增加值在全部工业增加值中的份额只有26.6%，1980年增长到42.6%，1996年达到50.8%。从就业结构来看，1975—2000年，台湾重工业就业比重由32.5%增长到45.8%；其中，金属及金属制品、机械设备与交通设备制造业的就业比重由16.3%增长到29.7%。1981年，机械、钢铁、化学品和石油炼制品在出口总额中达到32.3%。

表4.4 台湾制造业的增加值结构 单位：%

| 行业名称 | 1953年 | 1960年 | 1980年 | 1990年 | 1996年 |
|---|---|---|---|---|---|
| 轻工业 | 78.6 | 73.4 | 57.4 | 52.6 | 49.2 |
| 传统轻工业 | | | | | |
| 食品、饮料制造业与烟草加工业 | 33.1 | 31.7 | 13.1 | 10.7 | 9.0 |
| 纺织服装业，皮革制品业与制鞋业 | 23.9 | 16.4 | 17.4 | 12.6 | 9.1 |
| 木材加工业，家具制造业，造纸业与印刷业 | 13.3 | 13.7 | 8.0 | 7.0 | 4.7 |
| 非金属矿物制品业 | 4.1 | 8.0 | 4.9 | 4.6 | 3.9 |
| 高技术轻工业 | | | | | |
| 电子工业，精密仪器制造业 | 1.1 | 2.1 | 14.1 | 17.8 | 22.5 |
| 重工业 | 21.4 | 26.6 | 42.6 | 47.4 | 50.8 |
| 石油与化学工业 | 15.4 | 13.3 | 22.2 | 21.6 | 23.4 |
| 金属及金属制品，机械制造业与交通设备制造业 | 6.0 | 13.3 | 20.3 | 25.8 | 27.3 |

资料来源：王丽莉、文一，“中国能跨越中等收入陷阱吗？——基于工业化路径的跨国比较”，《经济评论》，2017年第3期。

## 4.4.4 韩国的经济结构转型升级路径拟合及其特征

韩国位于东亚朝鲜半岛南部，三面环海，西临黄海，与中国胶东半岛隔海相望，东南是朝鲜海峡，东边是日本海，北面隔着三八线非军事区与朝鲜相邻。总面积约10万平方千米，占朝鲜半岛总面积的45%，首都为首尔。北部属温带季风气候，南部属亚热带气候，海洋性特征显著，平均温度为6℃至16℃，年平均降水量1 500毫米左右。主体民族为朝鲜族，通用韩语（朝鲜语），2014年总人口约5 041.85万。韩国是世界上人口密度最大的国家之一，人口出生率和生育率均居世界低位，同时人口老龄化问题严重，是经济合作与发展组织（OECD）国家中青壮年劳动力人口下降最快的国家。自20世纪60年代以来，韩国政府实行了“出口导向型”开发经济战略，缔造了举世瞩目的“汉江奇迹”。韩国制造业与科技产业发达，除高速互联网服务闻名世界外，内存、液晶显示器及等离子显示屏等平面显示装置和移动电话都在世界市场中具领导地位。韩国拥有完善的市场经济制度，是20国集团和OECD成员之一，也是亚太经合组织（APEC）和东亚峰会的创始国。

韩国与中国台湾是战后全世界仅有的从低收入的农业经济转型升级到中等收入的工业经济再转型升级到高收入的现代经济的两个经济体。韩国采用了现实主义的方法进行产业升级，并且把战略调整为进入那些与自己潜在比较优势一致的产业。20世纪60年代韩国发展并出口的是服装、胶合板、假发等劳动力密集型产品。当资本逐渐积累，禀赋结构因为经济发展而改变时，韩国便向汽车等资本更为密集的产业升级。但是在升级初期，国内的生产主要集中在进口部件的装配上，这是劳动力密集型的生产，同时也是与当时韩国的比较优势相一致的。类似地，电子业起初主要生产家用电器，如电视、洗衣机、电冰箱等，之后才转向存储芯片的生产，这是信息产业中技术最简单的区段。韩国的技术提升迅速，其提升的速度同潜在比较优势变化的速度是一致的。这种变化也反映了有力的经济增长所带来的物质资本和人力资本的迅速积累，而增长之所以出现，是因为该国的主要产业部门时刻与该国现有的比较优势保持一致。

与中国的工业化路径类似，韩国工业化也遵循了从轻工业到重工业、从劳动力密集型工业到资本密集型工业、从生活消费品到生产资料的渐进的产业升级。20世纪50年代初到70年代中期，是韩国轻工业繁荣发展的阶段。自70年代末起，韩国开始进入重化工业化阶段。自50年代起，韩国优先发展投资少、技术设备简单、资金回收快的劳动力密集型工业，如食品加工业、纺织服装业、皮革制品业、制鞋业等。到50年代末，由于发达国家劳动力密集型制造业外移，国际市场对轻工业品需求旺盛。韩国政府抓住时机，积极推行出口导向型政策，利用其廉价劳动力优势，发展劳动力密集型产品出口。在国内外市场巨大需求的驱动下，韩国轻工业迅速发展壮大。表4.5展示了韩国制造业的增加值结构。1953—1960年，韩国轻工业增加值占全部制造业增加值的比重在80%以上，食品、饮料制造业与烟草加工业增加值占全部制造业增加值的比重在40%以上。1953—1973年的20年间，纺织服装业、皮革制品业与制鞋业的增加值占全部制造业增加值的比重都在30%以上。再看韩国制造业的就业结构，1961—1970年，韩国轻工业劳动力占全部制造业劳动力的比重在74%以上。从60年代到80年代的20年间，纺织服装业、皮革制品业与制鞋业的劳动力份额都在30%以上，是这一时期韩国最主要的生产与出口部门。1970—1980年，纺织与皮革制品的增加值由1 344亿韩元增长到19 765亿韩元，不考虑价格变化，年均增长率达到30.8%；纺织与皮革制品的总产值由5 217亿韩元增长到101 454亿韩元，年均增长率为34.7%。1962—1980年，纺织品的出口额由221.6万美元增长到219 755.8万美元，年均增长率为46.7%；服装出口额由111.8万美元增长到294 685万美元，年均增长率为54.9%。一个部门的规模化生产会创造对其他部门产品的大规模需求，从而引起其他部门的规模化生产，最后导致整个经济的机械化。随着韩国轻工业生产规模的扩大，工业企业对原材料、中间产品、机器设备与交通运输网络产生了巨大需求。到70年代末，韩国已经积累了足够的资金和技术实力，因而具备了发展资本密集型重工业的条件。在韩国政府的支持下，金属及金属制品、机器制造业、交通设备制造业以及石化工业快速增长。在1980—1990年的十年间，韩国工业增加值由85 188亿韩元增长到486 409亿韩元，不考虑价格变化，年均增长率为19%；其中，交通设备制造业的增加值由4 506亿韩元增长到58 845亿韩元，年均增长率为29.3%；金属及金属制品业的增加值由8 816亿韩元增长到69 935亿韩元，年均增长率为23%。如表4.5所示，1973—1990年，重工业增加值占全部制造业的比重由27.6%增长到47.9%；其中，金属及金属制品、机器与交通运输设备制造业增加值占全部制造业的比重由14.5%增长到33.6%。1970年，重工业劳动力占全部制造业的比重为25.7%，1990年增长到40.8%，2006年达到50.8%。在出口结构上，20世纪60年代初，食品加工业是韩国最主要的出口品，1961年其出口份额为36%。随后，纺织品出口快速增长，很快超越了食品工业。1962—1968年，纺织品、服装与鞋包出口额在总出口额中的比重由6.3%上升到40.7%。一直到1980年，纺织品、服装与鞋包的份额一直在35%以上，是这一时期韩国最主要的出口品。70年代末，韩国建立了钢铁和造船产业，90年代这些产品便晋升为韩国十大主要出口产品。韩国的半导体、计算机和汽车产业在80年代后期快速成长，90年代便成为韩国十大主要出口产品。1975年，韩国重工业品（不含石油及石油产品、电子电气）的出口份额为13.1%，1980年增长到24.3%，2000年达到41.6%。可见，韩国的主要出口产品也经历了从劳动力密集型和轻工业产品到资本密集型和技术密集型产品的转变。

表4.5 韩国制造业的增加值结构

单位：%

| 行业 | 1953年 | 1960年 | 1973年 | 1980年 | 1990年 | 2014年 |
|---|---|---|---|---|---|---|
| 轻工业 | 87.4 | 83.5 | 72.4 | 60.0 | 52.1 | 44.6 |
| 轻工业，除食品、饮料制造业与烟草加工业 | 47.0 | 50.1 | 54.7 | 46.7 | 42.2 | 38.6 |
| 传统轻工业 | | | | | | |
| 食品、饮料制造业与烟草加工业 | 39.1 | 31.7 | 14.6 | 10.7 | 7.2 | 4.5 |
| 纺织服装业，皮革制品业与制鞋业 | 33.3 | 35.9 | 32.4 | 23.2 | 13.4 | 5.1 |
| 木材加工业，家具制造业，造纸业与印刷业 | 11.6 | 11.0 | 8.8 | 4.8 | 5.0 | 2.8 |
| 非金属矿物制品业 | 1.5 | 2.4 | 5.1 | 6.4 | 6.5 | 2.7 |
| 高技术轻工业 | | | | | | |
| 电子工业，精密仪器制造业 | 0.6 | 0.8 | 8.4 | 12.3 | 17.4 | 28.0 |
| 重工业 | 12.6 | 16.5 | 27.6 | 40.0 | 47.9 | 55.4 |
| 石油与化学工业 | 5.4 | 7.1 | 13.1 | 19.9 | 14.3 | 15.6 |
| 金属及金属制品，机械制造业与交通设备制造业 | 7.2 | 9.4 | 14.5 | 20.2 | 33.6 | 39.7 |

资料来源：王丽莉、文一，“中国能跨越中等收入陷阱吗？——基于工业化路径的跨国比较”，《经济评论》，2017年第3期。

如果说中国是实现脱贫的典范中的典范，日本是实现赶超的典范中的典范，那么韩国一定是所有典范中的典范。直到1970年，韩国还是一个名副其实的穷国，其人均GDP不足美国的6%，但40年之后就达到美国的近一半。1965年的韩国不完全算是一个农业国，但其农业产值占GDP的比重也高达40%，可是到2012年这个比重只有微不足道的2.7%，完全实现了工业化。图4.27是韩国1970—2011年的非农产业转型升级发展战略路径。对数拟合（$R^2 = 0.922$）的非农产业结构转型升级的发展战略路径曲线为$I_{KOR,t} = 1.098+0.121\ 7\times\ln(E_{KOR,t})$，斜率和弹性分别为$\dfrac{\partial I_{KOR,t}}{\partial E_{KOR,t}}=\dfrac{0.121\ 7}{E_{KOR,t}}$，$\dfrac{\partial I_{KOR,t}}{\partial E_{KOR,t}}\dfrac{E_{KOR,t}}{I_{KOR,t}}=\dfrac{0.121\ 7}{I_{KOR,t}}$。相比于世界整体情况，以及发展典范样本中的其他国家和地区而言，韩国的发展战略路径非常稳健（拟合优度超过0.9），斜率和弹性都居中。因此，韩国的发展战略尤其应该引起重视。

图4.28是1970—2011年间韩国的工业发展战略路径，二次函数拟合（$R^2 = 0.924\ 5$）发展战略路径曲线为

$$I_{KOR,t} = 0.46\ 942+6.207\ 4\times E_{KOR,t}-7.139\ 83\times E^2_{KOR,t}$$

顶点和拐点分别为$I = 1.818\ 6$和$E = 0.434\ 7$。相较于世界样本，韩国工业升级发展战略路径的拐点出现得较晚而顶点略低，同样显示出稳健的特征。

图4.29是韩国1970—2011年间的服务业发展战略路径。对数拟合（$R^2 = 0.004$）

$$I_{KOR,t} = 0.768\ 67-0.001\ 47\times\ln\left(E_{KOR,t}\right)$$

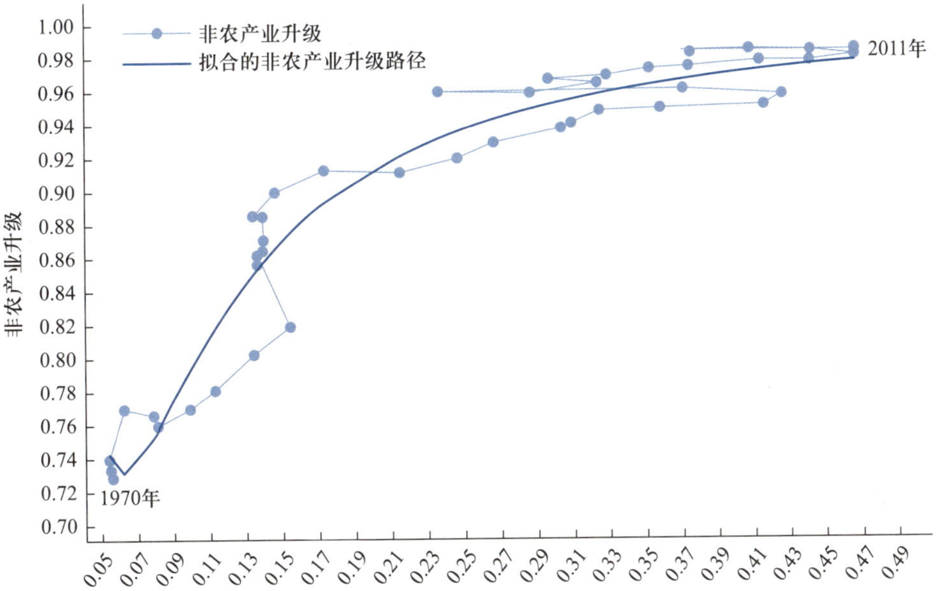


图4.27 韩国的发展战略路径（1970—2011年）及其拟合

斜率和弹性分别为 $\frac{\partial I_{KOR,t}}{\partial E_{KOR,t}}=\frac{0.001\,47}{E_{KOR,t}}$ 和 $\frac{\partial I_{KOR,t}}{\partial E_{KOR,t}}\frac{E_{KOR,t}}{I_{KOR,t}}=\frac{0.001\,47}{I_{KOR,t}}$，二者都很小，表明经济结构升级似乎主要依靠的是工业而非服务业。

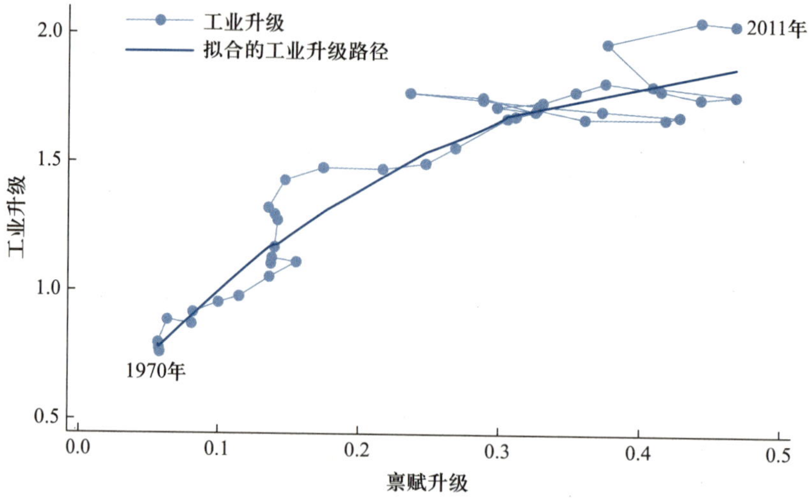


图4.28 韩国的工业发展战略路径（1970—2011年）及其拟合

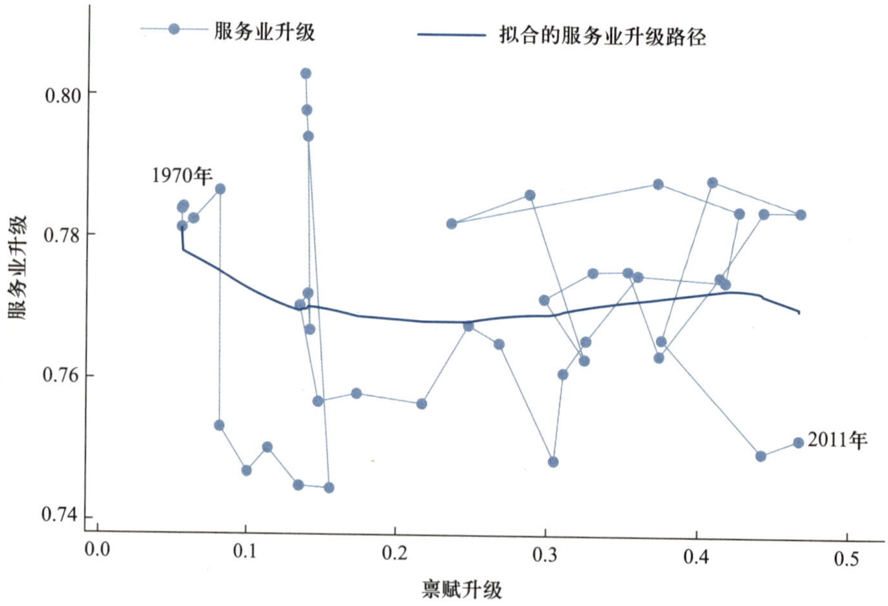


图4.29 韩国的服务业发展战略路径（1970—2011年）及其拟合

### 4.4.5 新加坡的经济结构转型升级路径拟合及其特征①

新加坡是东南亚的一个岛国，北隔柔佛海峡与马来西亚为邻，南隔新加坡海峡与印度尼西亚相望，毗邻马六甲海峡南口。土地面积仅有719.1平方千米，海岸线总长200余千米。国土除新加坡岛之外，还包括周围数岛。新加坡地处热带，平均温度在23℃至34℃之间，年均降雨量在2 400毫米左右。新加坡人口主要划分为四大族群：华人（汉族），74.2%；马来族，13.3%；印度裔，9.1%；欧亚裔/混血，3.4%。新加坡属外贸驱动型经济，以电子、石油化工、金融、航运、服务业为主，高度依赖美、日、欧和周边市场，外贸总额是GDP的4倍。经济长期高速增长，1960—1984年间GDP年均增长9%。新加坡的工业主要包括制造业和建筑业，2012年产值为1 085.5亿新元，占GDP的25.1%。制造业产品主要包括电子、化学与化工、生物医药、精密机械、交通设备、石油产品、炼油等产品。新加坡已经成为东南亚最大的修造船基地之一，以及世界第三大炼油中心。在服务业方面，批发与零售业、商务服务业、交通与通信业、金融服务业是新加坡服务业的四大重头行业。根据2014年的全球金融中心指数（GFCI）排名报告，新加坡是继纽约、伦敦、香港之后的第四大国际金融中心，同时也是亚洲重要的服务和航运中心之一。2012年金融业产值为2 780.7亿新元，占GDP的64.3%。新加坡以稳定的政局和廉洁高效的政府著称，是全球最国际化的国家之一。此外，新加坡是东盟成员国之一，也是WTO、英联邦以及APEC成员。

然而，回首历史，新加坡也曾历尽艰辛。新加坡没有农村，独立以后也是靠手工作坊起家，甚至在20世纪60年代还主要靠生产和出口假发从事原始积累。在政府的产业政策指导下，新加坡逐步从手工作坊产业升级为劳动力密集型规模化轻工业，再到重工业和金融业。1819—1959年，新加坡经历了140年的英国殖民统治。第二次世界大战之后，英国在亚洲的势力开始衰退，美国的势力开始扩张。经过多次谈判，1957年英国政府同意新加坡成为自治邦；1959年5月，李光耀于1954年发起成立的人民行动党参加在新宪制下举行的第一次自治邦议会大选，赢得了51个议席中的43席而获得执政权；6月，时年35岁的李光耀宣誓就任新加坡自治邦总理，人民行动党开始执政。在此之前，英国人并没有在新加坡建立一套完整的经济体系，只是利用新加坡自由港的历史地位，把其当作英国在远东的货物集散中心，转口贸易作为单一的经济形式占据新加坡经济的主导地位。当时，新加坡的日子很难过。因为没有制造业提供就业机会，老百姓找不到工作，失业率高达14%，因此，突破单一的转口贸易的经济结构，努力创造就业机会就成为新生政府面临的首要问题。李光耀说："我们从

① 本小节主要根据杨建伟所著的《新加坡的经济转型之路》（创意圈出版社，2015年版）一书整理而成。

1959年第一次执政开始，便一直扛着失业问题的包袱——那么多的年轻人在寻找工作，却没有工作可以应付他们的需求。”“经过几年的努力，我的内阁同僚们都知道，要生存的唯一办法是推行工业化。新加坡的转口贸易已经到达顶限，往后会进一步式微。印度尼西亚仍然跟我们对抗，马来西亚决意避开新加坡。我们想方设法，愿意尝试任何切实可行的点子，只要能制造就业机会，我们不必负债过日子就行。一位饮料制造商向我建议推动旅游业。这种行业属于劳动力密集型，需要厨师、女佣、侍应生、洗衣工人、干洗工人、导游、司机和制造纪念品的手工艺人，最理想的是发展这个行业所需的资金很少……令我感到欣慰的是，这个行业倒制造了不少的就业机会，给许多空空如也的口袋带来一些收入。它固然使失业人数减少，却无法彻底解决问题。”“为此，我们集中精力，设法招商到这里设立工厂。尽管新加坡只有200万人口，国内市场很小，我们却保护本地装配的汽车、冰箱、空调、收音机、电视机和录音机，希望日后这些产品当中有部分会在本地制造。我们鼓励本国商家开设小型工厂，制造植物油、化妆品、蚊香、发膏、金银纸，甚至是樟脑丸！我们也吸引了中国香港和台湾的投资者，到这里来开设玩具厂、纺织厂和制衣厂。”

伴随着新加坡从轻工业到重工业的产业升级过程，电子工业成为支柱产业，而且本身也经历了从生产消费型产品到投资型产品，从劳动力密集型产品到资本、技术密集型产品的转变。新加坡电子工业的成长可以分为三个阶段。在第一阶段，1960—1980年，新加坡利用廉价劳动力优势，生产简单的消费类电子产品，如电视机、收音机等。在这一时期，电子工业是劳动力密集型的，因此电子工业就业快速增长。电子工业职工人数的年均增长率在20世纪60年代为24.6%，在70年代为20.3%。到1980年，电子工业职工人数超过7万人，占制造业就业人数的1/4以上。随着新加坡劳动力成本的上涨，自1980年起，电子工业开始向资本、技术密集型转变。在第二阶段，1980—1990年，电子工业的就业增长率下降到5.5%。到80年代末，电子工业职工人数增长到12.3万，占制造业总劳动力人数的35%。在第三阶段，1990—1999年，电子工业的就业出现负增长，但工业增加值的年增长率仍高达11.2%。这一时期，电子工业以资本、技术密集型为主，劳动生产率年均增长13.1%，高于其他制造业部门。1996年，新加坡成为世界第三大电子产品出口国。1999年，新加坡电子工业的增加值接近GDP的10%，超过制造业增加值的44%，电子产品出口占总出口的60%以上，电子工业私人部门的研发投资占全国私人部门研发投资的55%。从产品结构来看，在第一阶段，新加坡吸引了飞利浦、松下等外商投资，依靠廉价劳动力，从事音频视频设备的加工装配。自第二阶段起，新加坡主要生产计算机及其外围设备，其增加值在1980—1990年的年均增长率接近40%。新加坡成为磁性硬盘驱动器、喷墨打印机、光盘与多媒体声卡等资本、技术密集型电子产品的最大生产国。其中，20世纪80年代末到90年代中期，新加坡生产了全世界超过一半的磁性硬盘驱动器。此外，在70年代，新加坡主要从事劳动力密集型的半导体装配与测试业务。自90年代中期起，在政府支持下，新加坡发展资本密集型的半导体芯片制造。因此，半导体行业的劳动生产率在第三阶段大大提高。显然，新加坡的电子工业经历了从劳动力密集型到资本、技术密集型的升级过程。作为支柱产业，电子工业带动上下游产业链发展，推动新加坡快速实现工业化与经济增长。

1998年，世界性的电子工业需求下降，加上新加坡劳动力成本过高的因素，许多跨国公司关闭或转移了新加坡的工厂，著名的裕廊工业园一夜之间冒出了许多空置的厂房。生产磁盘驱动器的巨型跨国公司希捷科技向中国搬迁了两家工厂，一家去东莞，一家去无锡，使得新加坡从原来占据世界磁盘驱动器总产量的73%跌到50%。面对变化了的外部环境，面对新兴工业国低劳动力成本的竞争，新加坡开始思考和着手调整经济结构和产业结构：减少对低端电子业的依赖，吸引和增加高端电子产业；不断瞄准世界新兴产业，通过引入新兴产业和本地培育，使产业结构不断调整升级；引进和发展生命科学和环境保护产业，打破新加坡的制造业在电子、精密机械、炼油、石化、造船等领域的局限；充分发挥新加坡洁净的空气和一流的生态环境的优势，引进生命科学、环境保护产业，并下大力气推动和促进其发展；发展和扩大水务产业，把新加坡打造成全球污水处理技术和产业的中心，把新加坡水资源的劣势转变为优势；发展教育产业，建立区域教育中心；继续用高薪政策吸引人才，希望把各界精英都吸收到政府中担任高级领导人，或者使他们成为医生、律师、会计师、大学教授、企业家、银行家等各界有能力并且诚实和品德优秀的杰出人物。

2002年，新加坡开始了新一轮的经济大转型，以求新、求变、实用主义的治国理念，使新加坡继续保持全球领先的竞争力：全方位检讨发展策略；引进和发展生命科学和环境保护产业；打破刻板形象：兴建两个赌场，首次举办F1夜间赛事；成功申办2010年世界首届青年奥运会；成功运作主权财富基金；与主要经济强国签订自由贸易协定。与此同时，新加坡以本国为圆心，以7小时的飞行距离为半径，制定了“7小时经济圈”的发展战略：在成功实现“总部经济”的战略之外，在该经济圈内继续巩固和打造若干区域中心，即世界贸易中心、海港转运中心、航空中心、会议中心、教育中心、医疗保健中心、国际医药中心、金融理财中心。7小时的飞行半径覆盖了东南亚各国以及香港、台北、北京、上海、东京、首尔、新德里、孟买、柏斯、墨尔本、悉尼等重要城市。

新加坡也因为最先提出了具有创意的“双边自由贸易协定”概念，获得WTO的高度赞赏和各国的积极响应。到目前为止，新加坡已经和美国、中国、日本、韩国、欧盟等十多个国家和地区签订了自由贸易协定。超前的经济政策，灵活的应对谋略，高效的行政手段，广泛的世界联系，为新加坡继续成为全球竞争力领先的经济体奠定了坚实的基础。

与日本一样，新加坡是为数不多的能够赶超世界前沿的国家。1970年时新加坡的人均GDP不足美国的1/5，但今天却与美国旗鼓相当。与中国香港一样，新加坡是一个自然资源匮乏的港口城市，其农业产值占比低下不足为奇。图4.30是新加坡1975—2011年间非

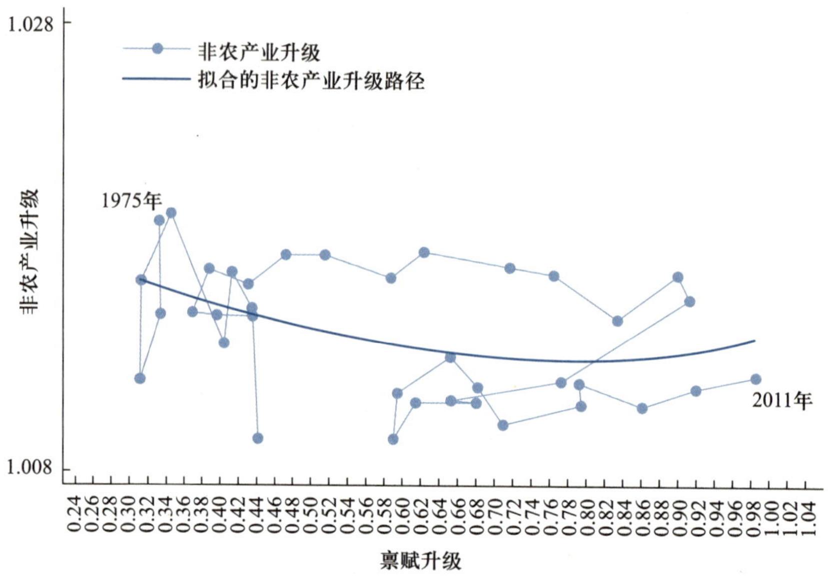


图4.30 新加坡非农产业转型升级的发展战略路径（1975—2011年）及其拟合

农业转型升级的发展路径。对数拟合（$R^2 = 0.15$）的发展战略路径曲线为$I_{SGP,\ t} = 1.012\ 3 - 0.003 \times \ln(E_{SGP,\ t})$，斜率和弹性分别为 $\frac{\partial I_{SGP,t}}{\partial E_{SGP,t}} = \frac{-0.003}{E_{SGP,t}}$，$\frac{\partial I_{SGP,t}}{\partial E_{SGP,t}} \frac{E_{SGP,t}}{I_{SGP,t}} = \frac{-0.003}{I_{SGP,t}}$。发展战略路径依然表现出随机游走特征。

图4.31是新加坡1975—2011年间工业发展战略路径。二次函数拟合（$R^2 = 0.80$）的发展战略路径曲线为

$$I_{SGP,t} = 0.109\ 26 + 3.552\ 92 \times E_{SGP,t} - 2.374\ 89 \times E_{SGP,t}^2$$

其顶点和拐点分别为$I = 1.438$和$E = 0.748$。即便与韩国相比，新加坡的顶点也较低，而拐点则较大，表明新加坡的工业升级发展战略路径比韩国要更为稳健。

图4.32是新加坡1975—2011年间服务业发展战略路径。对数拟合（$R^2 = 0.61$）的发展战略路径曲线为

$$I_{SGP,t} = 0.872\ 25 - 0.115\ 17 \times \ln\left(E_{SGP,t}\right)$$

其斜率和弹性分别为 $\frac{\partial I_{SGP,t}}{\partial E_{SGP,t}} = \frac{-0.115\ 17}{E_{SGP,t}}$ 和 $\frac{\partial I_{SGP,t}}{\partial E_{SGP,t}} \frac{E_{SGP,t}}{I_{SGP,t}} = \frac{-0.115\ 17}{I_{SGP,t}}$。在这里我们再一次看到，服务业在工业升级过程中进行了调整。

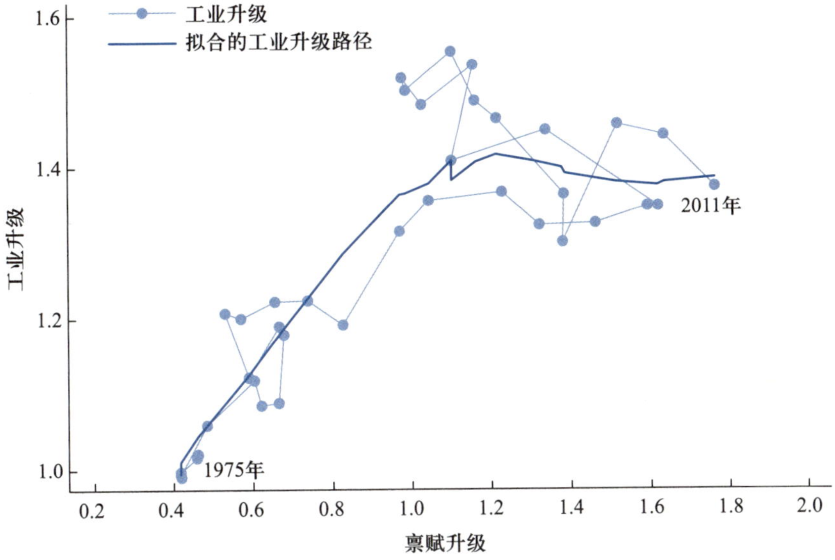


图4.31 新加坡的工业发展战略路径（1975—2011年）及其拟合

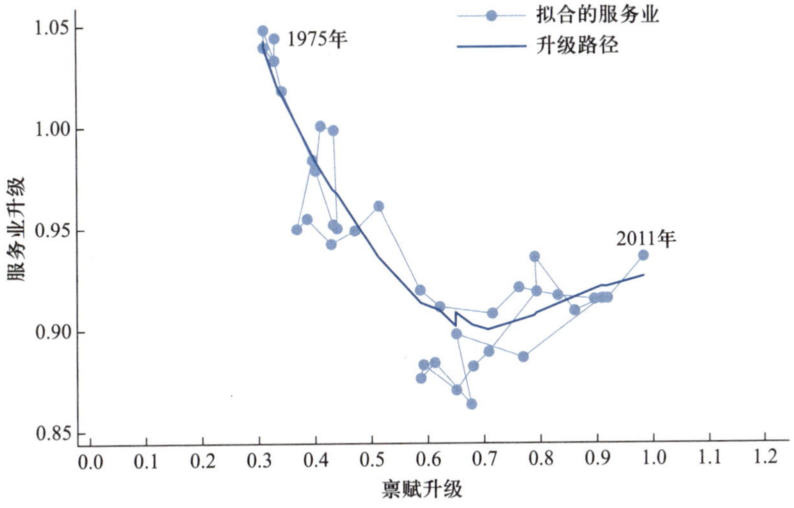


图4.32 新加坡的服务业发展战略路径（1975—2011年）及其拟合

### 4.4.6 日本的经济结构转型升级路径拟合及其特征①

日本位于亚洲东部、太平洋西北部。领土由北海道、本州、四国、九州四大岛及7 200多个小岛组成，总面积37.8万平方千米。日本东部和南部为太平洋，西临日本海、东海，北接鄂霍次克海，隔海分别和朝鲜、韩国、中国、俄罗斯、菲律宾等国相望。日本以温带和亚热带季风气候为主，夏季炎热多雨，冬季寒冷干燥，四季分明。全国横跨纬度达25°，南北气温差异十分显著。主体民族为和族，通用日语，总人口约1.26亿。第二次世界大战日本投降后，美国派军队占领日本。1947年，日本颁布新宪法，由天皇制国家变为以天皇为国家象征的议会内阁制国家。战后奉行“重经济、轻军备”路线，于20世纪60年代末一跃成为远东第一大经济强国。目前是仅次于美国、中国的世界第三大经济体。日本资源匮乏并极端依赖进口，发达的制造业是国民经济的主要支柱。科研、航天、制造业、教育水平居世界前列。此外，以动漫、游戏产业为首的文化产业和发达的旅游业也是其重要象征。日本在环境保护、资源利用等许多方面堪称典范，其国民普遍拥有良好的教育、较高的生活水平和素质。

日本的乡村工业化阶段酝酿了两个多世纪。在日本江户时代（1603—1868年），国内政治环境稳定，农产品贸易和乡村手工制造业得到全面发展。明治时代早期（1868—1890年），在政府主导下，日本基本完成以世界贸易为目的的乡村原始工业化。自18世纪早期起，由于农村地区靠近原材料、能源（水力）与来自农民家庭的廉价劳动力，日本的商业和制造业由城镇向农村转移。从18世纪到19世纪上半叶，日本35个城镇的人口平均减少了18%。相反，在这些城镇附近的农村地区，人口明显增长。制造业、贸易与运输业等非农劳动是日本农村家庭重要的收入来源。日本1843年对长州两省的调查显示，农民净收入的55%来自非农劳动。日本乡村制造业大多生产清酒、植物油、糖、丝绸、布、纸等生活消费品，企业一般规模很小，但乡村工业总产值巨大。在江户时代末期，城镇人口的衣食消费大多来自农村。例如，在1859年东京的丝绸产品有90%是农村生产的。商业与制造业在日本农村地区的发展，大大提高了广大农民的购买力与对工业制成品的需求。例如，从1875年到1895年，日本国内对布的需求增长了3倍，而农村地区的需求增长高于全国平均水平。②此外，乡村工业与商业的发展，能够培育农村劳动力的商业精神与工业技能，为日本开启工业化准备

---

① 本小节关于日本的经济结构转型升级历史主要根据：王丽莉、文一，“中国能跨越中等收入陷阱吗？——基于工业化路径的跨国比较”，《经济评论》，2017年第3期。

② Y. HaYami, *Toward the Rural-based Development of Commerce and Industry: Selected Experiences from East Asia*, World Bank, 1998.

了充足的劳动力大军。随着日本乡村工业的发展，劳动分工日益加强。到18世纪末，生产一般被分为几项独立的操作，由不同的家庭完成。日本的富农阶层是乡村工业的“企业家”或“中介人”，与英国17世纪的商人阶层扮演着相同的角色。他们充分了解市场的需求、当地产品的特征，以及劳动力的质量。这些富农为农民提供原材料和生产工具，雇用农民“就地”生产，然后把制成品分销到全国和世界各地。这种“包工制”（putting-out system）在18—19世纪的日本乡村非常普遍。日本很多乡镇在“包工制”下，生产小批量、差异化的棉纺织品，供应国内外市场。

日本在19世纪50年代的收入水平仅为同时期西方国家的1/3，但是仅用了50年的时间，日本就在1904年率先成为亚洲第一个工业国家。在1854年开放贸易后，日本政府实施了鼓励向西方世界学习先进技术和制度的政策，派遣包括半数日本内阁部长在内的高水平代表团在2年的时间内前往美国和欧洲学习。在1858年签订《安政条约》后，日本虽然丧失了控制关税的自由，但是日本政府却为现代化的基础设施建设提供了便利，并鼓励日本产业在实践中摸索。1870年东京和横滨之间的电报服务开通；1872年，日本历史上第一条铁路——横滨和新桥线开通；截至1900年，日本的铁路里程达到6 200千米。日本政府自19世纪后期开始通过进口现代机械和聘请成千上万的外国管理专家来积极引进国外的技术。在明治时期（1868—1912年），日本最主要的出口产品是丝、纱、茶叶和水产品等与本国比较优势相一致的产品。随着日本棉花产业的发展，对于棉花的进口逐年下降，并最终在1890年开始大量出口棉花、纱、布匹至邻近的亚洲国家。

第二次世界大战之后日本迅速从战争中恢复，从20世纪50年代中期的以农业和轻工业为主，开始逐步过渡到70年代末以重化工业为主，完成经济结构的现代化转型升级。1957年，日本第一产业创造的GDP为87 062亿日元，占GDP的16%。到1972年，日本第一产业创造的GDP为97 639亿日元，只占GDP的5%。在此期间，日本第一产业占比的下降实实在在地刻画了其农业的现代化转型升级。因此，日本1972年的第一产业GDP比1957年的绝对值增加了10 557亿日元，增长了12.1%。1960—1975年，动力耕耘机和农用拖拉机从51.4万台增加到392.1万台，增长了6.6倍；动力喷雾机从23.2万台增加到131.01万台，增长了4.6倍；农用汽车，包括三轮汽车从10.3万辆增加到110.6万辆，增长了10倍。农机拥有量的成倍增长使农业生产的机械化作业程度大大提高。1967年，水稻的机耕面积达96%，机械收割面积达80%，机械脱粒面积达98%。到20世纪70年代推广了小苗带土插秧机，解决了机械插秧问题，实现了农业生产的全面机械化。除农业机械化以外，日本在品种改良、栽培技术、农药和肥料的合理使用以及水利灌溉等各方面都达到了世界先进水平。受益于日本农业机械化程度的提高，1960—1984年农村人口从3 441万减少到2 049万，从总人口比重的36.8%下降到17%。农业就业人口从1 454.2万减少到565.7万，从总就业人数的22.3%下降到9.8%。

1957年，日本第二产业的GDP为127 758亿日元，1972年，第二产业创造的GDP为717 329亿日元，相对量增长了4.6倍，第二产业比重从1957年的23.5%提高到1972年的36.4%，增加了12.9个百分点。日本在1970年完成了从劳动力密集型轻工业向资本密集型重化工业的转型升级，重工业的比重超过轻工业的比重，分别为50.6%和49.4%。作为轻工业主导产业的食品和纺织行业分别从1957年占GDP的31.6%、10.5%下降到1972年的14.1%、4.7%，分别下降了17.5和5.8个百分点。然而以资本密集型为主的重化工业的比重则不断攀升。机电行业从1957年占GDP的11.0%提高到1972年的22.7%，增长了11.7个百分点，取代食品工业成为制造业中规模最大的部门。钢铁、电力、造船等产业的规模迅速扩大，石油、石化、家电、汽车等新兴产业相继诞生和发展，重化工业出现爆炸式增长态势。1955年到1970年，钢铁产量增长了10倍，铝增长了13倍，石油制品增长了19倍，水泥增长了5.4倍，发电量增长了4.3倍，电视机增长了100倍，小汽车增长了159倍。这使得日本成为名副其实的世界工业强国：造船长期位居首位，化纤、商业车（卡车、公共汽车）长期位居第二位；水泥1962年跃居第二位；钢铁1964年跃居第二位；电力1966年跃居第二位；石油制品1966年跃居第二位；合成橡胶1966年跃居第二位；小汽车1968年跃居第三位，1971年超过德国上升到第二位；水泥、塑料、彩电的产量在20世纪70年代跃居首位；计算机安装台数仅次于美国，居世界第二位。与前述中国目前的工业化实力一样，70年代之后日本强大的工业化实力使得其超过德国成为仅次于美国的世界第二大经济体。

在70年代开始向重工业化转移时，1970年日本的人均GDP约为美国的40%，堪称二战后中等收入国家跨越中等收入陷阱的发展典范。由于样本数据只覆盖了1970—2011年的数据，因此难以全面刻画日本200年来的工业化历程，尽管如此，也依然能够看出日本后工业化时代的经济结构转型升级路径特征。图4.33是1970—2011年间日本非农产业结构变迁的发展战略路径。对数拟合（$R^2 = 0.49$）的发展战略路径曲线为

$$I_{\mathrm{JPN},t} = 0.998\,9 + 0.008\,6 \times \ln\left(E_{\mathrm{JPN},t}\right)$$

斜率和弹性分别为 $\dfrac{\partial I_{\mathrm{JPN},t}}{\partial E_{\mathrm{JPN},t}} = \dfrac{0.008\,6}{E_{\mathrm{JPN},t}}, \dfrac{\partial I_{\mathrm{JPN},t}}{\partial E_{\mathrm{JPN},t}} \dfrac{E_{\mathrm{JPN},t}}{I_{\mathrm{JPN},t}} = \dfrac{0.008\,6}{I_{\mathrm{JPN},t}}$。

图4.34是1970—2011年间日本工业发展战略路径，二次函数拟合（$R^2 = 0.299$）的发展战略路径曲线为

$$I_{\mathrm{JPN},t} = 1.109\,1 + 0.321\,14 \times E_{\mathrm{JPN},t} - 0.088 \times E_{\mathrm{JPN},t}^2$$

图4.35是1994—2011年间日本服务业的发展战略路径。对数拟合（$R^2 = 0.27$）的发展战略路径曲线为

$$I_{\mathrm{JPN},t} = 0.909\,2 - 0.025\,6 \times \ln(E_{\mathrm{JPN},t})$$

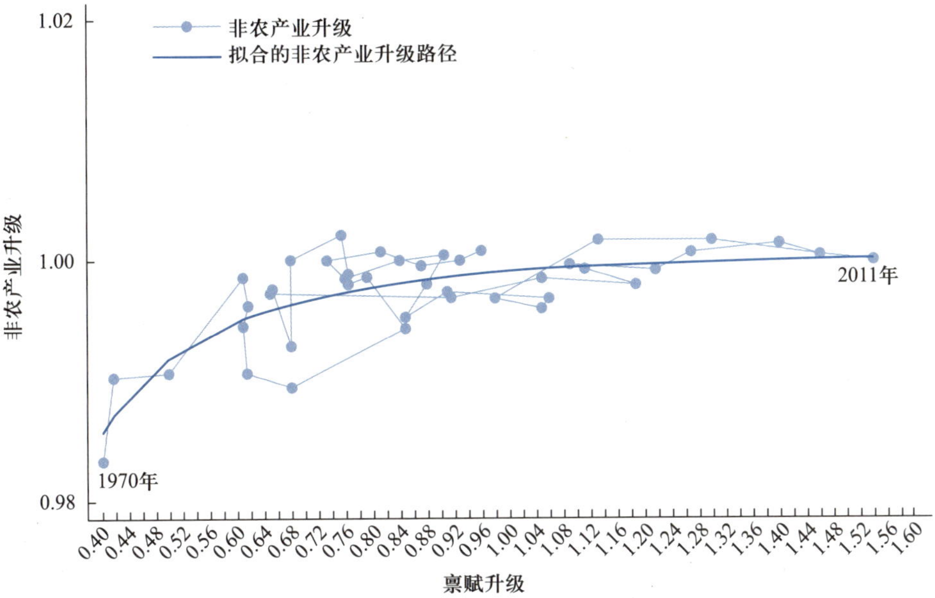


图 4.33 日本的非农产业发展战略路径（1970—2011 年）及其拟合

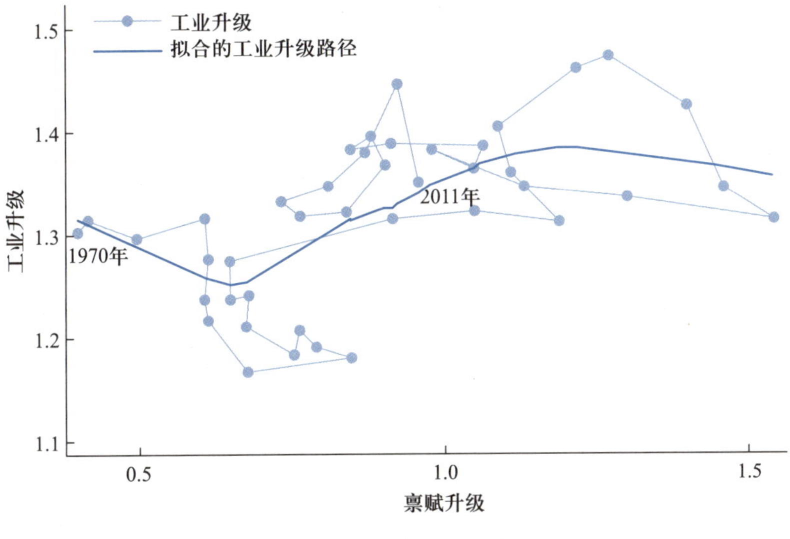


图 4.34 日本的工业发展战略路径（1970—2011 年）及其拟合

斜率和弹性分别为 $\dfrac{\partial I_{\mathrm{JPN},t}}{\partial E_{\mathrm{JPN},t}}=\dfrac{0.025\,6}{E_{\mathrm{JPN},t}}$ 和 $\dfrac{\partial I_{\mathrm{JPN},t}}{\partial E_{\mathrm{JPN},t}}\dfrac{E_{\mathrm{JPN},t}}{I_{\mathrm{JPN},t}}=\dfrac{0.025\,6}{I_{\mathrm{JPN},t}}$。

同中国香港一样，日本经济结构变迁的发展战略路径在 20 世纪 80 年代步入经济前沿之后就表现出强烈的随机游走特征。不过与中国香港有所不同的是，日本尽管通过战后成功的工业化实现了现代经济结构转型升级，但是在 1970 年日本的人均收入只有美国的 40% 左右，

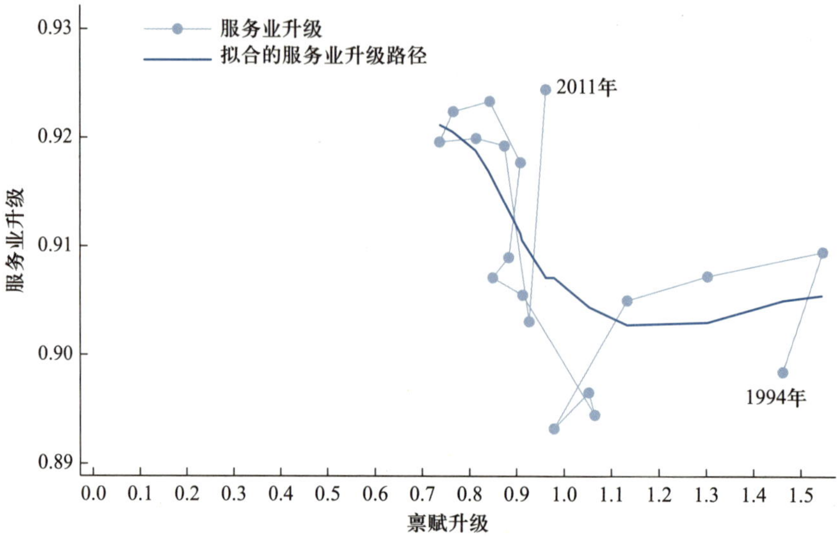


图 4.35 日本的服务业发展战略路径（1994—2011 年）及其拟合

产业结构升级依然有充足的后发优势，因此如图4.33所示的日本非农产业结构转型升级依然在70年代之后不断向世界前沿靠近，在1995年成功超过美国迈入世界前沿。

### 4.4.7 印度尼西亚的经济结构转型升级路径拟合及其特征①

印度尼西亚是东南亚国家，首都为雅加达。全国由17 000多个岛屿组成，是马来群岛的一部分，也是全世界最大的群岛国家，别称“千岛之国”。印度尼西亚与巴布亚新几内亚、东帝汶和马来西亚等国家相接，与泰国、新加坡、菲律宾、澳大利亚等国隔海相望，其疆域横跨亚洲及大洋洲。气候为典型的热带雨林气候，年平均温度25~27℃，无四季分别，年降水量1 600 ~ 2 200毫米。印度尼西亚资源丰富，矿产主要有石油、天然气、煤、锡、铝矾土、镍、铜和金、银等。印度尼西亚的石油、天然气和锡的储量在世界上占有重要地位，煤炭也是重要的出口品，已探明矿产储量为：石油500亿桶，天然气73万亿立方米，煤360亿吨。地热资源丰富，森林面积1.45亿公顷，约占国土总面积的74%。生物资源丰富。据不

① 关于印度尼西亚历史上的经济结构转型升级资料主要参考：日本海外贸易振兴会雅加达贸易中心，“印度尼西亚的工业化进展和对外贸易结构的变化”，《海外市场》（日本），1978年2月号。

完全统计，印度尼西亚约有40 000多种植物，同时渔业资源也十分丰富。2013年印度尼西亚总人口达2.48亿，是世界第四人口大国。有100多个民族，其中爪哇族47%，巽他族14%，马都拉族7%，华人3%~4%，此外还有米南卡保人、巴厘人等100多个民族的居民。民族语言200多种，通用印度尼西亚语。印度尼西亚是一个总统制共和国，人民协商会议为国家最高权力机关，由人民代表会议（即国会）和地方代表理事会共同组成。从1999年10月至今，人民协商会议对宪法进行了三次修改，主要包括规定总统和副总统只能连选连任一次、每任五年，减少总统权力、强化议会职能等。印度尼西亚是东南亚国家联盟创立国之一，也是东南亚最大经济体及20国集团成员国。

经历了350年的荷兰殖民统治后，印度尼西亚于第二次世界大战后宣告独立。独立后的印度尼西亚采取错误的发展战略走上计划经济体制，独立后20年，即到1965年，印度尼西亚的经济结构和荷兰殖民统治时期没有多大差别，依然以传统农业为主。如表4.6所示，1965年印度尼西亚的农业占GDP的比重高达59%，工业不足8%。在此之后一直到亚洲金融危机之前，都是印度尼西亚的发展黄金时期。按照增长与发展委员会的时期划定，1966—1997年是印度尼西亚超高速经济增长时期。印度尼西亚在20世纪70年代，轻纺工业得到快速发展，并奠定了工业化的基础。在1975年食品和纤维纺织就占工业的68%，其中包括制饼、调味品、饲料、饮料等在内的食品工业占到了工业的47%，纤维纺织有关的工业占21%。其后印度尼西亚在雅加达等五地设立了出口加工区，为投资于“外资法案”和“国内投资法案”所规定的开发项目的企业提供优惠待遇以资鼓励，出台了金融税收以及在海上运输方面的大量措施支持出口加工贸易。当然，时至今日印度尼西亚依然处在工业化的进程中，2013年其工业占GDP的比重为46.04%。

表4.6 印度尼西亚1965—1975年的产业结构

| | 1965年 | | 1970年 | | 1975年 | |
|---|---|---|---|---|---|---|
| | 产值（10亿盾） | 比重（%） | 产值（10亿盾） | 比重（%） | 产值（10亿盾） | 比重（%） |
| 农、林、渔业 | 13 928.70 | 58.75 | 1 575.00 | 47.15 | 4 045.00 | 33.18 |
| 矿业 | 528.80 | 2.23 | 172.60 | 5.17 | 2 483.00 | 20.37 |
| 工业 | 1 796.50 | 7.58 | 311.80 | 9.33 | 1 072.00 | 8.79 |
| 电气、煤气、下水道 | 5.40 | 0.02 | 15.00 | 0.45 | 60.00 | 0.49 |
| 建筑 | 437.20 | 1.84 | 100.30 | 3.00 | 550.00 | 4.51 |
| 运输、通信 | 518.70 | 2.19 | 95.80 | 2.87 | 521.00 | 4.27 |
| 商业、金融等 | 6 440.70 | 27.16 | 1 069.70 | 32.03 | 3 459.00 | 28.38 |
| 国内生产总值 | 23 710.00 | 100.00 | 3 340.20 | 100.00 | 12 190.00 | 100.00 |

资料来源：日本海外贸易振兴会雅加达贸易中心，“印度尼西亚的工业化进展和对外贸易结构的变化”，《海外市场》（日本），1978年2月号。

印度尼西亚虽然时下依然是发展典范样本中最穷的一个国家，2011年人均国内生产总值大约只有美国的7%，但是其产业结构升级极具典范性：1970年农业产值占国内生产总值的比重高达45%，但到2011年这个比重不足15%，从一个典型的农业国家转变为了非农业国。与中国一样，印度尼西亚作为一个贫穷的人口大国取得这样的发展绩效实属不易，堪称贫穷农业国发展的榜样。

图4.36是印度尼西亚1970—2011年的经济结构转型升级发展战略路径。对数拟合（$R^2 = 0.209$）的发展战略路径曲线为

$$I_{\mathrm{IDN},t} = 1.140\,5 + 0.099\,1 \times \ln\left(E_{\mathrm{IDN},t}\right)$$

斜率和弹性分别为 $\frac{\partial I_{\mathrm{IDN},t}}{\partial E_{\mathrm{IDN},t}} = \frac{0.099\,1}{E_{\mathrm{IDN},t}}$，$\frac{\partial I_{\mathrm{IDN},t}}{\partial E_{\mathrm{IDN},t}} \frac{E_{\mathrm{IDN},t}}{I_{\mathrm{IDN},t}} = \frac{0.099\,1}{I_{\mathrm{IDN},t}}$。印度尼西亚发展战略路径的斜率和弹性略微低于中国，但稍稍高于世界整体情况。可以直观地看到，相对而言20世纪70年代的经济结构转型升级较顺畅。

图4.37是印度尼西亚1970—2011年间的工业发展战略路径。二次函数拟合（$R^2 = 0.19$）曲线为

$$I_{\mathrm{IDN},t} = 1.286\,77 - 0.733\,8 \times E_{\mathrm{IDN},t} + 249.674\,4 \times E_{\mathrm{IDN},t}^2$$

可以直观地看到，70年代以及21世纪初期印度尼西亚工业化较为顺畅。

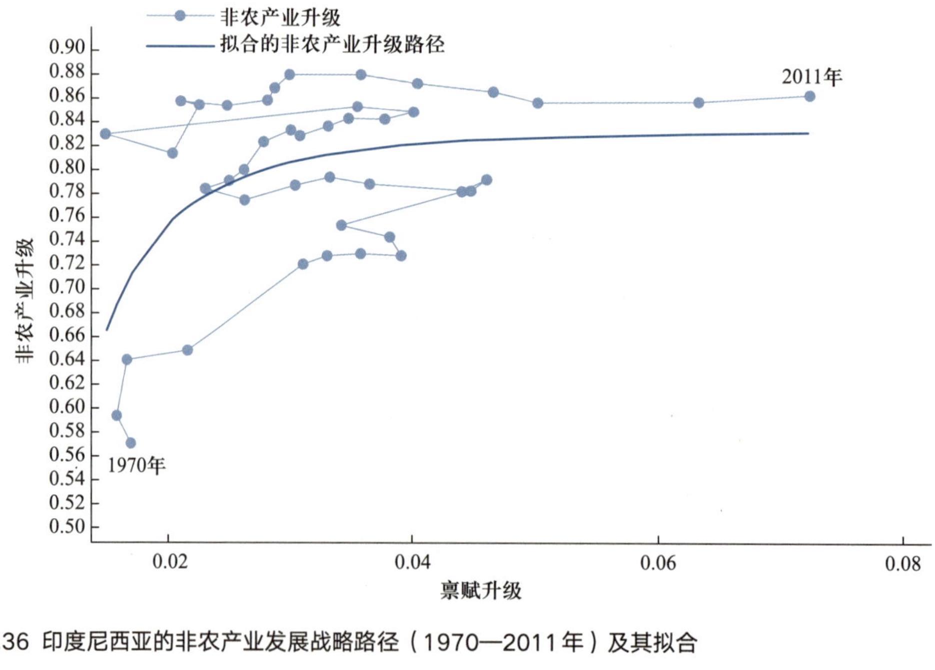


图4.36 印度尼西亚的非农产业发展战略路径（1970—2011年）及其拟合

图4.38是印度尼西亚1970—2011年的服务业发展战略路径，对数拟合（$R^2 = 0.07$）的发展战略路径曲线为

$$I_{\mathrm{IDN},t} = 0.44497 - 0.03134 \times \ln\left(E_{\mathrm{IDN},t}\right)$$

斜率和弹性分别为 $\dfrac{\partial I_{\mathrm{IDN},t}}{\partial E_{\mathrm{IDN},t}} = \dfrac{0.03134}{E_{\mathrm{IDN},t}}$，$\dfrac{\partial I_{\mathrm{IDN},t}}{\partial E_{\mathrm{IDN},t}} \dfrac{E_{\mathrm{IDN},t}}{I_{\mathrm{IDN},t}} = \dfrac{0.03134}{I_{\mathrm{IDN},t}}$。

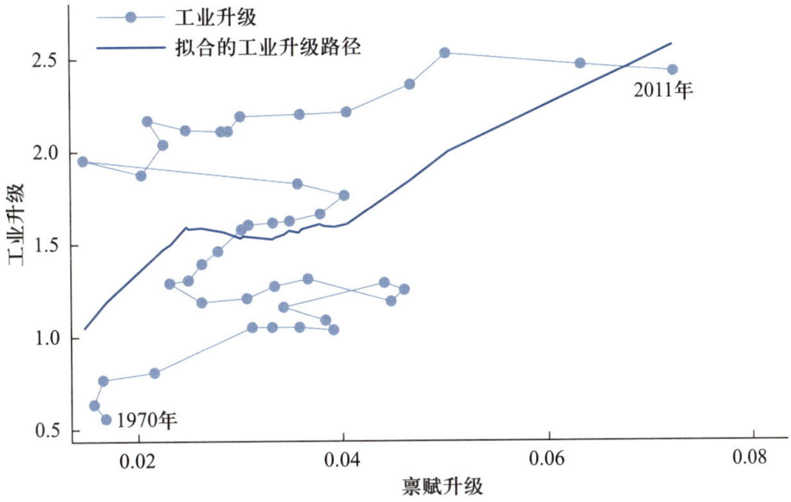


图4.37 印度尼西亚的工业发展战略路径（1970—2011年）及其拟合

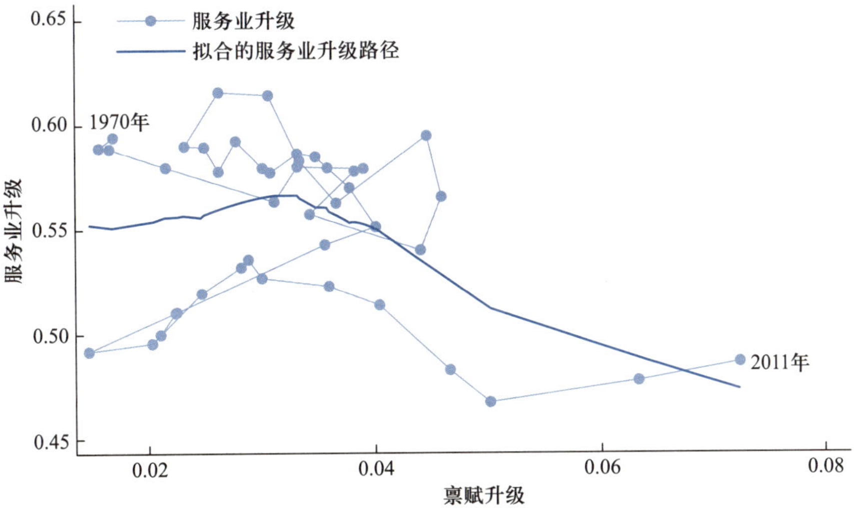


图4.38 印度尼西亚的服务业发展战略路径（1970—2011年）及其拟合

### 4.4.8 马来西亚的经济结构转型升级路径拟合及其特征①

马来西亚位于东南亚，首都为吉隆坡，联邦政府则位于布城。国土被南中国海分为两个部分：西马来西亚，位于马来半岛，北接泰国，南部隔着柔佛海峡，以新柔长堤和第二通道连接新加坡；东马来西亚，位于加里曼丹岛的北部，南接印度尼西亚。马来西亚属于热带雨林气候和热带季风气候，平均温度在26 ~ 30℃，全年雨量充沛。截至2015年，马来西亚总人口3 064万，其中马来人55%，华人24%，印度人7.3%，其他种族13.7%。马来语为国语，通用英语，汉语使用较广泛。伊斯兰教为国教，其他宗教有佛教、印度教和基督教等。国家元首是国王，政府首脑是总理。马来西亚是东南亚国家联盟的创始国之一，亚洲太平洋经济合作组织、英联邦和伊斯兰会议组织的成员。20世纪70年代前，马来西亚经济以农业为主，依赖初级产品出口。70年代以来不断调整产业结构，大力推行出口导向型经济，电子业、制造业、建筑业和服务业发展迅速。1987年起，经济连续10年保持8%以上的高速增长，为亚洲“四小虎”国家之一。1998年受亚洲金融危机冲击，经济出现负增长。通过稳定汇率、重组银行企业债务、扩大内需和出口等政策，经济基本恢复并保持中速增长。制造业是马来西亚最大的生产部门，2010年制造业总产值约为2 641.7亿美元，增加值为539.1亿美元，占GDP的比重达22.5%。马来西亚制造业以食品制造、电子电器业、木制品业、炼油业、橡胶产品业和非金属矿产品业为主。此外，旅游业和知识经济服务也发展迅速。增长与发展委员会认定的马来西亚黄金增长时期是1967—1997年的30年。1996年8月2日发行的德国《商报》称“马来西亚近期的经济读起来像一部成功的小说”。

马来西亚近现代的工业化也始于第二次世界大战之后。马来西亚在1958年刚刚独立之后的第二年便发布了《先驱工业法令》，为工业提供税收优惠，适度采取关税壁垒和一些领域的进口数量限额来保护国内的“幼稚工业”，初期的进口替代工业主要集中于满足国内市场的日用消费品工业。马来西亚的制造业占GDP的份额由1957年的11%上升到1968年的13%，制造业就业人数占总就业人数的比重由6%上升到9%。然而，随着这些日用工业受限于国内市场，1968年之后马来西亚开始将进口替代战略转变为出口导向型战略。1968年马来西亚政府发布了《奖励投资法案》，规定凡有助于发展出口工业、促进出口以及符合马来西亚经济发展需要的工业企业均可申请“新兴工业企业”的资格，获批后可享受2 ~ 8年的免税期，劳动力使用税减免，投资设厂地点优惠，以及减免出口税和所得税扣除等优惠政策。其后直到1986年马来西亚对《奖励投资法案》修订了七次，从各个方面大力促进出口

① 本节关于马来西亚经济结构转型升级的数据资料主要参考了马来西亚财政部历年的《马来西亚经济报告书》。

工业的发展。1971年4月，马来西亚政府颁布了《自由贸易区法令》，由政府投资建立工业区，出资修建工业区所必需的基础设施，如公路、通信、电力设施等；制定优惠的进驻政策，鼓励外资企业入驻工业区；被用于复出口的物品进口时免征关税，所得税也给予一定程度的减免；新增投资可享受更多的优惠；凡有80%以上产品出口的工业企业可以在自由贸易区设立“保税工厂”；凡生产出口品所需原材料部件的进口可免除关税。自1972年第一个自由贸易区在槟州南部的巴亚利巴（Byana Lepas）建成后，又陆续开辟了17个出口加工区，并在沙巴的拉布安岛设立了自由贸易港。马来西亚在20世纪六七十年代主要发展劳动力密集型出口产业。这一点直观体现在1969年马来西亚政府制定的“新工业发展战略”中，规划规定了其后工业化战略方向：① 为了扩大就业机会着重发展劳动集约型工业；② 设立投资委员会，负责促进工业化的进展；③ 政府介入工业化进程；④ 促进西马东海岸地区和东马的工业化；⑤ 各州政府对工业化进行协作；⑥ 加强对青少年的工业技术训练，等等。马来西亚的第二个五年计划（1971—1975年）也明确提出了出口导向的工业化方针，为面向出口工业企业的建立和发展制定了优惠政策，尤其是鼓励资金流向劳动力密集型面向出口的工业企业，并制定了一系列相应的税收、引资政策。在80年代马来西亚依然延续了轻工业优先发展的战略。1986年马来西亚政府制定了工业发展十年规划《马来西亚的中长期工业基本计划的概要（1986—1995年）》，即“大蓝图”，重点发展12个工业部门，如橡胶产品、棕油产品、木材产品、有色金属产品、电子电器、纺织产品等。

马来西亚在20世纪60至80年代的劳动力密集型出口产业发展战略极为成功，1970—1980年出口总额占国内生产总值的平均比重为44.5%，到1980年制造业产品出口已达63.19亿马元，占当年出口总额的22.4%。在出口的工业制成品中，电子电器的出口占第一位，1986年占工业制成品出口总额的53.5%，当时马来西亚已成为世界第三大半导体元件和空调机出口国；纺织品（包括服装和鞋类）是马工业制成品的第二大出口产品，1986年出口达16.44亿马元，居世界第十位，占出口工业制成品的11%。1970—1975年，制造业的增长率为11.6%，制造业在国内生产总值中的比重由1970年的13.4%上升到1980年的18.6%。1981—1985年，制造业年均增长率达5.2%，1986—1990年年均增长率达13.63%，1987年制造业在国内生产总值中的比重占22.5%，首次超过农业的比重21.9%，成功脱离农业经济成为一个工业经济国家。在成功实现了经济结构转型升级之后，其经济增长自然优异。1976—1979年马来西亚国内生产总值年平均增长率分别为11.6%、7.8%、6.7%、9.3%；整个20世纪80年代马来西亚国内生产总值年平均增长率高达8.4%。

马来西亚第二次经济结构转型始于90年代初期，开始推动劳动力密集型产业向资本和技术密集型产业转型升级。1991年2月28日，马哈蒂尔总理发表《马来西亚迈向前路》的工作报告，提出了要在2020年把马来西亚建成一个“充分发达的国家”，《2020年宏愿

（1991—2020年）》随之成为马来西亚的工业发展战略。1991年6月，马来西亚政府公布了《1991—2000年的国家发展战略》与《第二个长期发展计划》，指出了90年代发展战略方案的八项重要战略目标，主要是：促进主要经济部门之间的均衡发展，实现能够提高它们之间的互补性的最佳均衡发展；在不损害社会改组目标的前提下，培养工业发展所需要的生产效率高的工人与技术人员，发展科学与技术，提高具有战略意义的高科技与知识集约型技术的竞争能力，形成近代产业社会建设所必需的科技文化；为保持长期的持续的发展，必须注意到环境保护与生态平衡，等等。1996年5月，政府制定并公布了“第七个五年计划”，特别鼓励发展技术和资本密集型产业，提高出口产品附加值，促进出口工业向技术和资本集约型发展。在亚洲金融风暴之前，1990—1996年马来西亚同期制造业年平均增长率高达14%，制造业在国内生产总值中的比重由1990年的27%上升到1996年的34.5%。然而，由于劳动力成本上涨太快，致使马来西亚劳动力密集型出口产业迅速失去比较优势，在亚洲金融风暴前夕，资本和技术密集型替代产业尚未培育起来，因而在金融风暴中遭受重创，1967—1996年的增长奇迹一去不返。1997年马来西亚整体工资水平已达到劳动生产率的2倍，这对主要依赖于劳动力密集型出口产业的马来西亚的打击是致命的。1988年制成品出口总额中63%来自电器、电子和纺织工业，仅电子工业一项就占制成品出口总额的50%。马来西亚制造业出口额占出口总额的百分比由1992年的27%上升到1993年的30.1%，1995年制造业产品出口在出口总额中所占比重更是上升到79.6%；1996年工业制成品在出口总额中所占比重进一步提高到81%。当然，亚洲金融风暴并未中断马来西亚经济结构转型升级的继续推进。最为重要的举措便是，马来西亚政府在亚洲金融风暴之后继续通过多媒体超级走廊推动经济转型。马来西亚数码经济机构（MDEC）于1996年成立，至今共吸引投资2 830亿马元，成功打造3 881家具有多媒体超级走廊地位的资讯公司。过去20年马来西亚拥有多媒体超级走廊地位公司的总营业额达3 170亿马元，出口额达1 040亿马元。资讯工艺、多媒体创意、全球商业服务三个领域可申请多媒体超级走廊地位，获批后可享有许多优惠政策，包括外国投资者可控股、10年免税、聘请外国专业人才、资金可自由进出、无网络审查、享有MDEC的一站式服务等。每年平均有800家公司提出申请，250家可获批。

2011年马来西亚的人均收入水平依然只有美国的1/5多一点，马来西亚和后面要介绍的泰国虽然谈不上是耀眼的发展明星，但是在$\{E \in (0.08, 0.2), I \in (0.7, 0.9)\}$结构变迁发展区域上是模范，能在较高非农产业结构水平上继续升级产业结构，并能在较短时间内成功脱贫迈入中等收入国家行列。这两个国家也有着非常相似的发展战略路径。图4.39是马来西亚1970—2011年的非农产业发展战略路径，对数拟合（$R^2 = 0.22$）的发展战略路径曲线为

$$I_{\mathrm{MYS},t} = 1.132\ 2 + 0.136\ 2 \times \ln\left(E_{\mathrm{MYS},t}\right)$$

斜率和弹性分别为 $\frac{\partial I_{\mathrm{MYS},t}}{\partial E_{\mathrm{MYS},t}}=\frac{0.1362}{E_{\mathrm{MYS},t}}$，$\frac{\partial I_{\mathrm{MYS},t}}{\partial E_{\mathrm{MYS},t}}\frac{E_{\mathrm{MYS},t}}{I_{\mathrm{MYS},t}}=\frac{0.1362}{I_{\mathrm{MYS},t}}$。图4.40是马来西亚1970—2011年的工业发展战略路径。二次函数拟合（$R^2=0.23$）的发展战略路径曲线为

$$I_{\mathrm{MYS},t}=0.09166+15.7657\times E_{\mathrm{MYS},t}-29.47962\times E_{\mathrm{MYS},t}^2$$

其顶点和拐点分别为$I=2.1995$和$E=0.2674$，二者均介于中国和韩国之间。图4.41是马来西亚1970—2011年的服务业发展战略路径。对数拟合（$R^2=0.1319$）的发展战略路径曲线为

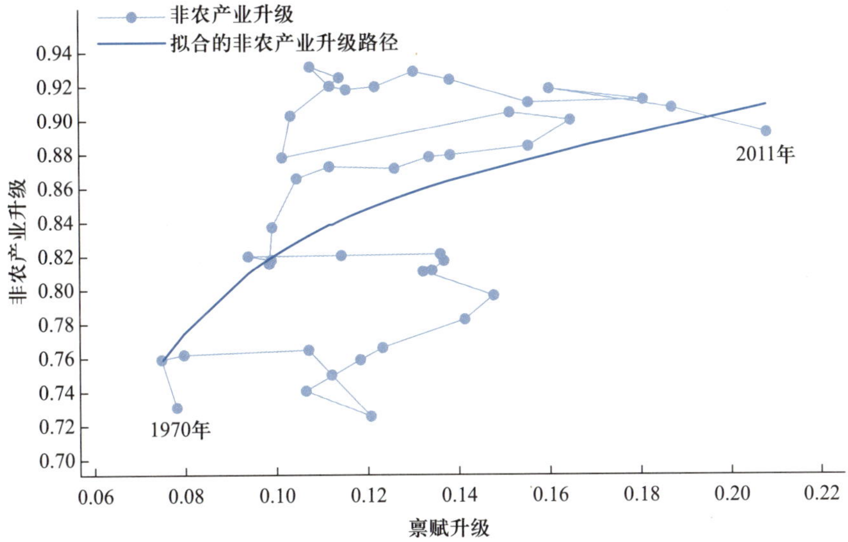


图4.39 马来西亚的非农产业发展战略路径（1970—2011年）及其拟合

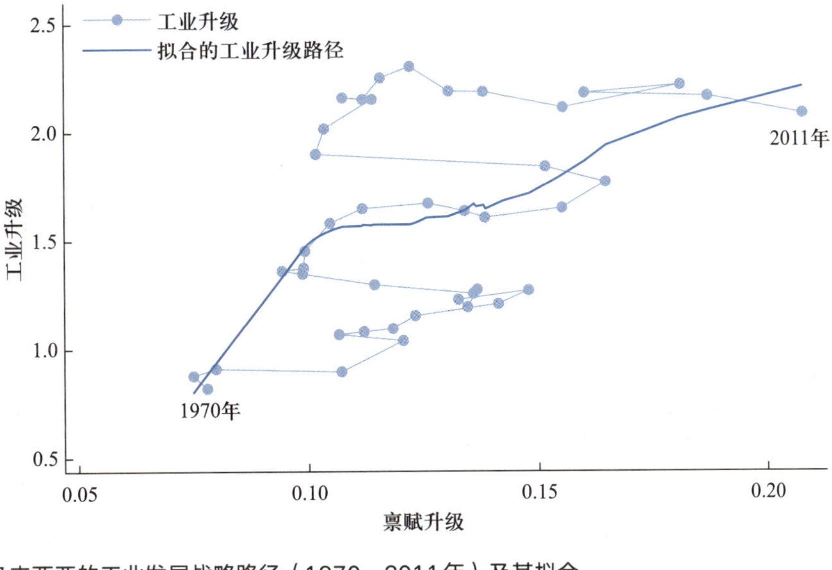


图4.40 马来西亚的工业发展战略路径（1970—2011年）及其拟合

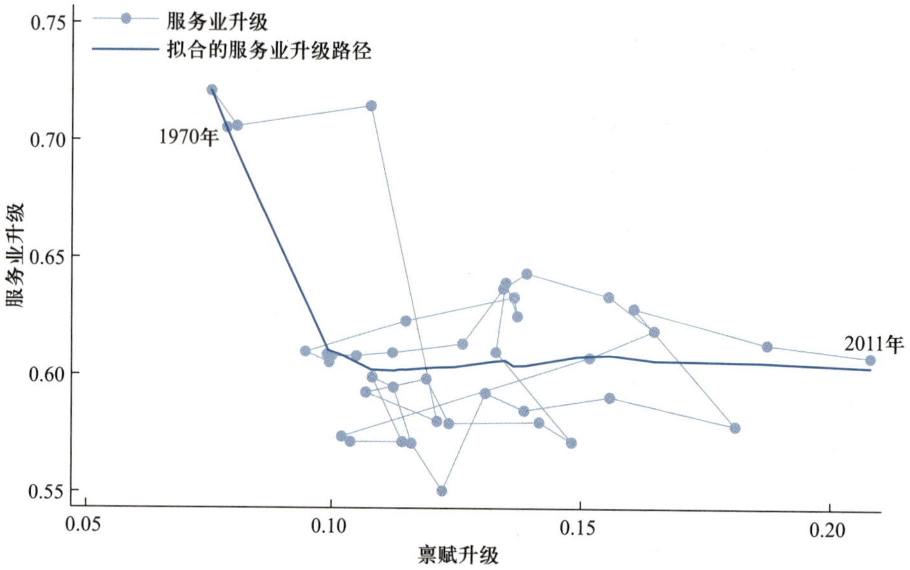


图4.41 马来西亚的服务业发展战略路径（1970—2011年）及其拟合

$$I_{\mathrm{MYS},t}=0.479\ 48-0.063\ 19\times\ln\left(E_{\mathrm{MYS},t}\right)$$

其斜率和弹性分别为 $\frac{\partial I_{\mathrm{MYS},t}}{\partial E_{\mathrm{MYS},t}}=\frac{0.063\ 19}{E_{\mathrm{MYS},t}}$ 和 $\frac{\partial I_{\mathrm{MYS},t}}{\partial E_{\mathrm{MYS},t}}\frac{E_{\mathrm{MYS},t}}{I_{\mathrm{MYS},t}}=\frac{0.063\ 19}{I_{\mathrm{MYS},t}}$。

## 4.4.9 泰国的经济结构转型升级路径拟合及其特征①

泰国是一个位于东南亚的君主立宪制国家，位于中南半岛中部，其西部与北部和缅甸、安达曼海接壤，东北是老挝，东南是柬埔寨，南边狭长的半岛与马来西亚相连。国境内大部分为低缓的山地和高原。属于热带季风气候，年均气温24 ~ 30℃，平均年降水量约1 000毫米。2014年3月，泰国总人口6 450万。全国共有30多个民族，其中泰族为主要民族，占人口总数的40%，其余为佬族、华族、马来族、高棉族以及一些山地民族。泰语为国语。90%以上的民众信仰佛教，马来族信奉伊斯兰教，还有少数民众信仰基督教、天主教、印度教和锡克教。泰国是东南亚国家联盟成员国和创始国之一，同时也是亚太经济合作组织、

① 关于泰国产业结构变迁历史的简要介绍可参考：吴文科，“泰国产业结构简析”，《亚太经济》，1993年第5期。

亚欧会议和世界贸易组织成员。在20世纪90年代经济发展较快，跻身亚洲“四小虎”之一。泰国是世界新兴工业国家和世界新兴市场经济体之一，制造业、农业和旅游业是泰国经济的主要产业。电子工业等制造业发展迅速，产业结构变化明显；汽车业是支柱产业，是东南亚汽车制造中心和东盟最大的汽车市场。泰国是亚洲唯一的粮食净出口国、世界五大农产品出口国之一。此外，泰国还是世界最闻名的旅游胜地之一。

与绝大多数发展中经济体一样，二战后的泰国也采取了进口替代的工业化战略，想以此实现农业国家的工业化。泰国在1947年的经济活动人口中农业占比高达84.8%，严重依赖于单一的稻米种植。1954年泰国出台了《鼓励工业发展法案》，1960年又出台了《鼓励工业投资法案》，通过一系列投资优惠政策吸引资本发展进口替代工业。就像新结构经济学所判断的那样，违背比较优势的进口替代战略在短期内能够通过投资拉动经济增长，但由于结构扭曲而无法长期持续发展。泰国在1951—1954年的国内生产总值就增长了13.6%。在进口替代发展战略期间，泰国制造业的比重由1951年的10%提高到1969年的15%，其中食品饮料等轻工业和石油冶炼、化工制品、机械制造在20世纪60年代都得到长足发展，但是由于违背比较优势的产业结构扭曲使得泰国在1947—1969年制造业占全部劳动力的比重仅仅提高了1.8%。由于制造业无法吸纳大量农业剩余劳动力，这些劳动力就只能涌入第三产业，尤其是旅游业，60年代泰国第三产业就业上涨了33.8%。然而，缺乏制造业基础的第三产业对提高劳动生产率并没有多大帮助。

从20世纪70年代开始，泰国开始将进口替代战略调整为出口导向型发展战略。泰国政府在《第三个国家经济社会发展计划（1972—1976年）》中明确提出出口导向工业化发展战略，强调加强发展出口贸易，尤其是发展面向出口工业和促进农产品多样化以及利用国内资源促进工业制成品国产化。与马来西亚等国促进出口产业的产业政策类似，1972年泰国也出台了《1972投资奖励法案》，规定凡是生产出口产品所需要的原材料进口就可以免除进口税，转口贸易商品也可以享受免除进口税的待遇，以及工业产品出口可以免除出口税和减免所得税。这种符合比较优势的劳动力密集型出口导向发展战略取得了成功。1973—1990年，泰国外贸出口平均增长18.7%，纺织品、集成电路与珠宝合计占总出口的比重从1979年的13.4%提高到1990年的23.9%，超过传统农业的出口总值，占制造业出口的32%。同期，塑料制品增长了23.6倍，家具增长了近30倍，人造花增长了近14倍，鱼罐头增长了41倍。在1972—1990年，泰国的第二产业比重从23.5%提高到32.8%，制造业部门在1985年首度超过农业成为最大的产业部门，农业比重从30.4%下降到14.4%，1972—1985年，第二产业就业人口增加了239万，从而实现了从农业经济向工业经济的转变。自然而然的结果便是，1972—1990年，泰国年均经济增长达到7.8%，第二产业增长率达到9.8%。

虽然泰国也在90年代初期就开始布局传统劳动力密集型产业的转型升级，着手发展计算机零部件、电器、集成电路、汽车及其零部件。但是，由于劳动力密集型产业失去比较优势的速度太快，而新兴的资本和技术密集型接替产业升级的速度跟不上，与马来西亚类似，再加上20世纪90年代初资本账户开放，外国投机资本大量流入催生了房地产泡沫，后又大量流出，导致泡沫破灭、货币急剧贬值，触发了亚洲金融风暴，遭受严重打击，1997年泰国工业增长率仅有4%。然而，亚洲金融风暴也同样没有阻止泰国的产业转型升级。在短短的7年中，泰国的汽车出口从1996年的1.4万辆飙升至2003年的23.5万辆，增加了15.7倍之多。1998—2003年，泰国汽车出口呈跳跃式增长，其平均出口量达到汽车生产总量的35.7%。2013年泰国电子产品出口中计算机产品占比达55.6%。

图4.42是泰国1970—2011年的非农产业发展战略路径，对数拟合（$R^2=0.48$）的发展战略路径曲线为

$$I_{\mathrm{THA},t}=1.240\ 1+0.135\ 4\times\ln\left(E_{\mathrm{THA},t}\right)$$

斜率和弹性分别为 $\dfrac{\partial I_{\mathrm{THA},t}}{\partial E_{\mathrm{THA},t}}=\dfrac{0.135\ 4}{E_{\mathrm{THA},t}}$，$\dfrac{\partial I_{\mathrm{THA},t}}{\partial E_{\mathrm{THA},t}}\dfrac{E_{\mathrm{THA},t}}{I_{\mathrm{THA},t}}=\dfrac{0.135\ 4}{I_{\mathrm{THA},t}}$。马来西亚和泰国发展战略路径的斜率和弹性比较接近韩国和中国，但较之非洲典范博茨瓦纳要温和，较之印度尼西亚要大很多。图4.43是泰国1970—2011年的工业发展战略路径。二次函数拟合（$R^2=0.55$）的发展战略路径曲线为

$$I_{\mathrm{THA},t}=-1.486\ 89+73.523\ 29\times E_{\mathrm{THA},t}-390.151\ 5\times E_{\mathrm{THA},t}^2$$

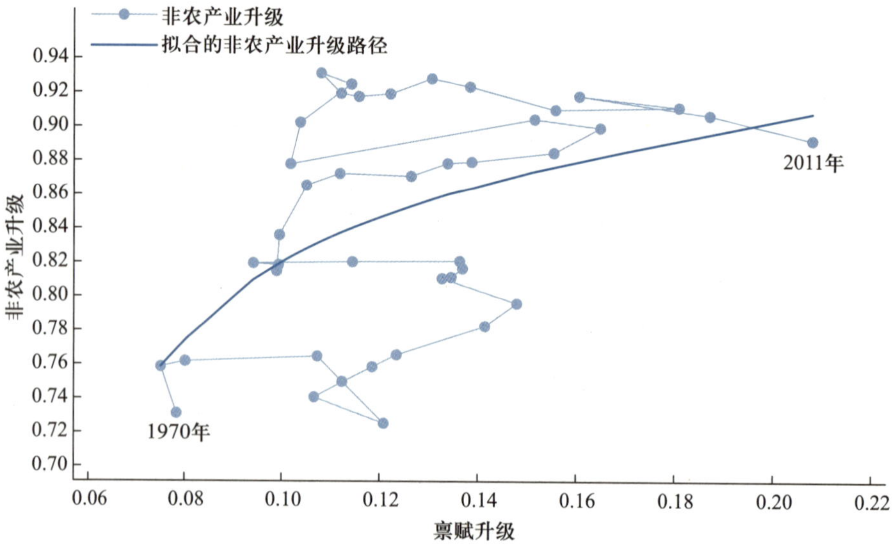


图4.42 泰国的非农产业发展战略路径（1970—2011年）及其拟合

其顶点和拐点分别为$I=1.976\ 9$和$E=0.094\ 2$，顶点与世界样本相比要略低一些，拐点则远小于世界样本而与中国接近，说明泰国的工业升级还是较快的。图4.44是泰国1970—2011年的服务业发展战略路径。对数拟合（$R^2=0.45$）的发展战略路径曲线为

$$I_{\mathrm{THA},t}=0.228\ 88-0.165\ 01\times\ln\left(E_{\mathrm{THA},t}\right)$$

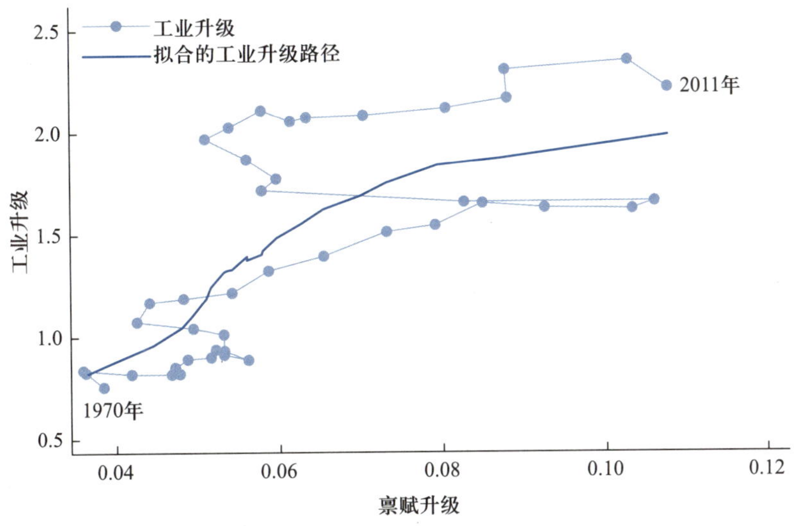


图4.43 泰国的工业发展战略路径（1970—2011年）及其拟合

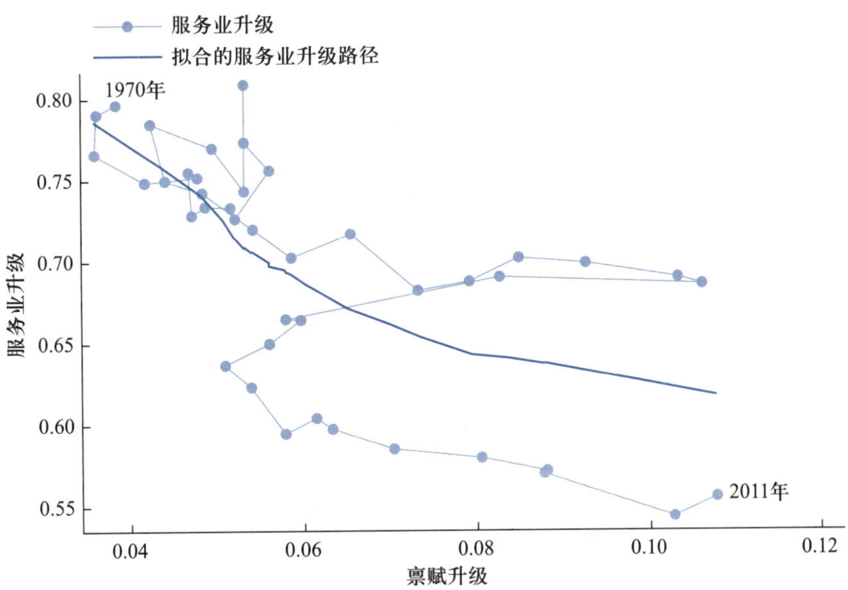


图4.44 泰国的服务业发展战略路径（1970—2011年）及其拟合

其斜率和弹性分别为 $\frac{\partial I_{THA,t}}{\partial E_{THA,t}}=\frac{0.165\ 01}{E_{THA,t}}$ 和 $\frac{\partial I_{THA,t}}{\partial E_{THA,t}}\frac{E_{THA,t}}{I_{THA,t}}=\frac{0.165\ 01}{I_{THA,t}}$。这与泰国早期由于进口替代战略导致制造业所无法吸收的大量农业剩余劳动力涌入第三产业尤其是旅游业，使得其产业结构虚高的历史是一致的。随着泰国劳动力密集型制造业的发展，这些劳动力再流入制造业，使得服务业下滑，进行正常调整。

### 4.4.10 阿曼的经济结构转型升级路径拟合及其特征①

阿曼位于阿拉伯半岛东南部，地处波斯湾通往印度洋的要道，西北接阿拉伯联合酋长国，西连沙特阿拉伯，西南邻也门共和国，东北与东南濒临阿曼湾和阿拉伯海。海岸线长1 700千米，国土面积30.95万平方千米，境内大部分是海拔200 ~ 500米的高原。除东北部山地外，均属热带沙漠气候。全年分两季：5月至10月为热季，气温高达40℃以上；11月至翌年4月为凉季，气温约为24℃。年平均降水量130毫米。2014年，阿曼全国人口总数为395.7万，其中本国人口221.3万，外籍常住人口174.4万。本国人口绝大多数是阿拉伯人，外来定居人口中印度人、伊朗人、巴基斯坦人等居多。阿曼是君主制国家，无宪法和议会，禁止一切政党活动，由苏丹颁布法律、法令和批准缔结国际条约与协定。

阿曼石油资源丰富，现已探明石油储量近7.2亿吨，天然气储量33.4万亿立方英尺。煤储量约3 600万吨，金矿储量约1 182万吨，铜储量约2 000万吨，铬100万吨，还有银及优质石灰石等。水产资源也非常丰富。但是，其最初依然是一个传统的农业经济国家。1970年，阿曼的人均国内生产总值只有美国的7%左右，20世纪80年代旋即成为中等收入国家。尽管阿曼是资源富足型国家，但是其结构变迁并未陷入“资源诅咒”。当然，阿曼在20世纪70年代的快速增长确实得益于其石油资源开发。60年代开始开采石油，目前仍以石油开采为主，油气田主要分布在西北部和南部的戈壁、沙漠地区。石油、天然气产业是阿曼的支柱产业，油气收入占国家财政收入的75%，占国内生产总值的41%。阿曼经济结构高度单一，有约40%以上的人口从事农、牧、渔业。②阿曼目前正在加速推进经济结构多元化转型升级。渔业历来是阿曼经济的重要组成部分，并被列为该国经济多元化改革中的五个驱动经济未来

① 关于目前阿曼经济多元化转型升级的资料主要参考 *The Report: Oman 2017*。

② 全国可耕地1 014平方千米，已耕地615平方千米，主要种植椰枣、柠檬、香蕉等水果和蔬菜。粮食作物以小麦、大麦、高粱为主，不能自给。

增长的关键行业之一。根据阿曼政府的规划，渔业产量将逐步提高20万吨，至2020年达到年产48万吨的水平，并新创造2万个就业岗位。目前在建的主要渔业项目包括位于杜库姆经济特区内的一个渔港和毗邻的渔业产业集群项目。矿业是另一个重点发展行业，其对阿曼GDP的贡献度为0.5%，未来增长空间巨大。目前，阿曼政府已出台了新的矿业法，以吸引更多外国和本地投资者进军该领域，开发当地的金、铜和稀土等矿产。此外，正在杜库姆经济特区内兴建的矿产品加工等设施也将进一步助力该行业的发展，提高矿业的整体收益水平。

新近发布的*The Report: Oman 2017*认为，实现经济多元化是阿曼政府的长期目标，从中短期来看，虽然国际油价复苏前景仍不乐观，但油气出口收入仍在阿曼的国民经济中发挥着至关重要的作用。2011—2014年，油气出口收入年均占到政府总收入的84%。为此，阿曼在近年继续着力扩大油气产能，目前年产原油量接近4亿桶。维持甚至增加产能的重要性不仅体现在国家收入方面，更在于油气勘探和开采活动是支撑阿曼国民经济活动（包括石化、冶金、海水淡化等）的基石，对于阿曼政府正在推行的多元化改革意义重大，为制造业等行业的发展提供了助力。例如，总耗资64亿美元的Liwa塑料化工一体化项目将成为阿曼制造业的旗舰项目，这一规划中的项目已收到了来自多家国际金融机构的融资支持，待2020年建成投产后，将成为该国首个聚乙烯生产厂，创造1.3万个就业岗位，并进一步支持其他使用聚乙烯为原材料的下游行业的发展。同时，阿曼看好东部非洲的经济快速增长前景，希望充分发掘自身地理位置优势和与该地区的历史传统关系，着力发展运输物流业，将该国油气领域上下游产品销往东非地区国家。阿曼出口信用保险机构（Export Credit Guarantee Agency，ECGA）总经理助理Imaadal-Harthy表示："得益于地理距离上的优势，阿曼正在东部非洲快速增长的经济体中寻找合作机会，并尤为关注埃塞俄比亚。"阿曼运输物流业最重要的发展项目就是中东部港口城市杜库姆的经济特区，其中包括了八个重要组成部分：杜库姆新港、工业区、住宅区、渔业码头、旅游中心、物流中心、中央商务区、教育培训区。杜库姆经济特区管委会（Special Economic Zone Authority Duqm，SEZAD）负责管理和规范区内的经济活动和项目发展。此外，占地95平方千米的al-BatinahSouth物流园区将是该国的另一个物流旗舰项目，致力于打造一个包含多式联运、轻工、商贸服务、仓储物流的地区枢纽。

阿曼旅游部希望至2020年将旅游业对GDP的贡献率提高至5%，并至2024年累计创造10万个就业机会。根据世界旅游及旅行理事会（World Travel & Tourism Council，WTTC）发布的《2016年旅游及旅行的经济影响》报告，阿曼旅游业直接产生的收入在2015年达到18亿美元（占GDP的2.5%），至2026年可增加到35亿美元（占GDP的3.4%）。如算上间接产生的收入，则该国旅游业在2015年营收额达到41亿美元（占GDP的5.7%），至2026年可达到79亿美元（占GDP的7.7%）。在就业方面，WTTC预测，旅游业目前直接创造5.3万个工作岗位，至2026年可累计创造8.1万个岗位。阿曼政府十分看中旅游业这一劳动力密集型行业在创造就业机会中的积极作用，目前有39个旅游项目正在建设实施，将为旅游业的未来增长奠定良好的基础。

尽管阿曼过去的经济结构转型路径也许对于大多数经济体而言不具有太多的可比性，但其是典型的资源型经济体，对于资源型经济体转型升级有一定的借鉴意义。图4.45是阿曼1970—2004年的非农产业发展战略路径，对数拟合（$R^2=0.84$）的发展战略路径曲线为

$$I_{\mathrm{OMN},t}=1.074\ 1+0.062\ 2\times\ln\left(E_{\mathrm{OMN},t}\right)$$

斜率和弹性分别为 $\dfrac{\partial I_{\mathrm{OMN},t}}{\partial E_{\mathrm{OMN},t}}=\dfrac{0.062\ 2}{E_{\mathrm{OMN},t}}$，$\dfrac{\partial I_{\mathrm{OMN},t}}{\partial E_{\mathrm{OMN},t}}\dfrac{E_{\mathrm{OMN},t}}{I_{\mathrm{OMN},t}}=\dfrac{0.062\ 2}{I_{\mathrm{OMN},t}}$。图4.46是阿曼1970—2004年的工业发展战略路径。二次函数拟合（$R^2=0.026$）的发展战略路径曲线为

$$I_{\mathrm{OMN},t}=2.304\ 1-1.297\ 35\times E_{\mathrm{OMN},t}+1.741\ 86\times E_{\mathrm{OMN},t}^2$$

图4.47是阿曼1970—2004年的服务业发展战略路径。对数拟合（$R^2=0.23$）的发展战略路径曲线为

$$I_{\mathrm{OMN},t}=0.788\ 92+0.173\ 95\times\ln\left(E_{\mathrm{OMN},t}\right)$$

斜率和弹性分别为 $\dfrac{\partial I_{\mathrm{OMN},t}}{\partial E_{\mathrm{OMN},t}}=\dfrac{0.173\ 95}{E_{\mathrm{OMN},t}}$ 和 $\dfrac{\partial I_{\mathrm{OMN},t}}{\partial E_{\mathrm{OMN},t}}\dfrac{E_{\mathrm{OMN},t}}{I_{\mathrm{OMN},t}}=\dfrac{0.173\ 95}{I_{\mathrm{OMN},t}}$。可以看到，虽然阿曼的收入水平大幅提高，但是其经济结构转型升级的路径还是相对于其他发展典范要紊乱得多。这在一定程度上表明阿曼的经济结构转型升级依然存在很多问题。

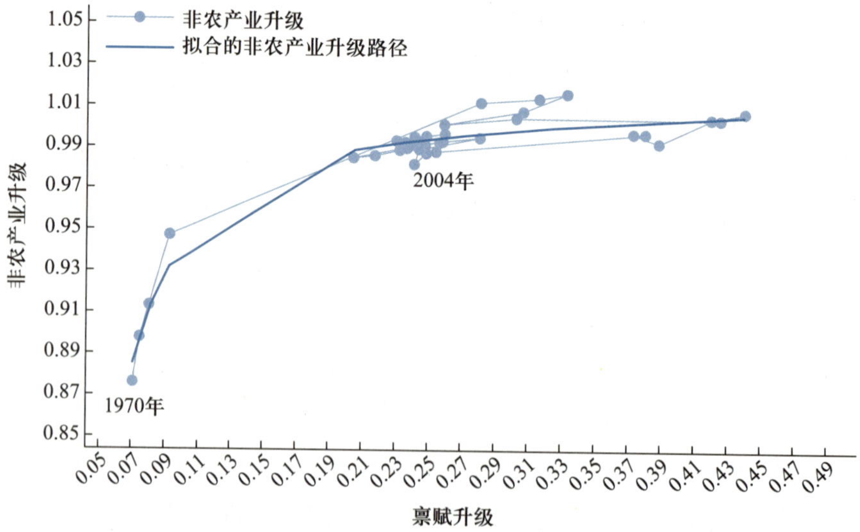


图4.45 阿曼的非农产业发展战略路径（1970—2004年）及其拟合

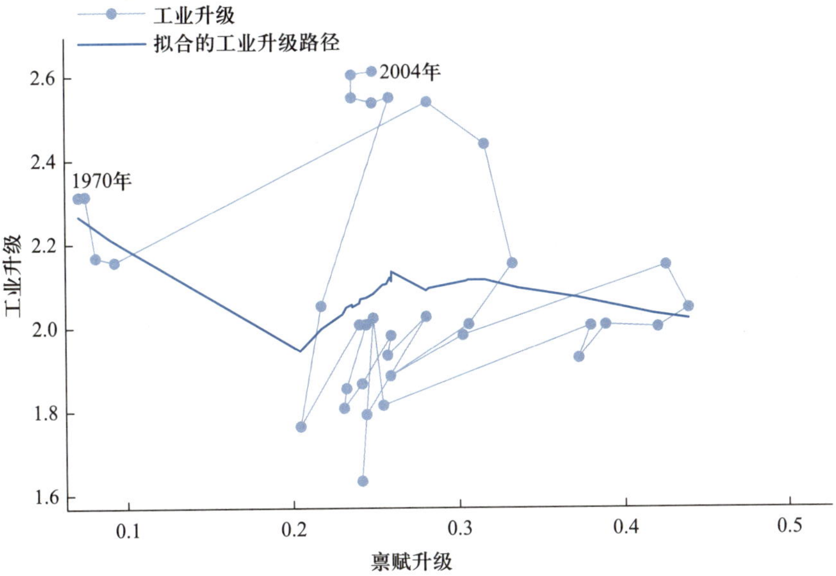


图4.46 阿曼的工业发展战略路径（1970—2004年）及其拟合

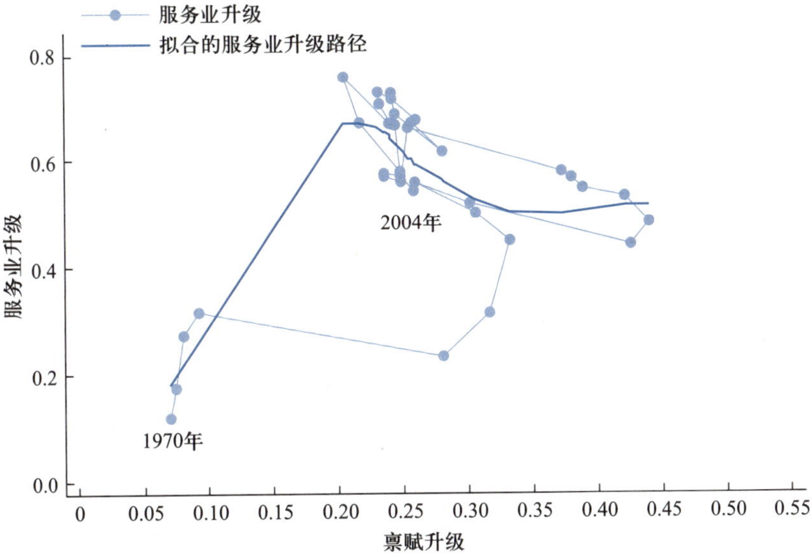


图4.47 阿曼的服务业发展战略路径（1970—2004年）及其拟合

### 4.4.11 马耳他的经济结构转型升级路径拟合及其特征①

马耳他位于南欧，毗邻意大利，位于意大利西西里岛以南90千米、突尼斯以东284千米、利比亚以北333千米。总面积316平方千米，相当于18个中国澳门的大小。马耳他属亚热带地中海式气候，冬季多雨，夏季高温干燥。全年平均气温21.3℃，最高气温40℃，最低气温5℃。年平均降水量560毫米。马耳他自然资源缺乏，除生产建筑用石灰岩外，无矿产资源，石油、天然气更是完全依赖进口。全国总人口42.15万，马耳他人占其中的95%以上，其余为阿拉伯人、意大利人、英国人等。天主教为马耳他的国教，信奉人数占98%，少数人信奉基督新教和东正教。官方语言为马耳他语和英语，同时意大利语也非常流行。马耳他实行共和国制，2004年加入欧盟，2008年加入欧元区。

如果说阿曼是典型的资源丰裕型经济体，其经济结构转型升级经验与问题对资源丰裕型经济体的转型升级有借鉴意义的话，那么马耳他则是典型的资源匮乏型“微型经济”的代表，其经济结构转型升级对这些微型经济体有借鉴意义。按照联合国贸易和发展会议、世界银行、英联邦秘书处等国际机构的常规标准，一般都选择以人口100万～150万作为微型经济体的门槛。②如果把标准定为100万的话，2011年世界范围内微型经济体有79个。因此，研究马耳他的经济结构转型升级从经济体数量上讲也颇具代表性。微型经济体面临的最重要的经济结构转型升级问题莫过于产业多元化。理由很简单，因为微型经济体体量小，产业相对单一，而如果一个经济体依赖于单一产业，则面临很大的风险。然而，尽管如此，如表4.7所示的一些微型经济体依然获得了成功。在表4.7的微型经济体中，马耳他的人均GDP2011年为1.92万美元，而中国澳门、冰岛和卢森堡的人均GDP则远远高于马耳他，分别为3.95万美元、4.16万美元和10.54万美元。增长与发展委员会在《增长报告》中认定的马耳他黄金增长期为1963—1994年，不过可以看到马耳他与遭受亚洲金融风暴的其他东亚发展典范不同，其在黄金增长期之后也取得了持续的发展，2010年成为国际货币基金组织列出的33个发达国家之一。而且，马耳他依然有充足的发展潜力。2011年，马耳他的人均收入水平只有冰岛的46%、中国澳门的48%、卢森堡的39%。因此，从成功的先例来讲，全球79个人口低于100万的微型经济体不会陷入人们所担心的“产业结构单一”陷阱。正如林毅夫在《新结构经济学》一书中批评迈克尔·波特的竞争理论时所指出的：“波特使‘竞争优势’这一名词

---

① 马耳他等微型经济体的产业多元化发展介绍可参考：曾忠禄，“微型经济产业多元化可行性研究”，《港澳研究》，2015年第4期。

② Crowards T, “Defining the Category of ‘Small’ States”, *Journal of International Development*, 2002, Vol.14, No.2, pp.143—179.

流行起来。基于他的论述，如果一个国家的产业符合如下四个条件，这个国家将在全球经济中获得竞争优势：（1）这些产业在生产中密集地使用该国丰富的、相对便宜的要素；（2）其产品拥有广大的国内市场；（3）每个产业形成一个产业集群；（4）每个产业的国内市场是竞争的市场。其中，第一个条件实际上意味着这些产业应符合由该国要素禀赋所决定的比较优势；而第三和第四两个条件仅当产业与该国要素禀赋相符时才会成立。因此，上述四个条件可以归结为两个相互独立的条件：比较优势与国内市场大小。而在这两个独立条件之中，比较优势又是最为关键的，因为如果一个产业符合该国的比较优势，该产业的产品就可以以全球为市场。这也是这个世界上很多最富有的国家都很小的原因。”①

表4.7 2011年一些代表性的高收入微型经济体

| 国家（地区） | 人口数量（万人） | 人均GDP（万美元） |
|---|---|---|
| 中国澳门 | 55.68 | 3.95 |
| 卢森堡 | 50.21 | 10.54 |
| 马耳他 | 41.76 | 1.92 |
| 冰岛 | 31.85 | 4.16 |

资料来源：CIA网站。

表4.8是2009年中国澳门、卢森堡、冰岛和马耳他按行业统计的就业人口构成，就业人口主要集中在服务业，分别占总就业人口的84%、77%、75%和74%。这四个经济体的第一产业和第二产业的就业人口分别占总就业人口的16%、23%、25%和27%。中国澳门就业人口最高的产业是包括博彩产业的“团体、社会及个人的其他服务”产业，该部门的就业人口占澳门总就业人口的23.7%（其中博彩业占19.8%，其他“团体、社会及个人的其他服务”占3.9%）。卢森堡就业人口最集中的行业是“不动产业务、租赁及向企业提供的服务”，该部门的就业人口占其总就业人口的17.2%。冰岛就业人口最集中的行业是“医疗卫生及社会福利”，该部门的就业人口占总就业人口的16.0%。马耳他就业人口最集中的行业是“批发及零售业；物品维修”，该部门的就业人口占总就业人口的比重为15.5%。除了众所周知的中

① 林毅夫，《新结构经济学：反思经济发展与政策的理论框架》，北京大学出版社，2012年版，第19页。

国澳门博彩业一枝独秀之外①，这些微型经济体整体的产业多元化程度还是相对较高的（见表4.9和表4.10）。澳门回归以后的2000年，特区政府的第一个《施政报告》就提出了经济多元化的问题。2001年的《施政报告》把离岸服务作为发展的重点，并提出通过博彩业带动酒店业、饮食业及会议展览业等。2003年《施政报告》中的“经济财政领域施政方针政策”，提出了“有选择地发展新兴产业”“推动本澳产业向适度多元化方向发展”的目标。该报告中提到的重点扶持产业包括离岸服务业、信息科技产业、会展业、创意产业、转口贸易和物流业。2004年提出的多元化的重点是离岸业务、医药产业、环保中介产业、航空物流业和会展业。从2003年起，中国澳门特区政府就开始对会展业、物流业、中医药产业加大投入。尽管如此，中国澳门的产业多元化效果并没有达到预期的设想，博彩业占GDP的百分比从

① 中国澳门向有“赌埠”之称，博彩业在澳门历史悠久。澳门起初也是禁赌的，但后来澳葡当局为解贸易急剧衰落、收入拮据之窘，实行公开招商设赌，向赌场征收“赌饷”，以开赌抽饷来增加收入。19世纪60年代中期，澳葡当局主要依靠赌饷和鸦片烟税，使得每年的财政收入增加到20多万元，并有约4万元的结余上交葡萄牙国库。1847年，澳门政府颁布法令，宣告赌博业合法化，揭开了赌业合法化的序幕，但当时并没有专营的赌场。20世纪30年代以后，澳门的博彩业改由政府与娱乐公司签订合约，实行专利经营。经营者必须向政府缴纳赌饷——博彩税，依约经营。1937年，高可宁、傅德荫合组的泰兴娱乐公司，开始实行赌博专营制度，此后澳门赌业发展初具规模。但泰兴公司经营不善，加上高、傅的继承人又不热衷赌业，澳门政府于是在20世纪50年代重新制定赌业管理办法，并公开竞标赌业管理权。1961年2月，葡萄牙海外部根据澳门当局的建议，批准在澳门正式开设博彩旅游业。1962年，由香港何鸿燊、叶汉合组的何氏澳门旅游娱乐公司竞标成功，获得赌业管理权。此后30多年，澳门的博彩业一直由何氏澳门旅游娱乐公司实行高度垄断经营。1997年7月，该公司与澳葡政府再次签订新修订的博彩专营合约，已把合约延期至2001年。2001年，澳门开放博彩业，澳娱属下的子公司澳门博彩股份有限公司投得其中一个博彩业牌照，澳门博彩股份2004年全年纯利达342亿元。澳门博彩业仍属专利经营性质，由政府开设。由于澳门以博彩旅游为主要经济支柱的现状是历史形成的，博彩业在澳门已有相当的基础，因此在今后相当长的历史时期内还将是澳门税收的重要来源。《中华人民共和国澳门特别行政区基本法》第118条规定：“澳门特别行政区根据本地整体利益自行制定旅游娱乐业的政策。”这就是说，澳门回归祖国之后博彩业依然保持原来的业态，但市场变大了之后又得到迅速发展。2000年特区政府博彩税收入达56.5亿澳门元；2001年特区政府收入博彩税达到60亿澳门元，仅次于1997年的61.5亿澳门元，居历史第二位。且在2000年突破入境游客数900万人之后又有一个跃进，2001年接待游客数突破1 000万人次，创下了史无前例的新高纪录。2002年更高达1 153万人次，不仅为旅游博彩业带来可观的收益，而且促进了相关产业的同步增长。它直接促进了酒店、餐饮、交通、金饰珠宝、古玩典当、娱乐服务、手信业的增长，甚至还吸纳了部分因制造业北移和建造业委顿而失业的工人，减少了因此而产生的震荡。更为可喜的是它还为沉寂多年的房地产市场注入了活力。2013年澳门的总就业人口为36.1万，其中博彩业为8.3万，占总就业人口的比重高达23%。而2003年，澳门赌权开放的第二年，澳门博彩业就业人口才占总就业人口的7.5%。2001年澳门的税收只有39.1%来自赌场博彩税，2013年该比重达到了76.3%。总之，澳门博彩业的成功发展得益于诸多因素，包括历史传统和超微型的自由港经济特征以及当地政府的有力扶持。澳门经济财政司司长谭伯源表示，对于未来澳门博彩业的发展，政府的态度是，任何经济范畴内需要关注的行业都会重视。博彩业的施政大方向是适度规模、规范管理、健康发展，推动博彩业朝规范化、专业化、国际化和可持续方向发展，实现扶助和“反哺”其他行业。管理博彩业方面，推行负责任博彩，会从多个方向考虑，包括：预防政策，注重宣传教育工作，要求营运商推行负责任博彩；治疗病态赌徒政策，设立中央辅导热线，统筹协调（五个）或将来设立的辅导中心；宣传教育公关政策，利用社区团体力量，做好负责任博彩的宣传推广，设立负责任博彩的网站，向有需要的人士提供更多的沟通渠道。在不同施政范畴合作上，提供意见和合作。（以上内容根据相关资料整理而成。）

2000年的25.9%上升到2013年的46.1%。除博彩业外，其他行业占GDP的比重都非常小，尤其是能够通过出口（货物出口和服务出口）带来收益的行业更是如此。这可能意味着，中国澳门的博彩业已经成为其根深蒂固的具有比较优势的产业，而其他产业的选择则因远离了这种产业基础而难以壮大。

表4.8 2009年中国澳门、卢森堡、冰岛和马耳他按行业统计就业人口构成（%）

| 行业 | 中国澳门 | 卢森堡 | 冰岛 | 马耳他 |
|---|---|---|---|---|
| 农、林、牧、狩猎、捕鱼及采矿业 | 0.3 | 1.5 | 5.2 | 2.0 |
| 制造业 | 5.4 | 9.9 | 11.9 | 15.1 |
| 电力、气体及水的生产及分配 | 0.3 | 0.5 | 0.9 | 2.2 |
| 建筑业 | 10.3 | 10.9 | 7.0 | 7.2 |
| 批发及零售业；物品维修 | 13.1 | 12.9 | 12.6 | 15.5 |
| 住宿、餐厅、酒楼及同类场所 | 13.8 | 4.6 | 4.6 | 8.2 |
| 运输、贮藏及通信 | 5.3 | 8.2 | 7.1 | 8.4 |
| 金融业务 | 2.4 | 11.7 | 4.7 | 3.7 |
| 不动产业务、租赁及向企业提供的服务 | 8.1 | 17.2 | 9.8 | 7.5 |
| 公共行政、防卫及强制性社会保障 | 6.4 | 5.1 | 5.5 | 9.0 |
| 教育 | 3.9 | 4.5 | 12.1 | 8.4 |
| 医疗卫生及社会福利 | 2.3 | 7.9 | 16.0 | 1.1 |
| 团体、社会及个人的其他服务 | 23.7 | 3.7 | 2.7 | 4.8 |
| 雇用佣人的家庭 | 4.9 | 1.5 | — | 0.1 |
| 国际组织及其他领土以外的机构 | 0.0 | 0.0 | 0.0 | 0.2 |
| 合计 | 100.0 | 100.0 | 100.0 | 100.0 |

资料来源：转引自曾忠禄、张冬梅，“产业多元化：微型经济体国际比较”，《经济地理》，2012年第9期。

表4.9 中国澳门与卢森堡、冰岛、马耳他各行业就业人口构成的熵指数和赫芬达尔指数（HHI）比较

| 年份 | 中国澳门 | | 卢森堡 | | 冰岛 | | 马耳他 | |
|---|---|---|---|---|---|---|---|---|
| | 熵指数 | HHI | 熵指数 | HHI | 熵指数 | HHI | 熵指数 | HHI |
| 2000 | 2.334 | 0.112 | 2.413 | 0.102 | 2.417 | 0.099 | 2.392 | 0.110 |
| 2005 | 2.328 | 0.112 | 2.405 | 0.101 | 2.416 | 0.099 | 2.417 | 0.103 |
| 2006 | 2.314 | 0.114 | 2.410 | 0.101 | 2.429 | 0.096 | 2.420 | 0.102 |
| 2007 | 2.288 | 0.122 | 2.405 | 0.102 | 2.432 | 0.096 | 2.428 | 0.100 |
| 2008 | 2.272 | 0.127 | 2.396 | 0.103 | 2.433 | 0.101 | 2.446 | 0.097 |
| 2009 | 2.292 | 0.124 | 2.400 | 0.103 | 2.403 | 0.101 | 2.442 | 0.097 |

资料来源：转引自曾忠禄、张冬梅，“产业多元化：微型经济体国际比较”，《经济地理》，2012年第9期。

表4.10 中国澳门与卢森堡、冰岛、马耳他GDP产业构成的熵指数和赫芬达尔指数（HHI）比较

| 年份 | 中国澳门 | | 卢森堡 | | 冰岛 | | 马耳他 | |
|---|---|---|---|---|---|---|---|---|
| | 熵指数 | HHI | 熵指数 | HHI | 熵指数 | HHI | 熵指数 | HHI |
| 2007 | 2.184 | 0.167 | 2.520 | 0.094 | 2.556 | 0.083 | 2.394 | 0.105 |
| 2008 | 2.183 | 0.166 | 2.476 | 0.101 | 2.553 | 0.082 | 2.377 | 0.108 |
| 2009 | 2.171 | 0.177 | 2.491 | 0.098 | 2.558 | 0.083 | 2.404 | 0.104 |

资料来源：转引自曾忠禄、张冬梅，“产业多元化：微型经济体国际比较”，《经济地理》，2012年第9期。

与中国澳门一样，马耳他的博彩业在政府的有意培育下也较为发达。马耳他很早就开始对远程赌博的基础设施进行大量投资。目前在远程游戏和博彩方面处于世界领先位置。自2001年彩票和其他博彩法生效以来，获得营业执照的公司从12家增至近250家，而网上博彩牌照的数量2012年达到了425家。这些公司直接雇用的员工超过5 000人，为他们服务的其他行业雇员达3 000多人。马耳他与网上博彩相关的行业包括电信运营商、数据中心运营商、律师、审计师、银行和支付机构。IT行业有超过200家公司在经营，这为马耳他的远程博彩行业的游戏开发提供了良好的技术环境、经验丰富的专业技术人员（尤其是分析和挖掘资料的专业人员）。世界网络博彩运营商有10%在马耳他落户，其中包括世界著名的网上博彩公司Betfair和Betsson。马耳他的网上博彩公司经营的博彩包括赌场博彩和技巧博彩、在线彩票、彩池设赌和扑克网络等，2011年博彩总收入达到马耳他GDP的7.82%。如果加上博彩业的支持产业，则整个行业对马耳他GDP的贡献达到了10%。① 马耳他旅游业也较发达，每年大约有130万游客，是国民的3倍多，旅游收入大约占其GDP的25%。2012年金融业对马耳他经济直接和间接贡献超过10亿欧元，占GDP的比重达12%，雇用的员工超过1万人。马耳他作为地中海的经贸中心，其金融行业的资本流入占马耳他外商直接投资的60%左右。然而，与中国澳门不同的是，马耳他的产业多元化则相对成功得多，有比较坚实的制造业基础，其船舶修理、飞机维修、建筑、食品饮料、药品制造、信息技术服务等产业优势突出。如图4.48所示，2012年马耳他的制造业占GDP的比重达16%，通信与科技占GDP的12%。马耳他正日益成为地中海地区优秀的制造业中心。马耳他制造业企业数目有4 000多个，雇用员工2万多人，占马耳他总劳动力的15%，制造业的出口额高达21.8亿欧元（同期中国澳门为12.5亿欧元）。马耳他自然资源匮缺，其制造业的发展主要依赖其劳动力。近年来，随着劳动力成本的升高，马耳他的制造业主要集中在高价值的资本与知识密集的高端制造业，包括半导体、制药、医疗设备、化工、塑料产品、电子机械设备等。马耳他制造业的很多公司都有很高的国际知名度，是高技术生产的

① Malta E-gaming Review 2013—2014.

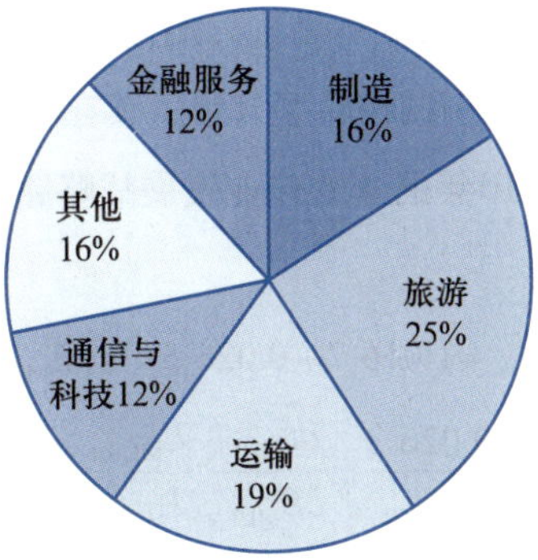


**图4.48 2012年马耳他的产业结构**

资料来源：Deloitte, *Malta*, *Essentials for Excellence*, 2013.

市场领袖，如迈梭电子（Methode Electronics）、特瑞堡公司（Trelleborg）、Abertax Quality公司等。如今马耳他的制造业劳动生产率很高，员工人均创造的价值达3.2万欧元，其中制药业更高达7.4万欧元。①2009年，在欧盟国家中，马耳他的中等科技和高科技产品出口位居第一，来自海外的许可和专利收入位居第二，在知识密集的行业的就业人口比重居第七位。②马耳他制造业最重要的行业是电子产业，2006年至2008年间，马耳他电子产业的销售超过9亿欧元，占制造业总销售额的41%。第二大制造业是制药业。目前马耳他的医药企业和相关的化工企业有81家，其中药物制剂企业10家。2012年，制药业出口价值为3.2亿美元，占当年GDP的4%，占制造业产值比重的10%；雇用的员工超过1 000人，占制造业员工总数的7%。制药业每年仅出口到欧洲的产品已超过1.5亿欧元（约合2.05亿美元）。2013年，工业产值占马耳他GDP的23%，其主要产品包括电子产品、机械设备、精密仪器、服装、食品饮料、化工产品等。约有2.2万人在制造业部门工作，其中约3 000人服务于电子部门。另外，马耳他的船运与空运业较发达，运输大约占马耳他GDP的19%。马耳他的海运业涵盖很广，其服务包括燃料仓库、维修、船只处理、转运及其他一些货物服务等。马耳他的空运服务业引入了大量的资金与鼓励机制，发展飞机维修保养业，致力于成为飞机保养、维修及翻新的领导者。马耳他于2006年通过了《商业游艇法》，从那时起马耳他就成为全球超级游艇最大的注册地之一。据2012年的统计，马耳他船舶登记数量位居欧洲之首、世界第七。在全球经济论坛《2014—2015年全球竞争力报告》中，马耳他在全球最有竞争力的144个国家中，排名47位。2015年，国际评级机构惠誉及穆迪将马耳他的国家评级评定为A级，这意味着该国经济稳定、安全系数高。

---

① Malta Council for Science and Technology, National Research Strategy for Manufacturing in Malta, 2012.

② 同上。

因此，就算是针对全球70余个人口不足百万的微型经济体而言，只要发展符合自身比较优势的产业并持续不断地推进经济结构转型升级，其在全球的竞争力依然不亚于其他人口大国。图4.49是马耳他1970—2010年的非农产业发展战略路径，对数拟合（$R^2 = 0.67$）的发展战略路径曲线为

$$I_{\mathrm{MLT},t} = 1.016\ 7 + 0.026\ 3 \times \ln\left(E_{\mathrm{MLT},t}\right)$$

斜率和弹性分别为 $\frac{\partial I_{\mathrm{MLT},t}}{\partial E_{\mathrm{MLT},t}} = \frac{0.026\ 3}{E_{\mathrm{MLT},t}}$，$\frac{\partial I_{\mathrm{MLT},t}}{\partial E_{\mathrm{MLT},t}} \frac{E_{\mathrm{MLT},t}}{I_{\mathrm{MLT},t}} = \frac{0.026\ 3}{I_{\mathrm{MLT},t}}$。与其他样本略微不同的是，马耳他的起点较高，是典型的中等收入国家实现向上升级的发展典范。图4.50是马耳他1970—2010年的工业发展战略路径。二次函数拟合（$R^2 = 0.54$）的发展战略路径曲线为

$$I_{\mathrm{MLT},t} = 0.371\ 5 + 11.304\ 84 \times E_{\mathrm{MLT},t} - 19.087\ 14 \times E_{\mathrm{MLT},t}^2$$

顶点和拐点分别为$I = 2.045$和$E = 0.296$，在发展典范当中与韩国较为接近，体现出稳健的工业升级风格。可以看到尤其是在20世纪七八十年代，马耳他的工业取得了持续的升级，奠定了其地中海制造业中心的地位。图4.51是马耳他1970—2010年的服务业发展战略路径。对数拟合（$R^2 = 0.323\ 7$）的发展战略路径曲线为

$$I_{\mathrm{MLT},t} = 0.911\ 54 + 0.224\ 1 \times \ln\left(E_{\mathrm{MLT},t}\right)$$

斜率和弹性分别为 $\frac{\partial I_{\mathrm{MLT},t}}{\partial E_{\mathrm{MLT},t}} = \frac{0.224\ 1}{E_{\mathrm{MLT},t}}$ 和 $\frac{\partial I_{\mathrm{MLT},t}}{\partial E_{\mathrm{MLT},t}} \frac{E_{\mathrm{MLT},t}}{I_{\mathrm{MLT},t}} = \frac{0.224\ 1}{I_{\mathrm{MLT},t}}$。与世界样本相比，近

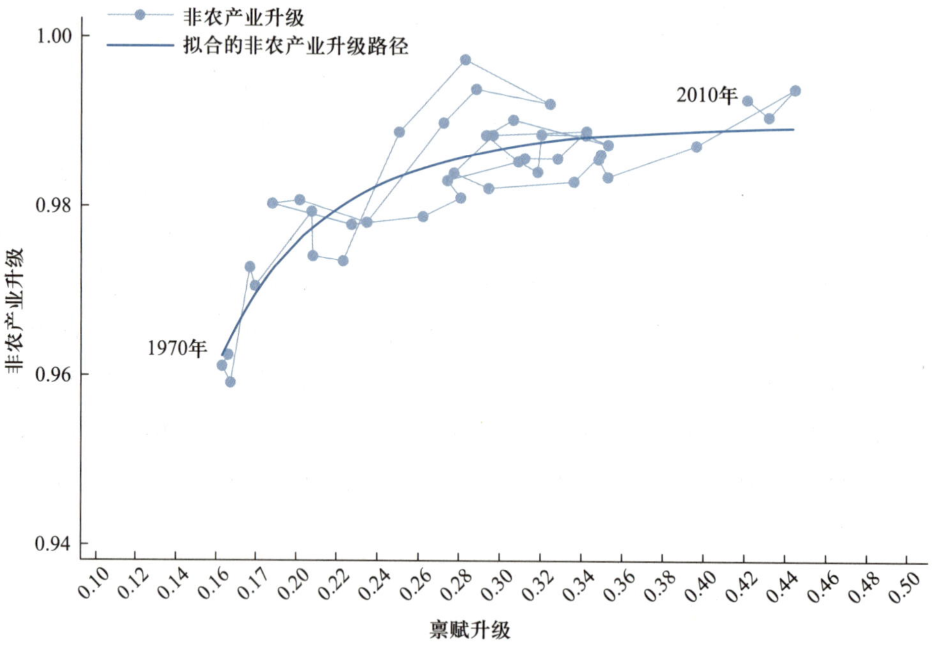


图4.49 马耳他的非农产业发展战略路径（1970—2010年）及其拟合

年来马耳他服务业升级发展战略路径的斜率和弹性都要大得多，表明其服务业升级较为迅速，这主要是前面所介绍的在21世纪初之后马耳他政府大力发展远程游戏博彩业与旅游业以及物流业之故。

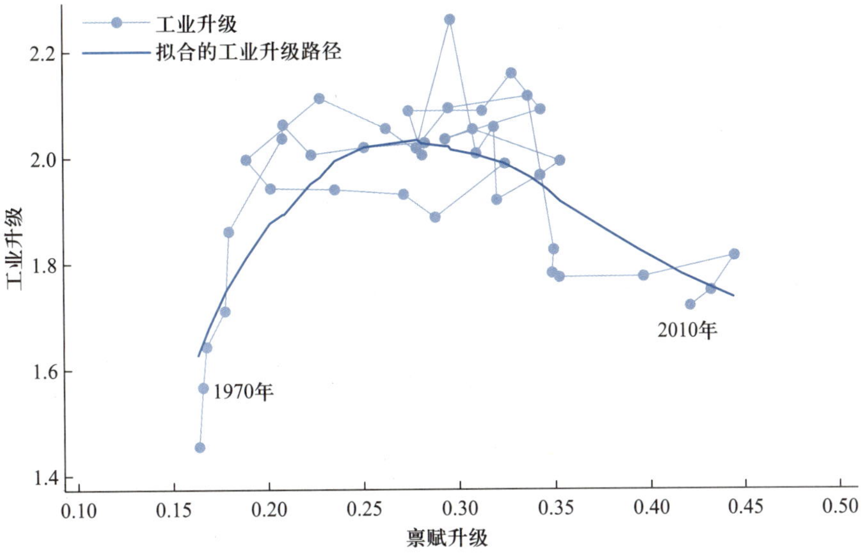


图4.50 马耳他的工业发展战略路径（1970—2010年）及其拟合

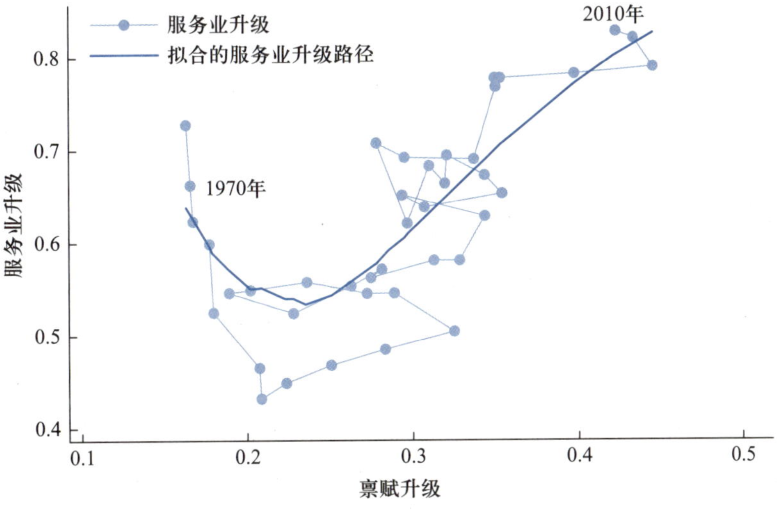


图4.51 马耳他的服务业发展战略路径（1970—2010年）及其拟合

### 4.4.12 博茨瓦纳的经济结构转型升级路径拟合及其特征[①]

博茨瓦纳共和国位于非洲南部内陆。该国地处南非高原中部的卡拉哈迪盆地，平均海拔约1 000米，国土面积581 730平方千米。东接津巴布韦，西连纳米比亚，北邻赞比亚，南接南非。大部分地区属热带干旱草原气候，西部为沙漠，属热带沙漠气候。年均气温21℃。年均降水量400毫米。博茨瓦纳实行总统内阁制，官方语言为英语，通用语言为茨瓦纳语和英语。2011年博茨瓦纳的人口为203.8万，茨瓦纳族（或称塞茨瓦纳族）是博茨瓦纳的主要民族，占总人口的79%；卡兰哈族占总人口的11%；巴茨瓦纳族占总人口的3%；另外，喀拉哈迪族和白人占7%。多数居民信奉基督新教和天主教，农村地区部分居民信奉传统宗教。目前博茨瓦纳是非洲经济发展较快、经济状况较好的国家之一。世界经济论坛在《全球竞争力报告》中将博茨瓦纳列为非洲两个最有竞争力的国家之一。

然而，从1966年独立到20世纪70年代初，博茨瓦纳是当时世界上25个最贫穷的国家之一。国家经济发展以农牧业，特别是原始粗放的农耕和放牧为主，80%的人口依靠农牧业为生，工业几乎是空白，仅有一座牛屠宰厂，交通运输只有一条产权属于罗得西亚的过境铁路和6千米的沥青公路，全国1/5人口靠国际救济粮生活。1968年建立国家经济咨询会议并出台了《过渡时期社会和经济发展计划》，恢复农牧业生产。1970年又成立财政和发展规划部，制定了发展农牧业的计划。经过数年的努力，博茨瓦纳的农牧业产量都显著提高。谷物产量独立前平均每年不足2万吨，而独立后的头10年平均每年为6万吨，最高年份达12万吨；养牛头数1966年为90万头，1972年已增至200万头。博茨瓦纳农业的发展为后续的经济发展奠定了一定的基础。

20世纪70年代中期至80年代末，博茨瓦纳的经济发展重心转向采矿业。博茨瓦纳的矿产尤其是钻石资源丰富。在此期间，博茨瓦纳政府实行了一套矿业政策：矿产权归国家所有；在政府的参与和监督下，主要由外国公司提供大部分资金、技术和管理经验及产品销售渠道；在勘探方面，发放探矿执照，限定勘探地区和完成期限；在收益方面，既保证国家从矿业发展中获得最佳利益，又要给予私人公司公平合理的利益；政府在矿业公司所占股份，视不同矿产的利润大小而定（如铜和煤矿分别为15%和25%，而钻石为50%）；政府代表参加董事会的决策和管理，实行监督。在1971—1983年的13年间，博茨瓦纳就与南非的德比尔斯公司、南非英美公司等跨国公司合资兴办了开采钻石、铜、煤等矿的公司。从70年代起，采矿业逐渐取代农牧业成为国民经济的支柱产业。1972年时矿产业收入已占GDP的11%，占政府收入的5%，占出口收入的44%；而1989年对应的比重分别增至51%、59%、89%。这段时

---

① 关于博茨瓦纳的一些历史资料可参考：徐人龙，《列国志——博茨瓦纳》，社会科学文献出版社，2000年版。

期是博茨瓦纳的黄金增长期，1970—1980年GDP年均增长率为14.5%，1980—1990年为10.3%。

由于长期依赖采矿尤其是钻石行业，博茨瓦纳在20世纪80年代末和90年代初也开始积极谋划产业多元化转型升级。博茨瓦纳政府在《第七个国家发展计划（1991—1997年）》中确定积极改变依靠钻石等矿产资源的状况，调整单一的经济结构，实行经济多元化，在保持矿业稳定发展的基础上，优先发展制造业、金融业、服务业和旅游业等，鼓励发展劳动力密集型产业。此后的第八（1997—2003年）、第九（2003—2009年）和第十（2009—2016年）个国家发展计划也延续了产业多元化发展战略。博茨瓦纳在此期间产业多元化的方向是发展轻工业，传统轻工业以畜产品加工为主，其次是饮料、金属加工和纺织等。由于博茨瓦纳的畜牧业以养牛为主，产值约占农牧业总产值的80%，有大量牛肉、皮革出口，后续博茨瓦纳发展成为非洲最大的畜产品加工中心之一，有现代化的大型屠宰厂和肉类加工厂，年屠宰能力为40万～50万头牛。近年来，汽车装配业发展很快，一度成为第二大创汇行业。在此期间，博茨瓦纳产业多元化取得了一定的成效，采矿业在博茨瓦纳国内生产总值中所占比重从1984年的51%降至2000年的33%左右。虽然远不及20世纪七八十年代超过两位数的经济增长，但博茨瓦纳在此期间的国民经济还是保持了稳步增长，国内生产总值在1990—2000年间年均增长率为4.9%，2000—2004年间年均增长率为5.5%。得益于持续的经济增长，博茨瓦纳人均国内生产总值在2000年达到3 647美元，已经成为中等收入国家。这个成绩在经济发展长期陷入低收入陷阱的非洲是成功的典范。

然而，博茨瓦纳的经济结构转型升级远未完成，依然任重道远。博茨瓦纳年轻人失业率依然很高，据博茨瓦纳官方消息，2011年12月发布的2009/2010博茨瓦纳核心福利指数（贫困）调查结果显示，博茨瓦纳失业人口与总劳力的比例达到17.8%，比2005/2006调查结果的17.5%略有上升。15—19岁人群失业率最高，为41.4%，20—24岁人群为34%。对于下一步的发展，按照新结构经济学的建议，博茨瓦纳可以继续发展劳动力密集型产业，进一步充实其产业多元化，吸纳劳动力，推进产业结构继续升级，进而获得持续的包容性经济增长。

发展典范中的博茨瓦纳，这个非洲的“虚拟变量”，不仅被增长与发展委员会重视，也引起了众多经济学家的注意。[①]20世纪70年代中期博茨瓦纳的人均GDP不足美国的6%，农

① 在2009年罗德里克主编的增长的国别分析《探索经济繁荣——对经济增长的描述性分析》一书中，阿西莫格鲁、约翰逊和罗宾逊从其著名的制度的历史计量分析视角专门为博茨瓦纳发展了一章长篇大论。他们认为，在博茨瓦纳的案例中，部落制度鼓励了人们广泛参与政治并限制了当权者的行为；殖民主义者直到殖民活动的晚期才对博茨瓦纳产生兴趣，因此英国殖民活动对博茨瓦纳的部落制度所产生的冲击相对有限；农村利益集团的相对强大使博茨瓦纳的地区比较优势和当权者的经济利益出现了部分交叠；最后（但并非最不重要）的一点在于博茨瓦纳独立后的执政者所展现出的明智且富有远见的领导才能。

业产值占GDP比重将近30%；但到21世纪初其人均GDP就接近美国的1/5，非农产值占GDP的比重高达97%。图4.52是博茨瓦纳1975—2011年的非农产业结构变迁路径及其拟合图。对数拟合（$R^2=0.51$）的非农产业结构变迁路径轨迹为

$$I_{\mathrm{BWA},t}=1.343\ 3+0.168\ 6\times\ln\left(E_{\mathrm{BWA},t}\right)$$

其斜率和弹性分别为$\frac{\partial I_{\mathrm{BWA},t}}{\partial E_{\mathrm{BWA},t}}=\frac{0.168\ 6}{E_{\mathrm{BWA},t}}$，$\frac{\partial I_{\mathrm{BWA},t}}{\partial E_{\mathrm{BWA},t}}\frac{E_{\mathrm{BEA},t}}{I_{\mathrm{BWA},t}}=\frac{0.168\ 6}{I_{\mathrm{BWA},t}}$。相对于世界整体的拟合情况而言，博茨瓦纳非农产业升级的步伐和弹性很大。图4.53是博茨瓦纳1975—2011年的工业产业结构变迁路径轨迹及其拟合图。我们采用二次函数拟合（$R^2=0.47$），拟合的工业产业结构变迁路径或战略路径曲线为

$$I_{\mathrm{BWA},t}=-0.165\ 04+36.771\ 6\times E_{\mathrm{BWA},t}-144.551\times E_{\mathrm{BWA},t}^2$$

顶点为$I=2.173\ 5$，拐点为$E=0.127\ 19$。与世界样本相比，博茨瓦纳工业升级拐点出现得较早，顶点值相近。图4.54是博茨瓦纳1975—2011年的服务业结构变迁轨迹及其拟合图。我们采用对数拟合（$R^2=0.18$），拟合的服务业发展战略路径为

$$I_{\mathrm{BWA},t}=0.914\ 73+0.130\ 05\times\ln\left(E_{\mathrm{BWA},t}\right)$$

其斜率和弹性分别为$\frac{\partial I_{\mathrm{BWA},t}}{\partial E_{\mathrm{BWA},t}}=\frac{0.130\ 05}{E_{\mathrm{BWA},t}}$，$\frac{\partial I_{\mathrm{BWA},t}}{\partial E_{\mathrm{BWA},t}}\frac{E_{\mathrm{BEA},t}}{I_{\mathrm{BWA},t}}=\frac{0.130\ 05}{I_{\mathrm{BWA},t}}$。

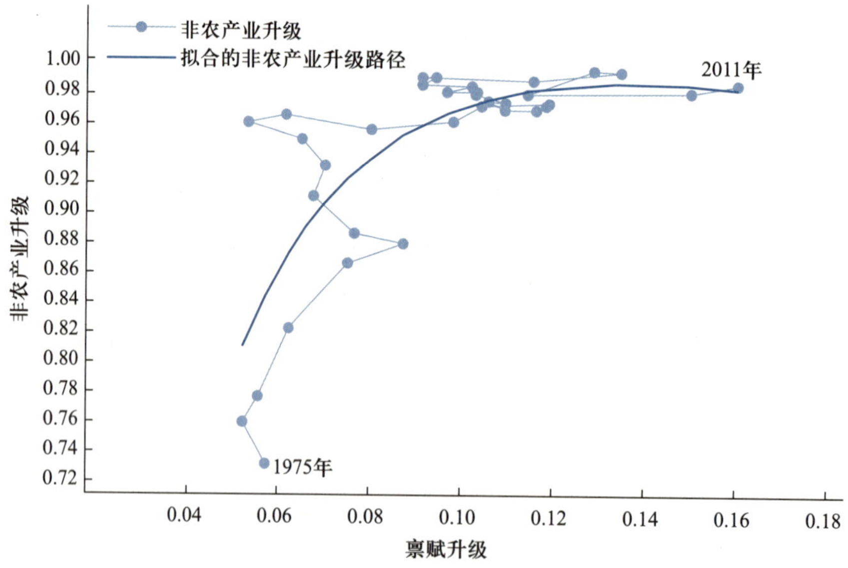


图4.52 博茨瓦纳的非农产业发展战略路径（1975—2011年）及其拟合

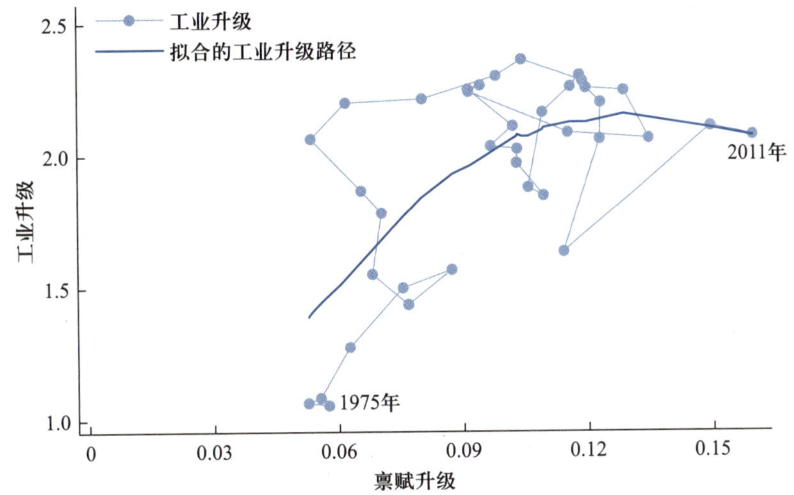


图4.53 博茨瓦纳的工业发展战略路径（1975—2011年）及其拟合

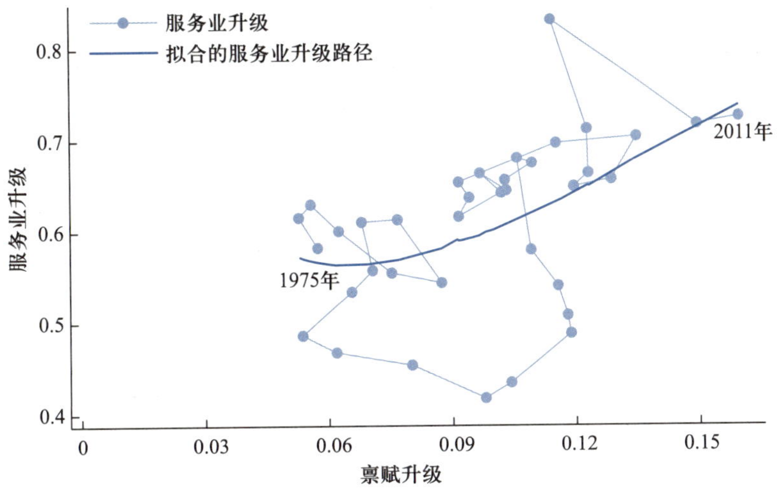


图4.54 博茨瓦纳的服务业发展战略路径（1975—2011年）及其拟合

### 4.4.13 巴西的经济结构转型升级路径拟合及其特征

巴西位于南美洲东南部，东临南大西洋，北邻法属圭亚那、苏里南、圭亚那、委内瑞拉和哥伦比亚，西界秘鲁、玻利维亚，南接巴拉圭、阿根廷和乌拉圭。海岸线长约7 400千米。领土面积851.49万平方千米，在世界上排行第五。巴西的地形主要分为两大部分：一部分是海拔500米以上的巴西高原，分布在巴西的中部和南部；另一部分是海拔200米以下的平原，主要分布在北部和西部的亚马逊河流域。巴西大部分地区处于热带，北部为热带雨林气候，中部为热带草原气候，南部部分地区为亚热带季风性湿润气候。亚马孙平原年平均气温25 ~ 28℃，南部地区年平均气温16 ~ 19℃。巴西总人口为2.01亿，其中白种人占53.74%，黑白混血种人占38.45%，黑种人占6.21%，黄种人和印第安人等占1.6%。国会由参、众两院组成，为国家最高权力机构。巴西拥有丰富的自然资源和完整的工业基础，国内生产总值位居南美洲第一，为世界第七大经济体。

巴西在1979年爆发第二次石油危机之后经济的高速增长戛然而止，因此增长与发展委员会在《增长报告》中只将巴西在1950—1980年的发展视为典范。虽然这段时间单纯从经济增长角度看巴西确实取得了较高的增长，但是巴西在20世纪70年代之后的经济结构转型升级却存在一定的问题，为其之后陷入中等收入陷阱埋下了隐患。巴西在1822年从葡萄牙独立之后，经过长期的发展，在二战后已经具备较好的发展基础。1950年巴西的工业比重就高达23.5%，其后的1950—1970年是巴西迅速工业化的20年，1960年工业比重增加到30.3%，1970年工业比重增加到35.4%。然而从20世纪70年代起，巴西工业化止步不前，1980年其工业比重衰退到34.1%，至今依然徘徊不前，如图4.55和图4.56所示。巴西工业化在80年代前后反差如此之大的根源在于巴西在70年代之后过早进入重工业化，这种违背比较优势的

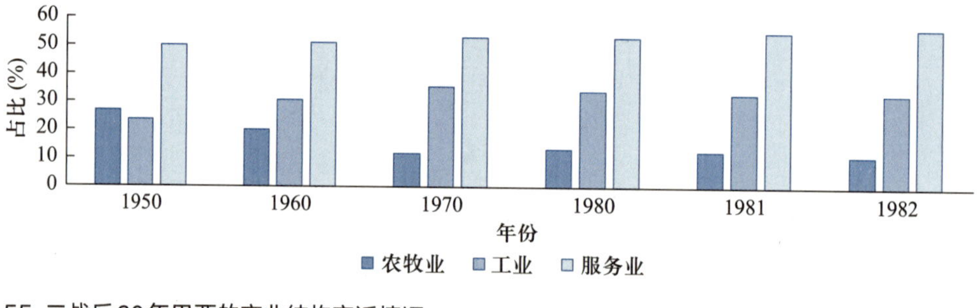


图4.55 二战后30年巴西的产业结构变迁情况

资料来源：1983年《巴西统计年鉴》。

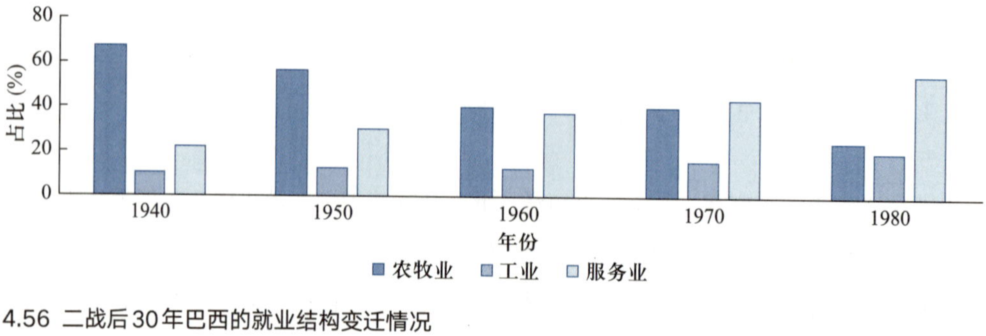


图4.56 二战后30年巴西的就业结构变迁情况

资料来源：1983年《巴西统计年鉴》。

经济结构转型升级发展战略严重受挫，经过40年之久的挣扎，以及各种政治制度改革，巴西仍然是一个中等收入国家。

回顾巴西经济结构变迁的历史，这个事实一目了然。二战后的20世纪50年代巴西采取了进口替代的工业化战略，但是其后的20年虽然有很强的重工业倾向，但是重工业的比重没有超过轻工业，到1970年轻工业的增加值占制造业增加值的比重为52%。70年代之后巴西在轻工业根基不牢时就发动了重工业赶超战略，优先发展冶金、机械、运输工具及石化产品。此后，重工业增加值在整个制造业增加值中的份额逐渐超过轻工业。重工业比重1974年为52.89%，1978年为54.9%，1979年为54%。图4.57展示了巴西在1963年、1975年与1980年的制造业结构与57个国家制造业分行业的增加值与就业份额平均值的比较。图4.58展示了巴西在1960年、1975年与1980年的制造业结构与57个国家制造业分行业的就业份额平均值的比较。在收入仍然偏低的情况下，巴西的食品、饮料制造业与烟草加工业，以及纺织服装业、制鞋业与皮革制品业这些劳动力密集型工业的增加值（以及劳动力就业）份额明显低于世界平均水平，而化学工业与石油工业，以及金属与金属制品、机器制造、电子与交通设备制造业等资本密集型工业的增加值（以及劳动力就业）份额明显高于世界平均水平。也就是说，巴西未能充分发展劳动力密集型轻工业，而是过早进入重工业化阶段。这种顺序颠倒

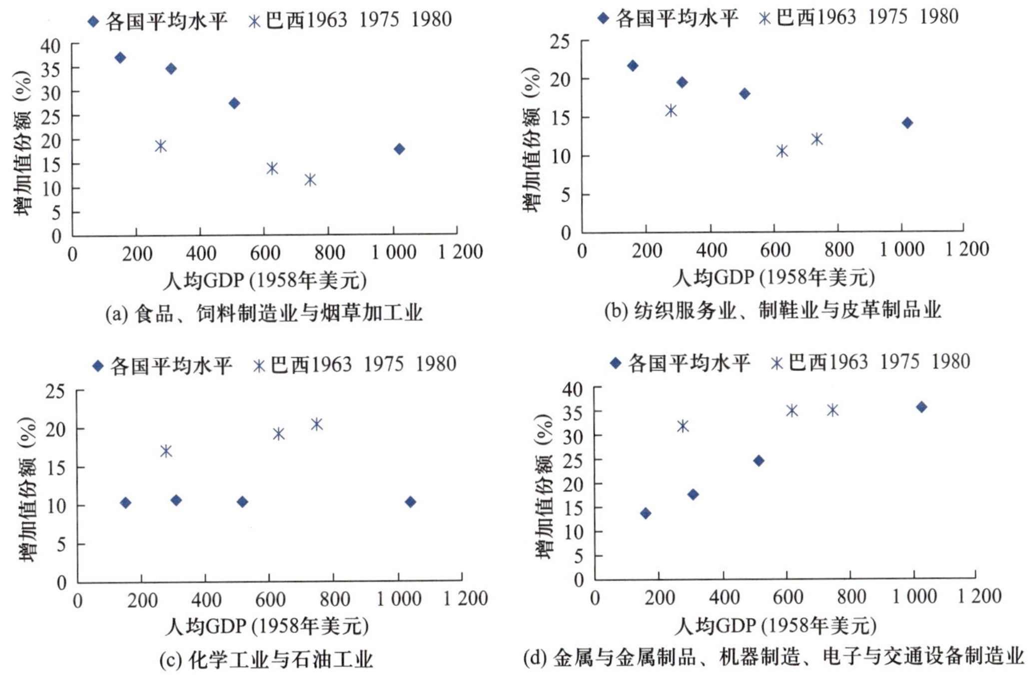


**图4.57 巴西制造业的产出结构**

资料来源：王丽莉、文一，“中国能跨越中等收入陷阱吗？——基于工业化路径的跨国比较”，《经济评论》，2017年第3期。

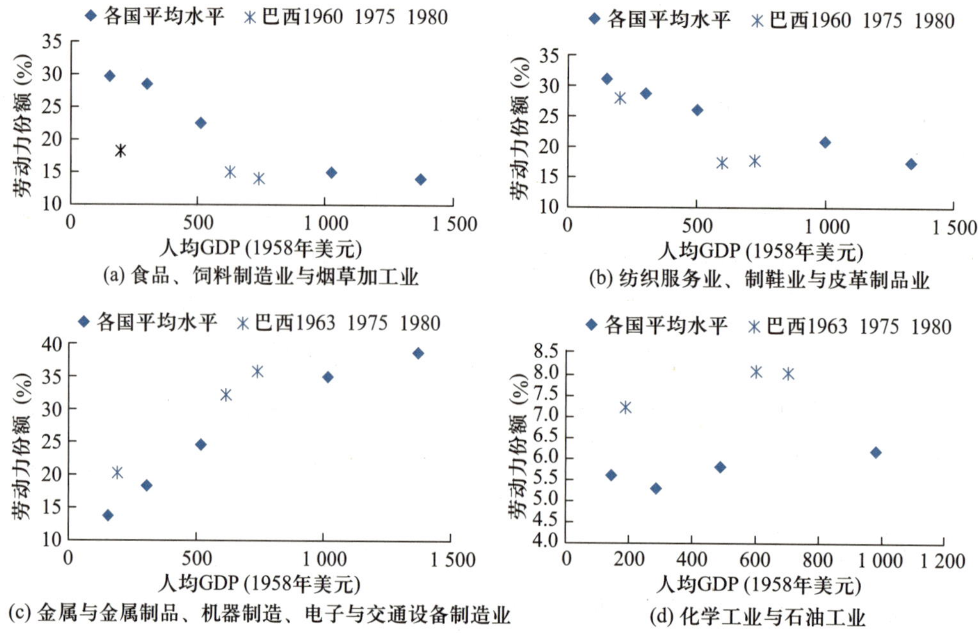


**图4.58 巴西制造业的就业结构**

资料来源：王丽莉、文一，“中国能跨越中等收入陷阱吗？——基于工业化路径的跨国比较”，《经济评论》，2017年第3期。

的发展路径，使得巴西的重型制造业不符合禀赋结构的比较优势，无法进入国际市场竞争，只能靠政府的补贴和保护勉强在国内市场生存，重工业的规模经济大，国内市场又无法充分消化其产能。例如，1965年，消费品工业设备利用率为65%，资本品工业设备利用率为53%。替代进口工业化的实行也造成了机器、设备与原材料进口的增加，以致国际收支恶化。例如，为了发展飞机制造业，1969年组建了巴西航空工业公司，引进国外先进技术，能独立生产十余种型号的飞机，成为世界重要的轻型飞机生产国。但是这些违背比较优势产业的企业大都没有自生能力。连续的亏损和债务负担迫使巴西进行经济改革。但与中国的改革不同，巴西在“华盛顿共识”指导下的经济改革期间，政府退出经济领域，放弃产业政策，出现“过早去工业化”现象，经济增长更加乏力，因此被困在中等收入陷阱中。巴西在短短几十年间的成败经历值得所有经济体引以为鉴。

上述巴西的历史事实也直观地体现在图4.59到图4.61的巴西经济结构转型升级轨迹图中。这个样本没有巴西在20世纪五六十年代的数据，但从70年代起可以看到巴西经济结构转型升级比较凌乱的步伐，这与前面第3章所刻画的其他陷入中等收入陷阱的拉美经济体的结构转型升级轨迹如出一辙。图4.59是巴西1970—2012年非农产业发展战略路径，对数拟合（$R^2=0.06$）的发展战略路径曲线为

$$I_{\mathrm{BRA},t}=0.969\ 4+0.018\ 2\times\ln\left(E_{\mathrm{BRA},t}\right)$$

斜率和弹性分别为 $\frac{\partial I_{\mathrm{BRA},t}}{\partial E_{\mathrm{BRA},t}}=\frac{0.018\ 2}{E_{\mathrm{BRA},t}}$，$\frac{\partial I_{\mathrm{BRA},t}}{\partial E_{\mathrm{BRA},t}}\frac{E_{\mathrm{BRA},t}}{I_{\mathrm{BRA},t}}=\frac{0.018\ 2}{I_{\mathrm{BRA},t}}$。相对于世界整体的拟合

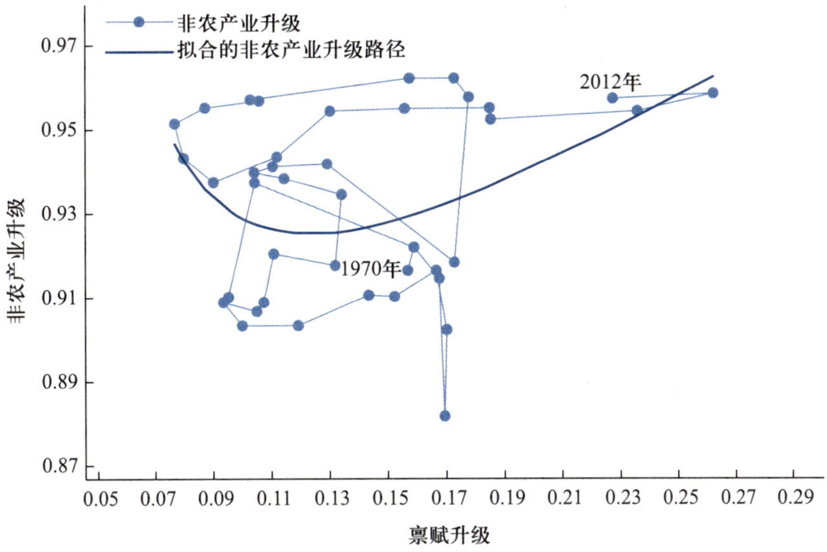


图4.59 巴西的非农产业发展战略路径（1970—2012年）及其拟合

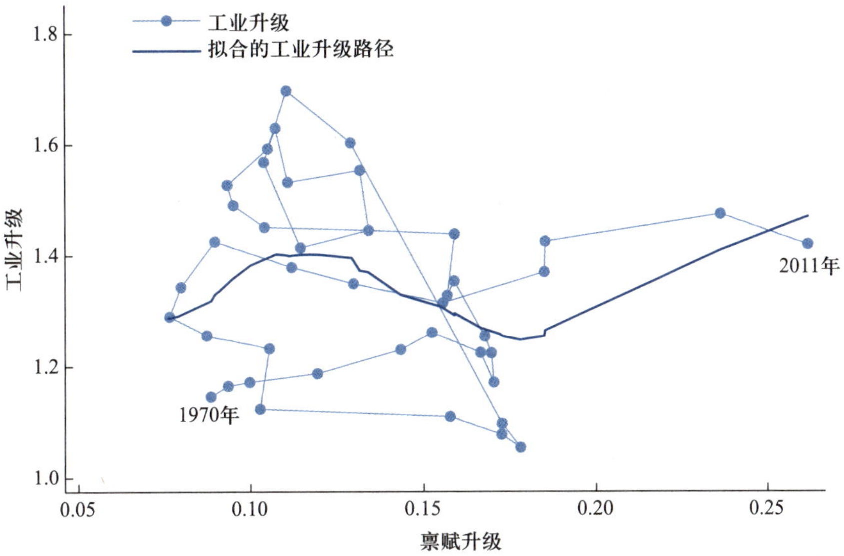


图4.60 巴西的工业发展战略路径（1970—2011年）及其拟合

情况而言，巴西产业升级的步伐和弹性很小。图4.60是巴西1970—2011年工业发展战略路径，二次函数拟合（$R^2 = 0.05$）的发展战略曲线为

$$I_{\mathrm{BRA},t} = 1.684\ 77 - 4.297\ 18 \times E_{\mathrm{BRA},t} + 11.982\ 3 \times E_{\mathrm{BRA},t}^2$$

顶点和拐点分别为$I = 1.299\ 5$和$E = 0.179\ 33$。相对于世界样本而言，巴西的工业升级拐点出现得较早，顶点值较低，表明巴西在工业升级的过程中过早去工业化。图4.61是巴西1970—2011年的服务业发展路径，对数拟合（$R^2 = 0.06$）的服务业发展战略路径曲线为

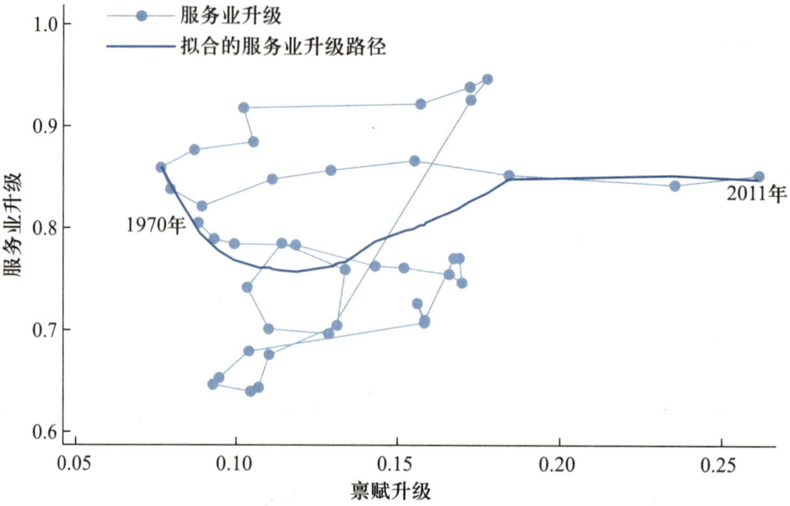


图4.61 巴西的服务业发展战略路径（1970—2011年）及其拟合

$$I_{\mathrm{BRA},t}=0.933\ 13+0.070\ 72\times\ln\left(E_{\mathrm{BRA},t}\right)$$

斜率和弹性分别为 $\frac{\partial I_{\mathrm{BRA},t}}{\partial E_{\mathrm{BRA},t}}=\frac{0.070\ 72}{E_{\mathrm{BRA},t}}$ 和 $\frac{\partial I_{\mathrm{BRA},t}}{\partial E_{\mathrm{BRA},t}}\frac{E_{\mathrm{BRA},t}}{I_{\mathrm{BRA},t}}=\frac{0.070\ 72}{I_{\mathrm{BRA},t}}$。

对于阿曼、博茨瓦纳和巴西这样的资源丰裕型经济体的转型升级，我们有必要再进一步从新结构经济学的角度予以分析和给出政策建议。[①]过去我们经常认为，人多资源少是发展的不利条件。可是从各国的实践经验来看，人少资源多的国家经济反而常常发展不起来，遭遇各种社会经济问题，出现了所谓的“资源诅咒”。为什么会出现这种现象？有几个方面的原因。第一，资源是埋在地底下的，埋在地底下的资源到底有多少、财富有多大并不是一眼就能看清楚的。如果资源由私营企业来开发，需要政府的批准，私营企业为了多获利，容易利用信息不对称，贿赂政府官员，以很低的价格取得资源开发的权利，因此，资源特别容易跟腐败联系在一起，导致收入分配不均，社会风气败坏，形成社会矛盾冲突，在这种状况下，经济当然也不容易发展得好。第二，资源的价格波动非常大。因为资源的供给弹性小，需求多的时候价格一年可以涨好几倍，但是需求少的时候资源的价格会跌得非常厉害。当它价格高的时候，政府的财政收入多，很容易造成政府大手大脚花钱，有的在福利的开支上特别多，有的在各种建设上到处铺摊子。等到价格下来想把福利支出减少会非常困难，赤字会急剧

① 林毅夫，“从‘资源诅咒’到‘资源祝福’：新结构经济学的视角”，北京大学新结构经济学研究中心讲稿，2017年。

增加；同样，建设铺得太大，到资源价格下跌时，到处是半拉子工程，浪费巨大。第三，资源是会枯竭的。资源枯竭以后资源所在城市、地区或国家如何继续发展？要是没有新的经济增长点，整个经济可能就会出现衰败的情形。第四，资源丰富的经济容易上马没有比较优势、赶超型的先进产业。一个发展中国家在经济发展过程当中经常会有快速追赶发达国家的良好愿望，要赶上发达国家，就需要有和发达国家一样先进的产业，这种产业看起来很先进，可是它违反了这个国家的比较优势，即使在政府的支持下能把它建立起来，这个产业中的企业在开放竞争的市场中没有自生能力，要让它们继续经营下去则需要靠政府不断保护补贴。有这样的产业固然令人骄傲，但是它的经营效率低，靠保护补贴生存，对收入水平的提高、人民生活福利的改善反而成为负担。而且，补贴容易造成权力寻租、腐败，以及政府被利益集团绑架的问题。资源越丰富的国家和地区，对这种产业投资的冲动、涉及的面、支撑的力度会越大，持续的时间会越长，这是资源成为经济发展的“诅咒”的第四个原因。

如何克服“资源诅咒”？主流经济学对上述问题目前的治理思路如下：针对资源容易产生腐败，就强调公开、透明，强调监管来防止腐败的出现。国际上有个组织，叫作资源开采透明国际组织，很多非洲的资源丰富国家，国内也有一些这样的非政府组织，在倡导公开、透明、监督，以此来减少腐败的可能性，世界银行也在推动这项工作。针对资源价格波动大的问题，则强调要未雨绸缪，当资源价格高的时候，收入多，只能用一小部分，绝大部分要储蓄下来，当资源价格低的时候，因为有储蓄，就可以用储蓄来承担福利支出或政府一些必要的公共支出。针对资源会枯竭的问题，在资源收益高的时候，要把大部分收入储蓄起来，变成金融资产，投资于国内、国际的股票市场或者政府债券，这些资产会有永续的收入，资源枯竭的时候可以靠这些永续收入来支持开支。从新结构经济学的角度来看，解决资源价格波动和枯竭的问题，还要多样化，增加非资源产业在经济中的比重，这样才能解决就业问题，并且“东方不亮西方亮”，可以减小资源价格波动对经济的冲击，并且，可以随资源存量的减少，逐渐转向非资源产业。但应该发展什么样的产业，主流经济学讨论得不多，并且从过去的发展经验来看，还经常会出现资源丰富的国家在发展非资源型产业时，容易热衷于发展一些赶超型的先进产业，而最终导致经济发展的不可持续，绩效比非资源型经济差的“资源诅咒”现象。

如何发展非资源产业？新结构经济学首先主张，发展的非资源型产业必须符合该经济体要素禀赋结构所决定的比较优势，这样才会有最低的要素生产成本，资源丰富的国家同样有大量的劳动力，劳动力资源也是具有比较优势的禀赋条件；其次，新结构经济学主张在竞争的市场中，以有为的政府动用资源收益中的一部分来消除限制具有比较优势的、多用劳动力的非资源型产业发展的软硬基础设施的瓶颈，以降低交易费用，使符合比较优势的产业能够迅速变成具有竞争优势的产业。至于如何选择具有比较优势的非资源型产业，以及如何针对不同的产业发挥有为政府因势利导的作用，则可以根据新结构经济学中增长甄别与因势利导的框架来进行（第10章将详细讨论）。能这样做的话，资源型的城市、地区和国家可用来完善软硬基础设施的资源会比资源短缺的城市、地区和国家更多，力度更大，经济发展转型的速度可以更快。这样资源就会从经济发展的"诅咒"变为经济发展的"祝福"。

## 4.5
## 寻找经济结构转型升级新结构经济学之路的最佳历史实践标杆①

虽然增长与发展委员会认定的这13个经济体并非完美无缺，都存在各种各样的问题，比如博茨瓦纳目前依然高度依赖于采矿业，巴西后来跌入了中等收入陷阱，其他经济体也不一定服气；但是有一点会让所有的争议都哑口无言——有谁还能够以7%的高速增长率持续增长25年之久？虽然经济增长不是目的，但却是实现发展最为重要的基础。如图4.62所示，持续的高速经济增长是由穷致富最快的途径。而且，上述13个战后发展样本有着广泛的代表性，博茨瓦纳和阿曼是资源富足型小国的发展典范，中国和印度尼西亚是劳动力富足型大

① 标杆管理（benchmarking）起源于20世纪70年代末80年代初美国学习日本的运动中，首开标杆管理先河的是施乐公司。1976年以后，一直保持着世界复印机市场实际垄断地位的施乐遇到了来自国内外特别是日本竞争者的全方位挑战，如佳能、NEC等公司以施乐的成本价销售产品且能够获利，产品开发周期、开发人员分别比施乐短或少50%，施乐的市场份额从82%直线下降到35%。面对着竞争威胁，施乐公司最先发起向日本企业学习的运动，开展了广泛、深入的标杆管理。施乐公司使用了"竞争标杆方法"这一概念和方法，这个方法是指：从生产成本、周期时间、营销成本、零售价格等领域中，找出一些明确的衡量标准或项目，然后将施乐公司在这些项目中的表现，与佳能等主要的竞争对手进行比较，找出了其中的差距，弄清了这些公司的运作机理，全面调整了经营战略、战术，改进了业务流程，很快收到了成效，把失去的市场份额重新夺了回来。在提高交付订货的工作水平和处理低值货品浪费大的问题上，同样应用标杆管理方法，以交付速度比施乐快3倍的比恩公司为标杆，并选择14家经营同类产品的公司逐一考察，找出了问题的症结并采取措施，使仓储成本下降了10%，年节省低值品费用数千万美元。

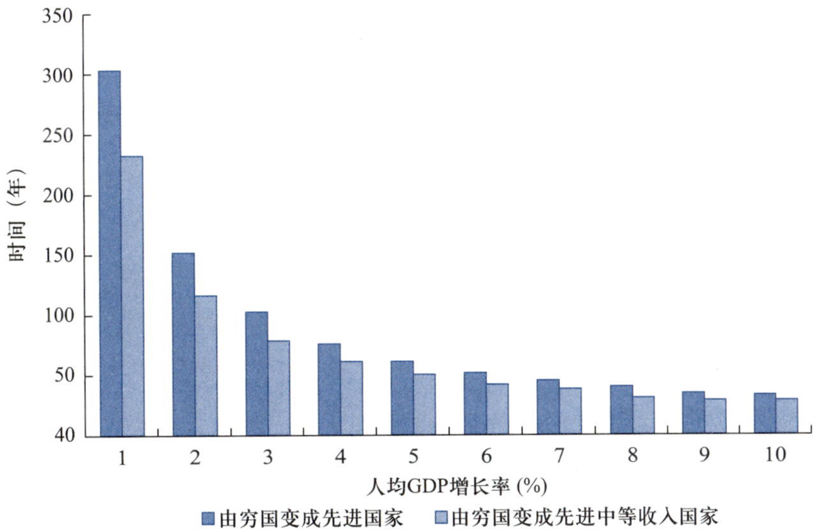


图4.62 步入高收入行列所需要的时间

国的发展典范，中国香港与新加坡是资源匮乏型港口城市的发展典范，日本和韩国是资源匮乏但劳动力富足型国家的发展典范，泰国和马来西亚是资源和劳动力均富足的中等规模国家的发展典范，马耳他则是微型经济的发展典范。除了样本中的中国，巴西也是“金砖国家”（还包括没有纳入样本的印度、俄罗斯、南非，“金砖国家”代表了全球最大的新兴经济体）。新结构经济学基于增长与发展委员会所概括的这些发展典范特征事实提供了一个逻辑自洽的新结构经济学诠释。接下来，我们把各个典范的经济结构转型升级的发展战略路径融合为一个样本，拟合一条新结构经济学主张的最佳实践发展战略路径标杆——这个标杆并不是以最发达国家为标准的。

在评价发展中国家结构变迁的发展战略时，标杆的选取是非常重要的。主流的发展经济学以发达国家为参照系，来看发展中国家缺什么（如结构主义所强调的现代资本、技术密集产业），或发展中国家做得不好的地方（如“华盛顿共识”所推动的私有化、市场化、稳定化），并以此作为改造发展中国家的依据。与其不同，新结构经济学主张应该看发展中国家现在有什么（即其要素禀赋），以及以此为基础能做好什么（即其比较优势），发展政策的目标是把现在能做好的做大做强，以此来实现逐步赶上和超越发达国家的目标。因此，我们以二战后这12个发展典范的发展战略路径作为标杆，而不是选取发达国家的战略路径作为标杆，来评价世界各个经济体的结构变迁的发展战略路径。

### 4.5.1 经济结构转型升级路径的最佳实践标杆：非农产业

表4.11是发展典范的非农产业结构变迁的样本的描述性统计，样本中禀赋水平从0.012 9到1.543、非农产业升级水平从0.57到1.02，非常广泛地覆盖了发展过程的各个阶段，有非常强的代表性。图4.63和图4.64是其分布的核密度图，图4.65是发展典范样本的散点图，图4.66是不同形式的拟合曲线。一般而言，按照第2、第3章所归纳的产业结构变迁一般规律特征而言，非农产业是一直随禀赋结构升级而不断攀升的。可以看到，线性拟合和指数拟合效果相对较低，$R^2$均不足0.4；对数、乘幂、多项式等拟合效果较好，$R^2$均接近0.7。可能正如阿德尔曼所言，发展过程绝对是高度非线性化的。[①]出于计算简便的考虑，同前面一样，我们不妨采取对数拟合：

$$I_{it}=f^{B}\left(E_{it}\right)=1.044\ 4+0.068\ 1\times\ln\left(E_{it}\right)$$

斜率和弹性分别为$\frac{\partial I_{it}}{\partial E_{it}}=\frac{0.068\ 1}{E_{it}}$，$\frac{\partial I_{it}}{\partial E_{it}}\frac{E_{it}}{I_{it}}=\frac{0.068\ 1}{I_{it}}$。有趣的是，相对于世界整个样本而言，增长与发展委员会认定的发展典范样本的发展战略路径的斜率和弹性要温和，大约只有世界样本的81.9%。当禀赋结构升级1单位时，发展典范的非农产业结构升级（0.068 1/$E$）个单位；当禀赋结构升级1%时，发展典范的非农产业结构升级（0.068 1/$I$）%。这似乎表明发展典范结构变迁的步伐相当稳健，并不激进。相对于这些发展典范的“循序渐进”的经济结构转型升级路径而言，其他发展中经济体反而“欲速则不达”。如前对国别经济结构转型升级路径的特征归纳所分析的，韩国就采用了现实主义的方法进行产业升级，并且把战略调整为进入那些与自己潜在比较优势一致的产业。20世纪60年代，韩国发展并出口的是服装、胶合板、假发等劳动力密集型产品。当资本逐渐积累，禀赋结构因为经济发展而改变时，韩国便向汽车等资本更为密集的产业升级。但是在升级初期，国内的生产主要集中在进口部件的装配上，这是劳动力密集型的生产，同时也是与当时韩国的比较优势相一致的。类似地，电子业起初主要生产家用电器，如电视、洗衣机、电冰箱等，之后才转向存储芯片的生产，这是信息产业中技术最简单的区段。韩国的技术提升是迅速的，其提升的速度同潜在比较优势变化的速度是一致的。这种变化也反映了有力的经济增长所带来的物质资本和人力资本的迅速积累，而增长之所以出现，是因为该国的主要产业部门时刻与该国现有的比较优势保持一致。[②]

---

① 阿德尔曼，“发展理论中的误区及其对政策的含义”，载《发展经济学前沿：未来展望》，中国财经出版社，2003年版。

② 林毅夫，《新结构经济学：反思发展理论与政策的理论框架》，北京大学出版社，2012年版，第73–74页。

表4.11 发展典范样本的禀赋升级与非农产业结构变迁样本的描述性统计

| 变量 | 观测值 | 均值 | 标准差 | 最小值 | 最大值 |
|---|---|---|---|---|---|
| 禀赋升级 | 453 | 0.261 459 9 | 0.286 922 4 | 0.012 860 5 | 1.542 937 |
| 产业升级 | 453 | 0.912 527 5 | 0.095 246 3 | 0.570 798 2 | 1.019 472 |

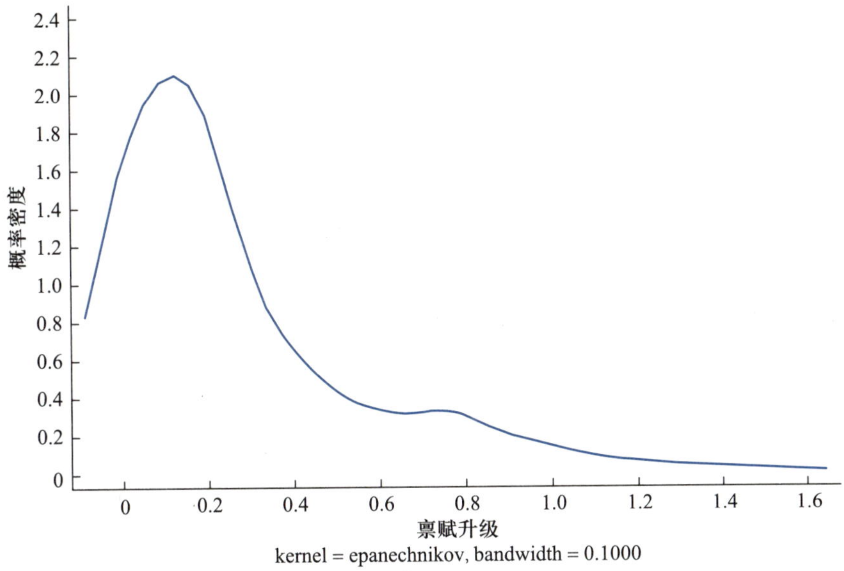


图4.63 发展典范样本禀赋升级的核密度图

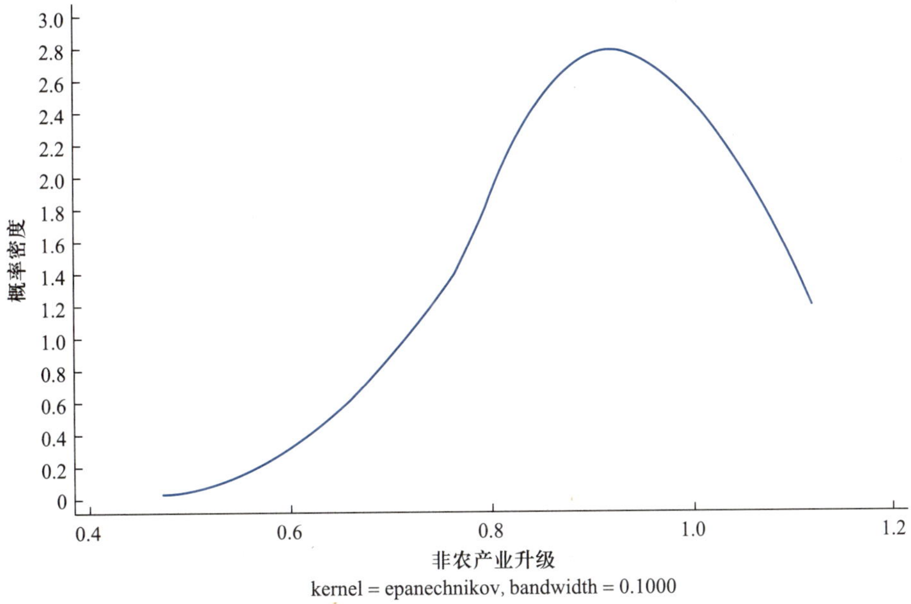


图4.64 发展典范样本非农产业升级的核密度图

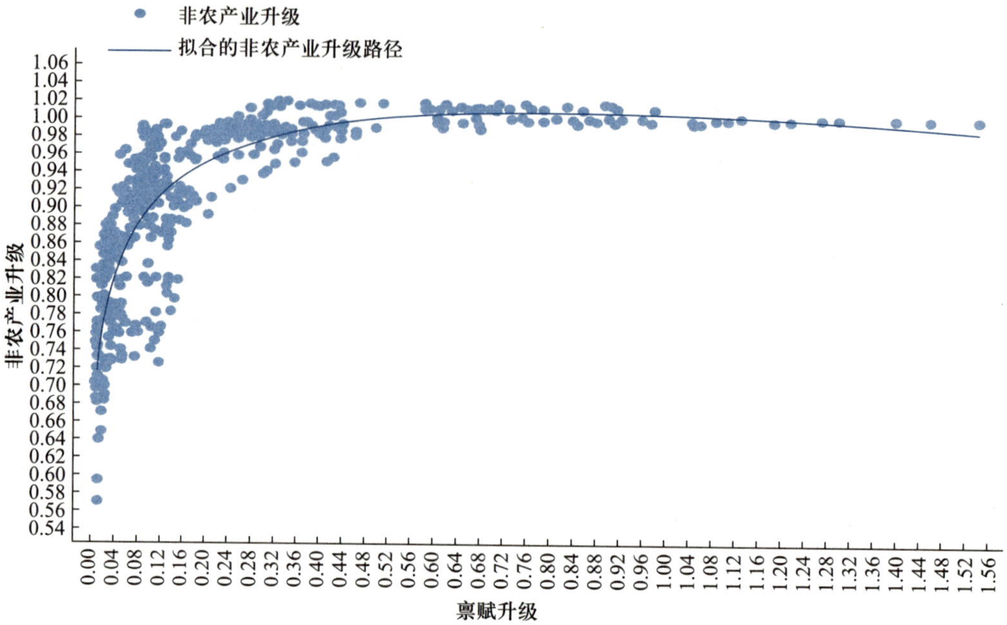


图4.65 12个发展典范的混合样本的非农产业发展战略路径（1970—2011年）

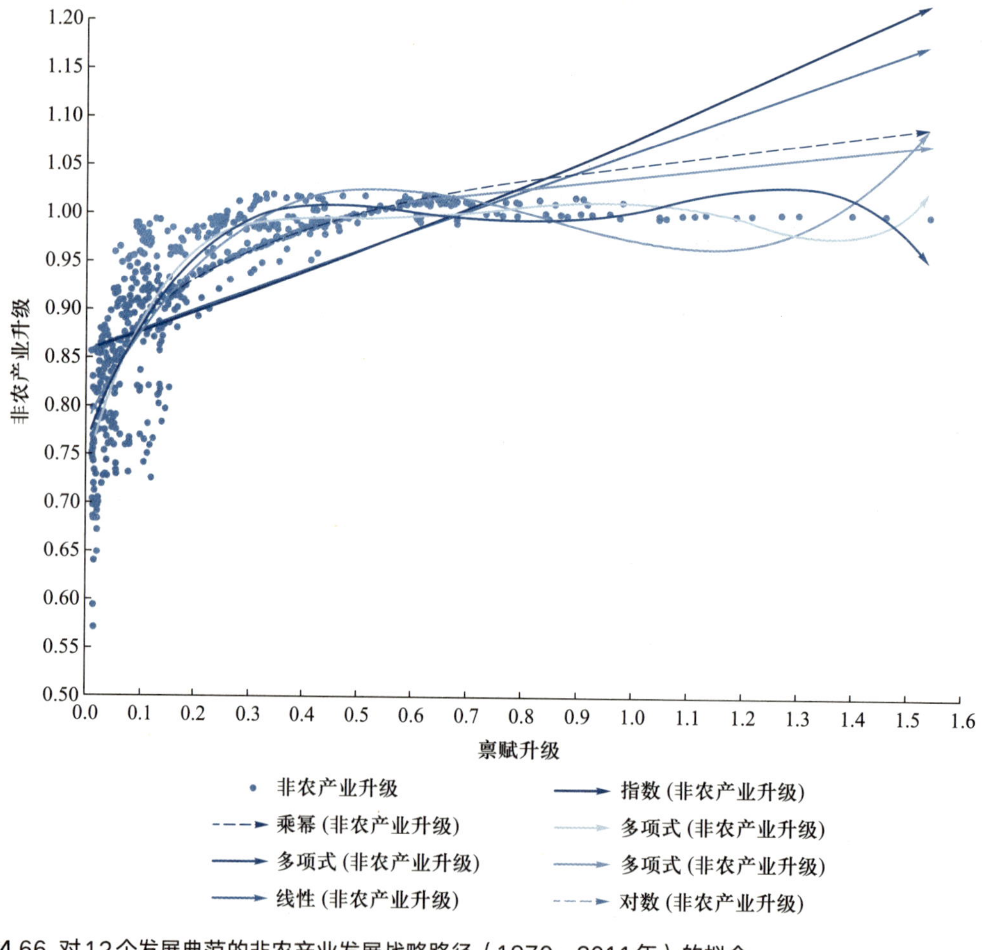


图4.66 对12个发展典范的非农产业发展战略路径（1970—2011年）的拟合

### 4.5.2 经济结构转型升级路径的最佳实践标杆：工业

与前面的方法类似，我们仍然通过对12个发展典范样本的产业结构升级之路来拟合工业的最佳实践发展战略路径标杆。表4.12是发展典范样本工业升级路径的描述性统计。同样，工业化升级水平从0.339到2.610，覆盖了整个发展阶段的广泛情况。图4.67是工业化升级分布的核密度图，图4.68是禀赋结构水平和工业化升级的散点图。图4.69是发展典范样本不同形式的拟合曲线。需要特别说明的是，按照第2、第3章所概括的产业结构变迁一般规律，随着一个经济体的禀赋结构不断升级，其工业占比会形成先升高后下降的倒U形曲线，然后在进入禀赋结构前沿后表现出随机游走的状态，因此我们在拟合时采取二次式拟合，并且在拟合时剔除了$E>1$的观测值。可以看到，线性拟合、乘幂、对数和指数拟合效果较差，而多项式拟合效果较好，$R^2$接近0.2。然而，相对于非农产业结构转型升级路径的拟合优度高达0.7而言还是非常低的，这在很大程度上反映了由于数据缺少的原因未能够覆盖日本、韩国等发展典范早期的工业化路径。二项式拟合的结果为

$$I_{it}^{\mathrm{NSE}}=f^{B}\left(E_{it}\right)=1.549\,537+0.906\,706\,3\times E_{it}-1.653\,191\times E_{it}^{2}$$

由于倒U形的路径特征，其斜率和弹性可能不是最重要的特征，我们采用顶点和拐点来刻画其路径特征比较合适。该拟合的工业化转型升级路径顶点为$I=1.673\,86$，拐点为$E=0.274\,23$。相对于全球样本的拐点（$E=0.766\,9$）和顶点（$I=2.006\,1$）而言，发展典范的顶点要低得多，但拐点要早得多。这意味着其他发展中经济体虽然采取了快速的工业化赶超，但是很晚才能实现工业化。同样再一次表明，发展典范采取循序渐进的工业化则成功了，而工业化赶超则欲速而不达。

表4.12 发展典范样本工业升级路径的描述性统计

| 变量 | 观测值 | 均值 | 标准差 | 最小值 | 最大值 |
|---|---|---|---|---|---|
| 禀赋升级 | 456 | 0.260 24 | 0.286 31 | 0.012 90 | 1.542 90 |
| 产业升级 | 456 | 1.573 17 | 0.471 44 | 0.339 21 | 2.609 51 |

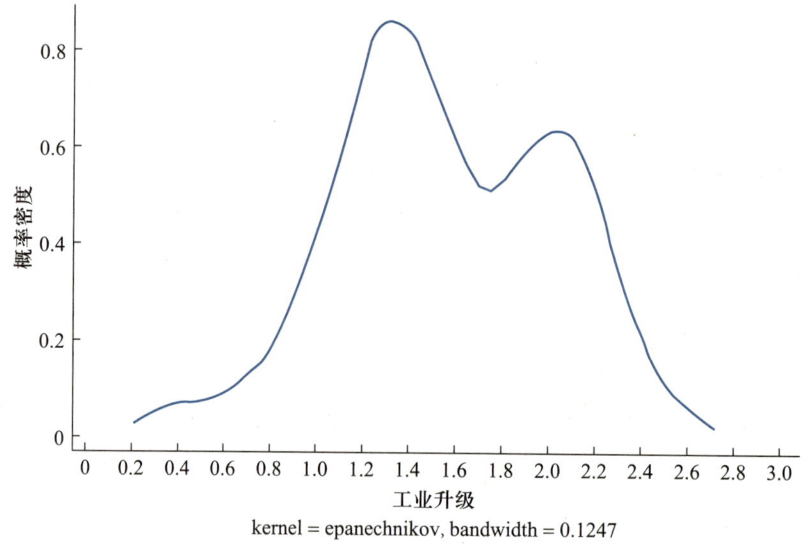


图4.67 发展典范样本工业升级的核密度图

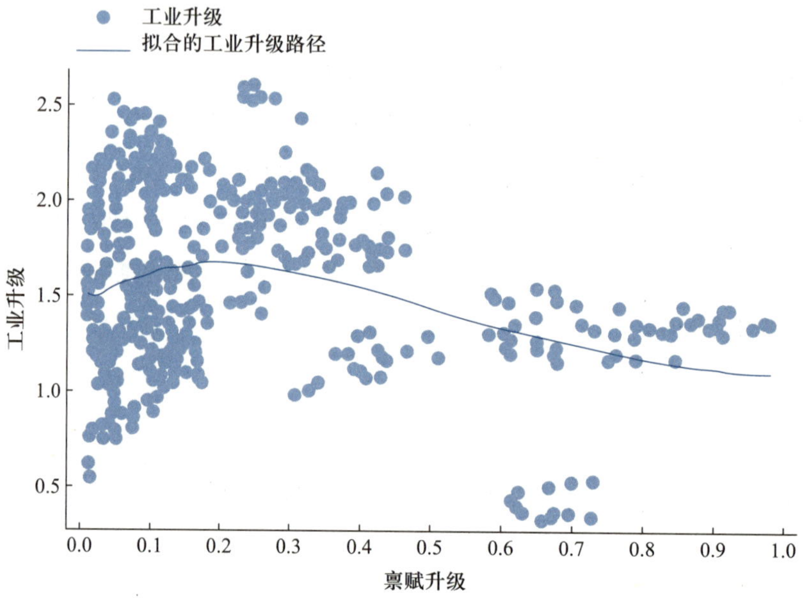


图4.68 12个发展典范的混合样本工业发展战略路径（1970—2011年，$E<1$）

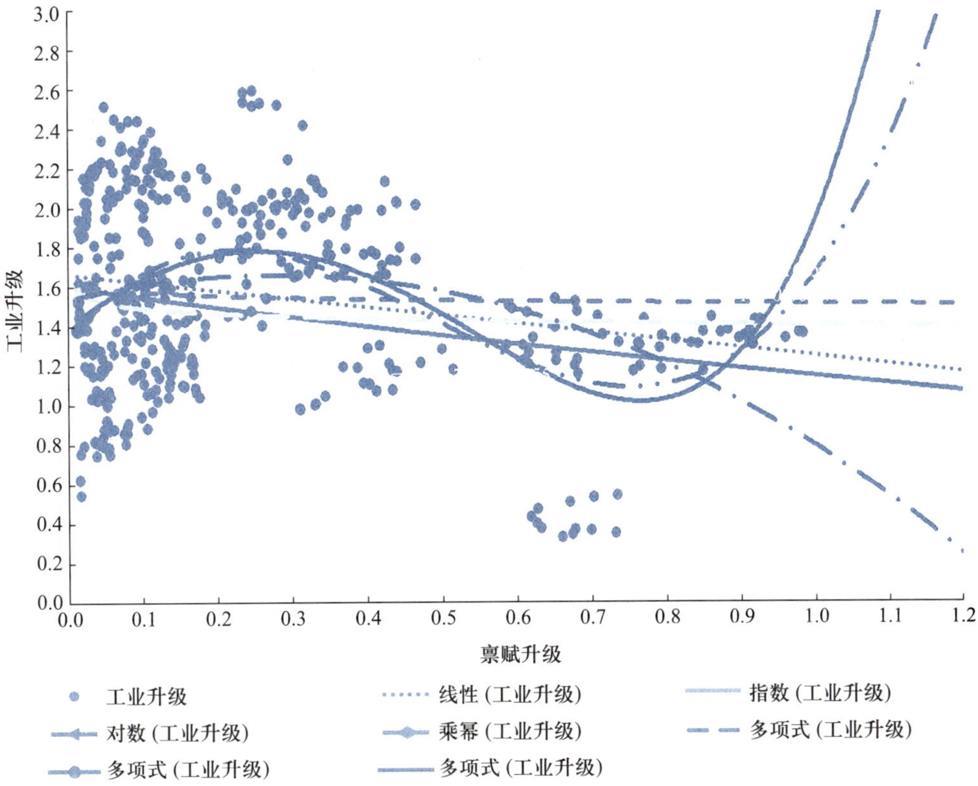


图4.69 对12个发展典范的工业发展战略路径（1970—2011年）的拟合

### 4.5.3 经济结构转型升级路径的最佳实践标杆：服务业

同样，按照第2、第3章所概括的产业结构变迁的一般特征，随着禀赋结构的不断升级，服务业占比也不断上升。我们也通过12个发展典范样本的服务业升级路径来拟合出一条最佳实践发展战略路径标杆。表4.13是发展典范样本服务业升级路径的描述性统计。服务业升级水平从0.118到1.207，覆盖了发展阶段的广泛情况。图4.70和图4.71分别是服务业升级水平分布的核密度图与禀赋结构升级水平的散点图。图4.72是发展典范样本不同形式的禀赋结构升级与服务业升级拟合曲线。可以看到，线性拟合、乘幂和指数拟合效果较差，而对数和多项式拟合效果较好，对数拟合的$R^2$均接近0.42，对数拟合结果为

$$I_{it}^{\text{NSE}} = f^{B}\left(E_{it}\right) = 0.897\ 196\ 9 + 0.106\ 003\ 2 \times \ln\left(E_{it}\right)$$

其斜率和弹性分别为 $\dfrac{\partial I_{it}}{\partial E_{it}} = \dfrac{0.106}{E_{it}}$，$\dfrac{\partial I_{it}}{\partial E_{it}}\dfrac{E_{it}}{I_{it}} = \dfrac{0.106}{I_{it}}$。因此，当禀赋结构升级1单位时，

发展典范的服务业比重上升（0.106/*E*）个单位；当禀赋结构升级1%时，发展典范的产业结构升级（0.106/*I*）%。相对于全球样本而言，发展典范的服务业转型升级的斜率和弹性要大，这可能反映出一个基本的事实：没有工业的支撑，服务业只是空中楼阁。正如前面对发展典范的国别经济结构转型升级梳理所归纳的基本事实，发展典范正是因为完成了工业化，有了坚实的工业化基础才能支撑起服务业的繁荣。

表4.13 发展典范样本的服务业升级的描述性统计

| 变量 | 观测值 | 均值 | 标准差 | 最小值 | 最大值 |
|---|---|---|---|---|---|
| 禀赋升级 | 432 | 0.229 524 | 0.253 808 | 0.012 900 | 1.542 900 |
| 产业升级 | 432 | 0.681 903 | 0.180 437 | 0.117 765 | 1.206 560 |

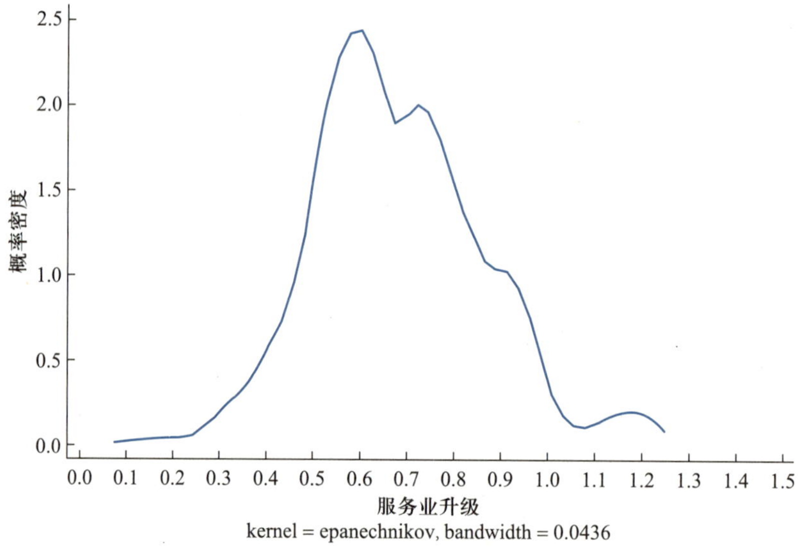


图4.70 12个发展典范样本服务业升级的核密度图

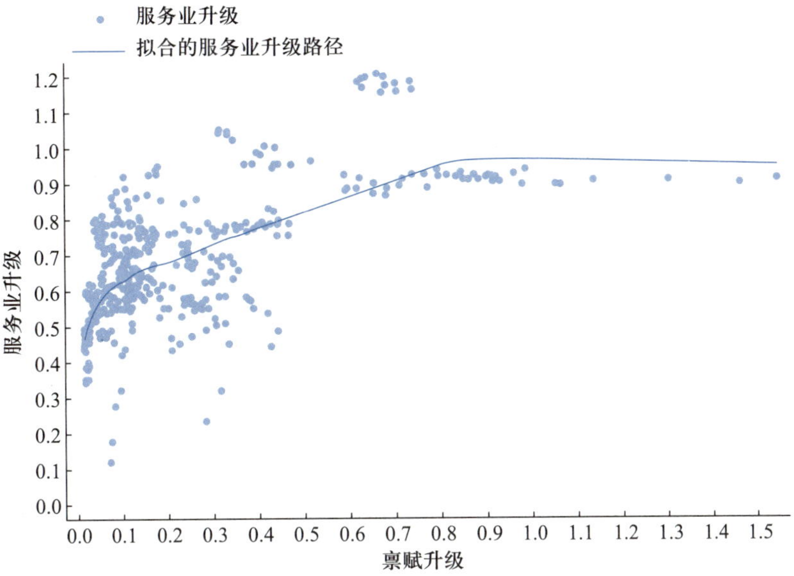


图4.71 12个发展典范的混合样本服务业发展战略路径（1970—2011年）

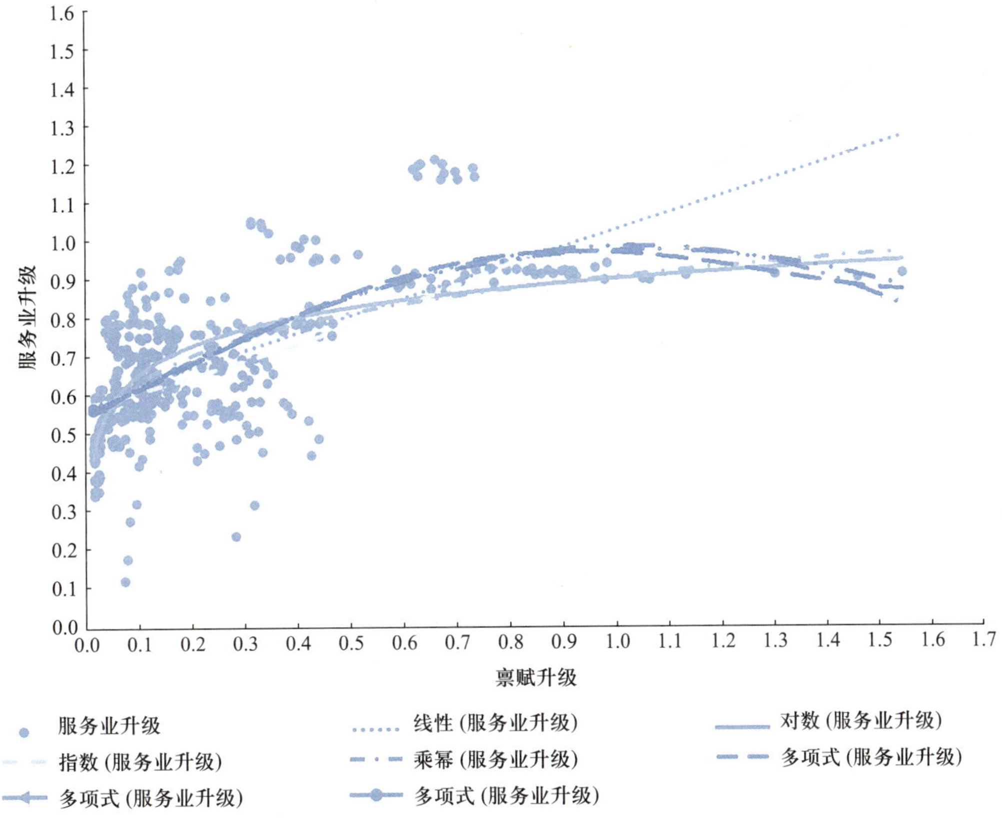


图4.72 对12个发展典范的服务业发展战略路径（1970—2011年）的拟合

# 4.6

# 加速禀赋结构升级的高储蓄率之谜的谜底：按照比较优势不断转型升级[①]

按照第1章第3小节所介绍的新结构经济学关于经济结构转型升级的理论框架，产业结构升级只是表象，背后的要素禀赋结构升级才是根本，而按照比较优势进行结构转型升级是积累资本进而改进禀赋结构最快的方式，这也是小步快跑的本质。这一新结构经济学的基本原理在上述二战后发展典范的结构变迁案例中得到了一目了然的彰显。主流的消费和储蓄理论难以给出解释，故又称之为“东亚高储蓄率之谜”，中国的故事也被单独称为“中国高储蓄率之谜”。然而，遗憾的是，目前的流行思潮对二战后发展典范尤其是东亚的高储蓄高投资现象嗤之以鼻，甚至将全球金融危机之过也归咎于它们。

诺贝尔经济学奖获得者Robert J. Shiller于2006年在*Project Syndicate*刊文对中美巨大的储蓄率差距之谜惊叹道：“中国的储蓄率是所有大国里最高的。中国的国民储蓄率（未被立即消费掉的国内产值百分比），包括公共储蓄和私人储蓄在内，大约是50%。恰恰相反，美国的储蓄率是所有大国里最低的，只占国内产值的约10%。其他所有国家几乎都处在这两极之间。储蓄率的差异至关重要，而且毫无疑问是目前中国年经济增长高于美国整整6个百分点的主要原因。如果人们把一半收入都用来储蓄，那么他们的资金投入就能够推动经济的快速发展。中国的储蓄在很大程度上是良性循环：快速的经济增长带来了高额储蓄，而高额储蓄反过来又支持了快速发展。中美储蓄率的差距几十年来一直在拉大。20世纪80年代初，中国的储蓄率是美国的2倍，而现在却是美国的5倍。这种变迁轨迹为何如此不同？”[②]

国际学术与政策界大都这样以美国作为参照系，对于中国储蓄率的普遍认识就是由于各种扭曲尤其是政府干预导致的“异常高的储蓄率”[③]。例如两位美联储前主席便表达了不

---

① 更多和更深入的内容可参考：林毅夫、付才辉，《新结构经济学导论》（上册），高等教育出版社，2019年版，第5章。

② Robert J. Shiller, “Thrifty China, Spendthrift America”, *Project Syndicate*, Aug 22, 2006.

③ Fehr, H. S. Jokisch, L. J. Kotlikoff, “Will China Eat our Lunch or Take Us out to Dinner? Simulating the Transition Paths of U.S., EU, Japan and China”, NBER Working Paper, NO.11668, 2005.

满。伯南克（Bernanke）指出，中国实行的“高储蓄、低消费”模式，是全球经济失衡的重要原因。[①]2008年全球金融危机爆发后，格林斯潘（Greenspan）也支持了上述观点。[②]这种认识也蔓延到国内，造成一种中国高储蓄率是不好的“弊端论”思潮，“高储蓄高投资”的中国发展模式受到广泛的批评，认为需要从“投资驱动”向“消费驱动”的增长模式转型，并逐步影响到国家政策。例如，樊纲等指出，中国较高的储蓄率以及储蓄—消费失衡是中国长期持续大规模贸易顺差的重要原因，从而带来中国内外经济比例失衡。[③]财政部国际司课题组也认为，“近10多年来，在全球经济高速增长的同时，世界主要经济体的国际收支失衡愈演愈烈。其中，美国的贸易逆差不断扩大，包括我国在内的东亚经济体、石油出口国的贸易顺差急剧膨胀……中国的贸易顺差屡创新高则是因为国内储蓄太高，国内消费由此受到抑制，产品只得出口到国外市场，又进一步加剧了经济增长对出口的过度依赖”。[④]李扬等也指出：“中国的储蓄率之高及其持续时期之长固然令人困惑，它所引发的一系列问题更为棘手。作为宏观经济运行中的供给面，高储蓄率显然构成当前我国经济运行中另外两个表现在需求面上的突出问题——居高不下的高投资和规模不断扩大的高顺差——的物质基础。2005年中国的投资率达到了43.4%，比1981年上升了11个百分点；而经常项目顺差占GDP的比重则在同年达到了4.5%的创纪录水平。问题的复杂性在于：无论高投资如何令人担心，亦无论巨额顺差引发的贸易摩擦如何让人不堪忍受，在国内消费率未能如愿提高的前提下，为了维持国民经济的正常运行，我们在一定程度上还须容忍它们的存在和发展。”[⑤]在政策层面，“十二五”规划和党的十八大报告中也分别指出，“要坚持扩大内需战略，保持经济平稳较快发展”，“要牢牢把握扩大内需这一战略基点，加快建立扩大消费需求长效机制，释放居民消费潜力”。在目前如火如荼的中美贸易摩擦背景下，这种“弊端论”思潮更加深入人心，即所谓的“三高病”。我们忍不住沉思：究竟是根深蒂固的由发达国家学界以发达国家的经验做参照引领的传统观念出了问题，还是真实世界出了问题？我们思考的答案倾向于前者。与这些思潮恰恰相反，前述二战后发展典范的案例与新结构经济学的理论吻合：如果一个经济体按照比较优势发展，其产品在全球市场上都有竞争力，必然能够创造最大的出口，实现最大的经济剩余，取得最大的投资回报，

① B. Bernanke, “The Global Savings Glut and the US Current Account Deficit”, The Homer Jones Lecture, St. Louis, Missouri, 2005, April 14.

② A. Greenspan, “The Fed Didn’t Cause the Housing Bubble”, *Wall Street Journal*, 2009, March 11.

③ 樊纲、魏强、刘鹏，“中国经济的内外失衡和财税改革”，《经济研究》，2009年第1期。

④ 财政部国际司课题组：“企业储蓄率偏高的原因、影响及对策”，《中国财政》，2009年第8期。

⑤ 李扬、殷剑峰：“中国高储蓄率问题探究——1992—2003年中国资金流量表的分析”，《经济研究》，2007年第6期。

可供储蓄的经济剩余和储蓄倾向都最大，因此高储蓄率是必然的而且也是合理的结果，而且，这样高的储蓄为资本积累和产业向资本更高、技术更先进的产业升级提供了必要的物质基础。

如图4.73所示，中国改革开放之后的储蓄率经历了大幅度的上升，从改革开放初期的35%左右上升到目前的50%左右。不仅中国如此，如图4.74所示，东亚的日本、韩国、新加坡的储蓄率均远超过美国和世界平均水平。值得注意的是，在20世纪70年代初，新加坡和美国的储蓄率差不多，都只有20%多一点，但其后的30年间，新加坡的储蓄率超过50%，而美国依然保持在20%左右。韩国与美国的储蓄率差距变迁类似，在20世纪80年代初，二者也相差无几，但其后的20年间，韩国的储蓄率升至40%左右，将近美国的2倍。中美储蓄率差距在近20年不断拉大的趋势类似于新加坡和美国在20世纪七八十年代的趋势，以及韩国和美国在20世纪八九十年代的趋势。从投资率的角度来看，东亚发展典范相对美国的逆袭更加耀眼。如图4.75所示，在20世纪60年代初，新加坡和韩国的投资率均低于美国，但其后的40年间远超美国。如图4.76所示，在20世纪70年代，东南亚和拉丁美洲的储蓄率很接近，但20年之后东南亚的储蓄率比拉丁美洲高20个百分点，对应的投资率也存在这个趋势。东亚与拉美之间的这种储蓄率和投资率变化趋势是那些高储蓄文化论者和特殊因素论者所无法解释的。[①]对此，新结构经济学一贯的解释便是，东亚由于采取遵循比较优势发展战略，由有效市场和有为政府共同推动结构持续升级，使得经济取得快速增长，创造大量可供储蓄的经济剩余，储蓄的回报率较高从而储蓄的边际倾向更强，因此出现了高储蓄率现象。与此相反，拉美由于在第二次世界大战以后采取进口替代的发展战略违背了比较优势，在20世纪80年代开始向市场经济转型时政府又采取“华盛顿共识”的“有限政府”主张，没有因势利导持续地推动经济结构持续升级，使得经济增长疲软，投资回报率低，可供储蓄的经济剩余以及储蓄倾向都比较弱，因此便出现了与东亚高储蓄现象的鲜明反差。总之，结构变迁越是违背比较优势（TCI指数越大），储蓄率越低，如图4.77和图4.78所示。其实，回顾美国的结构变迁历史，也有类似的故事。在19世纪40年代美国储蓄约占国民生产总值的14%，随着工业化的推进，储蓄率在19世纪中叶上升了5个百分点，到19世纪末又上升了4个百分点达到23%，大体上储蓄率上升了2/3。因此，如果能够好好审视自身的历史，前

---

① 类似的观点可追溯到韦伯。韦伯写道：当消费的限制和获利活动的解禁相结合，一种不可避免的实际效应就会显现出来：凭借禁欲主义的强制节俭来实现资本积累……在这个严谨的加尔文主义只统治了七年的国家（荷兰）里，越是严谨的宗教圈子，其生活方式就越节俭……与此同时，宗教禁欲主义的力量还为这些资产阶级商人提供了严谨、尽责又极为勤勉的工人，这些工人将工作视为上帝安排给他们的人生目标。（马克斯·韦伯，《新教伦理与资本主义精神》，马奇炎、陈婧译，北京大学出版社，2012年版，第174–178页）

面提到的几任美联储主席就不会妄加指责中国和其他新兴经济体的高储蓄率现象了。[1]其实，英国也如出一辙。例如，Madsen估算了英国过去8个世纪以来的私人储蓄率，如图4.79所示：工业革命之前英国的结构变迁处于马尔萨斯陷阱之中，储蓄率维持在较低的水平（在10%左右波动），工业革命之后英国持续的经济结构转型升级不断推高私人储蓄率，从10%一路升到30%。[2]

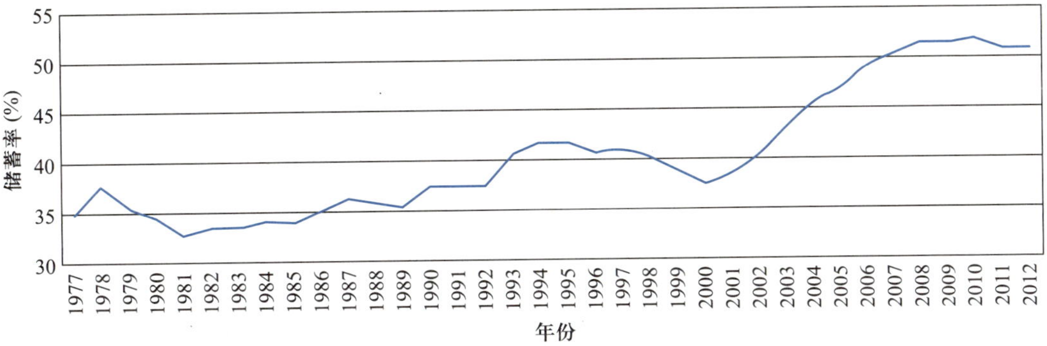


**图4.73 中国的储蓄率（1977—2012年）**

数据来源：国家统计局。

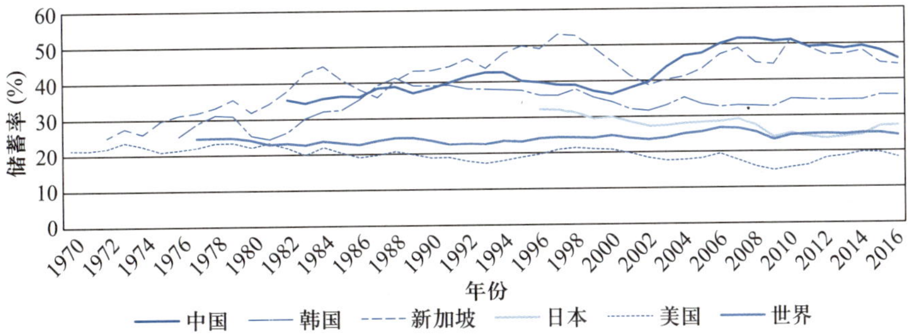


**图4.74 东亚发展典范与美国和世界的储蓄率比较**

数据来源：世界银行。

---

① 更多内容可参考：斯坦利·L. 恩格尔曼、罗伯特·E. 高尔曼主编，《剑桥美国经济史：漫长的19世纪》（第二卷），高德步等译，中国人民大学出版社，2018年版。

② Jakob Madsen, "Wealth and inequality over eight centuries of British capitalism", *Journal of Development Economics*, 2019, Vol.138, pp.246–260.

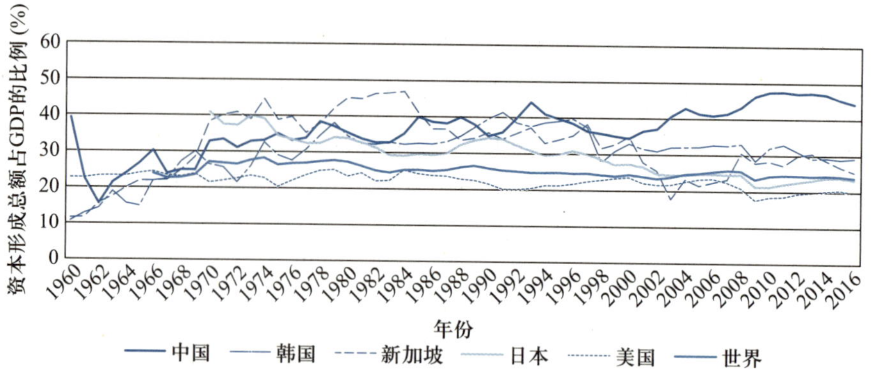


图 4.75 东亚发展典范与美国和世界的投资率比较

数据来源：世界银行。

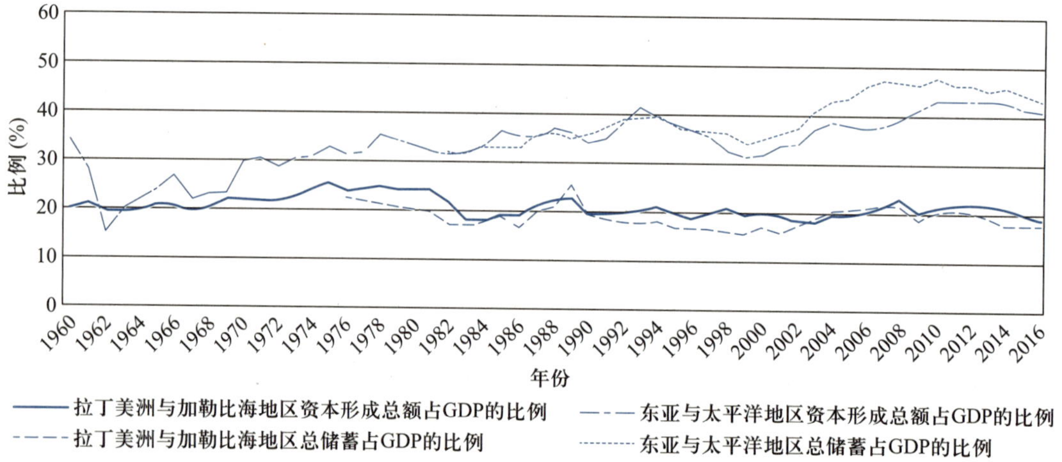


图 4.76 东亚与拉美的储蓄率和投资率比较

数据来源：世界银行。

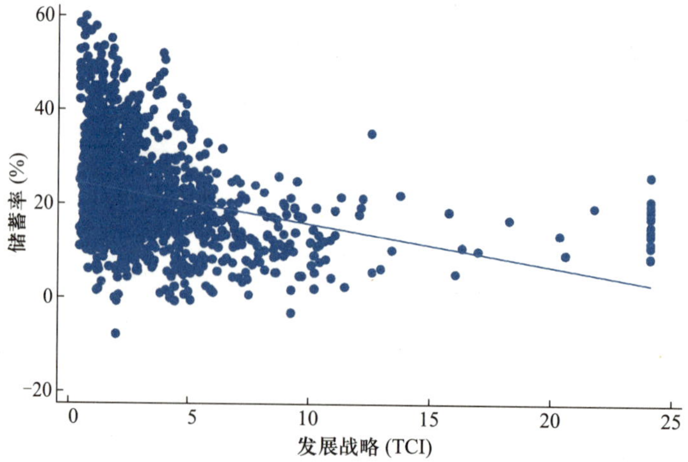


图 4.77 发展战略与储蓄率的全球跨国散点图

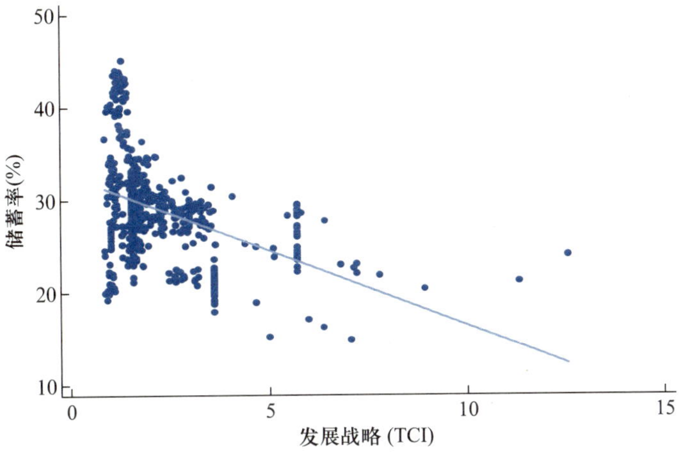


图4.78 发展典范经济体：发展战略与储蓄率的散点图

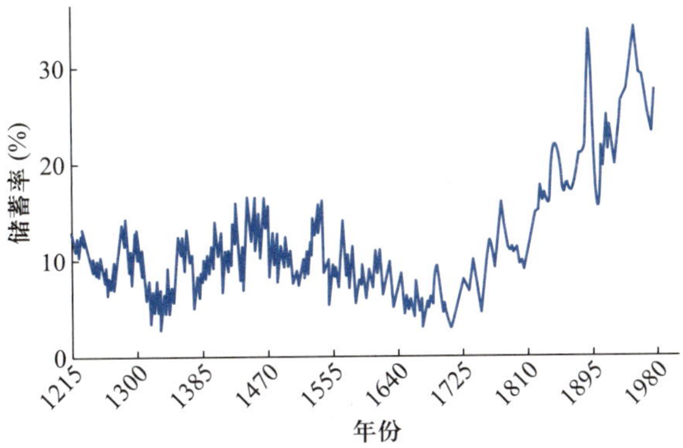


图4.79 英国过去8个世纪以来的私人储蓄率（9年移动平均值）

资料来源：Jakob Madsen, "Wealth and Inequality Over Eight Centuries of British Capitalism", *Journal of Development Economics*, 2019, Vol.138, pp.246-260.

# 第5章

# 监测世界经济结构变迁的轨迹

- 5.1 “尺有所短，寸有所长”
- 5.2 经济结构转型升级路径对最佳实践标杆的达标情况：非农产业
- 5.3 经济结构转型升级路径对最佳实践标杆的达标情况：工业
- 5.4 经济结构转型升级路径对最佳实践标杆的达标情况：服务业
- 5.5 世界经济结构转型升级趋势在不断好转
- 5.6 评价世界经济结构转型升级的效果
- 5.7 遵循比较优势进行持续的经济结构转型升级是经济发展成功的保证
- 5.8 违背比较优势的经济结构转型升级是导致发展陷阱的根源
- 5.9 违背比较优势的发展战略将错失全球化发展机遇

# 5.1

## “尺有所短，寸有所长”

任何事物从不同的标准看，可以得出不同的结论。然而，这个寻常的道理在主流发展思潮中却并不寻常。正如我们在第1章和其他章节中已经讨论过的，现在的主流经济学一般把发达国家的结构作为最优结构，忽视了不同发展程度国家产业结构差异的内生性，导致的结果就是20世纪50年代、60年代的结构主义，把发达国家的产业作为要发展的目标。80年代、90年代转型的时候，把发达国家市场经济制度结构当作最优结构，忽视了扭曲的内生性，直接把转型的目标作为转型的手段，导致的结果就是前面讲的，出发点非常好，效果非常差。以主流的现代经济学理论作为经济运行方方面面的指导原则，也同样会忽视了发展中国家和发达国家结构特性的差异而不适用。现代经济学的理论要在发展中国家发挥“认识世界、改造世界”的作用，就要求在理论中反映出发展中国家和发达国家结构差异和扭曲的内生性，并了解这些内生性对经济发展、转型和运行的影响，以及如何创造条件，为改变内生结果创造必要的条件。

在第5章中，与主流发展经济学的视角不同，我们并没有选取发达国家先进的产业结构作为标杆，而是将二战后发展典范结构变迁的最佳发展实践作为经济结构变迁路径的标杆。这个标杆的选取反映了新结构经济学的主张：看发展中国家现在有什么（即其要素禀赋），根据现在有的能做好什么（即比较优势），然后在政府的因势利导下帮助企业在市场中做大做强，以此积累资本，提升要素禀赋结构、比较优势、产业结构水平，来实现逐步赶上和超越发达国家的目标。这一部分我们将以此标杆为准绳，监测世界各个经济体（包括各个时期的前沿经济体）经济结构转型升级的经济结构变迁路径的达标情况。达标情况包括各个时期对标杆的偏离程度与达标程度，前者是绝对值，可以监测每一时期经济结构变迁的实际情况；后者是相对值，可以监测在不同时期经济结构变迁的动态调整情况。

## 5.2

## 经济结构转型升级路径对最佳实践标杆的达标情况：非农产业

### 5.2.1 非农产业结构转型升级偏离标杆程度的全球概况

回顾第3章的式（3.4）

$$\text{Deviation}_{it}=I_{it}-I_{it}^{\text{NSE}}=f\left(E_{it}\right)-f^{\text{NSE}}\left(E_{it}\right)$$

其中的$f^{\text{NSE}}$（$E_{it}$）是图1.26中的结构变迁的新结构经济学之路——其实也就是第4章我们所要寻找的结构变迁路径最佳实践标杆。式（3.4）计算的就是一个时刻具体的经济结构变迁路径对最佳实践标杆（新结构经济学之路）的偏离程度：

如果$\text{Deviation}_{it}>0$，那么表明非农产业结构过于先进，如图1.21中最优轨迹的上面部分；

如果$\text{Deviation}_{it}<0$，那么表明非农产业结构过于落后，如图1.26中最优轨迹的下面部分。

与前一章一样，我们选取便于计算而且拟合效度较好的发展典范的对数拟合标杆

$$I_{it}^{\text{NSE}}=f^{B}\left(E_{it}\right)=1.044\ 4+0.068\ 1\times\ln\left(E_{it}\right)$$

图5.1是全球样本的非农产业升级路径对拟合标杆的偏离程度$\text{Deviation}_{it}=f$（$E_{it}$）$-f^{\text{NSE}}$（$E_{it}$）分布的核密度图，大致接近于一个均值略低于零的正态分布，不过表现出明显的左部长尾。这表明，整体上看，相对于最佳实践路径而言，大部分非农产业升级路径的观测值集中在标杆附近并未过度偏离；选择过于先进的产业结构的结构变迁路径向上偏离程度分布和选择过于落后的产业结构的结构变迁路径向下偏离程度分布比较接近，但前者略低于后者，如图5.2所示。从我们的测算数据结果来看，中国从1970年非农产业结构向下偏离，到1980年非常接近非农产业结构的最优结构转型升级轨迹，然后又逐步出现向上的偏离；非洲不论在哪个时候经济体都严重地向下或向上偏离了最优非农产业转型升级轨迹；拉美则大体上与中国相反，先向上偏离然后逐步向下偏离；印度大体上长期向下偏离。

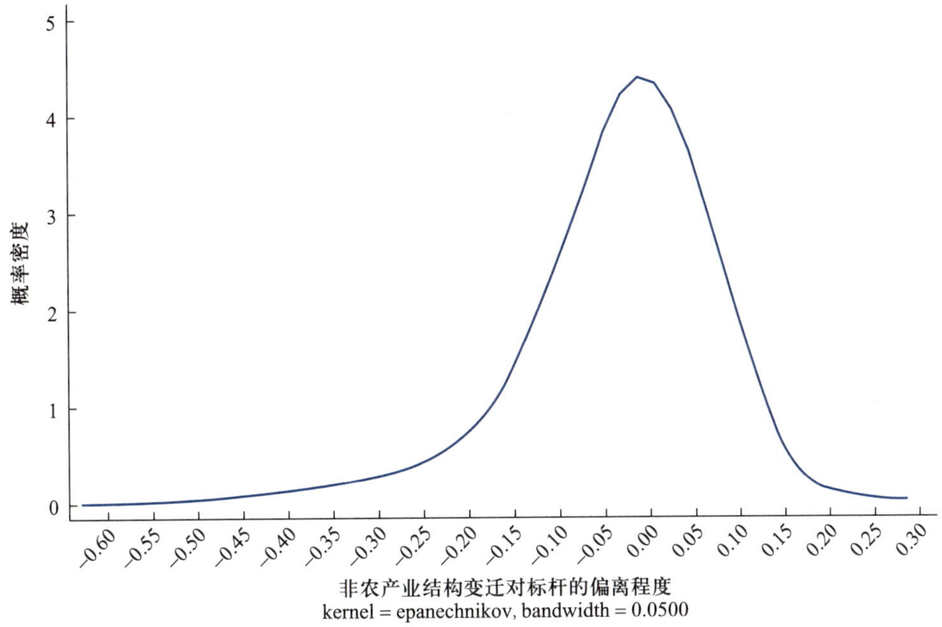


图5.1 世界180个经济体1970—2011年非农产业结构变迁对标杆的偏离程度分布的核密度

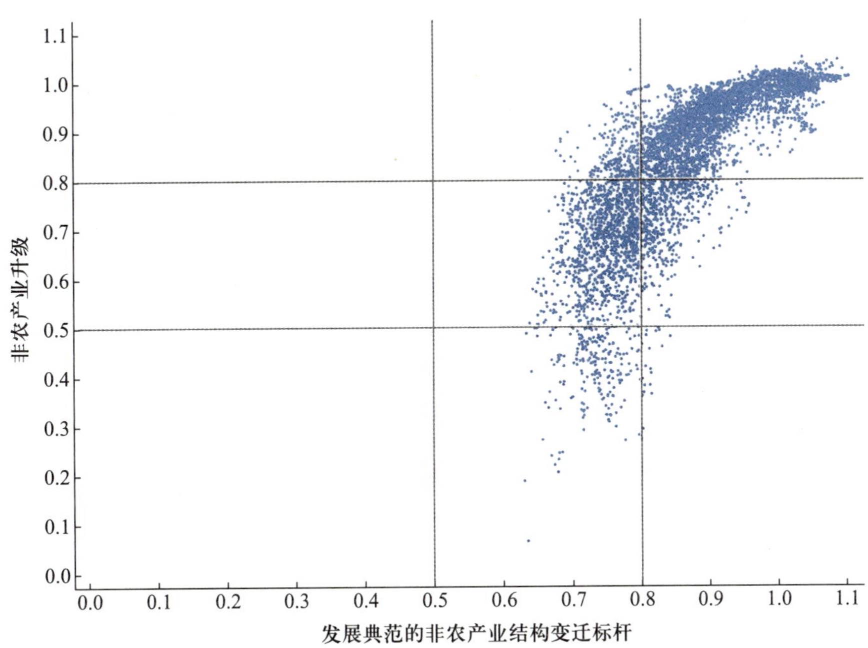


图5.2 世界180个经济体1970—2011年的非农产业升级路径与对应标杆的散点图

### 5.2.2 非农产业结构转型升级达标程度的全球概况

前一小节测算了世界各个经济体非农产业升级路径对标杆的偏离程度，这是一个绝对值。如前所示，不同发展阶段偏离标杆的绝对程度差别很大，尤其是诸多处于发展初级阶段的经济体，其赶超程度带来的偏离程度会很大，这种绝对偏离程度难以进行横向或纵向比较。接下来我们定义一个在各个阶段都相对可比的经济结构转型升级路径达标程度指标（%）：

$$I=\left(1-\frac{\text{Deviation}_{it}}{f^{\text{NSE}}\left(E_{it}\right)}\right)=\left(1-\frac{f\left(E_{it}\right)-f^{\text{NSE}}\left(E_{it}\right)}{f^{\text{NSE}}\left(E_{it}\right)}\right)\times 100 \tag{5.1}$$

结构变迁对标杆的偏离程度与结构变迁的达标程度这两个指标的区别不仅仅是绝对值与相对值的差别，还有着不同的应用功能。应用偏离度指标我们可以直接看到产业结构选择过于先进的程度（偏离度大于零）或过于落后的程度（偏离度小于零），达标程度指标则可以用来做跨国的比较。

同样，与前面一致，我们选取便于计算且拟合效度较高的非农产业升级路径发展典范的对数拟合标杆来监测各个经济体非农产业结构转型升级路径达标程度：

$$I_{it}^{\text{NSE}}=f^{B}\left(E_{it}\right)=1.549\ 537+0.906\ 706\ 3\times E_{it}-1.653\ 191\times E_{it}^{2} \tag{5.2}$$

按此可以测算全球180个经济体1970—2011年非农产业结构转型升级路径达标程度指数数据。根据我们的测算结果，中国的非农产业结构转型升级达标程度在逐步提高，1970年达标指数为85.49%，1980年达标指数提高到94.35%，1990年达标指数高达98.97%，其后的达标指数都在90%以上，这一时期也是中国经济结构转型升级最快与经济增长最快的时期。非洲有部分经济体的非农产业结构转型升级达标程度与中国一样在不断提高，如毛里求斯1976年的达标指数为89.32%，其后一直保持在93% ~ 99%的高得分值上，但是不少非洲经济体的达标指数却在恶化，例如津巴布韦在1970年的达标指数高达99.43%，其后一路下滑，2011年只有87.41%。

# 5.3

# –

# 经济结构转型升级路径对最佳实践标杆的达标情况：工业

## 5.3.1 工业结构转型升级偏离标杆程度的全球概况

同样采用式（3.4）来监测每个经济体的工业化转型升级对最佳实践标杆（新结构经济学之路）的偏离程度：

$$\text{Deviation}_{it} = I_{it} - I_{it}^{\text{NSE}} = f\left(E_{it}\right) - f^{\text{NSE}}\left(E_{it}\right) \quad (5.3)$$

如果$\text{Deviation}_{it} > 0$，那么表明工业化过于先进，如图1.21中最优轨迹的上面部分；

如果$\text{Deviation}_{it} < 0$，那么表明工业化过于落后，如图1.21中最优轨迹的下面部分。

与前一致，我们采用二次拟合

$$I_{it}^{\text{NSE}} = f^{B}\left(E_{it}\right) = 1.549\ 537 + 0.906\ 706\ 3 \times E_{it} - 1.653\ 191 \times E_{it}^{2} \quad (5.4)$$

对发展典范的工业升级之路进行拟合作为工业化的标杆。图5.3是全球样本的工业化路径对拟合标杆的偏离程度分布的核密度图，大致接近一个均值在−0.5左右的正态分布，并表现出明显的右侧长尾。图5.4是实际的工业化升级与对应的标杆的散点图，大部分实际值

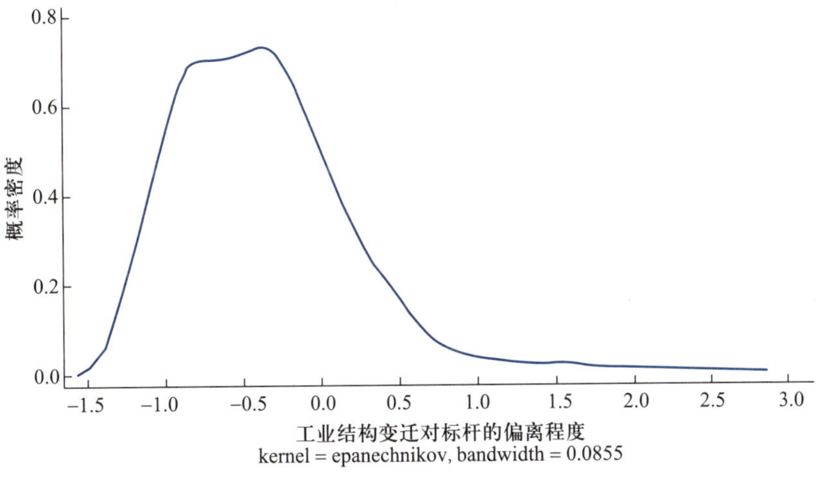


图5.3 世界180个经济体1970—2011年的工业变迁路径对标杆的偏离程度分布的核密度

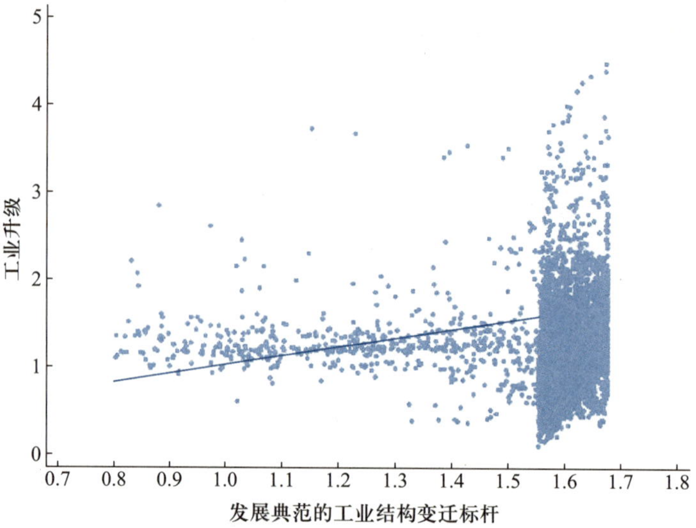


**图5.4 世界180个经济体1970—2011年的工业升级与对应标杆的散点图**

在标杆之下。这说明对于大多数经济体而言，在工业化过程中所面对的问题主要是产业结构中的工业比重过低，工业发展过于落后的问题，全球大部分经济体尚未有效实现工业化；同时，也有少数观测值相对于标杆的偏离程度大于1甚至大于2，表明这些国家存在工业过于赶超的问题。1970—2010年，绝大多数非洲经济体都长期存在向下偏离的情况，表明其艰难的工业化历程。中国的工业化则变化得非常剧烈，在20世纪70年代存在向下偏离的工业化落后情况，但是到21世纪之后则存在向上偏离，即工业化出现产能过剩的情况。

## 5.3.2 工业结构转型升级轨迹达标程度的全球概况

同前面一样，我们将工业结构转型升级偏离标杆程度的绝对值转化为达标程度指数的相对值。按此，可以得到工业化达标程度指数的测算结果。以中国为例，中国的工业化达标程度先是逐步提高，然后下降，1971年达标指数只有78.02%，1985年达标指数提高到92.89%，在20世纪90年代都维持在90%以上，但是在2008年全球金融危机之后达标指数下降到86.91%。80年代和90年代是中国工业化最为迅速的时期。非洲等经济体工业化达标指数整体上都比较低，难以启动工业化，即便是南非这样有大量白人移民的经济体在实现了一定程度的工业化之后也未能进行持续的工业化，南非1970年的工业化达标指数为73%，其后不断提高，1981年达到97%，然而在90年代至今其工业化达标指数长期低于80%。拉美的工业化达标指数与其中等收入陷阱相呼应，工业化水平长期徘徊。例如，阿根廷在20世纪70年代工业化达标指数就超过90%，然而其后的80年代和90年代工业化达标指数下滑到70% ~ 80%。

## 5.4

## 经济结构转型升级路径对最佳实践标杆的达标情况：服务业

### 5.4.1 服务业结构转型升级轨迹偏离标杆程度的全球概况

与非农产业和工业的转型升级检测一样，我们依然用实际的服务业结构转型升级轨迹与拟合的发展典范的服务业转型升级轨迹之间的偏离来监测每个经济体的服务业转型升级轨迹偏离程度：

$$\text{Deviation}_{it} = I_{it} - I_{it}^{\text{NSE}} = f\left(E_{it}\right) - f^{\text{NSE}}\left(E_{it}\right) \tag{5.5}$$

如果$\text{Deviation}_{it} > 0$，那么表明服务业升级过于先进，如图1.26中最优轨迹的上面部分；如果$\text{Deviation}_{it} < 0$，那么表明服务业升级过于落后，如图1.26中最优轨迹的下面部分。

与前面一致，我们仍旧选取发展典范的对数拟合标杆进行计算：

$$I_{it}^{\text{NSE}} = f^{B}\left(E_{it}\right) = 0.897\ 196\ 9 + 0.106\ 003\ 2 \times \ln\left(E_{it}\right) \tag{5.6}$$

图5.5是全球样本的服务业转型升级偏离程度分布的核密度图，大致接近一个均值在0.15左右的正态分布，并表现出明显的左侧长尾。这表明，相对于服务业最佳结构变迁路径而言，相当一部分服务业结构变迁路径的观测值对标杆有所偏离，且主要是服务业占比过高导致的结构变迁路径向上偏离，同时也有少数观测值的服务业发展占比过低导致服务业结构变迁路径向下偏离，图5.6所示的是实际服务业升级与标杆的散点图。

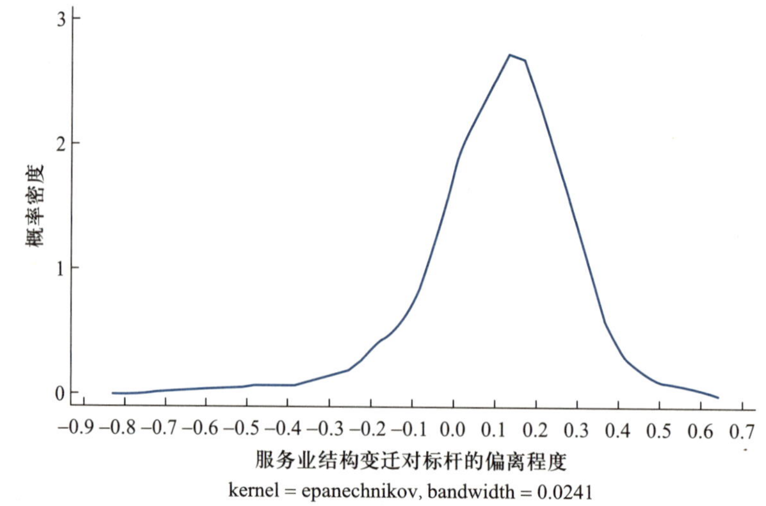


图5.5 世界180个经济体1970—2011年的服务业结构变迁路径对标杆的偏离程度分布的核密度

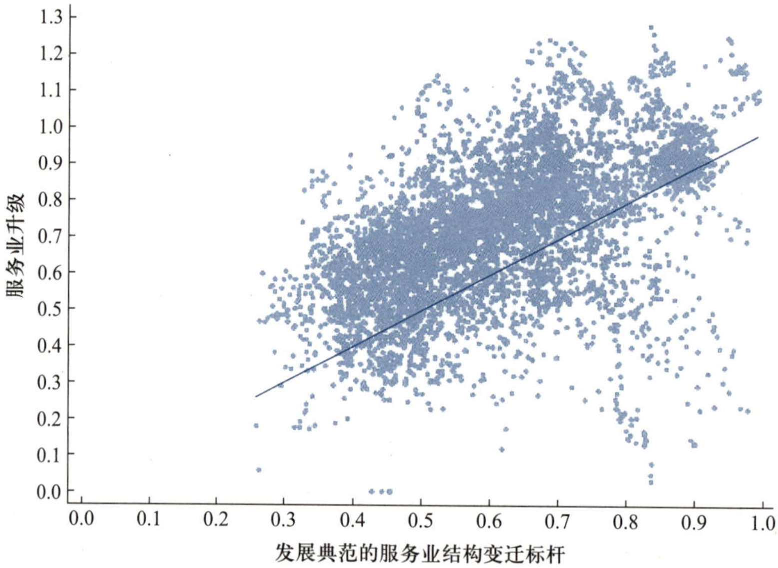


图5.6 世界180个经济体1970—2011年的服务业升级与对应标杆的散点图

### 5.4.2 服务业结构转型升级轨迹达标程度的全球概况

同前面一样，我们将服务业结构转型升级偏离标杆程度的绝对值转化为达标程度指数的相对值。据此，可以得到服务业达标程度指数的测算结果。以中国为例，中国的这个指标在1990年、2000年相对较高，说明服务业结构变迁达标程度较高。

## 5.5

## —

## 世界经济结构转型升级趋势在不断好转

回顾我们在第2章的讨论，主流的新古典增长理论有一个标准的收敛预测：初始收入水平越低，其后的经济增长就越快。然而，标准新古典总量生产函数预言的经济体总量层面的收敛在全球各个经济体之间的经验数据上是缺乏的。这也是建立在标准新古典总量生产函数基础上的新古典增长理论遭受质疑的原因。绝对收敛的缺失催生了条件收敛的概念，指的是诸如OECD国家以及一个经济体内部相对同质的地区之间出现的收敛。在现有文献中，条件收敛的“条件”相当含糊，泛指经济体之间存在异质性而不具有相同的稳态位置。而在新结构经济学中，这里的条件明确指的是产业结构转型升级。如果能够成功地实现持续的产业结构转型升级，那么，当收入水平逐渐向发达国家逼近，技术创新和产业升级越来越依靠于自主创新时，会出现罗德里克整理的跨国经验证据所显示的在制造业行业层面存在绝对收敛，如第2章的图2.23到图2.25所示。同时，总体的经济总量增长率也会出现向发达国家的增长率收敛，否则就不会出现收敛。[①]

按照经济结构转型升级达标指数所代表的新结构经济学之路，只要提高每个经济体转型升级的达标程度就会成功实现经济结构转型升级，促进经济增长收敛。令人欣慰的是，在经历了战后第一波结构主义发展思潮失败的教训之后，20世纪70—80年代，世界上诸多发展中国家进行了经济结构调整，将战后那些不切实际的赶超战略所扭曲的经济结构向符合比较优势的结构转型升级之路调整，因此出现了图5.7所示的世界非农产业结构转型升级达标指数的平均值大幅上升。然而，20世纪80—90年代由于受到第二波新自由主义“华盛顿共识”的误导，诸多发展中经济体未能发挥政府因势利导的作用，支持符合比较优势产业的不断出现，实现持续的经济结构转型升级，因此又出现了图5.7中世界非农产业结构转型升级达标指数的平均值徘徊不前，直到如专栏4.1所介绍的由于东亚奇迹和中国奇迹以及第二次世界大战后发展典范的成功，迫使包括世界银行在内的发展机构和各国政府不断反思主流的发展

① 林毅夫、付才辉，《新结构经济学导论》，高等教育出版社，2019年版，第4章。

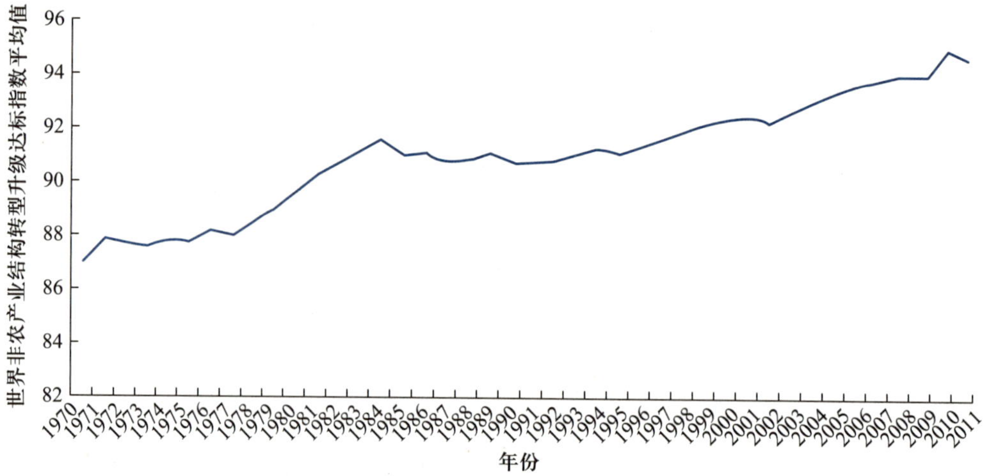


图 5.7 世界非农产业结构转型升级达标指数的平均值

思潮的合理性。得益于这种反思和东亚奇迹的示范效应，世界经济结构转型升级达标指数的平均值又不断得到提高。

## 5.6 —— 评价世界经济结构转型升级的效果

如我们反复强调的，经济发展的本质是人均收入的不断增加，其前提则是越来越高的劳动生产率水平。劳动生产率水平的提高有两个途径：一是通过技术创新，提高现有产业中产品的质量和生产效率；二是通过产业升级，将现有劳动力、土地、资本等生产要素配置到附加价值更高的产业，即转型升级（技术进步与产业升级）。自发展经济学诞生之日起，经济发展理论和政策都致力于推动落后经济体的产业结构升级，但是不同发展思潮的思路却极为不同。主流的发展经济学以发达国家为参照系，来看发展中国家缺什么（如第一代发展经济学——结构主义，强调发展和发达国家同样的现代化资本、技术密集产业），或发展中国家做得不好的地方（如第二代发展经济学——“华盛顿共识”，强调私有化、市场化、自由化，建立和发达国家同样的完善市场经济体系），并以此作为改造发展中国家的依据。第二次世界大战后，大多数遵循这些主流发展思潮的经济体都没能成功转型升级，但是有少数经济体并未按照主流发展思潮发展经济却取得了成功，如前述发展典范。

如果一个理论不能解释该理论所要解释的现象，或是根据该理论所做的选择、决策不能达到预期的目标，就应该进行反思，提出既能够解释现象，也能帮助政府、企业和个人进行决策，以达到预期目标的新理论。在这样的背景下，林毅夫提出新结构经济学，其主张应该看发展中国家现在有什么（即其要素禀赋），以及以此为基础能做好什么（即其比较优势），发展政策的目标是把现在能做好的做大做强，以此加速资本积累，提升要素禀赋结构、比较优势、产业结构，来实现逐步赶上和超越发达国家的目标。按照新结构经济学的基本原理，首先，在任意时点，给定的禀赋结构确定了比较优势，进而决定了最优的产业结构；其次，按照比较优势进行的产业升级将使经济剩余最大，进而禀赋结构升级最快；最后，禀赋结构升级之后，最优的产业结构也须升级。因此，我们想重申的是“比较优势遵循型方法在本质上是动态的……这意味着一个国家的经济发展也该务实地利用现有的、嵌入在一国的比较优势领域中的机会，当那些领域的比较优势被充分利用后，同时也要认识到产业升级的潜力”①。“遵循比较优势的发展方法对于贫穷国家的经济发展而言看起来或许是缓慢而令人沮丧的，但事实上，这种办法却是积累资本和提升要素禀赋结构的最快方法；并且，只要能得到更为发达的国家已经开发出来且依然存在于这些国家的技术，并进入这类产业，其产业结构升级速度还可加快。”②这一部分我们继续在前一部分基础上，估计经济结构转型升级的发展战略达标程度对经济结构转型升级本身的影响，以便对新结构经济学主张的发展方法有一个初步的定量认识。

---

① 林毅夫,《新结构经济学：反思经济发展与政策的理论框架》，北京大学出版社，2012年版，第129页。

② 同上，第23页。

### 5.6.1 经济结构转型升级达标程度绩效的评估模型 I 及其结果

我们建立如下的简单方程组（5.7）来简要估计发展战略达标程度对结构变迁的影响。如第3章所概括的经济结构转型升级的分析框架，禀赋升级（Endup）和产业升级（Indup）是经济结构转型升级的两个基本维度，因此需要如下方程组来捕获经济结构转型升级的发展战略达标程度（I）对经济结构转型升级本身的影响：

$$\begin{cases} \ln \text{Endup} = \alpha_0 + \alpha_1 \ln \text{I} + \varepsilon \\ \ln \text{Indup} = \beta_0 + \beta_2 \ln \text{I} + \nu \end{cases} \quad (5.7)$$

其中，$\varepsilon$与$\nu$是随机干扰项。弹性系数$\alpha_1$与$\beta_2$分别刻画了结构变迁达标程度（I）对禀赋升级和产业升级的影响。由于禀赋升级和产业升级也可能受到其他一些共同随机因素的影响，因此两个随机干扰项可能相关，所以我们采取方程组似不相关（SUR）进行估计。

表5.1是全球样本的估计结果，禀赋升级与产业升级对经济结构转型升级路径达标程度的弹性大约分别为5和1.4。表5.2是在发展早期阶段（人均收入水平低于美国的20%的阶段）的估计结果，禀赋升级与产业升级对经济结构转型升级的发展战略达标程度的弹性大约分别为3和1.2。这些简单估计结果是非常有弹性的，经济结构转型升级的新结构经济学之路对成功转型升级的重要性不言自明：越是按照新结构经济学主张的,在每个阶段都按照该阶段的禀赋结构所决定的比较优势发展其产业，产业升级速度就越快，反过来促进禀赋升级也就越快，如此积小胜为大胜的转型升级方法是成功转型升级的根本保证，如图5.8和图5.9所示。

表5.1 经济结构转型升级路径达标程度对经济结构转型升级影响的SUR回归结果：全球样本

| | （1）<br>ln Endup | （2）<br>ln Endup | （3）<br>ln Endup | （4）<br>ln Endup |
|---|---|---|---|---|
| ln uptst | 4.849*** | 5.147*** | 4.783*** | 5.077*** |
| | （36.95） | （39.12） | （36.67） | （38.81） |
| 年份 | | YES | | YES |
| 国别 | | | YES | YES |
| _cons | −24.39*** | 13.62*** | −23.80*** | 13.46*** |
| | （−41.21） | （4.46） | （−40.31） | （4.44） |
| *R*-sq | 0.192 0 | 0.214 1 | 0.204 4 | 0.225 6 |
| Chi2 | 1 364.98 | 1 564.43 | 1 475.04 | 1 672.69 |
| | ln Indup | ln Indup | ln Indup | ln Indup |
| ln uptst | 1.396*** | 1.394*** | 1.392*** | 1.389*** |
| | （119.95） | （117.81） | （119.91） | （117.71） |
| 年份 | | YES | | YES |
| 国别 | | | YES | YES |

续表

| | (1)<br>ln Endup | (2)<br>ln Endup | (3)<br>ln Endup | (4)<br>ln Endup |
|---|---|---|---|---|
| _cons | −6.492*** | −6.852*** | −6.454*** | −6.863*** |
| | (−123.68) | (−24.98) | (−122.79) | (−25.13) |
| $R$-sq | 0.714 7 | 0.714 8 | 0.717 1 | 0.717 2 |
| Chi2 | 14 388.15 | 14 394.40 | 14 558.24 | 14 566.47 |
| $N$ | 5 743 | 5 743 | 5 743 | 5 743 |

注：括号中是$t$统计量，$^*p < 0.05$，$^{**}p < 0.01$，$^{***}p < 0.001$。

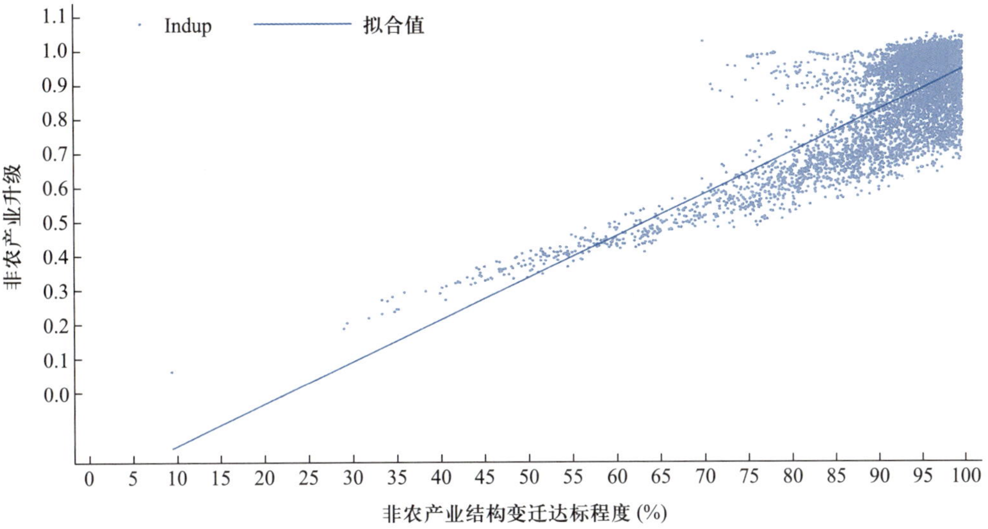


图5.8 经济结构转型升级路径的达标程度与产业结构升级的散点图：全球样本

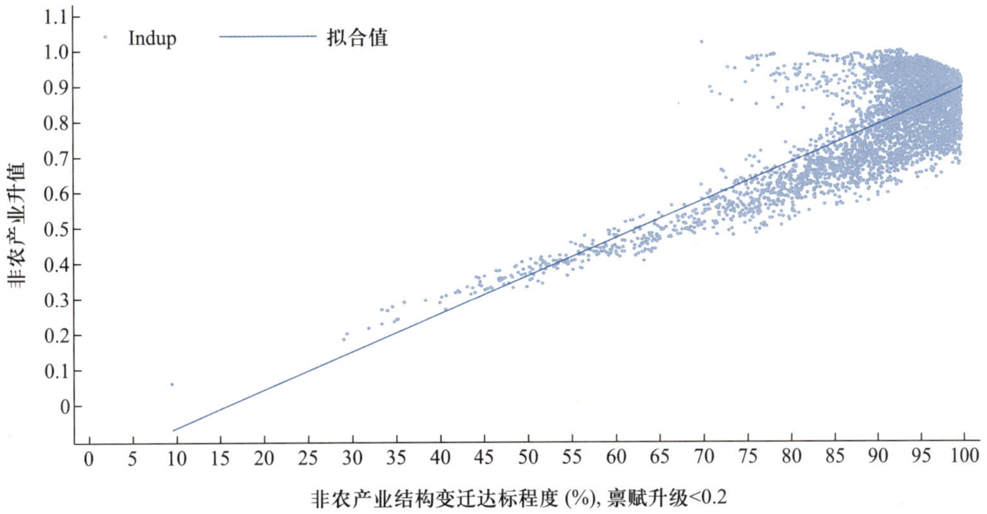


图5.9 经济结构转型升级路径的达标程度与产业结构升级的散点图：低收入阶段的样本

表 5.2 经济结构转型升级路径达标程度对经济结构转型升级影响的SUR回归结果：发展早期阶段的样本

| | (1)<br>ln Endup | (2)<br>ln Endup | (3)<br>ln Endup | (4)<br>ln Endup |
|---|---|---|---|---|
| ln uptst | 2.782*** | 3.066*** | 2.777*** | 3.060*** |
| | (29.86) | (32.99) | (29.82) | (32.95) |
| 年份 | | YES | | YES |
| 国别 | | | YES | YES |
| _cons | −15.74*** | 19.25*** | −15.64*** | 19.23*** |
| | (−37.65) | (7.92) | (−37.33) | (7.92) |
| $R$-sq | 0.176 5 | 0.216 7 | 0.178 1 | 0.218 0 |
| Chi2 | 891.60 | 1 150.86 | 901.44 | 1 159.95 |
| | ln Indup | ln Indup | ln Indup | ln Indup |
| ln uptst | 1.281*** | 1.268*** | 1.280*** | 1.267*** |
| | (104.88) | (101.84) | (104.92) | (101.87) |
| 年份 | | YES | | YES |
| 国别 | | | YES | YES |
| _cons | −6.009*** | −7.548*** | −5.995*** | −7.552*** |
| | (−109.66) | (−23.19) | (−109.18) | (−23.23) |
| $R$-sq | 0.725 6 | 0.727 1 | 0.726 3 | 0.727 8 |
| Chi2 | 10 998.78 | 11 082.60 | 11 038.00 | 11 124.30 |
| $N$ | 4 160 | 4 160 | 4 160 | 4 160 |

注：括号中是$t$统计量，$^{*}p < 0.05$，$^{**}p < 0.01$，$^{***}p < 0.001$。

## 5.6.2 经济结构转型升级达标程度绩效的评估模型II及其结果

前面的评估方法采纳的是似不相关对数线性方程组估算方法，然而经济结构转型升级的轨迹一般是高度非线性的，下面我们进一步采用非线性方程组（FGNLS）的估算方法来评价评估结果的稳健性。我们设定如下非线性方程组模型来评估经济结构转型升级的发展战略路径达标程度对经济结构转型升级影响的稳健性：

$$\begin{cases} \text{Endup} = \alpha_0 + \alpha_1 \text{I}^{\chi} + \varepsilon \\ \text{Indup} = \beta_0 + \beta_1 \text{I}^{\phi} + \nu \end{cases} \tag{5.8}$$

其中，$\varepsilon$与$\nu$是随机干扰项，参数$\chi$与$\phi$分别对应于模型（5.7）中的弹性系数$\alpha_1$与$\beta_1$，分别刻画了结构变迁路径达标程度（I）对禀赋升级和产业升级的敏感性响应（弹性）。表5.3是全球样本的FGNLS估计结果，参数$\chi$与$\phi$的估计值分别为5.86和1.57，比较接近模型（5.7）的弹性系数$\alpha_3$与$\beta_3$的SUR估计值5和1.4。表5.4是发展早期阶段的估计结果，对应的估计值为9和1.2。结论整体上是稳健的，也就是经济结构转型升级的发展路径达标程度越高的国家，要素禀赋结构和经济结构转型升级的速度越高。

表5.3 经济结构转型升级的达标程度对经济结构转型升级影响的FGNLS估计：全球样本

| | Coef. | Std.Err. | $z$ | $P>\|z\|$ | [95%Conf.Interval] | | $R$−sq | Obs |
|---|---|---|---|---|---|---|---|---|
| $\alpha_0$ | −0.023 054 6 | 0.022 077 8 | −1.04 | 0.296 | −0.066 326 2 | 0.020 217 1 | | |
| $q$ | 0.364 852 8 | 0.021 157 4 | 17.24 | 0.000 | 0.323 385 0 | 0.406 320 6 | | |
| $\chi$ | 5.864 348 0 | 0.750 924 9 | 7.81 | 0.000 | 4.392 562 0 | 7.336 133 0 | | |
| Endup（Endowment Upgrading） | | | | | | | 0.076 2 | 5 743 |
| $\beta_0$ | 0.052 839 3 | 0.032 823 1 | 1.61 | 0.107 | −0.011 492 8 | 0.117 171 4 | | |
| $\beta_1$ | 0.899 712 | 0.031 923 7 | 28.18 | 0.000 | 0.837 142 7 | 0.962 281 2 | | |
| $\phi$ | 1.572 106 0 | 0.084 195 5 | 18.67 | 0.000 | 1.407 086 0 | 1.737 126 0 | | |
| Indup（Industry Upgrading） | | | | | | | 0.617 5 | 5 743 |

表5.4 经济结构转型升级的达标程度对结构转型升级影响的FGNLS估计：
发展早期阶段（Endup < 0.2）

| | Coef. | Std.Err. | $z$ | $P>\|z\|$ | [95%Conf.Interval] | | $R$−sq | Obs |
|---|---|---|---|---|---|---|---|---|
| $\alpha_0$ | 0.018 400 5 | 0.002 287 1 | 8.05 | 0.000 | 0.013 917 8 | 0.022 883 2 | | |
| $\alpha_1$ | 0.080 678 5 | 0.002 577 5 | 31.30 | 0.000 | 0.075 626 7 | 0.085 730 3 | | |
| $\chi$ | 9.044 064 0 | 0.629 312 1 | 14.37 | 0.000 | 7.810 635 0 | 10.277 490 0 | | |
| Endup（Endowment Upgrading） | | | | | | | 0.177 5 | 4 160 |
| $\beta_0$ | −0.043 283 8 | 0.045 600 5 | −0.95 | 0.343 | −0.132 659 2 | 0.046 091 6 | | |
| $\beta_1$ | 0.942 484 3 | 0.044 500 6 | 21.18 | 0.000 | 0.855 264 7 | 1.029 704 0 | | |
| $\phi$ | 1.188 212 0 | 0.081 032 4 | 14.66 | 0.000 | 1.029 391 0 | 1.347 032 0 | | |
| Indup（Industry Upgrading） | | | | | | | 0.610 1 | 4 160 |

## 5.7

## 遵循比较优势进行持续的经济结构转型升级是经济发展成功的保证

总之，不论是第3章我们对世界每个经济体的经济结构转型升级的轨迹的测算，还是对陷入中等收入陷阱的拉美经济体以及二战后发展典范的经济结构转型升级轨迹的测评，都有一个共同的结论：但凡产业结构变迁在每一个阶段都遵循要素禀赋结构所决定的比较优势，循序渐进拾级而上的经济体大都能够成功实现经济结构转型升级，推动经济发展；而那些产业变迁违背比较优势，打乱产业升级次序的经济体，则难以实现持续的经济结构转型升级。当然，经济结构转型升级是一个不断持续的动态过程，过去符合比较优势的产业随着禀赋结构的升级，也会失去比较优势，需要进行产业升级以适应新的禀赋结构和比较优势的变化。这种经济结构转型升级持续保持比较优势的动态能力是非常关键的，也是非常难的，很少有经济体在每时每刻都按照比较优势进行经济结构转型升级。对于这一点，发展经济学家拉尼斯对东亚奇迹（大都是发展典范中的样本）的总结极具启发性："关键的和具有说服力的一点是决策者持久的可塑性，在过去40年，决策者总能够在每一个可以识别的增长转型的阶段对经济正在变化的需求做出相应的政策改变。由于这个可塑性，整个系统得以避免失去动力并能够在每一个阶段的末尾重新驶入轨道……每个十年有每个十年的挑战，每十年政府都能够做出政策的转变，用库兹涅茨的话来说，这些政策改变是为了适应而不是梗阻私人经济所要求的变化。"[①] 如图5.10和图5.11所示，在20世纪七八十年代，中国和韩国的经济结构转型升级当中非农产业升级的达标程度（Indup1）和工业升级的达标程度（Indup2）得到大幅度提高，经济结构转型升级不断向符合比较优势的轨道靠拢，然而有待改进的则是服务业升级的达标程度（Indup3）。韩国是1960年代以来经济发展最成功的国家，中国则是1980年代以来经济转型最成功的国家，从韩国和中国这两个国家

---

① Gustav Rains, "Another Look at the East Asian Miracle", *The World Bank Economic Review*, 1995, Vol.9, No.3, pp.509–565.

的经验来说，一个发展中国家在经济发展和转型的过程中，非农产业转型升级和工业转型升级的达标比服务业的达标更加关键。

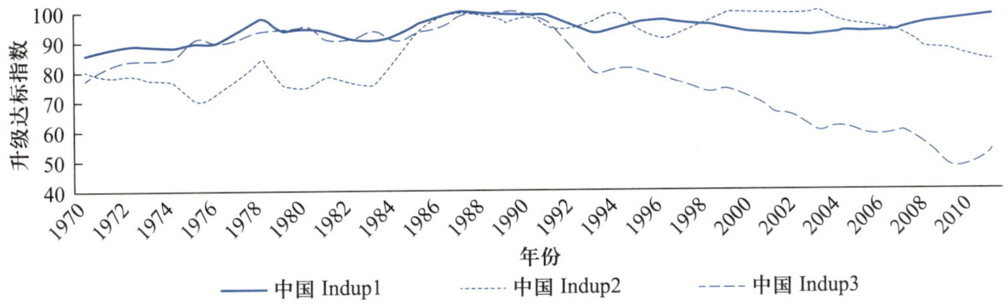


**图 5.10 中国经济结构转型升级路径的达标程度变化**

注：Indup1 表示非农产业升级达标指数；Indup2 表示工业升级达标指数；Indup3 表示服务业升级达标指数。

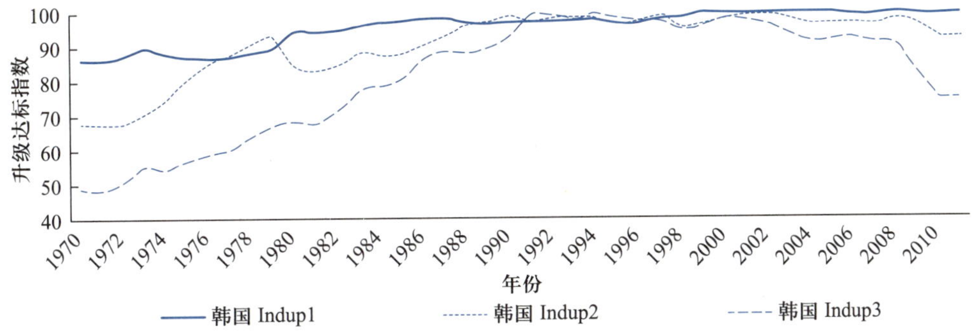


**图 5.11 韩国经济结构转型升级路径的达标程度变化**

注：Indup1 表示非农产业升级达标指数；Indup2 表示工业升级达标指数；Indup3 表示服务业升级达标指数。

# 5.8

# 违背比较优势的经济结构转型升级是导致发展陷阱的根源①

## 5.8.1 乡村原始工业化缺失与低收入陷阱

大多数非洲国家，尤其是撒哈拉以南的非洲国家经济增长缓慢，被困在贫困陷阱中。战后，非洲国家工业水平极端落后，靠出口农产品、矿物等初级产品换取外汇，进口外国工业品来维持经济生产和人民生活。为了摆脱殖民贸易型经济，许多非洲国家采取了结构主义的“进口替代”的工业化政策，企图“一步到位”地建立资本密集的大规模制造业，以本国生产的商品替代进口商品。然而，许多非洲国家的这一努力被昂贵的资本成本和国家高额的交通成本、较小的市场规模、有限的技能和工业技术所限制。由于经济发展不理想，20世纪90年代以来，在“华盛顿共识”的指导下，许多非洲国家进行结构性的政策调整，不断淡化国家在经济发展中所扮演的角色，推行新自由主义的经济和贸易自由化政策。在这一政策下，进口商品的关税被削减，更便宜的进口商品涌入国内市场，使现存的本土中小企业受到了进一步冲击。因为无法与外国商品竞争，许多公司被迫关门，国有公司被迫私有化。因此，即使众多的国际多边发展机构对非洲的大量援助并没有产生明显效果。按照产业结构转型升级的阶梯顺序，初级工业化的缺失是陷入低收入陷阱的根源。

因此我们看到，进口替代政策的“大推进”理论和“华盛顿共识”推崇的自由化，都没能帮助非洲国家逃脱贫困陷阱，反而使它们误入迷途、陷入困境。长期以来，撒哈拉以南的非洲国家或依赖矿产资源发展单一制造业，或试图在进口替代下建立大工业，或尝试推行自由化，或者依靠国外的人道主义援助。然而，这些非洲国家却没能充分调动本国广大的草根阶层，利用在低收入阶段廉价劳动力的比较优势，在政府的因势引导下，引进现代技术，发展能够进入国际大市场的现代化轻工业产品，无法实现从农业和资源产业向现代化制造业的

① 这一节的总结以及相关数据资料均转引自：王丽莉、文一，“中国能跨越中等收入陷阱吗？——基于工业化路径的跨国比较”，《经济评论》，2017年第3期。

转型，长期陷入贫困陷阱，这与私有产权和知识产权保护无关，而与政府是否发挥因势利导以克服结构转型的瓶颈限制有关。[1]图5.12到图5.14所示的是埃塞俄比亚、尼日利亚、卢旺达3个非洲经济体的例子，它们在经济结构转型升级上的达标程度整体上长期都很低。

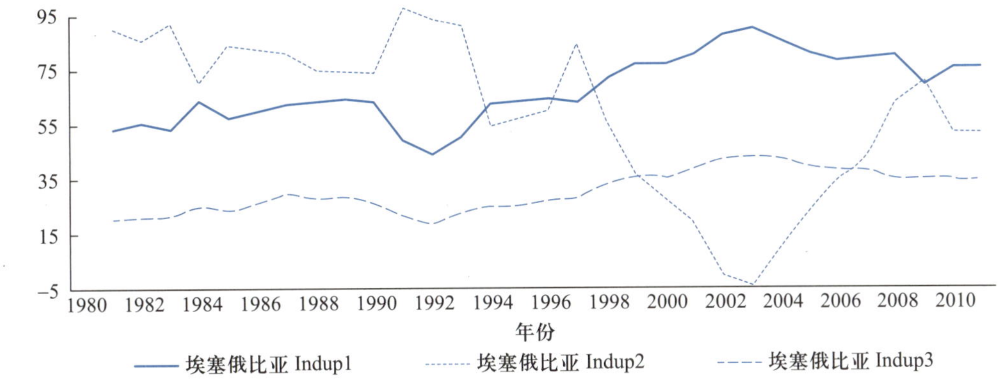


**图5.12 埃塞俄比亚经济结构转型升级路径的达标程度变化**

注：Indup1表示非农产业升级达标指数；Indup2表示工业升级达标指数；Indup3表示服务业升级达标指数。

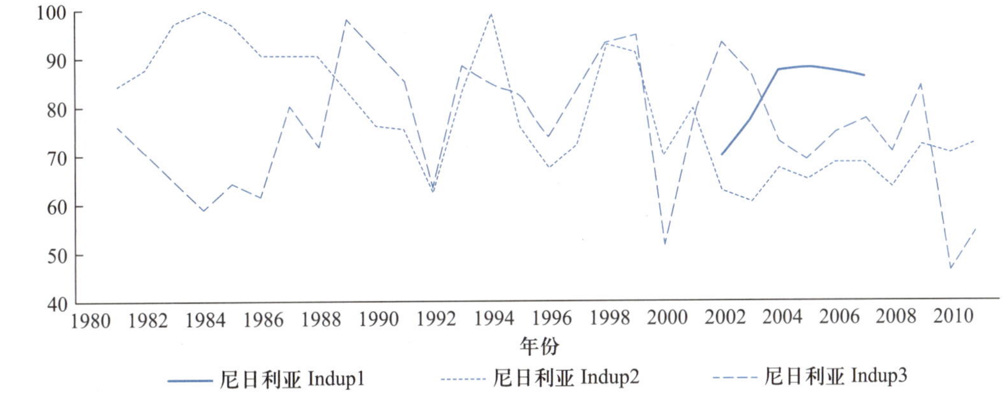


**图5.13 尼日利亚经济结构转型升级路径的达标程度变化**

注：Indup1表示非农产业升级达标指数；Indup2表示工业升级达标指数；Indup3表示服务业升级达标指数。

---

① Wen Yi and George Fortier, "The Visible Hand: The Role of Governmentin China's Long-Awaited Industrial Revolution"（"看得见的手：政府在命运多舛的中国工业革命中所起的作用"），美国联邦储备银行（圣路易斯分行）内部刊物《经济评论》，2016年第3卷第98期，第189–226页。

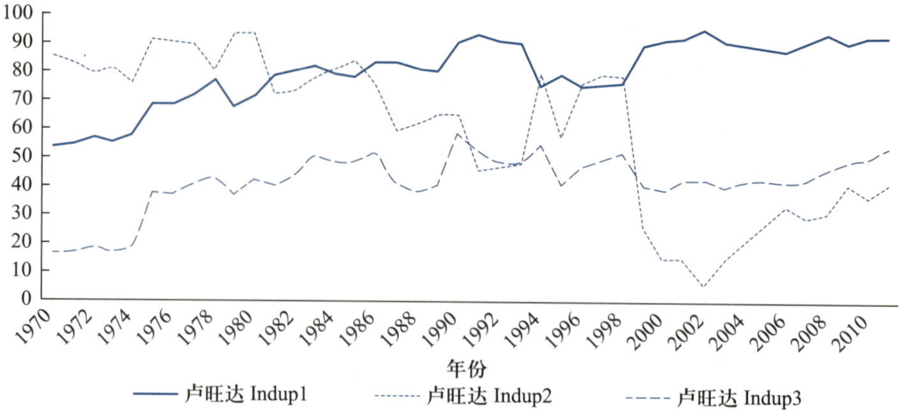


**图5.14 卢旺达经济结构转型升级路径的达标程度变化**

注：Indup1表示非农产业升级达标指数；Indup2表示工业升级达标指数；Indup3表示服务业升级达标指数。

## 5.8.2 违背比较优势的产业升级与中等收入陷阱

结构主义的代表人物之一哈佛大学的经济史学家格申克龙通过对德国、俄国等在19世纪经济发展的特殊经验进行比较分析，提出在落后国家动用国家银行向资本密集型生产方式跳跃的发展理论。由此衍生出的进口替代政策和“大推进”理论，令许多发展中国家陷入困境。尤其在二战后一些拉丁美洲国家和亚洲国家采取全面进口替代政策，封闭和限制自己产品的世界市场，由国内生产取代消费品尤其是重化工业品进口。虽然日用消费品的进口替代战略相对合理（因为这类产业属于劳动密集型，投资少，技术设备简单，符合当地比较优势，资本回收快），但也需要依靠国际大市场，才能使得比较优势充分发挥。而拉丁美洲的进口替代战略同时把国际市场封闭了，使得消费品生产的扩张受限于国内市场的规模。相对而言，在20世纪50年代末，韩国、中国台湾等亚洲经济体开始转向出口导向型战略，利用国际市场对廉价生活消费品旺盛的需求发展符合当地比较优势的劳动力密集型轻工业。这一出口导向的进口替代战略不仅大大扩大了市场，同时通过激烈的国际竞争训练了企业组织和管理，刺激了技术更新。同时，大多数拉丁美洲国家还采取了对耐用消费品、中间产品、机器设备等资本密集产品的进口替代，而这些产品不仅违反比较优势，而且需要的市场规模更大，资金和技术门槛更高。由此，在劳动力密集型轻工业没有得到充分发展，资本积累不够，比较优势没有发生根本性变化的情况下，拉丁美洲国家过早进入重工业化阶段。

过早开始重工业化不符合经济发展的内在规律。重工业往往需要巨大的固定资产投资，因而只有大规模生产才能降低成本、有利可图。然而，在工业化初期，有限的资本积累造成资本短缺，价格高，不足以支持在没有政府的保护补贴下对重工业的投资，而在政府保护补贴下的重工业的产品无法在国际市场上竞争，因此，也无法实现规模化生产。重工业产品比轻工业品更加需要国际大市场的支撑才能够达到规模和盈利，而这对产品质量和技术竞争能力的要求十分苛刻，这种竞争能力对于连轻工业都没有做好的拉丁美洲国家来说是不可能具备的，所以拉丁美洲国家的进口替代发展战略必败无疑。

按照前面类似的禀赋水平与产业级别两个维度，王丽莉和文一对比分析了拉丁美洲国家和"亚洲四小龙"的产业升级路径。[①]数据显示，1963—1969年韩国出口导向型劳动力密集型制造业的年均就业增长率高达11.7%。相反，在20世纪60年代继续实行内向型进口替代战略的拉丁美洲国家，就业几乎没有增长，但资本产出比大大提高。1960—1969年，中国台湾与韩国的平均资本产出比为1.7，而危地马拉、厄瓜多尔、巴拉圭的资本产出比达到3，玻利维亚、哥伦比亚、秘鲁的资本产出比达到3.5。1962—1970年，韩国制造品总出口额的年均增长率高达67%，非耐用消费品出口额的年均增长率高达75.7%。相比之下，在这一进口替代的黄金时期，拉丁美洲国家的出口增长远远低于轻工业品出口导向的韩国。其中，表现比较好的墨西哥在1962—1970年制造品总出口的年均增长率为11.8%，但非耐用消费品出口的年均增长率仅有5.8%。智利是所有拉丁美洲国家中表现得最为出色的国家，1962—1971年其制造品出口的年均增长率为13%，非耐用消费品的年均增长率为18%，不过这个出色表现与韩国和中国台湾也没法相提并论。

图5.15展示了重工业增加值份额的跨国比较。工业分行业增加值资料来源于CEPII数据库，人均实际GDP数据来自PWT9.0。我们以韩国为基准，比较各国的重工业份额。其中，重工业包含金属及金属制品业、机器制造业、交通设备制造业与石油化工业。1970—1990年，由于有了雄厚的轻工业基础，韩国现价重工业增加值在全部制造业中的份额由28%上升到47.9%。与之相比，在相同收入条件下，不重视轻工业出口的众多拉丁美洲国家与东欧国家的重工业增加值份额，则比相同收入水平的韩国高5%以上。其中，巴西（1963年、1990年）、厄瓜多尔（1990年）、玻利维亚（1980年）、墨西哥（1989年）、委内瑞拉（1980年）、阿根廷（1985年）、保加利亚（1997年）、波兰（1981年）、波黑（1991年）、土耳其（1981年）与阿塞拜疆（2001年）的重工业增加值份额比相同收入水平的韩国高10%以上；阿塞拜疆（2005年）、埃及（1991年）、委内瑞拉（1980年）、厄瓜多尔（1994年）、秘鲁（1985年）与玻利维亚（1988年）的重工业增加值份额比相同收入水平的韩国高20%左右。

与前面对经济结构转型升级绩效评估成果一样，王丽莉和文一也认为中等收入陷阱还可

---

① 王丽莉、文一，"中国能跨越中等收入陷阱吗？——基于工业化路径的跨国比较"，《经济评论》，2017年第3期。

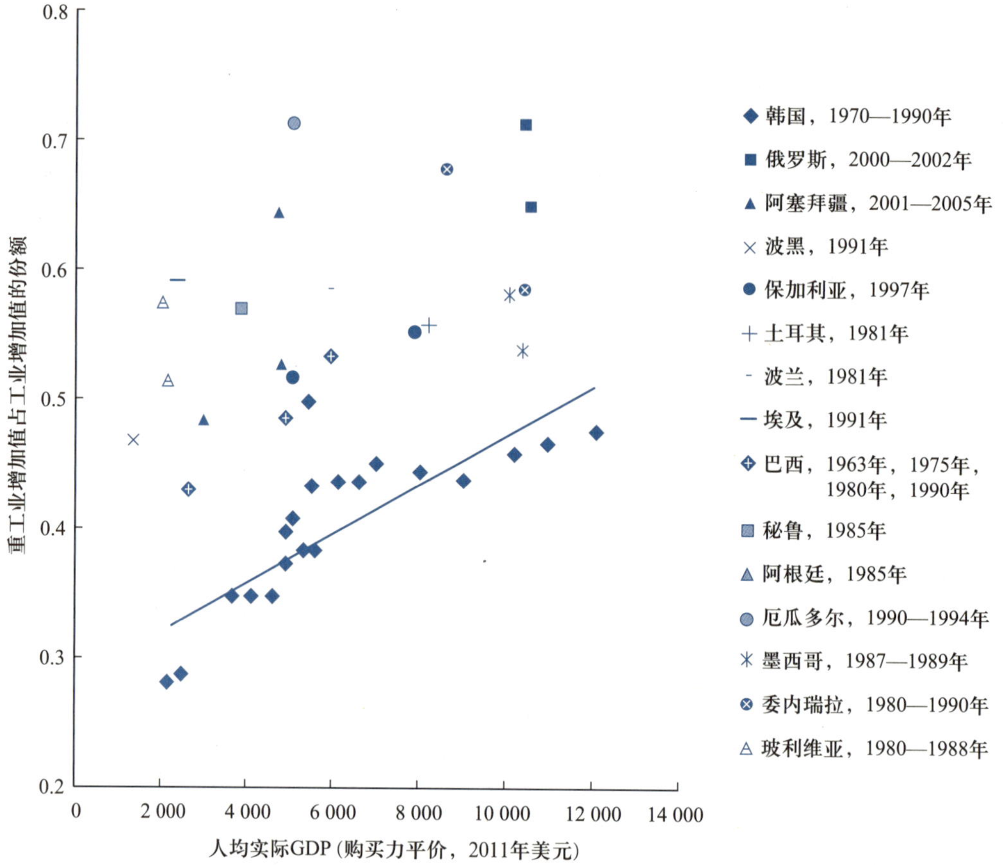


**图5.15 重工业增加值份额的跨国比较**

资料来源：王丽莉、文一，“中国能跨越中等收入陷阱吗？——基于工业化路径的跨国比较”，《经济评论》，2017年第3期。

以从产业升级速度与收入增长速度的关系来刻画。[①]过快的产业升级速度往往欲速则不达，导致收入增长速度放缓甚至绝对下降，这反过来又使得产业升级难以为继，出现倒退，造成一个恶性循环，为社会不稳和政治混乱埋下隐患。对于成功按照循序渐进方式实现产业升级的国家来说，它们的相对收入比（即相对于美国收入的收敛速度）应该是相对产业升级速度的增函数，即随着产业升级（主要是制造业）比率的提高，相对收入也提高，而且可能提高得更快，具有规模递增效应。根据王丽莉和文一的测算，如果相对收入比值超过0.7，表明成功跨越中等收入陷阱，进入发达国家行列。相反，对于产业升级失败的国家，这个单调上升的函数关系并不存在，相对收入比值停留在0.5以下，表明跌入中等收入陷阱，无法向发达国家收敛。

① 王丽莉、文一，“中国能跨越中等收入陷阱吗？——基于工业化路径的跨国比较”，《经济评论》，2017年第3期。王丽莉和文一的测算数据年份与《世界经济结构转型升级报告》的主要测算样本数据有细微的差别，但整体上基本一致。对于这里介绍的例子可参考第3章的测算。

我们可以回顾一下第4章所介绍的发展典范中的韩国、中国台湾和中国大陆的产业升级动力学。这三个经济体都在持续动态的产业升级过程中创造了持续的经济增长和追赶。例如，从1953年到2010年，韩国的相对非农就业份额从0.4（美国的40%）上升到0.98（美国的98%），代表了产业升级的速度。同时，韩国的相对人均实际收入由0.1（美国的10%）上升到0.72（美国的72%），说明产业升级带来了收入的持续稳定和急剧的增长。类似的，中国台湾在二战后的产业升级过程中也把相对收入从美国的10%左右提高到了70%以上，因此经济增长相对于产业升级的曲线呈现往上翘的弧形，而且十分平滑。中国大陆的表现在改革开放以前（1950—1980年）与韩国和中国台湾不同，相对收入没有随产业升级的提高而提高，一直停留在0.05（美国的5%）的水平，而且产业升级比值也来回摇摆。但是改革开放以后冲破了贫困陷阱，收入比值开始扶摇直上；当非农产业比值从美国的60%上升到90%左右时，相对收入也从美国的6%上升到美国的26%，顺利进入中等收入国家行列。中国大陆在整个20世纪50—80年代的表现是个例外：产业升级没有带来收入的增长和收敛，因为忽视了乡村原始工业化而直接投入重工业建设。但是在改革开放以后，这一现象迅速改观：循序渐进的产业升级直接带来了爆发式的收入增长和向发达国家的收敛，目前还未成为高收入国家。与韩国和中国台湾比较，当它们在横轴取值为90%左右时（即70年代末或80年代初），纵轴取值均为25%左右，与目前的中国大陆十分接近。因此可以预料，未来20 ~ 30年，如果中国大陆把非农产业相对于美国的比值提高到韩国与中国台湾目前的程度，即从90%上升到98%甚至更高（超过100%也是可以的），那么中国大陆的人均相对收入也可以从目前美国的25%左右提高到美国的70%左右，因为韩国和中国台湾达到这个水平也用了30年。与之相反，阿根廷、巴西、智利、秘鲁、哥伦比亚和委内瑞拉这些拉丁美洲国家，不仅没能持续地推进本国的产业升级，而且产业升级也没有带来相应的收入增长和向发达国家的收敛，因而陷入中等收入陷阱，经济发展长期徘徊不前，处于一种杂乱无章的混沌状态。这种拉美式产业升级与国民经济收入函数，是对中等收入陷阱的很好的刻画，如图5.16到图5.20所示。

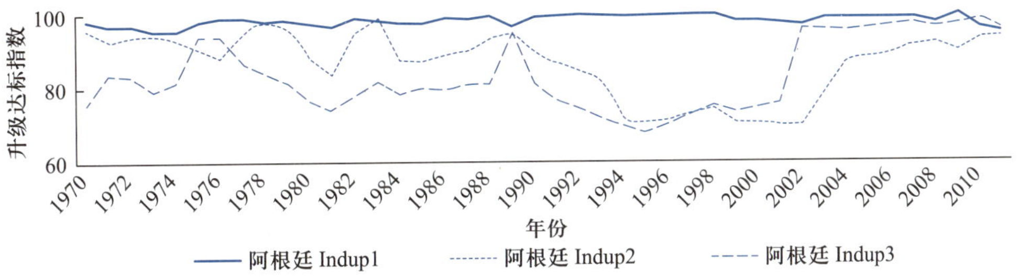


**图5.16 阿根廷经济结构转型升级路径的达标程度变化**

注：Indup1表示非农产业升级达标指数；Indup2表示工业升级达标指数；Indup3表示服务业升级达标指数。

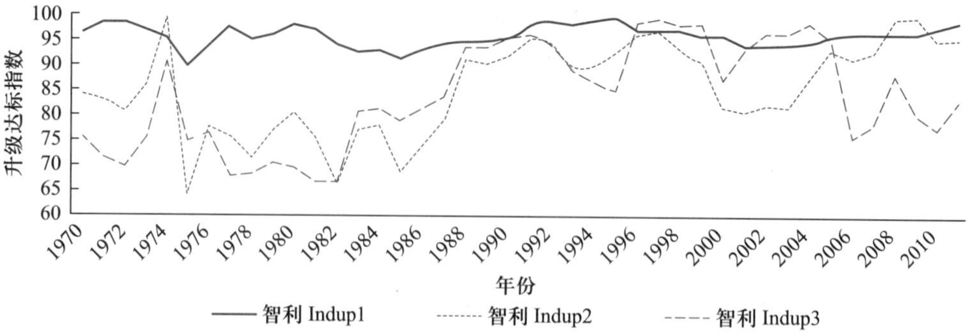


**图5.17 智利经济结构转型升级路径的达标程度变化**

注：Indup1表示非农产业升级达标指数；Indup2表示工业升级达标指数；Indup3表示服务业升级达标指数。

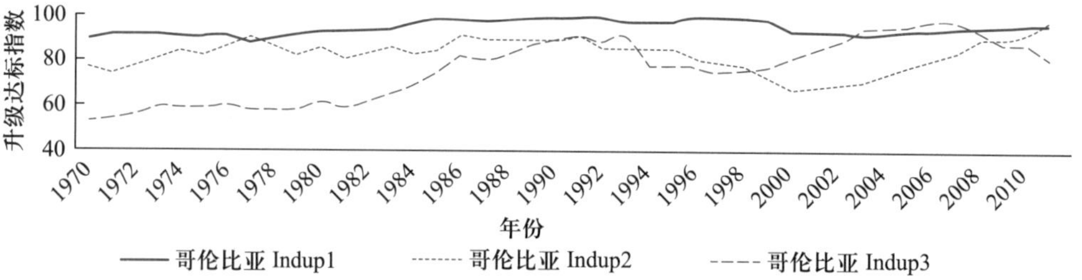


**图5.18 哥伦比亚经济结构转型升级路径的达标程度变化**

注：Indup1表示非农产业升级达标指数；Indup2表示工业升级达标指数；Indup3表示服务业升级达标指数。

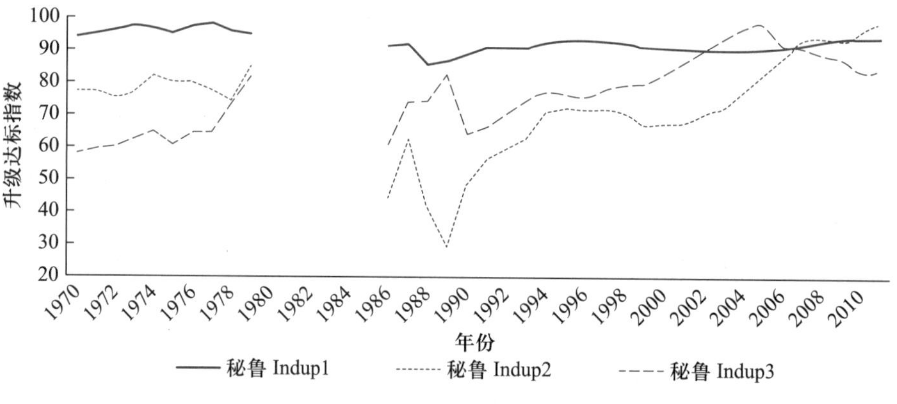


**图5.19 秘鲁经济结构转型升级路径的达标程度变化**

注：Indup1表示非农产业升级达标指数；Indup2表示工业升级达标指数；Indup3表示服务业升级达标指数。

阿根廷曾是拉美历史上最富有的国家，19世纪与美国没有显著差异，即便到了1950年，它与美国的人均收入比也在0.53左右。但是整个20世纪50年代和60年代没有任何起色，产业升级比率在87% ~ 90%，相对收入比率在45% ~ 55%。20世纪70—80年代，产业升级比率进步到90% ~ 92%，但是相对收入比率却几乎直线下降，在2000年降到只有美国人均收

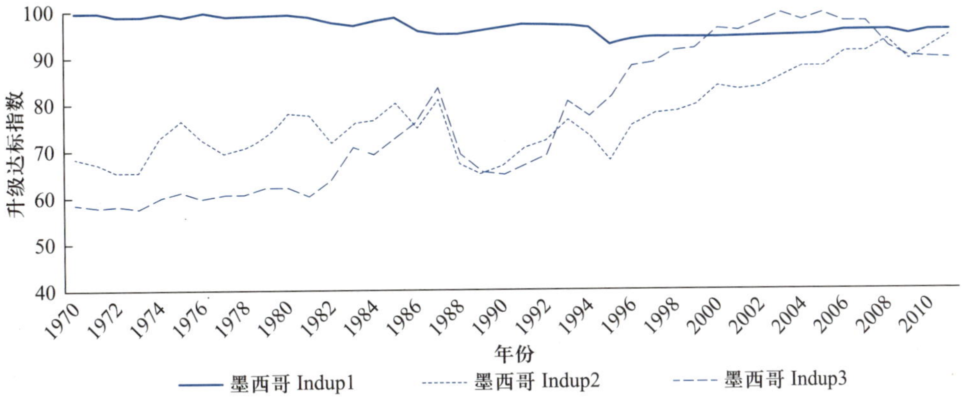


**图5.20 墨西哥经济结构转型升级路径的达标程度变化**

注：Indup1表示非农产业升级达标指数；Indup2表示工业升级达标指数；Indup3表示服务业升级达标指数。

入的25%，2010年有所回升，到了34%。再看我们已经在前面第4章中介绍过的巴西——这个拉美地区曾经的发展楷模和明灯。巴西1950年的产业升级指数为0.88，相对收入是美国的18%，正好处于一个跨越中等收入的门槛。在整个20世纪50年代到70年代末采纳进口替代战略期间，产业升级比较顺利，非农产业指数从不到0.18上升到1980年的0.96，相对收入指数从0.18上升到0.28。但是以重工业为主导的进口替代战略难以为继，巴西在80年代开始采纳"华盛顿共识"进行改革。结果巴西经济开始倒退和去工业化，产业升级指数从1980年的0.96降到2000年的0.95，收入指数从0.28降到0.19左右，之后由于中国经济的资源产品进口拉动上升到0.22。目前看来这个经济没有出现摆脱中等收入陷阱的希望。接下来我们看看智利，它在1950年的产业升级指数在0.955 ~ 0.96，但在之后的60年间一直在0.96 ~ 0.98，绕了一圈以后在2010年回到0.96。在这个失去的60年期间，它的收入指数从1950年的0.37下降到1986年的0.25，然后通过90年代一路上升又回到2000年的0.36，之后也是在中国进口带动下于2010年上升到0.45，但是产业没有获得升级（指数从0.965回到0.96），这是因为它向中国出口的主要产品是矿产资源和大豆。接下来的哥伦比亚和秘鲁也展现了类似的产业升级失败模式，产业升级指数到了0.9左右就开始出现问题。委内瑞拉是个特例，它从一个产业升级指数很高的高收入国家，退化为低中等收入国家。比如，它的产业升级指数在1968年高于0.99，相对收入指数当时是0.92，远远超过目前的韩国和中国台湾。但是之后几乎是直线倒退，在七八十年代尤其明显，产业升级指数在2003年为0.965，收入指数为0.23，从一个极高收入国家退化为一个低中等收入国家。

这些拉丁美洲国家的一个共同点，是在产业升级到了美国非农产业的90%左右时开始出现陷阱。它们没能同时推进产业升级和收入增长的原因，在于它们没能充分发展本国的劳动力密集型轻工业，积累资本改变比较优势使得重工业难以为继，而且，在劳动力密集轻工业发展不足的情况下，就业机会有限，失业率高，收入分配不平均，矛盾重重，带来社会不稳定，政治上左右摇摆，经济发展就更加困难。而产业升级失败以后，通过采纳放弃产业政策的“华盛顿共识”，进入“去工业化”阶段，从而陷入中等收入陷阱无法自拔。[①]如果我们用非农产业就业份额代替非农产业产值作为产业升级指数，得到的结论是一样的。它不仅再现了拉丁美洲国家的中等收入陷阱，以及亚洲“四小龙”是如何顺利突破中等收入陷阱的，而且体现了中国在改革开放前的发展模式难以为继，不可持续，但改革开放以后的发展模式却具有超越中等收入陷阱的趋势和能力。

中等收入陷阱还体现在出口结构的演变上。韩国与中国的出口结构呈现出如下共同特点：（1）正确的工业化进程开启后，初级农产品和原料产品的出口份额急剧下降，轻工业制成品的出口份额快速上升。例如，中国1985年初级产品的出口份额高达65%，到2002年下降到10%以下。（2）在韩国与中国工业化的前半段，纺织品、服装与鞋包这些劳动力密集型产品是最主要的出口品。韩国从1966年到1981年，中国从1992年到1999年，轻工业制品（不含食品）的出口份额一直在50%以上。韩国从1967年到1989年的20多年间，中国从1986年到1997年的10多年间，纺织品、服装与鞋包的出口份额都在30%以上。（3）韩国与中国在工业化的下半段（即完成第一次工业革命后），随着轻工业出口份额的逐渐下降，金属、机械制造、交通设备制造业等资本密集型重工业产品，以及高科技电子产品成为最主要的出口品。因此，两国的工业化经历了从轻工业品到重工业品的渐进轮替升级过程，因而具备国际竞争力和经济发展的可持续性。

相反，巴西、阿根廷、秘鲁以及经济改革后的俄罗斯的出口结构显示出两个特点：（1）出口偏向农副产品、石油资源等初级原料产品，工业制成品的出口比例偏低。例如，咖啡、茶、可可、香料及制品一直是巴西的第一大出口品，在1970年以前其出口份额在40%以上；1962—1985年，阿根廷的谷物出口一直在20% ~ 30%；而油气资源一直是俄罗斯最主要的出口品，2000年以来其出口份额高达50% ~ 60%。（2）对工业制成品的出口而言，这些国家跳过了劳动力密集型产品扩大出口的阶段，而偏向重工业产品出口。长期以来，巴西与阿根廷轻工业制品（不含食品）的出口额一直低于20%，俄罗斯甚至低于10%。然而，这些自上而下建立的重工业产品缺乏全球市场、自生能力与比较优势。例如，巴西、阿根廷的重工业产品以出口拉丁美洲国家为主，一些拉丁美洲国家在《安第斯条约》组织下，向受保护的协约国市场销售。因此，这些国家的出口品并不具备国际竞争力。

中国与韩国正是靠着出口大量的手工品和规模化生产的劳动力密集型轻工产品，积累资

---

① Dani Rodrik, “Premature Deindustrialization” , *Journal of Economic Growth*, 2016, Vol.21, No.1, pp.1–33.

本和外汇，才能为重工业进口昂贵技术创造必要条件，实现持续的产业升级和向重工业化阶段稳步迈进。这种出口导向式增长形成了一个正向反馈循环：通过出口规模化生产的产品来支持技术引进，继而用进口的先进技术生产更多的出口产品。这种靠参与世界制造业大循环的出口导向的正反馈系统，与巴西、阿根廷等拉丁美洲国家采纳“华盛顿共识”以后的发展战略形成鲜明对比：市场力量迫使拉丁美洲国家依赖农产品和自然资源的出口来支持工业化和技术引进。然而在原有的违反比较优势的产业失掉政府的保护补贴而不断退出的同时，由于缺乏政府对符合比较优势的产业发展的因势利导，而使得改革无法形成良性循环反馈系统。首先，农业资源开采都是土地密集型的，因此即便实现机械化耕作和资源开采，其规模报酬也非常有限。更重要的是，农业和矿业机械化减少了劳动力需求，而第一次工业革命的规模化生产则是提高劳动力需求。因此，尽管这种发展战略——依赖农产品或自然资源如矿石和石油的出口，符合拉丁美洲国家的比较优势，却不能带来规模化就业，也不能创造一大批企业家阶层和一个规模化国内市场来支持连续的产业升级和市场创造。如果没有引爆以劳动力密集型产业和全球贸易为特征的第一次工业革命，也就不会出现对能源、动力、运输和通信的基础设施的巨大需求市场和资金积累，从而也就不可能改变比较优势，支撑以规模化生产重工业产品为特征的第二次工业革命。结果是，大多数拉丁美洲国家虽然成功实现了农业和采矿部门的现代化（机械化），却无法完全实现轻工业和重工业部门的工业化和现代化，或建立具有国际竞争力的工业体系，因而陷入了中等收入陷阱。因此，跨越中等收入陷阱的方式应该是遵循比较优势，靠政府的因势利导帮助市场竞争的企业进行持续的经济结构转型升级，而非“华盛顿共识”下政府只扮演“守夜人”角色的自由市场经济。事实上，巴西在20世纪90年代就按照“华盛顿共识”实行了大规模的私有化，如表5.5所示，但是结果适得其反，整个90年代其增长率只有2.7%，相对于其黄金增长时期数据而言微不足道。这样的惨痛教训不得不引以为鉴。

表5.5 20世纪90年代（1991—1999年）巴西国有企业私有化情况　单位：百万美元

| 行业 | 企业数量 | 出售价格 | 转化的债务 | 合计 |
|---|---|---|---|---|
| 钢铁 | 8 | 5 562 | 2 625 | 8 187 |
| 石油化工 | 27 | 2 698 | 1 003 | 3 701 |
| 能源 | 3 | 3 907 | 1 670 | 5 577 |
| 铁路 | 6 | 1 697 | — | 1 697 |
| 矿业 | 2 | 3 305 | 3 559 | 6 864 |
| 电信 | 21 | 26 970 | 2 125 | 29 095 |
| 其他 | 14 | 2 442 | 344 | 2 786 |
| 联邦政府范围 | 81 | 46 581 | 11 326 | 57 907 |

续表

| 行业 | 企业数量 | 出售价格 | 转化的债务 | 合计 |
|---|---|---|---|---|
| 各州政府范围 | 26 | 23 724 | 5 311 | 29 035 |
| 共计 | 107 | 70 305 | 16 637 | 86 942 |

资料来源：Armando Castelar Pinheiro, Fabio Giambiagi, “The Macroeconomic Backgroundand the Institutional Framework of Brazilian Privatization” , in Armando Castelar Pinherio, Kiichiro Fukasaku eds, *Privatizationin Brazil: The Case of Public Utilities*, Brazilian Development Bank and OECD Development Center, 1999.

# 5.9

# 违背比较优势的发展战略将错失全球化发展机遇

## 5.9.1 全球化的历程与不同发展阶段国家参与全球化的概况

虽然在前现代，人类就开始全球迁徙，跨区域传播驯化与农耕技术，[①]千里迢迢互通有无，如古老的丝绸之路，但是由于前现代的生产力水平不高，经济剩余少，各国能够用于国际贸易的产品实际上并不多，而且道路交通不便，交易成本高，各地基本都是自给自足的自然经济。[②]一些研究显示，即便到了英国工业革命爆发半个世纪之后的1820年，世界生产的99%的商品还都没有进入国际贸易市场。[③]然而，全球化在此后就势如破竹。到战后初期，国际贸易已经是非常普遍的现象了，过去半个世纪以来，全球化尽管遭到了各种抵制，但依

① 贾雷德·戴蒙德，《枪炮、病菌和钢铁：人类社会的命运》，上海世纪出版集团，2006年版。

② 一些著作绘声绘色地描绘了国际贸易在人类历史上的灿烂传奇，可资参考的如：Kenneth Pomeranz, Steven Topik, *The World That Trade Created* (4th Edition). Routledge, 2017。

③ M. D. Bordo, A. M. Taylor, G. W. Williamson, *Globalization in Historical Perspective*. University of Chicago Press, 2005.

然一路高歌，如图5.21所示。

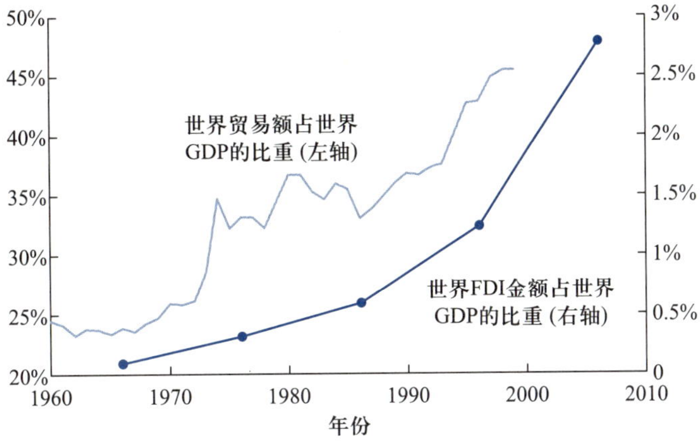


**图5.21 战后一路高歌的全球化**

注：世界贸易额是进出口额的加总。

资料来源：世界银行。

例如，1960年，不论是哪个发展阶段的经济体，货物和服务出口与进口分别占GDP的比重基本上都在10%左右。就出口比重来看，世界平均比重为11.88%，中低收入国家的比重为9.47%，中等收入国家的比重为9.38%，中高等收入国家的比重为9.4%，高收入国家的比重为12.79%。就进口比重来看，世界平均比重为12.19%，中低收入国家的比重为10.16%，中等收入国家的比重为10.04%，中高等收入国家的比重为9.65%，高收入国家的比重为12.96%。然而，在战后结构主义发展思潮的指引下，广大发展中经济体采取了“进口替代战略”，国际贸易止步不前，如图5.22所示。到1970年，出口比重方面，虽然世界平均比重提高到13.35%，但也只提高了1.47%，中低收入国家的比重下降到8.75%，中等收入国家的比重下降到8.64%，中高等收入国家的比重下降到8.14%，只有高收入国家的比重上升到15.02%。进口比重方面，虽然世界平均比重提高到13.37%，但也只提高了1.18%，中低收入国家的比重下降到9.57%，中等收入国家的比重下降到9.43%，中高等收入国家的比重下降到8.65%，只有高收入国家的比重上升到14.74%。后来学界的共识是，“进口替代战略”对经济增长的效果整体上不如“出口导向战略”，如表5.6所示。

表5.6 20世纪60年代初到80年代初出口导向型国家与进口替代型国家的年均经济增长率（%）比较

| 时期 | 进口替代型国家 | 出口导向型国家 |
|---|---|---|
| 1963—1973 | 5.8 | 6.6 |
| 1973—1976 | 5.3 | 5.5 |
| 1976—1979 | 4.6 | 8.1 |
| 1979—1982 | 2.6 | 2.4 |

续表

| 时期 | 进口替代型国家 | 出口导向型国家 |
|---|---|---|
| 1982—1984 | 1.7 | 5.3 |

资料来源：Bela Balassa, "Policy Responses to Exogenous Shocks in Developing Countries" , *American Economic Review*, 1986, Vol.76, No.2, pp.75–78.

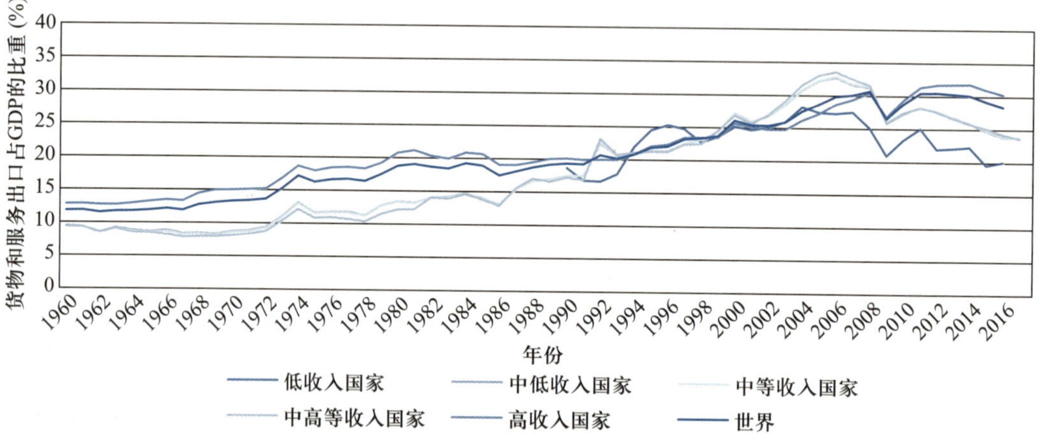


**图5.22 世界以及不同发展阶段国家的货物和服务出口占GDP的比重变迁趋势**

数据来源：世界银行。

其后，在新自由主义发展思潮的影响下，20世纪80年代开始了贸易自由化浪潮，到2008年全球金融危机前夕达到顶峰，如图5.22和图5.23所示。2008年，不论是哪个发展阶段的经济体，货物和服务出口与进口分别占GDP的比重基本上都上升到25% ~ 30%，总的贸易依存度达到60%左右。就出口比重来看，世界平均比重为30.77%，低收入国家的比重为25.14%，中低收入国家的比重为31.34%，中等收入国家的比重为31.43%，中高等收入国家的比重为31.64%，高收入国家的比重为30.54%。就进口比重来看，世界平均比重为30.17%，低收入国家的比重为41.32%，中低收入国家的比重为28.86%，中等收入国家的比重为28.69%，中高等收入国家的比重为27.04%，高收入国家的比重为30.7%。可以看到，到2008年时，高收入经济体由于经济结构中占比最高的服务业有许多是不可贸易的服务，因此，出口占GDP的比重只高于低收入国家，而低于其他发展阶段的国家；低收入国家的进口占GDP比重却是最高的，这就走到了曾经的"进口替代战略"的对立面。我们曾在第2章讲马尔萨斯陷阱时讨论过以进口维持生活是低收入国家的城市化超前的重要原因。2008年的全球金融危机对世界贸易确实造成了长久影响，到2016年也尚未恢复到危机前的水平。就出口比重来看，世界平均比重为28.52%，低收入国家的比重为20.12%，中低收入国家的比重为23.88%，中等收入国家的比重为23.95%，中高等收入国家的比重为24.28%，高收入国家的比重为30.34%。就进口比重来看，世界平均比重为27.69%，低收入国家的比重为38.19%，

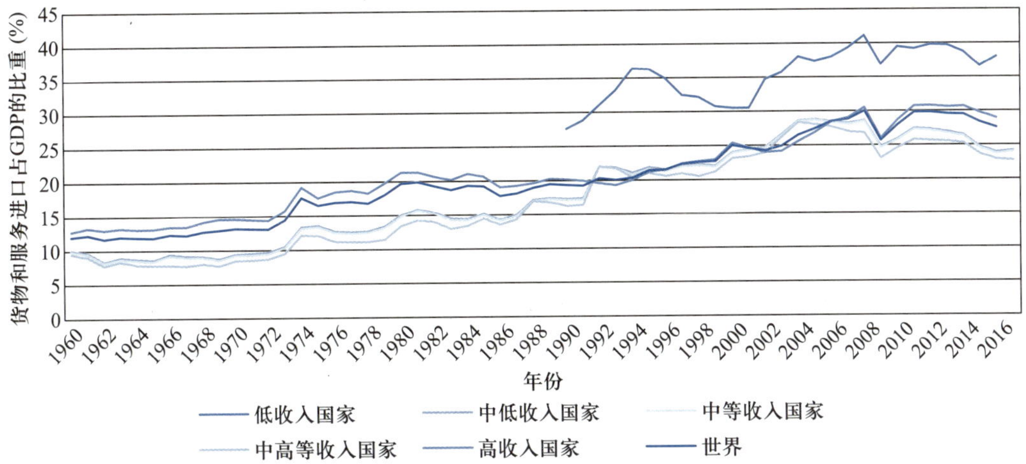


**图5.23 世界以及不同发展阶段国家的货物和服务进口占GDP的比重变迁趋势**

数据来源：世界银行。

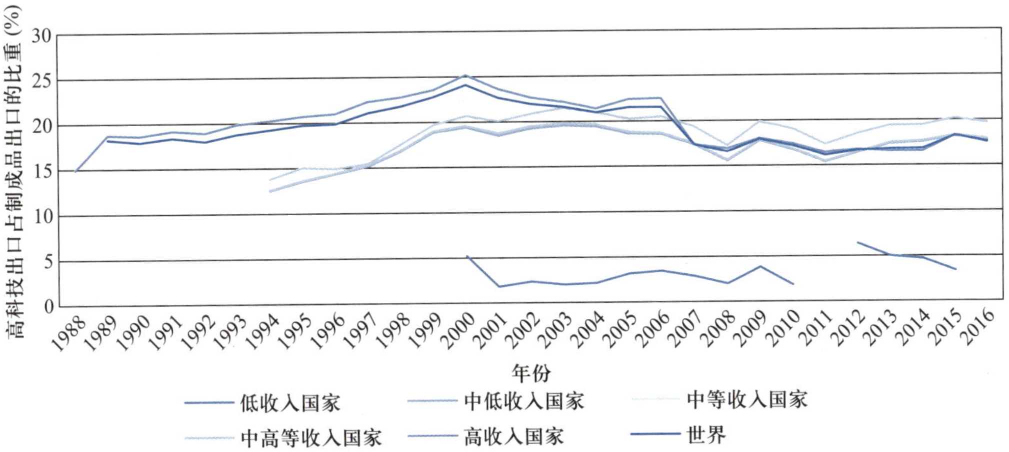


**图5.24 世界以及不同发展阶段国家的高科技出口占制成品出口的比重变迁趋势**

数据来源：世界银行。

中低收入国家的比重为24.08%，中等收入国家的比重为23.85%，中高等收入国家的比重为23.09%，高收入国家的比重为29.11%。当然，高收入国家长期以来出口结构与发展中经济体不同，例如，如图5.24所示，到1994年时，高科技出口占制成品出口的百分比，世界的平均比重是19.52%，高收入国家是20.54%，低收入国家是12.72%，中低收入国家的比重是12.82%，中等收入国家的比重是14.02%，中高等收入国家的比重是20.54%。然而，从20世纪90年代开始，一方面全球价值链兴起，另一方面一些发展中经济体也在加速促进贸易结构升级。到2016年，高科技出口占制成品出口的百分比上，世界平均比重下降到了17.88%，高收入国家的比重也下降到了17.81%，均低于其他发展阶段的国家，如中低收入国家的比

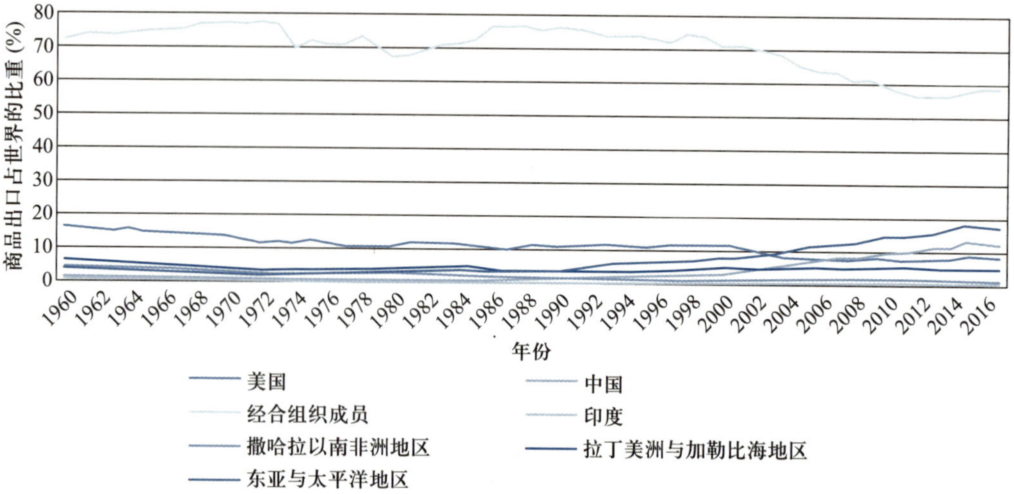


**图5.25 世界主要地区与经济体商品出口占世界的比重变迁趋势**

数据来源：世界银行。

重升高到18.08%，中等收入国家的比重也升高到18.2%，中高等收入国家的比重更是升高到19.95%。当然，前述概括仅仅是全球不同发展阶段上的国家货物与服务进出口变迁趋势的总体概括，图5.25概括了世界主要地区和经济体在世界中的贸易地位变迁。虽然中国等东亚经济体的贸易地位得到大幅度提升，如2017年中国商品出口占世界的12.7%，远超美国的8.68%，但是经合组织成员国依然主导全球商品出口，占比58.32%。

## 5.9.2 谜底揭晓：违背比较优势是很多发展中经济体无法利用外贸实现发展的根源

有很多经典的贸易理论能够解释很多贸易现象，但是却无法解释为什么很多发展中经济体无法利用外贸实现发展，而如第4章所讨论的战后的发展典范却借此实现了腾飞，也无法解释为何中国在改革开放之前和改革开放之后在利用外贸实现发展上有如此巨大的反差，本章最后一节我们将更详细地介绍中国的这一全球化经验。在新结构经济学的框架里，[①]选择

① 我们曾在第2章指出，经济学之父亚当·斯密的《国富论》诞生于大航海之后国际贸易盛行的年代。李嘉图继承了斯密的思想遗产，并进一步理论化，将斯密的绝对优势贸易理论拓展到相对比较优势贸易理论，建立了第一个现代贸易模型，即众所周知的“李嘉图模型”。李嘉图模型认为，即便一个经济体在所有产品的生产上的劳动生产率都比另一个经济体

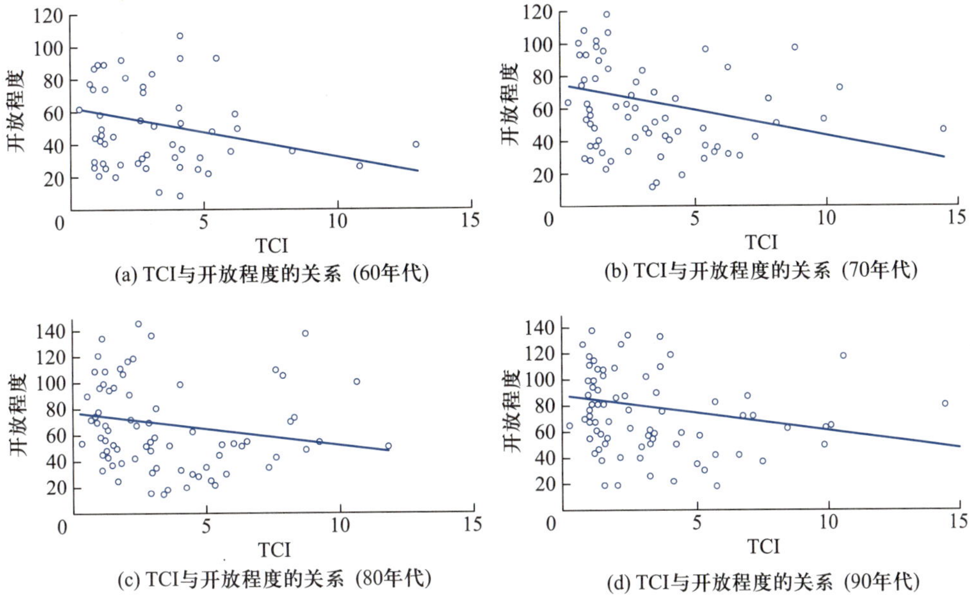


**图5.26 全球各个经济体的发展战略与开放程度（贸易依存度）**

资料来源：林毅夫,《经济发展与转型：思潮、战略与自生能力》，北京大学出版社，2008年版。

遵循比较优势的发展战略的国家将进口不具备比较优势的产品，同时出口具有比较优势的产品。对于这样的国家来说，开放程度是由国家是否遵循比较优势原则来发展所内生决定的，而不是外生决定进出口政策。如果欠发达国家的政府选择了违背比较优势的发展战略，试图以国内生产替代资本密集型制造品的进口，那么它的进出口贸易都将受到削弱，如图5.26所示。出口贸易受到削弱是因为资源会被从具有比较优势的产业转移出去，而且，为了促进不具有比较优势的产业的发展，本币价值会被高估，从而阻碍了出口。如印度和许多拉丁美洲

---

要低，即都没有绝对优势，但是只要在各种产品生产上的相对劳动生产率不同，依然可以选择专业化于相对劳动生产率高的产品并进行贸易来改善福利。用理性选择的话讲，便是“两害相权取其轻，两利相权取其重”。赫克歇尔和俄林的资源禀赋贸易理论，也就是新古典贸易理论（H-O模型）本质上是新古典经济学的资源配置理论，探讨了给定（相同）技术（生产函数）下贸易的跨国资源配置功能，因此得出与现实中资本和劳动价格事实不符的要素价格均等化结论。新贸易理论强调了技术上的规模经济与企业异质性对贸易的影响，但是其技术及其分布是外生的。新结构经济学与之不同，强调技术（生产函数）内生于要素禀赋，不同经济体要素禀赋不同内生决定了最优的技术（生产函数）也不同，对应的贸易结构也不同。因此，从分析思路上讲，新古典H-O模型可以视为给定技术（生产函数）下新结构贸易理论的退化特例，新贸易理论也可以视为给定外生的技术异质性下新结构贸易理论的退化特例。事实上，诸如萨缪尔森这样的经济学大师已经很敏锐地意识到如果新古典贸易理论中的技术（生产函数）出现各种变化的话，很多传统结论都将改变，尤其是基于资源配置效率的自由贸易观可能在结构变迁中会受到挑战。（Paul A. Samuelson, “Where Ricardo and Mill Rebut and Confirm Arguments of Mainstream Economists Supporting Globalization”, *Journal of Economic Perspectives,* Summer 2004, Vol.18, No.3, pp. 135–146.）

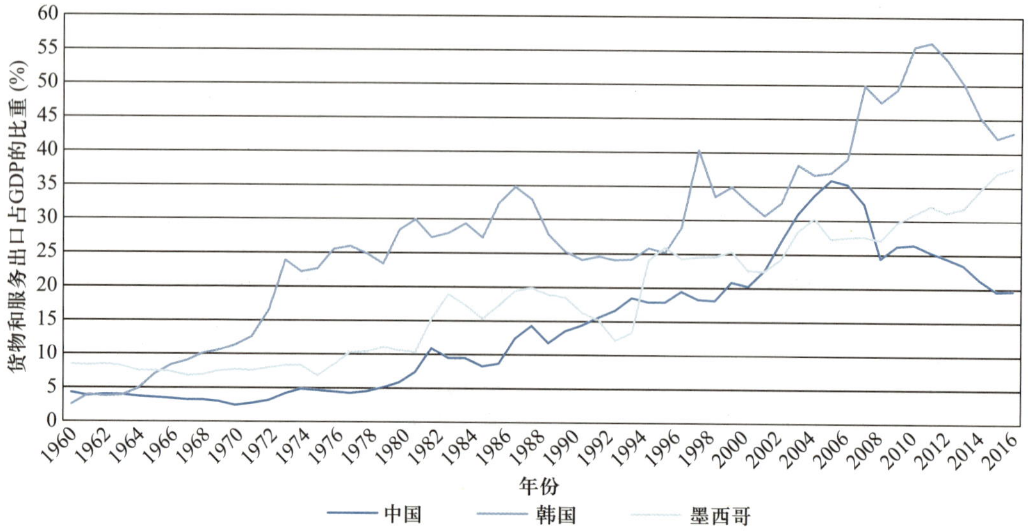


**图5.27 中国、韩国、墨西哥的货物和服务出口占GDP的比重比较**

资料来源：世界银行。

国家都属于这种情况。与选择了遵循比较优势的战略的国家相比，这些国家的增长绩效很不理想。欠发达国家的政府可能选择违背比较优势的战略，同时也鼓励优先发展的资本密集型产业扩大出口。在这种情况下，即使企业的产品拥有很高的出口比率并且技术进步的速度很快，出口也将不能促进经济的可持续发展。两位法国经济学家最近开展的一项跨国的新结构经济学实证研究支持了这一判断。①这两位学者观察到，从20世纪90年代以后，一些发展中经济体尝试努力促进出口多元化和复杂性（Export Diversification and Sophistication），尤其是吸引FDI和支持新兴产业涌现，但其可能远离了本国的要素禀赋。

因此，如果出口部门不符合比较优势，企业不具备自生能力，即便政府采取出口导向战略，可能也并不能取得符合比较优势的出口导向战略一样的效果，如中国、韩国和墨西哥的例子。②如图5.27所示，战后到20世纪80年代之前，中国和墨西哥的货物与服务出口占GDP的比重一直不足10%，中国则更低，只有5%左右；而韩国的比重从20世纪60年代初不足5%一直攀升到80年代初的30%左右，因此韩国的出口导向与中国、墨西哥进口替代的效果差

① Pauline Lectard & Eric Rougier, "Can Developing Countries Gain from Defying Comparative Advantage? Distance to Comparative Advantage, Export Diversification and Sophistication, and the Dynamics of Specialization". Cahiers du GREThA, 2017-14.

② 关于中国、韩国、墨西哥的比较案例分析更多内容可参考：付才辉，"不同的出口导向不同的效果：新结构经济学视角下的墨西哥与东亚的比较案例分析"，北京大学新结构经济学研究院工作论文，2018年。

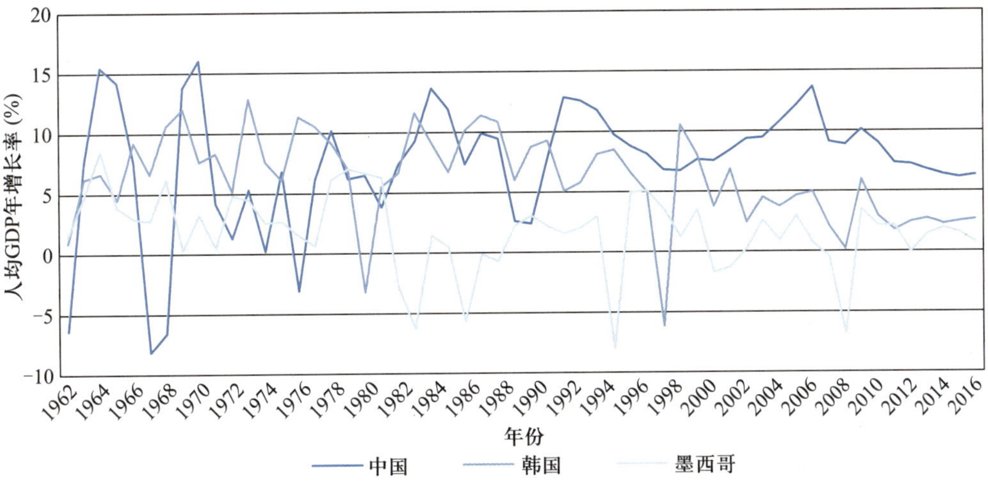


**图5.28 中国、韩国、墨西哥的基于不变价本币的人均GDP年增长率比较**

资料来源：世界银行。

异明显地反映在图5.27的经济增长率差异上。在20世纪80年代之后，中国和墨西哥都调整了出口战略，从进口替代转型到出口导向。墨西哥的货物与服务出口占GDP的比重从20世纪80年代初的10%左右上升到2017年的40%左右，尤其是1994年《北美自由贸易协定》生效之后，出口比重大幅提高。中国的比重从20世纪80年代初的5%左右上升到2008年全球金融危机前的35%左右。在此期间，中国、墨西哥都上升了大约30个百分点，然而与此对应的中国、墨西哥的经济增长率却迥异，如图5.28所示，中国实现了近两位数的增长率，与美国等发达经济体的收入差距不断缩小；而墨西哥的经济增长却不如进口替代时代，与美国等发达经济体的收入差距却不断扩大。如图5.29所示，墨西哥因此在1980—2000年经历了“失去的20年”，人均收入水平徘徊不前，跌入中等收入陷阱。与此相反，韩国与中国在第二次世界大战后的起点远低于墨西哥，但是在20世纪80年代中期韩国收入水平就超过了墨西哥。①

图5.30到图5.32分别选取服装、机械与交通设备三种出口类别对比了中国、韩国、墨西

① 包括罗德里克等全球化领域的学者认为东亚出口导向的成功取决于较高的初始条件，但这里给出的事实并非如此：Dani Rodrik, Gene Grossman and Victor Norman, “Getting Interventions Right: How South Korea and Taiwan Grew Rich”, *Economic Policy*, 1995, Vol.10, No.20, pp. 53–107.

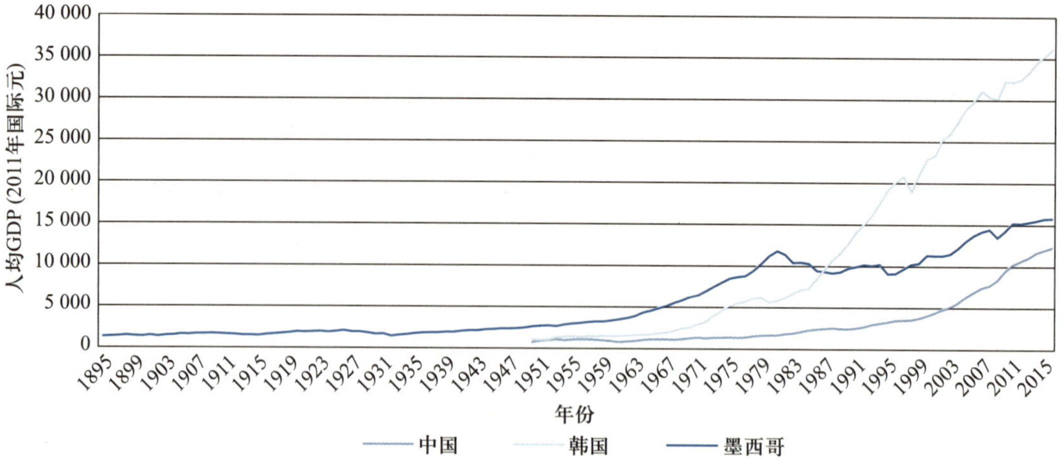


**图5.29 中国、韩国、墨西哥的实际人均GDP比较**

数据来源：Maddison Project Database（MPD）2018。

哥的RCA指数。[①]从图5.30中可以看到，在1994年《北美自由贸易协定》生效之前，墨西哥当时作为人口过亿的发展中经济体基本上放弃了服装这样的劳动力密集型产业的比较优势，而韩国在此之前却是充分利用了该比较优势；直到1994年《北美自由贸易协定》生效之后，墨西哥才开始释放劳动力密集型产业的比较优势，但程度却是蜻蜓点水，[②]而此时韩国的收入水平远超墨西哥，已经失去了劳动力密集型产业的比较优势；而中国在改革开放之后就一直大力释放劳动力密集型产业。与此相反，从图5.31和图5.32中可以看到，墨西哥在1980—2000年这20年间的机械出口RCA指数却超过了韩国和中国，交通设备出口RCA指数在20世纪80年代中期超过中国，在80年代末期超过韩国，直到21世纪初期又落后于韩国，这意味着不符合比较优势的出口扭曲程度方面，墨西哥超过了韩国和中国。[③]

因此，违反比较优势缺乏自生能力的企业的生存需要依靠国内市场的保护、银行的优惠贷款和其他的政策支持，这个国家的外汇储备会很少，并积累很多外债，使这个国家容易受

---

① RCA指数（Revealed Comparative Advantage Index），即显示性比较优势指数，是美国经济学家贝拉.巴拉萨（Bela Balassa）于1965年测算部分国际贸易比较优势时采用的一种方法，计算方法是通过该产业在该国出口中所占的份额与世界贸易中该产业占世界贸易总额的份额之比来表示。当然，RCA指数只是反映了出口相对状况，可能并未真正捕获一个经济体的禀赋结构状况。

②《北美自由贸易协定》的第一条便是关于纺织品关税的协定：在墨西哥占有劳动力优势的纺织品和成衣方面，除了取消一部分产品的关税外，对于墨西哥生产的符合原产地规则的纺织品和成衣，美国、加拿大取消其配额限制，并将关税水平从45%降到20%。这条协定有利于墨西哥发挥比较优势。

③《北美自由贸易协定》的第二条便是关于汽车产品关税的协定：对于汽车产品，美国、加拿大逐步取消了对墨西哥制汽车征收的关税，其中轻型卡车的关税从25%减到10%，并在5年内全部取消，重型卡车、公共汽车、拖拉机的关税则在10年内取消。墨西哥则将在10年内取消美国、加拿大汽车产品的关税及非关税壁垒，其中对轻型卡车在5年内取消关税。这意味着，墨西哥先被诱导出口不符合比较优势的产业，然后在没有自生能力的情况下被迫开放。这条协定对墨西哥极为不利。

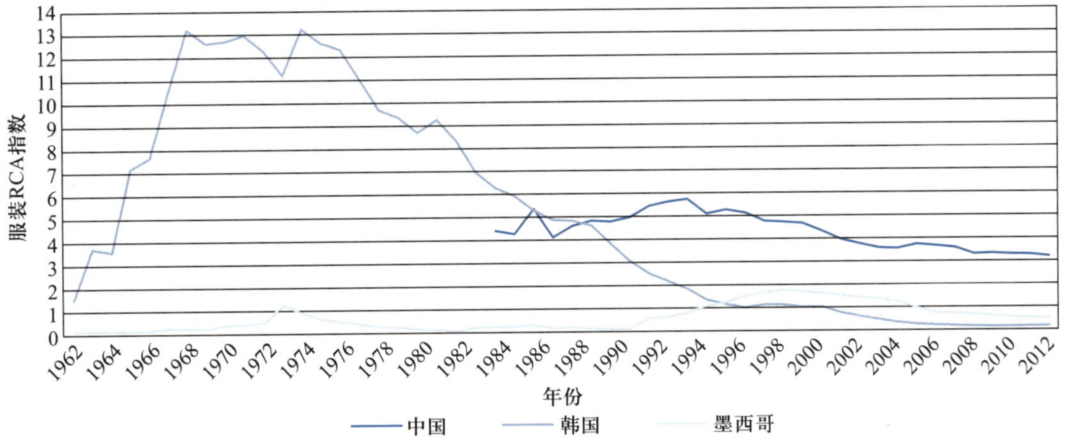


图5.30 中国、韩国、墨西哥的服装RCA指数比较

资料来源：根据COMTRADE数据计算。

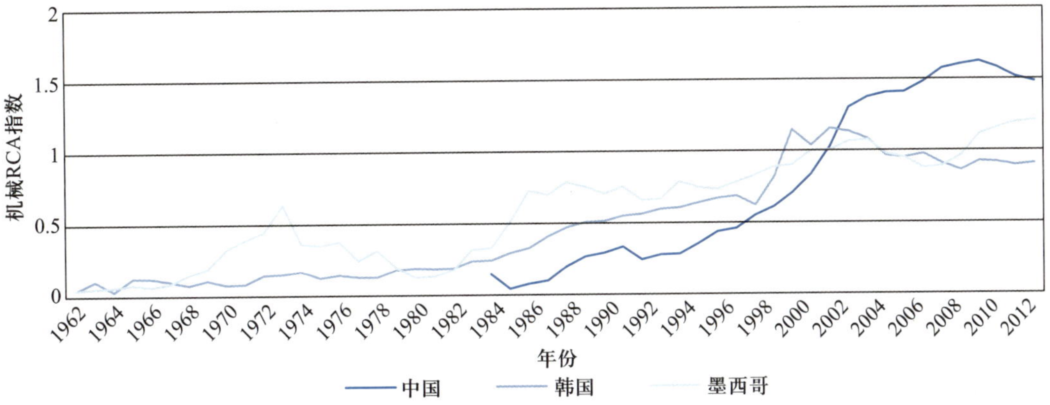


图5.31 中国、韩国、墨西哥的机械RCA指数比较

资料来源：根据COMTRADE数据计算。

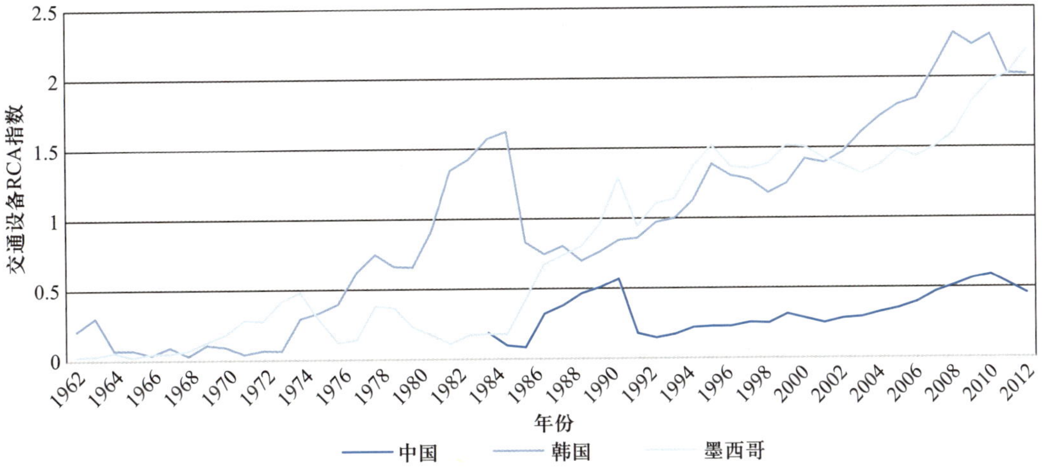


图5.32 中国、韩国、墨西哥的交通设备RCA指数比较

资料来源：根据COMTRADE数据计算。

到外部冲击的影响，这样的企业的出口也很难持续。与之相反，符合比较优势、具备自生能力的企业会有更多的出口倾向，创造更多剩余，进而提升禀赋结构，这反过来又促进出口升级，这正是后面我们将介绍的中国改革开放之后的贸易结构变迁。对于欠发达经济来说，选择违背比较优势的战略同时鼓励出口，可能要比选择违背比较优势的战略同时鼓励进口替代要好。然而，选择鼓励出口战略的经济整体绩效将比选择遵循比较优势战略的经济差。因此，并不是变更为出口导向的政策就是促进欠发达国家GDP增长的更好政策。此外，新结构经济学也认识到，许多发展中国家开始攀登产业阶梯的时候，往往面临着结构主义进口替代战略所留下的诸多扭曲。因此，新结构经济学建议贸易自由化应该采用渐进法。中国贸易体制的渐进式改革便是典型案例。以关税为例，事实上，在改革开放的早期，政府增加了对大部分商品的关税。到1982年，平均的法定关税率相当高，达到56%。1985年政府将这一水平减至43%，但之后的7年都在此水平。中国关税大幅度下降是从1992年开始的，平均关税逐渐下降了2/3。到2001年中国加入世界贸易组织前夕，关税才下降到15%左右。①

### 5.9.3 谜底揭晓：违背比较优势是很多发展中经济体无法利用外资实现发展的根源

除了国际贸易之外，国际资本也是全球化另外一个重要的维度。联合国贸易和发展会议（UNCTAD）每年都会发布《世界投资报告》，通过外商直接投资（FDI）的流入和流出来反映一个经济体的招商引资能力和资本出海的潜力。如图5.33所示，《2016年世界投资报告》发布的数据显示，2015年全球FDI表现出强烈的复苏态势，总体上涨了38%，达到1.762万亿美元，是2008年全球金融危机爆发至2015年的最高水平，然而整个体量的55%流入了发达经济体。②有种观点认为主要原因是，发达经济体的产业结构是资本相对密集型的，因此对资本的需求远超发展中经济体，使得大量资本流向发达经济体。③然而，我们也看到诸如

---

① 可参考Brandt和Rawski（2008）主编的《伟大的中国经济转型》（*China's Great Economic Transformation*）第16章"拥抱全球化"对中国渐进式开放历程的介绍。

② 这就是所谓的国际资本流动的卢卡斯之谜：主流理论认为发展中国家资本短缺，资本的回报率高，资本应该从发达国家流向发展中国家，但诺奖得主卢卡斯发现，在现实中资本却从大多数的发展中国家流向发达国家，参见：Robert Lucas, "Why Doesn't Capital Flow from Rich to Poor Countries?", *American Economic Review*, 1990, Vol.80, No.2, pp.92–96。

③ Jin Keyu, "Industrial Structure and Capital Flows", *American Economic Review*, 2012, Vol.102, No.5, pp.2111–2146.

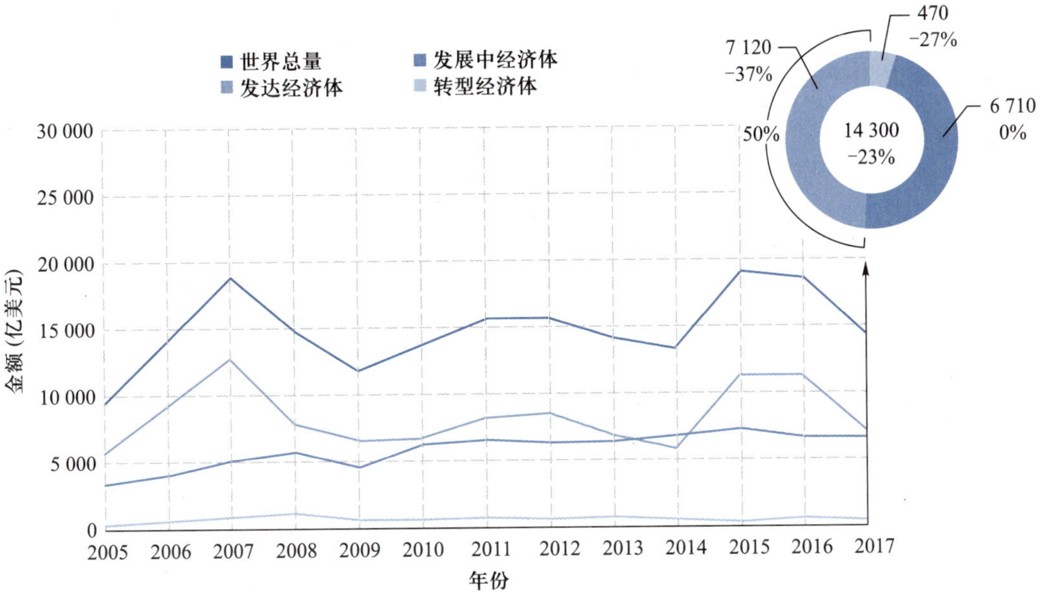


**图5.33 2005—2017年全球FDI流入情况**

资料来源：《2016年世界投资报告》。

亚洲新兴经济体，虽然大部分都是发展中经济体，但却是FDI流入最大的目的地。究其原因，是这些经济体按照比较优势进行了快速的经济结构转型升级，即便是劳动力密集型产业也可以获得超过发达经济体资本密集型产业的资本回报率而吸引外资。同样，当资本积累到一定程度，这些成功的经济体由于经济结构转型升级，还会迫使本国曾经具有比较优势的产业逐步失去比较优势而转移到海外，随之产生资本出海运营。[①]一些前述因发展战略违背比较优势而陷入低收入陷阱的非洲国家和陷入中等收入陷阱的拉丁美洲国家则截然相反。图5.34和图5.35便说明了这一破解“卢卡斯之谜”的成败经验。下一章我们将以全球制造业就业的变迁和转移为例，来估算和分析世界经济结构转型升级中的机遇。

新古典经济学无法解释上述国际资本流动现象，因此该现象被称为“卢卡斯之谜”。在新古典经济学中，由于缺乏结构与结构变迁，在外生给定的不变生产函数前提条件下，资本的边际产出进而边际报酬递减，这意味着发展中经济体的资本相对于发达经济体更加稀缺，其边

① 对此现象新结构经济学的解释是，如果一个发展中国家采取了违反比较优势的战略，不仅有权有势的富人从各种价格扭曲和行政干预中寻租获得的财富缺乏合法性，而且国内投资的资本回报率会低，资本就会外逃到发达国家。反之，如果按照比较优势发展，资本的回报率高，富人以及企业家才能从市场竞争中获得的财富有合法性，资本不仅不会外逃，而且还会流入。新结构经济学对“卢卡斯之谜”的这个解释在经验实证上和现实的经济现象一致。

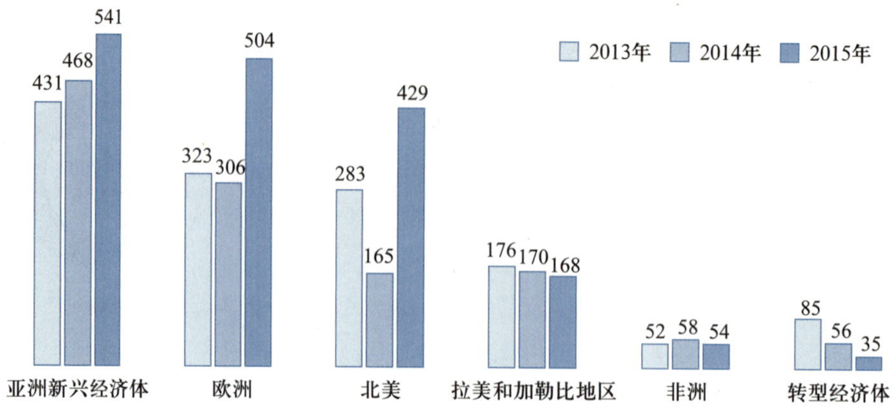


**图5.34 2013—2015年全球各主要地区FDI流入情况（单位：十亿美元）**

资料来源：《2016年世界投资报告》。

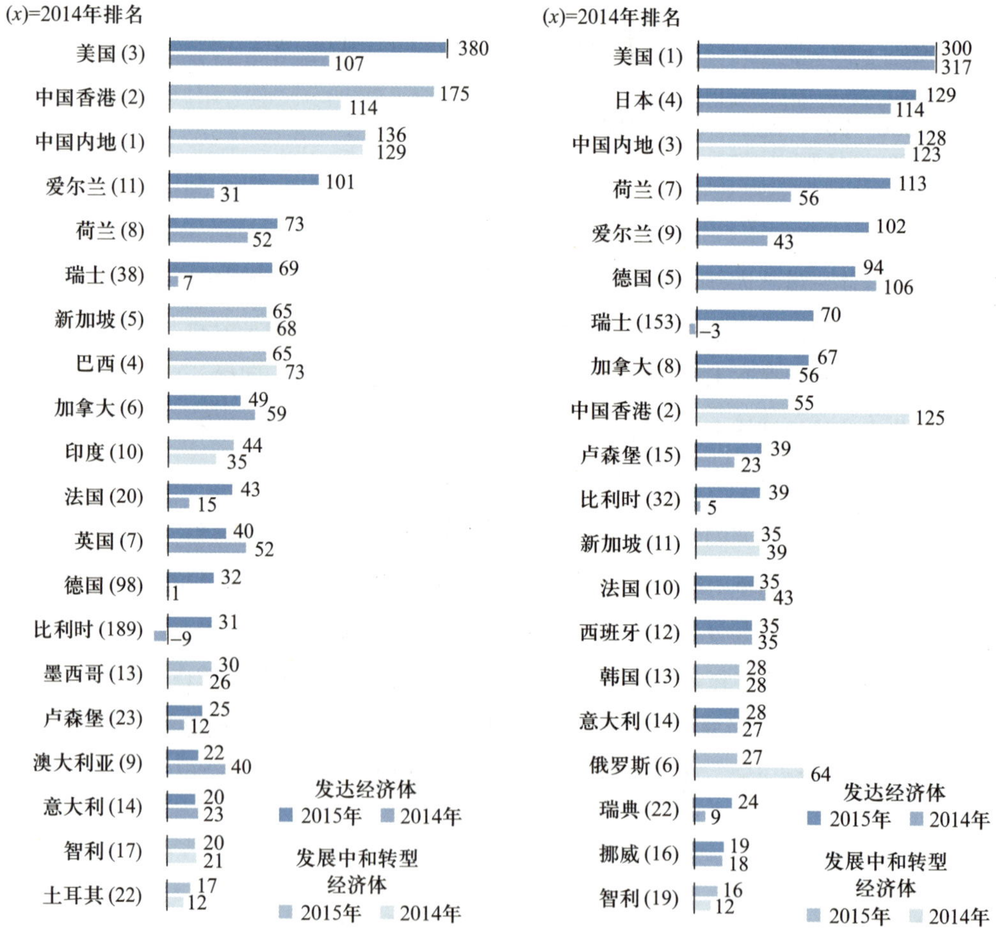


**图5.35 2014—2015年全球前20位FDI流入（左）和流出（右）目的地情况（单位：十亿美元）**

资料来源：《2016年世界投资报告》。

际报酬应该更高，因此资本理应从发达经济体流向发展中经济体。然而，这个新古典经济学的理论预测与现实截然相反。标准的新古典经济学理论无法解释上述现象，一些观点对其做了辩护。代表性的解释认为新古典经济学的基本理论没错，问题在于发展中经济体缺乏发达国家先进的技术和制度。例如，发展中经济体全要素生产率（TFP或C-D生产函数中的系数A，如第2章中的讨论）较低与产权常常没有保护以及腐败横行，政府缺乏信用拖欠借款，革命、政变和剥夺财产更为常见——这是典型的新制度经济学的观点。[①]然而，前面介绍的国际资本流动的一个典型经验特征事实便是，亚洲新兴经济体吸引的FDI超过了欧洲和北美洲，如中国内地和当年的“亚洲四小龙”吸引了巨大的FDI。而如第1章所介绍以及后面也将提及的，按照主流理论和流行思潮的看法，中国的全要素生产率和制度都与发达国家相去甚远。因此，为新古典经济学辩护的上述观点以及新制度经济学的观点也无法解释上述现象。从新结构经济学的角度可以为前述现象提供统一的解释。当一个发展中经济体按比较优势发展，一旦新古典经济学中生产函数内生于禀赋结构之后，持续的结构变迁使得资本回报率不会递减，就会产生更高的投资倾向和激励，除了自身的积累之外（回顾第4章对发展典范高储蓄率的讨论），还会吸引更多的外来投资。这就解释了我们所看到的诸如亚洲新兴经济体，虽然大部分都是发展中经济体，其产业结构在当时也都是劳动力密集型的，但却是FDI流入最大的目的地。根本原因就在于，这些经济体采取了比较优势发展战略，以及持续地进行了快速的经济结构转型升级，即便是劳动力密集型产业也可以获得超过发达经济体资本密集型产业的资本回报率而吸引外资。同样，当资本积累到一定程度，这些成功的经济体由于经济结构转型升级，还会迫使本国曾经具有比较优势的产业逐步失去比较优势而转移到海外，随之产生资本出海运营。这正是亚洲“四小龙”已经发生以及中国内地正在发生的情形。与此相反，如果一个发展中国家采取了违反比较优势的战略，不仅有权有势的富人从各种价格扭曲和行政干预中寻租获得的财富缺乏合法性，而且国内投资的资本回报率会低，资本就会外逃到发达国家。这也解释了前面的另外一个经验特征事实，即其他一些发展中经济体和转型经济体为什么吸引的FDI较少。当然，除了经济结构变迁遵循潜在比较优势之外，政府积极发挥因势利导作用，消除制约经济结构转型升级的软硬基础设施瓶颈也至关重要，如图5.36所示，这便是第7章的主题。

---

① 一些跨国实证研究貌似支持新制度经济学的观点（L. Alfaro, S. Kalemli-Ozcan & V. Volosovych, “Why doesn’t Capital Flow from Rich to Poor Countries? An Empirical Investigation”, *Review of Economics and Statistics*, 2008, Vol.90, No.2, pp. 347-368.），但是一旦把发达国家的样本剔除（因为以今天的眼光来看，发达经济体的制度质量无疑是高于发展中经济体的），或者控制了制度质量之后，长期来看发展中经济体依然存在“卢卡斯之谜”，也即这种新制度经济学观点并未实质性的被实证支持（Bilal Keskinsoy, “Lucas Paradox in The Long Run”, MPRA Paper, No. 78126, posted 6 April 2017）。

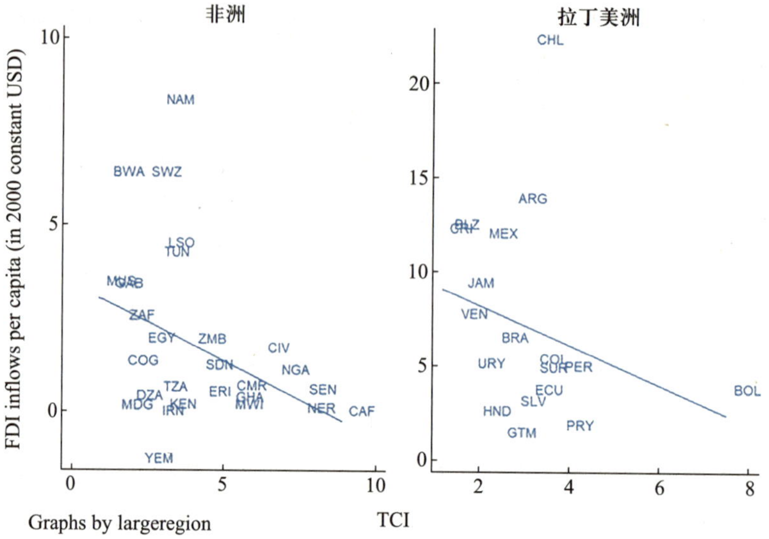


(a) 技术选择指数 (TCI) 和FDI流入

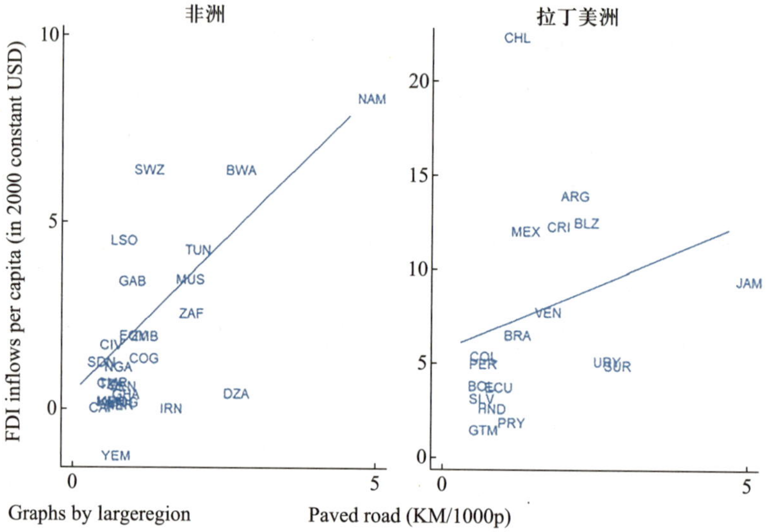


(b) 硬化道路和 FDI 流入

**图5.36 发展战略（TCI指数）、基础设施（道路）与FDI**

资料来源：Lin Justin Yifu, Wang Xin,“Development Strategy and International Capital Flows”，北京大学新结构经济学研究院工作论文，No.E2019003, 2019。

## 5.9.4 中国改革开放的经验——“两头在外”：发挥比较优势参与全球化实现结构转型

图5.37非常形象地概括了中国改革开放之后的全球化经验，那就是充分发挥各地（甚至是区、县一级的基层单位）的比较优势，面向全球市场，吸引外资，进而加速外贸，这一经验模式可以简单地称为充分利用国内国际两种资源和两个市场。回顾历史，中国错失了很多次全球化发展机遇。第二次世界大战之后，与诸多发展中国家一样，新中国成立以后采取了为赶超战略服务的进口替代战略。在此期间，中国在世界贸易中原本微不足道的地位进一步萎缩。例如，1953年中国的贸易量占世界贸易量的比重为1.5%，此后急剧下降到1977年的0.6%。1960年，中国货物和服务进口占GDP的百分比为4.43%，货物和服务出口占GDP的百分比为4.31%，然而到了1977年这两项比例依然分别维持在4.09%和4.3%。改革开放之后，中国将发展战略转轨到比较优势发展战略，相应的进口替代战略也转型为出口导向型战略，此后国际贸易一路高歌猛进。到2008年全球金融危机前夕的2007年，中国货物和服务进口占GDP的比重上升到26.72%，货物和服务出口占GDP的比重上升到35.39%，如图5.38所示。到2017年，中国商品出口占世界的12.7%，远超美国，成为世界第一大出口国。值得注意的是，与全球趋势一样，2008年全球金融危机对中国贸易造成了严重而持续的影响。在改革开放初期的1980年，初级产品占出口商品总额的比重为50.30%，工业制成品比重则只占49.70%。到2016年，中国出口结构发生了剧变，初级产品出口占出口商品总额的比重仅为5.01%，工业制成品出口比重则上升到94.99%。与此同时，在图5.33所示的2014—2015年

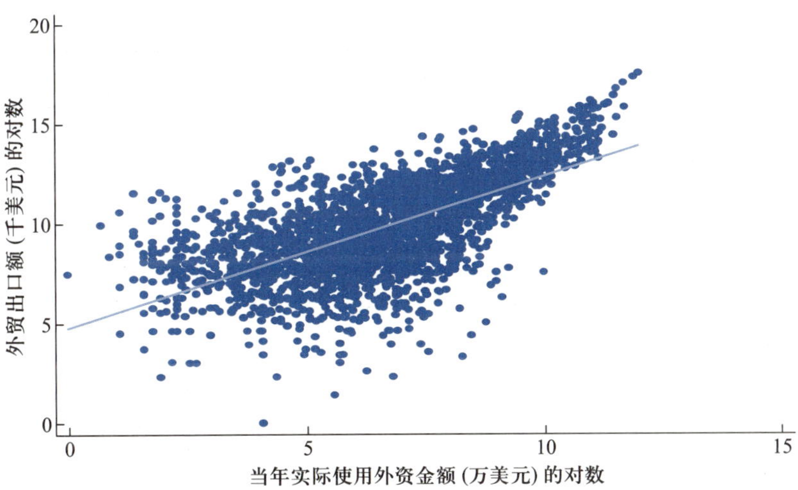


**图5.37 中国2 000余个区县近20年来（1997—2013年）的“两头在外”模式：外资与外贸**

资料来源：林毅夫、付才辉、赵秋运，《新结构县域战略管理：方法与案例》，北京大学新结构经济学研究院工作手稿，2019年。

位居全球前20位吸引FDI的经济体中，中国位居前列。图5.39则记录了改革开放后1984—2016年中国吸引外资从无到有再到位居世界前列的历程。关于更详细的中国招商引资扩大开放的讨论将在第8章介绍。

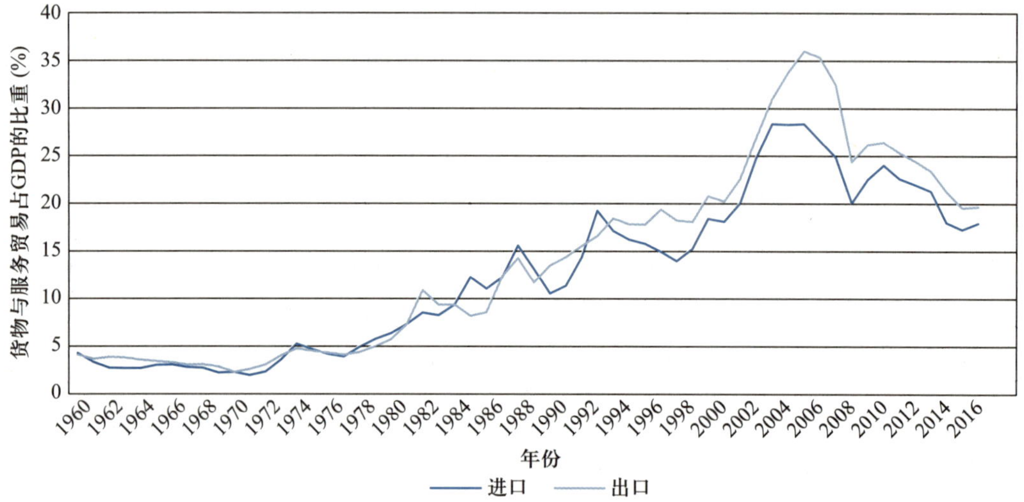


图5.38 中国的货物和服务进口与出口占GDP的比重变迁趋势

数据来源：世界银行。

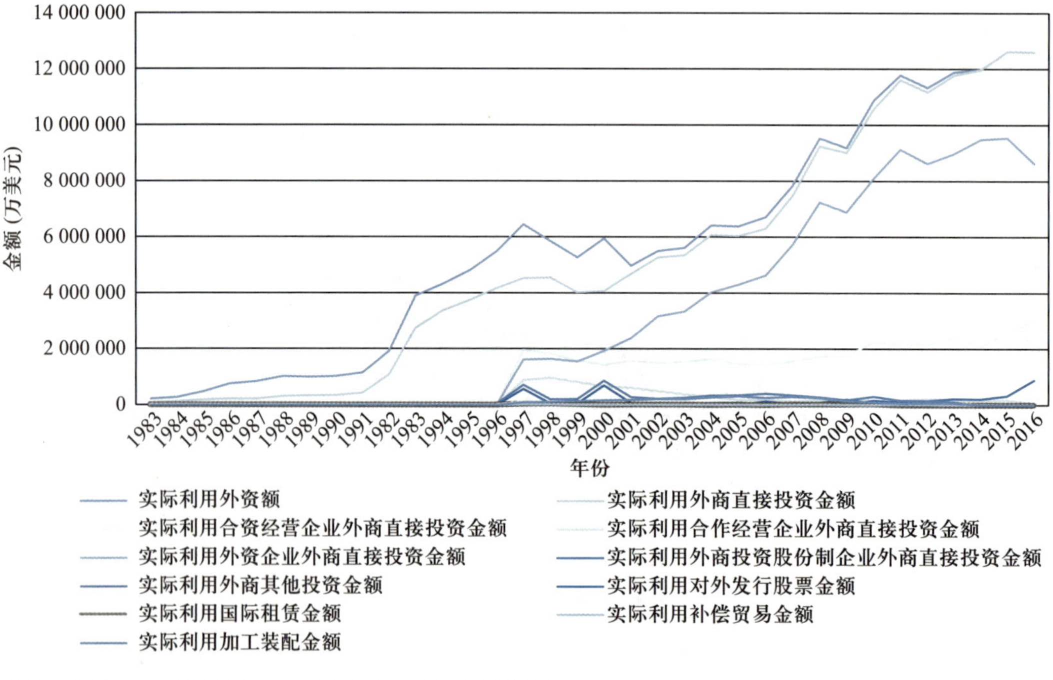


图5.39 改革开放后1984—2016年中国利用外资情况

数据来源：国家统计局。

# 第6章

# 世界经济结构转型升级中的机遇

第2章到第5章我们分析了经济结构变迁的轨迹，可以清晰地看到经济发展是一个持续的产业和技术升级过程，任何一个国家，无论处于何种发展阶段，如果能够在市场经济中由政府因势利导，帮助企业积极发展适应自身比较优势（由本国的要素禀赋结构决定）的产业，都可以成功推进这一发展过程。发展中国家取得杰出增长表现的秘诀是利用后来者优势，兴办与本国要素禀赋类似的快速发展国家曾发展的那些成熟产业。在全球化时代，低收入经济体经济转型的机遇比比皆是。众多新的增长极的出现（走向多极化世界，如第1章第2节的介绍）将给那些落后的国家带来机遇，使它们迈入快速工业化和结构转型的新时代。与此同时，身处世界前沿的经济体也在不断拓展结构变迁的边界，加速世界经济结构的变迁速度。本章将主要以制造业及其就业为例讨论在世界经济结构变迁中的发展机遇，因为就业是消除贫困降低失业的根本，是人类发展的基石。①

## 6.1

## 无工不富：制造业是世界财富的发动机和就业水池

如第2章所讨论的，工业化是人类步入现代社会的标志，而制造业又是工业化的主体。按照现代产业分类，工业中除了制造业还有一部分是矿业和建筑业。矿业是资源密集型产业，而建筑业伴随着城市化的发展而发展。如图6.1所示，就全球平均情况而言，一个经济体要想成为高收入经济体，发展制造业是基本途径。即便发达经济体到了今天，制造业尤其是高端制造业依然是经济结构的支柱。例如，2017年经合组织成员的制造业占GDP的比重达

① 林毅夫在《从西潮到东风》（第11章）以及《超越发展援助》（第6章）这两本著作中都对新兴经济体给低收入发展中经济体带来的产业转移机会所创造的就业数量做了初步的判断，《世界经济结构转型升级报告》在此基础上对全球每个经济体的制造业就业结构变迁所出现的缺口和剩余情况做了首次探索性估算。

14.34%，德国甚至高达20.64%。曾经创造东亚经济增长奇迹的日本和韩国以及新加坡至今依然以制造业立国，日本2016年制造业的比重为21.05%，韩国2017年制造业的比重为27.57%，新加坡2017年制造业的比重为17.97%。当今经济增长最具活力的经济体也是以制造业作为支撑，如东亚与太平洋地区2017年制造业比重为27.61%，中国2017年制造业占GDP比重达29.34%。与此相反，欠发达地区工业化的缺失也主要是制造业的缺失，如撒哈拉以南非洲地区2017年制造业占GDP的比重不足10%。当然，正如我们在第3章所讨论的，不同发展阶段制造业的结构是显著不同的。第二次世界大战后很多发展中经济体违反比较优势的激进工业化就适得其反，如果制造业结构变迁偏离比较优势过于激进也会适得其反。与制造业增加值结构变迁一样，就业结构变迁也是相对应的。图6.2展示了不同细分部门的制造业在不同发展阶段的变迁轨迹。服装、纺织、食品等劳动力密集型的轻工业往往是发展早期阶段的主导产业，而其他资本密集型的重工业和高技术产业往往是发展中后期阶段的主导产业。因此，劳动力密集型制造业是发展中经济体的就业源泉，[①]也是解决发展中国家贫困和失业之根本。

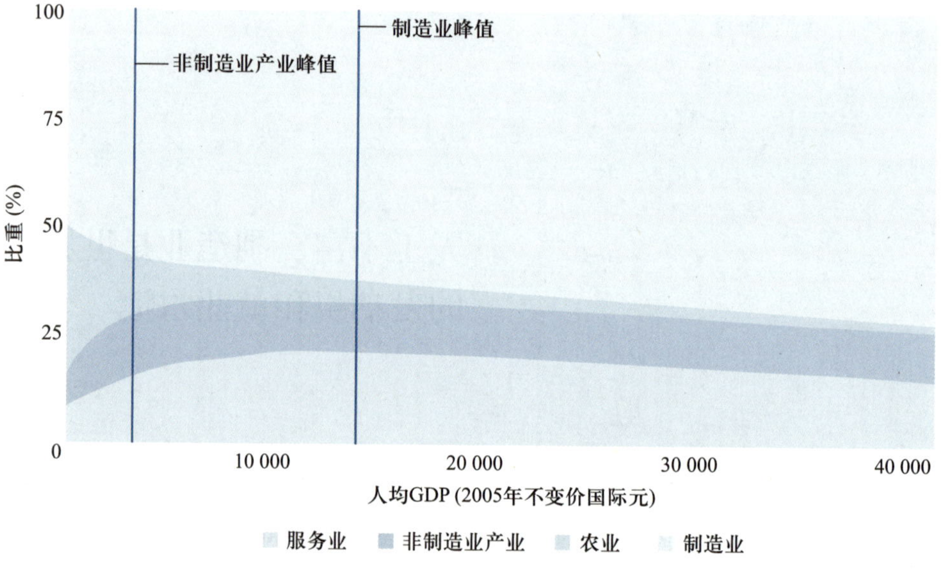


**图6.1 制造业是世界经济通往繁荣的必经之路**

资料来源：UNIDO, *Industrial Development Report 2013, Sustaining Employment Growth: The Role of Manufacturing and Structural Change*.

---

① UNIDO, *Industrial Development Report 2013, Sustaining Employment Growth: The Role of Manufacturing and Structural Change*.

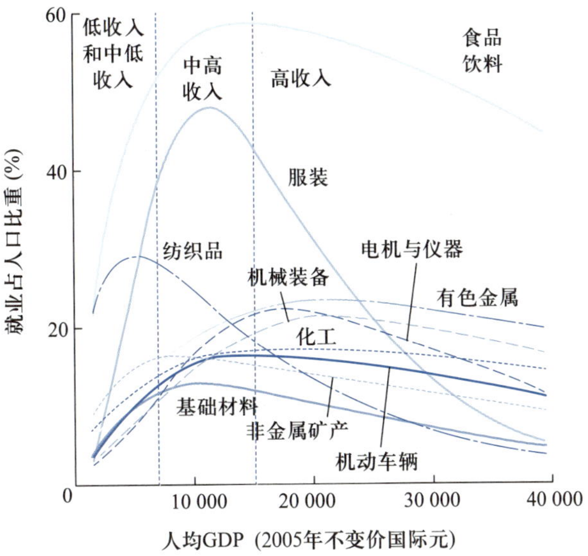


**图6.2 全球制造业细分行业结构变迁的特征事实**

注：图为95个经济体的混合数据。

资料来源：UNIDO, *Industrial Development Report 2013, Sustaining Employment Growth: The Role of Manufacturing and Structural Change*.

## 6.2

## 中国的脱贫成就与人类艰难的反贫困斗争：就业是发展的基石

在度量人类发展水平的联合国人类发展指数的三个维度指标中，以人均GDP度量的生活水平是最基础的，其对预期寿命和识字率与入学率有决定性影响。[①]正如2015年经济学诺贝尔奖得主安格斯·迪顿所批评的，一些观点认为我们对收入的重视程度过高了，美好的人生不只是拥有金钱，这大概是“少年不识愁滋味”！根据盖洛普咨询公司在全世界范围内开展的生活满意度调查数据，生活满意度与以人均收入度量的生活水平显著地正相关。生活在贫穷国家和地区的人们，通常对他们的生活总体水平非常不满意。与此相反，生活在高收入的国家和地区，人们不但拥有高收入，也认为自己的生活总体状况很好。在所有的国家和地区中，生活总体评价最差的是多哥这个世界上最穷的国家和地区之一，评价最好的是丹麦这个富裕的国度。[②]

我们在第3章讨论过人类通过工业革命跳出马尔萨斯陷阱，但是工业革命至今并未惠及全世界所有人，按每天生活费1.90美元（2011年购买力平价）衡量的贫困人口比例，1981年全世界依然高达42.1%，约一半的人口深陷贫困。过去40年来，人类消除贫困的成绩瞩目，2015年世界的贫困率下降到9.9%。然而，这一成就主要归功于中国，按照世界银行的这一标准和数据，1990年中国的贫困率高达66.2%，到了2015年骤然下降到0.7%。世界银行曾专门发布过报告——《推进更加包容、更可持续的发展》，对中国在扶贫方面取得的重大成就

---

① 联合国开发计划署（UNDP）在《1990年人文发展报告》中提出了人类发展指数（Human Development Index, HDI），用以衡量联合国各成员国经济社会发展水平，其包含三个维度四个指标：长寿水平（出生时预期寿命）、知识水平（成人识字率和综合入学率）和生活水平（实际人均GDP）。2010年后计算方式：1.预期寿命指数(LEI)=(LE−20)/(83.2−20)。2.教育指数(EI) =(√(MYSI × EYSI)−0)/(0.951−0)；2.1平均学校教育年数指数(MYSI)=(MYS−0)/(13.2−0)，2.2 预期学校教育年数指数(EYSI)=(EYS−0)/(20.6−0)。3. 收入指数(II)=(ln(GNIpc)−ln(163))/(ln(108211)−ln(163))。其中LE是预期寿命，MYS是平均学校教育年数（一个大于或等于25岁的人在学校接受教育的年数）、EYS是预期学校教育年数（一个5岁的儿童一生将要接受教育的年数），GNIpc：人均国民收入。HDI值为这三个基本指数的几何平均数。

② 安格斯·迪顿，《逃离不平等》，中信出版集团，2014年版。

给予大力称赞。报告显示，从1978年到2014年，中国人均收入增加了16倍，以每人每天生活费1.9美元（2011年购买力平价）计，中国的极端贫困发生率由1981年的88.3%大幅降至2013年的1.9%，超过8.5亿中国人摆脱贫困。联合国助理秘书长、联合国开发计划署助理署长也评价道，十八大以来，中国秉承开发式扶贫的理念，采取精准扶贫的措施，取得了显著成效。2012年到2017年，中国贫困人口减少近7 000万，相当于每分钟至少有26人摆脱了贫困；贫困发生率由10.2%下降到3.1%；贫困县数量实现了首次减少，减少了153个。创造了中国扶贫史上的最好成绩。精准扶贫的有效实施为中国和世界落实联合国《2030年可持续发展议程》及其17个可持续发展目标做出巨大贡献。中国在扶贫领域为其他国家树立了榜样。

然而，如图6.3所示，如果抛开中国的脱贫成就，全世界在新千年时的贫困率人口其实不减反增，人类反贫困的斗争愈发艰难。目前全球还有超过10亿人身处贫困。如图6.4所示，低收入国家的贫困率至今依然超过40%，数十年来基本上没有什么改善，中低等收入国家当今的贫困率也超过10%。如图6.5所示，当今世界贫困人口主要聚居在撒哈拉以南非洲地区，贫困率超过40%，另外就是南亚地区，2013年的贫困率高达16.1%。彻底战胜贫困犹如彻底战胜癌症一样艰难，即便是当今美国的贫困也没有完全绝迹，2016年的贫困率还有1.2%。当下，中国的精准脱贫与防范化解重大风险、污染防治是“三大攻坚战”，在相当一段时期内消除贫困依然会是中国人民的奋斗目标。彻底消除极端贫困也是世界银行等国际发展机构和全世界人民的目标。

中国脱贫成就的秘诀在于政府在市场环境中通过因势利导大力发展符合自身要素禀赋结

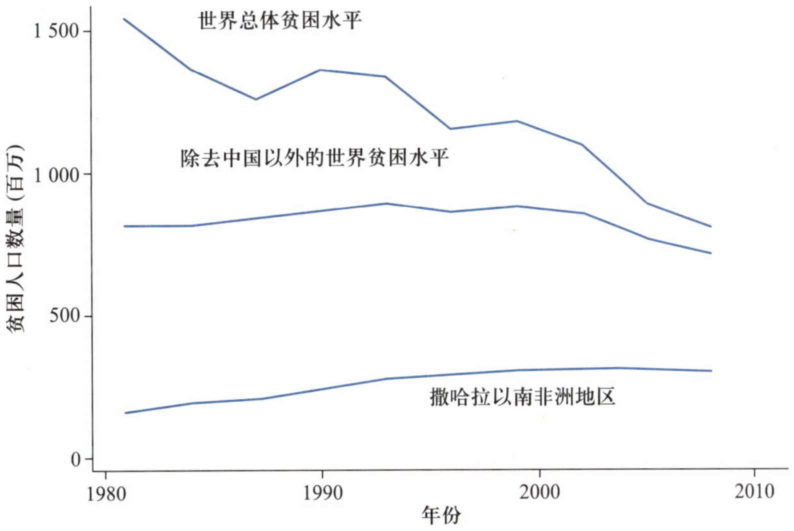


**图6.3 中国的脱贫成就对世界的贡献**

资料来源：安格斯·迪顿，《逃离不平等》，中信出版社，2014年版。

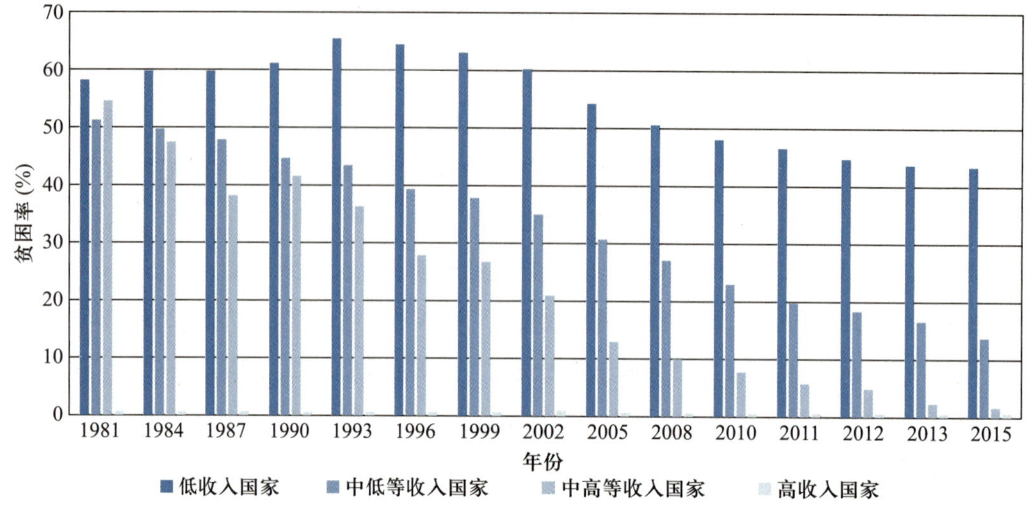


图6.4 不同发展阶段国家的贫困率

资料来源：世界银行。

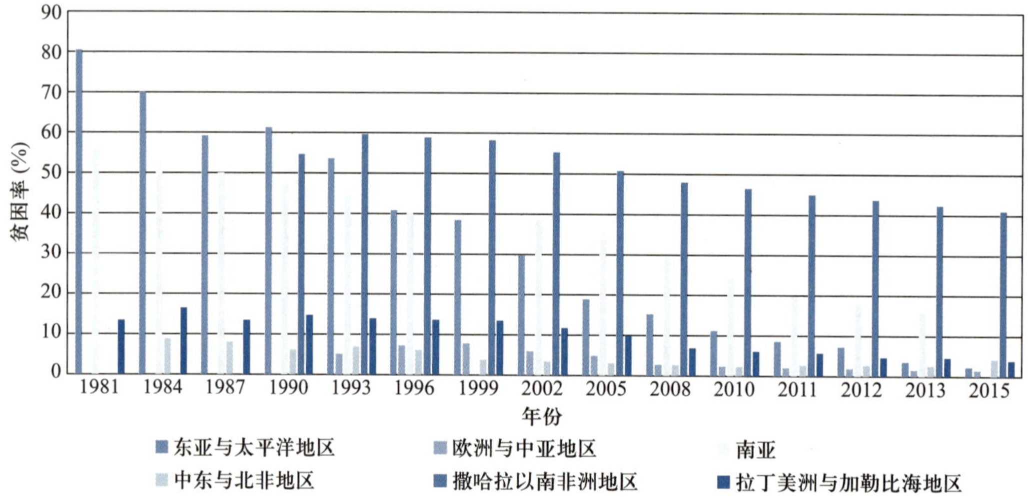


图6.5 不同地区的贫困率

资料来源：世界银行。

构的比较优势创造产业，进而创造大量就业。斯迪克（Siddique）的一项跨国比较分析就支持了新结构经济学的这一基本论断：发展战略越是违背比较优势（TCI指数越大），脱贫效果越差（贫困水平越高），如图6.6和表6.1所示。[①]

① A. B. Siddique, "Comparative Advantage Defying Development Strategy and Cross Country Poverty Incidence", *Journal of Economic Development*, 2016, Vol.41, No.4, pp.45–78.

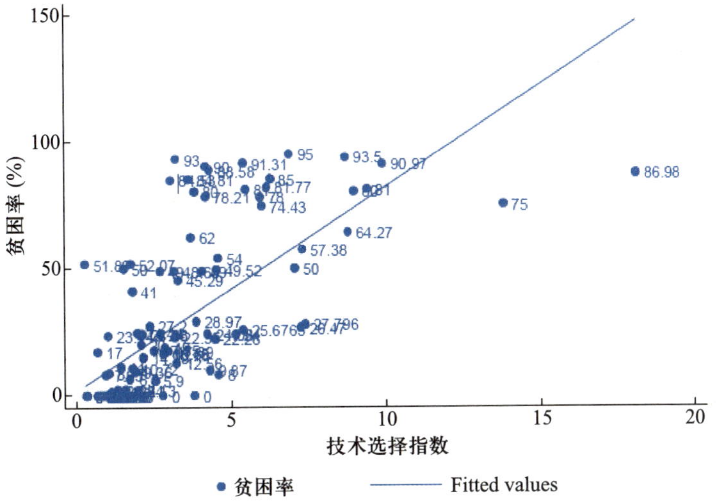


图6.6 结构变迁违背比较优势的程度（TCI指数）与贫困率的散点图

表6.1 结构变迁违背比较优势的程度（TCI指数）对贫困率影响的回归结果

| | Poverty 1.1 | Poverty 1.2 | Poverty 1.3 | Poverty 1.4 | Poverty 1.5 | Poverty 1.6 | Poverty 1.7 |
|---|---|---|---|---|---|---|---|
| Log of TCI | 29.65***<br>(3.246) | 28.528***<br>(3.240) | 29.079***<br>(3.687) | 28.225***<br>(3.844) | 22.096***<br>(6.348) | 13.597***<br>(6.333) | 8.122***<br>(2.835) |
| Growth rate of GDP per capita | | −2.413**<br>(1.204) | −2.505*<br>(1.342) | −2.456*<br>(1.317) | −0.716<br>(1.646) | 0.860<br>(1.520) | 0.752<br>(0.875) |
| Openness | | | 0.040<br>(0.060) | 0.024<br>(0.063) | −0.012<br>(0.065) | −0.047<br>(0.061) | −0.028<br>(0.041) |
| Landlock | | | | 6.216<br>(5.957) | 7.196<br>(6.993) | 8.850<br>(8.166) | 6.302*<br>(3.584) |
| Log of IEF | | | | | −65.783***<br>(23.259) | −37.186*<br>(20.902) | −16.899<br>(21.950) |
| Log of expropriatio & risk | | | | | | −57.926***<br>(12.639) | −50.691***<br>(8.962) |
| South Asia | | | | | | | 38.497***<br>(9.632) |
| Middle-East & North Africa | | | | | | | −12.142*<br>(6.327) |
| East Asia & Pacific | | | | | | | 8.750<br>(6.065) |
| Sub-Sahara & Africa | | | | | | | 31.505***<br>(6.541) |
| Latin America & Caribbean | | | | | | | −9.837**<br>(4.615) |
| Europe & Central Asia | | | | | | | −5.214<br>(5.101) |
| Constant | 2.375<br>(3.192) | 8.751*<br>(4.589) | 5.654<br>(7.942) | 6.378<br>(7.939) | 128.897**<br>(50.043) | 197.967***<br>(48.347) | 146.817***<br>(33.585) |
| $R^2$ | 0.53 | 0.55 | 0.55 | 0.55 | 0.54 | 0.62 | 0.87 |
| N | 113 | 109 | 107 | 107 | 85 | 76 | 76 |

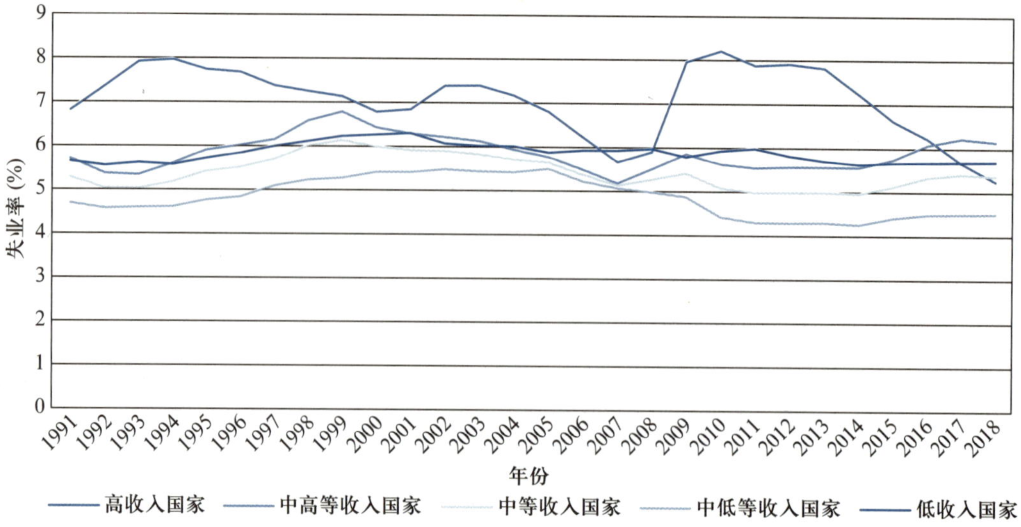


**图6.7 不同发展阶段国家的失业率**

资料来源：世界银行。

对个人来讲，就业是收入的基本来源。因此，世界银行《2013年世界发展报告》的主题就是“就业”。正如该报告所指出的，在发展中国家，就业是发展的基石，其回报远不仅限于收入。就减少贫困、让城市有效运作、为青年提供机会而言，就业至关重要。经过分析800余项调查和普查，《2013年世界发展报告》的团队估算出，虽然全世界就业人口超过30亿，但近有一半人从事农业、小型家庭企业或者临时性或季节性工作。这些就业岗位往往意味着微薄的收入和不健全的社会安全网，有时候社会安全网甚至完全缺失。仅青年就业问题而言，挑战就是惊人的。全世界有超过6.2亿的青年既不工作也没有求学，而处于闲散状态。在未来15年，全世界必须增加约6亿个就业岗位才能使就业率保持不变。如图6.7所示，失业问题始终困扰着所有发展阶段的国家，2018年高收入国家的失业率为5.26%，中高等收入国家的失业率为6.16%，中等收入国家的失业率为5.37%，中低等收入国家的失业率为4.5%，低收入国家的失业率为5.7%。如图6.8所示，失业问题也困扰着全球各个地区，2018年东亚与太平洋地区的失业率为4.05%，欧洲与中亚地区的失业率为7.06%，南亚的失业率为3.75%，中东与北非地区的失业率为9.98%，撒哈拉以南非洲地区的失业率为7.32%，拉丁美洲与加勒比海地区失业率为7.82%，北美的失业率为4.24%。然而，发展中国家的失业率很难准确度量。许多以农业和个体经营为主、社会安全网很不健全的发展中国家，失业率也可能很低。例如，在东欧和中亚地区，7个工人中有6个从事有工资收入的工作；而在撒哈拉以南非洲地区，5个工人中有4个是农民或者自我雇用。正如世界银行《2013年世界发展报告》所展示的那样，尽管不同地区、不同性别、不同年龄组在就业结构上存在巨大差异，但归根结底缺乏合适的就业机会是问题的根源。也如前世界银行行长金墉所言：“一个好就业岗位能够改变一个人的生活，而大量合适的就业机会能够改变整个社会。各国政府需要把就业放到促进繁荣和战胜贫困战略的核心。其中至关重要的一点是形成政府与私营部门的良好合作关系，因为私营部门为社

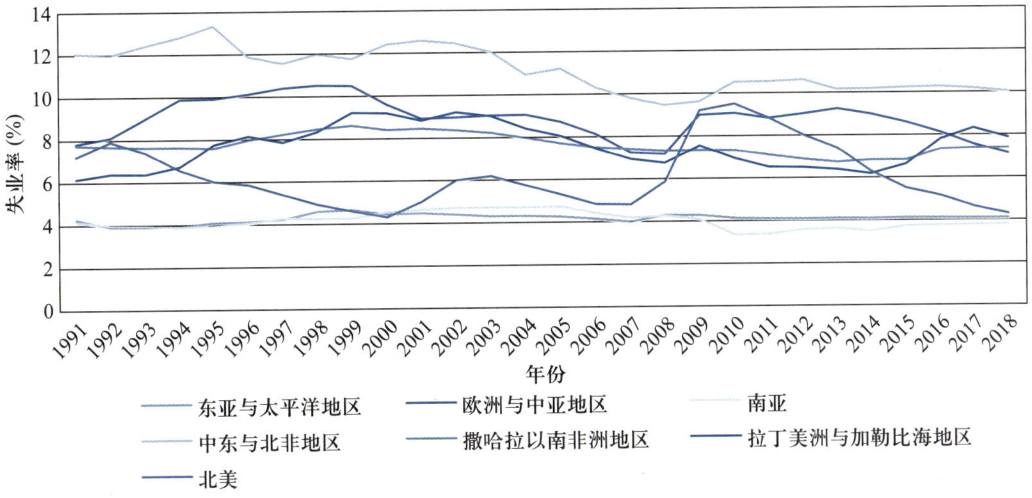


图6.8 不同地区的失业率

资料来源：世界银行。

会提供90%的就业岗位。因此我们需要寻找最佳方式来帮助小企业和农场成长。就业意味着希望，就业意味着和平，就业有可能脆弱国家变得稳定。”

# 6.3 – 全球制造业就业结构随禀赋结构变化而变化的一般规律与特征

## 6.3.1 全球制造业就业结构随禀赋结构变化而变化的一般规律

事实上，与产出的增加值相对应，就业结构也是产业结构变迁的另外一个方面。作为工业的构成，如图6.9所示，就全球整个制造业就业结构变迁特征而言，制造业就业结构随禀赋水平的提高而提高然后降低，是典型的倒U形或倒V形关系（可以回顾第3章对制造业细

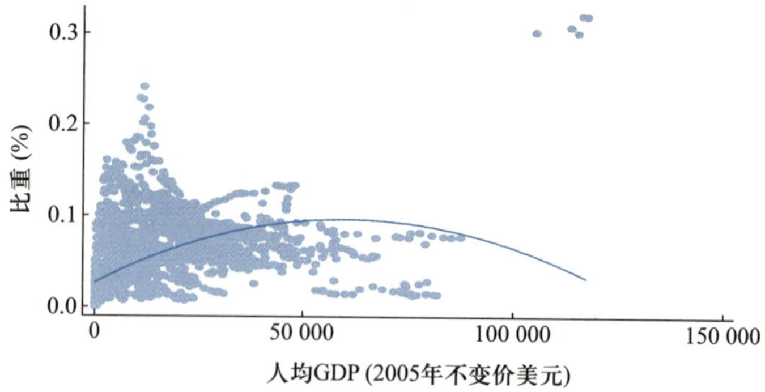


(a) 制造业就业人数占人口的比重

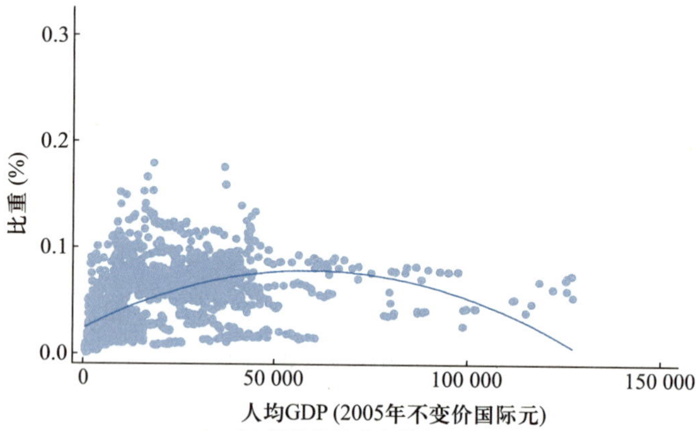


(b) 制造业就业人数占人口的比重

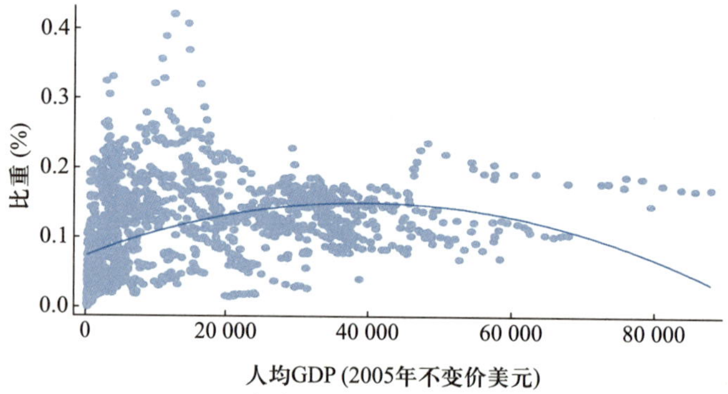


(c) 制造业就业人数占劳动力的比重

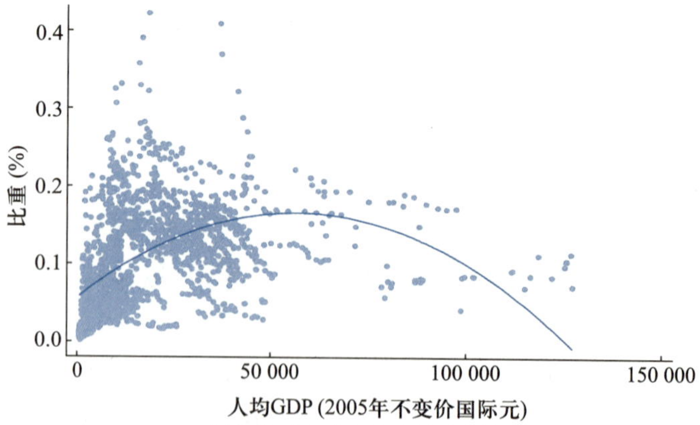


(d) 制造业就业人数占劳动力的比重

图6.9 制造业就业占比（占人口或劳动力的比重）与禀赋水平（人均GDP）的散点图

分产业变迁的讨论）。按照新结构经济学的基本理论，制造业就业结构由禀赋结构内生决定；禀赋结构的变化会使得过去符合比较优势的产业失去比较优势，对应产业的就业岗位过剩，且符合比较优势的产业得到发展而使得对应的就业岗位上升。因此，根据新结构经济学的理论和特征事实，设定如下的制造业就业结构基线估算方程①

$$\widetilde{\text{employees}}\text{ratio}(\text{gdp}) = \alpha + \beta \times \text{gdp} + \varphi \times \text{gdp}^2 + \gamma X + \varepsilon \tag{6.1}$$

其中，以制造业就业人数占人口的比重和制造业就业人数占劳动力的比重度量制造业就业结构，而不是以制造业就业人数占经济体的就业人数之比来度量，其原因是人口和劳动力相对于经济体总的就业人数是更加外生的变量；②作为一种综合性概括指标，我们以人均GDP（gdp）度量禀赋水平，这里同时采纳2005年不变价美元和不变价国际元两个口径的人均GDP；控制变量（$X$）主要选取相对外生的两个对制造业有着重要潜在影响的因素：自然资源（自然资源租金总额占GDP的百分比）和人口密度（每平方千米土地面积人数）。③

式（6.1）是按照禀赋结构预测的制造业就业结构基线，那么通过式（6.2）便可以估算出各个经济体制造业就业缺口或过剩值

$$\text{employeesgap}_{i,t} = \widetilde{\text{employees}}(\text{gdp}_{i,t}) - \text{employees}_{i,t} \tag{6.2}$$

其中，$\widetilde{\text{employees}}$（$\text{gdp}_{i,t}$）、$\text{employees}_{i,t}$分别是经济体$i$第$t$年的制造业就业人数按基线的预测值和实际值，二者相减得到的数值$\text{employeesgap}_{i,t}$就是符合要素禀赋结构所决定的比较优势的制造业就业缺口（如果$\text{employeesgap}_{i,t} \geqslant 0$）或失去要素禀赋结构所决定的比较优势的制造业中超过标准的就业（简称剩余劳动力）（如果$\text{employeesgap}_{i,t} \leqslant 0$）。

### 6.3.2 全球制造业就业结构分布与变迁概貌

除了制造业就业数据来自UNIDO 2013年数据，其余变量的数据均来自WDI 2014年数据，

---

① 采取不同的估算方程就会有不同的估算基线，这不仅受到变量度量方式，还受到不同控制变量的选择、不同的方程回归方式等问题的影响，这里仅提供了最基本的8条估算基线。

② 如UNIDO, Industrial Development Report 2013, Sustaining Employment Growth: The Role of Manufacturing and Structural Change。

③ 如N. Haraguchi, G. Rezonja, "Patterns of Manufacturing Development Revisited", UNIDO Working Paper, 2009。

表6.2 描述性统计

| 变量 | 观测值 | 均值 | 标准差 | 最小值 | 最大值 |
|---|---|---|---|---|---|
| 人均GDP（不变价美元） | 5 966 | 9 343.141 | 14 237.60 | 50 | 117 494 |
| 人均GDP（不变价国际元） | 3 026 | 15 788.38 | 18 415.48 | 142 | 127 236 |
| 制造业就业人数占人口的比重 | 4 316 | 0.049 424 4 | 0.106 289 1 | 0.000 034 6 | 2.477 744 |
| 制造业就业人数占劳动力的比重 | 1 952 | 0.112 023 4 | 0.236 509 5 | 0.000 144 1 | 3.792 000 |
| 自然资源租金总额占GDP的百分比 | 5 466 | 8.153 82 | 12.406 54 | 0 | 89.428 72 |
| 每平方千米土地面积人数 | 7 349 | 270.704 8 | 1 386.822 | 0.670 960 2 | 21 595.35 |

注：“制造业就业人数占人口的比重”与“制造业就业人数占劳动力的比重”的某些样本点大于1，本书的所有图形展示中去掉了大于0.5的少数异常值。

全球样本为1963—2010年的156个经济体的非平衡面板数据，表6.2是数据的描述性统计。如图6.10所示，从不同阶段不同经济体的角度来看，全球禀赋结构水平的分布差异巨大。在整个样本中，按照2005年不变价美元计算，禀赋结构水平最低的是1995年的利比里亚，人均GDP只有50美元；禀赋结构水平最高的是2008年的列支敦士登，人均GDP高达117 494美元，是1995年利比里亚禀赋结构水平的2 349.88倍。不过，尽管全球整体的禀赋结构水平分布都有所右移，但世界禀赋结构水平差距并没有明显缩小。与此相对应，如图6.11所示，各个经济体之间的制造业就业结构在不同的阶段也存在巨大的差异，但是不同地区或国家分布的变迁却迥异。[①]如图6.12所示，从整个分布来看，高收入OECD国家制造业就业人数占比从1963年到2010年不断左移，即不断减少，尤其是20世纪90年代以后左移幅度非常大。这一现象与发达国家去工业化的结构变迁密切相关，即制造业在就业中的比重持续下降而服务业在就业中的比重则持续上升，但正如后面的测算结果所示，发达经济体在目前也面临制造业的去空心化，再工业化的趋势明显。与发达国家去工业化密切相关的东亚太平洋地区的工业化浪潮，其制造业就业人数占比从1963年到2010年不断右移，即不断增加，从发达经济体去工业化过程中获益良多。例如，中国从改革开放之后制造业就业人数占比迅速攀升，在20世纪90年代中期迅速到达高峰然后逐步下降，进入21世纪初，再次攀升到现在的高峰，如后面的测算结果所示，中国将再次面临下调的趋势。撒哈拉以南非洲地区和拉丁美洲与加勒比海地区尽管制造业就业人数占比近年来有所扩张，但工业化进程非常缓慢。中东和北非、欧洲与中亚非OECD国家、南亚等地区的制造业就业占比在扩张—萎缩—再扩张的波动中没有表现出强劲的工业化趋势。它们的工业化均未能成功地从发达经济体去工业化过程中受益，但也正面临新一波工业化的绝佳窗口机遇期。

① 关于全球制造业结构分布的变迁更加详细的记录描述，可参见：UNIDO, Industrial Development Report 2013, Sustaining Employment Growth: The Role of Manufacturing and Structural Change。

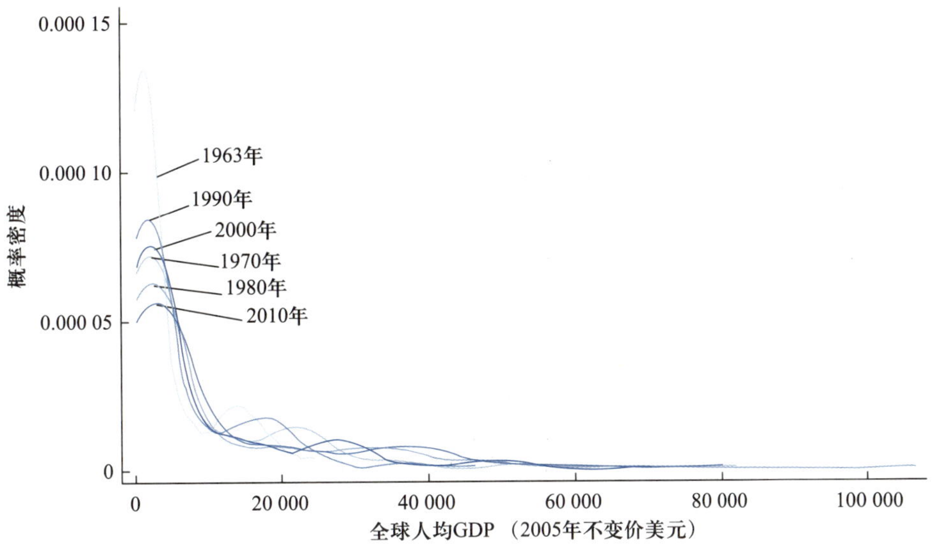


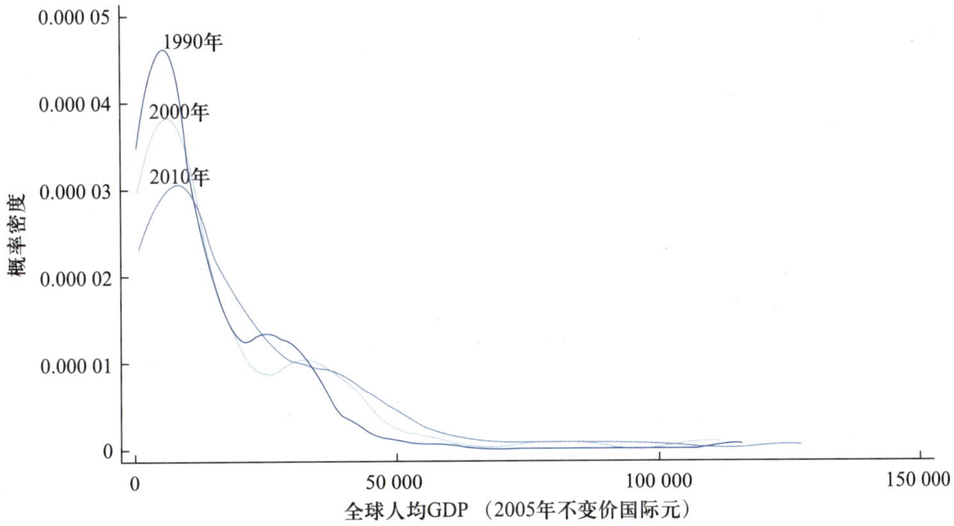


图6.10 全球禀赋水平的分布

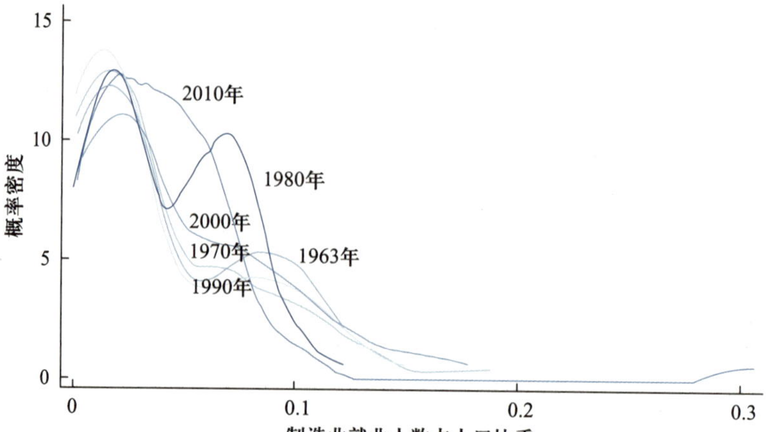


(a) 全球制造业就业人数占人口比重分布的变迁

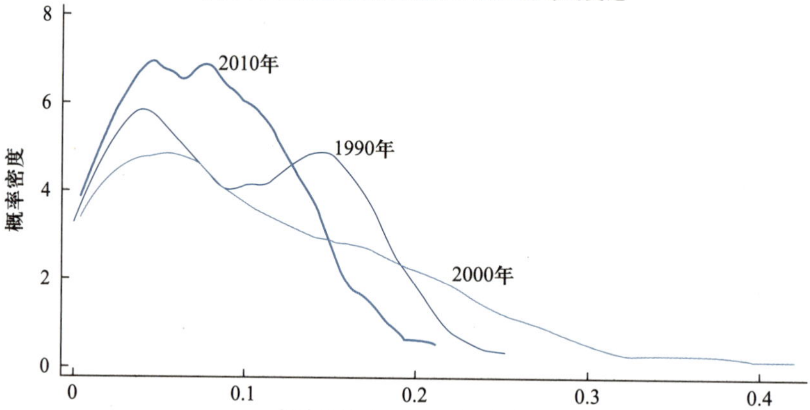


(b) 全球制造业就业人数占劳动力比重分布的变迁

图6.11 全球制造业就业结构的分布

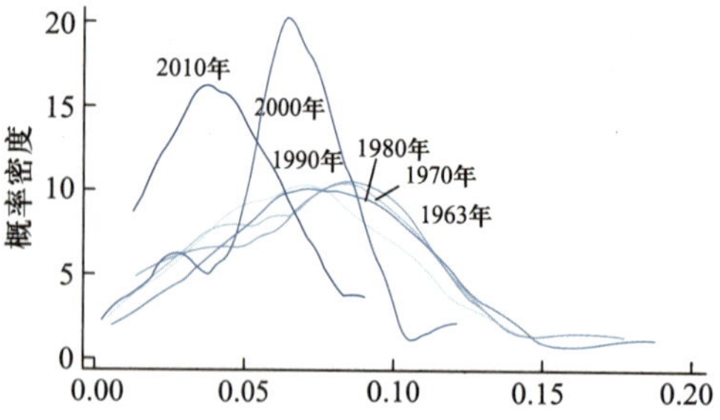


(a) 高收入经济体的制造业就业人数占人口比重分布的变迁

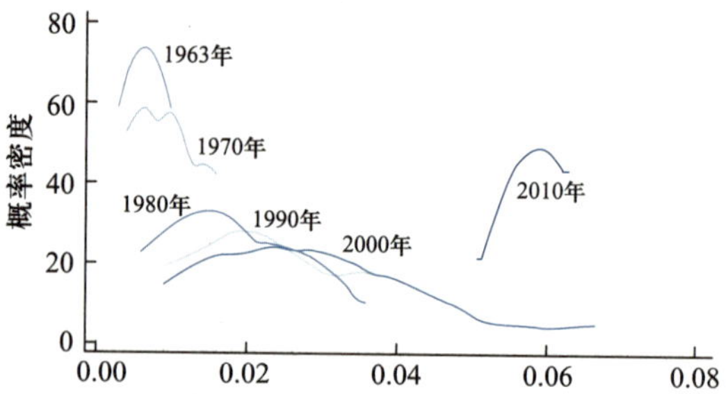


(b) 东亚和太平洋地区各个经济体制造业就业人数占人口比重分布的变迁

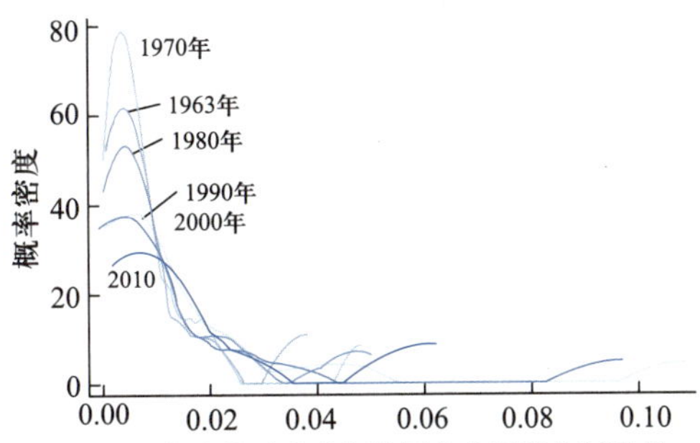


(c) 撒哈拉以南非洲地区各个经济体制造业就业人数占人口比重分布的变迁

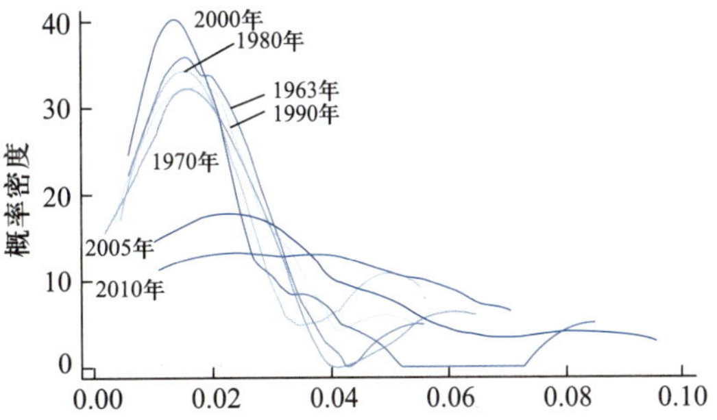


(d) 拉丁美洲与加勒比海地区各个经济体制造业就业人数占人口比重分布的变迁

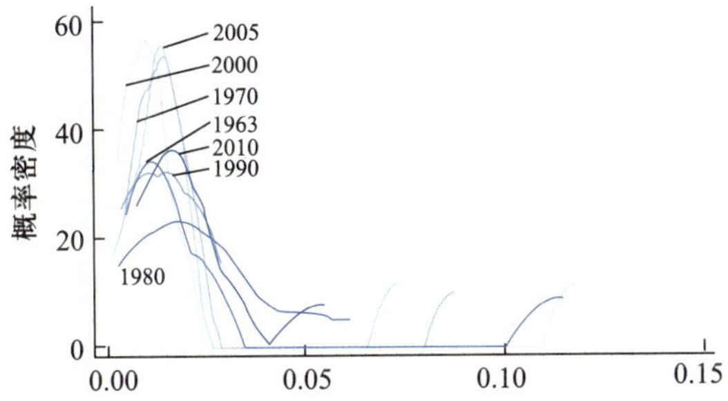


(e) 中东和北非地区各经济体制造业就业人数占人口比重分布的变迁

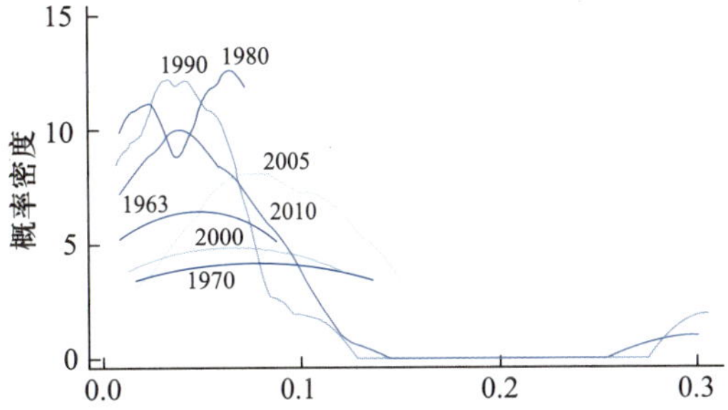


(f) 欧洲和中亚(非OECD)地区各经济体制造业就业人数占人口比重分布的变迁

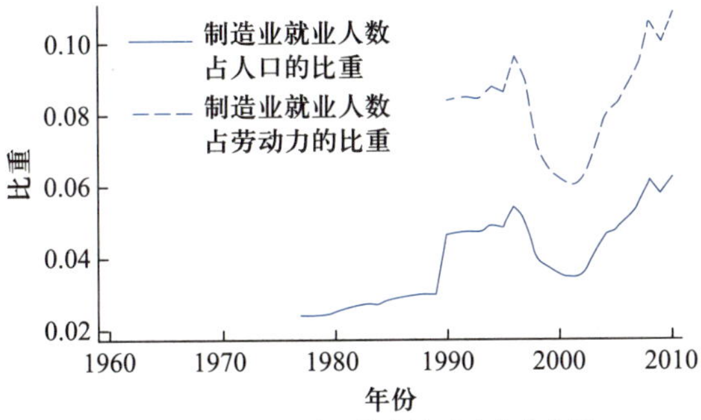


(g) 中国制造业就业比重分布的变迁

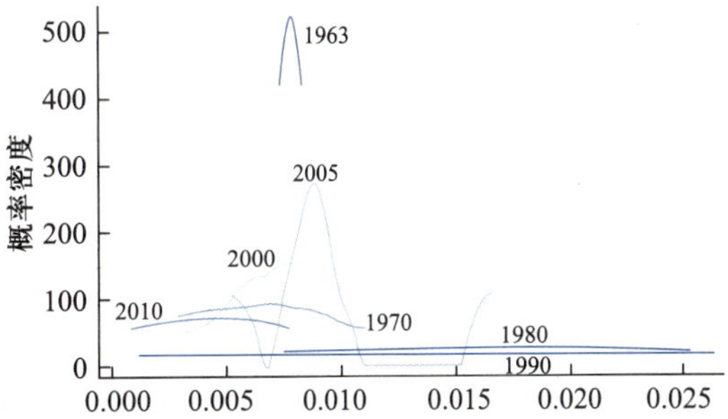


(h) 南亚地区各经济体制造业就业人数占人口比重分布的变迁

图6.12 全球各个地区与中国制造业就业占比分布的变迁（1963—2010年）

### 6.3.3 全球制造业就业结构变迁曲线及其就业缺口估算

表6.3是式（6.1）在8个口径数据下的回归结果，主要变量都非常显著。图6.13是根据该回归结果拟合的禀赋结构水平与制造业就业结构水平的8条基线。这些基线提供了一个经济体根据其禀赋结构变化对制造业就业比重的一个大致预测。据此可得全球156个经济体

1963—2010年按照前述估算方法估算的制造业就业低于标准与过剩（负数表示）情况的总量数据，从而预测全球各地区制造业就业结构变迁的趋势。尽管许多经济体的数据缺失非常严重，但还是能够提供非常丰富的信息。图6.14总结了全球各个地区制造业就业缺口分布的历史变化情况。

表6.3 制造业就业比重基线估算：以2005年不变价美元计算的人均GDP度量禀赋水平

| 项目 | 基线（1–1）制造业就业人数占人口的比重 | 基线（1–2）制造业就业人数占人口的比重 | 基线（2–1）制造业就业人数占劳动力的比重 | 基线（2–2）制造业就业人数占劳动力的比重 |
|---|---|---|---|---|
| 人均GDP（2005年不变价美元） | 0.000 002 42***<br>（32.32） | 0.000 001 86***<br>（24.41） | 0.000 004 41***<br>（19.26） | 0.000 003 73***<br>（16.12） |
| 人均GDP的平方 | $-2.01\times10^{-11}$***<br>（−16.13） | $-1.26\times10^{-11}$***<br>（−10.25） | $-5.43\times10^{-11}$***<br>（−12.46） | $-4.53\times10^{-11}$***<br>（−10.26） |
| 自然资源租金总额占GDP的百分比 | | −0.000 734***<br>（−14.35） | | −0.001 36***<br>（−11.40） |
| 人口密度（每平方千米土地面积人数） | | 0.000 003 82***<br>（13.22） | | 0.000 002 78***<br>（4.46） |
| 常数项 | 0.023 6***<br>（33.77） | 0.030 0***<br>（36.40） | 0.062 4***<br>（31.79） | 0.074 6***<br>（34.27） |
| Adj$R$-squared | 0.302 8 | 0.358 4 | 0.226 7 | 0.279 0 |
| Prob > $F$ | 0.000 0 | 0.000 0 | 0.000 0 | 0.000 0 |
| 观测值 | 3 919 | 3 511 | 1 898 | 1 878 |
| **项目** | **基线（3–1）制造业就业人数占人口的比重** | **基线（3–2）制造业就业人数占人口的比重** | **基线（4–1）制造业就业人数占劳动力的比重** | **基线（4–2）制造业就业人数占劳动力的比重** |
| 人均GDP（2005年不变价国际元） | 0.000 001 95***<br>（26.04） | 0.000 001 67***<br>（21.75） | 0.000 004 11***<br>（26.37） | 0.000 003 50***<br>（22.05） |
| 人均GDP的平方 | $-1.60\times10^{-11}$***<br>（−18.15） | $-1.21\times10^{-11}$***<br>（−13.26） | $-3.52\times10^{-11}$***<br>（−19.33） | $-2.67\times10^{-11}$***<br>（−14.27） |
| 自然资源租金总额占GDP的百分比 | | −0.000 702***<br>（−11.84） | | −0.001 54***<br>（−12.64） |
| 人口密度（每平方千米土地面积人数） | | 0.000 000 465<br>（1.55） | | 0.000 000 808<br>（1.31） |
| 常数项 | 0.018 7***<br>（17.18） | 0.025 4***<br>（21.41） | 0.044 7***<br>（19.86） | 0.059 5***<br>（24.40） |
| Adj$R$-squared | 0.297 7 | 0.342 6 | 0.293 2 | 0.342 3 |
| Prob > $F$ | 0.000 0 | 0.000 0 | 0.000 0 | 0.000 0 |
| 观测值 | 1 899 | 1 879 | 1 878 | 1 858 |

注：括号中是$t$统计量，*$p < 0.05$，**$p < 0.01$，***$p < 0.001$。

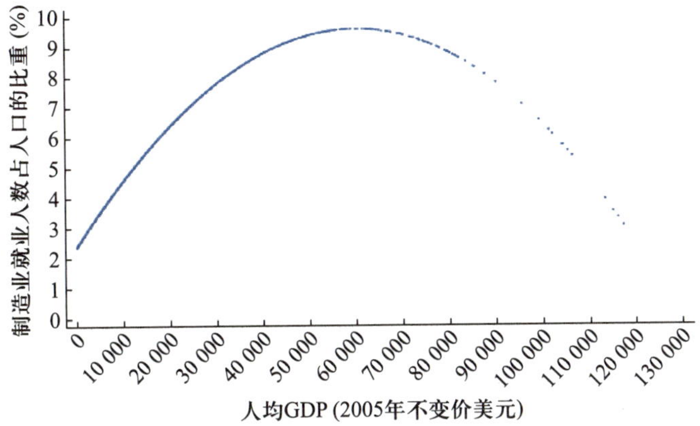


(a) 基线1-1 (无控制变量)

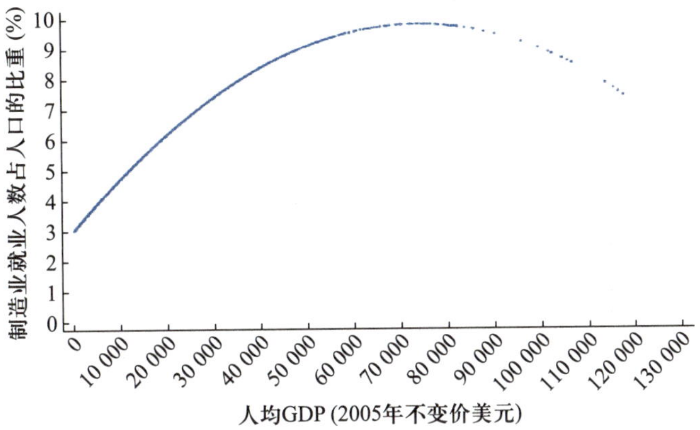


(b) 基线1-2 (控制自然资源和人口密度)

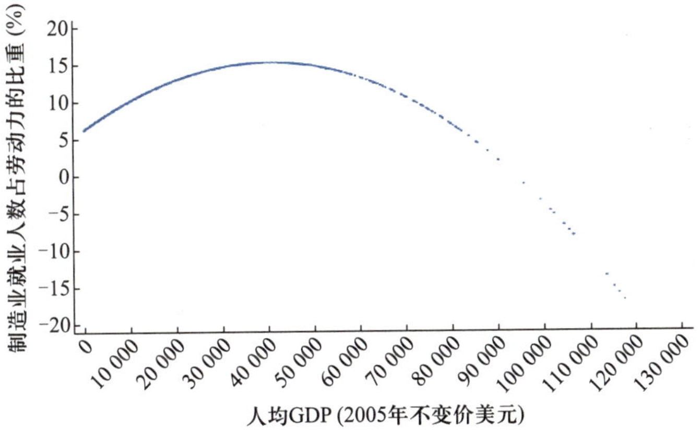


(c) 基线2-1 (无控制变量)

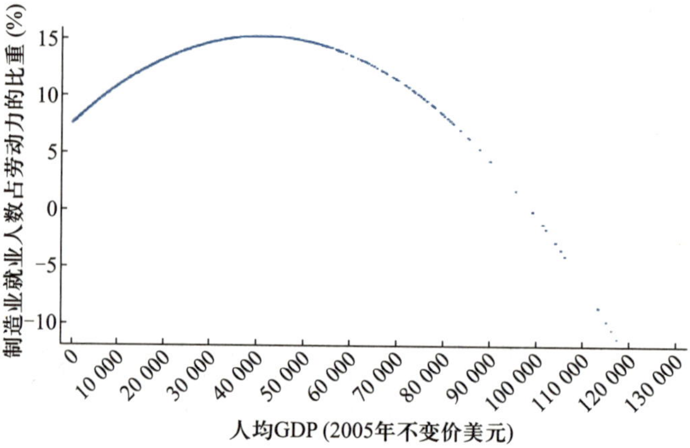


(d) 基线2-2 (控制自然资源和人口密度)

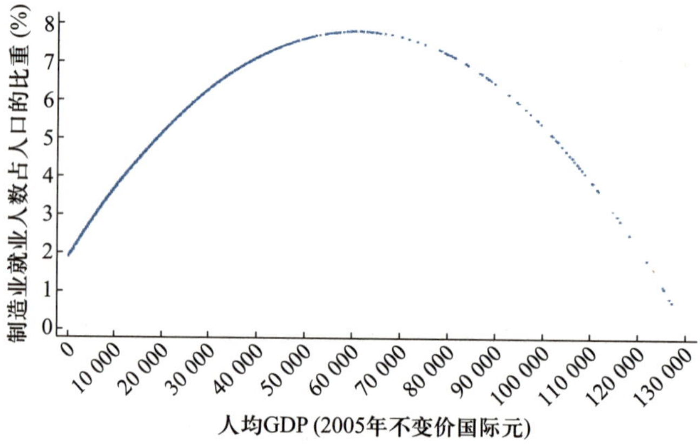


(e) 基线3-2 (无控制变量)

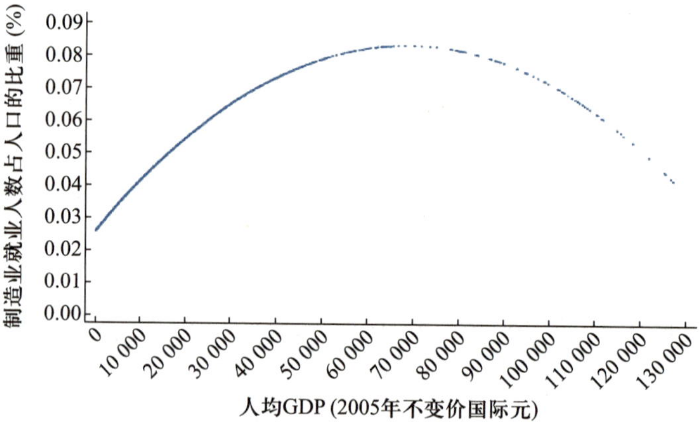


(f) 基线3-2 (控制自然资源和人口密度)

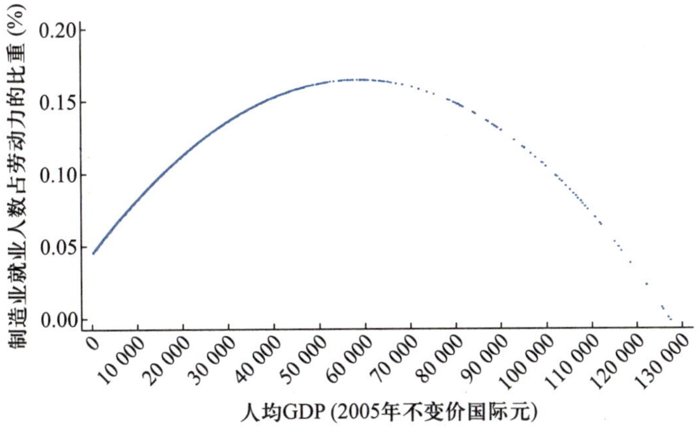


(g) 基线4-1 (无控制变量)

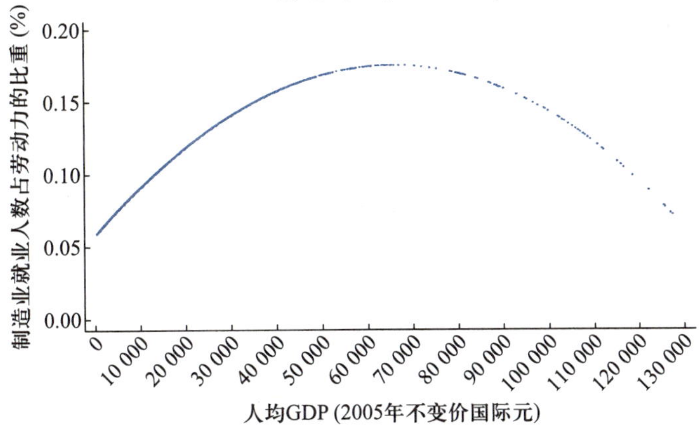


(h) 基线4-2 (控制自然资源和人口密度)

图6.13 禀赋水平与制造业就业人数比重的基线拟合

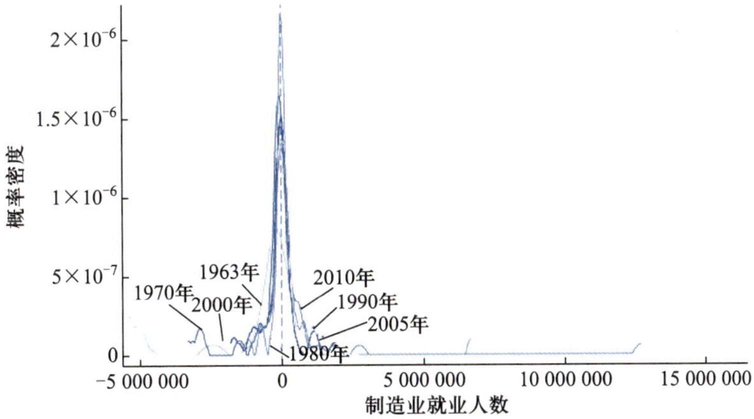


(a) 高收入OECD国家制造业就业缺口分布变迁

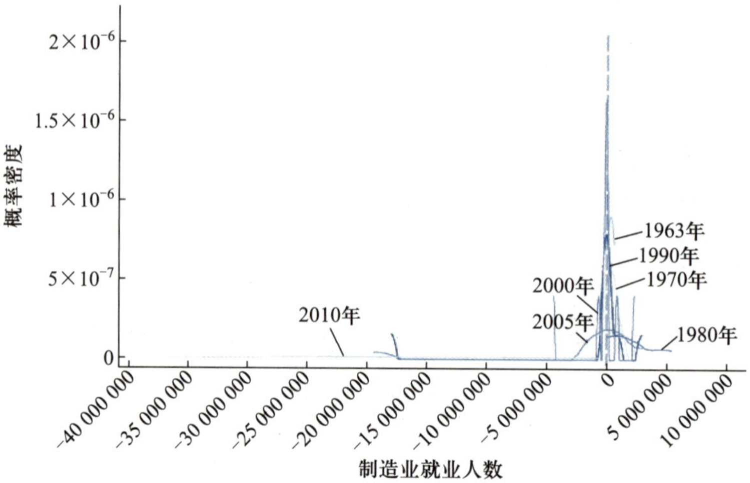


(b) 东亚和太平洋地区各经济体制制造业就业缺口分布的变迁

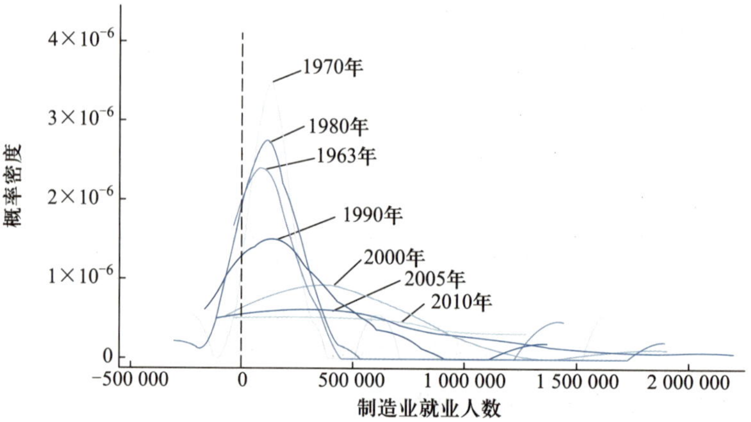


(c) 撒哈拉以南非洲地区各经济体制造业就业缺口分布的变迁

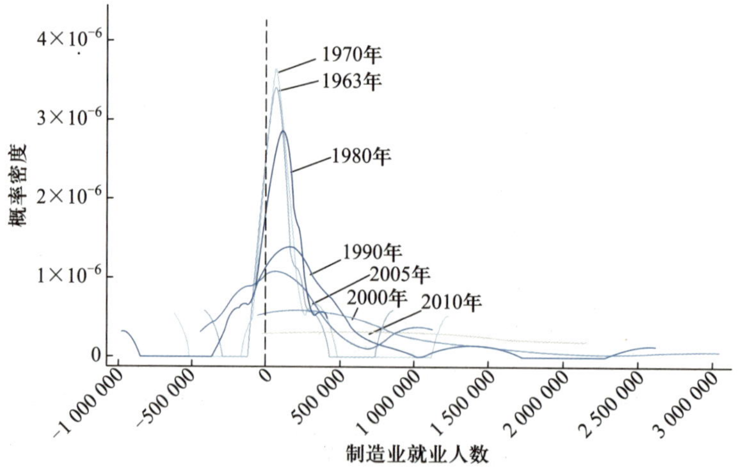


(d) 拉丁美洲与加勒比地区各经济体制造业缺口分布的变迁

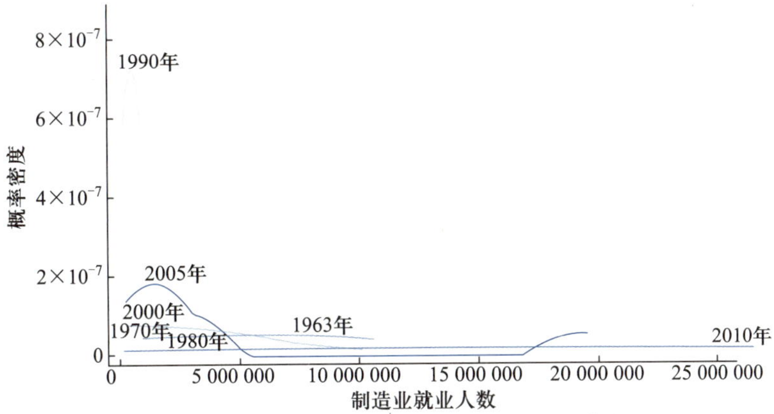

(e) 南亚地区各经济体制造业就业缺口分布的变迁

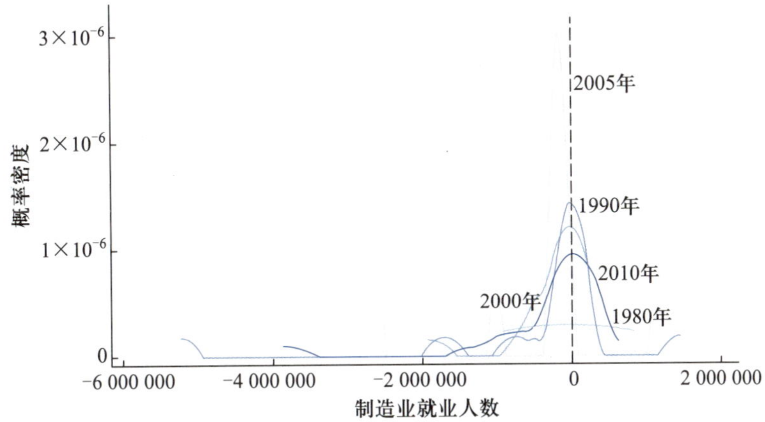

(f) 欧洲和中亚 (OECD) 地区制造业就业缺口分布的变迁

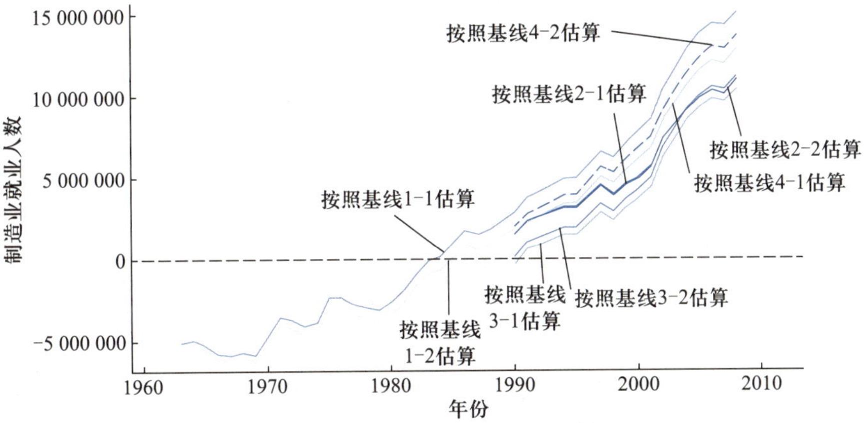

(g) 美国制造业就业缺口估算

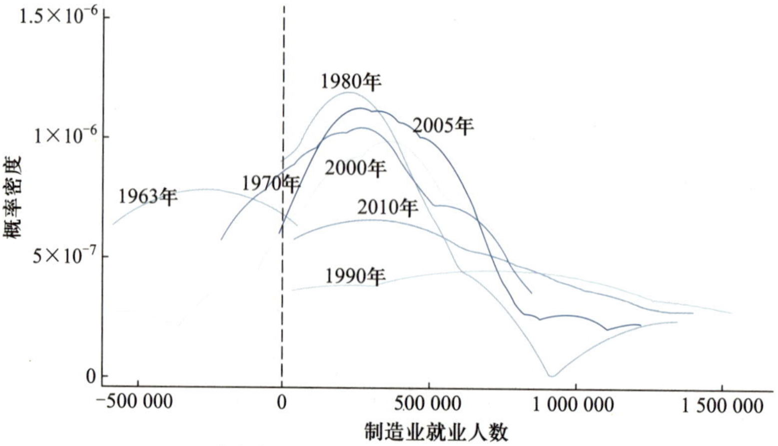


(h) 中东和北非地区各经济体制造业就业缺口分布的变迁

图6.14 全球各个地区以及美国制造业就业缺口分布变迁（1963—2010年）

# 6.4

# 全球各地区制造业就业结构变迁趋势

## 6.4.1 持续不断的亚洲“雁行模式”：东亚奇迹的秘密[①]

本书在第3章介绍经济结构变迁的次序特征时曾指出过，尽管库兹涅茨和罗斯托等早期

① 侯丹丹应用产品空间模型在产品层面也测算了亚洲金融危机之后（1998—2014年）亚洲的“雁行模式”。其测算结果显示，在亚洲金融危机之后，东亚经济体间产业发展的阶梯性尚存；随后东亚产业发展的梯度性显著削弱，后发经济体的赶超趋势明显增强（侯丹丹，“后‘雁行模式’时期东亚产品空间结构演化研究”，《国际经贸探索》，2018年第6期，第50–66页）。

的发展经济学家们描绘了结构变迁的一些重要特征事实，格申克龙也描绘了西欧诸国的追赶过程，但是日本经济学家赤松要对于日本的研究对发展中国家而言可能更有价值，因为日本在经济发展起步时的收入水平远远落后于西方国家。赤松要在1932年就发表了一篇具有开创价值的论文，但直到20世纪60年代才被翻译成英文，其中讨论了他首次提出的“雁行模式”在经济发展中的作用，其含义是“大雁组成一个倒V字阵形往前飞”①。“雁行模式”描述了后进国家的工业化发展次序，主要关注三个维度：产业内部、产业之间以及国家（地区）之间的劳动分工。产业内部的维度观察的是特定发展中国家的产品变化周期，一开始进口某种产品，然后走向国内生产与进口相结合，最后走向出口。产业之间的维度观察的是特定发展中国家的各种产业的出现和发展顺序，产业种类出现多元化和升级，从消费品走向资本品，从简单产品走向复杂产品。国际劳动分工的视角关注的是某些产业从发达国家向发展中国家转移，发展中国家的经济逐渐与发达国家趋同。与一些已有的研究在产品和行业层面对“雁行模式”的识别一样②，在我们的样本期内（1963—2010年）也能够识别出制造业总量层面的亚洲“雁行模式”，如表6.4和图6.15所示。按照基线1-1和基线1-2的估算，日本从20世纪60年代到90年代初期，制造业就业一直处于过剩状态，在60年代有将近500余万个失去比较优势的过剩制造业就业岗位可以转移出去，到90年代初期这一数字也在100万个左右。因此，亚洲的第一波“飞雁”便出现在日本与落后日本不太远的韩国、新加坡、马来西亚、中国香港、中国台湾之间，在20世纪六七十年代日本失去比较优势的制造业转移到存在符合潜在比较优势的制造业低于标准的亚洲“四小龙”，创造了第一波东亚奇迹。随着亚洲“四小龙”等先行者的成功，其收入水平不断提高，资本积累使得禀赋结构不断升级，从而制造业从过去的缺口变成过剩。在20世纪八九十年代便产生了从亚洲“四小龙”向中国内地、越南、印度尼西亚等其他亚洲经济体转移潜在失去比较优势但符合后者潜在比较优势的制造业，这便是第二波东亚“雁行模式”，创造了第二波东亚奇迹。③随着亚洲“飞雁”创造的两波经济发展奇迹，目前日本和亚洲“四小龙”等经济体早已进入高收入经济体

---

① Kaname Akamatsu, “A Historical Pattern of Economic Growth in Developing Countries”, *The Developing Economics*, 1962, 1, pp.3-25.

② 除了赤松要的研究，日本政策研究大学院大学（GRIPS）为2002年GRIPS发展论坛（GRIPS Development Forum in 2002）准备的一份文件也在具体的服装、高铁、普通电视机、录像机、高清电视机等产品层面上展现了亚洲的“雁行模式”。在跨国制造业细分行业层面的行业周期也可以视为雁行模式的体现，如 N. Haraguchi, G. Rezonja, “Patterns of Manufacturing Development Revisited”, UNIDO Working Paper, 2009。甚至美国最发达的制造业中细分行业也能够识别出有规律的行业周期，如Jiandong Ju, Justin Yifu Lin, Yong Wang, “Endowment Structure, industrial dynamics, and economic growth”, *Journal of Monetary Economics*, 2015, 76, pp.244-263。关于“雁行模式”的一个概括性阐述可参考林毅夫的《从西潮到东风》第9章“结构性变化的机制与收益”。

③ 可参考世界银行发布的《东亚奇迹》和林毅夫等所著的《中国的奇迹》对这些故事的阐述。

表 6.4 基线 1−1 和基线 1−2 估算下的亚洲的两次“雁行模式”

| 年份 | 日本 | | 新加坡 | | | 韩国 | | | 马来西亚 | | | 中国 | | | 越南 | | | 印度尼西亚 | | |
|---|---|---|---|---|---|---|---|---|---|---|---|---|---|---|---|---|---|---|---|---|
| | 基线1−1估算 | 基线1−2估算 | 与日本工资比 | 基线1−1估算 | 基线1−2估算 | 与日本工资比 | 基线1−1估算 | 基线1−2估算 | 与日本工资比 | 基线1−1估算 | 基线1−2估算 | 与韩国工资比 | 基线1−1估算 | 基线1−2估算 | 与韩国工资比 | 基线1−1估算 | 基线1−2估算 | 与韩国工资比 | 基线1−1估算 | 基线1−2估算 |
| 1963 | −5 448 661 | −5 256 248 | 102 | 15 362 | 23 997 | 38 | 340 098 | 496 606 | | | | | | | | | | | | |
| 1964 | −5 394 298 | −5 238 448 | 91 | 13 014 | 22 045 | 24 | 363 904 | 523 696 | | | | | | | | | | | | |
| 1965 | −4 624 767 | −4 485 957 | 80 | 9 279 | 18 396 | 20 | 303 557 | 466 966 | | | | | | | | | | | | |
| 1966 | −4 698 042 | −4 597 510 | 76 | 6 838 | 15 948 | 21 | 255 602 | 421 155 | | | | | | | | | | | | |
| 1967 | −4 667 492 | −4 609 852 | 67 | 1 409 | 10 410 | 23 | 200 144 | 368 764 | | | | | | | | | | | | |
| 1968 | −4 683 525 | −4 682 683 | 58 | −10 532 | −1 785 | 23 | 130 738 | 301 097 | 42 | 131 630 | 190 569 | | | | | | | | | |
| 1969 | −4 798 678 | −4 847 770 | 56 | −33 084 | −24 678 | 25 | 86 264 | 257 420 | 37 | 132 090 | 192 359 | | | | | | | | | |
| 1970 | −5 070 976 | −5 109 226 | 49 | −52 762 | −44 761 | 24 | 84 823 | 256 568 | 32 | 122 616 | 184 139 | | | | | | | 26 | 2 301 261 | 3 010 113 |
| 1971 | −4 762 854 | −4 819 287 | 45 | −69 170 | −61 518 | 22 | 128 907 | 301 236 | 27 | 113 804 | 176 604 | | | | | | | 27 | 2 353 707 | 3 079 852 |
| 1972 | −4 685 402 | −4 779 375 | 40 | −94 178 | −87 009 | 17 | 19 560 | 193 455 | 23 | 91 926 | 155 695 | | | | | | | 35 | 2 326 089 | 3 069 523 |
| 1973 | −4 594 441 | −4 727 971 | 39 | −117 572 | −110 820 | 15 | −119 277 | 52 624 | 19 | 34 580 | 99 049 | | | | | | | 36 | 2 399 868 | 3 160 290 |
| 1974 | −4 129 812 | −4 247 884 | 39 | −122 068 | −115 517 | 16 | −234 287 | 62 852 | 20 | 40 140 | 105 558 | | | | | | | 40 | 2 484 871 | 3 262 788 |
| 1975 | −3 802 230 | −3 930 624 | 42 | −110 260 | −103 830 | 15 | −325 822 | −154 203 | 20 | 34 714 | 101 865 | | | | | | | 44 | 2 476 542 | 3 272 695 |
| 1976 | −3 546 874 | −3 694 798 | 39 | −117 153 | −111 072 | 19 | −576 139 | −407 884 | 19 | 7 635 | 75 308 | | | | | | | 41 | 2 470 581 | 3 285 273 |
| 1977 | −3 084 549 | −3 253 728 | 34 | −125 243 | −119 539 | 20 | −733 007 | −568 068 | 17 | 898 | 69 456 | 21 | 147 660 | 5 796 632 | | | | 38 | 2 568 595 | 3 401 052 |
| 1978 | −2 850 330 | −3 046 433 | 28 | −145 461 | −140 288 | 20 | −878 902 | −717 096 | 14 | −26 333 | 43 233 | 18 | −37 862 | 5 980 650 | | | | 30 | 2 630 163 | 3 480 233 |
| 1979 | −2 610 859 | −2 835 702 | 32 | −166 382 | −161 838 | 26 | −843 108 | −683 661 | 17 | −56 947 | 13 263 | 16 | −52 238 | 6 036 308 | | | | 20 | 2 677 123 | 3 545 579 |
| 1980 | −2 564 063 | −2 802 698 | 36 | −177 019 | −173 212 | 25 | −764 579 | −599 997 | 18 | −96 500 | −25 364 | 19 | −706 668 | 5 451 612 | | | | 26 | 2 665 531 | 3 551 732 |
| 1981 | −2 471 873 | −2 732 482 | 39 | −165 088 | −161 655 | 24 | −721 551 | −558 733 | 17 | −141 808 | −69 642 | 16 | −1 654 800 | 4 575 128 | | | | 30 | 2 719 297 | 3 623 446 |
| 1982 | −2 242 929 | −2 521 147 | 47 | −151 605 | −148 303 | 27 | −728 461 | −568 468 | 21 | −85 777 | −12 362 | 14 | −2 612 532 | 3 704 770 | | | | 34 | 2 747 071 | 3 672 507 |
| 1983 | −2 242 235 | −2 536 293 | 50 | −141 245 | −138 709 | 26 | −782 239 | −629 004 | 32 | −46 115 | 28 550 | 14 | −3 050 010 | 3 348 990 | | | | 28 | 2 793 039 | 3 736 241 |
| 1984 | −2 145 873 | −2 463 811 | 53 | −137 613 | −135 840 | 27 | −852 984 | −705 973 | 23 | −35 530 | 40 154 | 13 | −2 887 034 | 3 582 072 | | | | 25 | 2 811 672 | 3 772 840 |
| 1985 | −2 014 415 | −2 366 000 | 53 | −116 901 | −115 022 | 26 | −900 630 | −758 813 | 23 | −3 886 | 74 778 | 11 | −4 108 986 | 2 426 048 | | | | 26 | 2 418 152 | 3 398 822 |
| 1986 | −1 885 630 | −2 251 477 | 35 | −109 196 | −107 497 | 18 | −1 124 768 | −993 731 | 15 | 5 582 | 86 901 | 10 | −4 847 752 | 1 762 126 | | | | 24 | 2 504 215 | 3 502 605 |
| 1987 | −1 552 090 | −1 938 805 | 30 | −130 516 | −129 934 | 19 | −1 306 530 | −1 187 634 | 13 | −16 802 | 66 410 | | −5 483 762 | 1 217 342 | | | | 16 | 2 498 108 | 3 514 131 |
| 1988 | −1 384 943 | −1 805 826 | 28 | −169 289 | −169 810 | 22 | −1 339 846 | −1 233 731 | 10 | −75 702 | 8 411 | | −6 131 270 | 655 416 | | | | 13 | 2 310 920 | 3 343 400 |
| 1989 | −1 217 049 | −1 661 286 | 34 | −171 890 | −173 425 | 31 | −1 250 743 | −1 151 809 | 11 | −147 529 | −62 470 | | −5 764 788 | 1 101 380 | | | | 10 | 2 224 912 | 3 271 538 |
| 1990 | −1 350 734 | −1 816 332 | 41 | −174 477 | −176 961 | 35 | −1 091 394 | −1 003 923 | 11 | −265 852 | −180 042 | | −24 900 000 | −18 000 000 | | | | 7 | 1 926 898 | 2 987 067 |
| 1991 | −1 367 912 | −1 844 867 | 42 | −172 623 | −175 766 | 37 | −906 933 | −832 510 | 11 | −375 927 | −289 766 | | −25 900 000 | −18 900 000 | | | | 7 | 1 701 569 | 2 774 585 |
| 1992 | −1 121 646 | −1 601 527 | 44 | −163 355 | −167 240 | 36 | −727 518 | −660 408 | 12 | −408 896 | −322 445 | | −26 100 000 | −19 000 000 | | | | 7 | 1 486 804 | 2 573 350 |
| 1993 | −828 198 | −1 309 038 | 42 | −146 491 | −151 928 | 34 | −730 637 | −672 303 | 11 | −499 010 | −412 841 | | −26 400 000 | −19 200 000 | | | | 7 | 1 329 105 | 2 428 547 |
| 1994 | −171 336 | −655 385 | 58 | −142 241 | −149 135 | 47 | −682 130 | −637 539 | 14 | −542 587 | −456 709 | | −28 400 000 | 21 200 000 | | | | 7 | 1 195 965 | 2 307 303 |
| 1995 | 38 734 | −451 571 | 60 | −135 644 | −143 429 | 51 | −598 432 | −568 780 | 14 | −669 681 | −584 564 | | −27 600 000 | −20 400 000 | | | | 9 | 949 490 | 2 070 940 |
| 1996 | 370 103 | −127 300 | 72 | −121 241 | −129 943 | 62 | −457 725 | −440 549 | 18 | −681 001 | −596 976 | | −34 600 000 | −27 400 000 | | | | 8 | 1 020 281 | 2 151 708 |
| 1997 | 613 199 | 111 615 | 79 | −103 879 | −113 745 | 60 | −188 317 | −181 283 | 20 | −572 150 | −488 279 | | −29 900 000 | −22 600 000 | | | | | | |
| 1998 | 642 916 | 145 239 | 79 | −89 732 | −98 836 | 43 | 113 403 | 135 106 | | | | | −17 600 000 | −10 300 000 | 9 | 978 507 | 1 440 900 | 6 | 1 198 423 | 2 379 111 |
| 1999 | 1 084 810 | 587 177 | 68 | −67 230 | −77 417 | 47 | 67 858 | 68 457 | 15 | −563 299 | −471 763 | | −13 700 000 | −6 456 464 | | | | 6 | 1 162 227 | 2 360 893 |
| 2000 | 1 390 767 | 887 368 | 68 | −56 915 | −68 587 | 52 | 43 599 | 26 367 | 14 | −743 526 | −653 249 | | −11 700 000 | −4 432 640 | 5 | 390 517 | 864 392 | 6 | 1 124 656 | 2 336 643 |
| 2001 | 2 031 777 | 1 526 976 | 74 | −54 895 | −66 172 | 54 | 123 573 | 97 351 | 20 | −549 195 | −456 061 | | −10 200 000 | −2 914 520 | | 161 696 | 640 487 | 8 | 1 180 723 | 2 407 532 |
| 2002 | 2 643 049 | 2 136 953 | 78 | −59 626 | −71 642 | 64 | 180 974 | 138 430 | 21 | −621 140 | −527 974 | | −10 800 000 | −3 568 880 | | −213 583 | 269 568 | 7 | 1 299 197 | 2 539 907 |
| 2003 | 2 901 416 | 2 391 308 | 76 | −49 334 | −62 254 | 68 | 213 878 | 165 185 | 20 | −607 356 | −514 613 | 8 | −16 400 000 | −9 177 108 | | −538 429 | −51 094 | 9 | 1 491 188 | 2 745 447 |
| 2004 | 3 167 166 | 2 653 176 | 73 | −40 422 | −54 844 | 69 | 251 319 | 191 409 | 19 | −616 856 | −525 336 | 8 | −24 500 000 | −17 300 000 | | −842 181 | −350 723 | 6 | 1 545 331 | 2 812 654 |
| 2005 | 3 241 891 | 2 726 294 | 76 | −37 083 | −52 592 | 82 | 245 417 | 176 228 | 20 | −713 464 | −622 466 | 8 | −26 500 000 | −19 400 000 | | −1 016 333 | −520 965 | 6 | 1 755 415 | 3 034 793 |
| 2006 | 3 340 392 | 2 823 402 | 86 | −30 229 | −46 951 | 95 | 279 064 | 198 012 | 19 | −726 648 | −636 474 | 8 | −30 000 000 | −23 000 000 | 4 | −1 287 160 | −788 140 | 6 | 1 359 910 | 2 651 414 |
| 2007 | 3 258 652 | 2 740 776 | 93 | −29 845 | −47 793 | 109 | 702 580 | 608 877 | 21 | −775 394 | −686 742 | 9 | −34 300 000 | −27 400 000 | 4 | −1 627 165 | −1 124 738 | 5 | 1 593 452 | 2 895 360 |
| 2008 | 3 188 620 | 2 671 248 | 88 | −46 706 | −65 224 | 87 | 814 317 | 714 716 | 21 | −1 536 625 | −1 448 634 | 14 | −42 700 000 | −35 900 000 | 6 | −1 766 569 | −1 260 445 | 7 | 1 883 382 | 3 195 777 |
| 2009 | 3 311 994 | 2 800 993 | 82 | −23 798 | −42 369 | | | | | −634 030 | −541 848 | | −37 500 000 | −30 900 000 | | −1 885 680 | −1 375 837 | | 2 109 733 | 3 434 423 |
| 2010 | 3 586 140 | 3 070 249 | 84 | 9 379 | −10 946 | | | | | −704 967 | −615 592 | | −43 300 000 | −36 800 000 | | −2 164 080 | −1 650 998 | | | |

注：工资为制造业平均工资（以不变价美元计算，下同），工资比例为百分比。

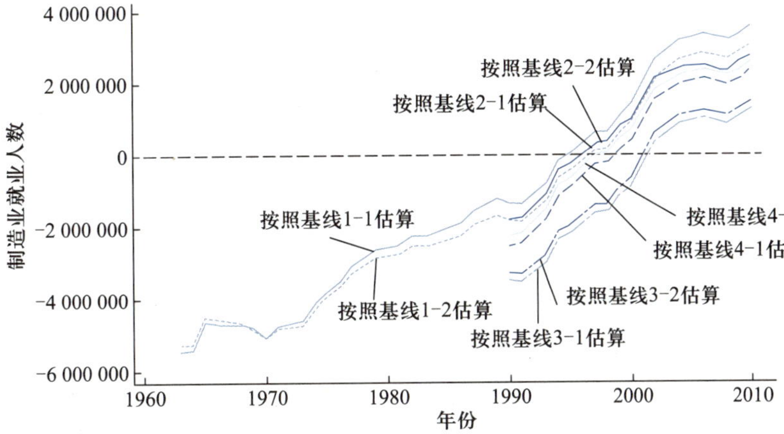


(a) 日本制造业就业缺口估算

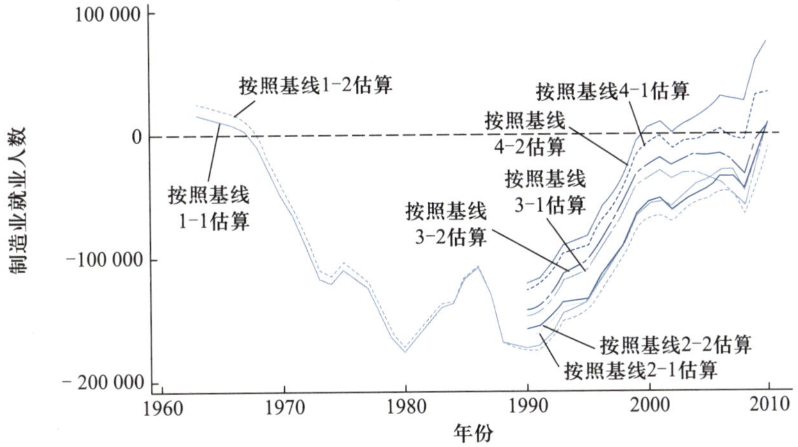


(b) 新加坡制造业就业缺口估算

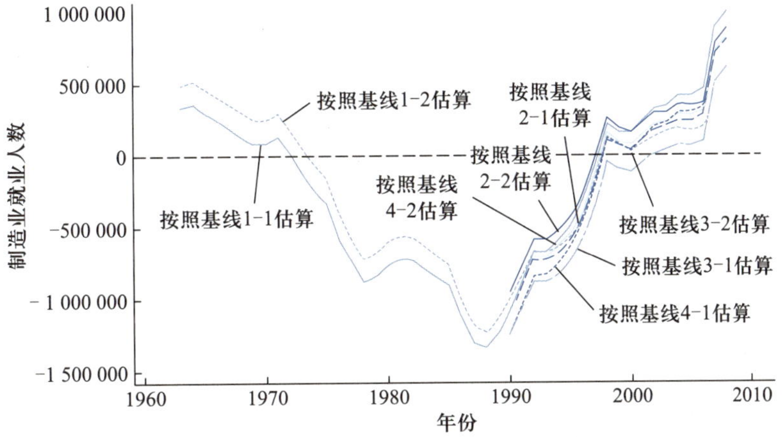


(c) 韩国制造业就业缺口估算

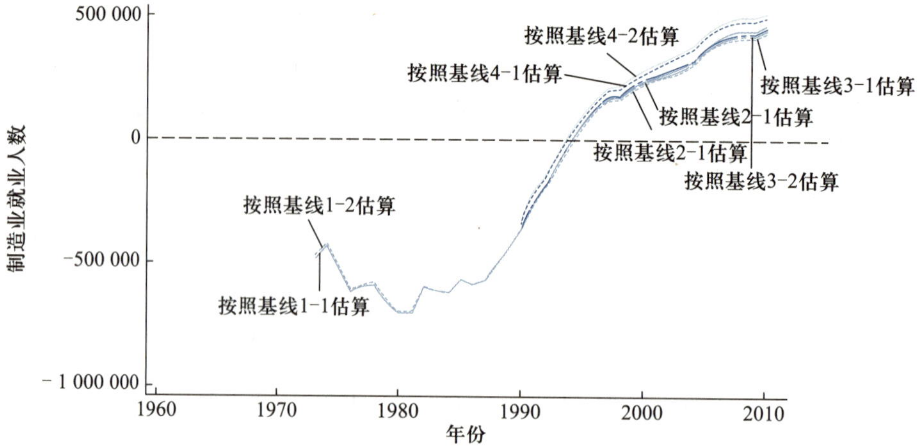


(d) 中国香港制造业就业缺口估算

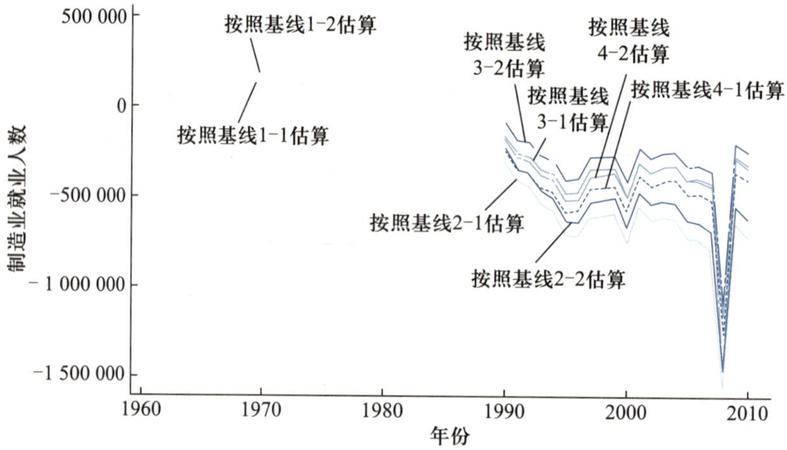


(e) 马来西亚制造业就业缺口估算

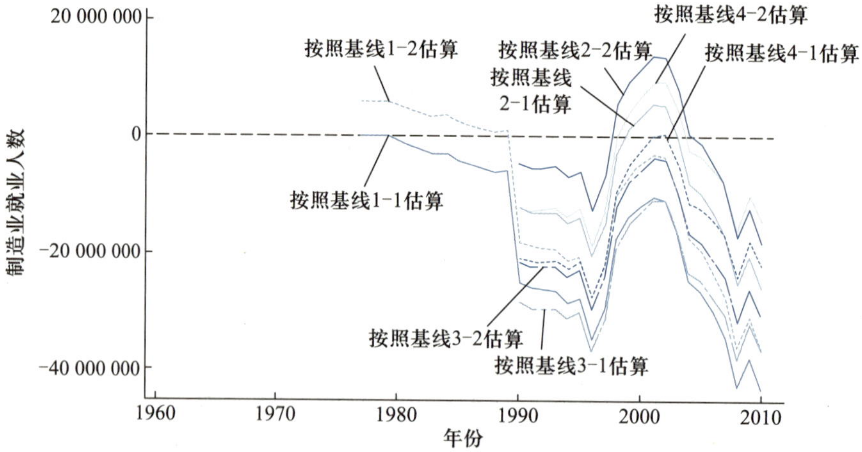


(f) 中国制造业就业缺口估算

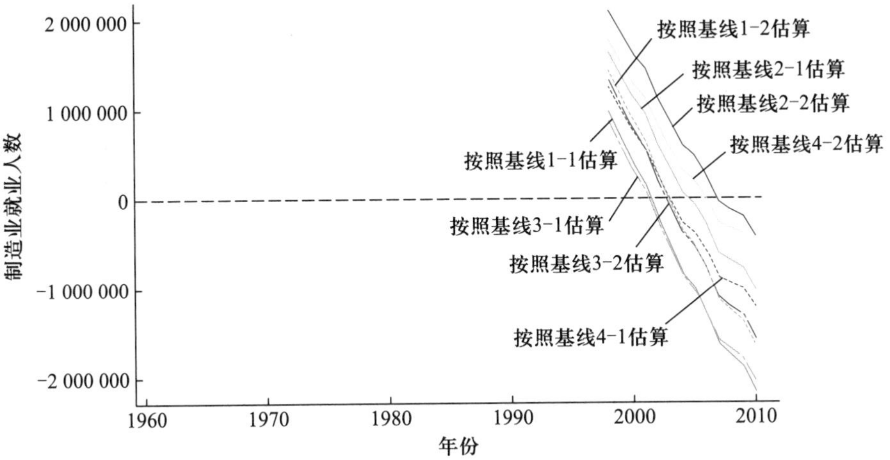


(g) 越南制造业就业缺口估算

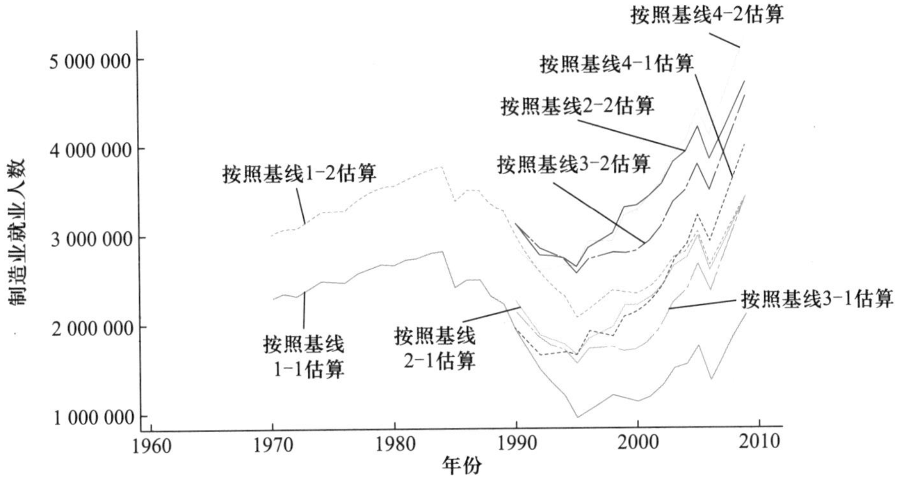


(h) 印度尼西亚制造业就业缺口估算

图6.15 亚洲的“雁行模式”

行列，其在去工业化之后又开始面临再工业化的问题；而中国内地、越南等第二波亚洲“雁行模式”中曾经的产业承接经济体，由于高速发展，收入水平不断提高、资本不断积累、工资水平不断上涨，使得过去承接的符合比较优势的制造业又失去比较优势，产生了大量过剩制造业就业岗位。当然，由于经济体所处水平不同以及产业细分的差异，亚洲内部的“雁行模式”并未结束。本章6.7节还会继续细化东亚“雁行模式”的讨论。例如，在第9章讨论“一带一路”时提到的泰中罗勇工业园、中国印尼综合产业园区青山园区、中柬西哈努克港经济特区，就是在继续的东亚“雁行模式”的案例。

上述持续不断的亚洲“雁行模式”其实就是东亚奇迹的秘密所在。从图6.16中，这个秘密一览无余：盘旋在东亚和太平洋地区的雁阵不断通过“两头在外”吸收失掉比较优势产业中的“剩余劳动力”——制造业出口与进口占商品出口的百分比从20世纪80年代到今天一直维持在60% ~ 80%左右，而且出口比重大于进口比重，出口比重保持不断上升的趋势，进

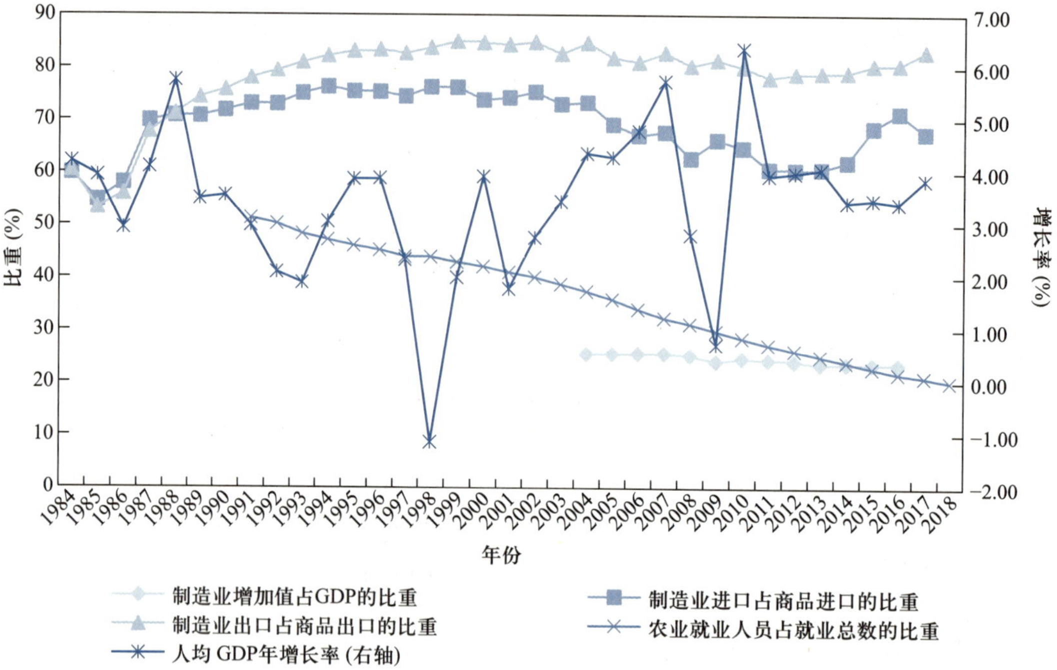


**图6.16 东亚与太平洋地区制造业各项指标比重、剩余劳动力（农业就业人口）与经济增长**

数据来源：世界银行。

口比重保持不断下降的趋势；农业就业人员占就业总数的百分比从20世纪90年代超过50%持续下降到2017年的20%左右。2018年东亚和太平洋地区的劳动力[①]高达12.6亿人次，因此我们有充分的理由认为其制造业会继续保持良好的发展态势，继续成为世界最具活力的制造业中心。东亚的“雁行模式”可以为后面将介绍的南亚和撒哈拉以南非洲地区利用世界经济结构变迁引致的全球劳动力密集型制造业迁徙的窗口机遇期提供借鉴。如表6.5所示，在过去60年中，东南亚一些发展中国家，如印度尼西亚、柬埔寨、马来西亚、菲律宾、泰国、越南的制造业增加值增长率甚至持续性地超过两位数，堪称“雁行模式”下发展制造业的奇迹。近些年来，越南的举措令人瞩目，进一步大力开放有比较优势的领域，如表6.6所示。

① 按照国际劳工组织的标准，本书中所指的劳动力总数包括所有年满15周岁、符合国际劳工组织对从事经济活动人口所作定义的群体：所有在特定阶段为货物和服务的生产提供劳力的人员。既包括就业者，也包括失业者。虽然各国在对待武装部队、季节工或兼职工的做法有所不同，但一般而言劳动力包括武装部队、失业者、首次求职者，但是不包括料理家务者和非正规部门的其他无偿看护和工人。

表6.5 1962—2018年印度尼西亚、柬埔寨、马来西亚、菲律宾、泰国、越南的制造业增加值增长率（%）

| 国家 | | | 1962 | 1963 | 1964 | 1965 | 1966 | 1967 | 1968 | 1969 |
|---|---|---|---|---|---|---|---|---|---|---|
| 印度尼西亚 | | | 12.27 | 1.37 | −1.89 | −1.37 | −0.84 | 1.97 | 3.31 | 8.80 |
| 菲律宾 | | | 4.18 | 5.37 | 7.50 | 3.39 | 4.17 | 7.18 | 8.71 | 6.29 |
| 泰国 | | | 10.26 | 11.63 | 9.38 | 8.57 | 16.67 | 11.28 | 12.16 | 7.23 |
| 国家 | 1970 | 1971 | 1972 | 1973 | 1974 | 1975 | 1976 | 1977 | 1978 | 1979 |
| 印度尼西亚 | 14.22 | 9.66 | 13.50 | 5.17 | 3.28 | 16.15 | 12.30 | 9.68 | 13.73 | 11.23 |
| 马来西亚 | — | — | 12.59 | 10.17 | 22.52 | 10.37 | 2.95 | 18.51 | 10.59 | 9.27 |
| 菲律宾 | 3.62 | 8.03 | 6.79 | 5.76 | 14.74 | 3.97 | 2.77 | 5.79 | 6.36 | 6.62 |
| 泰国 | 12.92 | 15.95 | 10.84 | 13.41 | 15.65 | 6.35 | 5.71 | 15.23 | 14.50 | 8.57 |
| 国家 | 1980 | 1981 | 1982 | 1983 | 1984 | 1985 | 1986 | 1987 | 1988 | 1989 |
| 印度尼西亚 | 18.60 | 22.17 | 10.16 | 1.22 | 2.20 | 22.05 | 11.19 | 9.29 | 10.61 | 11.99 |
| 马来西亚 | 11.34 | 9.22 | 4.72 | 5.60 | 7.87 | 12.29 | −3.83 | 7.53 | 13.40 | 16.99 |
| 菲律宾 | 4.68 | 4.18 | 1.95 | 1.60 | −0.32 | −10.11 | −7.90 | 1.81 | 5.57 | 9.52 |
| 泰国 | 8.40 | 2.85 | 6.28 | 2.65 | 11.19 | 6.20 | −1.37 | 9.84 | 16.04 | 17.93 |
| 越南 | — | — | — | — | — | — | — | 12.62 | 11.65 | 7.08 |
| 国家 | 1990 | 1991 | 1992 | 1993 | 1994 | 1995 | 1996 | 1997 | 1998 | 1999 |
| 印度尼西亚 | 9.20 | 12.50 | 9.60 | 10.14 | 9.35 | 12.36 | 10.88 | 11.59 | 5.25 | −11.44 |
| 柬埔寨 | — | — | — | — | — | — | 17.50 | 12.53 | 27.51 | 15.15 |
| 马来西亚 | 20.32 | 15.29 | 14.00 | 7.00 | 14.58 | 11.37 | 11.36 | 18.18 | 10.12 | −13.42 |
| 菲律宾 | 5.81 | 2.66 | −0.44 | −1.73 | 0.75 | 5.01 | 6.77 | 5.58 | 4.22 | −1.13 |
| 泰国 | 16.03 | 15.67 | 11.72 | 11.30 | 16.24 | 8.38 | 11.18 | 5.71 | 0.87 | −8.38 |
| 越南 | −12.88 | −6.34 | 5.62 | 13.72 | 9.53 | 9.33 | 13.55 | 13.59 | 12.83 | 10.20 |
| 国家 | 2000 | 2001 | 2002 | 2003 | 2004 | 2005 | 2006 | 2007 | 2008 | 2009 |
| 印度尼西亚 | 3.92 | 5.98 | 3.30 | 5.29 | 5.33 | 6.38 | 4.60 | 4.59 | 4.67 | 3.66 |
| 柬埔寨 | 19.72 | 30.29 | 15.20 | 14.41 | 12.30 | 17.66 | 9.72 | 17.43 | 8.88 | 3.12 |
| 老挝 | — | — | 12.10 | 12.97 | 5.63 | 15.12 | 10.33 | 13.55 | 13.70 | 9.17 |
| 缅甸 | — | — | 21.84 | 28.71 | 22.04 | 24.69 | 21.94 | 27.17 | 20.89 | 19.28 |
| 马来西亚 | 11.67 | 18.31 | −4.27 | 4.12 | 9.16 | 9.56 | 5.20 | 7.43 | 9.01 | −0.71 |
| 菲律宾 | 1.70 | 5.52 | 2.70 | 3.03 | 3.68 | 5.24 | 5.04 | 4.09 | 3.57 | 4.31 |
| 泰国 | 9.81 | 3.31 | 1.96 | 8.82 | 10.16 | 7.46 | 4.21 | 5.61 | 7.23 | 2.39 |
| 越南 | 7.99 | 11.68 | 11.35 | 11.60 | 11.53 | 10.86 | 12.92 | 13.36 | 12.37 | 9.78 |
| 国家 | 2010 | 2011 | 2012 | 2013 | 2014 | 2015 | 2016 | 2017 | 2018 | |
| 印度尼西亚 | 2.21 | 4.74 | 6.26 | 5.62 | 4.37 | 4.64 | 4.33 | 4.26 | 4.27 | |
| 柬埔寨 | −15.51 | 29.56 | 16.17 | 6.86 | 9.82 | 6.65 | 9.22 | 7.05 | 6.34 | |
| 老挝 | 5.78 | 3.71 | 10.39 | 9.93 | 3.52 | 9.75 | 4.42 | 3.15 | 4.43 | |
| 缅甸 | 18.58 | 35.80 | 10.81 | 8.32 | 9.54 | 9.46 | 9.90 | 9.31 | 10.26 | |
| 马来西亚 | −8.32 | 6.64 | 5.44 | 4.42 | 3.41 | 6.10 | 4.81 | 4.42 | 6.03 | |
| 菲律宾 | −4.80 | 11.16 | 4.73 | 5.39 | 10.26 | 8.29 | 5.67 | 7.00 | 8.55 | |

续表

| 国家 | 2010 | 2011 | 2012 | 2013 | 2014 | 2015 | 2016 | 2017 | 2018 | |
|---|---|---|---|---|---|---|---|---|---|---|
| 泰国 | −3.31 | 11.37 | −4.83 | 6.90 | 1.90 | 0.06 | 1.66 | 2.30 | 2.61 | |
| 越南 | 2.76 | −21.84 | 14.08 | 9.05 | 7.22 | 7.41 | 10.60 | 11.90 | 14.40 | |

资料来源：世界银行。

表6.6 2018年越南数千类进出口商品关税将降为零

| 文件 | 2018年越南关税情况 |
|---|---|
| 越南-韩国自贸区协定 | 2018年对纺织原辅料、鞋类、家用电器、机械设备、电子产品和零配件、电线、电缆线、汽车、汽车配件等产品实现关税自由化 |
| 越南-日本自贸区协定 | 2018年共有456项税目实施零关税，集中于脂肪、糖、机械设备等 |
| 东盟-中国自贸区协定 | 2018年从5%与10%减为零关税的商品包括：鸡肉、咖啡、原料茶、食品加工、纺织品服装、电器与电子设备等 |
| 亚欧经济同盟自贸区协定 | 至2018年有5 535项税目实施零关税，同时2018年内有3 720项税目降为零关税，如：乳及乳制品、汽车及其零配件、钢铁及其制品 |
| 东盟经济共同体 | 越南基本完成2015年东盟关税消减，到2018年剩余7%的税目商品将采用具有灵活性的税率，上述商品主要集中于汽车摩托车及其零配件、植物油、热带水果、冰箱、空调、乳品与乳制品等 |
| 区域全面经济伙伴关系协定 | 2017年谈判完成度80% |
| 越南-欧盟自贸区协定 | 将于2019年启动，欧盟将对越南取消99%的关税，越南承诺保护169种欧洲食品和饮料产品只从欧盟进口 |

资料来源：越南通讯社，天风证券研究所。

### 6.4.2 南亚与撒哈拉以南非洲地区急需发展劳动力密集型制造业来脱贫

与东亚的制造业处于过剩情况恰好相反，南亚与撒哈拉以南的非洲地区面临工业化制造业缺口较大。非洲是各个经济体制造业缺口最为密集的地方，而南亚的印度则是制造业缺口最多的国家。如图6.17所示，按照不同基线估算，印度制造业就业缺口在1 500万以上。巴基斯坦按照8条基线估算的平均制造业就业缺口在300万以上，阿富汗、尼泊尔也零星有些制造业就业缺口，但体量不大（图6.18）。南亚和撒哈拉以南非洲地区是全球贫困率最高和贫困人口最多的地区，是人类反贫困斗争最艰苦的地区。如前文所指出的，这些地区缺乏就业岗位是贫困的根源，而就业岗位的缺乏源于没有发展符合其潜在比较优势的劳动力密集型产业。2018年南亚地区有7.049 4亿劳动力，撒哈拉以南非洲地区有4.284 8亿劳动力。2018年南亚的失业率为3.75%，撒哈拉以南非洲地区的失业率为7.32%，也就是说南亚的失业劳动力就有2 643.5万人——这与前面的制造业就业缺口估算数据在量级上是吻合的，撒哈拉以南非洲地区的失业劳动力就有3 136.5万人。南亚和撒哈拉以南非洲地区之所以出现这种状况，主要是第二次世界大战后至今工业化极其缓慢，如图6.19所示，南亚地区的制造业增加值占GDP的百分比在1960年是14.35%，到了2017年依然只有14.82%，可以说是停滞不前。撒哈拉以南非洲地区也同样如此，制造业增加值占GDP的百分比1981年为16.66%，到了2017年反而下降到10.1%，萎缩了6个百分点，如图6.20所示。相应地，无法进入制造业的大量劳动力只能停留在低生产率的农业部门，2018年南亚农业就业人员占就业总数的百分比高达42.05%，撒哈拉以南非洲地区更是高达57.02%。这急需发展劳动力密集型制造业来创造就业岗位吸纳这些失业劳动力。

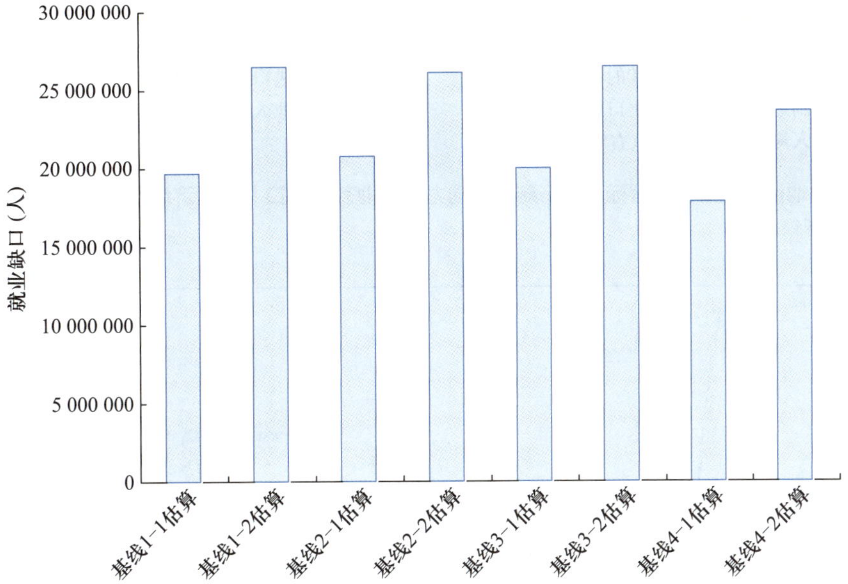

图6.17 按照8条基线估算的印度2005—2009年平均制造业就业缺口数量

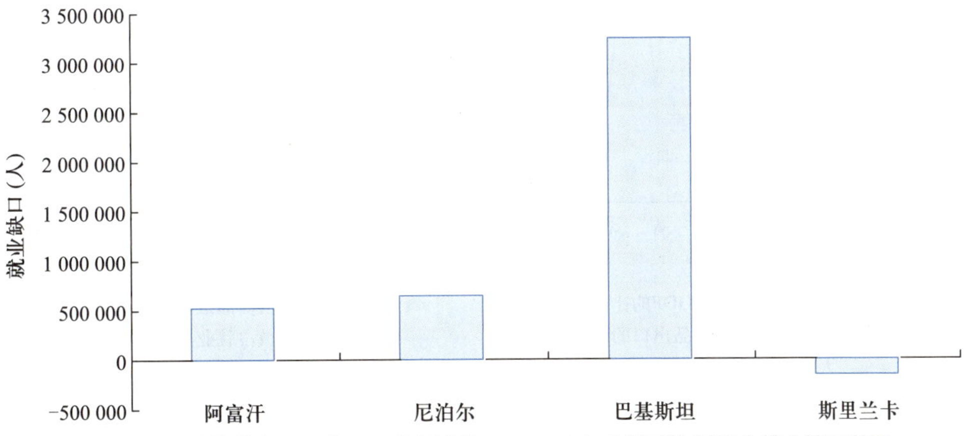

图6.18 按照8条基线估算的中亚及南亚一些经济体2006—2010年平均制造业就业缺口数量

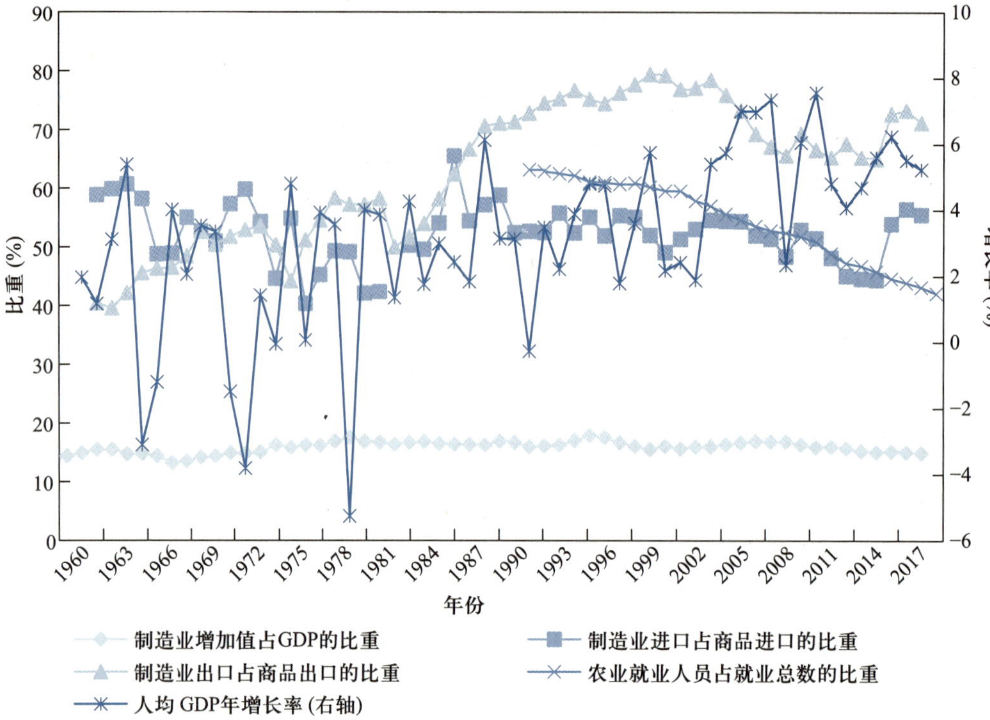


图6.19 南亚地区制造业各项指标比重、剩余劳动力（农业就业人口）与经济增长

数据来源：世界银行。

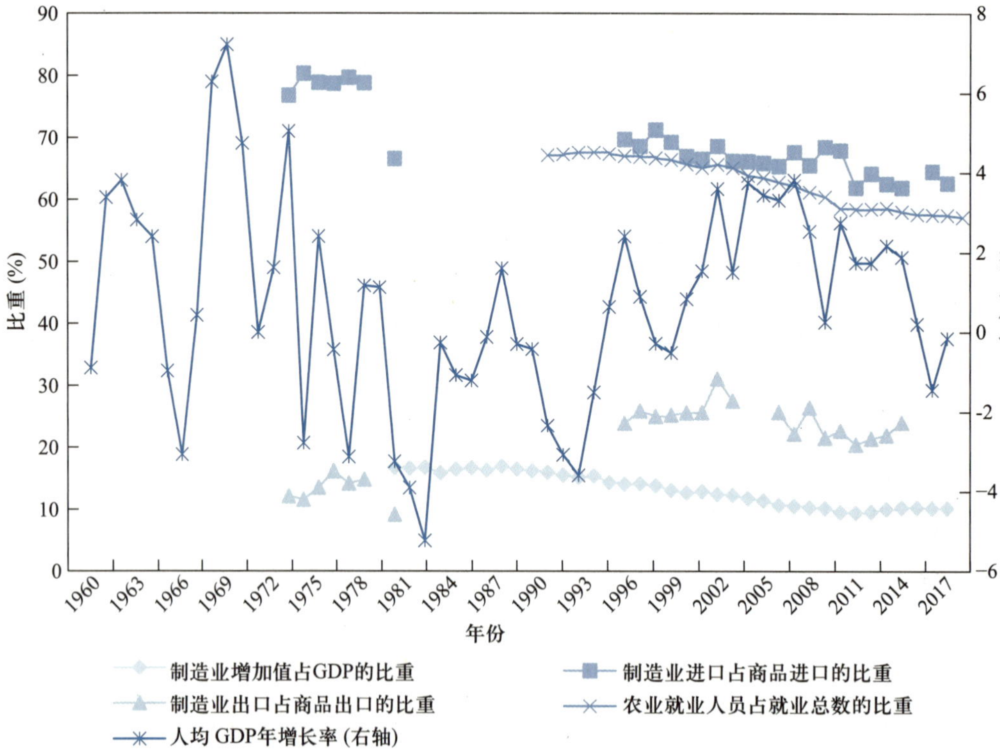


图6.20 撒哈拉以南非洲地区制造业各项指标比重、剩余劳动力（农业就业人口）与经济增长

数据来源：世界银行。

### 6.4.3 中东与北非以及拉美需要转型升级制造业以摆脱中等收入陷阱

与南亚和撒哈拉以南非洲地区极度欠发达不同，拉丁美洲与加勒比海地区以及中东与北非地区整体发展水平处于中等偏上。2018年，南亚的人均GDP只有1 842.26美元，撒哈拉以南非洲地区的人均GDP只有1 573.61美元，而拉丁美洲与加勒比海地区的人均GDP达到9 274.78美元，即便不包括高收入国家也达到8 350.11美元，中东与北非地区人均GDP也达到7 372.27美元，但不包括高收入国家只有3 791.75美元——也是南亚和撒哈拉以南非洲地区的2倍有余。另一个不同之处是，劳动力规模相差悬殊，2018年，拉丁美洲与加勒比海地区的劳动力有3.142 1亿人次，中东与北非的劳动力只有1.528 5亿人次。然而，即便整体上都是中等偏上经济体，但是拉美和中东、北非实现中等收入的方式极为不同。拉美其实在19世纪经济已经起飞，较早接入工业化。如图6.21所示，1965年拉美制造业增加值占GDP的比重就高达23.21%，然而东亚却在21世纪初才达到此水平——因此东亚有保持谦虚的理由，然而此后拉美深陷“中等收入陷阱”，制造业增加值占GDP的比重在2017年只有13.09%，萎缩了10个百分点。因此，拉美的发展问题是在第3章和第5章已经讨论过的，需要持续转型升级制造业以摆脱“中等收入陷阱”，如图6.27和表6.7所示。中东和北非一些富裕经济体

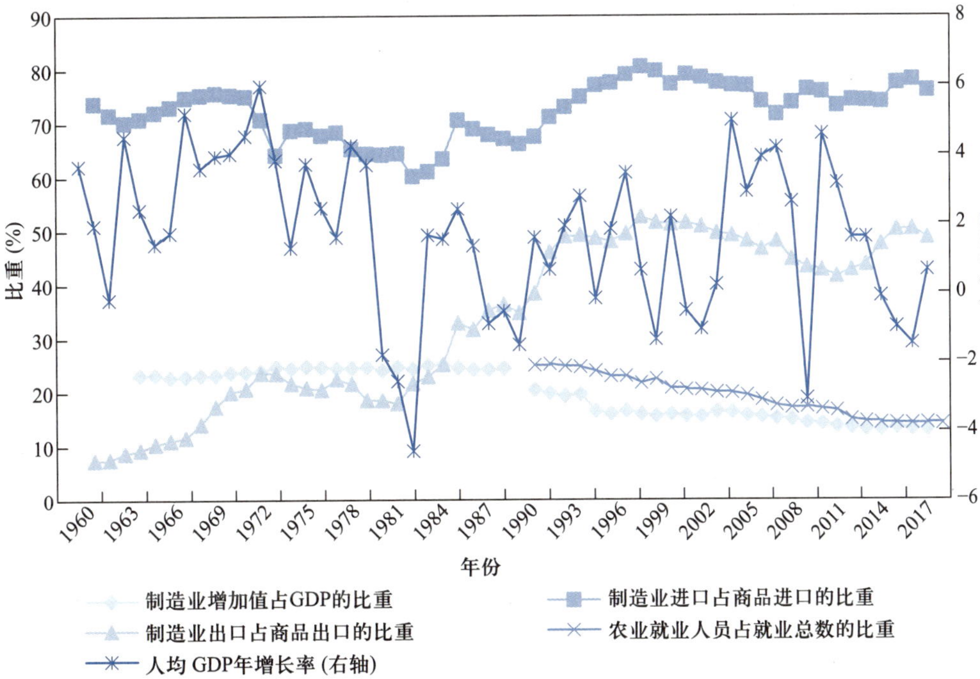


图6.21 拉丁美洲与加勒比海地区制造业各项指标比重、剩余劳动力（农业就业人口）与经济增长

数据来源：世界银行。

表6.7 拉丁美洲与加勒比海地区（不包括高收入）一些国家21世纪以来制造业增加值增长率（%）

| 国家 | 2000 | 2001 | 2002 | 2003 | 2004 | 2005 | 2006 | 2007 | 2008 | 2009 | 2010 | 2011 | 2012 | 2013 | 2014 | 2015 | 2016 | 2017 | 2018 |
|---|---|---|---|---|---|---|---|---|---|---|---|---|---|---|---|---|---|---|---|
| 伯利兹 | 6.83 | 24.34 | 0.04 | 1.65 | −0.28 | 12.38 | 0.41 | 30.46 | 3.24 | 4.37 | 28.10 | −8.19 | −2.59 | −7.57 | −19.39 | −7.50 | −14.65 | −7.54 | 1.00 |
| 玻利维亚 | 2.93 | 1.79 | 2.69 | 0.25 | 3.81 | 5.58 | 3.00 | 8.09 | 6.09 | 3.66 | 4.81 | 2.59 | 3.68 | 4.75 | 6.09 | 4.03 | 4.58 | 6.18 | 3.29 |
| 巴西 | −1.86 | 5.69 | 0.71 | 2.09 | 2.66 | 9.08 | 2.24 | 1.23 | 6.14 | 4.15 | −9.26 | 9.19 | 2.25 | −2.38 | 3.01 | −4.69 | −8.48 | −5.57 | 1.68 |
| 哥伦比亚 | −8.37 | 11.65 | 2.91 | 2.14 | 4.90 | 7.94 | 4.48 | 7.29 | 7.76 | 0.36 | −3.66 | 1.88 | 5.59 | 0.83 | 1.51 | 2.89 | 2.01 | 2.78 | −1.97 |
| 哥斯达黎加 | 2.14 | 3.19 | −0.57 | 3.47 | 1.37 | 4.02 | 3.59 | 4.05 | 2.83 | −2.29 | −7.99 | 6.26 | 2.98 | 3.36 | 0.11 | 0.81 | −5.09 | 4.51 | 3.41 |
| 古巴 | 7.19 | 5.15 | −0.60 | 0.15 | −1.98 | 2.48 | 9.50 | 4.66 | 9.65 | 5.22 | 0.91 | 1.09 | 3.95 | 2.19 | 2.06 | −3.61 | 6.28 | −5.20 | −1.07 |
| 多米尼克 | −17.30 | 7.41 | −5.83 | −11.28 | 9.48 | 7.02 | −2.56 | 5.36 | −4.02 | −12.23 | −2.62 | −1.46 | −5.87 | 5.62 | 3.26 | −6.80 | −9.51 | −20.93 | −15.40 |
| 多米尼加 | 8.10 | 4.71 | −3.31 | 4.57 | 0.90 | 6.10 | 6.42 | 0.83 | 1.71 | 5.02 | −5.18 | 8.94 | 3.53 | 0.78 | 2.99 | 4.95 | 4.12 | 4.24 | 3.30 |
| 厄瓜多尔 | −8.23 | 17.24 | 2.28 | 1.77 | −0.19 | 4.40 | 4.53 | 4.11 | 3.16 | 9.11 | −0.77 | 2.40 | 6.39 | 4.09 | 2.16 | 0.21 | −0.81 | −0.88 | 3.57 |
| 格林纳达 | 11.11 | 2.99 | 1.07 | 6.40 | −2.33 | −16.15 | 18.88 | −2.55 | 1.76 | −4.93 | −5.27 | 3.89 | −0.14 | −0.22 | −2.26 | 1.56 | 3.65 | 4.55 | 2.70 |
| 危地马拉 | 2.53 | 1.86 | 1.11 | 1.14 | 2.65 | 5.44 | 2.54 | 3.80 | 2.85 | 1.77 | −1.98 | 3.47 | 2.85 | 2.45 | 5.24 | 3.15 | 3.45 | 3.56 | 2.11 |
| 圭亚那 | 6.71 | −11.71 | 0.00 | 2.27 | −2.22 | 0.00 | 11.97 | 5.20 | 75.51 | −4.28 | 4.29 | 0.26 | 6.81 | 2.38 | 7.92 | 10.71 | 5.47 | −9.54 | 4.19 |
| 洪都拉斯 | 2.25 | 3.14 | 3.85 | 7.76 | 6.41 | 4.04 | 7.00 | 4.55 | 5.02 | 3.39 | −8.15 | 4.52 | 4.40 | 1.80 | 3.37 | 3.03 | 3.95 | 2.91 | 4.03 |
| 海地 | −2.99 | −0.53 | 0.11 | 1.60 | 2.34 | 0.39 | 2.74 | −3.56 | 1.28 | −0.10 | 4.47 | −15.16 | 17.76 | 7.08 | 2.17 | 2.64 | 4.48 | 1.51 | 1.09 |
| 牙买加 | −3.87 | −1.20 | −0.77 | −1.88 | −0.42 | 1.91 | −3.94 | −1.62 | 1.31 | −0.78 | −4.77 | −4.21 | 1.70 | −0.17 | −0.42 | −0.76 | 2.00 | 1.94 | 2.00 |
| 圣卢西亚 | 0.01 | −2.12 | 0.10 | −4.28 | 2.46 | 17.07 | −1.98 | 2.08 | 1.83 | 5.22 | 1.81 | 2.90 | 1.63 | 6.42 | 8.86 | −0.82 | 0.66 | 3.83 | 0.05 |
| 墨西哥 | 2.86 | 6.48 | −2.83 | −2.40 | −0.67 | 3.35 | 2.17 | 4.67 | 0.61 | −1.37 | −10.13 | 8.71 | 3.16 | 3.94 | 0.53 | 3.99 | 3.03 | 1.50 | 2.90 |
| 尼加拉瓜 | 6.95 | 4.30 | 5.85 | 2.07 | 2.44 | 9.01 | 5.61 | 6.41 | 3.74 | 1.37 | −5.48 | 8.90 | 9.85 | 10.22 | 6.53 | 7.57 | 1.12 | 2.82 | 5.15 |
| 秘鲁 | −1.39 | 5.55 | 0.87 | 6.64 | 3.90 | 7.45 | 6.58 | 7.27 | 10.55 | 8.52 | −6.46 | 10.12 | 8.33 | 1.27 | 5.25 | −1.05 | −0.90 | −0.55 | −0.25 |
| 巴拉圭 | −0.51 | −2.77 | 0.46 | −0.18 | 0.90 | 2.08 | −0.17 | 1.62 | −0.01 | 7.30 | −3.81 | 4.90 | 4.03 | 3.11 | 7.67 | 6.99 | 5.21 | 4.57 | 8.38 |
| 萨尔瓦多 | 1.42 | 1.89 | 1.49 | 0.41 | −0.03 | −1.54 | −1.15 | 2.89 | 2.11 | 5.41 | −4.14 | 1.88 | 4.17 | 1.50 | 0.39 | 1.62 | 3.31 | 1.31 | 3.45 |
| 苏里南 | −8.90 | 59.77 | 12.47 | −3.70 | 5.64 | 10.68 | 10.23 | −2.42 | 1.94 | 9.19 | −11.47 | 12.02 | 1.76 | −18.12 | 8.72 | −8.13 | 1.06 | 7.25 | 2.97 |
| 圣文森特和格林纳丁斯 | −0.88 | −9.41 | −4.08 | −2.72 | 7.85 | −2.71 | 7.33 | −0.36 | −6.03 | 2.62 | −8.13 | −4.93 | 4.92 | −4.32 | −4.06 | 6.01 | 1.87 | 1.94 | 3.22 |
| 委内瑞拉 | −7.32 | 4.80 | 0.27 | −13.74 | −7.41 | 23.86 | 6.01 | 7.33 | 3.24 | −9.13 | −6.45 | −3.43 | 3.82 | 1.79 | −0.30 | −7.22 | — | — | — |

注：根据不变价本币计算的制造业增加值的年增长率，总数根据2010年不变价美元计算。

资料来源：世界银行。

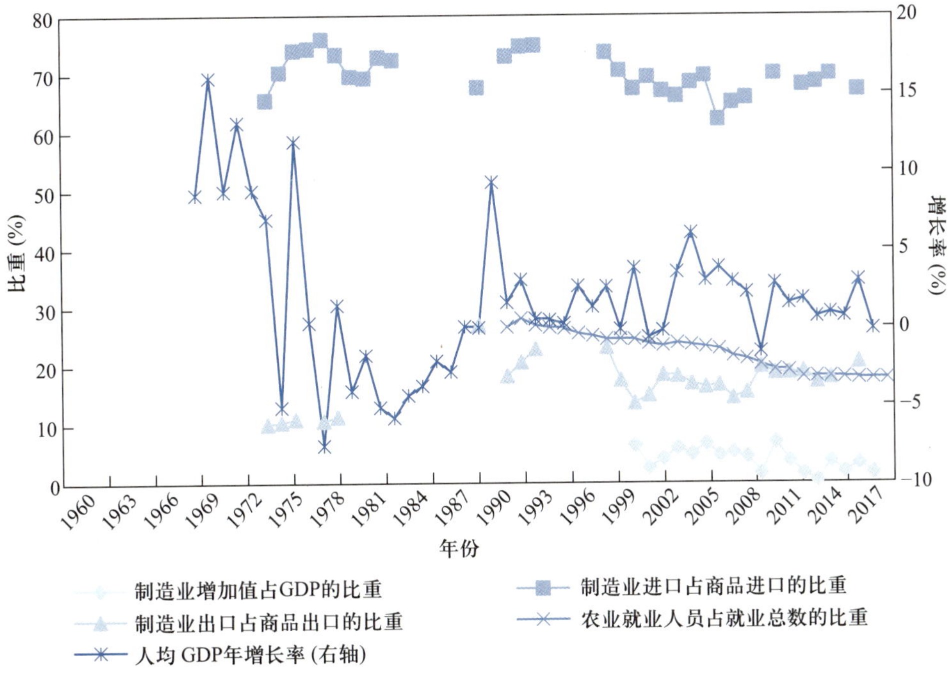


图6.22 中东与北非地区制造业各项指标比重、剩余劳动力（农业就业人口）与经济增长

数据来源：世界银行。

主要依靠石油和资源，而另外一些资源匮乏型经济体收入水平就低很多。典型的例子是本书在第4章中介绍的阿曼，不过阿曼在摆脱资源依赖进行产业多元化方面颇为成功，这也是未来中东资源型国家转型的方向，如图6.22和表6.8所示。

### 6.4.4 欧洲和中亚地区需要调整违背比较优势的制造业重获竞争优势

工业革命率先爆发于欧洲的英国，其后渐次在欧洲大陆传播开来。虽然东欧和中亚相对于工业发达的西欧来讲工业化程度逊色得多，但是相对于东亚和太平洋地区的工业化进程则早得多，制造业有一定的基础。[①] 如图6.23所示，在20世纪60年代初，欧洲和中亚地区制造业出口占商品出口的百分比就超过70%，而东亚和太平洋地区在20世纪80年代末期才达到这一水平。在经济转型后的1991年，欧洲和中亚地区的制造业增加值占GDP的百分比曾达

① 关于欧洲工业化史的简要介绍可参考：萧国亮、隋福民，《世界经济史》，北京大学出版社，2007年版。

表6.8 中东与北非地区（不包括高收入）一些国家和地区21世纪以来制造业增加值增长率（%）

| 国家（地区） | 2000 | 2001 | 2002 | 2003 | 2004 | 2005 | 2006 | 2007 | 2008 | 2009 | 2010 | 2011 | 2012 | 2013 | 2014 | 2015 | 2016 | 2017 | 2018 |
|---|---|---|---|---|---|---|---|---|---|---|---|---|---|---|---|---|---|---|---|
| 吉布提 | — | — | — | — | — | — | — | — | — | — | — | — | — | — | — | 49.81 | −7.32 | 11.35 | 8.02 |
| 阿尔及利亚 | — | 3.56 | −0.40 | 4.35 | 6.88 | 3.89 | 5.23 | −0.94 | 0.61 | −1.06 | −3.67 | −0.81 | −1.04 | −1.27 | −2.91 | 0.75 | 1.84 | 6.03 | 0.07 |
| 埃及 | 9.67 | 7.85 | 3.63 | 4.20 | 1.72 | 2.39 | 4.43 | 5.80 | 12.80 | 7.32 | 1.68 | 3.78 | −0.84 | −0.54 | 2.27 | 4.77 | 3.06 | 0.76 | 2.06 |
| 伊朗 | 10.17 | 11.94 | 13.69 | 12.54 | 10.50 | 4.10 | 10.50 | 7.93 | 1.98 | 3.12 | 8.11 | 10.50 | 5.65 | −4.08 | −5.25 | 7.99 | −4.64 | 6.86 | 5.31 |
| 伊拉克 | 5.64 | −4.47 | 9.21 | −8.85 | −28.53 | −22.29 | −1.10 | 10.50 | 6.25 | 6.70 | 35.99 | 6.34 | 2.33 | 2.10 | −11.32 | −22.20 | −25.70 | 5.90 | — |
| 约旦 | 7.37 | 6.76 | 8.42 | 19.33 | 2.83 | 16.92 | 7.78 | 11.25 | 9.17 | 5.13 | 1.99 | 2.02 | 4.04 | 2.35 | 1.93 | 1.49 | 1.34 | 1.15 | 1.02 |
| 黎巴嫩 | −0.90 | 0.00 | 1.90 | 5.20 | 3.90 | 3.83 | 5.18 | 1.47 | 19.47 | 7.62 | −2.35 | 6.42 | 1.36 | 1.10 | 4.35 | −5.69 | −4.78 | −6.56 | −12.70 |
| 摩洛哥 | 3.12 | 3.08 | 2.10 | 3.62 | 2.08 | 0.58 | 3.74 | 3.32 | 4.12 | 6.78 | −2.99 | 8.42 | 6.79 | 1.78 | −0.72 | 4.13 | 2.31 | 0.73 | 2.19 |
| 约旦河西岸和加沙 | −5.17 | −4.45 | −1.12 | −23.81 | 35.04 | −0.81 | 25.61 | −26.58 | 12.36 | 32.52 | 7.98 | 9.65 | −2.36 | 17.61 | 4.29 | −5.45 | −7.75 | 6.19 | 1.81 |
| 突尼斯 | 6.99 | 5.74 | 6.86 | 0.82 | 0.74 | 2.40 | 1.31 | 4.07 | 8.68 | 4.30 | −0.97 | 7.02 | −2.71 | 2.05 | 1.68 | 0.86 | −0.02 | 0.29 | 0.79 |
| 也门 | — | — | 3.00 | 3.86 | 3.94 | 6.79 | 7.97 | 5.11 | 5.30 | 4.80 | 2.00 | 4.40 | −12.50 | 4.00 | 4.00 | 1.00 | −12.51 | −10.54 | −6.56 |

注：根据不变价本币计算的制造业增加值的年增长率，总数根据2010年不变价美元计算。

资料来源：世界银行。

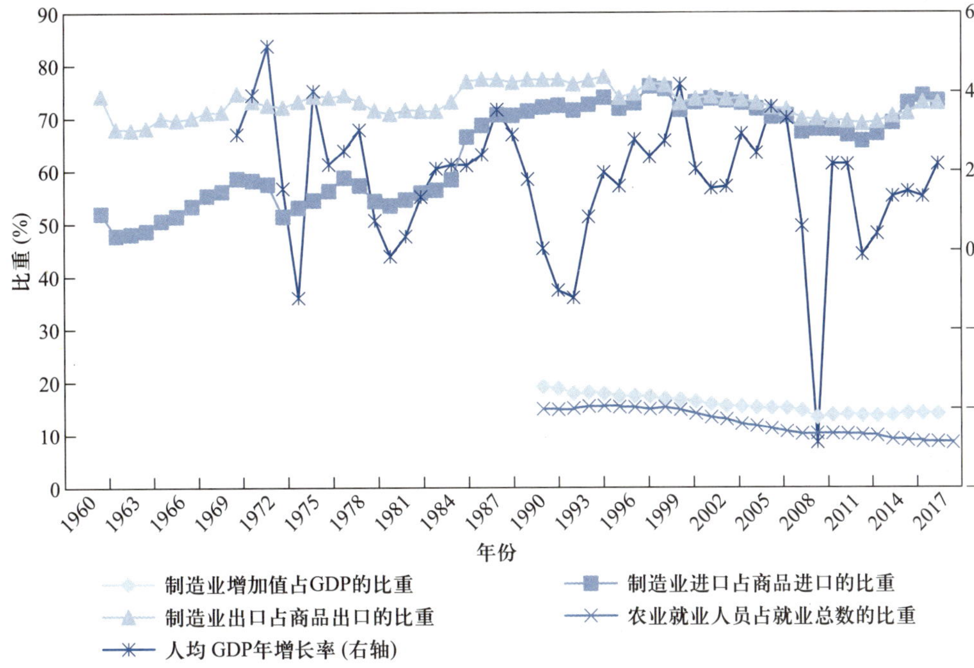


**图6.23 欧洲与中亚地区制造业各项指标比重、剩余劳动力（农业就业人口）与经济增长**

数据来源：世界银行。

19.2%。然而，正如本书在第1章第3小节中所讨论过的，受害于“休克疗法”，东欧和中亚经济转型遭遇滑铁卢。如图6.23所示，从1991年起欧洲和中亚地区的制造业增加值占GDP的比重一路下滑至今，下降了5个多百分点，时下略有复苏迹象，但势头微弱，过去5年来增加了不到1个百分点。如表6.9所示，欧洲与中亚地区（不包括高收入国家）在2008年的全球金融危机中制造业遭到了严重冲击，制造业增加值下滑严重，亚美尼亚下滑了7.11%，阿塞拜疆下滑了12.60%，保加利亚下滑了9.25%，波斯尼亚和黑塞哥维那下滑了5.46%，白俄罗斯下滑了2.20%，格鲁吉亚下滑了6.72%，哈萨克斯坦下滑了2.80%，吉尔吉斯斯坦下滑了9.31%，摩尔多瓦下滑了21.92%，黑山下滑了29.06%，罗马尼亚下滑了6.62%，俄罗斯下滑了14.62%，塞尔维亚下滑了4.52%，土耳其下滑了8.89%，乌克兰下滑了20.90%。这些经济体此后的制造业复苏也非常缓慢，而且波动不定。

究其原因，主要是其制造业发展违背比较优势比较严重，并且政府没有发挥应有的因势利导作用消除制造业发展的瓶颈，进而导致其在国际市场上缺乏竞争力。[①] 如图6.23所示，其制造业出口占商品出口的百分比从20世纪90年代初到全球金融危机之前萎缩了将近10个

①《经济政策改革学刊》（Journal of Economic Policy Reform）2015年第2期专门展开了转型经济学与新结构经济学之间关系的讨论（Transition economics meet new structural economics），其中一些文章专门实证研究了东欧这些转型经济体违背比较优势发展战略与经济增长关系，可资参考。

表6.9 欧洲与中亚地区（不包括高收入）部分国家20世纪90年代转型至今的制造业增加值增长率（%）

| 国家 | 1991 | 1992 | 1993 | 1994 | 1995 | 1996 | 1997 | 1998 | 1999 | 2000 | 2001 | 2002 | 2003 | 2004 | 2005 | 2006 | 2007 | 2008 | 2009 | 2010 | 2011 | 2012 | 2013 | 2014 | 2015 | 2016 | 2017 |
|---|---|---|---|---|---|---|---|---|---|---|---|---|---|---|---|---|---|---|---|---|---|---|---|---|---|---|---|
| 阿尔巴尼亚 | — | — | — | — | — | — | -32.30 | 41.40 | 13.00 | 6.90 | 5.80 | 4.20 | 19.30 | 6.00 | 13.90 | 13.00 | 12.70 | -5.00 | 2.90 | 11.60 | 10.50 | -15.70 | 9.80 | 9.40 | 5.00 | 4.30 | 13.46 |
| 亚美尼亚 | -4.00 | -59.70 | 8.90 | 9.60 | 2.60 | 1.10 | 1.30 | -2.23 | 5.40 | 6.60 | 9.84 | 17.25 | 16.98 | -2.54 | 8.84 | -0.46 | 1.59 | 0.90 | -7.11 | 12.10 | 13.70 | 4.10 | 7.70 | 6.00 | -5.50 | 11.10 | 5.90 |
| 阿塞拜疆 | — | — | -19.67 | -28.57 | -20.00 | -10.71 | 0.80 | -11.70 | -9.10 | -42.13 | 4.10 | 8.20 | 14.00 | 10.50 | 16.30 | 9.00 | 10.20 | 7.10 | -12.60 | 7.20 | 7.40 | 4.70 | 5.80 | 4.10 | 7.70 | -1.60 | -1.80 |
| 保加利亚 | — | — | — | — | — | — | — | — | -9.34 | 17.92 | 5.20 | 6.94 | 11.11 | 2.32 | 7.66 | 9.62 | 15.64 | 2.11 | -9.25 | -1.80 | 10.09 | 2.52 | -2.66 | 6.13 | 4.83 | 5.97 | 6.10 |
| 波斯尼亚和黑塞哥维那 | — | — | — | — | — | — | — | — | — | — | — | — | — | — | — | 14.33 | 10.64 | 6.41 | -5.46 | 7.21 | -0.04 | -0.80 | 5.01 | 4.30 | 6.39 | 5.39 | 8.20 |
| 白俄罗斯 | 0.53 | -8.65 | -9.46 | -16.60 | -10.20 | 4.71 | 17.59 | 10.51 | 8.71 | 6.38 | 7.24 | 6.16 | 10.36 | 19.65 | 14.40 | 13.60 | 8.30 | 14.70 | -2.20 | 10.80 | 9.79 | 6.95 | -5.23 | 0.65 | -6.34 | -0.05 | 6.95 |
| 格鲁吉亚 | — | — | — | — | — | — | — | — | — | — | — | — | — | 7.50 | 13.55 | 16.03 | 15.84 | -2.18 | -6.72 | 12.12 | 12.05 | 9.62 | 8.02 | 2.87 | -1.16 | 4.20 | 3.03 |
| 哈萨克斯坦 | — | — | — | — | — | — | — | — | — | — | 13.70 | 7.60 | 7.90 | 10.10 | 7.10 | 7.90 | 7.60 | -3.00 | -2.80 | 13.60 | 7.50 | 3.00 | 2.90 | 1.60 | 0.20 | 1.80 | 6.10 |
| 吉尔吉斯斯坦 | -0.29 | -25.61 | -23.07 | -36.08 | -24.70 | 4.70 | 59.45 | 7.92 | -5.72 | 4.10 | 9.07 | -10.88 | 17.84 | 2.20 | -16.83 | -14.15 | 6.34 | 21.21 | -9.31 | 11.33 | 5.20 | -27.97 | 46.96 | -2.86 | -6.25 | 5.85 | 7.59 |
| 摩尔多瓦 | — | — | — | — | — | -1.70 | -13.20 | -16.38 | -6.08 | 15.94 | 17.81 | 2.63 | 12.67 | 7.09 | -3.02 | -4.31 | -1.25 | 1.15 | -21.92 | 10.75 | 12.60 | 1.80 | 9.20 | 8.10 | 3.60 | 2.80 | — |
| 北马其顿 | -15.22 | -15.80 | -14.40 | -7.00 | -8.91 | 4.97 | -6.07 | 0.50 | 2.45 | 10.12 | -5.69 | 2.95 | 9.12 | 7.15 | 10.55 | 12.60 | -12.90 | -2.01 | 4.12 | -0.19 | 12.13 | -1.17 | 9.63 | 21.53 | 4.96 | -1.53 | 1.54 |
| 黑山 | — | — | — | — | — | — | — | — | — | — | 32.22 | -4.44 | -6.39 | 5.61 | 5.46 | 4.50 | -24.07 | -5.39 | -29.06 | -5.89 | 10.74 | -12.88 | 6.52 | -2.05 | 5.96 | -4.11 | 34.23 |
| 罗马尼亚 | — | — | — | — | — | 7.34 | -7.09 | -6.63 | -1.96 | 8.37 | 10.45 | 6.00 | 5.67 | 9.11 | 3.65 | 8.19 | 0.72 | 16.07 | -6.62 | 1.56 | 7.26 | -14.39 | 7.89 | 6.46 | 4.48 | 6.38 | 9.07 |
| 俄罗斯 | — | — | — | — | — | — | — | — | — | — | — | — | 8.80 | 8.05 | 4.44 | 6.57 | 7.52 | -2.12 | -14.62 | 8.61 | 8.59 | 4.57 | 0.71 | 0.75 | -4.63 | 1.15 | 0.09 |
| 塞尔维亚 | — | — | — | — | — | -0.48 | 2.32 | 3.69 | -19.42 | 28.42 | -9.65 | -5.89 | 0.96 | 3.71 | -0.04 | 1.90 | 9.47 | 3.33 | -4.52 | -0.33 | 1.86 | 7.66 | 5.67 | -2.06 | 1.87 | 2.16 | — |
| 塔吉克斯坦 | -2.00 | -23.30 | -17.80 | -31.40 | -13.60 | -23.90 | -2.00 | 8.20 | 5.00 | — | — | — | — | — | — | — | — | — | — | — | — | — | — | — | — | — | — |
| 土耳其 | 2.38 | 5.77 | 9.30 | -7.64 | 13.91 | 7.11 | 11.45 | 1.17 | -5.54 | 7.06 | -8.89 | 4.01 | 9.80 | 13.24 | 9.63 | 9.83 | 6.75 | 0.50 | -8.89 | 9.60 | 20.02 | 2.26 | 9.31 | 6.10 | 5.90 | 3.84 | 9.13 |
| 乌克兰 | -10.83 | -11.85 | -22.12 | -37.52 | -11.20 | -4.02 | -2.98 | 0.00 | 5.50 | 12.80 | 11.72 | 8.90 | 18.20 | 14.60 | 3.00 | 9.20 | 12.80 | -4.90 | -20.90 | 14.50 | 3.29 | -2.27 | -9.91 | -8.63 | -15.23 | 3.67 | 5.05 |
| 乌兹别克斯坦 | — | — | — | — | — | -0.09 | 3.40 | -1.12 | 2.04 | -1.32 | 4.98 | 0.50 | 1.03 | 2.00 | 2.00 | 32.58 | 12.12 | 10.96 | 4.54 | 11.70 | 5.78 | 8.80 | 9.06 | 8.26 | 7.60 | 6.70 | 4.00 |
| 科索沃 | — | — | — | — | — | — | — | — | — | — | — | — | — | — | — | — | 9.69 | 15.37 | 11.46 | 1.77 | -5.72 | 14.94 | 6.50 | -1.30 | 4.84 | 2.79 | 3.05 |

资料来源：世界银行。

百分点。中亚和东欧少部分经济体，如哈萨克斯坦、塔吉克斯坦、阿塞拜疆、土耳其等的制造业只存在数十万就业缺口，相对而言量级比较小（见图6.24）。而诸如俄罗斯、乌克兰、白俄罗斯、罗马尼亚、保加利亚等东欧经济体由于过去的重工业赶超战略积累了过多的违背比较优势的制造业，制造业也面临过剩的情况（见图6.25）。这种性质不同于东亚“雁阵模式”下的制造业过剩情况，后者是由于要素禀赋结构变化导致比较优势变化所致。一个引起广泛关注的案例是中国企业收购乌克兰航空发动机公司。2019年2月21日，据乌克兰基辅邮报报道称，中国企业成功收购乌克兰“动力沙皇”马达西奇公司。早在2015年12月，大公网、搜狐财经等媒体发表报道称，天骄航空与重庆市政府签署战略合作协议，天骄航空动力产业基地已于2015年年底开工建设，基地以航空发动机研发生产为主线，产品规划涵盖涡轴发动机、涡桨发动机、涡扇发动机、桨扇发动机和民用燃气轮机等多型号产品。由于欧洲和中亚地区的剩余劳动力较少，例如目前农业就业人员占就业总数的百分比不足10%，比东亚和太平洋地区低10个百分点，发展大规模的劳动密集型制造业不太现实。出路在于调整违背比较优势的制造业重获竞争优势。东欧和中亚的这些曾经失败的转型经济体目前正借“一带一路”的东风，积极结合自身的资源禀赋进行产能合作发展比较优势产业，同时发挥政府作用消除软硬基础设施瓶颈，有望走出“休克疗法”下的转型痛苦。这些内容将在本书第7章进一步介绍。

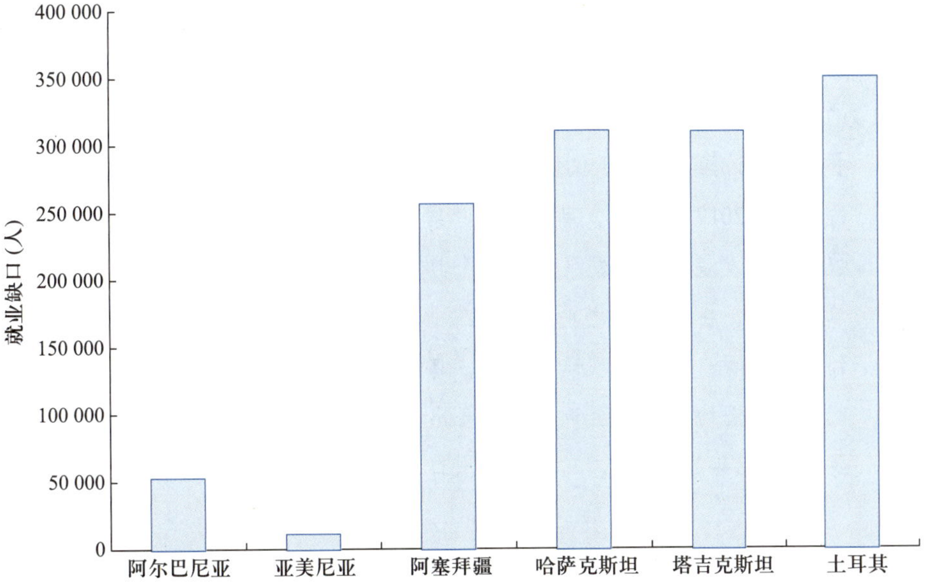


图6.24 按照8条基线估算的欧洲和中亚一些非高收入经济体2006—2010年平均制造业就业缺口数量

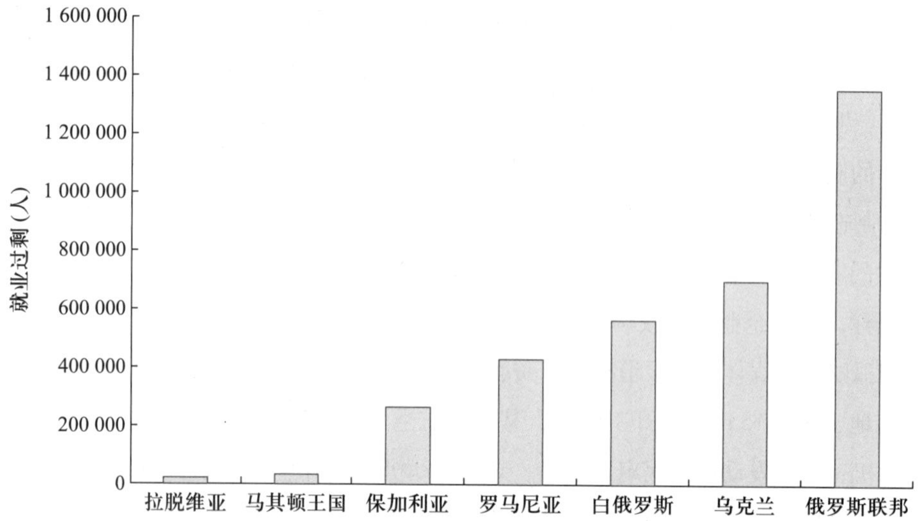


图6.25 按照8条基线估算的欧洲和中亚一些非高收入经济体2006—2010年平均制造业就业过剩数量

专栏6.1

白金（棉花）之国的产业转型升级[①]

1991年8月31日独立的乌兹别克斯坦拥有约3 300万人口，国土面积近45万平方千米，是全球仅有的2个“双内陆国”之一。支柱产业可以用4个“金”概括——黄金、白金（棉花）、乌金（石油）、蓝金（天然气）。作为世界排名第6的棉花生产国和排名第2的棉花出口国，乌兹别克斯坦拥有“白金之国”的美誉，如今该国不满足于仅仅出口原料，还想进行产业升级，对外出口附加值更高的产品。2017年12月，乌兹别克总统米尔济约耶夫签署了一份总统令，旨在加快纺织业发展，将其发展成为一个具有高科技水平的劳动密集型产业，并以出口为导向，在2021年之前使纺织工业产值增长60%，2025年之前将出口额提升到70亿美元。为了实现这个目标，乌兹别克斯坦宣布从2020年开始停止出口棉花。米尔济约耶夫甚至声称“不会出口一千克棉花，所有都要用于国内产业发展”。2018年1—11月，乌兹别克出口的棉纤维下降到11万吨，而纺织品出口则

① 本专栏根据《海外探客》的相关报道资料整理而成。

乌兹别克斯坦的白金（棉花）

比2017年同期增长15%，出口额近12亿美元。2018年，乌兹别克的棉花占中国进口量的4%，是排名第5位的棉花来源地。按照米尔济约耶夫的说法，再过1年乌兹别克斯坦将不再对华出口棉花。其实这个趋势早就已经显现，2016年从乌兹别克斯坦进口的棉花只有9.3万吨，比往年的30万吨骤降不少。旅游业是乌兹别克斯坦经济发展的重要支柱。为了促进这一产业的繁荣，乌兹别克也做出不少努力，具体措施是通过将30天免签证制度扩大到45个国家和地区（同时将电子签证系统扩大到76个国家和地区）、加快基础设施建设、提高服务水平。到2025年，乌兹别克斯坦希望能够利用国内7 300多处文化遗迹吸引至少900万外国游客，并将旅游业占GDP的比重提升到5%。

同时，乌兹别克斯坦政府于2016年聘请林毅夫教授为顾问，为乌兹别克斯坦利用其大量劳动力和皮革业的优势发展制鞋业工业园区与招商引资提供咨询和建议。

### 6.4.5 高收入经济体的再工业化与拓展世界前沿的产业政策

绝大多数高收入经济体由于经历了后工业化，制造业就业也面临较大的缺口。如图6.26所示，在21世纪之后高收入经济体的制造业增加值占GDP的比重大约维持在15%。除一贯注重制造业基础的德国积累了大量的制造业基础，可能面临剩余之外，老牌的G7集团成员法、美、日、英、意、加等国无一例外都面临制造业缺口。这也是德国推出工业4.0以及美国大张旗鼓地鼓励制造业回流的原因。然而，除了老牌工业国家面临再工业化，存在制造业就业缺口的基本事实，我们也可以看到图6.27中的另外一个基本的事实：发达国家的制造业年均工资水平非常高。因此，发达经济体的再工业化与发展中经济体工业化产生的制造业缺

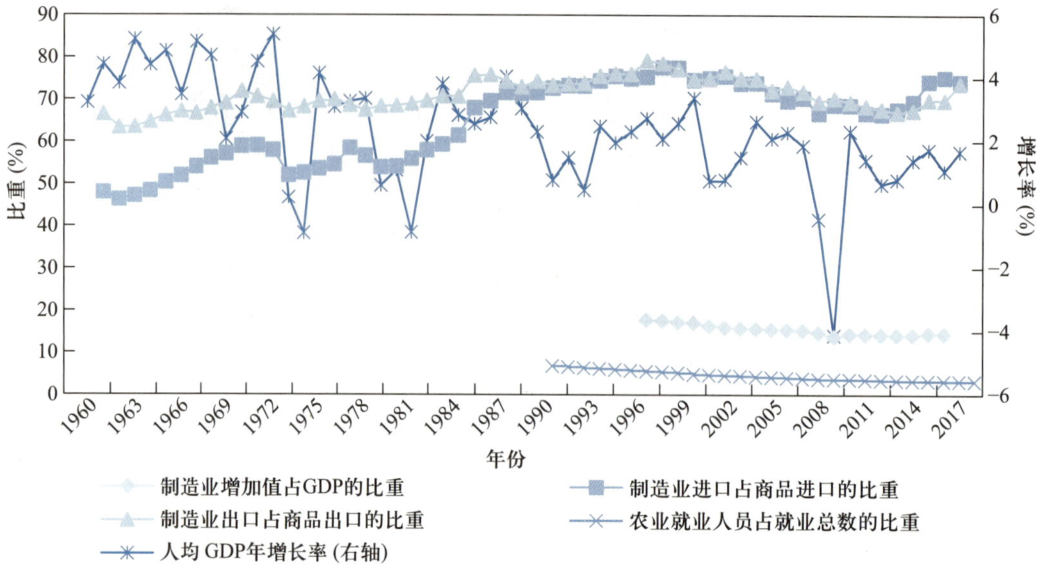


**图6.26 高收入国家制造业各项指标比重、剩余劳动力（农业就业人口）与经济增长**

数据来源：世界银行。

口的性质完全不同：发达经济体的制造业就业缺口由于产业级别高，所需的劳动力往往是高技能的，而非发展中经济体一般的劳动力，尽管2018年高收入国家有6.261 7亿劳动力，但是其中的农业就业人员占就业总数的百分比只有3%。所以，发达经济体再工业化不会导致其大规模的制造业从发展中经济体回流到发达经济体。发达经济体也需要持续的转型升级创造更高级别的制造业提高劳动生产率，才能够为高工资的高技能劳动力创造就业。因此，包括美国和欧洲在内的发达国家近年来相继启动了推动本国制造业转型升级拓展世界技术前沿的创新战略，并采取了一些具有实效的产业政策。例如，2019年2月19日，德国经济与能源部（BMWi）和法国经济部联合发布了《面向二十一世纪欧洲工业政策之法德宣言》（A Franco-German Manifesto for a European industrial policy fit for the 21st Century）。①

① 在德国与法国同其他国家讨论的基础上，根据2018年12月的“工业之友”（Friends of the Industry）声明，法国和德国认为未来的欧洲工业战略应围绕几个方面展开：① 大规模投资创新领域。只有创造、发展和生产新的技术，才能取得成功。因此，需要制定欧洲技术融资战略。这一战略应在InvestEU（欧盟大型投资基金项目）的范围之内，同时还需要相关经验丰富的欧盟机构（如欧洲投资基金（EIF））的参与，这些机构能利用私有资本满足初创公司和创新技术公司的股权要求，更加注重突破性创新。即在欧盟创新理事会（EIC）的框架下，支持欧洲层面的高风险深层技术项目（例如在医疗、能源、气候、安全和数字技术领域），给予项目经理更大的自主权，使他们能够自上而下地进行高风险技术投资，同时可以采用最好的私有专长技术和科技。这些原则一部分已经在欧盟创新理事会的2019—2020试点计划“先

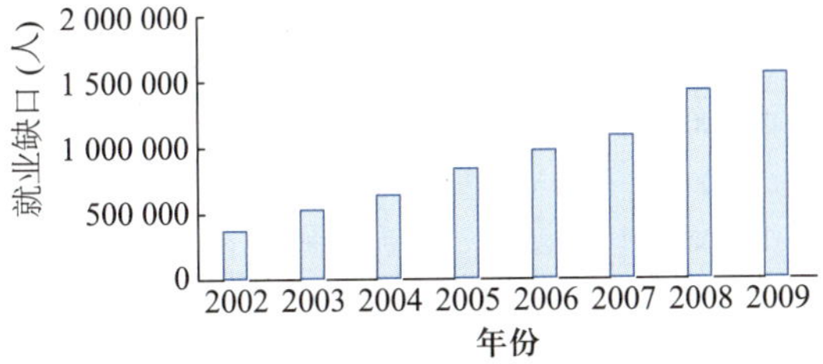


(a) 法国制造业就业缺口

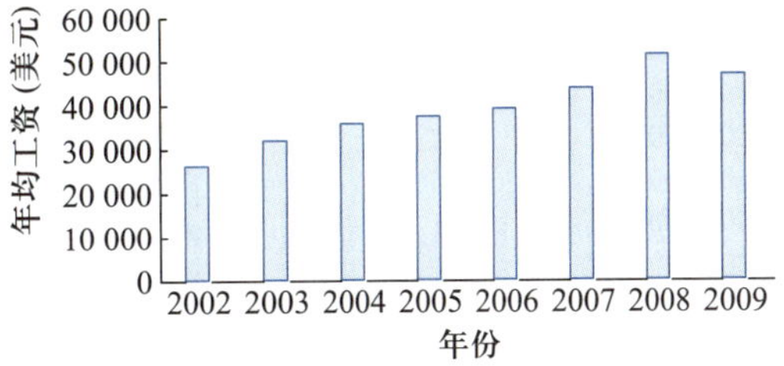


(b) 法国制造业年均工资

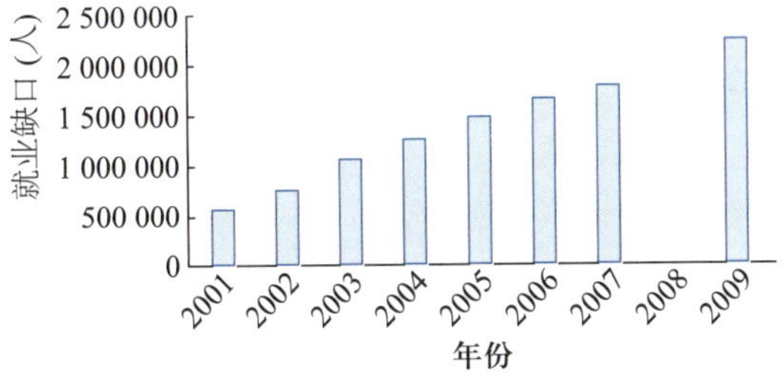


(c) 英国制造业就业缺口

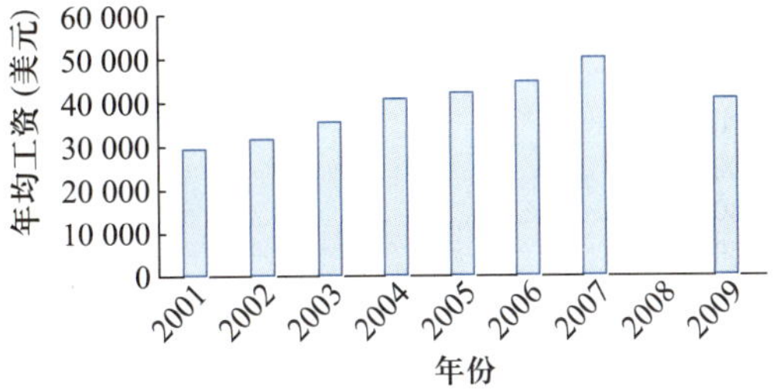


(d) 英国制造业年均工资

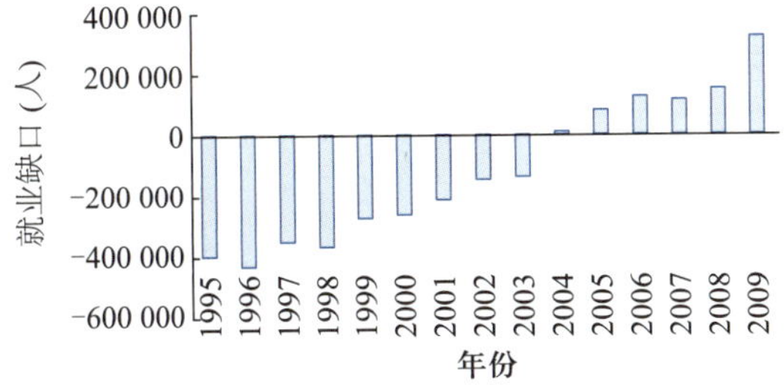


(e) 意大利制造业就业缺口

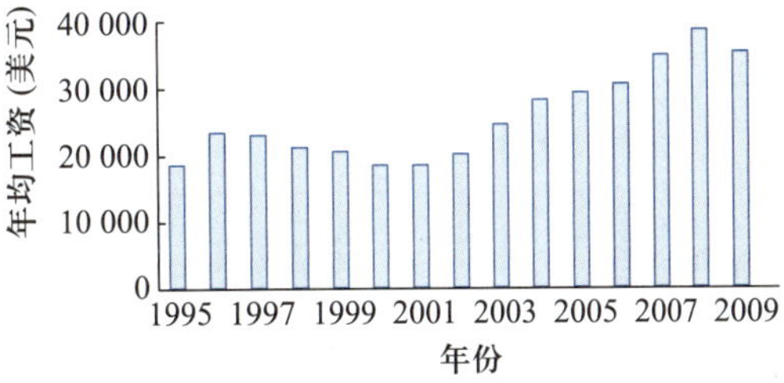


(f) 意大利制造业年均工资

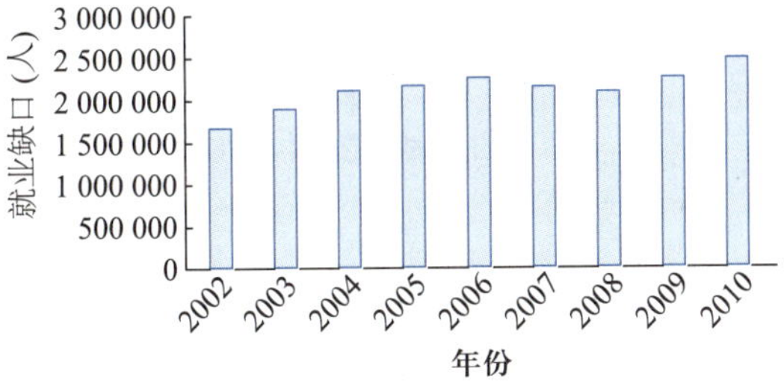


(g) 日本制造业就业缺口

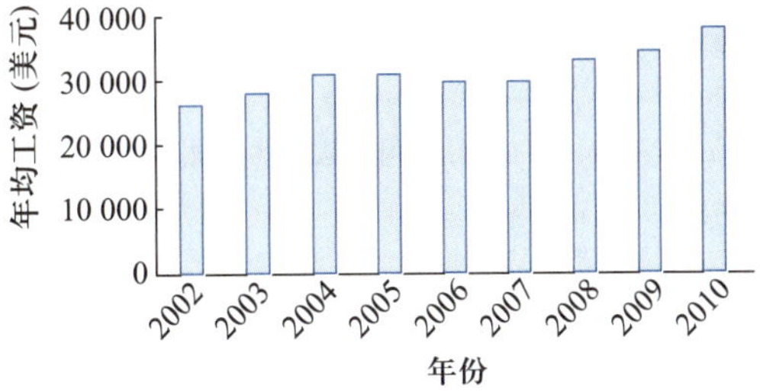


(h) 日本制造业年均工资

---

进研究探路者计划"（Pathfinder）中落实了，但仍应在欧盟创新理事会的最终提案中予以加强。② 成为人工智能技术的世界领导者。法国和德国会加强在人工智能（AI）领域的合作，实现欧盟在人工智能协调计划中体现的愿景。两国同意推动法德在人工智能的研发及应用方面的合作，通过结构性地巩固合作关系来促进共同的研究与创新网络。这一网络应解决将人工智能的研究运用到商用的难题，包括医疗、运输和机器人领域。为此，经济各部的工作组在讨论人工智能合作时，应重点关注四个话题：数据共享、跨境试验区、实现研究成果商用的最佳做法、技术与道德标准。③ 确保能够生产突破性/尖端技术。这需要在欧洲培育从研究到第一次工业部署的技术。通过首个欧洲共同利益重要项目（IPCEI），欧洲正在培育微电子技术。现在法国和德国希望为新一代电池技术制定第二个欧洲共同利益重要项目。法国和德国在此重申其目标，即确定包括汽车制造商在内的可靠财团，以便在2019年第一季度末之前做出决定。法国和德国会全力争取将新一代电池技术纳入欧洲共同利益重要项目，以便在2019年上半年尽快获得欧委会的批准。在许多其他领域，这种欧洲合作也是合理的、必不可少的，例如氢、低碳工业流程、智能医疗与网络安全。确保金融市场支持工业创新。这就是为什么欧洲要建立资本市场联盟（Capital Markets Union）并给予工业更容易融资的机会，尤其是当它们规模扩大的时候。

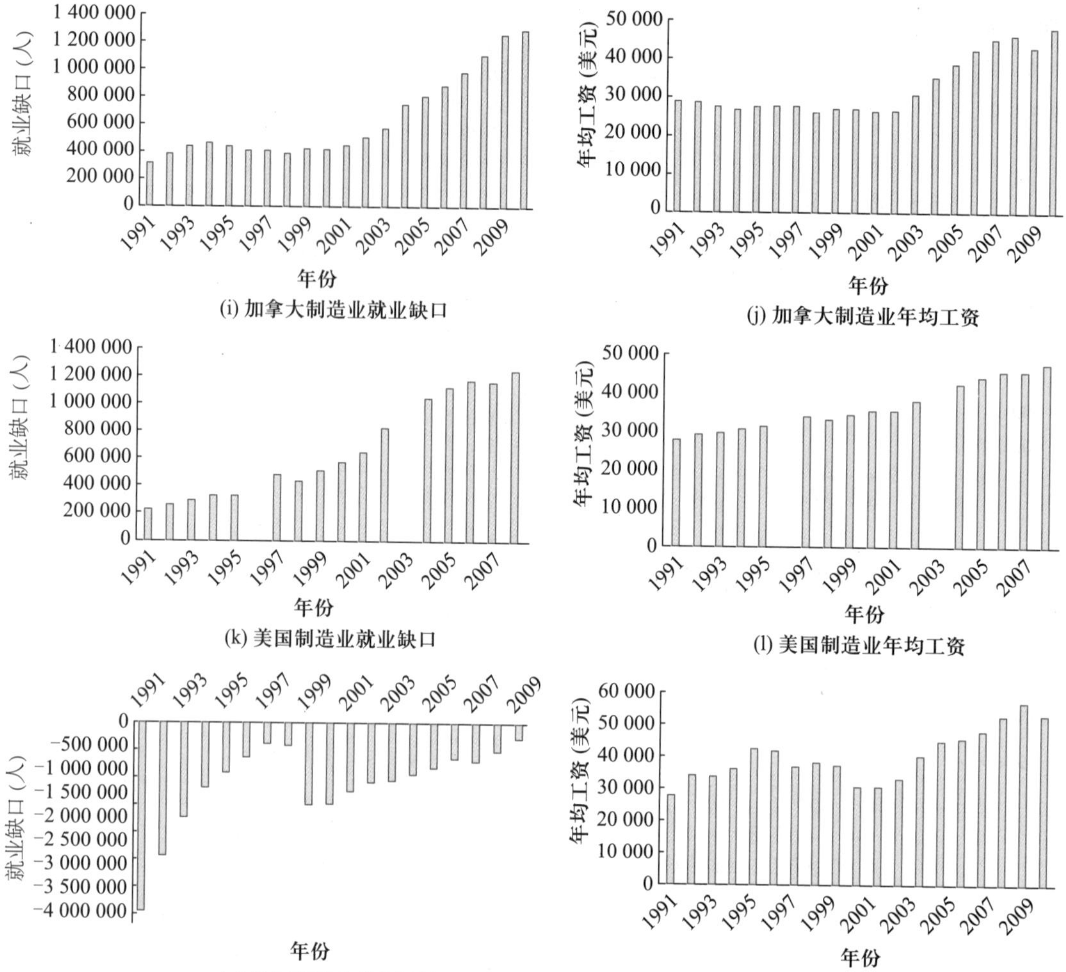


(i) 加拿大制造业就业缺口　(j) 加拿大制造业年均工资

(k) 美国制造业就业缺口　(l) 美国制造业年均工资

(m) 德国制造业就业缺口　(n) 德国制造业年均工资

注：图中空缺表示数据缺失。

**图6.27　G7集团成员国的工资水平与制造业就业缺口估算情况**

这里需要进一步指出的是，处于前沿内部的发展中国家的政府，其核心作用是在有效的市场的基础上发挥积极有为的因势利导作用消除各种制约，帮助有企业家精神的企业充分利用结构变迁的后来者优势，形成竞争优势，加速经济发展。对于中等发达国家，多数产业和发达国家仍有差距，少数产业则可能接近或已经达到国际先进水平，若有新技术或新产品企业需要自己开发，发展中国家的政府则需要和技术产业都已经处于国际前沿的发达国家的政府一样，对开发新技术、新产品所需的基础科研给予支持，具体措施包括科研基金、税收优惠、授权、国防合同以及政府采购政策，等等。[①]同样，发达国家的政府由于可用于支持基

① 对于当今发达国家历史上政府鼓励创新采取过的诸多政策梳理可参考林毅夫和蒙加的概述（Lin et al., "Growth Identification and Facilitation: The Role of the State in the Dynamics of Sturctural Change", *Development Policy Review*, 2011, 29(3), pp. 259–310）。

础科研的资金总量有限，只能有选择性地支持那些对国防安全、经济发展影响最大的基础科研，这种支持会决定企业的产品和技术开发的方向，并且还会用税收和政府采购等来支持特定的新技术、新产品的发展，并用政府资金支持特定的创新企业。所以，从本质上来说，发达国家的创新政策实际上也是一种产业政策。以乔布斯为例，1976年苹果I型计算机的推出是建立在20世纪60—70年代以美国政府的公共资金支持的计算技术的研发成果上，2001年的iPod和其后iPhone的推出也是建立在政府资金支持而研发出来的卫星定位、声控和大规模储存等新技术上的，乔布斯的天才在于把这些新技术组合开发成消费者喜爱的新产品。值得一提的是，苹果公司在未上市之前，除了得到风险投资的资金之外，也得到美国小企业局50万美元的风险股本投资。同样,Google核心的计算技术也是来自于政府资助的研究项目。① 因此，即便是发达国家主流经济学家所批评的，发达国家自身也依然实践着其历史上司空见惯的产业政策。②

### 6.4.6 世界经济结构变迁中的工作性质变迁和就业结构极化

本章关于制造业就业结构变迁的讨论以及前面一些章节关于世界经济结构变迁次序特征的讨论，都暗含了不同行业在要素禀赋结构需求上存在各种差异——其实这也是新结构经济学的要素禀赋结构需求原理——对应于给定时点上要素禀赋结构给定但可随时间变动的要素禀赋结构供给原理。然而，纵观世界经济结构变迁的历程，任何一个行业及其就业岗位的性

① 对政府支持的基础研究在美国现居全球领先地位的航天、信息、生化、纳米、医药等各种新技术、新产品的开发中所发挥的重要作用感兴趣的读者可参考Mariana Mazzucato的论述（The Entrepreneurial State: Debunking Public vs. Private Sector Myths），也可参考奥巴马政府时期美国国家创新战略报告（A Strategy for American Innovation: Driving towards Sustainable Growth and Quality Jobs, 2009）。Howell的最新实证研究就利用美国能源部设立的小企业研发创新补贴项目（SBIR），采用断点回归（Sharp RD）方法研究了研发补贴对企业创新的影响。他的研究发现：研发补贴提高了企业（特别是中小企业和初创企业）获得风险投资的概率；促进了企业创新产出（表现为高质量专利的增加）和创新成果转化（表现为企业营业收入的增加）。此外，研究补贴也有助于企业良好的运营和存续。进一步地，研究指出，研发补贴对企业创新的影响是通过资助企业进行新技术可行性实验，为企业提供“试错”的机会，降低研发的不确定性实现的（Howell, Sabrina T. , "Financing Innovation: Evidence from R&D Grants". *American Economic Review*, 2017，107 (4)，pp. 1136–1164. ）。

② 美国最好的产业政策就是让全世界相信美国没有（有效的）产业政策。对于美国产业政策的虚伪性，下面这篇文章阐述得淋漓尽致：Robert H. Wade, “The American paradox: ideology of free markets and the hidden practice of directional thrust”，*Cambridge Journal of Economics,* 2017, 41(3), pp. 859–880.

质都在不断变迁。例如，纺织行业曾经是18世纪和19世纪初最先进的资本密集型产业，但如今却成为劳动最密集的产业之一。同样，电子产业，如收音机、电视机、洗衣机、电冰箱、微波炉等家电产业，在20世纪也曾经是最先进的产业，而如今与很多当前的高科技产业相比，也只是成熟的、附加值较低的产业。即便是前面专栏提到的半导体产业，由于产业链的细分，芯片设计与芯片封装测试存在很大的技术差距，前者依然由美国、日本、韩国和中国台湾等发达经济体主导，而封装测试等早已转移到中国大陆与其他东亚国家。在当今日新月异的科技革新中，行业和工作的性质也在加速变迁。例如，2013年世界银行发布的旗舰报告的主题是通过创造就业消除贫困，但在6年之后的2019年，不得不由于人工智能等新一轮通用技术的革新影响将旗舰报告的主题聚焦于工作性质的变革。正如《世界发展报告2019：工作性质的变革》所指出的，从远古时代的狩猎，到农耕社会的春播秋收，再到工业时期的流水线生产，“工作”的概念一直被不断重新定义。这一次次的技术革新，伴随着生产方式变更，都不可避免地引发劳动力市场的恐慌，英国19世纪的破坏机器卢德运动就是最好的写照。然而回顾历史，技术造成的失业通常只是短暂阵痛，随后而来的往往是新兴就业机会、生产力提高与社会进步。[①]近十年，以人工智能为代表的技术爆炸正在重塑新一轮社会经济格局。零人工干预的借贷平台、分拣货物机器人、零工经济等新工作方式、工作形态不胜枚举。这些创新极大地改变了就业市场形势，也引发了社会各界对于未来工作的思考和探讨。该报告也指出：人力资本投资迫在眉睫，终身学习在急速变化的时代必不可少，社会情感技能（如领导力、团队合作能力、创造力）等软实力尤为重要；数字经济时代涌现的平台企业拓宽了市场边界，使弱势群体更便利地参与市场交易，共享市场经济繁荣。与此同时，平台企业也带来了新的监管挑战。许多跨国企业，尤其是平台科技公司，纷纷利用监管套利进行避税，全球企业税制迫切需要升级；政府需要进一步加强社会保障和社会保险，辅之以劳动力市场机构改革以促进劳动力跨行业转移和再就业。

如果一些劳动者跟不上上述工作性质的变迁则会出现工作降级，而一些劳动者通过获得更高的工作技能适应新的工作，这样就有可能出现所谓的“就业极化”。欧盟Eurofound（2008，2011，2013）发布了欧盟的就业结构变迁情况，一个具有典型特征事实的发现是“就

① Acemoglu和Restrepo关于美国的实证研究得出了令人悲观的结果：人工智能一方面可能产生替代效应（displacement effect），另一方面可能会创造新的劳动就业岗位从而产生相应的生产力效应（productivity effect）。他们利用美国1990—2007年的劳动力数据，结合IFR（The International Federation of Robotics）提供的美国各产业使用机器人的数据，发现投入高科技虽然会提高劳动生产率，但同时对于就业率和工资有负向的影响。具体而言，每1 000名工人增加1个机器人，最高可让4名工人失业，或是工人工资下降0.71%（Acemoglu D, Restrepo P., “Robots and Jobs: Evidence from US Labor Markets”, NBER Working Papers, 2017）。

业极化”或“工作极化”现象。[①]如图6.28所示，在产业或技术变迁过程中，中间工资水平的岗位数量减少得更多，高工资水平与低工资水平的岗位数量增长更快或减少更少，呈现出“中间低、两边高”，尤其是2008—2010年全球金融危机期间表现更加如此。当然，不同的国家也表现出不同的模式。如图6.29以及图6.30所示，一些经济体表现出就业结构升级的趋势，有的表现出降级的趋势。美国与欧盟的整体情况类似，在20世纪90年代后开始出现就业结构的两极分化，如图6.31和图6.32所示。[②]但是需要注意的是，在20世纪90年代之前，美国的就业结构表现出升级模式。对于发达经济体出现的就业结构极化现象，主要的解释是技术进步对常规任务型工作的替代以及信息技术兴起后外包任务变得容易。[③]一些研究发现中国的就业结构变迁也在一定程度上呈现了如欧美经济体近年来出现的工作极化现象。在更加微观的个体层面，一些研究也发现我国的就业结构变迁也在一定程度上呈现了工作极化现象，但更多的是反映了经济转型与发展阶段的变化，尤其是就业结构升级。[④]屈小博和程杰利用2005年全国1%人口抽样调查、2010年第六次全国人口普查和全国流动人口动态监测调查数据，采用就业岗位分析方法进行的研究发现了一些就业结构变迁的典型特征事实：中国整体就业结构变动呈现正在“升级”模式，但不同行业就业岗位变动特征存在一定差异。[⑤]例如，2005—2010年，制造业中最低收入岗位出现绝对减少，中等收入岗位增长最多，接近1 300万，中高和高收入岗位数量也分别增长约500万，制造业正在经历一个明显的升级过程。区域层面就业结构呈现多样化和有序递进，东部经济发达省份就业升级较快，中高或高收入岗位增长相对更多，符合中国发展阶段与产业升级的特征。但是，最近几年农民工就业结构变化的“两极化”（polarization）收入倾向已初露端倪，最低和中低收入岗位的就业增长率为负，尤其中低岗位大幅减少，中等收入岗位增幅较小，中高和最高收入岗位增长更多。这与我国近些年禀赋结构变化所引发的产业结构变迁有关。低人力资本的农民工可能会在产业结构升级过程中被边缘化，这需要引起政策重视。[⑥]

---

① ERM Report 2008–More and Better Jobs: Patterns of Employment Expansion in European, Eurofound; Shifts in the Job Structure in Europe during the Great Recession, Eurofound; Employment Polarization and Job Quality in the Crisis: European Jobs Monitor 2013, Eurofound.

② David Autor, “The Polarization of Job Opportunities in the U.S. Labor Market: Implications for Employment and Earnings” , *The Center for American Progress and the Hamilton Project*, 2010.

③ David H. Autor and David Dorn, “The Growth of Low-Skill Service Jobs and the Polarization of the US Labor Market” , *American Economic Review,* 2013, 103(5), pp. 1553–1597.

④ 吕世斌、张世伟，“中国劳动力‘极化’现象及原因的经验研究”，《经济学（季刊）》，2015年第2期，第757–778页。

⑤ 屈小博、程杰，“中国就业结构变化：‘升级’还是‘两极化’？”，《劳动经济研究》，2015年第1期。

⑥ 付才辉、林民书、赖小琼，“产业升级、民工进城与城乡收入差距”，《产业经济评论》，2013年第4期。

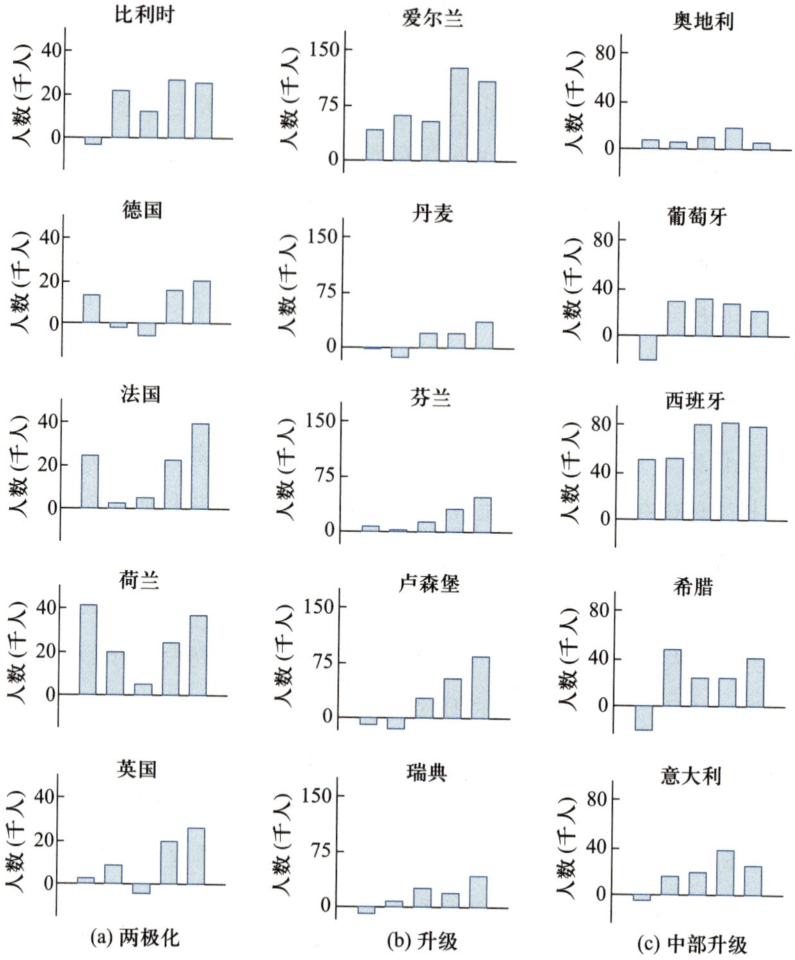


**图6.28 1995—2007年欧盟国家按工资分五等分的就业结构**

资料来源：European Labor Force Survey.

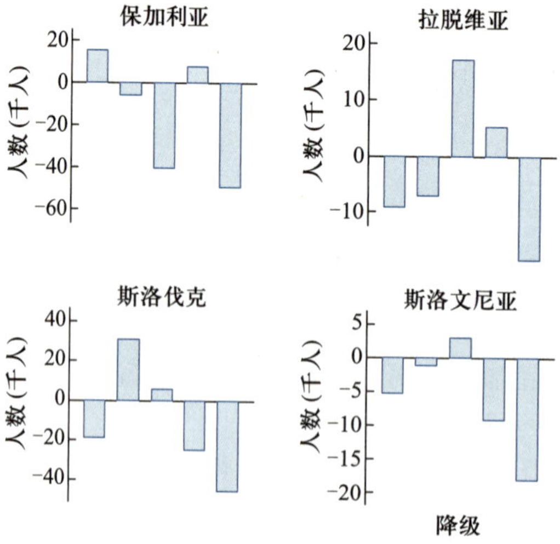


**图6.29 2011—2012年东欧部分国家按工资五等分的就业结构**

资料来源：Eurofound（2013）.

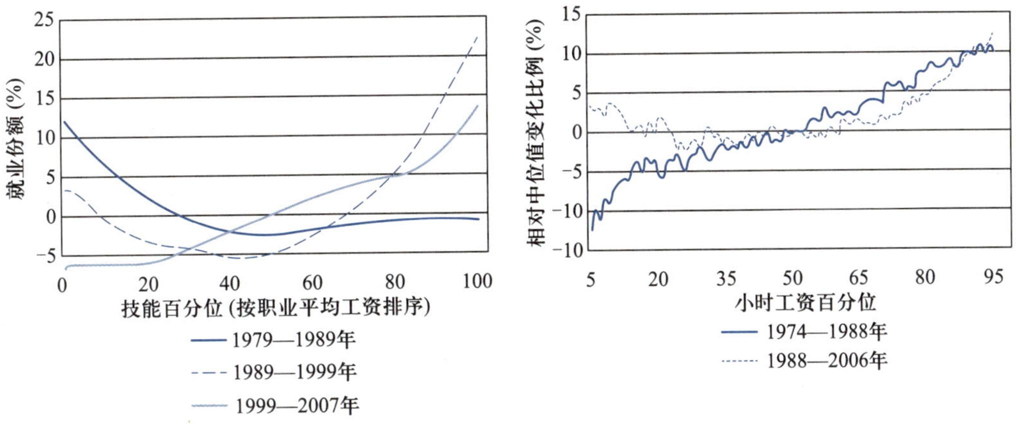


图6.30 1979—2007年美国按照技能等级划分的就业份额变迁（左）与小时工资相对中位值变化（右）

资料来源：Autor（2010）.

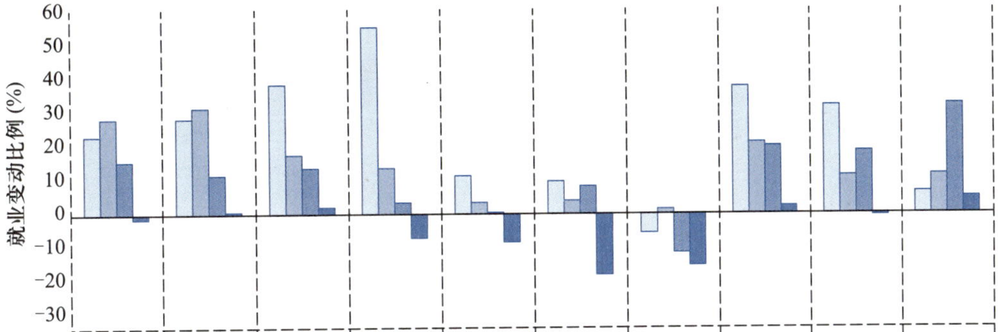


| | 经理 | 专业人员 | 技术人员 | 推销员 | 办公管理 | 生产、工艺和修理 | 操作者、制造商和工人 | 保护性服务 | 厨师、建筑和清洁 | 个人护理服务 |
|---|---|---|---|---|---|---|---|---|---|---|
| 1979—1989年 | 22% | 28% | 37% | 54% | 11% | 10% | -5% | 36% | 31% | 7% |
| 1989—1999年 | 27% | 30% | 17% | 14% | 3% | 4% | 1% | 20% | 11% | 12% |
| 1999—2007年 | 15% | 11% | 14% | 4% | 1% | 8% | -11% | 20% | 18% | 31% |
| 2007—2009年 | -19% | 0% | 2% | -7% | -8% | -17% | -15% | 2% | 0% | 5% |

图6.31 1979—2009年美国按照职业类型分类的就业变迁

资料来源：Autor（2010）.

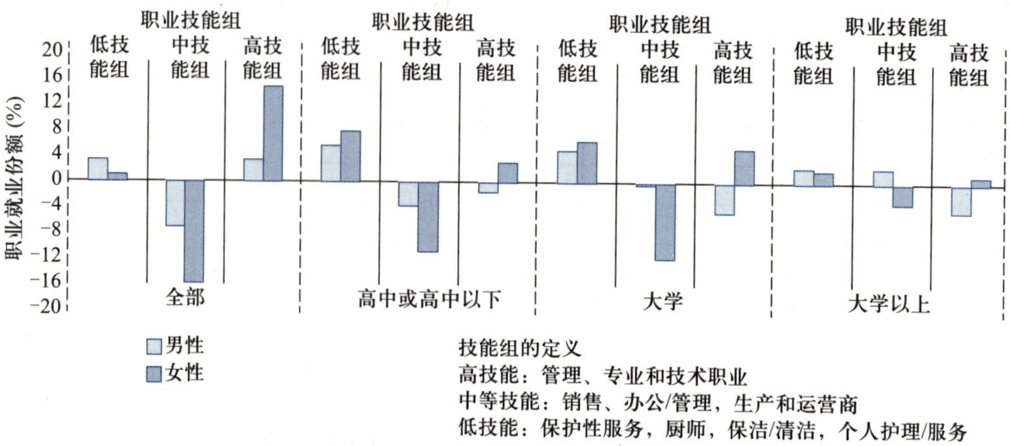


**图6.32 1979—2007年美国按照教育和性别划分的职业就业份额变迁**

资料来源：Autor（2010）.

# 6.5

# –

# 全球制造业差序格局与南南合作的产业基础以及中国的地位

## 6.5.1 全球制造业差序格局①

在全球制造业结构变迁中，每个经济体面临的制造业就业，不论是低于标准还是超过水平，对于每个经济体而言都是发展机遇：面临低于标准的经济体可以从合适的面临超过水平

①“差序格局”一词是中国社会学的奠基人费孝通提出的，旨在描述亲疏远近的人际格局，如同水面上泛开的涟漪一般，由自己延伸开去，一圈一圈，按与自己距离的远近来划分亲疏。

的经济体中引进合适的产业；同样，面临超过水平的经济体也可以向合适的经济体转移合适的产业。因此，问题的关键就在于每个经济体如何在全球制造业变迁大格局中找到合适的位置。根据中国的经验，最重要的是解放思想、实事求是，既正确认识自己，也正确认识别人。所谓正确认识自己，就是客观全面地了解本国的基本国情和条件，包括所处的发展阶段，所具有的自然资源、劳动力、资金等禀赋条件；也要了解过去和现在发展面临的主要问题及其产生的主要原因，等等。所谓正确认识别人，就是对世界上处于不同发展阶段的不同类型的国家做出系统分析，并对本国与这些国家之间的关系，包括可比性、差异性、互补性等，做出客观判断。其中，特别重要的是对本国和其他国家的要素禀赋及其结构和相对价格，或者说对不同国家的相对比较优势及其阶段性特征进行深入细致的研究。这是不同国家之间相互学习和借鉴的基本前提。①

用公式（6.3）来测度在全球制造业结构变迁格局中任何一个经济体与其他经济体之间的关系：首先，将每个时点上的经济体分为两类，一类是面临制造业就业低于标准的经济体（例如$\text{empgap}_i > 0$），一类是面临制造业就业超过水平的经济体（例如$\text{empgap}_j < 0$）；其次，一般而言禀赋水平比较高的经济体不会从禀赋水平比较低的经济体引进后者失去比较优势的产业或者后者向前者转移失去比较优势的产业，只会是禀赋水平比较低的经济体从禀赋水平比较高的经济体引进后者失去比较优势的产业或者后者向前者转移失去比较优势的产业；最后，可以通过如图6.33所示的夹角来度量这两类经济体之间的亲疏关系：夹角越大，说明两个经济体之间的禀赋水平越接近，产业引进或者产业转移的适合程度也越高；反之，适合程度就越低。图6.34就展示了以制造业工资水平差异所刻画的这种禀赋水平差异，其决定了全球制造业的差序格局，如图6.35所示。

$$\theta_{ijt} = \arctan\frac{\text{empgap}_{it} - \text{empgap}_{jt}}{\text{wage}_{jt} - \text{wage}_{it}} \tag{6.3}$$

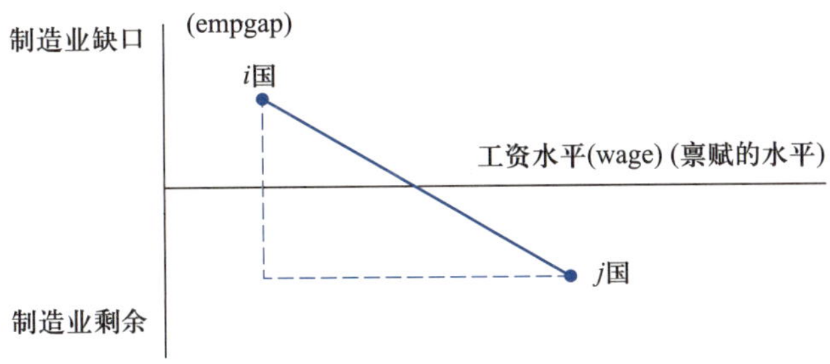


图6.33 全球制造业差序格局的度量

① 林毅夫，“中国经验对新兴经济体的启示”，《人民日报》，2016年4月24日。

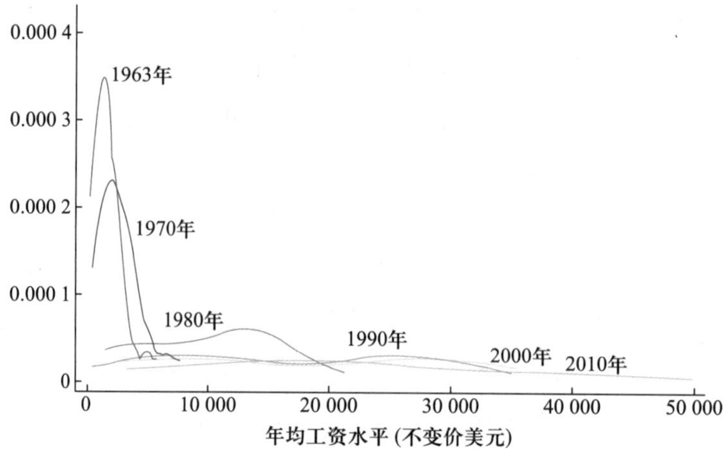


(a) 高收入经济体制造业年均工资水平分布的变迁

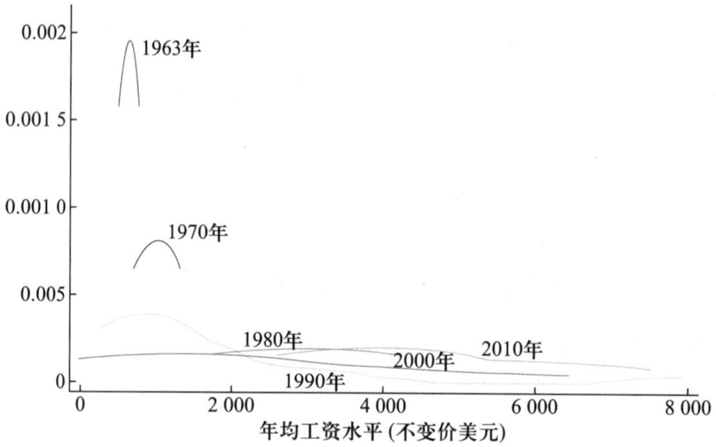


(b) 欧洲和中亚 (非高收入) 经济体制造业年均工资水平分布的变迁

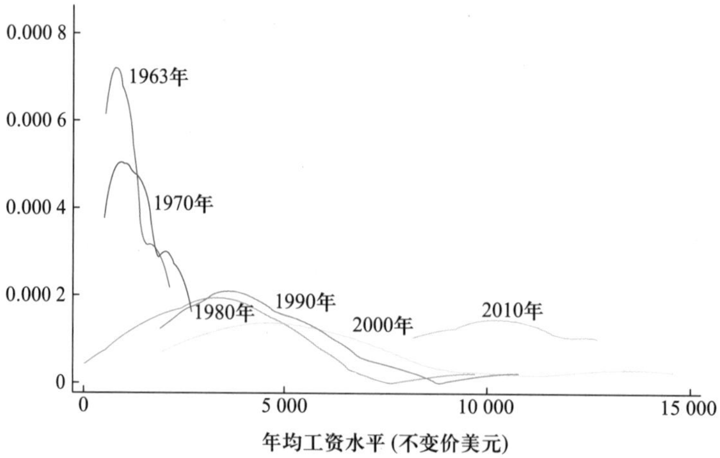


(c) 拉丁美洲和加勒比地区经济体制造业年均工资水平分布的变迁

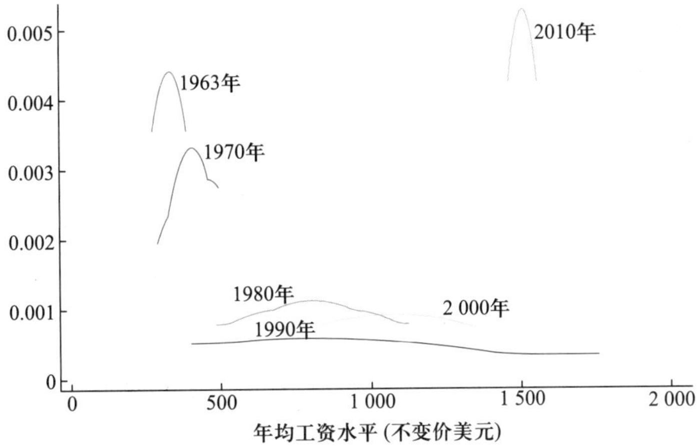

(d) 南亚地区制造业年均工资水平分布的变迁

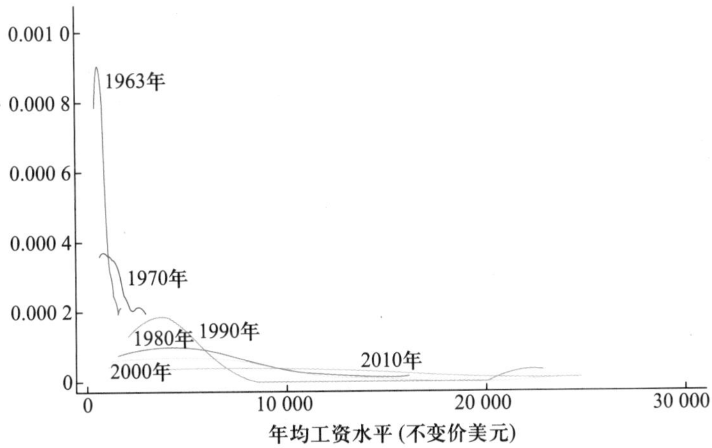

(e) 中东和北非地区制造业年均工资水平分布的变迁

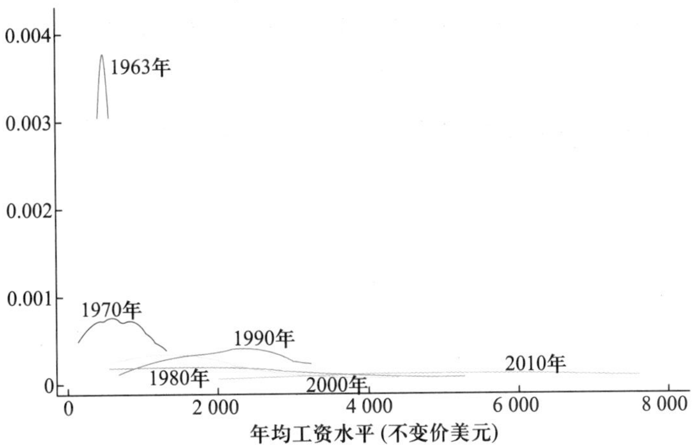

(f) 东亚和太平洋地区制造业年均工资水平分布变迁

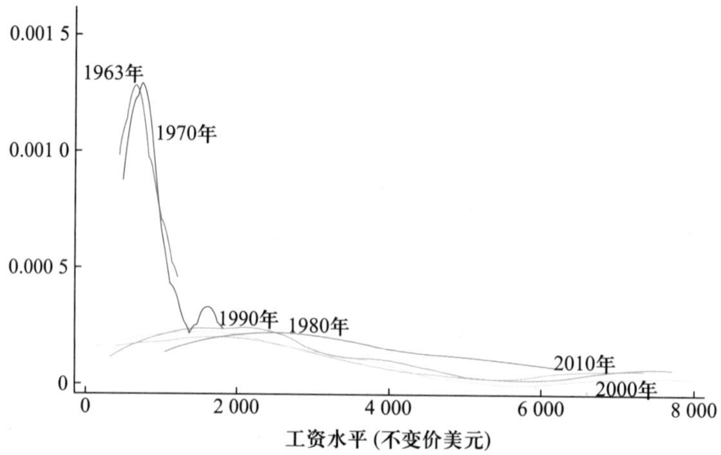


(g) 撒哈拉以南非洲地区制造业年均工资水平分布的变迁

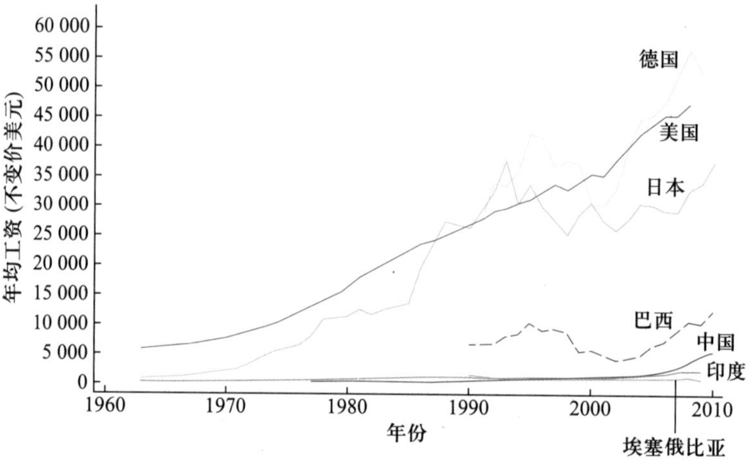


(h) 中国、印度、埃塞俄比亚、巴西、德国、日本与美国的制造业年均工资

图6.34 全球各个地区以及代表性国家的制造业年均工资水平（不变价美元）分布的变迁（1963—2010年）

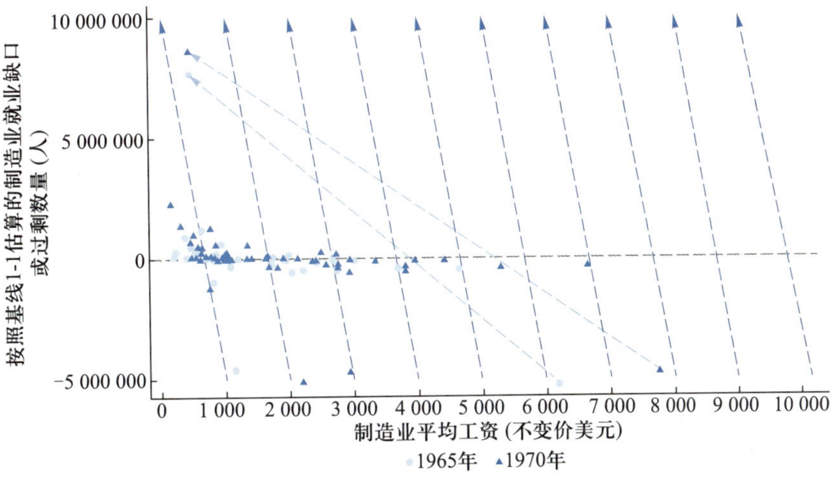


(a) 全球制造业差序格局及其变迁（1965—1970年）

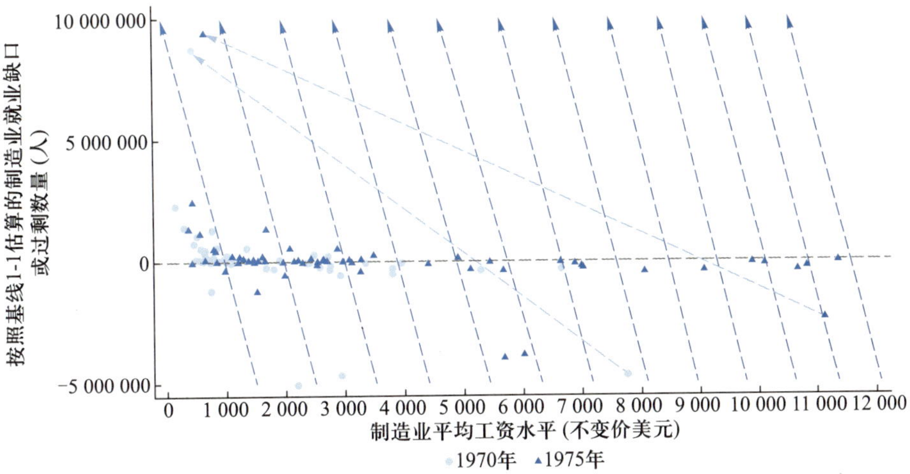


(b) 全球制造业差序格局及其变迁（1970—1975年）

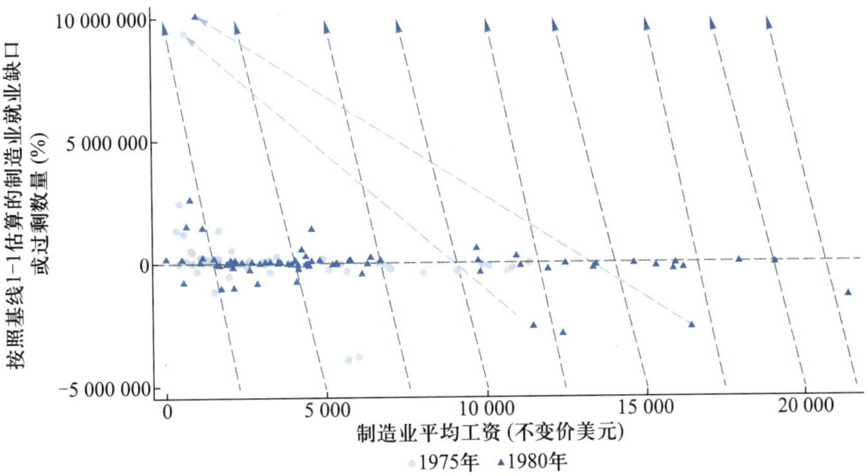


(c) 全球制造业差序格局及其变迁（1975—1980年）

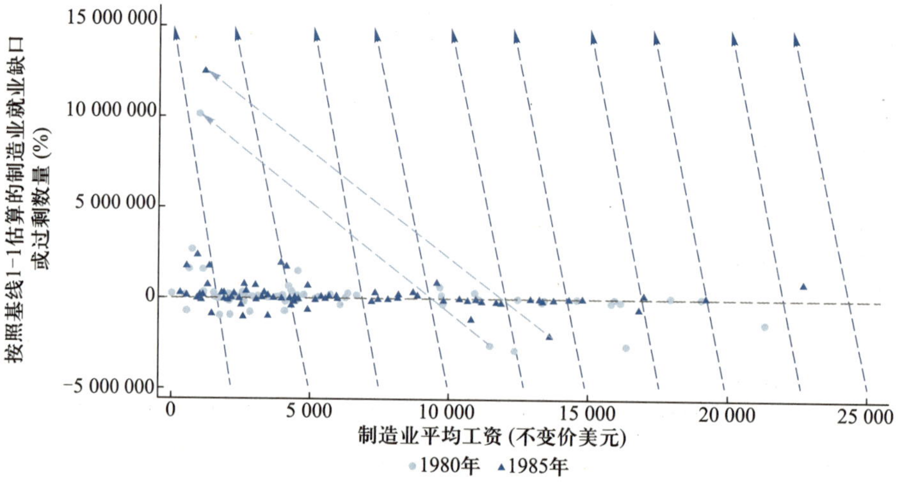

(d) 全球制造业差序格局及其变迁(1980—1985年)

图6.35 全球制造业差序格局度量示例

### 6.5.2 南北合作的产业基础：以中美为例

美国前总统奥巴马在发表2015年国情咨文时指出："我们深信我们能逆转外包浪潮，在国内创造新的就业机会。"新任美国总统特朗普发表的制造业回流的主张也引起了极大的关注。媒体长篇累牍地报道了美国制造业回流的案例，指出回流原因包括中国工人工资快速增长、美国工人工资增长缓慢、海运运费降低等。波士顿咨询（BCG）发布了一系列研究报告，认为制造业回流是一个很重要的趋势，预计将会有相当大的增长；在其2012年4月主导的一项网上调查中，发现产值在100亿美元以上的企业中，有37%正在着手或考虑将其产品生产从中国移回美国；2014年4月，波士顿咨询又发布了一份制造业竞争力指数的报告，美国排名第二，仅次于中国，该指数关键的四大影响因素包括工资、生产率增速、能源成本和汇率。[①] 然而，一份来自彼得森国际经济研究所的政策研究报告发现，并没有证据表明美国企业有普遍回流趋势，但确实在全球发生了漂移。如果将外包业务定义为美国跨国公司从中国子公司的进口，2011年美国对中国的外包业务有小幅下降，但2012年又恢复到2010年的水平；同时，美国对泰国、巴西、菲律宾等其他国家的外包业务增加了。2010—2012年，美国对中国

① 波士顿咨询（BCG），*The Shifting Economics of Global Manufacturing*.

的外包业务停滞不前时，对墨西哥的外包业务却增长了17%。证据显示，企业里低技术含量、更常规的工作被外包出去，但高附加值的业务却在美国国内得到进一步的扩张。[①]根据美国劳工部发布的制造业十个最大类别子行业过去十年来就业份额的变化数据，即便是在严格的制造业定义下，增长最快的行业类别是建筑设计、商业和金融、管理、计算机、销售等，更为传统的制造业岗位就业降幅最大，在制造业总就业中大约占一半的份额——鉴于制造部门整体就业只占美国总就业中8.8%的份额，这意味着传统制造业就业在美国总就业中大概只有4.6%的份额。

按照我们前面的估算，美国等发达经济体的制造业确实由于再工业化的问题面临较大的就业缺口，但是按照前面关于全球制造业差序格局的分析，以及基于图6.36所示的美国的制造业工资水平目前大约是中国的4倍的事实，制造业从发展中经济体回流到美国等发达经济体的说法却是伪命题。正如彼得森国际经济研究所的这份政策研究报告所言："美国企业回流的倡导，反映了回归传统制造业的愿望，但这却忽视了制成品生产组织的诸多重要变革，同时也忽视了伴随而来的机遇。说到制造业，我们不应该再浮现工人在生产线上装配产品的场景，如今制造业就业的增长，尤其是高工资、高附加值的岗位，更多是集中在如产品设计、分销、供应链管理等领域。事实上，相对外包量小的公司，将业务更多外包出去的美国跨国公司，它们在美国的就业岗位、产出、资本支出、研发支出的增幅更大。因此，美国制造业和服务业目前欣欣向荣，而这并非因为企业的回流，相反，外包是美国企业保持竞争力的一个要素。"[②]因此，除了贴近市场，即便美国存在一些回流的案例，其原因也不会仅仅是为了应对中国劳动力薪酬的上涨，更多的是为了享受美国工人更高的技能等资源禀赋。因此，按照全球制造业差序格局布局全球生产链是南北经济体保持持续竞争力的基础。

事实上也是如此。首先，从中美双方直接投资角度来看，中美的经济互补性非常强。高盛最近的一份研究报告显示，1990—2015年，美国企业在中国投资达2 280亿美元，中国企业在美投资达640亿美元，美国企业在中国投资的金额大约是中国企业在美国投资的30倍以上。从投资的具体方式和行业来看，美国企业在中国的投资主要集中于IT和通信行业、化学行业、材料行业。美国企业在中国投资的方式主要有两种：第一是设立工厂（大约为71%），第二是收购（大约为29%）。过去25年间，有1 300家美国企业在中国设立了工厂，其中有430家企业的投资额超过5 000万美元，有56家企业的投资额超过10亿美元。中国企业在美国的投资则主要集中在能源企业和房地产行业，不过近年来中国对于美国科技行业的

① Lindsay Oldenski, "Reshoring by US Firms: What Do the Data Say?", *Policy Review*, 2015, No. PB 15-14.

② 同上。

投资也越发增多。过去25年间，中国企业进行了1 200笔交易，其中85%是发生在过去5年。与美国不同，中国企业在美国大概90%的投资都用于收购。

图6.37和图6.38记录了最新的情况，反映出中美之间的结构性差异。

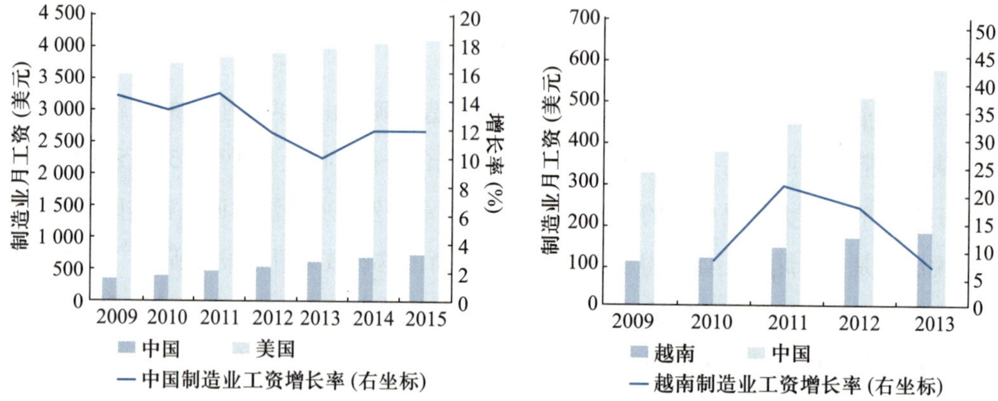


**图6.36 中国与美国（左）以及中国与越南（右）的制造业月工资水平及其增幅比较**

资料来源：国际劳工组织；高盛GIR。

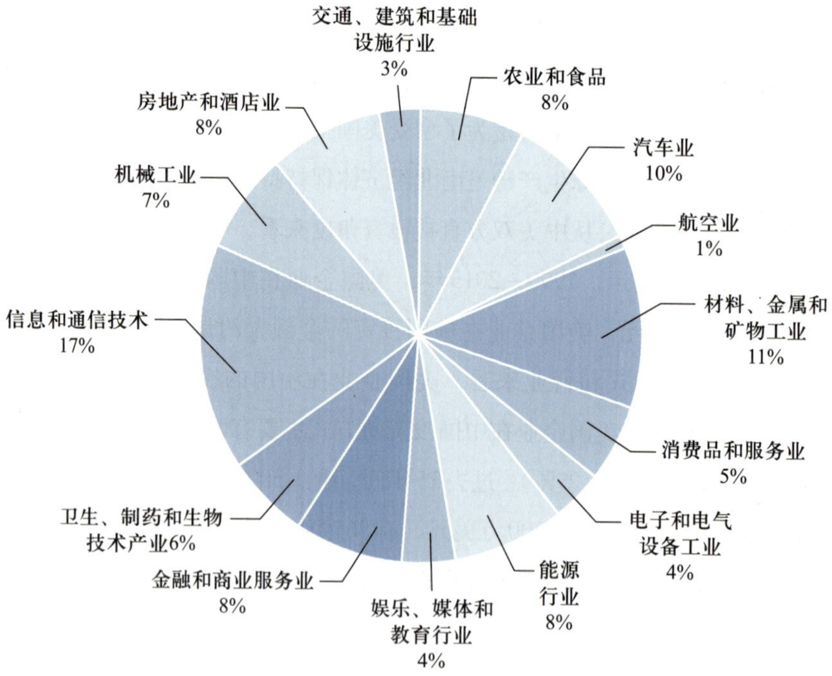


**图6.37 1990年—2019年6月美国企业在中国直接投资的行业分布**

资料来源：荣鼎集团(Rhodium Group)和美中关系全国委员会。

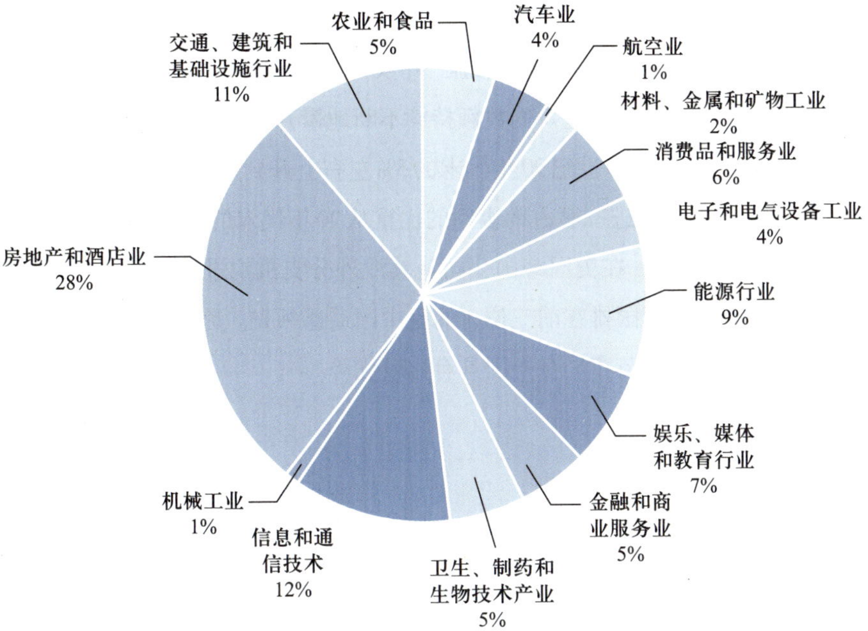


**图6.38 1990年—2019年6月中国企业在美国直接投资（FDI）的行业分布**

资料来源：荣鼎集团（Rhodium Group）和美中关系全国委员会。

其次，从中美贸易角度来看，中美产业互补性也非常强。美国2015年从中国进口4 800亿美元货物，相比2000年增长4 000亿美元，年复合增长率达11%。总体而言，过去25年间，中国对美国进口无论从具体数额，还是从比例上看，都有了较大增长，这也是中国对美国贸易顺差迅速增长的重要原因。中国2015年从美国进口约1 150亿美元货物，这意味着美国对中国的贸易逆差为3 650亿美元。2015年美国占据了中国总出口额的18%，而中国对美国的出口占据了中国GDP的3%。2015年，中国在科技和电气设备行业对美国的出口额达1 360亿美元，过去15年间的复合增长率达13%。不过，美国对全球的出口在过去15年间的复合增长率仅为1%。美国的同期全球进口总额仅为3 000亿美元。2000年，美国的全球进口总额为4 000亿美元，年复合增长率为-2%。而从比例上看，在某些特定行业，如玩具行业和伞业，中国占据美国进口额的80% ~ 90%。中国在鞋业、家具业和电子行业也占据了美国进口总额非常高的比例。美国对中国的主要贸易顺差来自交通行业和农业。美国对中国出口比例最大的产品是飞机及相关组件，美国占据中国飞机及相关组件进口的63%。美国在汽车行业对中国出口也比较多，但是比例相对较低，仅占中国汽车进口的20%左右。因此，可以看到，美国从中国进口也就是中国出口到美国的产品相对而言依然是劳动力密集型产品或者是技术密集型以及资本密集型产品通过劳动力密集型组装后再回到美国；与此相反，美国出口到中国也就是中国从美国进口的产品相对而言是资本密集型和技术密集型的制造业产品和土地密集型的农产品。整体上，这种贸易模式符合古老的要素禀赋结构决定的比较优势法则。

最后，从跨国公司的生产布局角度来看，中美产业互补性依然非常强。如图6.39所示，美国跨国公司过去十多年从海外进口的数额持续不断地攀升，美国跨国公司从其海外分支机构进口额占销售额的比重从20世纪90年代末的5%左右上升到2010年后的6%左右，美国跨国公司从其海外非分支机构进口额占销售额的比重从90年代末的4.5%左右上升到2010年后的8%左右。如图6.40所示，在美国跨国公司从其海外分支机构进口额的来源地分布中，目前中国内地、中国香港和泰国排在前三位，而且中国遥遥领先。因此，从跨国公司微观企业的理性决策而言，将生产环节布局在中国具有比较优势。

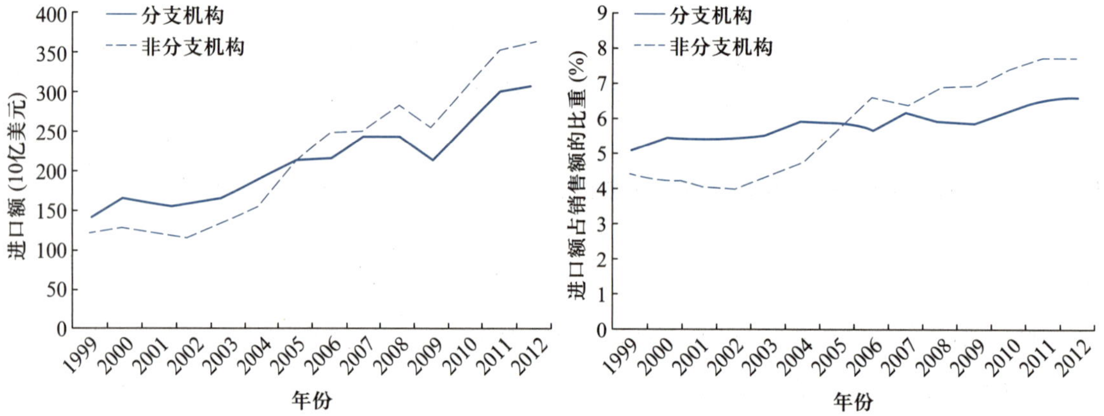


**图6.39 美国跨国公司从其海外分支机构与非分支机构进口额及其占销售额的比重**

资料来源：美国经济分析局。

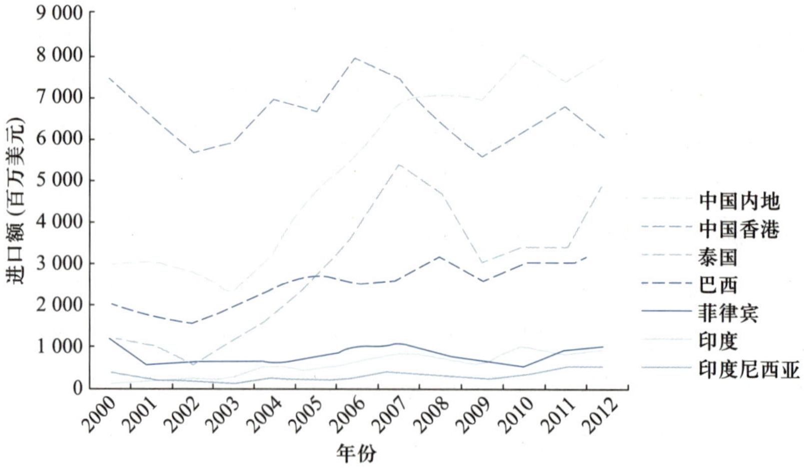


**图6.40 美国跨国公司从其海外分支机构进口额的来源地分布**

资料来源：美国经济分析局。

总之，中美之间互补的经济特征事实符合新结构经济学的理论，中美如果能够持续认识到并持续推进这种互补性，加强投资和贸易合作，对于中国和美国都是巨大的发展动力。然而，美国新任总统特朗普高举“保护主义”大旗，在竞选和就任之后的一系列宣示和举措违背了这样的基本道理和事实。2017年3月31日，特朗普就在白宫签署了两份有关美国贸易政策的行政命令。特朗普当天表示，此举意在重振美国的制造业。然而，特朗普没有找对美国问题的症结，没有看清问题，所以开出的“药方”也是错误的。他所采取的措施不仅不能保护他想保护的那部分选民，而且可能让问题更糟糕。实际上并不是中国抢走了美国的就业机会，因为中国卖给美国的这部分劳动力密集型产品，美国几十年前就已经不生产了。20世纪60年代，它们主要是日本在生产，后来转移到亚洲“四小龙”，然后才是在中国内地生产（本章最后将介绍电子信息产业在70年代从美国转移到日本和亚洲“四小龙”，然后在90年代开始转移到中国内地的情况，可供佐证）。所以，不是中国今天才抢了美国蓝领工人的就业岗位，而是生产这些产品不符合美国的比较优势。按照前面章节所讨论的产业结构变迁规律，诸如美国这样的发达国家由于禀赋结构水平的不断升级，产业结构随之不断升级，早在20世纪60年代中后期，第三产业的比重就超过50%。产业结构随禀赋结构的变迁也反映在贸易结构上。如图6.41所示，虽然美国总的贸易赤字从20世纪70年代开始逐渐扩大到2006年前后的峰值，但是贸易赤字主要来源于商品贸易赤字，服务贸易则始终盈余而且数额不断扩大。正是由于商品贸易赤字，使得中美贸易赤字也不断扩大，如图6.42所示。然而，中美贸易赤字则实际是前面所讨论的由要素禀赋结构变迁所驱动的东亚雁阵模式在贸易结构上的反映。如图6.43和图6.44所示，美国与中国的贸易赤字和美国与东亚地区贸易赤字以及中国

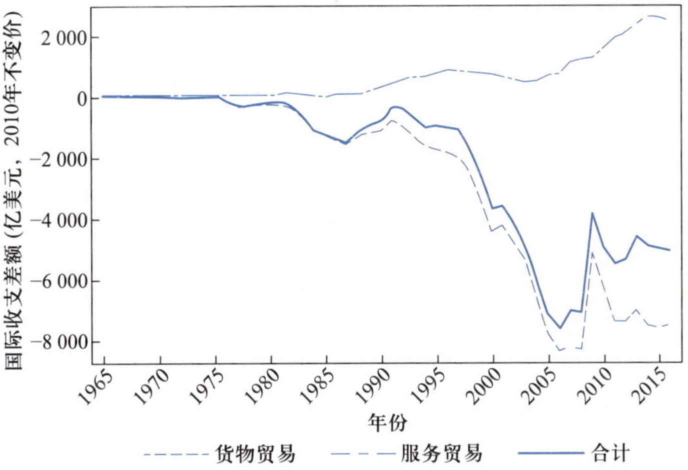


**图6.41 美国1965—2016年的贸易赤字结构变迁情况**

资料来源：美国商务部普查局。

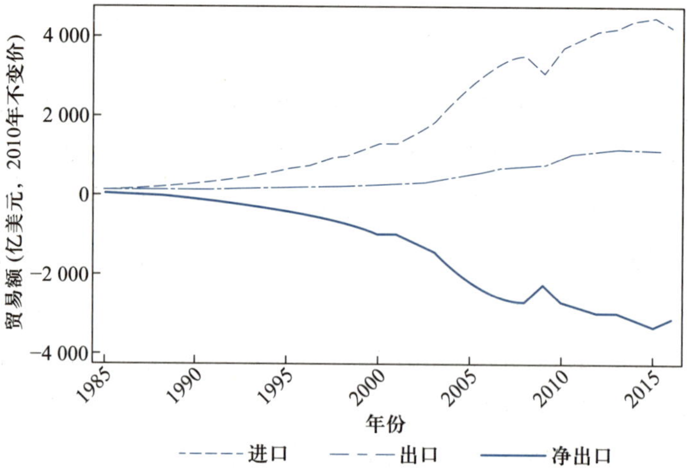


图6.42 1965—2016年美国对中国的双边贸易赤字结构变迁情况

资料来源：美国商务部普查局。

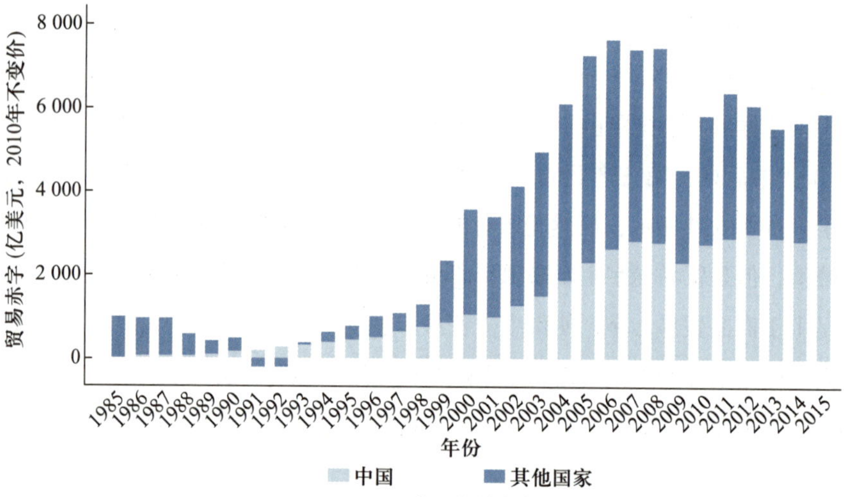


(a) 美国贸易赤字

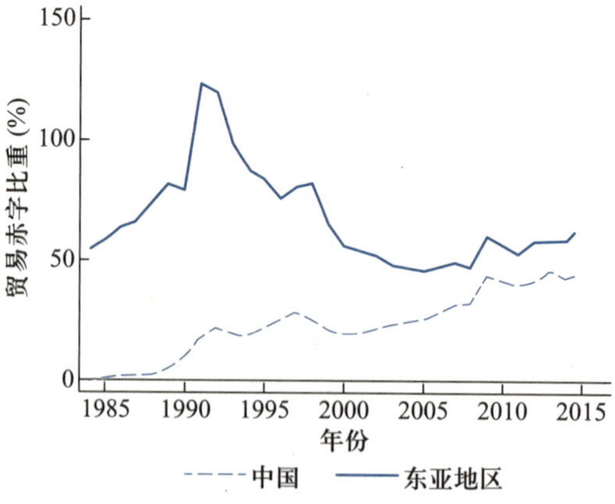


(b) 贸易赤字比重

图6.43 美国贸易赤字中结构

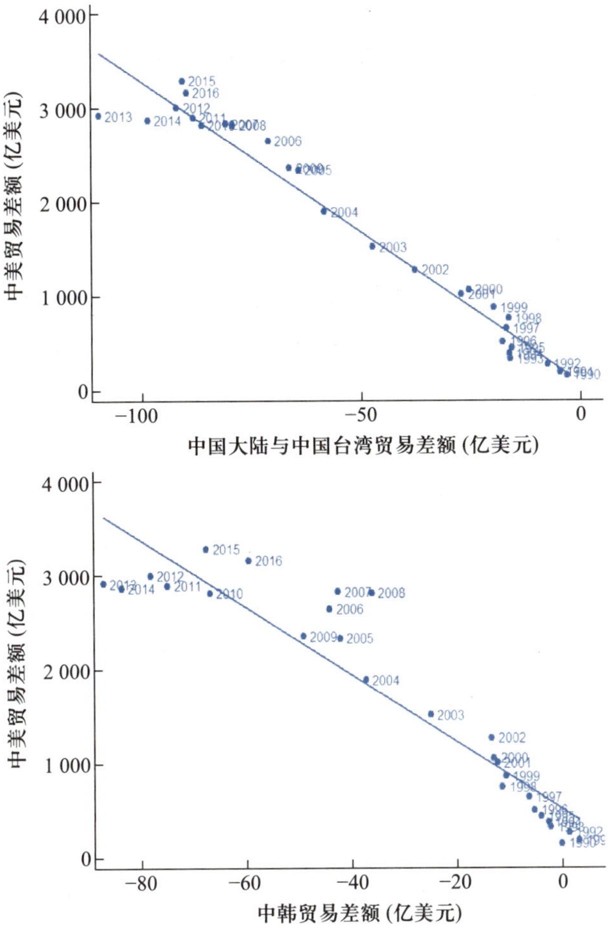


图6.44 中美贸易赤字与中国大陆和中国台湾贸易赤字（左）、中国与韩国贸易赤字的散点图

与东亚地区的贸易赤字是此消彼长的，尤其是在制造业不同部门之间。①因此，中美贸易关系的状况是全球经济结构变迁的基本规律所决定的。

① Lin Justin Yifu & Wang, Xin, “Trump economics and China-US trade imbalances”, *Journal of Policy Modeling*, 2018, Vol. 40, No.3, pp.579–600.

### 6.5.3 南南合作的产业基础：以中非为例①

然而，尽管有研究报告指出前述发达经济体制造业回流的伪命题，深刻认识到全球制造业差序格局中南北合作的产业基础，但是主流理论却严重忽视了南南合作的产业基础。例如，第二次世界大战后主流的结构主义思潮主张低收入的发展中经济体直接发展发达经济体的先进产业。按照新结构经济学的理论，以及前面估算的全球制造业差序格局，每一个面临制造业就业低于标准的低收入发展中经济体适合发展的产业并不是发达经济体最先进的产业，反而是收入水平略高的中等收入经济体失去比较优势的产业，尤其是中国。这就是南南合作的产业基础。

按照新结构经济学的基本原理，一个经济体符合比较优势的学习对象的目标产业一定不能过度背离自身的禀赋结构所决定的比较优势。一个经验法则是目标经济体的人均收入水平大致是自身的1~3倍，或是与20~30年前人均收入处于同一水平，在过去数十年快速发展的经济体。过去失败的经济体之所以失败，最为重要的根源在于不顾自身比较优势去学习与赶超收入水平远远超过自己的发达经济体。因此，对于当今的中低收入经济体整体而言，发达经济体并不是适宜的学习对象，反而是中国这样的新兴经济体才是合适的学习对象。如图6.36中所示的中国与美国以及中国与越南的制造业月工资水平差距，目前美国制造业工人一个月大概能挣4 000美元，而中国制造业工人一个月大概能挣700~750美元，但随着中国的劳动力成本上升，中美之间的劳动力成本差额正在下降，而且中国的劳动力成本大大高于越南等国家。美国与非洲15个经济体的人均工资水平之比大多高达上百倍，美国产业的复杂性和资本密集度过高，根本不适合大多数亚非拉中低收入经济体这样以劳动力相对富裕为禀赋结构特征的经济体，整体上只适合中等偏上的经济体。相对于美国与非洲而言，在前述制造业测算数据中可以看到，中国与非洲15个经济体的人均工资水平之比没有美国与其之比那样离谱，但是绝大多数非洲经济体的人均工资水平又比中国低很多。这意味着中国而非过于先进的发达经济体才是亚非拉中低收入经济体合适的学习对象，而且对于中国逐渐失去比较优势的劳动力密集型产业尤其是制造业具有成本优势。

中国经济在改革开放之后历经了数十年的高速增长，极大地促进了其禀赋结构的升级。禀赋结构的升级促进了产业升级和技术进步，中国20年、15年、10年前主要的出口产品将逐步失去比较优势。如图6.45到图6.47所示，1994年，鞋、玩具、皮箱、针织外套和女式外套这5项劳动力密集型低技术产品占到了中国全部出口的23.11%。这些劳动力密集型产业非

---

① 林毅夫在《从西潮到东风》和《超越发展援助》两本著作中详细阐述了新结构经济学理论框架下的南南合作的产业基础，供进一步参考。

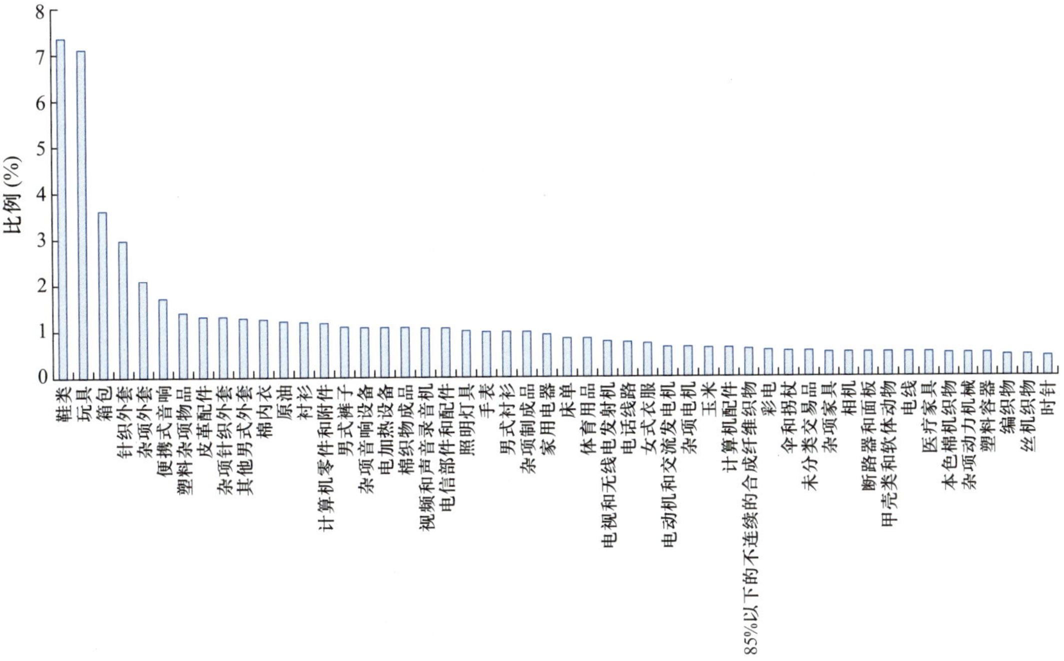


图6.45 1994年中国前50位出口产品及其占总出口的比例（20年以前）

资料来源：UN Comtrade.

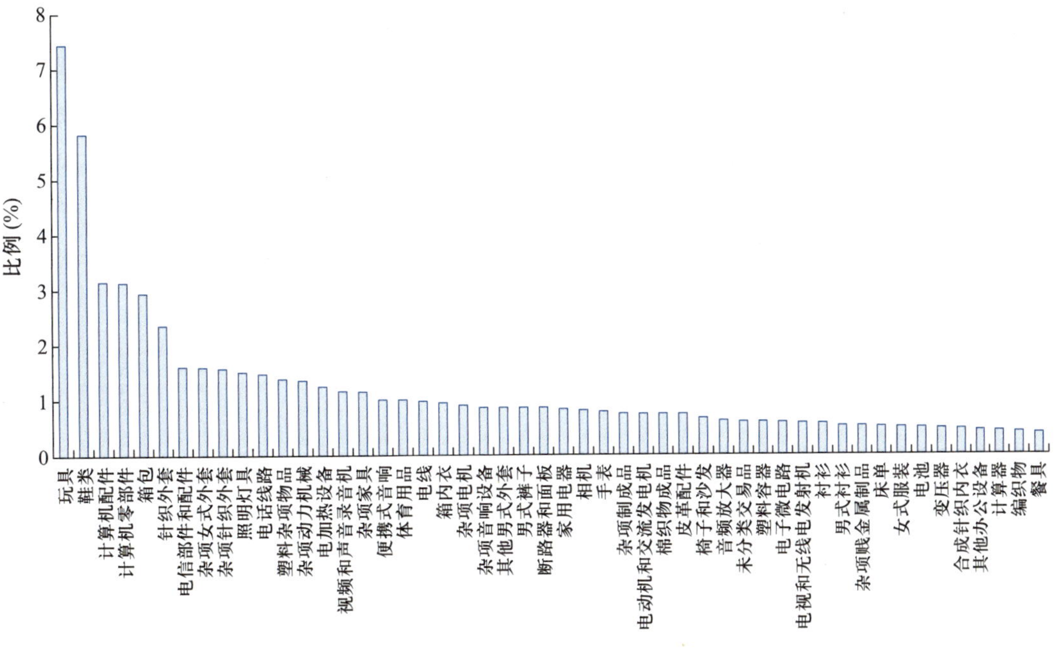


图6.46 1999年中国前50位出口产品及其占总出口的比例（15年以前）

资料来源：UN Comtrade.

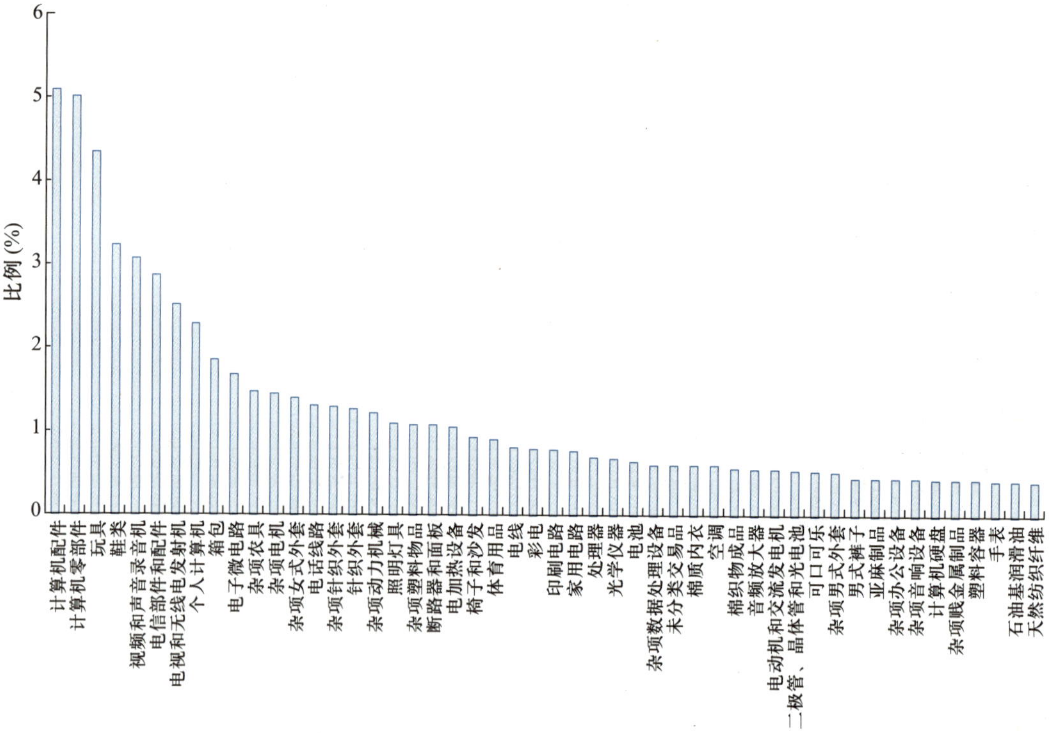


**图6.47 2004年中国前50位出口产品及其占总出口的比例（10年以前）**

资料来源：UN Comtrade.

常符合非洲乃至全球的低收入经济体禀赋结构决定的比较优势。低收入经济体只有大规模承接中国等新兴经济体逐步失去比较优势的劳动力密集型产业才能创造经济剩余，改善禀赋结构，逐步实现产业升级和技术进步。如果广大低收入经济体现在以美国为学习目标，因为美国的经济复杂性较高，如图6.48所示，美国20年前主要的出口品是大型飞机、微电子、交通运输设备零部件、汽车、处理器等资本和技术密集型产品，这必然违背低收入经济体的比较优势，后果会适得其反。

### 6.5.4 中国在南南合作中的地位：“领头龙模式”

正如林毅夫在2011年的WIDER年度演讲中指出的，全球经济结构转型升级将出现一个重大的差异：中国的经济体量远远大于引导之前的经济结构转型升级的亚洲经济体，中国是

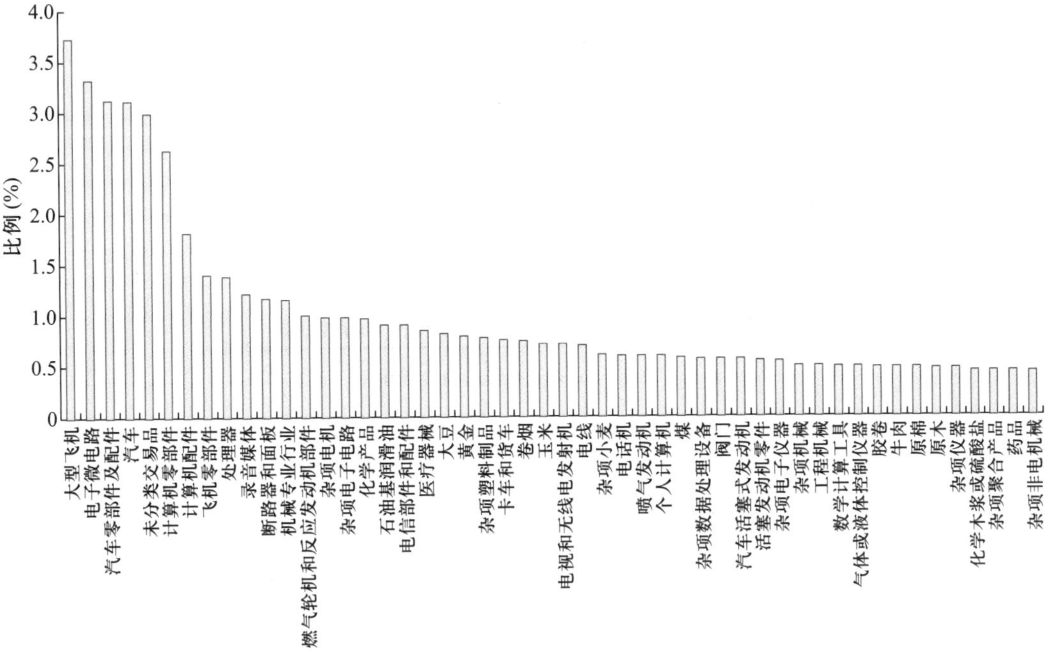


**图6.48 美国20年以前的前50位出口产品（1994年）**

资料来源：UN Comtrade.

一条领头龙而非仅仅是一只头雁。[①]如表6.10所示，中国目前的制造业雇用了1.24亿人，其中将近8 500万人在劳动力密集的加工制造业部门。林毅夫的这个判断与本书的估算是非常吻合的。如图6.49所示，亚洲过去两次“雁行模式”的头雁有待转移的失去比较优势但符合追随者潜在比较优势的制造业就业缺口是百万量级的，但是中国目前有待转移的失去比较优势的制造业就业剩余是千万量级的。按照上述8条基线估算，中国在2006—2010年5年间平均失去比较优势的制造业就业缺口就在1 100万~3 800万的量级之间，如图6.50所示。与此同时，如果参照韩国历史上制造业就业结构比重探底的时期，中国目前也即将处于制造业就业结构探底的阶段，因此，中国将会为其他劳动力富裕型的低收入经济体释放出全球历史上空前的发展机遇。如果全世界的发展中经济体与中国的经济结构转型升级进行对接，那么将产生巨大的动力，这是全球发展不可错失的机遇。例如，目前低收入经济体的总人口不足10亿，制造业在国内生产总值中的比例只有10%多，制造业就业人数也就1 000万左右，可想

① Lin Justin Yifu, “From Flying Geese to Leading Dragons: New Opportunities and Strategies for Structural Transformation in Developing Countries” , *Global Policy*, 2012, 3(4), pp. 397–409. Vandana Chandra, Justin Yifu Lin, Yan Wang, “Leading Dragon Phenomenon: New Opportunities for Catch-up in Low-Income Countries” , *Asian Development Review*, 2013, 30(1), pp. 52–84.

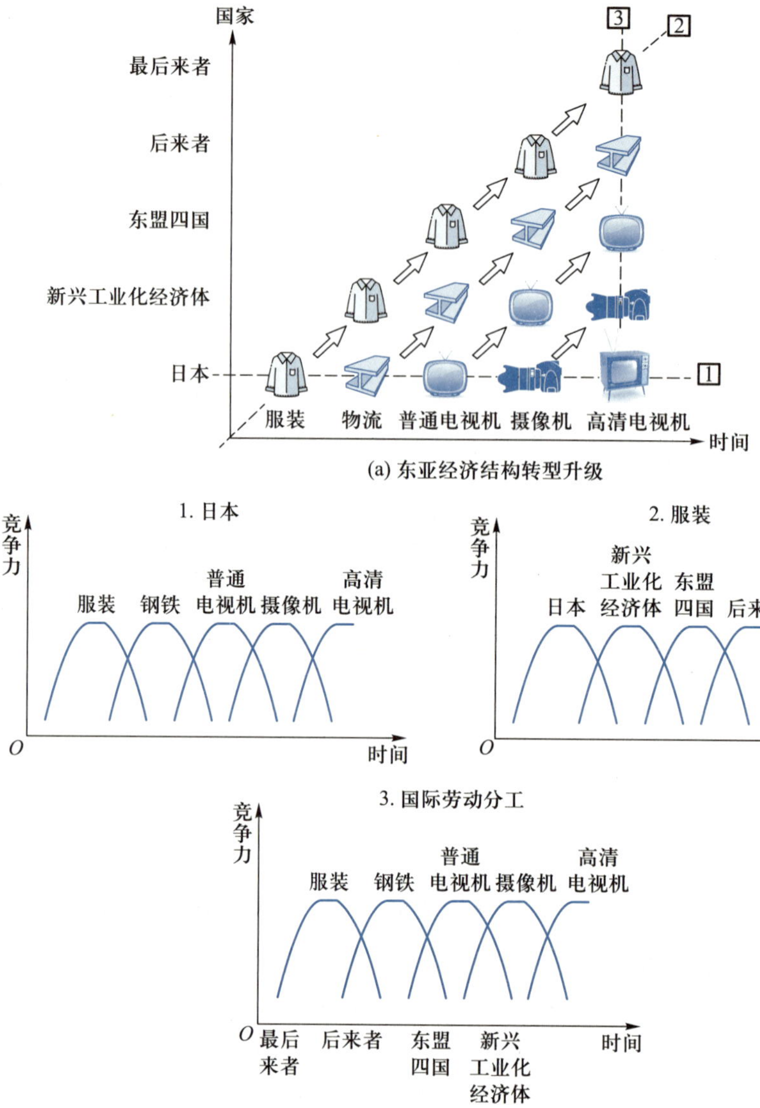


(a) 东亚经济结构转型升级

(b) 日本产业转移带来的“东亚奇迹”

图6.49 亚洲的“雁行模式”

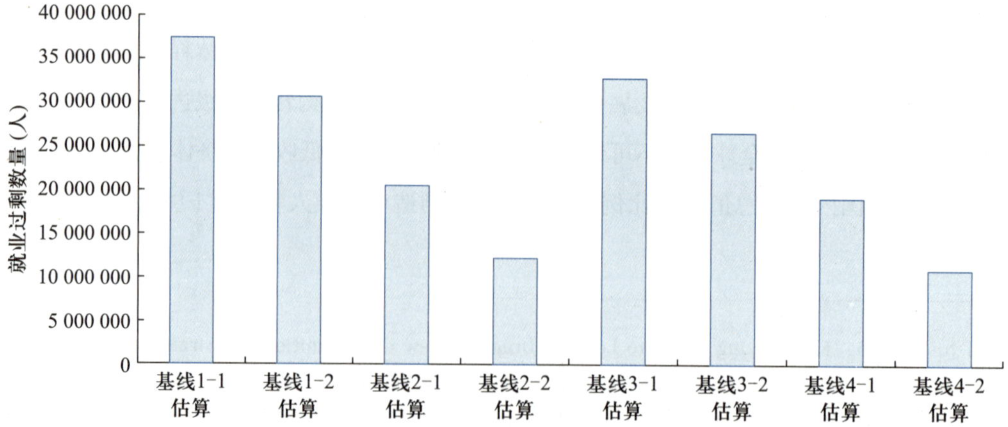


图6.50 按照8条基线估算的中国2006—2010年5年平均失去比较优势的制造业就业过剩数量

而知中国这数千万有待转移的劳动力密集型产业将使全球低收入经济体的制造业就业人数翻几番。中国庞大的失去比较优势的劳动力密集型产业一旦转移到非洲，非洲的发展问题将迎刃而解。虽然在2010年之前，中非由FDI形式的转移产业还微不足道，但这个时代在此之后将迅速开启。世界各个经济体如何与中国的经济结构转型升级进行对接将是第8章的主题。

表6.10 中国、日本和韩国在类似发展水平上的制造业

| 国别 | 年份 | 人均国内生产总值 | | 制造业 | | |
|---|---|---|---|---|---|---|
| | | 2000年不变价美元 | 2005年购买力平价美元 | 在附加值中的比重（%） | 在劳动力中的比重（%） | 就业人数（百万） |
| 日本 | 1960 | 5 493 | 6 976 | 35 | 20.0 | 9.7 |
| 韩国 | 1982 | 3 709 | 6 123 | 25 | 14.6 | 2.3 |
| 中国 | 2009 | 2 206 | 6 200 | 43 | 17.7 | 85.0 |

资料来源：林毅夫，《从西潮到东风》，中信出版社，2012年版，第147页。

如前面的量化估算显示的结论一样，过去20年后进国家的工业化发展次序仍然在亚洲延续。例如，中国在20世纪90年代早期已经成为鞋类和玩具等轻工业产品的主要生产国（见表6.11），日本当时仍然是重要的玩具生产国，但很明显已经在向更复杂的游戏品种的阶梯爬升，如任天堂公司和索尼公司的产品等。作为当时的低收入国家，中国有大量的鲜活动物产品出口。到21世纪后，中国得以爬升到更加复杂的制造业层次，取代了日本在塑料、电视机、电子产品及部件等领域的世界出口份额。韩国在20世纪90年代还是鲜活动物产品的重要出口国，但此后逐渐退出了这一初级产品部门。印度在鞋类制品市场的份额落后，但已在逐渐提高。

劳动和产品的国际分工提供了另一种观察雁行模式的视角。例如，鞋类制品的历史统计数据揭示了先进国家与后进国家各自的比较优势指数，给“雁行模式”理论提供了有力证明（见表6.12）。20世纪60年代早期，处于轻工业发展阶段的日本在鞋类制品上拥有比较优势。后来，其他国家开始在国际市场上扩大份额。当然这些变化与“雁行模式”描述的动态过程并非一模一样。实际历史数据总是掺杂着噪声，因为复杂程度不同、资本和技术密集度不同的产品在统计时往往被不加区分地集中到一个类别中。政府干预也可以造成产业结构偏离比较优势所决定的最优模式。但总体而言，实际情况基本符合理论的描述。

表6.11 亚洲的“雁行模式”——部分产业的国家排名（1992年与2008年）

| 国别 | 鲜活动物产品 | | 药品 | | 鞋类制品 | | 钢铁 | |
|---|---|---|---|---|---|---|---|---|
| | 1992年 | 2008年 | 1992年 | 2008年 | 1992年 | 2008年 | 1992年 | 2008年 |
| 中国 | 1 | 1 | 2 | 3 | 1 | 1 | 3 | 1 |
| 印度 | 5 | 4 | 3 | 1 | 4 | 2 | 4 | 4 |
| 日本 | 3 | 3 | 1 | 2 | 5 | 5 | 1 | 2 |
| 韩国 | 2 | 5 | 4 | 4 | 2 | 4 | 2 | 3 |
| 泰国 | 4 | 2 | 5 | 5 | 3 | 3 | 5 | 5 |

| 国别 | 塑料制品 | | 电子机械、部件 | | 电视机 | | 玩具 | |
|---|---|---|---|---|---|---|---|---|
| | 1992年 | 2008年 | 1992年 | 2008年 | 1992年 | 2008年 | 1992年 | 2008年 |
| 中国 | 3 | 1 | 3 | 1 | 3 | 1 | 1 | 1 |
| 印度 | 5 | 5 | 5 | 5 | 5 | 5 | 5 | 5 |
| 日本 | 1 | 2 | 1 | 2 | 1 | 2 | 2 | 2 |
| 韩国 | 2 | 3 | 2 | 3 | 2 | 3 | 3 | 4 |
| 泰国 | 4 | 4 | 4 | 4 | 4 | 4 | 4 | 3 |

注：排名根据出口产品的国际标准产业分类的两位数目录数据。

资料来源：United Nations Statistics Division 2011.

表6.12 亚洲各经济体在鞋类制品上的比较优势（1962—2000年）

| 1962年 | 1965年 | 1970年 | 1975年 | 1980年 | 1985年 | 1990年 | 1995年 | 2000年 | 其他 |
|---|---|---|---|---|---|---|---|---|---|
| 日本 | 日本 | | | | | | | | 其他中等收入经济体和低收入经济体加入 |
| 中国大陆 | 中国大陆 | 中国大陆 | 中国大陆 | 中国大陆 | 中国大陆 | 中国大陆 | 中国大陆 | 中国大陆 | |
| | 中国台湾 | 中国台湾 | 中国台湾 | 中国台湾 | 中国台湾 | 中国台湾 | | | |
| | 韩国 | 韩国 | 韩国 | 韩国 | 韩国 | 韩国 | | | |
| | 巴基斯坦 | | | | | | | | |
| | | 菲律宾 | 菲律宾 | 菲律宾 | | | | | |
| | | | 泰国 | 泰国 | 泰国 | 泰国 | | | |
| | | | 印度尼西亚 | 印度尼西亚 | 印度尼西亚 | | | | |
| | | | 印度 | 印度 | 印度 | | | | |
| | | | | 越南 | 越南 | | | | |
| | | | | 斯里兰卡 | 斯里兰卡 | | | | |
| | | | | 缅甸 | | | | | |
| | | | | 孟加拉国 | | | | | |
| | | | | 斐济 | | | | | |
| | | | | 柬埔寨 | | | | | |

注：反映的比较优势的计算方法是，鞋类制品在某个经济体的出口中的比重除以鞋类制品在全球出口额中的比重。如果该比例大于1，则这个经济体就表现出了在鞋类制品上的比较优势。除中国以外，其他经济体按收入水平顺序排列。

资料来源：United Nations Statistics Division 2011.

# 6.6

## 他山之石：日本和中国重庆如何把握全球电子信息产业转移的机遇

半导体产业是电子信息产业的基础，代表着当今世界最先进的主流技术发展。半导体产业于20世纪50年代起源于美国，之后共经历了三次大规模产业转移。第一次是在20世纪70年代末期，从美国转移到了日本，第一次转移后日本成为世界半导体的中心。第二次是20世纪80年代末至90年代初，产业从日本转移到了韩国、中国台湾和新加坡等地，形成了世界范围内美国、韩国、中国台湾等国家和地区多头并立的局面。第三次是21世纪以来，中国大陆由于具备人力资本和市场等多方面的优势，正在承接第三次大规模的半导体产业转移（见图6.51）。

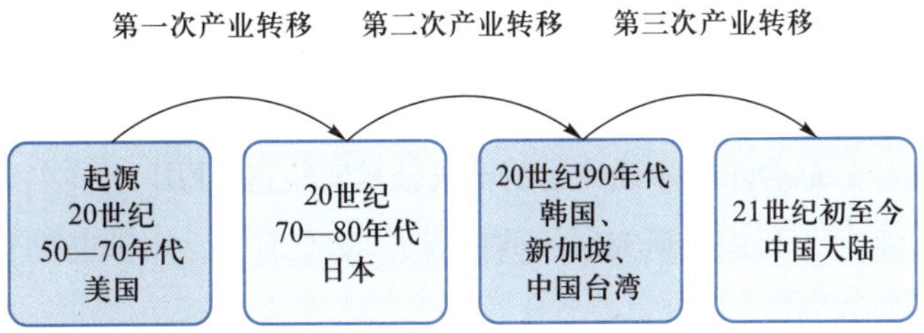


图6.51 半导体产业的全球产业转移

### 6.6.1 日本如何把握始于美国的半导体产业转移机会①

日本半导体企业的发展依次经历了崛起（20世纪70年代）、鼎盛（20世纪80年代）、衰落（20世纪90年代）、转型（21世纪初）四个阶段（见图6.52）。

① 本小节关于日本的案例根据广发证券发展研究中心行业研究报告《日本半导体产业发展历程解读》（2016）整理。

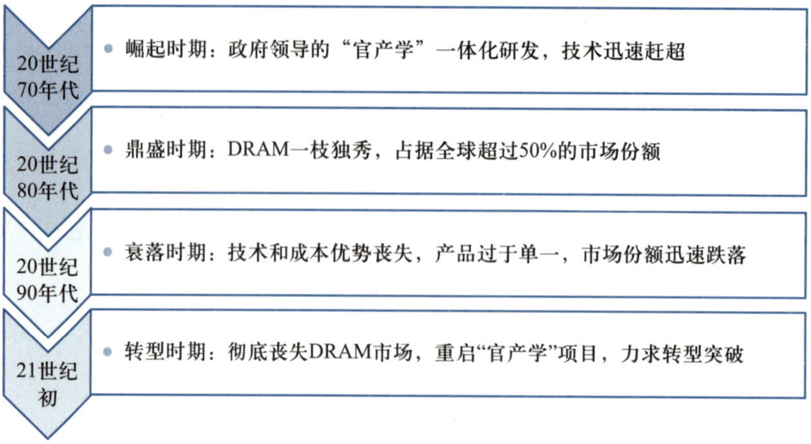


图6.52 日本半导体产业发展历程

崛起：20世纪70年代，VLSI研发联合体带动技术创新

20世纪70年代初，日本半导体产业整体落后美国十年以上。70年代中期，日本本土半导体企业受到两起事件的严重冲击。一件事是日本1975年、1976年在美国压力下被迫开放其国内计算机和半导体市场；另一件事是IBM公司开发的被称为未来系统（Future System，F/S）的新的高性能计算机中，采用了远超日本技术水平的一兆的动态随机存储器。1976—1979年在政府引导下，日本开始实施具有里程碑意义的、超大规模集成电路的共同组合技术创新行动项目（VLSI）。该项目由日本通产省牵头，以日立、三菱、富士通、东芝、日本电气五大公司为骨干，联合了日本通产省的电气技术实验室（EIL）、日本工业技术研究院电子技术综合研究所和计算机综合研究所，共投资了720亿日元，用于进行半导体产业核心共性技术的突破（见图6.53）。

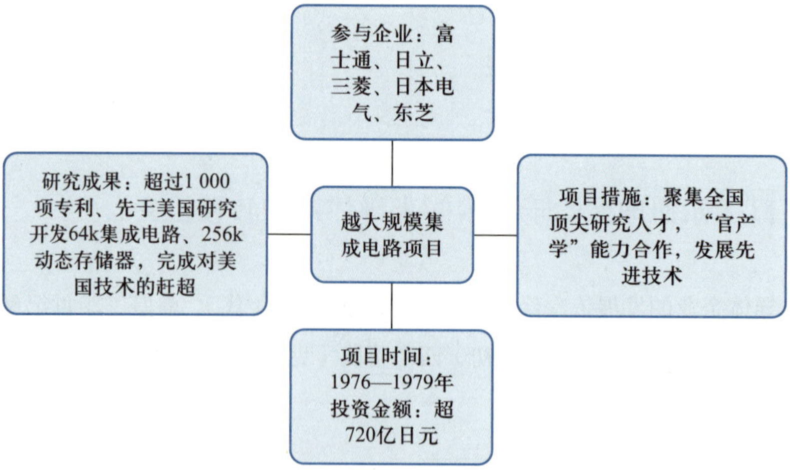


图6.53 VLSI项目实施情况

VLSI项目是日本“官产学”一体化的重要实践，将五家平时互相竞争的计算机公司以及通产省所属的电子技术综合研究所的研究人才组织到一起进行研究工作，不仅集中了人才优势，而且促进了平时在技术上互不通气的计算机公司之间的相互交流、相互启发，推动了全国的半导体、集成电路技术水平的提高，为日本半导体企业的进一步发展提供了平台，令日本在微电子领域上的技术水平与美国并驾齐驱。项目实施的4年内共取得了1 000多项专利，大幅度提升了成员企业的VLSI制作技术水平，日本公司借此抢占了VLSI芯片市场的先机。同时政府在政策方面也给予了大力支持。日本政府于1957年颁布《电子工业振兴临时措施法》，支持日本企业积极学习美国先进技术，发展本国的半导体产业。1971年、1978年分别颁布了《特定电子工业及特定机械工业振兴临时措施法》《特定机械情报产业振兴临时措施法》，进一步巩固了以半导体为核心的日本信息产业的发展（见表6.13）。

表6.13 日本的相关产业政策

| 时间 | 政府出台政策 | 内容 |
|---|---|---|
| 1957年 | 《电子工业振兴临时措施法》 | 规定了政府在发展日本电子工业中的作用、有关推动措施，有效地促进了日本企业在学习美国先进技术的基础上，积极发展本国的半导体产业 |
| 1971年 | 《特定电子工业及特定机械工业振兴临时措施法》 | 进一步秉承了《电子工业振兴临时措施法》的宗旨，强化了发展以半导体为代表的电子产业的力度。该法的实施成功地帮助日本企业通过加强自身研发、生产能力，有效地抵御了欧美半导体厂商的冲击，进而使日本半导体制品不断走向世界 |
| 1978年 | 《特定机械情报产业振兴临时措施法》 | 进一步加强了以半导体为核心的信息产业的发展 |

鼎盛：20世纪80年代，依靠低价战略迅速占领市场

该阶段，日本半导体产业的主要竞争力是产品的成本优势和可靠性。日本半导体产业的崛起以存储器为切入口，主要是DRAM（动态随机存取存储器）。到20世纪80年代，受益于日本汽车产业和全球大型计算机市场的快速发展，DRAM需求剧增。而日本当时在DRAM方面已经取得了技术领先，日本企业此时凭借其大规模生产技术，取得了成本和可靠性的优势，并通过低价促销的竞争战略，快速渗透美国市场，并在世界范围内迅速取代美国成为DRAM主要供应国。随着日本半导体的发展，世界市场快速洗牌，到1989年日本芯片在全球的市场占有率达51%，美国仅36%，欧洲占11%，韩国1%，其他地区1%。80年代，日本半导体行业在国际市场上占据了绝对的优势地位（见图6.54）。截至1990年，日本半导体企业在全球前10位中占据了6位（见表6.14），前20位中占据了12位。日本半导体产业达到鼎盛时期。

衰落：20世纪90年代，技术和成本优势丧失，市场份额迅速跌落

从微电子行业的世界技术发展趋势来看，进入20世纪90年代，在美国掀起了以压缩技

术为核心的技术革命，以PC（个人计算机）为代表的新型信息通信设备快速发展，但日本在该领域未有足够的准备。同时日本在DRAM方面的技术优势也逐渐丧失，成本优势也被韩国、中国台湾等地取代。PC取代大型主机成为计算机市场上的主导产品，也成为DRAM的主要应用下游。不同于大型主机对DRAM质量和可靠性（可靠性保证25年）的高要求，PC对DRAM的主要诉求转变为低价。DRAM的技术门槛不高，韩国、中国台湾等地通过技术引进掌握了核心技术，并通过劳动力成本优势，很快取代日本成为主要的供应商。1998年韩国取代日本，成为DRAM第一生产大国，全球DRAM产业中心从日本转移到韩国。之后，韩国一面继续维持DRAM的生产大国地位，一面开发用于数字电视、移动电话等的SOC（系统级芯片），双头并进（见表6.15）。而中国台湾通过不断增加投资，建成了世界一流的硅代工公司——台积电和联电，开发了一种新的半导体制作模式，同时积极研发，在部分尖端技术上已经可以与日本齐头并进。该阶段，日本半导体产品品种较为单一（过于集中在DRAM上），产品附加值低；同时未跟上世界技术潮流，日本半导体产业在该阶段受到重创。截至2000年，日本DRAM份额已跌至不足10%（见图6.55）。

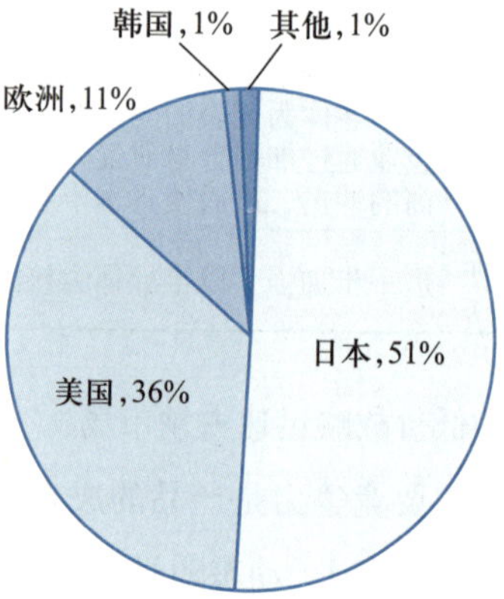


图6.54 1989年半导体芯片的市场份额

表6.14 1990年全球十大半导体企业

| 排名 | 公司 | 销售额（亿美元） |
|---|---|---|
| 1 | NEC | 48 |
| 2 | 东芝 | 48 |
| 3 | 日立 | 39 |
| 4 | 英特尔 | 37 |
| 5 | 摩托罗拉 | 30 |
| 6 | 富士通 | 28 |
| 7 | 三菱 | 26 |
| 8 | TI | 25 |

续表

| 排名 | 公司 | 销售额（亿美元） |
|---|---|---|
| 9 | 飞利浦 | 19 |
| 10 | 松下 | 18 |

表6.15 韩国DRAM技术完成对日、美的赶超

| 时间及差距 | 产品类型 | | | | | | |
|---|---|---|---|---|---|---|---|
| | 64K | 256K | 1M | 4M | 16M | 64M | 256M |
| 美、日开发时间 | 1979年 | 1982年 | 1985年 | 1987年年末 | 1990年年初 | 1992年年末 | 1994年年中 |
| 韩国开发时间 | 1983年 | 1984年 | 1986年 | 1988年年初 | 1990年年中 | 1992年年末 | 1994年年初 |
| 技术差距 | 4年 | 2年 | 1年 | 6个月 | 3个月 | 同时 | 领先 |
| 韩国投产时间 | 1983—1984年 | 1984—1985年 | 1985—1988年 | 1988—1990年 | 1990—1992年 | 1992—1996年 | 1996—1997年 |

资料来源："从模仿到创新"，《韩国半导体考察报告》。

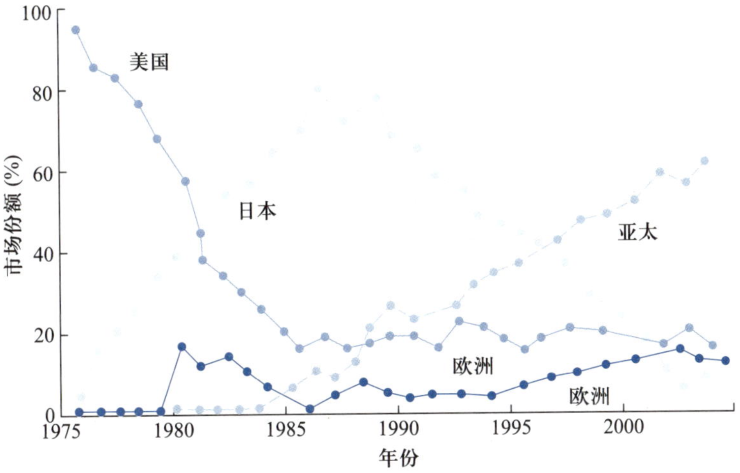


图6.55 DRAM市场份额变化

转型：21世纪初，合并整合与转型SOC

为挽回半导体产业的颓败之势，日本半导体企业首先进行了结构性改革。除Elpida外所有其他的日本半导体制造商均从通用DRAM领域退出，将资源集中到了具有高附加值的系统集成芯片等领域。2000年NEC、日立的DRAM部门合并，成立Elpida，东芝于2002年卖掉了设在美国的工厂，2003年Elpida合并了三菱电机的存储器部门。但Elpida于2012年宣告破产，2013年被美光购并，标志着日本在DRAM的竞争中彻底被淘汰。另一方面，日本重新开启了三个较大型的"产官学"项目——MIRAI、ASUKA和HALCA（见图6.56）。三

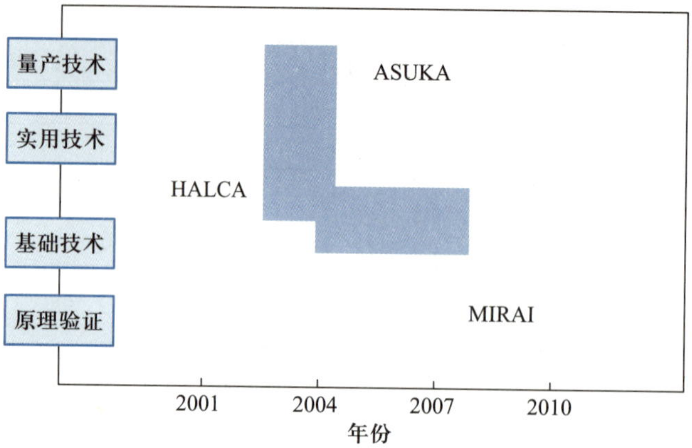


图6.56 日本三大半导体开发计划的关联

个项目都于2001年开启，以产业技术综合研究所的世界级超净室（SCR）作为研发室，ASUKA项目由NEC、日立、东芝等13家半导体厂家共同出资700亿日元，时间为2001—2005年，主要研制电路线宽为65纳米的半导体制造。

目前世界半导体产业进入到寡头时代，竞争格局相对稳定。尽管日本企业在半导体设备行业中的份额日益减少，但在半导体的一些其他细分行业以及半导体材料领域，仍保持着优势地位。DRAM领域主要的生产商是三星、Hynix和Micron（包括收购的原日本Elpida）；NAND领域是东芝（与Sandisk合资的四日市工厂）、三星和Micron；半导体制造设备是TEL、Screen、日立高科等；半导体材料是JSR、TOK、信越等；晶圆有信越、SUMCO等。

### 6.6.2 中国重庆如何把握电子信息产业在全球和国内的产业转移机会

如图6.51所示，半导体产业大概在2000年前后转移到中国沿海地区，尤其是长三角和珠三角地区。在2008年全球金融危机之后，由于沿海劳动力成本的极速上升，半导体产业中的劳动力密集型产业区段开始迁移到内陆地区。重庆把握住了此次机会，改变了20多年来沿海地区加工贸易大进大出的发展方式，在内陆地区创新发展了大规模的加工贸易。下面是时任重庆市市长黄奇帆的总结，从中可以看到一个国家内部的地方政府是如何发挥因势利

导作用，把握住全球产业结构变迁的机遇从而获得快速发展的：[1]

中国从20世纪80年代末开始在沿海地区开展加工贸易，最初是大进大出的“三来一补”，以后就形成了比较稳定的加工贸易发展方式。到2014年年底，中国的加工贸易占全部进出口的45%左右，也就是说，中国4万亿美元进出口当中，有1.8万亿美元是加工贸易形成的产值。沿海的加工贸易有两个特点：第一，它的产业链很短。比如一台计算机，如果产值是500美元的话，它的零部件、原材料一般占整个计算机产值的50%，即250美元；它的零部件、原材料从全世界运到中国沿海，又从中国沿海把整机销售到全世界，整个物流运输、仓储、销售环节占100美元；然后品牌商的研发以及售后服务一般占75美元；所以500美元中最后在中国沿海的加工贸易只留下75美元的总装，也就是占15%左右增加值的这一块，这是沿海加工贸易的一个特点。第二，由于它两头在外，原材料、零部件在外，在沿海加工，加工完了销售在外，所以它大进大出的物流结构的特点，决定了它一般只能在沿海，所以过去二十几年，中国所有加工贸易几乎99%在沿海，内陆几乎是零，原因就是这个，物流成本以及物流的时间，使得加工贸易放在内陆不合算，无法进行。沿海加工贸易发展二十几年来，由于中国沿海劳动力成本、各种要素结构在发生变化，所以最近几年，不少加工贸易订单转到越南等东南亚国家，都是沿海方便大进大出的地区。如何既能保持这一块的经济，又能克服既有的缺陷？重庆进行了研究，形成了两个路数，改变了沿海加工贸易的两个薄弱环节。第一，延伸产业链，把加工贸易的“微笑曲线”大部分留在重庆。重庆现在生产的每台计算机，其产值的70%都在重庆，这和沿海地区总装6 000多万台计算机，产值可能只有15%、20%的情况不同，现在除了总装这75美元留在重庆，零部件、原材料80%在重庆生产，所以250美元中的200美元落地重庆。第三块就是产品的销售结算，跨国公司销售结算的这一块现在也留在重庆。重庆向国家提出了申请，国家外管局、人民银行等有关部门都同意了重庆的试点，推动了重庆这一块的业务，重庆离岸金融结算2011年结算了200多亿美元，2012年有400多亿美元，2013年是600多亿美元，2014年到800多亿美元，2015年预计会有1 000亿美元。总而言之，离岸金融结算，是一个加工贸易的主要结算方式，重庆把这件事也抓起来了。这样三块加起来有350多美元，占一台计算机500美元的70%。因此，重庆的加工贸易效益比较好。现在经济比较低迷，电子产业一般效益都是下降的，但2015年1—4月，重庆电子产业利润却上涨了66%。为什么能有这样好的效益？就是和创新了加工贸易发展方式有关，零部件、原材料大量本地化，前几年860多个零部件厂陆续在建，现在正在大

① 本部分根据时任重庆市市长黄奇帆2015年6月13日在中国经济新常态与深化综合改革国际研讨会暨中国留美经济学会2015年度国际学术研讨会上的发言整理。

批投产，一下子把物流成本都降低了。第二，凡是要搞的加工贸易品种，都要形成集群，叫作三个集群。（1）零部件、原材料、整机上中下游产业链形成了集群——5+6+860，即五大品牌商、六大整机商、860多家零部件厂商都集聚在重庆。（2）同类项产品、同类企业在重庆形成了集群。在中国沿海，富士康、仁宝、纬创、英业达、广达等企业，基本上各个省你占两个，他占两个，一山不容二虎，互相分隔开来。现在中国沿海所有加工贸易总装厂都到了重庆，各种计算机、网络终端产品的品牌商也到了重庆，形成了集群。6大整机商生产了全球网络终端产品的90%，这样一来就形成了一个好的格局，东方不亮西方亮，这个企业订单少了，那个企业就多了，对重庆来说总体平衡，年年上升。（3）物流运输、销售结算等生产性服务业与制造业的集群。重庆的集群方式就是产业链整合的模式，克服了沿海加工贸易的两个薄弱环节，取得了成功。2014年重庆笔记本电脑的产量是6 300万台，全球是2亿台，重庆占1/3，沿海地区所有的产量也是6 000多万台。可以这么说，中国制造的笔记本电脑占全球2/3，重庆占1/3，沿海占1/3，一个世界级的笔记本电脑基地在重庆诞生。党的十八届三中全会决定的第七章，讲到了中国下一步的内陆开放中有一个条款，就是要转变沿海的加工贸易发展方式，推动整机加零部件垂直整合一体化的方式，在内陆开展加工贸易。这段话充分肯定了重庆的做法。

# 第7章

# 克服世界经济结构转型升级的瓶颈①

① 本章的初稿主要来自林毅夫和付才辉所著的《世界经济结构转型升级报告》第8章的相关内容，同时也吸收了林毅夫及其合作者所著的《从西潮到东风》第二部分“走向复苏的共赢之路”、《超越发展援助》第5章“利用中国的比较优势来解决非洲的基础设施瓶颈”、《战胜命运》第1和第7章的相关内容。关于政府在经济结构变迁中作用的更深入的讨论可参考：林毅夫、付才辉，《新结构经济学导论》，高等教育出版社，2019年，第9章。

## 7.1

## 基础设施：是障碍也是随手可牵的“替罪羊”

如第1章第3节所述，新结构经济学认为经济发展的本质是一个经济结构持续不断转型升级的过程，在每一个发展水平上都涉及产业升级来提高生产力水平以及相应的软硬基础设施的改善来降低交易成本。例如，在农业发展阶段，大量产品是用于生产者自身的消费，对外部投入和市场的依赖小，很少的剩余通常在临近的集市交换，因此对基础设施服务的需求较少。随着各国的工业化，生产更多转向制造业，规模经济更加突出，产品主要是为其他人生产，机器设备、汽油、柴油、煤炭要从外地甚至外国的厂家购买，也需要有电力的供给。由于市场范围扩大，良好的基础设施对于安全及时地向市场购买投入和提供产品和服务都至关重要。因此，在经济发展过程中，随着从农业到制造业、从简单制造业到高级制造业的变迁，一国的生产规模及投入品和产品的市场的范围越来越大，对运输和电力等基础设施的需求也越来越大。如图7.1所示，全球各个经济体的基础设施（通过永续盘存法估算的公共资本）与制造业发展存在非常强烈的相关性。也正如我们在第6章所估算的全球各个经济体的制造业缺口所显示的那样，很多经济体无法填补其符合潜在比较优势的制造业缺口的重要原因就是缺乏发展相应产业的基础设施。然而，与私人投资不同，基础设施有巨大的外部性，如果政府不发挥强大的因势利导作用来建设或协调基础设施投资，这将成为经济结构转型升级的瓶颈。一些成功的经济体正是因为政府发挥了应有的作用解决了基础设施瓶颈，才推动了经济结构转型升级，而那些不成功的经济体则面临普遍的基础设施瓶颈。

对于如何使发展中国家的经济表现得到改善，很多经济学家会给出一个最为常见的政策前提，即基础设施的数量和质量。至少自亚当·斯密以来，经济学家们就认定交通基础设施的建设对推动经济发展和消除贫困发挥着重要的作用。最开始是在Aschauer[①]、Sanchez-

① D. Aschauer, “Is Public Expenditure Productive?” *Journal of Monetary Economics*, 1989, Vol.23: 177–200.

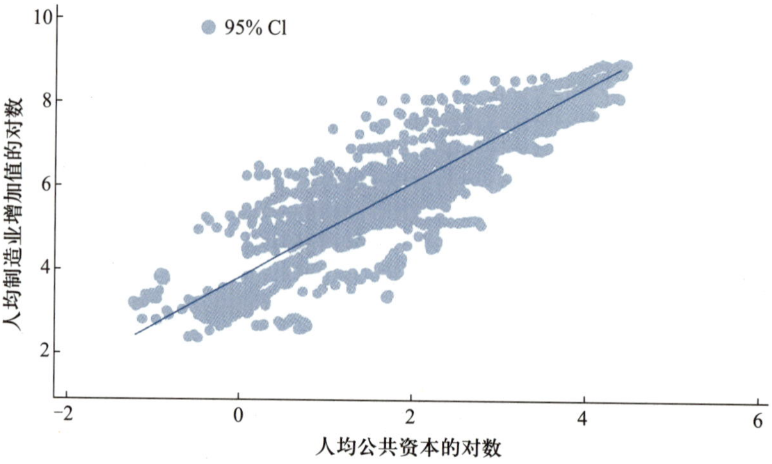


**图7.1 全球各个经济体的基础设施（通过永续盘存法估算的公共资本）与制造业发展的相关性**

资料来源：Anders Isaksson, " Public Capital, Infrastructure and Industrial Development ", Research and Statistics Branch Working Paper, 15/2009.

Robles[①]和Canning[②]的论文中，研究人员提供了令人信服的理论和实证分析，对于基础设施所起的作用予以肯定。尽管关于具体在什么样的条件下基础设施才能发挥作用的实证观点还远没有定论，但是广为接受的共识是，在适当的条件下，基础设施的发展可以促进增长和平等——这两者都有助于减少贫困。基础设施服务——包括我们在第2章最后一节所讨论的各种制度安排（软基础设施），更重要的作用是可以降低交易成本和其他成本，从而使人们更有效地利用现有的生产性投入。此外，基础设施服务"会影响投资调整成本、个人资本的耐久性以及卫生和教育服务的需求和供给。如果运输、电力或电信服务不存在或不可靠，企业将会面临额外费用的可能（例如购买发电机组），也会给采用新技术造成障碍。好的运输条件会增加劳动力市场的有效规模"。[③]

传统智慧有一个共识，所有经济体都严重依赖于各种基础设施和投资去改善现有条件和经济表现，从而使劳动力和货物更高效、更安全地到达国内和国际市场。一个国家如果追求繁荣，向往能为它的人民提供一个良好的生活水平，就需要具备有效的运输、卫生、能源和

---

① B. Sanchez-Robles, "Infrastructure Investment and Growth: Some Empirical Evidence." *Contemporary Economic Policy* 1998. Vol.16: 98–108.

② D. Canning, "The Contribution of Infrastructure to Aggregate Output." Policy Research Working Paper No. 2246. World Bank, 1999.

③ Jean-Jacques Dethier. "Infrastructure in Africa" . In Célestin Monga and Lin Justin Yifu(eds.), *The Oxford Handbook of Africa and Economics: Volume 2: Policies and Practices*, Oxford University Press, 2015.

通信系统。良好的公路、铁路、港口和机场是必不可少的，这是为了农业、工业、矿业、旅游业等重点行业的可持续增长——对发展中经济体来说这些尤为重要。良好的交通基础设施还能让更多的人享受到健康和教育等重要的社会服务。可以说，在大多数国家，如果没有一个运作良好的交通运输系统，经济活动将会陷于停顿。例如，麦肯锡的一份研究报告估算，从2016年到2030年，每年需要在基础设施建设方面投资GDP的3.8%才能支撑预期中的经济增长。①

无论对长期还是短期的经济发展，交通运输基础设施都会带来可观的经济收益。用于建造、维护或扩张道路和铁路网络的投资可以有效地增强经济效率，提高生产率，加快经济活动的增长。这些投资也是建筑行业和原材料生产行业的就业支撑，就职于这些行业的员工生活支出的增加对整个经济体会产生积极的连锁反应。短期效应可能因经济的不同阶段而有所差异。在一个经济周期的顶峰期，当经济运行达到或接近全部潜能的极致时，基础设施项目的就业收益可能会因为这些工人从其他生产性活动中转移出来而被抵消掉一部分，公共资金的投资也会“挤出”一些私人投资。②但是，在就业不足和失业率仍然很高的状况下，世界各地经济的运行一般会显著低于其完全就业潜能。在产能过剩的情况下增加建筑材料的支出以及新雇工人的个人消费，几乎不太可能分流其他用途的货物或材料。事实上，如果大量资源闲置，将它们用于基础设施投资的机会成本就会大大减少。因此，在全球经济仍然有大量未充分利用的资源，包括超过2亿的求职人员的情况下，做出这样的投资是有高价值的。

然而，许多发展中国家的基础设施仍不完善，这限制了它们的增长和在全球经济中的贸易能力。亚洲的基础设施建设资金仍有巨大的缺口。亚洲开发银行2017年发布的报告《满足亚洲基础设施建设需求》预测，亚洲及太平洋地区（亚太地区）若保持现有增长势头，到2030年其基础设施建设需求将超过22.6万亿美元（每年1.5万亿美元）。若将气候变化减缓及适应成本考虑在内，此预测数据将提高到26万亿美元，即每年1.7万亿美元。拉丁美洲和加勒比地区的情况也不是很好。Calderon和Servén对这一地区基础设施的有效存在、品质、可使用性与其他地区的基准指标进行了比较，重点关注电信、电力、地面交通、水和卫生设施。总的来说，他们发现的证据表明，相对于其他工业化和发展中地区的“基础设施差距”在20世纪八九十年代被拉开了，他们对这一地区基础设施差距的量化增长成本也进行了估计。③

---

① McKinsey & Company, *Bridging global infrastructure gaps*, 2016.

② Executive Office of the President, *Recent Examples of the Economic Benefits from Investing in Infrastructure*, White House, 2011 November.

③ Cesar A Calderon, Luis Servén. “Infrastructure in Latin America”, World Bank Policy Research Working Paper No. 5317, May 1, 2010.

与其他地区相比，非洲国家的基础设施面临更加艰巨的挑战。非洲国家的基础设施，尤其是能源和交通基础设施存量较小，而且，它们的信息和通信技术的潜力也没有得到充分的利用。匮乏的基础设施导致大多数非洲国家商业的交易成本较高。根据非洲开发银行的研究结果估测，基础设施的不足至少使非洲的年增长减缓了2%。相反，如果有充足的基础设施，非洲的企业可以实现高达40%的生产率增长。农业部门的情况更是令人担忧，Juma指出："非洲大陆无法养活自己，不能激发农村创业，探其究竟，很大一部分原因在于其薄弱的基础设施（交通、能源、水利灌溉和电信）。大多数的非洲农村人口并没有生活在全年道路通达的地区，于是，他们也就没有能力参与任何有意义的创业活动。平均而言，在中等收入的非洲国家，约有60%的农村人口居住在距离四季可通达道路2千米以内的位置。例如在肯尼亚，大约只有32%的农村人口能达到这一标准，在安哥拉为31%，马拉维为26%，坦桑尼亚为24%，马里为18%，而埃塞俄比亚则低至10.5%。"①

遗憾的是，太多的专家从这些诊断中得出错误的结论。能够正确地识别问题并不一定代表对它的意义和启示具有正确的理解。我们常常需要谨慎地理解阿尔伯特·爱因斯坦的话："如果我有一个小时来解决一个问题，我会用55分钟思考问题，然后用5分钟思考答案。"尽管基础设施差距问题必须得到解决，但是很多发展专家做出的假设是不正确的，他们认为差距必然阻碍发展中国家开启经济持续增长的进程。

基础设施落后的确是经济表现的主要约束因素，但这并不是经济转型不可逾越的障碍，尤其是在今天经济全球化的条件下：去中心化的全球价值链、与日俱增的自由贸易、灵活的资金流动和技术工人的迁移。经济发展和基础设施建设可以并行发展，相助互济。在人类历史上没有一个国家是在全国都拥有良好的基础设施之后才开启它的经济发展进程——18世纪末的英国绝对不是，19世纪初的美国当然也不是，而在20世纪末只有一个非常小的高速公路网络的中国，自然就更不是这种情况了。的确，非洲地区的基础设施差距成为经济增长和社会福利的主要瓶颈，但是，如果说只有填补这一差距之后经济才有可能成功发展，这个观点显然是不正确的——事实上，在非洲大陆，即使人均GDP达到10万美元，这个差距也会一直存在。基础设施的开发和维护是一个需要政策制定者持续关注的问题，美国总统特朗普就曾要求国会批准2万亿美元的预算以改善基础设施，也就是说，即使是高收入国家也需要伴随着技术创新、产业升级的需要，不断完善相应的基础设施。

此外，许多专家和政策制定者倾向于采取通用的、昂贵的、不切实际的解决方案，因为他们认为基础设施的差距是经济表现不佳的元凶，只有这个问题得到解决，持续增长才有可

① Calestous Juma, "Poor Infrastructure Is Africa's Soft Underbelly", *Forbes*, 2012, October 25.

能发生。按照亚洲开发银行的估算，2010—2020年，亚洲国家整体基础设施的投资需求为8万亿美元，即每年7 300亿美元，其中的68%是新增产能的投入，32%用于维护和更换现有的基础设施。[①]这些数字的确惊人，在2017年的亚洲开发银行报告中，这一数字进一步被调整为每年1.7万亿美元。非洲国家的基础设施缺口估计达每年930亿美元。[②]而在南非——大家公认的非洲大陆上最发达的国家，其基础设施的需求仍然很大，仅此一个国家，2012年政府公布的数据是3年970亿美元的耗资计划，用以改善道路、港口和运输网络条件，以提升煤和其他矿物的可得性。这项投入超出了埃塞俄比亚、坦桑尼亚和莫桑比克三国年GDP的总和。

"华盛顿共识"的拥护者认为经济增长是一个线性的和目的论的过程，在经济增长动态过程启动之前，所有的基础设施障碍都需要排除，他们普遍推荐的政策改革，是要将基础设施行业大规模私有化，并向其投入更多的公共和私人资金。[③]这样的建议涉及诸多漫无目的的政策和非常广泛的改革方案，往往由于政治上的原因而难以实现，所产生的结果是否是积极的也未可知。

在发展中国家普遍存在的基础设施政策的瑕疵，折射出了"华盛顿共识"框架所规划的改革方案是不切实际和令人沮丧的。在财政和行政资源有限的情况下，没有一个国家愿意严格地执行那个长长的被认定为经济增长发生条件的改革清单。每项改革可能会有其独特的意义，也可能不会有。如果不划分优先级，这几十个甚至数百个政策处方在政治上是不可行的，也并不能直击那些约束潜在比较优势行业的真正痛处。这就是为什么成功的发展中国家通常对这些所谓的处方并不盲从。此外，世界银行发布的《营商环境报告》排名中存在的莫名其妙的前后矛盾，也说明了其提议的改革方案是令人质疑的。全球经济发展表现顶尖的一些国家，其营商便利度的评估在过去的20年中始终排名很低：巴西排名第132位，越南第98位，中国第91位，落后于哈萨克斯坦、阿塞拜疆、突尼斯、白俄罗斯和瓦努阿图等明星经济体。[④]而如第1章专栏1.3所述，非洲发展最快、吸引外商在制造业直接投资最快的埃塞俄比亚的营商环境指数却急剧恶化。

表7.1列出了在过去的20年里增长最快的30个经济体，证据表明，那些用流行指标衡量的营商环境质量似乎都不重要，因为除了新加坡和马来西亚，其余经济体的营商指标评分

---

① Asian Development Bank and Asian Development Bank Institute (ADB/ADBI), *Infrastructure for a Seamless Asia*. Tokyo: ADB/ADBI, 2009.

② L. Andres, D. Biller, M. Herrera Dappe, *Reducing Poverty by Closing South Asia' s Infrastructure Gap*, World Bank, 2013.

③ V. Foster, C. Briceño-Garmendia, *Africa' s Infrastructure. A Time for Transformation.Paris and*, A copublication of the Agence Française de Développement and the World Bank, 2010.

④ World Bank, *Doing Business,* 2013.

居然都相当差！一个更务实的做法是政府将有限的资源和执行能力用于打造“模范园区岛”，或精心挑选拥有良好的基础设施和商业环境的地区（即使是在整体的基础设施和商业环境不善的国家），充分挖掘和利用经济体的潜在比较优势，促进有竞争力产业的兴起。下面我们便进一步讨论中国的案例和基础设施建设经验。

表7.1 不良商业环境中的出色经济表现：增长水平前30位的国家或地区（1992—2012年）

| 国家（地区） | 1992—2012年平均实际GDP增长率 | GDP表现排名 | 2012年营商便利指标排名 | 2013年营商便利指标排名 |
|---|---|---|---|---|
| 赤道几内亚 | 19.2 | 1 | 164 | 166 |
| 中国内地 | 10.1 | 2 | 99 | 96 |
| 波斯尼亚和黑塞哥维那 | 10.8 | 3 | 130 | 131 |
| 利比里亚 | 10.4 | 4 | 149 | 144 |
| 佛得角 | 9.3 | 5 | 128 | 121 |
| 中国澳门 | 8.9 | 6 | | |
| 不丹 | 7.8 | 7 | 146 | 141 |
| 卡塔尔 | 7.6 | 8 | 45 | 48 |
| 越南 | 7.4 | 9 | 98 | 99 |
| 柬埔寨 | 7.4 | 10 | 135 | 137 |
| 老挝 | 7.3 | 11 | 163 | 159 |
| 乌干达 | 7.2 | 12 | 126 | 132 |
| 莫桑比克 | 7.2 | 13 | 142 | 139 |
| 印度 | 7.0 | 14 | 131 | 134 |
| 安哥拉 | 7.0 | 15 | 178 | 179 |
| 埃塞俄比亚 | 6.9 | 16 | 124 | 125 |
| 乍得 | 6.8 | 17 | 189 | 189 |
| 卢旺达 | 6.6 | 18 | 54 | 32 |
| 新加坡 | 6.5 | 19 | 1 | 1 |
| 巴拿马 | 6.3 | 20 | 61 | 55 |
| 缅甸 | 6.2 | 21 | 182 | 182 |
| 多米尼加 | 6.0 | 22 | 112 | 117 |
| 马来西亚 | 6.0 | 23 | 8 | 6 |
| 加纳 | 6.0 | 24 | 62 | 67 |
| 约旦 | 5.9 | 25 | 119 | 119 |
| 布基纳法索 | 5.9 | 26 | 154 | 154 |
| 科威特 | 5.9 | 27 | 101 | 104 |
| 孟加拉国 | 5.8 | 28 | 132 | 130 |
| 斯里兰卡 | 5.7 | 29 | 83 | 85 |
| 阿塞拜疆 | 5.7 | 30 | 71 | 70 |

资料来源：林毅夫、蒙加，《战胜命运》，北京大学出版社，2017年版，第29-30页。

# 7.2

# 从局部到整体渐进式改善基础设施：中国经验①

## 7.2.1 政府能力与基础设施建设

正如我们在第4章所回顾的战后发展典范的经济结构转型升级的历史轨迹所展示的鲜明案例那样，中国在战后与绝大多数发展中经济体一样采取了结构主义主张的赶超战略，以政府主导来推动经济结构变迁，但最终以失败告终。我们在第1章就开宗明义地指出结构主义主张的赶超战略违背了比较优势，违背比较优势的产业是没有自生能力的，在竞争的市场中无法自发建立，只有靠政府直接动员资源、配置资源、扭曲各种价格信号、给予市场垄断的计划经济体制才能把这种产业建立起来。林毅夫早在1994年出版的《中国的奇迹》一书中就详细分析了中国战后采取违背比较优势的赶超战略所内生的计划经济体制及其随着发展战略向比较优势转变而进行的改革。在图7.2中，我们可以看到在1978年之前中国赶超战略时代的政府错误干预程度非常深，例如大多数企业不仅固定资产投资依靠政府的财政拨款，而且流动资金也如此。然而，中国在改革开放之后并没有按照新自由主义所主张的那样完全放弃政府干预，在发展战略从赶超战略转向比较优势战略之后，政府依然发挥了积极的作用。如果不深刻理解新结构经济学与结构主义和新自由主义在思想和理论上的根本不同之处，就很难理解中国改革开放前后经济结构转型升级以及政府作用的这种本质差别。

如图7.2所示，在改革开放之后，政府转变了执行赶超战略的计划经济体制，例如政府直接增拨企业流动资金占GDP的比重几乎可以忽略不计，但是中国政府的财政支出占GDP

---

① 关于新结构区域或空间经济学的更多内容可参考：林毅夫、付才辉，《新结构经济学导论》，高等教育出版社，2019年版，第14章。

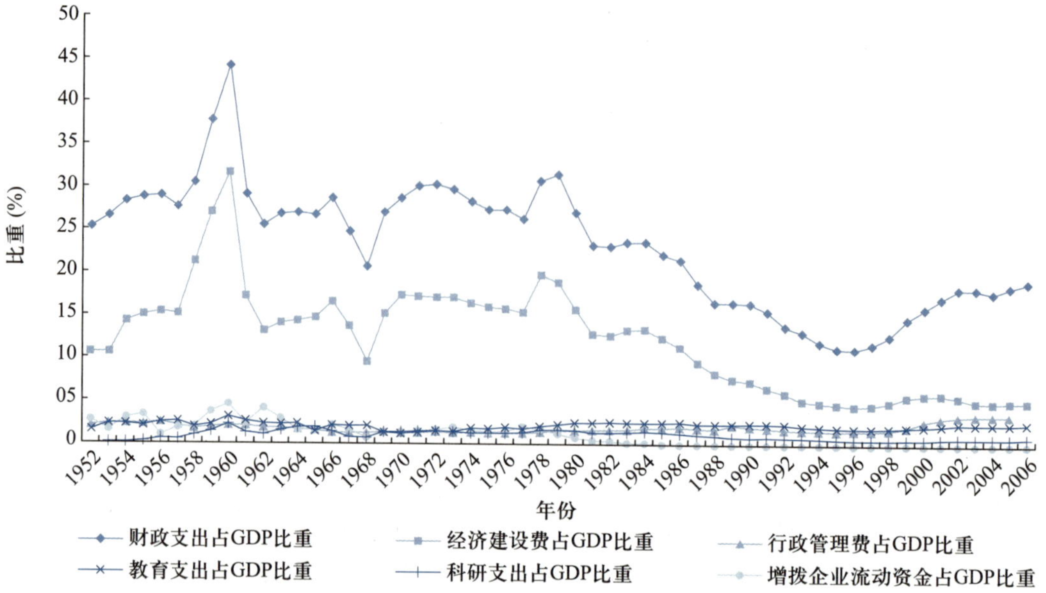


**图7.2 中国的政府财政支出结构变化**

资料来源：《新中国六十年统计资料汇编》，《中国财政年鉴》（历年）。

的比重依然很高，关键是用于经济建设的经费占GDP的比重远远超过了其他财政支出。财政支持除通过采取产业政策的方式直接扶持某些符合潜在比较优势的产业外，中国政府财政支出中的经济建设经费很大一部分是用于大规模的基础设施建设。金戈采用世界银行经济基础设施界定口径，利用1953—2002年“电力、煤气及水的生产和供应业”“地质勘查业、水利管理业”“交通运输、仓储及邮电通信业”三个科目的固定资产投资，以及2003—2008年“电力、燃气及水的生产和供应业”“交通运输、仓储和邮政业”“信息传输、计算机服务与软件业”“水利、环境和公共设施管理业”四个科目的固定资产投资数据估算了中国基础设施资本存量。[①]如图7.3所示，中国在1995年之前，基础设施资本存量指数与国内生产总值指数几乎是重合的，但1995年之后，基础设施资本存量的增长速度明显超过了GDP增长，两个指数之间逐渐拉开了差距。图7.4展示了中国基础设施基本建设投资占全部政府基本建设投资的比例，可以看到中国政府确实在改革开放之后持续不断地加大了基础设施建设。同时，也如林毅夫和王燕所判断的，近年来中国的基础设施建设是“超前”的。因为在中国这样的快速增长的经济体中，劳动力和土地成本上升很快，当下进行修建高速公路等基础设施建设比十年后修建要便宜得多，而且基础设施是具有很大正外部性的公共品，传统世界银行

① 金戈，“中国基础设施资本存量估算”，《经济研究》，2012年第4期。

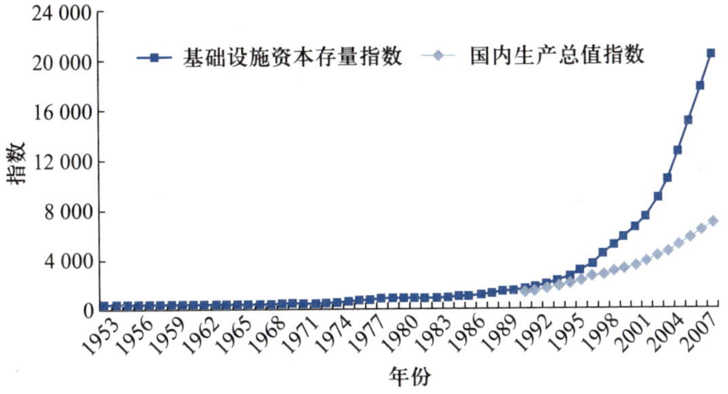


**图 7.3 中国国内生产总值指数与基础设施资本存量指数（1953 年 =100）**

资料来源：金戈，“中国基础设施资本存量估算”，《经济研究》，2012 年第 4 期。

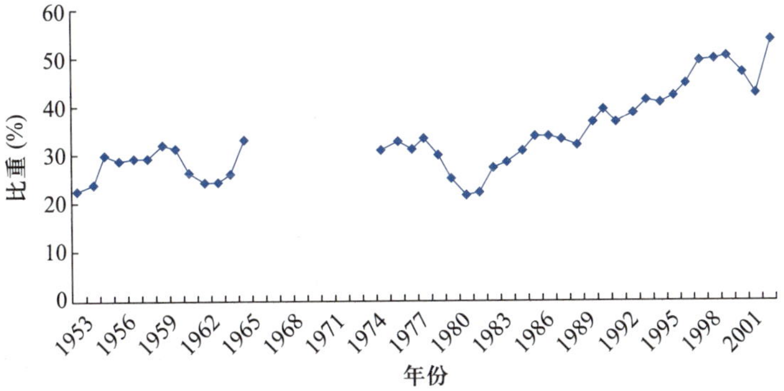


**图 7.4 中国基础设施基本建设投资占全部政府基本建设投资的比重**

资料来源：金戈，“中国基础设施资本存量估算”，《经济研究》，2012 年第 4 期。

的成本 – 收益分析不足以计算公共品的溢出效应，尤其是考虑在一个大国以及次大陆中的交通网络等基础设施的规模经济。[①]中国的大规模基础设施建设在持续推动经济结构转型升级上发挥了显著作用。

### 7.2.2 中国的经济开发区变迁及其效果

即便政府能力再强，任何一个国家也不可能在全国范围内普遍地改善各种普适性的软硬

① 可进一步参见林毅夫，王燕，《超越发展援助》，北京大学出版社，2016 年版，第 5 章。

基础设施。发展中国家的政府必须采取务实的方法利用其有限的资源和实施能力来推动具有比较优势行业的技术创新和发展，这样才能保持相对较低的生产要素成本。为了降低企业的交易成本，政府可以创建具有良好基础设施和营商环境的工业园区或经济特区。在全球产业周期变化背景下，每个不同发展水平的经济体都可以识别其面临的全球产业窗口机遇期，通过工业园区的局部渐进式改革消除瓶颈，承接符合禀赋结构决定的潜在比较优势的产业转移，充分利用后发优势迅速走上持续的经济发展之路。中国就是鲜活的案例。在1979年向市场经济转型时，营商环境差，基础设施落后，投资环境糟糕。按照"华盛顿共识"的建议，应该一步到位，而不应优先支持特定部门和地区。相反，中国政府动员其有限的资源和实施能力建立了经济特区和工业园区。工业园区通过俗称的"三通一平"（通电、通路、通水、土地平整）、"五通一平"（通电、通路、通水、通信、排水、土地平整）、"七通一平"（通电、通路、通水、通信、排水、热力、燃气、土地平整）等方式快速地消除了硬性的基础设施瓶颈。在特区和园区内部，基础设施瓶颈得以缓解，营商环境也变得富有竞争力。虽然在转型初期有低成本的劳动力，但是中国缺乏利用这个优势生产具有合格质量的劳动力密集型出口产品的知识。为了克服这些困难，中国各个地区的各级政府四处寻求国外投资者，鼓励他们在经济特区和工业园区内投资。通过采取这种办法，中国迅速建立起了劳动力密集型的轻工业，成为"世界工厂"（第8章将进一步介绍）。在局部地区取得的成功为政府改善其他地方的基础设施和消除扭曲提供了资源和条件。这不仅是中国，而且也是东亚其他经济体发展成功的奥秘。图7.5展示了中国经济特区对跨国公司、外资和外贸的巨大促进作用。

中国开发区本身也是一个持续不断的结构变迁过程，最早始于东南沿海的4个经济特区。在经济特区成功经验的基础上，逐步根据经济发展的需要，在全国范围内建立了经济技术开发区、高新技术产业开发区、出口加工区、保税区和边境经济合作区等不同类型的经济开发区。中国开发区的历程可分为四个阶段：

1. 1979—1983年：起步阶段，设立经济特区

1979年4月，邓小平首次提出要兴办"出口特区"，而后在1980年3月，"出口特区"更名为"经济特区"。1979年，广东省深圳、珠海和汕头三座城市获得了设立经济特区的资格，随后在1980年福建省厦门市也获批设立经济特区。4个经济特区的选址很有讲究：首先，都在东南沿海，远离政治中心北京，受中央计划经济的干涉较小，当地政府在设计和实施优惠政策上有更大的自由；其次，与港澳台和东南亚地区有特殊的地缘关系和血缘关系，社会联系紧密，贸易往来频繁。首批4个经济特区取得的成绩是巨大的，以深圳市为例，在1980到1984年，深圳市的年均复合经济增速约为54%。在吸引外资方面，经济特区也不负众望，1984年，4个经济特区吸引的国外投资占全国总量的26%。此外，在特区之内还形成了运行良好的劳动力、土地、资本和科技市场。例如深圳市建立了中国第一个劳动力市场，而在

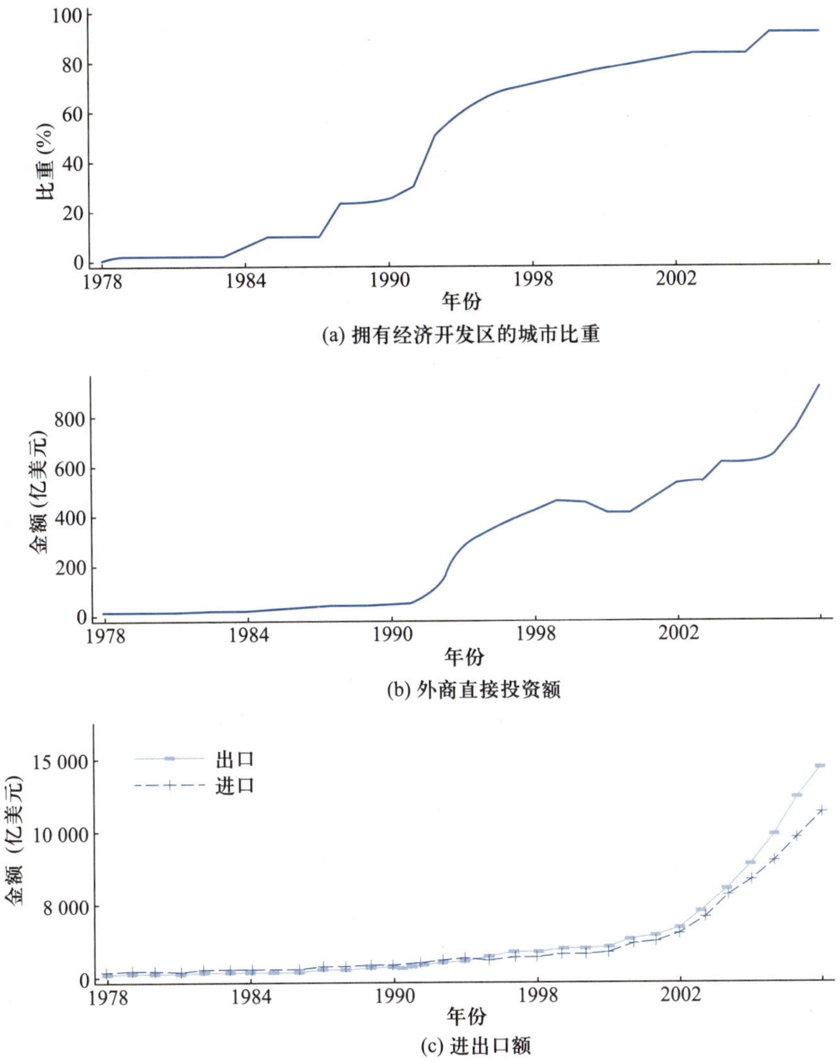


**图7.5 中国经济特区对跨国公司、外资和外贸的促进作用**

资料来源：D.Z. Zeng, Building Engines for Growth and Competitiveness in China: Experience with Special Economic Zones and Industrial Clusters, World Bank, 2010.

当时的特区之外是不合法的。今天，全世界最著名的经济特区非深圳莫属，其短短40年间从一个没有自然资源和缺乏基础设施的贫穷、寂静的小渔村转变为经济体量超过亚洲“四小龙”之一的中国香港。相比较于我们在第4章所总结的战后13个发展典范的结构变迁案例，深圳的结构变迁案例或许更加精彩绝伦，如专栏7.1的简要介绍。

2. 1984—1991年：初步发展阶段，设立沿海开放城市

1983年年底和1984年年初，邓小平两次视察深圳、珠海和厦门的经济特区，充分肯定了设立经济特区的成功经验，回京后于1984年2月24日就对外开放和特区工作发表了重要

讲话，提出“除现在的特区外，可以考虑再开放几个港口城市，如大连、青岛。这些地方不叫特区，但可以实行特区的某些政策”①。随后在1984年，14个沿海开放城市先后获批，这14个全国首批沿海开放城市获得了建立国家级经济技术开发区（简称经开区）的资格，并在开发区内施行4个经济特区适用的优惠政策。这14个城市在成为沿海开放城市之前就有很好的工业基础和高质量的劳动力市场，跻身中国最发达的地区之列。1985年，这14个沿海开放城市的工业产出占全国总量的21.8%。在这一阶段，除了经济技术开发区之外的另外一类重要的国家级开发区——高新技术产业开发区（简称高新区）也应运而生。1988年8月，火炬计划开始实施，创立高新区是被明确列入火炬计划的重要内容。在火炬计划的推动下，各地区纷纷结合当地的特点和条件，积极创办高新区，1988年设立的中关村科技园是我国的第一个高新区。这一阶段的另外一件突破性事件发生在1984年11月，上海批准3M公司成立了一家独资子公司，这是在我国经济特区以外成立的第一家外商独资企业，而在当时还没有相关的法律允许经济特区之外的城市可以这么做。

3. 1992—2002年：快速发展阶段，全面深入内陆

1992年，邓小平第二次视察南方并发表重要讲话，为中国的招商引资和对外开放带来了新的发展契机。开放格局由仅仅集中在沿海发达地区，向内陆地区全面深入发展，各类开发区和开放区域在全国范围内普及开来。邓小平视察南方之后不久，浦东新区在上海成立。同年5月，中央四号文件指示，计划在长江流域的5个城市、9个沿海城市和所有的省会城市建立国家级开发区，四号文件还允许在零售业和服务部门尝试引进外资，并减少了行政限制。18个国家级经开区在1992至1993年间获批，17个国家级经开区在2000至2002年间获批，这35个经开区大多建立在内陆省份。

4. 2003—2014年：规范发展阶段

在经历了上一阶段的快速发展之后，2003年之后中国的开发区进入了规范、平稳的发展阶段，期间经历了一次大范围的清理整顿。开发区的设立取得了重大的成功，同时，建立开发区也成为地方政府吸引投资、发展当地经济的“常规武器”。通过官员在不同地区间的调动，设立和管理开发区的经验也在不同地区之间传播，给尚未设立开发区的地区提供经验。一大批低级别的开发区在这一阶段的早期在全国各地建立起来。一方面，中央政府给予国家级开发区的优惠政策不适用于低级别的开发区，但另外一方面，中央政府不直接监督管理低级别的开发区，由地方政府直接监督管理，而地方政府有动机给予当地的低级别开发区以更优惠的政策来吸引投资，因此低级别开发区建设泛滥、参差不齐。为此，国家发改委、国土

---

①《改革开放三十年重要文献选编》（上），人民出版社，2008年版，第319页。

资源部、建设部和商务部共同发布文件，全面调查开发区违规使用土地的情况。根据《中国开发区审核公告目录（2006年版）》，截至2006年，国家级开发区共计222家，其中包括经济技术开发区49家、高新技术产业开发区53家、保税区15家、出口加工区58家、边境经济合作区14家以及33家其他类型的国家级开发区。

5. 2014年至今：转型升级阶段

2014年《国务院办公厅关于促进国家级经济技术开发区转型升级创新发展的若干意见》发布，提出：要努力把国家级经开区建设成为带动地区经济发展和实施区域发展战略的重要载体，成为构建开放型经济新体制和培育吸引外资新优势的排头兵，成为科技创新驱动和绿色集约发展的示范区。国家级经开区要在发展理念、兴办模式、管理方式等方面加快转型，努力实现由追求速度向追求质量转变，由政府主导向市场主导转变，由同质化竞争向差异化发展转变，由硬环境见长向软环境取胜转变。东部地区国家级经开区要率先实现转型发展，继续提升开放水平，在更高层次参与国际经济合作和竞争，提高在全球价值链及国际分工中的地位。中西部地区国家级经开区要依托本地区比较优势，着力打造特色和优势主导产业，提高承接产业转移的能力，防止低水平重复建设，促进现代化产业集群健康发展。强化土地节约集约利用，国家级经开区必须严格土地管理，严控增量，盘活存量，坚持合理、节约、集约、高效开发利用土地。加强土地开发利用动态监管，加大对闲置、低效用地的处置力度，探索存量建设用地二次开发机制。省级人民政府要建立健全土地集约利用评价、考核与奖惩制度，可在本级建设用地指标中对国家级经开区予以单列。允许符合条件且确有必要的国家级经开区按程序申报扩区或调整区位。规范招商引资。国家级经开区要节俭务实开展招商引资活动，提倡以产业规划为指导的专业化招商、产业链招商。加强出国（境）招商引资团组管理，加大对违规招商的巡查和处罚力度。严格执行国家财税政策和土地政策，禁止侵占被拆迁居民和被征地农民的合法利益。不得违法下放农用地转用、土地征收和供地审批权，不得以任何形式违规减免或返还土地出让金。这一时期的转型升级还主要是清理中国过去几十年开发区建设过程中不合时宜的问题以适用新时期发展所需要的规范化。为深入贯彻落实《中共中央 国务院关于构建开放型经济新体制的若干意见》，2017年发布《国务院办公厅关于促进开发区改革和创新发展的若干意见》，指出当前全球经济和产业格局正在发生深刻变化，中国经济发展进入新常态，面对新形势，必须进一步发挥开发区作为改革开放排头兵的作用，形成新的集聚效应和增长动力，引领经济结构优化调整和发展方式转变。在新时代，中国为构建开放型经济深度参与全球化，加快了国家级新区的建设。

国家级新区，是由国务院批准设立，承担国家重大发展和改革开放战略任务的综合功能区。新区的成立乃至开发建设上升为国家战略，总体发展目标、发展定位等由国务院统一进行规划和审批，相关特殊优惠政策和权限由国务院直接批复，在辖区内实行更加开放和优惠的特殊政策，鼓励新区进行各项制度改革与创新的探索工作。国家级新区是中国于20世纪90年代初期设立的一种新开发开放与改革的大城市区。1992年10月上海浦东新区成立，1994年3月天津滨海新区成立，2010年6月重庆两江新区成立，2011年6月浙江舟山群岛新区成立，2012年8月兰州新区成立，2012年9月广州南沙新区成立，2014年1月陕西西咸新区成立、贵州贵安新区成立，2014年6月青岛西海岸新区成立、大连金普新区成立，2014年10月四川天府新区成立，2015年4月湖南湘江新区成立，2015年6月南京江北新区成立，2015年9月福州新区成立、云南滇中新区获批成立，2015年12月哈尔滨新区成立，2016年2月长春新区成立，2016年6月14日江西赣江新区成立。截至2016年6月，中国国家级新区共18个。

### 专栏7.1
### 中国深圳：全世界最著名经济特区的40年结构变迁案例①

深圳是中国改革开放40余年最大放异彩的缩影。1979年中国的人均GDP只有423元人民币，按当年美元计算为184美元，2016年飞跃到53 935元人民币，按当年美元计算达8 123美元，按不变价计算是1979年的21.1倍；1979年深圳的人均GDP只有606元人民币，合264美元，2016年飞跃到167 411元人民币，合25 213美元，按不变价计算是1979年的45.7倍。深圳现在的地区生产总值已经

① 深圳特区符合中国的渐进式发展改革的特征，这不同于前世界银行首席经济学家保罗·罗默提出的“宪章城市”设想，后者由于在范围太大的一个城市全盘复制“太先进的制度”而无法实施。保罗·罗默是著名的内生增长理论的开创者，2018年的诺贝尔经济学奖得主，与主流经济学家一样，其认为制度对于经济增长至关重要。在2009年录制的TED讲座中，为了简单地说明体制的重要性，他展示了来自美国太空总署的图片。在相邻地区辉煌灯火的衬托下，朝鲜和海地犹如两个黑洞。罗默教授认为滋生这些黑洞的根本原因是体制。那么如何使这些黑洞出现光明呢？他从中国香港的巨大成功中得到了启示：能否在其他国家或地区复制中国香港的成功经验？理论上来讲，任何一个发展中国家都可以划出一块地，让给某个民主政治及经济发展高度完善的国家去管理（比如挪威或加拿大）。他称这个设想为宪章城市（Charter Cities）。洪都拉斯于2012年9月宣布推出宪章城市计划，并与国外投资者签订了备忘录。在这一切看来十分顺利的时候，罗默教授作为洪都拉斯宪章城市“公开委员会”主席突然与其他成员共同发布公开信申明不再与洪都拉斯政府有任何官方联系。洪都拉斯总统虽然曾签署“公开委员会”五位成员的任命书，被赋予任命“特首”、维护政策制定中的公正透明等权力，但该任命却未经过政府正式发布（其中原委一直没有公开），因此从法律上来讲，该委员会尚未存在。当该委员会向洪都拉斯政府索取上述备忘录的细节时竟然无法获得。罗默教授等认为在此环境下，“公开委员会”已无法继续开展工作，故而退出。

超过了香港。这些发展水平巨大改善的背后是深圳产业结构魔幻般的变迁，从一个以农业为主的小渔村变幻为国际工业化之都。1979年的深圳农业占GDP的比重高达37%，人均农业总产值为405元，是人均工业总产值220元的近2倍；到了2010年，深圳的农业基本消失了，其贡献可以忽略不计，2016年人均农业总产值只有区区144元，不到人均工业总产值的万分之六。这就是工业化提升人均收入魔术般的力量，深圳2016年的人均工业总产值高达245 180元，第二产业比重从1979年的20.5%上升到2005年的53.4%。改革开放前20年深圳完成了以劳动力密集的轻工业为主导的工业化，其后20年则完成了以资本和技术密集的工业为主导的工业化转型。1979年，深圳轻工业占工业总产值的88.5%，资本密集工业比重只有11.5%；到2000年，资本密集工业的比重达55.3%，已经超过轻工业比重的44.7%。当然，由于存在产业内升级，劳动力密集产业和资本密集型产业内部都在不断升级，所以即便到2016年深圳的劳动力密集型产业占工业的比重依然达22.3%。与此同时，随着工业化的推进，服务业须与之适应，第三产业比重也不断提高。不过，直到国际金融危机爆发的2008年深圳的第三产业比重才首度超过50%，2016年达到60%。这新增的近10个百分点，意味着深圳在国际金融危机之后涌现了大量新兴产业。2009年深圳的新兴产业增加值为2 215.03亿元，其中新一代信息技术产业为1 111.76亿元，文化创意产业为576亿元，互联网产业为125.20亿元，新材料产业为117.89亿元，生物产业为142.73亿元，新能源产业为141.46亿元。到2018年，战略性新兴产业增加值合计9 155.18亿元，占地区生产总值比重为37.8%。其中，新一代信息技术产业增加值4 772.02亿元，数字经济产业增加值1 240.73亿元，高端装备制造产业增加值1 065.82亿元，绿色低碳产业增加值990.73亿元，海洋经济产业增加值421.69亿元，新材料产业增加值365.61亿元，生物医药产业增加值298.58亿元。（上述数据来自2018年深圳统计公报）

### 7.2.3 为何经济特区通常未能形成有竞争能力的产业集群[①]

除了中国外，经济开发区有着悠久的历史，也盛行于全世界。1547 年，意大利的里南那港被正式命名为自由港，成为世界上第一个现代意义的开发区。1937年，纽约建立了一个经济特区；1942年，波多黎各建立了另一个经济特区；1959年，在爱尔兰的香农机场又建立了一个经济特区；1960年，冰岛和中国台湾也建立了经济特区。经济特区被一些后来者如韩国、中国台湾等加以有效利用，以建立产业集群、效仿发达国家的经济发展战略，甚至在经济繁荣的竞赛中赶超这些发达国家。世界其他地区的一些发展中国家也成功建立了不同类型的运转良好的经济特区，从而推进各自的出口和增长战略，并创造了许多需求迫切的就业机会，刺激了本国的产业升级。这方面比较著名的案例当属哥斯达黎加的英特尔工业园，以及洪都拉斯、萨瓦尔多、孟加拉国、越南和毛里求斯的加工出口区。世界各个地区的发展中国家使用工业园、加工出口区、经济特区等作为吸引国际直接投资以及实现经济转型的主要手段。Farole指出经济特区使多米尼加共和国创造出超过10万个制造业的就业岗位，并使其经济迅速摆脱了对农业的依赖。[②]卡塔尔也启动了经济特区以使其从以油气为主导的经济——这使该国成为世界上最富裕的国家之一，但仍受动荡的全球油价制约——转向以知识为基础的经济。埃塞俄比亚走的是同样的路线，主要是为了解决它的物流困境（基础设施）以及试验新的治理模式，从而给予投资者更大的灵活性，允许他们在本国具备比较优势的轻工制造业雇用工人。发达的工业化经济体同样在联邦、州及地方各级利用各种形式的经济特区来吸引投资者、刺激经济以及创造就业。[③]根据国际劳工组织的调查报告，全球仅出口加工区的数量就从1986年的176个增长至2003年的3 000余个，分布国家亦从47个增长到116个。[④]根据世界银行的调查报告，截至2008年共有119个发展中国家和转型国家设立了超过2 300个各类开发区。[⑤]

目前全球存在大约4 500个这样的经济特区，但只有少数得到了预期的结果。对大多数

---

① 更详细的内容可参考：林毅夫、蒙加，《战胜命运》，北京大学出版社，2017年版，第7章。

② T. Farole, “Special Economic Zones: What Have We Learned?” Voxeu.org, 2011, September 28.

③ 对美国联邦经济开发区（federal urban empowerment zone (EZ) program）的一项实证研究可参考：Matias Busso, Jesse Gregory and Patrick Kline, “Assessing the Incidence and Efficiency of a Prominent Place Based Policy”, *American Economic Review*, 2013, Vol. 103, No. 2, PP. 897–947.

④ ILO, “Employment and Social Policy in Respect of Export Processing Zones”, International Labour Organization, GB.286/ESP/3, 2003, March.

⑤ G. Akinci, J. Crittle, “Special Economic Zones: Performance, Lessons Learned, and Implications for Zone Development”, World Bank, 2008.

国家而言，建立、运营经济特区的收益成本比率一直令人失望。个人所得税、许可费和服务费、由开发商缴纳的公用土地的销售和租赁费、从经济特区销往国内关税区的进口关税和产品税、用于诸如港口和电厂等设施的特许经营费，以及企业所得税（估定额）总计只有微不足道的数额。同时，经济特区产生的走私机会造成的进口关税和费用损失，企业从国内关税区搬入经济特区而减少的税收收入，基础设施（通常是非定向的）和经常性开支（主要是公共部门员工的工资，这些员工是运行和监管经济特区所必需的）等公共投资往往意味着政府的巨大花费。即便在中国，某些举措也没能吸引有竞争力的企业或者形成就业，政府不得不对它们进行重新设计。[①]几十年来，许多经济特区的确失败了，政策制定者们不知道如何正确地运行它们，于是只好放弃。这样一来，经济特区在主流经济学界往往被贬斥为单纯的幻想，或者更糟，被称为"中国式"事件——平常又并非那么下意识的口气里带有政治和意识形态的轻蔑之意。

没有什么比这个更不符合事实了。首先，正如历史记录明确表明的，经济特区不是中国独创的。实际上，邓小平于1978年起就在尽其所能地积极寻求新的思想和有益的政策，将意识形态之争放在一边，并道出"不管黑猫白猫，捉到老鼠就是好猫"的名言。1980年，一些中国官员被派往世界各地观察和研究经济特区的运行模式。参观完一些国家之后，他们来到爱尔兰，并在那里受到了启发："代表团听取了关于世界上第一家免税店的介绍，这是一个专注于机场的基础设施项目，也是一个实行低税率和自由贸易的经济特区。代表们赞赏香农开发区的务实做法。……爱尔兰从不鼓吹自己的意识形态议程。香农的政府工作人员将精力集中在就业创造、实践培训和技能传授上，并为每个新企业的发展需求提供便利。这就是那只'捉到老鼠的猫'。访问过世界上各种类型的经济特区之后，香农模式以及新加坡模式成为仅有的两个中国决定效仿的经济特区。"[②]

更重要的是，经济特区已经成为吸引FDI、建立各种类型的集群或者工业区的最有效渠道，它们使大型或者小型经济体都可以充分利用全球贸易的新模式。如果碎片化生产（正如上文所强调的那样）在可预见的未来确实是全球交易的"新常态"，那么即使是那些基础设施落后、人力资源有限或者治理不善的国家也可以找到务实的解决方案，将其经济定位为全球供应链中可信赖的商业环境。成功的经济特区不仅可以解决这类问题，而且能够成为在国

① X. Zhang, "Clusters as an Instrument for Industrial Policy: The Case of China." Paper presented at the International Economic Association (IEA)—World Bank Roundtable "New Thinking in Industrial Policy" at the World Bank, 2012, May.

② P. Quigley, "Why Do China' s Leaders Love Visiting Shannon?" Business ETC—Economy, Technology, and Companies, 2012, February 23.

内各个行业的企业（小型企业或大型企业）与跨国公司之间建立商业联系的最佳阵地。

经济学家和政策制定者对大多数经济特区失灵的原因也给出了五花八门的解释——每个单独拿出来看的话都讲得通，但若将它们放在一起来看的话就非常令人困惑了。它们包括对于经济特区思想的全面性否定，即“商业中的政府官僚主义”—— 一种主要基于意识形态原因的观点。[①]这一观点认为这些是“政治优先”，通常会导致产生所谓的“白象效应”，[②]治理不善问题，缺乏制度框架和政治承诺，执行能力薄弱，以及不适当的监管和评价机制等。[③]

这些对于经济特区高失败率的解释，都倾向于将问题产生的原因和其症状或结果混为一谈。尽管许多类型的错误可以解释发展中国家的政策制定者在复制来自中国和一小部分其他国家的经济特区成功经验方面的无能，根本问题往往存在于战略选择方面。建立成功的经济特区的一阶条件是挑选“正确的”行业——并不一定是最“现代的”或者最令人振奋的，体现领导人政治野心的行业，而是那些符合当地要素禀赋结构所决定的比较优势的行业，因此它们能够迅速发展为具有竞争优势的行业。正如Farole所指出的：“单就一个特殊的经济特区体制、一个有说服力的总体规制，甚至一套全面建成的基础设施来说，其存在本身越来越难以在吸引投资、创造就业以及对当地经济形成外溢效应方面有所作为。相反，真正能够决定成败的是经济特区计划在特殊背景下的关联性，以及这些项目在不断推进的基础上被设计、实施以及管理的有效性。”[④]

回顾过去，经济特区表现不佳的主要原因似乎在于人们相信它们是随机出现的。大多数经济特区辜负了政策制定者的期待，是因为它们没有找准合适的行业定位，或者它们过于广泛的通病使它们无法吸引足够的有竞争力的企业。在许多发展中国家，试图创建经济特区的政策制定者们没有正确思考在一个日益全球化的经济中本国经济成功发展所需要的条件，以及怎样最有效地发掘经济中具有比较优势的产业，通过经济特区提供必要的基础设施和营商环境使其迅速变成竞争优势的产业集群。贫穷国家通常面临阻碍私人部门发展的两大制约因素：高生产要素成本（对于高技能劳动力和资本而言）以及高交易成本（主要由于落后的基础设施、不良的商业环境和薄弱的行政能力）。它们又往往由于政治俘获和权力寻租而加剧。

---

① World Bank, *Bureaucrats in Business: The Economics and Politics of Government Ownership*, Oxford University Press, 1995.

② Special Economic Zones: Political Priority, Economic Gamble, *Economists*, 2015, April 4.

③ D. Z. Zeng, “SEZs in Africa: Putting the Cart in Front of Horse?” *Let’ s Talk Development*, 2012, April 9.

④ T. Farole, “Special Economic Zones: What Have We Learned?” Voxeu.org, 2011, September 28.

得益于劳动力和资本的全球化与自由流动，高生产要素成本在近几十年来普遍下降，即便在偏远的地方也是一样。2015年，一个国家，像玻利维亚，如果需要训练有素的工程师，就可以从墨西哥或西班牙吸引大量这样的人才，而成本比1970年还要低。同样，斯里兰卡如今比30年前更容易从卡塔尔或马来西亚（拥有充足的主权财富基金）吸引到私人资本。但是对于大多数低收入国家而言，要想规避高要素成本约束，使得经济发展成功的可能性最大，最好的方法是制定旨在利用其唯一具有竞争力的要素成本（低技能劳动力和土地）的发展战略。如果经济发展战略与国家的比较优势保持一致，同时各种要素（低技能劳动力、土地或者自然资源）得到广泛使用，就可以切实降低要素成本。因此，如果被选中并且被吸引进入经济特区的行业主要是那些很好地利用了低技能劳动力的行业，那么第一个制约因素就被消除了。

要消除第二个制约因素，发展中国家可以将经济特区打造为优秀园区，普遍存在的问题，如基础设施问题、不良的商业环境以及薄弱的治理和行政能力等，在那里都可以得到有效的解决（对一个拥有有限财政资源和行政能力的政府而言，在一个经济特区的地理范围内提供一流的基础设施以及打击官僚作风和腐败，比在全国范围内进行确实要容易得多）。

然而，要想消除第二个制约因素，确保经济特区的有效运行，在优秀园区内经营的企业首先必须符合当地的要素禀赋结构所决定的比较优势，在经济上具有自生能力，同时园区提供的条件和政策激励必须有助于它们之间的合作和竞争，形成产业集群以降低物流等交易成本。因此，经济特区最好一开始就被设想为当地某个具有比较优势产业的工业园区（“专业化”的经济特区），政府向园区内的所有企业提供这个产业发展所必须要有的基础设施。一般性的经济特区会吸引来自不同行业的企业，不仅不容易形成具有竞争力的产业集群，而且，这些企业往往需要不同的基础设施，这就要求政府进行巨额投资，也使得经济特区的可持续发展面临更大的挑战。

被吸引到经济特区中的企业往往违背了本国的比较优势，不具有自生能力，因此，若没有一套强有力的保护政策就无法生存。在大多数情况下，政策制定者们要么以他们的个人喜好或者政治原因来确定行业，要么没有积极努力地去甄别出那些可能最适合本国要素禀赋结构的行业（即劳动密集型行业）。他们认为那些愿意加入经济特区或者出口加工区的外国企业将会创造就业，这样至少是聊胜于无。缺失甄别战略可能会造成的后果之一，就是经济特区里出现很多单独的小企业，它们来自关联性甚小的不同行业。考虑政府财政预算的有限和公共投资计划的薄弱，很少有政府能够向它们提供特定行业所需要的基础设施支持。

还有，经济特区的地点选择经常不是最佳的。一些经济特区建立在港口城市，那些城市本身就是增长极或者靠近交通枢纽；另外一些则建立在孤立或者偏远的地区，选择这些地区并非基于经济学上的考虑，而是为了争取政治支持。对于少数愿意到这些地区建厂的企业来说，这导致了生产和交易成本的增加。然而，减少交易成本尚未成为战略重点的一部分。由于在行业挑选上的随意性和政府财政资源的有限性，很多这样的经济特区有时甚至连最基本的公用设施和服务都不能提供。这说明政府并未积极发挥它们不可或缺的因势利导作用。它们没有为特定行业提供基本的基础设施，往往等待（无望中白等）符合入驻条件的企业投入资金，支持园区内的电力、供水或者通信设施建设。它们没有对企业在本行业中进行设计和生产所共同需要和使用的资金进行协调（如存储设备）。

另一个主要问题是经济特区能够产生的商业交易容量有限。在同一经济特区内从事不同行业的一小部分企业，针对的是狭小的国内市场，而非广大的国家市场，很难产生足够数量的商业交易，以达到实现马歇尔外部性所必需的临界规模，并使得该区域的企业成为全球市场可信赖的合作伙伴。在当今的世界经济中，那些有能力以最低价格从供应商那里获得原料和中间产品及服务的企业，通常是那些处于世界贸易网络中的企业——通过大量买入，它们处于更为有利的地位去获得最佳的单位成本。因此，那些拥有许多不同行业或是针对国内市场的经济特区，当需要为单一企业配售原料和中间产品及服务时，就会处于劣势。换句话说，即使一个经济特区拥有与经济的比较优势相一致的行业，企业在经济上具有自生能力，但如果它试图同时发展过多不同的行业和商业活动，从而不能为企业赢得足够广大的市场，那么它仍然会失败——这样的经济特区实际上摊薄了自己的利益。

总之，要消除第二个制约因素（即高交易成本）就必须发展能够产生同一行业的大量企业集群、并且针对国际市场的经济特区，这样才能实现规模经济，降低物流成本，提高产业内的知识溢出以及其他集聚效应。而且，经济特区生产的产品如果能够在国际市场竞争，也就一定能够在国内市场竞争。反过来，如果生产的产品不能在国际市场竞争，那么，也很难在没有保护的状况之下在国内市场和进口产品竞争。在许多发展中国家的政府只是凭借对各行各业的广泛财政激励措施创建了通用的经济特区，并没有在产业集聚的过程中进行因势利导出口产业，而要做到这一点，需要政府为特定行业提供基础设施，处理集聚过程中不时出现的协调性和外部性问题，也需要有明确的招商引资政策，把以出口为导向的生产企业招引来成为经济特区的支柱企业。

还有一个常常导致许多发展中国家的经济特区项目失败的一阶战略性错误是其推进者（政府或私人部门参与者）没能在这些优秀园区和其他国内企业之间建立有效的商业连接。他们没有考虑一直处于发展过程核心位置的政治经济问题。就其本质而言，渐进的经济发展战略是建立在对最有前途的潜在增长力量进行的战略选择和地理定位基础上的，这必然产生赢家和输家，至少在短期内会是如此。因此，有必要促进快速的成功（就时间和结果而言），建立企业后向和前向关联以缓和社会紧张。在一些国家，当地商业团体对经济特区持怀疑态度，将其视为地理区域和封闭的“特殊俱乐部”，在这里发生的是不透明的商业活动，通常与外国企业和一小部分与统治阶级保持良好关系的商界领袖有关。例如，据报道，在印度这个联邦法律和各邦法律法规常常重叠适用的国家，补贴和税收激励在经济特区内遭到滥用，为建立特区发起的征地活动也常常引发抗议。

### 7.2.4 建立成功的经济特区和工业园区的一些指导性原则①

为了使经济特区的成功率最大化（使它们成为通往产业和技术升级、可持续发展以及就业增加的主要工具），发展中国家应该在挑选所要发展的行业时更加谨慎，确保为符合当地比较优势，能够迅速在国内外市场形成竞争优势的具有发展潜力的企业配备必要的基础设施，纠正很多国家以往的扭曲和低效表现，其所采用的政策和制度框架要能对经济增长产生正确的激励，并且强化与国内经济的联系。相比创建一般性的、目标宽泛的经济特区，发展中国家更应考虑建设配备专门设施的园区，以满足特定行业和部门的需求，这种园区被称为基于集群的工业园区（CBIP）。如何发展这类园区将取决于要推动的是哪一个行业，这些产业应该与本国已有的或潜在的比较优势保持一致。②根据这类园区为满足目标行业的独特需求而配备的专门设施的不同，它们可能是旨在支持与航空有关的商业活动（例如水果、蔬菜或者

---

① 本小节内容转引自：林毅夫、蒙加，《战胜命运》，北京大学出版社，2017年版，第7章。

② 经济开发区既是一种区域经济现象，也是一种基于地点（place-based）的产业政策（E. L. Glaeser, J. D. Gottlieb, "The Economics of Place-Making Policies", *Brookings Papers on Economic Activity*, 2008, No. 1, pp. 155–239）。基于集群的工业园区应以转变潜在或现有的比较优势成为竞争优势为主要目标，为产业链延伸和产业升级提供支持，由此通过物资、金融和人力资本等要素的积累，来促进比较优势的动态变化。然而，许多政策制定者把比较优势的动态变化和动态的比较优势的概念搞混，不知道支持潜在或现有的比较优势产业的发展是加速比较优势动态变化的基础，在建立这些工业园区时产业选择过于雄心勃勃，如同在某些国家所表现的那样。这种细微差别是非常重要的。根据动态比较优势理论来制定政策的国家通常试图帮助企业进入本国在未来具有比较优势的行业。在非洲，由于禀赋结构的限制，即使政府提供协调和外部性补偿，那些具有动态比较优势的产业中的企业在一个竞争的市场上也还不具备自生能力，需要不断的保护补贴才能建立起来和维持生存，结果一直处于所谓的"婴儿期"。相对而言，基于集群的工业园区应该着眼于帮助企业进入那些已经显现或具有潜在比较优势的行业。在这种设计下，一旦政府提供了先行者的外部性赔偿和必要的基础设施与营商环境，这些企业将立即具备自生能力，不再需要补贴或保护。即便在局部区域的园区层面上也不能违背比较优势，一些实证研究支持这一点。陈钊和熊瑞祥利用1998—2007年中国工业企业微观数据，结合倍差法考察了国家级出口加工区在成立之初对所选择的主导产业的扶持政策是否有效，以及比较优势在其中扮演的角色。他们的研究发现，平均而言，一个城市出口加工区的出口鼓励政策使得受扶持行业内企业的出口额显著提高约11%。进一步的分样本研究表明，上述政策效果在那些原先就不具备比较优势的行业中并不存在，而对那些原先具备比较优势的行业，出口鼓励的扶持能使行业内企业的出口增长约13.1%。对上述政策动态效果的考察表明，产业政策的效果在那些有比较

切花出口）的基于机场的经济特区，也可能是旨在促进离岸活动的农副产业甚至只是金融服务区。

对入驻基于集群的工业园区的行业应该仔细进行甄选，这些行业应与每个国家已有的或潜在的比较优势相一致，以确保它们尽可能地将最充裕的要素（通常是低技能劳动力）物尽其用，并能够在政府只提供先行者激励、软硬基础设施完善的情况下，不需要政府的保护和补贴即可以在国际市场上保持竞争力。至少在初始阶段，它们应该开展劳动密集型、装配导向型的生产活动，如纺织品、服装、鞋类、电气和电子产品等的生产。在这样的行业中，活动范围还要进一步扩展，不仅包括生产和加工，也应包括诸如仓储或转运等商业服务与专业服务。

对所有的投资者（国外的和国内的）应该一视同仁。因此，应该执行适当的法律法规、规章制度来减少政府激励措施被扭曲的可能性。此外，对所有选中的行业应该实行单独的一套财政激励措施，不论其地理位置所在（位于经济特区内部还是外部）。全世界的政治领导人现在都面对着前所未有的社会政治挑战，它们来自日益增多的、要求严格的、（通常是）受过良好教育的民众。事实上，如果不能迅速交付可见的成就，尤其是在就业方面，维护执政地位的代价就变得非常高了。随着发展中国家新一届更加务实的领导人的出现，政策制定者们可能会对选举政治更为敏感，也会对他们所选择的经济政策更加负责。

基于具有比较优势的出口集群工业园区与整个国民经济容易相融合，出口企业可以使用当地私人部门提供的各种产品和服务，这样政府在给工业园区提供先行者激励和软硬基础设施的支持时更容易在政治上和社会上被接纳，而且因为它们在商业活动中积极与国内企业（特别是中小型企业）进行利益共享，能够更有效地建立可持续和包容性增长的基础。对

---

优势的行业呈现出逐年递增的趋势，在那些没有比较优势的行业则始终不显著。所使用的倍差法符合同趋势假设，表明产业政策的制定过程中并不存在事先的挑选赢家行为。（陈钊、熊瑞祥，“比较优势与产业政策效果——来自出口加工区准实验的证据”，《管理世界》，2015年第8期，第67–80页；Chen Zhao, Poncet Sandra, Xiong Ruixiang, “Inter-industry relatedness and industrial-policy efficiency: Evidence from China’s export processing zones,” *Journal of Comparative Economics*, Vol. 45, No. 4, pp. 809–826.）。李力行和申广军利用中国城市–行业层面的数据对经济开发区的设立与产业结构变动的关系进行了实证研究。他们利用2004年和2008年的中国工业企业数据库，构造了产业结构变动指标和行业集中度指标，并与城市数据匹配，得到了包含280个地市级行政区、30个两位数行业的样本。实证分析发现，经济开发区的设立可以解释短期内产业结构变动的20% ~ 30%。利用不同样本和不同设定的进一步检验表明，经济开发区对产业结构变动的作用十分稳定。一般而言，经济开发区在设立之初就确定了要重点吸引和扶助哪些行业的发展，我们称之为经济开发区的“目标行业”。经济开发区这种行业偏向的特征，促进了产业结构向目标行业聚集。数据分析显示，当某一行业被设定为开发区的目标行业，该行业增长速度、行业集中度等各类经济指标会提高9%~15%，在地区工业总量中的份额会提高20% ~ 30%。因此，针对目标行业的产业政策对于该行业的发展大有裨益。进一步的实证研究也发现，当设置的目标行业符合当地的比较优势时，经济开发区的积极作用尤为明显。（李力行、申广军，“经济开发区、地区比较优势与产业结构调整”，《经济学（季刊）》，2015年第2期，第885–910页）

于任何一个吸引了具有较强出口竞争潜力的私人企业从而很有可能获得成功的经济特区而言，没有什么要比被（误）认为是腐败政治家和外国企业家之间进行黑幕交易的国内飞地更糟的了。与当地的小企业和其他参与者（例如学术机构）共建经济和社会关系网络，有助于减少外国投资者到发展中国家投资时所面对的猜疑和抱怨。

基于集群的工业园区要抢先解决国内不可避免的批评、社会恐慌以及其他政治经济问题，应该努力在建立之后迅速创造成果。若想最有效地做到这一点，新创建的园区必须快速创造出制造业就业机会，吸收大量低技能劳动力。其推进者应该鼓励园区内的企业与当地企业建立联系，这样园区就可以作为成功案例催化更广泛的改革，并与地方政府和商业协会进行合作，推动国际劳工组织劳动标准的实行。信息交流的确是很重要的，对于贫穷国家处于劳动力阶层的大多数人而言，如果不在这样的工业园区里就业，就意味着要从事生产率低下、收入微薄的非正式工作，在城市地区不完全就业，或者在农村地区从事低收益且高风险的农业工作，甚至失业，永远陷入贫困陷阱之中。即便只有最低程度的正规教育，许多毫无技能的工人仍然可以受雇于工业园区，专门从事基本的组装操作，并为工业化文明的引进和建立打下基础。从中长期发展来看，基于集群的工业园区的战略重点应该放在务实的基础上，随着人力资本、金融资本、国内外市场联系的社会资本的积累，以可行的节奏向高价值生产活动迈进，从而提升产业结构的水平。只有不断促进劳动力技能的发展，将产业和技术升级作为园区内企业发展的终极目标，上述战略目标才有可能实现。

基于集群的工业园区还面临一个重要问题，那就是公共部门和私人部门在园区的设计、所有权及管理方面的角色分配。在一个国家或地区，刚从农业经济向现代化经济转型时，各种基础设施严重不足，营商环境也不适合于出口型制造业的需要，此时为了启动工业化，工业园区所需的各项基础设施应该由国家财政或国际发展机构的援助来建设，并由政府通过立法给园区提供特殊的政策环境，成立独立管理机构来负责招商引资，管理经营。当一个国家已经启动了工业化的进程并且有了成功的出口型工业园，可以逐渐往公私合营，直至私营方向发展，从纯粹的政府投资经营，改为建立公私合作的伙伴关系，公共部门提供诸如道路等场外基础设施，场内基础设施所需的资金由公私合作提供。政府部门可以直接为建设园区内的基础设施和设备提供财政支持或担保。私人部门的参与可以采取不同的形式：与政府建立共担风险、共享利益的基本合作伙伴关系，签署特许协议，采取“建设—拥有—运营”（BOO）、“建设—运营—转让”（BOT）或“建设—拥有—运营—转让”（BOOT）等安排。基于集群的工业园区的成功模式包括一系列的合同类型，往往伴随着公私合作关系随时间的变化。近期流行的一种模式与“股权转移”安排有关，它允许政府园区的一个私人合约经理在其达到预定的业绩水平的条件后行使股票认购权。

即便是设计良好的私营的工业园区，也要获得来自最高级别政府机构的强有力的政治承诺，支持其改善商业环境、迅速消除执行过程中的所有障碍，才有可能获得成功。一个为此做准备的好的制度框架可以是一个跨部门的委员会，由一位颇具威信的政治“支持者”领导，以推进事情的完成。这位领导者还应该成为园区开发者和企业与所有政府机构之间沟通的主要对接者，并能够对来自商业界的要求做出迅速、有效的回应，还要与政治压力绝缘，不取悦国内任何政治支持者。

当有在工业园成功发展起来的产业集群的示范效应以后，若政府愿意为私人园区开发者寻找可以租赁的地块、提供权属保证时，以工业园经由公私合营或私人企业建立产业集群就不再那么困难了。在许多贫穷国家，法律框架使得政府机构对土地的分配权具有长期影响力。各国政府都不愿意交出土地分配权，政府控制以历史和社会公平的理由被合法化，而这种控制的存在，为权力寻租和官僚专断提供了空间。国家所有权，特别是对土地重新分配的权力，使得公民和商人只能听从地方官僚机构的行政独断，因为他们掌握着土地分配的大权。基于集群的工业园区通过为所有利益相关者带来快速成功、改善他们的集体福利，为渐进实行土地改革提供了一个很好的机会。即使是埃塞俄比亚和坦桑尼亚等在历史上长期强烈抵制土地私有化和个人土地产权的国家，也都在考虑改变它们的土地所有制政策——这是进步的标志，也表明这些国家意识到这可能是经济发展最可行的选择。

为广泛地扩大园区内的工业设施和生活设施建设，政府或公私合作双方不仅要考虑到特定行业的工厂和基础设施，还应考虑一系列服务设施，例如高速通信和互联网服务、通用保税仓库设施、培训设施、保养和维修中心、产品展示区、现场通关和贸易物流设施、园内住宿、园内银行、医疗诊所、购物中心、儿童看护设施等。发展一个集群园区，使其成为集工业、商业、居住及休闲于一体的，而非单一性的园区，使得开发者们将其潜在的收入来源多样化，并以其他活动较高的利润抵消某些商业活动中的利润亏损。在东亚许多运行良好的私人园区里，多达半数的年度总收入来自商业支持服务及其他形式的收入。

## 7.3

—

## 世界基础设施建设概况：进展、趋势与缺口

现在世界各国已经认识到了策略性地改进基础设施对于经济社会结构转型的重要性。前面也提到一些研究甚至定量估算了世界基础设施建设投资缺口，下面将进一步分类别、分地区对世界基础设施建设的现状、趋势与缺口进行概括性介绍。

### 7.3.1 基础设施的分类与进展

按照世界银行在《世界发展报告1994——为发展提供基础设施》中给出的定义，基础设施可以划分为经济基础设施（economic infrastructure）和社会基础设施（social infrastructure）两大类。经济基础设施是指长期使用的（long-lived）工程构筑、设备、设施及其为经济生产和家庭所提供的服务，具体包括公共设施（public utilities，如电力、通信、管道煤气、自来水、排污、固体垃圾收集与处理）、公共工程（public works，如大坝、水利工程、道路）以及其他交通部门（如铁路、城市交通、港口、河道和机场）三种类型。社会基础设施则主要包含教育和卫生保健。在新结构经济学中，基础设施可分为软件和硬件基础设施。软件基础设施包括制度、条例、价值体系以及其他社会和经济安排等，硬件基础设施包括高速公路、港口、机场、电信系统、电网和其他公共设施等。软件基础设施和硬件基础设施只有和各发展阶段产业的技术、规模和风险特征相符合，才能降低交易费用，使得该阶段具有潜在比较优势的产业变为在国内外市场的竞争优势。软硬基础设施的完善对于任何发展阶段都是至关重要的，而且只有通过各种资源的投入才能获得。由于各个发展中国家都已经在教育、金融、法律等方面进行了许许多多现代化的努力，相对而言，目前在绝大多数发展中国家把潜在比较优势的产业变为竞争优势的瓶颈制约是硬件基础设施。因此，接下来主要对一组包括水、电、交通、电信、互联网、能源等最基本的硬件基础设施在内的基础设施建设情况以及缺口进行概括性介绍。此外，鉴于新冠疫情

（COVID-19）巨大的全球破坏性影响，我们在这些经济基础设施外也简要概括介绍世界医疗卫生等社会基础设施建设情况。

在现代社会，基础设施系统及其价值的衡量也变得更加复杂，投资的选择和决策也变得复杂和多样化。那些仅有狭窄街道和一个水资源系统的时代已经一去不复返了，现在横跨城市和地区的基础设施网络系统为社会提供能源、水资源、运输和更多服务。这些系统之间通过网络进行连接，其可靠性会影响到从国防到新生儿等人类社会的方方面面。① 尽管如此，为简化起见，我们通过一些简单的指标及其对应的世界银行提供的数据来直接观察上述基础设施类别在世界的建设水平和分布状况。例如，可以用获得改善水源的人口所占百分比来观察水利基础设施建设情况，用人均耗电量来观察电力基础设施建设情况，用人均集装箱码头吞吐量来观察海运基础设施建设情况，用人均铁路总里程来观察铁路基础设施建设情况，用人均航空运输量来观察航空基础设施建设情况，用每100人所拥有的电话线路数量来观察电信基础设施建设情况，用固定宽带互联网用户数来观察互联网基础设施建设情况，用人均能源使用量来观察能源基础设施建设状况。这些指标一方面直接反映了基础设施拥有水平，另一方面也可以间接反映实际获取的基础设施服务水平。

#### 7.3.1.1 全球水利基础设施建设进展概况

水利基础设施广泛涉及与生产生活用水需求、利用水资源、防治水患等相关的公共设施。人类建设水利基础设施的历史非常古老。例如，在本书第二作者的家乡几千年前就建有举世闻名的都江堰水利工程。约公元前256年，战国时期秦国蜀郡太守李冰率众修建位于岷江上的都江堰水利工程，至今依旧在灌溉田畴，是造福人民的伟大水利工程。其以年代久、无坝引水为特征，是世界水利文化的鼻祖。这项工程主要由鱼嘴分水堤、飞沙堰溢洪道、宝瓶口进水口三大部分和百丈堤、人字堤等附属工程构成，科学地解决了江水自动分流（鱼嘴分水堤四六分水）、自动排沙（鱼嘴分水堤二八分沙）、控制进水流量（宝瓶口与飞沙堰）等问题，消除了水患。在20世纪末其灌溉面积达到66.87万公顷，灌溉区域已达40余县。由于水利基础设施对于农耕的极端重要性，中国历朝历代都非常重视水利工程。时至今日，中国依然设有水利部，负责保障水资源的合理开发利用，负责生活、生产经营和生态环境用水的统筹和保障，按规定制定水利工程建设有关制度并组织实施。

获取淡水的水利基础设施，不仅是所有生产的基础，也是人类起码的生活基础。水利对

---

① 尼尔 · S. 格里格，《PPP与基础设施融资》，机械工业出版社，2017年版。

农业尤为重要。目前在世界大部分地区，超过70%的淡水用于农业。到2050年，要养活地球上的90亿人口，据估计农业产量需要增加50%，水提取量需要增加15%。全世界过去20多年来在获得改善的水源方面取得了巨大的成就。[①]1990年世界不能获得改善水源的人口所占百分比依然高达24%，到2014年下降到了9%；中国和印度这两个人口最多的国家1990年有30%左右的人口不能获得改善的水源，但到2014年下降到5%左右。[②]当今世界获得改善的水源不再是普遍的问题，但是对于非洲而言依然是严峻的问题，将近一半的人口不能获得改善的水源。除此之外，农村地区获得改善的水源方面依然还有很大的改善空间。在发达国家，能获得改善水源的人口所占比重已经非常高，水利基础设施相对饱和，但由于其水利基础设施建成时间久远，也需要改造升级。例如，英国伦敦的主要供水管道中至少有20%已有超过150年的历史。

#### 7.3.1.2 世界电力基础设施建设进展概况

电力是以电能作为动力的能源，发明于19世纪70年代。电力的发明和应用掀起了第二次工业化高潮，成为18世纪以来人类历史上发生的三次科技革命之一，从此科技改变了人们的日常生活。事实上，我们在日常生活中已经将“水电”合为一体来称呼，如同水一样，电力也成为生产生活的必需品。20世纪出现的大规模电力系统是人类工程史上最重要的成就之一，是由发电、输电、变电、配电和用电等环节组成的电力生产与消费系统。它将自然界的一次能源通过发电动力装置转化成电力，再经输电、变电和配电将电力供应到各用户。产生电力的方式包括火力发电（煤）、太阳能发电、大容量风力发电技术、核能发电、氢能发电、水力发电、垃圾焚烧发电等。

近40多年来，世界的电力基础设施得到了巨大的改善。1971年世界人均耗电量为1 200千瓦时，到2013年达到3 014千瓦时，足足增长了1.5倍。[③]然而，当今发展中经济体的电力基础设施建设依然是发展的一大瓶颈。2013年最不发达国家（联合国分类）的人均耗电

---

① 获得改善的水源是指从改善的水源合理获得足够用水的人口比例。改善的水源包括诸如接入家庭的输水管线，公共水管，蓄水池，受到保护的井、泉以及雨水收集。未经改善的水源包括售水机、水罐车、未加保护的井和泉。合理地获得水源意味着每人每天从距离居所1千米范围内的水源可获取至少20升水。

② Blakeslee等研究了印度水资源日益短缺的影响，他们发现水井干涸导致农场收入和财富急剧持续下降，几乎没有农业适应的证据。然而，这有可能推动劳动力向非农产业转移，特别是在制造业较为发达的地区。(David Blakeslee, Ram Fishman and Veena Srinivasan, “Way Down in the Hole: Adaptation to Long-Term Water Loss in Rural India”, *American Economic Review,* 2020, Vol. 110, No. 1, pp. 200–224.)

③ 耗电量用发电厂和热电厂的发电量减去输配电和变电损耗以及热电厂自用电量得出。

量仅为191千瓦时，中低收入国家为1 888千瓦时，中等收入国家为2 009千瓦时，均远低于世界平均水平。相对于中高等收入国家人均耗电量的3 404千瓦时、高收入国家的9 084千瓦时，还有巨大的增长空间。从地区来看，2013年人均耗电量北美最高，为13 241千瓦时，其次是欧洲与中亚地区，为 5 429千瓦时，东亚与太平洋地区为3 568千瓦时，均高于世界平均水平；而中东与北非地区为2 880千瓦时，拉丁美洲与加勒比海地区为2 118千瓦时，南亚为673千瓦时，撒哈拉以南非洲地区为488千瓦时，均低于世界平均水平。根据世界银行企业调查网站的数据，2015年企业在一个典型月份里经历的电力中断（次数）在埃塞俄比亚为8.2次、印度尼西亚为0.5次，电力中断导致的价值损失占销售额的比例在埃塞俄比亚为6.9%、越南为2.2%、印度尼西亚为1.9%。2012年全球绝大多数经济体的所有人口基本上全部通电，但南亚和非洲依然有很多人口未能通电，印度有21%的人口尚未通电，非洲大部分经济体有超过一半的人口尚未通电。2014年全球依然有超过10亿人口没有通电。发达经济体在战后几十年电力基础设施建设力度较大，例如，在美国中等寿命的煤炭发电厂的投产时间已超过40年。

#### 7.3.1.3 世界海运基础设施建设进展概况①

海运，即海洋运输，是国际物流中最主要的运输方式，它是指使用船舶通过海上航道在不同国家和地区的港口之间运送货物的一种方式。集装箱运输的兴起和发展，不仅使货物运输向集合化、合理化方向发展，而且节省了货物包装用料和运杂费，减少了货损货差，保证了运输质量，缩短了运输时间，从而降低了运输成本。海洋运输的运量大，海运费用低，航道四通八达，是其优势所在。事实上，15世纪在西方发生的两件大事就是大洋航道的开拓和新大陆的发现。目前国际贸易总运量中的2/3以上是利用海上运输完成的，这足以说明海运基础设施对于贸易的重要性。

2015年全球十大集装箱港“俱乐部”入门门槛为1 400万标箱（TEU，20英尺集装箱），目前全球年吞吐量1 500万标箱以上港口共9个，2 000万标箱以上港口共5个，比上年多出1个，3 000万标箱以上港口为2个。2015年港口集装箱吞吐量统计前十名依次为：上海港、新加坡港、深圳港、宁波－舟山港、香港港、釜山港、青岛港、广州港、迪拜港、天津港。前十大港口，中国包揽七席。当然，仅仅靠集装箱吞吐量大还不能成为国际航运中心。航运经纪服务、航运工程服务、船舶管理服务、海事法律服务、航运金融服务和船舶维修服务等

① 内陆国家并没有海运基础设施。

航运服务是国际航运中心重要的软基础设施。根据《新华－波罗的海国际航运中心发展指数报告（2015）》，2015年全球前十位国际航运中心分别为新加坡、伦敦、香港、鹿特丹、汉堡、上海、迪拜、纽约、釜山、雅典。亚洲占四席，分别是新加坡、香港、上海、釜山，其中上海位列全球十大国际航运中心的第六位。综合对比2014年的情况，总体较为稳定，略有微调。其中，雅典入围前十，东京被挤出前十梯队。新加坡、伦敦、香港依旧处于前三名绝对领先地位。上海反超迪拜，跃居第六。此外，青岛、宁波－舟山、天津、广州、大连、深圳、厦门也跻身国际航运中心行列。航运服务排在全球前十位的港口城市依次为伦敦、新加坡、香港、上海、雅典、迪拜、汉堡、纽约、东京和孟买。其中，伦敦、新加坡和香港在航运服务能力上具有不可撼动的优势地位，稳居前三名，上海、雅典航运服务发展迅猛，而迪拜、纽约等城市排名有所下滑。除了这些世界级港口和航运中心的更替变迁，世界整体的海运也随着国际贸易的飙升而迅速发展，世界集装箱码头吞吐量在过去十多年间已经翻了一番多，2000年不足2.5亿TEU，到2014年已经超过6.5亿TEU。然而，目前世界海运依然是发达经济体所主导的，2014年高收入国家的集装箱码头吞吐量占世界的48.54%。从地域来看，东亚与太平洋地区以及欧洲与中亚地区占有绝对主导地位，其集装箱码头吞吐量占世界的80%。发达经济体长期占据海上贸易的主导权，不过诸多发展中经济体依然还有巨大的发展空间。

#### 7.3.1.4 世界铁路基础设施建设进展概况

铁路运输是两种最重要的陆上运输方式，如果配置得当，铁路运输可以比公路运输在运载同一重量客货物时节省五至七成的能量。而且，铁轨能平均分散火车的重量，令火车的载重力大大提高。铁路运输由于受气候和自然条件的影响较小，且运输能力及单车装载量较大，在运输的经常性和低成本性上占据了优势，再加上有多种类型的车辆，使它几乎能承运任何商品，可以不受重量和容积的限制，而这些都是公路和航空运输方式所不能比拟的。归纳起来，铁路运输的主要特征包括运输能力大、运行速度快、运输成本低、运输经常性好、能耗低、通用性好、机动性差、投资大、建设周期长、占地面积少。因此，铁路是所有交通基础设施中最为重要的方式。

英国是第一个拥有路轨运输的国家。1804年，理查·特里维西克在英国威尔士发明了第一台能在铁轨上前进的蒸汽机车。第一台取得成功的蒸汽机车是乔治·斯蒂芬森在1829年建造的“火箭号”。19世纪20年代，英格兰的史托顿与达灵顿铁路成为第一条成功的蒸汽火车铁路。后来的利物浦与曼彻斯特铁路更显示了铁路的巨大发展潜力。铁路很快便在英国和世界各地通行起来，且成为世界交通的领导者近一个世纪，直至飞机和汽车发明后铁路的重要性才降低。高架电缆在1888年发明后，首条使用接触网供电的电气化铁路在1892年启用。第二次世界大战后，以柴油和电力驱动的列车逐渐取代蒸汽推动的列车。20世纪60年代起，多个国家均建设了高速铁路。而货运铁路亦连接至港口，并与船运合作，以集装箱运送大量货物，大大降低了成本。现在全球200多个国家和地区中，有144个设有铁路运输（包括全世界最小的国家梵蒂冈在内），其中约90个国家和地区提供客运铁路服务。铁路依然是世界上载客量最大的交通工具，拥有无法取代的地位。当然，随着高铁以及信息技术的使用，铁路运输基础设施本身也在不断升级。①

世界铁路总里程从20世纪90年代初的94万千米上升到目前的超过100万千米。从地区分布来讲，2014年欧洲和中亚地区37.6万千米，北美28万千米，东亚和太平洋地区12.7万千米，撒哈拉以南非洲地区5.96万千米，中东和北非地区3.2万千米，南亚2.8万千米，拉美和加勒比海地区1万千米。从不同收入水平的经济体的铁路里程构成来看，2014年最不发达国家（联合国分类）有3.1万千米铁路，低收入国家有2万千米铁路，中等收入国家有50.1万千米铁路，中高等收入国家有34.8万千米铁路，高收入国家有53.5万千米铁路。从铁路基础设施的绝对量上讲，发展中经济体是远远低于发达经济体的。

#### 7.3.1.5 世界航空基础设施建设进展概况

航空输运是使用飞机及其他航空器运送人员、货物、邮件的一种运输方式，具有快速、机动的特点，是现代旅客运输，尤其是远程旅客运输的重要方式，也是国际贸易中的贵重物品以及精密仪器、市场销售周期特别短的商品（如鲜花、海鲜、时尚服装等）运输所不可缺的。航空运输的主要优点是速度非常快，缺点是运输费用相当高。投资额度和运输成本都比较高，固定成本方面包括开拓航线、修建机场和机场维护需要大量资金；可变成本也比较高，主要是由于燃料、飞行员薪水、飞机的维护保养等方面的支出很大。航空运输的基础设施主要包括航路、航空港、飞机和通信导航设施等。航路是根据地面导航设施建立的走廊式保护

---

① 自1997年以来，中国实施了6次铁路提速，这可以看做是交通基础设施质量改善的一次自然实验。周浩和郑筱婷选取京广线和京沪线作为铁路提速代表，构造了1994—2006年提速铁路线沿途站点和其他未提速站点相对应的城市一级面板数据，利用倍差法系统考察了其对经济增长的影响。他们的研究发现，铁路提速促进了沿途站点的经济增长。在整个铁路提速期间，相对于未提速站点，铁路提速将提速站点的人均GDP增长率提高了约3.7个百分点；同时，在铁路提速后期，其对经济增长的促进作用更为明显。可参考：周浩、郑筱婷，“交通基础设施质量与经济增长：来自中国铁路提速的证据”，《世界经济》，2012年第1期。

空域，是飞机航线飞行的领域。其划定是以连接各个地面导航设施的直线为中心线，在航路范围内规定上、下限高度和宽度。对在其范围内飞行的飞机，要实施空中交通管制。航空港是民用飞机场及有关服务设施构成的整体，是飞机安全起降的基地，也是旅客、货物、邮件的集散地。飞机是主要的载运工具。机型选用根据所飞航线的具体情况并考虑整体经济技术性能而定。通信导航设施是沟通信息、引导飞机安全飞行并到达目的地安全着陆的设施。

航空运输的历史也非常悠久，始于1871年。当时普法战争中的法国人用气球把政府官员和物资、邮件等运出被普军围困的巴黎。1918年5月5日，飞机运输首次出现，航线为纽约—华盛顿—芝加哥。同年6月8日，伦敦与巴黎之间开始定期邮政航班飞行。20世纪30年代有了民用运输机，各种技术性能不断改进，航空工业的发展促进了航空运输的发展。第二次世界大战结束后，在世界范围内逐渐建立了航线网，以各国主要城市为起讫点的世界航线网遍及各大洲。1990年世界定期航班完成总周转量达2 356.7亿吨千米。近40年来世界航空运输量增长了2倍，注册承运人全球出港量来从1975年的不足1 000万上升到2015年的超过3 000万。从航空运输的特征就可以知道这种高资本密集型的基础设施主要适合于发达经济体。2015年高收入国家的航空运输量（注册承运人全球出港量）占世界的比重高达62.3%，OECD国家的航空运输量占世界的比重高达61.2%。

在所有的国际航线之中，长距离航线的经济作用尤为突出。一方面，因为短途的航线往往仅能促进较小区域相似经济体的整合，并且与其他运输方式还存在着替代关系，但6 000英里①以上长途航线则能够连接全球。另一方面，由于长距离航线需要更换更大的运输工具，如1970年开始投入运营的波音747飞机②，因此长距离航线在运营收益方面与短距离航线也有较大的区别。Campante和Yanagizawa-Drott（2018）利用国际民航组织（ICAO）提供的1989—2014年期间按独立航段统计的国际航线定期航班信息，从中选出200个国家中819个城市的主要机场、航程在2 000英里以上的航班信息，由此确定城市之间各年直飞航班连接的情况，并依据与之相连的城市构建了给定城市的网络中心性。以1989和2014年航线数量为例，可以发现航线数量在6 000英里处有明显的下降，说明6 000英里以上的长途航线有其特殊之处，在全球经济发展中扮演中特殊的角色。他们进一步研究了远程航线对经济活

① 1英里合1.609 3千米。

② 2019年4月4日，波音公司CEO米伦伯格表示，随着埃航事故调查初步报告的发布，“很明显，737 MAX8的自动防失速系统（MCAS）导致了两起致命空难。在这两起事故中，飞机的自动防失速系统（MCAS）为了回应错误的迎角信息而启动”。将近半年内，印度尼西亚狮子航空公司和埃塞俄比亚航空公司各有一架波音737 MAX8型客机坠毁，合计致死346人；全球超过300架波音737 MAX系列客机继而停飞，多个国家和地区停飞或禁飞这些客机。

跃度[①]和商业联系[②]以及资本流动的影响，其结论总体来说，航线连接对商务联系有显著影响，会增加外国持有公司的数量和两地的商务事件，促进人员和资本流动，长距离航线可以转化为经济动力，但最贫穷的国家除外。[③]这一实证研究反映出对于不同发展阶段的国家来讲，不同类型的航空基础设施的作用是不同的，这类似于前面提到的高铁对于中国不同层级的地区的影响是不同的结论。

#### 7.3.1.6 世界电信基础设施建设进展概况

与水电、海陆空运输基础设施一样，通信基础设施所实现的人与人或人与自然之间通过某种行为或媒介进行的信息交流与传递也是生产生活的基本需要。电报是一种最早用电的方式来传送信息的、可靠的即时远距离的现代化通信方式，它是19世纪30年代在英国和美国发展起来的。电报信息通过专用的交换线路以电信号的方式发送出去，该信号用编码代替文字和数字，通常使用的编码是莫尔斯编码。现在，随着电话、传真等的普及应用，电报已很少被人使用了。现在被广泛使用的通信方式是电话。早在18世纪欧洲已有“电话”一词，用来指用线串成的话筒（以线串起杯子）。电话的出现要归功于亚历山大·格拉汉姆·贝尔。贝尔于1876年3月申请了电话的专利权。[④]历史上对电话的改进和发明包括：碳粉话筒、人工交换板、拨号盘、自动电话交换机、程控电话交换机、双音多频拨号、语音数字采样等。近年来的新技术包括：ISDN、DSL、网络电话、模拟移动电话和数字移动电话等。然而，现代的电子通信系统即电信网已经非常复杂，它是构成多个用户相互通信的多个电信系统互联的通信体系，是人类实现远距离通信的重要基础设施，利用电缆、无线、光纤或者其他电磁系统，传送、发射和接收、文字、图像、声音或其他信号。电信网由终端设备、传输链路和交换设备三要素构成，运行时还应辅之以信令系统、通信协议以及相应的运行支撑系统。电信终端设备一般装在用户处，提供由用户实现接入协议所必需的功能的设备（电信端点）。它的作用是将语音、文字、数据和图像（静止的或活动的）信息转变为电信号或电磁信号发出去，并将接收到的电或电磁信号复原为原来的语音、文字、数据和图像信息。典型的终端

① 以美国国家海洋和大气管理局（NCEI-NOAA）提供的1992—2010年的夜间灯光数据衡量。

② ORBIS数据库报告了523 702家具有跨国持有关系的公司的坐标等信息，以及GDELT数据库报告了1979年1月至2013年3月期间主体跨国并距离机场100英里以内的31 000条重要商务事件记录。

③ Filipe Campante & David Yanagizawa-Drott, “Long-range Growth: Economic Development in the Global Network of Air Links”, *The Quarterly Journal of Economics,* 2018, Vol.133, No.3, pp. 1395–1458.

④ 2002年6月15日，美国国会269号决议确认安东尼奥·穆齐为电话的发明人。穆齐于1860年首次向公众展示了他的发明，并在纽约的意大利语报纸上发表了关于这项发明的介绍。

设备有电话机、移动电话机、无线寻呼机、数据终端机、计算机、传真机、电视机等。有的终端本身也可以是一个局部的或小型的电信系统，它们对公用电信网来说，就作为终端设备接入，如用户交换机、ISDN终端、局域网、办公室自动化系统、计算机系统等。电信传输设备是将电信号或电磁信号从一个地点传送到另一个地点的一种设备。它构成电信网中的传输链路，包括无线电和有线电传输设备。无线电传输设备有短波、超短波、微波收发信机和传输系统，以及卫星通信系统（包括卫星和地球站设备）等。有线电传输设备有电缆、光缆等传输系统，以及装在上述系统中的各种调制解调设备、脉码调制设备。终端和中继附属设备、监控设备等，也属于传输设备。电信交换设备实现一个呼叫终端（用户）和它所要求的另一个或多个终端（用户）之间的接续的设备和系统，是构成电信网中节点的主要设备。它包括各种电话交换机、数据交换机、移动电话交换机、分组交换机、宽带异步转移模式交换机等。网络技术是电信网宏观上的软件部分。它包括网络拓扑结构、网内信令、协议和接口，以及网络技术体制、标准等，是业务网实现电信服务和运行支撑的重要组成部分。

近几十年来全球电信基础设施建设取得了巨大成就。尽管在电话已经被发明了将近一个世纪之后的20世纪70年代，全球绝大多数人依然被排除在电话的世界之外，不过到了21世纪初叶，全球各个经济体每100人所拥有的电话线路数量已经接近20条。[①]然而，目前绝大多数发展中经济体的人口依然没有进入电话时代，2015年低收入经济体每100人所拥有的电话线路数量只有0.86，撒哈拉以南非洲地区也只有1.1。

#### 7.3.1.7 世界互联网基础设施建设进展概况

以互联网的全球化普及为重要标志的信息革命被视为第四次工业革命。互联网是网络与网络所串联成的庞大网络，这些网络以一组通用的协议相连，形成逻辑上单一且巨大的全球化网络，在这个网络中有交换机、路由器等网络设备，各种不同的连接链路，种类繁多的服务器和数不尽的计算机、终端，可以将信息瞬间发给千里之外的人，是信息社会的基础。从2000年开始互联网在全球迅速兴起，全球固定宽带互联网用户（每100人）2015年超过10%。这主要得益于由美国政府发起的20世纪信息高速公路这一全球基础设施的兴建。1992年2月，美国总统布什发表的国情咨文中提出计划用20年的时间耗资2 000亿～4 000亿美元以建设“美国国家信息基础设施”（NII），作为美国发展政策的重点和产业发展的基础。1993年，美国政府正式宣布实施国家信息基础设施建设，旨在以因特网为雏形，兴建信息时代的高速公

① 2005年以后，每百人拥有的电话路线下降是因为固线电话被移动电话取代。

路，使所有的美国人方便地共享海量的信息资源。互联网基础设施不但为其他相关生产活动奠定了基础，本身也形成了庞大的互联网产业——以现代新兴的互联网技术为基础，专门从事网络资源搜集，互联网信息技术的研究、开发、利用，信息商品的生产、贮存、传递和营销，可为经济发展提供有效服务的综合性生产活动的产业。

然而，互联网在全球的普及程度差别也是巨大的，2015年，美国每100人有31.53人是固定宽带互联网用户，而低收入经济体每100人只有0.31人是固定宽带互联网用户，撒哈拉以南非洲地区每100人只有0.54人是固定宽带互联网用户。中国这个世界上人口最多的经济体是拥抱互联网非常积极的国家，2000年每100人只有0.002人是固定宽带互联网用户，而2015年这一比例高达18.56，迅速拥抱了信息化时代。与前面几种类型的基础设施不同，几乎全球各地区以及不同收入水平的经济体都在积极开展互联网基础设施建设，至今方兴未艾。①

#### 7.3.1.8 世界能源基础设施建设进展概况

能源亦称能量资源或能源资源，是指可产生各种能量（如热能、电能、光能和机械能等）或可做功的物质的统称，包括煤炭、原油、天然气、煤层气、水能、核能、风能、太阳能、地热能、生物质能等一次能源和电力、热力、成品油等二次能源，以及其他新能源和可再生能源。不论处于哪一次工业革命，能源都是所有工业革命的基础。过去数十年中，全球能源基础设施得到了一定的改善。然而，如同工业化在全球的分布极不均匀一样，作为工业化最为重要的能源基础设施在全世界的差距也是巨大的，2013年高收入国家人均能源使用量为4 765千克石油当量，而最不发达国家（联合国分类）只有351千克石油当量，前者是后者的13.6倍。2015年北美的人均能源使用量为6 944千克石油当量，是撒哈拉以南非洲地区的10倍，也是中国这样快速工业化国家的3倍。

然而，随着环境问题的日趋严峻，与能源基础设施建设整体水平相对应的是能源结构和能源效率的不断调整。从可持续发展的角度讲，可再生能源以及清洁能源对世界能源基础设施建设尤为重要。根据能源是否可再生可分为可再生能源和不可再生能源。凡是可以不断得到补充或能在较短周期内再产生的能源称为再生能源，反之称为非再生能源。风能、水能、

① 为了展示互联网对非洲就业的影响有多快，Hjort和Poulsen利用海底互联网电缆逐渐抵达非洲海岸以及陆地电缆网络的地图，对来自12个国家的3个数据集的双重差分估计显示其对就业率的正面影响。样本范围内的影响是由高技能职业的就业增加推动的，但受教育程度较低的工人的就业增加较少。一些国家的公司级数据表明，其增加了公司进入、生产力和出口，也有助于创造更多的净就业机会，整体上使得平均收入增长。（Jonas Hjort, Jonas Poulsen, “The Arrival of Fast Internet and Employment in Africa”, *American Economic Review*, 2019, Vol.109, No.3, pp. 1032–1079）

海洋能、潮汐能、太阳能和生物质能等是可再生能源，煤炭、石油和天然气等是非再生能源。地热能基本上是非再生能源，但从地球内部巨大的蕴藏量来看，又具有再生的性质。根据能源消耗后是否造成环境污染可分为污染型能源和清洁型能源，污染型能源包括煤炭、石油等，清洁型能源包括水力、电力、太阳能、风能以及核能等。传统的不可再生且可造成环境污染的化石燃料能耗在持续不断地下降，而可替代能源和核能占能源使用总量的百分比在持续不断地上升，目前将近10%。同时能源效率也在不断提升。王冬等基于新结构经济学的理论框架分析了自1978年改革开放以来，中国能源结构转型的原因。其结果表明，从长期来看，整个经济体的资本深化程度是导致能源结构转型的原因，反之则不然。基于Johanson协整检验和误差修正模型（VECM）的脉冲响应分析进一步验证了，在长期中，能源结构内生于经济体的禀赋结构，即资本深化是决定能源结构的原因。而短期中，来自人均资本侧的外部冲击导致的调整期大约为五年，这与中国五年规划的政策周期基本一致。长期中，中国的能源转型是由资本深化（即禀赋结构变化）驱动技术进步偏向于资本密集型的新能源所导致的，产业政策的冲击（如五年规划）可以促进这个过程。[①]他们的研究表明，产业政策要更好地消除与新能源投资相关的市场摩擦，通过诸如税收减免、减少信息不对称、促进技术标准化、建立公平有效竞争市场、支持绿色金融等政策措施，在提升资本深化水平的同时，促进能源技术创新和应用，把“资本深化”的过程变成“资本绿化”的过程，从而推动能源结构转型。这一能源转型的中国模式可能对其他发展中国家同样具有启示意义。

#### 7.3.1.9 世界医疗卫生基础设施建设进展概况

前面介绍的八类基础设施基本上都是硬件基础设施，下面我们介绍一类重要的软件基础设施：医疗卫生基础设施。除了间接得益于人均收入水平提升之外，正是直接得益于医疗卫生基础设施的改善，全世界的预期寿命在战后大幅提升。[②]1960年，世界人口的预期寿命只有52.58岁，2017年大幅上升到72.38岁。这在我们第2章介绍的马尔萨斯传统社会是不敢想象的。例如，1800年世界人口的预期寿命为30岁，比狩猎-采集社会时的35岁还要短。[③]

---

① Wang Dong, Amin Mugera, Ben White, “Directed Technical Change, Capital Intensity Increase and Energy Transition: Evidence from China”, *The Energy Journal*, 2019, Vol. 40.

② David E. Bloom, David Canning, “The Health and Wealth of Nations”, *Science*, 2000, Vol. 287, No. 5456, pp. 1207-1209.

③ 大卫·克里斯蒂安，《极简人类史：从宇宙大爆炸到21世纪》，中信出版社，2016年版。

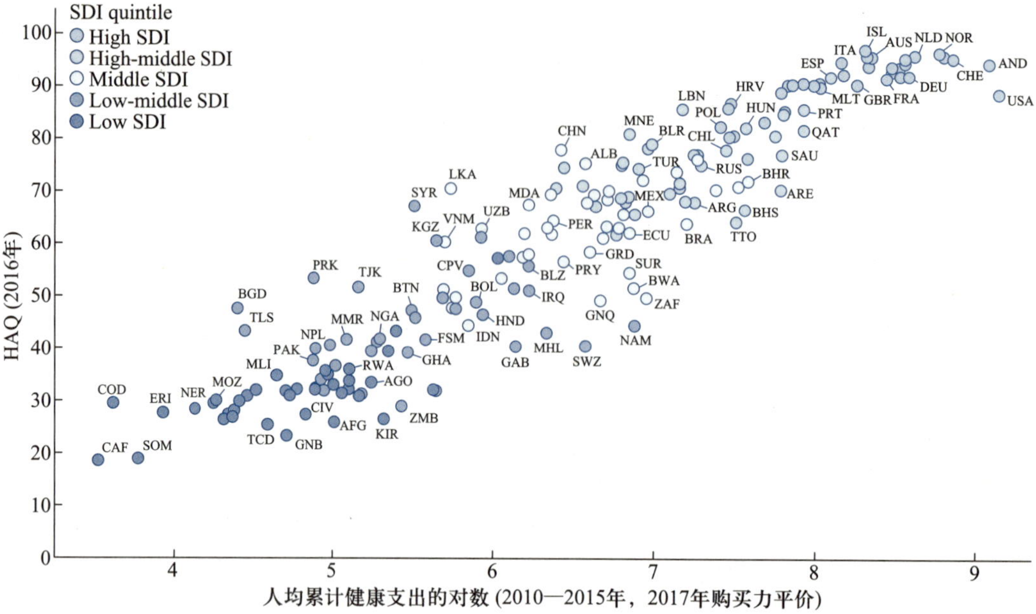


**图7.6 2010—2015年人均累计健康支出与2016年医疗可及性和质量指数**

资料来源：The Lancet（2018）。

事实上，疾病与瘟疫恰恰是马尔萨斯时代平衡人口与社会的重要机制。[①]医疗卫生等社会基础设施与前面那些经济基础设施一样，都是随着经济发展而逐步完善（如图7.6所示），当然反过来又影响经济社会发展。例如，20世纪初，美国南部地区40%的学龄儿童感染了钩虫病，洛克菲勒卫生委员会随后在该地区发起了治疗和教育运动，钩虫感染水平较高的地区在干预后的入学率、出勤率和识字率都有较大提高，并对长期人力资本积累都产生了正面影响。[②]然而，随着世界人口的急剧增加，所需要的医疗卫生基础设施变得越来越紧张。例如，世界每千人医院床位数在1970年是3.08张，1985年上升到4.13张，但是随着人口增长，2000年

① 一项研究探讨了中世纪晚期的黑死病对英国发展的深远影响与新结构经济学视角一致：黑死病导致人口外生地锐减—人口锐减改变人地禀赋结构（从土地稀缺变成劳动稀缺）—人地禀赋结构改变导致农业结构变迁（土地密集的畜牧业相对劳动密集的种植业占比变大）；种植业相对畜牧业而言是体力活，女性在畜牧业上相对更有比较优势—农业结构变迁导致女性就业结构变迁—女性就业结构变迁导致其婚姻结构变迁：女性开始变得晚婚晚育—婚姻结构变迁又导致人口结构变迁：女人晚婚晚育导致人口出生率下降—人口结构变迁又反过来导致禀赋结构变迁：工资水平变得越来越高。（Nico Voigtländer and Hans-Joachim Voth, "How the West 'Invented' Fertility Restriction." *American Economic Review*, 2013, Vol. 103, No. 6, pp. 2227–2264）

② Hoyt Bleakley, "Disease and Development: Evidence from Hookworm Eradication in the American South" .*The Quarterly Journal of Economics*, 2007, Vol. 122, No. 1, pp.73–117.

又下降到2.88张，2011年也只维持在2.7张。

然而，比医疗卫生基础设施世界性短缺更头疼的是，发展中国家与发达国家巨大的医疗卫生基础设施差距。根据医学期刊《柳叶刀》发布的2016年全球医疗可及性与质量指数（HAQ指数）[①]，2016年，HAQ指数排名最高的国家冰岛为97.1分，而排名最低的国家中非共和国仅18.6分。在本书第1章末尾所举的瑞士和布隆迪的例子中，瑞士的HAQ指数为96分，排名第7，布隆迪的HAQ指数为27分，排名第187。毫无疑问，在如此悬殊的医疗卫生条件下，布隆迪与瑞士在预期寿命上的差距令人咋舌：2016年布隆迪只有57岁，而瑞士高达83岁。在HAQ指数的评估中，中国从1990年的42.6分，到2000年的53.3分，再到2016年的77.9分，取得了巨大的进步，在全球范围内进步显著，尤以2000年以来提升最为迅速。1990年，中国排名仅为第110位，经过25年，2015年中国进步到了第60位，进步的幅度位居全球第3位。到2016年，比上年跃升了12位，成为中等SDI（sociodemographic index，社会人口学指数）国家中进步最大的国家之一。中国作为世界上人口最大的发展中国家，在医疗卫生基础设施建设上的这一成就实属不易。尽管如此，面对如此庞大人口的健康需求，中国与世界其他国家一样，医疗卫生基础设施建设提升空间巨大。例如，2018年，中国公共卫生领域的财政支出1.6万亿元，仅占GDP的1.7%。

## 7.3.2 基础设施的评估与缺口

### 7.3.2.1 基础设施随发展阶段不断升级

按照新结构经济学关于基础设施的基本论断，基础设施需要随着产业结构的升级而升级，否则就会成为经济结构转型升级的瓶颈，并且在经济结构转型升级过程中基础设施投资需要适当超前。与第6章对制造业缺口的估算一样，对基础设施缺口的估算目前也没有一个非常精确的方法。由于影响基础设施需求和供给的因素非常多，除了社会经济与人口等因

① GBD 2016 Healthcare Access and Quality Collaborators, "Measuring performance on the Healthcare Access and Quality Index for 195 countries and territories and selected subnational locations: a systematic analysis from the Global Burden of Disease Study 2016", *The Lancet*, 2018, Vol. 391, No. 10136, pp. 2236–2271.

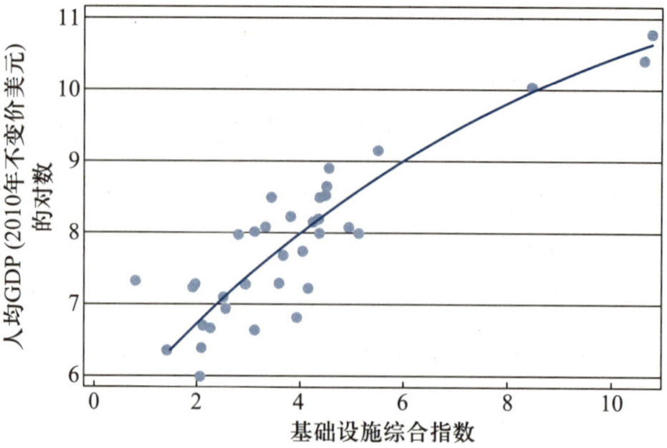


**图7.7 人均GDP与基础设施综合指数的散点图**

资料来源：Asian Development Bank, *Meeting Asia' s infrastructure needs*, 2017.

素之外，甚至还包括气候因素。①因此，不论采取哪种估算方法，结果都只能算是"鸟瞰"（birds-eye view）。②在亚洲开发银行2017年的报告中，对基础设施投资需求估算的基准方程中，除了人均GDP外，还纳入了农业占GDP的比重、工业占GDP的比重、城市化等经济结构变量以及人口密度。从前面的章节讨论中，我们知道农业GDP的占比重、工业化、城市化等经济结构变量与人均GDP是密切相关的，甚至是高度相关的，因此将这些变量一起放入估算方程中其实也是高度共线性的，综合反映了不同发展阶段的不同基础设施需求。当然，即便是整体层面上，基础设施需求随发展阶段的变化也不是线性的，如图7.7和图7.8所示。总的趋势上，基础设施需求的增加会对应于人均GDP的增加，但制造业增加对导致最多的基础设施需求的增加，农业和服务增加导致的基础设施需求的增加则较少，如图7.9所示。不同类型的基础设施对应于不同发展阶段的产业结构的需求则差异性更大。

### 7.3.2.2 全球基础设施投资的近期状况

2014年在澳大利亚布里斯班举行的G20峰会已经充分认识到基础设施建设对于经济社会

① M. Fay, T. Yepes, "Investing in Infrastructure: What is Needed from 2000 to 2010?", Policy Research Working Paper. No. 3102. World Bank, 2003. F. Ruiz-Nunez, Z. Wei, "Infrastructure Investment Demands in Emerging Markets and Developing Economies", Policy Research Working Paper. No. 7414, World Bank, 2015.

② Asian Development Bank, *Meeting Asia' s infrastructure needs*. Mandaluyong City, Philippines: Asian Development Bank, 2017.

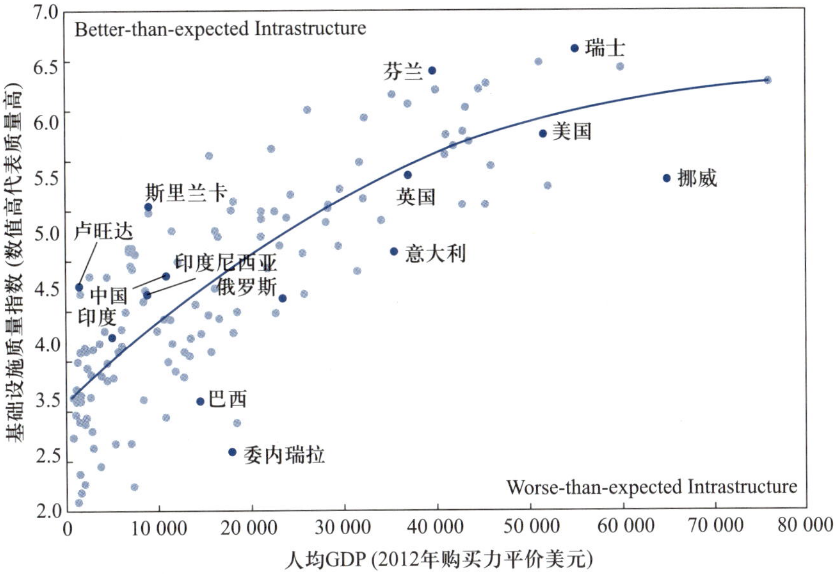


**图7.8 人均GDP与基础设施质量指数的散点图**

资料来源：McKinsey & Company, *Bridging global infrastructure gaps*, 2016.

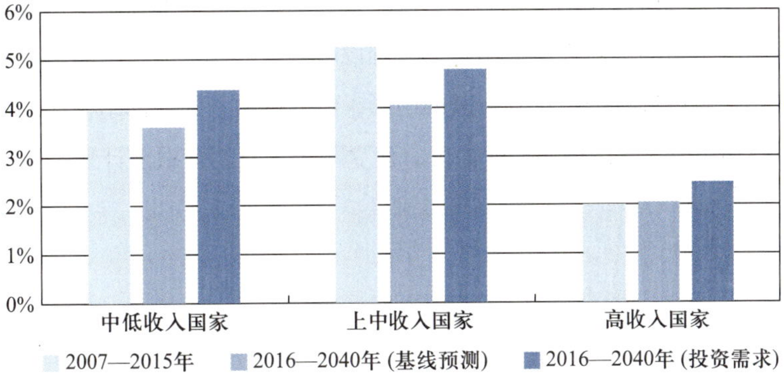


**图7.9 不同发展阶段的国家的基础设施投资需求占GDP的比重：实际水平（2007—2015）与预测水平**

资料来源：G20倡议的全球基础设施中心发布的《全球基础设施展望》。

结构转型的重要性，并专门发布了全球基础设施倡议推进全球基础设施建设，参见专栏7.2。根据G20全球基础设施倡议建立的全球基础设施中心于2017年发布了《全球基础设施展望》（Global Infrastructure Outlook），按照统一的口径评估了全球50个国家7个部门到2040年的基础设施投资需求。电力、公路、电信、铁路、水利、港口和机场这7个部门的基础设施投资从2007年的1.8万亿美元上升到2015年2.3万亿美元（按照2015年汇率计算），年均增长率为2.9%，平均每年为2万亿美元。如图7.10所示，这与世界经济增长大致维持在一个相互平衡的水平，近十年来全球基础设施支出占GDP的比重大致维持在3%上下，占总固定投

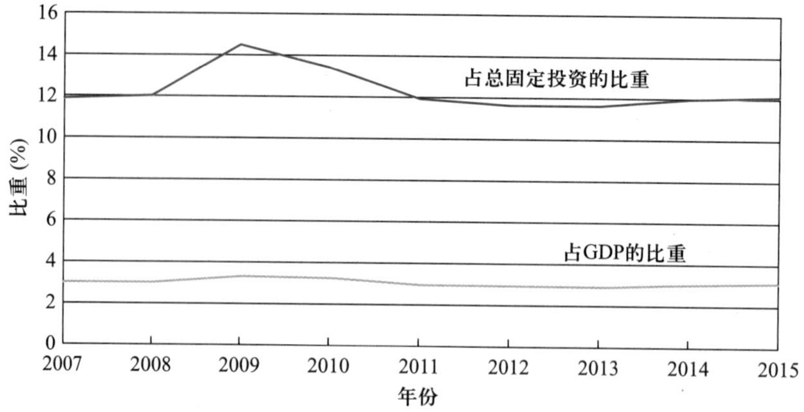


**图7.10 全球基础设施支出占GDP的比重和占总固定投资的比重（2007—2015年）**

资料来源：G20倡议的全球基础设施中心发布的《全球基础设施展望》。

资的比重大致维持在12%上下。但是基础设施投资体现了一定的逆周期性，全球基础设施投资占总固定投资的比重在2008年国际金融危机之后出现了大幅度增加，2009年达到15%。这符合新结构经济学的“超越凯恩斯主义”的主张：[①]在经济萧条时投资基础设施既可以缓解短期下行压力，也可以为长期增长创造条件。事实上，早在国际金融危机爆发伊始，时任世界银行首席经济学家的林毅夫就提出全球基础设施投资倡议来解决国际金融危机和世界发展问题。为了扫除金融危机给全世界带来的阴影，给发达国家的内部结构性改革创造外部空间，林毅夫2009年2月9日在华盛顿就提议，建立一个富有“马歇尔计划”精神的全球恢复

① Lin Justin Yifu, “Beyond Keynesianism: The Necessity of a Globally Coordinated Solution”, *Harvard International Review*, 2009, Vol.31, No.2, pp.14-17. Lin Justin Yifu, “Beyond Keynesianism: Global Infrastructure Investments in Times of Crisis,” *Journal of International Commerce, Economics and Policy*, 2012, Vol.3, No.3. Lin Justin Yifu, “Global infrastructure initiative and global recovery”, *Journal of Policy Modeling*, 2013, Vol. 35, No. 3, pp.400–411. Lin Justin Yifu, Wang Yan, “Beyond the Marshall Plan: A Global Structural Transformation Fund”, Submitted to the High Level Panel on the Post-2015 Development Agenda, 2013.

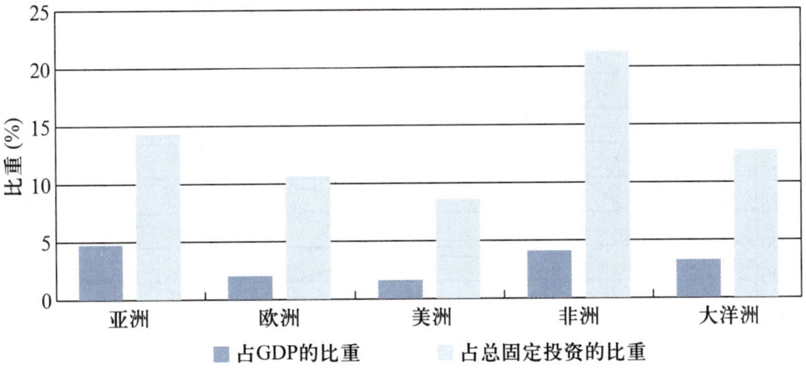


**图7.11 全球各地区的基础设施支出占GDP的比重和占总固定投资的比重（2007—2015年平均）**

资料来源：G20倡议的全球基础设施中心发布的《全球基础设施展望》。

基金。[①]

全球各地区中，2007—2015年基础设施支出占GDP的比重最高的是亚洲地区，近5%；占总固定投资的比重最高的是非洲地区，超过20%，如图7.11所示。亚洲基础设施投资从2007年到2015年增加了50%，这其中中国的贡献超过了一半。与此相反，欧洲受困于政府债务困境，基础设施投资不断萎缩。如图7.12所示。因此，亚洲在全球基础设施投资中的份额从2007年的49%上升到2015年的59%，而同期欧洲下降了6个百分点，美洲下降了4个百分点。在基础设施各个类别中，电力和公路的支出占到总的基础设施支出的2/3，电信和铁路占到1/8，剩下的一小部分是水利、港口和机场，如图7.13所示。上述全球基础设施投资的地区和类别结构，其实充分反映了亚洲尤其是中国快速的工业化对基础设施的需求。

---

① 马歇尔计划（The Marshall Plan），官方名称为欧洲复兴计划（European Recovery Program），是1947年6月5日美国国务卿乔治·马歇尔在哈佛大学发表演说时首先提出的援助欧洲经济复兴的方案，故名马歇尔计划。该计划正式启动于1947年7月，并整整持续了4个财政年度。在计划实施期间，西欧各国通过参加经济合作发展组织总共接受了美国援助合计130亿美元，其中包括金融、技术、设备等各种形式的援助。该计划对欧洲国家的发展和世界政治格局产生了深远的影响。Giorcelli在一项新近的实证研究中从微观企业层面评估了当年马歇尔计划的绩效。马歇尔计划有一个子项目是美国技术援助和生产力计划（The United States Technical Assistance and Productivity Program），旨在向欧洲企业管理者提供到美国学习先进管理经验的机会及提供贷款购买设备。根据《生产力计划》（1952—1958），美国为意大利经理组织了到美国公司的管理培训旅行，并向意大利公司提供技术先进的机器。该项目原定在意大利五个地区实行，但由于预算突然削减，援助计划缩小到五个省，最终申请成功的企业数量较原计划大大减少。在研究设计上，将申请成功的企业设定为处理组，将同一地区的其余企业作为对照组，基于DID方法比较这两组企业在援助计划前后的绩效，进而识别管理策略对企业绩效的影响。Giorcelli的实证研究发现，与被预算削减排除在外的企业相比：在该计划实施后的至少15年里，将经理派驻美国的意大利企业的业绩有所增长；接受新机器的企业业绩有所增长，但随着时间的推移趋于平稳；管理和新机器是相辅相成的。（Michela Giorcelli，“The Long-Term Effects of Management and Technology Transfers”，*American Economic Review*，2019，Vol. 109，No. 1，pp. 121–152）

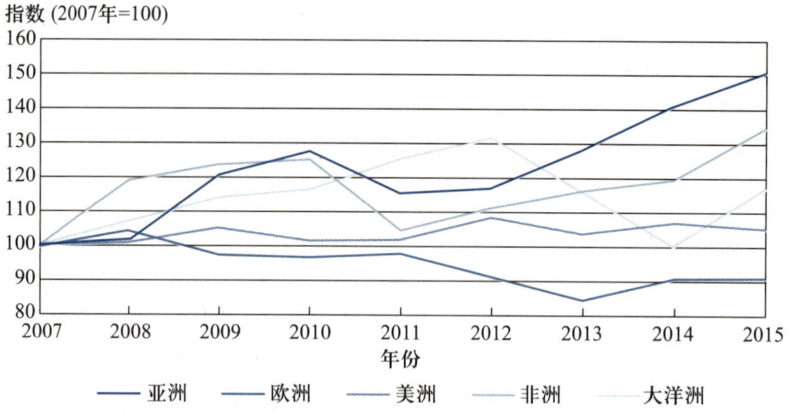


**图7.12 全球各地区的基础设施投资指数（2007—2015年）**

资料来源：G20倡议的全球基础设施中心发布的《全球基础设施展望》。

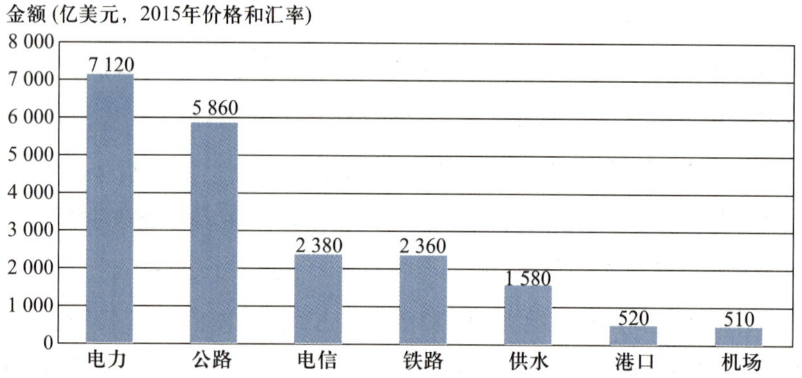


**图7.13 全球各类基础设施支出（2007—2015年平均）**

资料来源：G20倡议的全球基础设施中心发布的《全球基础设施展望》。

### 7.3.2.3 全球基础设施投资的未来缺口

前面介绍的是已经实现的世界基础设施支出与投资，《全球基础设施展望》也估算了到2040年基础设施投资缺口。其方法是，先按照每个国家的经济增长与人口的变化对基础设施投资趋势做基线预测（current trends），然后再参照最佳实践国家的标准（the performance of their best performing peers），并控制每个国家的特征差异来预测基础设施投资需求（investment need），前者不足后者的部分就是基础设施投资缺口。[①]如果按照目

① 详细的具体内容参见《全球基础设施展望》的技术附录。

前经济增长与人口变化预测，全球基础设施投资在2040年将达到3.8万亿美元，比2015年将增加67%，平均每年3.2万亿美元；然而，如果参照最佳实践国家的标准来预测，全球基础设施投资需求在2040年将增加到4.6万亿美元，平均每年为3.7万亿美元。这意味着到2040年全球基础设施投资缺口达8 000亿美元，平均每年的缺口达5 000亿美元。

图7.14显示了全球各地区基础设施投资的累计和平均需求。如图7.15所示，按照基线预测，亚洲基础设施需求占59%，比美洲高17%，比欧洲高16%。但是，如图7.16所示，美洲和非洲的投资缺口最大，分别超出基线预测的47%和39%。这意味着，美洲和非洲相对于最佳实践国家的标准而言基础设施严重拖后腿，例如美国占了美洲一半的缺口。从绝对量上看，亚洲和美洲占全球基础设施投资缺口的3/4。对于最不发达的非洲地区，到2040年，基础设施投资需求，按基线预测需要累计4.3万亿美元，按最佳实践国家的标准则需要累计6万亿美元，也就是每年2 400亿美元，差不多占到其GDP的6%，而世界的平均水平在3%上下，如图7.17所示。在基础设施各个类别中，图7.18显示了其投资的累计和平均需求。如图7.19所示，电力和公路投资需求占比最大，按照基线预测二者占到7类基础设施总投资需求的65%，占GDP的比重超过2.2%（如图7.20所示）；如果按照参照最佳实践国家的标准，二者占到67%。基础设施投资需求最大的是公路和港口，超出基线预测的30%。

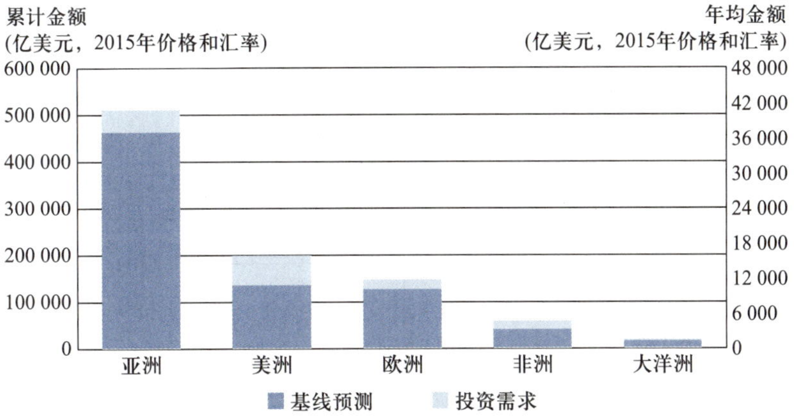


**图7.14 全球各地区2016—2040年的基础设施投资需求**

资料来源：G20倡议的全球基础设施中心发布的《全球基础设施展望》。

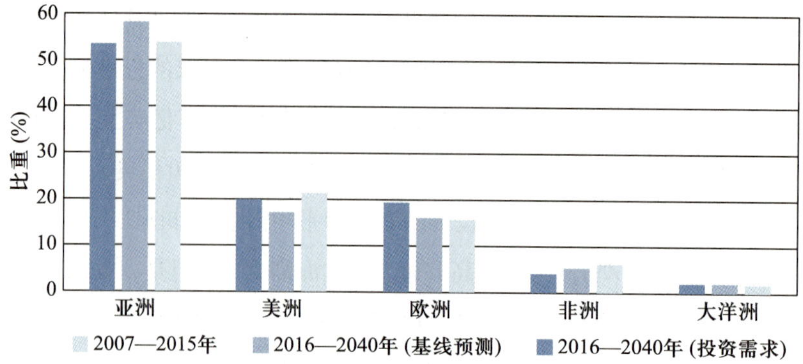


图7.15 全球基础设施投资需求（2007—2040年）的地区份额

资料来源：G20倡议的全球基础设施中心发布的《全球基础设施展望》。

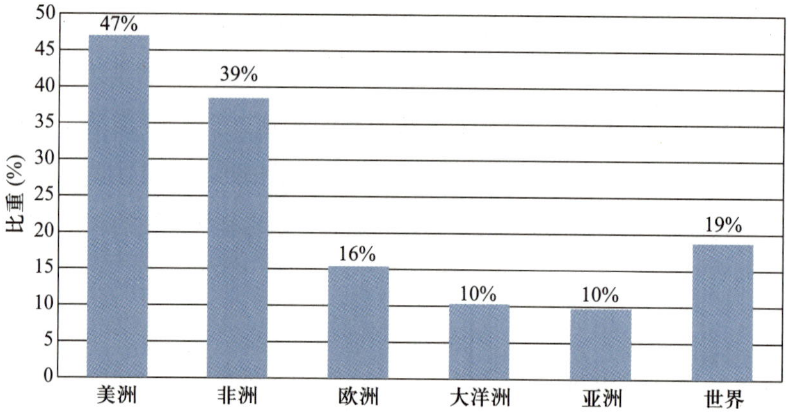


图7.16 全球各地区的基础设施投资缺口（2016—2040年）

资料来源：G20倡议的全球基础设施中心发布的《全球基础设施展望》。

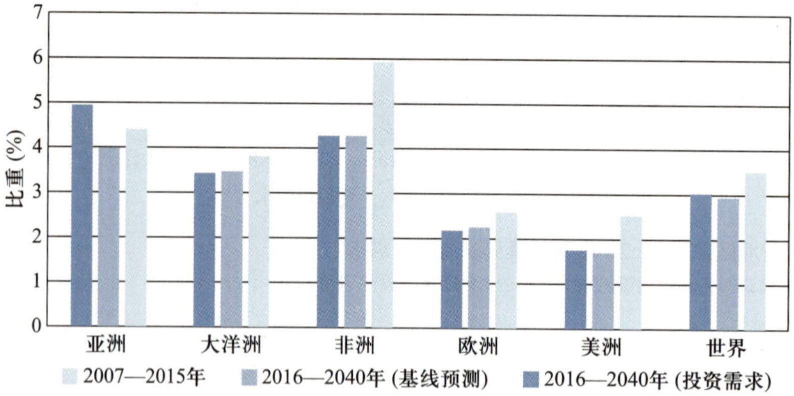


图7.17 全球各地区基础设施支出占GDP的比重（2016—2040年平均）

资料来源：G20倡议的全球基础设施中心发布的《全球基础设施展望》。

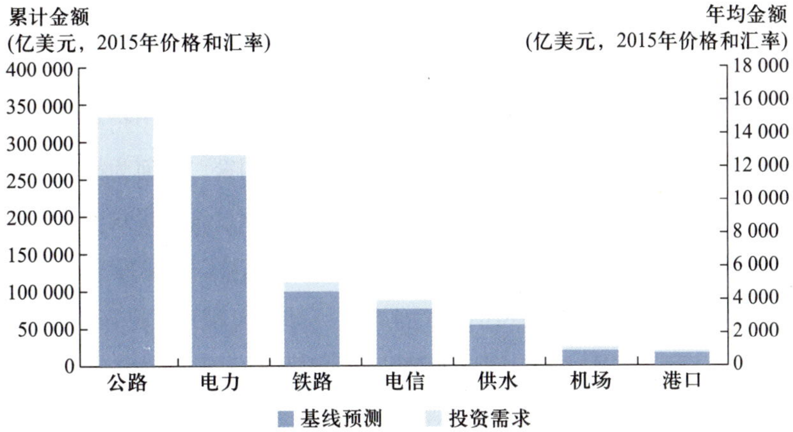


图7.18 全球基础设施投资（2007—2040年）的分类份额

资料来源：G20倡议的全球基础设施中心发布的《全球基础设施展望》。

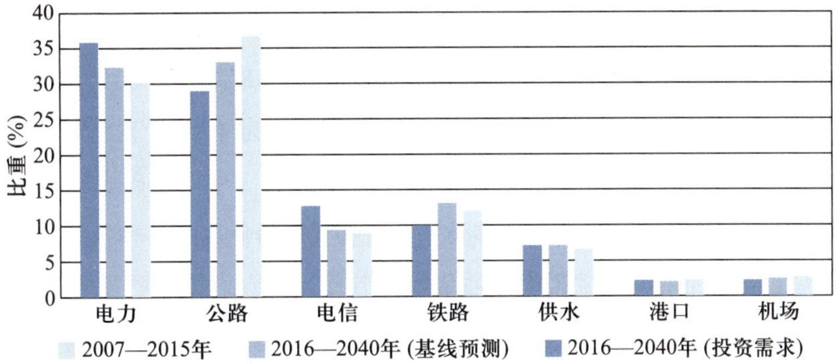


图7.19 全球基础设施投资（2007—2040年）的分类份额

资料来源：G20倡议的全球基础设施中心发布的《全球基础设施展望》。

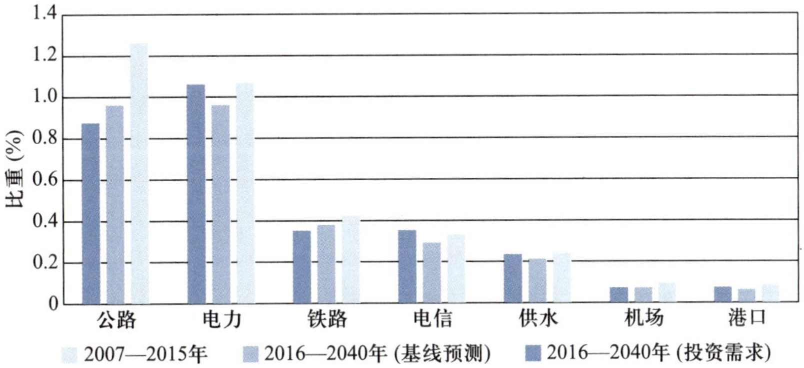


图7.20 全球各类基础设施支出占GDP的比重（2007—2040年）

资料来源：G20倡议的全球基础设施中心发布的《全球基础设施展望》。

#### 7.3.2.4 为全球基础设施投资缺口融资[①]

面对如此巨大的基础设施投资需求和缺口，我们在本章开门见山指出的策略性地改善基础设施至关重要。尽管如此，不论是发展中国家还是发达国家，如何为如此巨大的基础设施投资需求融资，填补投资缺口，都是非常棘手的问题。基础设施除了众所周知的外部性特征之外，还具有规模大、周期长、资本密集和沉没成本高的特点，需要很长时间才能建成并产生收益。基于这种基础设施投资的长期性特征维度，林毅夫和王燕将资本分为"耐心资本"和"非耐心资本。[②]耐心资本大致定义为投资于一种"关系"的资本，其中的投资方愿意看到被投资方在未来获得发展，从而获得可观的回报。例如，父母对孩子进行教育投资，风险投资家对具有潜力的创新展开投资，企业家对实体经济领域进行创业投资，金融家对公司（项目）的非上市股权注入资金。这些投资者关注的不是短期回报，而是期望能在投资项目得到发展或扩大规模时收获长期的未来收益。耐心资本所有者类似于股权投资者，但愿意将资金长期投入实体经济领域、非上市公司或非上市的基础设施项目。在这个定义中，"耐心"的期限是什么？耐心资本（适用于基础设施投资项目）的成熟期可能会达到10年或更长，这取决于"关系"的性质。按照常规定义，风险投资一般为 7 年，直接投资则达到10年以上。利用经合组织的"机构投资者和长期投资"项目，表7.2中对基础设施融资工具进行了分类。这些工具的覆盖范围非常全面，涉及了政府和代理所使用的各种债务、股权和风险缓解工具。该表最后添加了一列来说明耐心资本及其作用，它们是基础设施融资工具的买方（出资方）。第一，耐心资本高度依赖能够把公民长期积蓄转化为可贷资金的国内银行部门和机构投资者。因此，应鼓励商业银行、投资银行、主权财富基金、养老基金等的发展，因为它们在基础设施融资中能发挥重要作用。第二，在将国内公共储蓄转变成国际长期开发资金（耐心资本的一部分）的过程中，国际多边金融机构（如世界银行）、区域开发银行以及双边捐助开发银行（基金）发挥着关键的作用。因此，设立亚洲基础设施投资银行和金砖国家新开发银行等机构，以及丝路基金和其他基础设施基金应受到欢迎和支持。这些机构均是耐心

---

① 基础设施资产的资本市场相对复杂、非标准化，而且缺乏流动性。关于基础设施融资更丰富的技术细节性讨论可参考：尼尔 · S. 格里格，《PPP与基础设施融资》，机械工业出版社，2017年版。

② Lin Justin Yifu and Wang Yan, "The New Structural Economics: Patient Capital as a Comparative Advantage", *Journal of Infrastructure, Policy and Development*, 2017, Vol. 1, No. 1, pp.4–23. 亦可参考该论文的中文版：林毅夫、王燕，"新结构经济学：将'耐心资本'作为一种比较优势"，《开发性金融》，2017年第1期，第3–15页。

资本的提供者。[①]第三，非上市的股权类工具或非上市的基础设施基金（不容易进行交易）非常适合于耐心资本。应创造更多的此类工具（基金）。与短期资本（如对冲基金）交易频繁的短期债务工具相比，这些更适用于基础设施。第四，“耐心资本”与创业资本（直接投资）存在极强的关联，因此在实体经济领域，新的想法、创新、国际知名品牌、冒险和勤奋都是使这种资本转化为投资项目、实现发展的重要元素。各国政府应通过改善投资环境吸引外国直接投资，鼓励私营部门参与基础设施、经济特区、生态工业园、生态城市以及实体经济领域或制造行业的直接投资。理论概念和操作工具上虽如此，但是现实中的基础设施融资模式五花八门，即便是相同类别的基础设施在不同国家或地区采取的融资模式也可能完全不同。以PPP模式为例，一些发达国家（澳大利亚、加拿大、美国与英国）基础设施投资中的PPP融资模式占比差异非常大，如图7.21所示。英国近些年来比较流行采取此模式，但美国却并不流行。[②]

---

① 开发性银行往往是政策性银行，这里可以看到产业政策通过基础设施对产业结构变迁产生影响的渠道，相关讨论可参见：徐佳君，“作为产业政策抓手的开发性金融:新结构经济学的视角”，《经济评论》，2017年第3期，第70—80页。茹弘用国家开发银行的数据实证发现政策性金融对私人企业产生了正面和负面两种效应：一方面使得私人企业受益于基础设施贷款的溢出效应，另一方面在同行业中对国企的贷款会产生的挤出影响。（Ru Hong, “Government Credit, a Double-Edged Sword: Evidence from the China Development Bank”，*The Journal of Finance*, 2018, Vol. 73, No. 1, pp. 275–316）

② 龚强等的研究揭示了在不同发展阶段，地方政府推广PPP模式的不同最优策略。在中国，20世纪90年代尝试开展PPP模式时，由于PPP项目数量较少且市场对基础设施需求旺盛，地方政府的最优策略是事前给予社会资本优厚条款，待社会资本进入后，再以施加公共品负担的形式提高公共福利，避免社会资本获得过高的私人利益。不同于过去，当前PPP模式被作为防范地方债务风险和稳定地方投资的重要政策工具，但当前中国基础设施水平和产业发展水平已大幅提升，如果地方政府仍然事后对社会资本施加公共品负担，将严重弱化社会资本的进入激励，引发PPP项目落地难、实施效率低等问题。当前地方政府的最优策略是通过合理界定自身权力边界，减少地方政策的"时间不一致性"，唯此才能提高社会资本的进入激励，让PPP模式缓解地方财政压力、保障公共品供给的重要作用得以充分发挥。可参考：龚强、张一林、雷丽衡，“政府与社会资本合作（PPP）：不完全合约视角下的公共品负担理论”，《经济研究》，2019年第4期。关于中国的案例研究可参考：吉富星，《中国PPP模式的案例解析》，中国财政经济出版社，2017年版。

表7.2 基础设施融资工具分类以及耐心资本的作用

| 资产类别 | 基础设施融资工具 | | | 市场工具 | 买房/出资方 |
|---|---|---|---|---|---|
| | 工具 | 基础设施项目 | 企业资产负债表 | 资金池 | 耐心资本或短期资本 |
| 固定收入 | 债券 | 项目债券 | 公司债券、绿色债券 | 债券指数、债券基金（ETF） | 拥有耐心资本或非耐心资本的所有参与者 |
| | | 市政、子主权债券 | | | |
| | | 绿色债券、伊斯兰债券 | 次级债券 | | |
| | 贷款 | 直接投资贷款、银团项目贷款、资源融资基础设施贷款（RFI） | 对基础设施企业的直接投资贷款、银团贷款、证券化贷款（ABS）、抵押贷款债券（CLO） | 债券基金（GPS）、贷款指数、贷款资金 | 耐心资本：多边开发银行、双边捐赠资助银行或基金、半公共资助投资银行或公司、一些国家开发银行 |
| 混合 | 混合 | 夹层融资 | 可转换债券 | 夹层债务基金、混合债券基金 | 混合参与者 |
| 股权 | 上市 | 收益公司 | 上市的基础设施和公用事业股票、封闭式基金、房地产投资信托基金（REIT）、IIT、MLP | 上市的基础设施股票基金、指数、信托基金、ETF | 耐心资本：主权财务基金、养老基金及其他 |
| | 未上市 | 对基础设施项目股权的直接投资、公私合营（PPP） | 对基础设施企业股权的直接投资 | 未上市的基础设施基金 | 耐心资本：主权财富基金、养老基金、创业资金、直接投资、拟设立的全球结构转型基金 |

资料来源：林毅夫、王燕，“新结构经济学：将‘耐心资本’作为一种比较优势”，《开发性金融》，2017年第1期，第3–15页。

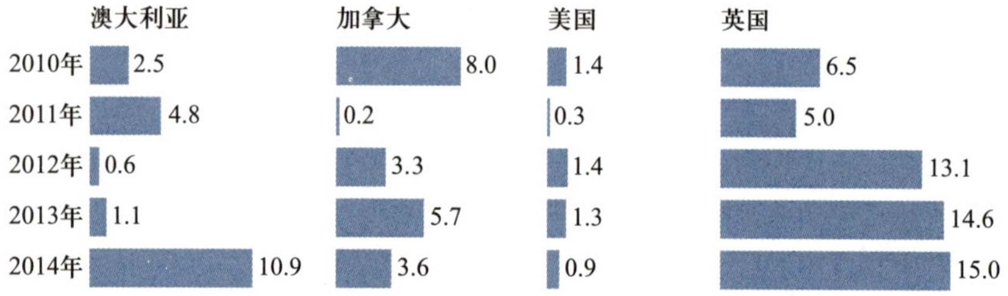


图7.21 一些发达国家（澳大利亚、加拿大、美国与英国）基础设施投资中的PPP融资模式占比（%）

资料来源：McKinsey & Company, Bridging global infrastructure gaps, 2016.

**专栏7.2**

**G20全球基础设施倡议**

1. 考虑到投资对刺激需求、提高生产率和促进经济增长的重要作用，全球基础设施倡议应是一个旨在提高公共和私人部门基础设施投资的多年期工作计划。

2. 该倡议将成为我们履行创造促进投资（尤其是高质量基础设施和中小企业投资）的良好环境承诺的重要途径。根据该倡议，我们将通过执行全面增长战略和布里斯班行动计划（Brisbane Action Plan）的核心举措，改善成员国投融资环境。

3. 我们同意在投资领域采取一系列自愿和率先垂范的示范做法，以推动并优化高质量投资和便利机构投资者的长期项目融资，包括自愿执行G20/OECD高级别的机构投资者长期项目投融资原则。

4. 我们将通过该倡议鼓励包括透明的证券化在内的市场融资，尤其是为中小企业服务。这些行动将帮助我们实现吸引更多私营部门资金用于基础设施投资和中小型企业的目标。我们也开始将基础设施作为一类固定资产评估其发展。我们将继续同多边开发银行合作，并鼓励各国开发银行，通过优化资产负债表的方式提供额外贷款。

5. 我们还同意采取行动降低投资壁垒，增加投资就绪项目的可获得性，帮助在投资者与项目间牵线搭桥和改善政策传递渠道，具体包括如下举措：

（1）建立致力于为政府、国际组织、开发银行、国家基础设施机构和私人部门提供汇总和分享基础设施项目和融资信息的知识共享网络；

（2）解决事关投资者的关键性数据缺失问题；

（3）开发有效方法执行自愿和率先垂范的高质量投资的G20示范做法，包括规范化项目识别、准备和采购的相关文件；

（4）通过分享最佳实践做法，改善政府官员针对基础设施的体制安排能力；

（5）建立与国家和多边开发银行数据库相连接的基础设施项目综合数据库来增加投资机会，在潜在投资者与项目间牵线搭桥。

6. 作为全球基础设施倡议行动的一部分，多边、区域和国别开发银行将通过自身的基础设施倡议和持续努力优化资产负债表，并与私营部门合作。总之，这些努力应有助于提高对发达经济体、新兴市场、发展中和低收入经济体的高质量基础设施投资。

## 7.4

## 发达经济体的基础设施投资：改造升级[①]

从前面的基础设施建设概况梳理以及缺口评估结果来看，发达经济体的主要特征有如下几个方面：发达经济体基础设施建设水平较高，遥遥领先于世界，远超发展中经济体；除了21世纪初叶才大举兴起的互联网基础设施外，传统的基础设施，如水力、电力、交通基础设施等，相对饱和但是需要大力改造，而电信、互联网、能源等基础设施并未饱和，需要继续加大投资。因此，总体上来看，欧洲和美洲的基础设施投资占GDP的比重目前比较低，对于前述7类基础设施，美国2007—2015年平均只有1.5%，欧洲2007—2015年平均只有2.2%，二者在全球都处于最低水平。与此同时，发达国家由于处于较高的发展阶段，其基础设施需求结构与发展中国家也会有所不同。

事实上，发达国家已经意识到基础设施投资对于重整其经济的重要性。欧洲委员会很强调持续进行基础设施投资的重要性，早在2006年发布的《面向2030年基础设施》报告中就估计欧盟在2011—2020年需要2.1万亿～2.8万亿美元的基础设施投资才能保持足够的竞争力。[②]根据《全球基础设施展望》，按照目前的趋势，2016—2040年欧洲基础设施投资需求为12.8万亿美元，按照最佳实践标准则需要14.8万亿美元，主体是电力和公路，如图7.22和图7.23所示。相对于世界平均的基础设施需求架构而言，欧洲在铁路和电信上的需求相对更大，如图7.24所示，这可能反映了欧洲对改造升级传统交通通信基础设施的需要。[③]

根据《全球基础设施展望》，按照目前的趋势，2016—2040年美国基础设施投资需求为8.5万亿美元，按照最佳实践标准则需要12.4万亿美元，即每年达4 940亿美元，主体是公路和电力，如图7.25和图7.26所示。相对于世界平均的基础设施需求架构而言，美国在公路和

---

① 进一步可参考：林毅夫、余江，《从西潮到东风》，中信出版社，2012年版，第6章"超越凯恩斯主义"。

② OECD, Infrastructure to 2030: Telecom, Land Transport, Water and Electricity. Pairs, 2006.

③ 关于德国19世纪末期和20世纪初期的交通基础设施建设对后续就业和工资等劳动力市场长期影响的研究可参考：J. Möller, M. Zierer. 2018. "Autobahns and jobs: A regional study using historical instrumental variables" Journal of Urban Economics 103:18–33.

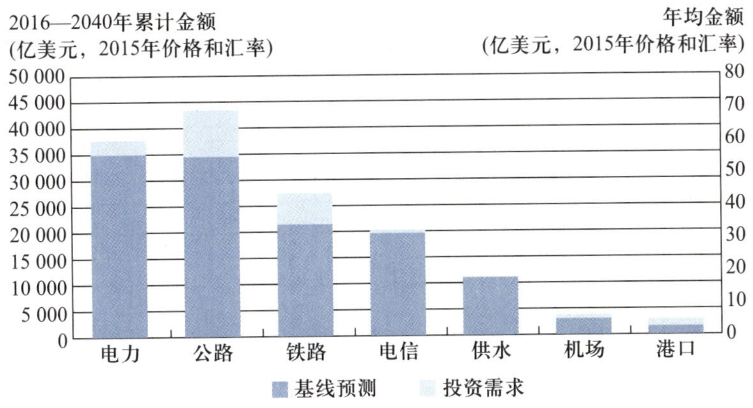


图7.22 欧洲各类基础设施投资需求

资料来源：G20倡议的全球基础设施中心发布的《全球基础设施展望》。

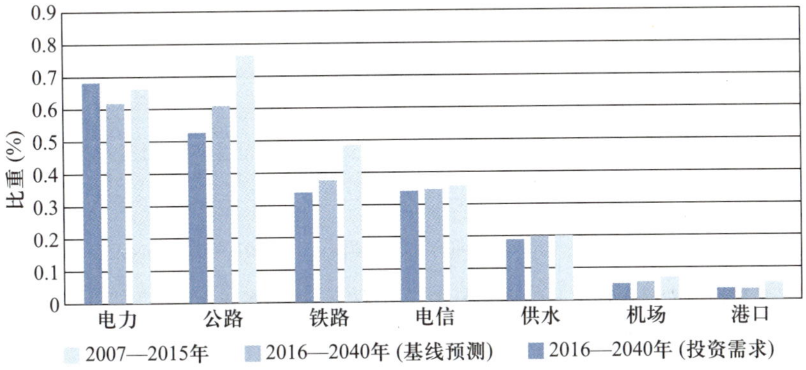


图7.23 欧洲各类基础设施投资需求占GDP的比重（2016—2040年平均）

资料来源：G20倡议的全球基础设施中心发布的《全球基础设施展望》。

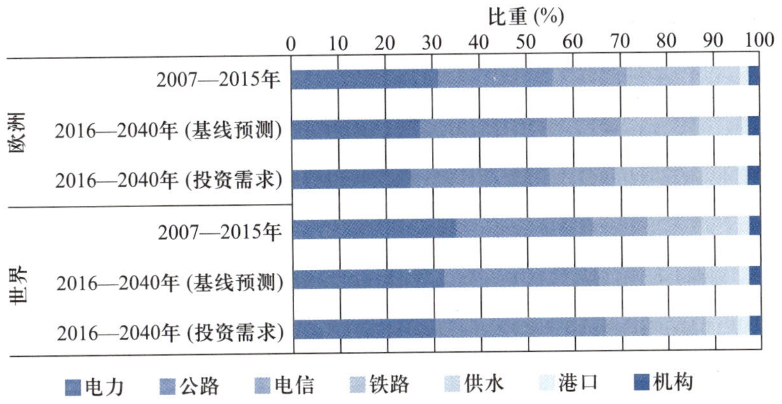


图7.24 欧洲与世界的基础设施投资结构比较

资料来源：G20倡议的全球基础设施中心发布的《全球基础设施展望》。

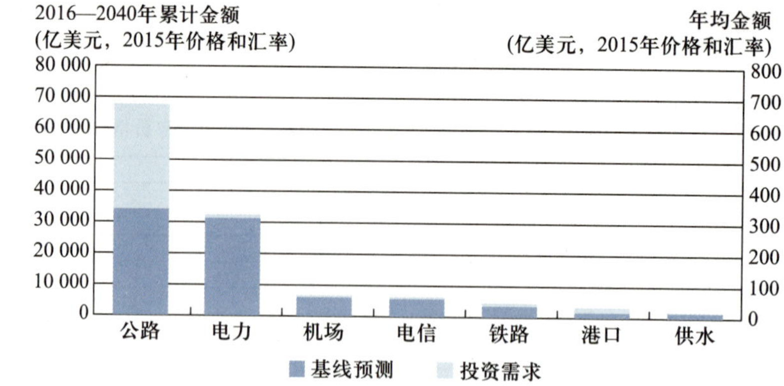


**图7.25 美国各类基础设施投资需求**

资料来源：G20倡议的全球基础设施中心发布的《全球基础设施展望》。

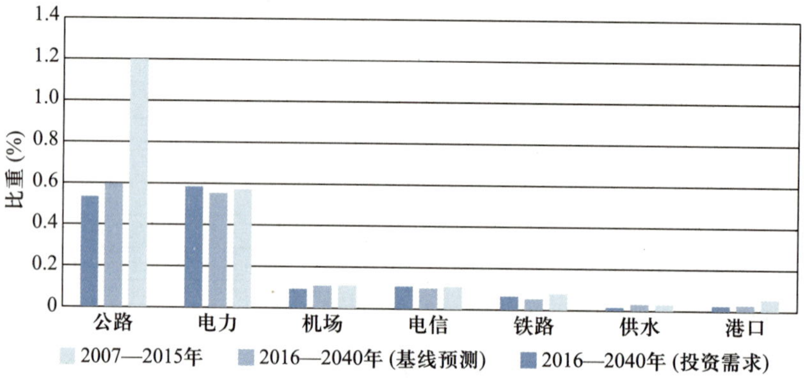


**图7.26 美国各类基础设施投资需求占GDP的比重（2016—2040年平均）**

资料来源：G20倡议的全球基础设施中心发布的《全球基础设施展望》。

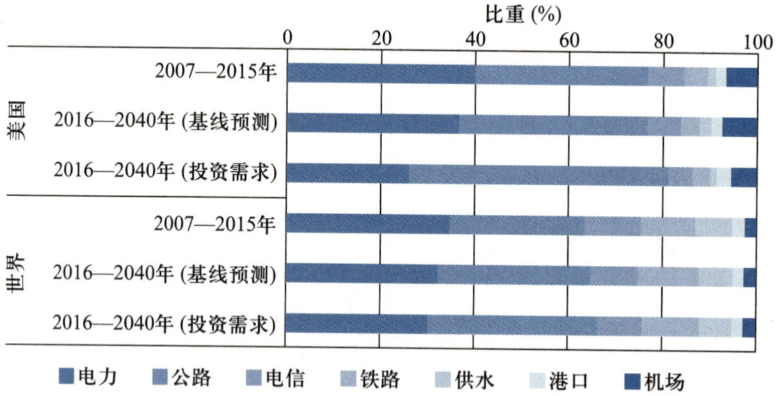


**图7.27 欧洲与世界的基础设施投资结构比较**

资料来源：G20倡议的全球基础设施中心发布的《全球基础设施展望》。

机场的需求相对更大，如图7.27所示，这可能反映了美国对改造升级传统公路交通与航空基础设施的需要。

根据美国土木工程师协会的评估，美国要耗费10年时间进行基础设施修补和重建工程，所需资金超过3.3万亿美元。而根据目前的政府资金规模，这项耗资巨大的工程将有至少1.4万亿美元的缺口；如果这项工程被拖到2040年完成，资金的缺口将高达5万亿美元以上。该协会预计，如果不进行基础设施建设，那美国将要付出的代价可能更大。到2025年，因为落后的基础设施建设拖累商业贸易、高昂的交通设施维修费用，以及对经济其他领域所产生的影响将为美国国内生产总值带来超过4万亿美元的损失，并将造成250万个工作机会的流失。这个数字可能是最高的估计值，不过美国的许多政府机构也确认了大规模基础设施维护和升级的需要。万亿基础设施改造计划是美国总统特朗普2016年的竞选和施政纲要的核心。

1919年，年轻的陆军中校德怀特·艾森豪威尔需要56天才能指挥汽车运输部队跨越华盛顿特区到加利福尼亚州奥克兰的3 250英里旅程。他当时报告说，车队压坏了桥梁，卡车在雨天陷入泥泞，某些道路不能满足快速舒适的旅行需要。后来，当上总统的艾森豪威尔推动了1956年《联邦高速公路促进法案》（Federal Aid Highway Act），期望对美国经济发挥超出计算结果的影响——例如给制造业和建筑业创造就业岗位，打开农村地区的开发前景等。100年过去了，道路、桥梁、电网、能源管道早已遍布美国50个州，然而现在却年久失修，需要进行“大修大补”。美国道路与交通建设商协会（American Road & Transportation Builders Association）2016年的一项研究发现，美国60万座桥梁中有近10%存在结构性缺陷。每个州都独自对桥梁进行检查，以确定桥梁是否存在不足（包括那些跨越河流和小溪的桥梁以及跨越高速公路的桥梁）。这导致一个独特的问题——需要创造一套州与州之间一致的标准。艾奥瓦州拥有最大数量的“有结构缺陷”的桥梁，当地超过20%（超过5 000座）的桥被划入这一类，据美国国家桥梁库存数据库的数据，这意味着桥梁“有一个或多个结构缺陷需要注意”；内布拉斯加州的问题是老桥太多，当地每5座桥中就有1座是20世纪30年代初建造的；特拉华州的桥梁虽然现代化得多，但是该州75%“有结构缺陷”的桥梁是在过去50年内建造的。

美国拥有超过160 000英里的铁路、76 000座铁路桥和800个隧道，由数百家运营商提供客运和货运服务。数以百万计的乘客（主要在东北地区）依靠美国铁路公司提供通勤服务。美国第一条铁路诞生于1830年，铁路时代已被汽车和飞机取代。100多岁的铁路更新不多，高铁技术几乎一片空白。

美国的航空公司是世界上最繁忙的航空公司。在2016年11月初的3天时间里，追踪实况空中交通的Flightradar24软件显示，超过160 000个航班到达或离开美国机场。最繁忙的线路是在芝加哥和纽约、洛杉矶和旧金山、洛杉矶和芝加哥之间。根据2016年Skytrax世界机场奖的数据，美国最好的机场是丹佛国际机场，排名全球第28位，纽约肯尼迪机场排在第59位，洛杉矶国际机场则排在第91位。与此同时，亚洲、太平洋、欧洲和中东的机场排名持续上升。

美国陆军工程兵团的数据显示，美国海外贸易中有95%以上通过港口完成，根据世界航运协会的数据，洛杉矶港和长滩港位列世界前25个最繁忙的港口，东海岸的几个港口位列前50名。然而，2015年全球前10位国际航运中心，美国只有纽约入选。

在美国有超过3 300个电力公司和约7 700个电厂为用户提供电力。电力通过超过160 000英里的高压输电线路进入美国的每个角落。《华尔街日报》报道称，有专家将美国的电网描述为一个由输电和配电设施（某些可以追溯到19世纪）拼凑、打满补丁的公用事业，这一系统将最终崩溃，除非投资数千亿美元改善。“当我们开始建造所谓的电网时，托马斯・爱迪生并没有坐下来制订一个全国性的计划，但我们还是建起了电网。”美国土木工程师协会基础设施委员会奥托・林奇这样表示。但是几十年来这些线路一直承载着比它们设计更重的负载。“到目前为止，美国的电网比世界上任何其他国家都更加捉襟见肘。”他说。

在美国有大约150 000英里的石油管道和超过150万英里的天然气管道。自2010年以来，水力压裂技术的繁荣使得宾夕法尼亚州、西弗吉尼亚州、俄克拉荷马州和西得克萨斯州的天然气产量增加，这也扩大了管道基础设施的需求。美国大部分石油和天然气的生产来自墨西哥湾，而近半数的炼油能力则位于墨西哥湾沿岸。石油天然气需要基础设施，以便于将它们从一个地方运输到另一个地方，但这一点却不容易，北达科他输送管道的争议表明了在几百英里内建设一条管道的困难。此外，近来一些石油和天然气管道事故也表明，美国需要更好的管道管理和维护。

除了欧洲和北美洲的发达国家之外，大洋洲的澳大利亚也类似。根据《全球基础设施展望》，澳大利亚需要增加以下投资方可满足未来20年的发展需求即：铁路建设650亿美元，港口建设560亿美元，电网建设210亿美元，通信建设100亿美元。事实上，澳大利亚政府于2106年已经正式宣布《澳大利亚基础设施规划》，针对未来15年内澳大利亚基础设施领域面临的需求与挑战，重点提出了93项优先建设项目，并对各级政府发展基础设施提出了78项建议，内容涵盖改扩建悉尼、墨尔本等首府城市的轨道交通，霍巴特等老城区翻新改造，大力发展收费公路，扩建大型机场枢纽，改革电力、供水、宽带等领域的融资和运营方式。

## 7.5

## 发展中国家的基础设施投资：消除瓶颈[①]

前述对发展中经济体基础设施建设概况的梳理最重要的事实便是其基础设施存量低得惊人，不过相对于其发展阶段而言对基础设施的需求也较低。以非洲地区为例，根据《全球基础设施展望》，按目前的趋势，到2040年的基础设施投资需求为4.3万亿美元，也即每年1 740亿美元；按照最佳实践的标准，到2040年的基础设施投资需求为6万亿美元，即每年2 400亿美元。绝大多数发展中经济体依然面临严重的水电短缺与道路不足，很多人口依然没有进入工业化和信息时代。全球有大约14亿人没有电力，8.8亿人没有安全的饮用水，26亿人无法获得基本的卫生服务，估计有10亿农村居民的住所与全天候道路的距离在2千米以上。基础设施的瓶颈不但影响到数十亿人的生活质量，还增加了交易成本，限制了生产率和产品质量的改善，从而打击了创业活动，削弱了企业的竞争力。在撒哈拉以南的非洲国家，这一问题尤其突出，那里每年的人均电力消耗量仅为124千瓦时（南非除外），仅能在每天为每个人提供6个小时的照明。由于电力匮乏且不可靠，许多企业自己发电，平均成本超过发电厂的3倍。例如在贝宁、布基纳法索、冈比亚、马达加斯加、莫桑比克、尼日尔和塞内加尔，企业的能源成本超过总成本的10%，而中国的企业仅为3%。电力匮乏造成的损失相当于中位数的坦桑尼亚企业销售额的10%，而中国仅为1%。许多撒哈拉以南的非洲居民还因此被隔绝在本国市场和全球市场之外。尽管有2/3人口住在农村地区，并且许多国家是内陆国，撒哈拉以南非洲国家的路网密度却是全球最低的。因此不足为奇的是，这里的交通成本极高，相当于企业间接成本的16%。在未来，发展中国家对基础设施服务的需求还将快速增长，从中期来看，发展中国家的人均GDP将达到5%的增速。随着世界人口在2050年接近90亿，以及更多的人口迁往城市居住，全球的建筑存量预计到2050年还将翻番。发展中国家的基础设施建设非常必要而且需求旺盛。因此，对于发展中国家而言，尤其是欠发达经济体，基础设施建设还处于最基本的水、电、路需求阶段。以非洲地区为例，根

① 进一步可参考：林毅夫、余江，《从西潮到东风》，中信出版社，2012年版，第6章“超越凯恩斯主义”。

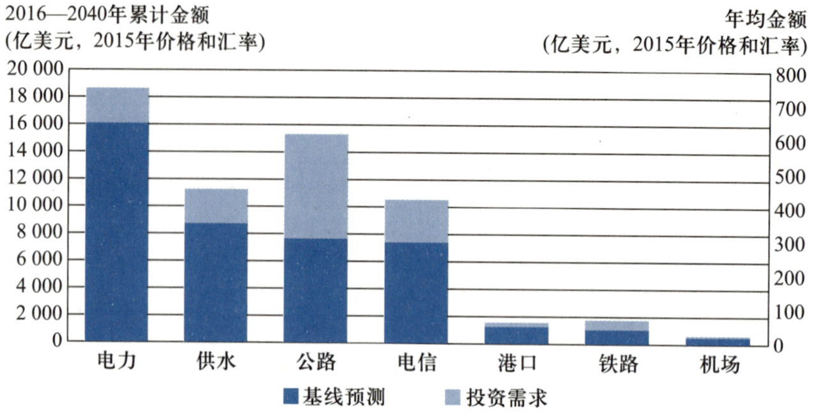


**图7.28 非洲各类基础设施投资需求**

资料来源：G20倡议的全球基础设施中心发布的《全球基础设施展望》。

据《全球基础设施展望》，基础设施投资需求最大的三类便是电力、供水和公路，如图7.28到图7.30所示。

基础设施不仅是增长的副产品，还将成为经济发展的驱动力。经济发展是个持续技术创新、产业升级和多样化以及结构变化的过程。在农业发展阶段，大量产品是用于生产者自身的消费，用于市场交换的比例和数量少，因此对基础设施服务的需求较少。随着各国的工业化，生产更多地转向制造业，规模经济更加突出，产品主要是为其他人生产。由于市场范围扩大，良好的基础设施对于安全及时地向市场提供产品和服务，并且让工人能够获得最合适的岗位工作都至关重要。良好的基础设施还能支持可持续的发展，最大幅度地减轻自然灾害的破坏，提高公共交通的可靠性，这些对于适应全球气候变化以及随之而来的自然灾害的增多都非常关键。基础设施的改善会通过多个渠道影响一个国家的产出。在建设期，基础设施投资会给地方经济带来就业机会和经济增长。完工后，基础设施会改进生产率，促进私人资本的形成（通过提高投入的边际生产率或降低交易成本来提高私人投资的预期回报率），加快产业集群的出现等。基础设施还有利于改进健康和教育状况。例如在摩洛哥，随着全天候道路的建成，妇女和儿童在收集柴火等家务劳动方面的时间减少，使得女童的入学率从1985年的28%提高到1995年的68%。当地居民去医院和卫生中心的次数翻番，健康指标也大为改善。例如一项研究估计，2001—2005年和1991—1995年相比，基础设施投资使发展中国家的年均增长率提高了1.6个百分点，南亚更是达到2.7个百分点。如果撒哈拉以南的非洲国家能把它们与印度和巴基斯坦之间的基础设施差距缩小一半，中非的低收入国家的经济增长率平均能提高2.2个百分点，东非和西非国家能提高1.6个百分点。类似的是，如果拉美国家把基础设施提高到其他中等收入国家（如保加利亚和土耳其）的平均水平，其经济增长

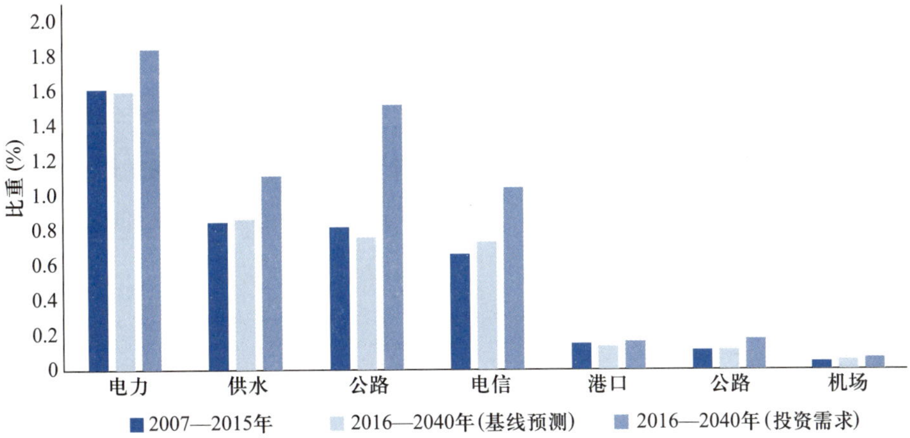


**图 7.29 非洲各类基础设施投资需求占 GDP 的比重（2016—2040 年平均）**

资料来源：G20 倡议的全球基础设施中心发布的《全球基础设施展望》。

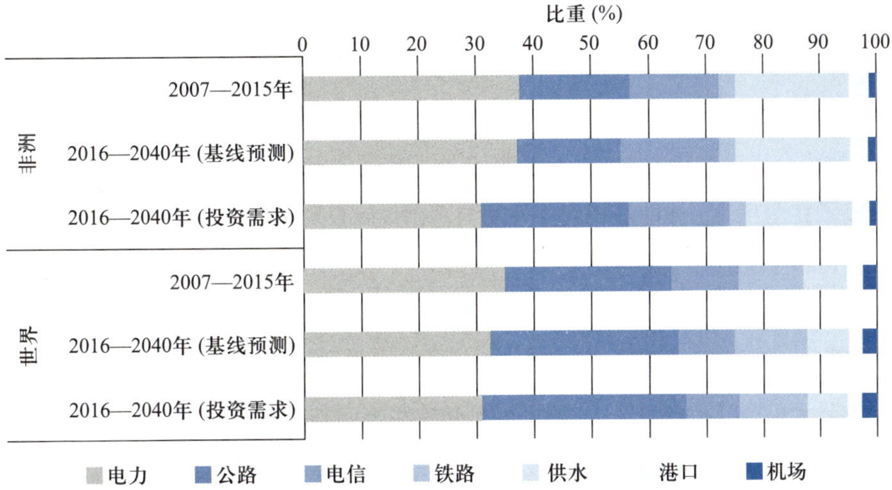


**图 7.30 非洲与世界的基础设施投资结构比较（2016—2040 年）**

资料来源：G20 倡议的全球基础设施中心发布的《全球基础设施展望》。

率每年可望提高 2 个百分点。[①] 中国便通过高速公路和高铁建设快速促进了经济发展，[②] 而且高铁建设势头随着“一带一路”倡议的推进将有增无减。

---

① Cesar Calderon, Luis Serven, “Infrastructure and Economic Development in Sub-Saharan Africa”, *Journal of African Economies*, 2010, No.19, i13–87.

② B. Faber, “Trade Integration, Market Size, and Industrialization: Evidence from China’s National Trunk Highway System”, *The Review of Economic Studies*, 2014, Vol.81, No.3, pp.1046–1070.

# 7.6
# —
# 对发展中国家关键的是比较优势产业与基础设施建设良性互动

相对于发达经济体而言，发展中经济体的基础设施存量较小，而且往往是经济结构转型升级的瓶颈，因此整体上发展中经济体基础设施投资回报率较发达经济体高，尤其是那些通过基础设施建设成功推动经济结构转型升级的经济体，基础设施投资回报率是最高的。在快速实现经济结构转型升级时期的亚洲"四小龙"便是成功的案例，如图7.31和图7.32所示。因此，亚洲"四小龙"以及前面所介绍的中国的经验对广大发展中国家最重要的启示，不在于单单强调基础设施建设的重要性，而在于策略性地动员有限的资源有针对性地改善发展第6章所介绍的符合比较优势的潜在比较优势产业所需要的基础设施，只有比较优势产业与基础设施形成了良性互动，才能获得经济发展与基础设施投资回报的"鱼和熊掌兼得"。否则，可能出现"鱼和熊掌兼失"的恶性局面。①

例如，前面我们提到全球10亿人居住在铺设道路2千米以外的地方，而其中1/3的人在印度。截至2001年，印度超过60万个村庄未通公路。印度政府基于糟糕的道路连接性是农村发展的最大障碍这一想法，从2000年起开始实施一项"总理的乡村道路项目"（Prime Minister's Village Road Program）。该工程主要铺设乡村支路从而连接村庄到外围主路，到2015年该项目已经花费400亿美元为将近20万个村庄铺设了全天候道路。世界银行的几位经济学家评估了这一项印度版的"村村通路"工程，结论非常悲观：其显著提升了交通服务，但是在居民资产、农业投资以及消费等维度的影响乏善可陈，除了导致劳动力流失之外。②同样，尽管高铁是现阶段最高水平的铁路交通基础设施，但是对于不同发展阶段的经

---

① 关于这一新结构经济学假说的一份来自中国数据的实证检验可参考：Xiao Ke , Lin Justin Yifu, Fu Caihui, Wang Yong, "Transport Infrastructure Development and Economic Growth in China: Recent Evidence from Dynamic Panel system-GMM Analysis", Working Paper, Institute of New Structural Economics at Peking University, 2020.

② Sam Asher, and Paul Novosad, "Rural Roads and Local Economic Development", *American Economic Review*, Vol. 110, No. 3, pp. 797–823.

济体的影响是不同的，对于高收入经济体的作用可能大于低收入经济体。例如，自2008年以来，由于高铁的开通，中国许多县告别了没有火车站的历史，这为研究高铁建设与县域经济发展的因果关系提供了很好的案例。张俊选取了2008—2013年首次开通高铁的县作为处理组，使用匹配倍差法考察了高铁开通对“高铁县”经济发展带来的影响。其基于卫星灯光数据的研究发现，第一，高铁开通对县级市和县经济发展带来不同影响，高铁开通对县级市经济增长贡献为34.64%，而对县的经济增长影响不明显；第二，高铁开通促进了“高铁县”投资的增加，平均而言“高铁县”的固定资产投资增加了37%，约合10.86亿元；第三，高铁开通对“高铁县”产业结构则没有产生显著的影响。①柯潇等利用1990—2013年中国地级城市数据，通过采用Hsiao，Ching and Wan的面板数据政策评估方法②，基于城市之间经济增长的横截面关系，构建了高铁沿线城市在没有开通高铁假想情形下的经济增长预测，从而估计出高铁开通带来的政策效应。其研究发现，高铁开通给各个城市带来的政策效应与该城市的地理位置、基础设施配套以及经济结构等特征紧密相关。总体来说，一方面，工业化程度较高、服务行业吸收劳动力较强和配套基础设施较好的城市，高铁开通对经济增长起到的作用更大。而另一方面，地方保护主义政策则降低了高铁带来的正面作用。文章还发现，在高铁建设和高铁开通阶段，高铁给城市带来的收益不同。③不过，高铁在中国是最近十几年才开通，对一个地区的经济发展和产业结构变迁的影响可能还需经过一段更长的时间才能完全显现。④

---

① 张俊，“高铁建设与县域经济发展——基于卫星灯光数据的研究”，《经济学季刊》，2017年第4期。

② C Hsiao, H. S. Ching, S.K. Wan, “A panel data approach for program evaluation—Measuring the benefits of political and economic integration of Hong Kong with mainland China”, *Journal of Applied Econometrics*, 2012, Vol, 27, No. 5, pp. 705–740.

③ Xiao Ke, Chen Haiqiang, Hone Yongmiao, Cheng Hsiao, “Do China’s high-speed-rail projects promote local economy?—New evidence from a panel data approach”, *China Economic Review*, 2017, Vol. 44, 203–226.

④ Donaldson利用印度殖民地时期形成的铁路网数据发现铁路交通基础设施通过降低贸易成本进而增加贸易量提高了长期收入水平。可参考：Dave Donaldson, “Railroads of the Raj: Estimating the Impact of Transportation Infrastructure”, *American Economic Review*, 2018, Vol. 108, No. 4–5, pp. 899–934.

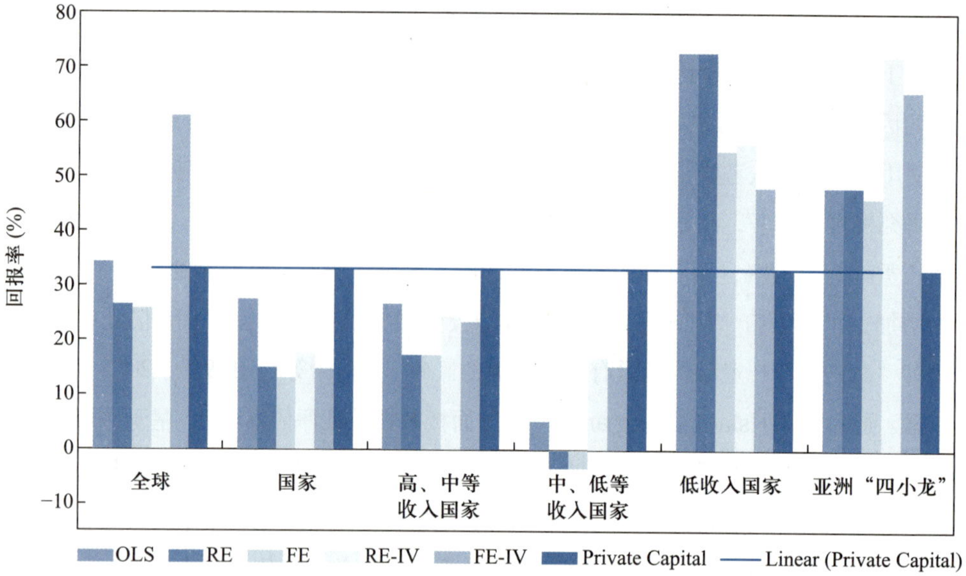


**图7.31 基础设施投资（公共资本）从制造业获得的回报率估算**

资料来源：Anders Isaksson, "Public Capital, Infrastructure and Industrial Development", Research and Statistics Branch Working Paper, 15/2009.

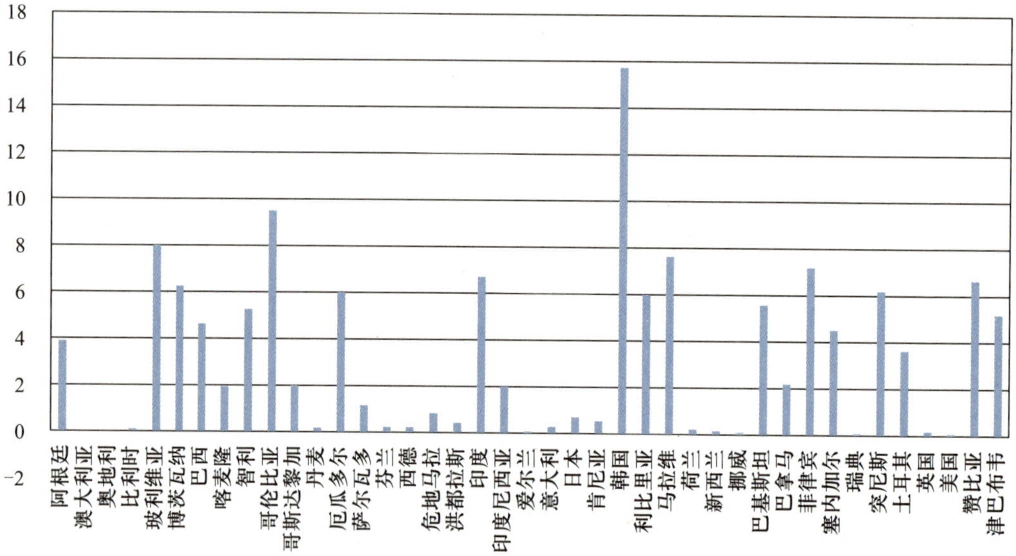


**图7.32 世界一些经济体（基础设施）修路的产出弹性（1960—1990年）**

资料来源：D. Canning and E. Bennathan, "The Social Rate of Return to Infrastructure Investments", Policy Research Working Paper No. 2390, DECRG, World Bank, 2000.

# 第8章

# 世界经济结构转型升级中的中国

- 8.1 中国在世界经济结构转型升级中的方位
- 8.2 中国在世界经济结构转型升级中的力量
- 8.3 中国与发达国家经济结构转型升级的匹配
- 8.4 中国与发展中国家经济结构转型升级的匹配
- 8.5 新时期中国融入世界构建开放型经济新体制的战略体系

前面的一些章节我们已经介绍了中国在世界经济结构变迁中举足轻重的作用，如第6章中所讨论的以中美为例的南北合作以及以中非为例的南南合作。与此同时，前面一些章节也回顾了中国参与世界经济的历程，如第5章所讨论的中国改革开放前错失但之后利用全球化发展机遇的经验教训。[①] 例如，1953年中国的贸易量占世界贸易量的比重为1.5%，此后却进一步下降到1977年的0.6%。1960年，中国货物和服务进口占GDP的比重为4.43%，货物和服务出口占GDP的比重为4.31%，然而到了1977年这两项比重依然分别维持在4.09%和4.3%。改革开放之后，中国将发展战略转轨到比较优势发展战略，相应地将进口替代战略转型为出口导向型战略，此后国际贸易一路高歌猛进。到2008年国际金融危机前夕的2007年，中国货物和服务进口占GDP的比重上升到26.72%，货物和服务出口占GDP的比重上升到35.39%。2010年，中国成为全球最大出口国，2013年成为全球最大贸易国。然而，正如经济学家罗德里克（Rodrik）开门见山地指出的，金融危机后，全球经济面临两难选择：一方面，发达国家为了维持全球经济稳定并防止贸易保护主义反弹，必须竭力控制大规模经常账户失衡，以避免金融危机再次出现；另一方面，发展中国家为保持经济高速发展，希望扩大国际贸易中的市场份额。解决这两个问题的挑战集中体现在中美双边关系上，欧美发达国家认为中国通过低估人民币汇率获得巨大的贸易盈余，而中国则担心人民币升值会损害出口，到时，不仅有损经济增长，更有可能影响到国内社会稳定，甚至也会反过来影响全球经济。那么，解

---

① 中国参与早期经济全球化的历史可参考李伯重教授的著作《火枪与账簿：早期经济全球化时代的中国与东亚世界》（生活·读书·新知三联书店，2017年版）。15世纪末至17世纪是经济全球化大潮出现和迅速发展的阶段，即早期经济全球化时代（回顾第2章和第3章的相关内容）。这个时代的特征是“火枪与账簿”。火枪代表了军事革命导致的新型暴力，账簿则意味着对商业利益的积极追求。早期经济全球化的出现和发展，导致东亚世界原有的秩序被打破，出现了前所未有的大变局。在这个历史的十字路口，中国未能抓住机遇，从而不得不再等上两个世纪，才又在新的国际环境中重新开始近代化的进程。新中国成立后的70年，中国与世界经济的联系发生了沧桑巨变：从1949年新中国成立到1978年中共十一届三中全会决定改革开放，这一阶段中国发展战略的定位是以自力更生为主，以争取外援为辅；从1978年确定对外开放基本国策到2001年加入世界贸易组织，这是中国走上对外开放发展道路的开始；从2001年加入世界贸易组织到2012年中共十八大召开，这是中国加入世界贸易组织后的发展阶段，中国与世界经济的关系发生历史性变化，成为世界经济增长的最主要贡献者；从2012年中共十八大召开后至今，这一阶段在延续了上一阶段中国对世界经济推动作用的同时，突出表现为以“一带一路”建设为重点的深度联系（第9章将专门讨论）。更多关于新中国成立70年来与世界的经济联系的概括可参考：张幼文，“70年中国与世界经济关系发展的决定因素与历史逻辑”，《世界经济研究》，2019年第7期。

决方案是什么？①

本章中我们将继续在前面对世界经济结构变迁讨论的基础上，系统梳理中国与世界经济结构的关系，寻求共同繁荣的长远而根本的出路。这对中国和世界都至关重要。进入了新时代的中国对世界的影响，从未像今天这样全面、深刻、长远；世界对中国的关注，也从未像今天这样广泛、深切、聚焦。2019年新中国成立70周年之际，国务院新闻办公室发布了《新时代的中国与世界》白皮书，以中、英、法、俄、德、西、阿、日8个语种与世界沟通。②麦肯锡全球研究院甚至估算了中国与世界经济关系的价值，其研究报告认为，到2040年，中国和世界其他经济体彼此融合有望创造22万亿～37万亿美元经济价值，相当于全球经济总量的15%～26%。总之，世界其他经济体和中国加强合作，将会创造出巨大的经济价值。③中国目前的经济规模和进一步与世界融合的空间见表8.1。

表8.1 中国目前的经济规模和进一步与世界融合的空间

| | 中国的经济规模 | 进一步与世界融合的空间 |
|---|---|---|
| 贸易 | 中国自2013年以来一直是全球第一大贸易国，2017年占全球货物贸易的11.4% | 中国2017年的服务贸易额仅占全球总量的6.4%左右 |
| 企业 | 中国拥有110家《财富》世界500强上榜企业，数量与美国相当 | 这些企业的收入仍然主要来自国内市场（海外营收仅占18%，而标普500企业的平均比例为44%） |
| 资本 | 中国拥有庞大的金融系统（全球第一大银行系统、第二大股票市场、第三大债券市场） | 跨境流动（美国的流动规模是中国的3～4倍）和外资参与度相对有限（银行、股票和债券市场外资占比尚不足6%） |
| 人员 | 中国是全世界最大的留学生（在2017年高等教育阶段国际学生中占比17%）和出境游客（出境游2018年达到1.5亿人次，居全球之首）来源地 | 人员流动的地理区域仍然较为集中（约60%的留学生前往美国、澳大利亚和英国），移民中国的外国人仅占全球移民总数的0.2% |
| 技术 | 中国投入巨资开展研发（2018年以2 930亿美元的研发支出位居全球第二） | 仍然需要进口技术（仅3个国家就为中国贡献了一半以上的技术进口）和进口知识产权（中国的知识产权进口额是出口额的6倍） |
| 数据 | 中国拥有全球最大的网民群体（规模超过8亿人），产生了海量数据 | 跨境数据流动的规模很有限（位居全球第八，但仅为美国数据流动的20%） |

① 认为中国低估人民汇率以增加出口、积累外汇储备的观点见：Dani Rodrik, “Making Room for China in the World Economy,” *American Economic Review*, Vol. 100, No. 2, pp. 89–93. 上述观点依据的是巴拉萨-萨缪尔森效应，根据这个理论，一个国家的可贸易部门生产率提高，出口增加，会带来不可贸易部门的需求和工资上涨，导致物价水平上升和真实汇率升值，但是，中国在2001年加入世界贸易组织以后，可贸易部门生产率大幅提高，出口迅猛增加，外贸盈余大增，汇率并无升值。其实，这是因为中国大量的农村剩余劳动力进入不可贸易部门抑制了工资上涨的结果，并非中国政府故意抑制汇率升值来增加出口。见：Ju Jiandong, Lin Justin Yifu, Liu Qing and Shi Kang, “Structural changes and the real exchange rate dynamics”, *Journal of International Money and Finance*, 2020, Vol.107, available online 12 April 2020。

② 由人民出版社、外文出版社分别出版。

③ 麦肯锡全球研究院，《中国与世界：理解变化中的经济联系》，2019年7月。

续表

| | 中国的经济规模 | 进一步与世界融合的空间 |
|---|---|---|
| 环境影响 | 中国在可再生能源方面的投资占全球的45% | 依然是全球最大的碳排放源（占全球年总排放量的28%） |
| 文化 | 中国正在大举投资提升全球文化影响力（2017年，全球票房排名前50的电影有12%在中国拍摄了内容，而2010年仅为2%） | 文化影响力仍然有限（电视剧出口额仅为韩国的1/3） |

资料来源：麦肯锡全球研究院，《中国与世界：理解变化中的经济联系》，2019年7月。

# 8.1

# 中国在世界经济结构转型升级中的方位

## 8.1.1 中国的经济体量将重回世界第一

根据经济史学家麦迪逊的研究，在19世纪20年代，中国的经济总量仍然占当时世界经济总量的1/3，但是，在那之后急遽下降。1949年，中国经济总量占世界的比重只剩4.2%；到1978年，当中国开始从计划经济向市场经济转型时，其经济规模只回升到4.9%。按照汇率法计算，2019年中国GDP总量为14.5万亿美元，占全球的比重超过16%，仅次于美国位居第二。如果按照购买力平价法计算，中国在2014年便是全球最大的经济体，其经济总量不但远超日本，而且与美国和整个欧盟的体量不相上下。与GDP总量相称，中国目前不但是全球最大的制造业大国和工业专利大国，也是全球最大的贸易大国，以及第二大对外投资国。2019年，全年国内生产总值99.1万亿元，全年货物进出口总额31.54万亿元，其出口17.23万亿元，进口14.31万亿元，按美元计分别为4.58万亿美元、2.49万亿美元、2.08万亿美元。根据《2014年中国对外直接投资统计公报》数据，中国对外投资流量达1 231.2亿美元，首超日本成为世界第二大对外投资国。2018年实际使用外商直接投资金额8 856亿元，全年对外非金融类直接投资额7 974亿元。因此，尽管（按照汇率计算）与美国的经济总量有一定差距，但中国与美国已经是两个对世界经济结构转型升级有举足轻重影响的大国。

### 8.1.2 中国的经济发展水平世界居中

除了体量大，决定中国在世界经济结构转型升级中角色的另一个重要特征是其经济发展水平位居中等。按国际货币基金公布的数据，2019年中国人均国内生产总值为10 099美元，在统计的192个国家中居于第70位，低于欧美发达经济体，但又高于印度和非洲等诸多发展中经济体。中国目前按美元计算的人均GDP仅为美国的15.5%。除了人均收入水平，与禀赋结构水平更加贴近的一个指标是平均工资水平。与人均GDP一样，中国的工资水平现阶段也处于中间位置。中国改革开放后较长一段时期的平均工资水平远低于各大洲的主要发达国家，如大洋洲的澳大利亚、欧洲的德国、亚洲的日本和北美洲的美国，甚至非洲的南非，也远低于同属东亚的亚洲“四小龙”的工资水平。正如第6章所讨论过的，中国改革开放之后充分利用了这一低工资的比较优势迅速发展劳动力密集型产业，启动了持续的经济增长。现阶段，中国的收入水平以及对应的工资水平则远高于诸多“一带一路”沿线国家及非洲国家的水平。

中国经过改革开放后40多年的高速发展已经步入中等收入国家行列，禀赋条件发生了较大的变化，如图8.1所示。对应地，禀赋结构决定的中国产业结构也发生了相应的变化。随着劳动人口数量逐渐下降和资本存量加速上升以及由此带来的要素相对丰裕度变化，中国经济的总供给结构将发生调整。根据范志勇和赵晓男对1981—2011年的统计数据的估算，当给定其他条件不变时，随着劳动力资源日益稀缺和资本存量增加，中国将生产更多投资品，减少消费品和出口品的生产。这意味着随着要素相对丰裕度的改变，中国供给结构将出现系统性调整。[①]正如第6章所测算的，由于禀赋结构的升级，中国存在大量失去比较优势的劳动力密集型产业，这个数据按照不同口径估算都有数千万之巨。但与此同时，相对于发达国家的禀赋结构水平，以及如与发达国家的人均收入水平差距所揭示的（回顾第1章的相关内容），中国的禀赋结构水平依然远离世界前沿，故产业结构都有很大的转型升级空间。第10章我们将进一步讨论中国这样的发展水平居中但体量巨大以及内部异质性很大的经济体的五

① 范志勇、赵晓男，“要素相对丰裕度改变与中国供给结构调整”，《世界经济》，2014年第8期。

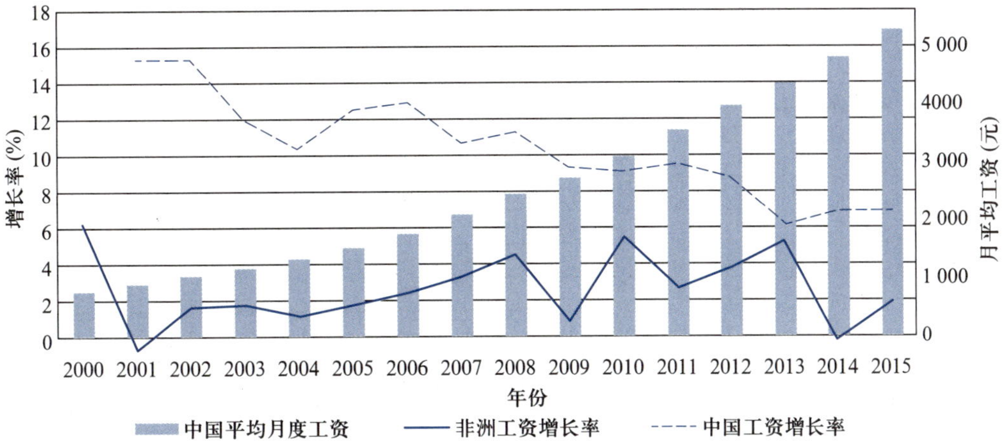


**图8.1 过去十几年来中国的工资水平及其上涨率（以及非洲的工资变化）**

资料来源：国际劳工组织，Global Wage Report 2018/19。

类产业——领先型、追赶型、转进型、弯道超车型、战略型产业的因势利导方式。

### 8.1.3 中国经济结构层次的复杂多样性

当然，与世界其他经济体相比，中国还有一个显著的经济结构特征，那就是经济结构层次复杂而多样。中国是世界上人口最多，经济结构变迁最剧烈的发展中经济体。首先，在区域经济结构层面上，中国有32个省、直辖市、自治区，300余个地市，近3 000个区县，这些地区之间的禀赋结构水平差距非常大，对应的生产结构也千差万别。整体上而言，中国东部地区的禀赋结构水平远高于全国平均水平，中部的禀赋结构水平次之，西部的禀赋结构水平最低。以省级比较为例，如图8.2所示，2018年相对于北京人均地区生产总值达14万元（现价人民币）而言，只有上海市、天津市、江苏省、浙江省大致与其相当，分别为其96.27%、86.09%、82.14%、70.35%，相对发达的东部福建省、广东省、山东省，也只有其65.04%、61.62%、54.39%，宁夏回族自治区、湖南省、海南省、河南省、河北省、新疆维吾尔自治区、四川省、青海省、江西省、安徽省、山西省、黑龙江省、西藏自治区则不足其40%，内蒙古自治区、重庆市、湖北省、陕西省、吉林省、辽宁省也不足其50%，广西壮族自治区、贵州省、云南省、甘肃省则不足其30%。在最细分区域——近3 000个区县层面，

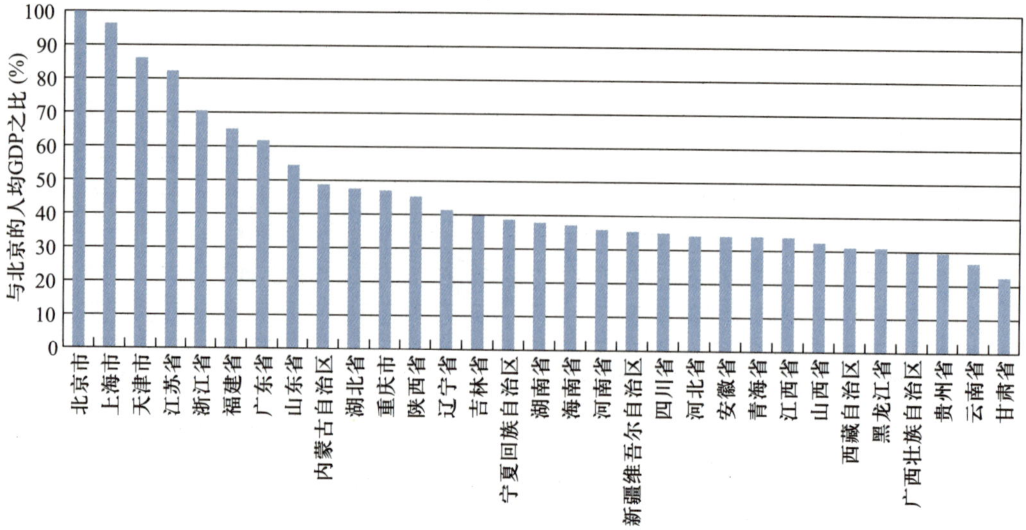


**图8.2 2018年中国内地各个省份相对于北京的人均GDP（%）**

数据来源：国家统计局。

这种禀赋结构的差异还会进一步被放大，如图8.3所示。[①]各种各样的区域发展样板都可以观察到，如图8.3中的各种散点：高收入且高增长，高收入且低增长，中等收入且高增长，中等收入且低增长，低收入且高增长，低收入且低增长，等等。在城乡之间，2019年中国有8.5亿城镇人口和5.5亿农村人口，城市居民人均可支配收入达到42 359元，而农村居民人均可支配收入只有16 021元。中国偏远地区的农村贫困人口是目前扶贫攻坚的重点。

对应于巨大的区域经济结构差异的是中国产业结构的多样性。按照联合国统计署的产业分类，中国是唯一一个产业门类齐全的国家。目前，在中国的产业结构中，既有生产率水平处于世界前沿的领先型产业，也有前面提到的由于要素禀赋结构的变化而逐步失去比较优势的劳动密集型产业，当然绝大部分产业的生产率水平还处于世界前沿内部（第10章我们将专门讨论这些产业类型）。因此，中国内部区域之间的巨大差异以及产业结构的多样性使得中国嵌入世界经济结构转型升级的程度更加密切和复杂，几乎全世界任何经济体的经济结构

① 有鉴于此，我们在第6章讨论的世界制造业迁徙的“雁阵模式”也会发生在中国内部这些差异极大的地区之间。例如，曲玥等采用中国制造业规模以上企业数据，从县级经济体的水平上考察了中国制造业是否发生“飞雁”模式的转移。其研究发现，产业聚集的效应在2004年以前一直发挥着促使产业向东部沿海地区集聚的重要作用，而在这之后该效应的效果逐渐下降，表现为制造业特别是劳动密集型产业出现向中西部内陆地区移转的趋势。此时，企业的综合经营成本上升和要素成本的提高逐渐成为诱致产业转移的重要因素。（曲玥、蔡昉、张晓波，“‘飞雁模式’发生了吗？——对1998—2008年中国制造业的分析”，《经济学（季刊）》，2013年第3期）

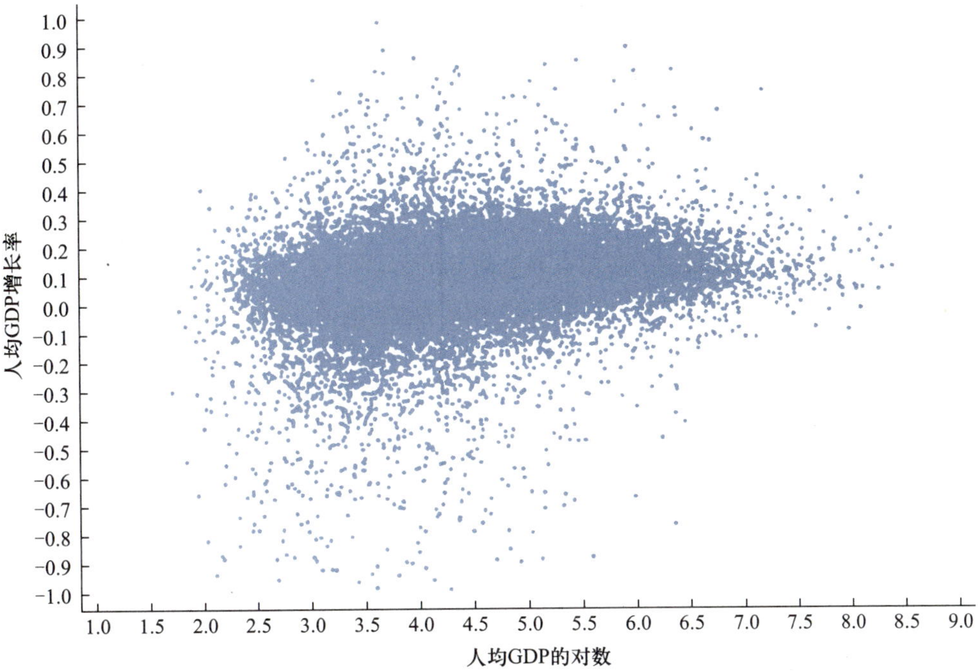


**图8.3 1998—2013年中国各个区县的收入水平与经济增长的组合**

资料来源：根据历年《中国县域统计年鉴》测算绘制。

转型升级都可以找到与中国的匹配之处——回顾第5章图5.37所示的中国各个区县“两头在外”模式（外资与外贸）的散点图。总之，如果将中国的经济结构转型升级与全球经济格局匹配起来，不论对世界还是对中国自己都将会产生巨大的能量。

### 8.1.4 中国与世界的经济结构深度耦合

如本章开篇所介绍的，整个计划经济时代由于中国采取了违背比较优势的进口替代战略，不但未能融入世界经济，反而与其脱钩。那个时期中国在世界贸易中的角色微不足道，1953年中国的贸易量占世界贸易量的比重只有1.5%，到1977年进一步下降到0.6%。从贸易依存度（进出口总额占GDP的比重）上看也微不足道：1960年为8.74%，到1977年依然维持在8.39%。改革开放之后，中国迅速融入世界经济，贸易依存度在国际金融危机之前的2007年就上升到62.11%。2011年12月11日是中国加入世界贸易组织10周年纪念日，这一天国务院发表了《中国的对外贸易》白皮书，指出中国已经与世界更加紧密地联系在一起，有力推动了中国的现代化建设，也促进了世界的繁荣与进步。改革开放后，中国全方位发展对外贸易，与世界上绝大多数国家和地区建立了贸易关系。贸易伙伴已经由1978年的几十个国家和地区发展到2010年的231个国家和地区。欧盟、美国、东盟、日本、金砖国家等成为中国主要贸易伙伴。中国加入世界贸易组织之后到国际金融危机爆发前，中国进一步融入世界经济的速度超过世界平均的开放水平。例如，2000年至2009年，中国出口量和进口量年均增长速度分别为17%和15%，远远高于同期世界贸易总量3%的年均增长速度。中国不仅加强了与发达国家的经济融合，也与新兴市场和发展中国家加速融合。例如，2005年至2010年，中国与东盟货物贸易占中国货物贸易比重由9.2%提高到9.8%，与其他金砖国家货物贸易所占比重由4.9%提高到6.9%，与拉丁美洲和非洲货物贸易所占比重分别由3.5%和2.8%提高到6.2%和4.3%。图8.4和图8.5是2015年中国内地对全世界的进口和出口目的地分布。到2010年，中国关税总水平就已经降至9.8%，其中农产品平均税率降至15.2%，工业品平均税率降至8.9%。关税约束率自2005年起一直维持在100%。在世界贸易组织服务贸易分类的160个分部门中，中国在2010年就已经开放了100个，开放范围已经接近发达国家的平均水平。2020年4月1日，中国全面开放了金融业，这意味着中国向世界敞开了最后一扇门。麦肯锡全球研究院的“MGI连接指数”根据商品、服务、金融、人员和数据流动情况对各个经济体的参与度进行了排名，结果显示，中国2017年的连接程度位居全球第9。但如前文表8.1所示，中国与世界未来还有巨大的融合空间。因此，至关重要的便是弄清楚中国经济的体量与特征以及如何与世界每个经济体的经济结构转型升级进行准确匹配以释放全球发展的巨能。

总之，尽管受到各种各样的因素的阻碍，中国经济与世界经济的关系已经发生了剧烈的结构性变化，深度融合在一起。把中国经济发展看作“威胁”和“挑战”，试图把中国挤出全球产业链、供应链、价值链，使中国与世界经济“脱钩”，既不可行，而且有害。例如，

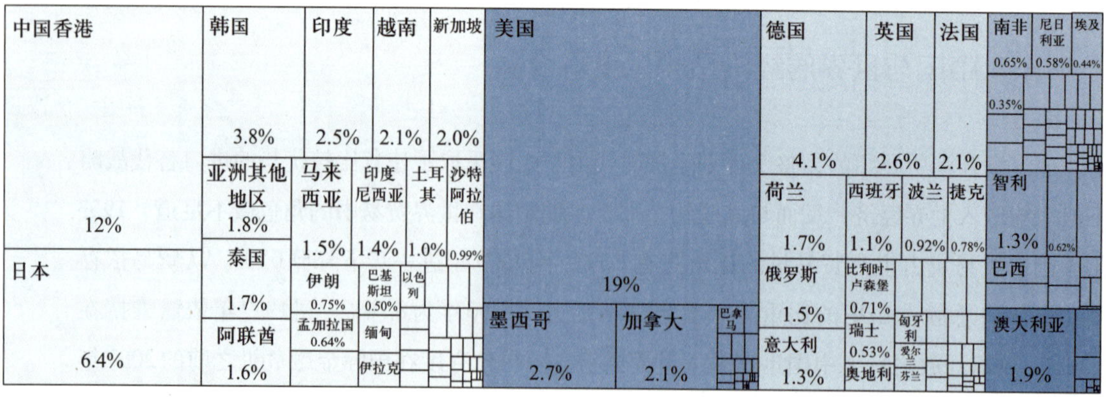


图8.4 2015年中国内地出口目的地分布

资料来源：经济复杂性研究中心。

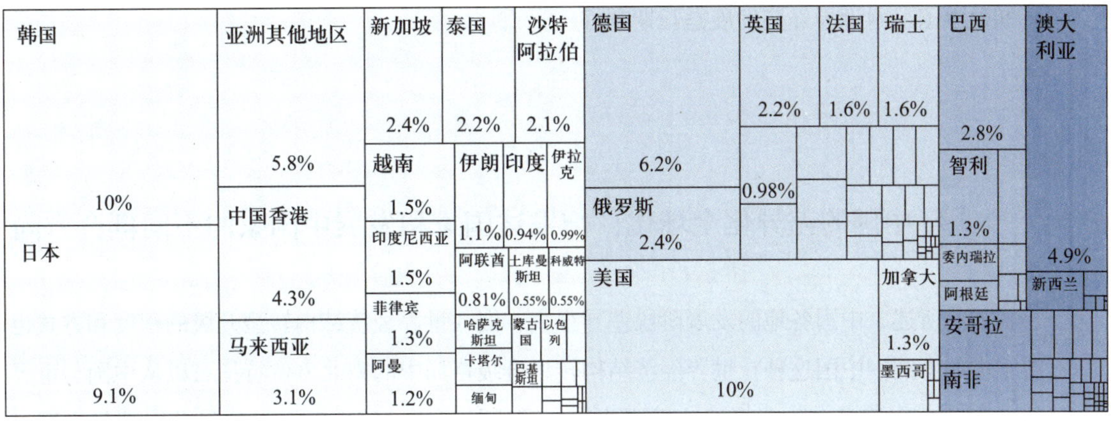


**图8.5 2015年中国内地进口目的地分布**

资料来源：经济复杂性研究中心。

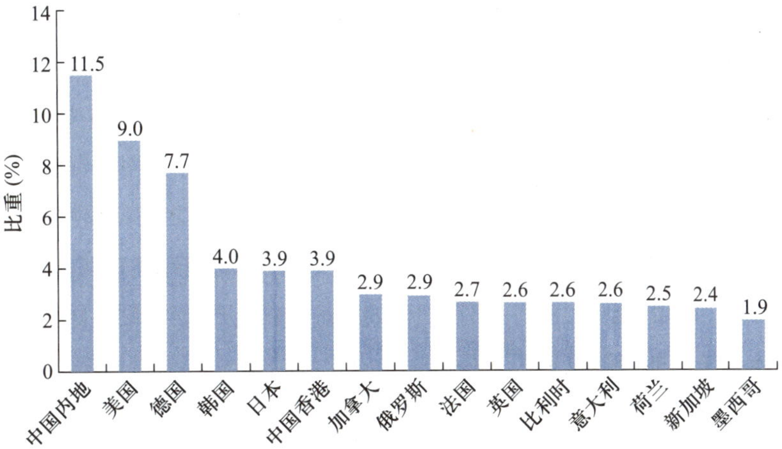


**图8.6 世界主要经济体中间产品出口占世界的比重**

数据来源：UN Comtrade.

2018年占全球货物出口额52%的中间产品出口额达9.7万亿美元，① 其中中国的比重为11.5%，超过美国的9%和德国的7.7%，如图8.6所示。② 经济运行更稳定、增长质量更高、增长前景

① 2018年全球中间产品出口额占全球货物出口额超过一半意味着目前世界的产品内分工体系已经形成和全球价值链体系已经处于主导地位，这使得世界上几乎开放发展的国家都融入了世界经济的产业分工体系、产品分工体系、技术分工体系、市场分工体系和价值分工体系，世界各国经济相互依赖、相互依存。

② 从图8.6中可以看到目前中国、美国和德国对全球价值链体系的支配角色。鞠建东基于全球生产、贸易结构呈现出三足鼎立的状态，提出了与此相适应，以美、中、德为核心国的北美自贸区、欧盟、华夏共同体的G3新框架，很可能代表了一个全球经济治理体系的未来。可参考：鞠建东、余心玎，"'一体两翼、三足鼎立'：贸易新常态、治理新框架、开放新战略"，《清华金融评论》，2016年第11期。

可期的中国，对世界经济发展是长期利好。①

### 8.1.5 中国的差异化全球化：与发达国家和发展中国家的不同耦合方向

如前所述，中国各地的发展阶段差异很大，嵌入世界经济结构转型升级的程度和方式也有很大的不同。中国这种在世界经济结构转型升级格局中的南北方位特征可以从中国与世界的经贸关系中管窥。欧美等发达经济体与中国比较优势的巨大互补性使得其依然是中国最大的贸易伙伴和招商引资目标以及重要的对外投资目的地。尽管在贸易摩擦不断的情况下，2016年和2018年欧盟和美国占中国内地出口比重分别高达34.6%和35.6%，占进口比重达21.6%和25.2%。2017年在中国内地实际投入外资金额排名前十位的国家和地区依次为中国香港（989.2亿美元）、新加坡（48.3亿美元）、中国台湾（47.3亿美元）、韩国（36.9亿美元）、日本（32.7亿美元）、美国（31.3亿美元）、荷兰（21.7亿美元）、德国（15.4亿美元）、英国（15.0亿美元）、丹麦（8.2亿美元）合计1 246亿美元，占实际使用外资总额的95.1%。2015年年底，中国对外直接投资存量中发达经济体占比14%，而北美洲和欧洲占比就达12.4%。后面将进一步通过外贸和外资来梳理讨论中国与发达国家经济结构的匹配情况。

与此同时，随着中国“一带一路”倡议的推进，以及产业伴随对外直接投资的转移，发展中经济体与中国的经贸投资关系将进一步强化。例如，2017年中国对亚洲、非洲和拉丁美洲的对外直接投资流量分别达1 100亿美元、41亿美元、141亿美元。总之，如第6章所讨论的南北合作与南南合作的产业基础一样，以制造业对外投资为例，中国在发达经济体的制造业投资主要是为了贴近其市场和学习其先进的技术管理经验等，而中国在发展中经济体的制造业投资则主要是转移劳动力密集型产业。例如，2015年年底，中国对欧洲直接投资存量中制造业占比达19.2%，排在所有行业的第二位；中国对非洲直接投资存量中制造业占比达13.3%，排在所有行业的第三位。反过来，中国又将为这些比中国发展水平低的发展中国家生产的大量劳动密集型产品提供巨大的消费市场。事实上，早在2010年，中国就已经对36个已建交最不发达国家原产的4 700多个税目商品实施进口零关税，约占全部税则税目的60%。自2008年以来，中国一直是最不发达国家第一大出口市场，早在2010年中国自最不发达国家的货物进口总额就约占这些国家出口总额的1/4。

---

① World Bank, “Global Economic Prospects: Heightened Tensions, Subdued Investment” , 2019.

因此，正是中国这种发展阶段位居中等但经济体量庞大的快速发展的大国特征，让中国成为推动世界经济结构转型升级的中流砥柱。对于老牌的发达国家来讲，中国将成为其高质量产品与服务以及高端产业产品和投资与技术转移的最为重要的市场；对于发展中国家来讲，中国将成为其初级产品最重要的市场以及劳动力密集型产业转移承接与产能合作最为重要的伙伴。不论是发达国家还是发展中国家，中国经济由于处于中等收入水平阶段，对二者形成的都是比较优势互补，合作共赢的机会大于竞争。同样，对于中国经济结构转型升级而言，一方面需要将失去比较优势的劳动力密集型产业转移到禀赋结构水平更低的发展中经济体；另一方面也需要加快“腾笼换鸟”，促进原有产业就地升级以及从禀赋结构水平更高的发达国家引进新技术和新产业，以培育和促进新兴产业的逐步壮大。因此，中国与发达国家和发展中国家的这种经济互补性格局决定了其耦合的不同方向。这种比较优势的互补性也决定了中国未来不同于发达国家单向的全球化方式。

### 8.1.6 中国与世界经济联系的多样性：不同国家不同行业与中国的不同联系

正如我们在前面7章中所展示的，世界经济结构的多样性远非发达经济体和发展中经济体这样简单的二元划分，全世界每个国家的禀赋结构及其对应的产业结构都千差万别，中国各个地区、各行各业也千差万别。因此，世界与中国的经济联系必然也是多样性的。麦肯锡全球研究院对73个经济体和20个行业的分析证实了这一结论，不同地区和行业对中国经济的依存度存在较大差异，如图8.7和图8.8所示。[①]国家层面的依存度体现在各个经济体对中国的进口（国内产值出口到中国的比例）、出口（来自中国的进口额占国内消费总额的比例）和资本（来自中国的外商直接投资占国内投资总额的比例）的依存度。自2007年以来，在其研究的73个经济体中，有69个经济体的国内产值相对于中国进口的依存度上升；有72个经济体的国内消费相对于中国出口的依存度上升；还有58个经济体的国内投资相对于中国资本的依存度上升。总的来讲，地理位置邻近中国、资源贸易占比较高，并且参与跨境资本流动的国家对中国经济的依存度最高。具体来讲，亚洲经济体与中国的联系因区域供应链而越发紧密。亚洲国家对中国经济的依存度一直在上升，尤其是那些对中国出口比重较大的国

---

① 资料来源：麦肯锡全球研究院：《中国与世界：理解变化中的经济联系》，2019年。

家。它们往往通过全球价值链与中国建立了紧密的联系，对中国贸易在国内产值中占比很高。例如，新加坡的与中国的贸易额（包括进口和出口）几乎占其国内产值的30%。马来西亚、新加坡、菲律宾这三个国家的最大贸易伙伴都是中国。其中一些经济体对中国资本的依存度也同样明显。例如，2013—2017年，马来西亚从中国获得的外商直接投资相当于其国内投资总额的6%，在新加坡则为5%。资源丰富的国家更依赖中国的需求。对外出口自然资源的国家显著依赖中国的需求。以南非为例，对中国出口额目前已占其国内总产值的15%，而2003—2007年这一比率仅为2%。与之相似，对中国出口额目前已占澳大利亚总产值的16%，先前这一比率仅为4%。仅铁矿石出口一项就占澳大利亚对中国出口总额的48%（矿产和金属共计占到出口总额的84%），澳大利亚采掘业21%的产出都流向了中国。一些新兴经济体和体量较小的成熟经济体也高度依赖中国的投资。举例而言，2013—2017年，埃及从中国获得的外商直接投资相当于其国内投资总额的13%，巴基斯坦则为8%。又如，中国不只是非洲最大的贸易伙伴，也是其最大的基础设施融资来源和第三大国外援助来源。相比之下，大型发达经济体对中国经济的依存度较低。从国内经济体量的角度考虑，发达经济体（尤其是西欧和北美各国）在贸易和投资方面对中国的依存度相对较低。对中国出口额通常在其总产出中占比不足5%，从中国进口额在其国内消费中的占比也不足5%。另外，来自中国的外商直接投资占其国内投资的比例更低于1%。然而，如前所讨论的，过去以及现阶段中国对发达国家的贸易和资本依存度却较高。2018年欧盟和美国占中国内地出口比重达35.6%，占进口比重达25.2%。对中国投资前十几位的地区几乎都是发达经济体。当然，中国对发达国家的依存度也存在不同。例如，中国去海外的留学生六成都集中在美国、英国和澳大利亚。

麦肯锡全球研究院也选取了20个可贸易性较强的基础产业和制造业，综合分析了全球各国对中国消费、生产和进出口的依存度，如图8.8所示。由于中国的经济体量极为庞大，几乎所有行业都在一定程度上依存于中国：在20个行业当中，中国有17个行业的消费份额在全球总消费中占比超过20%。根据贸易依存度可将行业归纳为5个类别，中国在电子、机械和设备领域已经全面融入全球价值链。在这些深度整合的贸易领域当中，中国的角色既是供应方，也是市场。中国在这些领域的高占比反映出中国已经高度融入全球贸易——中国占全球出口总额的17% ~ 28%，占全球进口总额的9% ~ 16%。中国在这些领域的产出占比也很可观，全球份额高达38% ~ 42%。对于贸易属性极高的轻工制造和劳动密集型产业而言，全球各国高度依赖中国的产出，所以中国当之无愧地被称为“世界工厂”。中国在全球轻工制造领域（例如纺织品和服装）的份额甚至高达52%。在很多情况下，全球各国也高度依赖于中国的出口：中国占据了全球纺织品和服装出口总额的40%，家具出口总额的26%。随着中国的工业化不断取得进展，全球上游产业对中国的依存度均有所提高。那些为进一步加工提供原材料的行业都要依赖中国的进口。中国制造业的增长大幅提升了对原材料和中间

依存度 最低 最高

| 类型 | 国家 | 对中国出口占国内产值比例(%) | | 对中国进口占国内消费比例(%) | | 来自中国的外商直接投资占国内总投资额比例(%) | |
|---|---|---|---|---|---|---|---|
| | | 2003—2007年 | 2013—2017年 | 2003—2007年 | 2013—2017年 | 2003—2007年 | 2013—2017年 |
| 地理位置依存度 | 韩国 | 8 | 11 | 4 | 6 | <1 | <1 |
| | 马来西亚 | 8 | 11 | 5 | 11 | <1 | 6 |
| | 菲律宾 | 12 | 8 | 6 | 14 | 6 | <1 |
| | 新加坡 | 10 | 11 | 12 | 18 | 2 | 5 |
| | 越南 | 3 | 11 | 6 | 13 | 3 | 1 |
| 资源依存度 | 澳大利亚 | 4 | 16 | 3 | 7 | <1 | 3 |
| | 智利 | 5 | 13 | 3 | 10 | <1 | <1 |
| | 哥斯达黎加 | 9 | 9 | 2 | 5 | 3 | <1 |
| | 加纳 | <1 | 8 | 5 | 18 | <1 | 4 |
| | 南非 | 2 | 15 | 2 | 6 | <1 | 3 |
| 资本依存度 | 埃及 | <1 | <1 | 3 | 5 | 1 | 13 |
| | 巴基斯坦 | <1 | 1 | 3 | 7 | 2 | 8 |
| | 秘鲁 | 4 | 7 | 1 | 5 | 2 | 6 |
| | 葡萄牙 | <1 | 2 | <1 | 3 | <1 | 3 |
| 发达经济体 | 美国 | <1 | 2 | 3 | 6 | <1 | <1 |
| | 德国 | 2 | 4 | 2 | 3 | <1 | <1 |
| | 日本 | 4 | 5 | 3 | 5 | <1 | <1 |
| | 英国 | <1 | 2 | 2 | 5 | <1 | 2 |

图8.7 世界不同国家对中国的不同依存度

资料来源：麦肯锡全球研究院，《中国与世界：理解变化中的经济联系》，2019年。

品（用于加工成最终商品）的需求，人均收入的增长也推升了中国的整体商品需求。2003—2007年，中国贡献了全球采掘业进口额的7%，2013—2017年这一比例更升高到21%。与前几类行业相反，在另一些全球贸易属性较强的行业中，中国并不是主要参与者。在一些着重于服务快速增长的本地需求且有本地成分要求的行业，尽管这些行业的贸易强度很高，但并不太依赖中国。以制药行业为例，中国的贸易额仅占全球药品出口总额的4%，进口总额的3%。同样，虽然汽车领域的贸易强度较高，但中国的贸易额仅占全球出口总额的3%、进口总额的7%。当然，中国对这些行业都有相当庞大的潜在需求。当然，没有加入全球贸易的“本地自产自销”行业对中国和其他外部国家的依存度往往都较低。尽管贸易强度相对较低，但中国仍在其中一些行业占据了很大份额。举例而言，中国的金属制造行业占据了全球出口总额的23%，农产品行业则占据了全球进口总额的18%。

低 … 高

| 类型 | 行业名称 | 贸易强度 | 中国占全球出口总额的比例(%) | | 中国占全球进口总额的比例(%) | |
|---|---|---|---|---|---|---|
| | | | 2003—2007年 | 2013—2017年 | 2003—2007年 | 2013—2017年 |
| 高度整合 | 计算机、电子和光学产品 | | 15 | 28 | 12 | 16 |
| | 电气设备 | | 16 | 27 | 7 | 9 |
| | 其他机械和设备 | | 7 | 17 | 8 | 9 |
| 高度依存于中国的出口 | 纺织、服装和皮革 | | 26 | 40 | 5 | 5 |
| | 家具、安全、消防等 | | 17 | 26 | 2 | 4 |
| | 其他非金属矿产 | | 11 | 22 | 5 | 8 |
| | 橡胶和塑料 | | 10 | 19 | 5 | 7 |
| | 基础金属 | | 8 | 13 | 8 | 8 |
| 高度依存于中国的进口 | 采掘业 | | 1 | 1 | 7 | 21 |
| | 化工 | | 4 | 9 | 9 | 12 |
| | 纸和纸制品 | | 3 | 9 | 6 | 12 |
| 对中国的贸易依存度很小的全球价值链 | 其他运输设备 | | 3 | 6 | 3 | 5 |
| | 制药 | | 2 | 4 | 1 | 3 |
| | 机动车及拖车 | | 1 | 3 | 2 | 7 |
| | 焦炭和成品油 | | 2 | 4 | 4 | 6 |
| 自产自销 | 食品、饮料和烟草 | | 3 | 4 | 3 | 6 |
| | 金属制品 | | 14 | 23 | 3 | 5 |
| | 木材及木制品 | | 11 | 22 | 2 | 3 |
| | 印刷和媒体 | | 8 | 18 | 2 | 4 |
| | 农业、林业和渔业 | | 5 | 5 | 7 | 19 |

图8.8 技术、劳动密集型商品和资源价值链对中国的贸易依存度

资料来源：麦肯锡全球研究院，《中国与世界：理解变化中的经济联系》，2019年。

# 8.2

# 中国在世界经济结构转型升级中的力量

## 8.2.1 中国是世界经济增长的引擎

1979—2019年，中国经济以年均9.3%的速度快速发展，成为全球经济增长的重要引擎。2008年，全球遭遇严重金融危机，世界经济受到重创，中国采取一系列有效措施成功应对危机，经济迅速回升向好，并持续保持中高速增长，成为世界经济增长的主要稳定器和动力源。2016年到2018年的三年，中国经济总量连续跨越70万亿元、80万亿元和90万亿元大关，2019年达到99.1万亿元，占世界经济的比重接近16%。2013—2018年，中国对世界经济增长的平均贡献率超过28.1%。2013—2016年，如果没有中国因素，世界经济年均增速将放缓0.6个百分点，波动强度将提高5.2%。[①]麦肯锡全球研究院发布报告认为，2000—2017年，世界对中国经济的综合依存度指数从0.4逐步上升至1.2，中国贡献了全球制造业总产出的35%。[②]

我们认为，中国在2008年开始还有20年年均增长8%的潜力，2010年开始经济增长下滑主要原因是外部性和周期性影响。由于发达国家未进行必要的结构性改革，增长会长期低于往年3% ~ 3.5%的增长率，抑制收入和消费的增长，减少进口需求，抑制中国的出口。未来中国的增长主要靠内需。中国作为中等收入国家还有巨大的投资于产业升级和技术创新的空间，中国也有足够的财政政策空间和储蓄支持投资，创造就业，增加收入和消费，在8%的

① 中华人民共和国国务院新闻办公室，《新时代的中国与世界》，人民出版社，2019年版。

② 麦肯锡全球研究院，《中国与世界：理解变化中的经济联系》，2019年。

增长潜力下，中国有可能在2030年以前靠内需的增长维持6%的左右的增长。[①] 中国新产业新业态快速崛起便是其经济结构快速转型推动经济增长有力佐证。2018年，高技术制造业、战略性新兴产业和装备制造业增加值分别比上年增长11.7%、8.9%和8.1%；新能源汽车、智能电视、锂离子电池和集成电路行业分别比上年增长66.2%、17.7%、12.9%和11.2%；信息服务业同比增速高达30.7%，其中移动游戏、网络购物、约车平台、旅游平台、大数据云计算等子行业增速达30% ~ 50%，每个子行业都诞生了一批独角兽企业（第10章中将进一步介绍）。

### 8.2.2 中国拥有全球最具活力的消费市场

中国拥有全球最具活力的庞大消费市场，既是“世界工厂”，也是“全球市场”。中国有14亿人口，4亿中等收入群体，市场规模全球最大。中国消费空间和潜力巨大，并且消费结构也处在快速升级的过程中。改革开放初期中国居民的消费主要是解决温饱，而今将全面实现小康。例如，1978年城镇和农村恩格尔系数分别高达57.5%和67.7%，2018年这一数据下降到27.7%和30.1%。按照世界银行的统计，2018年最终消费总额全球为62.6万亿美元，中

① 1978—2016年，中国经济平均每年增长速度是9.6%，但是从2010年以后逐年下滑，2016年为6.7%。原因是什么呢？学界主要有两种不同的看法：一种认为是由中国的内部性、体制性、结构性的原因造成的，另一种则认为2010年以后的增长速度下滑主要是外部性和周期性因素造成的。中国有没有体制性、机制性、结构性的问题？当然有。因为中国不但是一个发展中国家，还是一个转型中国家，而且中国是用渐进双轨的方式来转型的，所以拿标准的经济理论模型来看，中国必然有很多体制性、机制性、结构性的扭曲。但是这些扭曲是长期存在的，应该说我们的改革是在不断深化的，与20世纪八九十年代那些体制机制性的扭曲来比，应该是越来越少的，而不是越来越多的。因此，说2010年以后中国的体制性、机制性的问题更严重了，这个看法说不过去。更重要的是，中国的经济不能只看中国，因为中国现在按照购买力平价计算已经是世界第一大经济体，并且是全世界第一大贸易国，中国的经济表现会影响世界，同样，世界的经济表现也会影响中国。以全球的眼光来看，2010年以后中国的经济增长速度持续下滑，更多的是外部性、周期性因素。我们可以看一看其他金砖国家或者是跟中国同样发展程度的发展中国家的情况。中国经济增长率从2010年的10.6%下降到2016年的6.7%，其他的金砖国家，比如俄罗斯，2010年的增长速度是4.5%，2015年是−2.8%，2016年是−0.2%。巴西2010年的增长速度是7.6%，2015年是−3.8%，2016年是−3.6%，同样下滑，而且幅度比中国大。印度2010年的增长速度跟中国同一个水平，达到10.3%，2015年是7.9%，高于中国的6.9%。但是有两个原因必须考虑：一是印度2012年的增长速度下滑到5.1%，中国维持在7.3%，印度下滑的幅度比中国大，有触底反弹的因素；二是2014年年底印度调整统计方式，使经济增长率增加了1个百分点。如果把上述两个因素去掉以后，印度2015年的增长速度并不比中国高。2016年，中国是6.7%的增长，印度则是6.6% 的增长，所以，印度从2010年以来整体增长态势与中国一样。但考虑触底反弹和统计方法两个因素，其实印度下滑幅度比中国大。另外，土耳其在2010年的时候，经济增长速度是8.9%，2011年是10.1%，2016年是3.3%。更详细的分析讨论可参考：Lin Justin Yifu, Wan Guanghua and Peter J. Morgan, “Prospects for a Re-acceleration of Economic Growth in the PRC” , *Journal of Comparative Economics*, 2016, Vol.44, No.4, pp.842−853。

国为7.3万亿美元，约占全球总额的11.7%。最终消费总额已经相当于欧元区国家总水平的71.8%左右。根据《中国统计年鉴》的数据，2019年中国居民人均消费支出21 559元，城镇居民人均消费支出28 063元人民币，农村居民人均消费支出13 328元。根据《2019年国民经济和社会发展统计公报》的数据，全年最终消费支出对国内生产总值增长的贡献率为57.8%。2019全年社会消费品零售总额41.2万亿元，其中城镇消费品零售额35.13万亿元，乡村消费品零售额6.03万亿元。按消费类型统计，商品零售额36.49万亿元，餐饮收入额4.67万亿元。2019年实物商品网上零售额达8.5万亿元。未来15年（到2035年），中国进口商品和服务将分别超过30万亿美元和10万亿美元。①

根据经济学人智库预测，随着产业与就业的转移，中小城市经济与居民收入将出现增长，其针对286个地级市的统计分析显示，到2030年地级市的居民人口中，高收入的比例将大幅增加，地级市中的富裕城市将越来越多，中高收入人群的分布将保持扩大，如图8.9所示。事实上，日益庞大的中产阶层已经使中国成为诸如汽车、智能手机等产品全球最大的消费市场。另外，中国的消费也变得越来越前卫和开放。例如，阿里巴巴公司"双十一"大数据显示，中小城市"双十一"购买人群占比逐渐提升，且这一趋势仍然在强化中。2017年阿里巴巴公司年货节数据显示，中小城市和农村对洋年货的消费偏好在显著提升，尤其是在消费升级代表的母婴品类方面，农村消费者在海外母婴产品的消费金额占洋货总消费金额的比例

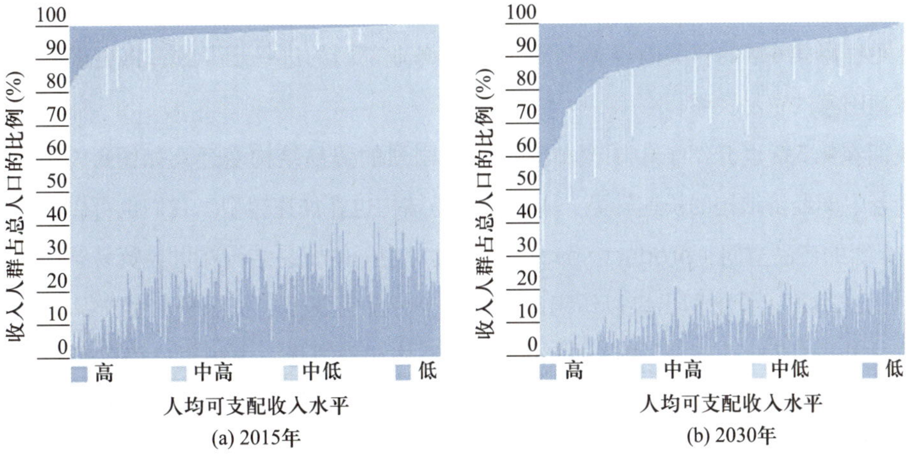


**图8.9 2015年与2030年（估计）中国地级市人均可支配收入分布情况**

注：分布为占总人口的百分比，经过灰色收入调整后，2015年不变价。

资料来源：经济学人智库。

① 麦肯锡全球研究院：《中国与世界：理解变化中的经济联系》，2019年。

达50.23%（同期城市消费者该比重仅为25.69%）。此外，城市数据亦显示出了三、四、五线城市的消费潜力。偏好洋货消费的前十位城市中，包括一线城市的北京、上海，二线城市的沈阳，三线城市的昆明、哈尔滨、乌鲁木齐，以及四、五线城市的抚顺、克拉玛依、巴音郭楞蒙古自治州、石河子。这反映出中小城市对商品品质、品牌、产地的要求正在逐步提高。

### 8.2.3 中国将长期居于全球最大的贸易国

我们在第5章已经介绍了中国改革开放之后充分利用国内国际两种资源和两个市场大获成功的全球化经验。在2010年中国就成为最大出口国，2013年成为最大贸易国。尽管近年来中国的贸易增长趋势下滑明显，但依然是全球最大的贸易大国，而且在可预见的未来，这个地位将难以撼动。2015年中国占据了全球货物贸易份额的15%，将近位居第二、第三位的美国和德国之和。2018年中国货物进出口总额30.5万亿元，比上年增长9.7%；出口16.42万亿元，增长7.1%；进口14.09万亿元，增长12.9%。货物进出口顺差2.33万亿元，比上年减少5 217亿元。全年服务进出口总额5.24万亿元，比上年增长11.5%。其中，服务出口1.77万亿元，增长14.6%；服务进口3.47万亿元，增长10.0%。服务进出口逆差1.7万亿元。中国这种货物贸易顺差和服务贸易逆差的结构与美国截然相反，反映了二者比较优势的巨大差异和互补性（可回顾第6章的相关内容）。未来中国服务业部门的进一步开放，将更进一步强化中国与发达国家的贸易关系。

我们在第5章也介绍了中国改革开放以来剧烈的贸易结构变迁，如图8.10和图8.11所示。随着中国经济结构的快速转型，中国的贸易结构也在加速转型。我们也可以进一步利用第3章介绍的产品空间（product space）①工具对中国的贸易结构在世界贸易结构中的方位进行对比：2000年，中国出口以纺织品、鞋帽等劳动密集型、资源密集型产品为主，位于产品森林外围；2005年，产品森林核心－外围结构初现雏形，中国出口仍以劳动密集型为主，但所占比重逐年下降，开始缓慢发展核心地带的资本密集型产品；2011年，中国密集生产核心地带的"机械设备集群""综合化学品集群"的技术密集型产品，并保持强劲的增

① C. A. Hidalgo, B. Klinger, A.-L. Barabasi, R. Hausmann, "The Product Space Conditions the Development of Nations", Science, 2007, Vol.317, No.5837, pp.482–487。

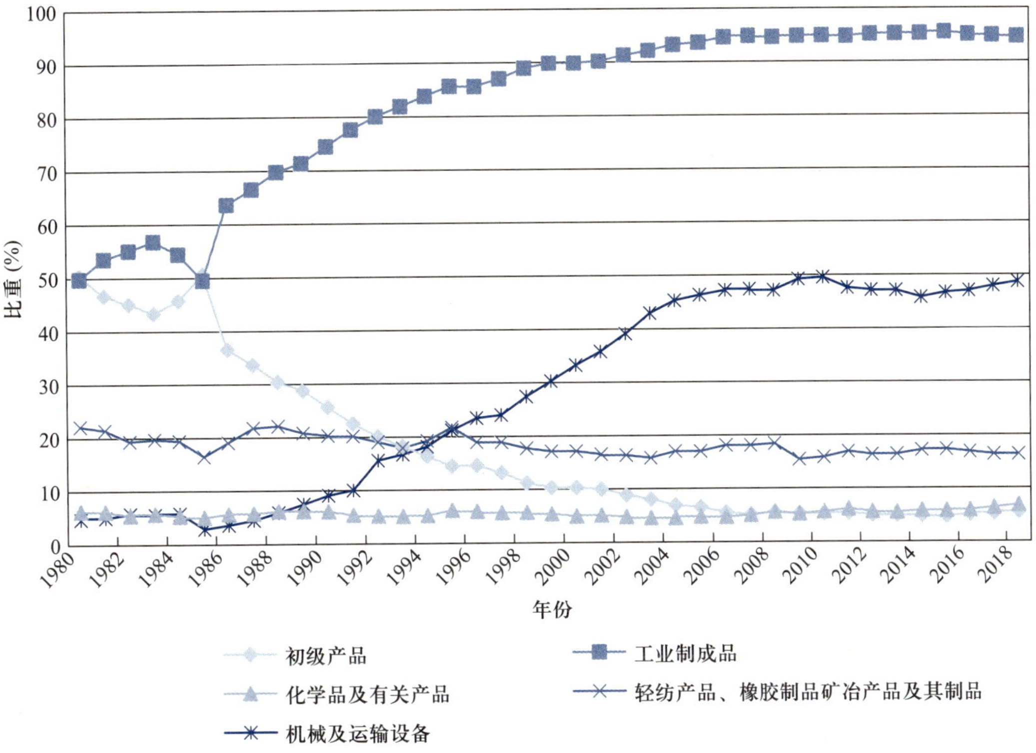


**图8.10 1980—2018年来中国出口结构变迁**

资料来源：国家统计局。

长势头，这反映出中国正着力发展先进技术行业，从重“量”走向重“质”。[①]中国目前的纺织纱线、织物及制品、服装及衣着附件、鞋类、家具及其零件等劳动力密集型产品的出口正在逐步减少，食品及主要供食用的活动物以及矿物燃料、润滑油及有关原料的进口正在逐步增加，正成为全球最大的能源进口国，这将进一步强化发展中国家或资源富裕型国家与中国的贸易关系。到2016年，中国加工贸易只占货物出口额的34%，高新技术产品占货物出口额的比重达29%，机电产品占货物出口额的比重达58%。2015年高科技出口额（现价美元），中国为5 586.06亿美元，美国为1 556.41亿美元，德国是1 997.18亿美元，高科技出口占制成品出口的比例中国为25.75%，美国为19.01%，德国为16.67%，法国为26.85%。2015年中国计算机出口比重最大，占比7.9%。2016年中国出口了19.06亿块液晶显示板、12.72亿部手持或车载无线电话、15.93亿台自动数据处理设备及其部件。然而，目前中国内地的出口依

① Shan Li, Xun Li, Haohui Chen, Wei Lang, “China’s export evolution in the dynamic global product space from 2000 to 2011”, *Current Science*, 2019, Vol. 117, No. 3.

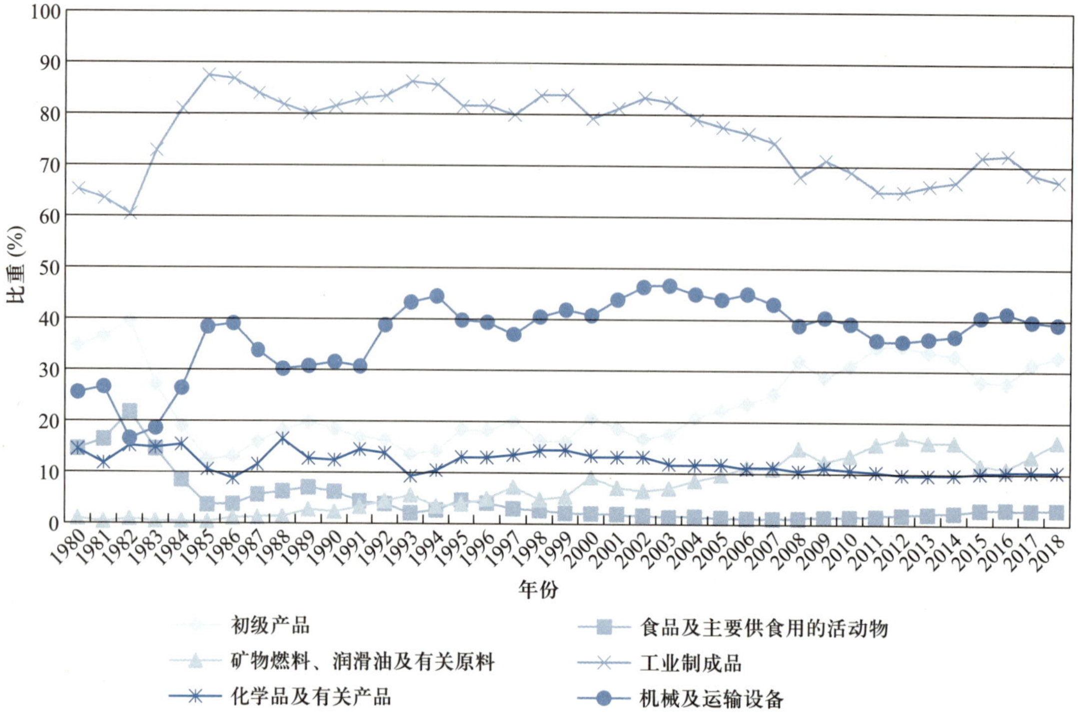


图8.11 1980—2018年来中国进口结构变迁

资料来源：国家统计局。

然高度依赖于欧盟、美国、中国香港和日本，这同时也意味着世界其他经济体与中国内地的贸易关系有巨大的发展空间。2018年中国高新技术产品进口额达44 340亿元（约6 500亿美元），增长12.2%。另外，值得一提的是，2018年中国进口了4 176亿个集成电路，数量上增长了10.8%，总价值20 584亿元（约3 000亿美元），价值上增长了16.9%，超过原油的进口价值的15 882亿元（约2 300亿美元）。这充分反映出中国作为中高等收入水平国家的处境，在高新技术商品上对发达国家的依赖。总之，中国目前的贸易结构显示，不论在传统劳动密集型产业，还是在高新技术产业方面，中国既与发达国家也与发展中国家存在巨大的比较优势互补以及产业技术合作的空间。

### 8.2.4 中国是全球最具投资吸引力的地区

2017年，中国的外商投资流量达1 363亿美元，占全球的比重上升到9.5%，长期以来（连续26年）中国位居发展中经济体吸引外资之首（回顾第5章第5.8节关于国际资本流动的讨论内容)。中国不断优化的营商环境、不断扩大的国内市场、完整的工业门类以及高素质的劳动力,给国外生产者、投资者提供了更加广阔的空间、更加优质的营商环境,[①]中国将继续保持最具吸引力的投资目的地地位。例如,中国正在实行高水平的贸易和投资自由化、便利化政策,制定《外商投资法》,全面实施准入前国民待遇加负面清单管理制度,持续放宽市场准入,着力打造对外开放新高地(本章8.5节将进一步讨论)。中国加大知识产权保护力度,进一步完善体制机制、法律法规,健全与国际经贸规则接轨的创新保护体系,为广大投资者和权利人提供更加有力有效的保护。2018年全年外商直接投资(不含银行、证券、保险领域)新设立企业60 533家,比上年增长69.8%。实际使用外商直接投资金额8 856亿元,增长0.9%,折1 350亿美元,增长3.0%。联合国贸发会议《2019年世界投资报告》显示,2018年全球外国直接投资延续了下滑趋势,规模较上年下降了13%,但中国实现了逆势增长,继续稳居全球第二大外资流入国地位。[②]

由于中国劳动生产率不断攀升,工资水平不断上涨,2016年工资水平已经超过大部分拉美等中等收入经济体。由于中国资本相对劳动变得越来越丰富,为顺应这种禀赋结构的变化,外商直接投资结构在中国也发生了相应的变化。例如,2016年,尽管在体量上制造业吸引外资的规模依然占将近1/4,位居各行业首位,但是却下降了6.1%。一般性居民服务业也下降了25%。利用外资结构向产业链高端环节转移,2016年信息传输、计算机服务和软件业实际使用外资增长128.0%,租赁和商务服务业增长67.8%。2018年全年高技术制造业实际使用外资898亿元,增长35.1%。尽管如此,抛开庞大的国内市场不谈,中国相对于发达国家而言工资水平依然相对较低,同时有完备的供应体系和生产设施,因此中国依然是中等技术密集和资本密集型产业最佳的全球生产基地。例如,中国的劳动力资源近9亿人,就业人员7亿多,受过高等教育和职业教育的高素质人才1.7亿,每年大学毕业生800多万,人才红利巨大。事实上,中国的外商投资企业依然在延续过去加工贸易“大进大出”“两头在外”的特征,只是产业结构发生了巨大变化。未来中国在吸引外资方面依然具有巨大的前景,如图8.12所示,2017年中国离美国2 754亿美元的外商投资流量还有很大的追赶空间。

---

① 根据世界银行《2019年营商环境报告》,中国在全球190个经济体中排名第46位,比上年大幅提升32位,尤其是在登记财产和执行合同方面排在第6位。

② 联合国贸发会议(UNCTAD),《2019年世界投资报告》(*World Investment Report 2019*),2019年。

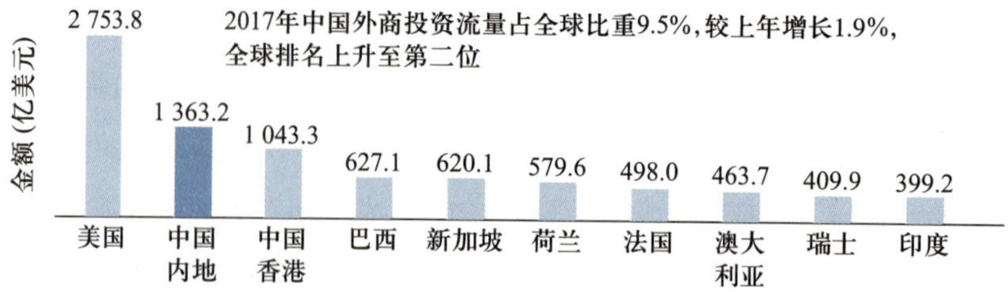


**图8.12 2017年全球十大外商投资流入国家或地区**

数据来源：联合国贸发会议，《2018年世界投资报告》。

### 8.2.5 中国拥有最具实力的工业化能力与基础设施建设能力

中国快速推进的工业化进程所带来的巨大产能进入海量的规模经济时代，贡献了全球制造业总产出的35%。如图8.13所示，不论是相对于进入后工业阶段的高收入经济体，还是相对于中低等收入经济体，中国制造业占GDP的比重都是最高的。中国确实是毫无争议的全球制造业大国。根据我们在第1.2节介绍的新结构经济学基本原理，当一个国家在经济发展过程中拾级而上时，由于资本设备的不可分性，该国生产的规模效应也在扩大，该国企业的规模更大，需要更大的市场。如果无法得到全球市场的释放，大都会产生产能过剩。因此，重要的不单单是去产能，还应该扩大全球市场，拉动需求。随着收入水平的进一步提高，有些产业失掉了比较优势，中国已经将推动"三去一降一补"作为推进供给侧结构性改革的主要政策抓手，推动高质量发展，以调整优化中国的产业结构。在中国失掉比较优势的转进型产业恰好是其他发展中经济体工业化所迫切需要的。正如2015年6月9日李克强在会见联合国工业发展组织总干事李勇时表示的，中国将积极开展国际产能合作，带动中国装备"走出去"。这既是中国经济发展到今天的客观需要，契合发展中国家工业化和发达国家再工业化的需求，也是扩大南南合作、深化南北合作的重要途径。

随着工业化实力的提升以及要素禀赋结构的升级，中国大部分技术行业均与全球标准整合。[①]国际标准化组织（ISO）已经发布了2.5万余项国际标准，国际电工组织（IEC）和国际电信联盟（ITU）分别发布了9 200项和4 800余项国际标准。截至2019年3月，根据全国

① 侯俊军、钟灵子，"要素禀赋结构与标准供给——基于中国制造业行业面板数据的实证研究"，《湖南大学学报（社会科学版）》，2019年第4期，第66–72页。

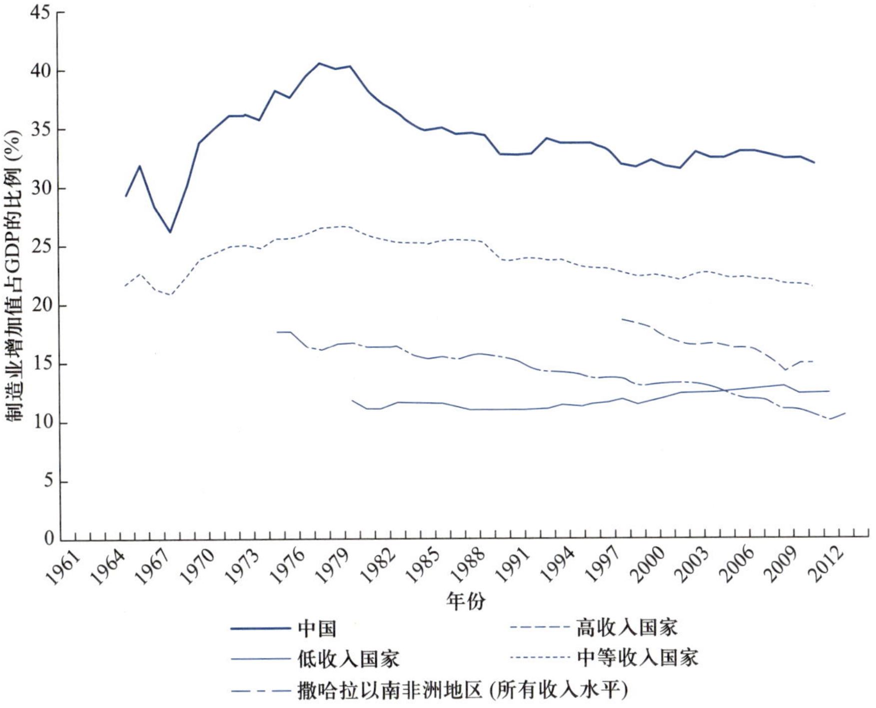


**图8.13 中国的制造业比重与不同收入水平国家的比较**

资料来源：世界银行。

标准信息公共服务平台的统计数据，我国已制定和实施的现行国家标准有36 150项，行业标准有62 739项，地方标准有41 447项，合计达到14万项。为了衡量中国与世界在技术链上的融合程度，麦肯锡全球研究院从11个领域择取了81项技术进行研究。研究发现，中国对其中超过90%的技术均采用了全球标准，如图8.14所示。

前面第7章第2节我们已经回顾并介绍了中国基础设施建设的整体情况，中国在20世纪90年代之后基础设施建设速度快于国内生产总值的增长速度，获得了超前发展。具体而言，如图8.15所示，中国在过去几十年间完成了水、电、海陆空交通、电信、互联网与能源基础设施的大规模建设，取得了旷世成就，被戏称为“基建狂魔”。截至2011年年底，中国发电装机达10.63亿千瓦，年发电量4.73万亿千瓦时，发电量跃居世界第一。2013年中国进入全球500强的电力企业达到9家，位居世界第一。中国电力企业在海外电源开发、电网运营、资源并购、电工装备、工程总包等领域不断取得突破。2015年度全球港口集装箱吞吐量统计排名依次为上海港、新加坡港、深圳港、宁波－舟山港、香港港、釜山港、青岛港、广州港、迪拜港、天津港，中国港口包揽七席。上海港以超过3 500万标箱的吞吐量遥遥领先，增势明显，排名第二的新加坡港吞吐量为近3 000万标箱，有不小的降幅。2012年新加坡港

|  | 行业/领域 | 评估的技术 | 采用全球标准的比例 | 拥有国内供应商的比例 | 中国供应商可以在技术上提供优于全球领导者或可以与之媲美的比例 |
|---|---|---|---|---|---|
| 基础材料 | · 采矿<br>· 钢铁 | 7 |  |  |  |
| 化工 | · 油气<br>· 日用化工及特殊化工<br>· 纺织 | 12 |  |  |  |
| 电子元件 | · 显示屏<br>· 集成电路 | 8 |  |  |  |
| 电动汽车 | · 纯电动汽车<br>· 插电式混合动力汽车 | 7 |  |  |  |
| 交通运输 | · 高铁<br>· 航运 | 10 |  |  |  |
| 消费电子产品和互联网 | · 消费电子产品<br>· 数字支付<br>· 无人机 | 11 |  |  |  |
| 设备 | · 手术机器人<br>· 工业机器人 | 4 |  |  |  |
| 制药和生物科技 | · 小分子药物<br>· 生物分子药物 | 6 |  |  |  |
| 人工智能 | · 语音识别<br>· 人脸识别<br>· 无人驾驶 | 5 |  |  |  |
| 下一代技术 | · 量子技术<br>· 5G<br>· 太空 | 8 |  |  |  |
| 基因组学 | · 基因分型<br>· 基因测序<br>· 基因编辑 | 3 |  |  |  |
| 总计 |  | 81 | >90% | 60%~80% | 40%~60% |

**图8.14 中国大部分技术行业均与全球标准整合**

资料来源：麦肯锡全球研究院，《中国与世界：理解变化中的经济联系》，2019年。

与上海港差距为80余万标箱，2013年扩大到100余万标箱，2014年差距再拉大到约140万标箱，而2015年更将差距锁定在560万标箱左右。2015年深圳港完成集装箱吞吐量2 420.4万标箱，连续三年稳坐全球第三的位置。2013年，深圳港首次超越香港港，跃居全球第三，其后逐渐扩大与第四名香港港的差距，世界第三的位置牢牢站稳。截至2019年年底，中国铁路总里程为13.98万千米，占全球的6.35%，其中高铁为3.5万千米，占全球的2/3，堪称世界一流。中国的基础设施建设能力不仅体现在其目前的体量上，更多地在于中国在如此短的时间内完成了如此浩大的系列基础设施工程。这种能力足以消除每个经济体经济结构转型升级面临的基础设施瓶颈。新时期，中国已经开始了新一轮知识和技术密集型的新型基础设施建设，如5G、人工智能、工业互联网和物联网等。[①]

事实上，中国的基础设施建设能力目前已经广泛服务于全球。以通信基础设施建设为例，以中国电信、中国移动、中国联通、华为等为主体的全球知名的信息通信企业，已经成为中国通信行业对外投资的主力军。[②]中国电信与全球100多家领先互联网运营商建立了互联，中国电信、中国移动和中国联通已跻身世界500强企业。中国移动已与468家运营商（涉及257个方向）建立漫游合作关系，其中已与191家运营商（涉及163个方向）开通LTE漫游业务。中国联通2017年实际完成境外投资总规模2.9亿元，国际业务实现收入72.2亿元，同比增长23.1%。至2017年年底，境外自有PoP总数增至49个，连同vPoP共计112个，连接亚太、美洲、欧洲等70个主要国家和地区。在基础资源建设方面，2017年全年国际海缆新增3.5T，达到16.2T，覆盖国家和地区26个；跨境陆缆新增3T，达到10.6T，连接国家和地区13个。在设备制造方面，华为等已成长为世界一流企业，海外收入占比超过50%，服务全球170多个国家。华为已成为全球最大的电信设备商。中国的手机品牌占全球的市场份额已达40%，在全球的研发中心超过16个。通信工程建设方面，中国通信服务公司在海外43个国家和地区设立了子公司或办事处，业务覆盖非洲、亚洲、拉丁美洲和中东60多个国家和地区。在互联网服务方面，互联网企业国际化拓展取得积极成效，投融资持续活跃。阿里巴巴、百度、腾讯等企业纷纷走出国门，进军国际市场，业务范围覆盖扩展到全球，业务体系愈加庞大。行业生态加速重构，产品国际化输出成效显著，国际影响力快速提升，资本投入持续活跃，投融资市场持续复苏。阿里巴巴正在全球范围内推动eWTP（全球电子商务平台）的实现，通过互联网创造的新实体经济，促进普惠贸易发展，支持全球80%的小企业进入全球市场；腾讯微信产品全球月活跃用户数突破10亿大关。[③]

---

① 新型基础设施和传统基础设施在供给侧所影响的具体生产技术和在需求侧所涉及的投资的产业来源构成上均存在差别，可参考：郭凯明、潘珊、颜色，“新型基础设施投资与产业结构转型升级”，《中国工业经济》，2020年第3期，第63—80页。

② 然而，遗憾的是，美国对中兴、华为等中国企业采取了无理的抵制。

③ 上述资料来自：商务部，《中国对外投资发展报告2018》，2018年。

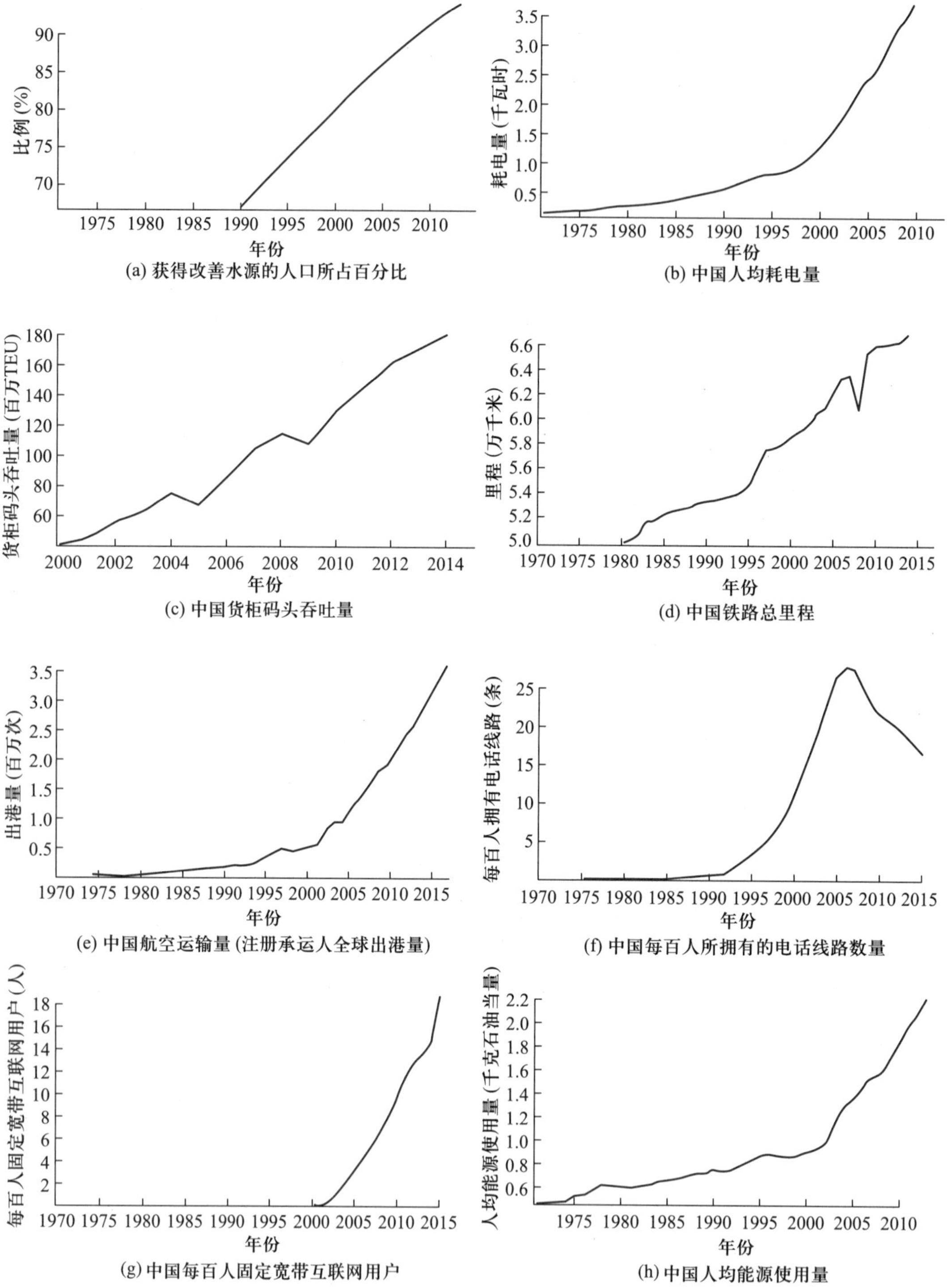


**图8.15 中国过去几十年的水、电、海陆空交通、电信、互联网与能源基础设施建设情况**

资料来源：世界银行。

### 8.2.6 中国已经成为净资本输出国并位居对外投资流量大国[①]

相对于全球外国投资持续低迷的形势，中国对外直接投资流量强势上扬，堪称全球化的中流砥柱。如图8.16所示，2002—2015年中国对外直接投资年均增幅高达35.9%，2015年对外投资流量达1 456.7亿美元，占全球总额的9.9%，仅次于美国（2 999.7亿美元），首次位列世界第二（日本1 286.5亿美元，位居第三位）。回首2002年，中国仅位居全球第26位。2017年，中国对外投资进行了如前所述的战略性调整，同比下降了19.3%，对外直接投资流量1 582.9亿美元，全球占比11.1%，对外投资流量位居全球第三位，继续保持发展中国家对外直接投资第一的地位。2017年的投资存量位列全球第二，对外直接投资存量全球占比接近6%。[②]不过，相对于美国依然以77 990亿美元的对外直接投资存量继续位居全球第一的状况，中国依然有很大的成长空间。

中国于2016年首次成为净资本输出国，如图8.17所示。2014年，中国非金融领域对外直接投资6 321亿元（约合1 028.9亿美元），比上年增长14.1%。2018年，中国非金融类对外直接投资1 205亿美元，同比增长0.3%。如表8.2所示，近年来对外投资结构也发生了巨大变化。2014年流向制造业的投资只有不到70亿美元，低于采矿业的193.3亿美元，但2015年就发生了历史性的变化，流向制造业的投资高达143.3亿美元，同比增长105.9%，远超采矿业的108.5亿美元，其中流向装备制造业的投资为70.4亿美元，同比增长154.2%，占制造业对外投资的49.1%，占同期总投资额的6%。2016年，流向制造业的投资为310.6亿美元，同比增长116.7%，其中流向装备制造业的投资178.6亿美元，是上年的2.5倍，占制造业对外投资的57.5%，占同期总投资额的10.5%。尽管中国在投资流量增长速度和投资结构转型升级上势头惊人，但是中国对外投资的全球化时代才刚刚开始，未来的潜力不可估量，成为全球最大的资本输出国指日可待。截至2014年年底，全球对外直接投资存量为25.9万亿美元，基本保持上年年末规模水平。同期，中国对外投资存量为8 826.4亿美元，占全球的3.4%，居全球第8位，比上年提升3位，首次步入全球前十行列。然而，中国对外直接投资存量同发达国家相比仍有较大差距，仅相当于美国当期存量的14%，德国和英国当期的55.7%，法国当期的69%，日本当期的74%。2017年，中国对外投资出现了大幅下滑，主要是国家调控过热的对外投资所致。2018年，中国对外投资趋于稳定，并向“一带一路”沿线国家倾斜。2018年，中国对外非金融类直接投资额7 974亿元，比上年下降1.6%，折1 205亿美元，增

---

① 关于中国对外投资的一些实证研究可参考：黄益平、何帆、张永生，《中国对外直接投资研究》，北京大学出版社，2013年版。

②《2017年度中国对外直接投资统计公报》。

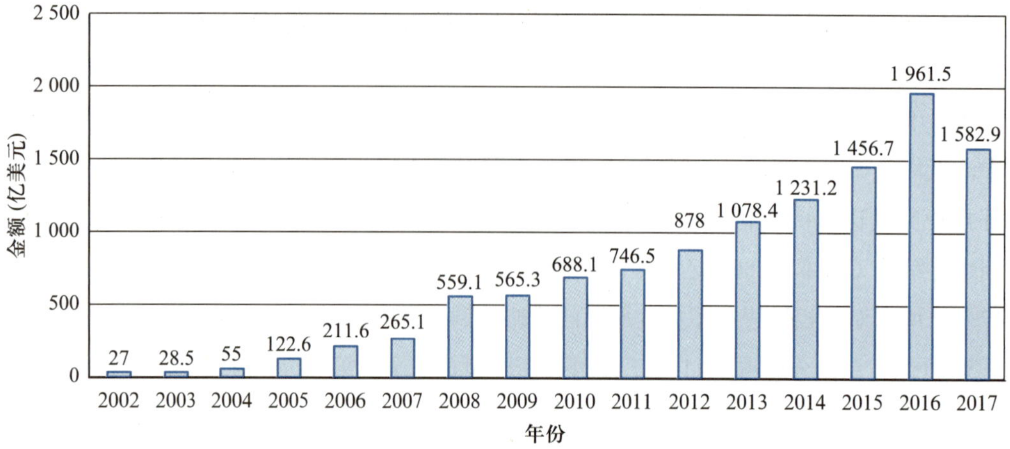


**图8.16 2002—2017年中国对外直接投资流量变化趋势**

资料来源：商务部，《2018年中国对外投资发展报告》，2018年。

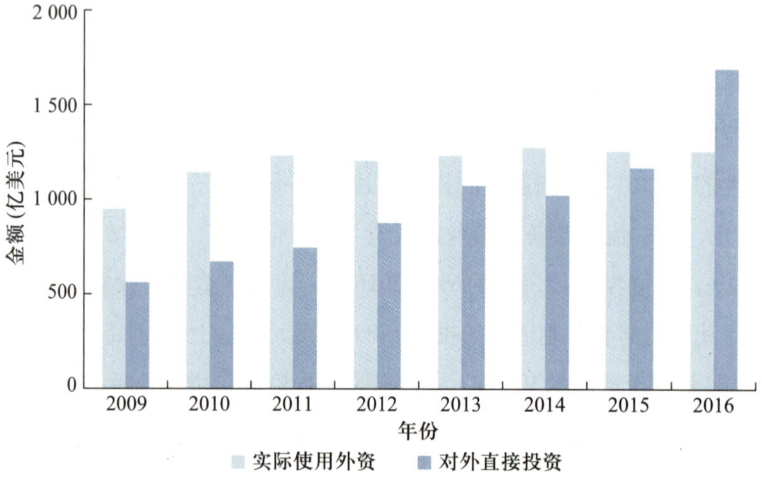


**图8.17 2009—2016年中国双向直接投资对比**

资料来源：历年《中国对外直接投资统计公报》与《国民经济和社会发展统计公报》。

长0.3%。其中，对“一带一路”沿线国家非金融类直接投资额156亿美元，增长8.9%。全年对外承包工程完成营业额11 186亿元，比上年下降1.7%，折1 690亿美元，增长0.3%。对“一带一路”沿线国家完成营业额893亿美元，增长4.4%，占对外承包工程完成营业额比重为52.8%。对外劳务合作派出各类劳务人员49万人。因此，中国的对外投资很大程度上反映了前一小节所介绍的中国所拥有的工业化能力与基础设施建设能力对世界经济的积极影响。

表8.2 2014—2016年中国非金融领域对外直接投资额及其增长率 单位：亿美元

| 行业 | 2014年 | | 2015年 | | 2016年 | | 2017年 | | 2018年 | |
|---|---|---|---|---|---|---|---|---|---|---|
| | 金额 | 增长率（%） | 金额 | 增长率（%） | 金额 | 增长率（%） | 金额 | 增长率（%） | 金额 | 增长率（%） |
| 总计 | 1 028.9 | 14.1 | 1 180.2 | 14.7 | 1 701.1 | 44.1 | 1 201 | −29.4 | 1 205 | 0.3 |
| 农、林、牧、渔业 | 17.4 | 19.2 | 20.5 | 17.8 | 29.7 | 44.9 | 22 | −25.9 | 18 | −18.2 |
| 采矿业 | 193.3 | −4.1 | 108.5 | −43.9 | 86.7 | −20.1 | 83 | −4.4 | 92 | 11.3 |
| 制造业 | 69.6 | −19.8 | 143.3 | 105.9 | 310.6 | 116.7 | 191 | −38.5 | 188 | −1.6 |
| 电力、热力、燃气及水生产和供应业 | 18.4 | 36.3 | 27.9 | 51.6 | 25.3 | −9.3 | 32 | 26.5 | 32 | 0 |
| 建筑业 | 70.2 | 7.5 | 45.0 | −35.9 | 53.1 | 18.0 | 73 | 37.5 | 74 | 1.4 |
| 批发和零售业 | 172.7 | 26.3 | 160.2 | −7.2 | 275.6 | 72.0 | 249 | −9.7 | 106 | −57.4 |
| 交通运输、仓储和邮政业 | 29.3 | 17.2 | 30.9 | 5.5 | 36.2 | 17.2 | 30 | −17.1 | 58 | 93.3 |
| 信息传输、软件和信息技术服务业 | 17.0 | 100.0 | 57.8 | 240.0 | 203.6 | 252.3 | 103 | −49.4 | 68 | −34.0 |
| 房地产业 | 30.9 | 45.8 | 90.6 | 193.2 | 106.4 | 17.4 | 22 | −79.3 | 40 | 81.8 |
| 租赁和商务服务业 | 372.5 | 26.5 | 416.7 | 11.9 | 422.7 | 1.4 | 349 | −17.4 | 446 | 27.8 |

注：分项只列出了部分项目，故分项加总与总计不等。

资料来源：2014—2018年《国民经济和社会发展统计公报》。

# 8.3

# 中国与发达国家经济结构转型升级的匹配

## 8.3.1 充分利用中国与高收入经济体互补的比较优势深化合作

在当今的世界经济格局下，中国与发达经济体之间依然存在着巨大的、互补的比较优势。中国现在的人均收入水平按照购买力平价计算也只不过是高收入经济体的1/5左右。发达国家产业链中相对劳动力密集的环节依然会放在中国生产，中国依然会是这方面对发达国家主要的出口国。中国业已成为全球最大的市场，必然是发达国家最为重要的出口市场和投资地。例如，根据2017年的统计，中国的手机销量占全球销量的40%，电动车销量占64%，半导体消费占46%。中国市场已经为很多发达国家高科技企业提供了重要的增长机遇。根据摩根士丹利资本国际指数（MSCI），美国信息技术领域有14%的营收来自中国。以集成电路和光学设备领域为例，中国的进口额高达国内产值的5倍。2008年国际金融危机之后，发达经济体增长疲软和全球贸易受到抑制，是2010年以后中国经济增长出现持续下滑的主要原因。中国与传统老牌工业强国以及高收入经济体之间依然有着非常强的相互依赖性，彼此之间难以脱钩。[①]中国可以充分利用这种大国之间的合作互补基础创造有利的全球稳定环境，但前提是必须理顺各种合作关系，而不是盲目地违背比较优势进行赶超，引起不必要的恶性竞争。习近平2019年访问欧洲诸国时就强调了这一点。从经济体量上看，2018年高收入国家的GDP（2010年不变价美元）占世界的64%，中国占13%，二者合计占77%。因此，中国与高收入国家之间的经济关系不仅对各自双方而且对全世界都举足轻重。

① 可回顾第1章1.2节所介绍的中国与主要发达国家（美国、日本、德国、法国）间的经济体量和贸易流量。

### 8.3.2 发达国家依然是中国通过学习利用后来者优势的对象

我们在本章开篇就已经指出了中国转型升级在全球范围内的定位，相对而言，发达国家依然是中国学习的对象。整体上，发达国家处于世界经济前沿，技术水平全面领先。中国整体上处于世界经济前沿内部，除了部分领先型和换道超车型产业之外，主要产业还是追赶型的（如专栏8.1介绍的装备制造业，我们也将在第10章进一步讨论）。例如，2015年中国研发支出占GDP的比例虽然已经达到2.015%，但依然低于美国的2.725%、德国的2.826%、瑞典的3.306%，每百万人中研究人员数量，中国是902.96人，美国是3 866.96人，德国是40 773.77人，瑞典是5 255.86人，澳大利亚是4 530.73人。技术链是最复杂的价值链之一，尤其需要各方通力协作，事实上中国早已深度融入其中，并占据了相当大的全球进出口份额。因此，中国在产业升级与技术进步上依然有巨大的追赶空间，亦即有充足的后来者优势可以利用。这也符合中国的比较优势。相对于主要的工业强国工资水平，中国在发达国家产业链的劳动力密集型环节依然具备巨大的比较优势。并且，如前所述，随着收入水平的提高，一国过去符合比较优势的产业也将逐渐失去比较优势，发达国家也不例外，这是都是后发国家可以引进吸收的后来者优势。当然，发达国家可能出于各种考虑阻碍中国向发达国家学习。例如，受特朗普政府采取的保护主义政策影响，2017年中国对美国的直接投资骤降了62.2%。但是，这种保护主义的做法需要权衡其经济得失，如果得不偿失，发达国家也不会采取此类政策。例如，2017年中国对欧洲的直接投资就同比增长72.7%。

### 8.3.3 去发达国家投资促进中国与发达经济体的经济结构转型升级

发达经济体处于全球产业链的前沿，在转型升级的各个维度上都为后发国家提供了可资借鉴的学习机会，即发展中经济体具有充足的后来者优势。目前中国产业正处在转型升级的关键时期，尤其是对于追赶型产业的转型升级，欧美发达经济体由于经济复苏缓慢，中国每年为世界贡献30%左右的市场规模的扩张，欧美企业在中国增加投资以扩大在中国的市场份额，和中国企业并购欧美优质企业提升技术和品牌、拓宽渠道，是中国追赶型产业结构转型升级的一条途径。在当今的全球经济环境下，中国各地政府的招商引资和企业到海外并购有了更多的机会，这些投资也是帮助发达经济体快速复苏的重要力量。这种将中国的市场和效率与发达国家的优势资产结合的方式是推动全球经济快速复苏的途径之一。与此同时，根据第7章对全球基础设施缺口情况的评估，发达国家有大量老旧的基础设施需要改造升级，而中国的基础设施建设能力可以帮助发达经济体升级其基础设施。

根据联合国贸发会议发布的《2019年世界投资报告》，2018年全球外国直接投资下滑，但中国吸引外资总量却逆势上涨近4%，占全球外国直接投资总额的比重超过10%，继续保持全球第二大外资流入国地位。在全球并购市场上，中国也已经成为一支重要的力量，2016年中国企业跨境并购的金额超过所有其他国家，跃居世界第一。原来由国有企业主导的海外并购逐渐转换成以民营企业为主导，民营企业海外并购数量及交易额实现同比增长至少五成，热衷于对技术创新、品牌和市场的并购，进军欧美发达国家。按照《世界投资报告》的统计口径，2014年中国企业境外并购项目数为331个，并购金额达395.80亿美元，项目平均投资规模达到1.2亿美元。从商务部发布的数据来看，2014年中国企业境外并购项目达到595个，金额达到569亿美元，其中直接投资并购金额达到324.8亿美元，占当年境外并购总额的57.08%，境外融资244.2亿美元，占并购总额的42.92%。2015年中国企业共实施境外并购项目579起，涉及62个国家（地区），实际交易总额544.4亿美元，其中直接投资372.8亿美元，占并购交易总额的68.5%、当年中国对外直接投资总额的25.6%，境外融资171.6亿美元，占并购金额的31.5%。2015年中国企业境外投资并购涉及制造业、信息传输/软件和信息技术服务业、采矿业、文化/体育和娱乐业、租赁和商务服务业等18个行业大类，相比2014年新增了水利/环境和公共设施管理类并购项目。从并购金额上看，制造业137.2亿美元，同比增长13.4%，位居首位，涉及137个项目；信息传输/软件和信息技术服务业84.1亿美元，同比增长135.6%，位列次席。2015年中国内地企业境外投资并购项目分布在全球62个国家（地区），从实际并购金额上看，美国、开曼群岛、意大利、中国香港、澳大利亚、荷兰、以色列、百慕大群岛、哈萨克斯坦、英国位列前十。

#### 8.3.3.1 中国在北美洲的投资及其与北美洲的经济结构匹配情况①

以美国和加拿大两国为主的北美洲在世界经济结构中整体处于塔尖层次，经济体量巨大而且发展水平高。2018年北美洲的GDP（2010年不变价美元）占世界的24%。尽管受到中美贸易摩擦的影响，2019年美国依然占据了中国出口的16.7%，仅次于欧盟。北美的产业发达，技术实力雄厚，人力资本和物资资本以及能源充沛，研发能力突出。中国对北美地区的投资

① 由于主要讨论的是发达国家，这里关于北美洲的数据不含墨西哥。

一直保持良好势头，直到最近特朗普政府挑起的中美经济摩擦为止，如图8.18所示。[①]北美洲是中国企业境外并购主要的目的地之一。2017年，中国企业对北美洲企业的并购活动仍然较为活跃，领域更加广泛，国别以美国为主。2017年，中国企业共对美实施并购项目82个，实际交易金额120.3亿美元。但是，从实际并购金额看，美国由2016年的榜首退居第二位。

截至2017年年底，中国在北美洲的投资存量为869.1亿美元，占中国对外直接投资存量的4.8%，主要分布在美国（77.5%）、加拿大（12.6%）。中国位于北美洲的境外企业超过5 900家，占境外企业总数的15.1%，主要分布在美国、加拿大。中国内地企业在美国设立的境外企业数仅次于中国香港，排名第二。2017年，中国对北美洲的投资存量主要分布在5个行业领域：制造业（22.4%），采矿业（16.9%），租赁和商务服务业（14.7%），金融业（12.2%），信息传输、软件和信息技术服务业（7.6%）。这5个行业投资存量合计为642.7亿美元，所占比重高达73.8%。2017年，中国对美国投资从存量行业分布情况看，制造业以172.8亿美元高居榜首，占对美投资存量的25.6%；租赁和商务服务业110.02亿美元，占16.3%；金融业91.41亿美元，占13.6%；信息传输、软件和信息技术服务业65.91亿美元，占9.8%；批发和零售业51.75亿美元，占7.7%；房地产业44.69亿美元，占6.6%；采矿业占5.2%；科学研究和技术服务业占4.9%；文化/体育和娱乐业占3.5%。

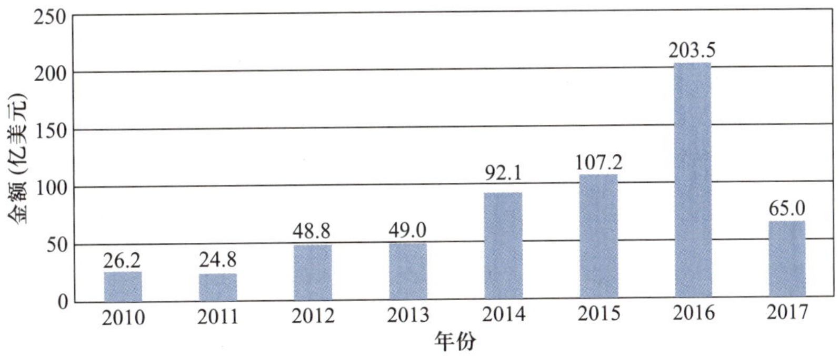


**图8.18 2010—2017年中国对北美洲直接投资流量**

数据来源：商务部，《中国对外投资报告2018》，2018年。

① 2018年以来，特朗普政府对包括中国在内的主要贸易伙伴加征关税，特别是对中国发起贸易战，并利用其国内法规对中兴通讯采取制裁措施，严重影响了中美关系的正常发展。2019年中国对美国的出口下降了8.7%，进口下降了17.1%。受中美贸易争端影响，中国企业对美国的投资降幅较大，且未来一定时间内仍将持续这一趋势。

中国企业在北美洲的投资领域广泛，涉及制造业、能源、农产品、基础设施、金融业、服务业等多个领域。传统上，中国对美投资集中在制造业、批发贸易和金融等领域。近年来中国对美投资日益关注高技术及高端服务业，出于缩短与国际先进企业技术差距的考量，越来越多的中国企业将投资目标定位于产业链和技术阶梯的高端，倾向于收购品牌技术或投资于高附加值的行业领域。2017年11月，中美签下的经贸合同总金额高达2 535亿美元，其中能源领域的合同金额逾1 600亿美元，大部分集中在中国对美国能源、基础设施的投资方面。未来随着中国增加来自美国的能源和农产品进口，以及特朗普政府推行大规模基础设施更新计划，中国可能更多投资于美国的能源、农产品和基础设施等领域。（专栏8.1介绍了2017年中国中车集团在芝加哥建设首家地铁车辆制造厂改造升级美国基础设施的案例。）但近期，特朗普政府对涉及美国核心利益的外国投资更为敏感，预计随着美国《外国投资风险评估现代化法案》的实施，中国对美高技术投资可能受到更多的阻碍，如表8.3所示。①中国对加拿大的投资行业也日益多元化，私营企业逐步成为中国对加投资的重要力量，能源、矿业成为投资重点领域，且投资力度持续加大。同时，中国企业还向清洁技术、航空航天、民用核能、农业科技等新兴合作领域拓展。②

① 根据2015年美国外国投资审查委员会（CFIUS）向美国国会提交的年度报告数据，2009—2015年，共有770份涉及“担保交易”的通知被提交，CFIUS对其中的40%进行了审查，其中42%属于制造业，32%属于金融、信息和服务领域。2013—2015年，中国公司提交的通知最多（74份）。2018年8月13日，经美国总统特朗普签署，美国《外国投资风险评估现代化法案》（FIRRMA）正式生效。该法案从以下几方面扩大了CFIUS的审批权限。第一，从“控制”到“非被动投资”。长期以来，CFIUS的审查范围包括可能导致外国对美国企业或资产实现“控制”的交易。即外方投资者无论是否持有51%的所有权，只要是拥有“实质的”所有权和在公司重大事项上拥有决定权，都会被认为是达到了控制标准，就要接受CFIUS的安全审查，其他情况则可以不受CFIUS审查的限制。但根据FIRRMA的规定，本来已经涵盖很宽泛的“控制”被进一步扩大，需要接受CFIUS审查的外国投资类型更多。这些被格外关注的交易类型包括有：（1）外国人买卖或者租赁军事基地和国家安全设施附近的地产；（2）外国人对涉及关键技术、关键基础设施、保存或搜集美国人个人信息的美国公司的投资；（3）故意逃避或规避CFIUS审查的交易。而想要不受CFIUS管辖，外国投资要满足以下要求：（1）不是收购；（2）不允许外国投资者获得企业的非公开技术信息或任何未向所有投资者开放的其他信息；（3）不赋予外国投资者在企业管理机构中指定董事、董事会观察员或类似职位的权利；（4）除了通过股票投票外，外国投资者不会参与公司业务的管理、治理或运营；（5）外国投资者和企业之间没有平行战略伙伴关系或其他物质财务关系；（6）符合CFIUS通过细则法规建立的其他标准。除此之外，《外国投资风险评估现代化法案》还要求外国投资者对CFIUS审查从自愿申报到强制申报。这样严苛的条件，恐怕很少会有企业接受。考虑到实践中CFIUS的决定实质上是不受美国法院司法审查（总统的决定是最终决定），其影响可能会超过历史上美国颁布过的其他对外投资限制的法律。关于美国外资安全审查制度的变迁、修改及影响的梳理可参考：沈伟，“美国外资安全审查制度的变迁、修改及影响——以近期中美贸易摩擦为背景”，《武汉科技大学学报（社会科学版）》，2019年第6期；钟红、吴丹，“美国《外国投资风险评估现代化法案2018》影响研究”，《国际贸易》，2019年第1期。

② 商务部，《中国对外投资报告2018》，2018年。

表8.3 近年因CFIUS审查被阻止并购的中国投资交易

| 年份 | 买方 | 标的 | 行业 |
|---|---|---|---|
| 2005 | 中国海洋石油有限公司 | 美国优尼科公司 | 能源 |
| 2008 | 中国华为公司联合贝恩资本 | 美国电信设备制造商 | 通信 |
| 2009 | 中国西色国际投资有限公司 | 美国优金采矿公司 | 能源 |
| 2010 | 中国唐山曹妃甸投资公司 | 美国光纤制造商安科 | 通信 |
| | 中国鞍山钢铁集团 | 美国钢铁发展公司 | 制造业 |
| | 中国华为 | 美国服务器技术公司 | 通信 |
| 2016 | 中国金沙江创投财团 | 荷兰皇家飞利浦旗下Lumileds公司（含美国业务） | 制造业 |
| 2017 | 中国TCL集团 | 美国Novatel Wireless旗下MIFI | 通信 |
| | 中国四维图新联合腾讯、新加坡政府投资基金 | 荷兰数字地图供应商HERE（含美国业务） | 地图 |
| | 中国海航集团 | 美国全球鹰娱乐有限公司 | 娱乐 |
| | 中国忠旺集团 | 美国爱励铝业 | 制造业 |
| 2018 | 中国蚂蚁金服集团 | 美国速汇金公司（Money- Gram） | 金融 |
| | 中国大北农科技集团 | 美国种猪销售公司（Waldo Genetics） | 农业 |
| | 中国蓝色光标 | 美国大数据营销公司（Cogint） | 互联网 |
| | 中国重型汽车集团 | 美国UQM科技股份有限公司 | 制造业 |
| | 中国海航资本 | 美对冲基金公司天桥资本（SkyBridge Capital） | 金融 |

资料来源：中华人民共和国国务院新闻办公室，《关于中美经贸摩擦的事实与中方立场》，2018年9月。

正如中国政府在2018年发表的《关于中美经贸摩擦的事实与中方立场》白皮书中所阐述的，中国是世界上最大的发展中国家，美国是世界上最大的发达国家。中美经贸关系既对两国意义重大，也对全球经济稳定和发展有着举足轻重的影响。中美两国建交以来，双边经贸关系持续发展，利益交汇点不断增多，形成了紧密合作关系，不仅使两国共同获益，而且惠及全球。特别是进入21世纪以来，在经济全球化快速发展过程中，中美两国遵循双边协定和世界贸易组织等多边组织的规则，拓展深化经贸合作，基于比较优势和市场选择形成了结构高度互补、利益深度交融的互利共赢关系。双方通过优势互补、互通有无，有力促进了各自经济发展和产业结构优化升级，同时提升了全球价值链效率与效益，降低了生产成本，丰富了商品种类，极大促进了两国企业和消费者利益。①例如，中国是美国飞机和大豆的第一大出口市场，汽车、集成电路、棉花的第二大出口市场。2017年美国出口中57%的大豆、

① 中华人民共和国国务院新闻办公室，《关于中美经贸摩擦的事实与中方立场》，2018年9月。

25%的波音飞机、20%的汽车、14%的集成电路、17%的棉花都销往中国。中美双边贸易互补性强。美国居于全球价值链的中高端，对中国出口多为资本品和中间品，中国居于中低端，对美国出口多为消费品和最终产品，两国发挥各自比较优势，双边贸易呈互补关系。2017年中国向美国出口前三大类商品为电机电气设备及其零附件、机械器具及零件、家具寝具灯具等，合计占比为53.5%。中国从美国进口前三大类商品为电机电气设备及其零附件、机械器具及零件、车辆及其零附件，合计占比为31.8%。机电产品在中美双边贸易中占重要比重，产业内贸易特征较为明显。中国对美出口的“高技术产品”，大多只是在中国完成劳动密集型加工环节，包含大量关键零部件和中间产品的进口与国际转移价值。总之，正如我们在第6章所讨论的，中美之间的经济结构是互补的，中美经贸关系可以实现双赢，美国贸易逆差的原因不在中国，不在东亚，而是在美元是国际储备货币以及美国家庭低储蓄高消费的生活方式。①

### 专栏8.1
### 中国中车集团在芝加哥建设首家地铁车辆制造厂

1863年横贯北美大陆的美国太平洋铁路开工时，吸引了大批华人前来寻找工作。他们作为社会底层的工人用血和泪完成了全程3 000多千米的历史上第一条跨洲铁路。155年后的今天，远在大洋彼岸的中国中车四方股份公司（简称中车四方）以投资客的身份在芝加哥建厂，并雇用当地工人生产、组装芝加哥地铁！

中车四方在2016年3月以低于竞争对手2.26亿美元的竞标价，中标芝加哥846辆、金额总价13亿美元的地铁车辆项目，勇夺芝加哥最贵地铁订单。2017年3月16日，中车四方在芝加哥南部举办建厂动工仪式。总投资1亿美元、占地275亩的厂区，预计在2019年年初完工，并投入使用。该厂房的破土动工，也标志着中国地铁出口发达国家最高纪录订单的生产正式启动。中车四方在芝加哥南部开设新厂，是50年来捷运系统列车的生产首次回归芝加哥。同时，也成为芝加哥30多年来的首家地铁车辆制造厂。制造业的落户，给芝加哥注入了新鲜血液，每年不低于168辆地铁车辆的生产，也为当地带来至少170个就业机会，以

① 林毅夫，“中国的新时代与中美贸易争端”，《武汉大学学报（哲学社会科学版）》，2019年第2期。

及可观的税收。据中标协议，该笔订单需要满足“购买美国”要求，也就是说本地化率达到60%，并在当地进行组装，芝加哥建厂的契机也在于此。“新厂建成后生产的地铁车辆，将在美国完成转向架组装和车辆总装及调试，根据成本核算，车辆的本土化比例达到了60%以上。”中车四方美国公司总经理刘成永介绍，除在美国采购的部分部件外，车体总组焊是在位于青岛的中车四方完成的。在芝加哥生产的新车，不仅有美国“户口”，还带有浓浓的中国血统、中国技术。芝加哥（北纬41.8度）位于密歇根湖畔，与中国乌鲁木齐、沈阳等城市同处高纬度地区，气候严寒，多大风天气。中车四方将把已经成熟的耐高寒技术应用在芝加哥地铁车辆上，以保证地铁的安全运行和乘客的舒适度。

芝加哥拥有全美第二大公共交通系统，1892年开始运行地铁，目前共有8条地铁线，总长达170千米，贯穿芝加哥地区，年载客量约240万人次。目前行驶在芝加哥的地铁还有30年前的2600系老旧车型，车厢内部陈旧，噪音大。预计2020年首批新型7000系列地铁车辆投入使用后，芝加哥将拥有全美最新的地铁。在芝加哥体验中国高铁的舒适感，不再是遥远的畅想。这一最新案例验证了中国参与美国基础设施改装升级的互补性。

#### 8.3.3.2 中国在欧洲的投资及其与欧洲的经济结构匹配情况

虽然同是发达地区，欧洲的国家结构比北美要多元化得多，①不会如美国一样单边设置经济摩擦就会严重遏制中国在北美的投资和贸易。中欧双方积极推动“一带一路”倡议与欧洲投资计划对接，推进一批基础设施互联互通建设和国际产能合作项目落地，将有力促进中国与欧洲经济结构的深度融合。欧盟连续14年是中国第一大贸易伙伴（2019年欧盟占中国出口的17.2%和进口的13.3%），中国则是欧盟第二大贸易伙伴。以实际使用外资累计金额计，欧盟是中国第五大投资来源地。欧盟还是中国累计第一大技术供应方。中欧经贸关系已经成

① 西欧和北欧远比东欧和南欧发达，并且经济结构也存在巨大的差异，自然与中国的经济结构关系非常不同。此外，中国在欧洲的经济关系也受到欧洲不同国家的影响。例如，刘作奎通过分析中国在巴尔干地区（包括塞尔维亚、黑山、波斯尼亚和黑塞哥维那、克罗地亚、保加利亚、罗马尼亚、阿尔巴尼亚、北马其顿、希腊、土耳其）的9项投资案例，总结了中国企业在巴尔干地区投资的动机、特点、进展以及可能产生的影响和存在的问题。其发现中国在巴尔干地区的投资虽然显著增长，但并没有改变欧盟在巴尔干地区的主导地位。未来，中国在巴尔干地区的投资会受到欧盟因素、国内外营商环境、地缘风险、融资方式等影响。（刘作奎，“一带一路”倡议下中国对巴尔干地区的投资现状及影响——基于实地调研案例分析，《欧亚经济》，2019年第3期）

为当今世界最为重要的对外经济关系之一。[①]

欧洲尤其是发达的西欧地区，在世界经济结构中也处于顶尖位置，其产业结构和技术水平层次高，是中国可以学习的重要对象，但中国的基础设施建设能力则可以帮助欧洲基础设施升级，因此在产业和基建的实体经济领域有很强的互补性。欧洲在物流、生物技术、信息通信、生物医药等行业对中国企业和投资者具有巨大吸引力。中国企业出于转型升级的需要，通过并购欧洲优质资产获得先进技术、投资于先进管理模式下的高附加值产业等提高国际竞争力，更为东道国经济发展注入强大动力，解决资金链不畅的问题，并创造大量就业。随着中国企业开始在全球价值链的高端领域布局和发力，预计未来一段时间，高端制造业、高科技等行业将成为中国企业海外投资并购的热点，尤其是新一代信息技术领域，如人工智能、大数据、云服务等领域的直接投资和并购将增多。然而，尽管欧洲不像现在的美国那样大张旗鼓地为抵制向中国进行技术转移而进行严格投资审查，但一些欧洲国家也心存戒心。刘国全的研究发现，在战略资源获取型的海外并购当中，相对于私有制而言，国有企业的所有制形式会降低并购成功率，而在整个欧洲地区来说，制度稳定性、经济自由度、文化差异性等要素对于并购成败的影响并不明显，目标企业的科技含量会削弱海外并购成功率，同时会对企业所有制形式要素产生调节作用。[②]

事实上，欧洲地区是中国企业并购的主要目的地之一。2017年，中国企业对外投资并购金额前10位国家和地区中，3个属于欧洲地区，依次为瑞士、德国、英国。主要并购项目包括：中国化工集团421亿美元收购瑞士先正达公司 98.06%股权，是2017年中国企业“走出去”实施的最大海外并购项目，同时也是当年全球跨境并购第二大项目；中国国家电网公司完成与希腊国家电网公司的股权交割，以3.2 亿欧元收购了希腊国家电网公司24%的股权；中国投资有限责任公司收购了伦敦希思罗机场10%的股份；北京建工集团获得了曼彻斯特“空港城”的建设参与权；中远海运港口有限公司2亿欧元收购西班牙诺特姆港口公司51%的股份。2016年10月，中远海运港口有限公司就收购了意大利瓦多码头控股公司40%的股权。自双方开展合作以来，瓦多码头控股公司的经营状况持续改善，2018年公司利润增长了16%。2019年3月，中意两国正式签署政府间关于共同推进“一带一路”建设的谅解备忘录。位于意大利利古里亚大区的瓦多港，目前已经成为“一带一路”倡议延伸至中南欧

① 更系统的中欧经济关系历史变迁的梳理可参考：车文娇，《中国欧盟经贸关系发展研究》，东北财经大学2009年博士论文。新中国70年来的中欧关系回顾可参考：丁纯纪、吴楠，“中欧关系70年：成就、挑战与展望”，《世界经济与政治论坛》，2019年第6期。

② 刘国全，《战略资源获取型海外投资模式及并购成败的影响因素研究——以中国企业在欧洲的并购为例》，东北财经大学2017年硕士论文。

的门户港口，在中资推动下，这里实现了运营与建设的跨越式发展。瓦多港所在的小城瓦多利古雷则位于靠近利古里亚大区中心的临海处，距工业重镇都灵和米兰分别只有140千米和190千米，对于意大利北部的经济发展至关重要。每年约50万吨水果从非洲、中美洲及南美洲等地运至瓦多港，由这里进入欧洲。随着工业品、生活用品及其他货物的涌入，新码头的货源结构将变得更加多元，原有以水果为货运主体的单一结构将因此改变。而瓦多港也将成为集冷藏码头、输油码头和半自动化集装箱码头为一体的多功能港口，这也是意大利第一个半自动化集装箱码头。截至2015年11月底，在建的境外经贸合作区中有25个位于欧洲地区。2014年，东风汽车公司8亿欧元收购法国标致雪铁龙集团14.1%的股份也是一个耀眼的制造业并购项目。

截至2017年年底，中国企业在欧洲43个国家和地区设立了境外机构，覆盖率达87.8%，仅次于亚洲。在欧洲设立境外企业近4 200家，占境外企业总数的10.7%，主要分布在俄罗斯、德国、英国、荷兰、法国、意大利等国家。截至2017年年底，中国在欧洲地区投资存量为1 108.6亿美元，占中国对外直接投资存量的6.1%，主要分布在英国（203.2亿美元）、荷兰（185.3亿美元）、卢森堡（139.4亿美元）、俄罗斯（138.7亿美元）、德国（121.6亿美元）、瑞士（81.1亿美元）、瑞典（73.1亿美元）、法国（57亿美元）、挪威（20.8亿美元）、意大利（19亿美元）等国家。中国对欧洲地区投资涉及近20个行业领域，从投资存量上看主要分布在5个行业领域，依次为制造业（30.8%）、采矿业（20.3%）、金融业（16.0%）、租赁和商务服务业（9.6%）以及批发和零售业（4.7%）。上述5个行业投资存量合计901.4亿美元，占中国对欧洲投资存量的81.4%。其中，制造业增幅较大，占比比上年提高10.7个百分点。中国对欧盟投资存量的主要行业领域依次为：制造业246.2亿美元，占28.6%，主要分布在瑞典、德国、英国、荷兰、法国等；金融业171.3亿美元，占19.9%，主要分布在卢森堡、英国、德国、法国等；采矿业141.3亿美元，占16.4%，主要分布在荷兰、卢森堡、比利时等；租赁和商务服务业99.2亿美元，占11.5%，主要分布在英国、卢森堡、德国、法国、荷兰等；批发和零售业44.9亿美元，占5.2%，主要分布在法国、德国、卢森堡、英国、荷兰等。中国对俄罗斯投资的主要行业领域依次为：采矿业65.9亿美元（47.5%）、农林牧渔业27.0亿美元（19.5%）、制造业15.7亿美元（11.3%）、租赁和商务服务业9.2亿美元（6.7%）、金融业4.9亿美元（3.5%）。

#### 8.3.3.3 中国在大洋洲的投资及其与大洋洲的经济结构匹配情况

大洋洲的澳大利亚、新西兰等虽然是发达国家，但是其经济体量较小，产业结构较为单一以及产业层次不如欧美。因此，中国在大洋洲的投资较少。截至 2017年年底，中国对大洋洲直接投资存量为417.6亿美元，占中国对外直接投资存量的2.3%。但是，从发展战略层面来看，“一带一路”倡议当中的21世纪海上丝绸之路，其中有一个方向就是伸向南太平洋。2017年，国家发改委和国家海洋局联合发布《“一带一路”建设海上合作设想》，提出共建中国—大洋洲—南太平洋蓝色经济通道。澳大利亚和新西兰都是这条经济通道上最具代表性的两个国家。目前，中国与澳大利亚和新西兰均签署了自由贸易协定（FTA），而且正在致力于打造协定的“升级版”。中国连续数年成为澳大利亚和新西兰第一大货物贸易伙伴，重要出口市场和进口来源地。中国的工业制成品在大洋洲地区受到广泛欢迎，而大洋洲地区也是世界上重要的农产品、矿产品产地，在中国市场有巨大的需求。[①]随着“一带一路”建设与澳大利亚“北部大开发”计划的战略对接，未来中国与大洋洲国家经贸投资合作关系将朝着多领域、多层次、多形式方向发展，合作潜力将逐步释放，投资规模将稳步增长。2005—2015年，澳大利亚成为中国全球直接投资的第二大目的国。2013—2015年，中国成为澳大利亚第一大海外直接投资来源国。截至2017年年底，中国在大洋洲设立境外企业约1 300家（澳大利亚约1 000家），占境外企业总数的3.5%，覆盖大洋洲12个国家（地区），覆盖率为50%。它们主要分布在澳大利亚、新西兰、巴布亚新几内亚、萨摩亚、斐济等国。2017年，中国设立境外企业数量的国家（地区）排名中，澳大利亚由第四位上升到第三位，在中国企业对外投资并购额前十位国家中排名第八位，吸引中国企业并购投资超过50亿美元。2017年，中国对澳大利亚直接投资流量42.42亿美元，占对全球投资流量总额的2.7%，占对大洋洲投资流量的83.1%。对澳投资存量为361.75亿美元，占中国对外直接投资存量总额的2%，占对大洋洲投资存量的86.6%。同时，澳大利亚在中国对发达国家（地区）直接投资存量排名中位列第三，占比15.8%。

正如前面所介绍的，大洋洲尤其是澳大利亚的资源型产业对中国的依赖度很高，这一点也反映在中国在大洋洲的投资上。截至2017年年底，中国企业在大洋洲投资存量主要分布在5个行业领域（占83.2%）：采矿业投资223.8亿美元（53.6%）、房地产业44.3亿美元（10.6%）、租赁和商务服务业投资31.3亿美元（7.5%）、金融业投资28.4亿美元（6.8%），制造业19.6亿美元（4.7%）。2017年，中国对澳大利亚的投资从主要流向看，采矿业投资14.3亿美元，占33.7%；租赁和商务服务业投资5.45亿美元，占12.8%；金融业投资5.03亿美元，占11.9%；房地产业投资4.93亿美元，占11.6%；制造业投资4.7亿美元，占11.1%；农林牧

① 澳大利亚矿产和农业资源丰富，铁矿石、煤炭、黄金、铀、锌、铅、铝土、锰、石油、天然气、页岩气等产量居世界前列，农业高度现代化、机械化，是全球第四大农产品出口国。澳大利亚已探明的铁矿石资源约有160亿吨，勘探开发较为成熟。澳大利亚是世界最大的煤炭出口国，黑煤地质储量约为575亿吨（工业经济储量为397亿吨），居世界第六，褐煤地质储量约为418亿吨（工业经济储量为376亿吨），占全球褐煤储量的20%，居世界第二。

渔业占5.1%；建筑业占3.6%。截至2017年年底，中国对澳大利亚直接投资存量主要行业为：采矿业205.94亿美元，占56.9%；房地产业41.02亿美元，占11.3%；租赁和商务服务业28.9亿美元，占8%；金融业24.42亿美元，占6.7%；制造业15.64亿美元，占4.3%；批发和零售业9.58亿美元，占2.6%；交通运输、仓储和邮政业8.89亿美元，占2.5%。从这些数据中可以看到，尽管中国对大洋洲和澳大利亚的投资最主要的依然是资源型行业，但是已经逐步多元化，这意味着中国在促进大洋洲经济结构的多元化。中国的投资在大洋洲尤其是澳大利亚也涉及基础设施领域。例如，招商局集团以8.75亿澳元获得澳大利亚纽卡斯尔港口的99年租赁权，山东岚桥集团5.06亿澳元获得达尔文港99年租赁使用权，国家电网收购当地电网公司的股权。这些都将有助于改善大洋洲的基础设施（可回顾第7章的相关内容）。

### 8.3.4 从发达国家“引进来”促进中国与发达经济体的经济结构转型升级[①]

#### 8.3.4.1 中国“引进来”及其与中国的经济结构匹配情况

如我们在第5章图5.39中所展示的，中国实际利用外资金额从1983年的22.61亿美元一路飙升到2018年的1 349.66亿美元。从发达国家招商引资是中国在改革开放之后经济快速发展最为重要的推动力之一，也是中国推动发达国家经济结构转型升级最为重要的推动力之一。中国对发达国家在实体经济领域的开放，不但使得发达国家充分利用了中国劳动力丰富的比较优势和庞大的市场，也使得中国引进了新技术，培育了新产业，迅速地促进中国经济结构转型升级。2005年，《商务部关于全面提高外商投资促进工作水平的指导意见》（商资发〔2005〕340号）中就指出了引进外资对中国经济发展的重要性：“党的十一届三中全会以来，我国将吸收外资作为对外开放基本国策的重要内容。20多年的实践证明，吸收外资加速了国内、国外两种资源和两个市场的融合，带入了现代管理经验和市场营销理念，引进了大量资金、适用技术，增强了自主研发能力，培养了大批人才，创造了更多的就业机会，增加了国家税收和外汇收入。吸收外资大大推进了我国开放型经济的形成与发展，加速了经济结构的调整和产业升级，增强了国家经济实力和国际竞争力，促进了思想解放和观念更新，对社

① 本小节的数据资料主要来自商务部发布的《中国外商投资报告》，更详细的内容资料可参考该系列报告。

会主义市场经济的建立和法律体系的建设起到了重要作用。”

1979年春天成立的中外合资企业北京航空食品有限公司，拉开了中国改革开放之后外商投资企业在中国雨后春笋涌现的序幕。截至2017年年底，全国累计设计外商投资企业高达约90万家，其中外商独资企业占据半壁江山。如图8.19所示的新增企业分布，在1992年之后掀起了一波外商投资企业高潮，1993年新增外商投资企业数量高达8.3万家，创历史之最；在2001年中国加入世界贸易组织之后开启了第二波高潮，2002—2007年外商投资企业新增数目年均超过3万家。即便在2008年国际金融危机之后，中国近十年来年均新增外商投资企业数目也超过2万家。在这些近百万家外商投资企业中，既有肯德基这样的遍布大街小巷的大众餐饮企业，也有特斯拉这样的高端智能制造工业企业，也有沃尔玛、宜家、高盛和摩根士丹利等全球商业、金融巨头。当然，这些外商投资企业的行业分布并非随机，而是随中国经济结构变迁的韵律而跳动。在20世纪80年代，中国鼓励来料加工和进料加工贸易，以加工贸易为主的制造业是吸引外资企业的主要行业。直到2008年国际金融危机爆发时，随着中国经济结构向服务业转型，服务业的新增外商企业开始超过制造业，如图8.20所示。1998—2017年，累计新增外商投资企业中制造业占49.7%，批发和零售位居第二占17.1%。这些外商投资企业反过来又推进了中国与世界经济的深度联系，除了前面已经多次介绍的外资外，贡献了中国外贸的半壁江山。如图8.21所示，外商投资企业进出口总额从2000年的2 367.14亿美元飙升到2018年的近2万亿美元，为中国创造的贸易顺差从2000年的21.69亿美元迅速上升到2007年的1 355.78亿美元，2018年依然维持在1 040.25亿美元，大致贡献了中国贸易顺差的一半。

中国改革开放之后堪称按照比较优势迅速转型升级吸引外资的典范。中国的经验与新结构经济学理论事实上已经破解了第5章提到的卢卡斯之谜。所谓的卢卡斯之谜是指：主流理论认为发展中国家资本短缺，资本的回报率高，资本应该从发达国家流向发展中国家，但卢卡斯发现，在现实中资本却从大多数的发展中国家流向发达国家。对此现象新结构经济学的

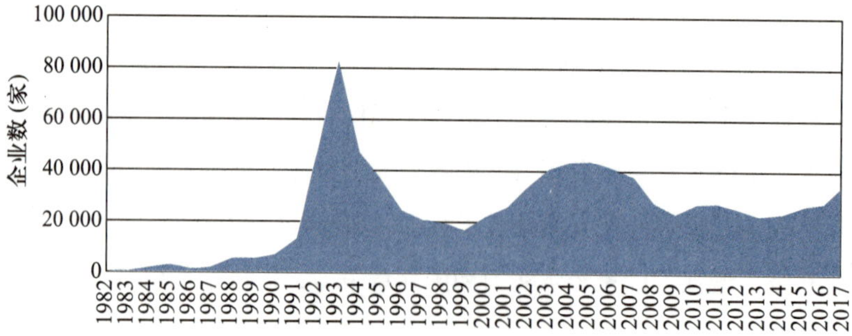


**图8.19 改革开放以来中国外商投资企业新增数目**

数据来源：商务部，《中国外商投资报告2018》，2018年。

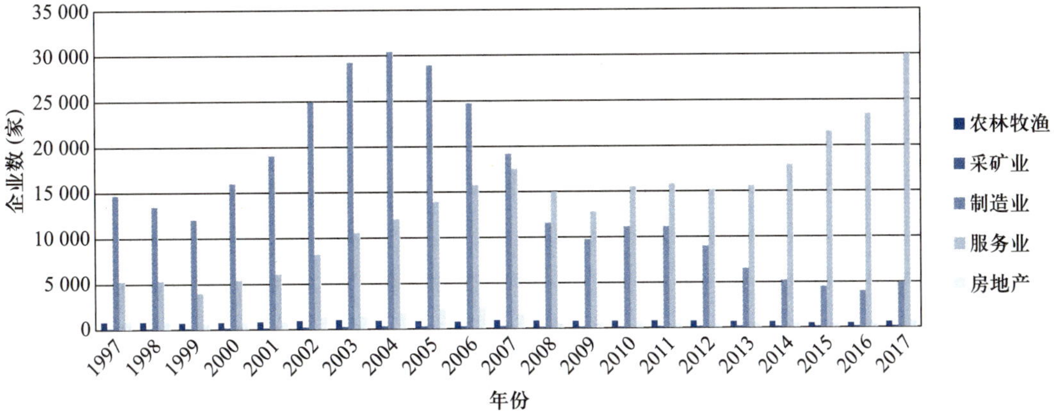


**图8.20 近20年来中国外商投资企业的行业分布**

数据来源：商务部，《中国外商投资报告2018》，2018年。

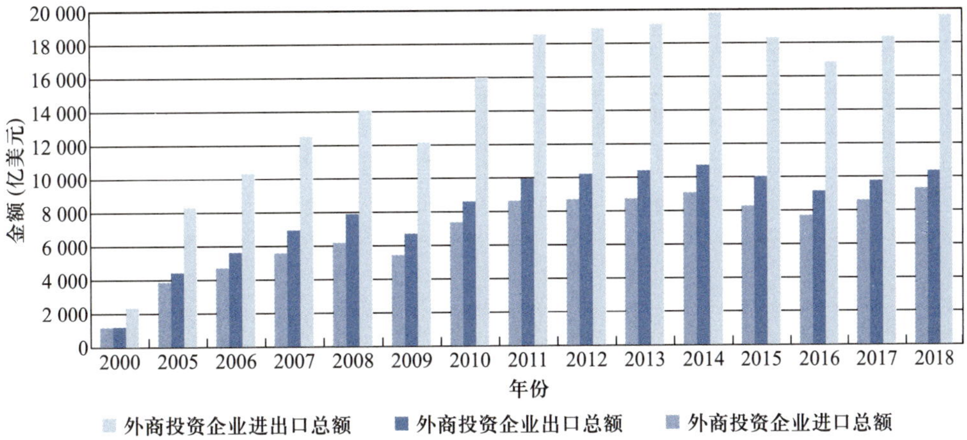


**图8.21 近20年来外商投资企业进出口总额**

数据来源：国家统计局。

解释是，如果一个发展中国家采取了违反比较优势的战略，不仅有权有势的富人从各种价格扭曲和行政干预中寻租获得的财富缺乏合法性，而且国内投资的资本回报率会低，资本就会外逃到发达国家。反之，如果按照比较优势发展，资本的回报率高，富人以企业家才能从市场竞争中获得的财富具有合法性，资本不仅不会外逃，而且还会有资本流入[①]。从中国利用

① Lin Justin Yifu and Wang Xin, “Development Strategy and International Capital Flow” , INSE Working Paper Series, E2019003, 2019.

外资的方式以及外商投资模式及产业布局就可以看到中国与外商皆大欢喜的双赢格局。外商投资主要通过在制造业投资以及在零售业并购的方式充分利用了中国劳动力丰富的禀赋结构资源（如表8.4所示）以及庞大的国内市场（回顾本章前面的讨论），中国则充分借助外资发挥了比较优势，利用了后来者优势，迅速推进了经济结构转型升级。例如，2017年外商投资企业以占全国不到3%的企业数目和不到4%的固定资产投资，雇用了6%的城镇就业人员，创造了全国近一半的对外贸易、1/4的规模以上工业企业利润、1/5的税收收入。当然，随着中国经济结构的转型升级，外资也随之不断升级并发挥了领军作用。例如，2017年高技术产业利用外资占了约30%，与2012年相比提高了近14个百分点。2016年外商投资企业投入研发人员61.7万人，占全国的22.8%；投入研发经费2 419.3亿元，占全国的22.1%；有效发明专利数量14.7万件，占全国的19.1%；产品或工艺创新高出全国平均水平6.4个百分点；占了全国80%的高技术产品出口份额。事实上，外商投资已经成为影响中国经济社会各方面的一股极为重要的力量。①

表8.4 2011—2016年外商投资企业户均吸纳就业能力与全国企业平均水平比较

| 指标 | | 2011年 | 2012年 | 2013年 | 2014年 | 2015年 | 2016年 |
|---|---|---|---|---|---|---|---|
| 外商投资企业 | 数量合计（个） | 230 115 | 243 453 | 202 389 | 231 954 | 237 456 | 203 836 |
| | 就业人员合计（万人） | 2 149 | 2 215 | 2 963 | 2 955 | 2 790 | 2 666 |
| | 户均企业吸纳就业（人） | 93 | 91 | 146 | 127 | 117 | 131 |
| 全国企业 | 数量合计（个） | 7 331 200 | 8 286 654 | 8 208 273 | 10 617 154 | 12 593 254 | 14 618 448 |
| | 就业人员合计（万人） | 35 914 | 37 120 | 38 240 | 39 310 | 40 410 | 41 428 |
| | 户均企业吸纳就业（人） | 49 | 45 | 47 | 37 | 32 | 28 |
| 外商投资企业吸纳就业是全国平均的倍数 | | 1.9 | 2.0 | 3.1 | 3.4 | 3.7 | 4.6 |

注：整体比重中的外商投资企业包括港澳台商投资企业。
数据来源：国家统计局，《2017年中国统计年鉴》。

① 关于外商投资对中国经济增长、产业结构、技术进步、劳动力市场、金融市场、对外开放、区域发展、环境污染、制度建设等一系列议题的相关研究已经多如牛毛，感兴趣的读者可去查阅文献。

#### 8.3.4.2 中国各行业“引进来”推进转型升级的情况

中国改革开放之后率先在加工贸易领域引进外资，主要集中在劳动力密集型出口导向的制造业，这符合中国当时的比较优势。这一趋势一直到中国加入世界贸易组织之后达到顶峰。例如，2005年中国制造业实际利用外商直接投资金额占比超过70%，与之相对比的是2005年批发和零售业实际利用外商直接投资金额占比不足2%。2008年国际金融危机之后，外资在中国的行业结构随着中国的禀赋结构的变化而发生了阶段性变化，展现出两个新趋势：服务业逐步取代制造业成为吸引外资的主要行业（目前形成了第二产业与第三产业三七开的格局），资本和技术相对密集的制造业逐步取代劳动密集型制造业成为吸引外资的主要制造业。具体如图8.22和表8.5所示。

中国制造业实际利用外商直接投资金额占比从2009年的51.95%下降到2010年的46.90%，首次下降到一半以下，但是，到2018年依然占30.51%，达411.7亿美元，如图8.23所示。虽然制造业吸引外资的整体比重有所下降，但制造业的外资结构在不断升级。例如，2017年中国高技术制造业新设立外商投资企业1 032家，实际投资金额98.9亿美元，其中：电子及通信设备制造业新设立外商投资企业623家，实际投资金额64亿美元；医药制造业新设立外商投资企业126家，实际投资金额21.4亿美元。服务业实际利用外商直接投资金额占比则从2005年的24.7%上升到2017年的67.9%，达889.8亿美元，如图8.24所示。其中，2007—2016年房地产业实际利用外商直接投资金额占比平均达到了20%左右。租赁和商务服务业实际利用外商直接投资金额占比从2007年的5.38%上升到2018年的13.98%，批发和零售业实际利用外商直接投资金额占比从2007年的3.58%上升到2018年的7.24%，信息传输、计算机服务和软件业实际利用外商直接投资金额占比从2007年的1.99%上升到2018年的8.64%，科学研究、技术服务和地质勘查业实际利用外商直接投资金额占比从2007年的1.23%上升到2018年的5.05%。与制造业外商投资不断升级一样，服务业的外商投资也在不断升级。例如，

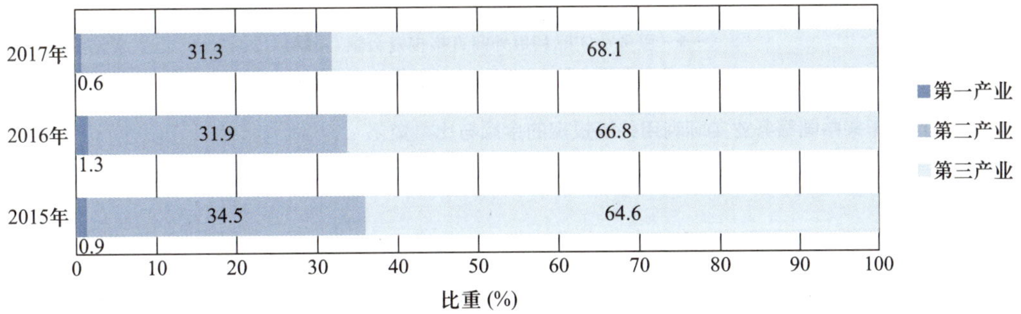


图8.22 目前中国外商投资的三次产业结构分布格局

数据来源：商务部，《中国外商投资报告2018》，2018年。

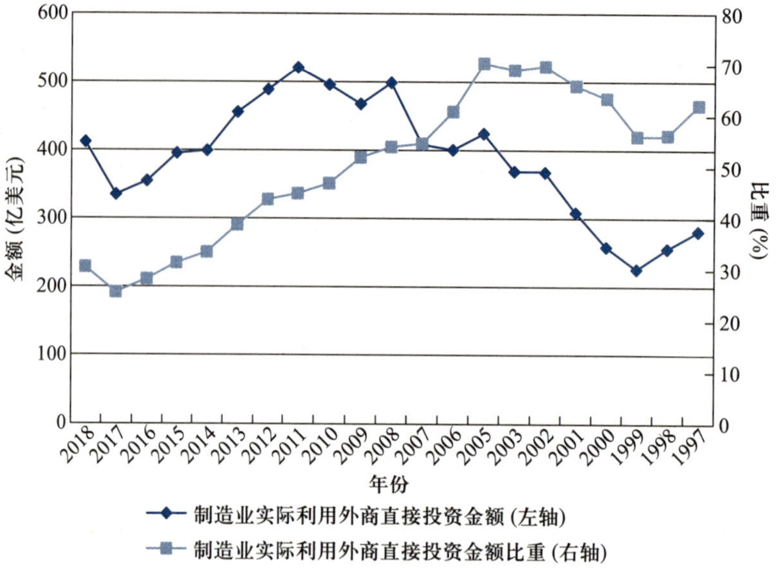


图8.23 近20年来中国制造业实际利用外商投资的金额与比重变化

数据来源：国家统计局。

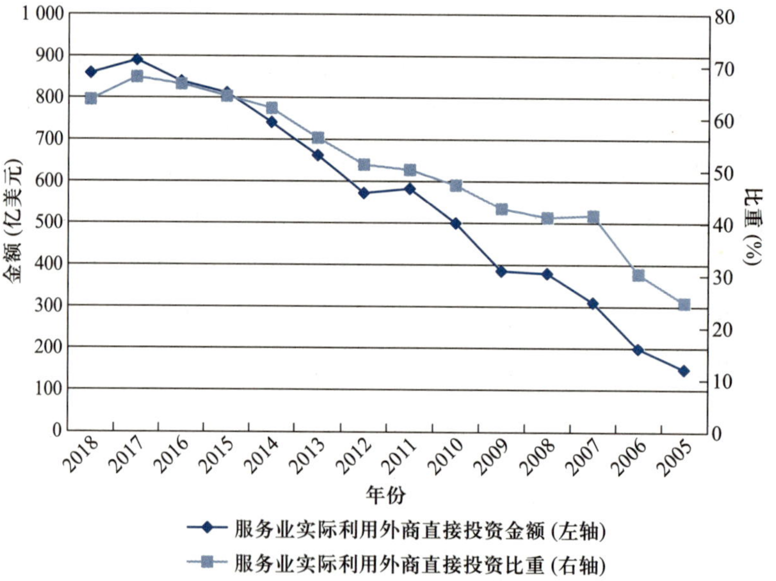


图8.24 近20年来中国服务业实际利用外商投资的金额与比重变化

资料来源：国家统计局。

表8.5 2005—2018年中国各行业实际利用外商直接投资金额占比（%）

| 行业 | 年份 | | | | | | | | | | | | | |
|---|---|---|---|---|---|---|---|---|---|---|---|---|---|---|
| | 2005 | 2006 | 2007 | 2008 | 2009 | 2010 | 2011 | 2012 | 2013 | 2014 | 2015 | 2016 | 2017 | 2018 |
| 农、林、牧、渔业 | 1.19 | 0.91 | 1.24 | 1.29 | 1.59 | 1.81 | 1.73 | 1.85 | 1.53 | 1.27 | 1.21 | 1.51 | 0.82 | 0.59 |
| 采矿业 | 0.59 | 0.70 | 0.65 | 0.62 | 0.56 | 0.65 | 0.53 | 0.69 | 0.31 | 0.47 | 0.19 | 0.08 | 0.99 | 0.91 |
| 制造业 | 70.37 | 60.89 | 54.66 | 54.00 | 51.95 | 46.90 | 44.91 | 43.74 | 38.74 | 33.40 | 31.32 | 28.17 | 25.57 | 30.51 |
| 电力、燃气及水的生产和供应业 | 2.31 | 1.95 | 1.43 | 1.84 | 2.35 | 2.01 | 1.83 | 1.47 | 2.07 | 1.84 | 1.78 | 1.70 | 2.69 | 3.28 |
| 建筑业 | 0.81 | 1.05 | 0.58 | 1.18 | 0.77 | 1.38 | 0.79 | 1.06 | 1.04 | 1.04 | 1.23 | 1.97 | 2.00 | 1.10 |
| 交通运输、仓储和邮政业 | 3.00 | 3.02 | 2.68 | 3.09 | 2.81 | 2.12 | 2.75 | 3.11 | 3.59 | 3.73 | 3.32 | 4.04 | 4.26 | 3.50 |
| 信息传输、计算机服务和软件业 | 1.68 | 1.63 | 1.99 | 3.00 | 2.50 | 2.35 | 2.33 | 3.01 | 2.45 | 2.30 | 3.04 | 6.70 | 15.96 | 8.64 |
| 批发和零售业 | 1.72 | 2.72 | 3.58 | 4.80 | 5.99 | 6.24 | 7.26 | 8.47 | 9.79 | 7.92 | 9.52 | 12.60 | 8.76 | 7.24 |
| 住宿和餐饮业 | 0.93 | 1.26 | 1.39 | 1.02 | 0.94 | 0.88 | 0.73 | 0.63 | 0.66 | 0.54 | 0.34 | 0.29 | 0.32 | 0.67 |
| 金融业 | 0.36 | 0.45 | 0.34 | 0.62 | 0.51 | 1.06 | 1.65 | 1.90 | 1.98 | 3.50 | 11.85 | 8.17 | 6.05 | 6.45 |
| 房地产业 | 8.98 | 12.50 | 22.86 | 20.12 | 18.66 | 22.68 | 23.17 | 21.59 | 24.49 | 28.96 | 22.96 | 15.60 | 12.86 | 16.65 |
| 租赁和商务服务业 | 6.21 | 6.42 | 5.38 | 5.48 | 6.75 | 6.74 | 7.23 | 7.35 | 8.81 | 10.44 | 7.96 | 12.80 | 12.77 | 13.98 |
| 科学研究、技术服务和地质勘查业 | 0.56 | 0.77 | 1.23 | 1.63 | 1.86 | 1.86 | 2.12 | 2.77 | 2.34 | 2.72 | 3.59 | 5.17 | 5.22 | 5.05 |
| 水利、环境和公共设施管理业 | 0.23 | 0.30 | 0.36 | 0.37 | 0.62 | 0.86 | 0.74 | 0.76 | 0.88 | 0.48 | 0.34 | 0.33 | 0.43 | 0.35 |
| 居民服务和其他服务业 | 0.43 | 0.77 | 0.97 | 0.62 | 1.76 | 1.94 | 1.62 | 1.04 | 0.56 | 0.60 | 0.57 | 0.39 | 0.43 | 0.42 |
| 教育 | 0.03 | 0.04 | 0.04 | 0.04 | 0.01 | 0.01 | 0.00 | 0.03 | 0.02 | 0.02 | 0.02 | 0.07 | 0.06 | 0.05 |
| 卫生、社会保障和社会福利业 | 0.07 | 0.02 | 0.02 | 0.02 | 0.05 | 0.09 | 0.07 | 0.06 | 0.05 | 0.06 | 0.11 | 0.20 | 0.23 | 0.22 |
| 文化、体育和娱乐业 | 0.51 | 0.37 | 0.60 | 0.28 | 0.35 | 0.41 | 0.55 | 0.48 | 0.70 | 0.69 | 0.63 | 0.21 | 0.53 | 0.39 |

资料来源：根据国家统计局数据计算。

2017年中国高技术服务业新设立外商投资企业5 990家，实际使用外资金额260.7亿元，其中：信息服务业新增外商投资企业3 392家，实际投资金额209.7亿美元；科技成果转化服务业新设立外商投资企业1 991家，实际投资金额32.9亿美元。2008年国际金融危机之后，中国的金融业开放令人瞩目，金融业实际利用外商直接投资金额占比从2009年的0.51%上升到2018年的6.45%。

在农业领域，中国利用外资的形式可以分为两个阶段：第一个阶段主要是国际援助形式，第二阶段才是具有商业性质的外商投资。[①]20世纪90年代中期以前，中国农业利用外资主要以世界银行、亚洲开发银行、国际农业发展基金会、联合国粮农组织、世界粮食计划署、欧洲共同体、联合国开发计划署等国际组织及政府间的借款或无偿援助等间接投资方式为主，一度占到了中国农业利用外资的80%以上。到1997年，农、林、牧、渔业实际利用外商直接投资金额虽然只有6.3亿美元，但占全部实际利用外商直接投资金额的1.4%。此后的十年，中国农业吸引外商直接投资的增幅不大，1997—2006年的年均实际利用外商直接投资金额只有7.6亿美元。但此后的10年是中国农业吸引外商直接投资的黄金时期，2007—2016年的年均实际利用外商直接投资金额达17亿美元，如图8.25所示。截至2015年年底，农业领域累计设立外商投资企业24 094家，占全国累计外商投资企业数的2.88%；实际使用外资金额197.42亿美元，占全国累计吸收外资金额的1.53%。徐玉波梳理了外商直接投资流入对中国农业经济、农产品贸易、农民收入等均能产生积极的促进作用。[②]孙致陆和李先德根据1994—2010年的省际面板数据的经验分析，发现农业领域外商直接投资对中国农业技术效率和农业技术进步均具有显著的正向影响。[③]当然，也有研究指出，外资在中国农业领域的研发会产生负向的溢出效应，不断拉大本土企业与外资企业研发水平的差距，有利于外资企业建立技术优势，逐渐形成垄断。[④]在新时期，中国农业也发生了巨大的转型升级，需要高质量引进来。例如，《全国农业现代化规划（2016—2020年）》在提高农业引进来质量方面指出："加强先进技术装备引进，鼓励引进全球农业技术领先的企业、机构和管理团队。推行准入前国民待遇加负面清单管理模式，鼓励外资投向现代农机装备制造业、特色产业、农产品加工业、农业废弃物资源化利用。"

---

① 吕立才、熊启泉，"我国农业利用FDI30年:实践及理论研究进展"，《国际贸易问题》，2010年第2期。

② 徐玉波，《农业利用外商直接投资对中国农业的影响》，中国农业科学院博士论文，2012年。

③ 孙致陆、李先德，"农业FDI提升了中国农业全要素生产率吗——基于面板数据随机前沿函数模型的分析"，《国际商务（对外经济贸易大学学报）》，2014年第3期。

④ 马述忠、陈颖、王笑笑，"农业FDI对中国粮食安全的动态影响研究——基于种业研发能力视角"，《管理世界》，2013年第7期。

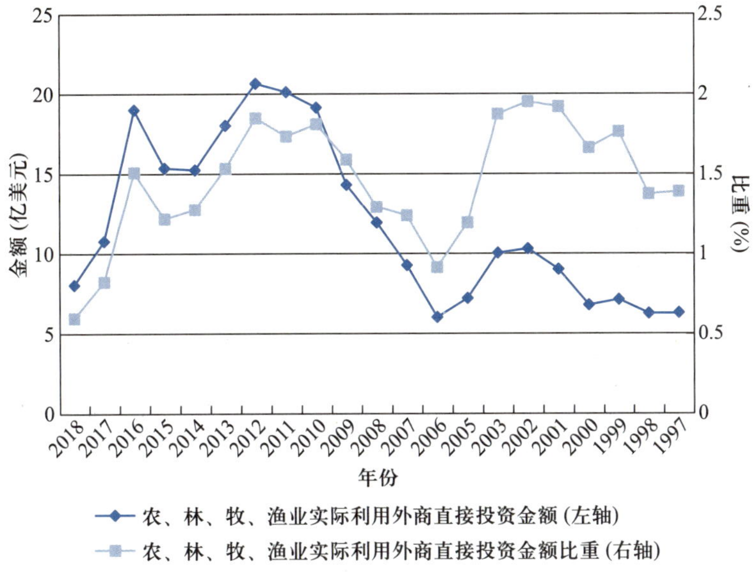


**图8.25 近20年来中国农业实际利用外商投资的金额与比重变化**

数据来源：国家统计局。

最后，通过前面对中国各行业引进外资的梳理，我们也可以看到一些重要的结构变化规律：外商投资结构随着具有比较优势的产业结构变化而变化。中国农业一开始并不具备自生能力，利用外资的形式更多是国际援助性质的无偿贷款，因此最初的外商投资主要集中在劳动力密集型的制造业，然后随着中国经济结构转型升级，外商投资又向服务业集中。有意思的是，服务业外商直接投资可能与制造业外商直接投资有密集的联动关系。唐保庆以1988—2006年美国对中国的直接投资数据，检验了生产者服务业外商直接投资与制造业外商直接投资之间的关系，如图8.26所示，结果表明，流入东道国的制造业外商直接投资明显受到来自母国的生产者服务业外商直接投资的追逐。[①]因此，不同发展阶段，服务业外商直接投资的效果必然不同。[②]

① 唐保庆，“生产者服务业FDI追逐制造业FDI吗？”，《财贸研究》，2009年第5期。

② 华广敏，“高技术服务业FDI对中美制造业效率影响的比较分析——基于中介效应分析”，《世界经济研究》，2013年第3期。

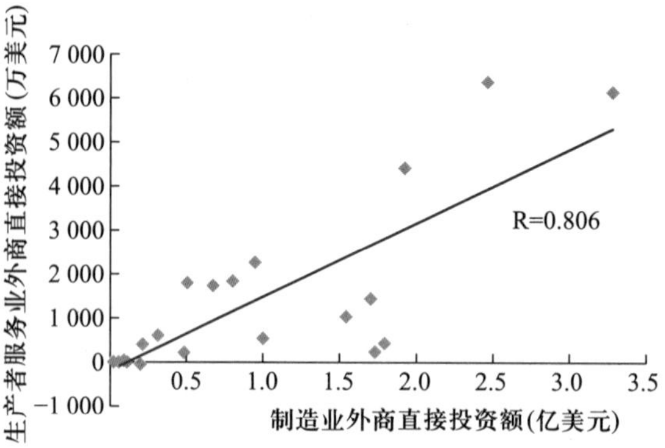


**图8.26 1988—2006年美国对华的生产者服务业外商直接投资额与制造业外商直接投资额的联动变化**

资料来源：美国经济分析局（BEA），转引自：唐保庆，“生产者服务业FDI追逐制造业FDI吗？”，《财贸研究》，2009年第5期。

## 专栏8.2
## 中国装备制造业的追赶历程[①]

装备制造业又称装备工业，主要是指资本品制造业，是为满足国民经济各部门发展和国家安全需要而制造各种技术装备的产业的总称。按照国民经济行业分类，其产品范围包括机械、电子和兵器工业中的投资类制成品，分属于金属制品业、通用装备制造业、专用设备制造业、交通运输设备制造业、电气装备及器材制造业、电子及通信设备制造业、仪器仪表及文化办公用装备制造业7个大类185个小类。

装备制造业是为国民经济和国防建设提供生产技术装备的制造业，因此被视为制造业的核心组成部分甚至是国民经济发展特别是工业发展的基础。装备制造业的发展水平被直接用来衡量工业化水平的高低。装备制造业是典型的资本密集型和技术密集型以及人力资本密集型行业。装备制造业从生产通用类装备（如农用机械、工程机械），到生产基础类装备（如机床、工装），再到生产成套类装备（如石油、化工、煤化工、盐化工成套设备等），乃至更高级的生产安全保障类装备和高技术关键装备（如军事、航空航天装备等），其厂房成本、设备成本、材料成本、研发成本、人力成本等开支都十分巨大，投资规模动辄上亿元，以十亿、

① 本专栏来自：林毅夫、付才辉，《世界经济结构转型升级报告》，北京大学出版社，2017年版。

百亿元观，也不鲜见。所以装备制造业是十足的资本密集型产业。装备制造业的生产过程对技术和智力要素的依赖大大超过其他行业。比如，生产数控机床、大规模集成电路；微电子和电力电子器件、仪器仪表、自动化控制系统；矿产资源的井采及露天开采设备；大型火电、水电、核电成套设备；民用飞机、高速铁路、地铁及城市轨道车，汽车、船舶等先进交通运输设备；大型科学仪器和医疗设备；先进大型的军事装备，通信、航管及航空航天装备；等等。这些产品技术含量高、生产工艺精密，组织过程复杂，对研发水平、技术实力、知识产权投入方面的要求都很高，所以装备制造业又可谓技术密集型产业。与能够标准化生产降低对劳动力技能和知识水平要求的批量化轻工业生产模式不同，装备制造业所生产的产品，如矿产资源的井采及露天开采设备，石油化工成套设备，电力成套设备，船舶、地铁、航空航天、军事装备等，其生产组织过程都非常复杂，主要是通过按单制造、非标制造、项目制造等模式进行的，而这些生产组织模式与最终消费品制造业的生产组织模式极为不同。最终消费品制造业的产品多可进行批量化、流水线生产，而装备制造业几乎不存在由少数几个工人看管数条生产线便可以使生产过程运转顺利的情况。按单制造、非标制造、项目制造模式中存在着大量的定制化采购、定制化设计、定制化生产组织、定制化装配工作，以及过程中的技术工艺变更、生产计划调整等事项，这些都需要靠人力介入进行解决，没有一成不变的、按钮式控制的“傻瓜式”生产过程。

由于装备制造业是典型的资本、技术与人力资本密集型重工业，时至今日依然是资本相对劳动丰裕的发达经济体的比较优势产业，发展中经济体难以望其项背。当前世界主要装备制造业大国的基本格局未发生明显改变，仍以美、日、德、法、意、英等发达国家为主，占全部总产值的70%。高端产品、关键核心技术被发达国家掌控，短期内其他国家难以超越。例如，根据2016年度《世界机械500强》的数据，世界机械500强企业仍主要集中在发达国家，格局基本稳定。美国、日本分别有138家、101家企业入选榜单，中国内地占95个席位，蝉联第3。前10强中，德国占3席，美国占2席，日本占2席，中国内地、韩国、中国台湾各占1席；前3位由日本、德国、中国占据。可以看到，老牌机械强国的竞争力仍然突出，德国、法国进入500强的企业总数虽不多，但进入百强的企业占三成左右，并均在行业领域优势突出。德国企业平均规模最大，平均销售收入38.9亿美元。亚洲国家除日本外，韩国机械企业很有竞争力，有12家企业上榜，虽然数量不多，但平均销售收入达352.4亿美元，超过了德国，且一半的企业进入百强。中国内地共有95家企业入选，排在前3位的分别是上汽、一汽和东风汽车，分别排在第3、第20和第23位。大部分入选企业都排在200名以后。从行业分布来看，世界装备制造企业遍布17个行业，以电工电器行业为首，机动车及零部件制造行业紧随其后，这两大行业优势明显，占据总榜单前10位中的9席。其中，排名前3位的企业分别是德国大众、丰田汽车和上汽，分别占据机动车及零部件制造行业的前3位。

2013年，中国装备制造业产值规模突破20万亿元，是2008年的2.2倍，年均增长17.5%，占全球装备制造业的比重超过1/3，稳居世界首位。2014年，中国装备制造业产值规模突破22万亿元，占全球装备制造业的比重超过1/3，连续5年居世界首位；出口额达6.8万亿元，占全部工业产品出口的56.8%。目前，中国工程机械行业业务覆盖170 多个国家和地区，产品已经出口到200多个国家和地区，2017年出口首次跨越200亿美元大关，海外营业收入及出口占企业营业收入的比重达到25%左右，已成为全球工程机械市场主要供应商之一，是工程机械产品门类最齐全、种类最多的国家。中国的这一成绩并非一夜间取得的，而是历经了数十年的发展。然而，这一过程也非常曲折。事实上，在2000年之前，中国的装备制造业由于禀赋结构水平太低以及轻纺工业尚未充分发展，而不具备比较优势和国内市场，对世界前沿的追赶大都违背了比较优势。如图8.27所示，1980年到2000年的20年间，中国的装备制造业增加值始终超不过美国的10%。而且，利用新结构转型升级的“前沿距离－产业份额”矩阵和联合国工业发展组织（UNIDO）制造业的数据测算①，整个装备制造行业以及各个细分行业即便短暂地在某些年份的劳动生产率上有异常的赶超，但是其相对份额却无法提高，即便能够在技术上赶超，也是没有竞争力的，无法持续地促进产业结构转型升级。但是在2000年之后，由于中国禀赋结构的大幅度改善，比较优势提升，以及充分实现了轻纺工业的发展，对装备制造业产生了巨大的需求，中国的装备制造业持续转型升级，如图8.28所示。在图8.29中，中国装备制造业下属的7个细分行业中，除了办公室、会计和计算机械的制造的劳动生产率没有持续向前沿收敛，其他所有行业在劳动生产率和体量上都持续收敛。这是对第2章第2.4节所讨论的结构转型升级收敛性的一个生动说明。

① 新结构转型升级的“前沿距离－产业份额”矩阵是由付才辉开发的用来识别一个经济体的某种产业是领先型、追赶型、退出型等产业类型的诊断工具，参见：付才辉，“新结构经济学理论及其在转型升级中的应用”，《学习与探索》，2017年第4期。

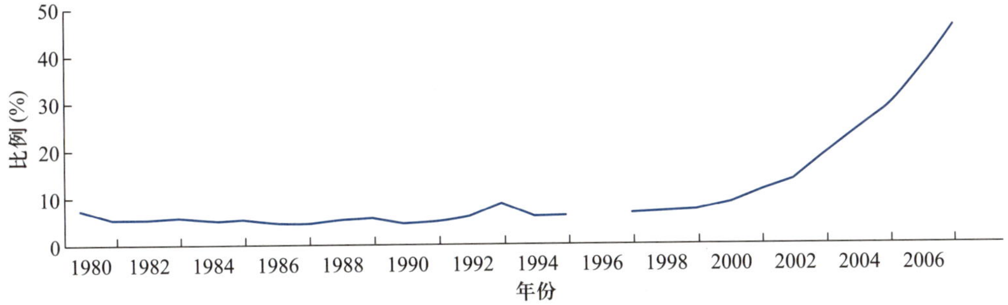


**图8.27 美国装备制造业增加值与中国之比**

资料来源：根据UNIDO数据计算。

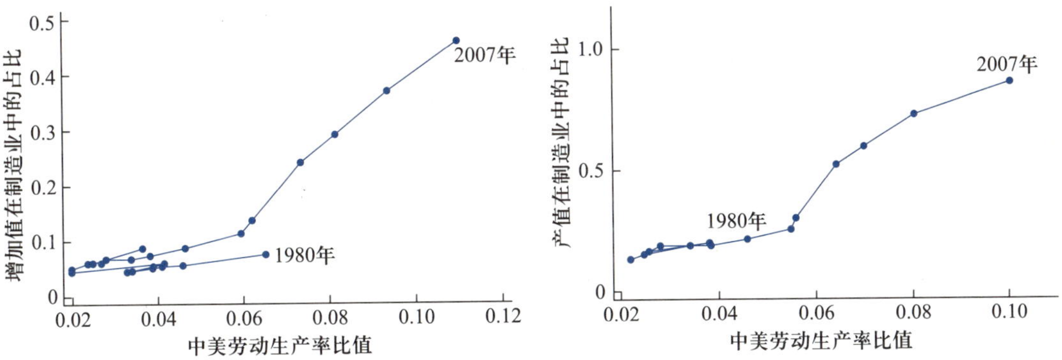


**图8.28 中国装备制造业的“前沿距离－产业份额”追赶矩阵**

资料来源：根据UNIDO数据测算。

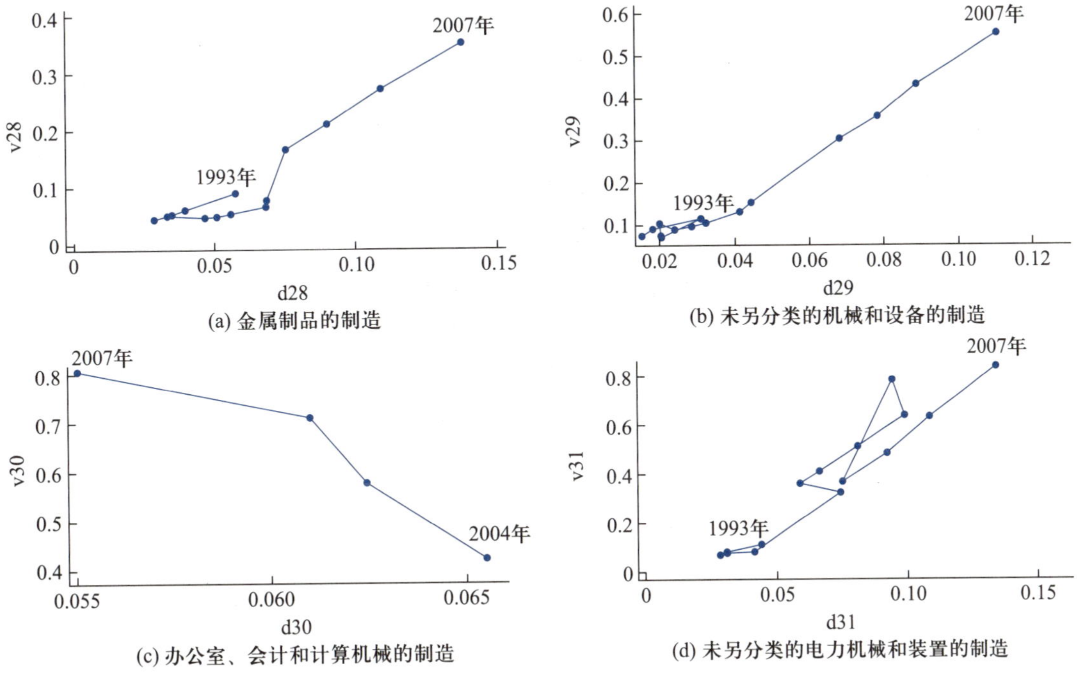

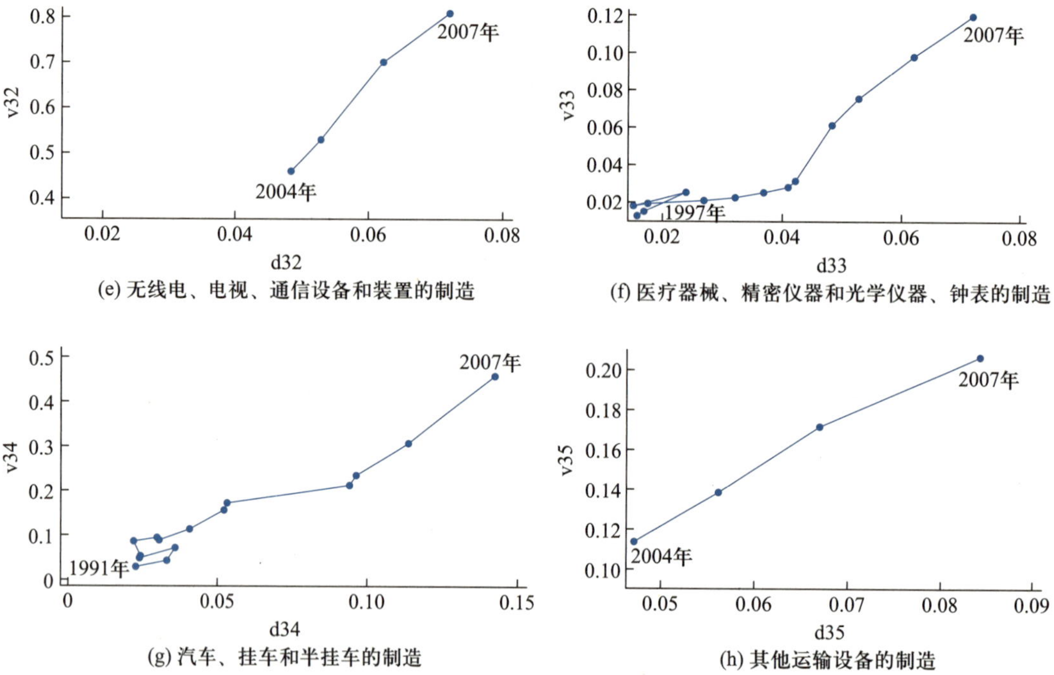


**图8.29 中国装备制造业细分行业的“前沿距离－产业份额”追赶矩阵**

资料来源：根据UNIDO数据测算。

### 8.3.4.3 中国各地区“引进来”及其与当地经济结构匹配情况[①]

如本章开头对中国地区之间的经济体量和发展水平巨大差异的介绍，相应地，其外商投资水平差别也非常显著。由于中国的改革开放始于沿海地区，特别是广东省（回顾第7章对中国沿海经济特区尤其是深圳的介绍），因此这些地区最先获得了外商投资，广东省率先获得了港资，江苏则获得台资较多。如图8.30所示，1993年，广东省的外商投资企业投资总额达131.49亿美元，占全国34.4%的份额，一枝独秀。到中国加入世界贸易组织之后，外商投资已经遍布沿海省份了，例如2002年东部沿海的广东省继续独领风骚地获得了24.69%

① 与引资相伴的引智也是中国各地区引进来的重要内容。魏浩和袁然将中国制造业企业的微观数据与省市的国际人才流入数据相结合的实证研究发现，国际人才流入可以显著促进中国企业研发投入，但这种效应因地区差异和企业异质性有所不同。更多实证内容可参考：魏浩、袁然，“国际人才流入与中国企业的研发投入”，《世界经济》，2018年第12期，第144−166页。与人才引进相反的是人才流失，如果发展中国家或地区经济结构不能顺利升级，就不能创造相应的就业岗位（回顾第6章的相关内容），英雄就无用武之地，必然造成人才流失。对于发展中国家的人才流失问题，可参考Frédéric Docquier and Hillel Rapoport, “Globalization, Brain Drain, and Development”, *Journal of Economic Literature*, 2012, Vol. 50, No. 3, pp. 681−730。

的外商投资份额，上海市和江苏省紧随其后分别获得13.37%和13.11%的份额，辽宁省获得了6.94%，福建省获得了6.21%，山东省获得了4.92%，北京市获得了4.75%，浙江省获得了4.51%，天津市获得了3.82%，这九个省份的外商投资份额超过八成。这一格局一直维持到今天，只是部分地区出现了新的局部变化。例如，2008年国际金融危机之后，广东省首当其冲，受到较大影响，2009年的外商投资份额下降到16.39%，被江苏省超过，后者获得了18.49%的外商投资份额，长三角的浙江省也获得了6.8%的外商投资份额。不过，近十年来，珠三角地区加速了经济结构转型，广东省又重新获得了最多的外商投资份额，2017年的外商投资企业投资总额达1 762亿美元，占全国的份额超过1/4。2017年，长三角的江苏省、上海市、浙江省的外商投资企业投资总额合计占全国的份额超过了30%。因此，珠三角和长三角已经是中国名副其实的对外开放高地。2019年印发的《粤港澳大湾区发展规划纲要》和《长江三角洲区域一体化发展规划纲要》都明确提出进一步提升粤港澳大湾区和长三角一体化地区在对外开放中的支撑引领作用，建立与国际接轨的开放型经济新体制，建设高水平参与国际经济合作新平台。在北方，京津冀协同发展战略提出以来，京津冀地区也加大了对外开放的力度，尤其是北京率先开展服务业扩大开放综合试点。2017年，北京的服务业实际利用外资比重超过九成；京津冀三地新设外商企业数目达2 383家，实际使用外商投资283.5亿美元。

与珠三角、长三角和京津冀形成鲜明对比的是，中西部和东北地区长期以来吸引的外资微不足道。例如，安徽省、江西省、陕西省、广西壮族自治区、山西省、内蒙古自治区、吉林省、云南省、黑龙江省、贵州省、宁夏回族自治区、甘肃省、新疆维吾尔自治区、青海省、西藏自治区不但外商投资比重低而且还处于下滑趋势，外商投资企业投资总额从1993年的10%下降到2017年的9%。截至2015年年底，东部地区设立外商投资企业700 587家，实际使用外资13 991.2亿美元，分别占全国总量的83.78%和85.19%；中部地区累计设立外商投资企业87 443家、实际使用外资金额1 338.85亿美元，分别占全国总量的10.45%和8.15%；西部地区设立外商投资项目数48 374个，实际使用外资1 093.15亿美元，占全国的比重分别为5.78%和6.66%。现阶段，这也意味着，中国中西部地区的开放潜力尚未充分释放。随着东部地区的经济结构转型升级，以及中西部地区工业化迅速推进和基础设施的逐步完善，中西部地区的进一步开放势在必行。如图8.31所示，2009年，东部地区省份向服务业主导的经济结构迈进，中西部大多数省份的工业增加值占GDP的比重达到40%左右。中西部地区的工业化既能继续吸引外资也可以通过外资推进工业化。陈艳莹和董旭选取中国省级细分行业面板数据，利用存量调整模型，对服务业与制造业的外国直接投资区位选择的差异进行了研究。他们的结果表明：与经济发达国家不同，处于转轨阶段的中国制造业的外国直接投资存量调整到均衡水平的速度快于服务业；服务业和制造业跨国公司在中国投资时，服务业看重市场规模和基础设施水平，受集聚因素的影响不显著，制造业则看重市场规模和劳动力成本，倾向于投资到产业集聚度高的地区。[①]此外，政府发挥因势利导作用，改善软硬基础设施，也会进一步加速中西部地区吸引外资。[②]2017年2月17日，国家发改委和商务部发布了新修订的《中西部地区外商投资优势产业目录（2017年修订）》，进一步扩大中西部地区的对外开放力度。下一章将专门介绍的“一带一路”倡议就有利于中国中西部地区的对外开放，目前已经取得初步成效。

专栏8.3

江苏太仓德国中心引进来的案例[③]

自1993年第一家德国企业克恩－里伯斯（太仓）有限公司落户以来，到2014年太仓新区已入驻德资企业230多家，项目总投资近20亿美元，注册资本近10亿美元，年工业总产值近300亿元人民币。截至2014年年底，德企亩均产值800多万元人民币，亩均税收50万元人民币，人均税收10万元人民币，万元产值能耗仅为0.021吨标准煤，使太仓成为中国德资发展最好、密度最高、经济效益最明显的地区之一，被誉为“中国德企之乡”。近年来，太仓德企以每年20家的速度递增，而且90%以上德企完成了增资扩产。

● 档次升级，率先实践工业4.0。在中国制造业升级换档的当下，作为最早提出工业4.0的制造业大国，德企对于工业4.0的实践，无疑是中国企业学习的榜样。在主营机床业务的德企通快（中国）有限公司，钣金加工“工业4.0”的全过程是：工作人员点开iPad中的“TruTops Fab”生产管理软件，输入相关产品参数，一个订单便生成了。点开这个订单，每一道工序的成本、价格都清楚呈现。

① 陈艳莹、董旭，“服务业与制造业对华FDI区位选择的差异——基于存量调整模型的实证研究”，《世界经济研究》，2013年第3期。

② 例如，陈海波和陈赤平以交通运输能力为门槛，利用2006—2013年中国224个城市构建面板门槛模型，结果发现当城市交通运输能力低于低门槛值（0.215）时，FDI对制造业发展具有显著的抑制作用，而当交通运输能力高于高门槛值（0.720）时，FDI对制造业发展表现为显著的促进作用。从异质性角度看，在城市公路运输能力门槛条件下，FDI对制造业发展的影响存在显著的“N”形特征；而在铁路和水路运输能力门槛条件下，FDI对城市制造业发展则表现为“U”形影响；航空运输能力对FDI影响制造业发展不存在门槛效应。因此，各城市要积极完善水陆空各大交通运输体系，提升制造业对FDI的吸收能力，促进制造业发展和升级。更详细的实证研究可参考：陈海波、陈赤平，“FDI、交通运输能力与制造业发展：基于224个城市的面板门槛模型的实证分析”，《世界经济研究》，2018年第6期。

③ 本专栏根据太仓招商网的资料和《中国县域经济报》的报道整理而成。

经过自动编程后，订单进入生产环节。车间各种钣金加工机床也安装有生产管理软件，生产调度人员调用程序，机床即按照指令生产。作为管理者，只需坐在办公室里，通过一个iPad，就能对订单进行实时管理并监控生产过程。最近太仓市委、市政府出台《关于进一步深化全市对德合作工作的实施意见》，太仓将推动德国工业4.0模式与落实中国制造2025规划充分融合，在太仓移植生根，努力建立国内领先的以自动化、智能化、精细化生产为主导的先进制造业基地。

● 结构升级，服务性企业加快落户。第二产业规模聚集到一定程度，必将带动第三产业发展，特别是服务于第二产业的生产性服务业。近两年来，德国资本投资太仓的结构也开始发生变化，越来越多的德资服务性企业开始来到太仓。太仓迅捷信息技术有限公司是进驻太仓的第一家德资服务业企业，自2010年进入太仓以来，客户已经发展到60多家，除德企外，还有瑞士、奥地利等德语国家企业，分布在整个亚太地区。其公司主要业务是为德企架设性能优良的全球网络，为工业4.0数据保驾护航。德国工业4.0的重要内涵之一就是生产设备上的各种传感器实时产生大量数据，传送到服务器上进行汇总和分析，为生产流程的优化和运营提供数据支持。2015年，太仓新引进的德企中，约1/3是商贸服务性企业。不仅如此，此前在太仓投资制造业的一些德企，也开始进入服务业。翰备机械部件（太仓）有限公司在太仓注册成立了博睿纳贸易公司。据公司相关负责人介绍，翰备机械部件公司主要从事生产制造，而博睿纳贸易公司则将深挖中国市场，开展进出口贸易，拓展在华业务领域。世界第八家、中国第三家德国中心在太仓正式运行。跟随其步伐，一些德国的市场调研服务业企业、会计师事务所和律师事务所已经明确将到太仓发展。

● 配套升级，刚柔并济“五星服务”。“刚”，是指硬件设施。考虑德国企业多是家族式的中小企业，在经营方面十分谨慎稳妥，在投资初期一般选择先租用厂房。为此，太仓投资3亿元建立了占地300亩[①]的中德中小企业工业园，专门用来引进装备制造、汽车零部件、生物医药等产业领域的德国中小科技企业，目前已经有12家德企签约入驻14栋厂房。同时，太仓建立了3.6万平方米的德国留学生创业园，主要孵化信息技术、新材料、精密机械、环保科技等高科技创业企业，打造集高科技企业研发、技术创新和产品中试的公共平台和产业载体，目前已有22个项目落户，均代表着行业细分领域的领先水平。此外，太仓还建立了

① 1亩约合666.7平方米。

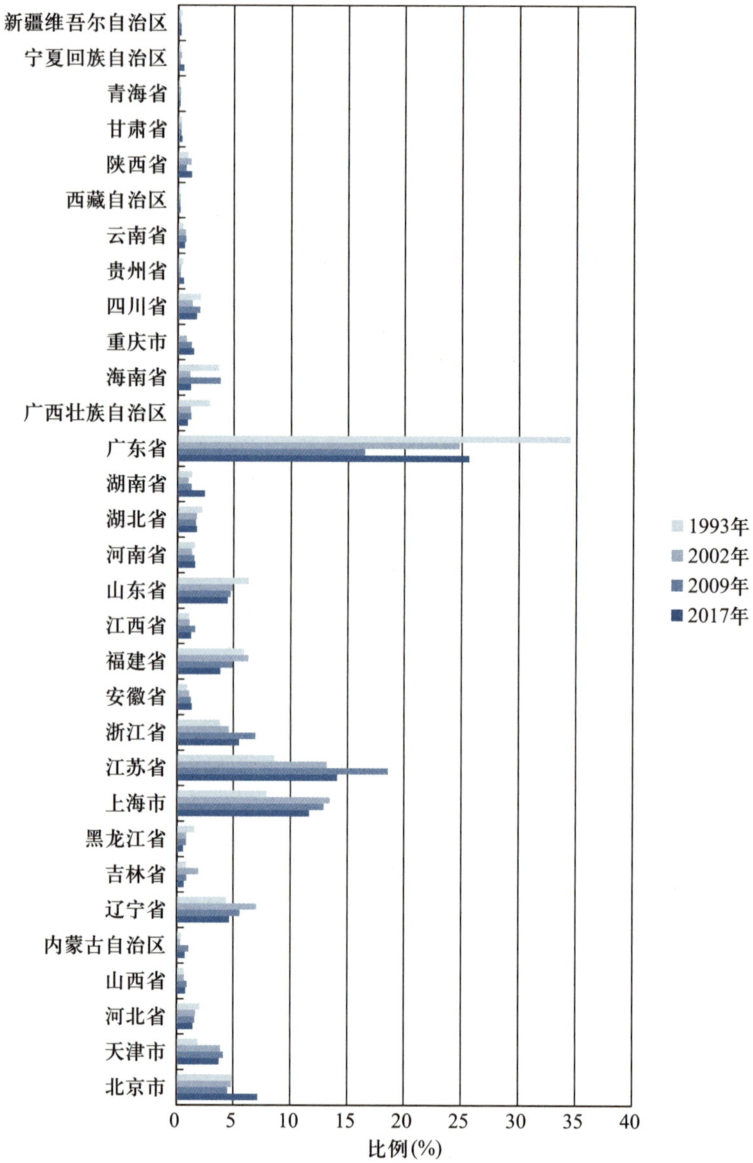


**图 8.30 中国内地各省份外商投资企业投资总额份额变迁**

数据来源：根据国家统计局数据测算。

太仓驻德国办事处、中国德国商会驻太仓办事处两大双向沟通平台，推动德企进驻中国市场并稳步发展。“柔”，则是指软件服务。太仓坚持“无事不扰，有求必应”的服务理念，根据企业实际需要，积极提供个性化服务，及时解决德企遇到的各种问题。为了满足德企人才需求，自 2001 年开始，太仓借鉴德国“双元制”教育模式，创办了太仓德资企业专业技术工人培训中心，AHK-上海、健雄职业技术学院专业技术工人培训中心，舍弗勒（中国）培训中心，海瑞恩（太仓）培训中心等多个职业教育培训机构，成为我国最大的“德国职业资格”考试和培训基地，培养了上万名企业急需的技能型人才。AHK中德双元制职业教育示范推广基地在太仓建立，舍弗勒双元制应用本科项目正式启动，进一步为德资企业深耕太仓奠定了人才基础。

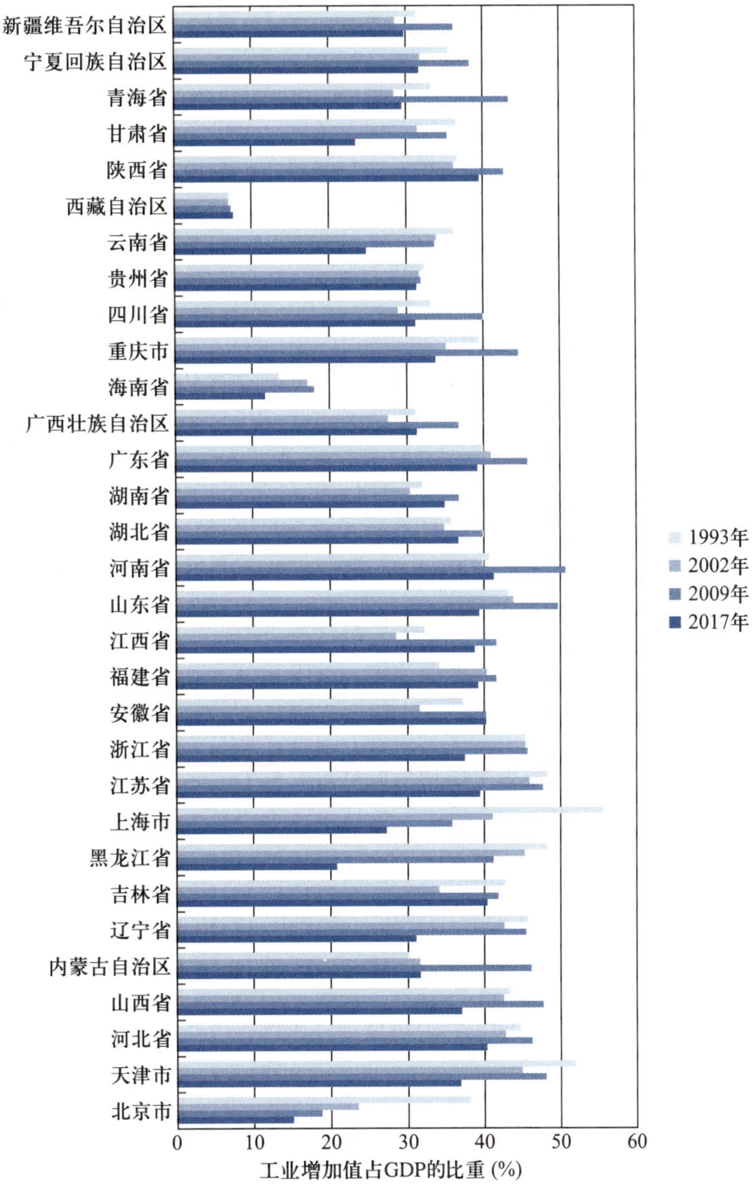


**图8.31 中国内地各省份的工业化进程**

资料来源：根据国家统计局数据测算。

## 8.4

## —

## 中国与发展中国家经济结构转型升级的匹配

### 8.4.1 中国能带给发展中经济体的产业转移机会与基础设施建设能力

按照在第1章已经介绍过的新结构经济学的基本原理，经济发展的本质是收入水平的不断提高，而收入水平的提高本质上则是劳动生产率的提高。劳动生产率的提高取决于技术创新和产业升级，技术创新和产业升级所提升的生产力潜力的发挥依赖于软硬件基础设施的不断完善。经济发展就是劳动生产率水平不断提高，技术创新和产业升级不断进行，同时软硬基础设施不断完善的过程。硬件基础设施，包括港口、道路与电力、电信等；软件基础设施，则是指金融制度、法律体系等。怎样让这个过程持续良性地发展下去？如同我们在第2章到第6章所揭示的全球历史经验事实一样，很重要的就是产业升级的过程要符合一个国家的比较优势，同时实现符合比较优势的技术创新和技术引进。而在这个过程中，有许多事情企业没有能力做，尤其是基础设施与产业政策，政府却是可以有所作为的。简单来讲，对于今天广大低收入与中等收入的发展中经济体来讲，最要紧的事莫过于寻找符合其潜在比较优势的产业，也就是从当前的要素禀赋结构来说具有要素生产成本低的比较优势，但是因为没有合适的软硬基础设施，交易费用太高，在市场上还没有竞争力的产业，为这样的产业消除软硬基础设施的瓶颈制约，将其变成现实的比较优势，即在国内外市场上具有竞争力的产业。

历史发展到今天，中国40多年激动人心的快速结构转型升级在符合比较优势行业和基础设施建设两个方面都给亚非拉等发展中经济体创造了前所未有的福音。林毅夫和王燕在2016年出版的《超越发展援助》一书中提出，南南发展合作的时代已经来临。[①]中国能够为

① 林毅夫、王燕,《超越发展援助》，北京大学出版社，2016年版。

发展中经济体的经济结构转型升级提供理念、隐性知识和经验以及发展融资和投资。随着真实工资在中国的不断上升，中国会将其部分制造业岗位与对外直接投资一起迁移到其他发展中经济体。[①]任何低收入国家如果能够把握住轻型制造业转移的机会，就能够获得几十年的强劲增长，从而创造就业、消除贫困，成为一个中等收入甚至高收入经济体，就像我们在前面的章节中所梳理的历史经验事实一样。我们在第7章已经估算了这种由全球经济结构转型升级带来的制造业就业机会，按照不同的口径，中国都能够为低收入经济体提供可待转移的数千万制造业就业机会。例如，以第一次工业革命的旗舰产业——轻纺行业为例，中国目前的体量将近全世界的一半，如表8.6所示。事实上，由中国带领的全球发展的“领头龙”模式已经在悄然快速发生。如表8.7所示，2013年全球服装出口分布格局就发生了巨大变化，东南亚、南亚、非洲等发展中经济体迅速崛起。

表8.6 2012年十国纺织品、服装、皮革产品体量

| 排名 | 国家 | 产出（亿美元） | 全球占比（%） |
|---|---|---|---|
| 1 | 中国 | 10 584.71 | 42.39 |
| 2 | 印度 | 1 438.01 | 5.76 |
| 3 | 土耳其 | 1 257.13 | 5.03 |
| 4 | 意大利 | 1 045.29 | 4.19 |
| 5 | 美国 | 838.75 | 3.36 |
| 6 | 韩国 | 770.25 | 3.08 |
| 7 | 巴西 | 714.89 | 2.86 |
| 8 | 日本 | 514.33 | 2.06 |
| 9 | 印度尼西亚 | 360.91 | 1.45 |
| 10 | 德国 | 285.91 | 1.15 |
| 合计 | | 17 810.18 | 71.33 |

资料来源：根据WIOD数据库《世界投入产出表（2012）》相关数据整理所得。

① 一项实证研究显示，最低工资的上涨可以解释2001—2012年中国对外直接投资增长的32.3%。对于生产性更强的企业、拥有外资所有权的企业、劳动密集型行业的企业、沿海地区的企业以及面向生产的外国直接投资项目，对中国最低工资上涨更加敏感。更详细的实证研究可参考：Fan Haichao, Lin Faqin, Tang Lixin, “Minimum Wage and Outward FDI from China”, *Journal of Development Economics*, 2018. Vol.135, pp. 1–19。

表8.7 2013年各国服装出口额及显性比较优势指数（RCA）

| 国家 | 地域 | 服装出口额（亿美元） | 总出口额（亿美元） | 服装出口占比（%） | RCA |
|---|---|---|---|---|---|
| 柬埔寨 | 东南亚 | 50.21 | 92.48 | 54.29 | 21.651 38 |
| 斯里兰卡 | 南亚 | 45.11 | 99.77 | 45.21 | 18.032 49 |
| 毛里求斯 | 非洲 | 7.59 | 18.97 | 40.01 | 15.958 43 |
| 萨尔瓦多 | 中美洲 | 20.72 | 54.58 | 37.96 | 15.140 32 |
| 尼加拉瓜 | 中美洲 | 12.75 | 41.56 | 30.68 | 12.229 55 |
| 马达加斯加 | 非洲 | 4.03 | 17.53 | 22.99 | 9.171 384 |
| 巴基斯坦 | 南亚 | 53.53 | 250.23 | 21.39 | 8.530 849 |
| 约旦 | 西亚 | 11.42 | 67.63 | 16.89 | 6.731 432 |
| 突尼斯 | 非洲 | 28.42 | 170.59 | 16.66 | 6.644 161 |
| 马其顿 | 欧洲 | 6.36 | 42.66 | 14.91 | 5.945 340 |
| 阿尔巴尼亚 | 欧洲 | 3.34 | 23.31 | 14.33 | 5.707 530 |
| 越南 | 东南亚 | 173.61 | 1 319.55 | 13.16 | 5.247 052 |
| 危地马拉 | 中美洲 | 13.18 | 100.52 | 13.11 | 5.227 523 |
| 吉尔吉斯斯坦 | 中亚 | 1.05 | 8.09 | 12.98 | 5.159 597 |
| 斐济 | 大洋洲 | 0.58 | 4.84 | 11.98 | 4.772 184 |
| 土耳其 | 西亚 | 155.82 | 1 484.08 | 10.50 | 4.187 229 |
| 尼泊尔 | 南亚 | 0.76 | 8.63 | 8.81 | 3.521 393 |
| 中国 | 东亚 | 1 766.29 | 22 089.27 | 8.00 | 3.188 852 |
| 佛得角（万美元） | 非洲 | 427.90 | 6 917.73 | 6.19 | 2.466 813 |
| 摩尔多瓦 | 东欧 | 0.99 | 16.19 | 6.11 | 2.430 282 |

资料来源：联合国商品贸易统计数据库（UN Comtrade Database）。

正如我们在第4章梳理中国经济结构转型升级的历史轨迹时所展示的那样，诸如纺织服装这类轻纺工业在20世纪70～90年代是中国内地承接日本和韩国以及中国香港此类产业转移的追赶型产业。中国成功地把握住了此次发展机会，取得了巨大成功，如图8.32所示。而今随着中国劳动力工资水平的不断上扬，此类曾经的追赶型产业又变成退出型产业，中国又需要继续“腾笼换鸟”进行转型升级。如图8.33和图8.34所示的用联合国工业发展组织制造业数据所识别的产业类型的“前沿距离－产业份额”矩阵，进入21世纪之后中国的纺织服装行业占制造业的比重在持续下滑，但生产率水平在不断提高。中国此类正在失掉比较优势的劳动力密集转进型产业正是其他收入水平较低的发展中经济体典型的追赶型产业。

2009年林毅夫在担任世界银行首席经济学家兼高级副行长期间，倡议以全球大规模基础设施投资计划帮助发达国家走出2008年的金融危机。林毅夫指出，发达国家陷入金融危机，需要进行结构性改革才能真正复苏。但是结构性改革会压低消费、扩大失业，在政治上面临很大阻力。此次危机在发达国家同时爆发，传统上当一个国家发生危机时所用的以货币

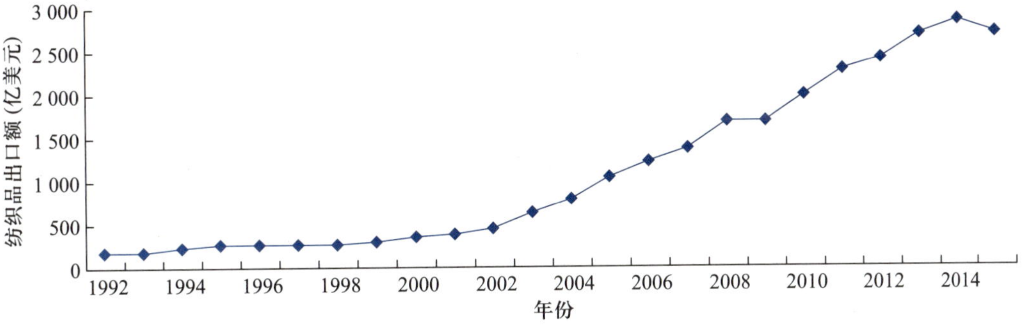


图8.32 1992—2015年中国纺织品出口额

资料来源：联合国商品贸易统计数据库（UN Comtrade Database）。

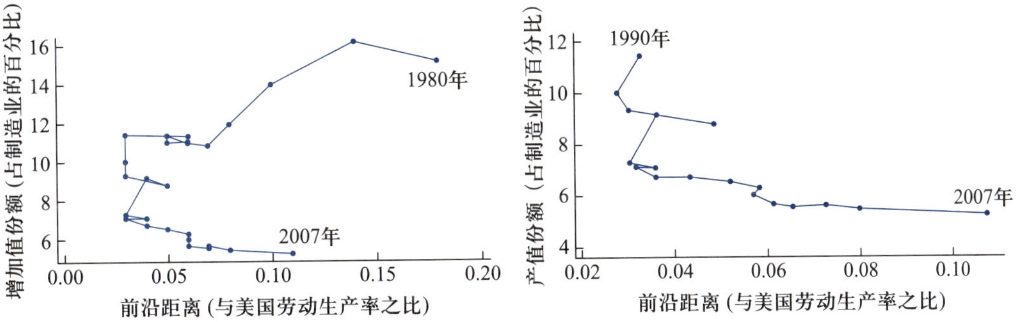


图8.33 1980—2007年中国纺织业的前沿距离（与美国纺织业劳动生产率的比值）与制造业份额矩阵（左为增加值份额，右为产值份额）

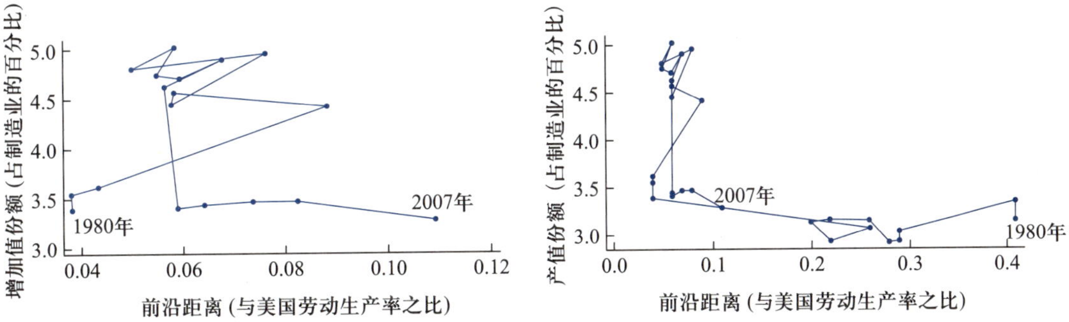


图8.34 1980—2007年中国服装制造业的前沿距离（与美国服装制造业劳动生产率的比值）与制造业份额矩阵（左为增加值份额，右为产值份额）

贬值增加出口来创造国内改革的空间，以及以国际援助渡过难关等方法都无济于事。因此林毅夫提出一个全球复兴计划，主要内容是对发达国家特别是发展中国家的基础设施进行大量投资。这些基础设施投资不仅会促进所在国的经济增长，还会拉动其他国家包括发达国家的出口，其效果等同于货币贬值增加出口，只要规模过大，发达国家可以乘势进行结构性改革。之所以提出这个计划，是因为发达国家的基础设施还有改进空间，中国以外的发展中国家的基础设施非常差。发达国家的退休基金、中国及石油输出国的外汇储备大量购买政府债券，收益率很低，不如用于基础设施投资。上述建议在提出以后，被越来越多的人接受。2010年，20国集团首尔峰会将帮助发展中国家建设基础设施列为共识的第一项，后来的峰会对此也多次强调。2014年，20国集团布里斯班峰会发表了全球基础设施倡议（回顾第7章的相关内容）。如今中国通过“一带一路”倡议率先推进，为全球做出了榜样。中国之所以能够发起“一带一路”倡议，源于中国在过去数十年中开展了规模浩大的基础设施建设，积累了基础设施建设、融资与运营管理的丰富经验。中国不但为发展中经济体如何快速消除基础设施瓶颈提供了经验，而且还为发展中经济体的基础设施建设提供了新的机会。这些基础设施建设则能为发展中国家消除增长瓶颈，帮助发展中国家抓住中国劳动力密集产业转移的窗口机遇期，实现工业化、现代化，消除贫困，提高收入，进一步为发达国家扩大出口市场。

### 8.4.2 中国对亚洲的投资及其与亚洲的经济结构的匹配情况①

在此，我们不妨先回顾一下第7章介绍的亚洲基础设施缺口情况。按照全球基础设施中心2017年发布的《全球基础设施展望》的预测，亚洲基础设施需求占全球的份额59%，比美洲高17%，比欧洲高16%，到2040年每年的基础设施投入需求在40 000亿美元上下。因此，亚洲是中国“一带一路”倡议的主战场，而“一带一路”的重点是基础设施互联互通。第9章我们将专门讨论“一带一路”如何助力世界经济结构转型升级。世界最大的自贸区也即将在东亚出现。《区域全面经济伙伴关系协定》（RCEP）谈判于2012年由东盟发起，长跑8年即将全面落地，成员包括东盟10国、中国、日本、韩国、澳大利亚、新西兰和印度。RCEP涵盖全球47.4%的人口，32.2%的GDP，29.1%的贸易额以及32.5%的投资额。除了印度，15

① 亚洲也是中国最重要的贸易市场。2019年，东盟占中国出口的14.4%，占中国进口的13.6；日本占中国出口的5.7%，占中国进口的8.3%；韩国占中国出口的4.4%，占中国进口的8.4%。

个RCEP成员国已经结束全部20个章节的文本谈判以及实质上所有的市场准入问题的谈判，有望在2020年签署协定。二战后世界经济的中心从欧洲转移到北美，1960年北美的GDP占世界的42.6%，加上欧盟，欧美的GDP总和占到世界的近7成。二战后的东亚被认为是最没有发展希望的地区，然而随着日本的迅速复兴以及亚洲“四小龙”的快速崛起，逐步改善了东亚的经济地位，东亚与太平洋地区GDP的世界占比从1960年的11.18%持续上升1994年的26%，接近当时北美的比重；1997年亚洲金融危机使东亚经济严重受挫，其GDP占世界的比重在2007年时下跌到只有21%。2008年国际金融危机使欧美经济严重受挫，北美的GDP占世界的比重下降到25.92%，欧盟的比重下降到21.85%，东亚经济由于中国的强劲带动，其GDP占世界的比重迅速上升到2018年的30.2%，已经超过北美或欧盟的比重。然而，欧美以不到世界1/10的人口创造的GDP总和至今依然占到世界的一半，东亚的比重相差近20个百分点，还有巨大的追赶空间。

亚洲地区是中国对外直接投资存量最多的目标市场。截至2017年年底，中国内地企业在亚洲46个国家和地区设立了境外分支机构，亚洲的境外企业覆盖率达97.9%，居全球首位。中国内地企业在亚洲地区设立的境外企业数量超过2.2万家，占境外企业总数的56.3%，主要分布在中国香港、新加坡、日本、越南、韩国、印度尼西亚、老挝、泰国、柬埔寨、马来西亚、阿拉伯联合酋长国、蒙古国等。截至2017年年底，中国在亚洲地区的投资存量为11 393.2亿美元，占中国对外直接投资存量的63%。众所周知，中国香港是中国内地开放的桥头堡，与中西方的桥梁，中国内地在亚洲的对外投资和前面介绍的外商投资大都通过中国香港进出。截至2017年年底，中国内地企业在中国香港的直接投资存量为9 812.7亿美元，占亚洲地区存量的86%。新加坡、印度尼西亚、中国澳门、哈萨克斯坦、老挝、韩国、巴基斯坦、缅甸、柬埔寨是位居中国内地企业对外直接投资存量第二至第九位的国家与地区。这里可以看到，如果除去中国香港，中国内地企业对亚洲地区的投资存量依然相对较低，对亚洲发展中地区的直接投资潜力巨大。截至2017年年底，中国企业对亚洲国家和地区的投资主要集中在5个行业领域，依次为租赁和商务服务业（44.8%）、批发和零售业（13.5%）、金融业（12.3%）、采矿业（7.0%）以及制造业（6.4%）。上述5个行业投资存量合计为9 569.2亿美元，所占比重高达84.0%。对东盟10国投资存量行业主要包括：租赁和商务服务业（19.6%），制造业（17.5%），批发和零售业（13.3%），采矿业（11.6%），电力、热力、燃气及水的生产供应业（10.8%）。制造业是中国对东盟涉及国家最广泛的行业，投资额上亿美元的国家包括越南、泰国、印度尼西亚、新加坡、柬埔寨、马来西亚、老挝、菲律宾、缅甸。这在一定程度上反映出我们在第7章测算的还在继续的亚洲“雁行模式”。截至2015年11月底，在建的境外经贸合作区中有28个位于亚洲地区。

亚洲是中国对外承包工程的传统市场。2014年，中国对亚洲承包工程业务保持增长，新签合同额842.2亿美元，同比增长18.7%；完成营业额648.4亿美元，增长0.7%；分别占当年新签合同总额和完成营业额总额的43.9%和47%按照新签合同额排序，主要国别市场包括：沙特阿拉伯（94.7亿美元）、伊朗（65.1亿美元）、伊拉克（63.8亿美元）、印度尼西亚（51.9亿美元）、马来西亚（43.3亿美元）。前十大国别市场新签合同额合计为512.1亿美元，占当年亚洲总额的60.8%。按完成营业额排序，主要国别市场包括：沙特阿拉伯（59.5亿美元）、伊拉克（49亿美元）、印度尼西亚（45.8亿美元）、巴基斯坦（42.5亿美元）、越南（39.8亿美元）。前十大国别市场完成营业额合计为387.6亿美元，占当年亚洲总额的59.8%。这些都反映了中国对亚洲基础设施建设的贡献。

### 8.4.3 中国对非洲的投资及其与非洲的经济结构匹配情况[①]

正如我们在第6章和第7章所讨论过的，非洲目前面临的最大发展难题莫过于劳动密集型产业的缺失导致的就业问题，以及基础设施的缺失导致的发展瓶颈问题。长远来讲，中非合作无疑对解决这两大难题提供了出路。[②]14亿中国人民同12亿多非洲人民的携手发展将是人类历史上最精彩的南南合作诗篇。[③]2015年中非合作论坛约翰内斯堡峰会以来，中国全面落实约翰内斯堡峰会上确定的中非"十大合作计划"：一大批铁路、公路、机场、港口等基础设施以及经贸合作区陆续建成或在建设之中，中非和平安全、科教文卫、减贫惠民、民间交往等合作深入推进，中国承诺提供的600亿美元资金支持都已兑现或作出安排。习近平在2018年中非合作论坛北京峰会又宣布，在推进中非"十大合作计划"基础上，同非洲国家密切配合，未来3年和今后一段时间重点实施"八大行动"：实施产业促进行动，实施设施

① 关于中国与中东和北非地区的基础设施合作的一些梳理可参考：魏敏，"'一带一路'框架下中国与中东基础设施互联互通问题研究"，《国际经济合作》，2017年第12期，第58–63页；姜英梅，"中东国家基础设施建设与'一带一路'合作前景"，《阿拉伯世界研究》，2019年第2期，第91–104页。

② 一些实证研究发现过去非洲的FDI净流入对非洲的经济增长都没有显著影响。从增长核算的角度以及通过对撒哈拉以南非洲国家其他经济增长决定因素的检验，发现劳动力人均资本存量的变化对撒哈拉以南非洲国家的增长具有持续而显著的正向影响。这意味着过去的非洲FDI尚未对产业发展与基础设施难题产生实际效果，需要进一步加强中非合作解决这两大问题。相关的实证研究可参考：Zhang J., Alon I. and Chen Y., "Does Chinese investment affect Sub-Saharan African growth?" , *International Journal of Emerging Markets*, 2014, Vol. 9 No. 2, pp. 257–275。

③ 中非合作作为最重要的南南合作，如我们在第6章所讨论的，有其必然的经济逻辑。一些实证研究发现，中国对非洲国家的投资不存在偏好性，而主要取决于目标国经济、市场及能源储量。可参考：董艳、张大永、蔡栋梁，"走进非洲——中国对非洲投资决定因素的实证研究"，《经济学（季刊）》，2011年第2期。

联通行动，实施贸易便利行动，实施绿色发展行动，实施能力建设行动，实施健康卫生行动，实施人文交流行动。为推动“八大行动”顺利实施，中国愿以政府援助、金融机构和企业投融资等方式，向非洲提供600亿美元支持，其中包括：提供150亿美元的无偿援助、无息贷款和优惠贷款，提供200亿美元的信贷资金额度，支持设立100亿美元的中非开发性金融专项资金和50亿美元的自非洲进口贸易融资专项资金，推动中国企业未来3年对非洲投资不少于100亿美元。同时，免除与中国有外交关系的非洲最不发达国家、重债穷国、内陆发展中国家、小岛屿发展中国家截至2018年年底到期未偿还政府间无息贷款债务。

截至2017年年底，中国企业在非洲地区的52个国家开展了投资，投资覆盖率为86.7%，设立的境外企业超过3 400家，占境外企业总数的8.7%，主要分布在赞比亚、尼日利亚、埃塞俄比亚、南非、肯尼亚、坦桑尼亚、加纳、安哥拉、乌干达等。中国在非洲地区的投资存量为433亿美元，占中国对外投资存量的2.4%，其中在南非的直接投资存量达到74.7亿美元，位居非洲首位。中国对非洲地区的投资存量主要分布在5个行业领域，依次为建筑业（29.8%）、采矿业（22.5%）、金融业（14.0%）、制造业（13.2%）以及租赁与商务服务业（5.3%）。2017年，中国流向非洲对外直接投资41.1亿美元，同比增长70.8%，是五大洲中增长最快的目标市场。

中国企业在非洲建设境外经贸合作区开创了中非合作的新模式。截至2015年11月底，在建的境外经贸合作区中有20个位于非洲地区。其中，赞比亚中国经贸合作区是中国在非洲地区设立的第一个境外经贸合作区，也是赞比亚政府宣布设立的第一个多功能经济区，该区累计投资近15亿美元，已有35家企业入驻。此后，中国企业在埃塞俄比亚建设了东方工业园，在埃及建设了苏伊士经贸合作区，在尼日利亚建设了莱基自由贸易区等一批经贸合作区。境外经贸合作区已成为中国对非集群式投资的重要平台。

非洲是中国对外承包工程的主要市场。2014年，中国对非洲承包工程业务保持增长，新签合同额754.9亿美元，同比增长11.3%，与中国当年对全球新签合同总额11.7%的增速基本持平；完成营业额529.7亿美元，增长8.6%，大大高于中国当年对全球完成营业总额3.8%的平均增速；分别占当年在各国（地区）新签合同总额和完成营业额总额的39.4%和37.2%。按照新签合同额排序，主要国别市场包括：尼日利亚（177.1亿美元）、阿尔及利亚（97.5亿美元）、肯尼亚（53.5亿美元）、埃塞俄比亚（50.8亿美元）、安哥拉（34.7亿美元）。前十大国别市场新签合同额合计为532.2亿美元，占当年非洲总额的70.5%。按完成营业额排序，主要国别市场包括：埃塞俄比亚（68.3亿美元）、安哥拉（64亿美元）、阿尔及利亚（63.3亿美元）、尼日利亚（45.3亿美元）、刚果共和国（25.3亿美元）。前十大国别市场完成营业额合计为363.2亿美元，占当年非洲总额的68.6%。习近平在2018年中非合作论坛北京峰会上宣布，中国决定和非洲联盟启动编制《中非基础设施合作规划》；支持中国企业以投建营一体化等模式参与非洲基础设施建设，重点加强能源、交通、信息通信、跨境水资源等合作，同非方一道实施一批互联互通重点项目；支持非洲单一航空运输市场建设，开通更多中非直航航班；为非洲国家及其金融机构来华发行债券提供便利；在遵循多边规则和程序的前提下，支持非洲国家更好利用亚洲基础设施投资银行、新开发银行、丝路基金等资源。

根据林毅夫和王燕的估算，2001—2010年，非洲从中国融资的168个基础设施工程项目中（见图8.35），有将近63%的项目都与非洲的瓶颈匹配。[①]中国参与的这些基础设施项目很大程度上缓解了非洲经济结构转型升级的瓶颈，使得（尤其是通过园区形式进一步降低特定产业或区域的基础设施瓶颈（表8.8））符合潜在比较优势的产业发展成为可能。根据《非洲华侨周报》2017年3月22日的报道，在过去2年中，中国已为非洲创造了近3万个工作岗位，因而成为为非洲人民提供最多就业机会的国家。标准银行集团的经济学家杰里米·史蒂文斯说："就在非的项目投资数量而言，中国排名第七位，但它向非洲人民提供的就业岗位数量却是其他国家遥不可及的。"大多数就业机会来自中国民营企业。一方面，中国对非投资主要集中于劳动力密集型产业；另一方面，非洲国家把劳动就业作为优先发展项，而中国公司愿意雇用当地劳动力。以肯尼亚为例，2016年3月，世界银行发布了政策研究工作报告，报告称2003年至2015年，中国通过对肯直接投资所创造的工作岗位数量在该国排名第五，93%的驻肯中资企业都会雇用当地员工。这12年里，肯尼亚的每个海外直接投资项目平均创造100个工作岗位，而中国对肯直接投资的每个项目平均创造167个工作岗位。此外，60%的驻肯中资企业会为当地员工提供工作技巧、安全防范和医疗卫生知识的常规培训。非洲如果像当年中国改革开放之初那样积极主动地去把握中国大量失去比较优势的劳动力密集型产业转移机会，以及积极有为地建设消除产业发展的基础设施瓶颈，那么非洲取得像中国近40年来那样的快速发展指日可待。[②]

---

① 更详细内容参见：林毅夫、王燕，《超越发展援助》，北京大学出版社，2016年版，第5章附录5.1。

② 对中国制造业对外直接投资与非洲工业化之间的关系和实践的一项评估可资参考：Lu Feng, Liu Xiaoguang, "Africa's industrialization and China's OFDI in the manufacturing sector: rationales and practices", *China Economic Journal*, 2018, Vol. 11, No. 2, pp. 126–150。

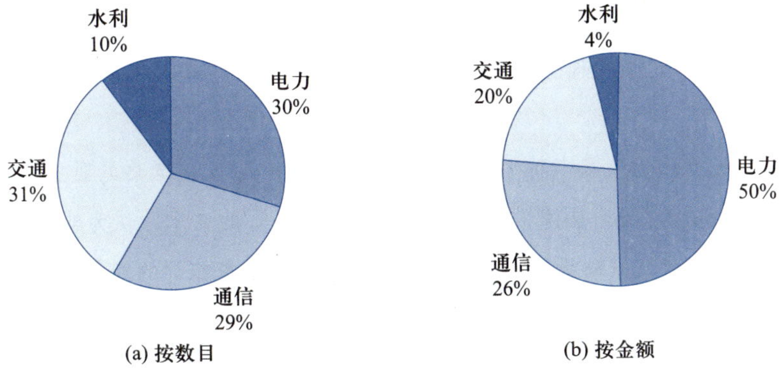


图8.35 2001—2010年间非洲从中国进行中国的基础设施融资情况

资料来源：World Bank-PPIAF Chinese Projects Database.

表8.8 中国在非洲的一些境外园区案例

| 年份 | 所在国 | 名称 | 投资主体 | 磋商主体 | 认证 |
| --- | --- | --- | --- | --- | --- |
| 2003 | 赞比亚 | 赞比亚中国经济贸易合作区 | 赞比亚政府、中国有色集团 | 非洲政府－中国国企 | 国家级 |
| 2006 | 尼日利亚 | 尼日利亚莱基自贸区 | 尼日利亚拉各斯政府、中非基金、中国铁建、南京江宁经开区、中土集团 | 非洲政府－中国国企 | 国家级 |
| 2007 | 埃塞俄比亚 | 埃塞俄比亚东方工业园 | 江苏永元投资有限公司 | 中国民企 | 国家级 |
| 2008 | 埃及 | 埃及苏伊士经贸合作区 | 中非基金、天津经开区（泰达）、埃及政府等 | 非洲政府－中国国企 | 国家级 |
| 2010 | 津巴布韦 | 农垦津巴布韦经贸合作区 | 津巴布韦国防部、安徽农垦集团 | 非洲政府－中国国企 | 省级 |
| 2011 | 莫桑比克 | 莫桑比克贝拉国际经贸合作区 | 鼎盛国际投资（由安徽省外经建设集团设立） | 非洲政府－中国国企 | 省级 |
| 2012 | 南非 | 海信南非家电工业园 | 海信集团、中非基金 | 中国民企 | 无 |
| 2015 | 乌干达 | 辽沈工业园 | 辽宁省政府支持的乌干达张氏集团、辽宁中大集团 | 非洲政府－中国省政府－中国民企 | 省级 |
| 2017 | 埃塞俄比亚 | 湖南阿达玛工业园 | 湖南省政府、埃塞俄比亚政府、中地海外、三一重工 | 非洲政府－中国省政府－中国民企 | 省级 |
| 2017 | 吉布提 | 吉布提自贸区 | 招商国际、吉布提政府 | 非洲政府－中国国企 | 无 |

资料来源：赵祚翔、吴昕月、李浩民，“一带一路”倡议下中非产能合作的机制和实践——基于新结构经济学的视角，《国际贸易》，2018年第4期，第45-49页。

## 专栏8.4
## 非洲的基础设施建设投资机会①

银行投资专家卡特·戴维斯于2017年2月28日在坦桑尼亚主流媒体《卫报》上发表题为“7个国家欢迎基础设施建设投资”的文章，认为非洲国家领导人认为发展现代化基础设施对经济增长至关重要，但是非洲的能源、网络和运输成本仍是全球最高的。虽然许多官员都怀有改造和建设基础设施的雄心壮志，然而现实中因2015年和2016年经济不景气，公共财政支出有限，壮志难酬。在非洲，私营部门投资参与基础设施建设成为大势所趋。每年的基础设施建设资金缺口超过900亿美元，一些私人投资在积极地寻找机会。包括黑石（Blackstone）、阿布拉吉（Abraaj）在内的私募投资机构，认为非洲的基础设施建设充满商机，都组建了专业的团队，关注潜在的项目，特别是电力项目。可以预见，2017年将有更多的私募基金参与其中。

●塞内加尔。塞内加尔具有国际航运和区域陆运优势。目前塞内加尔已经开始着手建设达喀尔港，以替代日渐老化和拥挤的旧港，新港将带动这个国家高速发展。塞内加尔是西非最稳定的民主国家，但经济上比较落后。2016年，塞内加尔经济增速为6.5%，是该国10年内的最高增速。而新港是高速发展的动力之一，电力的发展将是带动经济发展的引擎。目前塞内加尔发电成本高，因为50%以上依靠生物能源。近期发现的油气资源，特别是大储量海上油气的发现，是建设天然气发电厂的契机。投资者投资电力领域对塞内加尔至关重要。

●科特迪瓦。科特迪瓦2017年时的总统瓦塔拉曾任国际货币基金组织经济学家，预算部部长西斯拥有经商经验，二人都认为加强基础设施建设对科特迪瓦的经济发展至关重要。西斯部长宣布到2020年，政府计划累计投入600亿美元发展基础设施，其中68%将来源于私营部门，80%以上的公私合营（PPP）模式将用于运输、电信和能源等关键基础设施领域。科特迪瓦政府的承诺正在逐步落实。2015年的经济增速为10%。截至2016年年初，电力装机容量已超过2 000兆瓦，国家发电公司功不可没，对私营公司的投资补贴也不容忽视。目前科特迪瓦已开始向贝宁、布基纳法索、加纳、马里和多哥出口电力。独立供电商增加等因素，有助于电力部门继续发展。

① 本专栏根据坦桑尼亚《卫报》2017年2月28日发表的“7个国家欢迎基础设施建设投资”一文整理而成。

● 喀麦隆。喀麦隆电力短缺，包括首都雅温得在内的大城市也缺电。电力短缺是制约喀麦隆经济发展的主要瓶颈。喀麦隆总统比亚承诺通过建设发电厂缓解电力缺口，包括即将投入运营的Memve'ele和Mekin发电厂，此外还有多个建设中的发电站。同时比亚总统还要求其国家电网公司加强电网管理。比亚总统表示，目前喀麦隆正在充分发掘自身潜力，推进工业化进程，需要更多的电力供应和输变电线的改造升级。

● 乌干达和坦桑尼亚。乌干达和坦桑尼亚是东非的“潜力股”。两国在电力领域均有投资机会，特别是天然气发电项目。乌干达决定放弃肯尼亚而选择与坦桑尼亚在原油管线项目上合作，索马里青年党的恐怖威胁是原因之一。选择坦桑尼亚意味着项目成本的上升，这对于面临财政困难的乌干达是不小的挑战。同时，坦桑尼亚在马古富力总统的领导下，实行紧缩的财政政策，将直接（和间接）地影响对基础设施的投资。为什么说这两个国家是“潜力股”呢？因为两国都需要引入私人资本发展电力，同时两国也拥有包括天然气在内的发电燃料资源。乌干达的卡鲁玛和伊希姆巴水力发电站与坦桑尼亚的姆特瓦拉天然气项目都是标志性项目。然而这些项目仍不足以支撑两国5%的经济增速。此外，两国的管道、公路、机场等领域也需要投资，以配合经济发展。

● 刚果民主共和国。由于矿业公司不断发展壮大，刚果民主共和国的电力短缺问题更加突出，输变电线的升级改造也成为必需。刚果民主共和国超过45%的公司自备发电机，以应对频繁停电造成的电力短缺问题。估计刚果民主共和国的水力发电潜力为50 000兆瓦。现实是存在大量的投资机会，但是对于处于初级阶段的刚果民主共和国基础设施建设领域，仍有许多地方需要加强学习。

● 尼日利亚。作为非洲最大的天然气供应国，现在仍无法实现天然气发电。尼日利亚政府正在努力改善电力状况。例如，2015年，尼日利亚电力管理委员会提高了商业、工业和居民用电的价格。在对私人投资电力领域进行多次讨论后，目前的情形对独立发电商更有利。但尼日利亚人在经济下行压力下，仍要求政府提供合理电价，因此投资者仍然比较犹豫。本国货币贬值也加剧了这一趋势。

### 8.4.4 中国对拉丁美洲的投资及其与拉美的经济结构匹配情况

2014年年底和2015年年初墨西哥通信和交通部宣布中国中标其高铁项目并旋即宣布取消中标，这一被称为中国高铁“走出去”真正意义上的“第一单”充满戏剧性，也反映了拉丁美洲进行大规模基础设施建设的挑战性，但这无法阻挡经济发展要求所内生的趋势。正如我们在第3章到第6章对全球每个经济体的经济结构转型升级轨迹的追踪评估所显示的那样，诸多拉丁美洲经济体之所以陷入中等收入陷阱，主要是由于没有持续的经济结构转型升级，而这又源于产业升级次序颠倒以及政府没有发挥因势利导作用积极主动地去消除产业发展面临的软硬基础设施瓶颈。中国的发展日益后来居上。如图8.36所示，中国近年来制造业工资水平和总体工资水平已超过拉美。这意味着中国诸多劳动密集的产业区段相对拉美而言已逐渐失去比较优势，这对拉丁美洲而言也意味着机会，需要积极主动地向中国招商引资并帮助中国企业进入。在合作政策层面，截至2017年年底，中国与拉丁美洲形成了“全面合作伙伴关系+全面战略伙伴关系+战略伙伴关系+多种友好关系”立体化大格局，其中，中国与巴西、墨西哥、阿根廷、智利、秘鲁、委内瑞拉、厄瓜多尔7国建立了“全面战略伙伴关系”，与哥斯达黎加、乌拉圭建立了“战略伙伴关系”。2016年11月中国政府发布的《中国对拉美和加勒比政策文件》指出，要推动中拉全面合作伙伴关系再上新台阶，新阶段的总目标是中拉成为携手发展的命运共同体，深入推进中拉各领域合作，包括政治，经贸，社会，人文，国际协作，和平、安全、司法，整体合作，三方合作8个方面。

截至2017年年底，中国在拉丁美洲设立境外企业2 200多家，占中国境外企业总数的5.7%，覆盖拉丁美洲33个国家（地区），覆盖率为67.3%。主要分布在英属维尔京群岛、开曼群岛、巴西、墨西哥、智利、委内瑞拉、秘鲁、厄瓜多尔等。中国企业在拉丁美洲的并购投资活动以巴西为主，2017年，在中国企业对外投资并购额前十位国家排名中，巴西位列第四位，吸引中国企业并购投资近80亿美元。截至2017年年底，中国在拉丁美洲的投资存量主要分布在开曼群岛、英属维尔京群岛、委内瑞拉、巴西、阿根廷、厄瓜多尔、牙买加、秘鲁、特立尼达和多巴哥、墨西哥等。其中开曼群岛和英属维尔京群岛累计存量3 717.4亿美元，占对拉美地区投资存量的96.1%。由此可知，抛开离岸金融中心，其实中国投资真正进入拉丁美洲国家实体经济的相对较少。截至2017年年底，中国企业对拉丁美洲国家投资主要集中在5个行业领域，依次为信息传输、软件和信息技术服务业（48.2%）、租赁和商务服务业（19.8%）、批发和零售业（15.4%）、金融业（6.5%）、采矿业（2.3%）。上述5个行业投资存量合计为3 564.9亿美元，占总投资额的比重高达92.2%。其中信息传输、软件和信息技术服务业增速迅猛，占比相比上年上升了近30个百分点，排名超越租赁和商务服务业位居第一。

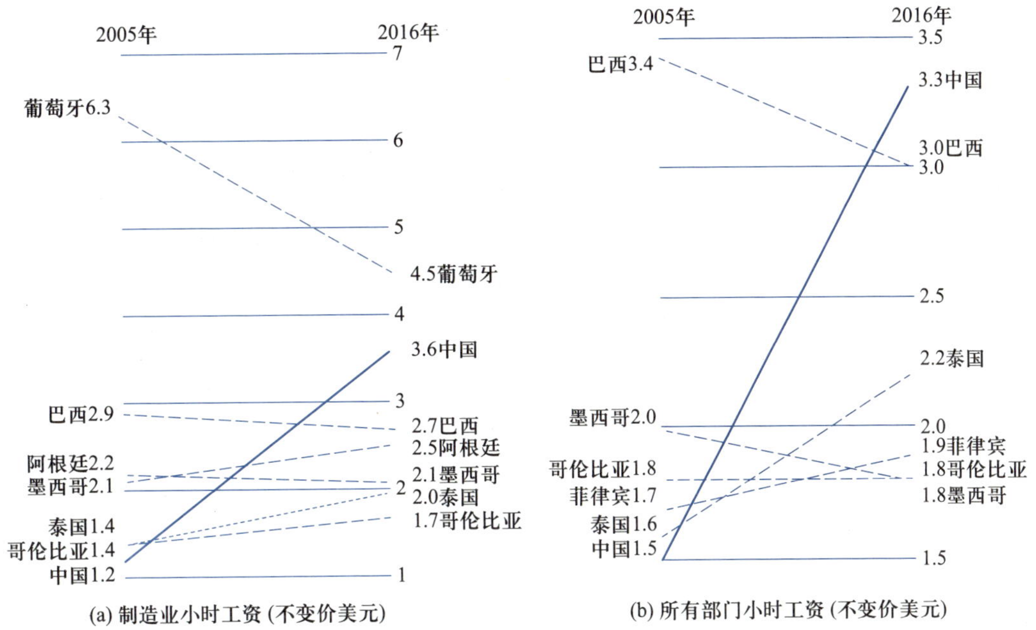


**图8.36 中国与拉丁美洲制造业工资水平和总体工资水平比较**

资料来源：Euromonitor International.

截至2014年年底，拉丁美洲是中国对外承包工程的重要市场。2014年，中国对拉丁美洲承包工程业务出现波动，新签合同额164.7亿美元，完成营业额131.8亿美元，分别占当年在各国（地区）新签合同总额和完成营业额总额的8.6%和9.3%。按照新签合同额排序，主要国别市场为：阿根廷（65.1亿美元）、委内瑞拉（43.2亿美元）、巴西（12.2亿美元）。前十大国别市场新签合同额合计为158.6亿美元，占当年拉丁美洲总额的96.3%。按完成营业额排序，主要国别市场为：委内瑞拉（50.1亿美元）、厄瓜多尔（24亿美元）、巴西（15亿美元）。前十大国别市场完成营业额合计为121.6亿美元，占当年拉丁美洲总额的92.3%。

## 8.5

## 新时期中国融入世界构建开放型经济新体制的战略体系

### 8.5.1 新时期中国融入世界构建开放型经济新体制的比较优势

按照新结构经济学的理论和全球与中国各地的经验（回顾第4章和第5章），如果一个经济体在发展战略中遵循自身的比较优势，那么它的经济就会是对外开放的，生产那些与现有禀赋结构相一致的产品和服务并出口至国际市场，进口那些不符合自身比较优势的产品和服务。这个经济体的贸易依存度内生于自身的比较优势，将会大于其他任何情况下的贸易依存度，并且由于投资回报率高，会吸引大于其他任何情况下的外来投资，同时伴随失掉比较优势产业的向外转移而进行对外投资。这个经济体将达到最有竞争力的状态，它的禀赋结构和产业结构将以可能的最快速度升级。在产业升级过程中，这个经济体能够通过向发达国家或地区借鉴技术和产业，充分挖掘自身的后来者优势，并实现比发达国家或地区更快的经济增长率，因为它的创新成本将小于那些已经处于全球技术前沿、需要依靠自己发明来取得新技术的发达国家或地区。因而，这个经济体将能实现与高收入国家或地区的收敛。从这个角度而言，通过对外开放利用世界市场是按照由一个经济体的禀赋结构决定的比较优势来推动产业升级的增长战略的结果。对外开放的全球和中国各地的经验以及新结构经济学的理论给我们的启示是清楚的：依靠比较优势（出口世界其他地方之所需，并为保持经济竞争力，按照禀赋结构的改变一步步升级其产业结构），利用后来者优势的潜力（在产业升级过程中从世界其他地区引进创意、技术和专业技能）。此外，这样的经济体由于有竞争力，经济剩余多，因投资回报高储蓄率也高，资本积累和禀赋结构升级的速度很快，过去符合比较优势的产业由于禀赋结构升级而逐渐失去比较优势，需要向比自己禀赋结构水平更低的其他经济体转移这些产业，因此对外投资也将随着经济的增长而不断增加。

改革开改之后的中国作为二战后为数不多的发展典范之一，便是这样的开放型经济体。中国是世界上最大的贸易国，长期位居发展中经济体吸引外资之首。21世纪初，中国对外投资流量只有20多亿美元，过去十多年来中国对外直接投资年均增幅超过30%，堪称神速。

这事实上是中国快速的经济结构转型升级的内在要求。一方面，中国由于快速的经济结构转型升级，劳动力水平大幅上升，工资水平增长迅猛，过去体量巨大的劳动力密集型产业逐步失去比较优势，需要向比中国收入水平低、劳动力密集型产业发展不够充分又有大量劳动力的经济体转移；另一方面，中国同样由于快速的经济结构转型升级，迫切需要向产业链高端攀爬，除国内自主创新和招商引资之外，去海外并购以及设立研发与生产运营机构，进行本国的逆向技术反馈，也是内在需求。如图8.37所示的2004—2014年中国三次产业对外直接投资比重与三次产业增加值比重，对外投资结构与国内产业结构变迁较为吻合。反映上述趋势更加明显的是图8.38所示的2004—2014年技术、资金和劳动力密集型行业对外直接投资流量规模和比重的走势。无论从投资规模还是从投资占比来看，劳动力密集型行业对外直接投资均高于技术和资金密集型行业，2004年中国劳动力密集型行业对外直接投资规模和比重分别为45.53亿美元和77.34%，同期技术和资金密集型行业对外直接投规模和比重仅为0.48亿美元和0.87%、0.85亿美元和1.55%。2014年，中国劳动力、技术和资金密集型行业对外直接投资规模分别达742.65亿美元、48.3亿美元和225.2亿美元，比重分别为60.33%、3.92%、18.29%，劳动力密集型行业对外直接投资占据中国同期对外直接投资规模的半壁江山。这一点确凿无疑地反映了中国快速的经济结构转型升级迫使大量的劳动力密集型产业向海外更低成本的地方转移。另外，技术密集型行业对外直接投资规模和比重均呈上升态势。2004年中国技术密集型行业对外直接投资流量为0.85亿美元，比重1.55%，2014年中国实现技术密集型行业对外直接投资流量225.2亿美元，比重升至18.29%。技术密集型行业对外直接投资的动机多数基于获取外部先进的技术资源和接近研发密集地域，并且通过企业间的内部渠道实现先进技术的逆向回流，促进母公司技术研发、吸纳和创新能力的提升，进而带动母公司所属行业和整体产业技术水平的提高和优胜劣汰，对于国内产业结构的升级换代起到重要的推进作用。有实证研究支持这一点。①

① 霍忻，《中国对外直接投资逆向技术溢出的产业结构升级效应研究》，首都经济贸易大学博士论文，2016年。

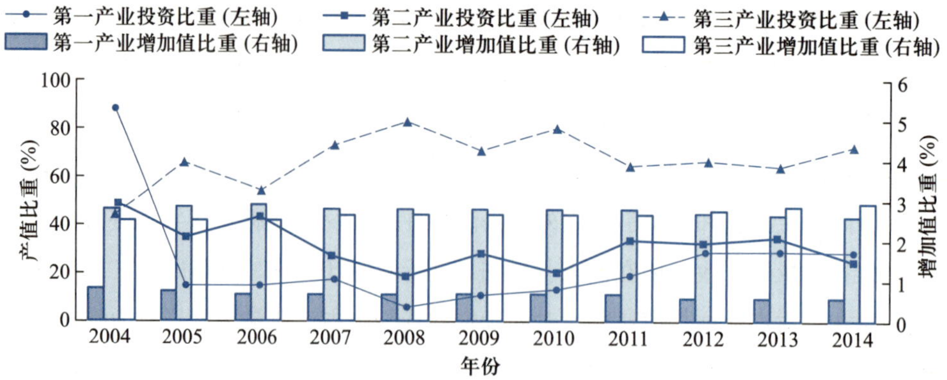


**图8.37 2004—2014年我国三次产业对外直接投资与增加值比重**

资料来源：历年《中国统计年鉴》《中国对外直接投资公报》。

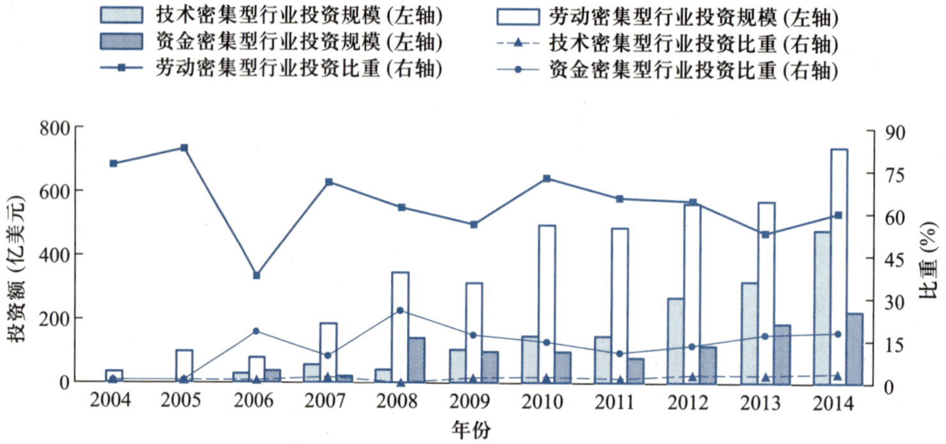


**图8.38 中国技术、劳动力和资金密集型行业对外直接投资走势**

注：技术密集型行业包括技术服务业、计算机和软件业，劳动力密集型行业包括制造业、交通运输业、批发零售业、商务服务业等行业，资金密集型行业包含金融业和房地产行业。

资料来源：霍忻，《中国对外直接投资逆向技术溢出的产业结构升级效应研究》，首都经济贸易大学博士论文，2016年。

## 8.5.2 新时期中国融入世界构建开放型经济新体制的战略架构与自贸区

中国由于自身和世界经济结构转型升级的内在要求，在新时期依然会继续采取更加开放的姿态融入世界，构建开放型经济体系，促进经济结构转型升级，只不过对应于快速的经济结构转型升级，贸易结构和投资结构也会发生快速的变化，尤其是相对于长期坚持的“引进来”而言，“走出去”在未来将更加突出，如图8.39所示的理论机制。2015年5月5日，中共中央和国务院印发了《关于构建开放型经济新体制的若干意见》(简称《意见》),这一纲领性文件绘制了中国新时期构建开放型经济体系的国家战略蓝图。《意见》重申了对外开放是中国的基本国策,在新的世界经济形势和国内新形势下要统筹开放型经济顶层设计,加快构建开放型经济新体制,进一步破除体制障碍,使对内对外开放相互促进,“引进来”与“走出去”更好结合,以对外开放的主动赢得经济发展和国际竞争的主动,以开放促改革、促发展、促创新,建设开放型经济强国,为实现“两个一百年”奋斗目标和中华民族伟大复兴的“中国梦”打下坚实基础。《意见》从11个方面对新时期中国构建开放型经济体系做了50条具体的顶层设计,重点包括:创新外商投资管理体制,如统一内外资法律法规,推进准入前国民待遇加负面清单的管理模式,完善外商监管体系,推动开发区转型升级和创新发展(可回顾第7章第7.2节的讨论内容);建立促进走出去战略的新体制,如确立并实施新时期走出去国家战略,推进境外投资便利化,创新对外投资合作方式,健全走出去服务保障体系,“引进来”和“走出去”有机结合(回顾本章关于中国与世界经济结构的匹配讨论);构建外贸可持续发展的新机制,如提高贸易便利化水平,培育外贸竞争新优势,建立健全服务贸易促进体系,实施质量效益导向型的外贸政策,健全贸易摩擦应对机制;优化对外开放区域布局,如建设若干自由贸易试验区(接下来将着重讨论),完善内陆开放新机制,培育沿边开放新支点,打造沿海开放新高地;加快实施“一带一路”倡议(第9章将专门讨论);拓展国际经济合作新空间,如坚持世界贸易体制规则,建立高标准自由贸易区网络,积极参与全球经济治理,构建多双边、全方位经贸合作新格局,建立国际经贸谈判新机制;构建开放安全的金融体系),如扩大金融业开放,推动资本市场双向有序开放,建立走出去金融支持体系,扩大人民币跨境使用,完善汇率形成机制和外汇管理制度;构建稳定、公平、透明、可预期的营商环境。

除了第7章介绍的中国国家级新区之外,新时期中国融入世界构建开放型经济新体制最重要的支撑平台或试验区当属自由贸易试验区。自由贸易区即通常所称的“境内关外”的特殊区域。[①]2013年9月29日成立的中国(上海)自由贸易试验区(简称上海自贸区)是中国第一个自贸区,面积28.78平方千米,涵盖上海市外高桥保税区、外高桥保税物流园区、洋山保税港区和上海浦东机场综合保税区4个海关特殊监管区域。上海自贸区成立至今已近七年,其成

① 20世纪50年代初,美国就明确提出:可在自由贸易区发展以出口加工为主要目标的制造业。20世纪60年代后期,一些发展中国家也利用这一形式,将它建成为特殊的工业区,并逐步发展成为出口加工区。20世纪80年代以来,许多国家的自由贸易区积极向高技术、知识和资本密集型发展,形成科技型自由贸易区。据不完全统计,截至2013年,全球已有1 200多个自由贸易区,其中15个发达国家设立了约425个,占35.4%;67个发展中国家共设立约775个,占65.6%。

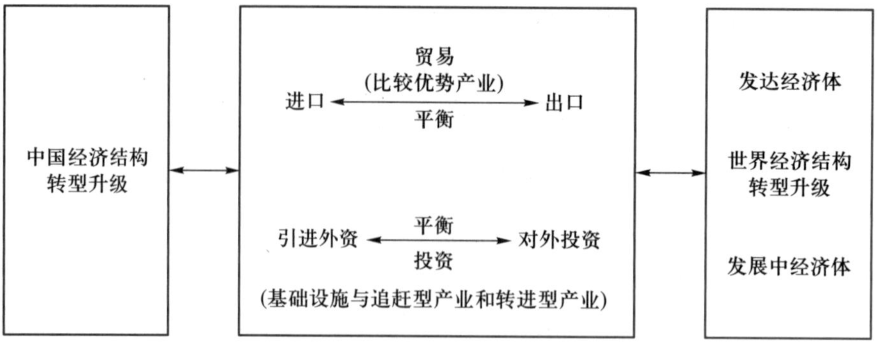


图8.39 中国与世界的深度融合：中国与世界经济结构转型升级的内在需求

效究竟如何呢？很多著作描述了其运作过程与制度细节，①也有不多的研究对其进行了实证检验，得到的结论都比较正面。例如，刘秉镰和王钺考察了上海自贸区的成立对区域创新能力的影响，利用合成控制分析技术，构建“反事实”样本，实证考察上海自贸区成立前后创新变量的实际值与“反事实”值之间的差距。他们的研究发现，上海自贸区的设立能够显著促进上海市创新水平的提升，如图8.40所示。②通过如图8.41所示的人力资本效应、竞争效应、溢出效应、贸易效应等微观、中观和宏观层面的影响，根据他们的估计，在整个事后窗口期内，上海自贸区成立对创新产生的影响的平均“处置效应”达到了15%。紧随上海自贸区之后，2014年12月，中国决定增设广东、天津、福建3个自由贸易试验区，覆盖了东部沿海的华北、华东、华南三大区域的核心经济带。这些自由贸易试验区秉承了中国改革开放的实践经验智慧，充当了试验田的作用。中国在2016年G20杭州峰会前公布了新增的7个自由贸易试验区，向全球发出一个明确的信号：中国支持贸易自由化，反对贸易保护主义。中国新一批自由贸易试验区的设立，就是在国家层面支持贸易自由化。2016年增设的7个自由贸易试验区，从沿海到内陆，代表了自由贸易试验区向纵深化发展，进一步对接高标准国际经贸规则，在更广领域、更大范围形成各具特色、各有侧重的试点格局，推动全面深化改革扩大开放。左思明基于倾向得分匹配和双重差分模型，采用2010—2015年中国31个省份的面板数据检验了自由贸易试验区建设对外商直接投资的影响。他的实证结果表明，自由贸易试验区显著地促进了该区域的外资流入，从而肯定了自由贸易试验区建设在促进外商直接投资中所起到的关键作用。③

① 一些相关著作可资参考：肖林，《国家试验——中国（上海）自由贸易试验区制度设计》，格致出版社，2015年版；周奇、张湧主编，《中国（上海）自贸试验区制度创新与案例研究》，上海社会科学院出版社，2016年版。

② 刘秉镰、王钺，“自贸区对区域创新能力的影响效应研究——来自上海自由贸易试验区准实验的证据”，《经济与管理研究》，2018年第9期。

③ 左思明，“自贸区建设对外商直接投资的影响——基于倾向得分匹配和双重差分法”，《制度经济学研究》，2018年第2期。

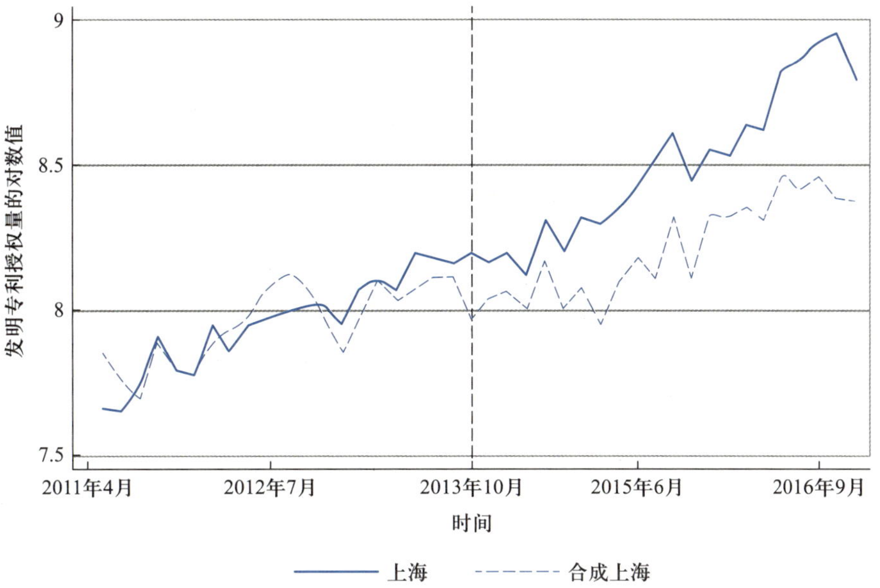


**图 8.40 上海自贸区对区域创新影响的估计**

资料来源：刘秉镰、王钺，“自贸区对区域创新能力的影响效应研究——来自上海自由贸易试验区准实验的证据”，《经济与管理研究》，2018 年第 9 期。

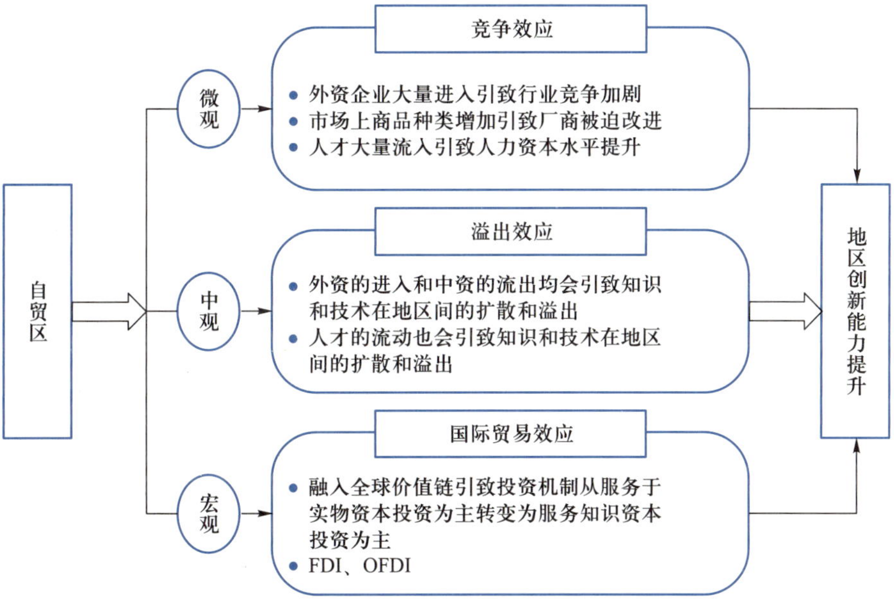


**图 8.41 上海自贸区提升区域创新的机制**

资料来源：刘秉镰、王钺，“自贸区对区域创新能力的影响效应研究——来自上海自由贸易试验区准实验的证据”，《经济与管理研究》，2018 年第 9 期。

# 第9章

# 『一带一路』助推世界经济发展

- 9.1 “一带一路”倡议的比较优势
- 9.2 “一带一路”倡议的内容与进展
- 9.3 “一带一路”倡议的产能合作与经贸合作区
- 9.4 “一带一路”倡议与经贸投资成效
- 9.5 “一带一路”倡议与企业转型升级
- 9.6 “一带一路”倡议与人民币国际化
- 9.7 提高“一带一路”沿线基础设施投资回报率与“耐心资本”
- 9.8 世界各国如何发挥比较优势参与“一带一路”
- 9.9 中国各地如何发挥比较优势参与“一带一路”

# 9.1

# —

# “一带一路”倡议的比较优势①

正如我们在第8章讨论的，改革开放以来，中国经济发展成就斐然。2013年，习近平提出“丝绸之路经济带”和“21世纪海上丝绸之路”倡议（简称“一带一路”倡议），这是展现新时代中国开放胸怀的伟大蓝图，将进一步推动全球化，传播中国的理念和经验，助推更多国家实现经济繁荣。2008年国际金融危机爆发以来，世界经济普遍陷入低迷，至今尚未完全复苏。与此同时，由于外部需求减弱、产能过剩比比皆是，世界经济转入低速增长，出现了“逆全球化”的潮流。主要表现为：一是各国间宏观政策协调难度加大，为加快经济复苏，各国利益诉求和政策着力点的差异日益显现；二是部分国家保护主义抬头，贸易壁垒逐渐增加；三是有些国家和利益群体把利益分配不均、贫富分化加剧错误地归咎于全球化，成为反全球化的主要力量。在此背景下，“一带一路”倡议以共商、共建、共享为原则，顺应并助推经济全球化、世界多极化、文化多样化与各国互联互通、包容互鉴、互利共赢的时代潮流，从中国自身发展经验出发，为解决世界发展难题贡献中国智慧，成为维护和推进全球化的一股清流。②

随着中国经济的快速发展和占世界经济比重的不断提升（回顾第1章第1.2节相关内容），中国对世界要承担的责任也就越来越多。中国文化一向强调所谓“己立立人，己达达人”，中国从一个低收入的贫穷落后的发展中国家，发展成为中等偏上而且可能很快成为高收入的国家，对于有相同命运的发展中国家，理应有新时代的大国担当。多年来的实践证明，“一带一路”倡议彰显中国的大国担当，是打造人类命运共同体的伟大创举。“一带一路”倡议是以中国经济实力和发展成功经验为基础的全球化方案。中国提出“一带一

---

① 相关背景可参考《推动共建丝绸之路经济带和21世纪海上丝绸之路的愿景与行动》的政策介绍，更多的理论分析可参考：林毅夫，“中华民族伟大复兴和‘一带一路’倡议”，《上海对外经贸大学学报》，2018年第6期。亦可参考林毅夫作为“一带一路”国际合作高峰论坛咨询委员会主席领衔发布的《共建“一带一路”：建设更美好的世界——“一带一路”国际合作高峰论坛咨询委员会研究成果和建议报告》。

② 世界银行研究组的量化贸易模型结果显示，共建“一带一路”将使“发展中的东亚及太平洋国家”的国内生产总值平均增加2.6%至3.9%（Francois de Soyres, The Growth and Welfare Effects of the Belt and Road Initiative on East Asia Pacific Countries, World Bank Group, October 2018 Number 4.）。

路”倡议具备四大优势[①]：

一是强大的基础设施建设实力。基础设施建设的重要性（回顾第7章的内容），不仅中国，其他国家包括美国也看到了。2011年，当时的美国总统奥巴马就提出“新丝绸之路”计划，倡导以基础设施的互联互通，把中亚五国跟阿富汗连在一起，在印度洋找到一个出海口。同年还提出“印太经济走廊”，用基础设施把印度洋和太平洋连在一起。这些倡议的内容和“一带一路”倡议相似，但是现在美国提出的“新丝绸之路”“印太经济走廊”国际反响一般，而“一带一路”倡议在国际上得到积极的反应。为什么会有这种差异呢？是因为在基础设施的建设上面，中国有比较优势，而且是可信的。在基础设施建设所需的钢筋、水泥、平板玻璃、电解铝方面，中国的产量超过世界的一半；中国拥有一支强大的基础设施建设施工队伍，在国际上可以最低价格提供同样的基础设施（可回顾第8章的相关内容）。美国基础设施建设的高峰时期是第二次世界大战后大建高速公路时，那时候它的基础设施建设能力非常强，现在已经衰落（可回顾第7章的相关内容）。

二是充足的外汇储备。如图9.1所示，中国过去20多年积累了大量的外汇储备，截至2019年1月，中国大约有3.087 9万亿美元（合2.204 6万亿SDR）的外汇储备。中国的外汇储备以往主要用于购买美国的政府债券或股票，但美国政府债券基本为零利率的局面在短期内不会改变，股市泡沫又十分巨大。加之多数发展中国家普遍面临基础设施落后导致的发展瓶颈，十分欢迎基础设施投资（回顾第7章相关内容）。在此状况下，只要项目选择、设计、施工、管理得当，外汇储备用于基础设施建设的回报率更高。而且未来中国每年的外汇储备还

---

① 李兵和颜晓晨使用1984—2014年全球双边贸易数据和全球恐怖袭击数据，运用引力模型分别考察了恐怖袭击对“一带一路”沿线国家出口和进口的影响。他们的实证结果表明，恐怖袭击显著降低了“一带一路”沿线国家的出口和进口；相对其他国家而言，恐怖袭击对中国与“一带一路”沿线国家之间的贸易的负面影响较小，这一效果不仅与美国、日本和德国这样的贸易强国比较非常明显，而且也比墨西哥这样的发展中国家略微明显；这一效果在2003年伊拉克战争发生之前并不明显，但是在伊拉克战争之后更为明显。这一方面表明中国从事外经贸实务人员具有勤劳勇敢、不惧死伤、勇于开拓进取的精神，另一方面也表明我国以和平共处五项原则为基础的外交政策使得我们更少遭到恐怖袭击的侵害，这两个方面共同构成了我国与“一带一路”沿线国家双边贸易的新比较优势。详细的实证研究可参考：李兵、颜晓晨，中国与“‘一带一路’沿线国家双边贸易的新比较优势——公共安全的视角”，《经济研究》，2018年第1期，第184-197页。

事实上，正如法赫迪·阿力什2017年3月25日在阿拉伯语的《伊拉夫报》上发表的文章所指出的：“中国奉行中立政策，不挑事，不制造对立，鼓励通过对话和协商解决分歧。同时中国也在伊拉克等被战争损毁的国家，默默开展基础设施的援建工作，这也让国际社会和阿拉伯世界对中国的政治智慧感到信任与佩服。”此外，由于中东地区很多国家正处在工业化、城市化的起步或加速阶段，加上年轻化的人口结构，对交通、通信、电力等基础设施的需求量巨大，这成为中国与中东国家共建“一带一路”、实现基础设施领域互联互通和互利共赢的重要契机。（魏敏，“‘一带一路’框架下中国与中东基础设施互联互通问题研究”，《国际经济合作》，2017年第12期，第58–63页；姜英梅，“中东国家基础设施建设与‘一带一路’合作前景”，《阿拉伯世界研究》，2019年第2期，第91–104页）

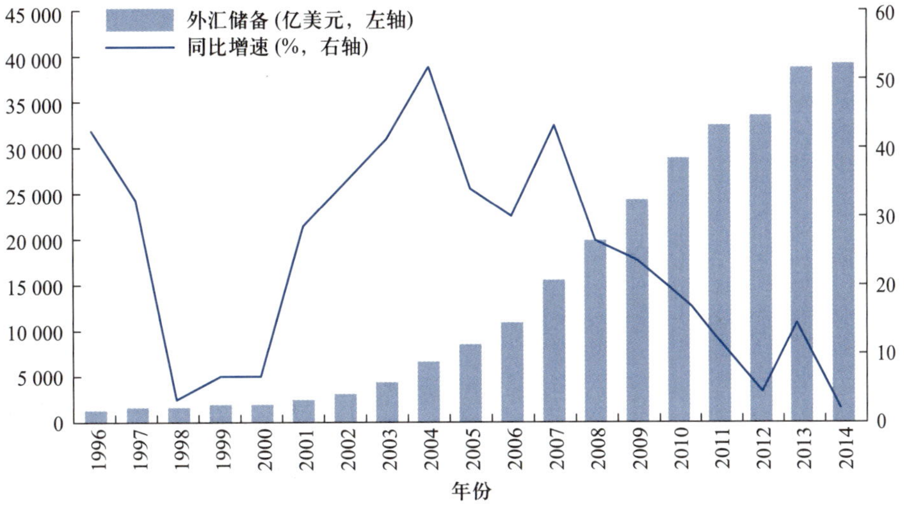


**图9.1 过去20多年来中国的外汇储备及其同比增长率**

资料来源：Wind数据库。

可能继续增加，[①]有足够的资金作为种子资金动员主权基金、退休基金和金融市场上的其他资金投资于“一带一路”所需的基础设施建设。

三是中国所处发展阶段的优势。基础设施建设以后是不是能致富，取决于有没有产业发展。改革开放以来，中国依靠劳动力密集型加工制造业的发展成为世界的工厂、最大的出口国。现在随着工资水平的不断上升，劳动力密集型加工制造业逐渐失去比较优势，需要转移到其他工资水平较低的国家。“一带一路”沿线大多数国家的人均GDP水平不及中国的一半，是承接中国劳动力密集型产业转移的好地方。通过“一带一路”的基础设施建设，帮助这些国家承接劳动力密集型产业，能够为其创造就业、增加出口。二战后的经验表明，只要抓住劳动力密集型产业国际转移的窗口机遇期，就能取得二三十年的快速发展，摆脱贫困，进入中等收入甚至是高收入经济体的行列（回顾第4章的内容）。二战后取得快速发展的发展中经济体，也为发达经济体带来了不断扩张的市场。20世纪60年代，日本的劳动力密集型产业向海外转移时，其制造业雇用人数的总体规模是970万人。20世纪80年代，亚洲“四小龙”的劳动力密集型加工产业向海外转移时，韩国整个制造业雇用人数的规模是230万人，中国台湾是150万人，中国香港不到100万人，新加坡是50万人。按照第三次工业普查数据，中国制造业雇用人数则高达1.24亿人，其中劳动力密集产业就达

① 国家外汇管理局公布的最新数据：2018年中国经常账户顺差491亿美元；储备资产因国际收支交易（不含汇率、价格等非交易因素影响）增加189亿美元，其中，外汇储备增加182亿美元；非储备性质的金融账户（含四季度净误差与遗漏）呈现顺差602亿美元。

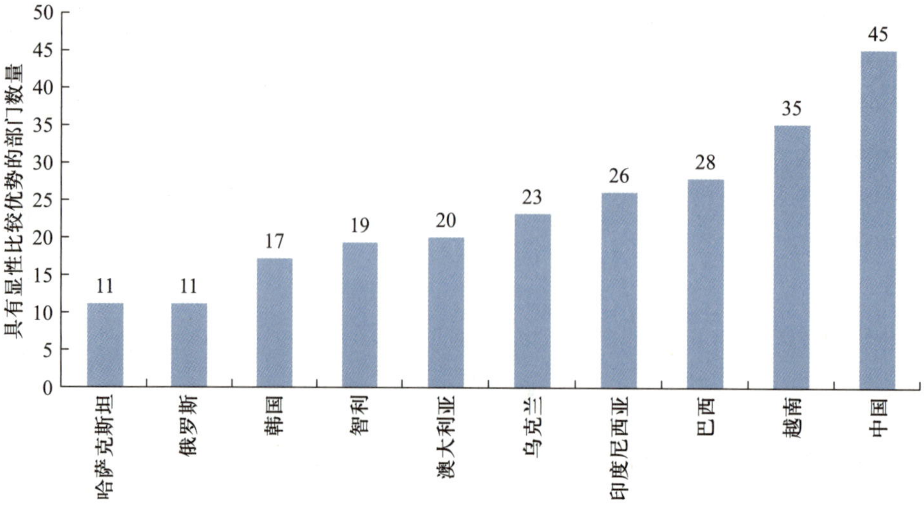


**图9.2 中国工业门类齐全，具有比较优势，有知识经验和能力来帮助其他发展中国家的产业转型升级**

注：柱状图上方的数字基于2010年或2011年，表示具有显性比较优势（RCA > 1）的部门的个数（这里我们使用了2位HS2分类代码（1996年版，共97个部门））。

资料来源：林毅夫、王燕，哈萨克斯坦报告[①]，第144页，基于世界银行WITS数据计算。

8 500万人，能够有足够的机会让“一带一路”沿线的所有发展中国家同时实现工业化和现代化（可回顾第6章的相关内容）。图9.2显示了2010—2011年我们选择的一些样本国家和部门（共97个部门）的显性比较优势（RCA > 1）的计算结果。在中等收入国家之间进行比较，自然资源丰富的俄罗斯和哈萨克斯坦只有11个部门具有显性比较优势（RCA > 1）。中低收入的亚洲国家，例如印度尼西亚和越南，具有更多的显性比较优势部门。中国在这一组中是工业门类最齐全、最多元化的国家，在97个部门中有45个都具有显性比较优势。所以，中国处在很有利的地位，有知识经验和能力来帮助其他发展中国家在其具有潜在比较优势的部门提高竞争力。

四是中国发展理念的优势。目前的主流理论一般都来自于发达国家，通常以发达国家为参照系，看发达国家有什么，发展中国家缺什么，或看发达国家能做好什么，发展中国家什么做不好，就主张发展中国家去发展发达国家拥有的，照搬发达国家的做法。出发点非常好，但由于未考虑前提条件和发展中国家本国国情，效果都很差。中国的经验是，解放思想、实事求是，既正确地认识自己，也正确地认识别人。正确认识自己，就是既要客观全面地了解

① 更多内容可参见2015年我们应亚洲开发银行邀请，运用“增长甄别因势利导”框架为哈萨克斯坦写的报告：Lin Justin Yifu and Yan Wang, “Catching Up:Structural Transformation and Diversification,” in Jesus Felipe ed., *Development and Modern Industrial Policy in Practice: Issues and Country Experiences*, Asian Development Bank and Edward Elgar Publishing, 2015.

自己国家的基本国情和条件，包括自己国家的发展阶段、自然资源、劳动力、资金条件，也要了解以前和现在的主要问题及其产生的原因，等等。正确认识别人，就是要对世界上处于不同发展阶段的不同类型的国家做出系统分析，并对自己国家与这些国家之间的关系包括可比性、差异性、互补性等做出客观判断。尤为重要的是，要对自己国家和其他国家的相对比较优势及其阶段性特征，做出深入细致的研究，不能简单照搬或模仿其他国家，尤其是条件和自己不同的发达国家的理论、政策和经验（回顾第1章第4节的内容）。

## 9.2

## “一带一路”倡议的内容与进展[①]

“一带一路”倡议始于2013年，2014年正式成为中国对外政策框架[②]，2015年完成顶层规划设计，2016年以来“一带一路”倡议已经进入全面落实阶段。“一带一路”倡议建设从无到有、由点及面，进度和成果超出预期。“一带一路”贯穿亚欧大陆，2015年“一带一路”沿线有64个国家，人口约44亿人，GDP为23万亿美元，分别占世界总量的63%和

① 推进“一带一路”建设工作领导小组办公室于2019年4月22日发布的《共建“一带一路”倡议：进展、贡献与展望》报告可供参考。此外，也可参考相关的一些最新评估研究报告，如：国家信息中心“一带一路”大数据中心，《“一带一路”大数据报告（2018）》，商务印书馆，2018年版；刘卫东等，《“一带一路”建设进展第三方评估报告（2013—2018）》，商务印书馆，2019年版。

② 相对于“长江经济带”和“京津冀一体化”空间战略，“一带一路”倡议有更大的全球化内涵。如储殷和高远所指出的：“一带一路”倡议在大方向基本清晰的情况下，在战略定位上仍然存在着三个有待进一步厘清的问题，包括：“一带一路”倡议是全球性的还是区域性的？“一带一路”应以多重双边伙伴关系为基础还是应以跨区域整合为基础？“一带一路”倡议应以西北方向为优先还是应以东南方向为优先？对这三个问题的诠释对于“一带一路”倡议的推进有着极为重要的意义。这一倡议虽然表现出了一定的全球性特征，但在本质上还是区域性的；其推进必须以多重双边伙伴关系为基础。（储殷、高远，“中国‘一带一路’战略定位的三个问题”，《国际经济评论》，2015年第2期）。

29%，贸易总量占全球的将近1/4。目前，“一带一路”涉及的国家已经延伸至西欧的英国、法国、德国等，非洲的南非，大洋洲的澳大利亚以及南美洲的国家和地区。事实上，“一带一路”倡议是中国的国际发展合作的载体，① 目前已经有100多个国家和国际组织参与到“一带一路”建设中。②

2013年9—10月，习近平正式提出包含“丝绸之路经济带”和“21世纪海上丝绸之路”的“一带一路”倡议；2014年12月，中央经济工作会议将“一带一路”与京津冀协同发展、长江经济带建设共同列为国家三大战略；2015年3月，国家发改委、外交部、商务部联合发布了《推动共建丝绸之路经济带和21世纪海上丝绸之路的愿景与行动》,《愿景与行动》是“一带一路”首次公布的总体的顶层设计和规划；2016年3月，“一带一路”被列入“十三五”时期主要目标任务和重大举措。政策逐层演进，由理念到框架，由框架到规划，由规划到深入实施。“一带一路”倡议提出以来，中国在国内外层面取得了一系列重要的政策进展。

国内方面，中央和部委层面各项具体推进措施不断出台，大部分“一带一路”省市已经出台“一带一路”专项政策，国家发改委、商务部等13个部门以及香港特区政府均已设立“一带一路”专门机构。亚洲基础设施投资银行（简称亚投行）是首个由中国倡议设立的多边发展机构。2015年2月召开的中央财经领导小组第九次会议就已明确亚投行的主要任务，是为亚洲基础设施和“一带一路”建设提供资金支持。亚投行和丝路基金均依照国际标准设立，两者对于跨境经济活动更具优势。亚投行法定资本1 000亿美元，创始成员国为57个，到2019年7月，成员已增加到100个。亚投行旨在促进亚洲地区基础设施和其他生产设施的发展建设，包括能源、交通、通信、农业基础设施、水利和水环境、环境保护、城市发展以及物流设施等方面。截至2016年9月底，亚投行公布了该行参与投资建设的六个项目，项目贷款额总计8.29亿美元，涉及孟加拉国、印度尼西亚、巴基斯坦、塔吉克斯坦和缅甸五个国家，涵盖能源、交通和城市发展等领域。六个项目中，除了孟加拉国的电力输送升级和扩容项目为亚投行独立提供贷款的项目，其余项目计划与世界银行、亚洲开发银行、欧洲复兴开发银行等其他多边开发银行以及商业银行进行联合融资。丝路基金成立于2014年12月29日，资金规模为400亿美元，首期资本金100亿美元，外汇储备（占比65%，通过梧桐树投资平台有限责任公司）、中国投资有限责任公司（占比15%，通过赛里斯投资有限公司）、中国进出口银行（占比15%）、国家开发银行（占比5%，通过国开金融有限责任公司）共同

---

① 刘卫东，“‘一带一路’战略的科学内涵与科学问题”,《地理科学进展》，2015年第5期。

② 更详细的实时信息参见中国一带一路网（https://www.yidaiyilu.gov.cn）；更丰富的数据与案例资料可参见“一带一路”研究与决策支撑平台（http://www.drcnet.com.cn/www/ydyl/）。

出资。丝路基金类似于私募股权，以股权投资为主，主要为“一带一路”框架内的经贸合作和多边互联互通提供融资支持，投资期限较长。丝路基金按照市场化、国际化、专业化的原则开展投资业务，可以运用股权、债权、基金、贷款等多种方式提供投融资服务，也可与国际开发机构、境内外金融机构等发起设立共同投资基金，进行资产受托管理、对外委托投资等。丝路基金在股权投资、资源开发、产能合作和金融合作等领域具备灵活性等优势。目前，丝路基金参与投资的项目涵盖巴基斯坦、哈萨克斯坦、俄罗斯、阿联酋、埃及、意大利等国，包括合作设立产能合作专项基金、投资企业及项目股权等。2017年1月，国家发改委同外交部、生态环境部、交通运输部、水利部、农业农村部、人民银行、国资委、林业局、银保监会、能源局、外汇局以及全国工商联、中国铁路总公司13个部门和单位共同设立“一带一路”PPP工作机制，旨在与沿线国家在基础设施等领域加强合作，积极推广PPP模式，鼓励和帮助中国企业走出去，推动相关基础设施项目尽快落地。

国外方面，习近平亲抓“一带一路”倡议，在2013年9月至2016年8月期间就访问了37个国家（亚洲18国、欧洲9国、非洲3国、拉美4国、大洋洲3国）。[①]2019年3月23日，习近平在对意大利进行国事访问期间，中意两国在罗马正式签署政府间关于共同推进“一带一路”建设的谅解备忘录，这是首个G7国家加入“一带一路”倡议。截至2018年8月，已有103个国家和国际组织同中国签署了118份“一带一路”方面的合作协议。2017年首届“一带一路”国际合作高峰论坛在北京成功举办，29个国家的元首和政府首脑出席，140多个国家和80多个国际组织的1 600多名代表参会。论坛279项成果中，到目前为止有265项已经完成或转为常态工作，剩下的14项正在督办推进，落实率达95%。[②]2019年4月25—27日，第二届“一带一路”国际合作高峰论坛在北京举行，37个国家的元首、政府首脑和来自150多个国家和90多个国际组织的近5 000名外宾参加，盛况空前。

战略衔接是“一带一路”成功走出去的重要一环。中国提出的“一带一路”倡议已经与沿线多国的国家发展战略实现对接，包括哈萨克斯坦“光明之路”、俄罗斯“欧亚经济联盟”、蒙古“草原之路”、欧盟“容克计划”、英国“英格兰北方经济中心”、韩国“欧亚倡议”、越南“两廊一圈”、澳大利亚“北部大开发”、东盟“互联互通总体规划”、波兰“琥珀之路”等。马来西亚、新加坡等国均设立“一带一路”专门机构，以管理协调“一带一路”相关事宜。马来西亚华人公会对华事务委员会设立“一带一路”中心。新加坡《联合早报》与新加坡工商联合总会设立“一带一路”专网。上海进出口商会、新疆生产建设兵团贸促会、土耳

① 关于习近平亲自推动“一带一路”倡议的报道可参见：“习近平与‘一带一路’”，中国一带一路网（https://www.yidaiyilu.gov.cn/xwzx/gnxw/6339.htm）。

② 上述信息来自国务院新闻办公室于2018年8月27日举办的新闻发布会。

其-中国工商业协会、吉尔吉斯斯坦工商会等近百家中外商会、企业发起设立“一带一路”贸易商联盟。联合国设立联合国海陆丝绸之路城市联盟（UNMCSR），是联合国内部唯一协调“一带一路”国际事务的专门机构。2017年3月17日，联合国安理会一致通过第2344号决议，呼吁国际社会通过“一带一路”建设加强区域经济合作，敦促各方为“一带一路”建设提供安全保障环境、加强发展政策战略对接、推进互联互通务实合作等。联合国安理会文件首次载入“构建人类命运共同体”的重要理念，体现了国际社会的共识，彰显了中国理念和中国方案对全球治理的重要贡献。

“一带一路”沿线各国资源禀赋各异，经济互补性较强，彼此可以合作的领域非常广阔。按照《推动共建丝绸之路经济带和21世纪海上丝绸之路的愿景与行动》的顶层设计，目前主要以政策沟通、设施联通、贸易畅通、资金融通、民心相通为主要内容，详见表9.1。①

表9.1 “一带一路”倡议的主要内容

| | |
|---|---|
| 政策沟通——加强政策沟通是“一带一路”建设的重要保障 | 加强政府间合作，积极构建多层次政府间宏观政策沟通交流机制，深化利益融合，促进政治互信，达成合作新共识。沿线各国可以就经济发展战略和对策进行充分的交流对接，共同制定推进区域合作的规划和措施，协商解决合作中的问题，共同为务实合作及大型项目实施提供政策支持。 |
| 设施联通——基础设施互联互通是“一带一路”建设的优先领域 | 在尊重相关国家主权和安全关切的基础上，沿线国家宜加强基础设施建设规划、技术标准体系的对接，共同推进国际骨干通道建设，逐步形成连接亚洲各次区域以及亚欧非之间的基础设施网络。强化基础设施绿色低碳化建设和运营管理，在建设中充分考虑气候变化的影响。抓住交通基础设施的关键通道、关键节点和重点工程，优先打通缺失路段，畅通瓶颈路段，配套完善道路安全防护设施和交通管理设施设备，提升道路通达水平。推进建立统一的全程运输协调机制，促进国际通关、换装、多式联运有机衔接，逐步形成兼容规范的运输规则，实现国际运输便利化。推动口岸基础设施建设，畅通陆水联运通道，推进港口合作建设，增加海上航线和班次，加强海上物流信息化合作。拓展建立民航全面合作的平台和机制，加快提升航空基础设施水平。加强能源基础设施互联互通合作，共同维护输油、输气管道等运输通道安全，推进跨境电力与输电通道建设，积极开展区域电网升级改造合作。共同推进跨境光缆等通信干线网络建设，提高国际通信互联互通水平，畅通信息丝绸之路。加快推进双边跨境光缆等建设，规划建设洲际海底光缆项目，完善空中（卫星）信息通道，扩大信息交流与合作。 |

① 更详细的内容可参考：《推动共建丝绸之路经济带和21世纪海上丝绸之路的愿景与行动》。

| | |
|---|---|
| 贸易畅通——投资贸易合作是“一带一路”建设的重点内容 | 宜着力研究解决投资贸易便利化问题，消除投资和贸易壁垒，构建区域内和各国良好的营商环境，积极同沿线国家和地区共同商建自由贸易区，激发释放合作潜力，做大做好合作“蛋糕”。沿线国家宜加强信息互换、监管互认、执法互助的海关合作，以及检验检疫、认证认可、标准计量、统计信息等方面的双多边合作，推动世界贸易组织《贸易便利化协定》的生效和实施。改善边境口岸通关设施条件，加快边境口岸“单一窗口”建设，降低通关成本，提升通关能力。加强供应链安全与便利化合作，推进跨境监管程序协调，推动检验检疫证书国际互联网核查，开展“经认证的经营者”（AEO）互认。降低非关税壁垒，共同提高技术性贸易措施透明度，提高贸易自由化、便利化水平。拓宽贸易领域，优化贸易结构，挖掘贸易新增长点，促进贸易平衡。创新贸易方式，发展跨境电子商务等新的商业业态。建立健全服务贸易促进体系，巩固和扩大传统贸易，大力发展现代服务贸易。把投资和贸易有机结合起来，以投资带动贸易发展。加快投资便利化进程，消除投资壁垒。加强双边投资保护协定、避免双重征税协定磋商，保护投资者的合法权益。拓展相互投资领域，开展农林牧渔业、农机及农产品生产加工等领域深度合作，积极推进海水养殖、远洋渔业、水产品加工、海水淡化、海洋生物制药、海洋工程技术、环保产业和海上旅游等领域合作。加大煤炭、油气、金属矿产等传统能源资源勘探开发合作，积极推动水电、核电、风电、太阳能等清洁、可再生能源合作，推进能源资源就地就近加工转化合作，形成能源资源合作上下游一体化产业链。加强能源资源深加工技术、装备与工程服务合作。推动新兴产业合作，按照优势互补、互利共赢的原则，促进沿线国家加强在新一代信息技术、生物、新能源、新材料等新兴产业领域的深入合作，推动建立创业投资合作机制。优化产业链分工布局，推动上下游产业链和关联产业协同发展，鼓励建立研发、生产和营销体系，提升区域产业配套能力和综合竞争力。扩大服务业相互开放，推动区域服务业加快发展。探索投资合作新模式，鼓励合作建设境外经贸合作区、跨境经济合作区等各类产业园区，促进产业集群发展。在投资贸易中突出生态文明理念，加强生态环境、生物多样性和应对气候变化合作，共建绿色丝绸之路。中国欢迎各国企业来华投资。鼓励本国企业参与沿线国家基础设施建设和产业投资。促进企业按属地化原则经营管理，积极帮助当地发展经济、增加就业、改善民生，主动承担社会责任，严格保护生物多样性和生态环境。 |
| 资金融通——资金融通是“一带一路”建设的重要支撑 | 深化金融合作，推进亚洲货币稳定体系、投融资体系和信用体系建设。扩大沿线国家双边本币互换、结算的范围和规模。推动亚洲债券市场的开放和发展。共同推进亚洲基础设施投资银行、“金砖国家”开发银行筹建，有关各方就建立上海合作组织融资机构开展磋商。加快丝路基金组建运营。深化中国—东盟银行联合体、上合组织银行联合体务实合作，以银团贷款、银行授信等方式开展多边金融合作。支持沿线国家政府和信用等级较高的企业以及金融机构在中国境内发行人民币债券。符合条件的中国境内金融机构和企业可以在境外发行人民币债券和外币债券，鼓励在沿线国家使用所筹资金。加强金融监管合作，推动签署双边监管合作谅解备忘录，逐步在区域内建立高效监管协调机制。完善风险应对和危机处置制度安排，构建区域性金融风险预警系统，形成应对跨境风险和危机处置的交流合作机制。加强征信管理部门、征信机构和评级机构之间的跨境交流与合作。充分发挥丝路基金以及各国主权基金作用，引导商业性股权投资基金和社会资金共同参与“一带一路”重点项目建设。 |

续表

| | |
|---|---|
| 民心相通——民心相通是“一带一路”建设的社会根基 | 传承和弘扬丝绸之路友好合作精神，广泛开展文化交流、学术往来、人才交流合作、媒体合作、青年和妇女交往、志愿者服务等，为深化双多边合作奠定坚实的民意基础。扩大相互间的留学生规模，开展合作办学，中国每年向沿线国家提供1万个政府奖学金名额。沿线国家间互办文化年、艺术节、电影节、电视周和图书展等活动，合作开展广播影视剧精品创作及翻译，联合申请世界文化遗产，共同开展世界遗产的联合保护工作。深化沿线国家间的人才交流合作。加强旅游合作，扩大旅游规模，互办旅游推广周、宣传月等活动，联合打造具有丝绸之路特色的国际精品旅游线路和旅游产品，提高沿线各国游客签证便利化水平。推动21世纪海上丝绸之路邮轮旅游合作。积极开展体育交流活动，支持沿线国家申办重大国际体育赛事。强化与周边国家在传染病疫情信息沟通、防治技术交流、专业人才培养等方面的合作，提高合作处理突发公共卫生事件的能力。为有关国家提供医疗援助和应急医疗救助，在妇幼健康、残疾人康复以及艾滋病、结核、疟疾等主要传染病领域开展务实合作，扩大在传统医药领域的合作。加强科技合作，共建联合实验室（研究中心）、国际技术转移中心、海上合作中心，促进科技人员交流，合作开展重大科技攻关，共同提升科技创新能力。整合现有资源，积极开拓和推进与沿线国家在青年就业、创业培训、职业技能开发、社会保障管理服务、公共行政管理等共同关心领域的务实合作。充分发挥政党、议会交往的桥梁作用，加强沿线国家之间立法机构、主要党派和政治组织的友好往来。开展城市交流合作，欢迎沿线国家重要城市之间互结友好城市，以人文交流为重点，突出务实合作，形成更多鲜活的合作范例。欢迎沿线国家智库之间开展联合研究、合作举办论坛等。加强沿线国家民间组织的交流合作，重点面向基层民众，广泛开展教育医疗、减贫开发、生物多样性和生态环保等各类公益慈善活动，促进沿线贫困地区生产生活条件改善。加强文化传媒的国际交流合作，积极利用网络平台，运用新媒体工具，塑造和谐友好的文化生态和舆论环境。 |

资料来源：根据《推动共建丝绸之路经济带和21世纪海上丝绸之路的愿景与行动》相关内容整理。

“一带一路”倡议的主要内容“五通”完全吻合新结构经济学的理论和世界经济结构转型升级的趋势：政策沟通——“一带一路”建设的重要保障；设施联通——“一带一路”建设的优先领域；贸易畅通——“一带一路”建设的重点内容；资金融通——“一带一路”建设的重要支撑；民心相通——“一带一路”建设的社会根基。按照新结构经济学的理论，一个经济体要想实现经济发展和提高人民收入有两个前提：第一个前提是必须不断按照比较优势的变化，升级产业技术，以此来提高劳动生产率水平；第二个前提是在这个升级过程当中，必须根据新的产业和技术的需要不断完善基础设施，以降低交易费用。而“一带一路”建设正好可以满足这些需求。消除发展瓶颈的基础设施和符合比较优势的产业是双轮，国际贸易和国际金融是基础设施建设和产业发展所需要的市场和金融，国家之间的政策合作以及社会互动是这些安排的基本保障。“一带一路”倡议的主要内容就犹如奥运会的五环会徽，如图9.3所示。可以预期，由于前面概括的中国经济的体量及结构特征与世界经济结构转型升级所需恰好对应，中国发起的“一带一路”倡议将利用中国的产业迭代和基础设施建设能力填补“一带一路”沿线经济体甚至世界经济结构转型升级的产业缺口和基础设施建设缺口。

事实上，近几年来，共建“一带一路”大幅提升了中国和沿线国家贸易投资自由化便利化水平，推动中国开放空间从沿海、沿江向内陆、沿边延伸，形成陆海内外联动、东西双向互济的全面开放新格局；中国同“一带一路”相关国家的货物贸易额累计超过5万亿美元，对外直接投资超过600亿美元，为当地创造20多万个就业岗位，中国对外投资成为拉动全球对外直接投资增长的重要引擎。2018年8月27日，习近平总书记在推进“一带一路”建设工作5周年座谈会上发表讲话时强调，过去五年“一带一路”完成了总体布局，绘就了一幅“大写意”，未来要在保持健康良性发展势头的基础上，推动共建“一带一路”向高质量发展转变，今后要聚焦重点、精雕细琢，共同绘制好精谨细腻的“工笔画”，这是下一阶段推进共建“一带一路”工作的基本要求。

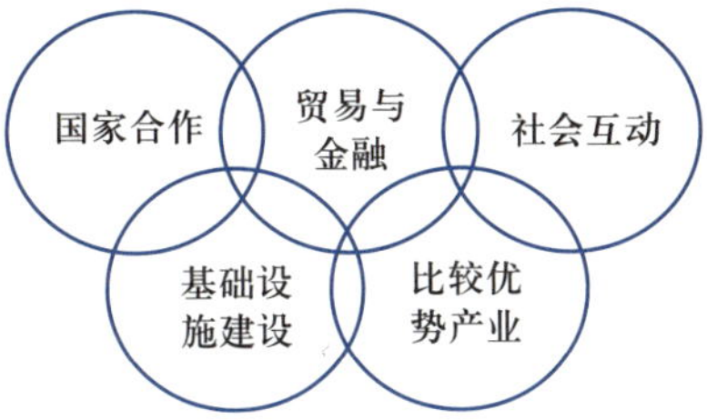


图9.3 “一带一路”倡议主要内容犹如“奥运会五环”

## 9.3

## “一带一路”倡议的产能合作与经贸合作区

包括产业转移与基础设施建设在内的产能合作以及合作的落地园区平台是合作的经济基础。产能合作是指产业和能力的输出，不是简单地把产品卖到国外，而是把产业整体输出到不同的国家去，帮助这些国家建立更加完整的工业体系、提升制造能力。2014年12月14日，中国总理李克强在哈萨克斯坦首都同哈总统纳扎尔巴耶夫、总理马西莫夫就中哈在钢铁、水泥、平板玻璃、装备技术等领域加强产能合作达成重要共识，商定把产能合作作为深化中哈合作的重点和亮点，这被视为推进国际产能合作的开端。2015年5月16日，国务院印发了《关于推进国际产能和装备制造合作的指导意见》（简称《意见》）。《意见》提出了推进国际产能和装备制造合作的指导思想和基本原则、目标任务、政策措施，是当前及今后一个时期推进国际产能和装备制造合作的重要指导性文件。《意见》提出，力争到2020年，与重点国家产能合作机制基本建立，一批重点产能合作项目取得明显进展，形成若干境外产能合作示范基地。推进国际产能和装备制造合作的体制机制进一步完善，支持政策更加有效，服务保障能力全面提升。形成一批有国际竞争力和市场开拓能力的骨干企业。《意见》提出的总体任务为，将与中国装备和产能契合度高、合作愿望强烈、合作条件和基础好的发展中国家作为重点国别，并积极开拓发达国家市场，以点带面，逐步扩展。将钢铁、有色、建材、铁路、电力、化工、轻纺、汽车、通信、工程机械、航空航天、船舶和海洋工程等作为重点行业，分类实施，有序推进。中国已与哈萨克斯坦、巴西、马来西亚、埃塞俄比亚等几大洲的15个国家签订了开展产能合作的框架协议或谅解备忘录，并正在与其他33个国家进行磋商。中国企业联合体与印度尼西亚国企联合体正式签署协议，合作建设印度尼西亚雅加达至万隆高速铁路，这标志着中国高铁“走出去”取得历史性突破；中老铁路成功举行开工奠基仪式；中泰双方签订政府间铁路合作框架文件，项目启动仪式即将举行；中国－中东欧合作的“旗舰项目”匈塞铁路也取得重要进展，中匈签署了政府间合作协议，中塞两国企业签署了项目总合同。目前中国已同哈萨克斯坦、埃及、埃塞俄比亚、巴西等40多个国家签署了产能合作文件，同东盟、非盟、拉美和加勒比国家共同体等区域组织进行合作对接，开展机制化产能合作。中国与法国、意大利、西班牙、日本、葡萄牙等国签署了第三方市场合作文件。“一带一路”产能合作主要涉及两类产业：基础设施建设的基建行业与劳动力密集型和富余产能的产业（也就是我们在第10章将讨论的转进型产业）。这两类产业事实上是相辅相成的，基础设施建设能够有效消除其他行业发展面临的瓶颈，而劳动力密集型产业和富余产能行业则主要是“一带一路”沿线发展中国家或地区解决就业和产业转型升级的主导产业（回顾第6章的相关内容）。

境外经贸合作区已成为推进“一带一路”国际产能合作的重要载体，以及中国企业“走出去”的平台和名片。中国企业在境外投资建设的境外经贸合作区，是以企业为主体，以商业运作为基础，以促进互利共赢为目的，主要由投资主体根据市场情况、东道国投资环境和引资政策等多方面因素进行决策。投资主体通过建设合作区，吸引更多的企业到东道国投资建厂，增加东道国就业和税收，扩大出口创汇，提升技术水平，促进经济共同发展。如第7章介绍的中国过去的成功经验一样，园区能够在小范围内快速提供对应产业集群所需要的软硬基础设施。这些“一带一路”沿线的合作区不仅使中国汽车、摩托车、机械、电子、化工、纺织、服装等优势产业在海外形成集聚效应，也降低了中国企业“走出去”的风险与成本。对于东道国而言，这些合作区能有效地在短期内解决基础设施瓶颈问题，吸引更多的中国企业前来投资建厂，不仅在增加就业、提高税收、扩大出口创汇等方面发挥了重要作用，还有力地推动了东道国工业化进程并促进了相关产业的升级。[①]“一带一路”倡议由于很好契合了沿线国家的需求，到2017年年末，中国企业共与44个国家建设了初级规模的境外经贸合作区99家，累计投资307亿美元，入驻企业4 364家，上缴东道国税费24.2亿美元，为当地创造25.8万个就业岗位。这些经贸合作区涉及的“一带”国家包括哈萨克斯坦、吉尔吉斯斯坦、乌兹别克斯坦、俄罗斯、白俄罗斯、匈牙利、罗马尼亚和塞尔维亚等；涉及的“一路”国家分布在东南亚、南亚和非洲地区。[②]表9.2概括了一些“一带一路”沿线国家境外经贸合作区的产业定位。从中可以看到，整体上的产业定位偏向于劳动力密集型和资源型产业，大体上符合当地的潜在比较优势。[③]与当年中国国内的园区主要由地方政府主动建设来招商引资不同，这些“一带一路”沿线的园区主要由私人企业尤其是投资国的私人企业建设，不但可以引入产业，还能提高当地的园区建设成效，这是多么难得的春风！[④]如果“一带一路”沿线的发展中经济体要想取得像中国过去40年的经济增长奇迹，那么在园区建设与产业转移以及基础设施建设上就应该更加积极。

由于同时融合基础设施建设和比较优势产业发展，中国境外经贸合作区能够产生立竿见影的效果。例如，南亚的“中巴经济走廊”（China-Pakistan Economic Corridor，CPEC）是“一带一路”倡议的样板工程和旗舰项目。“中巴经济走廊”目前以基础设施建设为主，

---

① 李嘉楠等通过倾向得分匹配的方法，结合签约国制度水平、经济发展情况与自然资源储备，量化分析了1999—2013年间境外经贸合作区对中国国际投资以及进出口贸易所产生的具体影响，试图填补该领域的文献空白。他们的研究发现：境外经贸合作区的建立能够显著提高中国对签约国的直接投资，其促进作用甚至大于双边投资协定和自由贸易区协定；境外经贸合作区对于中国的出口贸易具有替代作用。这一实证结果印证了境外经贸合作区正在发挥着符合战略预期的重要作用。（李嘉楠、龙小宁、张相伟，“中国经贸合作新方式——境外经贸合作区”，《中国经济问题》，2016年第6期）余官胜等从宏观上度量了中国对各东道国的企业对外直接投资进入速度，并通过实证研究发现，出于集群规避风险的目的，中国企业对外直接投资在总体上倾向于以更快的速度进入经济风险和政治风险较高的东道国；而在建有中国境外经贸合作区的东道国，风险则不影响企业对外直接投资的进入速度，间接反映出境外经贸合作区的风险规避功能。他们更进一步利用倾向得分匹配估计方法发现境外经贸合作区建设本身也能提升企业对外直接投资进入速度，直接反映出境外经贸合作区在“一带一路”建设中的重要性。（余官胜、范朋真、龙文，“东道国风险、境外经贸合作区与我国企业对外直接投资进入速度——度量与跨国面板数据实证研究”，《国际商务研究》，2019年第2期，第15-25页）

② 上述数据来自《中国对外投资发展报告2018》。关于中国境外经贸合作区实时资料信息可参考国务院发展研究中心信息网“一带一路”依据与决策支撑平台。

③ 有一些相关的境外经贸区案例研究可进一步参考：佘莉，“中埃苏伊士经贸合作区：背景、成效、发展机遇”，《国际经济合作》，2018年第7期；孟广文、王春智、杜明明、王继光、赵钏、鲁笑男、王红梅，“尼日利亚奥贡广东自贸区发展历程与产业聚集研究”，《地理科学》，2018年第5期；孟广文、隋娜娜、王雪，“赞比亚-中国经贸合作区建设与发展”，《热带地理》，2017年第2期。

④ 关于中国和非洲园区比较研究可参考：If Africa builds nests, will the birds come? Comparative Study on Special Economic Zones in Africa and China. 中国国际扶贫中心和UNDP，Working Paper Series No.06, 2015.

表9.2 一些“一带一路”沿线国家境外经贸合作区的产业定位案例①

| 合作区名称 | 成立年份 | 所在国 | 中方园区开发企业 | 主导产业 |
| --- | --- | --- | --- | --- |
| 苏伊士经贸合作区 | 1998 | 埃及 | 中非泰达投资股份有限公司 | 新型建材、纺织服装、高低压电器设备和石油装备 |
| 中俄（滨海边疆区）农业产业合作区 | 2004 | 俄罗斯 | 黑龙江东宁华信经济贸易有限责任公司 | 种植、养殖、农产品加工 |
| 泰中罗勇工业园 | 2005 | 泰国 | 华立产业集团有限公司 | 汽配、机械、家电 |
| 西哈努克港经济特区 | 2006 | 柬埔寨 | 江苏太湖柬埔寨国际经济合作区投资有限公司 | 纺织服装、五金机械、轻工家电 |
| 海尔－鲁巴经济区 | 2006 | 巴基斯坦 | 海尔集团电器产业有限公司 | 家电、汽车、纺织、建材、化工 |
| 莱基自由贸易区（中尼经贸合作区） | 2006 | 尼日利亚 | 云南省海外投资有限公司 | 以生产制造与仓储物流为主导，以城市服务与房地产为支撑 |
| 乌苏里斯克经贸合作区 | 2006 | 俄罗斯 | 康吉国际投资有限公司 | 轻工、机电（家电、电子）、木业 |
| 中国－印度尼西亚聚龙农业产业合作园 | 2006 | 印度尼西亚 | 天津聚龙集团 | 油棕种植开发、精深加工、收购、仓储物流 |
| 越南龙江工业园 | 2007 | 越南 | 前江投资管理有限责任公司 | 纺织轻工、机械电子、建材化工 |
| 赞比亚中国经济贸易合作区 | 2007 | 赞比亚 | 中国有色矿业集团有限公司 | 有色金属矿冶、现代物流、商贸服务、加工制造、房地产、配套服务和新技术产业 |
| 中国－印度尼西亚经贸合作区 | 2007 | 印度尼西亚 | 广西农垦集团有限责任公司 | 汽车装配、机械制造、家用电器、精细化工及新材料 |
| 中俄托木斯克木材工贸合作区 | 2008 | 俄罗斯 | 中航林业有限公司 | 森林抚育采伐、木材深加工、商贸物流 |
| 埃塞俄比亚东方工业园 | 2008 | 埃塞俄比亚 | 江苏永元投资有限公司 | 纺织、皮革、农产品加工、冶金、建材、机电 |
| 乌兹别克斯坦“鹏盛”工业园 | 2009 | 乌兹别克斯坦 | 温州市金盛贸易有限公司 | 建筑材料、真皮制品、灯具和五金制品、电机电器、农用机械、轻纺及纺织品 |
| 万象赛色塔综合开发区 | 2010 | 老挝 | 云南省海外投资有限公司 | 能源化工、农畜产品加工、电力产品制造、饲料加工、烟草加工、建材科技、物流仓储 |
| 匈牙利中欧商贸物流园 | 2011 | 匈牙利 | 山东帝豪国际投资有限公司 | 商品展示、运输、仓储、集散、配送、信息处理、流通加工 |
| 吉尔吉斯斯坦亚洲之星农业产业合作区 | 2011 | 吉尔吉斯斯坦 | 商丘贵友食品有限公司 | 种植、养殖、屠宰加工、食品深加工 |
| 中匈宝思德经贸合作区 | 2011 | 匈牙利 | 烟台新益投资有限公司 | 化工、生物化工 |

① 更详细的经贸合作区资料可参考国务院发展研究中心信息网“一带一路”依据与决策支撑平台。

续表

| 合作区名称 | 成立年份 | 所在国 | 中方园区开发企业 | 主导产业 |
|---|---|---|---|---|
| 俄罗斯龙跃林业经贸合作区 | 2013 | 俄罗斯 | 黑龙江省牡丹江龙跃经贸有限公司 | 林木采伐、粗加工和深加工、森林培育、森林采伐、精深加工、林产品展销交易、跨境物流运输 |
| 中国印尼综合产业园区青山园区 | 2013 | 印度尼西亚 | 上海鼎信投资（集团）有限公司 | 镍铁、不锈钢 |

资料来源：叶尔肯·吾扎提、张薇、刘志高，“我国在‘一带一路’沿线海外园区建设模式研究”，《中国科学院院刊》，2017年第4期。

中巴产能合作则以钢筋、水泥、建筑材料和装备制造业等进入当地市场的项目为主，[①]未来需要增加中国劳动力密集型加工出口产业项目，为巴基斯坦承接中国劳动力密集型加工出口产业转移提供支持。[②]根据世界银行的数据，巴基斯坦2018年有7 152万劳动力，农业就业人员占就业总数的百分比高达41.28%，制造业增加值占GDP的百分比只有11.98%，毫无疑问现阶段其主导的产业定位便是劳动力密集型产业。巴基斯坦2018年的人均GDP为1 547.85美元，只有中国的17.54%，按照新结构经济学的增长甄别与因势利导工具（GIFF）（第10章将详细介绍），中巴产业合作恰到好处。建设中的巴基斯坦工银－如意费萨拉巴德纺织服装工业园就将起到很好的效果。巴基斯坦工银－如意费萨拉巴德纺织服装工业园项目是“中巴经济走廊”项目之一，将在巴基斯坦旁遮普省费萨拉巴德市建设纺纱、面料、服装以及与之配套的2×135兆瓦电力项目，由中国工商银行、山东如意科技集团、巴基斯坦哈比银行等共同投资建设。该工业园将打造纺纱、染色、织布、整理、高端面料、服装、仓储、物流一体化，具有能源配套优势的棉纺服装产业链纺织工业园区。项目得到中国工商银行、中巴投资基金、中东投资基金及巴基斯坦金融机构多渠道支持，成为备受青睐的热点投资项目，成为产业与国际资本、金融资本成功结合的典型范例。又比如地处北非和中东地区的埃及2018年人均GDP为2 412.73美元，发展水平高于巴基斯坦，但也只有中国的27.33%，同样非常适合增长甄别与因势利导方法。埃及虽然有一定的制造业基础，如2018

① 已经建成的“巴基斯坦海尔－鲁巴经济区”已经实现了良好的效果。“巴基斯坦海尔－鲁巴经济区”是中国商务部批准建设的首个“中国境外经济贸易合作区”，也是巴政府批准建设的“巴基斯坦中国经济特区”。早在2006年11月26日，时任中国国家主席胡锦涛和巴基斯坦总理阿齐兹就共同为其揭牌。经济区一区规划面积33万平方米，二区启动2万平方千米。主导产业为家电、汽车、纺织、建材、化工等。该经济区以现有的巴基斯坦海尔工业园为基础进行扩建，海尔集团与巴基斯坦RUBA集团合资建设，中巴股比为55∶45。双方均以现金方式出资，共同购买土地、进行园区建设。经济区所在的巴基斯坦旁遮普省首府拉合尔市，近几年的GDP增长率平均达到8%以上。

② 林毅夫：关于把“中巴经济走廊”建设成“一带一路”和“人类命运共同体”倡议示范工程的提案（摘要与国家发改委的复文内容可参见《中国经贸导刊》2019年第6期）。

年制造业增加值占GDP的百分比为16.44%，但其农业就业人员占就业总数的百分比依然达24.48%。埃及苏伊士经贸合作区（天津）于2009年11月揭牌，2015年年底合作区起步区1.34平方千米就已全部建成，累计投资1.05亿美元，吸引包括宏华钻机和国际钻井材料制造公司、西电-Egemac高压设备公司、巨石（埃及）玻璃纤维公司在内的68家企业入驻，初步形成了石油装备产业园区、高低压电器产业园区、纺织服装产业园区、新型建材产业园区以及机械制造类产业园区，具备了完整产业链条。又比如东南亚的柬埔寨，2018年其人均GDP为1 384.42美元，比巴基斯坦发展水平还要低，只有中国的15.68%，同样非常适合增长甄别与因势利导方法。柬埔寨2018年有949万劳动力，农业就业人员占就业总数的百分比达25.74%，制造业增加值占GDP的百分比为16.2%。桑莎柬埔寨纺织工业园和西哈努克港经济特区的建设就为柬埔寨带来了立竿见影的效果。桑莎柬埔寨纺织工业园是山东桑莎集团投资6 000万美元在柬埔寨建设的占地2 250亩[①]的潍坊首家境外工业园区，成为以纺织服装企业为龙头，集保税仓库、纸箱厂、纱线生产区、面料加工区、针织服装制造区、梭织服装制造区、辅料生产区、物流及策划研发区于一体的工业园区。一期主要生产针梭织服装，二期主要是织布、印染。2016年上半年就已实现出口1 580万美元。西哈努克港经济特区由红豆集团为主导联合中柬四家企业共同开发建设，2008年奠基以来，已引入来自中国、欧美、日本等国家及地区的包括工业、服务业在内的企业81家，59家已生产经营，区内从业人员1.2万名。园区以纺织服装、五金机械、轻工家电等为主要发展产业，全部建成后，将入驻企业300家，形成10万产业工人、20万居住人口的宜居新城。

---

① 1亩=666.67平方米。

## 9.4

## —

## “一带一路”倡议与经贸投资成效①

中国与沿线国家经贸合作的步伐不断加快，双向投资保持较高水平。贸易方面，2013—2018年，中国与沿线国家货物贸易进出口总额超过6万亿美元，年均增长率高于同期中国对外贸易增速，占中国货物贸易总额的比重达到27.4%。其中，2018年，中国与沿线国家货物贸易进出口总额达到1.3万亿美元，同比增长16.4%。中国与沿线国家服务贸易由小到大、稳步发展。2017年，中国与沿线国家服务贸易进出口额达977.6亿美元，同比增长18.4%，占中国服务贸易总额的14.1%，

① 由国家信息中心编撰的《“一带一路”大数据报告2016》汇聚了各类数据约3 000亿条，构建了一套国别合作度指数和省（区、市）参与度指数对“一带一路”倡议的合作重点“政策沟通、设施联通、贸易畅通、资金融通、民心相通”进行了综合评估，对中国与“一带一路”沿线60多个国家之间国别合作情况进行数量化评价并形成综合测评指数。测评结果显示，在参评的64个“一带一路”沿线国家中，32个国家属于“有待加强型”，17个国家属于“逐步拓展型”，13个国家属于“快速推进型”，2个国家属于“深度合作型”。其中，俄罗斯、哈萨克斯坦、泰国、巴基斯坦、印度尼西亚位列前五名。测评结果显示，中国与“一带一路”沿线国家的政策沟通效果整体较好，政治互信明显增强，通信设施基本达到“互联互通”，而设施联通水平则呈现出明显的地域特征。泰国、新加坡、马来西亚与中国航空联通最好，俄罗斯、哈萨克斯坦、蒙古、缅甸与中国能源设施联通最好，巴基斯坦、老挝、俄罗斯、哈萨克斯坦、蒙古等与中国跨境通信设施联通最好。在贸易和投资方面，中国的对外投资合作较为顺利，国别合作项目和工程拓展势头良好，中国与俄罗斯、蒙古、东南亚国家的投资合作成效显著。目前，中国对外贸易增速有所放缓，资金融通水平在国别间具有明显差异，仅与东南亚国家之间的金融支撑环境建设相对较好，其他地区均有待加强。民心相通建设虽有明显成效，但需要强化深入持续的信息沟通以及更有针对性的舆论宣传。更详细的内容参见本章专栏9.1。省区市参与度指数围绕“基础—行动—效果”三个层面来构建系统评价模型及其方法体系，对全国31个省（区、市）参与“一带一路”建设情况及实施效果进行综合测评。结果显示，5个省（区、市）处于“低”水平，9个省（区、市）处于“中等”水平，12个省（区、市）处于“较高”水平，5个省（区、市）处于“高”水平，其中广东、浙江、上海、天津、福建、江苏、山东、河南、云南、北京在综合得分中位列前十。各省（区、市）的“一带一路”建设参与度水平存在较大差距，东部沿海地区的省市在综合评测中得分最高，而西北地区和西南地区则有待加强。与此同时，自“一带一路”倡议提出以来，各地“一带一路”政策环境优化，管理体制基本健全，政策文件陆续出台，资金保障力度逐步加强，相关设施配套建设加快，到境外推进园区建设逐渐增多，铁路、航空、公路、港口的联通水平不断增强。在对外投资方面，各地参与对外经贸合作积极性较高，对外直接投资势头良好，81.7%的省（区、市）对外直接投资额高于10亿美元，77.42%的省（区、市）对外直接投资增速高于20%。各地积极参与海外项目建设，山东、云南、广东、四川、北京五省（市）排位在前。各地参与“一带一路”建设的综合影响力开始显现，新疆、福建、广东、上海、北京五省（区、市）位列国内影响力前五，国外影响力方面则是上海、河南、北京、广东、浙江五省（市）位列前五。更详细的内容参见本章专栏9.2。这一节的数据资料主要根据《“一带一路”大数据报告》《“一带一路”贸易合作大数据报告》相关资料整理而成，这些系列数据报告可资参考。

比2016年提高1.6个百分点。目前，中国与“一带一路”沿线国家贸易额占中国与全球贸易额比重将近1/4（见图9.4）。在地域构成上来看，2013—2016年，中国对东南亚、中亚、南亚和欧盟进出口占比均有所提升，对南亚、中亚、西亚和北非地区进口额占比有所下降。出口方面，2013年以来，中国对东南亚、欧盟、南亚和中亚地区的出口占比有所上升，对日本出口占比有所下降，对西亚和北非占比相对平稳。东南亚、中亚和南亚三个区域出口额占中国总出口额的比重从14.8%上升到17.6%。其中，东南亚出口占比由10.7%上涨到12.2%，中亚和南亚两者占比由4.1%上涨到5.4%，西亚和北非出口占比保持在4%左右。进口方面，2013—2016年，中国对东南亚、欧盟、日本的进口额占比有所上升，对中亚和南亚地区、西亚和北非地区出口额占比下降。东南亚、南亚和中亚三地占比由13.3%上升到14.1%，主要为东南亚由10.6%上涨到12.4%，中亚和南亚占比则由2.8%下降到1.7%，西亚和北非占比由9%下降至5.87%。整体上，“一带一路”有助于缓和中国对美国的贸易依赖问题。在贸易结构上，中国与沿线经济体也有很大的互补优势，如图9.5和图9.6所示，例如中国对其最大的出口产品是电机、电气设备及其零件等，最大的进口产品是矿物燃料、矿物油及其蒸馏产品等。本章第8节将进一步讨论中国与“一带一路”沿线国家的比较优势互补性。

投资方面，2013—2018年，中国企业对沿线国家直接投资超过900亿美元，在沿线国家完成对外承包工程营业额超过4 000亿美元。2018年，中国企业对沿线国家实现非金融类直接投资156亿美元，同比增长8.9%，占同期总额的13.0%；沿线国家对外承包工程完成营业额893亿美元，占同期总额的53.0%。世界银行研究表明，预计沿线国家的外商直接投资总额将增加4.97%，其中，来自沿线国家内部的外商直接投资增加4.36%，来自经济合作与发展组织国家的外商直接投资增加4.63%，来自非沿线国家的外商直接投资增加5.75%。[①]对外

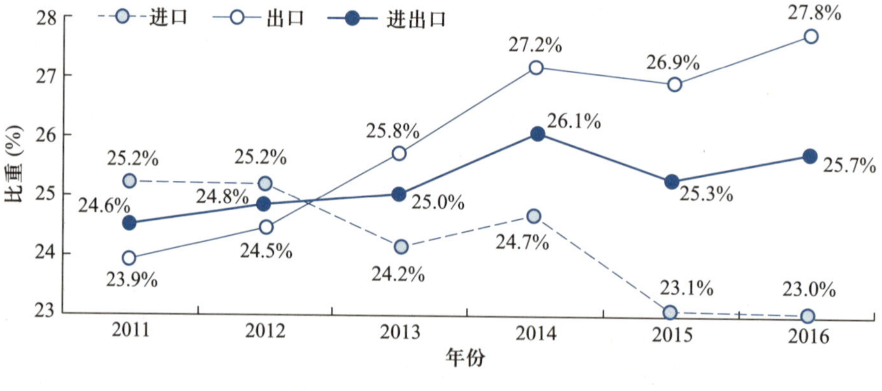


**图9.4 2011—2016年中国与“一带一路”沿线国家贸易额占中国与全球贸易额比重**

资料来源：国家信息中心，《“一带一路”贸易合作大数据报告2017》。

---

① Chen Maggie Xiaoyang, Lin Chuanhao. Foreign Investment across the Belt and Road Patterns, Determinants and Effects, World Bank Policy Research Working Paper 8607, October 2018.

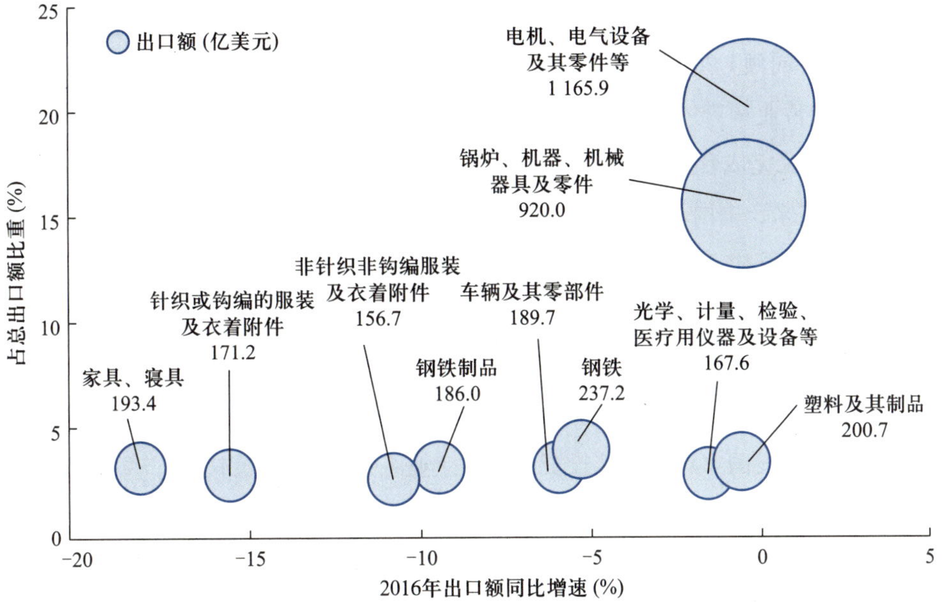


图9.5 2016年中国对“一带一路”沿线国家出口额前十位产品

资料来源：国家信息中心，《“一带一路”贸易合作大数据报告2017》。

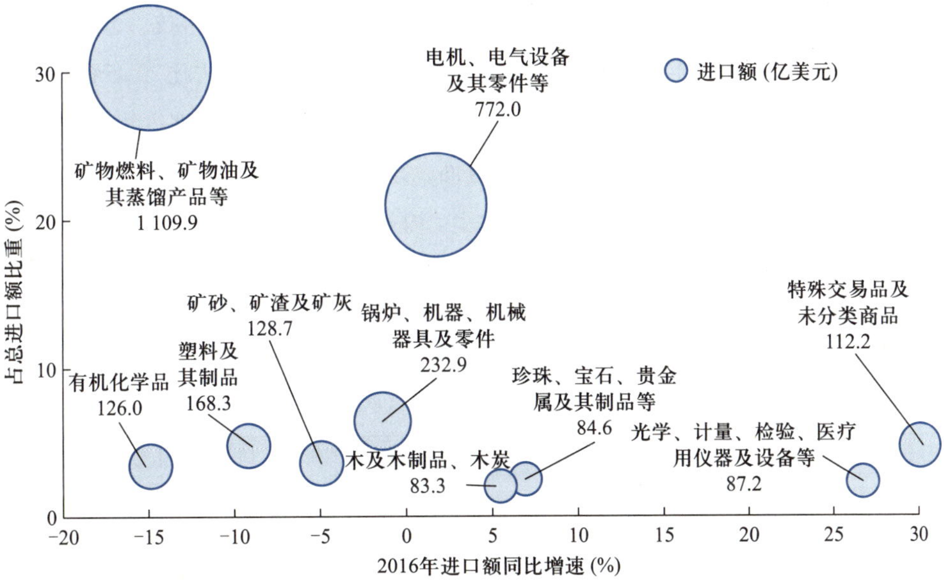


图9.6 2016年中国对“一带一路”沿线国家进口额前十位产品

资料来源：国家信息中心，《“一带一路”贸易合作大数据报告2017》。

承包工程方面，2016年中国企业在“一带一路”沿线61个国家新签对外承包工程项目合同8 158份，新签合同额1 260.3亿美元，占同期中国对外承包工程新签合同额的51.6%，同比增长36%；完成营业额759.7亿美元，占同期总额的47.7%，同比增长9.7%。2018年对“一带一路”沿线国家完成营业额893亿美元，增长4.4%，占对外承包工程完成营业额比重为52.8%。2013年以来，中国对东南亚、中亚和南亚等主要“一带一路”国家和地区直接投资总额大幅上涨，中国对三个区域的直接投资占世界总投资的比重亦有所上升。相对而言，中国对欧盟的直接投资则稳中趋缓。2014年和2015年三地总投资同比增速分别为12%和37%，主要为中国对东南亚的直接投资分别增长8%和87%（中国对东南亚国家的直接投资占比达80%以上）。“一带一路”除了大规模促进中国对外投资，还会吸引大量外资进入中国。2018年“一带一路”沿线国家对华直接投资新设立企业4 479家，增长16.1%；对华直接投资金额424亿元，增长13.2%，折合为64亿美元，增长16.0%。2005—2016年，中国世界范围内直接投资和建设合同规模14 859.1亿美元，“一带一路”倡议提出后中国对外投资增速加快，其中2015年对东亚①和西亚的投资分别增长150.31%和12.9%。行业层面，按照投资规模排名，主要分布在能源、交通运输、有色、房地产、科技、金融、农业、旅游和娱乐领域，其中能源投资规模5 946.1亿美元，占总投资的40%；其次是交通运输规模2 689.1亿美元，占总投资的18%。近两年对欧美的投资加速，对欧美的投资主要集中于科技、金融和旅游业。具体来看，如表9.3所示，能源投资方面主要集中在亚洲地区，西亚占比22.25%，东亚占比15.11%，欧洲占比9.79%，中东和北非占比9.18%。交通运输方面，欧洲占比19.11%，其次为西亚15.83%、中东和北非12.20%。房地产方面，东亚、中东和北非、欧美几个地区旗鼓相当。科技主要在欧美地区，两地占比60%以上。金融亦主要集中于欧美，两地占比70%以上。农业投资主要在欧洲和美国，中东和北非和东亚也有部分。旅游和娱乐主要投资于欧美，两地占比70%以上。“一带一路”相关投资主要是能源、交通运输、房地产和农业等领域。

表9.3 2005—2016年中国对“一带一路”地区及欧美直接投资和建设合同行业结构（%）

| 行业 | 中东和北非 | 东亚 | 西亚 | 欧洲 | 美国 | 其他 |
|---|---|---|---|---|---|---|
| 农业 | 12.25 | 10.66 | 9.69 | 21.94 | 14.74 | 30.73 |
| 能源 | 9.18 | 15.11 | 22.25 | 9.79 | 2.89 | 40.78 |
| 娱乐 | 16.33 | 4.34 | 0.00 | 36.63 | 35.76 | 6.94 |
| 金融 | 0.00 | 6.90 | 2.82 | 31.23 | 41.53 | 17.53 |
| 有色 | 4.68 | 13.18 | 11.32 | 2.12 | 1.06 | 67.64 |
| 房地产 | 17.54 | 17.71 | 5.65 | 16.26 | 15.98 | 26.88 |

① 美国American Enterprise Institute数据库的东亚标准为东亚、东南亚、中亚等地区。

续表

| 行业 | 中东和北非 | 东亚 | 西亚 | 欧洲 | 美国 | 其他 |
|---|---|---|---|---|---|---|
| 科技 | 2.09 | 7.69 | 9.26 | 33.43 | 32.38 | 15.16 |
| 旅游 | 5.82 | 5.80 | 3.20 | 25.02 | 50.71 | 9.45 |
| 交通运输 | 12.20 | 10.50 | 15.83 | 19.11 | 2.89 | 39.47 |

资料来源：朱振鑫、杨晓，《"一带一路"研究手册》，民生证券研究院研究报告，2017年。

"一带一路"倡议除了对中国和沿线国家的双边经贸关系产生积极影响之外，其实更广泛的影响在于通过改善基础设施和国际关系促进了所有沿线国家的对外经贸。2019年世界银行的三位经济学家对"一带一路"倡议的贸易效应进行了量化评估，他们的结果显示，基础设施建设配合贸易便利化的政策改革，"一带一路"建设能够显著降低贸易成本，促进"一带一路"沿线国家的贸易量。[①]根据他们的估算，在"一带一路"倡议之前，沿线国家的双边贸易所需的平均时间约为16天。[②]不同地区之间相差较大，东亚地区与其他地区的贸易时间较长，尤其以东亚－中欧以及东亚－西亚两条贸易路线成本最高。"一带一路"倡议之后，国家间贸易时间平均降低了0.5天（区间估计下限，假定"一带一路"实施后不改变交通方式）至0.7天（区间估计上限，假定"一带一路"实施后部分海上运输转变为铁路运输）。而不同地区之间的改善程度也各不相同，如表9.4所示，中亚与西亚区域内的运输成本得到了最大程度的降低。[③]跨区域的运输上，东亚－撒哈拉以南非洲与东亚－中亚西亚两条运输线的运输成本分别在区间下限与区间上限估计中得到最大程度的降低。在它们的泊松回归结果中，贸易时间每增加一天，出口数量平均降低5.2%；贸易条约每增加一个条款，出口数量平均增加1.9%；关税每增加一个百分点，出口数量平均降低1.8%。这意味着基础设施改善、贸易政策改革以及关税削减都非常有利于沿线国家出口。

当然，按照新结构经济学的理论，我们很自然可以看到，不同的地区、不同的国家、不同的产业肯定受到"一带一路"倡议影响的程度也不同。上述实证研究也支持这一看法：在地区层面，这种差异如表9.5所示。东亚太平洋地区、撒哈拉以南非洲受益最大，贸易量增长最多。

① Suprabha Baniya, Nadia Rocha, Michele Rut, "Trade Effects of the New Silk Road: A Gravity Analysis", World Bank Policy Research Working Paper 8694, 2019.

② 这项研究中定义的"贸易时间"（trading times）是物理距离、地理特征、交通方式与平均速度的函数。与传统意义的把货物从一个城市运输到另一城市所需时间的概念不同，该指标综合考虑了沿线基础设施的数量与质量、物理的运输障碍（沿线的地形复杂程度）以及人为的贸易摩擦（行政边界等），是对跨境贸易运输成本更为真实的测度。

③ 一些实证估计也发现，随着铁路和海运运输成本的降低，欧盟国家，特别是内陆国家，将从中受益良多。东欧和中亚也是如此，东南亚也是如此，只是程度较轻。（Alicia Garcia Herrero, Xu Jiawei, "China's Belt and Road Initiative: Can Europe Expect Trade Gains?", *China & World Economy*, 2017, Vol.25, No.6, pp. 84–99）

表9.4 “一带一路”倡议对地区之间贸易时间的平均改善程度（%）

（a）Lower-bound

| Avg. Change in time to trade (%) | CEE | CWA | EAS | MEA | SAS | SSF |
|---|---|---|---|---|---|---|
| Central and Eastern Europe | 0.7 | | | | | |
| Central and Western Asia | 2.9 | 19.4 | | | | |
| East Asia & Pacific | 2.9 | 5.6 | 5.2 | | | |
| Middle East & North Africa | 0.4 | 2.3 | 4.0 | 0.6 | | |
| South Asia | 1.4 | 1.9 | 6.0 | 1.5 | 2.9 | |
| Sub-Saharan Africa | 3.5 | 4.0 | 7.8 | 4.0 | 4.9 | 5.8 |
| Regional Average | 1.9 | 6.0 | 5.3 | 2.1 | 3.1 | 5.0 |

（b）Upper-bound

| Avg. Change in time to trade (%) | CEE | CWA | EAS | MEA | SAS | SSF |
|---|---|---|---|---|---|---|
| Central and Eastern Europe | 1.1 | | | | | |
| Central and Western Asia | 3.8 | 20.8 | | | | |
| East Asia & Pacific | 3.7 | 9.1 | 8.6 | | | |
| Middle East & North Africa | 3.1 | 4.2 | 5.1 | 0.8 | | |
| South Asia | 3.5 | 2.9 | 7.0 | 2.9 | 3.6 | |
| Sub-Saharan Africa | 5.8 | 8.9 | 8.6 | 4.4 | 5.4 | 6.3 |
| Regional Average | 3.5 | 8.3 | 7.0 | 3.4 | 4.2 | 6.6 |

资料来源：Baniyaet al.（2019）.

表9.5 “一带一路”倡议对地区之间贸易量的平均改善程度（%）

（a）Lower-bound

| Origin | CEE | CWA | EAS | MEA | SAS | SSF | Total |
|---|---|---|---|---|---|---|---|
| Central and Eastern Europe | 0.4 | 1.6 | 4.0 | 0.7 | 0.8 | 4.1 | 1.93 |
| Central and Western Asia | 2.2 | 8.3 | 4.3 | 1.2 | 0.3 | 3.7 | 3.34 |
| East Asia & Pacific | 5.1 | 6.4 | 1.5 | 5.2 | 4.6 | 10.2 | 5.48 |
| Middle East & North Africa | 0.7 | 0.7 | 5.0 | 0.0 | 0.1 | 3.1 | 1.60 |
| South Asia | 0.8 | 0.3 | 4.2 | 0.1 | 0.4 | 3.0 | 1.46 |
| Sub-Saharan Africa | 3.5 | 6.0 | 11.1 | 3.1 | 3.3 | 3.5 | 5.11 |

（b）Upper-bound

| Origin | CEE | CWA | EAS | MEA | SAS | SSF | Total |
|---|---|---|---|---|---|---|---|
| Central and Eastern Europe | 0.7 | 2.5 | 4.5 | 2.0 | 3.7 | 6.0 | 3.21 |
| Central and Western Asia | 3.4 | 10.2 | 10.6 | 3.7 | 0.8 | 6.9 | 5.93 |
| East Asia & Pacific | 5.5 | 12.6 | 2.2 | 12.0 | 5.7 | 12.8 | 8.45 |
| Middle East & North Africa | 1.7 | 1.8 | 8.7 | 0.1 | 1.1 | 3.3 | 2.78 |
| South Asia | 2.7 | 0.9 | 5.0 | 0.9 | 0.6 | 3.8 | 2.33 |
| Sub-Saharan Africa | 5.6 | 20.9 | 13.7 | 3.4 | 4.1 | 3.9 | 8.60 |

资料来源：Baniya et al.（2019）.

从区间估计的下限来看，东亚－撒哈拉以南非洲路线受益最大；从区间估计的上限来看，撒哈拉以南非洲－西亚受益最大。在国家层面，这种差异如图9.7所示，乌兹别克斯坦、伊朗、阿曼、马尔代夫与缅甸受益于“一带一路”建设最多，其贸易量增长幅度均超过7%。而中国、沙特阿拉伯贸易量的绝对增长最大。行业层面，这种差异如图9.8所示，木材与木制品、蔬菜制品行业受益最大，这两个行业的贸易量增加均超过60%。道理很简单，因为家畜、蔬菜、鲜果、粮食等农业相关产品需要及时将最终产品运送至消费者手中。“一带一路”沿线的很多发展中经济体农业占比很大，因此农林牧渔业都会受益良多。[①]例如，2018年11月举行的首届中国国际进口博览会（CIIE），共有130多个国家的企业参展，其中包括了58个“一带一路”沿线国家。在进博会期间，京东与果锐科技达成战略合作，果锐科技将为包括海囤全球在内的京东多个渠道供应来自非洲的商品。双方还将在国际供应链的跨境物流仓储、城市配送等方面展开深入合作，建立“一带一路”沿线国家商品进入中国的“绿色通道”。[②]2019年1月28日，乌干达AFRICHAIN天然芒果干、肯尼亚精品咖啡在京东海囤全球（原京东全球购）首发。自此，中国消费者可享受到来自东非高原的纯天然非洲食品。此次上线的芒果干，来自盛产优质大芒果的乌干达，采用农场种植－加工一体化的形式，将芒果做成了无添加、无防腐剂的芒果干，再用海、陆、空全程冷链联运的方式运送到国内。这种跨境全冷链的供应方式在国内尚属首次。[③]而金属、机械、塑料、化学等行业目前受益较小，贸易量增加小于5%。化学、黑色金属、橡胶与塑料制品行业需要及时将中间投入品投入生产以提高生产效率，这些行业未来也将极大受益于“一带一路”倡议的实施。

此外，按照新结构经济学的理论，我们也可以很自然地看到，不同阶段的不同类型基础设施的影响也是不同的。例如，张鹏飞基于引力扩展模型，聚焦于“一带一路”沿线亚洲国家交通基础设施和通信基础设施建设水平对其区域内贸易量的影响展开了实证分析。他的研究表明：当一国交通基础设施发展到一定水平后，通信基础设施的作用会越来越显著；不同收入水平国家之间的进口对基础设施建设水平要求不同，其中高等收入水平国家从中低等收入水平国家进口更加注重出口国的通信基础设施建设水平；中低等收入水平国家从高等收入水平国家进口更加注重出口国的交通基础设施建设水平；中低等收入水平国家之间的进口取

① 2017年5月首届“一带一路”国际合作高峰论坛以来，中国与沿线国家签署100多项合作文件，实现了50多种农产品食品检疫准入。中国和哈萨克斯坦、吉尔吉斯斯坦、塔吉克斯坦农产品快速通关“绿色通道”建设积极推进，农产品通关时间缩短了90%。

② 跨境电子商务等新业态、新模式正成为推动贸易畅通的重要新生力量。2018年，通过中国海关跨境电子商务管理平台零售进出口商品总额达203亿美元，同比增长50%，其中出口84.8亿美元，同比增长67.0%，进口118.7亿美元，同比增长39.8%。“丝路电商”合作蓬勃兴起，中国与17个国家建立双边电子商务合作机制，在“金砖国家”等多边机制下形成电子商务合作文件，加快了企业对接和品牌培育的实质性步伐。

③ 多款纯天然非洲食品在京东海囤全球首发，实现国内首个跨境全冷链运输，搜狐网。

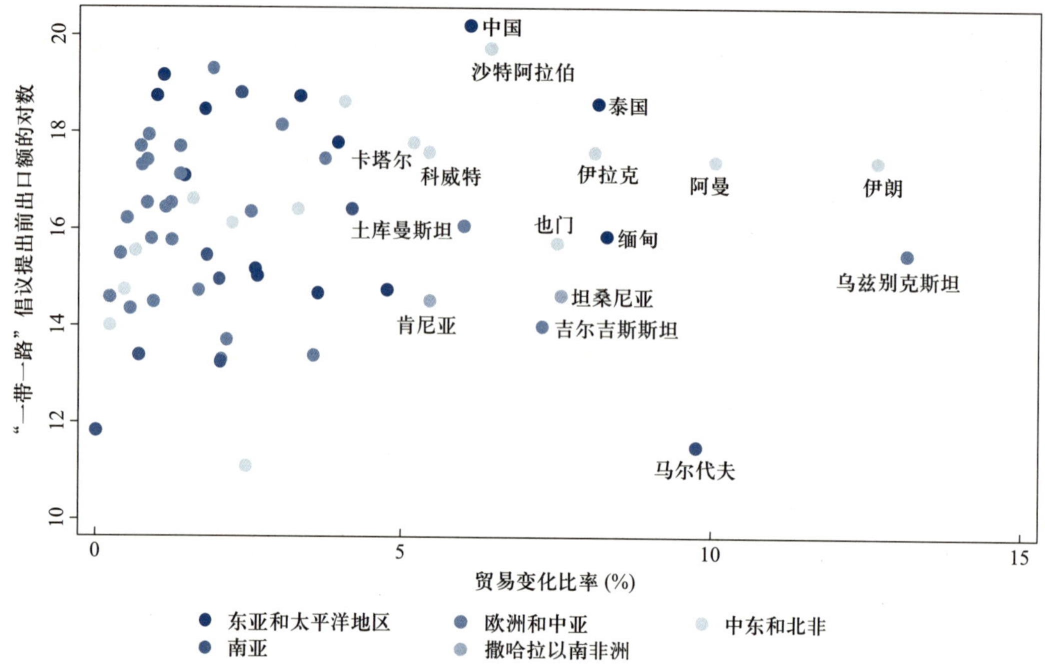


图9.7 "一带一路"倡议提出后沿线各国出口额的变化幅度

资料来源：Baniya et al.(2019).

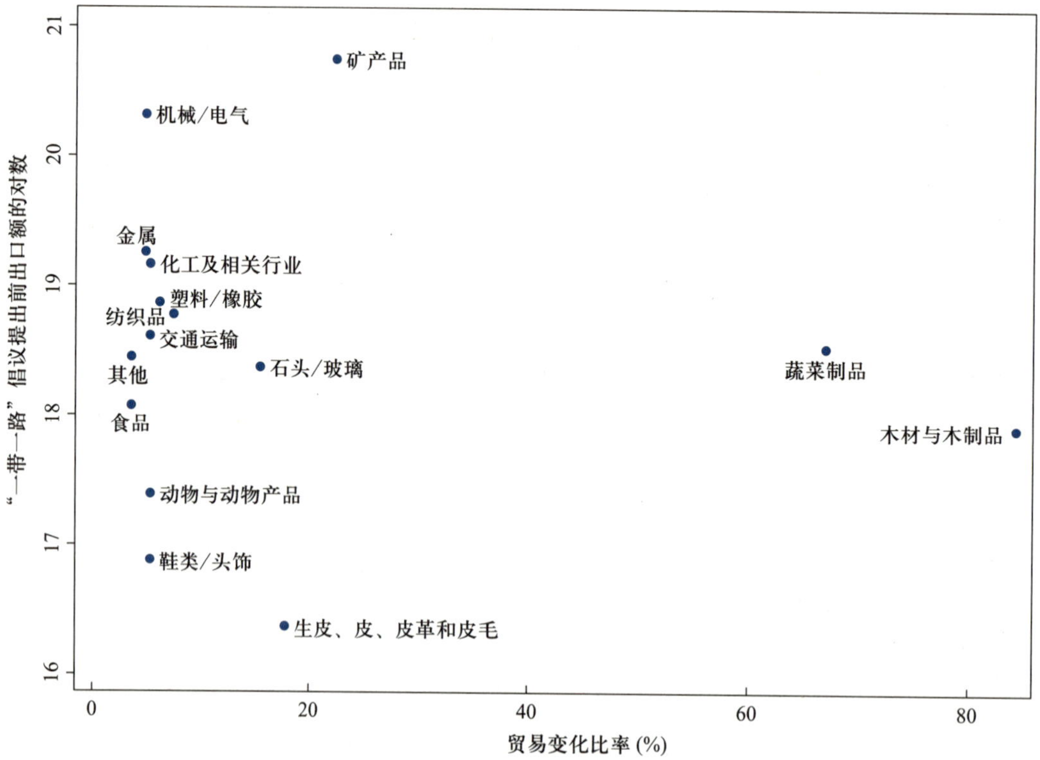


图9.8 "一带一路"倡议提出后沿线国家分产业部门出口额的变化幅度

资料来源：Baniya et al.(2019).

决于出口国的通信基础设施建设水平和交通基础设施建设水平，但是通信基础设施的经济效应强于交通基础设施。[①]胡再勇等则同样采用引力模型和面板数据模型分析了能源、交通、通信网络三类基础设施及其交互作用对“一带一路”沿线国家进口、出口以及域内双边贸易的影响。他们的研究结果表明：“一带一路”沿线国家能源基础设施和交通基础设施的进口效应、出口效应、双边贸易效应都为正；能源、交通、通信网络基础设施在国际贸易的两个方向上的作用大小不一致；不同类型基础设施的国际贸易效应大小也不一致；不同类型基础设施的交互作用对国际贸易的影响方向不确定。[②]

## 9.5

## “一带一路”倡议与企业转型升级

我们曾在第8章详细概括了中国与世界经济结构转型升级的状况与趋势，指出如果将中国与世界的经济结构进行深度匹配将释放巨大能量，不但可以推动发达国家的转型升级还能够推动发展中国家的发展，更关键的是也能够推动中国自身的经济结构转型升级。王桂军和卢潇潇采取更加微观的视角从企业层面实证研究了“一带一路”倡议对企业转型升级的影响。[③]他们利用2012—2017年中国A股上市公司数据，以对“一带一路”沿线国家实施直接投资的企业作为处理组，未实施对外直接投资的企业作为控制组，利用双重差分模型考察了“一带一路”倡议对中国企业升级的影响效应及作用机制，得到了几点重要的发现。“一带一路”倡

① 张鹏飞，“基础设施建设对‘一带一路’亚洲国家双边贸易影响研究：基于引力模型扩展的分析”，《世界经济研究》，2018年第6期。

② 胡再勇、付韶军、张璐超，“‘一带一路’沿线国家基础设施的国际贸易效应研究”，《数量经济技术经济研究》，2019年第2期。

③ 王桂军、卢潇潇，“‘一带一路’倡议与中国企业升级”，《中国工业经济》，2019年第3期，第43–61页。

议可以显著推动中国以全要素生产率和劳动生产率提高为表征的企业升级，如表9.6所示。他们进一步将中国产业分为新兴产业、成熟产业和瓶颈产业，并从研发创新视角分析“一带一路”倡议影响各产业中企业升级的作用路径的实证检验发现：“一带一路”倡议可以通过研发创新助推中国企业升级，且对瓶颈产业的企业升级影响最大，其次为新兴产业和成熟产业。他们估计，在“一带一路”倡议下，研发创新对新兴企业升级的效应值为0.146 2，对成熟企业升级的效应值为0.067 3，对瓶颈企业升级的效应值为0.276 2。[①]瓶颈企业转型升级的效用之所以较大，主要是其面临着产能严重过剩和技术瓶颈亟待突破的双重压力，企业生产效率相对低下，在“一带一路”倡议的政策红利下，一方面，企业通过“顺梯度”投资可以将富余产能有效转移并获得可观的交换价值来为企业研发创新提供充裕的资金支持；另一方面，企业通过“逆梯度”投资可以从国外发达经济体的企业引进先进技术手段，加以企业自身的自主研发快速突破技术瓶颈。综合以上两点，瓶颈企业在“一带一路”倡议的政策红利下可以获得技术进步的“第二种机会窗口”，使得企业成功进入“再生阶段”，企业生产效率会得到大幅度提高。此类企业所在的产业主要是前面提到的“一带一路”产能合作领域，也是第10章我们将讨论的转进型产业。此外，王桂军和卢潇潇还根据产权性质进行分样本回归，其结果显示，“一带一路”倡议可以同时助推国有企业和民营企业升级，这一结论意味着，在“一带一路”倡议稳步推进的过程中，中国经济发展形成了“国进民进”的新格局。

表9.6“一带一路”倡议对以劳动生产率量化的企业升级的影响

| | 劳动生产率（1） | 禀赋结构（资本劳动比）（2） |
|---|---|---|
| 企业分组变量×时间分组变量（处置效应） | 0.080 6** | 0.048 3 |
| | （2.160 6） | （0.993 7） |
| 企业规模（企业员工总数的自然对数） | −0.295 8*** | −0.254 9*** |
| | （−10.102 9） | （−6.654 3） |
| 企业年龄（企业成立时间的自然对数） | 0.776 5*** | 1.047 5*** |
| | （3.408 4） | （4.490 4） |
| 成长能力（营业收入增长率） | 0.548 9*** | −0.122 9*** |
| | （11.008 4） | （−2.995 0） |
| 资本结构（资产负债率） | −0.002 9** | 0.003 2** |
| | （−2.558 9） | （2.555 6） |
| 现金流量（现金流量净额与营业收入比） | 0.010 2*** | 0.002 1* |
| | （8.523 9） | （1.839 7） |

① 他们的另一项研究发现，“一带一路”倡议对中国企业创新的促进效应严重依赖于企业的对外直接投资。（王桂军、卢潇潇，“‘一带一路’倡议可以促进中国企业创新吗？”，《财经研究》，2019年第1期，第19–34页）

续表

| | 劳动生产率（1） | 禀赋结构（资本劳动比）（2） |
|---|---|---|
| 股权集中度（前十大股东股份占比） | 0.013 4*** | 0.001 4 |
| | （10.267 8） | （0.979 7） |
| 常数项 | 11.238 7*** | 11.281 0*** |
| | （18.444 3） | （17.691 8） |
| 年份效应 | Yes | Yes |
| 企业效应 | Yes | Yes |
| 省份 × 年份效应 | Yes | Yes |
| 观察值 | 12 414 | 12 414 |
| Adj-R2 | 0.234 5 | 0.139 8 |

资料来源：王桂军、卢潇潇，"'一带一路'倡议与中国企业升级"，《中国工业经济》，2019年第3期，第43-61页。

其实，"一带一路"倡议实施过程中"国进民进"的新格局是由各自的比较优势所决定的。基础设施行业投资具有很强的正外部性以及投资规模大、投资周期长的特征，因此目前中国央企是"一带一路"基础设施投资的主力军。这为中国民企"走出去"创造了完备的路线、交通、资源和产业园区等基础条件，形成"国企搭台，民企唱戏"的格局，国企和民企根据产业特征形成了"走出去"的合理分工。根据国资委新闻中心2015年7月14日发布的《"一带一路"中国企业路线图》，截至2014年年底，国资委监管的110余家央企中已有107家在境外共设立8 515家分支机构，分布在全球150多个国家和地区，其中80多家已在"一带一路"沿线国家设立分支机构。"十二五"以来，央企境外资产总额从2.7万亿元增加到4.6万亿元，年均增长12.2%，截至2014年年末央企境外资产总额、营业收入和利润总额分别占央企总体的12.7%、18.3%和8.6%。在电力领域，央企在境外建设的电站涵盖火电、水电、核电、风电和太阳能、生物质能发电等多种类型，在周边国家建成和在建的水电项目达17个，总装机容量近1 000万千瓦；在建材领域，央企在马来西亚、老挝、蒙古等国建设大量钢材、水泥、玻璃等建材生产线，其中水泥技术工程及装备全球市场占有率达到45%以上；在轨道交通领域，央企从设备出口装备运营维护起步，目前铁路装备已实现六大洲全覆盖，轨道车辆整车产品已进入北美发达国家市场。目前已有80多家央企在"一带一路"沿线国家设立分支机构，在促进基础设施互联互通方面，央企承担了大量"一带一路"倡议通道和战略支点项目的建设和推进工作，具体包括中俄、中哈、中缅原油管道，中俄、中亚、中缅天然气管道，俄罗斯等周边国家的10条互联互通输电线路以及中缅、中泰、中老铁路，中巴喀喇昆仑公路，斯里兰卡汉班托塔港等项目。随着2013年"一带一路"倡议明确提出之后，非国有企业海外投资步伐明显加快。非国有企业除了直接投资一般产业，也大量参与投资建设和运营海外工业园区。例如，作为中国企业最早"走出去"建立的境外经济贸易合作区之一，罗勇工业园开发有限公司中国国内投资主体中国华立集团，自2005年设立以来，已经聚集了80多家来自中国的企业在泰投资。2006年国有企业占比81%，2006—2015年国有企业占比逐渐降低，非国有企业逐步成为“走出去”的重要力量。2015年中国非金融类对外直接投资存量9 382亿美元，国有企业和非国有企业平分秋色，其中国有企业占50.4%，非国有企业占49.6%（见图9.9）。2017年年末，中国对外直接投资企业为25 529家，其中有限责任公司10 577家，占比41.4%，是当年中国对外投资最大、最活跃的主体。私营企业6 570家，位列第二，占比25.7%；股份有限公司2 790家，占比10.9%，位居第三；包括港、澳、台资企业在内的外商投资企业有2 134家，占比8.4%；国有企业1 422家，占比5.6%，比重较上年增加0.4个百分点；个体经营646家，占比2.5%；股份合作企业465家，占比1.8%；集体企业94家，占比0.4%；其他企业831家，占比3.3%。

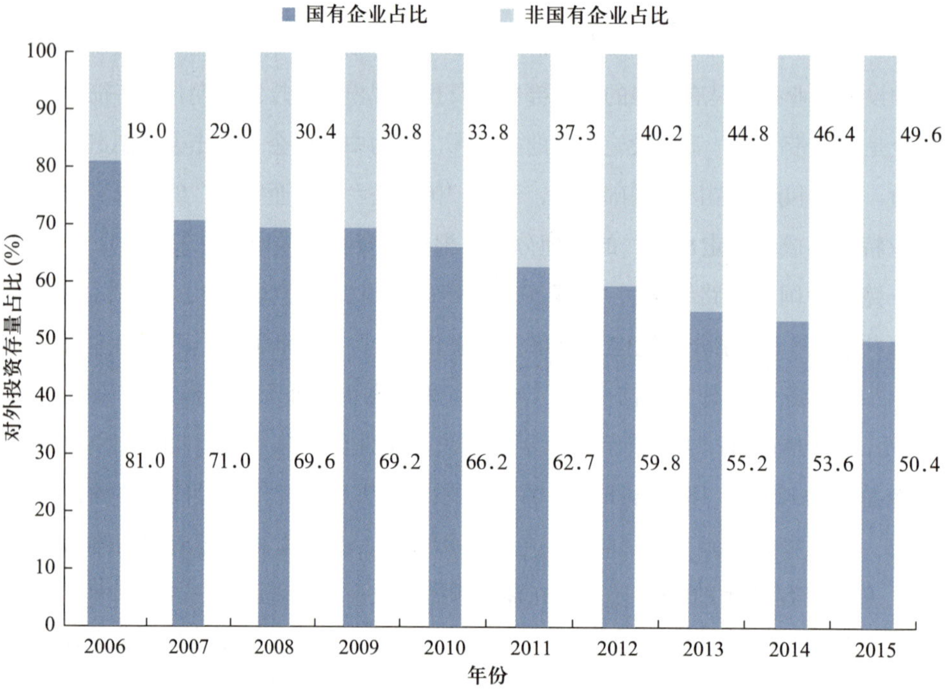


图9.9 2006—2015年中国国有企业和非国有企业对外投资存量占比情况

资料来源：《2015年度中国对外直接投资统计公报》。

## 9.6

## “一带一路”倡议与人民币国际化

中国从2009年就开始推动人民币跨境结算试点，但是到2017年12月人民币跨境支付量仅占国际支付的0.98%（SWIFT数据），人民币结算的贸易额占中国总贸易额的月均比例也仅为15.7%，这与中国的经济实力不符，人民币国际化有较大的潜力。如前文表9.1所示，包括人民币国际化在内的资金融通是“一带一路”建设的重要支撑。反过来，“一带一路”倡议其实也是人民币国际化最重要的支撑，这就催生了大量的相关思考，如图9.10所示。尽管对于人民币国际化的可行路径与方法仍然存在一定的争议，但在实践中“贸易结算+离岸市场”模式的人民币国际化已经取得了巨大成绩。①如前所述的“一带一路”在经贸等方面的广泛合作不仅给人民币的境外使用提供了空间，还会突破人民币国际化的路径。②例如，根据中国建设银行发布的《2018全球人民币国际化报告》，在受访企业中，70%的境外企业和90%的境内企业认为，“一带一路”将提升人民币在国际贸易中的使用，超过半数金融机构认为“一带一路”将提升人民币在国际投资领域的使用。事实上，中国已经先后与20多个沿线国家建立了双边本币互换安排，与7个沿线国家建立了人民币清算安排，与35个沿线国家的金融监管当局签署了合作文件。人民币国际支付、投资、交易、储备功能稳步提高，人民币跨境支付系统（CIPS）业务范围已覆盖近40个沿线国家和地区。截至2017年年末，境外机构和个人持有境内人民币金融资产总量增加至4.28万亿元，较2016年增加41.3%。然而，“一带一路”沿线国家的金融发展水平参差不齐，金融基础设施薄弱，这些都给人民币国际化推进增添了不少阻力。当然，加强“一带一路”国家金融基础设施合作建设是推进人民币国际化

① 殷剑峰，“人民币国际化：‘贸易结算+离岸市场’，还是‘资本输出+跨国企业’？——以日元国际化的教训为例”，《国际经济评论》，2011年第4期。

② 宗良，“‘一带一路’与人民币国际化协同效应研究”，《国际金融》，2017年第3期。

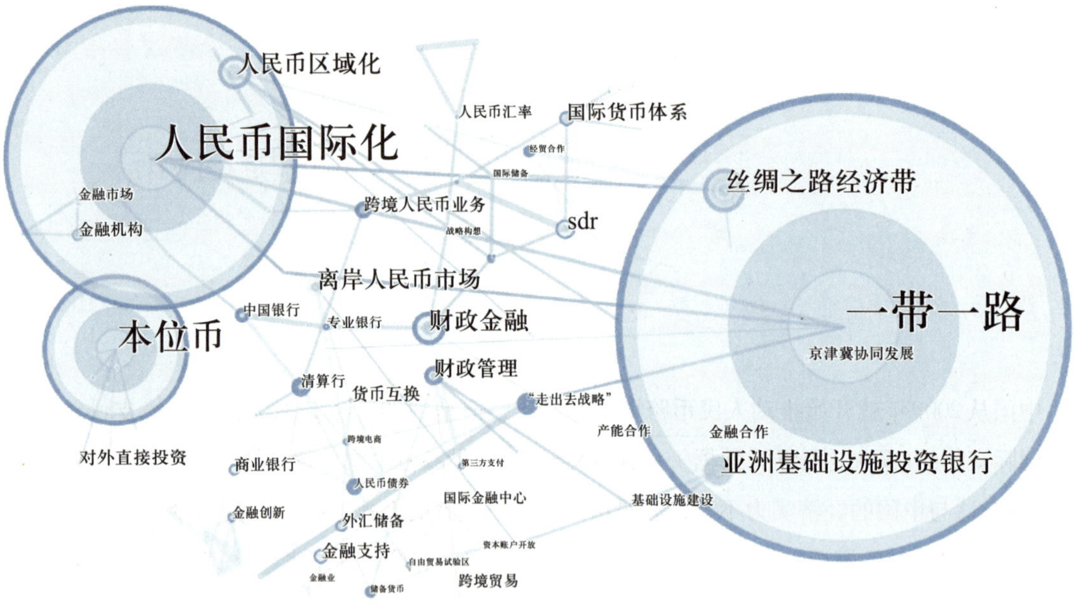


图9.10 "一带一路"倡议与人民币国际化中文研究文献关键词共现图谱(截至2018年)

资料来源:周雷、陈捷、赵子聪,"'一带一路'倡议与人民币国际化研究文献可视化分析——基于CiteSpace知识图谱软件的计量",《苏州市职业大学学报》,2018年第4期,第1–8页。

需要注意的一个重要方面。①但是,从新结构经济学角度来看,从要素禀赋结构出发深入思考基本理论逻辑可能更为关键,因为这是"一带一路"倡议下人民币国际化战略的基础。

吴文和龚婷做了这方面的理论初探。②他们首先概括了货币国际化的两大方式:一是资本输出(本币债权式国际化),二是贸易赤字(净进口)输出(本币债务式国际化)。虽然货币国际化可以获得国际铸币税的收益,③但实际只发生于本币贬值与本币债务式国际化相组合的情形,如果是本币升值与本币债务式国际化相组合的情形,对方债权国只需向货币发行国要求兑现(通过以其持有的本币购买发行国的商品或者进行投资),便可避免被征收国际

① 周小川,"'一带一路'建设多元化金融体系支持十分必要",《中国经济导报》,2018年第3期。然而,程炼基于货币搜寻模型考察了"一带一路"框架下金融基础设施合作可能对于人民币国际化产生的影响。其研究发现,改善东道国通用型金融基础设施对提高人民币可接受性的作用并不确定,甚至可能带来负面效果。当存在多个相互联通的人民币离岸市场时,提高某个区域的金融基础设施质量在促进人民币使用方面兼具"贸易创造"效应和区域间的"贸易转移"效应。当后者的规模足够大时,将可能改变人民币离岸市场的区域分布结构,对其他地区的人民币国际化进程产生不利影响。(程炼,"'一带一路'金融基础设施合作与人民币国际化",《区域与全球发展》,2018年第4期,第19–36页)

② 吴文、龚婷,"要素禀赋结构与货币国际化——基于新结构经济学视角的初探",《国际经济合作》,2018年第12期。

③ 陈雨露、王芳、杨明,"作为国家竞争战略的货币国际化:美元的经验证据——兼论人民币的国际化问题",《经济研究》,2005年第2期。

铸币税甚至可以获得利息，这是因为本币升值条件下的本币债务是沉重的。实际上，美元国际化初期主要是通过资本输出的方式，通过马歇尔援助计划让欧洲成为美元圈，这笔贷款充分利用了欧洲战后重建（破败的欧洲就如同一个发展中国家）所带来的高速经济增长机会大获其利。但当时美元坚挺，美元也并非以债务形式流出，也就没有所谓铸币税收益。反而美国要求欧洲用美元购买美国商品，在回收美元的同时形成了对欧洲的贸易顺差，借欧洲重建之机促进了美国实体经济的进一步发展。即便当前美元趋弱，美元债务式国际化成为一种新的获利工具，但仔细研究便可发现，美元债务式国际化相比美元债权式国际化仍然处于次要从属地位。这可从以下两个角度说明：首先，以美元债务式国际化的方式收取国际铸币税在道义上易被谴责，会遭到债权国家的激烈反对，受对方国家容忍度的制约，在方式上也只能采用“温水煮青蛙”的渐进式。一旦操作过激，债权国“玉石俱焚”式地抛售美元，会导致美元与美国金融市场的崩溃。资本输出的投资收益在当前的国际经济秩序规则下却合理合法，利润空间也很大。只要美国的要素禀赋结构与被投资国家或地区存在较大差异，美国的过剩资本就可以通过输出的方式获得远超本土投资的平均利润。除非发展中国家采取正确的比较优势战略并对其国家重大利益所在有清醒的认识，否则这种禀赋结构的差距会保持甚至扩大。这就说明对美元而言，债权式国际化比债务式国际化能带来更持久可观的利润。其次，从资金链的角度来看。通过铸币税所获资本也是再次投入到对外资本输出中，因为这些资本在美国国内也没有太好的获利机会。因此，债务式国际化主要是与债权式国际化相搭配使用，充当债权资本的“抽水机”，使得美国用于对外输出的资本更加充裕。

其次，吴文和龚婷运用我们在第1章第3小节所介绍的新结构经济学的基本原理对发达国家与发展中国家的资本流动进行了简要分析。[①]在发展中国家，由于其要素禀赋结构较低，即便结构转型缓慢，资本边际报酬递减的趋势是微弱的，如果结构升级效应超过报酬递减效应，就会呈现边际报酬递增的情形。与此同时，发达国家处于世界前沿，结构升级相对缓慢。因此，在大多数时候，发达国家的资本收益率低于发展中国家。在允许资本流动的国际环境下，发达国家的资本就会在利益的驱动下流向发展中国家。这一跨国资本流动的实质是扩大了发达国家可以利用的劳动力生产要素，但正因为资本为寻求高额利润而流动，而非劳动力为寻求高额利润而流动。发展中国家为外国资本所雇用的劳动力虽然可能获得略高于其他产业部门劳动力的平均报酬，但远低于发达国家中的劳动力报酬水平。如果发达国家的资本是以参股控股的形式对发展中国家的企业进行投资，其支付给当地劳动力的报酬更可能是按照当地标准。显然资本和劳动力两种要素中，资本在全球范围的流动性远大于劳动力，资本更具有全球属性，劳动力更具有国别属性。

---

① 吴文、龚婷，“要素禀赋结构与货币国际化——基于新结构经济学视角的初探”，《国际经济合作》，2018年第12期。

最后，吴文和龚婷据此认为：主权货币的国际化是与该主权国家的全球化资本输出相一致的，甚至可以说本币国际化只是表象，本国资本为寻求利润最大化而在全球范围内扩张，以寻求高于本国的获利机会才是目的与本质；由于本国资本的流出大多以本币为载体，这就表现出了本币国际化的外观，即既然债务输出不是货币国际化的关键，那么只能是资本输出。该假说的直接推论便是，美国对某国家或地区进行的资本输出规模与该国家或地区货币的美元化程度正相关。对货币美元化的理解是广义的，既包括美元直接在当地充当流通手段与当地货币相竞争甚至完全替代，也包括货币局制度，还包括类似中国的以外汇占款作为本国货币发行准备的情形。对于最后一种情形的货币美元化，其度量程度的指标是以外汇占款为准备的人民币发行量占总货币发行量的比例。又由于中国人民银行的外汇储备资产主要是通过企业贸易顺差结汇的方式积累，这一推论便与双顺差的现象吻合。如果该命题及其推论成立，那么正因为美国资本输出是美元国际化的基础，则凡是美国资本大量存在的地方都是美元国际化网络节点最强的地方（以二战后的欧洲和现在的东亚各国为代表），反之则相反。同时，正因为现在的中国还是资本相对比较稀缺的国家，所谓人民币国际化只能局限在区域化阶段，正确的人民币区域化方式是中国资本输出到要素禀赋结构较中国更低的国家或地区，而这正是当前“一带一路”倡议主要指向的世界经济带，与当年的国际板议案在经济战略方向选择上恰好相反。[①]只有当中国的比较优势由劳动力密集型转变为资本密集型时，人民币国际化才成为必需。因此，从要素禀赋结构较低的角度看，人民币属于“内秀”型的主权货币，在当前国内投资机会依然相对多于国外，资金回报相对较高，资本并不具有最强烈的对外输出驱动力的情形下，人民币国际化并不具有坚实的经济基础（当然出于资产配置的需要，部分资本出海也是一种合理需求，尤其是符合“一带一路”倡议的投资方向）。如此看来，自2015年以来，中国人民银行的外汇储备虽然从历史最高点大比例减少，但长期来说有利于人民币逐步摆脱美元陷阱，增强人民币生成机制的内生性与自主性，这反而夯实了人民币国际化的基础。未来，国际化的人民币是以人民币自身为意义，而非作为“小美元”（人民币在外汇市场被称为“小美元”）而存在，并不是美元国际化网络的一部分。因此，中国资本的流向定位应是国内或者禀赋结构更低的发展中国家，这当属于“一带一路”倡议的内在含义。

---

① 吴文和龚婷也从新结构经济学角度初步分析了国际板问题。国际板曾被视为推进人民币国际化的重要举措。一些学者认为美元国际化成功的重要原因是美国开放的资本市场，私人部门可以方便地在美国市场上投融资；建设国际板可以为外国优秀企业在中国上市融资提供便利，以此增加人民币的吸引力和接受度。然而按照比较优势理论，要素禀赋结构条件并不高的中国在总体上不应向欧美资本密集型企业提供融资（不排除细分市场中的特例）。美国市场为外国企业提供融资平台的做法符合美国经济的比较优势，因为其要素禀赋结构高，资本充裕。因此，如果简单地模仿，恰恰违背了比较优势战略。（吴文、龚婷，“要素禀赋结构与货币国际化——基于新结构经济学视角的初探”，《国际经济合作》，2018年第12期）

## 9.7

## 提高“一带一路”沿线基础设施投资回报率与“耐心资本”

基础设施投入不足是发展中国家经济发展的瓶颈，加快设施联通建设是共建“一带一路”的关键领域和核心内容。如第7章所测算的，目前“一带一路”沿线国家的基础设施发展普遍滞后于其经济发展，且无论在质还是量上均低于国际标准，仅在亚洲区域内就存在巨大的资金缺口。根据亚洲开发银行最新的预测，未来10年，亚洲基础设施投资需要17万亿美元，即每年需要新增投入1.7万亿美元基础设施资金。而2013年，亚洲除中、日、韩三大经济体外的GDP总额约为8万亿美元。根据世界银行统计，中低收入国家资本形成率占GDP的比重仅为1/4左右，其中用于基础设施投资方面的资金仅为20%左右，约4 000亿美元，融资存在巨大缺口。目前为亚洲基础设施建设提供融资的主要机构——亚洲开发银行2013年仅提供了210亿美元贷款，而即使把世界银行集团、发达国家ODA等都考虑在内，资金缺口依然难以得到弥补。为此，中国正在积极推动建设为“一带一路”解决融资缺口的新平台和新模式。目前的融资资金池包括：亚洲基础设施投资银行，其资本规模为1 000亿美元，其中中国出资400亿美元；丝路基金，首期规模为400亿美元，资金来源为外汇储备、中国投资公司、中国进出口银行、国开行，资本比例为65%、15%、15%、5%；金砖国家银行，资本金规模为1 000亿美元；上合组织开发银行。此外，中国将向南亚、上合组织、非洲分别提供200亿、50亿、300亿美元的信贷配套支持。区域性和国际性组织也为“一带一路”的基础设施建设提供部分资金。上述各种融资渠道目前能向“一带一路”跨境基础设施提供的融资规模为3 500亿美元左右，远远不能满足融资需求。为了撬动更多的民间资金，2017年年初，国家发改委会同外交部、环境保护部、交通运输部、水利部、农业农村部、人民银行、国资委、林业局、银保监会、能源局、外汇局以及全国工商联、中国铁路总公司13个部门和单位，共同建立“一带一路”PPP工作机制，与沿线国家在基础设施等领域加强合作，积极推广PPP模式，鼓励和帮助中国企业“走出去”，推动相关基础设施项目尽快落地。各国主权基金和投资基金发挥越来越重要的作用。近年来，阿联酋阿布扎比投资局、中国投资有限责任公司等主权财富基金对沿线国家主要新兴经济体投资规模显著增加。丝路基金与欧洲投资基金共同投资的中欧共同投资基金于2018年7月开始实质性运作，投资规模5亿欧元，有力促进了共建“一带一路”倡议与欧洲投资计划相对接。各类创新金融产品也不断推出，大大拓宽了共建“一带一路”的融资渠道。中国不断提高银行间债券市场对外开放程度，截至2018年年底，熊猫债发行规模已达2 000亿人民币左右。中国进出口银行面向全球投资者发行20亿人民币“债券通”绿色金融债券，金砖国家新开发银行发行首单30亿人民币绿色金融债，支持绿色丝绸之路建设。证券期货交易所之间的股权、业务和技术合作稳步推进。2015年，上海证券交易所、德意志交易所集团、中国金融期货交易所共同出资成立中欧国际交易所。上海证券交易所与哈萨克斯坦阿斯塔纳国际金融中心管理局签署合作协议，将共同投资建设阿斯塔纳国际交易所。

过去五年来，“一带一路”沿线的基础设施互联互通水平大幅提升，铁路、公路、港口、航空、能源、通信等基础设施合作建设方面得到大力推进。①

铁路合作方面：以中老铁路、中泰铁路、匈塞铁路、雅万高铁等合作项目为重点的区际、洲际铁路网络建设取得重大进展。泛亚铁路东线、巴基斯坦1号铁路干线升级改造、中吉乌铁路等项目正积极推进前期研究，中国－尼泊尔跨境铁路已完成预可行性研究。中欧班列初步探索形成了多国协作的国际班列运行机制。中国、白俄罗斯、德国、哈萨克斯坦、蒙古、波兰和俄罗斯7国铁路公司签署了《关于深化中欧班列合作协议》。截至2018年年底，中欧班列已经联通亚欧大陆16个国家的108个城市，累计开行1.3万列，运送货物超过110万标箱，中国开出的班列重箱率达94%，抵达中国的班列重箱率达71%。与沿线国家开展口岸通关协调合作、提升通关便利，平均查验率和通关时间下降了50%。

公路合作方面：中蒙俄、中吉乌、中俄（大连－新西伯利亚）、中越国际道路直达运输试运行活动先后成功举办。2018年2月，中吉乌国际道路运输实现常态化运行。中越北仑河公路二桥建成通车。中国正式加入《国际公路运输公约》（TIR公约）。中国与15个沿线国家签署了包括《上海合作组织成员国政府间国际道路运输便利化协定》在内的18个双多边国际运输便利化协定。《大湄公河次区域便利货物及人员跨境运输协定》实施取得积极进展。

港口合作方面：巴基斯坦瓜达尔港开通集装箱定期班轮航线，起步区配套设施已完工，吸引30多家企业入园。斯里兰卡汉班托塔港经济特区已完成园区产业定位、概念规划等前期工作。希腊比雷埃夫斯港建成重要中转枢纽，三期港口建设即将完工。阿联酋哈利法港二期集装箱码头已于2018年12月正式开港。中国与47个沿线国家签署了38个双边和区域海运协定。中国宁波航交所不断完善“海上丝绸之路航运指数”，发布了16+1贸易指数和宁波港口指数。航空运输方面。中国与126个国家和地区签署了双边政府间航空运输协定。与卢森

① 推进“一带一路”建设工作领导小组办公室，《共建“一带一路”倡议：进展、贡献与展望》，2019年。

堡、俄罗斯、亚美尼亚、印度尼西亚、柬埔寨、孟加拉国、以色列、蒙古、马来西亚、埃及等国家扩大了航权安排。5年多来，中国与沿线国家新增国际航线1 239条，占新开通国际航线总量的69.1%。能源设施建设方面。中国与沿线国家签署了一系列合作框架协议和谅解备忘录，在电力、油气、核电、新能源、煤炭等领域开展了广泛合作，与相关国家共同维护油气管网安全运营，促进国家和地区之间的能源资源优化配置。中俄原油管道、中国－中亚天然气管道保持稳定运营，中俄天然气管道东线将于2019年12月部分实现通气，2024年全线通气。中缅油气管道全线贯通。

通信设施建设方面：中缅、中巴、中吉、中俄跨境光缆信息通道建设取得明显进展。中国与国际电信联盟签署《关于加强“一带一路”框架下电信和信息网络领域合作的意向书》。与吉尔吉斯斯坦、塔吉克斯坦、阿富汗签署丝路光缆合作协议，实质性启动了丝路光缆项目。

然而，目前以基础设施建设为优先领域的“一带一路”受到的争议就主要集中在投资的回报率较低上。一种流行的辩护观点是，中国有庞大的外汇储备（见图9.1），与其购买美国超低回报的国债，还不如投资“一带一路”沿线国家和国内具有长期外部性的基础设施。从机会成本的角度讲，这种观点有一定的合理性。然而，从新结构经济学的角度讲，提高包括基础设施在内的投资回报率的方法便是改善软硬基础设施，促进具有潜在比较优势的产业变成有竞争优势的产业。如果符合潜在比较优势的产业由于基础设施建设消除了其瓶颈而得到快速发展，那么其在全球市场上不论是生产成本还是交易成本都是最低的，从而最具竞争力，产生的经济剩余也最多，因此不论是私人投资还是基础设施投资的回报率都是最大的。正如我们在第7章所测算的，整体而言发展中经济体的基础设施产出弹性要远大于发达经济体，而那些经济结构转型升级较为成功的发展中经济体（例如亚洲“四小龙”）的基础设施产出弹性更大。从图9.5所示的中国对“一带一路”沿线经济体的出口结构中可以看到，2016年中国出口的服装纺织以及家具等轻纺行业位居前十位，体量较大，但是处于快速的下降趋势（可回顾第8章的相关内容）。这意味着许多劳动力丰富的“一带一路”沿线的发展中经济体可以筑巢引凤、招商引资，支持当地企业等发展这些劳动力密集型的轻纺产业。因此，为了保证基础设施投资的回报率，符合潜在比较优势产业的发展必须跟上。后面我们将进一步介绍一些应用增长甄别与因势利导工具初步梳理的“一带一路”沿线国家可能甄别的潜在产业（更详细的案例在第10章介绍）。

除了通过促进“一带一路”沿线国家潜在比较优势产业发展来提高基础设施回报率之外，另一个非常重要的问题是要注意基础设施禀赋与一般的生产资本的异质性及其衍生的融资问题。在传统的新古典经济学中资本是同质的，不会存在货币与期限不匹配的问题——期限结构也是非常重要的金融结构维度，而新结构经济学则认为资本存在广泛的异质性，这种资本异质性与人力资本异质性一样，不但对产业升级与技术创新存在重要影响，而且还会对金融安排生产重要影响。这里我们特别强调基础设施禀赋的异质性及其对金融安排的影响。即便一个经济体具备相应产业的要素禀赋条件，但如果缺乏相应软硬基础设施，依然会存在瓶颈而只能成为潜在比较优势。基础设施除了外部性特征之外，基础设施项目还具有规模大、周期长、资本密集和沉没成本高的特点，需要很长时间才能建成并产生收益。基于这种基础设施资本的长期性特征维度，林毅夫和王燕将资本分为“耐心资本”和“非耐心资本（可回顾第7章的讨论）。[①]

国外净资产是度量“耐心资本”的一个很好的指标，它能揭示出口资本的比较优势，这包括但不限于“耐心资本”。包括中国、日本、韩国、新加坡在内的许多东亚国家都具有此类长期导向和“耐心资本”。与缺少大量“耐心资本”的国家相比，这些国家的国外净资产可能更多。从图9.11中可以发现，国外净资产与长期导向指数存在明显的正比关系。如果能对这一假设展开进一步的研究，再加上净外国直接投资（流出减去流入）和跨国并购等其他证据，那么可以认为这些国家均具有“耐心资本”比较优势。此外，储蓄率低的短期导向型国家将会发现自己的国外净资产地位在不断下降，而国外债务在持续上升。在所有“国家价值调查”中，中国凭借长期导向指数始终排在前五。很多东亚国家——如日本、韩国、印度尼西亚和新加坡——在长期导向指数中的排名也很靠前。与收入水平类似的国家相比，这些国家的基础设施能够获得更多的资金，因此建设得比较完善，这表明“耐心资本”至少属于一种潜在比较优势。但问题在于它是一种潜在比较优势，还是一种显性比较优势？在什么条件下，潜在比较优势可以转化为显性比较优势？图9.12显示国外净资产与储蓄率存在明显的正相关关系。此外，截至2015年年末中国估计拥有2.4万亿美元的国外净资产，目前排在第二位，仅次于日本的3.6万亿美元。国外净资产的增加来自经常账户盈余。截至2015年的4年间，中国的累计经常账户盈余达到了1万亿美元，远大于日本的2 000亿美元。如果这些趋势继续下去，中国到2020年将会成为最大的净债权国。过去20多年来，通过基础设施方面的投资，德国、日本、韩国和新加坡已成为在亚洲和非洲与发展中国家建立长期合作关系的楷模。中国正在学习和努力追赶。中国已开始使用自己的“耐心资本”比较优势，通过化解基础设施瓶颈来实现双赢。作为后来者，中国直到最近才将自己的“耐心资本”潜在比较优势转化为显性比较优势。在跨国并购方面，中国2008年才开始成为净供应国；在净对外直接投资（流出减去流入）方面，中国刚开始追赶。2015年，中国的对外直接投资为1 456亿美元，只略微超过流入。随着更多的企业走向世界，中国潜力很大。中国进行海外贷款

① Lin Justin Yifu and Wang Yan, The New Structural Economics: Patient Capital as a Comparative Advantage, *Journal of Infrastructure, Policy and Development*, 2017, Vol.1, No.1, pp.4–23.亦可参考该论文的中文版：林毅夫、王燕，“新结构经济学：将‘耐心资本’作为一种比较优势”，《开发性金融》，2017年第1期，第3–15页。

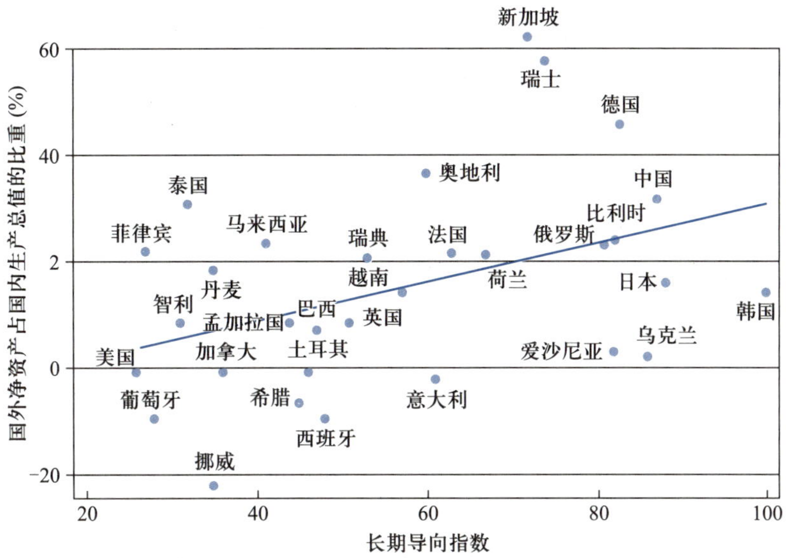


**图9.11 国外净资产占国内生产总值的比重和长期导向指数**

资料来源：林毅夫、王燕，“新结构经济学：将‘耐心资本’作为一种比较优势”，《开发性金融》，2017年第1期，第3–15页。

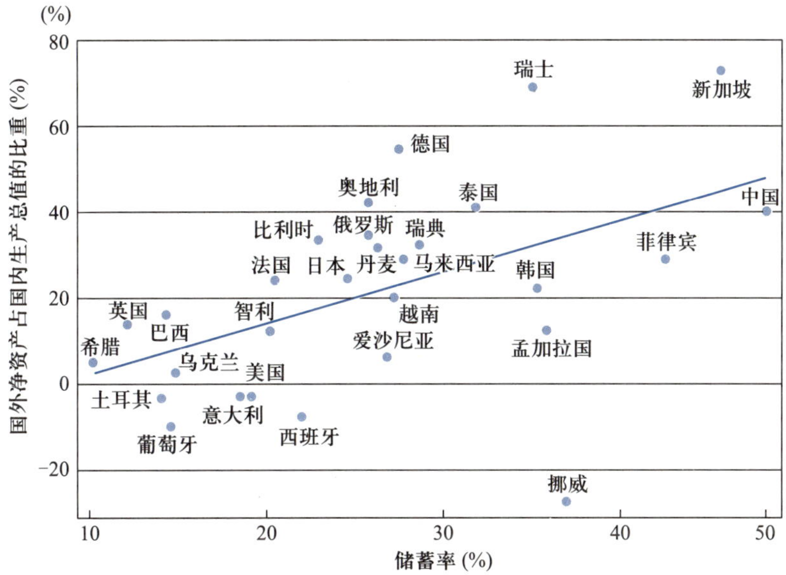


**图9.12 国外净资产占国内生产总值的比重和储蓄率（2015年）**

资料来源：林毅夫、王燕，“新结构经济学：将‘耐心资本’作为一种比较优势”，《开发性金融》，2017年第1期，第3–15页。

时，在着眼于一个国家的财产净值长期动态而不是短期流动性（如国际货币基金组织的债务可持续性框架）方面，中国的厄瓜多尔政策便是一个出色范例。这表现在将发展中国家的资产作为抵押，提供优惠和非优惠贷款进行投资——比如建立水力发电厂和缓解电力约束。长远来看，这些项目可以推动经济增长、创造就业机会。“打包”基础设施项目的能力也是基础设施融资的关键所在。从国家开发银行的芜湖项目开始，中国自20世纪90年代后期以来便独辟蹊径，提高了自己“打包”基础设施项目的能力，将营利和非营利项目“打包”在一起，实现双赢。这样做存在一些先决因素：投资银行具有长期导向和“耐心资本”，致力于同客户建立长期的合作关系，并期望客户能获得发展。中国这种以“耐心资本”为主的全球化完全不同于过去“非耐心资本”为主的全球化，这有助于包容性全球化。在新自由主义旗帜下，缺乏耐心的短期导向的外资游牧，事实上会对当地经济生态造成极大的破坏。[①] 与之相反，FDI中存在一些“耐心资本”，可持续性地促进当地要素禀赋升级。[②]

① 随洪光、余李、段鹏飞，“外商直接投资、汇率甄别与经济增长质量——基于中国省级样本的经验分析”，《经济科学》，2017年第2期，第59–73页。

② 例如，Branstetter对美国境内日资跨国公司的研究发现，日资企业对美国知识的使用和反馈加速了当地知识资本的演进与积累（Branstetter, L., “Is Foreign Direct Investment a Channel of Knowledge Spillovers? Evidence from Japan's FDI In the United States”，*Journal of International economics*, 2006, 68(2), pp. 325–344）。

# 9.8

# 世界各国如何发挥比较优势参与“一带一路”[①]

## 9.8.1 “一带一路”沿线国家与中国的贸易比较优势互补性

我们在第6章曾指出，与东亚“雁阵模式”不同，在新一轮全球经济结构变迁中，中国是广大发展中经济体的领头龙。[②]这个趋势在“一带一路”沿线国家中也不例外，中国现阶段不但体量最大而且比较优势互补性也很强。邹嘉龄和刘卫东采用社会网络的分析方法分析了“一带一路”沿线国家贸易网络的基本特征以及贸易网络组团的结构变化，贸易网络的核心边缘及其演化情况，并在最后对中国与东南亚国家的子贸易网络进行了核心边缘分析。他们的结果表明：“一带一路”沿线国家贸易网络密度增强，中国在“一带一路”沿线国家贸易网络中的核心度在逐渐提高，在2013年就已经成为最核心的国家，且在中国与东南亚国家构成的子贸易网络中，中国也成了最核心的国家，如表9.7所示。[③]杨文龙等采用复杂网络和地理统计方法，借助GIS、Pajek、Ucinet和数据库等技术手段，对“一带一路”贸易网络的拓扑性质、空间结构以及节点的邻近性进行了研究。他们的研究得到一些重要的结论：首先，“一带一路”沿线国家贸易网络具有小世界和无标度性质，遵循增长性和择优选择；其次，沿线国家贸易具有典型的“核心—边缘”等级性，中国对沿线国家产业升级和经济发展具有引领和带动作用。此外，还有一些重要特征，比如贸易网络是“混合型”结构，呈现枢纽辐射式为主、全连通式并存的联系模式，不同中心性空间分布差异显著。[④]

---

① 关于“一带一路”沿线地区的资源环境基础与社会经济背景可参考：刘卫东等，《共建绿色丝绸之路——资源环境基础与社会经济背景》，商务印书馆，2019年版。

② Vandana Chandra, Lin Justin Yifu and Wang Yan, “Leading Dragons Phenomenon: New Opportunities for Catch-Up in Low-Income Countries” , WB Policy Research Working Paper 6000, 2012.

③ 邹嘉龄、刘卫东，“2001—2013年中国与‘一带一路’沿线国家贸易网络分析”，《地理科学》，2016年11期。

④ 他们的拓展引力模型对“一带一路”沿线国家贸易网络具有较强的解释力，贸易关系存在大国效应和地理邻近效应，科研邻近和语言邻近是重要的推动力，制度邻近的影响呈显著负相关，文化邻近的正向作用相对较弱。因此，中国宜遵循“由近及远”的原则，重点强化对邻近国家的贸易渗透，再加强对沿线重点国家的贸易辐射，进而向重点国家的周边地区拓展，从不同空间层次制定差异化政策，发挥科研和语言邻近的推动作用，强化对沿线国家的文化渗透。（杨文龙、杜德斌、马亚华、焦美琪，“‘一带一路’沿线国家贸易网络空间结构与邻近性”，《地理研究》，2018年11期）

表9.7 2001、2007和2013年中国与“一带一路”沿线国家贸易网络节点核心度前十国家

| 2001年 | | 2007年 | | 2013年 | |
|---|---|---|---|---|---|
| 国家 | 核心度 | 国家 | 核心度 | 国家 | 核心度 |
| 新加坡 | 0.797 | 中国 | 0.623 | 中国 | 0.784 |
| 马来西亚 | 0.521 | 新加坡 | 0.506 | 新加坡 | 0.294 |
| 中国 | 0.188 | 马来西亚 | 0.333 | 马来西亚 | 0.231 |
| 泰国 | 0.164 | 印度 | 0.216 | 印度 | 0.214 |
| 印度尼西亚 | 0.093 | 印度尼西亚 | 0.210 | 印度尼西亚 | 0.179 |
| 菲律宾 | 0.080 | 泰国 | 0.195 | 俄罗斯 | 0.179 |
| 沙特阿拉伯 | 0.067 | 俄罗斯 | 0.178 | 沙特阿拉伯 | 0.177 |
| 印度 | 0.065 | 沙特阿拉伯 | 0.145 | 泰国 | 0.167 |
| 阿联酋 | 0.046 | 阿联酋 | 0.135 | 阿联酋 | 0.150 |
| 越南 | 0.046 | 伊朗 | 0.088 | 越南 | 0.143 |

资料来源：邹嘉龄、刘卫东，“2001—2013年中国与‘一带一路’沿线国家贸易网络分析”，《地理科学》，2016年11期。

徐梁通过构建贸易互补性指数（trade complementary index），①测算了中国2000—2014年与“一带一路”沿线国家的贸易互补性指数，如表9.8所示。他的测算结果显示，以动植物产品和食品等为代表的自然资源类产品，中国自身的出口比较优势正处于动态下降过程，与“一带一路”沿线国家的贸易中也体现了这个趋势，说明与各国的贸易关系不强；在能源贸易方面，中国本身属于能源较缺乏国家，仔细观察发现，对“一带一路”沿线国家的贸易互补程度差距明显，其中对东南亚、南亚互补程度最高，是最低的西亚的数倍，说明亚洲各地能源分布很不均匀，中国可以通过对能源出口政策调整达到国内能源储备的目的。钢铁制品在近10年来获得比较优势的动态提升后，成为中国出口的优势产品，与“一带一路”沿线国家的互补性较强，与沿线各国的贸易联系很紧密，在国家号召输出过剩产能以及亚投行对沿线国家基础建设的支持下，未来的钢铁制品的出口将维持一个长期良好的优势地位。化工基础产品出口的规模大、覆盖面广，基本上中国与各国的贸易互补性接近，对东南亚地区的出口明显高于其他地区，是最低的西亚地区的4倍多，这与东南亚和西亚的产业发展不同有关。药品的贸易互补性也在减弱，而且近年来减弱趋势明显，一方面与中国药企普遍研发

① 具体公式：$C_{ijk}=RCA_{ik}\times RCA_{jk}$。其中，$C_{ijk}$是商品$k$两国的贸易互补性指数；$RCA_{ik}$表示双边贸易中中国在出口商品上的比较优势；$RCA_{jk}$表示双边贸易$j$地区在进口商品$k$上的比较劣势，计算公式为$RCA_{jk}=(M_{jk}/M_{wk})/(M_{jt}/M_{wt})$，其中，$M_{jk}$为$j$地区进口商品$k$的金额，$M_{wk}$为世界进口商品$k$的金额，$M_{jt}$为$j$地区全部商品的进口总额，$M_{wt}$为世界全部商品进口总额。当某国出口产品的类别与另一国进口产品的类别越吻合，两国的贸易互补性指数就愈大。一般认为，当贸易互补性指数大于1时，说明两国的贸易互补性高，关系比较紧密，贸易潜力大，反之则相反。

表9.8 中国与“一带一路”沿线地区的贸易互补性指数

| 地区 | 年份 | 动、植物产品 | 食品 | 燃料和矿产品 | 能源 | 钢铁及其制品 | 化工产品 | 药品 | 机械电子设备 | 办公及电信设备 | 交通运输设备 | 纺织制品 | 服装制品 |
|---|---|---|---|---|---|---|---|---|---|---|---|---|---|
| 东南亚地区 | 2000 | 0.705 1 | 0.617 9 | 0.440 9 | 0.403 1 | 2.027 0 | 0.886 1 | 0.639 8 | 0.603 4 | 0.513 4 | 0.208 7 | 9.774 9 | 4.502 8 |
| | 2005 | 0.558 2 | 0.469 3 | 0.243 2 | 0.178 1 | 2.384 2 | 0.601 5 | 0.127 0 | 0.853 5 | 1.231 0 | 0.127 7 | 13.155 8 | 1.284 5 |
| | 2010 | 0.493 5 | 0.441 9 | 0.110 1 | 0.068 2 | 2.642 5 | 0.647 0 | 0.137 3 | 1.264 2 | 2.040 0 | 0.240 1 | 14.234 2 | 0.790 6 |
| | 2011 | 0.504 6 | 0.434 6 | 0.100 5 | 0.064 9 | 2.289 4 | 0.725 3 | 0.142 0 | 1.363 2 | 2.866 0 | 0.230 7 | 15.019 1 | 0.742 1 |
| | 2012 | 0.472 8 | 0.418 9 | 0.077 2 | 0.045 8 | 2.356 3 | 0.691 3 | 0.144 2 | 1.604 9 | 4.515 6 | 0.175 3 | 15.019 9 | 0.764 8 |
| | 2013 | 0.412 7 | 0.361 6 | 0.066 3 | 0.038 0 | 2.449 5 | 0.654 2 | 0.126 3 | 1.725 8 | 5.488 0 | 0.130 8 | 14.198 2 | 0.679 5 |
| | 2014 | 0.406 1 | 0.349 6 | 0.076 2 | 0.042 6 | 2.811 4 | 0.665 2 | 0.117 4 | 1.610 6 | 5.044 6 | 0.123 0 | 13.335 0 | 0.621 3 |
| 中亚地区 | 2000 | 0.869 4 | 1.078 7 | 0.393 8 | 0.332 6 | 2.424 4 | 0.577 8 | 0.450 7 | 0.777 8 | 0.399 6 | 0.280 0 | 0.929 7 | 0.527 6 |
| | 2005 | 0.454 8 | 0.541 7 | 0.186 6 | 0.144 8 | 2.687 0 | 0.388 5 | 0.174 2 | 1.408 2 | 0.765 1 | 0.342 3 | 0.971 6 | 0.633 1 |
| | 2010 | 0.418 1 | 0.495 9 | 0.085 9 | 0.071 5 | 1.967 3 | 0.532 6 | 0.291 3 | 1.769 8 | 1.206 5 | 0.593 3 | 1.352 3 | 1.022 3 |
| | 2011 | 0.807 7 | 0.953 5 | 0.159 2 | 0.127 3 | 3.548 1 | 0.929 5 | 0.378 7 | 3.003 9 | 2.929 9 | 1.134 5 | 2.936 5 | 2.230 7 |
| | 2012 | 0.674 7 | 0.783 3 | 0.116 5 | 0.081 7 | 5.118 6 | 0.832 8 | 0.370 7 | 2.970 4 | 2.832 9 | 1.200 4 | 3.080 6 | 3.723 0 |
| | 2013 | 0.309 6 | 0.358 2 | 0.065 0 | 0.049 4 | 3.269 3 | 0.444 9 | 0.213 1 | 1.497 1 | 1.524 0 | 0.527 2 | 1.590 1 | 2.218 0 |
| | 2014 | 0.320 9 | 0.368 5 | 0.042 8 | 0.026 4 | 2.361 6 | 0.462 6 | 0.196 9 | 1.496 8 | 1.355 0 | 0.518 0 | 1.708 4 | 2.372 8 |
| 南亚地区 | 2000 | 0.673 0 | 0.525 7 | 1.178 1 | 1.118 9 | 0.555 4 | 0.525 7 | 0.184 2 | 0.303 7 | 0.394 5 | 0.062 4 | 1.258 7 | 0.065 8 |
| | 2005 | 0.294 5 | 0.247 5 | 0.514 0 | 0.395 6 | 0.824 0 | 0.396 7 | 0.047 2 | 0.672 4 | 1.364 2 | 0.101 5 | 1.904 0 | 0.061 9 |
| | 2010 | 0.207 9 | 0.181 0 | 0.278 7 | 0.225 1 | 0.913 2 | 0.432 8 | 0.051 0 | 0.788 3 | 1.430 4 | 0.189 0 | 1.366 2 | 0.100 1 |
| | 2011 | 0.198 3 | 0.168 9 | 0.247 4 | 0.187 2 | 0.821 3 | 0.453 4 | 0.047 3 | 0.772 1 | 1.589 9 | 0.150 6 | 1.346 1 | 0.117 2 |
| | 2012 | 0.213 0 | 0.181 6 | 0.232 7 | 0.172 4 | 0.860 5 | 0.442 9 | 0.047 2 | 0.757 1 | 1.483 3 | 0.171 3 | 1.275 8 | 0.115 8 |
| | 2013 | 0.187 5 | 0.157 0 | 0.264 6 | 0.196 4 | 0.761 7 | 0.455 0 | 0.047 3 | 0.752 1 | 1.614 9 | 0.157 9 | 1.355 7 | 0.140 7 |
| | 2014 | 0.205 9 | 0.173 4 | 0.293 1 | 0.211 0 | 1.017 7 | 0.497 6 | 0.045 6 | 0.689 8 | 1.581 7 | 0.127 7 | 1.334 6 | 0.149 4 |

续表

| 地区 | 年份 | 动、植物产品 | 食品 | 燃料和矿产品 | 能源 | 钢铁及其制品 | 化工产品 | 药品 | 机械电子设备 | 办公及电信设备 | 交通运输设备 | 纺织制品 | 服装制品 |
|---|---|---|---|---|---|---|---|---|---|---|---|---|---|
| 中东欧地区 | 2000 | 0.659 0 | 0.463 5 | 0.592 4 | 0.411 3 | 1.551 5 | 0.781 2 | 0.626 5 | 0.750 7 | 0.783 5 | 0.327 8 | 4.320 3 | 0.756 4 |
| | 2005 | 0.310 5 | 0.209 7 | 0.331 7 | 0.164 8 | 1.579 0 | 0.578 6 | 0.196 1 | 1.102 0 | 1.161 5 | 0.320 3 | 5.354 2 | 0.959 9 |
| | 2010 | 0.282 9 | 0.205 5 | 0.209 9 | 0.138 2 | 1.703 3 | 0.594 3 | 0.189 1 | 1.257 6 | 1.080 7 | 0.575 1 | 6.043 8 | 2.271 7 |
| | 2011 | 0.298 1 | 0.226 9 | 0.170 1 | 0.104 3 | 1.621 1 | 0.635 9 | 0.169 5 | 1.302 2 | 1.120 9 | 0.614 2 | 5.781 2 | 2.032 6 |
| | 2012 | 0.281 2 | 0.221 6 | 0.156 0 | 0.094 7 | 1.807 1 | 0.603 6 | 0.138 2 | 1.222 3 | 1.230 6 | 0.484 7 | 5.127 5 | 1.591 7 |
| | 2013 | 0.240 2 | 0.188 5 | 0.146 2 | 0.091 1 | 2.053 2 | 0.594 4 | 0.128 1 | 1.253 8 | 1.329 7 | 0.421 9 | 4.756 4 | 1.564 1 |
| | 2014 | 0.260 1 | 0.208 9 | 0.163 1 | 0.097 3 | 2.257 5 | 0.648 8 | 0.129 5 | 1.160 0 | 1.338 9 | 0.395 5 | 4.826 8 | 1.515 8 |
| 独联体地区 | 2000 | 1.559 4 | 1.930 9 | 0.234 9 | 0.098 0 | 1.189 8 | 0.547 8 | 0.799 4 | 0.396 9 | 0.226 2 | 0.115 5 | 1.879 1 | 0.733 6 |
| | 2005 | 0.762 1 | 0.956 5 | 0.053 4 | 0.015 8 | 0.811 3 | 0.421 5 | 0.255 6 | 1.081 2 | 1.206 9 | 0.282 1 | 1.404 0 | 1.069 2 |
| | 2010 | 0.605 1 | 0.713 2 | 0.023 5 | 0.010 6 | 0.964 9 | 0.544 7 | 0.341 6 | 1.661 7 | 1.980 1 | 0.572 7 | 2.478 5 | 4.563 1 |
| | 2011 | 0.554 7 | 0.646 4 | 0.021 6 | 0.010 3 | 1.067 3 | 0.582 0 | 0.341 7 | 1.977 8 | 2.068 9 | 0.834 5 | 2.567 3 | 4.339 0 |
| | 2012 | 0.508 6 | 0.585 0 | 0.017 7 | 0.005 5 | 1.000 3 | 0.556 0 | 0.305 2 | 2.061 2 | 2.076 4 | 0.865 8 | 2.615 3 | 3.872 4 |
| | 2013 | 0.468 3 | 0.535 8 | 0.017 4 | 0.005 3 | 1.047 1 | 0.559 1 | 0.314 8 | 1.910 7 | 1.855 8 | 0.692 5 | 2.254 5 | 3.310 7 |
| | 2014 | 0.466 7 | 0.526 2 | 0.022 5 | 0.006 8 | 1.150 9 | 0.581 4 | 0.284 3 | 1.655 6 | 1.925 5 | 0.505 1 | 2.184 8 | 3.142 1 |
| 西亚地区 | 2000 | 0.486 0 | 0.622 1 | 0.036 1 | 0.010 7 | 0.510 8 | 0.216 5 | 0.150 9 | 0.377 2 | 0.275 2 | 0.169 1 | 3.946 8 | 1.556 2 |
| | 2005 | 0.345 8 | 0.426 6 | 0.047 8 | 0.006 8 | 1.043 2 | 0.190 5 | 0.042 2 | 0.880 7 | 1.326 1 | 0.234 2 | 3.333 5 | 2.314 3 |
| | 2010 | 0.232 9 | 0.278 8 | 0.022 3 | 0.007 0 | 0.913 2 | 0.179 1 | 0.044 7 | 0.878 5 | 0.764 3 | 0.413 8 | 1.962 8 | 1.841 4 |
| | 2011 | 0.233 1 | 0.279 8 | 0.023 6 | 0.006 2 | 1.027 1 | 0.201 0 | 0.051 2 | 0.897 0 | 0.749 5 | 0.438 0 | 1.979 2 | 1.869 0 |
| | 2012 | 0.235 8 | 0.279 1 | 0.020 7 | 0.005 2 | 1.190 1 | 0.199 9 | 0.048 8 | 0.915 6 | 0.770 7 | 0.417 7 | 2.057 8 | 1.870 5 |
| | 2013 | 0.204 2 | 0.238 4 | 0.019 7 | 0.005 2 | 1.244 7 | 0.192 6 | 0.044 9 | 0.908 3 | 0.825 4 | 0.355 4 | 1.951 9 | 1.788 5 |
| | 2014 | 0.180 0 | 0.206 7 | 0.022 5 | 0.005 6 | 1.325 4 | 0.173 8 | 0.038 2 | 0.740 6 | 0.594 8 | 0.293 7 | 3.946 8 | 1.572 8 |

资料来源：徐梁，“基于中国与‘一带一路’国家比较优势的动态分析”，《管理世界》，2016年第2期。

能力不强有关，另一方面缘于贸易壁垒。世界各国对药品的管制明显高于其他产品，如何提高出口药品的比较优势，充分利用中国的中医优势，应该是将来的突破口。机电产品和部分高新技术产品、运输设备等，已与“一带一路”沿线国家取得较强的贸易互补性。说明近年来国家调整产业结构，转变出口方式的战略已经初见成效，中国正逐渐将以往靠传统比较优势产业，向靠资本密集型和技术密集型产业的出口结构调整。南亚贸易互补指数目前略低于其余地区的一个可能的原因是，印度在相关行业产品的出口与中国类似，挤压了中国的市场空间。今后中国在继续保持比较优势的前提下，要着眼提高产品出口质量与自主研发比例，提高利润率。以纺织服装为代表的劳动密集型产业在各地区具有极强的贸易互补性，符合中国传统的出口比较优势产业。同时纺织制品的贸易互补性明显高于服装制品，在东南亚地区的表现尤其明显。纺织制品出口的多为原材料和初级产品，并不能完全代表服装产品，以东南亚地区为例，纺织品贸易互补指数数倍于服装制品贸易互补指数，可推测东南亚各国大量从中国进口纺织材料与初级产品，加工后自行出口。

### 9.8.2 “一带一路”沿线国家与中国的产业比较优势互补性①

我们在第6章所讨论的雁阵模式以及全球制造业差序格局其实已经在介绍产业比较优势互补性了，这里我们简要应用第10章将详细介绍的增长甄别和因势利导工具方法来简要概括“一带一路”沿线国家与中国的产业比较优势互补性。为简化讨论，我们不对“一带一路”沿线国家之间进行一一的案例分析，而只以中国作为目标国，其他国家作为学习国来讨论产业比较优势互补性。当然，中国作为世界上体量最大但发展水平居中而且地区差异极大的经济体，只将中国作为一个单一的同质分析单元明显欠妥——其他学习国也一样。下一节我们将把分析单元细分到省级层面，然后再看中国省级单位与“一带一路”沿线国家之间的产业比较优势互补性。与此同时，第10章将把中国的产业分成五种类型——领先型、追赶型、转进型、弯道超车型和战略型，分别讨论其不同的增长甄别与因势利导方法。因此，这里的讨论只涉及转进型产业，也即主要涉及前面讨论的产能合作领域中的劳动密集型产业（如图9.13所示）。

赵秋运和赵磊做了中国与“一带一路”沿线国家的增长甄别的练习。以中国整体作为产

---

① 本小节的内容主要来自：赵秋运、赵磊，“新结构经济学与‘一带一路’：转入国的筛选和转出产业的甄别”，《西部论坛》，2017年第6期。关于新结构经济学增长甄别与因势利导工具对“一带一路”应用更详细的内容可参考：钟飞腾，《“一带一路”建设中的产业转移：对象国和产业的甄别》，社会科学文献出版社，2016年版。

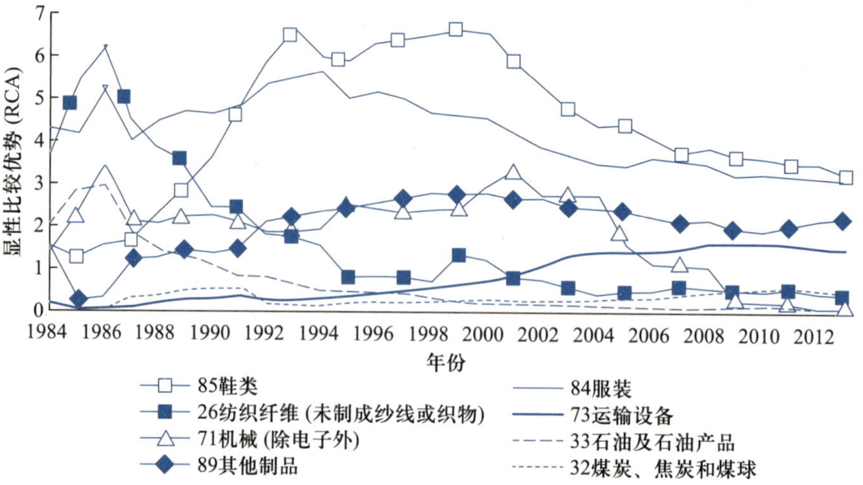


**图9.13 中国的显性比较优势：在劳动密集型出口部门的下降（1984—2013年）**

注：RCA=某一特定细分产业在一个经济体的出口中所占份额除以该产业在全球出口中所占份额。

资料来源：基于UN Comtrade数据计算，SITC Rev.1的2位码。

业转出国，选择合适的产业转移承接国，中国的人均收入需要为承接国的1～3倍，而“一带一路”沿线国家除巴勒斯坦和叙利亚没有相关数据以外，有28个国家的人均收入低于中国，35个国家的人均收入高于中国。所以，要从人均收入低于中国的各国中，筛选中国人均收入为其1～3倍国家。如表9.9所示，根据国际货币基金组织基于购买力平价（PPP）计算的人均GDP（现值国际元），2015年中国的人均GDP为14 017.43国际元，排除掉不符合条件的国家，共有21个国家符合要求。在选定对象国之后，需要确定合适的转移出产业。这就需要考虑转入国与中国的比较优势，对于劳动密集型、低技术产业而言，可以用把工资和就业作为衡量比较优势的主要指标。如表9.10和表9.11所示，在低技术制造业领域，对于“一带一路”沿线国家，其就业人数主要集中在食品与饮料、纺织品、服装三大产业中。中国低技术制造业领域的就业人数占比为34.39%，其他国家中，只有菲律宾就业人数占比小于50%，其他各国都在50%以上，主要为典型的劳动密集型产业发展中国家。其中食品与饮料产业的就业人数占比在约旦、埃及、格鲁吉亚、亚美尼亚、菲律宾的制造业中占据主导地位，在斯里兰卡也比较高，并且如表9.13所示，食品与饮料产业的人均工资，在埃及2012年为4 595美元，格鲁吉亚2013年为4 545美元，亚美尼亚2013年为3 460美元，斯里兰卡2012年为1 560美元，而中国在2010年为5 315美元。显然，这些国家是食品与饮料产业转移的理想国家。服装产业的就业人数占比在斯里兰卡、越南占据主导地位，在约旦、菲律宾也比较高，斯里兰卡2012年人均工资为1 254美元，越南2013年为2 588美元，约旦2013年为4 152美元，菲律宾2012年为3 142美元，中国2010年为4 337美元，所以这四个国家皆为服装产业转移的理想国家。阿尔巴尼亚的纺织品产业在2013年就业人数占比最多，人均工资为2 727美元，埃及的纺织品产业的就业人数占比在2012年也较高，人均工资3 980美元，而中国2010年为4 402美元，所以，阿尔巴尼亚和埃及比较适合纺织品产业的转移。而根据就业数据（表9.10和表9.11），中国在低技术产业中的就业人数占比略有减少，而其他14国中，除乌克兰、印度、菲律宾以外，其余11国的低技术就业占比都在50%以上，为典型的劳动密集型产业发展中国家。而在人均GDP突破1万美元后，非金属矿物产业、基本金属产业、金属制品产业的就业占比依次快速进入下降阶段，这些产业解决就业不如劳动密集型产业多，但劳动生产率高，容易获取资本，可以为东道国带来投资机遇。[①]中国的中等技术制造业的就业人数占比已经从2010年的32.09%下降到2015年的23%，随着人均收入的提高，其就业人数占比还会逐渐下降。而人均收入在1万美元以下并且中等技术就业人数占比低于中国的国家有菲律宾、越南，而根据表9.12，其工资水平也较符合要求，所以他们可以作为上述产业合适的转移承接国。

表9.9 2015年中国人均GDP为其1~3倍的国家 单位：国际元

| 国家 | 人均GDP | 中国/其他国家 | 国家 | 人均GDP | 中国/其他国家 |
|---|---|---|---|---|---|
| 中国 | 14 107.43 | 1.00 | 亚美尼亚 | 8 467.95 | 1.67 |
| 马其顿 | 14 009.14 | 1.01 | 不丹 | 8 200.67 | 1.72 |
| 塞尔维亚 | 13 671.43 | 1.03 | 乌克兰 | 7 970.752 | 1.77 |
| 蒙古 | 12 146.64 | 1.16 | 菲律宾 | 7 254.2 | 1.94 |
| 约旦 | 12 122.85 | 1.16 | 印度 | 6 161.62 | 2.29 |
| 埃及 | 11 849.63 | 1.19 | 乌兹别克斯坦 | 6 068.45 | 2.32 |
| 阿尔巴尼亚 | 11 300.82 | 1.25 | 越南 | 6 024.35 | 2.34 |
| 印度尼西亚 | 11 125.92 | 1.27 | 缅甸 | 5 468.76 | 2.58 |
| 斯里兰卡 | 10 566.19 | 1.34 | 老挝 | 5 309.41 | 2.66 |
| 波黑 | 10 491.8 | 1.34 | 摩尔多瓦 | 5 006.24 | 2.82 |
| 格鲁吉亚 | 9 629.96 | 1.46 | 巴基斯坦 | 5 000.01 | 2.82 |

资料来源：赵秋运和赵磊（2017）计算。

表9.10 2010—2013年中国与“一带一路”沿线8个国家中低技术制造业就业人数占比（%）

| 行业/产业 | 中国 | 约旦 | 埃及 | 阿尔巴尼亚 | 斯里兰卡 | 格鲁吉亚 | 亚美尼亚 | 菲律宾 | 越南 |
|---|---|---|---|---|---|---|---|---|---|
| 年份 | 2010 | 2013 | 2012 | 2013 | 2012 | 2013 | 2013 | 2012 | 2013 |
| 食品与饮料 | 8.06 | 23.04 | 22.77 | 14.34 | 19.63 | 34.74 | 38.33 | 20.15 | 10.8 |
| 烟草 | 0.25 | 0.94 | 1.66 | 0.24 | 0.42 | 0.53 | 4.19 | 0.81 | 0.24 |

① 钟飞腾，《“一带一路”建设中的产业转移：对象国和产业甄别》，社会科学文献出版社，2016年版。

续表

| 行业/产业 | 中国 | 约旦 | 埃及 | 阿尔巴尼亚 | 斯里兰卡 | 格鲁吉亚 | 亚美尼亚 | 菲律宾 | 越南 |
|---|---|---|---|---|---|---|---|---|---|
| 年份 | 2010 | 2013 | 2012 | 2013 | 2012 | 2013 | 2013 | 2012 | 2013 |
| 纺织品 | 7.98 | 1.35 | 12.83 | 25.92 | 6.96 | 0.44 | 0.57 | 2.04 | 2.23 |
| 服装 | 5.36 | 16.69 | 7.93 | — | 45.74 | 6.05 | 4.34 | 10.45 | 21.70 |
| 皮革制品 | 3.59 | 0.63 | 0.35 | 22.79 | 1.66 | 0.68 | 0.63 | 1.69 | 17.80 |
| 木制品 | 1.78 | 1.86 | 0.30 | 1.68 | 0.35 | 1.48 | 0.65 | 2.02 | 2.35 |
| 纸 | 1.91 | 2.35 | 2.31 | 5.68 | 1.18 | 1.06 | 1.39 | 1.73 | 2.03 |
| 印刷与出版 | 1.01 | 3.19 | 1.29 | — | 2.52 | 5.46 | 2.39 | 1.63 | 1.24 |
| 家具 | 4.45 | 7.16 | 2.11 | 4.64 | 3.44 | 3.39 | 4.17 | 4.05 | 8.14 |
| 低技术产业 | 34.39 | 57.21 | 51.55 | 75.29 | 81.9 | 53.83 | 56.66 | 44.57 | 66.50 |
| 焦炭与精炼石油 | 1.09 | 1.84 | 4.30 | — | 0.46 | — | — | 0.18 | 0.10 |
| 橡胶与塑料 | 4.17 | 3.22 | 3.13 | — | 8.97 | 3.21 | 3.03 | 4.73 | 3.84 |
| 非金属矿物 | 6.43 | 8.99 | 9.77 | 6.77 | 2.43 | 10.29 | 9.95 | 3.12 | 5.25 |
| 基本金属 | 7.25 | 2.00 | 6.36 | 8.75 | 0.58 | 14.25 | 7.68 | 1.96 | 1.48 |
| 金属制品 | 4.92 | 10.27 | 3.24 | — | 0.80 | 4.02 | 4.18 | 4.54 | 5.04 |
| 中等技术产业 | 32.09 | 36.48 | 36.95 | 22.71 | 15.28 | 38.31 | 35.02 | 19.43 | 18.6 |

资料来源：赵秋运和赵磊（2017）根据 UNIDO，Statistical Country Briefs（June 2016）整理。

表9.11 2014—2015年中国与“一带一路”沿线7个国家中低技术制造业就业人数占比（%）

| 行业/产业 | 中国 | 蒙古 | 约旦 | 埃及 | 阿尔巴尼亚 | 印度尼西亚 | 斯里兰卡 |
|---|---|---|---|---|---|---|---|
| 年份 | 2014 | 2014 | 2015 | 2014 | 2015 | 2015 | 2014 |
| 食品与饮料 | 9.17 | 29.94 | 22.81 | 22.95 | 13.35 | 18.20 | 19.60 |
| 烟草 | 0.25 | 0.26 | 1.06 | 1.68 | 0.41 | 7.30 | 0.42 |
| 纺织品 | 5.56 | 16.47 | 1.23 | 12.04 | 27.51 | 10.53 | 6.95 |
| 服装 | 5.24 | 5.91 | 17.29 | 8.05 | 0 | 11.16 | 45.68 |
| 皮革制品及鞋类 | 3.45 | 2.02 | 0.68 | 0.33 | 24.58 | 5.05 | 1.65 |
| 木材制品 | 1.61 | 5.93 | 1.8 | 0.31 | 1.76 | 4.86 | 0.35 |
| 纸 | 1.57 | 1.15 | 2.22 | 2.63 | 6.14 | 2.64 | 1.18 |
| 印刷及出版 | 1.09 | 6.82 | 3.13 | 1.68 | 0 | 1.02 | 2.52 |
| 家具 | 4.44 | 1.75 | 6.91 | 1.61 | 4.76 | 6.88 | 3.44 |
| 低技术产业 | 32.38 | 70.25 | 57.13 | 51.28 | 78.51 | 67.64 | 81.79 |
| 焦炭和精炼石油 | 1.10 | 0.76 | 1.78 | 4.75 | 0 | 0.16 | 0.46 |
| 橡胶及塑胶 | 3.88 | 1.52 | 3.15 | 3.19 | 0 | 8.11 | 8.96 |
| 非金属矿物 | 6.75 | 13.39 | 8.97 | 8.62 | 6.53 | 3.66 | 2.42 |
| 基本金属 | 6.96 | 4.85 | 1.96 | 6.04 | 8.60 | 1.34 | 0.57 |
| 金属制品 | 4.31 | 3.38 | 9.59 | 3.30 | 0 | 3.26 | 0.80 |
| 中等技术产业 | 23.00 | 23.90 | 25.45 | 25.90 | 15.13 | 16.53 | 13.21 |

续表

| 行业/产业 | 波黑 | 格鲁吉亚 | 亚美尼亚 | 乌克兰 | 菲律宾 | 印度 | 越南 |
|---|---|---|---|---|---|---|---|
| 年份 | 2015 | 2015 | 2014 | 2015 | 2015 | 2015 | 2014 |
| 食品与饮料 | 14.78 | 37.96 | 40.57 | 21.41 | 21.82 | 13.41 | 9.89 |
| 烟草 | 0.54 | 0.51 | 4.58 | 0.28 | 0.63 | 3.45 | 0.20 |
| 纺织品 | 4.99 | 0.45 | 0.34 | 1.04 | 2.30 | 11.58 | 3.95 |
| 服装 | 8.05 | 6.19 | 6.11 | 2.93 | 10.04 | 7.59 | 21.49 |
| 皮革制品及鞋类 | 11.37 | 0.55 | 0.37 | 1.17 | 1.61 | 2.41 | 18.36 |
| 木材制品 | 8.90 | 1.84 | 0.79 | 2.14 | 2.00 | 0.59 | 2.09 |
| 纸 | 2.10 | 1.19 | 1.53 | 1.89 | 2.33 | 1.91 | 1.76 |
| 印刷及出版 | 1.35 | 5.16 | 2.43 | 1.43 | 2.05 | 1.21 | 1.16 |
| 家具 | 8.02 | 3.85 | 3.58 | 3.34 | 4.25 | 2.59 | 7.99 |
| 低技术产业 | 60.10 | 57.70 | 60.30 | 35.63 | 47.03 | 44.74 | 66.89 |
| 焦炭和精炼石油 | 2.34 | 0 | 0 | 1.78 | 0.20 | 0.85 | 0.10 |
| 橡胶及塑胶 | 3.85 | 3.97 | 3.11 | 3.08 | 5.24 | 4.57 | 4.33 |
| 非金属矿物 | 3.10 | 9.58 | 8.47 | 5.49 | 3.26 | 7.43 | 4.63 |
| 基本金属 | 6.08 | 13.93 | 8.36 | 12.33 | 1.89 | 7.56 | 1.41 |
| 金属制品 | 11.58 | 3.52 | 3.63 | 5.03 | 4.13 | 5.23 | 4.79 |
| 中等技术产业 | 26.95 | 31.00 | 23.57 | 27.71 | 14.72 | 25.64 | 15.26 |

资料来源：赵秋运和赵磊（2017）根据 UNIDO，Statistical Country Briefs（June 2016）整理。

表9.12 2010—2013年中国与“一带一路”沿线8个国家中低技术制造业人均工资　单位：美元

| 行业/产业 | 中国 | 约旦 | 埃及 | 阿尔巴尼亚 | 斯里兰卡 | 格鲁吉亚 | 亚美尼亚 | 菲律宾 | 越南 |
|---|---|---|---|---|---|---|---|---|---|
| 年份 | 2010 | 2013 | 2012 | 2013 | 2012 | 2013 | 2013 | 2012 | 2013 |
| 食品与饮料 | 5 315 | 7 542 | 4 595 | 3 482 | 1 560 | 4 545 | 3 460 | 6 529 | 3 009 |
| 烟草 | 14 974 | 8 420 | 7 443 | 2 711 | 4 086 | 6 688 | 4 740 | 10 032 | 6 624 |
| 纺织品 | 4 402 | 4 454 | 3 980 | 2 727 | 1 641 | 4 172 | 3 589 | 3 415 | 3 215 |
| 服装 | 4 337 | 4 152 | 2 275 | — | 1 254 | 2 811 | 2 179 | 3 142 | 2 588 |
| 皮革制品 | 4 194 | 5 510 | 1 594 | 2 812 | 1 219 | 2 596 | 2 976 | 2 657 | 2 492 |
| 木制品 | 4 285 | 2 505 | 3 241 | 2 934 | 1 085 | 4 179 | 2 479 | 2 553 | 2 201 |
| 纸 | 4 982 | 10 652 | 4 814 | 3 801 | 1 697 | 4 946 | 3 076 | 4 238 | 2 904 |
| 印刷与出版 | 4 649 | 7 897 | 5 503 | — | 2 038 | 4 829 | 3 190 | 3 592 | 2 981 |
| 家具 | 4 388 | 3 921 | 2 685 | 2 935 | 1 549 | 4 069 | 3 125 | 3 706 | 2 706 |
| 焦炭与精炼石油 | 8 315 | 13 934 | 19 593 | — | 5 478 | — | — | 40 783 | 6 558 |
| 化学及化工产品 | 5 842 | 15 385 | 8 265 | 4 836 | 1 780 | 6 977 | 4 203 | 8 727 | 4 654 |
| 橡胶与塑料 | 4 752 | 7 142 | 4 097 | — | 1 733 | 3 685 | 3 129 | 4 120 | 3 171 |
| 非金属矿物 | 4 518 | 6 136 | 4 451 | 4 870 | 2 583 | 4 902 | 4 099 | 6 291 | 2 931 |
| 基本金属 | 7 475 | 8 555 | 8 263 | 3 697 | 2 559 | 6 007 | 8 079 | 6 962 | 3 103 |
| 金属制品 | 4 924 | 4 470 | 4 226 | — | 1 492 | 4 796 | 4 307 | 5 145 | 3 068 |

资料来源：赵秋运和赵磊（2017）根据 UNIDO，Statistical Country Briefs（June 2016）整理。

专栏9.1

一带一路沿线国家参与情况[①]

按照最初的规划，“一带一路”倡议涉及60多个国家和地区，现在已超出预期，有100多个国家和国际组织参与到“一带一路”建设中。2019年3月，习近平主席访问欧洲期间，作为G7成员国的意大利加入“一带一路”倡议。2019年4月，李克强总理访问欧盟期间，欧盟重申支持“一带一路”倡议。根据《共建“一带一路”倡议：进展、贡献与展望》报告显示，截至2019年3月，中国政府已与125个国家和29个国际组织签署173份合作文件。共建“一带一路”国家已由亚欧延伸至非洲、拉美、南太等区域。读者可关注时政了解“一带一路”沿线国家的最新参与情况。

根据《“一带一路”大数据报告2016》测算的中国与“一带一路”沿线国家合作程度高低指数，俄罗斯和哈萨克斯坦两个国家处于深度合作阶段，排名前两位；快速推进程度国家主要为东南亚国家、巴基斯坦和内蒙古；逐步拓展程度国家主要为阿拉伯国家及部分东南亚国家；有待加强型国家主要为东欧国家。未来有较大潜力的国家分布在东南亚、中亚、西亚和北非。基本情况如下。

1. **东北亚**

**蒙古。**2014年8月，两国签署《中华人民共和国和蒙古国关于建立和发展全面战略伙伴关系的联合宣言》，双方认为应大力发展政治领域，经贸领域，教育、卫生、文化、人文领域以及国际、地区合作等。

**俄罗斯。**2015年5月，中俄双方共同签署并发表了《关于丝绸之路经济带建设与欧亚经济联盟建设对接合作的联合声明》，“一带一路”与“欧亚经济联盟”实现对接，双方达成共识，优势互补。

**蒙古、俄罗斯。**2015年7月，三国签署《关于编制建设中蒙俄经济走廊规划纲要的谅解备忘录》，明确了三方联合编制《建设中蒙俄经济走廊规划纲要》的总体框架和主要内容。下一步将抓紧把三方发展战略对接落实到具体合作领域和项目上来，推进中蒙俄经济走廊建设走向深入。

**日本。**2016年11月，中国国际经济交流中心与日本经济团体联合会达成联合声明，指出双方愿意进一步推进包括亚洲地区的基础设施及“一带一路”建设

① 本专栏根据《“一带一路”大数据报告》《“一带一路”研究手册》《中国对外投资公报》等相关资料整理而成。

等重大项目在内的第三方市场合作。

2. **中亚**

**哈萨克斯坦。**哈萨克斯坦是丝绸之路经济带的关键节点，共建丝绸之路经济带的构想也正是2013年9月在哈萨克斯坦首次提出的。此后，2014年双方签署了28项价值230多亿美元的基础设施合同。2014年12月，两国签署《中华人民共和国国家发展和改革委员会与哈萨克斯坦共和国国民经济部关于共同推进丝绸之路经济带建设的谅解备忘录》，提出发展和加强区域间互联互通，促进和深化丝绸之路经济带沿线有关交通、经贸、旅游、投资及其他合作领域的经济活动。2016年10月，双方签订《中国和哈萨克斯坦关于“丝绸之路经济带”建设与“光明之路”新经济政策对接合作规划》，实现“丝绸之路经济带”建设与“光明之路”新经济政策的战略对接，中哈两国将在四个领域总共30项内容上进行全面务实合作。

**土库曼斯坦。**2014年5月，两国签署《中华人民共和国和土库曼斯坦关于发展和深化战略伙伴关系的联合宣言》，提出双方将共同推动“丝绸之路经济带”建设，在金融、铁路、农业、能源、安全等多领域加强合作，研究开展合作的方式并启动具体合作项目。

**乌兹别克斯坦。**2015年6月，两国签订《关于在落实建设“丝绸之路经济带”倡议框架下扩大互利经贸合作的议定书》，提出进一步全面深化和拓展两国在贸易、投资、金融和交通通信等领域的互利合作，重点推动大宗商品贸易、基础设施建设、工业项目改造和工业园等领域的项目实施，实现双边经贸合作和共建“丝绸之路经济带”的融合发展。

**塔吉克斯坦。**2015年9月，两国签订《关于编制中塔合作规划纲要的谅解备忘录》，明确了共同编制《中塔合作规划纲要》的总体框架和主要内容，以共建丝绸之路经济带为契机，继续扩大和深化投资、贸易、产业、人才等各领域务实合作，共同推进中国—中亚—西亚经济走廊建设。

3. **东南亚**

**缅甸。**2014年11月，两国发表《中华人民共和国与缅甸联邦共和国关于深化两国全面战略合作的联合声明》，提出加强海洋经济、互联互通、科技环保、社会人文等各领域务实合作，支持缅甸农村和农业发展，建立两国政府电力合作机制，继续加强金融、海洋经济、互联互通、科技环保等领域的合作。

**马来西亚。**2015年11月，两国发展《中华人民共和国和马来西亚联合声明》，提出两国加强产能和装备制造合作潜力巨大，继续推动“两国双园”协调发展，共同探讨推进钢铁、船舶、通信、电力、轨道交通等重点领域合作。

**老挝。**2016年5月，两国发表《中老联合声明》，指出加强发展战略对接和产能合作，推动中国“一带一路”倡议和老挝“变陆锁国为陆联国”战略、中国“十三五”规划和老挝“八五”规划有机结合，密切配合尽早共同编制完成“一带一路”建设合作规划纲要，采取切实措施促进两国产能与投资合作。

**柬埔寨。**2016年10月，中柬两国发表《中华人民共和国和柬埔寨王国联合声明》，签署了31项合作协议，确立了2017年双边贸易规模达50亿美元的切实目标，习近平特别提出要着力打造西哈努克港经济特区，并签订了《关于确认并共同推动产能与投资合作重点项目的协议》《关于实施中柬友谊医院大楼项目的立项换文》《关于编制共同推进“一带一路”建设合作规划纲要的谅解备忘录》《关于联合开展水利项目合作谅解备忘录》等文件。

**孟加拉国。**2016年10月，在中国商务部和孟加拉国出口促进局、孟加拉国工商联合会举办的“中国－孟加拉国企业贸易对接会暨签约仪式”上，双方企业签署了13项贸易协议，合同金额达1.86亿美元，涉及海产品、皮革、黄麻纱线等孟方优势产品。2016年10月，两国发表《中华人民共和国和孟加拉人民共和国关于建立战略合作伙伴关系的联合声明》，双方同意扩大和深化贸易和投资合作，将基础设施、产能合作、能源电力、交通运输、信息通信、农业作为中孟务实合作的重点领域加以推进，鼓励两国有关企业加强合作。2016年10月，习近平对孟加拉国进行国事访问期间，中孟双方签署了共建“一带一路”以及产能、能源、信息通信、投资、海洋、防灾减灾、人文等领域的合作文件。

**4. 南亚**

**马尔代夫。**2014年12月，两国签署《中华人民共和国商务部和马尔代夫共和国经济发展部关于在中马经贸联委会框架下共同推进“21世纪海上丝绸之路”建设的谅解备忘录》，推动中马自贸区建设，并将通过经贸联委会进一步加强对华互利合作，增加鱼类等产品对华贸易。

**尼泊尔。**2014年12月，两国签署《中华人民共和国商务部和尼泊尔政府财政部关于在中尼经贸联委会框架下共同推进“丝绸之路经济带”建设的谅解备忘录》，宣布正式启动双边自贸协定联合可行性研究，双方同意成立工作组，尽快就共同关注的领域开展全面研究。

**巴基斯坦。**巴基斯坦是“一带一路”的标杆国家之一，早在2014年，中巴两国就决定共建中巴经济走廊，是“一带一路”的旗舰项目。2015年4月，两国发表《中华人民共和国和巴基斯坦伊斯兰共和国关于建立全天候战略合作伙伴关系的联合声明》，双方同意以中巴经济走廊为引领，以瓜达尔港、能源、交通产业合作为重点，形成“1+4”经济合作布局。2015年4月，习近平总书记前往巴基斯坦国事访问期间，双方签下了51项合作协议和备忘录，其中超过30项协议、备忘录与中巴经济走廊相关，涉及机场、高速、电力、铁路等项目。其中，比较关键的4项谅解备忘录包括瓜达尔港国际机场、瓜达尔港东湾高速公路、卡拉奇—拉合尔高速公路和喀喇昆仑公路第二阶段升级的项目；电力项目包括50兆瓦的达乌德风电项目、50兆瓦的萨察尔风电项目、Zonergy 900兆瓦的电力工业园区和100兆瓦的吉姆普尔风电场项目等；铁路方面包括中国国家铁路局和巴基斯坦铁道部之间关于卡拉奇—白沙瓦线（ML1）升级和巴基斯坦铁路赫韦利杨干散货中心的联合可行性研究的框架协议。

5. 中东欧

**白俄罗斯。**2015年5月，习近平对白俄罗斯进行国事访问期间，双方签署了总价值约157亿美元的近20份经济合作协议（“丝绸之路经济带”合作议定书），并共同签署了《中华人民共和国和白俄罗斯共和国友好合作条约》和《中华人民共和国和白俄罗斯共和国关于进一步发展和深化全面战略伙伴关系的联合声明》，强调两国将采取措施扩大贸易规模，为对方商品、服务、技术、资本准入创造良好条件。2016年9月，两国签署《中华人民共和国政府与白俄罗斯政府共同推进“一带一路”建设的措施清单》，该措施清单涵盖交通物流、贸易投资、金融、能源、信息通信、人文等领域相关措施或项目，是推动中白在“一带一路”框架下开展务实合作的第一份路线图，也是指导两国务实合作的重要框架性文件。

**匈牙利。**2015年6月，两国签订《中华人民共和国政府和匈牙利政府关于共同推进丝绸之路经济带和21世纪海上丝绸之路建设的谅解备忘录》，是中国同欧洲国家签署的第一份此类合作文件。双方希望以签署政府间谅解备忘录为契机，使匈牙利成为“一带一路”建设在欧洲的重要支点；以共同建设匈塞铁路为契机，使匈牙利成为欧亚物流的重要枢纽；以增强两国高度互信为契机，使匈牙利成为中欧友谊的重要桥梁。

**罗马尼亚。**2015年10月，两国签署了“第比利斯‘一带一路’论坛”联合声明，旨在加强“一带一路”沿线国家政府之间经济层面的对话，发展各国之间的双边经济合作以及与国际和地区的金融机构的合作。

**中东欧多国。**2015年11月，结合“一带一路”倡议和《中欧合作2020战略规划》，中国和中东欧16国制定“16+1合作”中国规划图，共同发表《中国—中东欧国家中期合作规划》，推动“16+1合作”提质增效，其中一半国家与中国签署了共建“一带一路”合作备忘录。

**波兰。**2015年11月，两国签署《中华人民共和国政府与波兰共和国政府关于共同推进“一带一路”建设的谅解备忘录》，提出加强“一带一路”与“可持续发展计划”对接，共同组织编制中波合作规划纲要，开展和深化互利合作。2016年6月，两国发表《中华人民共和国和波兰共和国关于建立全面战略伙伴关系的联合声明》。中波视彼此为长期稳定的战略伙伴，将在中国提出的“丝绸之路经济带”和“21世纪海上丝绸之路”以及波兰提出的“可持续发展计划”框架下共同推动经贸、金融、交通物流、基础设施建设、民航、能源、农业、电子商务、科技、环保等领域双边合作。

**捷克。**2016年3月，两国发表《中华人民共和国和捷克共和国关于建立战略伙伴关系的联合声明》。双方将以两国政府签署的共建“一带一路”谅解备忘录为基础，加强“一带一路”与各自发展战略和政策的协同，开展和深化互利合作。2016年4月，两国签署《中华人民共和国政府和捷克共和国政府关于共同编制中捷合作规划纲要的谅解备忘录》，双方商定在基础设施建设、产业投资、贸易、能源资源、科技与研发、金融、运输与物流、医疗保健、航空、标准与认证、文化、体育、教育等领域加强合作。

**塞尔维亚。**2016年6月，两国发表《中华人民共和国和塞尔维亚共和国关于建立全面战略伙伴关系的联合声明》，将以两国政府签署的共建“一带一路”谅解备忘录为基础，充分把握“一带一路”建设带来的重要机遇，推动双方各自发展战略的对接，进一步加强两国能源和交通基础设施建设、产能合作、农业等领域的务实合作。

**斯洛伐克。**2016年10月，丝绸之路国际总商会与斯洛伐克工商联合会签署了在“一带一路”倡议框架下深化合作的战略合作协议，中东欧是“一带一路”在欧洲的落脚点，斯洛伐克位于欧洲中部，是连接东西欧市场的桥梁和通往巴尔干地区的门户，斯洛伐克将成为“一带一路”合作的重要合作伙伴。此外，2015年中国分别与塞尔维亚、捷克、斯洛伐克、保加利亚等多国签署政府间共同推进“一带一路”建设的谅解备忘录。

**6. 西亚与北非**

**卡塔尔。**2014年11月，两国发表《中华人民共和国和卡塔尔国关于建立战略伙伴关系的联合声明》，双方认为应充分利用两国经贸互补优势，促进双边经贸关系和相互投资，扩大在基础设施建设、各项工业和高科技领域，特别是交通、路桥、铁路、电信、国有企业、先进技术转移便利化等多种形式的互利合作，建立能源与替代能源领域长期全面的战略合作关系，扩大两国在银行、金融市场等金融领域的合作等。

**南非。**2015年12月，中国和南非签署了价值419亿元人民币的26项双边合作协议，其中包括：中国工商银行与非洲最大银行标准银行集团签署了总金额为100亿兰特的兰特发债合作协议，中国出口信用保险公司为南非国家交通运输集团提供25亿美元的授信额度用于设备购买，中国国家开发银行为南非电力公用事业提供5亿美元贷款支持电站建设。

**科威特。**2014年6月，科威特首相对中国进行友好访问，期间与中方签订了《科中关于丝绸之路经济带和科威特丝绸城建设合作谅解备忘录》以及《科中能源合作协议》《科中基础设施项目投资合作协议》《科中航空合作协议》等10份合作协议。

**格鲁尼亚。**2015年3月，两国签署"丝绸之路经济带"合作的备忘录，提出将在中格经贸合作委员会框架内，共同推进"丝绸之路经济带"建设的经贸合作，全面提升贸易、投资、经济技术合作和基础设施互联互通水平。

**土耳其。**2015年11月，两国签署"一带一路"建设谅解备忘录，指出双方应该积极利用丝路基金和亚洲基础设施投资银行等平台，创新合作渠道和模式，实现共同发展和共同繁荣。

**阿塞拜疆。**2015年12月，两国签订《中阿关于共同推进丝绸之路经济带建设的谅解备忘录》，标志着两国务实合作迈入新阶段。此外，双方签署《中阿关于共同推进丝绸之路经济带建设的谅解备忘录》及经贸、司法、民航、教育、交通、能源等领域双边合作文件。

**沙特阿拉伯。**2016年1月，两国发表《中华人民共和国和沙特阿拉伯王国关于建立全面战略伙伴关系的联合声明》，提出双方愿继续本着互利共赢原则，开展务实合作，扩大相互投资，进一步深化基础设施领域合作，重点做好铁路、道路桥梁、通信、港口等方面的互利项目，加强产能政策协调与对接，推动技术转让、产业升级和经济多元化。

**埃及。**2016年1月，两国签署《中华人民共和国政府和阿拉伯埃及共和国政府关于共同推进丝绸之路经济带和21世纪海上丝绸之路建设的谅解备忘录》以及电力、基础设施建设、经贸、能源、金融、航空航天、文化、新闻、科技、气候变化等领域多项双边合作文件，并为中埃苏伊士经贸合作区二期揭牌。这一项目将引进纺织服装、石油装备、摩托、太阳能等100家企业，可以为埃及创造1万多个就业机会。2016年1月，两国签署《中华人民共和国和阿拉伯埃及共和国关于加强两国全面战略伙伴关系的五年实施纲要》，从政治经贸、军事和安全、能源油气产业合作等10个大项目80个分项，对中埃关系未来五年发展与合作做了详细的规划安排。

**伊朗。**2016年1月，两国签署《中华人民共和国政府和伊朗伊斯兰共和国政府关于共同推进丝绸之路经济带和21世纪海上丝绸之路建设的谅解备忘录》，以及能源、产能、金融、投资、通信、文化、司法、科技、新闻、海关、气候变化、人力资源等领域多项双边合作文件。

**7. 其他**

**南美洲多国。**2015年5月，李克强总理出访拉美四国——巴西、哥伦比亚、秘鲁、智利，签署了矿产、能源、农业金融等领域的多项合作文件，并与巴西、秘鲁签署了横跨大西洋和太平洋的“两洋铁路”的可行性研究合作文件。

## 9.9 中国各地如何发挥比较优势参与“一带一路”

中国的开放是先从东部沿海地区展开的。因此，改革开放40余年事实上使得东部沿海地区比内陆尤其是西部地区更加开放。国家提出“一带一路”倡议的目的之一就是要让中西部地区更加开放，缩小地区之间由于历史上的开放政策导致的过大发展差距。2015年国家发改委等发布的《推动共建丝绸之路经济带和21世纪海上丝绸之路的愿景与行动》圈定了重点涉及的省份有18个，其中“一带”涉及新疆、陕西、甘肃、宁夏、青海、西藏、云南、广西、重庆、内蒙古、黑龙江、吉林和辽宁13个省、市、区，“一路”涉及福建、上海、广东、浙江和海南5个省、市。在过去，“一带”涉及的西部和东北地区不论在经济还是社会方面的开放程度都远低于“一路”涉及的东部地区，如表9.13和表9.14所示。[①]其原因主要是经济水平相对较低与基础设施相对落后以及开放政策差异所致。[②]“一带一路”倡议通过国家的力量正在逐步改善中西部地区的基础设施和开放政策以及国际环境，然而各地要借助开放促进经济发展的根本还在于发挥自身的比较优势。我们在第6章中介绍的重庆案例以及河南郑州的“空中丝路”便是内陆地区发挥比较优势参与“一带一路”的成功典型。

表9.13 “一带”与“一路”沿线省、区、市2003—2014年开放度对比

| 区域 | 2003 | 2004 | 2005 | 2006 | 2007 | 2008 | 2009 | 2010 | 2011 | 2012 | 2013 | 2014 |
|---|---|---|---|---|---|---|---|---|---|---|---|---|
| “一带” | 1.53 | 1.68 | 1.76 | 1.85 | 2.18 | 2.00 | 1.93 | 2.12 | 2.23 | 2.64 | 2.15 | 2.27 |
| “一路” | 6.23 | 6.56 | 6.73 | 6.91 | 7.41 | 6.71 | 6.43 | 7.27 | 8.05 | 7.20 | 6.94 | 7.20 |

资料来源：伍凤兰、马忠新，“‘一带’与‘一路’沿线18个省区市对外开放度的比较研究”，《云南社会科学》，2017年第1期。

表9.14 “一带”与“一路”沿线各省、区、市平均开放程度对比

| 区域 | 内蒙古 | 青海 | 辽宁 | 吉林 | 广西 | 重庆 | 云南 | 西藏 | 陕西 | 甘肃 |
|---|---|---|---|---|---|---|---|---|---|---|
| 开放度 | 1.74 | 0.89 | 3.66 | 1.93 | 2.08 | 2.18 | 2.81 | 2.33 | 1.92 | 1.70 |
| 区域 | 黑龙江 | 新疆 | 宁夏 | 上海 | 浙江 | 福建 | 广东 | 海南 | “一带” | “一路” |
| 开放度 | 2.10 | 1.88 | 1.17 | 10.16 | 4.23 | 5.47 | 8.86 | 6.12 | 2.03 | 6.97 |

资料来源：伍凤兰、马忠新，“‘一带’与‘一路’沿线18个省区市对外开放度的比较研究”，《云南社会科学》，2017年第1期。

中国各个地区之间的巨大差异在世界经济结构变迁中本身也是一种独特的比较优势，每个地区都可以发挥自身比较优势接入“一带一路”，在国家层面也可以进一步形成协同效应。赵秋运和赵磊做了一个初步的测算，如表9.15所示，根据国际货币基金组织基于购买力平价（PPP）计算的人均GDP（现值国际元），2015年天津市人均GDP最高，为30 465.64国际元，其次为北京30 052.79国际元，上海29 290.58国际元，与“一带一路”沿线国家比较，分别

① 在伍凤兰和马忠新的测算研究中，选择了2个一级指标和9个二级指标来综合评价开放度。经济开放度包括5个子指标：出口总额与国内生产总值的比值、进口总额与国内生产总值的比值、外资企业进出口总额与国内生产总值的比值、外资企业的投资额与国内生产总值的比值、对外投资额与国内生产总值的比值。社会开放度包括5个子指标：接待入境人数与人口总数的比值、涉外婚姻数与人口总数的比值、国际旅游外汇收入与国内生产总值的比值、外资所投资的星级酒店与人口数的比值。然后他们用主成分分析法合成了开放度指标。（伍凤兰、马忠新，“‘一带’与‘一路’沿线18个省区市对外开放度的比较研究”，《云南社会科学》，2017年第1期）

② 朱廷珺和孙睿采用因子分析法测算了“一带一路”沿线西部省份2003—2013年的经济开放度，并采用DEA包络线分析西部各省开放型经济运行效率，发现其总体经济开放度低于全国平均水平，部分省份经济开放程度与运行效率脱节，开放度受经济水平、基础设施、国家政策等因素影响较大。（朱廷珺、孙睿，“‘一带一路’沿线西部省份开放型经济运行效率研究”，《经济经纬》，2016年第2期）

排在第13位、第14位、第16位。除过缺少数据的巴勒斯坦和叙利亚，还有50个国家的人均GDP低于这三个直辖市。而作为人均GDP最低的甘肃，人均GDP7 383.60国际元，排在第80位，其后还有15个国家。

表9.15 2015年中国31个省、市、区与“一带一路”沿线国家收入水平比较　　单位：国际元

| 排序 | 经济体 | 人均GDP | 排序 | 经济体 | 人均GDP | 排序 | 经济体 | 人均GDP |
|---|---|---|---|---|---|---|---|---|
| 1 | 卡塔尔 | 132 098.69 | 33 | 保加利亚 | 19 097.27 | 65 | 河南 | 11 040.27 |
| 2 | 新加坡 | 85 253.24 | 34 | 广东 | 19 048.92 | 66 | 斯里兰卡 | 10 566.19 |
| 3 | 文莱 | 79 586.96 | 35 | 辽宁 | 18 442.49 | 67 | 波黑 | 10 491.80 |
| 4 | 科威特 | 70 165.99 | 36 | 黎巴嫩 | 18 239.84 | 68 | 四川 | 10 377.68 |
| 5 | 阿联酋 | 67 616.88 | 37 | 山东 | 18 107.81 | 69 | 江西 | 10 363.28 |
| 6 | 沙特阿拉伯 | 53 624.40 | 38 | 阿塞拜疆 | 17 993.43 | 70 | 安徽 | 10 158.13 |
| 7 | 巴林 | 50 094.93 | 39 | 白俄罗斯 | 17 654.17 | 71 | 广西 | 9 930.40 |
| 8 | 阿曼 | 44 628.28 | 40 | 伊朗 | 17 251.25 | 72 | 山西 | 9 853.92 |
| 9 | 以色列 | 33 656.08 | 41 | 土库曼斯坦 | 16 444.54 | 73 | 格鲁吉亚 | 9 629.96 |
| 10 | 塞浦路斯 | 32 785.46 | 42 | 黑山 | 16 123.14 | 74 | 西藏 | 9 029.92 |
| 11 | 捷克 | 31 549.49 | 43 | 泰国 | 16 097.35 | 75 | 亚美尼亚 | 8 467.95 |
| 12 | 斯洛文尼亚 | 31 007.44 | 44 | 伊拉克 | 15 474.23 | 76 | 贵州 | 8 422.64 |
| 13 | 天津 | 30 465.64 | 45 | 马尔代夫 | 14 922.76 | 77 | 不丹 | 8 200.67 |
| 14 | 北京 | 30 052.79 | 46 | 重庆 | 14 764.66 | 78 | 云南 | 8 128.87 |
| 15 | 斯洛伐克 | 29 720.06 | 47 | 吉林 | 14 416.15 | 79 | 乌克兰 | 7 970.75 |
| 16 | 上海 | 29 290.58 | 48 | 湖北 | 14 294.24 | 80 | 甘肃 | 7 383.60 |
| 17 | 爱沙尼亚 | 28 591.85 | 49 | 中国 | 14 107.43 | 81 | 菲律宾 | 7 254.20 |
| 18 | 立陶宛 | 28 359.10 | 50 | 马其顿 | 14 009.14 | 82 | 印度 | 6 161.62 |
| 19 | 波兰 | 26 455.27 | 51 | 塞尔维亚 | 13 671.43 | 83 | 乌兹别克斯坦 | 6 068.45 |
| 20 | 希腊 | 26 448.70 | 52 | 陕西 | 13 439.76 | 84 | 越南 | 6 024.35 |
| 21 | 马来西亚 | 26 314.80 | 53 | 宁夏 | 12 361.50 | 85 | 缅甸 | 5 468.76 |
| 22 | 匈牙利 | 26 221.99 | 54 | 蒙古 | 12 146.64 | 86 | 老挝 | 5 309.41 |
| 23 | 俄罗斯 | 25 410.92 | 55 | 约旦 | 12 122.85 | 87 | 摩尔多瓦 | 5 006.24 |
| 24 | 江苏 | 24 831.64 | 56 | 湖南 | 12 064.91 | 88 | 巴基斯坦 | 5 000.01 |
| 25 | 拉脱维亚 | 24 712.17 | 57 | 埃及 | 11 849.63 | 89 | 孟加拉国 | 3 606.65 |
| 26 | 哈萨克斯坦 | 24 267.90 | 58 | 青海 | 11 641.06 | 90 | 柬埔寨 | 3 487.46 |
| 27 | 浙江 | 21 910.65 | 59 | 海南 | 11 518.58 | 91 | 吉尔吉斯斯坦 | 3 362.61 |
| 28 | 克罗地亚 | 21 581.43 | 60 | 河北 | 11 359.71 | 92 | 塔吉克斯坦 | 2 749.40 |
| 29 | 罗马尼亚 | 20 786.86 | 61 | 阿尔巴尼亚 | 11 300.82 | 93 | 也门 | 2 670.61 |
| 30 | 土耳其 | 20 437.79 | 62 | 新疆 | 11 297.91 | 94 | 尼泊尔 | 2 465.23 |
| 31 | 内蒙古 | 20 064.26 | 63 | 黑龙江 | 11 135.93 | 95 | 阿富汗 | 1 947.00 |
| 32 | 福建 | 19 179.58 | 64 | 印度尼西亚 | 11 125.92 | | | |

资料来源：赵秋运、赵磊，“新结构经济学与‘一带一路’：转入国的筛选和转出产业的甄别”，《西部论坛》，2017年第6期。

从国内31个省、市、区对“一带一路”沿线国家的贸易额看（见表9.16），广东、江苏、浙江、北京、上海与“一带一路”沿线国家贸易额位居前五。北京、上海、海南、黑龙江、内蒙古、吉林存在贸易逆差。华东、华南、华北是与沿线国家开展贸易合作的主要地区。从中国各主要区域与“一带一路”沿线国家整体贸易额来看，2016年，华东地区最高，达3 616.2亿美元，占比为37.9%；华南地区为2 842.8亿美元，占比为29.8%；华北地区为1 408.4亿美元，占比为14.8%；中部地区、西南地区、东北地区、西北地区贸易额较小，均在600亿美元以下。华东地区、华南地区和华北地区合计占比达82.5%，是我国与“一带一路”沿线国家开展贸易合作最重要的地区。华东、华南是向沿线国家出口的主要地区。从出口看，华东地区和华南地区占据我国向“一带一路”沿线国家出口额的前两位，合计占比达72.1%。其中华东地区为2 430.9亿美元，占比为41.4%；华南地区为1 803.7亿美元，占比为30.7%。7个区域出口较2015年均出现了下降，其中西南地区向沿线国家出口下降了31.4%，东北地区下降了23.5%；其他地区降幅在6%以内。华东、华南、华北是自沿线国家进口的主要地区。从进口看，华东地区、华南地区和华北地区占据了我国自“一带一路”沿线国家进口额的前三位，合计占比达85.2%。其中，华东地区为1 185.3亿美元，占比为32.4%；华南地区为1 039.1亿美元，占比为28.4%；华北地区为893.8亿美元，占比为24.4%。西南地区自沿线国家进口大幅增加20.0%；西北地区维持不变；华北、中部、东北下降明显，降幅超过10%；其他地区降幅较小。在各地对外投资情况方面，从表9.17可以看出国内各地对外投资的整体情况，东部沿海整体上领先。这很大程度上与东部经济结构转型升级目前处于“腾笼换鸟”阶段有关，“走出去”的需求强烈。就目前国内各个地区的发展阶段而言，借助“一带一路”，东部地区将更多侧重于对外转移产业和海外并购，中西部地区将更多侧重于吸引外资和对外贸易（可回顾第8章的相关讨论）。例如，深处西部内陆的四川省，2018年全年实际利用外资754.3亿元，比上年增长28.7%。2018年全年进出口总额飙升到5 947.9亿元，比上年增长29.2%；出口额3 334.8亿元，增长31.4%；进口额2 613.1亿元，增长26.5%。四川贸易的爆炸性增长与蓉欧快铁物流建设不无关系。[①]总之，处于不同经济结构转型升级阶

① 中欧班列运行初期，一直面临着回程货源短缺的难题，导致运输成本居高不下。2013年3月8日，中欧班列首次迎来回程班列。目前国内多条中欧班列均已实现双向常态化开行，运输成本不断下降。例如，2015年“渝新欧”开行达257班（去程156班、回程101班），实现双向常态化运行，运输成本进一步从2013年的每千米每个集装箱0.7美元（1美元约合6.78元人民币）下降至0.5美元，不断接近海运价格。2014年4月8日，中欧班列首次从货运专列升级为公共班列，货源种类进一步拓展。以“渝新欧”为例，此前货源主要为笔记本电脑、数码打印机等IT产品。据统计，2015年“渝新欧”承运的商品中，IT产品和非IT产品各占50%。其中，去程货源包括笔记本电脑、服装、日用品、咖啡豆等多个品类，回程货源包括汽车整车及零部件、化妆品、酒类、高档母婴用品等。

段的地区需要找准自身的比较优势，才能最大限度地参与全球化并从中受益。

表9.16 2016年中国31个省、市、区与“一带一路”沿线国家贸易情况　　单位：亿美元

| 省、市、区 | 进出口 | | 出口 | | 进口 | |
|---|---|---|---|---|---|---|
| | 贸易额 | 排名 | 贸易额 | 排名 | 贸易额 | 排名 |
| 广东省 | 1 995.6 | 1 | 1 294.9 | 1 | 700.7 | 2 |
| 江苏省 | 1 098.9 | 2 | 774.1 | 3 | 324.5 | 4 |
| 浙江省 | 1 052.0 | 3 | 876.5 | 2 | 175.5 | 6 |
| 北京市 | 958.5 | 4 | 197.4 | 7 | 761.0 | 1 |
| 上海市 | 842.0 | 5 | 402.5 | 4 | 439.5 | 3 |
| 山东省 | 623.6 | 6 | 377.8 | 5 | 245.8 | 5 |
| 福建省 | 490.1 | 7 | 336.3 | 6 | 153.8 | 7 |
| 广西壮族自治区 | 304.2 | 8 | 159.0 | 9 | 145.2 | 8 |
| 辽宁省 | 240.1 | 9 | 132.2 | 11 | 107.9 | 9 |
| 天津市 | 232.9 | 10 | 164.1 | 8 | 68.8 | 12 |
| 重庆市 | 181.0 | 11 | 109.2 | 13 | 71.7 | 11 |
| 新疆维吾尔自治区 | 146.9 | 12 | 134.9 | 10 | 12.1 | 23 |
| 河北省 | 144.5 | 13 | 128.7 | 12 | 15.8 | 21 |
| 云南省 | 134.3 | 14 | 73.2 | 19 | 61.1 | 13 |
| 安徽省 | 123.0 | 15 | 97.4 | 15 | 25.6 | 19 |
| 河南省 | 121.7 | 16 | 91.7 | 17 | 29.9 | 18 |
| 江西省 | 119.8 | 17 | 104.6 | 14 | 15.1 | 22 |
| 黑龙江省 | 116.9 | 18 | 31.9 | 21 | 85.0 | 10 |
| 湖北省 | 115.8 | 19 | 97.3 | 16 | 18.5 | 20 |
| 四川省 | 113.9 | 20 | 77.7 | 18 | 36.2 | 16 |
| 内蒙古自治区 | 72.5 | 21 | 24.4 | 24 | 48.1 | 14 |
| 湖南省 | 63.2 | 22 | 52.0 | 20 | 11.1 | 26 |

张祥建等采用PSMDID方法，以2008—2017年中西部地区的面板数据，实证检验了中欧班列开通对内陆地区贸易增长的影响效应及其传导机制。研究发现：（1）中欧班列显著促进了内陆地区的贸易增长，对开通地区的贸易增长影响更大，并且这种增长效应呈现出先高后低再高的阶段性动态特征。（2）中欧班列的开通有助于降低运输成本和交易成本，提高外资和内资吸引力，促进产业结构和产业布局的优化调整，为中西部地区的贸易进出口增长提供内生动力。（3）进一步对区位异质性分析后发现，内陆自由贸易区、货源地节点和运输通道的贸易水平受中欧班列的影响更大，中欧班列强化了内陆自由贸易区的资源要素汇聚功能，放大了货源地节点的“虹吸效应”和运输通道的“辐射效应”。因此，在把握中欧班列开通带来的贸易便利化的同时，应优化中欧班列的运输线路布局，建立地区货源协调机制，充分发挥内陆自由贸易区的对外开放枢纽作用和中欧班列的辐射带动效应。详细的实证研究可参考：张祥建、李永盛、赵晓雷，“中欧班列对内陆地区贸易增长的影响效应研究”，《财经研究》，2019年第11期。

续表

| 省、市、区 | 进出口 | | 出口 | | 进口 | |
|---|---|---|---|---|---|---|
| | 贸易额 | 排名 | 贸易额 | 排名 | 贸易额 | 排名 |
| 海南省 | 53.0 | 23 | 13.6 | 28 | 39.4 | 15 |
| 吉林省 | 46.3 | 24 | 14.0 | 27 | 32.4 | 17 |
| 山西省 | 36.7 | 25 | 25.4 | 23 | 11.3 | 25 |
| 陕西省 | 34.7 | 26 | 28.0 | 22 | 6.7 | 27 |
| 甘肃省 | 27.9 | 27 | 16.5 | 26 | 11.4 | 24 |
| 贵州省 | 23.6 | 28 | 20.3 | 25 | 3.3 | 28 |
| 宁夏回族自治区 | 11.0 | 29 | 8.3 | 29 | 2.7 | 29 |
| 青海省 | 7.0 | 30 | 6.4 | 30 | 0.6 | 30 |
| 西藏自治区 | 4.8 | 31 | 4.6 | 31 | 0.2 | 31 |

资料来源：国家信息中心《"一带一路"贸易合作大数据报告2017》。

表9.17 2007—2015年中国各地对外投资流量　　单位：万美元

| | 2007年 | 2008年 | 2009年 | 2010年 | 2011年 | 2012年 | 2013年 | 2014年 | 2015年 |
|---|---|---|---|---|---|---|---|---|---|
| 一、中央合计 | 1 958 488 | 3 598 284 | 3 819 275 | 4 243 698 | 4 502 314 | 4 352 693 | 5 632 449 | 5 247 617 | 2 781 752 |
| 二、地方合计 | 525 341 | 587 633 | 960 250 | 1 774 542 | 2 356 036 | 3 420 576 | 3 641 489 | 5 472 587 | 9 360 410 |
| 北京市 | 15 295 | 47 299 | 45 185 | 76 614 | 117 503 | 168 855 | 413 010 | 727 353 | 1 228 033 |
| 天津市 | 7 993 | 8 200 | 20 992 | 34 132 | 40 706 | 67 495 | 112 020 | 414 637 | 252 654 |
| 河北省 | 5 394 | 5 363 | 21 993 | 53 237 | 46 363 | 57 809 | 92 757 | 121 865 | 94 030 |
| 山西省 | 8 347 | 2 702 | 33 295 | 7 926 | 18 319 | 30 966 | 56 483 | 30 491 | 18 611 |
| 内蒙古自治区 | 4 235 | 6 190 | 15 547 | 8 042 | 12 825 | 51 845 | 40 880 | 110 969 | 40 447 |
| 辽宁省 | 12 833 | 10 600 | 75 786 | 193 566 | 114 384 | 276 260 | 129 499 | 147 902 | 212 204 |
| 其中：大连市 | 6 542 | 4 427 | 46 384 | 163 229 | 74 591 | 203 087 | 104 450 | 57 481 | 134 920 |
| 吉林省 | 8 322 | 10 673 | 29 814 | 21 340 | 20 493 | 29 641 | 75 240 | 33 310 | 65 823 |
| 黑龙江省 | 17 851 | 22 797 | 12 131 | 23 780 | 23 834 | 72 405 | 77 338 | 65 531 | 42 388 |
| 上海市 | 52 266 | 33 714 | 120 869 | 158 468 | 183 802 | 331 517 | 267 524 | 499 225 | 2 318 288 |
| 江苏省 | 51 899 | 49 384 | 85 061 | 137 119 | 225 383 | 313 050 | 302 001 | 406 983 | 725 000 |
| 浙江省 | 40 346 | 38 768 | 70 226 | 267 915 | 185 287 | 236 023 | 255 276 | 386 170 | 710 816 |
| 其中：宁波市 | 5 253 | 22 515 | 21 097 | 39 460 | 75 573 | 63 839 | 84 468 | 103 663 | 251 456 |
| 安徽省 | 5 079 | 6 051 | 5 782 | 81 365 | 53 089 | 71 043 | 91 055 | 38 029 | 206 747 |
| 福建省 | 36 847 | 16 169 | 36 582 | 53 495 | 53 028 | 85 705 | 95 249 | 105 064 | 275 743 |
| 其中：厦门市 | 19 099 | 4 159 | 12 389 | 22 881 | 15 276 | 23 400 | 26 463 | 26 523 | 99 523 |
| 江西省 | 1 536 | 2 587 | 2 265 | 9 470 | 18 833 | 37 316 | 38 091 | 73 853 | 100 457 |
| 山东省 | 18 928 | 47 478 | 70 441 | 189 001 | 247 339 | 345 621 | 426 472 | 391 590 | 710 983 |
| 其中：青岛市 | 4 898 | 1 547 | 10 472 | 46 197 | 23 466 | 91 985 | 102 267 | 121 749 | 127 774 |
| 河南省 | 7 036 | 13 127 | 12 075 | 11 864 | 28 251 | 34 117 | 58 971 | 54 692 | 131 284 |

续表

| | 2007年 | 2008年 | 2009年 | 2010年 | 2011年 | 2012年 | 2013年 | 2014年 | 2015年 |
|---|---|---|---|---|---|---|---|---|---|
| 湖北省 | 903 | 350 | 4 116 | 8 061 | 70 903 | 49 687 | 52 011 | 67 161 | 63 596 |
| 湖南省 | 14 088 | 25 446 | 100 568 | 27 477 | 117 628 | 99 499 | 56 970 | 78 449 | 112 370 |
| 广东省 | 114 101 | 124 251 | 92 298 | 159 977 | 363 350 | 528 821 | 594 288 | 1 089 671 | 1 226 250 |
| 其中：深圳市 | 92 433 | 76 375 | 41 447 | 60 878 | 113 306 | 336 833 | 300 814 | 598 933 | 645 920 |
| 广西壮族自治区 | 2 620 | 3 844 | 8 169 | 18 682 | 16 714 | 27 240 | 8 134 | 22 864 | 45 091 |
| 海南省 | 122 | 82 | 6 072 | 22 179 | 121 999 | 32 012 | 81 731 | 88 708 | 120 119 |
| 重庆市 | 8 713 | 10 448 | 4 747 | 36 109 | 40 125 | 52 960 | 34 655 | 76 676 | 149 638 |
| 四川省 | 29 120 | 8 107 | 10 740 | 69 097 | 56 341 | 59 509 | 58 447 | 138 223 | 118 730 |
| 贵州省 | 51 | 25 | 522 | 289 | 2 033 | 2 025 | 20 815 | 8 764 | 6 539 |
| 云南省 | 13 641 | 28 467 | 27 008 | 51 339 | 24 845 | 104 046 | 83 036 | 126 195 | 94 648 |
| 西藏自治区 | — | — | — | 29 | 216 | 2 | 22 | 385 | 29 681 |
| 陕西省 | 2 058 | 14 063 | 22 462 | 26 055 | 44 816 | 60 784 | 30 789 | 41 411 | 62 408 |
| 甘肃省 | 15 364 | 35 808 | 1 852 | 10 176 | 64 917 | 138 209 | 43 182 | 27 321 | 12 293 |
| 青海省 | 110 | 202 | 209 | 138 | 173 | 1 280 | 3 596 | 1 601 | 7 826 |
| 宁夏回族自治区 | 569 | 502 | 1 509 | 711 | 1 295 | 6 421 | 8 626 | 33 883 | 108 959 |
| 新疆维吾尔自治区 | 8 535 | 6 934 | 18 057 | 4 776 | 31 474 | 43 123 | 31 579 | 54 832 | 61 077 |
| 新疆生产建设兵团 | 21 139 | 7 999 | 3 877 | 12 111 | 9 768 | 5 189 | 1 742 | 8 780 | 7 679 |
| 合计 | 2 483 829 | 4 185 917 | 4 779 525 | 6 018 240 | 6 858 350 | 7 773 269 | 9 273 938 | 10 720 204 | 12 142 162 |

资料来源：《2015年度中国对外直接投资统计公报》。

事实上，《推动共建丝绸之路经济带和21世纪海上丝绸之路的愿景与行动》也正是这样强调的：推进“一带一路”建设，中国将充分发挥国内各地区的比较优势，实行更加积极主动的开放战略，加强东中西互动合作，全面提升开放型经济水平。各地区具体如下：

（1）西北、东北地区。发挥新疆独特的区位优势和向西开放重要窗口作用，深化与中亚、南亚、西亚等国家交流合作，形成丝绸之路经济带上重要的交通枢纽、商贸物流和文化科教中心，打造丝绸之路经济带核心区。发挥陕西、甘肃综合经济文化和宁夏、青海民族人文优势，打造西安内陆型改革开放新高地，加快兰州、西宁开发开放，推进宁夏内陆开放型经济试验区建设，形成面向中亚、南亚、西亚国家的通道、商贸物流枢纽、重要产业和人文交流基地。发挥内蒙古联通俄蒙的区位优势，完善黑龙江对俄铁路通道和区域铁路网，以及黑龙江、吉林、辽宁与俄远东地区陆海联运合作，推进构建北京－莫斯科欧亚高速运输走廊，建设向北开放的重要窗口。

（2）西南地区。发挥广西与东盟国家陆海相邻的独特优势，加快北部湾经济区和珠江－西江经济带开放发展，构建面向东盟区域的国际通道，打造西南、中南地区开放发展新的战略支点，形成21世纪海上丝绸之路与丝绸之路经济带有机衔接的重要门户。发挥云南区位优势，推进与周边国家的国际运输通道建设，打造大湄公河次区域经济合作新高地，建设成为面向南亚、东南亚的辐射中心。推进西藏与尼泊尔等国家边境贸易和旅游文化合作。

（3）沿海和港澳台地区。利用长三角、珠三角、海峡西岸、环渤海等经济区开放程度高、经济实力强、辐射带动作用大的优势，加快推进中国（上海）自由贸易试验区建设，支持福建建设21世纪海上丝绸之路核心区。充分发挥深圳前海、广州南沙、珠海横琴、福建平潭等开放合作区作用，深化与港澳台合作，打造粤港澳大湾区。推进浙江海洋经济发展示范区、福建海峡蓝色经济试验区和舟山群岛新区建设，加大海南国际旅游岛开发开放力度。加强上海、天津、宁波－舟山、广州、深圳、湛江、汕头、青岛、烟台、大连、福州、厦门、泉州、海口、三亚等沿海城市港口建设，强化上海、广州等国际枢纽机场功能。以扩大开放倒逼深层次改革，创新开放型经济体制机制，加大科技创新力度，形成参与和引领国际合作竞争新优势，成为“一带一路”特别是21世纪海上丝绸之路建设的排头兵和主力军。发挥海外侨胞以及香港、澳门特别行政区独特优势作用，积极参与和助力“一带一路”建设。为台湾地区参与“一带一路”建设作出妥善安排。

（4）内陆地区。利用内陆纵深广阔、人力资源丰富、产业基础较好优势，依托长江中游城市群、成渝城市群、中原城市群、呼包鄂榆城市群、哈长城市群等重点区域，推动区域互动合作和产业集聚发展，打造重庆西部开发开放重要支撑和成都、郑州、武汉、长沙、南昌、合肥等内陆开放型经济高地。加快推动长江中上游地区和俄罗斯伏尔加河沿岸联邦区的合作。建立中欧通道铁路运输、口岸通关协调机制，打造“中欧班列”品牌，建设沟通境内外、连接东中西的运输通道。支持郑州、西安等内陆城市建设航空港、国际陆港，加强内陆口岸与沿海、沿边口岸通关合作，开展跨境贸易电子商务服务试点。优化海关特殊监管区域布局，创新加工贸易模式，深化与沿线国家的产业合作。

## 专栏9.2
## 中国各地参与一带一路情况[①]

正如我们在前面所指出的，“一带一路”倡议不仅仅是区域战略，是中国新时期的全球化新型平台，全国各地都在积极参与。按照《推动共建丝绸之路经济带和21世纪海上丝绸之路的愿景与行动》的最初规划，“一带一路”直接涉及的国内区域整体分为西北6省（区）、内陆1市、西南3省（区）、东北3省、东南5省五大区域。各省在“一带一路”建设中的重要性和所发挥的作用不同，新疆和福建是“一带一路”的关键省区，其中，新疆是“丝绸之路经济带核心区”，福建是“21世纪海上丝绸之路核心区”。目前，“一带一路”各省、市、区大都制定了本地对接“一带一路”倡议的相关举措，其中西北6省、区以及福建、广东和黑龙江等关键省份均出台了专项规划和实施方案。其中，新疆、青海、甘肃、陕西、宁夏、内蒙古、黑龙江、福建、广东、湖南和江西等省、区出台了总体规划/实施方案/建设方案/行动计划等；甘肃、重庆、广西、上海、广东、浙江和海南等省、市、区将其列入“十三五”规划。一些省、市、区的举措和成效简要概括如下。

**新疆。**新疆作为丝路经济带核心地区，打造“五大中心”，即区域性交通枢纽中心、商贸物流中心、金融中心、文化科教中心和医疗服务中心是重中之重，目前“五大中心”专项规划也已提上日程。2016年4月，出台《新疆国税局关于落实“一带一路”发展战略要求做好税收服务与管理工作的意见》，提出了新疆国税局服务“一带一路”建设十项具体措施，推动企业“走出去”。2016年3月，《新疆生产建设兵团参与建设丝绸之路经济带的实施方案》完成，提出促进基础设施互联互通、打造八大进出口产业基地、打造经贸合作平台、实施“走出去”战略、完善城镇嵌入式布局、密切人文交流、提升医疗服务水平、增强金融支撑能力、当好生态卫士及构建开放型经济体制机制等十项任务。2016年10月，出台《丝绸之路经济带创新驱动发展试验区总体规划纲要》，提出试验区建设以丝绸之路经济带核心区建设为中心，先行先试探索具有新疆特色的创新道路、创新模式和创新机制，引领示范构建创新型经济体系，打造丝绸之路经济带核心区发

① 本专栏根据中国“一带一路”网及《“一带一路”大数据报告》《“一带一路”研究手册》《“一带一路”贸易合作大数据报告2017》等相关资料整理而成。

展新动能，带动全面建成创新型新疆。

**青海**。2015年12月，通过《青海省参与建设丝绸之路经济带与21世纪海上丝绸之路实施方案》，包括构建对外开放通道，打造西宁、海东和格尔木三个对外开放节点城市，打造“澜沧江-湄公河源头风情文化旅游”线路，建设10个国际商城和进口生活馆，在重点国家和地区建设中国（青海）特色商品国际营销中心，以及在机场开设口岸免税商店6项举措。2016年出台《青海省人民政府关于推进国内贸易流通现代化建设法治化营商环境的实施意见》，2017年出台《青海省人民政府关于贯彻落实国家自由贸易区战略的实施意见》，2018年出台《青海省深入推进“一带一路”建设高质量发展实施意见》。受益于“一带一路”建设，青海省一些资源特色商品首次出现出口。2018年青海省进口14.9亿元，出口31.1亿元。

**甘肃**。2014年5月，出台《丝绸之路经济带甘肃段建设总体方案》，提出着力构建兰州新区、敦煌国际文化旅游名城和“中国丝绸之路博览会”三大战略平台，重点推进道路互联互通、经贸技术交流、产业对接合作、经济新增长、人文交流合作、战略平台建设等六大工程，进一步提升兰（州）白（银）、酒（泉）嘉（峪关）、金（昌）武（威）、平（凉）庆（阳）、天水、定西、张掖、敦煌等重要节点城市的支撑能力，努力把甘肃省建设成为丝绸之路的黄金通道、向西开放的战略平台、经贸物流的区域中心、产业合作的示范基地、人文交流的桥梁纽带。2015年3月，出台《丝绸之路经济带甘肃段“6873”交通突破行动实施方案》，指出集中力量开展“6873”交通突破行动，即：从2015年起用6年时间，完成投资8 000亿元以上（公路建设5 000亿元、铁路建设3 000亿元、民航建设400亿元），建成公路、铁路70 000千米以上（公路67 000千米、铁路3 400千米），实现全省对内对外公路畅通、铁路联通、航路广通三大突破，从根本上解决交通发展不足的问题。2015年12月，出台《甘肃省参与丝绸之路经济带和21世纪海上丝绸之路的实施方案》，明确提出围绕一大构想，着力构建三大平台、六大窗口、八大节点城市，推进五大重点工程建设的发展战略。该实施方案共有5个附件，分别是《甘肃省参与建设丝绸之路经济带和21世纪海上丝绸之路2015—2016年度工作要点》《甘肃省参与建设丝绸之路经济带和21世纪海上丝绸之路项目清单》、六大经济走廊、多国同甘肃省建设友好关系及设立合作窗口产业园区表、甘肃省推进“一带一路”建设战略走向示意图和“丝绸之路经济带”甘肃段建设规划示意图。2016年1月，《甘肃省国民经济和社会发展第十个五年规划纲要（草案）》提出将丝绸之路经济带甘肃黄金段建设成为甘肃未来五年主攻的10

项重大任务之一，提出甘肃“十三五”将建设兰州国际港务区，兰州中欧货运班列编组枢纽和物流集散中心，兰州、敦煌、嘉峪关三大空港，兰州、武威、天水三大陆港，打造面向“一带一路”的综合经济走廊和物流集散大枢纽。

**陕西。**2013年9月，与丝绸之路经济带沿线的意大利、伊朗、乌兹别克斯坦、亚美尼亚、印度、葡萄牙、西班牙等9个国家共同发布了《共建丝绸之路经济带西安宣言》，将通过建立城市间共享的信息平台，以及信息的有效传播，在商贸、旅游、农业、教育、科技、文化等方面探求新的合作方式，共同建设“丝绸之路经济带”。2015年7月，出台《陕西省“一带一路”建设2015年行动计划》，提出促进互联互通建设、密切交流合作、加强科技教育合作、深化经贸领域合作、搭建对外开放平台、加强生态环保合作、创新金融合作方式等工作目标，并提出《丝绸之路经济带中国（陕西）自由贸易试验区总体方案》。此后，2016年、2017年、2018年、2019年连续四年发布了年度行动计划。2016年发布《陕西省推进建设丝绸之路经济带和21世纪海上丝绸之路实施方案（2015—2020年）》。2018年发布《关于加强和规范“一带一路”对外交流平台审核工作的通知》《陕西省推进绿色“一带一路”建设实施意见》《陕西省标准联通共建“一带一路”行动计划》《西安建设“一带一路”综合改革开放试验区总体方案》。陕西省提出大力发展“三个经济”（枢纽经济、门户经济、流动经济），建设“一带一路”五大中心（交通商贸物流中心、国际产能合作中心、科技教育中心、国际文化旅游中心、丝绸之路金融中心），打造内陆改革开放新高地。五年来陕西省取得了“一带一路”的实际成效，对沿线国家进出口贸易额从2013年的243.2亿元增长到2018年的389.26亿元，对外投资从2013年的2.9亿美元增长到2018年的6.47亿美元，在沿线国家完成对外承包工程营业额从2014年的7.24亿美元增长到2018年的26.55亿美元，2013年始发“长安号”国际货运班列，2018年开行1 235列；2018年西咸国际机场旅客吞吐量超过4 460万人次，国际旅客量增速位居全国十大机场之首。

**宁夏。**2015年7月，通过《关于融入“一带一路”加快开放宁夏建设的意见》，提出以打造丝绸之路经济带战略支点为主攻方向，先行先试“一带一路”重大项目合作方式，着力提升开放型经济产业支撑能力，着力提升基础设施互联互通能力、开放平台辐射带动能力、市场主体国际竞争能力、人文经贸互融互动能力。2015年11月，《宁夏参与丝绸之路经济带和21世纪海上丝绸之路建设规划》提出要拓展对外开放通道，集中精力打造陆上、网上、空中“三条丝绸之路”，加快建设国际化综合交通枢纽；并且要加强外向型园区培育，依托综合保税区、清真产业园区、慈善产业园区等平台，主动对接阿拉伯国家贸易或产业园区。要促进贸易便利化，探索内陆地区自由贸易新模式。打通宁夏对外快速通道，加强与出海通道合作，将向西开放优势转化为开放发展动力，先行先试，推进开放宁夏建设。

**内蒙古。**2014年12月，《创新同俄罗斯、蒙古国合作机制实施方案》提出，内蒙古自治区要利用3～5年的时间，初步建成以满洲里、二连浩特等口岸及城镇为主体，内连经济腹地、外接俄蒙的充满活力的沿边经济带的目标。2015年，《参与建设“丝绸之路经济带”实施方案》编制完成，提出建设海路联运的新型业态，打通珠恩嘎达布其—毕其格图口岸铁路，连通锦州港、营口港。2016年4月，《中国“一带一路”中的内蒙古丝绸之路经济带》和《内蒙古建设国家向北开放桥头堡和沿边经济带规划领导工作用图》编制完成，围绕以“双核、多点”为依托的沿边开发开放经济带、自治区腹地主要城市（园区）辐射支撑区以及以沿边经济带、连通俄蒙和我国腹地的六大经济走廊，解读了自治区建设国家向北开放桥头堡和沿边经济带的规划内容，展示了自治区16个正式对外开放口岸和19个边境旗（市）的电力、水利、信息等基础设施建设情况，反映了口岸进出口、口岸周边物流园区、工业园区、互市贸易区建设及其主要加工产业以及境外主要矿产资源分布情况，呈现了建设国家向北开放桥头堡和沿边经济带规划区域内的公路、铁路、航空水运等交通网络。

**重庆。**2014年11月，通过《关于贯彻落实国家“一带一路”战略和建设长江经济带的实施意见》，提出要深入实施五大功能区域发展战略，以建设长江上游综合交通枢纽为支撑，从着力构建大通道立体交通体系、打造内陆开放高地、增强战略支点集聚辐射功能、培育特色优势产业集群、推进城市群建设、构筑长江上游生态安全屏障等方面着手，促进经济转型升级、提质增效，将重庆建设成为长江经济带西部中心枢纽、西部开发开放重要战略支撑和内陆开放高地。2016年9月，发布《重庆市现代商贸服务业发展“十三五”规划》，指出“十三五”期间，重庆将基本建成“一带一路”重要的流通节点城市和长江上游地区现代商贸中心。实施五大功能区域发展战略与“一带一路”倡议深度融合，包括都市功能核心区、都市功能拓展区、城市发展新区、渝东北生态涵养发展区、渝东南生态保护发展区。

**四川。**2015年发布《四川省参与建设丝绸之路经济带和21世纪海上丝绸之路实施方案》，2016年建立四川省“一带一路”建设重大项目储备库，2017年出台《关于贯彻落实“一带一路”国际合作高峰论坛精神务实推进四川“一带一路”建设的实施意见》，2018年印发《四川省推进国际产能合作三年行动指引（2018—2020年）》。四川提出以“一带一路”建设引领全面开放合作，强化以“一带一路”与长江经济带重要节点功能，打造国际航空枢纽和国际铁路港，提升投资贸易便利化水平，构建“四向拓展、全域开放”立体全面开放新格局。目前四川省在提升国际综合交通枢纽功能方面成效卓著，已建成出川大通道31条，成都双流国际机场开通国际地区航线114条。截至2019年3月底，中欧班列（成都）累计开行超过3 300列，境外站点数达25个。泸州港和宜宾港为重点建设港口，五年间新开通12条集装箱航线。四川省对沿线国家进出口额从2013年的1 206.9亿元增长到2018年的1 652.2亿元。截至2018年，四川省对外承包工程营业额为228亿美元。例如，哈罗格兰德大桥工程就是四川省与挪威签署的基础设施建设重点工程。四川在自贸区建设和产业合作平台建设方面也成效卓著。四川全面创新改革试验区在全国推广16条经验，位居全国之首，中国（四川）自贸区形成400余个创新实践案例。打造了中德创新产业合作平台、中法生态园、中韩创新产业园、新川创新科技园、中意文化创新园区、中德中小企业合作园等国别合作园区，已落地一大批企业和项目。这些举措也加快了四川引进来建设开放型经济体的步伐。例如，2018年四川利用外资达114亿美元，对外投资达163.8亿美元。

**西藏。**2015年11月，《西藏自治区南亚大通道建设规划》签署，提出西藏“十三五”建设南亚重大通道：建设国家面向南亚开放重要通道，提升与毗邻国家互联互通水平，提升与周边省区互联互通水平，加强对外经贸文化合作交流。

**云南。**2015年印发了《关于加快建设我国面向南亚东南亚辐射中心的实施意见》《云南省五大基础设施网络建设规划（2016—2020年）》《云南省与周边国家基础设施互联互通实施方案》；2016年印发了《关于支持沿边重点地区开发开放若干政策措施的实施意见》《建设面向南亚东南亚科技创新中心专项规划》《关于建设面向南亚东南亚金融服务中心的实施意见》《云南建设面向南亚东南亚人文交流中心规划（2016—2020年）》《提升金融创新能力建设面向南亚东南亚金融服务中心》；2018年国家发改委印发了《关于支持云南省加快建设面向南亚东南亚辐射中心的政策措施》；2019年印发了《云南省新时代扩大和深化对外开放若干意见》以及综合交通枢纽体系建设。跨境贸易便利化、重大项目金融支持力度、科教文化医疗卫生跨境合作、跨境农业等15个实施方案。在一些专项规划中云南融入“一带一路”也作为重点。例如，2016年9月，《云南省会展产业“十三五”发展规划纲要》提出，会展产业发展是云南主动融入和服务于国家“一带一路”倡议的必然选择，力争到2020年，把云南建设成为在国内有更大影响力、在国际上有更高认知度的重要会展举办地，将昆明建设成为面向“两亚”的会展之城，将滇中地区建设成为西部会展产业集聚区，将云南建设成为会展产业强省。除了这些政策规划之外，云南“一带一路”建设也取得切实成效。例如，在基础设施互联互通方面，中亚（滇越）国际联运班列自2017年12月首次开行以来累计开行超过千列，累计开通客货航运线总数达434条，中老泰铁路、中越铁路、中缅铁路、中老公路、中越公路、中缅公路等交通基础设施以及电力、管道、线缆等基础设施加速推进。

**广西。**2016年1月，《广西壮族自治区国民经济和社会发展第十三个五年规划纲要》通过，提出建设衔接“一带一路”重要枢纽、建设“一带一路”产业合作基地、建设“一带一路”重要服务平台、建设“一带一路”人才交流纽带、建设“一带一路”区域金融中心。

**黑龙江。**2014年12月，《“中蒙经济走廊”黑龙江陆海丝绸之路经济带建设规划》制定，提出建设：“四带”，即哈大齐（满）产业聚集带、哈牡绥东产业聚集带、哈佳双同产业聚集带、哈绥北黑产业聚集带；“一环”，即沿边环形产业集聚带，以漠河、塔河、呼玛、孙吴、逊克、嘉荫、萝北、绥滨、同江、抚远、饶河、虎林、密山等边境县镇为节点；“一外”，即境外产业园区。2016年印发了《关于建设“龙江丝路带”加快形成对外开放新格局的若干意见》《黑龙江关于落实〈推进“一带一路”建设科技创新工作专项规划〉的实施方案》；2017年出台《关于印发黑龙江绥芬河—东宁重点开发开放试验区建设若干政策的通知》；2018年出台《绥芬河—东宁重点开发开放试验区建设总体规划》《面向欧亚物流枢纽建设规划》。“三桥一岛一索一管道”建设取得实质性进展，2013—2018年哈欧、哈俄班列累计开行800列，“哈绥俄亚”陆海联运累计开行144列，对俄航线累计开通13条。

**吉林。**2016年3月，《关于支持通化市建设向南开放窗口的若干意见》出台，明确提出建设通化国际内陆港务区，全面对接丹东港，使其成为向南开放窗口的核心平台。2016年8月，《吉林省国家税务局吉林省地方税务局助力企业“走出去”服务行动计划》《“走出去”企业税收服务指南》（中韩双语）出台，持续完善助力企业“走出去”、服务企业“走下去”的工作体制、运行机制和工作措施，全力打造境外税收服务与管理工作新格局。

**辽宁。**2015年3月，发布《辽宁企业走进“一带一路”投资指南》，介绍“一带一路”沿线39个国家的具体投资情况，以及辽宁省境外投资机构在当地的联系方式，为企业走进“一带一路”沿线重点国家铺路搭桥。2015年6月，出台

《关于贯彻落实“一带一路”战略推动企业“走出去”的指导意见》，明确提出了6项保障措施：推进口岸通关便利化、创新走出去方式、加大政策扶持力度、完善服务体系、加强风险防范和建立协调机制。辽宁省确定以俄蒙和中东欧为重点工作方向，以推进境外工业园区建设为突破，引导企业创新“走出去”的方式。“走出去”的重点任务包括：三大通道建设、拓展对外产业投资、推进境外经贸合作区建设、带动对外贸易发展、推进境外资源开发、提高对外承包工程的规模和水平、加大境外科技型企业的并购力度、培育境外合作主体。

**福建。**2015年11月，发布《福建省21世纪海上丝绸之路核心区建设方案》，提出打造从福建沿海港口南下，过南海，经马六甲海峡向西至印度洋，延伸至欧洲的西线合作走廊；从福建沿海港口南下，过南海，经印度尼西亚抵达南太平洋的南线合作走廊；结合福建与东北亚传统合作伙伴的合作基础，积极打造从福建沿海港口北上，经韩国、日本，延伸至俄罗斯远东和北美地区的北线合作走廊。截至2018年年底，全省沿海建成万吨级以上泊位181个，开通集装箱国际航线127条，通达50多个国家的近140个港口。截至2018年年底，全省新批对外投资企业2 594家，中国肯尼亚经贸合作园、柬埔寨中柬工业园、越南福东工业园等9个境外经贸合作园区纳入商务部境外经贸合作园统计。2018年福建与沿线国家进出口贸易额达3 946.2亿元，增长10.68%。

**上海。**上海正在制定对接“一带一路”建设规划。2016年2月，《上海市国民经济和社会发展第十三个五年规划纲要》指出，“十三五”时期，上海要着力加强“四个中心”与自贸试验区建设、“一带一路”和长江经济带等国家战略的深度结合。一是进一步推进国际金融中心建设，二是进一步推进国际航运中心建设，三是进一步推进国际贸易中心建设。

**天津。**针对“五通”，天津分别出台了《天津市人民政府和蒙古国交通运输发展部关于深化经贸合作谅解备忘录》《天津市推动落实〈中欧班列建设发展规划（2016—2020年）〉实施方案》《关于实施企业“走出去”战略促进对外投资合作健康有序发展行动方案（2017—2020年）》《天津市“走出去”企业海外投资保险统保平台三年工作方案（2018—2020年）》《关于推进我市职业院校在海外设立“鲁班工坊”试点方案》《天津市“一带一路”科技创新合作行动计划（2017—2020年）》。目前天津已开通21世纪海上丝绸之路集装箱班轮航线超过40条，涉及沿线国家40多个港口。

**广东。**2015年6月，发布《广东省参与建设“一带一路”的实施方案》，提出九大领域的合作设想，即九项重点任务，分别是促进重要基础设施互联互通、提升对外贸易合作水平、加快产业投资步伐、推进海洋领域合作、推动能源合作发展、拓展金融业务合作、提高旅游合作水平、密切人文交流合作、健全外事交流机制。为切实推进方案实施，制定了《广东省参与“一带一路”建设重点工作方案（2015—2017年）》，一共40项工作，以及《广东省参与“一带一路”建设实施方案优先推进项目清单》，一共有68个项目，总投资达550多亿美元，涵盖了基础设施建设、能源资源、农业、渔业、制造业、服务业六个领域。

**浙江。**2016年10月，《浙江省开放型经济发展“十三五”规划》通过，提出推进舟山航空口岸开放和波音项目建设，成为国家“一带一路”建设的重要战略支点；打造以金华—义乌为重点，连接“一带一路”的战略支点；创建以温台为龙头的民企民资参与“一带一路”建设先行区；建设一批“一带一路”沿线国家的农林渔合作开发地。以“一带一路”沿线国家主要节点城市和港口为重点，推动浙江企业依托大型投资项目在境外布局建设一批经贸合作区。

**海南。**2015年3月，海南代表团向第十二届全国人大三次会议提交《关于支持海南在国家21世纪海上丝绸之路战略中更好地发挥桥头堡作用的建议》，提出将海南打造成“21世纪海上丝绸之路”的重要战略支点，承担起海上丝路桥头堡的作用。2016年3月，《海南省国民经济和社会发展第十三个五年规划纲要》中提出全面融入国家“一带一路”倡议，推动海南与沿线国家和地区港口、航空交通基础设施互联互通，推进临港经济区、临空经济区建设，致力于将海南打造成“一带一路”国际交流合作大平台、海洋发展合作示范区、中国（海南）-东盟优势产业合作示范区。

**江苏。**2015年印发《江苏省参与“一带一路”建设行动计划》，2016年印发《江苏省推进国际产能和装备制造合作三年行动计划（2016—2018）》，2017年印发《江苏省中欧班列建设发展实施方案》，2018年印发《江苏省委省政府关于高质量推进“一带一路”交汇点建设的意见》。江苏省以深化国际产能合作为重点，积极探索“重资产投资运营”和“轻资产管理输出”境外园区建设新路径新模式。江苏省2018年对“一带一路”沿线国家进出口占全国的11.6%。累计开行中欧（亚）班列5 434列，形成“连新亚”“苏满欧”“宁亚”“宁欧”等线路。值得一提的是，江苏省2017年7月就成立了江苏“一带一路”投资基金，首期基金规模30亿元。2015年年底建立了“走出去”政治风险统保平台，截至2018年年底，平台共承保项目482个，承保金额134.17亿美元。

**湖南。**2015年8月，《湖南省对接“一带一路”战略行动方案（2015—2017年）》出台，提出以长沙为节点城市，以重点区域、重大项目、重点平台、重要机制建设为依托，以提升全面开放水平、扩展经贸合作领域、扩大人文交流为重点，着力实施“六大行动”（装备产能出海行动、对外贸易提升行动、引资引技升级行动、基础设施联通行动、合作平台构筑行动、人文交流拓展行动），完善“五大机制”（项目推进机制、金融财税扶持机制、人才保障机制、风险防控机制，工作协调机制），建设80个左右的重大项目，总投资3 000多亿元，将湖南打造成“一带一路”的重要腹地和内陆开放的新高地。2015年湖南省又密集出台《湖南省参与建设丝绸之路经济带和21世纪海上丝绸之路的实施方案》《推进国际产能和装备制造合作的实施意见》《湖南省对接“一带一路”战略推动优势企业“走出去”实施方案》；2017年印发《关于加快推进国际产能合作的意见》《湖南省推进国际产能和装备制造合作三年行动计划（2018—2020年）》《关于大力实施创新引领开放崛起战略的若干意见》；2018印发《关于加快推进开放崛起专项行动的通知》。截至2018年年底，中欧班列（长沙）累计发运494列。湖南省对沿线国家进出口从2013年的344.2亿元增长到2018年的802.6亿元。截至2018年，湖南省对外承包工程累计营业额170.57亿美元。巴基斯坦卡拉奇—拉合尔高速公路项目就是湖南省与巴基斯坦签署的路桥重点工程。湖南省也成立了“一带一路”产业促进基金，规模200亿元。

**湖北。**湖北省对接“一带一路”倡议分别出台了《湖北省参与建设丝绸之路经济带和21世纪海上丝绸之路的实施方案》《湖北省深度融入“一带一路”建设重点任务分工方案》《中欧班列（武汉）建设发展规划（2016—2020年）》《标准联通“一带一路”湖北行动计划（2018—2020年）》等政策措施。2018年中欧班列（武汉）共计发运423列。江海联运五年累计开行近400个班次。湖北省对沿线国家进出口总值从2013年的100.5亿美元增长到2018年的124.4亿美元，对沿线国家开展工程项目营业额从2013年的34.3亿美元增长到2018年的46.1亿美元。湖北省建设了哈萨克斯坦湖北工业园区、伊朗北斗科技园、中国比利时科技园、莫桑比克农业产业园等境外产业园区。

**江西。**2015年5月，《江西省参与丝绸之路经济带和21世纪海上丝绸之路建设实施方案》出台，提出要依托国内国际大通道，重点谋划三大战略走向，突出重点区域，体现江西特色，发挥地方优势，畅通陆上通道，连接海上通道，构建空中走廊，拓宽数字通道，融入“一带一路”建设。

**山东。**2015年出台参与建设“一带一路”实施方案，2016年出台关于稳定外贸增长的意见，2017年出台推进国际产能合作的实施意见，2018年出台推动全省欧亚班列统筹发展的意见和融入“一带一路”大战略齐鲁丝路行的意见。

2018年实现了全省欧亚班列统一运营，全年共开行“齐鲁号”欧亚班列369列，累计开行欧亚班列1 100余列。山东省在引导优势产能和高端装备走出去方面成效显著，2014—2018年在沿线国家完成对外承包工程营业额超过2 000亿元。山东省目前有13个境外经贸合作区。

**河南。**2015年发布《河南省参与建设丝绸之路经济带和21世纪海上丝绸之路实施方案》，2016年发布《河南省参与建设“一带一路”工作领导小组主要职责和议事规则》，2017年印发《郑州—卢森堡“空中丝绸之路”建设专项规划（2017—2025年）和工作方案》，2018年印发《郑州国际航空货运枢纽战略规划》。河南省提出“空中丝绸之路”，把提升交通物流枢纽功能作为突破口，以郑州—卢森堡“空中丝绸之路”建设为引领，统筹推进空中、陆上、网上、海上丝绸之路“四路协同”，走出一条内陆地区开放型经济发展的新路子。河南省按照比较优势和资源禀赋推动产业国际化布局，不断扩大电子、汽车装备制造出口规模，积极进口先进设备和能源资源，构建“优进优出”贸易发展格局。郑州机场在全球前20位货运枢纽机场中开通15个航点，国际枢纽航线网络初步形成；中欧班列（郑州）在境外形成覆盖24个国家126个城市的集疏网络，中欧班列累计开行超过2 000列，郑州机场已开通56条国际地区客货航运线。河南省对沿线国家进出口从2013年的104.4亿美元增长到2018年的176.8亿美元；利用沿线国家外资从2014年的6.31亿美元增长到2018年的11.7亿美元；截至2018年，对外承包工程累计营业额86.2亿美元。目前，郑州航空港经济综合实验区年产手机近3亿部，基本建成全球重要的智能手机生产制造基地和国际货物集散分拨中心。河南自贸试验区入驻企业已超过5万家。河南已建成5个海关特殊监管区域和9个功能性口岸，成为内陆地区指定口岸数量最多、功能最全的省份。

# 第10章

# 世界经济的繁荣稳定包容之路①

① 本章可以看成是全书总结性的政策建议和对世界经济繁荣稳定的期待，更详细的政策建议请参见《新结构经济学》《从西潮到东风》《繁荣的求索》《超越发展援助》和《战胜命运》等著作中关于政策建议部分的论述。

## 10.1

## 战胜命运

本书的第一作者林毅夫于第二次世界大战结束不久后的20世纪50年代初期生于中国台湾，当时的中国台湾像多数非洲国家一样贫穷落后。本书的第二作者付才辉生于20世纪80年代中期的中国四川省，此时的中国大陆与本书第一作者出生时的中国台湾一样贫穷落后，而这时的中国台湾已经成长为一个新兴工业化经济体，后被誉为亚洲“四小龙”之一。2008年，中国大陆的经济已奇迹般地实现了像中国台湾那样的腾飞。本书第一作者也成为第一位来自发展中国家的世界银行首席经济学家。世界经济格局在短短40年间发生剧变（回顾第1章）。如此梦幻般的经历让我们确信贫困并非宿命。一个国家即便深陷贫困陷阱的泥沼长达数个世纪，也能够骤然改变命运，踏上快速发展转型之路，在一两代人之间摆脱贫困，实现工业化、现代化。[①]

就在40多年前，中国要比撒哈拉以南非洲的大多数国家穷得多，人均GDP仅有156美元（1978年），不足撒哈拉以南非洲国家平均值（492美元）的1/3（31.83%）。1985年，中国人均GDP（295美元）也只与埃塞俄比亚（232美元）和卢旺达（280美元）相当。到1990年，中国仍然是低收入国家，以购买力平价计算的人均收入比撒哈拉以南非洲国家平均值低30%。但时至今日（2019年），中国已经是中等收入国家，人均GDP超过10 000美元，是撒哈拉以南非洲国家平均值的5倍多。中国占全球GDP中的比重接近16%，成为仅次于美国的第二大经济体。这个13亿人口的大国并没有多余的石油、可可、咖啡、棉花、木材、钻石或铀矿可供出口，却取得了惊人的发展成就。中国在过去40多年快速增长得益于融入世界经济迅速而持续的经济结构转型升级。在1978年启动经济改革时，中国还主要是个体农业经济体。即便到1990年，中国仍然有74%的人口居住在农村，初级产品在GDP中的比重占到27%。到2009年，这些数据分别下降到53%和11%。中国的出口产品结构也出现了类似的变化，1990年，初级产品在商品出口中占很大比重，到2009年中国成为世界第一出口大国时，95%以上的出口是制造品。中国在过去40多年取得的巨大成就来自严格执行务实的经济发展与转型战略，该战略从劳动密集型产业开始，逐级而上，向资本密集型产业升级，每

① 林毅夫，《新结构经济学》序言，北京大学出版社，2014年版。

个发展过程都基于中国自身的要素禀赋结构所决定的比较优势。中国从计划经济向市场经济的转型采取的是两方面策略：第一，采取双轨制改革办法，在维持稳定的同时实现有活力的转型，给转型前建立的不符合比较优势的资本密集型老产业部门中缺乏自生能力的国有企业提供转型期保护，同时放开转型前受到抑制的符合比较优势的劳动力密集型产业的进入，并且以工业园、招商引资等局部性、针对性措施消除软硬基础设施的瓶颈因势利导其发展；第二，作为后进国家，在放开准入的部门中国选取的经济发展战略充分利用了沿着雁行模式道路前进的后来者优势（回顾第4章）。[①]与此相反，绝大多数发展中经济体在第二次世界大战后采取违背比较优势的赶超战略，结果适得其反，欲速而不达，反而造成了经济结构根深蒂固的扭曲，为可持续的结构转型升级埋下隐患，在转型期政府则既取消了对原来赶超部门的保护补贴导致经济崩溃，也放弃了对新的符合比较优势部门的因势利导，而难于出现新的有竞争力的产业（回顾第2章到第5章）。

在全球产业周期变化背景下，每个不同发展水平的经济体都可以识别其面临的全球产业窗口机遇期（回顾第6章），通过政府因势利导消除限制新的符合比较优势的产业变成竞争优势的软硬基础设施"瓶颈"（回顾第7章），承接符合禀赋结构决定的潜在比较优势的产业转移，充分利用后来者优势，迅速走上持续的经济发展之路。以中国为例，在1979年向市场经济转型时，营商环境差，基础设施落后，投资环境糟糕。按照"华盛顿共识"的建议，应该一步到位，而不应该优先支持特定部门和地区。相反，中国政府动员了其有限的资源和实施能力建立了特定地域范围内的经济特区和工业园区。在经济特区和工业园区内部，基础设施"瓶颈"得以缓解，营商环境也变得富有竞争力。在转型初期，虽然中国有低成本的劳动力，但是缺乏利用这个优势生产具有合乎国际市场所需质量的劳动力密集型出口产品的知识。为了克服这些困难，中国各个地区的各级政府四处寻求海外拥有生产及管理技术和国外销售渠道的投资者，鼓励他们在经济特区和工业园区内投资。采用这种办法，中国迅速建立起了劳动力密集型的轻工业，成为"世界工厂"，进而拥有了改变世界经济格局的力量（回顾第8章）。同时，在局部地区取得的成功为政府积累了越来越多的资金和经验，为改善经济特区、工业园区等先行区域之外的地方的基础设施和消除扭曲提供了资源和条件，进而在更大范围内进行经济结构转型升级。这不仅是中国，而且也是东亚其他经济体发展成功的奥秘（回顾第4章）。中国的快速成功不但是对经济学理论本身的重构，而且对世界经济的发展思路和发展机会都将产生深远影响（回顾第1章、第8章及第9章）。[②]

---

① 关于中国经济更详细的内容请进一步参见：林毅夫，《解读中国经济》，北京大学出版社，2018年版。

② 可参见国际知名学术出版商Taylor & Francis于2017年3月在其官方网站上报道的林毅夫发表在*Area Development and Policy*上的文章"The Rise of China and Its Implications for Economics and Other Developing Countries"。

## 10.2

## —

## 发展没有前提条件但理论和政策有[①]

2017年3月，中国颇具声望的媒体《财经》杂志在对林毅夫的一次专访[②]中开门见山地问道："第二次世界大战结束以后，发展经济，实现现代化，成为发展中国家自身的主要任务，发达国家也给予各种援助，但是在整体和平的70余年里，为什么真正成功地从低收入国家、中等收入国家迈入高收入国家行列的为数极少？发展经济学应该如何反思？"林毅夫一针见血地回答道："确实，到目前为止，只有韩国和中国台湾两个经济体从低收入迈入到高收入，中国大陆则有可能在2025年前后成为第三个；1960年时的101个中等收入经济体，到2008年时也只有13个跨过门槛成为高收入经济体，其中8个是原本收入差距就不大的西欧周边国家或石油生产国，另外5个是日本和亚洲'四小龙'。绝大多数发展中国家没有缩小和发达国家的差距。但是，从我在世界银行工作期间访问许多发展中国家时的观察，不是这些国家的国民不努力，也不是这些国家的领导人不希望国家繁荣。问题是，迄今为止这些国家在西方主流理论的指引下和国际发展机构的帮助下所制定的政策都未能使得它们走向繁荣。相反，少数几个比较成功的国家或地区，当初主流理论认为它们推行的政策是错误的。原因在于这些主流理论来自于发达国家，以发达国家作参照系。第二次世界大战结束以后，大部分发展中国家摆脱了殖民统治，在第一代领导人的领导下追求现代化，冀图民富国强。怎么才能民富？当时的主流经济理论认为，要和发达国家的人民一样富，劳动生产力水平就需跟发达国家一样高，产业技术必须处于同一水平。怎么才能国强？国防产业必须跟发达国家一样先进。于是，发展中国家努力去建设和发达国家相同的先进产业，实行'进口替代'政策。问题是，先进产业都是资本密集型的，发展中国家的最大短板就是资本短缺。用'田忌赛马'的故事作比喻，就相当于用自己的'下马'跟人家的'上马'赛跑，肯定会输。在开放竞争的市场上这种产业不能靠市场的力量自发产生，只能靠政府的各种以扭

---

① Lin Justin Yifu, Célestin Monga, *Beating the Odds: Jump-Starting Developing Countries*, Princeton University Press, 2017.

② 马国川，"专访林毅夫：新结构经济学更有力量"，《财经》，2017年3月20日。

曲市场价格信号和直接干预资源配置为代价的保护、补贴才能建立起来。从理论上看，实行进口替代似乎天经地义，实践却失败了。遗憾的是，即使到今天许多发展中国家的知识精英还受到这种思路的影响，老跟着发达国家发展自己没有比较优势的先进产业。20世纪80年代以后，主流理论变成了新自由主义。发展中国家为什么搞不好？新自由主义认为，是因为没有发达国家的完善市场制度、先进治理体系，国家干预太多，造成了许多扭曲。于是实行私有化、市场化、自由化，想通过'休克疗法'来消除在推行进口替代战略时形成的各种干预、扭曲。从内部逻辑来看，有扭曲就会有资源错配和寻租，经济绩效就会低；从事实来看，转型中国家经济发展不好，普遍存在扭曲、资源错配和寻租的问题。所以，这个理论也很有说服力，很容易为每个人的直觉所接受。但是这些落后和扭曲有内生性，发展中国家的许多制度和发达国家比看起来是落后的，但是，经济基础决定上层建筑，在发展中国家那些看似落后的制度，在发展中国家的条件下却是有效的。例如，发展早期农村偏远地区的集市贸易，隔三差五才有一次市场交易，和发达国家城市里每天都有交易的超市、百货公司相比看似落后，但是，在经济交易量很低的农村，这种集市贸易却是有效的制度安排。同样，转型中国家存在的许多扭曲是为了保护补贴进口替代战略下建立起来的违反比较优势产业中缺乏自生能力企业的需要而存在的，仅仅去除表面的落后和扭曲是不够的。例如，以前违反比较优势建立起来的产业，一旦取消保护补贴，企业就会垮台，造成大量人员失业，国防安全也可能受到威胁。世界银行和欧洲开发银行的大量实证研究证明，在苏联、东欧转型国家私有化以后，为了让那些违反比较优势的大型企业继续生存以维持社会稳定和保障国防安全，政府给予的保护补贴反而比原来更多，但效率更低。还有，转型以后，一切都由市场来解决。但是经济发展必须不断有新产业出现，新产业必须要有先行者，先行者是否成功除了企业家的努力，还取决于软硬基础设施是否合适。事实上市场不能解决这些问题。例如，南美洲的智利在20世纪70年代推行'华盛顿共识'以后，各种扭曲消除得很彻底，被称为是'华盛顿共识'的模范生。但是，旧的产业垮台了，新的产业如果没有合适的软硬基础设施，交易费用会太高，在开放的市场中没有竞争力，也不会自发涌现。软硬基础设施的完善需要政府协调不同企业来投资，或是政府自己来做，市场解决不了这些问题。所以，智利在过去30多年，新的产业一直没有成长起来，失业问题严重，收入差距扩大，一直没有缩小和美国的差距。特别是从计划经济向市场经济转型的国家，主流理论认为，必须全面进行私有化、市场化、自由化，一次性把所有扭曲取消掉。但是这样做的国家经济基本都崩溃了，增长停滞，危机不断，少数几个比较成功的，如中国、越南、柬埔寨，推行的都是渐进式改革。在东欧国家中表现最好的两个国家——波兰和斯洛文尼亚，在苏联国家中表现最好的两个国家——乌兹别克斯坦和白俄罗斯，大型国有企业也一直没有私有化。当时，主流学界认为这种渐进的'双轨制'改革，继续以扭曲来保护旧的产业，同时放开对新产业的市场准入，结果会比原来的计划经济还糟。但是，这些推行最糟转型方式的国家经济表现反而最好。”

来自西方主流的这些理论听起来头头是道，可惜，都没有帮助发展中国家实现民富国强，而且，发展中国家和发达国家的差距反而越来越大。任何理论的成立都有明的和暗的前提条件，如果前提条件不同，即使理论本身的逻辑很严谨，按理论来做政策也必然会有“淮南为橘，淮北为枳”的问题。所以，在运用一个理论时，必须把理论中明的和暗的前提条件弄清楚，确定这些条件在现实中是否存在，而不能因为运用某个理论没有达到预期的效果就说是“歪嘴和尚念错经”。发展中国家按发达国家的经来念基本是没有成功的，总不能说发展中国家的和尚都嘴歪吧？另外，也有少数成功的国家念的却被认为是“错”的经。那么，到底是和尚嘴歪，还是经错了？

自然科学的理论一向是如果按照理论的要求去做，必然能够获得理论所预期的结果，否则这样的理论是不会被接受的。社会科学的理论也应该是这样。最近，林毅夫提出“唯成乃真知”，倡导“知成一体”。经济学作为一门社会科学，其目的是帮助人们“认识世界、改造世界”，如果按照理论的认识去做，不能得到理论所预期的结果，那一定是理论有问题。一个理论在发展中国家实践，不能带来理论所预期的效果，那么很有可能是理论本身就没有把发展中国家的问题和条件认识清楚。现在的经济学主流理论主要是总结于发达国家的经验现象，其明的前提条件是按发达国家的情况来设定的，并且，还暗含了发达国家的法律社会等条件，而发展中国家的条件和发达国家并不一样。由于前提条件不一样，把经济学的主流理论应用于发展中国家，怎么会得到理论所预期的效果？更何况，发达国家的条件也总是在变，理论也跟着在变，所以如果发达国家的理论在发达国家都不一定适用，在发展中国家怎么能够保证适用呢？这同“鞋子不合脚，不能削足适履，该换的是鞋子”是一个道理。因此，理论的作用在于帮助人们“认识世界、改造世界”，如果原来的理论不适用，那就应该进行理论创新，深入了解所要解决的问题的性质和背后的原因，提出新的理论。总结于发达国家的主流理论不适用于发展中国家，要理论适用于发展中国家必须从发展中国家的经验和教训出发，总结发展中国家各种问题和现象背后的因果逻辑，提出新的理论体系，将其作为发展中国家解决问题的参照系，这样成功的概率才会比较高。新结构经济学就是这样的一种努力。

与西方主流发展思潮不同，新结构经济学主张应该从每个发展中国家或经济体现在有什么（即其要素禀赋）出发，规划在此基础上能做好什么（即其比较优势），把现在能做好的做大做强，以此实现逐步赶上甚至超越发达国家的目标。不论基础设施和营商环境天生多么糟糕，任何发展中国家都可以即刻走上动态持续的经济结构转型升级推动增长之路。发展中国家的政府必须采取务实的方法，利用其有限的资源和实施能力来推动具有比较优势行业的技术创新和发展，这样才能保持相对较低的生产要素成本。为了降低企业的交易成本，政府可以创建具有良好基础设施和营商环境的工业园区或经济特区。这就是在新结构经济学的思想和思路下如何填补第6章所测算的每个经济体符合潜在比较优势的产业缺口，以及如何消除第7章所测算的制约潜在比较优势产业发展的基础设施瓶颈的方法。

按照新结构经济学的基本原理，一个国家或者地区经济发展的本质是人均收入和生活水平的不断提高，其前提则是越来越高的劳动生产率水平。劳动生产率水平的提高有两个途径：一是通过技术创新，提高现有产业中产品的质量和生产效率（产业内升级）；二是通过产业升级，将现有劳动力、土地、资本等生产要素配置到附加价值更高的产业（产业间升级）。根据新结构经济学的分析，这两者的实现需要有"有效的市场"和"有为的政府"的共同作用。在理论上讲，"市场有效以政府有为为前提，政府有为以市场有效为依托"。

"有效的市场"的重要性在于，引导企业家按照要素禀赋结构所决定的比较优势来选择技术和产业，生产出来的产品在国内国际市场的同类产品中，要素生产成本才会最低，如果同时有合适的软硬基础设施，交易成本也会低，这样就会最有竞争力，企业才可能获得最大利润，整个经济才有机会创造最大的剩余和资本积累，使得比较优势从劳动力密集或自然资源密集逐渐向资本密集提升，为现有产业、技术升级到资本更为密集、附加价值更高的新产业、新技术提供物质基础。企业家会按照要素禀赋所决定的比较优势来选择产业和技术的前提，是必须有一个能够很好地反映各种要素相对稀缺性的价格体系。如果有这样的价格体系，企业为了自己的利润和竞争力，就会按照要素禀赋所决定的比较优势来选择合适的技术和产业，这种价格体系只有在充分竞争的市场中才会存在。所以，新结构经济学主张，一个经济体要发展好，必须要有一个"有效的市场"。

然而，由于经济发展不是静态的资源最优配置，而是一个技术不断创新、产业不断升级，以及硬的基础设施和软的制度环境不断完善的结构变迁过程，在这个过程中必须对技术创新和产业升级的先行者给予外部性的补偿，以及根据新的产业的需要协调相应的软硬基础设施的完善，这些工作仅能由政府来做，所以必须要有一个"有为的政府"，经济结构才能顺利按照要素禀赋结构和比较优势的变化变动。因此，"有效的市场"和"有为的政府"是经济快速可持续发展的两个最重要的制度前提。

尽管市场机制如此重要，在发展过程中，政府仍应积极主动发挥作用，为产业升级和多样化提供便利。首先，做出产业升级和多样化的决定从来不是一个显而易见的选择。一个先驱企业可能因为新产业缺乏互补的生产要素或足够的基础设施而失败，又或者仅仅因为目标产业与本国经济的比较优势不相符而不能成功。因此，产业升级和经济多样化可能更像是一个高代价的"试错练习"，即使这个试错练习具有后来者优势。为了在竞争性市场上取得成功，发展中国家的企业需要如下信息：处于全球产业前沿内的哪些产业与本国的潜在比较优势相符。这个信息具有与公共品一样的性质，信息的收集和处理成本是巨大的。然而，信息一旦形成，允许一个企业分享既得信息的边际成本就为零。因此，政府可通过投资于信息的收集和处理，利用将有关新兴产业的信息免费提供给企业等方式来为企业提供便利。另外，新产业的选择还可能以路径依赖的方式，通过特定的人力资本和社会资本的积累，来塑造未来的经济增长潜力。当然，在分析这些信息并将信息告知公众方面，政府肯定比各个私营企业做得更好。

其次，技术创新、产业多样化和产业升级通常伴随着对企业资本和技能的要求而变化，也伴随着市场范围和它们对基础设施的需求而变化，而后者是由在此过程中生产活动所体现的演进性质所决定的。换句话说，产业升级和多样化通常伴随着对软硬基础设施的要求而变化。例如，在经济发展过程中，随着从农业到制造业、从简单制造业到高级制造业的变迁，一国的生产规模和市场范围越来越大，对运输和电力的需求也越来越大。单个企业无力内部化这些设施的提供，也难以统筹不同部门间企业的协作来满足这些持续增长的需求。即使一些大企业愿意为该国的公路或电网建设提供资金，为确保一致性、效率，并防止随着经济增长可能出现的自然垄断，政府协调也是必要的。在低收入国家，小规模、劳动力密集型的农业和制造业，除了硬件基础设施，企业不需要劳动力有多么熟练、融资和市场体系有多么成熟，但是，当经济发展到现代制造业的阶段，企业就需要高技能的劳动力、一次性设备投资所需的巨额资金、流动资本和出口融资，以及新的市场规划了。然而，很多单个企业无力内部化所需的软件基础设施的变化。这就又需要政府来提供或者协调这些经济部门的变化，从而为单个企业的升级和多样化提供便利。

最后，创新是产业升级和多样化进程的基础，但它本质上是一个非常冒险的行为。即便政府愿意并能够提供必要的信息和协调来帮助企业，仍不能保证企业一定成功。企业可能因为目标产业太过先进或市场太小，又或是供应链的瓶颈，软硬基础设施不完善而失败。但即使是这些失败的案例，也会给其他企业提供有用的信息，表明该目标产业是不合适的，应重新审视。因此，先驱企业付出的失败代价，也可以为其他企业提供有价值的信息。而如果它们成功了，那么它们的经历更是向其他企业提供了信息外部性，证明新产业与经济新的比较优势相一致，进而激励更多新企业进入该产业。然而，随着大量新企业的进入，先驱企业可能享有的租金就会被消除。从单个企业的角度来看，成为先驱企业的动力是被抑制的，因为失败的成本太高，而成功的优势有限，二者是不对称的。除非能对先驱企业所创造的信息外部性进行补偿，否则鲜有企业有动力去成为先驱企业。最终，产业的升级和多样化及经济增长的步伐就会受到阻碍。在处于全球产业前沿的发达国家中，成功的先行者通常被授予专利，使之在一段时间内享有创新所带来的垄断租金。对于发展中国家来说，新产业很可能是处于全球产业前沿之内的一个成熟产业。从而先驱企业难以因为先进入新产业而获得专利。因此，政府对甘愿冒险进入新产业的先驱企业做出一些激励是正当合理的。

发达国家的产业处于全球前沿上，其产业升级和多样化依赖于自身通过试错过程所创造的新知识。相比之下，处于赶超过程的发展中国家处于全球产业前沿内部，具有后来者优势。换句话说，发展中国家可以借鉴发达国家的现有技术和产业来进行产业升级和多样化。这种方法比发达国家企业所用的方法成本更低、风险更小。因此，在一个致力于建设市场体制的发展中国家中，如果企业知道如何利用后来者优势的潜力，而且政府又积极主动地在产业升级和多样化过程中提供信息、协调和外部性补偿，那么该国的增长速度就可以比发达国家快得多，达到与高收入国家趋近的目标。实际上，18世纪前的英国，19世纪的德国、法国和美国，20世纪的北欧国家、日本、韩国、新加坡、马来西亚、中国台湾和东南亚其他经济体都是这样发展起来的。

## 10.3
## –
## 繁荣之路可操作的因势利导方法①

按照新结构经济学的上述理论，在有效的市场中，政府必须发挥有为的作用，来克服在经济转型升级中的外部性和协调的问题。政府的资源和执行能力是有限的。按照“华盛顿共识”及新自由主义的看法，政府应该把全国的基础设施都建设好，把全国的各种法制、营商环境都完善好，不应该对任何地区或产业有偏向，并认为把这些工作做好了，新产业和新技术就会自发地涌现。这种想法的意愿是好的，但是有一个问题，发展中国家基础设施普遍不好，要把全国的基础设施都完善，有那么多资源吗？如果没有那么多资源，就必须按毛泽东所讲的，集中优势兵力打歼灭战，按对经济发展可做出最大贡献的产业发展的需要，把一个

① 通俗而翔实的完整介绍可细读：林毅夫，《繁荣的求索》，北京大学出版社，2012年版（英文版Lin Justin Yifu, *The Quest for Prosperity: How Developing Economies Can Take Off*, Princeton University Press, 2012）。

局部区域搞好，降低其交易费用，那个局部区域的经济就能够快速发展，然后，星星之火可以燎原，从一点发展，带动全面发展，这是个很实事求是的哲学思想（回顾第7章）。

这种策略性地使用资源的方式，必须了解要发展什么产业，这些产业所需要的软硬基础设施有哪些，在哪里建立工业园区合适。这种针对特定产业在特定地区提供因势利导措施的举措就是所谓的产业政策。从历史经验来看，没有不用产业政策而取得成功的国家，也没有不用产业政策而维持领先的国家，而更多的是，实行产业政策失败的国家。为什么会这样？我们发现绝大多数产业政策失败是因为违反了比较优势。违反比较优势有两种可能性：一是，发展中国家违反比较优势，通常是过度赶超，想在资本极端短缺的情况下去和发达国家直接竞争，发展资本或技术密集型产业。二是，发达国家的产业政策失败的原因正好是相反的，有些产业已经失掉比较优势了，如农业或一些加工业，但是为了维持就业，还给它很多支持，像在欧盟，每头奶牛每天政府补贴2欧元。这两者都是违反比较优势的表现。违反比较优势的结果会怎么样？企业在开放竞争的市场中没有自生能力，就必须给予保护补贴。一给予保护补贴，就导致两个结果：一个是资源错误配置，另一个是寻租腐败。在这种状况下，产业政策当然会失败。从新结构经济学的角度来看，产业政策若想取得成功，就要帮助企业进入到一个要素生产成本比较低的产业，也就是从要素禀赋结构来看具有比较优势的产业。但国际上的竞争是总成本的竞争，总成本还包括交易成本。交易成本取决于交通基础设施、法治环境、金融服务等是否合适。如果不合适，交易成本会特别高。因此，即使这个产业是符合比较优势的，要素生产成本低，但交易成本太高，总成本也就太高，还是没有竞争力。这样的产业在新结构经济学中被称为具有潜在比较优势的产业。产业政策的目的是什么？就是把那些具有潜在比较优势，但因为交易成本太高，在国内外市场中还不具有竞争优势的产业，经由政府帮助改善基础设施和金融法治环境，把交易成本降低。如果能把交易成本降低，这个产业就能马上从具有潜在比较优势变成具有竞争优势，这是产业政策的目的。

在经济结构转型升级的过程中，如何在“有效的市场”环境中发挥“有为的政府”的作用，推动产业从中低端向中高端及将来从中高端向高端升级，实现可持续的中高速增长？不论是像第4章中所介绍的阿曼这样的微型经济体，还是像中国这样的中等收入发展中大国①，

① 中国是世界上人口最多的经济体，地区之间发展差异巨大，而且不同特征的产业门类众多，按照联合国统计署的产业分类，中国是唯一一个产业门类齐全的国家。

以及波兰这样的高收入转型经济体，[①]在具体产业发展战略上，按照每个经济体或地区、每个产业在全球的前沿距离及新技术的研发周期可将各个经济体的产业分成5种不同类型，政府因势利导的作用各有差异。

### 10.3.1 追赶型产业的因势利导方法

中国和其他中等收入增长极国家即将从低技能制造业向更高层次转型，这对贫穷国家来说是个宝贵机遇，包括撒哈拉以南的非洲国家（全球51个低收入国家中有37个位于该地区）。“一带一路”沿线与非洲等发展中国家需要通过紧紧抓住中国这个“领头龙”国家产业转移和产能合作的良机促进经济结构转型升级。如果各国的政策制定者能充分利用后来者优势，促进本国发展适合自身比较优势的产业，这将是完全可能实现的。增长甄别与因势利导工具（the Growth Identification and Facilitation Framework，GIFF）是新结构经济学的追赶型产业发展的应用工具，可以帮助发展中国家的政策制定者识别哪些产业拥有潜在的比较优势，并促进有竞争力的私人部门的发展。

以中国为例，在整个国家层面上而言，2019年中国的人均GDP虽然达到10 000美元，但是依然只有美国的15%、英国的22%、德国的20%、法国的23%、意大利的28%、加拿大的20%、日本的23%（回顾第1章和第8章）。这种人均GDP的差距反映的是劳动生产率水平的差距，代表中国现有产业的技术和附加值水平，比发达国家同类产业的水平低，处于追赶

---

① 2003年波兰的失业率一度高达20%，2004年后失业率开始有所下降，但至今仍在10%附近徘徊。因为与德国和美国的人均收入差距，有大量的波兰人去西欧国家寻找工作。这种情形跟20世纪80年代爱尔兰的情形非常像（参见专栏10.2）。2015年10月，波兰法律与公正党赢得大选,并重新组阁新政府，力图振兴波兰经济。欧洲深处债务危机泥潭，波兰执政者希望向东看，寻找波兰复兴的机会。波兰的人均GDP只有德国的三分之一、美国的四分之一，还处在追赶的过程中，经济发展、人均收入水平的提高是产业不断升级、人均劳动生产力水平不断提高的结果。新结构经济学的五种产业划分,对波兰的产业政策和发展计划有参考借鉴的价值。2016年2月16日，波兰副总理莫拉维茨基（后升任总理）代表政府推出被称为“莫氏计划”的“负责任发展规划”，自此之后波兰媒体多次以“莫拉维茨基和林毅夫”为标题发表评论文章。“莫氏计划”是法律与公正党领导的新一届政府为落实竞选时的承诺而制定的波兰未来经济发展目标及其实现路径的总体方案，反映了新一届政府将积极有为地推动经济发展，扶持具有比较优势的产业，采取适当政策，提升波兰产业竞争优势的“经济哲学”。在这一框架引导下，2017年波兰以欧盟10%的人口创造了欧盟70%的新增就业，是过去两年欧盟国家中创造就业最多、经济发展最好的国家。更详细的内容可参考：Lin Justin Yifu and Alojzy Z. Nowak, *New Structural Economics for Less Advanced Countries*, University of Warsaw Faculty of Management Press, 2017; Lin Justin Yifu and Alojzy Z. Nowak, *New Structural Policy in an Open Market Economy*, University of Warsaw Faculty of Management Press, 2018.

阶段。中国的汽车、高端装备业、高端材料即属于这种类型（回顾第8章专栏8.1）。对于追赶型产业，中国各地政府和金融机构可以在资金融通和外汇获取上支持所在地的合适企业，像吉利汽车、三一重工那样，到海外并购同类产业中拥有先进技术的企业，作为它们技术创新、产业升级的来源。发达国家自2008年的国际金融危机以来，经济发展乏力，很多拥有先进技术的企业经营不好，低价求售，出现了许多好的并购机会。在没有合适的并购机会时，各地政府也可以提供方便，支持所在地的企业像华为、中兴那样，到海外设立研发中心，直接利用国外的高端人才来推动技术创新。另外，各地政府也可以筛选中国每年从发达国家大量进口的高端制造业产品，根据其地区比较优势，创造这些产业所需的基础设施，改善营商环境，到海外招商引资，把那些高端制造业产品的生产企业吸引到国内来设厂生产。中国现在的GDP规模约占世界的16%，在新常态下，每年6.5%左右的增长意味着中国每年对世界的贡献可达到将近1个百分点，现在世界每年的经济增长在3% ~ 4%，也就是说，中国每年对世界市场容量扩张的贡献率达到30%左右。如果地方政府能够根据这些高端制造业的需要提供合适的基础设施、人才培训、营商和法治环境，国外许多高端生产企业，会有很高的积极性到国内设厂生产，以满足中国不断扩大的需求（回顾第8章），并以中国为基地生产供应世界各地的市场。江苏省太仓市的中德企业合作园区2012年被工信部授予“中德中小企业合作示范区”，到2014年年底吸引了220家德国企业入园，投资总额达20亿美元，就是一个很好的案例（回顾第8章的专栏8.2）。在中高端产业的招商引资上，中国仍处于大有作为的机遇期。因此，追赶型产业发展战略依然是中国各地目前最主要的战略选择，对于发展水平比中国低的国家更加毋庸赘言，发展水平比中国高的国家只要不是处于世界前沿也都适用，如前面提到的波兰及专栏10.2所介绍的爱尔兰。正因为如此，我们在后面以各个发展阶段的国家为例再做进一步的介绍。

新结构经济学为追赶型产业制定了操作性很强的增长甄别与因势利导工具（GIFF）——“两轨六步法”，如图10.1所示。下面做简要介绍：①

第一步：选择正确的目标经济体。政策制定者应该选择那些二三十年来增长强劲、与本国具有相似禀赋结构的经济体或地区作为目标。例如，发展中国家或地方的政府可以确定一份可贸易的产品和服务的清单。这些产品和服务应满足如下条件：人均收入高于本地区约100%，过去二三十年来高速增长国家中的商品，已超过10~20年的成熟的商品和服务。这些产品和服务部类或许能成为符合本地潜在比较优势的新产业。对于发展中地区实现产业升级和多样化并利用后发优势来说，这是最重要的原则。这是因为，在动态增长的经济中，工资

① 读者可下载本书附录的联合国工业发展组织（UNIDO）对GIFF的一个技术说明手册参考。

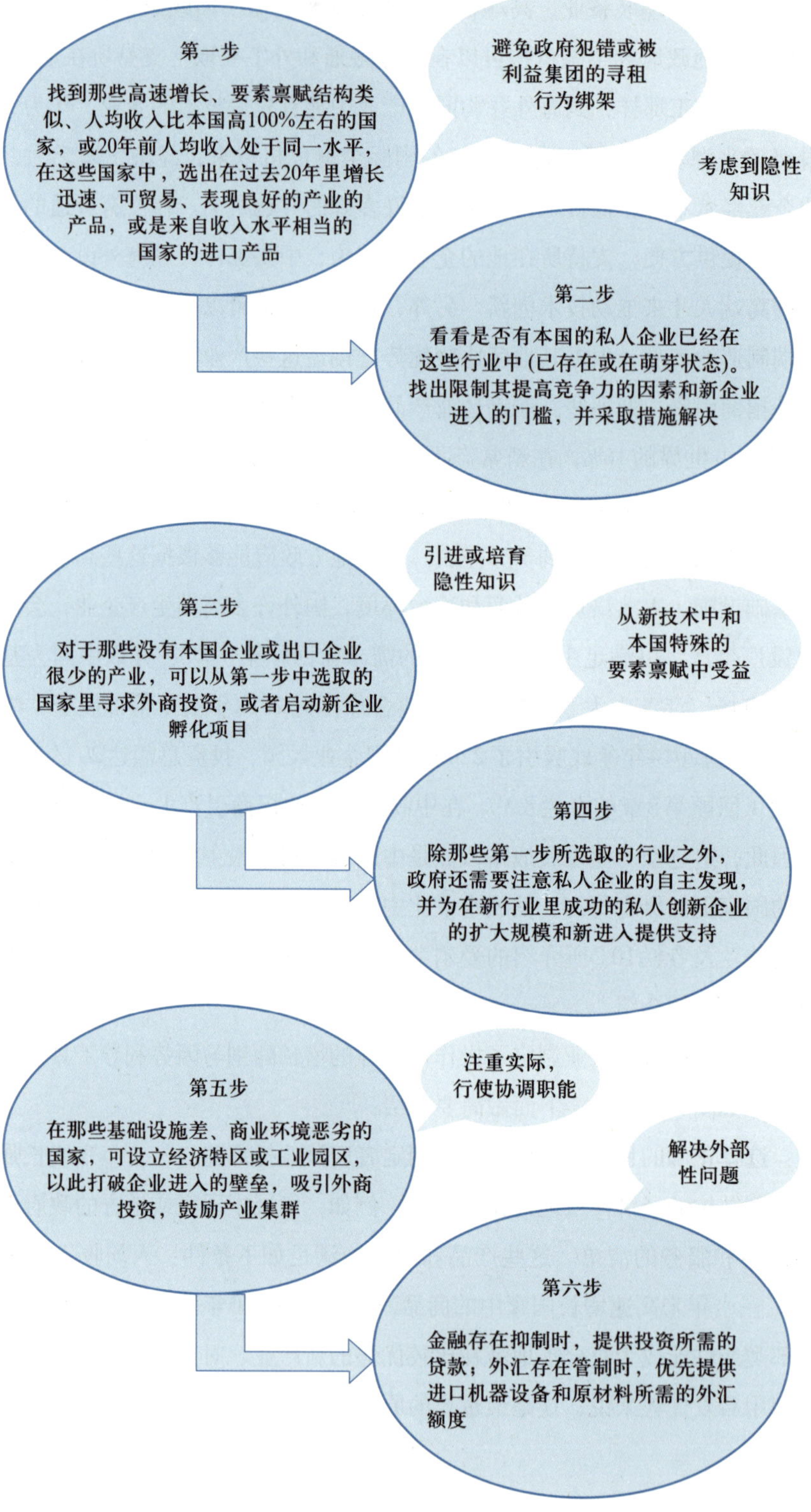


图10.1 追赶型产业的增长甄别与因势利导“两轨六步法”

率增长迅速，这就有可能导致该经济体生产多年的产业开始失去比较优势。因此，该产业就会在具有类似要素禀赋结构且工资较低的国家中具有潜在比较优势。该原则还意味着，当一国的收入水平达到最发达国家收入水平的50%时，它将越来越难以甄别可能符合其潜在比较优势的产业。因此，政府应该改为采用后面所要介绍的支持领先型产业发展的政策。

**第二步：协助解决当地已经进入上述所甄选出来的产品和服务的私人企业在提高产品质量和竞争力时所遇到的瓶颈障碍**。分析本地的私人企业在哪些产业已经比较活跃，并检查可能阻碍它们提升产品质量与提高效率或阻碍其他企业进入该产业的障碍。各国政府可以先在一些地区试点实施相应的政策以去除此类障碍，取得效果和经验后再推广到其他合适的地区。

**第三步：招商引资吸引外来投资者**。对于那些没有本国企业和出口企业很少的产业，鼓励上述作为参照系的国家生产此类产品的企业来投资，这些企业可能希望把生产向更低收入水平的国家或地区转移，降低劳动力成本。当地政府还可以实施孵化计划，来鼓励此类产业的创业活动。

**第四步：壮大本地优势产业**。除了第一步需要政府通过参照目标经济体甄别潜在的比较优势，每个国家都有一些特殊的禀赋，能生产出受国内国际市场欢迎的产品，同时，新技术也可能带来一些新的产品或服务，这两类不包括在第一步的机会清单中，因此，政府还需要关注本地私人企业的自我发现，帮助这些已经发现新商机的企业消除扩大规模的瓶颈障碍，以进一步做大做强。

**第五步：迅速搭建发展平台**。在一个基础设施落后、商业环境不佳的地区或国家,设立经济特区或产业园区以及其他平台来克服企业进入和外国投资的障碍。大多数低收入国家的政府由于预算和能力的限制不能在全国范围内提供良好的基础设施和营商环境，这些特区可以集中政府有限的资源，创造有利的商业环境，建立产业园区或特区还能促进产业集群的形成，进一步降低交易费用。(回顾第7章)

**第六步：为目标产业提供必要的激励**。给予目标产业的领先企业一定时限的税收优惠,在存在金融抑制时提供必要的信贷以支持投资,在存在外汇管制时给予必要的外汇额度以进口机器设备、原材料,以补偿市场领先者创造的外部性,并鼓励企业形成产业集群。由于通过鉴定的目标产业符合本地的比较优势，企业有自生能力，只要政府供合适的软硬基础设施，企业自己管理好，就应该在竞争的市场上有盈利。因此，这样的激励措施在时间和财务成本上应该是有限的。为防止出现寻租和政治俘获,政府还须避免采取可能导致垄断租金、高关税或其他扭曲的激励措施。

需要特别说明的是，上述“增长甄别与因势利导工具”不是完全由政府主导的政策工具，其融合了经济结构转型升级的基本原则，即“有效的市场”和“有为的政府”。GIFF的第一步“产业甄别”最重要的作用不仅仅是挑选符合本地区潜在比较优势的产业，更重要的是防止政府采取不切实际的“跨越式”赶超战略，避免政府太冒进，这是过去绝大多数发展中国家产业政策失败的原因，同时，也是为了避免企业以发展某种先进的产业为理由向政府寻租。第二步到第四步，是企业自己的选择，而不是政府指定的，政府只是有针对性地“顺水推舟”。

### 10.3.2 领先型产业的因势利导方法

对于像中国这样的中等偏上收入国家，它的有些产业，像白色家电、高铁、造船等，其产品和技术已经处于国际领先或已接近国际最高水平。这些领先型产业必须依靠自主研发新产品、新技术，才能继续保持国际领先地位。自主研发包括两种不同性质的活动：新产品、新技术的“开发”和新产品、新技术开发所需的“基础科研的突破”。企业开发的新产品、新技术可以申请专利，这类活动理当由企业自己来进行（图10.2展示了美国近一个世纪以来的专利数目变迁）。但是，基础科研不仅投入大、风险高，其产品是论文等，多数属于社会公共知识，企业一般没有从事这项工作的积极性。没有基础科研的突破，新产品、新技术的开放就将成为无源之水，所以，政府必须在基础科研上负主要责任。像美国这样的发达国家的产业，领先型产业的技术创新和产业升级所需的基础研究，绝大多数是由美国国家科学基金会资助高校或是由美国国家健康研究院、国防部、能源部等政府机构及其支持的科研机构来进行的（图10.3展示了近80年来美国的研发支出及其构成变迁），欧洲、日本等发达地区及国家也以政府的资金支持类似的机构来进行这方面的基础研究。例如，一项新近的实际研究显示，美国能源部设立的小企业研发创新补贴项目（SBIR）就起到了很好的效果。通过研发补贴提高了企业（特别是中小企业和初创企业）获得风险投资的概率，促进了企业创新产出（表现为高质量专利的增加）和创新成果转化（表现为企业营业收入的增加）。研发补贴也有助于企业良好的运营和存续。研发补贴对企业创新的影响通过资助企业进行新技术可行性实验，为企业提供“试错”的机会，降低研发的不确定性实现。[①]其实，美国早在1982年就通过了执行至今的《小企业创新发展法案》，并推出了面向中小企业的创新计划。它要求美国联邦政府研发经费超过1亿美元的部门，都要拿出一定比例的经费，来扶持中小企业的成果转化。[②]

① Sabrina T. Howell, “Financing Innovation: Evidence from R&D Grants”, *American Economic Review*, 2017, Vol.107, No.4, pp.1136–1164.

② 林雪萍、金东寒，“美国如何为技术创新‘端茶送水’？”，《瞭望》新闻周刊，2019年3月11日。

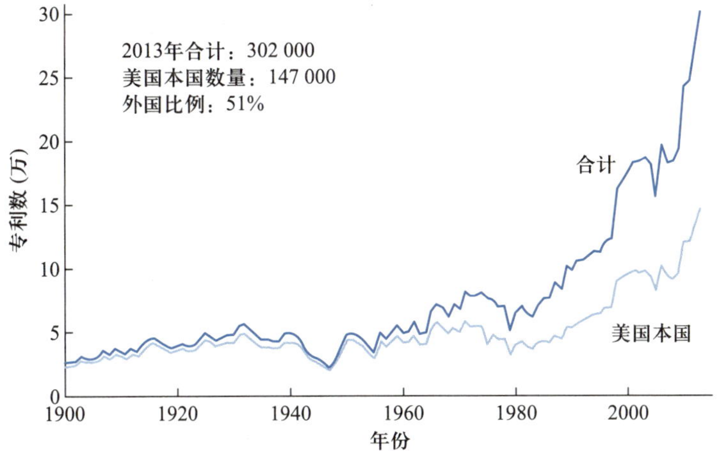


**图10.2 美国的专利数目**

资料来源：C. I. Jones, Chapter 1 - The Facts of Economic Growth, in John B. Taylor, Harald Uhlig eds., Handbook of Macroeconomics, Elsevier, 2016, Vol.2, pp.3-69.

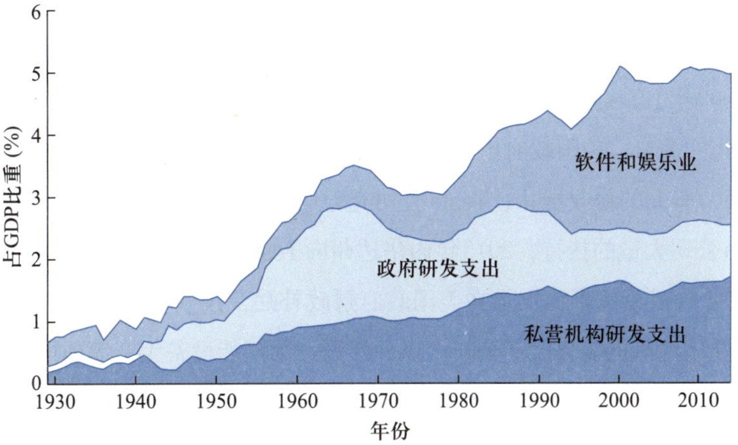


**图10.3 美国的研发支出及其构成**

资料来源：C. I. Jones, Chapter 1 - The Facts of Economic Growth, in John B. Taylor, Harald Uhlig eds., Handbook of Macroeconomics, Elsevier, 2016, Vol.2, pp.3-69.

在中国上海投资建立特斯拉工厂并在美国发射火箭的“科技明星”企业家马斯克相信大家并不陌生，然而对其商业帝国如何受益于美国产业政策的背后故事却鲜为人知。杨柯巍和张原最近就马斯克的发展做了细致的研究[①]，详情如下：马斯克旗下SpaceX、特斯拉（Tesla）、SolarCity三家公司，在发展过程中均获得了来自美国政府的大力支持。SpaceX公司在美国政府技术转移与政府采购扶持下渐成航天“巨兽”。作为全球唯一掌握了航天器发射回收技术的私营企业，目前SpaceX公司估值已超过200亿美元。在创业初期，SpaceX公司面临着关键技术短缺、市场需求不足和资金匮乏等诸多困难。美国国家航空航天局（NASA）和美国空军通过专利转让以及技术指导等方式，给予了SpaceX公司大量的技术扶持和转移，解决了其关键技术短缺的问题。例如，SpaceX公司的“猎鹰”系列火箭的发动机采用了“阿波罗”计划登月舱发动机的喷管技术。NASA也分别在2008年、2014年给予SpaceX公司价值16亿美元、26亿美元的合同，2017年又采购4次载人发射服务，以政府采购的方式解决了SpaceX公司市场需求不足和资金匮乏的问题。同样，在美国政府低成本融资、优惠税收等支持下，Tesla公司成为新能源汽车产业的“领头羊”。Tesla公司以独有的电池技术和自动驾驶技术，在汽车制造产业异军突起，引领新能源汽车产业发展，目前市值已高达500亿美元。同样，在能源革命的道路上高歌前行的Tesla，也曾遭遇资金短缺的发展“瓶颈”。2009年，Tesla公司获得了美国能源部4.65亿美元的低息贷款，以低成本融资渡过了资金最紧张的关口。美国政府出台新能源汽车的消费税收抵免政策，消费者购买新能源汽车可享受7 500美元的税收抵扣，Tesla公司充分运用税收优惠手段提升实际收益。州政府也给予了Tesla公司大量的扶持，2015年内华达州向Tesla公司提供了980公顷土地免费使用权及13亿美元税收减免优惠。也是在美国政府财政补贴及税收优惠支持下，SolarCity公司成为全美最大住宅太阳能装备生产公司。工厂建设、太阳能设备生产等前期巨大的投入，成为SolarCity公司面临的最大难题。2009—2011年，美国联邦政府通过可再生能源现金返还补贴政策，以财政资金给予SolarCity公司共计5.1亿美元补贴。同时，美国联邦政府还通过30%（2017年降至10%）的投资税收抵免，以及五年期加速折旧等税收优惠手段帮助SolarCity公司解决资金困境。另外，州政府也为SolarCity提供电价补贴、绿色电力及净计量电价等其他优惠政策。我们在第6章第6节提到的家喻户晓的苹果公司也如出一辙，美国类似的例子比比皆

① 更多内容可参考：杨柯巍、张原，“美国产业政策如何‘照亮’马斯克商业帝国？”，《瞭望》新闻周刊，2019年4月10日。

是。[①]除了美国，欧洲一些国家的创新政策也值得借鉴。例如，德国的研发支出与制造业增加值占GDP的比重多年来一致领先于其他发达国家（如表10.1所示），不过制造业比重领先程度远远超过研发支出比重的程度，这表明了其奇高的创新效率。德国也因此在经济竞争力与就业民生方面在发达国家中处于领先地位（可回顾第6章第6.4节的相关内容）。

表10.1 1997—2016年德国的研发支出比重与制造业比重在发达国家中的领先情况

（a）研发支出占GDP的比例（%）

| | 1997 | 1998 | 1999 | 2000 | 2001 | 2002 | 2003 | 2004 | 2005 | 2006 |
|---|---|---|---|---|---|---|---|---|---|---|
| 德国 | 2.18 | 2.21 | 2.33 | 2.39 | 2.39 | 2.42 | 2.46 | 2.42 | 2.42 | 2.46 |
| 高收入国家 | 2.16 | 2.17 | 2.24 | 2.30 | 2.33 | 2.29 | 2.27 | 2.22 | 2.24 | 2.27 |
| 经合组织成员 | 2.14 | 2.15 | 2.22 | 2.27 | 2.30 | 2.24 | 2.24 | 2.19 | 2.20 | 2.23 |
| | 2007 | 2008 | 2009 | 2010 | 2011 | 2012 | 2013 | 2014 | 2015 | 2016 |
| 德国 | 2.45 | 2.60 | 2.73 | 2.71 | 2.80 | 2.87 | 2.82 | 2.87 | 2.92 | 2.94 |
| 高收入国家 | 2.27 | 2.36 | 2.42 | 2.39 | 2.40 | 2.43 | 2.42 | 2.46 | 2.46 | 2.51 |
| 经合组织成员 | 2.23 | 2.32 | 2.40 | 2.36 | 2.39 | 2.41 | 2.40 | 2.44 | 2.45 | 2.49 |

（b）制造业增加值占GDP的比例（%）

| | 1997 | 1998 | 1999 | 2000 | 2001 | 2002 | 2003 | 2004 | 2005 | 2006 |
|---|---|---|---|---|---|---|---|---|---|---|
| 德国 | 20.30 | 20.50 | 20.14 | 20.73 | 20.51 | 19.98 | 20.06 | 20.28 | 20.31 | 20.93 |
| 高收入国家 | 17.55 | 17.37 | 16.99 | 16.87 | 16.11 | 15.76 | 15.60 | 15.51 | 15.32 | 15.24 |
| 经合组织成员 | 17.73 | 17.54 | 17.13 | 17.00 | 16.18 | 15.71 | 15.52 | 15.48 | 15.31 | 15.29 |
| | 2007 | 2008 | 2009 | 2010 | 2011 | 2012 | 2013 | 2014 | 2015 | 2016 |
| 德国 | 21.09 | 20.25 | 17.88 | 19.97 | 20.57 | 20.42 | 20.18 | 20.59 | 20.76 | 20.64 |
| 高收入国家 | 15.08 | 14.55 | 13.64 | 14.23 | 14.15 | 14.04 | 13.93 | 13.99 | 14.39 | 14.31 |
| 经合组织成员 | 15.13 | 14.63 | 13.65 | 14.18 | 14.16 | 14.08 | 13.96 | 14.01 | 14.43 | 14.34 |

数据来源：世界银行。

德国制造业成功的关键是在市场环境下通过有为政府的领先型产业政策培育了大量高水平的产业集群，尤其是在生物技术、智能制造、有机电子、碳纤维等领域的15个世界级领先集群，集聚了尖端的企业、人才、科研机构等资源。根据一份调查研究报告显示，德国遴选培育集群的赛马机制、设立集群的促进机构、建立分类施策的治理体系，以及发挥政府引导作用，是德国产业集群取得成功的重要经验[②]：

在遴选培育集群方面，德国的集群不是通过国家意志的相马机制遴选，而是只需政府制

① 对政府支持的基础研究在美国现在居全球居领先地位的航天、信息、生化、纳米、医药等各种新技术、新产品的开发中所发挥的重要作用感兴趣的读者可参考：Mariana Mazzucato, *The Entrepreneurial State: Debunking Public vs. Private Sector Myths*, Anthem Press, 2013。

② 中国工信部赛迪研究院，“德国培育世界级产业集群有何高招？”，2019年。

定宏观战略目标、资金支持方式等顶层设计，实际集群的形成、管理和发展，基本上都由区域内各主体自行组织，联邦政府资助的集群最后通过竞赛方式遴选而出。“领先集群”充分发挥集群的自主性和主动性，在众多集群中通过竞赛好中选优。

在设立集群的促进机构方面，德国集群促进机构虽然大部分由政府引导发起，但并不是政府的派出机构，也不代表某些企业利益，是介于市场与政府之间中立的“第三方”，原则上是非营利性组织，在运营的不同阶段会得到政府不同比例的资金资助。以巴伐利亚州“机电一体化产业集群”为例，集群促进机构发挥其精准服务集群成员的纽带作用，以企业需求为中心构建各方高度协作的网络化体系，打通政策链创新链、产业链、资金链，形成良好的集群治理结构。第一，在打通政策链方面，2005年政府支持成立了集群促进机构，召集研究所、机电学院、企业、工商会、中介组织等加入集群成为会员，共同申报政府资助的集群项目，从而推动来自科技界、产业界和社会各界的协同合作。第二，在打通创新链方面，促进机构注重使集群内机电研究所的研发成果与企业实际生产需求相结合，同时推动各研究所互相沟通科研进展，以解决共性问题，实现研究成果的共享，从而有效解决科研机构、大学和企业之间研发和产业化信息不对称问题。第三，在打通产业链方面，促进机构定期与企业沟通，提供关于产品、技术、市场等方面的信息，加强集群内产业链上下游企业间的互助合作，同时加强有竞争关系的企业的相互合作，共同应对来自外部的竞争。第四，在打通资金链方面，利用促进机构的资源和威望，积极促进集群内企业与金融机构、风险投资机构进行合作，为资金供给方提供企业优质项目信息。总之，通过多种多样的活动和精准服务，促进机构将有合作关系和竞争关系的各方通过共同目标整合在一起，成为维系集群各方的重要纽带。

在建立分类施策的治理体系方面，为了实现提高优势产业领域的国际竞争力和区域差异化平衡发展两大目标，德国集群政策的演变基本遵循如下路径：先促进单个产业发展，再促进区域协调发展，然后再促进多产业、多区域创新发展，最后促进集群合作发展。例如，20世纪90年代，德国提出了以“生物区域”为代表，促进单个产业国际竞争力的计划。此时德国虽然在生物技术方面已具备一定优势，但科技界与产业界互不结合问题突出，与美国相比落后20年，与英国相比落后10年。借鉴美、英两国发展产业集群的经验，德国1995年启动了该计划，从17名参赛者中确定4个获胜者，给予5年共1.5万亿德国马克的资金支持，从而解决和改善了科研成果在本地实现商业化的问题。1990年两德统一后，德国以“创新区域”为代表，提出着眼于区域协调发展的计划。此时德国东部落后于西部的差距日益显现，1999年起实施该计划，要求参赛者只能来自新设立的联邦州，当时共有444个参赛项目，竞赛选出25个予以支持。这对缩小东西差距，实现区域协调发展起到了重大作用。2000年以后，德国提出以“创新能力中心计划”为代表，提升多产业、多区域差异化创新发展的计划。此时德国将生物技术产业化的经验推广到培育其他产业集群的发展中，更多的州开始致力于培育高水平的产业集群。比如，“领先集群”计划既关注新兴产业，也关注传统成熟产业，注重在全国不同区域打造最有国际影响力的集群。目前德国已拥有遍布全国的集群计划项目640个。近年来，德国提出了协调集群间过度竞争的合作网络计划。大量的集群计划有效激发了企业尤其是东部企业的创新精神，但也带来了区域过度竞争和政府资源的浪费。合作网络计划有目的地支持企业和企业相关设施之间的地区合作，发起更多联合倡议，从而提升了区域合作竞争力，并建立了集群联系的信息网络和沟通机制。

在发挥政府引导作用方面，德国政府采取主动制定政策和间接参与的形式，发挥集群在国家制造业体系建设中的重要性，致力于打造集群发展的利益共同体，有效纠正集群合作中的市场失灵。对此应发挥政府资金的引导作用，加强对集群发展的引导和扶持。比如最早的生物计划，政府总资助额为7 500万欧元，主要面向生物技术的新创企业，虽然支持力度不算太大，但打消了众多企业和投资者的顾虑，使得大量的风险投资涌入支持生物技术发展中。同时要通过政府力量为地方提供更多智力支撑。政策的重点由对大学和公立科研机构以及企业的单独促进，转变到促进产、学、研联合方面，重点支持研究机构与企业结成创新联盟。比如，政府在原来相对落后的巴伐利亚州建立了一些知名应用型大学的分校，支持创新资源与该州的实际产业发展需求有机融合起来，这些科研资源会源源不断地提供后备力量，从而为该州提供创新支撑。在15个领先集群中，弗劳恩霍夫协会都布局有专业的研究所，部分集群内有多个研究所，政府会投入大量资金用于研究所公共研发支出，并在集群内将成果转化为企业的商业化价值。另外，政府应始终以资助企业为中心保持市场导向。企业是政府资助的重要对象，有一部分企业会直接受益于政府对集群的资金支持。据统计，领先集群中1 685个成员企业中，获得直接补贴的有573个。此外，对获得政府资金的集群项目会要求企业1∶1配套资金投入，政府资金主要用于技术研发，产业化部分主要由各类企业配套投入，从而使得实现商业价值部分更多的由市场主体决定。

因此，中国这样的发展中国家自然也必须采取同样的方式来支持领先型产业的新技术和新产品开发所需的基础科研。各国的中央和地方政府可以用财政拨款设立科研基金，支持所在地领先型产业的企业与科研院校协作进行基础科研，支持企业开发新产品、新技术。中央和地方政府也可以以资金支持相关行业的企业组成共用技术研发平台，攻关突破共用技术“瓶颈”，在此基础上再各自开发新产品、新技术。在企业新技术和产品开发取得突破后，中央和地方政府也可以通过采购帮助企业较快地形成规模化生产，以降低单位生产成本，提高产品的国际竞争力。领先型产业需要到世界各地建立销售、加工生产、售后服务等网络，以开发市场；中央和各地政府也需要在人才培训、资金、法律、领事保护上给予相关企业必要的支持以助力其海外拓展。

### 10.3.3 转进型产业的因势利导方法

转进型产业因为国内经济的发展，要素禀赋结构变化，工资水平上升，而丧失了比较优势（回顾第9章）。对于中国而言，劳动力密集型的出口加工业是最典型的第一类产业（回顾第8章和第6章）。这类产业最主要的成本是工资成本。到2020年“十三五”结束，实现中共十八大提出的两个“翻一番”目标，加上人民币升值，普通工人的月工资可能会上升到1 000美元。这类产业在中国失掉比较优势是不可逆转的趋势。面对这种挑战，中国劳动力密集型出口加工产业中的一部分企业可以升级到品牌、研发、品管、市场渠道管理等高附加值的“微笑曲线”的两端。从事生产加工的多数企业则只能像20世纪60年代以后的日本和80年代以后的亚洲“四小龙”同类产业中的企业那样，利用其技术、管理、市场渠道的优势，转移到海外工资水平较低的地方去创造第二春，把中国的GDP变为GNP，否则必然会因竞争力丧失、海外订单流失而被淘汰掉。这些加工企业在海外的成功也将给中国相关产业中附加价值比较高的中间部件和机器设备的生产企业提供海外市场，成为中国产业转型升级的拉动力。中国各种劳动力密集型出口加工产业，绝大多数在一些市、县形成产业集群，这些产业集群所在地的地方政府可以采取以下两种因势利导的政策：一是提供设计、营销方面的人才培训、展销平台等，鼓励一部分有能力的企业转向“微笑曲线”的两端，经营品牌的企业则可以对其新产品开发的费用给予和高新产业研发费用一样在税前扣除的待遇；二是协助所在地加工企业抱团出海，提供信息、海外经营人才培训、资金支持，以及和承接地政府合作设立加工出口园区等，帮助企业利用当地廉价劳动力资源优势来提高竞争力，创造企业的第二春。随着中国国内工资水平的上涨，许多20世纪八九十年代转移到中国内地的台资、港资、韩资劳动力密集型加工出口企业已经转移出去，中国内地自己的劳动力密集型加工出口企业则因为不熟悉国外投资环境，缺乏海外经营管理人才而仍滞留国内。劳动力密集型加工出口产业集群所在地的政府，可以给企业提供适合发展加工出口产业的国家信息；和承接地政府做好对接，帮助它们学习中国的招商引资经验，设立工业园区，营造良好的投资和经营环境；会同行业协会因势利导，协助中国的企业抱团到那里投资。商务部、外交部等中央部委和国家进出口银行、国家开发银行、中非发展基金等金融机构也要在投资保护、签证便利和金融服务上给走出去的企业以必要的支持。根据这一思路，中国劳动力密集型加工出口业应向何处转移？由于中国是一个13亿人口的大国，第三次工业普查显示，整个制造业的从业人员高达1.25亿人。对人口规模相对较小的越南、柬埔寨、老挝、孟加拉国等国而言，中国的劳动力密集型加工产业稍微往那些国家转移，马上就会带动当地工资和中国一样迅速上涨，实际上这正是近些年来那些国家出现的情形。从人口和劳动力供给而言，非洲现在有11亿人口，大量是富余的农村年轻劳动力，和中国20世纪80年代初的状况一样，目前的工资水平仅为中国的1/10到1/4，是承接中国劳动力密集型出口加工产业最合适的地方。但一个地方要成为现代制造业加工出口基地，除了工资水平低，当地的生产企业还必须具备比较现代化的管理水平和技术能力，以及国际买家对当地企业的产品质量和按时交货有信心。非洲国家现在遇到的发展“瓶颈”是，基础设施薄弱，国际买家对非洲企业的管理、技术、产品质量和按时交货的能力缺乏信心。如果中国中央政府和劳动力密集加工企业所在的地方政府在“一带一路”和“中非命运共同体”的合作框架下，能够帮助非洲国家学习和吸取中国在招商引资方面的经验，设立工业园区改善基础设施，提供“一站式”服务，以发展产业集群的方式将中国的劳动力密集加工企业吸引过去，非洲也能快速发展起来。(回顾第1章专栏1.3)

将转进型产业与前面的第一种追赶型产业比较，可以发现一国的转进型产业恰好是该国被作为学习目标对象的国家的追赶型产业。如果从产业转移的角度讲，转进型产业针对的是产业转出国，追赶型产业对应的则是产业转入国。比如，前面我们以中国为例所讨论的这些转进型产业，恰好是收入水平比中国低，符合其潜在比较优势国家的追赶型产业。在此，我们不妨回顾第9章对“一带一路”沿线国家与中国的产业比较优势互补性的讨论。林毅夫和王燕在《超越发展援助》一书中以中国和非洲为例，将这种南南合作关系比喻为攀登结构转型“大山”的队友，相互促进彼此的经济结构转型升级。[①]这种基于比较优势互补性的学习转型合作伙伴关系，类似中国人奉行的“三人行，必有我师”，完全不同于南北发展援助的援助者和受援者之间的关系，二者的经济激励机制不同。《超越发展援助》一书中列举了大量的这种中非合作案例。除了我们在本书中反复提及的劳动密集型产业外，还有农业和基础设施以及服务业的大量案例。例如，1979年之后，中国在农业领域实现了高产，利用这个经验和比较优势，中国资助了非洲农业技术示范中心的建设，传递了适宜的农业和技术。[②]例如，中国过去往往采取劳动密集型的技术而不是采用资本密集型的技术来修铁路，这种经验就用到了非洲坦赞铁路。[③]另一个医疗健康服务业的案例便是中国现在家喻户晓的青蒿素的故事，其低廉的成本拯救了数百万非洲人的性命，中国科学家屠呦呦因此贡献而荣获诺贝尔奖。事实上，这种类型的合作关系也适用于“一带一路”倡议。

---

① 林毅夫、王燕，《超越援助》，北京大学出版社，2016年版，第4章（英文版Lin Justin Yifu and Wang Yan, *Going Beyond Aid: Development Cooperation for Structural Transformation*, Cambridge University Press, 2016）。

② D. Brautigam, *Will Africa Feed China?* Oxford University Press, 2015.

③ Lin Justin Yifu, Célestin Monga, *The Oxford Handbook of Africa and Economics (I/II)*, Oxford University Press, 2015.

### 10.3.4 换道超车型产业的因势利导方法

此类产业的特征是人力资本需求高、研发周期短。相对于一种新药的研发周期可能历时10年以上，成本投入高达10亿美元，信息、通信产业的软件、手机等，研发周期仅为几个月到一年，属于人力资本需求高、研发周期短的“换道超车型”新兴产业。这种产业又分成重资产和轻资产两类，前者需要大量资本投入，如三星研发的存储器，华为研发的麒麟芯片以及程控交换机；后者资本投入不多，如互联网运用、游戏软件或者像以现有可用的硬件为基础来开发新手机的小米那样。对于中国而言，在这类产业的发展上，拥有国内市场巨大、科技人才多和完备的生产加工能力能够把概念迅速变成产品等优势，并已经出现了阿里巴巴、腾讯、华为、小米等成功的企业。各地政府可以针对这类企业发展的需要，提供孵化基地，加强知识产权保护，鼓励风险投资，制定优惠的人才和税收政策，[①]支持国内和国外的创新性人才创业，利用中国的优势，推动“换道超车型”产业在当地的发展。除了中国，其他具备类似潜在人力资本比较优势的经济体也可以采取类似的因势利导政策（如图10.4所示，在城市层面的现代经济中，人口数量与专利数量几乎高度一致。）

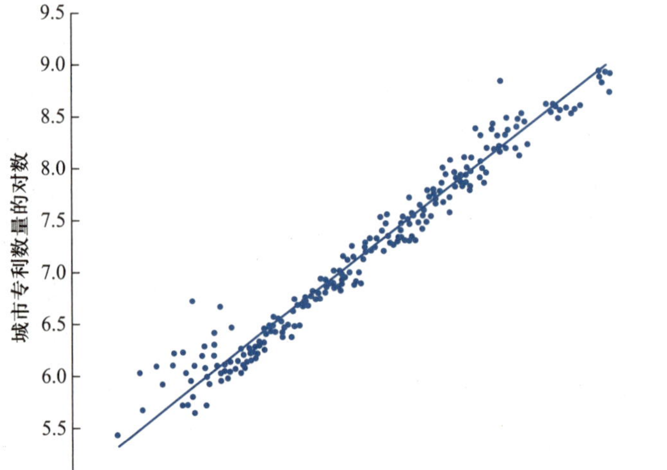


**图10.4 人口规模与城市专利数量**

资料来源：杰弗里·韦斯特，《规模——复杂世界的简单法则》，张培译，中信出版社，2018年版。

① Keun Lee，*Schumpeterian Analysis of Economic Catch-up: Knowledge，Patch Cratation，and the Middle-inomce Trap*，Cambridge University Press，2012.

重资产的换道超车产业给在该产业已经经营多年的成功企业赶超全球同行业领袖提供了机会，例如，三星对日本存储芯片企业的赶超，华为对诺基亚、西门子程控交换机的赶超。[①]轻资产的换道超车产业则给新创业的企业提供了天地，中国由于人多、天才多、国内市场大、配套产业齐全，在弯道超车的轻资产产业上独显优势，拥有数量最多的市场估值超过10亿美元的独角兽公司。2018年全球独角兽企业的地域分布：中国数量第一，共205家，占比47.79%；美国第二，共149家，占比34.73%；其他数量较多的国家包括英国、印度、德国、韩国，分别占比3.5%、3.03%、1.86%、1.40%。中国这205家独角兽企业的累计估值达到9 573亿美元，美国149家独角兽企业的累计估值达到5 548亿美元，中美两国占全球比重为88.83%。这些独角兽企业是典型的人力资本密集型创业企业。据对中国独角兽企业的调查报告显示，企业创始人整体高学历、理工科专业背景的人数最多，共49人，占比达到54.4%。他们具备电子、计算机、通信等专业领域的知识和工作经验，对行业的发展和技术的革新有着较深的理解，这与独角兽企业中互联网和IT行业的比重较高十分吻合。[②]对中美独角兽企业的研究证实了前述中国在换道超车的以人力资本投入为主的短周期产业，因国内人才多、市场大、硬件配套产业齐全而具有潜在比较优势的看法，同时也证伪了新制度经济学把西方政治制度作为创新的前提的观点。这一现象背后恰好反映了过去10年来中国要素禀赋结构的变迁，人力资本禀赋在结构变迁中的作用日益凸显，如图10.5所示。

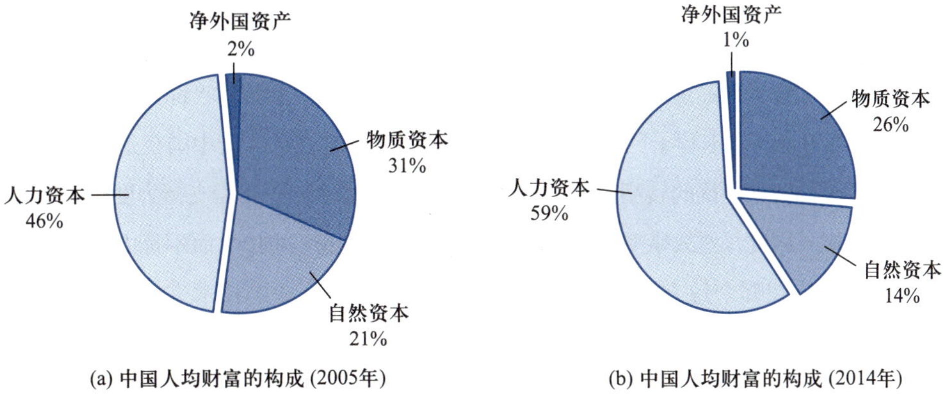


**图10.5 中国近2005年与2014年禀赋结构的变迁**

资料来源：World Bank,"The Changing Wealth of Nations: Measuring Sustainable Development in the New Millennium", Environment and Development, World Bank, 2011; Glenn-Marie lange, Quentin Wodon, Kevin Carey,"The Changing Wealth of Nations 2018: Building a Sustainable Future", World Bank, 2018, p.222.

---

① Keun Lee, *Schumpeterian Analysis of Economic Catch-up: Knowledge, Patch Cratation, and the Middle-inomce Trap*, Cambridge University Press, 2012.

② 可参考：清科研究中心，《2018年中国独角兽企业研究报告》；德勤，《中美独角兽研究报告》。

### 10.3.5 战略型产业的因势利导方法

这类产业的特性和换道超车型产业正好相反，通常不仅资本非常密集，而且，研发周期长，投入巨大，往往不符合比较优势，企业没有自生能力，但是其发展关系到一个国家的国防安全或经济安全，大飞机、航天、超级计算机、核心芯片产业等即属于这种类型。战略型产业有一个特性，即它不能完全依靠市场，需要有政府的保护补贴才能发展起来。过去在发展早期，经济总体规模小，这类产业规模大、配套产业多，发展起来在经济中所占的比重会很多，政府的保护补贴只能通过对各种要素价格的扭曲和给予市场垄断的间接方式来实现。这是发展中国家普遍采取计划经济体制来发展该类产业，造成了诸多根深蒂固的扭曲的原因。目前，中国作为一个中等偏上收入的经济大国，这类产业在国民经济中的占比已经不大，今后应该像发达国家一样由财政直接拨款来补贴这类企业。对于国防安全产业，在美欧等发达国家，不论民营（如在美国）还是国有（如在欧洲），都由政府财政直接拨款来支持。除了和国防安全相关的军工企业之外，一些战略型新兴产业，其产业发展方向非常明确，国内又有很大的市场需求，例如，一些核心芯片，如果没有国家的支持，中国的企业发展这样的产业还非常缺乏竞争力。但是，没有这些核心技术可能会出现“卡脖子”的问题而影响到经济安全，由国家财政支持来攻关，从长期动态的角度来看则有其经济合理性。例如，在第8章中我们曾提到，2018年中国进口了4 176亿个集成电路，数量上增长了10.8%，总价值20 584亿元，价值上增长了16.9%，超过原油进口价值的15 882亿元。这充分反映出中国作为中高等收入水平国家的处境，在高新技术商品上对发达国家的依赖（2018年总的高新技术产品进口额达44 340亿，增长12.2%），存在很多“卡脖子”的技术清单。与此同时，这也意味着中国在这些战略新兴产业方面具有巨大的方向明确的转型升级空间。由于这些战略型产业所需支持力度较大，地方政府可能难以负担，因此，对战略型产业的扶持是国家行为，应该由中央而不是由地方财政来承担。这类产业落户在哪个地方，会间接地促进那个地方配套产业的技术进步和产业升级，所以，各地政府可以支持鼓励配套产业的发展，并改善基础设施、子女教育、生活环境等软硬条件，来争取战略型产业落户当地，以实现战略型产业和当地产业转型升级的双赢。

专栏10.1

借力全球化：通往成功的路线图[①]

尽管有非关税措施的阻碍，但是总体来讲，全球贸易的长期趋势对于发展中国家而言依然是非常积极的。而且，如果考虑全球生产系统的结构转变，以及发达经济体和发展中经济体之间巨大的双赢机会，全世界平均关税的总体下降趋势不太可能回卷。这种演化过程的最好证明是许多产品在不同国家在同一时间被制造出来，全球贸易因此不再仅仅是在本国生产单独的产品和服务并在国际市场上进行交换的国家之间的一系列交易，而更多的是协同以及合作关系，甚至是在竞争更加激烈的世界环境下。制造业已经逐步演变为一个全球供应链网络，在该网络中，各个生产阶段总是发生在具有最高成本有效性的地方——无论它们在世界的哪个角落。[②]

在过去的几十年中，全球贸易的组成已经发生了深刻的变化，这证实了新模式的出现。直到第二次世界大战结束前，原材料和农业产品对工业产品的交易还在国家间的商业交易中占主导地位。自1945年以来，制造产品或其零部件已经成为贸易的主要部分，其价值已经从1900年占世界贸易的40%增长到2000年的75%，与此同时，农产品占全球贸易的比重也在持续下降（见图10.6）。这种变化也反映在从国与国之间进行本土产品的买卖，到国际上进行由相互竞争的经济体联合生产的产品的交易的转变。这种转变使高强度的保护主义政策的空间越来越小。

全球价值链日益增强的主导地位，以及为发展中国家提供的机遇不仅仅是一种推测和假说。如今，有大量的经验证据表明，发展中国家在全球贸易中扮演着新锚点的角色，并在全球经济的快速增长中充当潜在的承载工具。统计人员必须重新设计价值链中每个国家的国民核算体系，以体现不同国家之间以及世界不同地区之间的产业互动。要完成这样烦琐的工作就必须构建一个大型的国际投入产出矩阵，其中包括一项最终产品或服务在生产和消费之前发生的所有产业间贸易行为。这项工作还要求适当协调每一个贸易伙伴的国民账户，以及对贸易产品和

---

① 本专栏资料来自：林毅夫、塞勒斯汀·孟加，《战胜命运》，北京大学出版社，2017年版，第七章。更详细的讨论可参考该书。

② R. Baldwin, Global Supply Chains: Why They Emerged, Why They Matter, and Where They Are Going, CEPR Discussion Paper, No. 9103. London: Centre for Economic Policy Research, 2012.

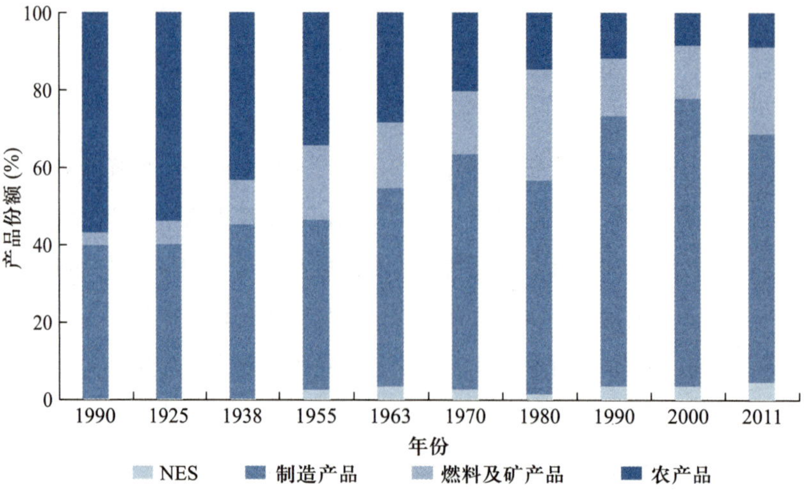


**图10.6 百年变迁与机遇：世界商品出口的产品份额，1900—2011年**

注：NES（不另详述）是指：（1）低价值的贸易；（2）贸易伙伴名称未知或伙伴分配出现错误。四舍五入导致各分项加总不等于100。

资料来源：WTO, World Trade Report 2013.

服务的用途进行详细分析，也就是被用于消费还是投资，或是在一个新的生产过程中被进一步使用。

衡量全球价值链中多种贸易投入产出流的实证分析是必要的，却也很有挑战性，因为这需要不同国家及行业的详细数据。参与全球价值链的任一国家均同时采用中间进口投入（进口增值）以及本国国内增值以生产产品和服务。贸易经济学家经常采用的一种直接方法是观察A国的出口（或最终需求），该出口可以分为两部分：一部分体现国内生产增值，另一部分体现从其他国家获得的进口增值。对全球价值链的完整分析还应该考虑到以下事实，即一国的出口不只是由最终产品构成，也可以包括被其他国家用作生产（及出口）投入的中间产品。

为了衡量A国在全球价值链中的参与，至少下面两个要点是应该考虑的：（1）该国在出口中使用的国外增加值（FVA）份额，并计为A国总出口额中的一个比重（这是A国参与全球价值链下游生产程度的一个指标，因为它衡量了A国在生产出口产品过程中使用外国投入的情况）。（2）A国被世界其他所有国家作为中间投入吸收为出口增加值的国内增加值（DVX）份额，并为A国总出口额中的一个比重（这是A国参与全球价值链上游生产程度的一个指标，因为它衡量了其投入——增加值——在其他国家生产及出口的产品和服务中的使用情况）。因此，全球价值链参与度指标是将一国用在本国出口中的国外增加值（FVX）与提供给他国出口的国内增加值（DVX）结合起来，取其总和并计算其在总出口额中的占比。

通过使用上述计算框架，Foster-McGregor等[①]揭示了世界范围内各地区1995年、2000年、2005年及2010年度的全球价值链参与度。[②]他们的实证分析显示了一些有趣的事实。他们证实，全球价值链参与度随着时间的推移在全球大多数地区都有增长，出口份额作为多阶段全球价值链过程的一部分，由1995年的14%增长至2010年的近50%。唯一例外的是，参与度在中美洲和加勒比地区有某种下降的倾向（见图10.7）。

不出意外，发达国家，尤其是欧盟，深度参与到全球价值链中（见图10.7）。东亚和东南亚较为深入地参与其中，西亚稍逊，这也都是符合预期的。或许非洲经济在全球价值链参与中的攀升，是证明即使低收入国家也可以在全球贸易中表现良好的最振奋人心的证据。1995年，非洲的全球价值链参与度约为所有地区参与度的平均值（大约41%），但其主要参与环节为上游生产（即为其他国家提供中间投入产品），而非下游生产（出口加工）。1995—2010年间非洲地区的全球价值链参与度增长率也与所有国家相似：其间，非洲的全球价值链参与度增长了19.9%，而所有国家整体增长了20.5%。

对于发展中国家而言，最鼓舞人心的消息或许是从按部门分类进行全球价值链的实证分析中所得到的事实（见图10.8）。平均而言，高科技行业占所有国家全球价值链参与度的58%，其中发达国家的这一比重更高，为62%，中美洲为69%。亚洲的高科技行业占全球价值链参与度的比重位于平均数附近，其中南亚和西亚的数据要落后于东亚和东南亚。最引人注目的是非洲的产业贡献，其第一产业的比重为26%，两个服务部门（高科技与低科技）的比重均为约20%，两个制造部门（高科技与低科技）的比重均为约17%，似乎各部门相当均衡。但是，相对其他国家制造业产品和服务在全球价值链参与度中的比重（平均为66%），非洲的这一比重（33%）要远远落后于其他地区。除此之外，只有西亚和加勒比地区的这一比重低于40%。

对这个总体积极形势持怀疑态度者仍然观察到，即便让自己的企业参与全球

---

① N. Foster-McGregor, F. Kaulich, R. Stehrer, Global Value Chains in Africa, UNU-MERIT Working Papers, 2015.

② 该数据来自用UNCTAD的Eora数据库构建的全球价值链参与指标。该数据库提供了世界范围内的跨地区投入产出表，同时提供了1970—2011年间向187个国家报告的国际投入产出表；报告了基于不同国家的25~500个行业的信息。Foster-McGregor等使用的是1995—2010年间25个部门的数据库，使用的数据是在这一层面上对所有187个国家进行整合并一致报告的基础价格数据。

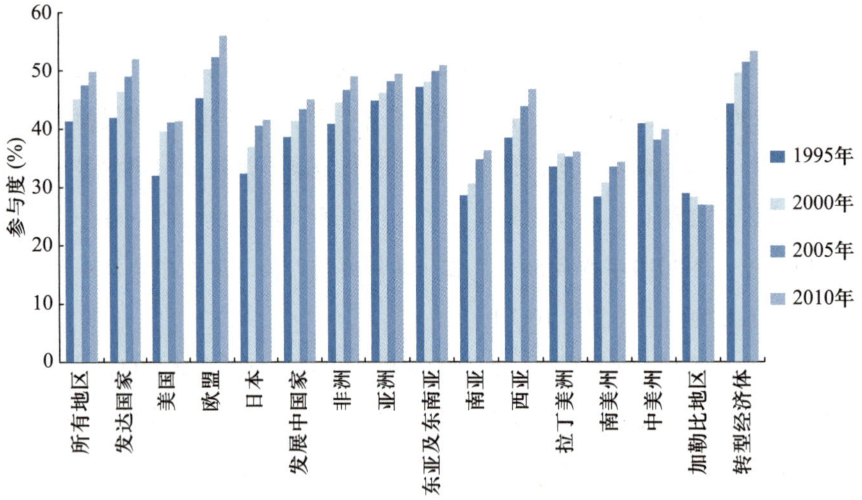


图10.7 各地区全球价值链参与度（1995—2010年）

资料来源：N. Foster-McGregor, F. Kaulich, R. Stehrer, Global Value Chains in Africa, UNU-MERIT Working Papers, 2015.

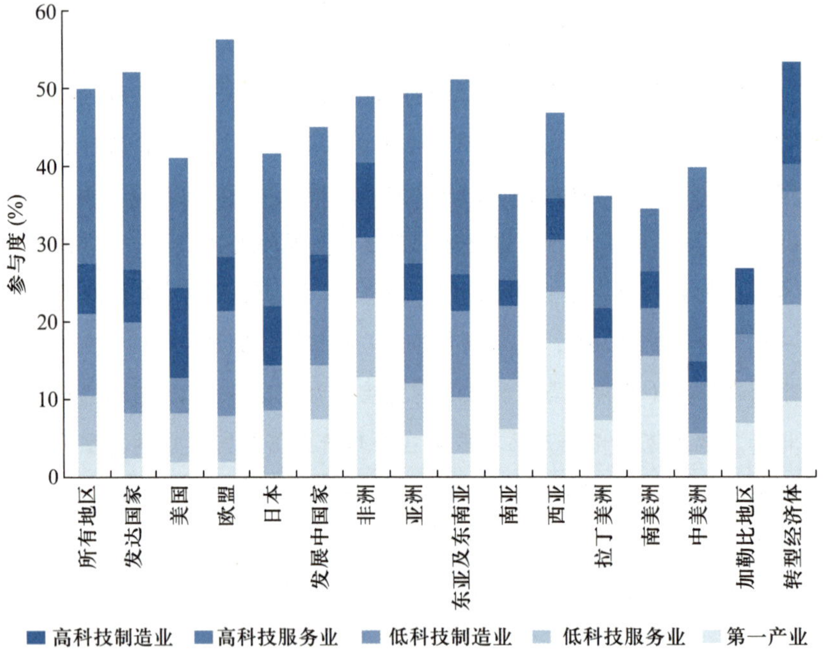


图10.8 各地区及各行业的全球价值链参与度（2010年）

资料来源：N. Foster-McGregor, F. Kaulich, R. Stehrer, Global Value Chains in Africa, UNU-MERIT Working Papers, 2015.

价值链，也不能保证一个贫穷的经济体最终保持高速增长。比如，他们会指出孟加拉国等国的经历，这些是劳动密集型产业（纺织、服装）发展良好的国家，但似乎受困于全球价值链的低增值环节，在这些环节进行创新或技术转移的可能性几乎为零。的确，世界经济经历了许多加速增长的阶段，但这些阶段并未使得低收入国家和高收入国家之间的经济差距缩小。Hausmann等指出，自19世纪中叶以来，有80个这样的经济增长加速时期，他们认为这种增长加速时期极难预测。据此他们得出了悲观的结论，即绝大多数的增长加速是与经济增长文献中的标准决定因素无关的，同时大多数经济改革事件并未产生增长加速。①的确，一个经济发展战略在一开始获得成功是可能的，甚至培育出有竞争力的企业、创造就业机会并对一国的经济增长做出贡献，但是，这个经济战略最终会因为未考虑到保持产业和技术的持续升级而失败。这就引出了一个更广泛的问题，即经济发展战略的有效性，该战略必须不断变化以反映变化的经济要素禀赋结构，并根据制度和要素要求而做出调整。那些在推动生产、发展贸易方面获得成功，并将贸易作为经济增长的一个稳定、可靠来源的国家，通常会为其最有竞争力的行业建立企业集群。这些国家的做法通常是切实保证了政府能够创造条件使国内外投资者建立强有力的合作关系，并培育出可以在国际市场上获得成功的企业。

① R. Hausmann, L. Pritchett, D. Rodrik, “Growth Accelerations”, *Journal of Economic Growth,* 2005, Vol.10, No.4, pp.303-329.

## 10.4

## 因势利导方法促进经济发展的全球案例[①]

### 10.4.1 发达国家的案例[②]

我们在第1章和第4章介绍了二战后有两个经济体——中国台湾和韩国，从贫困的农业经济体如何沿着新结构经济学主张的发展道路进行经济结构转型升级成为高收入经济体，堪称发展典范中的典范。即便如此，韩国这样的高收入国家依然需要通过因势利导方法以继续保持和取得新的国家竞争优势。[③]孙瑾和刘文革根据世界银行WDI数据库，选取人均GDP等指标筛选要素禀赋结构相似的国家进行了比较。人均资本存量反映资本和劳动力禀赋，自然租金比反映自然资源禀赋，三次产业占比反映一国产业结构。如表10.2所示，发达国家中德国、法国、日本和韩国的要素禀赋结构较相似。德国、法国、日本的人均GDP均为约4万美元，比韩国约2万美元的人均GDP高一倍，可作为韩国学习的"指南针"。当然，韩国作为一个高收入经济体，尽管与德国、法国、日本相比存在这样的差距，但其诸如汽车和芯片等产业是处于全球领先的，需要采取领先型产业因势利导方法继续获取国家竞争优势。韩国的目标国中，德国是世界上贸易顺差占比排名第一位的国家。[④]对应地，在表10.3中可以看到几个明显的结构变迁趋势。首先，20年前的主要出口产品和如今差不多，不过药品（联合国HS编码30）和航空器、航天器及其零件（88）却从原来的排名第10位左右大幅上升到前5位，2008—2012年间德国的纸或纸板制品（48）的生产和出口减少，法国的有机化学品（29）的生产和出口减少，转向大力发展航空器产业，并且随着大宗商品价格的上涨，矿物

---

① 有很多应用该因势利导政策框架进行的案例练习可供参考，读者也可自行进行类似的案例分析。

② 这一部分案例主要来自：孙瑾、刘文革，"国家竞争优势产业甄别与升级——基于新结构主义经济学方法"，《国际贸易》，2014年第4期，第11-17页。

③ 关于新结构经济学对在发展的高级阶段如何转型升级的讨论可进一步参考：林毅夫，《繁荣的求索》第9章，北京大学出版社，2012年版。

④ 中国则排在第二位，但是中国的人均GDP只有德国的1/10。

燃料产品的出口额位居前10位。其次，日本这20年来排名前10位的出口产品不变，产业结构保持不变，基本没有产业升级，并且服务贸易出口占世界比重连续下降，这也部分解释了日本“失去的20年”的原因。与德国和法国相比，日本排名前10位的产品没有药品和航空器。最后，相比之下，人均收入相对较低的韩国产业结构升级较明显，在1993—1997年，韩国的化学纤维长丝、针织和非针织的服装及衣着附件等还是主要的出口产品，但是20年后这些纺织类产品退出了韩国的主要出口产品之列，取而代之的是有机化学品（29）及光学、照相、电影、计量、检验、医疗或外科用仪器及设备、精密仪器及设备（90）等产品。目前，韩国和日本的主要出口产品非常相似，但是这里只给出了HS2位码大类商品，根据UN Comtrade数据库，韩国未来可以按照日本每一部门大类下的细分商品比重指导其进行部门产业内升级，并以德国和法国为参照系指导其进行产业间升级。

表10.2 德法日韩的要素禀赋结构与产业结构（2008—2012年平均值）

| 国家 | 人均GDP（美元） | 人均资本存量（美元） | 劳动力（人） | 自然租金比 | 第一产业占比（%） | 第二产业占比（%） | 第三产业占比（%） |
|---|---|---|---|---|---|---|---|
| 德国 | 42 144.9 | 6 424.7 | 42 185 186 | 0.27 | 0.79 | 30.71 | 68.50 |
| 法国 | 41 191.9 | 6 560.7 | 29 792 228 | 0.08 | 1.90 | 18.87 | 79.22 |
| 日本 | 42 683.7 | 7 235.3 | 66 039 776 | 0.04 | 1.16 | 26.14 | 72.69 |
| 韩国 | 20 301.1 | 5 305.3 | 25 071 653 | 0.07 | 2.68 | 39.83 | 57.49 |

资料来源：孙瑾和刘文革（2014）根据WDI数据库计算。

表10.3 德、法、日、韩在不同时期排名前10位的出口产品

| 出口产品（HS2位码） | 1993—1997年 | | | | 2008—2012年 | | | |
|---|---|---|---|---|---|---|---|---|
| | 德国 | 法国 | 日本 | 韩国 | 德国 | 法国 | 日本 | 韩国 |
| 矿物燃料、矿物油及其蒸馏产品，沥青物质，矿物蜡（27） | | | | | √ | √ | | √ |
| 有机化学品（29） | √ | √ | √ | | √ | | √ | √ |
| 药品（30） | √ | √ | | | √ | √ | | |
| 塑料及其制品（39） | √ | √ | √ | √ | √ | √ | √ | √ |
| 橡胶及其制品（40） | | | √ | | | | √ | |
| 纸及纸板，纸浆、纸或纸板制品（48） | √ | | | | | | | |
| 钢铁（72） | √ | √ | √ | √ | √ | √ | √ | √ |
| 钢铁制品（73） | √ | | √ | √ | √ | | √ | √ |
| 核反应堆，锅炉，机器、机械器具及其零件（84） | √ | √ | √ | √ | √ | √ | √ | √ |

续表

| 出口产品（HS2位码） | 1993—1997年 | | | | 2008—2012年 | | | |
|---|---|---|---|---|---|---|---|---|
| | 德国 | 法国 | 日本 | 韩国 | 德国 | 法国 | 日本 | 韩国 |
| 电机、电气设备及其零件，录音机及放声机、电视图像、声音的录制和重放设备及其零件、附件（85） | √ | √ | √ | √ | √ | √ | √ | √ |
| 车辆及其零件、附件，但铁道及电车道车辆除外（87） | √ | √ | √ | √ | √ | √ | √ | √ |
| 航空器、航天器及其零件（88） | | √ | | | √ | √ | | |
| 船舶及浮动结构体（89） | | | √ | √ | | | √ | √ |
| 光学、照相、电影、计量、检验、医疗或外科用仪器及设备、精密仪器及设备，上述物品的零件、附件（90） | √ | √ | √ | | √ | √ | √ | √ |
| 饮料、酒及醋（22） | | √ | | | | √ | | |
| 非针织或非钩编的服装及衣着附件（62） | | | | √ | | | | |
| 化学纤维长丝（54） | | | | √ | | | | |
| 针织或钩编的服装及衣着附件（61） | | | | √ | | | | |

注：2008—2012年德国钢铁（72）和钢铁制品（73）出口并列第10位。
资料来源：孙瑾和刘文革（2014）根据UN Comtrade数据库计算整理而得。

### 专栏10.2
### “欧洲乞丐”的转型升级

当1845年、1847年两场大饥荒接踵而至的时候，100多万人被活活饿死，140万人背井离乡。到1925年时，已经有580万人移居国外。存活下来的人，不到当时人口的一半，仅剩下400万人左右。这个国家就是爱尔兰——数百年来一直以出国移民潮、悲情诗人、饥荒、内战和矮精灵而闻名于世的国家。到1962年，爱尔兰的年度移民依然达到净流出109 734人。1960年，爱尔兰的人均GDP只有法国的50%，美国的23%。尽管在1973年爱尔兰和丹麦、英国一起加入了欧盟，但这一年爱尔兰的人均GDP只有德国的48%、美国的36%。1988年，英国《经济学家》杂志以爱尔兰作为封面故事，文章题目为“欧洲的乞丐”，当年爱尔兰的人均GDP只有德国的60%，美国的50%。爱尔兰自1960年代起就采取了鼓励出口的政策，但是不针对特定产业，一直无法形成有竞争力的产业集群，1980年代末以后，爱尔兰改变了过去的政策，只针对软件、制药、电子和化工

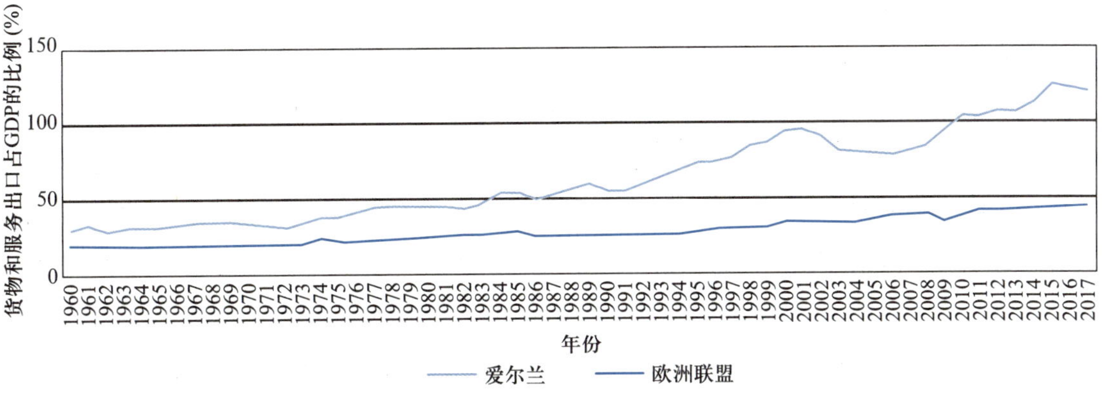


**图10.9 爱尔兰与欧盟出口占GDP比重的比较**

数据来源：世界银行。

产业给予优惠政策，并积极到人均GDP高一倍左右的美国、德国、瑞士等国家招商引资，迅速将这些产业发展成为具有竞争优势的产业集群。1998年对外进出口突破1 000亿美元大关，2001年达1 500亿美元，如图10.9所示。以信息产业为例，根据经济合作与发展组织的研究报告，2000年爱尔兰软件出口就已达85亿美元，超过美国成为世界第一大软件出口国。目前在欧洲市场上，43%的计算机、60%的配套软件都是在爱尔兰生产的。1996年以来，大量的社会资金和风险资本、外国资本及跨国软件公司进入爱尔兰软件产业，爱尔兰国内从事软件业的公司由1995年的390多家，急剧增加到2000年的780多家。目前，爱尔兰是摩托罗拉、IBM、英特尔等公司在欧盟总部的所在地，世界10大软件公司有7家在爱尔兰设立公司，有的还设立了研究开发中心。过去爱尔兰大量出口劳动力，现在它却感到劳动力紧缺，不得不引进人才。仅2000年就有近5万人移居爱尔兰，其中7 000多人来自英国，长期流落异国的爱尔兰人及其后裔也纷纷返回故里。2002年的移民达到净流入199 949人。1999年爱尔兰的人均GDP超过了德国，2003年超过美国，2017年爱尔兰的人均GDP高达69 330美元，比美国的59 531美元高出16.5%，爱尔兰在1980年代末以来发展的成功被称为“凯尔特老虎”（Celtic Tiger）。①

① Kieran Allen, *The Celtic Tiger: The Myth of Social Partnership in Ireland*, Manchester University Press, 2000; Sean O Riain, “The Flexible Development State: Globalization, Information Technology and the ‘Celtic Tiger’”, *Politicas & Society*, 2000, 28(2), pp. 157–193.

### 10.4.2 亚洲发展中国家的案例①

孙瑾和刘文革对亚洲发展中国家做了案例分析。如表10.4数据结果显示，亚洲劳动密集型国家马来西亚、泰国、印度尼西亚、菲律宾和越南的要素禀赋结构较相似。马来西亚的人均GDP将近9 000美元，约是泰国的1.8倍，同时，马来西亚的人均资本存量也是泰国的约1.8倍。印度尼西亚的人均GDP为2 885美元，不过印度尼西亚的自然资源禀赋和马来西亚相似。对于资源和劳动力都丰富的国家，资源丰富型国家和劳动力丰富型国家都可作为比较对象，因此印度尼西亚也可以向马来西亚学习。菲律宾的人均GDP为2 168美元，菲律宾和印度尼西亚都可以作为越南的学习榜样，且这三个国家人均资本存量相近。根据联合国UN Comtrade数据库核算出的这5个国家排名前10位的产品，可以发现只有人均GDP最高的榜样国家马来西亚的光学、照相、电影、计量、检验、医疗或外科用仪器及设备、精密仪器及设备（90）产品出口位列前10位。泰国生产的车辆及其零件、附件，铁道及电车道车辆除外（87），出口排名第4位，不同于其他国家的主要出口产品还包括肉、鱼等制品（16）和谷物（10）等，泰国已经具备一定的工业基础和生产潜力，未来可以向马来西亚学习，进行更高技术水平的产业升级。印度尼西亚的劳动力丰裕，且自然资源丰富，主要出口矿物燃料（27）、矿砂（26）、铜及其制品（74），此外非针织服务也是主要出口产品。印度尼西亚是世界第四人口大国，大量人口将可以强有力地支撑内需，带动经济快速发展。但是印度尼西亚的工业产业亟待升级，可以向泰国学习，印度尼西亚的汽车普及率仅为8%（2008年泰国为31%），处于亚太12个国家及地区倒数第二的水平，且印度尼西亚的家电普及率尚处于较低状态。这也使得中国企业赴印度尼西亚投资，在纺织、石化、电子信息等产业都存在较多的机会。菲律宾的车辆及其零件、附件（87）产品出口排名第三位，此外针织服务（61）也是其主要出口产品，下一步产业升级也可以学习泰国。越南主要出口服装鞋帽，62、64、61类产品排名前5位，此外还主要出口农产品，应该向菲律宾学习。

亚洲收入较低的国家斯里兰卡、老挝、巴基斯坦、柬埔寨和孟加拉国要素禀赋结构相似。相对来说，这些国家劳动力数量较少、产业结构中农业还占有较高比重，除了斯里兰卡之外，其他国家人均资本存量偏低，人均收入在700~1 100美元，均可以向斯里兰卡学习。根据联合国UN Comtrade数据库核算出这5个国家排名前10位的主要出口产品，发现和前面所列国家有明显的不同，出口的主要产品为服装和农产品，而非机电产品和工业制成品。这些国家都是工

---

① 孙瑾、刘文革，“国家竞争优势产业甄别与升级——基于新结构主义经济学方法”，《国际贸易》，2014年第4期，第11–17页。

表10.4 马来西亚、泰国、印尼、菲律宾和越南的禀赋结构与产业结构（2008—2012年平均值）

| 国家 | 人均GDP（美元） | 人均资本存量（美元） | 劳动力 | 自然租金比 | 第一产业占比(%) | 第二产业占比(%) | 第三产业占比(%) |
|---|---|---|---|---|---|---|---|
| 马来西亚 | 8 991.6 | 1 523.23 | 12 128 567 | 12.66 | 10.38 | 42.12 | 47.49 |
| 泰国 | 4 989.0 | 832.12 | 38 914 501 | 4.58 | 10.47 | 39.11 | 50.42 |
| 印度尼西亚 | 2 885.0 | 402.58 | 114 631 713 | 11.44 | 14.84 | 47.35 | 37.81 |
| 菲律宾 | 2 168.2 | 279.40 | 39 105 092 | 2.83 | 12.64 | 31.92 | 55.44 |
| 越南 | 1 372.4 | 325.28 | 50 999 488 | 14.35 | 19.64 | 37.84 | 42.51 |

资料来源：孙瑾和刘文革（2014）根据WDI数据库计算。

业基础十分薄弱、经济结构单一的农业国家。目前，斯里兰卡已经摆脱最不发达国家身份，步入中低等收入国家行列，这主要源于斯里兰卡政府的一些产业政策所推动。参照表10.5，首先，确定具有与巴基斯坦、柬埔寨、孟加拉国等国家相似的要素禀赋结构且人均GDP高于它们一倍的斯里兰卡蓬勃发展的贸易品产业：针织和非针织服装，橡胶制品，珍珠、宝石、贵金属制品，书籍，电机，船舶，制粉工业品，核反应堆零件等。其次，分析这些国家在国内已经寻找、成功实现自我发现或者增长迅速、具有较大的就业影响并可以更快增长的产业，如柬埔寨的橡胶制品、车辆及其零件和孟加拉国的核反应堆零件等，参照斯里兰卡这些大类产品的细分产品生产进一步进行产业内的升级。再次，确定那些目前本国不具有比较优势，但是需要少量投资及政府扶持可以发展的具有潜在比较优势的产业，如电机、电气设备及其零件，录音机及放声机，电视图像、声音的录制和重放设备及其零件、附件，以及船舶及浮动结构体等。孙瑾和刘文革的上述案例分析是对第6章所量化分析的东亚“雁阵模式”的很好说明。

表10.5 斯里兰卡、巴基斯坦、柬埔寨与孟加拉国2011年排名前十的出口产品

| 排序 | 斯里兰卡 | 巴基斯坦 | 柬埔寨 | 孟加拉国 |
|---|---|---|---|---|
| 1 | 针织服装等（61） | 棉花（52） | 针织服装等（61） | 针织服装等（61） |
| 2 | 非针织服装（62） | 其他纺织制成品；成套物品；旧衣着及旧纺织品；碎织物（63） | 书籍、报纸、印刷图画及其他印刷品；手稿、打字稿及设计图纸（49） | 非针织服装（62） |
| 3 | 橡胶及其制品（40） | 谷物 | 车辆等（87） | 鱼等（3） |
| 4 | 天然或养殖珍珠、宝石、贵金属及其制品；仿首饰（71） | 针织服装等（61） | 鞋靴、护腿和类似品及其零件（64） | 其他植物纺织纤维；纸纱线及其机织物（53） |
| 5 | 书籍等（49） | 非针织服装（62） | 橡胶及其制品（40） | 其他纺织制成品（63） |
| 6 | 电机等（85） | 矿物燃料等（27） | 非针织服装（62） | 生皮及皮革（41） |

续表

| 排序 | 斯里兰卡 | 巴基斯坦 | 柬埔寨 | 孟加拉国 |
|---|---|---|---|---|
| 7 | 船舶及浮动结构体（89） | 皮革制品；鞍具及挽具；旅行用品、手提包及类似容器；动物肠线（蚕胶丝除外）制品（42） | 谷物（10） | 棉花（52） |
| 8 | 制粉工业产品；麦芽；淀粉；菊粉；面筋（11） | 化学纤维短纤（55） | 木及木制品；木炭（44） | 矿物燃料等（27） |
| 9 | 其他植物纺织纤维；纸纱线等（53） | 盐；硫磺；泥土及石料；石膏料、石灰及水泥（25） | 天然或养殖珍珠等（71） | 鞋靴、护腿和类似品及其零件（64） |
| 10 | 核反应堆零件等（84） | 塑料及其制品（39） | 烟草、烟草及烟草代用品的制品（24） | 核反应堆零件等（84） |

资料来源：孙瑾和刘文革（2014）根据 UN Comtrade 数据库计算整理而得。

### 10.4.3 非洲发展中国家的案例

下面用一个具体国别案例来说明GIFF在非洲的应用，也是对第1章专栏1.4的进一步补充说明讨论。2015—2016年，应联合国工发组织邀请，北京大学新结构经济学研究院运用GIFF为埃塞俄比亚甄别目标行业，受到东道国的欢迎。具体方法就是前面所介绍的六个步骤。这里只讨论第一步骤的两个分步：第一是选择目标国家，即学习的对象；第二是选择目标行业和部门，评估在目标国家哪些部门的显性比较优势正在下降，它们的企业正在寻找向海外转移的机会。表10.6和表10.7是其分析结果。表10.6显示了可供选择发展中国家的人均收入（以2011年购买力平价计算的人均GDP）并与埃塞俄比亚各年人均收入相比（%），同时我们还要看看这些国家人均GDP增长的业绩以及GDP增长率。

表10.6显示了三点重要信息：埃塞俄比亚是非洲最有活力的国家，1990年时从极低的起点起步——人均GDP（PPP）仅为653国际元，近年来它的人均GDP增长相当迅速，超过了同样位于非洲的加纳。该国与亚洲发展中国家的收入差距日益缩小——与孟加拉国相比从2000年的258%到2013年的214%——但赶超的速度有待加强。发展中国家在短短30年期间进行快速赶超是完全可能的。在表10.6的可比国家中，加纳在1990年是较为富有的，但是亚洲国家发展的速度更快，现在它们比加纳更为富裕。这些亚洲国家的发展思路是值得仔细研究的。孟加拉国、柬埔寨、加纳、越南、印度，这些国家最初入选是因为它们的经济都相

当有活力，人均收入水平在埃塞俄比亚的200% ~400%区间。中国入选为目标国之一是因为在20多年前，即1990年，中国的人均GDP只是埃塞俄比亚的228%，它在15~20年前的发展经验还是非常相关的。再者，由于中国劳动力成本上升，它的劳动密集型产业正在寻求海外投资的机会，试图像日本、韩国当年所做的那样，将工厂转移到劳动力充裕、劳动成本低廉的国家去。这就为低收入的发展中国家创造了通过吸引外商直接投资进行赶超的机会。

表10.6 GIFF第一步：埃塞俄比亚可选择的目标国家

| 国家 | 人均GDP（2011年购买力平价国际元） | | | | | | 人均GDP年均增速（%） | GDP年均增速（%） |
|---|---|---|---|---|---|---|---|---|
| | 1990年 | 与埃塞俄比亚相比（%） | 2000年 | 与埃塞俄比亚相比（%） | 2013年 | 与埃塞俄比亚相比（%） | 1990—2013年 | 1990—2013年 |
| 埃塞俄比亚 | 653 | 100 | 623 | 100 | 1 336 | 100 | 3.20 | 6.27 |
| 孟加拉国 | 1 239 | 190 | 1 606 | 258 | 2 853 | 214 | 3.69 | 5.44 |
| 柬埔寨 | 1 004 | 154 | 1 368 | 220 | 2 944 | 220 | 5.56 | 7.73 |
| 加纳 | 1 892 | 290 | 2 240 | 359 | 3 864 | 289 | 3.07 | 5.68 |
| 越南 | 1 501 | 230 | 2 650 | 425 | 5 125 | 384 | 5.39 | 6.83 |
| 印度 | 1 812 | 278 | 2 600 | 417 | 5 238 | 392 | 4.69 | 6.39 |
| 中国 | 1 488 | 228 | 3 609 | 579 | 11 525 | 863 | 9.03 | 9.92 |

注：由于柬埔寨1990年人均GDP数据缺失，用1993年数据代替。
数据来源：根据世界银行WDI数据集的数据计算。

完成了上述的第一步之后，我们又计算了中国、印度、越南等国家的显性比较优势（用SITC-3位数代码分类），用线性回归看看哪些产业的比较优势正在显著下降。由于篇幅有限，我们仅仅以这三个国家为例，列出那些RCA下降的产业。从事这些产业的企业正在向海外转移其生产出口能力，这就为具有类似要素禀赋的发展中国家（埃塞俄比亚）创造了学习和赶超的机会。如果某一产业在三国中有两个国家的RCA均为下降趋势并且在统计上显著，我们就将该行业选为目标行业。

表10.7列出了我们为埃塞俄比亚甄别的8个目标行业作为它的潜在比较优势。

政府收到报告之后或会采用上述六步法中的一些政策。该表显示，我们仅仅用三个国家历年出口数据计算的显性比较优势及其变化，就可以简明扼要地选出可供埃塞俄比亚选择的8个行业，即皮革业、制鞋业、纺织类日用品、金属类日用品、自行车等非机动车辆、制衣业、旅行包手提包旅行用具、刀具炊具等行业，均为劳动密集产业。这些产业都是显性比较优势在中国、印度等国下降的产业，也是中外企业含跨国公司要重新选址转移（relocate）的产业，由此给埃塞俄比亚的进入创造了机会。当然，这仅仅是GIFF六步法中的第一步。在我们的报告中还详细研究了埃塞俄比亚的国内工业发展状况、投资环境、工业园的进展，

表10.7 运用GIFF为埃塞俄比亚甄别目标行业：8个目标行业

| SITC code | 行业 / 产品名称 | 越南：比较优势下降的行业 | 中国：比较优势下降的行业 | 印度：比较优势下降的行业 | 是否被选为埃塞俄比亚的目标行业 |
|---|---|---|---|---|---|
| 611 | 皮革业 | 0 | 1 | 1 | 是 |
| 656 | 纺织类日用品 | 0 | 1 | 1 | 是 |
| 696 | 刀具炊具等 | 0 | 1 | 1 | 是 |
| 697 | 金属类日用品 | 0 | 1 | 1 | 是 |
| 733 | 自行车等非机动车辆 | 1 | 1 | 1 | 是 |
| 831 | 旅行包手提包等旅行用具 | 1 | 1 | 1 | 是 |
| 841 | 制衣业（除毛皮以外） | 0 | 1 | 1 | 是 |
| 851 | 制鞋业 | 1 | 1 | 1 | 是 |

注：1=显性比较优势下降且统计上显著，0=显性比较优势未下降。
资料来源：王燕、申晓芳、华晓峰，北大新结构中心与联合国工发组织合作报告（2016）。

以及政府的作用（含优惠政策）。

目前埃塞俄比亚的制造业发展相当迅速，创造了大量工作岗位（可回顾第1章的专栏1.4）。相对于国际金融危机爆发后的2009年，2017年埃塞俄比亚的制造业增加值占GDP的百分比提高了1.7个百分点，2016年制造业出口占商品出口的百分比提高了3.88个百分点，2017年农业就业人员占就业总数的百分比下降10.5个百分点。2009—2017年制造业增加值年增长率平均高达13.57%，人均GDP年增长率平均高达7.28%。这个案例告诉我们，包括撒哈拉以南非洲在内的发展中国家无须坐等所有的发展条件都具备了才行动。如果政府能够采取前述务实的发展方法，那么，随着中国的发展，工资的增长，比较优势的变化，来自中国潜在的8 500万的劳动力密集加工出口制造业工作机会将使几乎所有低收入国家实现如中国和其他东亚国家在过去数十年那样的动态增长。中国也正在和埃及、埃塞俄比亚、毛里求斯、尼日利亚与赞比亚建立经贸合作区。中国逐渐失去比较优势的巨大的劳动力密集型产业是广大低收入经济体新一轮国际发展的窗口机遇期，而中国发展经验却是把握住发展机遇的方法。

总之，上述新结构经济学关于中国及亚洲和非洲国家，以及专栏10.2所介绍的欧洲爱尔兰的案例分析和实践应用，回答了第1章最后提出的问题——人类发展思想的最大挑战：布隆迪如何转型升级为瑞士。

## 10.5

## 结束语：过去、现在与未来

至此，我们用新结构经济学之笔（第1章）绘制了一幅跌宕起伏的世界经济结构变迁历史画卷，勾勒了世界经济发展的轮廓与脉络。这幅画卷从过去到现在再到未来徐徐铺开：第2—3章的时间尺度覆盖了整个人类漫长的经济结构变迁以及近现代以来的世界经济结构变迁，第4—5章的时间尺度覆盖了战后至今的世界经济结构变迁，第6—7章则顺应历史变迁趋势而面对当下世界经济发展的关键问题（产业发展与基础设施建设），第8—9章则聚焦当下中国与世界经济的结构关系，第10章面向未来为没有贫困、和平、共享繁荣的人类社会提供政策方案。

正如这幅画卷所描绘的，世界经济发展一路走来坎坎坷坷，未来也注定不能一帆风顺，但人类依然勇往直前。正当我们要为本书划上句号之时，突如其来的新冠疫情（COVID-19）正在疯狂地肆虐全球，使得尚未完全从国际金融危机阴霾中走出来的世界经济雪上加霜，将造成的世界经济萧条可能超过20世纪初叶的“大萧条”。正如林毅夫等20名医疗专家和经济学家在《致G20首脑的抗疫公开信》（The COVID-19 pandemic: A letter to G20 leaders）中所指出的，在发达经济体艰难应对COVID-19疫情传播的同时，新兴国家和发展中国家正面临着对人类生命、社会凝聚力和经济破坏的前所未有的集体威胁。全球性的抗疫必须在公共卫生和经济政策两条战线上展开。2020年3月26日，G20领导人首次以视频方式举行应对新冠肺炎特别峰会，取得了三项重要应对成果：一是各方承诺及时分享信息，保障医疗物资供应，采取一切必要措施共同抗击疫情，维护全球公共卫生安全。二是各方同意为发展中国家特别是最不发达国家抗疫提供支持，同时完善全球公共卫生体系，为应对未来传染病疫情作好准备。三是各方承诺维护全球经济金融稳定，提振市场信心，保障就业民生，减少疫情对全球贸易和供应链的冲击。此次G20特别峰会通过了启动总额5万亿美元的经济计划，以应对疫情对全球社会、经济和金融带来的负面影响，并支持各国中央银行采取措施促进金融稳定和增强全球市场的流动性。正如此次G20特别峰会公报最后所强调的，战胜疫情比以往任何时候都需要采取全球团结和国际合作，相信紧密的合作有助于克服困难，并为保护人类生命、恢复全球经济稳定和实现强劲、可持续、平衡和包容性增长奠定坚实的基础。全球抗疫，世界发展，已然一家，谁也不能独善其身，唯有同舟共济，人类才有美好的未来。

# 本书关键名词

北美自由贸易协定

North American Free Trade Agreement (NAFTA)

超前城市化

Over-urbanization

城市化

Urbanization

出口导向

Export-oriented

创新结构

Innovation structure

达标程度

Up to standard

大分流

Great divergence

大萧条

The great depression

大洋洲

Oceania

德国

Germany

低收入国家

Low-income countries

第二次世界大战

World War II

第三世界

The third world

电力基础设施

Electricity infrastructure

电信基础设施

Telecommunications infrastructure

东欧

Eastern Europe

东亚

East Asia

东亚奇迹

The East Asian Miracle

东亚与太平洋地区

East Asia and the Pacific

多极世界

A multipolar world

俄罗斯

Russia

二十国集团

The Group of Twenty (G20)

发达国家 / 发达经济体
Developed countries/developed economies
发展典范
Outstanding case for development
发展理论
Development theory
发展思想
Development thought
发展陷阱
The development of Trap
发展战略
Development strategy
发展中国家 / 发展中经济体
Developing countries/developing economies
纺织业
Textile industry
非农产业
Non-agricultural industries
非洲
Africa
服务业
Services
福利社会
Welfare society
高储蓄率之谜
Myth of high savings rate
高收入国家
High-income countries
工业
Industry
工业革命
The industrial revolution
工业化
Industrialization
工业社会
Industrial society
公司治理
Corporate governance
古典经济学
Classical economics
官僚制度
Bureaucracy
国际货币基金组织
International Monetary Fund (IMF)
国际经济秩序
International economic order
国家级新区
State-level new development area
过剩产能
Excess capacity
海运基础设施
Maritime infrastructure
韩国
South Korea
航空基础设施
Aviation infrastructure
荷兰
Nether Lands
后工业社会
Post-industrial society
后来者优势
Latecomer advantage
互联网基础设施
Internet infrastructure
华盛顿共识
Washington consensus
换道超车型产业
“Corner overtaking” industries
基础设施
Infrastructure
基础设施建设能力
Infrastructure construction capacity

基础设施瓶颈
Infrastructure bottleneck
基础设施缺口
Infrastructure gap
基础设施投资
Infrastructure investment
基础设施投资回报率
Return on infrastructure investment
吉布提
Djibouti
计划经济
The planned economy
技术创新
Technology innovation
技术进步
Technical progress
渐进式改革
Gradual reformation
教育制度
The education system
结构变迁
The structure change
结构变迁方程
Structural change equation
结构变迁轨迹
Structural transition trajectory
结构扭曲
The structure distortion
结构主义
Structuralism
进口替代
Import substitution
经合组织成员国（OECD国家）
Organization for Economic Co-operation and Development (OECD)
经济结构转型升级
Economic structure transformation and upgrading
经济开发区
Economic development zone
经济收敛
Economic convergence
经济特区
Special economic zones
经济停滞
Economic stagnation
经贸合作
Economic and trade cooperation
竞争优势
Competitive advantage
旧石器
Paleolithic
就业
Employment
就业结构
Employment structure
就业结构极化
Employment structure polarization
就业缺口
The employment gap
卡尔·海因里希·马克思
Karl Heinrich Marx
开放型经济新体制
The new system of open economy
康乾盛世
Kang-Qian flourishing age
可变总量生产函数
Variable aggregate production function
可持续发展
Sustainable development
恐怖主义
Terrorism

拉丁美洲
Latin America
拉丁美洲与加勒比海地区
Latin America and the Caribbean
劳动分工
The division of labor
劳动密集型产业
Labor-intensive industry
劳动生产力
Labor productivity
劳工制度
The labor system
历史唯物主义
Historical materialism
林毅夫
Justin Yifu Lin
领头龙模式
Lead dragon pattern
领先型产业
Leading edge industries
卢卡斯之谜
Lucas paradox
马尔萨斯陷阱
Malthusian trap
马耳他
Malta
马来西亚
Malaysia
马铃薯
Potato
煤炭
Coal
美国工业革命
American industrial revolution
棉花
Cotton
民主制度
Democracy
墨西哥
Mexico
耐心资本
Patient capital
南北合作
North-south cooperation
南南合作
South-south cooperation
南亚
South Asia
内生增长
Endogenous growth
能源基础设施
Energy infrastructure
农耕时代
Agrarian age
农业
Agriculture
农业社会
Agricultural society
奴隶贸易
The slave trade
欧佩克
Organization of Petroleum Exporting Countries (OPEC)
欧洲和中亚地区
Europe and central Asia
贫困
Poverty
贫困陷阱
Poverty trap
七国集团（G7）
Group of Seven (G7)
前现代社会
Pre-modern society

轻工业

Light industry

圈地运动

Enclosure movement

全球化

Globalization

全球价值链

Global value chain

全球金融危机

Global financial crisis

全球经济治理

Global economic governance

全球竞争力报告

Global Competitiveness Report

全球贸易

Global trade

全球治理体系

Global governance system

人口大爆炸

Population explosion

人类命运共同体

A community of shared future for mankind

人民币国际化

Internationalization of RMB

日本

Japan

瑞士

Switzerland

撒哈拉以南非洲地区

Sub-Saharan Africa

三次产业

The three industries

社会福利

Social welfare

生产函数

Production function

生产结构

Production structure

失业

Unemployment

石油危机

The oil crisis

世界经济格局

World economic pattern

世界经济结构转型升级

The world economy structure transformation and upgrading

世界贸易组织（WTO）

World Trade Organization (WTO)

世界银行（WB）

World Bank (WB)

市场经济

The market economy

水利基础设施

Water infrastructure

司法制度

The legal system

斯德哥尔摩陈述

The Stockholm Statement

苏联解体

The collapse of the Soviet Union

泰国

Thailand

铁路基础设施

Railway infrastructure

脱贫

Anti-poverty

外贸

The foreign trade

外资

Foreign direct investment (FDI)

违背比较优势

Comparative advantage defying (CAD)

乌兹别克斯坦
Uzbekistan
西蒙·史密斯·库兹涅茨
Simon Smith Kuznets
西欧
Western Europe
习近平
Xi Jinping
显性比较优势
Revealed Comparative Advantage (RCA)
现代化
Modernization
新大陆
The New World
新古典经济学
Neoclassical economics
新加坡
Singapore
新结构经济学
New structural economics
新兴经济体
Emerging economies
新制度经济学
New institutional economics
新自由主义
Neoliberalism
休克疗法
Shock therapy
修昔底德陷阱
Thucydides' trap
亚当·斯密
Adam Smith
亚非拉
Asia, Africa and Latin America
亚洲基础设施投资银行
Asian infrastructure investment bank
亚洲"四小龙"
Asian tigers
雁行模式
Flying geese
要素禀赋
Factor endowments
"一带一路"
The Belt and Road
"一带一路"倡议
The Belt and Road Initiative
印度尼西亚
Indonesia
英国工业革命
British industrial revolution
营商环境
Doing business
有为政府
The facilitating government
有效市场
The efficient market
原始工业化
Proto-industrialization
原始积累
Primitive accumulation
约翰·梅纳德·凯恩斯
John Maynard Keynes
增长报告
Growth Report
增长核算
Growth accounting
增长甄别与因势利导工具（GIFF）
Growth identification and facilitation framework (GIFF)
战略型产业
Strategic industries
蒸汽机
The steam engine

知识产权
Intellectual property rights
殖民掠夺
Colonial rob
制造业
Manufacturing
中等收入国家
Middle-income countries
中等收入陷阱
Middle income trap
中东与北非地区
Middle East and North Africa
中国
China
中国工业革命
China's industrial revolution
中国共产党
Communist Party of China(CPC)
中国奇迹/中国的奇迹
Chinese miracle
中国深圳
Shenzhen, China
中国台湾
Taiwan, China
中国香港
Hong Kong, China,
中国重庆
Chongqing, China
重工业
Heavy industry
专利
Patent
专利结构
Patent structure
转进型产业
Comparative advantage-losing industries
转型经济体
Transitional economies
装备制造业
Equipment manufacturing
追赶型产业
Catching up industries
资本密集型产业
Capital intensive industry
资源密集型产业
Resource intensive industry
自贸区
Free trade zone
自生能力
Viability
遵循比较优势
Comparative advantage following (CAF)

## 附录1

–

## 联合国新结构“增长甄别与因势利导”技术手册

扫描二维码下载

## 附录2

–

## 新结构经济学全球包容性可持续结构转型指数

扫描二维码下载

## 郑重声明